HISTORY OF THE IRISH PARLIAMENT

1692–1800

BOYLE (0210)

Speaker: Henry Boyle, 1st Earl of Shannon, 1682–1764
Time as Speaker: 1733–56
Painting by Stephen Slaughter, oil on canvas, 1744
(WOA 2613)

HISTORY OF THE
IRISH
PARLIAMENT
1692–1800

COMMONS, CONSTITUENCIES
AND STATUTES

EDITH MARY JOHNSTON-LIIK

VOLUME
III

ULSTER HISTORICAL
FOUNDATION

The Ulster Historical Foundation is pleased to acknowledge the contribution of the Department of Culture, Arts and Leisure, Belfast, and the Office of the Taoiseach, Dublin, towards this publication.

Over the many years during which the research for this publication was undertaken, financial and material assistance was provided by a large number of organisations. These include: the Australian Research Council; the British Academy; the Department of Economic Development, NI (under its Action for Community Employment scheme); the Esme Mitchell Trust; the Leverhulme Trust; the Public Record Office of Northern Ireland; the Queen's University of Belfast; the School of Irish Studies Funds; the University of Sheffield and Macquarie University Research Funds.
All assistance is gratefully acknowledged.

FRONT ENDPAPER: *The Irish House of Commons*, 1780
by Francis Wheatley courtesy Leeds City Council
BACK ENDPAPER: Key to the front endpaper painting by Francis Wheatley
reproduced in *The Lady the House*, 1906, courtesy Belfast Central Library

First published 2002
by the Ulster Historical Foundation
12 College Square East, Belfast BT1 6DD
www.ancestryireland.com

Copyedited by Brendan O'Brien and Moira Johnston
Design by Dunbar Design
Typeset by December Publications
Printed by ColourBooks Limited, Dublin
Bound by William Clowes Limited, England

Set in Adobe Garamond
11point text on 13.5 leading
printed on 90 gsm Munken Pure paper
bound in dark green Wintan Lorca Bonded leather
with dark green Snowden cloth

SERIES CONTENTS

INTRODUCTION
TO THE
MEMBERS OF THE
IRISH HOUSE OF COMMONS

THE MPs'
ENVIRONMENT

THE IRISH PARLIAMENT MET FOR THE FIRST TIME on 18 June 1264 at Castledermott, and for the last time in the Parliament House in Dublin on 2 August 1800. From 1707 it was the only parliament in the British Empire with the medieval structure of King (represented by the Lord Lieutenant), Lords and Commons. In their introduction to *The Irish Parliament in the Middle Ages*, H. G. Richardson and G. O. Sayles wrote that: 'The kings of England brought to Ireland a two-fold gift, imperfect perhaps but of inestimable worth – parliament and the Common Law.' They also pointed out that it was *gesta Dei per Francos*,[1] for the Irish, like the British parliament, was part of the European parliamentary movement of the thirteenth century. In fact the first meeting of the Irish parliament preceded that of the English parliament – if only by a few months. The Irish parliament developed in parallel with the English parliament and in the eighteenth century it adjusted both to contemporary British practices and to Irish conditions. Before 1692 its meetings, like those of the English parliament, were erratic and peripatetic; for instance, the parliament that passed Poynings' Law, the statute which, until 1782, required all legislation to have the prior approval of the Irish and English Privy Councils before it came before the Irish parliament, was passed at a parliament meeting at Drogheda.

The seventeenth century was a period of enormous social change and disruption. Beginning with the Flight of the Earls and the Plantation of Ulster, it ended with the confiscations following William III's victories at Londonderry, the Boyne, Aughrim and finally Limerick. Although each of these added its own psychological consequences to the eighteenth century, they were preceded by much greater changes, as between 1641 and 1660 there was a major change in landholding.[2] Confiscated land was used to pay war speculators and some 35,000 soldiers. Wars are expensive and civil wars particularly so, as their costs both materially and otherwise have to be met within the society where they occur. Parliament had to pay its victorious troops and this was

---

[1] H. G. Richardson and G. O. Sayles, *The Irish Parliament in the Middle Ages* (Philadelphia 1964) p. 280. G. O. Sayles was later Professor of History at Belfast.
[2] S. J. Connolly, *Religion, Law and Power: The Making of Protestant Ireland, 1660–1760* (Oxford 1992) pp. 13–14.

done by grants of land confiscated from their opponents. Often these were quite small amounts and inevitably some recipients were glad to sell their grants and receive hard cash in these troubled times, while others collected small holdings into often scattered estates. In 1660 royalists demanded a restoration of their property and some adjustments were made to meet their demands. Nevertheless, the result was a chaotic lottery to which the Acts of Settlement (1662) and Explanation (1665) attempted to give a veneer of order and legality. Ultimately, the uneasy result of these arrangements was that between 1641 and the Revolution in 1688 the percentage of land owned by Roman Catholics dropped steeply: while religion and landholding cannot be precisely determined, this was a very considerable change in land ownership, most of which took place during the Commonwealth and proved irreversible at the Restoration.

It has been calculated that the pattern of landholding which emerged resulted in about 2,000 estates, mostly of between 2,000 and 4,000 acres.[3] The majority of these estates were not compact and often comprised parcels of land, and of political influence, in different counties. Apart from institutional holdings, estates were fluid entities as ownership of various portions changed with inheritance, marriage, sale or purchase. After 1700 this scattered pattern of landholding continued as estates were for the most part acquired by marriage or inheritance. Among the larger institutional landholders were the Established Church, Dublin University and, in the north, the Irish Society. The impact of the seventeenth-century changes is illustrated by Figure 1, which shows that even after the Flight of the Earls and the Plantation of Ulster, nearly 60 per cent of the land, the country's basic source of wealth and social status, was still in Catholic hands in 1641; by 1688 this had fallen to 22 per cent and by 1703 to 14 per cent. The Williamite confiscation added only about 8 per cent to the total confiscation. Although the confiscations following the Treaty of Limerick were restrained, they were the final instalment of a continual attrition over 150 years, and the penal laws of Queen Anne's reign led to even further if gradual reductions. By 1778 Catholic proprietors were in receipt of only 1.5 per cent of the rental of Ireland – £60,000 out of a total rental estimated at £4,000,000. This was largely as a result of the gavelling clause in the penal statute, 2 Anne, c. 6.This, 'an Act to prevent the further growth of popery', was the most severe of the penal laws for the non-conforming secular society. It was confirmed in 1709 by 8 Anne, c. 3. These acts contained a gavelling clause which not only prevented Catholics from amassing land but led to partible inheritance, while the oaths required of officeholders ensured that only members of the Established Church would be able to participate in government.

[3] D. Dickson, *New Foundations: Ireland 1600–1800* (Dublin 1987) pp. 103–4.

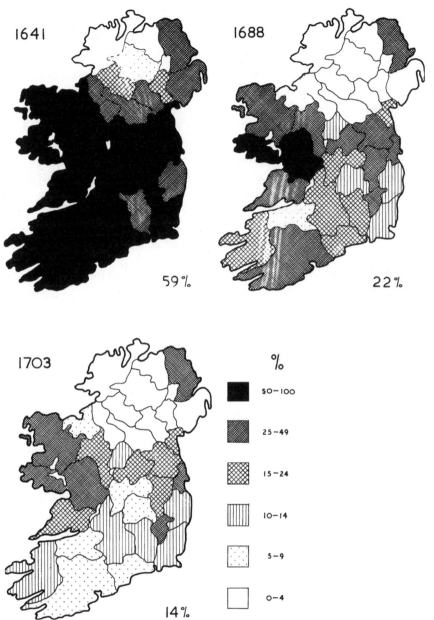

Maps by J. G. Simms showing the proportion of land owned by Catholics in Ireland according to counties in 1641, 1688 and 1703. The effect of the Cromwellian confiscation, as modified at the Restoration, is indicated by the first and second maps, and the effect of the Williamite confiscation by the second and third maps. (Source: T. W. Moody and F. X. Martin (eds), *The Course of Irish History*, 3rd edn (Cork, 1994) p. 201. Used by permission of the family of the late J. G. Simms and with the consent of Radio Telefís Éireann.)

'The laws against popery have so far operated,' remarked Lord Townshend in 1772, 'that at this day there is no popish family remaining of any great weight from landed property.' Townshend's statement was extreme for there were some, for example the Brownes, Lords Kenmare, who had the good fortune to produce a single son and heir in succeeding generations during the penal period. The following extract from Lord Kenmare's notes on his estate in the 1750s illustrates both his discretion and the problems which confronted even a fortunate Catholic landlord. He writes that:

> If ever my family should be capable of purchasing this farm [Clounmelane] would deserve it best of any in Kerry as it is surrounded on every side by our lands. It was offered to be sold me by McMahon the tenant at my coming of age but I ever avoided meddling in purchases as I scarce know the trustee I would depend on and wrangles or roguery on this head might stagger a man in the most determined resolution of (what is in all matters the most essential) his religion.[4]

Occasionally, friendly Protestants nominally held land in trust for Catholics and some families had Catholic and Protestant branches. This 'trusteeship' was illegal, so that not only did the Catholic owner have no security against fraud, but both the owner and the trustee ran the risk of being discovered by an informer.[5] Catholic landlords, however, could and did exert electoral influence through their Protestant tenants.

Then there were the 'reluctant conformists' – for example, De Latocnaye, visiting Galway in 1796, reported that:

> Nearly all the inhabitants in this district are Catholics, rich as well as poor; only the rich submitted, formerly to the Anglican form, in order that they might possess their goods in peace, and, now, in order that they may be eligible for election to Parliament. Thirty years ago the proprietor of a very fine estate called Oranmore, fearing that some cousin might turn Protestant in order to filch it from him, sought the bishop and offered to renounce the superstitions of the Church of Rome. 'What motives my son' said the pastor 'urge you to enter the fold of the faithful …?' 'Oranmore' replied the convert, and to all the customary questions he had but the single word – 'Oranmore' – for answer.[6]

The hope was that if the father was a reluctant conformist the children would conform automatically. In an overwhelmingly Catholic community this was a questionable assumption.

Those who retained their faith and remained in Ireland – many left for the continent – often lived in reduced circumstances, mindful of past glories. Arthur Young, visiting

---

[4] *IMC Kenmare*, p. 193.
[5] Ibid., p. xi.
[6] De Latocnaye, *A Frenchman's Walk through Ireland* (Dublin 1797; trans. Belfast, 1917) p. 146; *see also* J. Brady and P. J. Corish, 'The Church under the Penal Code', in P. J. Corish (ed.), *A History of Irish Catholicism* (Dublin 1971) vol. 4, p. 2.

Roscommon in 1776, commented on the formality of one of the leading Gaelic lords: 'O'Connor, the direct descendant of Roderick O'Connor, who was King of Connacht ... [whose] possessions formerly so great are reduced to £300 or £400 a year receives presents of cattle etc. upon various occasions. They consider him as the Prince of a people involved in one common ruin.'[7] Possibly these cattle were the vestiges of the traditional dues of a Gaelic chief. Some years later De Latocnaye also commented on the 'ceremonious respect' accorded to the O'Connor, adding that: 'I have been told his domestics serve him kneeling' and that 'the crown of gold of the last monarch is said to be in the possession of the family, although there are those who think it has been disposed of to a jeweller.'[8]

A completely new social elite had emerged and it was these new men who formed the majority in the eighteenth-century Irish parliament. The interregnum of the 1650s brought, in support of parliament and the Lord Protector, a great influx of speculators and adventurers of various kinds. The conquistador Bernal Diaz[9] (whose works were translated by an Irish MP, Maurice Bagenal St Leger Keating (**1135**)) said that men went to the new world to serve God and the king and to grow rich as most men desire to do. These words, with slight adjustments, could equally be applied to the men who came to Ireland in the train of Cromwell and his armies. After the death of Cromwell many of those who had come to prominence during his regime were quite happy to support the restored monarchy so long as they could retain their newly acquired possesions.[10] However, those who had supported the monarchy looked for restitution in view of their proven loyalty. The wily Charles II, making supportive gestures to both sides, left this problem to the wisdom of the Irish Restoration Parliament called in 1661.

The situation was impossible, and its resolution in the Act of Settlement 1662 and the Act of Explanation in 1665 proved haphazard and inevitably unsatisfactory. Parliament was dissolved in 1666 and this was the last predominantly Protestant parliament which met before 1692. But Charles was without a legitimate heir, and the aggrieved could hope that their wrongs might be rectified under his Catholic brother and heir apparent. Before this could be achieved James II had alienated his English subjects and made Ireland a theatre of a European war, which enabled William III and his wife, James II's Protestant daughter, Mary II, to consolidate their positions. Not only was the status quo of Charles II's land settlement retained but it was consolidated by a further wave of confiscations.

---

[7] Arthur Young, *A Tour in Ireland* (London 1780) vol. 1, p. 219.

[8] De Latocnaye, op. cit., p. 286.

[9] Bernal Diaz (*Conquest of New Spain*, ed. J. M. Cohen, Harmondsworth 1963) wrote of his deceased comrades: 'They died in the service of God and of His Majesty, and to give light to those who sit in darkness – and also to acquire that wealth which most men covet'; various translations paraphrase this quotation from the Spanish in different ways.

[10] A. Clarke, *Prelude to Restoration in Ireland* (Cambridge 1999) gives a detailed interpretation of this difficult period.

Meanwhile the uncertainty continued: William and Mary were childless and by 1700 all of Anne's large family had died. In 1701 the English parliament had passed the Act of Settlement, 11 & 12 Will. III, c. 2, which settled the English crown on the Electress Sophia of Hanover, a grand-daughter of James I. In 1541, 33 Henry VIII, c. 1 declared that the King of England was *ipso facto* King of Ireland (interestingly, this act was brought before parliament in both Irish and English). Thus the English Act of Settlement also applied to Ireland. Nevertheless, no one was quite sure what would happen when Anne died. Thus an integral part of the problem was the long uncertainty over the succession and with it the finality of the land settlement. This lasted certainly until 1746, and the perceived threat even longer. Throughout the century nothing aroused such fear as that attainders might be reversed and estates restored to their former owners – despite the fact that as the years passed unscrambling changes in landholding would have been virtually impossible. In the 1730s Lord Clancarty, who was a British naval officer and governor of Newfoundland from 1733 to 1735, endeavoured to persuade the British cabinet in 1736 to consider a bill to reverse his father's attainder and restore his family estates, which had an income estimated at £60,000 p.a. When this became known in Ireland panic ensued and Archbishop Boulter warned Newcastle that:

> I can assure your Lordship anything of this nature will be a great blow to the Protestant interest here, and will very much shake the security Protestants think they now have of the enjoyment of their estates … and I think the affair of the last importance to the Protestant interest here.[11]

Clancarty's appeal was rejected and he joined the Jacobites in France: subsequently he was implicated in the 1745 rebellion and died in exile. His was not the only, though perhaps the most prominent case. For instance, in 1755 Sir Thomas Prendergast (**1725**) appealed to the House of Commons for protection against the O'Shaughnessys who, since 1731, had been seeking a reversal of the estate of Gort granted to his father (**1724**) for 'discovering' the 1696 plot against William III. The House of Commons resolved to proceed against all such claimants 'as persons endeavouring to lessen the Protestant interest of this kingdom'. As late as 1789 Fitzgibbon, counselling caution at the time of the Regency Crisis, reiterated this fear when he reminded the House that:

> the only security by which they hold their property, the only security they have for their present constitution in Church and State, is the connexion of the Irish crown with, and its dependence upon the crown of England … when we speak of the people of Ireland it is a melancholy truth that we do not speak of the great body of the people. This is a subject on which it is painful to me to be obliged to touch in this assembly … the ancient nobility of this kingdom have been hardly treated. The Act

[11] *Boulter Letters*, vol. 2, pp. 118–20.

by which most of us hold our estates was an Act of violence – an Act subverting the first principles of the common Law in England and Ireland. I speak of the Act of Settlement; and that gentlemen may know the extent … I will tell them that every acre of land which pays quit rent to the crown is held by title derived under the Act of Settlement.[12]

Although the Commonwealth immigrants had brought with them a considerable diversity of religious opinion, the Restoration and especially the Revolution Settlement decided, not entirely for religious reasons, that despite its paucity of numbers (probably not more than 10 per cent), the established Church of Ireland would be Anglican.[13] Its position was confirmed by the penal code which affected Catholics and Dissenters in varying ways and to varying degrees. Based on religious discrimination, these laws had widespread social, political and economic consequences for Catholic landholding. But they also reflected the insecurity of the Protestants with their memories of the rebellions and uncertainties of the seventeenth century. Land was the key not only to economic but also to social and political power, both locally and nationally. In 1844, when the laws affecting Catholic ownership and acquisition of land had been repealed for over 60 years, the Devon Commissioners still found their influence pervasive, commenting that 'They interfered with almost every mode of dealing with landed property by those who professed that religion, and by creating a feeling of insecurity directly checked their industry.' They added that the political implications of the laws during their enforcement had boomeranged on the Protestant landlords by restricting their choice of tenant 'for in letting their estates they were to a great degree confined in the selection of their tenants, to those who alone could enjoy any permanent tenure under them and were exclusively entitled to the elective franchise'.[14] Until 1778, only protestants could hold a tenancy for life or lives which carried with it the vote, but until 1793 Catholics so qualified could not exercise the franchise.

The vast majority of the population in Leinster, Munster and Connacht were Catholics. Since the Reformation Ireland has had two ecclesiastical hierarchies, and by the eighteenth century these had been joined by other denominational administrations, most notably that of the Presbyterian Church in Ireland. The Church of Ireland 'by law established' was Anglican in form and was, although subsequently disestablished in 1869, merged with the Church of England in 1800. The two hierarchies, Catholic and Anglican, were territorially similar but not identical. While both churches used the traditional diocesan system, the dioceses were variously united for purposes of ecclesiastical administration; for example, the Church of Ireland united

---

[12] *Irish Parliamentary Debates*, 20 February 1789, quoted in J. A. Froude, *The English in Ireland in the Eighteenth Century* (London 1872–4) 2nd edn, vol. 2, 1881, pp. 552–4. Fitzgibbon is referring to the 1662 Act of Settlement, 14 & 15 Chas II, c. 2.

[13] See A. Ford, J. McGuire and K. Milne (eds), *As by Law Established: the Church of Ireland since the Reformation* (Dublin 1995).

[14] *Report from Her Majesty's Commissioners of Inquiry into the State of the Law and Practice in Respect of the Occupation of Land in Ireland* (Earl of Devon, chairman) HC 1845 (605), p. 7.

the dioceses of Cork and Ross, and the Catholic Church the dioceses of Cloyne and Ross.

The Church of Ireland, as the established or official church, exercised secular judicial and administrative functions which affected the everyday lives of Anglicans and non-Anglicans alike, for instance over matters affecting family life such as marriages and wills. The parish was an important unit of civil as well as of ecclesiastical administration. Acts of parliament often assigned to the vestry responsibilities in connection with such secular duties as the oversight of rates, beggars, police and the watch. Until 1760 the parish was responsible for local roads – an unpopular task, though probably not as unpopular as the Church's role in collecting tithes and granting probate on wills. Protestant non-conforming churches were organised on congregational rather than strictly territorial lines. The most numerous protestant dissenting denomination was the Presbyterian Church in Ireland – its title reflecting its links with the wider reformed community and in particular with its 'established' parent church in Scotland. Largely concentrated in the province of Ulster, they deeply resented the dominant legal position of the Church of Ireland and attempted with some success to exercise ecclesiastical jurisdiction over their adherents on questions of faith and morals. Nevertheless, Presbyterian authority, like that of the Catholic Church, was based on moral and community pressures, not the force of law.

These pressures were often strong, and the implicit dichotomy that this created between communal attitudes and the law of the land has remained one of the long-standing issues in Irish history. For instance, in 1719 Archbishop King wrote to the Archbishop of Canterbury about the basic reason for retaining the penal law against the Presbyterians, emphasising that:

> The true point between them and the gentlemen is whether the Presbyterians and lay elders in every parish shall have the greatest influence over the people, to lead them as they please, or the landlords over their tenants. This may help your Grace in some degree to see the reason why the Parliament is so unanimous against taking off the test.[15]

The fear, not without substance, was that the close-knit structure of Presbyterianism would create a state within a state. Presbyterians were seriously affected as regarded marriages, education and membership of corporations. Although excluded from the boroughs, they retained the county franchise and the right to sit in parliament.[16] As early as the 1690s Sir Richard Cox, while paying lip-service to toleration for 'all friends

---

[15] BL Add. MS 6117; King, *A Great Archbishop of Dublin, William King DD*, p. 218.

[16] It is for this reason that, in this study, 'Protestant (as by law established)' refers to Anglicans and 'protestant' to all protestant denominations. Presbyterian marriages were considered invalid – in some respects as late as 1844, *Regina v. Willis* – and as wills etc. were probated in the church courts this affected questions of legitimacy and inheritance. Marriages conducted by Catholic priests were invariably legal throughout the penal period.

to the State', was anxious to maintain an exclusively Anglican ascendancy. People might go to heaven as they pleased but only through the portals of the Established Church might they enter the government, practise law or enter Dublin University. To this end he moved that Presbyterians be excluded from all public offices, civil or military.

The Presbyterians owned little land outright and Presbyterian landowners, with some notable exceptions, usually conformed within a generation or two. For the Catholic landowners the situation was much more severe. No Catholic sat in parliament from 1692 to 1828. No Catholic, or protestant married to a Catholic, could vote from 1727 until 1793, and it is possible that the 1727 act only clarified and consolidated a widely existing tradition. Nevertheless, despite their vicissitudes the remnants of the old Irish nobility did retain a separate identity, often reinforced and emphasised by their European connections. The ascendancy, as the new Protestant elite came to be called, were always conscious of their presence and in 1778 Arthur Browne, a lawyer and Fellow of Trinity College, expressed their fears, when, speaking on the anti-terrorist Whiteboy Act, 27 Geo. III, c. 15, he stated that whereas: 'in other countries the land title is purchase, here it is forfeiture. The old proprietor feeds the eternal memory of his ancient claim. The property of this country resembles the thin soil of volcanic countries, lightly spread over subterraneous fires.'[17] This view was confirmed by reports of the descendants of once great families still bequeathing their former estates to their sons.[18] This is often characteristic of a people who feel that they have been deprived by military rather than economic means – a similar tradition existed among Moors expelled from Granada by the Catholic Sovereigns in 1492 and the Spanish driven out of Jamaica by the British in 1654.

The final débâcle of the 1690s left the Irish Catholics without effective leadership until the rise of the Catholic middle class in the mid and late eighteenth century and ultimately the growing influence of the Catholic Church in the nineteenth century. Nevertheless, isolation and alienation contributed to a retrospective pride in an identity with an ancient and heroic race. Even at the end of the eighteenth century it was observed that: 'Everyone in Ireland is a gentleman, or was a gentleman or is related to a gentleman.' The ascendancy were always very conscious of, and scared of, the fractured society over which they presided.

Despite fictional representations, there was no stereotype eighteenth-century Irish landlord. As a class they varied considerably from the great nobleman with estates scattered throughout the British Isles to the country gentleman living on his single estate. In addition, variations in intellect and personality ensured a multiplicity of role models. For example, Dennis Daly (**0570**), MP for Co. Galway 1768–90, and John Fitzgibbon (**0749**), MP for Dublin University 1778–83, Kilmallock 1783–9 and later Lord Chancellor, were known to possess exceptionally fine libraries, while

[17] *Parliamentary Register*, Dublin, vol. 7, p. 229.
[18] Young, op. cit., p. 300.

another aspect of Irish life was represented by the Fordes of Seaforde (**0780–0783**), Co. Down, 'where the hounds circulate briskly in the morning and the bottle in the afternoon'.[19] The extreme formality of the Duke of Leinster's (**0745**), MP for Dublin city 1767–73, establishment at Carton was in complete contrast with the scene of exhausted bacchanalia which greeted Sir Jonah Barrington (**0087**, MP for Tuam 1790–7 and for Clogher 1798–1800) when he paid a surprise visit to his brother's hunting lodge.[20]

In looking at such varied personalities it would be difficult to disagree with Sir Lewis Namier's view of the reasons that attracted men to parliament:

> Men went there 'to make a figure' … The 'figure' of their daydreams differed with their rank and profession, with age, temperament and circumstances; but so much was common to practically all – the seat in the House was not their ultimate goal but a means to ulterior aims.

Nor should the social dimension of a seat in parliament be ignored: 'To be out of parliament is to be out of the world and my heart is set in being in it', wrote the victorious Admiral, Lord Rodney, to Lord George (Sackville) Germain (**1835**) in 1780.[21] Dublin became the focus of social as well as political life especially during the parliamentary season, which lasted approximately eight months in every second year from 1703 to 1781 and every year thereafter until 1800. During this period balls, dinners, receptions and all manner of entertainments crowded the social calendar and membership of parliament naturally opened many doors, even apart from those of the Castle, which was at the centre of this social whirl. The Irish stage was smaller than the British one, its limitations greater, but the same ambitions, modified by harsher circumstances, inspired members of a like society and a similar way of life. Membership of parliament conferred privilege, prestige and frequently professional or personal advantage on its possessor.

Although the MPs belonged to a narrow and an exclusive class, it would be incorrect to regard their activities as wholly self-centred. In 1700 the country had minimal infrastructure but the infrastructure which they established was to last, with little change, for the next 150 years. They encouraged the building of a network of toll and other roads and they supported the first commercial canal, the Newry canal (1731–41), in the British Isles. Dublin, with its wide streets and classical buildings, shows their sophisticated interest in architecture and town planning, as do the villages adjoining many of their estates, for example, Monivea in Co. Galway, Westport in Co. Mayo and Hillsborough and Castlewellan in Co. Down. This interest was also

[19] W. Crawford, *Letters of an Irish Land-Agent* (PRONI) p. 41; various Fordes of Seaforde sat in the Irish parliament for nearly 50 years.
[20] J. Barrington, *Personal Sketches* (1836 edn) pp. 42 *et seq.* Barrington's descriptions were often subject to exaggeration; D. Guinness and W. Ryan, *Irish Houses and Castles* (London 1971) pp. 187–8.
[21] L. B. Namier, *The Structure of Politics at the Accession of George III* (London 1957) pp. 1–2.

displayed in their town and country houses with their magnificent interior decoration. The Royal Dublin Society, 1731, and the Royal Irish Academy, 1785, both date from this century and there were many local improving societies. In addition they gave numerous grants to Dublin University, where many of the members had been educated, going on to the Inns of Court in London, where they received varying degrees of legal training, equipping some for their subsequent role as Justices of the Peace and others for distinguished legal careers. On their return to Dublin they were enrolled in the King's Inns and called to the Irish Bar. Apart from these specific outlets the law was an important general training for a wide range of positions.

Some MPs sent their children to English public schools: Eton, Harrow and Westminster were the most popular. These school connections were often long-lasting and had far-reaching political ramifications. In 1768 Lord Kildare (0745), then on the Grand Tour, wrote to his mother the Duchess of Leinster that: 'Lord Fitzwilliam, Mr Charles Fox and Mr Price arrived yesterday, but they propose going in a few days. We are about ten English at present, and eight of us were at Eton together. It is amazing how one picks up our old Eton acquaintances abroad. I dare say I have met above forty since I have been in Italy.'[22] Private tutors were widely used. The best known Irish 'public' school was Kilkenny College, founded or refurbished in 1667 by the 1st Duke of Ormonde, but there were also the Royal Schools founded as part of the Plantation of Ulster; probably the most famous of these was the Royal School at Armagh where Castlereagh was educated. There were many private foundations which produced various grades of education for a variety of practical and academic purposes. In 1747 the Irish parliamentarians gave the first grant for elementary education in the British Isles, although with that proselytising element which was part of virtually all eighteenth-century support for education.[23]

The Irish MPs were not immune to the social problems so clearly exposed around them. Health was a major concern, as is reflected in the number of Dublin hospitals which date from the eighteenth century. The first maternity hospital in the British Isles was established in Dublin in 1745. In 1765 parliament attempted to establish a nationwide system of county infirmaries. As early as 1767 it authorised, 7 Geo. III, c. 15, the Dublin Society to use part of its grant for establishing a *pharmacopoea pauperum* 'for dispensing medicines to the poor of the city of Dublin according to a plan laid down by John Wade, Chemist'. In 1792 the Belfast Dispensary was advertising for support and in 1793 a dispensary was established in Tandragee, Co. Armagh. By the 1780s the dispensary movement was established, and by the close of the century Dublin and other large cities had a number of hospitals and charitable institutions of various kinds.

---

[22] *IMC Leinster Correspondence*, vol. 3, p. 529.
[23] 19 Geo. II, c. 3 – this was the grant to the charter schools and it was continued by subsequent parliaments; education and religion were not separated in the eighteenth century and denominational education has had a long history in both Ireland and Great Britain.

With the establishment of the Dublin Workhouse in 1703, followed by similar, less ambitious, institutions in other large towns, MPs tried with dubious success to control the problems created by poverty and abandoned children; provision for the latter was made in the Foundling Hospital at first attached to the Dublin Workhouse but later separated from it. Another problem was created by the lack of a Poor Law, which in England made the poor of the parish the responsibility of the parish. This meant that in Ireland the poor roamed the country begging or looking for work and often spreading epidemic disease.

Towards the end of the century the MPs responded to the demands of John Howard for prison reform, establishing the system of the inspectorate,[24] which was later so important in enforcing the British Factory Acts. They gave public support, both local and national, to the improvement of agriculture and the development of industry. Until 1757 the Dublin Society, through which many of these grants were channelled, actually met in the grand committee room in the Parliament House.[25] Ireland was a poor country and the MPs realised that free enterprise was unlikely to succeed without state support, although this encouragement was limited and never enough. Moreover the awarding of parliamentary grants was fraught with local jealousies, often reflected in the conflicting demands of the local MPs. Inevitably this spread what finance was available far too thinly for it to realise its full potential. Not all of their plans succeeded, or succeeded as they intended, but their successes and failures should be viewed in the light of their very limited resources, for most of these parliamentarians were new men with no accumulated wealth or resources to fall back on, while the country had only limited prospects of commercial development or mineral exploitation.

The basic wealth of the country was land, and the landed estate had both a social and an economic position. It lay at the centre of the social structure of the country during the eighteenth century and, although there are many interpretations of what constitutes the eighteenth century in Ireland, this fact was undisputed. For instance, the parliamentary century dates from 1692 to 1800 but the social and economic interpretation favours the longer view from the Restoration to the 1840s famine, and attitudes to landed estates come under this broader definition. Dr Dickson, reviewing Dr Maguire's *The Downshire Estates*, has remarked that 'Irish historians have been slow to come to terms with the social institution of the landed estate and to disentangle it from the politics of tenant-right and of "landlordism". Inhibited by memories of the mid-nineteenth century demographic disaster, few have wished to be seen to be rushing to demote the landed estate to humbler levels of demonology, where it could be examined clinically and dispassionately.'[26] Yet a balanced understanding of both

---

[24] O. MacDonagh, *The Inspector-General: Sir Jeremiah Fitzpatrick and the Politics of Social Reform, 1783–1802* (London 1981).

[25] H. F. Berry, *A History of the Royal Dublin Society* (1915) p. 88.

[26] D. Dickson, *Studia Hibernica* (1973) p. 190; quoted in *Ir. Econ. & Soc. Hist.* (1989), Crawford, 'The significance of the landed estate in Ulster society in the seventeenth and eighteenth centuries'. Most of the published research has been done on Ulster estates.

aspects of landholding is essential for any real understanding of Ireland in the eighteenth century and of the circumstances which led to so terrible a débâcle. Such débâcles were not unique to Ireland but were a part of both Irish and European societies before industrialisation; for instance, the crisis of the early 1740s was probably as severe[27] as that of the 1840s, and the severe Finnish famine of 1867 followed the Irish one.

It is the pre-eminent importance of the estate which has given it its place in this study[28] and its specific reference in the biographies. The issues can best be illuminated through a study of individual estates, but many estates did not keep good records and many estate records were lost in the great land transfers of the post-famine era. One important category of estate records is the correspondence between absentee landowners and their generally conscientious agents. But are the records which have survived the atypical records of the better administered estates? This may well be the case, but fortunately there is a counterbalance. Historians have a valuable point of reference in what is probably the most thorough investigation of a pre-industrial society in Western Europe – the mass of evidence taken on oath from upwards of 1,100 'persons of every class and condition' and appended to the *Report from Her Majesty's Commissioners of Inquiry into the State of the Law and Practice in Respect of the Occupation of Land in Ireland*, commonly called the *Devon Report*. It refers to conditions in the year 1844, but many of the customs and traditions described in the report were indisputably present in the eighteenth century, although often in an embryonic and therefore a less dangerous form.

After 1815 the agrarian scene was increasingly distorted by the runaway increase in population – estimated at approximately 30 per cent between 1800 and 1841.[29] Furthermore, such distortions drew force from a failure to industrialise and the agricultural slump which followed the Napoleonic wars. At this time the peculiar structure of Irish society, and the order of magnitude these problems assumed in certain areas, gave prominence to conditions which were not in themselves unique to Ireland. Evidence of them is to be found in Scotland[30] and in similar societies in Europe and elsewhere.

The Devon Commissioners considered that many of the distinctive features of Irish landholding had their origins in the consequences of the confiscations and plantations of the sixteenth and seventeenth centuries on the relatively undeveloped state of the country. At this time large grants of undeveloped land were made on the understanding that their recipients would settle them with protestant English or Scottish migrants,

---

[27] L. M. Cullen, *The Emergence of Modern Ireland, 1600–1900* (London 1981) pp. 168–71.

[28] Most of the detail for the estates has been unearthed by Dr Malcomson, and it should always be borne in mind that an estate was a living, changing entity.

[29] Exact figures for the Irish population before 1822 are a matter of much speculation, and this is particularly true of the eighteenth century.

[30] See M. W. Flinn, 'Malthus, emigration and the potato in North-West Scotland, 1770–1870', in L. Cullen and T. C. Smout (eds), *Comparative Aspects of Irish and Scottish Economic and Social History*, pp. 47–64, esp. p. 56.

who would become exemplary tenants and loyal subjects. However, the Commissioners found that these undertakings had been only partly fulfilled and with varying results: for instance, 'in Munster the plantation was more imperfectly carried out … and a class of undertakers … became the landlords of the native peasantry … producing for that reason comparatively little change' in the population, while 'the extensive settlement of Scotch and English in the counties of Ulster, has introduced habits and customs which give a different character to that province from other parts of the island.'[31]

The Commissioners also found that the homogeneity which characterised English agrarian society was unknown in Ireland. Marc Bloch, comparing England to France, thought that in France the application of Roman law to local traditions 'confirmed and reinforced the idea of perpetuity which was already implicit in the right of real property traditionally exercised by the tenant over his house and fields'.[32] In this respect it is interesting to note that the concept of 'tenant right' was particularly strong in Ulster, where it may reflect Scottish law, which, like French, was based on Roman law. However, while the Scots provided the largest influx of tenant migrants, the largest land transfer occurred in the mid-seventeenth century and many of these Cromwellian settlers formed a 'small proprietary' who, the Devon Commissioners noted, 'being generally resident exercised an influence on the relations of society different from that produced by the large and absent grantees of former reigns'.[33] Many of those who rose from these origins to the eighteenth-century peerage could trace their ancestors no further back than to the mid-seventeenth century, although great efforts were often made to extend their claims further backwards, even in some cases to the Norman conquest. Amiens Street in Dublin is a reflection of such a baronial claim (*see* **2024**).

The rise in land values during the eighteenth century encouraged a more competent and professional approach to land surveying,[34] but even at this more sophisticated level of quantification there were three different types of measurement. The most universal measure was the Irish or plantation acre and five Irish acres equalled eight English, imperial or statute acres. The English acre was the principal unit of land measurement in two places: firstly, in a horseshoe shaped area around Belfast, which included south Antrim, north Down, Armagh, north Cavan and east Tyrone; and secondly in west Waterford and east Cork where, for example, the great Burlington–Devonshire estates, which had once belonged to Sir Walter Raleigh, were measured in English acres. In the Ulster counties of Antrim, Down, Tyrone, Donegal and

---

[31] *Devon Report*, op. cit., p. 7; see also P. Roebuck, 'The economic situation and functions of substantial landowners 1600–1815: Ulster and Lowland Scotland compared', in R. Mitchinson and P. Roebuck, *Economy and Society in Scotland and Ireland*, pp. 81–92, esp. p. 90.

[32] M. Bloch, *French Rural History* (Berkeley 1966) p. 129.

[33] Devon Report, op. cit., p. 7.

[34] W. Greig, *General Report on the Gosford Estates in Co. Armagh 1821* (PRONI, 1976). This refers to the Acheson (**0002**) estates.

Londonderry, the variously called Scotch or Cunningham acre was widely used. It was slightly smaller than the Irish acre and slightly larger than the statute acre, as five Cunningham acres equalled seven statute acres. It was not unknown for nearby estates to be measured in different types of acre. For instance, although the Cunningham acre was the most usual measurement throughout the north, the Caledon estate in south Tyrone and south Armagh was measured in Irish acres, while the nearby south Tyrone Ranfurly estate was measured in English or statute acres.

A small consolidated estate, such as R. L. Edgeworth's (**0688**) in Co. Longford, could be administered by a resident landlord himself. But larger and more complicated estates were usually administered through one or more agents.[35] Permission to hold a market could be a valuable asset, depending on its popularity and the duties and tolls that it engendered. The place name most used on an Irish estate was that of the townland. This is usually recorded in estate papers and interpreting them presents obvious problems, particularly as Irish estates were often made up of bits and pieces of land (and townlands) scattered, sometimes widely, through a number of counties. This sometimes gave their owner political interests far beyond the county in which he normally resided.

A brief look at land divisions and administrative units will help to clarify the origins, often lost in antiquity, of strange place names and administrative units. By the eighteenth century the four traditional provinces had no political or administrative significance, and only a vestigial ecclesiastical one, reflected in the four archbishoprics – Armagh, Dublin, Cashel and Tuam – whose holders were respectively the Primate of all Ireland, the Primate of Ireland, the Primate of Munster and the Primate of Connacht. By the beginning of the seventeenth century the four provinces had been divided into the 32 counties of modern Ireland. In Ulster, the northern province, there were nine counties: Donegal, Londonderry, Antrim, Down, Armagh, Tyrone, Fermanagh, Cavan and Monaghan. Leinster, the most prosperous of the provinces, contained the eastern counties of Louth, Meath, Dublin, Wicklow, Wexford, Carlow, Kildare, Westmeath, Longford, King's County (Offaly), Queen's County (Leix) and Kilkenny. Munster, the southern province, comprised the south and south-west counties of Waterford, Cork, Kerry, Limerick, Tipperary and Clare. In the west, Connacht, the poorest of the provinces, claimed, with the exception of Clare, the counties lying to the west of the river Shannon – Galway, Mayo, Sligo, Leitrim and Roscommon. The counties were divided into a random number of baronies and parishes; for example, Co. Antrim had eight baronies and 77 parishes, Co. Galway 16 baronies and 116 parishes, Co. Cork 16 baronies and 269 parishes and Co. Kilkenny nine baronies and 127 parishes. The county, with these subdivisions, formed the basic unit of government. The focus of the county was the county town, the legal and

---

[35] The way the system worked is very clearly shown in W. A. Maguire, *The Downshire Estates in Ireland, 1801–45* (1972) and W. H. Crawford and B. Trainor, *Aspects of Irish Social History 1750–1800* (PRONI, 1969); there are a number of other similar studies.

administrative centre of local government, the meeting place of the Grand Jury and Quarter Sessions and the venue of the Assize judges on circuit from the central courts in Dublin.

The principal centre of local government in the eighteenth century was the county, and to be governor or Custos Rotulorum of your county was the ultimate recognition of your standing in it. But the county was only the final tier in a series of social and administrative units. Older divisions, baronies and parishes, although they might run across county boundaries, continued to be used in the exercise of local and central government; for instance, the basic revenue, the Hearth Tax, was collected by centrally appointed collectors, who were assigned specific baronies, while the parish, although an ecclesiastical division, was also the grassroots unit of secular administration. All of these units, including the counties, varied considerably in size. Behind the counties and baronies lay older and more variable designations of place and area. The most persistent of these was the townland.

Everybody in Ireland lived (or lives) in a townland. It appears in the title deeds even of town houses, while in rural areas it was the universally accepted definition of place, associated with a man's name during his lifetime and when he died recorded on his tombstone. There are about 62,000 townlands in Ireland. Approximately 5,000 of these begin with the prefix 'Bally' and other common prefixes are 'Kil', 'Lis' and 'Tully'. Frequently the names of townlands reflect a curious mixture of Celtic imagination and English clerical error in recording complex Irish names. Some random examples of townland names are Kilrats, Ballymorran, Tullycore, Roughan, Carron, Shilnavogie, Cushybracken, Lisbeg and Tattynuckle. Furthermore, and adding to the confusion, in the eighteenth century spelling was not standardised as regards either personal or place names.[36]

Townlands are of a wide range of sizes, shapes and descriptions. They vary from as much as 2,000 acres, usually in mountainous regions, to under five acres, and average about 300 acres. Their variable size has frequently baffled the administrator; for instance, the census officials in 1821 listed barony, townland, ploughland and gneeve as existing definitions of areas of land and more than 80 years later the compilers of the 1904 census embarked on the dubious exercise of trying to convert these into logically definable areas, viz. 12 gneeves = 1 ploughland; 4 ploughlands = 1 townland, and 30 townlands = 1 barony. But even this is only a cumulative arrangement of variable measurements. This lack of uniformity probably relates to the importance not of the quantity of land but of its productivity. For instance, Lord George Hill found in nineteenth-century Gweedore, Co. Donegal, that 'The land is never let, sold or devised by the acre, but by "a cow's grass", although a cow's grass, as it varies according to the quality of the land, comprises … a rather indefinite quantity.'

---

[36] People did not spell names consistently – not even father and son (e.g. Cleere/Clere, **0421, 0422**). Pearce/ Peirce/Pierce, Taylor/Taylour and Smith/Smyth were often used interchangeably. The general rule in the biographies is to use the spelling first entered in *CJ Ire.*, while keeping families together.

Nevertheless, for practical purposes all townlands in the area were divided into 'cow's grass' and then subdivided into various smaller divisions referred to as a foot, a half-foot or 'cleet'.[37] Arthur Young, writing in the 1770s, commented that in the parish of Tooavister on the coast of Co. Kerry: 'They have a way of taking land by the ounce ... an ounce is the sixteenth part of a gineve, and is sufficient for a potato garden.'[38] The potato garden was the all-important source of food in a country which depended on subsistence agriculture to feed a rapidly rising population.

Throughout this period Ireland remained overwhelmingly rural, dependent on pastoral and arable agriculture and, mainly along the coast, fishing. Apart from Dublin and Cork most towns were small. Commercial life was restricted and industrialisation had made little impact. Such minerals as there were were poor in quality; for example, coal was found near Kilkenny, at Ballycastle (*see* **0197**) in Co. Antrim and at Coalisland in Co. Tyrone. Iron ore was found at Arigna, near Lough Allen, and great efforts were made to use it commercially, but, although iron ore is a commonly found mineral, commercially viable iron ore is not so common; the ore usually comes mixed with less desirable elements which either make smelting difficult or the final product unusable. Furthermore, the coal used for smelting often adds further chemicals as well as other problems. Ireland had, certainly by the middle of the century, virtually exhausted her supplies of wood for charcoal smelting. MPs were quite prepared to invest in entrepreneurial ventures and anxiously looked for minerals on their estates. In 1793 Peter La Touche (**1207**) made an expensive, and profitless, investment in the Arigna ironworks.

Textiles, the usual manufacture of a pre-industrial society, were, in the case of wool, restricted by English legislation and the mercantalist system. The exception to this was the linen manufacture, which developed in Ulster but failed, despite special encouragement, to develop to the same extent in the rest of Ireland, although many landlords, for example Robert French of Monivea (**0834**),[39] tried to encourage it. For a mixture of honour and patronage MPs sought to belong to the Linen Board, which regulated and encouraged the trade. After the country recovered from the famine of the 1740s there was an increasing abundance of under-utilised labour, but neither the capital to create nor the resources to sustain an industrial development such as that taking place in contemporary Britain. Nor was there the necessary infrastructure. The peasants often paid their rent by goods or labour. Many were still bound by manorial obligations, grinding their corn at the lord's mill, attending his manor court and paying him dues such as an inheritance tax, known as a heriot. Much trade was still done by barter and in certain areas tradesmen's tokens were used instead of specie.

Land, though the basic, was not the only source of wealth. For instance, Joseph Leeson's (**1213**) wealth came from his father, 'a fanatic brewer' who made a fortune.

---

[37] G. Hill, *Facts from Gweedore* (Dublin 1845) pp. 26–7.

[38] Young, op. cit., vol. 1, p. 347.

[39] D. A. Cronin, *A Galway Gentleman in the Age of Improvement: Robert French of Monivea, 1716–79* (Dublin 1995).

His son built Russborough and became Earl of Milltown. Six members of the great banking house of La Touche (**1203–1208**) sat in parliament. Four members of the Alexander family (**0027–0030**), East India and Londonderry merchants, and three members of the Stewart family (**2001, 2006, 2009**), from a similar commercial background, all sat in parliament. But all hastened to turn their wealth into landed property.

Theoretically, all land belonged to the sovereign – this was tangibly reflected in the various dues, such as Crown Rents and Quit Rents, which applied to land redistributed as a result of successive confiscations. Apart from this technicality, there were two commercial ways of acquiring the ownership of land in eighteenth-century Ireland: purchase in 'fee-simple' or a lease in perpetuity, which was a halfway house, part sale, part lease. Marriage and inheritance were by far the most usual methods for the transfer of land regardless of how it had been originally acquired. The Devon Commission reported that the expression 'tenure of land' might be used with reference either to the landlord's ownership or 'to the interest which an occupying tenant has in his farm'.[40] Even before regional variations in the type and quality of the soil or the political potential of the inhabitants imposed their own patterns, landholding in Ireland was complicated, and a variety of leases emerged to cover these complexities.

The upheavals of the sixteenth century had created enormous social problems. The population was small and large areas of the country either had been destabilised or were underdeveloped. Under these circumstances most landlords gave long leases at fixed rents in the expectation, often expressly stated in the leases, that the tenant would provide the buildings, fencing and drainage as well as plant trees. Leases were of three basic types: for the duration of a specified life or lives, for a fixed term of years, or for lives with a concurrent, or an additional, term of years. Often leases were renewable but at an increased rent. From 1704 to 1771 a Catholic could only hold a lease for a maximum term of 31 years. In 1771 this period was extended to 61 years for the reclamation of bogland, and all restrictions were finally lifted in 1778.

Contemporary English leases were usually for five or 21 years, but good landlord–tenant relations brought a *de facto* security of tenure, along with assistance in improving the farm, and for tenants who met their obligations there were other substantial advantages. This system provided the infrastructure necessary for development and gave the landlord better control over his land, allowing him to adjust rents gradually to meet altered land values and inflation. But in Ireland during the latter part of the eighteenth and the early nineteenth centuries, inflation and rapidly rising land values compounded the problems inherent in the traditionally long Irish leases. A major problem with Irish leases was not their brevity but their length. Theoretically a lease could last over 100 years. When a long lease fell in and another was granted, changes were abrupt and rents rose in sharp, steep steps rather than in long gradual absorbable

[40] *Devon Report*, op. cit., p. 12.

increases;[41] consequently rents could vary greatly between neighbours. One way round this was to 'fine it down' or compound for a lower rent by paying a lump sum, but this required the leaseholder to be a man of substance. Not surprisingly, sudden even if anticipated large rent increases caused resentment, particularly when neighbouring unexpired leases remained at a lower level. At the same time, any attempt to shorten the span of leases was construed as a threat to tenure. This could create social unrest, as did any large 'fines' required to reduce the rent demands on the new leases, and communal pressures could be strong in an alienated society. Thus the enduring ramifications of an anachronistic leasing system prevented reform of the system of land tenure in Ireland.

However, while the economic circumstances of individual landlords were as various as the class itself, De Latocnaye was probably correct when he remarked of the resident landlords that: 'nearly all the rich, I am told, spend more than their incomes, and are obliged to resort to ruinous expedients to keep up style.'[42] Family responsibilities, building and politics accounted for much if not all and more of the landlord's income. Some rebuilding was probably essential given the wars of the seventeenth century, but possibly not on the ambitious scale so often attempted. Moreover, encumbrances upon an estate were cumulative, not only as regards debts and mortgages but also with regard to family responsibilities. 'There are some owners of very large estates,' observed Wakefield, 'who have not a shilling income, the whole of their fortune being absorbed either by the payment of a mother's jointure, the fortunes bequeathed to brothers and sisters, or debts contracted by themselves, or left them by their predecessors.'[43]

As the land was the basic source of the landlord's income, his best hope of improving it was to expand his estates and increase their productivity. The Dublin Society, founded in 1731, was the forerunner of many local and national societies aimed at 'improvements' of various kinds. However, these invariably required money and the ability to persuade a conservative tenantry, so poor that they could not afford to make a mistake, to adopt them. Apart from wealth acquired from family sources or through good management, where did the money for land purchases or improvements come from? Prior to the Roman Catholic Relief Act of 1778, Catholics could not hold mortgages on land and there were few Irish nabobs or wealthy heiresses. But a

---

[41] See P. Roebuck, 'Rent movement, proprietorial incomes and agricultural development, 1730–1830', in P. Roebuck (ed.), *Plantation to Partition, Essays in Ulster History in Honour of J. L. McCracken* (Belfast 1981) esp. p. 91; Maguire, op. cit., p. 39; W. Crawford, 'Landlord tenant relations in Ulster', *Irish Economic and Social History*, vol. 2 (1975) esp. table on p.13; R. J. Dickson, *Ulster Emigration to Colonial America* (Belfast 1966); D. Dickson, PhD thesis (Dublin University) appendix, p. 2.

[42] De Latocnaye, op. cit., p. 20.

[43] E. Wakefield, *An Account of Ireland, Statistical and Political* (Dublin, 1812) vol. 1, p. 245; P. Roebuck, 'Landlord indebtedness in Ulster in the seventeenth and eighteenth centuries', in J. M. Goldstrom and L. A. Clarkson (eds), *Irish Population, Economy and Society: Essays in Honour of the Late K. H. Connell* (Oxford 1981) pp. 134–54; D. Hayton, 'Ireland and the English ministers' (unpublished PhD thesis, Oxford University, 1975) pp. 10–11. In 1715 the Earl of Granard had an income of £2,000 p.a. and debts of £12,000 and Lords Bellew, Bellomont, Blayney, Roscommon and Granard were in receipt of government pensions.

considerable amount of money was borrowed in England either directly or indirectly; for example, when a landlord had an estate in England as well as in Ireland he could borrow money against his English property. Irish property was not a particularly popular collateral, although it could be used. In 1779 Lord Lieutenant Buckinghamshire, concerned about the financial drain of interest payments out of Ireland, wrote to the Secretary of State Lord Weymouth to point out that: 'As the gentlemen of Ireland are not more economical than those of England, they have charged their estates with mortgages, the interest of which is, in very few instances, paid here. The interest of the national debt stands in a similar predicament.'[44] Much of this indebtedness had been created by building, politics, extravagant lifestyles and family commitments.

Land was the usual security for loans. Landlords, bankers, merchants and insurance companies all borrowed and lent money on land, while a reputable landlord often held small sums borrowed from local people, who felt that the landlord was safer than the bank. For example, in 1738, a widow Smith wished to lend Judge Ward (**2181**) the sum of £800,[45] and in 1783 Thomas Knox (**1188**), later 1st Earl of Ranfurly, thanking the wealthy linen draper, Thomas Greer of Dungannon, for his offer of a £200 loan, wrote that: 'I will only accept it if I can be sure of paying it back and could only do this if you will increase the amount to be lent to me to £1,000, which would cover all my requirements. Let me know if I can have £600 more in February.'[46] In 1810 the 3rd Marquess of Downshire borrowed from the Belfast merchants Hugh Crawford, John Robinson and Robert Linn, £13,000, £10,000 and £7,000 respectively and a further £10,000 from the Coleraine merchant, Robert Kyle.[47]

The usury laws against excessive interest were in force throughout the eighteenth century and to some extent curbed the excesses of market supply and demand. At the beginning of the century interest had been as high as 10 per cent, the official ceiling for lending decreed in 1635 by 10 Chas, 1 c. 22. In 1704 the maximum chargeable interest was reduced, by 2 Anne, c. 16, to 8 per cent, and in 1722, 8 Geo. I, c. 7, further reduced the permissible rate to 7 per cent. The final adjustment for the century was made by 5 Geo. II, c. 7, which decreed that all arrangements that involved an interest charge in excess of 6 per cent 'shall be utterly void'. The official rate in England was 5 per cent but scarcity and the exchange rates militated against the Irish pound, as Irish currency was devalued against the pound sterling. Ireland did not have a mint, and an almost constant shortage of specie ensured that all sorts of coins were in circulation. They were valued in accordance with their presumed metal content and traders carried small pocket scales to value by weight the coins of assorted currencies

[44] PRO SP63/465, 28 May 1779 ff. 21 *et seq.*
[45] PRONI D/2092/1/5/36, 8 May 1738.
[46] PRONI D/1044/677A.
[47] Maguire, op. cit., p. 101, see also p. 95.

that they were offered. Naturally this system retarded economic development and encouraged fraud and forgery. There was a similar problem with standardising weights and measures, and 'official' weights and measures were placed in major market towns in an attempt to benefit trade by standardising them throughout the country.

As a class the Irish landlords were not good financial managers, and debts tended to get piled up against mortgages on their estates. As early as 1761 the Irish House of Commons passed by a majority of 12 – albeit in a thin House on the last day of the parliamentary session – the heads of a bill to allow Catholics to invest money in mortgages on land. Subsequently, the bill was rejected by the British Privy Council, who considered that it might endanger Protestant control over land with consequent political implications. Nevertheless, pressure to allow Catholics to invest capital in land continued. In 1771 concessions in the length of lease and local taxes were made for reclamation of bogs, an action indicative of the growing shortage of land as well as shortage of capital for improvements. But the administration was still reluctant to allow direct investment in mortgages for, as Lord Townshend pointed out, 'It would give the Popish creditors such a control over those who are in debt as may in particular times operate very strongly'.[48] Another unsuccessful attempt, sponsored by Thomas Maunsell (1371), was made in February 1774. Finally in 1778 Luke Gardiner (0842) successfully introduced a bill allowing Catholics to purchase and hold land on the same *de facto* terms as Protestants.

Indebtedness was cumulative, often carried from generation to generation. Encumbered estates were not easily disposed of and, as selling the estate was the final admission of bankruptcy, it was usually desirable to sell the whole estate as speedily as possible to met the escalating demands of creditors. Thus by 1844 the Devon Commissioners found that 'It now rarely happens that land in Ireland is brought into the market for sales in lots of a moderate or small size' and they attributed this to the fact that 'estates are so generally encumbered by family settlements or otherwise' that the delay and difficulty of dividing them tended to outweigh the higher price which would almost certainly be obtained from smaller lots. This prevented the rising commercial class from acquiring an attachment to the land and diverting their resources into its development, for while land was a 'store of value' it was also an asset which required a 'cash flow' for its maintenance and to utilise its potential.[49] Hence the liquidity of a landlord's financial position, as well as his personality, ability and ambitions, bore a direct relation to the management of and the income from his estate. Shortage of capital for emergencies and improvements was always a major problem, both for the landlord at the top and the peasant who actually worked the land at the bottom of the agrarian pyramid. By the end of the eighteenth century the

---

[48] W. E. H. Lecky, *History of Ireland in the Eighteenth Century* (London 1892) vol. 2, p. 193.
[49] PRONI T2541/1A1/2/34, Nisbitt to Abercorn 1750: 'The purchase of lands are greatly advanced in this country particularly small estates, as there are so many people of middle rank has got money.'

foundations of the road to the Encumbered Estates Act (1849) had already been laid.[50]

An eighteenth-century estate was in many ways a family concern. Although primogeniture ensured that the estate went to the eldest male child, thereby keeping the core of the family's wealth intact, other members of the family also had a claim to provision from it. In default of surviving sons, daughters could inherit the family property, but not, unless there was a special remainder, any of their father's titles. Thus it was possible for the family fortune to become separated from the family title, leaving the possessor of the title inadequate resources to sustain his dignity. For instance, the 5th Viscount Allen found himself in this position as the 'family estate went between Lady Maine (Mayne) and Lady Carysfort, daughters to a former Lord Allen'.[51] While this was a very clear-cut example, the failure of a direct male heir inevitably produced changes, especially when an estate was variously divided among a number of co-heiresses. The Rochfort–Loftus case had such an origin.

A landlord had a duty to provide for his wife, the widows of his predecessors, his brothers and sisters and his own children. This was done by settling parts of the estate in the hands of trustees so that the income would provide jointures, or annuities, for the widows, suitable dowries for the daughters and portions for the younger sons. Once made, these settlements could only be altered by act of parliament. The further expense and the publicity which this involved made it an expedient of last resort. It has been estimated that during the eighteenth century half of the land of England was held under strict settlement.[52] The available evidence indicates that the situation in Ireland was more extreme, particularly as less support could be drawn from sources other than the land. The effect of these settlements was to make the landlord a tenant for life of the family estate and their intention was to ensure that it would pass intact to his eldest son, upon whose coming of age and marriage the various settlements would be rearranged to the same end for the next generation.

Estates could not be entailed for the following generation while the heir was a minor, but on his majority he, as the interested party in the last entail, could agree to alterations being made before the estate was again tied up. Further adjustments were made when he married or remarried to absorb the dowry, ensure the jointure of the bride and make provision for any children apart from the heir that might be born to the marriage. About 1780 the heir of the French family of Co. Roscommon came of age and his father requested his permission to sell for £12,780 his Sligo estate, which then had a rent roll of £710 p.a. The son refused consent and in 1809 was receiving

---

[50] See F. S. L. Lyons, *Ireland since the Famine* (London 1971) pp. 14–15, 35; also L. M. Cullen, *An Economic History of Ireland since 1660* (1972) p. 138; J. S. Donnelly Jr, *Landlord and Tenant in Nineteenth-Century Ireland* (Dublin 1973) pp. 49–50.

[51] *Proceedings of the Royal Irish Academy*, 56 C 3, p. 281.

[52] Maguire, op. cit., pp. 84–5; H. J. Habakkuk, 'Marriage settlements in the eighteenth century', *Transactions of the Royal Historical Society*, vol. 30 (1950). See also G. E. Mingay, *English Landed Society in the Eighteenth Century* (London 1963) pp. 32–6.

from it an income of £2,000 p.a. – as a result of a combination of changes in leasing policy and the rapid escalation of rents in the intervening period.[53]

Marriage was usually considered the best opportunity to improve the family fortune. Some attention was usually given to the personal aspects of the arrangement, as affection and respect were normally considered desirable. The marriage settlement legalised the agreement made between the couple, or more often their families. Its terms usually reflected the addition made to the fortune of the bridegroom's family by the dowry of the bride. Traditionally, the mother's dowry, or an equivalent, was earmarked to provide dowries or fortunes for the younger children of the marriage and her jointure was usually assessed as an annual allowance amounting to 10 per cent of her dowry,[54] but it could be more. These complex arrangements were often the cause of family dissensions, as in the case of the settlements made in 1684 on the marriage of Sir Nicholas Browne, 2nd Viscount Kenmare, with his cousin, Helen Browne, which resulted in law suits spanning nearly a century.[55] The chances of the couples achieving matrimonial happiness do not appear to have been markedly less than those whose marriages were established on other expectations. Lady Caroline Fox wrote to her sister, Lady Kildare: 'I own I pity those most who are parted after a long time of tenderness, friendship and affection; it is being divided from oneself, one may say.'[56] Couples conformed to the mores of their class and, particularly when both were young at the time of the marriage, they very often grew together, and there are some touching memorials to long and affectionate unions.[57]

Marriages were essentially long- or short-term lotteries with potential credits as well as debits. This was clearly shown in the marriage fortunes of the Hill family. In 1747, Wills Hill, 1st Earl of Hillsborough and 1st Marquess of Downshire, married Lady Margaretta FitzGerald, the daughter of the 19th Earl of Kildare. She brought her husband the unusually large dowry of £20,000 and her marriage settlement arranged for the conventional jointure of 10 per cent – £2,000 p.a. – with a portion of £10,000 each for any younger children. Lady Hillsborough died in 1766 leaving, besides a son and heir, two daughters whose fortunes, as stipulated in the marriage settlement, exactly matched their mother's dowry.[58] Two years later Lord Hillsborough remarried. His second wife, Mary, *suo iure* Baroness Stawell, died in 1780, again obviating the need for a jointure as she predeceased him by 13 years and there were no children by this marriage. In the same year Lord Hillsborough had a windfall. On

---

[53] Wakefield, op. cit., vol. 1, p. 275.

[54] Maguire, op. cit., pp. 84–5.

[55] *IMC Kenmare*, pp. 41–2.

[56] *IMC Leinster*, vol. 1, p. 195.

[57] The Lennox sisters (daughters of the 2nd Duke of Richmond), Caroline, Emily, Louisa and Sarah married at 21, 15, 15 and 17 years respectively. Their correspondence (*IMC Leinster*, 3 vols) gives an intimate portrait of the everyday life of an aristocratic family. In St Patrick's Cathedral there is a memorial to Elizabeth, Viscountess Doneraile, daughter of Joseph Deane (**0603**) and wife of Hayes St Leger, 4th Viscount Doneraile (**1855**), recording a happy if childless marriage.

[58] Maguire, op. cit., p. 86.

the death of Charles Dunbar he inherited the Blessington estate and parliamentary borough, which had belonged to his great-great grandfather, the seventeenth-century Primate Michael Boyle. Despite the fact that he did better on the marriage market than most of his contemporaries, when Lord Hillsborough, then 1st Marquess of Downshire, died in 1793 his debts amounted to £69,660.[59]

The 2nd Marquess of Downshire (**1016**) married in 1786. His bride, Mary Sandys, was one of the richest heiresses in Great Britain or Ireland. She brought her husband the Edenderry estate in King's County, the Dundrum estate in Co. Down, Easthampstead Park in Berkshire, a large sum of money invested in the funds and further expectations. These splendid additions to the family property were reflected in two settlements, one on the marriage in 1786 and another three years later, which fixed Lady Hillsborough's jointure at £5,000 p.a. and the provision for the younger children at £20,000 for one child, £15,000 each for two children and £40,000 to be divided between three or more children. The 2nd Marquess also had a windfall. He was the reluctant, but the largest, single beneficiary from the compensation given for the disfranchisement of parliamentary boroughs by the Act of Union, receiving £55,486 12s 9d (£52,500 plus £2,986 12s 9d interest). Nevertheless, when he died, aged 48, in 1801 the family debt had increased to £325,212 and of this £33,837 was owed to tradesmen and other casual debtors. Subsequently the total debt was reduced to the still enormous sum of £269,726 by the £55,486 compensation which was paid after his death.[60]

Widely scattered estates immediately introduce the question of absenteeism, which was endemic from the way Irish estates were acquired. No landlord could live on all his estates at once. Nevertheless, personal supervision or at least a frequent presence was desirable. Although it was obviously important for the economy of the locality if he spent his money and kept up his residence there, and even better if he occupied it, perhaps the real question was whether he spent his money in Ireland or drained it abroad. This was a problem throughout the century, but it became a much greater one after the Union.

If the Downshire family were lucky in marriage and the size of their families, the same could not be said of the ducal house of Leinster, who provided an illustration of the extent to which family commitments could encumber an estate.[61] The story, though complicated, is instructive. In 1747 James, 20th Earl of Kildare (**0734**), married Lady Emily Lennox, daughter of Charles, 2nd Duke of Richmond and a great-granddaughter of Charles II. It was rumoured that Lady Emily, who was not only well connected but one of the greatest beauties of the century, brought her husband 'not a shilling'.[62] This was unlikely, as the traditional dowry of a ducal daughter appears to have been £10,000

[59] Ibid., p. 90.
[60] Ibid., p. 91.
[61] A. P. W. Malcomson, *The Pursuit of the Heiress: Aristocratic Marriage in Ireland 1750–1820* (UHF, 1982) pp. 4, 9–11 gives considerable detail about a number of marriage arrangements.
[62] Ibid., p.10.

and in his will her father made similar dowries for his younger unmarried daughters a first charge on his estate – a commitment which the 3rd Duke punctiliously acknowledged in 1758, when his sister, Lady Louisa, married the wealthy Thomas Conolly (**0459**), writing that: 'As Mr Conolly will expect to have Lady Louisa's fortune on the day of the marriage, I must have it ready.'[63] A further reason to suspect that Lady Emily had a similar dowry to her sisters is the large building programme which the Earl of Kildare inherited from his father and which he continued; both Carton and Kildare (Leinster) House were built at this time. Moreover, Lord Kildare's sister, Lady Margaretta FitzGerald, married Lord Hillsborough in the same year, 1747, and she brought her husband the large dowry of £20,000. Possibly the rumour arose because an English viscounty was added to the FitzGerald titles at this time, most probably as a reward for Lord Kildare's support during the recent Stuart rebellion,[64] but gossip preferred the story that George II had dowered his god-daughter with English title. Subsequently, the personal qualities and family connections of the bride made their contribution to the much desired marquessate and dukedom to which Lord Kildare was successively elevated in 1761 and 1766.

Lady Emily's marriage settlement provided for the very large jointure of £3,000, later increased to £4,000, which eventually became a charge on the Leinster estates for over 40 years. Furthermore the 1st Duke and Duchess had 23 children, six of whom died in infancy, leaving provision to be made from the estate for the remainder, ten of whom reached their majority. When the duke died in 1773 the dowager duchess had the guardianship of their younger children[65] and she was entitled to an allowance of £400 for the education and maintenance of each of them. This appears to have been a customary allowance for minors, as it was the amount paid to Lady Holland and the duchess, then Lady Kildare, for the maintenance of their younger sisters following the death of their parents. In 1774 the dowager duchess remarried and as her new husband (**1571**), who had been tutor to her sons, was not a wealthy man, provision had to be found for him and the two daughters of this marriage – in the event only one survived. In 1776 Lady Louisa Conolly wrote to warn her sister that their brother, the Duke of Richmond, was going to scold her for her extravagance 'as he has no notion of your not saving money for them'.[66]

William (**0745**), 2nd Duke of Leinster, upon whom these financial responsibilities descended was a well-meaning but not over-intelligent country gentleman, highly conscious of his position as premier peer of Ireland and, at that time, its only duke.[67] He inherited a financial position that would have defeated better managers than himself. He had to find jointures not only for his mother but also for his grandmother,

[63] Ibid., p. 11. The duke had to sell land to raise the money for his sister's dowry. £10,000 was also the dowry for each of the two daughters of the 3rd Duke of Devonshire on their marriages to Lord Duncannon and John Ponsonby (Chatsworth MSS).

[64] *IMC Leinster*, vol. 1, p. ix: he offered to raise and equip a regiment at his own expense.

[65] *IMC Leinster*, vol. 2, pp. 133–4; Guinness and Ryan, op. cit., p. 186; Malcomson, op. cit., p. 4.

[66] *IMC Leinster*, vol. 3, p. 195.

[67] E. M. Johnston, *Ireland in the Eighteenth Century* (Dublin 1974) pp. 262–3.

the Dowager Lady Kildare,[68] who died in 1780, having survived her husband for 36 years. At the same time portions, dowries and maintenance had also to be provided for his younger siblings. He married a gentle and rather colourless heiress, Emilia St George,[69] and they proceeded to have a large family – eight daughters and five sons. Not surprisingly, the 2nd Duke worried about money all his life: 'He is mighty queer about money,' observed his wealthy and childless aunt, Lady Louisa Conolly, 'and his distress about it is I am sure the foundation of all that he does.' On another occasion she wrote to her sister, the Duchess Emily, 'I hope you get your money remitted but William, I believe, is as ill off as his neighbours, and it's really wonderful how people go on.'[70]

Considerations of ambition and snobbery occasionally compounded the financial complexities of these arrangements. In 1777 John, Lord Crosbie (**0534**) married the eldest daughter of Lord George Sackville (Germain) (**1835**) and Lord George stipulated that 'as is usual' the bride's dowry, in this case £10,000, or an equivalent should be used to make provision for any younger children of the marriage. This arrangement did not prevent the bridegroom's family from making use of the money in the interim, and Lord Crosbie remarked to his father that it would provide his sisters with dowries equal to that of Lady Anne Talbot! Emulation was not the only peripheral consideration as Lord Crosbie, in persuading his father to agree to the particularly large jointure of £2,000, 20 per cent instead of 10 per cent of the bride's dowry, wrote: 'Don't you think that my marrying in this manner will mortify the narrow envious people of Kerry?' By 1784 John Crosbie, now Earl of Glandore, was in such severe financial straits that he petitioned the Irish House of Lords to allow him to bring in a private bill in order to break the entail and to enable him to sell part of his estate in order to satisfy his creditors. However, in 1785 he was at least partly rescued as Lady Glandore's father died and left her £3,000 p.a.[71]

Usually marriages observed the strict hierarchical basis of eighteenth-century property-oriented society. Exceptions might, however, be made in cases of well-connected poverty and respectable, if not so well-connected, wealth. For instance, Mary Granville, Mrs Pendavers, and subsequently Mrs Delany, had reluctantly consented to her family's wishes over her first marriage, which balanced her connections against her poverty and her bridegroom's wealth. Visiting Dublin in March 1731/2 Mrs Pendavers wrote to her sister that: 'Miss Burton ... is since married to Lord Netterville, – a fop and a fool, but a lord with a tolerable estate, who always wears fine clothes; she had £9,000 for her fortune, with a pretty person much in vogue'; nearly 30 years later she commented on the marriage in 1759 of the parents of the future Marquess Wellesley and Duke of Wellington, remarking that: 'She [Ann Hill] has

---

[68] *IMC Leinster*, vol. 1, p. 184. His father, the 1st Duke, had also to make provision for his mother and his grandmother, who died in 1758 aged 93.
[69] Ibid., vol. 2, pp. 162–3.
[70] Ibid., vol. 3, pp. 182, 310.
[71] *IHS*, vol. 15, pp. 39–40, D. Large, 'Wealth of greater Irish landowners'; Malcomson, op. cit., pp. 7, 9, 11–12.

£6,000 and the family estate settled on her in case her brother has no children; Lord Mornington settles £1,400 jointure on her with £500 a year pin money; his estate is now £8,000 and will be £10,000 in two or three years more.'[72] These arrangements were the gossip of a small society in which everybody either knew, or knew of, everybody else. In 1794 a former Lord Lieutenant, the Earl of Carlisle, warned a future one, Earl Fitzwilliam, that 'The whole town of Dublin is one large family or company under one roof and everything is known and made the subject of conversation immediately after it happens.'[73]

It was a *cause célèbre* when Emily, Dowager Duchess of Leinster, who was in effect the leader of Irish society, decided to marry her children's tutor, an obscure and penniless Scot called William Ogilvie, for this marriage had none of the conventional ameliorating features. Gossip abounded, much of it vicious, but the ducal houses of Leinster in Ireland and Richmond in England liked Ogilvie and closed ranks behind the Duchess, although her brother, who had not at the time of the engagement met Mr Ogilvie, expressed some concern, considering that 'In the common order of things any inequality between husband and wife generally tended to make them less happy.' However, as head of the family he decreed that they should keep any reservations 'to ourselves', and Lady Louisa Conolly remarked to her sister the duchess that 'You hurt your rank in the world, in my opinion that is all you do; and if you gain happiness by it, I am sure you make a good exchange.' Another sister, the shortly to be divorced Lady Sarah (Bunbury), thought that she should 'be married at Goodwood at your brother's house *dans la face de l'univers*, and not smuggle the marriage abroad, as if you were ashamed of it'.[74] The dowager duchess was herself more cautious. She was married at Toulouse and for some years afterwards she and her husband lived with their own and the younger FitzGerald children in the chateau at Aubigny which Louis XIV had given to her great-grandmother, Louise de la Keroualle, the French mistress of Charles II. The Duchess, like her sister, Lady Holland, and her brother, the 3rd Duke of Richmond, was liberal and tolerant in outlook. She was a dominant influence on her children and particularly on her most famous son, Lord Edward FitzGerald (**0730**).

One of the reasons why marriage settlements had to be made so carefully, and only finalised almost immediately before the marriage took place, was to protect the bride and her dependants from an unscrupulous husband. On her marriage a woman's property, unless it had been legally safeguarded, became her husband's, whose reciprocal duty was to provide for her and their children. The marriage settlement made this contractually binding. Under these circumstances, elopements were a serious problem for the bride and for her family, particularly if she was an heiress. They became even

[72] Lady Llandover (ed.), *The Autobiography and Correspondence of Mary Granville, Mrs Delany* (London 1861–2) ser. 1, vol. 1, p. 341; ser. 1, vol. 3, pp. 536, 539.
[73] Quoted in R. B. McDowell, *Ireland in the Age of Imperialism and Revolution 1760–1801* (Oxford 1979) p. 28.
[74] *IMC Leinster*, v. II pp. 127, 136–7; v. III p. 94.

more so when the penurious and unscrupulous as well as the irresponsible among the gentry and squireens sometimes formed clubs to recover their fortunes through abducting and forcibly marrying heiresses. Of one such club it is recorded that:

> They had emissaries and confederates in every house, who communicated information of particulars – the extent of a girl's fortune … domestic arrangements and movements. When a girl was thus pointed out the members drew lots, but more generally tossed up for her, and immediate measures were taken to secure her for the fortunate man by all the rest. No class of society was exempt from their visits.[75]

These marriages were usually performed by canonically ordained but renegade priests known as couple-beggars. In 1745 the Irish parliament, declaring that previous laws 'have been found wholly ineffectual', passed an act, 19 Geo. II, c. 13, making marriages between Protestants, or Protestants and Catholics, performed by a Catholic priest null and void and reiterated that the celebrant of such marriages was committing a capital offence; indeed, few years earlier, on 29 November 1740, Edward Sewell, a couple-beggar, had been hanged.[76] Nevertheless, irregular marriages were sufficiently common to necessitate safeguarding against the social disruption which would occur if already existing unions were declared illegal. Thus a parallel act was passed to safeguard the civil consequences of such irregular unions.

At the root of the whole problem of marriages were questions of property and inheritance, which made the legitimacy of the children of particular importance. As the real problem lay with the financial necessities of the abductors and sometimes with the youth and inexperience of the heiress, the custom continued regardless of any legislative attempts to prevent it. Since 1634, parliament had repeatedly, and ineffectually, legislated against this well-established custom. Finally, in 1780, the abduction of the Kennedy sisters, two co-heiresses aged 14 and 15, brought matters to a head and indicated changing social mores, for the abductors were tried at the Kilkenny Assizes, found guilty and executed. The case was tried before John Scott (**1891**), then the Attorney General and an assize judge, who declared that if this case was not treated with the full rigour of the law no similar family could exist in tranquillity and no heiress would be safe.[77]

The decision was not popular, as the hard-riding and hard-drinking squireens, who were the main participants in this activity, enjoyed the popular admiration of the anti-establishment peasantry. This was seen in the McNaughton case. The story, which has gone down in Ulster tradition as that of 'half-hung McNaughton', began with the

[75] *CJ Ire.* vol. 3 (1719) Petition of Rebecca White; Delany Correspondence, op. cit., vol. 2, pp. 348–53; see also C. Maxwell, *Town and Country in Ireland under the Georges* (London 1940) p. 22.

[76] S. Connolly, *Priests and People in Pre-Famine Ireland 1780–1845* (Dublin 1982) p. 200 *et seq.*; J. Brady, *Catholics and Catholicism in the Eighteenth-Century Press* (Maynooth 1965) p. 62.

[77] Lecky, op. cit., vol. 1, pp. 371 *et seq.* esp. pp. 377–8 n.; Froude, op. cit., vol. 1, pp. 465 *et seq. Eighteenth-century Ireland* vol. 9 (1994) pp. 7–43, J. Kelly, 'The abduction of women of fortune in eighteenth-century Ireland'.

forcible abduction of an heiress. It ended with the trial and conviction of her abductor for her murder, as, during the abduction, the 15-year-old heiress was killed while protecting her father, Andrew Knox (**1175**). McNaughton, the abductor, was condemned, but at his execution the rope broke, whereupon, refusing the crowd's assistance to aid his escape, he declared that he would not be known as a 'half-hanged man' and the execution was duly completed.[78]

Divorce in the eighteenth century was rare and could only be achieved by a private act of parliament. Marriages were too complex to be easily dissolved. Apart from any ecclesiastical considerations, the social stigma was considerable, for divorce attacked the foundations of a society based on hereditary right and property. The Duchess of Leinster's sister, Lady Sarah Lennox (Bunbury) was divorced in 1776, some seven years after she had left her husband, and her sister Lady Louisa Conolly told the Duchess with some relief that the bill's passage through the British parliament had coincided with the notorious bigamy trial of Elizabeth Chudleigh, Countess of Bristol *alias* Duchess of Kingston, writing that: 'This talk is lucky for us at this time as it drowns Sarah's bill of divorce which is to have the second reading tomorrow. I feel very awkward being in town while it is going on.'[79] This story had a happy ending, as after 12 years in seclusion living 'a life of penitence' she married, in 1781, Col. George Napier. Their marriage was a happy one and of their eight children the three eldest sons were generals: Sir Charles, Sir George and Sir William Napier.

Heiresses with large fortunes were comparatively rare in Ireland and the rich City of London heiress portrayed by Hogarth virtually unknown. It has been estimated that of the 151 marriages contracted by Irish peers alive in 1783, only six were definitely and a further eight possibly in this category.[80] In 1697, Lady Peyton despaired of her son Kean O'Hara finding a good wife in Sligo – 'that is to say a wife with money'[81] – although she voiced a generally held opinion when she remarked that such 'parties' were numerous in England. The desirability of marrying for money was quite openly admitted throughout the social spectrum: for example, the *Limerick Chronicle* of 17 October 1768 reported the marriage of the Rev. John Madress, Chancellor of the diocese of Ross, to Miss Baldwin, 'a most amiable lady with a large fortune'. In 1738 John, 5th Earl of Cork and Orrery, announced his marriage to a friend, declaring that 'I am the happiest man in the world! Yesterday Miss Hamilton gave me with the usual ceremony, her hand and heart. A heart filled with love and a hand with money. What a turn of fortune is here.'[82] Margaret Hamilton was one of the great Irish heiresses of the century and her fortune included the Caledon estate which her son sold, in 1776, to James Alexander (**0029**), later 1st Earl of Caledon.

---

[78] H. Boylan, *A Dictionary of Irish Biography* (3rd edn, Dublin 1998) p. 257. See Andrew Knox (**1175**), MP for Co. Donegal 1743–68.
[79] *IMC Leinster*, op. cit., vol. 3, p. 198
[80] Large, op. cit.
[81] PRONI, O'Hara MSS T2812/4/205, 263.
[82] E. C. Boyle (ed.), *The Orrery Papers* (2 vols, London 1902) vol. 1, p. 240.

Two of the most famous land sales in the eighteenth century were of Ulster estates: the Colvill estate at Newtown(ards), Co. Down, in 1744 and, in 1776, the Hamilton–Orrery estate at Caledon, Co. Tyrone. Coincidentally, both estates were bought by merchants with Londonderry connections, from capital accrued in the East India trade. The Colvill estate belonged to Robert Colvill (**0453**), the step-son of Brabazon Ponsonby (**1696**), 1st Earl of Bessborough, who administered the estate and the parliamentary borough of Newtown both during Colvill's minority and in his wild, unbalanced majority. In 1721 Colvill made a will in favour of his infant half-brother, John Ponsonby (**1702**), but in 1744, under the influence of his mistress, he sold the estate for £42,000 to Alexander Stewart, a rich, ambitious Belfast flax-merchant. Stewart had inherited an estate in Co. Donegal from his older brother, but the bulk of his wealth came from his wife and cousin, Mary Cowan, daughter and heiress of both her father, Alderman Cowan of Londonderry, and more importantly her brother, Sir Robert Cowan, a former Governor of Bombay. Her fortune was estimated at nearly £100,000.[83]

This sale was probably a considerable blow to Colvill's ambitious stepfather, who in 1743 had negotiated the marriage of his son, John, with Lady Elizabeth Cavendish, daughter of the Lord Lieutenant, the 3rd Duke of Devonshire – four years earlier he had married his eldest son to her sister. When the marriage was arranged, the Newtown(ards) estate would undoubtedly have formed part of John Ponsonby's expectations. The sale was the prelude to a series of bitter and expensive legal battles between the Stewarts and the Ponsonbys over the control of the parliamentary borough of Newtown(ards), which the Ponsonbys retained, although the town was built on Stewart's estate.[84]

One of the largest estate auctions in the century, that of the Caledon estate of the Earl of Cork and Orrery, was advertised to take place at the Globe Coffee House, Essex Street, Dublin on 1 September 1775 between 12 noon and 2 p.m. The purchaser was James Alexander (**0029**), a Londonderry merchant who was that most desired of purchasers, an East India 'nabob'. The sale was finalised on 18 January 1776, when the estate of 8,810 statute acres in counties Tyrone and Armagh changed hands for £96,500 with a down payment of £20,000 – a purchase price of nearly 30 years the value of the rental, estimated at £3,250 gross and £3,115 net.[85] Land prices were high in 1775 but the 30-year valuation took into account the fact that the estate was let at probably about 50 per cent of its potential rental and as the leases fell in a considerable increase in the rental could be expected. Furthermore, the estate was in the north and it had political value accruing from its mainly protestant tenantry, who could be given leases for lives and thereby enfranchised. Alexander's political position was further

[83] A. P. W. Malcomson, 'The Newtown Act of 1748: Revision and Reconstruction', *IHS*, vol. 18 (1973) pp. 317–18.

[84] *HMC Charlemont I*, p. iii. See also Malcomson, op. cit., pp. 313–44; A. P. W. Malcomson, 'The Politics of "Natural Right": the Abercorn Family and Strabane Borough', *Historical Studies*, vol. 10, pp. 43–90.

[85] PRONI D2433/32/2, D2433/1/100.

strengthened – he sat in parliament for the prestigious seat of Londonderry – by his subsequent purchase of Banagher borough, speedily exchanged for Newtown(ards). By 1790 he had a peerage and by 1800 an earldom. James Alexander was the ancestor of the Earls of Caledon and the Earls Alexander of Tunis and Errigal; Alexander Stewart's son Robert (**2008**) was the 1st Marquess of Londonderry and his son, Alexander's grandson, was Lord Castlereagh (**2009**).

Money from Irish commercial ventures was also reflected in land transfers. The career of Nicholas Lawless (**1209**), 1st Baron Cloncurry, illustrates the centrality of the possession of land to social advancement. His father had been a successful Dublin clothier and Nicholas Lawless was 'well versed in the commerce of money'. In 1775 he purchased the 3,683 acre estate of Abington, Co. Limerick for £26,000. The value of an estate was usually calculated as a multiple of so many years' rental, thus, as the gross rental of the Abington estate was £982, he paid approximately 26 $^{1}/_{2}$ years for its purchase. However, the rental was subject to certain encumbrances, such as a jointure, or widow's annuity, of £300 p.a. and a quit rent, a due paid to the Crown, of £30 p.a. Estimating his purchase on its net rather than its gross return, he had paid nearly 40 years' purchase. Not surprisingly he considered it 'a dear bargain', particularly as he was obtaining 4 per cent from government debentures and 5 per cent from other investments.

However, rents rose in the years following the American war and by 1793 Nicholas Lawless, now Lord Cloncurry, had an unencumbered income from Abington of £1,104. In addition he could calculate with satisfaction his 'other valuables, my peerage worth £10,000 [*sic*], my house in Merrion Square worth £4,000, and my plate and books which cost more than £2,000'. He had been made a baronet in 1776 and for the next two parliaments he purchased his return for the borough of Lifford from the Earl of Erne.[86] During this time he earnestly pursued a peerage, which he ultimately obtained in 1790. Success of this kind reinforced a widespread faith in the value of land and parliamentary influence and Lawless's faith was almost certainly echoed by two other newly arrived peers, Lords Londonderry and Caledon. Although the Irish honours bubble collapsed in the years following the Union, the land boom continued, with temporary fluctuations, until after the Napoleonic wars, when land prices collapsed in the severe post-war recession.

Both James Alexander and Sir Nicholas Lawless purchased in 1776 when the land market was high. Subsequently the American war and the economy slump depressed the price of land. There were, of course, regional exceptions to this generalisation, particularly in Munster where the provision trade flourished in wartime. At this time Richard Hare, a leading Cork provision merchant, bought a major part of the estate

---

[86] Large, op. cit., pp. 29–30; E. M. Johnston (ed.), 'Members of the Irish Parliament, 1784 7', *Proceedings of the Royal Irish Academy*, 71 C 5, pp. 162, 190, 213; Cloncurry, *Personal Recollections of the Life and Times of Valentine, Lord Cloncurry* (Dublin 1850) pp. 2, 5–6. Lawless later bought Mornington House in Merrion Street, which he rented to Lord Castlereagh at the time of the Union.

of the 3rd Earl of Kerry for £49,000.[87] His son William (**0966**) was created Earl of Listowel. But in Ulster the war adversely affected the linen trade, and in 1779, when the Edmondstone estate in Co. Antrim came on the market, the asking price was 25 years and Edmondstone remarked that this was 'very considerably less than I would have sold it for 3 years ago'. In the end he accepted £24,625 sterling instead of the £26,250 sterling which he had originally asked, and this he computed at 'under 21 years purchase'. He requested payment in 3 per cent government securities which he was willing to accept 'as at 60', thereby securing a 5 per cent return on his capital without the problems and risks of managing an Irish estate.[88]

Although Edmondstone did not obtain the price he had anticipated, he did not make an unduly unfavourable sale, as Arthur Young reported that at this time land sold at 20 years in Limerick, Clare, Sligo and Tipperary and at 21 or 22 years' purchase in Mayo and Kilkenny. It might be argued that an Ulster estate had advantages, and when Arthur Annesley sold his Co. Down estate a few years later, in 1784, he sold at 18 years' purchase and his neighbour, Lord Hillsborough, considered this to be the current price for 'most eligible lands' in 'various parts of this kingdom'.[89]

Edmondstone wanted a safe trouble-free investment, but other sales were forced through the lack of basic capital for the improvements essential to make the estate viable, bad management and, in some cases, sheer profligacy. One exasperated agent remarked that 'the general dissipation of our nobility and gentry has qualified them much better to sell estates than to purchase.' One of the more spectacular profligates was the Earl of Barrymore who, having come of age in 1789, had by 1791 mortgaged his estates to the London banker Thomas Hammersley. Four years later he died having, in the brief period of his majority, through horses, gaming, conviviality and various other diversions, amassed debts to the amount of £150,000.[90]

From about the middle of the century, there was a demand for small estates from the rising middle-class protestant merchants. Pressure had also been building up from wealthy Catholic merchants and the first of the major Catholic Relief Acts, the 1778 act, allowed the purchase of 999-year leases or virtual fee simple. Recognising this phenomenon, Arthur Annesley's agent vainly tried to persuade Annesley to sell in small blocks rather than as a whole on the grounds that nabobs, or wealthy cash purchasers were rare, but there were an increasing number of moderately wealthy businessmen, particularly in that linen-dominated area, who were anxious to become landed gentry and were increasingly frustrated by their inability to purchase small estates.[91] As early as 1750 Nathaniel Nisbitt had told Lord Abercorn that in the Co. Donegal hinterland of Londonderry 'The purchase of lands are greatly advanced in

---

[87] Dickson, PhD thesis (Dublin University) pp. 80–89, the sale was finalised in 1783; see also J. G. Alger, 'An Irish absentee and his tenants', *EHR* (1895).
[88] PRONI D2651/2/1,2, 11 & 25 July 1779.
[89] Young, op. cit., vol. 1, pp. 78, 237, 259, 295, 288, 391; Crawford, *Ir. Agent*, op. cit., p. 56.
[90] See Dickson, PhD thesis (Dublin University) pp. 80–89.
[91] Crawford, *Ir. Agent*, op. cit., p. 57.

this country particularly small estates, as there are so many people of middle rank has got money.'[92] This indication of a growing middle class was an important feature of Irish society in the second half of the eighteenth century and land purchases reflected the prosperity accruing from Ireland's major commercial enterprises, linen in Ulster and provisions in Munster, while land around Dublin, with the metropole's multiplicity of variously sized businesses, was always at a premium.

Throughout the eighteenth century, many landlords were anxious to purchase small acreages to round off their estates, and details of such purchases are to be found in estate papers. For example, in 1745 John Colhoun purchased for Lord Abercorn a small parcel of about 75 acres let at £22 p.a. with 15 years on the leases. He paid £535 or slightly over 24 years' purchase. Sixty-five years later in 1810, Lord Downshire's agent purchased the 221 acre estate of North Tyrella, near Downpatrick, for £9,310 or 24^{1}/2 years' purchase of a rent-roll of £381, although this purchase was encumbered with an annuity of £150 for the lifetime of a 73-year-old lady.[93] These small sales frequently offered opportunities for considerable chicanery. In 1800 Earl Macartney (**1302**) was considering adding to his Co. Antrim estate at Lisanoure near Ballymoney, and his agent informed him that the vendor's law agent had told him that 'If you should give him £500 you should get the lands perhaps £1,000 cheaper than you would do otherwise' and he backed up his offer by quoting other examples of similarly fraudulent activity.[94]

Apart from purchasing an estate outright or in fee simple, another way was to purchase a lease in perpetuity. Leases held in perpetuity separated the beneficial ownership from the possession of an estate. These leases reflected the difficulty of raising a large capital sum, representing the true value of the estate, in a poor country where land had only a limited appeal to external buyers. They overcame the market problem of raising large capital sums by an arrangement amounting to a lump sum coupled with a perpetual fixed annuity. Leases could be bought and sold within the term of the lease and there was nothing to prevent a landlord from selling an estate leased in perpetuity. For instance, in 1738, Lord Burlington sold to Sir Richard Heathcote, one of his creditors, a large estate, already let in perpetuity for £3,000 p.a., around Cappoquin on the borders of Counties Cork and Waterford. Sir William, a London businessman, purchased it for £53,300 sterling or £60,000 Irish, thus securing a 5 per cent return on his capital.[95] There is no record of Sir William ever visiting his estate nor, apart from curiosity, was there any reason why he should regard it as anything other than a fixed-income investment. The owner of an estate leased in perpetuity had nothing to do with the actual management of the estate, although his 'annuity' was an extra charge upon it. The purchaser of a lease in perpetuity became

---

[92] PRONI T2541/1A1/2/34.
[93] PRONI T2541/1A1/1B/53, 16 June 1745; Maguire, op. cit., p. 12.
[94] PRONI T2541/1A1/2/34.
[95] A. P. W. Malcomson, 'Absenteeism in eighteenth-century Ireland', *Irish Economic and Social History*, vol. 1 (1974) p. 18.

the *de facto* landlord, while the grantor of the lease remained the *de iure* owner of the same estate. Nevertheless, if a perpetuity lease was granted by an absentee to local people, there was still an immediate drain of a large sum of money out of the area. For instance, there is some evidence that even a comparatively wealthy county like Cork was at least temporarily affected by the drain of money created by Lord Burlington's leasing fines in the decade 1728–38, when he raised the enormous sum of £280,000, mainly from local men who wished to buy either long or perpetuity leases.[96]

Irish leases could be measured either in years or in lives. For most of the century leases for lives could only be held by protestants. They were considered equivalent to a freehold and as such they had political as well as economic implications. A lease for lives – often for three lives – ran for the lifespan of the longest survivor. This caused problems, as a 'life' could move or even emigrate and no one would know when a lease ran out. A perpetuity allowed lives to be replaced as those originally named, and their successors, died. Any life, public or private, could be named and usually the lessee chose the names to be inserted. In the case of a lease in perpetuity the lessee was responsible for inserting new lives and complying with the attached conditions. The original 'fine', or down payment, for such a lease was high, but not as high as an outright sale and the subsequent fine, which was specified in the original lease, for the insertion of additional lives was often nominal. The Devon Commission referred to these leases as: 'the landlords' tenure in Ireland … a species of tenure, scarcely known elsewhere, which prevails very extensively in that country, one-seventh of Ireland being said to be held under it. We allude to the tenure by lease for lives, with a covenant of perpetual renewal on payment of a fine, sometimes merely nominal upon the fall of each life.'[97]

A complex illustration of absenteeism, selling in fee simple, leasing in perpetuity, marriage and inheritance is the Burlington–Devonshire estates in Counties Cork and Waterford. At the beginning of the eighteenth century Charles, 3rd Earl of Cork and 2nd Earl of Burlington, sold part of the Munster estates, which had originally belonged to his grandfather, the great earl. He died in 1704 leaving his son and heir a minor. Richard Boyle, 4th Earl of Cork and 3rd Earl of Burlington, a spectacular and gifted patron of the arts, was to be hailed as the 'new Maecenas'. An enthusiastic collector, his zeal manifested itself early as he returned from the Grand Tour bringing 878 trunks and crates containing the start of his famous collection. He married an English heiress and lived in England; Burlington House commemorates both his name and his interests. However, his aesthetic taste was far superior to his talents for business management as in gratifying it he exhausted the income from his great estates. Moreover, his agents were dishonest and his accounts irregularly made up. In 1737 he sold in fee simple the Clonakilty estate, including the patronage of the parliamentary borough of Clonakilty, for £17,000 to his kinsman, Henry Boyle, then Speaker of the

---

[96] Dickson, PhD thesis (Dublin University) pp. 80 *et seq.*
[97] Devon Report, op. cit., p. 13.

House of Commons and later 1st Earl of Shannon. At that time Lord Burlington's rents were estimated to be £80,000 in arrears, 'of which,' a contemporary declared, 'he will see little or nothing, the tenants being gone off and not to be found, which proceeded from his several agents being underhand'.[98] On his death, in 1753, his still vast estates, English and Irish, passed to the heirs of his sole surviving child, the Marchioness of Hartington, and to her heirs the Dukes of Devonshire.[99]

Many of these perpetuities were, like the Burlington leases, early eighteenth-century grants, which had been made in times of recession to provide the landlord with immediate money at a cost that either the locality could sustain or the foreign purchaser was willing to pay. Rents had been depressed in the 1730s, and there had been the panic created by Lord Clancarty's unsuccessful attempt to have his father's attainder reversed and his estates in Counties Cork and Kerry restored.[100] The 1740s had opened with severe famine and this was followed by the political uncertainties of the 1745 rebellion. Landlords did not expect the marked improvements in rents and land values that came in the second half of the century, let alone their rapid escalation during the period of the French and Napoleonic wars. Little was known about inflation, long leases were customary and landlords were usually short of money. However, as the century progressed, the chief landlords became increasingly aware of the widening gap which separated the actual from the nominal return on the land that they, or their ancestors, had leased in perpetuity. In 1776 Arthur Young found that Lord Antrim's vast estate of 173,000 acres was let for £8,000 p.a. but 'relet for £64,000 a year by tenants that have perpetuities, perhaps the cruelest instance in the world of carelessness for the interests of posterity. The present Lord's father granted those leases.'[101] By the beginning of the nineteenth century Wakefield considered that the head rent was not one-twentieth of the gross rent for the same estate. Similar reports were current throughout Ireland: for instance, Wakefield also discovered that Lord Doneraile's father let an estate of £2,000 'for ever' and lived to see it relet at a profit rent of £18,000 p.a.; and in Co. Kerry, 'Lord Powis had the fee of a large estate which at present produces £30,000 per annum. In 1734, one of his ancestors leased it "for ever" at £1,900 per annum and a fine of £6,000.'[102]

Inevitably, as some landlords felt inadequately recompensed for their continuing equity in the estate, they began to look for loopholes in the leases which might allow them to regain control of their estates. In 1775 there was a classic example of such a challenge in the case of *Murray v. Bateman*, which occurred about the time that Young was recording these ever-growing discrepancies. Murray, the titular owner of an estate,

[98] Dickson, PhD thesis (Dublin University) pp. 80 *et seq.*
[99] The Dowager Countess of Burlington, d. 1758, possibly had a life interest in the estates as on her death the Duke of Devonshire received many letters congratulating him on his Burlington inheritance, see PRONI Chatsworth MSS T3158/1602, T3158/1603, T3158/1604.
[100] Boulter, *Letters*, vol. 2, p. 119; Lecky, op. cit., vol. 1, p. 460.
[101] Young, op. cit., vol. 1, p. 146.
[102] Wakefield, op. cit., vol. 1, p. 253.

challenged the possession of his tenant, Bateman, who held a perpetuity lease for lives renewable but had failed to perform his contractual obligations, having been dilatory in inserting new lives and in paying the accompanying fine. Murray, the landlord, reclaimed the estate on the ground that the lease was void as the obligations specified in it had not been met. Bateman's failures were a common occurrence, and Lord Chancellor Lifford gave judgment for the defendant on the grounds of 'an old Irish equity'. The plaintiff (Murray) appealed to the British House of Lords, then the final court of appeal for Irish cases, where, according to the Irish Attorney General, John Scott, 'the subject is not understood' and the British Lords of Appeal, dominated by the formidable Lord Chief Justice Mansfield, upheld the appeal.[103]

This decision shook the whole system of landholding in Ireland to its foundations, as the majority of these tenants had sub-tenants – 'Between the actual proprietor and the occupant of the land there are frequently no less than four or five progressive tenants' – each of whose leases depended on the validity of that of his superior in the 'cascade'. Furthermore, many of the estates leased in perpetuity were encumbered with family provisions such as jointures. Faced with potential chaos, the Irish parliament passed 19 & 20 Geo. III, c. 30, commonly known as the Tenantry Bill. This statute restored the 'old Irish equity', stating that:

> Great parts of the lands in this kingdom are held under leases for lives with covenants for perpetual renewals upon payment of certain fines ... and whereas ... those deriving under them have frequently neglected to pay or tender such fines within the times prescribed ..., and whereas many such leases are settled to make provision for families and creditors, most of whom must be utterly ruined if advantage shall be taken of such neglects ... in such cases [they should be relieved] against the lapse of time upon giving adequate compensation ... where no fraud appears to have been intended.

The Irish parliament was sharply divided and the bill passed in both Houses by the narrowest of margins – two votes in the House of Commons and a single vote in the House of Lords.

Entry into the governing class depended not simply on wealth, but on wealth combined with the ownership of land. Between 1704 and 1778 the penal laws placed severe restrictions on Catholics' acquiring land by either purchase or lease in perpetuity. Despite the market restrictions, there was, in the course of the century, a considerable transfer of land mainly into the hands of local people and often from absentee proprietors. Irish land, never regarded as a particularly attractive or secure investment for British capital, became even less so as the agrarian violence, beginning about 1760, led to increasing social tension and finally erupted in the 1798 rebellion. This prevented much-needed capital for agrarian investment from coming into the country. Instead rents collected by absentees and increasingly purchase money drained capital out of

---

[103] M. O'Connell, *Irish Politics and Social Conflict in the Age of the American Revolution* (Philadelphia 1965) pp. 266–81, esp. pp. 267–8, 276–7. See *Devon Report*, op. cit., p. 13.

the country, although absentees often sold to local people to whom land was a tangible, if troublesome, investment.

By the latter half of the eighteenth century the vast majority of Irish landlords were in debt, and often for spectacular amounts. Debts were inherited along with estates and indebtedness became cumulative. As early as 1715 the Earl of Granard had an income of £2,000 p.a. and debts of £12,000. At the end of the century, as previously noted, the 1st Marquess of Downshire (died 1793) left debts amounting to £69,660 and his son the 2nd Marquess (**1016**) (died 1801, MP for Co. Down 1776–93) debts of £325,212, subsequently reduced to the still enormous sum of £269,726 by the £55,486 paid in Union compensation.[104] Many private acts of the Irish parliament were an attempt to rearrange entails and manage indebtedness.

By the end of the century, the Leinster predicament was that of an increasing number of the Irish nobility. The family business was too small to support the family, but what alternatives were available? Business was considered socially beneath them, although business fortunes were perfectly acceptable as dowries or *nouveaux riches* husbands for moderately dowered daughters. The armed forces, particularly the army, were a favoured career for younger sons. In 1775 Lord Lieutenant Harcourt wrote to Lord North that:

> My private reasons for adopting Major Skeffington (**1932**) are, I will confess, founded in the exigence of the moment. He is brother to the late Lord Massareene. He is in Parliament. His two nephews (**1931**, **1935**) are in Parliament also … If Major Skeffington is not gratified I cannot expect his own or his nephews support; and a defection of three which to us makes a difference of six voices will … be highly prejudicial to His Majesty's government in this Kingdom.[105]

Letters like this one are numerous. There were fewer naval officers, although some eminent ones. At the 1776 general election Lord Charles FitzGerald (**0728**) was returned for Co. Kildare and in 1779 Lord Lieutenant Buckinghamshire wrote to Lord Weymouth that: 'The Duke of Leinster was with me this morning ... I rather think he is coming round, if he does, his brother the Seaman being promoted is a Point insisted upon.'[106] In default of male heirs estates could pass to daughters, thus it was possible for the family estates to become separated from the family title, leaving its inheritor with insufficient resources to maintain his dignity.[107] These necessitous

---

[104] D. Hayton, 'Ireland and the English Ministers' (unpublished Oxford University PhD thesis, 1975) pp. 10–11; Maguire, op. cit., pp. 90–91.

[105] Harcourt Papers, vol. 10, pp. 16–18; see also E. M. Johnston, *Great Britain and Ireland 1760–1800* (Edinburgh 1963) pp. 240–44.

[106] PRO SP63/467, f. 45.

[107] G. O. Sayles, 'Contemporary sketches of the members of the Irish parliament in 1782', *Proceedings of the Royal Irish Academy*, 56 C 3, p. 281. Lord Allen had a pension of £600 p.a. granted in 1770. The four previous Viscounts Allen had all been MPs, while Lady Mayne's husband was both a British and an Irish MP: see A. P. W. Malcomson, *Pursuit of the Heiress: Aristocratic Marriage in Ireland 1750–1820* (Belfast 1982) for a discussion of the Allen marriage, to which the eventual heiress was Elizabeth Proby, Lady Carysfort and her heirs. For private statutes see TCD Library 186s 39–40.

peers were often considered a claim on government and positions and pensions were usually found for them. In 1782 Lord Aylmer ('has no property – much distressed – has applied for a pension') was given a pension of £400 p.a. Another case where a pension was combined with an honourable occupation was that of Viscount Ranelagh, who 'has a pension of £400 p.a., but in addition ... is chairman to the Committees of Lords, £2,000 per session'. One peer, Lord Strangford, attempted to sell his vote on the Rochfort–Loftus trial for £200.

The family borough was often a lever for making provision for younger sons for whom the family estate could not make adequate provision. For these a government job, the Established Church or the army could provide a suitable living and all were assisted and advanced by the family's political influence.[108] Indeed, the family's standing was often considered to be reflected in the amount and quality of the patronage which its members received. 'His expectations cannot be very high,' wrote Lord Annaly recommending Mr Smyth, the son of the MP for Mullingar, 'as he is not in parliament but there are many places in my Lord Lieutenant's gift, which are fit for a gentleman yet may not be the object of a Member of Parliament's desire.'[109] In 1769 Lord Townshend stressed the political importance of places in the Revenue worth £300–£400 p.a. 'requiring no particular skill or attendance on the Revenue (as may be sought by members of parliament)'!

Military positions were particularly sought. 'My intention is ... to bring Arthur into parliament' wrote his brother, the future Marquess Wellesley (**2215**), of the future Duke of Wellington (**2210**) asking, in 1787, for a post as aide-de-camp 'on pay'; otherwise Arthur was destined for India. Lord Mornington had succeeded his father (**2215**) as 2nd Earl of Mornington in 1781. He had a large family of siblings whom he proceeded to establish. In 1783 he returned his brother William (**2216**), although under age, for the family borough of Trim. William inherited the Ballyfin, Queen's County estate of his cousin, William Pole (**1690**) and entered the British parliament for East Looe; next in line was his brother Arthur, barely of age in 1790 when he was returned for Trim. Meanwhile Henry had come of age and in 1795 he sat for a few months for Trim, his return had been the result of the Place Act which had allowed Clotworthy Taylor (**2039**) to resign by accepting the office of Escheator of Munster in order to replace his brother Lord Bective (**2051**) as MP for Co. Meath.

All four Wellesley brothers got UK peerages and a fifth was chaplain to the queen. A career in the Established Church was certainly helped by belonging to a politically significant family; for instance, Lord Tyrone had originally been against the augmentation of the army in 1768 but 'It was thought prudent to alter his way of

---

[108] For the importance of the family unit in both British and Irish politics see L. B. Namier, *England in the Age of the American Revolution* (London 1961) p. 19 and A. P. W. Malcomson, *John Foster: The Politics of the Anglo-Irish Ascendancy* (Oxford 1978) p. 1.

[109] BL Add. MSS 40,179, f. 21, Lord Annaly to Lord Nugent, father-in-law of the then viceroy Lord Temple, 12 August 1782. Sir Skeffington Smyth was MP for Mullingar 1779–83, Belturbet 1783–90 and Galway Borough 1790–7. I have not been able to trace this son, who probably *d.s.p.* young.

thinking by giving his brother a good living.'[110] Church patronage was complicated by English demands,[111] particularly for bishoprics and high ecclesiastical office, but parliamentary influence was useful here also; every Lord Lieutenant's correspondence is full of such arrangements. There were very few medical doctors, and the more eminent of these had state appointments of some kind. Sir Patrick Dun (**0665**), Sir Edward Barry (**0090**) and William Clement (**0409**), the Vice Provost and Regius Professor of Physic at Dublin University, were probably the best known. Medicine appears to have been largely, though not entirely, the province of Catholics and Dissenters.

For lawyers parliament was the obvious road to advancement, whether to the Bench or a more minor position. The law was also also a suitable training for either 'a man of business', such as Lord Tyrone's (**0113**) brother, John Beresford (**0115**), who was eventually First Commissioner of the Revenue, or for a less talented MP who simply wished for a small administrative post. Minor legal placemen were numerous, but for anyone with his eyes on the Bench a seat in parliament was essential, for as Lord Townshend remarked, 'The lawyers of eminence here are always in Parliament.'[112] The law also offered the best opportunity for a career based on unconnected talent, and, in the case of Provost Hely-Hutchinson (**1001**),[113] political ability.

In 1792 John O'Neill (**1592**), MP for Co. Antrim, and Thomas Conolly (**0459**), MP for Co. Londonderry, both declared that there were 110 placemen or pensioners in the Irish House of Commons.[114] Until the 1793 Place Act MPs did not have to seek re-election on accepting a place of profit under the Crown. Similarly, once elected only death or elevation to the peerage or bench allowed an MP to retire. After 1793 an MP could apply for the Escheatorship of one of the four provinces and this allowed him not only to retire but to change his seat. It also allowed government to rearrange the House to secure the passing of the Union in 1800, so that a measure intended to purify the House led to its destruction.

Heads of families sought peerages (or advancement in the peerage), lucrative sinecures and other advantages. For all of these parliamentary influence was a necessity, while the law, the church and the armed forces were the principal career openings for younger sons. In addition there was a certain amount of grace and favour patronage; for instance,

[110] PRONI DOD 572/1/6 20 February 1769, Townshend to Macartney; Historical Manuscripts Commission, *Fortescue I* Mornington to W. W. Grenville, 31 October 1787; BL Add. MSS 24,138 f. 126; see Johnston, *Great Britain and Ireland*, op. cit., pp. 214 *et seq.* for various examples of parliamentary favours.
[111] O. MacDonagh, W. F. Mandle and Pauric Travers (eds), *Irish Culture and Nationalism, 1750–1950* (London 1983); E. M. Johnston, 'Problems common to both Protestant and Catholic churches in eighteenth-century Ireland', gives a brief overview of church affairs.
[112] *Cal. HO Papers* 1766–9, no. 690.
[113] John Hely-Hutchinson was probably the most notorious pluralist in Ireland: see Lecky, op. cit., vol. 2, no. 1. Lord North said that 'If you were to give him the whole of Great Britain and Ireland for an estate he would ask the Isle of Man for a potato garden.' Lecky described him as a man of 'brilliant and versatile ability'. He ended his career as Provost of Dublin University and Secretary of State for Ireland (a sinecure); his wife was created Baroness Donoughmore, and by 1800 their son was an earl.
[114] Lecky, op. cit., p. 82.

in 1783 Lord Keppel wrote to Lord Temple on 'the subject of Marine Commissions intended in compliment to the Government of the Lord Lieutenant of Ireland ... you will find how rigidly I have been constantly in reserving fifteen Commissions of Second Lieutenants of Marines for your Recommendation the same number that the Duke of Portland was indulged with.' There was a similar arrangement with the East India Company.[115] Despite their reputation for high living most peers and commoners were acutely conscious of their financial position and spent much of their time juggling settlements, dowries, portions and mortgages in order to remain solvent while maintaining the standard of life which their rank and position decreed.

At almost every point the Irish parliament modelled itself on the Westminster parliament,[116] and the members were extremely sensitive regarding their rights and privileges. The great points of freedom of speech and freedom of access to the Crown by the Speaker had long since been won, but the question of the extent of the privilege of freedom from arrest and its potential abuse remained. This freedom derived from the fact that parliament was called by the sovereign to consult with him or her on the business of the kingdom. Therefore those elected for this purpose should be free from arrest by the ordinary courts so long as their services were required, a privilege which was extended to their servants, although in 1715 the House ordered that only domestic or menial servants were protected and then only if they were not Roman Catholics.[117] In 1695 the House called upon Captain Corker to explain why he had granted protection to one John Shelley as his menial servant. Shelley was the receiver of Corker's rents and in this respect the House agreed that he was a menial servant but ruled that when he was sued '*in autre droit* [he] has not any protection of this House'.[118]

The privilege was an old one, dating back to the reign of Edward IV, when a statute of 1463, 3 Edw. IV, c. 1, 'An act whereby the lords and commons of Parliament hath priviledge for certain days before and after the said Parliament', stated that for 40 days before and after the said parliament no member 'should be impleaded, vexed nor troubled by no means'. During the reign of Henry VIII it arose in the case of George Ferrers, an MP whose arrest in 1543 brought the personal wrath of Henry VIII, who summoned the Chancellor, the Judges, the Speaker and some of the most prominent MPs to declare that the king was at the apex of his power in parliament and that 'Whatsoever offence or injury, during that time is offered to the meanest member of the House is to be judged as done against our person and the whole court of Parliament' and that as parliament was the supreme court of the land all inferior courts must give way before it.[119] By the beginning of the eighteenth century interpretations of 3 Edw.

[115] BL Add. MS 40,177, f. 154; PRONI D572/1/50, NAI IA:41:134.

[116] See P. D. G. Thomas, *The House of Commons in the Eighteenth Century* (Oxford 1971; reprint 1992). The Speakership was perhaps more important in Ireland where the Speaker was *primus inter pares*, but otherwise there was little difference.

[117] E. Porritt and A. Porritt, *The Unreformed House of Commons* (1903) vol. 2, p. 460.

[118] *CJ Ire.* (Bradley ed.) vol. 2, pp. 655, 657, September 1695.

[119] T. F. T. Plucknett (ed.), *Taswell-Langmead's Constitutional History* (11th edn, 1960) p. 250; there are many other descriptions of this famous event.

IV, c. 1 had created a number of uncertainties between the normal jurisdiction of the state and the jurisdiction of parliament. Furthermore, as parliament began to meet more frequently this privilege became increasingly liable to abuse. An attempt was made to control and clarify it by a statute of 1707, 6 Anne, c. 8, 'an act for explaining and limiting the Privileges of Parliament'. This statute confirmed the 40 days before, during adjournments and 40 days after the prorogation or dissolution of parliament. At the same time a plaintiff was not to be debarred from prosecuting his suit by the statute of limitations; distress for rent, duty or services were excluded from privilege; and privilege did not extend to MPs in their capacity of guardians, trustees or executors, nor to Crown debtors.

In 1728 a further attempt, 1 Geo. II, c. 8, was made to control this by reducing the time within which MPs might be sued before and after the meeting of parliament to 14 instead of 40 days: after 14 days they might be sued, subjected to judgments, etc. but they could not be arrested during the 40 days before or after the meeting of parliament. In effect the plaintiff's action was delayed but not prevented by privilege of parliament. Freedom from imprisonment for debt was a valuable privilege[120] and, as Primate Boulter pointed out when the bill came before the House of Lords, 'Several of our Lords are very much in debt and value themselves in paying nobody, were from the first very much against the bill.'

Parliament had powers over its own members and over those who it felt had behaved in a derogatory or disrespectful fashion towards it. These powers were usually expressed by brief imprisonment by the Serjeant-at-Arms, the executive officer of the House, under the direction of the Speaker, a fine, an apology and a reprimand by the Speaker during which, particularly in the earlier part of the century, the defendant was usually required to kneel at the bar of the House and express penitence. In cases of extreme annoyance a member might be expelled[121] permanently or otherwise, depending on how seriously his offence was judged. This was rare – there were only about eight cases in all, and none between 1717 and 1753. The last case was that of Arthur Jones-Nevill (**1125**), the Surveyor General, who was expelled in 1753 because the House considered that he had not obeyed its resolution regarding the repair of barracks and had thereby 'acted in manifest contempt of the authority' of the House. This expulsion, at the height of the Money Bill crisis, was carried by 124 to 116 votes and the process was really resurrected in order to attack the government.

Reasons for expulsion were various. For example, John Asgill in 1703 had written a book entitled *An Argument proving that according to the covenant of eternal life revealed in the scriptures man may be translated from hence into that eternal life without passing through death although the human nature of Christ himself could not be thus translated til he passed through death.* This was adjudged wicked and blasphemous, and the author

---

[120] See Namier, *Structure of Politics at the Accession of George III*, op. cit., pp. 60–61.
[121] See Volume 2, 'Members censured and expelled', for the names of those expelled and the reasons for their expulsion.

was 'to be expelled from this House and be forever hereafter incapable of being chosen, returned or sitting a Member in any succeeding Parliament of this kingdom'. The book was to be burnt by the common hangman both outside the gates of parliament and outside the city hall; the House ordered that 'the Sheriffs of the City of Dublin be required to see the same done accordingly'.

Privilege was gradually whittled away until by 1772, 11 & 12 Geo. III, c. 12, 'an act for further preventing delays of justice by reason of privilege of parliament', admitted that the previous acts had proved insufficient and that actions or suits or processes were not to be delayed by privilege of parliament. This act was originally in force for seven years but it was subsequently extended. By this statute there was little left except freedom from arrest, which continued until the Union,[122] although as the indebtedness of the Irish parliamentarian grew, there were occasional regrets at the diminution of privilege. For example, John Beresford told his friend Lord Auckland at the time of the Union debates in 1799 that: 'Lord Ormonde and Lord Westmeath are in debt, and the traders to whom they are indebted sent in their bills, and not being paid directly, they have procured executions. The goods were actually advertised before the execution was laid on. This is going rather far.'[123] The merchants, accurately gauging the effect of the Union on their business, were exceedingly anxious to prevent it, while necessitous parliamentarians were most likely to vote for it.

In conclusion, there can be no clearer indication of the vast changes brought about by the social upheaval of the seventeenth century than the fact that every eighteenth-century Speaker came from a family which had emerged from obscurity in the seventeenth century, usually during the interregnum. The Levinges (**1230**) were a post-Restoration family originally from Derbyshire; Rochfort (**1806**), Speaker in 1695, was the son of Prime Iron Rochfort, a lieutenant-colonel in Cromwell's army (executed for killing another officer in a duel); Brodrick's (**0237**) father, Sir St John Brodrick, had received large grants of land in Co. Cork under the Protectorate and also for his part in the Restoration; Conolly (**0460**) was reputed to have come from humble Irish origins and made his wealth as possibly the most successful land speculator of the post-Revolution period; Sir Ralph Gore (**0872**) was the descendant of a late sixteenth-century alderman of London who had eight sons, some of whom sought their fortune in Ireland and obtained grants of land in the north and west of Ireland in the early seventeenth century. Henry Boyle (**0210**), Gore's successor, was a descendant of Richard Boyle, Earl of Cork, the great Cork and Waterford land speculator and entrepreneur of the early seventeenth century, whose son, Lord Broghill, figured prominently during the Protectorate. John Ponsonby's (**1702**) ancestor was colonel of a regiment of horse under Cromwell and obtained two grants of land at the Act of Settlement; the ancestors

---

[122] See PRONI (or Library of Congress) Cavendish Debates: on 18 May 1778 Speaker Pery pointed out that this act took away all privileges of parliament in suits and actions brought against MPs.
[123] *Beresford Correspondence II*, p. 200, Beresford to Auckland 26 January 1799; for the impact of the Union on Dublin see C. Maxwell, *Dublin under the Georges* (London, rev. edn 1956) pp. 92–3.

of Pery (**1671**), his successor, came to Ireland about 1650 because a Nicholas Pery had met, in London, a Miss Sexton and it was through her that Speaker Pery acquired his Limerick estates.[124] John Foster (**0805**), the last Speaker of the Irish House of Commons, did not date his ancestry further back than the mid-seventeenth century.

Many early eighteenth-century MPs were rough and tough; for instance, the behaviour of Francis Flood (**0760**), the grandfather of Henry Flood, was such that he was expelled from the House, though not for long. By 1800 their descendants had been transformed into elegant gentlemen and patrons of the arts, as was indicated by the foundation of the Royal Irish Academy, while men like Castlereagh (**2009**) and Wellington (**2210**) are exemplars of their political and military abilities. Very few MPs who sat in the parliaments of William III had any previous parliamentary experience. The Restoration parliament of Charles II had been dissolved in 1666 after failing to achieve the impossible, namely to resolve the problems arising from the redistribution of land during the Commonwealth. The parliament of James II which met from 7 May to 18 July 1689 was preoccupied with the same problem as perceived by the Catholics who had been dispossessed by the Cromwellian redistribution of land. There were probably only about six MPs who sat in both the parliaments of James II and William III.

---

[124] I am greatly indebted to Dr A. P. W. Malcomson for this information, which came from Lord Limerick. It is in a speech which he made in Limerick in 1995 and is published in *Georgian Limerick* (Limerick 1996).

ACHESON – CURTIS

A

ABERCORN, Earl of: *see* HAMILTON

0933 Hamilton, Rt Hon. James, 1st Baron
Mountcashell and Viscount Strabane [I], 6th Earl
of Abercorn [S] (his great-grandson, John James,
was 9th Earl and 1st Marquess of Abercorn), MP
Co. Tyrone 1692–3, 1695–9

0001 ACHESON, Rt Hon. Sir Archibald

MP for TCD 1741–60; Co. Armagh 1761–8–76;
Enniskillen 1776 [r. Killyleagh 1768]

> b. 1 Sept. 1718; d. 5 Sept. 1790 at his seat,
> Gosford Castle, Co. Armagh
> HONOURS: PC, sworn 7 May 1770.
> PEERAGES: Suc. as 6th Bt [S] 1749; cr. Baron
> Gosford 20 July 1776, Viscount Gosford 20 June
> 1785.
> FAMILY/BACKGROUND: Son of Sir Arthur Acheson,
> 5th Bt (0003) and Anne, dau. of Rt Hon. Philip
> Savage (1889).
> MARRIED: [1740] Mary, yst dau. of John
> Richardson of Rich Hill, Co. Armagh, who
> survived him.
> CHILDREN: Rt Hon. Arthur, 1st Earl of Gosford
> (0004); Anna Marie, m. (1) Alexander Boyd of
> Ballycastle, Co. Antrim, (2) Rev. Henry Maxwell;
> Nichola, m. Michael Obins of Castle Obins, Co.
> Armagh; son (b. 16 Mar. 1749/50; d. yg); Julia
> Henrietta, m. Alexander McAuley of Glenville,
> Co. Antrim; Lucinda, m. (1) Thomas St George
> (1850), (2) Jeremiah French; Mary, m. Hugh
> Montgomery of Castle Hume, Co. Fermanagh;
> Sophia (d. unmar.).
> EDUCATION: Entered TCD 17 Jan. 1736, LLD
> 2 Mar. 1742.
> CAREER/OCCUPATION: Governor of the Workhouse
> & Foundling Hospital 1749–79; High Sheriff of
> Co. Armagh 1751, Deputy Governor 1756–71;
> High Sheriff of Co. Cavan, patent 19 Feb. 1761;
> Trustee of the Linen Board for Leinster 1760–89;
> *Governor of Erasmus Smith's Schools and other
> Charities 1764–89; *Trustee of the Inland
> Navigation for Ulster May 1768; *Commissioner
> of the Tillage Act for Ulster 1769–84; Director of

the Royal Corporation for working the Collieries
of Ireland.

POLITICAL ACTIVITY: He began his parliamentary
career in 1741, representing the university, and
was nominated for 86 committees between 1741
and 1760. At the 1761 election he was returned
for Co. Armagh, where he had a large estate, and
he represented that county for the next 15 years.

Armagh was a northern county dominated by
the linen industry. Its numerous protestant inhabitants ensured that it had a larger than average
electorate, probably between 2,000 and 3,000 in
the 1760s. Furthermore, political influence in the
county was divided between major landowners
such as the church, the Brownlows (0265) and
Lord Charlemont and numerous substantial, if
smaller, landowners. Acheson increased his political influence by marrying the daughter of one of
the latter, John Richardson of Rich Hill, while his
sister married Dr Walter Cope, Bishop of Ferns;
the Copes were another Armagh family. This fragmented influence ensured periodic electoral conflict.

It is possible that Acheson's espousal of the
Country party in the 1750s, as reflected in his
votes for the expulsion of Arthur Jones-Nevill
(1125) and against the Money Bill, owed something to the activities of the unpopular Primate
Stone in Co. Armagh politics as well as to the issues involved. Moreover, the protestant voters,
who had to be freeholders or tenants for life, enjoyed exceptionally long leases (often for up to
three lives) and the independence that this afforded. The economic success of the linen industry not only gave a degree of independence to the
weavers, but allowed the linen factors to exercise
a degree of influence over them apart from that of
the landlords.

From 1755 the *Almanacks* list Acheson as a
member of the Royal Dublin Society, and in December 1765 he was appointed to the committee
to inquire into the public works necessary to the
nation. Acheson originally came in for Co. Ar-

magh by an alliance with the Brownlows, but in 1768 he insured his election through a double return, being also returned for Killyleagh, Co. Down. As one of the Co. Armagh members Acheson had to pay attention to the various interests in this complex county; in 1769 it was noted that he was 'rather inclined to government but he courts popularity. Wants to be made a Privy Counsellor. To be spoken to on interesting questions.' He voted against the augmentation of the army in 1768, but three years later was a supporter of the address to Lord Lieutenant Townshend.

By 1773 he was more interested in pursuing a peerage than upholding the traditional views of the country gentleman MP, for by 1772 he was a Privy Counsellor, and noted as a 'steady friend to government'. He was recommended for a peerage, and for the next few years he voted for the government on all substantial measures. The Absentee Tax was an 'open', if managed, vote, and the government did not insist on its supporters' voting for the 1772 act allowing Catholics a 61-year lease to reclaim bogland, 11 & 12 Geo. III, c. 21, or the 1774 act that allowed Catholics to take an oath of allegiance to the king, to disavow any temporal authority of the pope within the realm, and to deny the alleged doctrine that Catholics need not keep faith with protestants, 13 & 14 Geo. III, c. 22. In 1775 it was noted that he was looking for an employment of £200 p.a. for his son-in-law and that Lord Harcourt had given to his recommendation a Distributor of Stamps and subsequently a Hearth Money Collection.

Following the 1776 election, when he was returned for Enniskillen, he was created Lord Gosford. In the House of Lords, while he gave the impression of independence, he generally supported the government and in 1788 he was created a viscount. Noting the viscounty, one of the 1788 Parliamentary Lists mentioned that he was 'a little hurt about affair with late Bishop of Ferns – he did not behave quite right – but it is just', adding that nevertheless he was a supporter of government. This refers to his relation Dr Walter Cope, who died on 31 July 1787. In 1784 Lord Lieutenant Northington had written to his successor, the Duke of Rutland, recommending not only that Gosford be advanced to a viscounty but

that 'His brother-in-law the Bishop of Ferns was the only bishop out of four who hold boroughs, that gave his two seats to the nomination of His Majesty's government, a conduct which certainly deserves to be noticed.' As he was not promoted, Gosford possibly felt that the bishop had not been adequately 'noticed'.

By the late 1780s the social unrest that was to make Armagh such a flashpoint in the 1790s had already made its appearance; Lord Gosford wrote in February 1788 to reassure the Lord Lieutenant 'that the riotous conduct of the People was not general throughout this County, and in many parts where the riot has prevail it has ceased … Several of the Rioters have inditements found against them and five have been several months in Jail, who must be tryed for their lives next Assizes … The Assizes are very near at hand, Good Juries, and punishments adequate to their crimes being inflicted, may open the eyes of the lower Order of the People, and strike terror in the minds of the more wealthy, if any such are underhand concerned, which I hope they are not.'

This involvement of the minor gentry was a serious problem not only in Armagh – it was also a feature of the rural disturbances in Cork and elsewhere (*see* 1082). Interestingly, Gosford points out that even if the government decided to restore order – and the only way to do this was by force of arms – 'I do not know where fodder could be had for Even one Troop of Dragoons, at this advanced Season of the year.' The logistics of control were not always easy. Shortly after, Lord Gosford provoked a severe reaction by illegally arming Catholics to protect his property. He died in 1790, before the problem reached its climax in the 1795 'Battle of the Diamond'.

DIVISION LISTS:
    1749 (1) voted against the election of James Digges La Touche (♦♦♦♦).
    1753 (1) voted for the expulsion of Arthur Jones-Nevill (**1125**).
    1753 (2) voted against the Money Bill.
    1768 (1) voted against army augmentation.
    1771 (1) voted for Lord Townshend as Lord Lieutenant.
    1771 (2) voted against Sir Lucius O'Brien's (**1558**) motion for retrenchment.

1772 (2) voted against a Short Revenue Bill.

1773 (1) voted for the Absentee Tax.

1773 (2) voted against an untaxed press.

1774 (1) voted for the Stamp Bill.

1774 (2) voted against Catholic relief.

1775 (1) voted against the pro-American amendment to the Speech from the Throne.

ESTATES/RESIDENCE: Markethill, Co. Armagh (main country residence); Sackville Street, Dublin, 1795–9 (this property was valued at £2,000); Arvagh, Co. Cavan. It was estimated in 1789 that there were 200 (protestant) freeholders on his estates.

SOURCES: PRONI D/302; PRONI D/1606/1/139 Gosford Papers, Election Calculations [June 1789]; PRONI T/906 (1 and 2) Acheson pedigree; PRONI T/1584 Pinkerton transcripts p. 73, 15 Nov. 1763, p. 90, 6 May 1766, 9 Aug. 1766; (W. H. Crawford ed.) *General Report on the Gosford Estate in Co. Armagh* [PRONI 1976]; McCracken thesis; GEC *PB*; Burke *PB* (1921) p. 995 [b. 1717 but *DJ infra* gives 1718]; *Alum. Dub.; Index to Irish Privy Counsellors, 1711–1910*; Hughes, *Pat. Officers*; M. Kelleher, *List of Members of the Dublin Society, 1731–1800* (Dublin, 1982); *HMC Stopford-Sackville I* p. 196 Primate to Lord G. Sackville, 16 Apr. 1753 [referring to Sir A. Acheson's 'strange behaviour'], *HMC Rutland III* p. 76, *The Dublin Gazette* 6 Mar. 1742; *BNL*, 23 Mar. 1749, 27 Dec. 1765, 23 June 1767; *Pue's Occurrences* 19 Jan. 1751; *Almanacks*; *DJ* 5 Mar. 1751, 9–11 Sept.1790; *FJ* 14–17 May 1768; D. Dickson (ed.), *The Gorgeous Mask* (Dublin, 1987), pp. 41–2; Parliamentary Lists, 1769 (1), 1772 (2), 1773 (1), (2), 1774 (1), 1775 (1), 1776 (2), 1777 (1), 1782 (1), 1784 (1), 1787 (1), 1788 (1).

0002 ACHESON, Rt Hon. Archibald

MP for Co. Armagh 1797–1800; [UK] 1800–7

b. 1 Aug. 1776; d. 27 Mar. 1849 at Gosford Castle, Co. Armagh

HONOURS: PC [UK] 3 Sept. 1834, GCB (Civil) 19 July 1838.

PEERAGES: Styled Lord Acheson 1806–7; suc. as 2nd Earl of Gosford 1807; cr. Baron Worlingham [UK] 13 June 1835, Rep. Peer 1811–49.

FAMILY/BACKGROUND: Son of Rt Hon. Arthur Acheson, 1st Earl of Gosford (0004) and Millicent (d. 1825), dau. of Lieut.-Gen. Edward Pole.

MARRIED: [20 July 1805] Mary (d. 1841), o. dau. and h. of Robert Sparrow.

CHILDREN: Archibald, 3rd Earl of Gosford, m. [1832] Theodosia, only dau. of John Chambre Brabazon, 10th Earl of Meath; Mary, m. James Hewitt, 4th Viscount Lifford; Millicent, m. Henry Bence Jones; Olivia; Annabella.

EDUCATION: Entered Oxford (Christ Church) 22 Jan. 1796, MA 26 Oct. 1797.

CAREER/OCCUPATION: Governor of Co. Armagh 1790, 1798, 1805; Trustee of the Linen Board for Leinster 1799 (f.); Lord-in-Waiting 1831–4; Governor of Lower Canada 1835–8; Custos Rot. Co. Armagh, patent 24 or 25 Mar. 1800, 1818; Lord Lieutenant of Co. Armagh 1831–49; Vice-Admiral of the Province of Ulster.

MILITARY: Major, Armagh Militia 1798, Colonel 1801; Captain of the Yeomen of the Guard July–Nov. 1834, Apr.–June 1835.

POLITICAL ACTIVITY: His political career began with his return for Co. Armagh in the 1797 general election. He was as ardently against the Union as his father (0004) was for it, voting against it in both 1799 and 1800. As a county MP he continued to represent Co. Armagh immediately after the Union, and was again returned in 1802 and 1806. His sister Mary's marriage to Lord William Bentinck in 1803 connected him with the Duke of Portland. His father had been made a UK peer in 1806 and on his death the following year, Lord Acheson went to the House of Lords as 2nd Earl of Gosford. He was expected to support Pitt's second ministry, but Co. Armagh was an area of strong sectarian feeling and on 14 May 1805 he voted against the Catholic claims.

In 1815 he was described as 'a good natured and venerable little fellow … without political or personal pretensions'. After 1820 he went over to the Whigs. In 1835 Lord Melbourne nominated him Governor of Lower Canada (Quebec). This was a poisoned chalice, as Gosford had relatively little experience in political administration and was appointed at a time of particular difficulty owing to the constitutional demands of the movement led by Jean Louis Papineau, the Speaker of the Legislative Assembly. The Legislative Assembly was dominated by French Canadians and the Legislative Council by English Canadians. Their disagreements, which long preceded the arrival of Gosford, who tried to be conciliatory, erupted into open rebellion in 1837. Gosford was recalled early in 1738. He received the thanks of the ministry and was made a GCB (Civil).

DIVISION LISTS:
1798 (1) voted against Sir Laurence Parsons'(**1636**) motion for an investigation into 'the present discontents'.
1799 (1) voted against the Union – 'Has £4,000 p.a. in landed property or is heir apparent to it'.
1800 (1) voted against the Union.

ADDITIONAL INFORMATION: He was a member of the Dublin Society from 1798 and had a lifelong interest in agriculture and promoting the linen manufacture, which dominated the economy in Co. Armagh. In 1821 he commissioned William Greig to prepare a detailed report on his Co. Armagh estate, which is an important document in the context of pre-famine estate management in Ireland even if, as Professor F. M. L. Thompson remarks, it was 'a large stone which sank almost without trace in the pond of Gosford estate management'.

ESTATES/RESIDENCE: Gosford Castle, Markethill, Co. Armagh (main country residence); Sackville Street, Dublin (this was valued at £2,000 in the 1790s, when his expenditure in Dublin was estimated at £1,000 p.a., but would have fallen considerably in value in the early nineteenth century); Arvagh, Co. Cavan. Lord Gosford acquired through his marriage to Mary Sparrow the estate of Worlingham in Suffolk.

The 2nd Earl began the building of Gosford Castle around 1820. It was said to have cost c. £80,000. The Gosford estate consisted originally of all or part of the manors of Baleek, Coolmalish and Drumorgan, Co. Armagh and comprised c. 32 townlands. The rental of the Armagh estates was £3,770 in 1792 and £7,354 in 1815, in part a reflection of various purchases of land that appear to have been made in the interim. After deducting these additions the rental is £6,108, giving a wartime inflation of c. 62%. In the late 1820s the Armagh estate was expanded by the purchase of most of the property of the Richardson family of Rich Hill and, in 1829, all the surviving property of the Graham family of Ballyheridan. These comprised c. 44 townlands in whole or in part.

In Co. Cavan the family owned the manor of Carrowdownan, comprising c. 23 townlands – part of which was the town of Arvagh. The rental of the Cavan estate was £2,704 in 1816 and it contained 6,680 statute acres in 1838.

In 1818 the debts outstanding on the security of all estates totalled c. £45,000, on which the annual interest payment was £2,700. In addition there were annuities of £1,083. Rents nominally produced £10,476 p.a., but actual receipts in 1817 were £6,600, possibly reflecting the post-war slump. These conjectures are complicated by the length of leases. On this estate in the late eighteenth century they were usually for three lives and averaged c. 64 years.

In 1883 the estates consisted of 12,177 acres in Co. Armagh and 6,417 in Co. Cavan, worth a total of £17,934 p.a.

SOURCES: PRONI D/1606/7C/1 and /6D/9 Gosford Papers [Cavan estate rental, 1816–17 and Richmond's survey of the Cavan estate, 1838]; GEC *P*; Burke *PB* (1906) p. 714; Hughes, *Pat. Officers*; W. H. Crawford (ed.), *General Report on the Gosford Estate in Co. Armagh* [PRONI 1976] pp. 8, 23–4; M. Kelleher, *List of Members of the Dublin Society, 1731–1800* (Dublin, 1982); *HP 1790–1820*; D. Dickson (ed.), *The Gorgeous Mask* (Dublin, 1987), pp. 41–2; *Almanacks*; Parliamentary Lists, 1799 (3), 1800 (3); *DNB* Supplement I.

0003 ACHESON, Sir Arthur

MP for Mullingar 1727–49

b. 26 Jan. 1688; d. 8 Feb. 1749
HONOURS: Suc. as 5th Bt [S] 1701.
FAMILY/BACKGROUND: Son of Sir Nicholas Acheson, 4th Bt (**0005**) and Anne, dau. of Thomas Taylor.
MARRIED: [Oct. 1714] Anne, o. dau. of Rt Hon. Philip Savage (**1889**).
CHILDREN: Rt Hon. Sir Archibald, 1st Viscount Gosford (**0001**); Capt. Arthur (Royal Irish Carabineers), m. Jane dau. of John King (**1160**) (she m. (2) Abraham Creighton, 1st Baron Erne (**0515**)); Anne, m. [1742] Walter Cope, Bp of Ferns and Leighlin; Nichola, m. Robert French (**0834**).
EDUCATION: School: Mr Martin; Royal School: Armagh, 26 Jan. 1688; entered TCD 25 May 1706, BA 1709.
CAREER/OCCUPATION: High Sheriff of Co. Armagh 1728; *Governor of the Workhouse 1733–d.; *Commissioner of the Tillage Act for Ulster 1735–d.; Governor of Co. Armagh 1746–d.

POLITICAL ACTIVITY: On 13 December 1715 the Lords Justices wrote to Secretary Stanhope objecting to Sir Arthur Acheson becoming Chancellor of the Exchequer (his father-in-law, Philip Savage

(1889), wanted to resign the Chancellorship and sell it to Acheson) on the grounds that he had shown disaffection to the Hanoverian succession and was 'extremely disagreeable to all the King's friends in this country'.

On 24 December 1715 the Lords Justices wrote again to Stanhope on the occasion of Acheson producing letters patent constituting him Chancellor of the Exchequer and a Privy Counsellor. The Lords Justices deferred executing the letters until their previous objections had been fully considered. They again stated the uneasiness in Ireland over the promotion of a man 'who has ever been esteemed a professed Jacobite'. Then on 5 January 1716 the Lords Justices again wrote to Stanhope urging reconsideration of Acheson's appointment, and on 22 January they wrote that 'We are very thankful for His Majesty's goodness in leaving the place of Chancellor of the Exchequer to our recommendation.' On 30 January 1716 they recommended Sir Ralph Gore (0872) to the post.

He appears to have been nominated for only 13 committees during a parliamentary career of 22 years.

ADDITIONAL INFORMATION: Dean Swift stayed with the family eight months after the death of Stella, and described his host's 'quiet and indolent ease' as follows:

> Such is the fate of Gosford's knight,
> Who keeps his wisdom out of sight,
> Whose uncommunicative heart,
> Will scarce one precious word impart,
> Still rapt in speculations deep,
> His outward senses fast asleep,
> Who while I talk a song will hum,
> Or with his fingers beat the drum,
> Beyond the skies transports his mind,
> And leaves a lifeless corpse behind.

ESTATES/RESIDENCE: Markethill, Co. Armagh; Carrowdownan and Arvagh, Co. Cavan; Nova Scotia, Canada. The Co. Cavan estate contained 12,000 acres in 1714 let for £300 p.a. and worth £500. *The Commons Journals*, 7 October 1737, in an account of payments made on King's Letters, reveals that Acheson 'in full satisfaction and discharge of all claims and demands whatsoever, on account of several sums of crown rent which he and his ancestors have paid in their own

wrong, for lands in the County of Armagh' received £1,276 3s 4d on 7 May 1736.

His receiver Mr Lorimer was killed in a duel, 21 April 1738.

His daughter-in-law, Jane née King (the wife of his son Arthur, died 1758) received per year £137 rent out of Argonnell, and £51 out of Portadown, until her death in 1800. She married Abraham Creighton, 1st Baron Erne (0515), and was again widowed, thereby acquiring two jointures. Some adjustment must have been made in these jointures or Lady Erne became confused as to their source and amount, as from her calculations of her income in 1798 it appears that the Portadown rent came from Lord Erne, along with £100 and £170 (the latter from a Strabane property), and that Lord Gosford paid her £100 plus £183 [*sic*] out of Argonnell – 'Both jointures', £601. She also had £545 from the interest on mortgages. Widowhood in these circumstances was not uncomfortable.

SOURCES: PRONI D/302; *CJ Ire.* (Bradley ed.) vol. 6 p. 729; PRONI D/1606 Gosford Papers; PRONI T/448 pp. 174, 183, 196, 217, TSPI 1715–16; PRONI T/ 1584 Pinkerton transcripts p. 19, 10 July 1753; McCracken thesis; (W. H. Crawford ed.) *General Report on the Gosford Estate in Co. Armagh* [PRONI 1976]; GEC *B*; TCD House of Lords Appeals: Printed Case Papers, 1711–39, 202 r. 31, 184; *Alum. Dub.*; M. L. Ferrar, *Register of the Royal School* (Armagh, 1933); *Coll. Gen.*; *Dublin Weekly Journal* 20 Jan. 1728; *Dublin Newsletter* 22 Apr. 1738; NLI MS 15360/2, 15360/5 Erne Papers, Account between Robert Peebles and Lady Erne, MS Calculations 1798, 24 Feb. 1799; *Almanacks*.

0004 ACHESON, Rt Hon. Arthur

MP for Old Leighlin 1783–90, 1790

b. *c.* 1745; d. 14 Jan. 1807
HONOURS: PC, sworn 13 Feb. 1793, suc. as 7th Bt [S].
PEERAGES: 2nd Viscount Gosford 1790, cr. Earl of Gosford 1 Feb. 1806.
FAMILY/BACKGROUND: Son and h. of Sir Archibald Acheson, 1st Viscount Gosford (0001) and Mary, dau. of John Richardson of Rich Hill, Co. Armagh.
MARRIED: [Mar. 1774] Millicent (b. 1825), dau. of Lt. General Edward Pole.
CHILDREN: Rt Hon. Archibald, 2nd Earl of Gosford (0002); Arthur (d. yg); Arthur Pole (d. yg); Lieut.-Col. Edward (Coldstream Guards); Olivia, m. [14 Mar. 1797] Brig.-Gen. Robert

Bernard Sparrow of Tanderagee, Co. Armagh;
Mary, m. [19 Feb. 1803] Lord William Bentinck;
Millicent, m. Rev. J.H. Barber.
EDUCATION: Entered TCD 6 Apr. 1762.
CAREER/OCCUPATION: Governor of Co. Armagh,
patent 5 Oct. 1790; Customer of Dingle,
Skerries, Malahide and Wicklow, patent, 29 Aug.
1795.
MILITARY: Colonel of Co. Armagh Militia 1793.

POLITICAL ACTIVITY: According to his obituary in
the *Belfast Newsletter* he 'lived for many years, after he was married, on the continent and was considered one of the most elegant and well-bred men
of the age'. He was returned by his uncle Dr Cope,
Bishop of Ferns, at the desire of Lord
Northington's administration. He supported government and his father's (0001) desire for an advance in the peerage. This was achieved in 1785
when Sir Archibald was created Viscount Gosford.
In parliament he opposed both Flood's motion
for parliamentary reform and, by his absence, the
Commercial Propositions.

He was influenced by Lord Northington but,
against the latter's advice, he supported the election of John Foster (0805) as Speaker in 1785.
This was important, as the support of the northern county MPs was influential in Foster's success. As he wanted a place or pension in 1788, his
behaviour was described as 'strangely doubtful'.
This ambiguity was clarified as he supported the
opposition and voted for a regency in 1789. He
seems to have been sincerely attached to the
Whigs, and, after his succession to the House of
Lords in 1790, he was noted as being in opposition. Nevertheless, he gave a voluntary and strong
support for the Union, although his son (0002)
opposed it. Feeling in Co. Armagh against the
Union had been so strong that many Union supporters felt that silence was the best course. However, Chief Secretary Castlereagh was informed
that 'Lord Gosford has taken much pains to write
letters, and consult with those gentlemen who
agreed in sentiment with him.' Gosford was offered an earldom for his services and refused it;
eventually he accepted it after the Whigs came
into office in 1806.

DIVISION LISTS:
    1783 (1) voted against Flood's (0762)

motion for parliamentary reform.
1785 (1) voted against the Commercial
Propositions.
1789 (1) voted for a regency.
1790 (2) absent.

ESTATES/RESIDENCE: Gosford Castle, Markethill, Co.
Armagh; Great Britain Street, Dublin; Arvagh, Co.
Cavan; Pultney Street, Bath. His Co. Armagh rental
was at least £3,808 in 1795 – a figure that relates to the
two biggest components of the 8,000 Irish acre Co.
Armagh estate, the Manors of Coolmalish and Baleek,
but leaves out the recently acquired ([?]c. 1785) Hamilton's Bawn etc. property (715 statute acres).

SOURCES: PRONI D/1606/7/4 and /6B/4, 8, 9 Gosford
Papers [Rent and Remittance book, 1791–9, and maps
of Hamilton's Bawn, 1785, Coolmalish and Baleek,
1818]; (W. H. Crawford ed.) *General Report on the
Gosford Estate in Co. Armagh* [PRONI 1976]; PRONI
T/1584 Pinkerton transcripts, p. 181, 11 Mar. 1744;
RCBL P80/1/1, Parish Registers of St Thomas, Dublin; GEC *P*; Burke *PB* (1906) p. 715; *Alum. Dub.*; *Index to Irish Privy Counsellors, 1711–1910*; Hughes *Pat.
Officers*; J. Kelly, *Prelude to Union* (Cork, 1992) pp. 192,
207; *Cornwallis Corr.* vol. 3 p. 50 [date of earldom is
incorrect]; *FJ* 25–7 Apr. 1793; *BNL* 23 Jan. 1807 [says
he was above 60 years of age at his death]; Parliamentary Lists, 1783 (2), 1784 (1), (2), (3), 1785 (1), (2),
(4), 1787 (1), 1788 (1), 1789 (1), 1790 (1), 1791 (1),
1798 (1), 1800 (1).

0005 ACHESON, Sir Nicholas

MP for Co. Armagh 1695–9

b. 1655–8; d. 1701
HONOURS: Suc. as 4th Bt [S] 1685.
FAMILY/BACKGROUND: Son of Sir George Acheson,
3rd Bt, and his first wife Nichola [m. 1654], dau.
and co-h. of Robert Hannay, 1st Bt, of Scotland.
MARRIED: [1686] Anne, o. dau. of Thomas Taylor
of Kells, Co. Meath.
CHILDREN: Sir Arthur, 5th Bt (0003); Nichola
Anne, m. (1) [7 Nov. 1706] Sir William
Johnston, son of Richard Johnston (1109), (2)
William Montgomery (?Acheson Moore (1449)).
CAREER/OCCUPATION: Sheriff of Co. Armagh 1685,
1695; Governor of Co. Armagh 1699.

POLITICAL ACTIVITY: He followed the country line,
voting in 1695 against Lord Chancellor Porter,
who was accused by some MPs of favouring

Catholics; in 1696 he signed the Association for the protection of William III in the country.

ESTATES/RESIDENCE: Markethill, Co. Armagh; Arvagh, Co. Cavan.

SOURCES: PRONI D/302; PRONI T/618/326 Crossle Papers [says his dau., Henrietta (*sic*), wid. of William Johnston m. (2) William Montgomery]; PRONI MIC/315/8/50 Blackwood pedigrees; GEC *B*; Burke *PB* (1921) p. 955 [says his father m. twice (1) 1654 and (2) 1659 hence his d. of b.]; Simms' cards; *Coll. Gen.*; *JRSAI* vol. 55 (1925) pp. 37, 40, H. A. S. Upton, 'A List of Governors and Deputy Governors of Counties in Ireland in 1699'; Parliamentary Lists, 1695 (1), 1696 (1).

0006 ADAIR, Robert

MP for Philipstown 1727–37

b. *c.* 1682; d. 31 July 1737, having 'had one of his legs cut off above the knee for a mortification and died soon after'
FAMILY/BACKGROUND: Son of Charles Adair of Cloonbary, Co. Longford, and Elinor, dau. of John Cooke of Co. Westmeath.
MARRIED: [13 Apr. 1703] Jane, dau. of Rev. John Forster.
CHILDREN: Johnny (d. unmar.); Forster, m. [3 Nov. 1748] Eliza, dau. of Sir George Ribton, 1st Bt; Nicholas; Anne, m. Hon. William Molesworth (**1420**); Dorcas, m. [June 1742] Galbraith Holmes (n.d.e. Banagher 1734–5); Elizabeth, m. [1738] John Lambert; Elinor, m. [1742] William Hudson; Jane; Arkison; Charles; Ignata; John; William Forster; Dorothy.
CAREER/OCCUPATION: ?Searcher, Limerick, patent 21 Mar. 1715, 26 Oct. 1727; a famous wine merchant.

POLITICAL ACTIVITY: He was listed on 17 committees during his ten years in parliament. In 1707 he gave land to build the established church in Ballymena.

ESTATES/RESIDENCE: Hollybrook (or Holybrook), Co. Wicklow; Peter Street, Dublin.

SOURCES: PRONI D/1430/E/18 Clarke Papers; PRONI T/277 Abstract of Will p. 139; PRONI T/559 vol. 20 p. 291, Burke, extract pedigrees; McCracken thesis; Hughes, *Pat. Officers*; Smyth, *Law Officers*; J. H. Bernard (ed.), *The Register of St Patrick, Dublin, 1677–1800* (Parish Register Society of Dublin, 1907) p. 16; *JRSAI*

vol. 30 (1900) p. 189, F. E. Ball, 'Tully, Rathmichael, Kilternan, and Other Places in South County Dublin'; *Ir. Gen.* vol. 7 no 3 (1988) pp. 265, 367, A. Dusek, 'Baptisms in St Bride's, Dublin 1633–1724'; *Pue's Occurrences* 6 Aug. 1737 [says he died 1 Aug.].

0007 ADAMS, John

MP for Fore 1692–3

b. 1634; d. *post* 1703
FAMILY/BACKGROUND: Eldest son of Rev. Randall Adams (Puritan minister) and Mary, dau. of John Archdale of Dareham, Suffolk.
MARRIED: (1) [1665] Mary, eldest dau. of Rev. George Creighton, Rector of Kinawley, Co. Fermanagh; (2) [1671] Elizabeth, dau. and h. of William Wiseman of Rollstone Manor, Writtle, Essex, wid. of Oliver Raymond (settlement dated 12 Aug. 1671); (3) [1685] Penelope, dau. of John Burgoyne of Patton Bedfordshire (settlement dated 15 Oct. 1685).
CHILDREN: Randall; Elizabeth; Raymond.
CAREER/OCCUPATION: Commissioner for granting a supply to William III 1695 and 1697; High Sheriff of Co. Westmeath, patent, 4 Dec. 1673; Member of Grand Jury 1703.

POLITICAL ACTIVITY: Little is known of his parliamentary activities. The parliament was in session only from 5 October to 3 November 1692, when it was prematurely prorogued prior to its dissolution on 26 June 1693 without ever meeting again.

ESTATES/RESIDENCE: Ledwithstown (Ledwichtown, Ledestown), Ballymahon, Co. Longford. The house was designed in 1746 and attributed to Richard Castle. The family of Adams, originally from Lincolnshire, settled in Co. Westmeath in 1642 and acquired considerable estates which eventually amounted to some 3,500 acres. In 1694 John petitioned for 'some land' in lieu of the £7,000 worth of damage that, he claimed, the garrison at Mullingar had inflicted on his estates during the recent war. His second marriage brought a large amount of property in England, where he mostly resided after 1694, renting out his home at Ledwithstown. In 1715 his son Randall sold the Ledwithstown estate to Major John Lyons (**1291**) of Grangemellon, Co. Kildare.

SOURCES: NLI MS 391; *Cal. SP Dom.* 1694–5 (London, 1906) p. 167; Hughes, *Pat. Officers*; *Grand Juries Co. Westmeath* (1853) reprinted by John Charles Lyons, Ledestown, vol. 1, App. p. 1; *Analecta Hibernica 10* (1941) pp. 251–86, P. Walshe, 'The Adams Rental';

Desmond Guinness (ed.), *Irish Georgian Society News-letter* (Spring l983) pp. 7–8.

0008 ADARE (*alias* ADAIR), Sir Robert

MP for Antrim B. 1692–3

b. Feb. 1659; d. 9 Feb. 1745
FAMILY/BACKGROUND: Only son of William Adair of Ballymena, Co. Antrim, and Anne Helen, dau. of Colonel Walter Scott of Hartwoodburn (she married (2) Archibald Edmonstone of Broadisland, Co. Antrim).
MARRIED: (1) [15 Aug. 1688] Penelope dau. of Rt Hon. Sir Robert Colvill (**0452**); (2) [1705] Martha? Colvill (d. Aug. 1705); (3) [Oct. 1705] Anne McAuley; (4) [9 Feb. 1721] Arabella Ricketts.
CHILDREN: (1) Capt. (of Horse) William Robert, m. Catherine Smallman of Ludlow, Salop.
(2) [?25 Mar. 1753] Anne dau. of Alexander McAuley (**1307**).
(3) Robert; Alexander (d. yg).
CAREER/OCCUPATION: Deputy Governor of Co. Antrim *c.* 1690; High Sheriff of Co. Antrim 1695, 1726, Sheriff 1725.
MILITARY: Raised a regiment of Foot for William III and was made a Knight on the battlefield at the Boyne, 1 July 1690.

POLITICAL ACTIVITY: Probably none. This parliament sat only from 5 October to 3 November 1692. It was prematurely prorogued and was not recalled before its dissolution on 26 June 1693.

ESTATES/RESIDENCE: Ballymena, Co. Antrim; Kinhilt, Wigtown, Scotland. The Adair estate eventually comprised 22 townlands including the townparks of Ballymena and Ballymena town. In 1779 Young reckoned the then Mr Adair's rental at £2,000. The estate had an estimated 4,300 acres in 1789. In 1807 its estimated rental was £1,938.

SOURCES: PRONI D/302 [calls him Bt 1726]; PRONI D/929/F3/2, D/2779, T/818/1, T/1310/3 Adair Papers [survey of the estate by James Williamson 1789, and rental 1807–9]; PRONI D/1430/E/18 Clarke Papers [says his mother's name was Anne-Helena; there is some confusion about the order of his wives, although there is general agreement that there were four and that he was succeeded by the son of his 1st wife, Penelope Colvill]; PRONI T/1584 Pinkerton transcripts, p. 14, 31 July 1752; RCBL T34, Extracts from the Parish Registers of St Andrew's, Dublin; Burke *PB* (1900) p. 16;

C. Dalton (ed.), *English Army Lists and Commission Registers, 1661–1714* (London, 1896) vol. 3 p. 167 [gives a Capt. Adair in Viscount Lisburne's Regiment of Foot 1690]; J. Foster (ed.), *Members of Parliament, Scotland 1357–1882* (London, 1882) p. 5; *Coll. Gen.*; Young, *Tour in Ire.*, vol. 2 App. p. 83; *Ir. Builder* 15 Apr. 1887, 'St Audoen's Church, Corn Market: Its History from its Foundation to the Present Time'; *JRSAI* vol. 55 (1925) pp. 37, 43, H. A. S. Upton, 'A List of Governors and Deputy Governors of Counties in Ireland in 1699'.

ADARE, Baron and Viscount: *see* QUIN

1753 Quin, Valentine Richard, Baron Adare, Viscount Mount-Earl, Viscount Adare and Earl of Dunraven, MP Kilmallock 1799–1800

0009 ADDERLEY, Thomas

MP for Charlemont 1752–60; Bandon 1761–8–76; Clonakilty 1776–83–90–1

b. *c.* 1713; d. 28 May 1791
FAMILY/BACKGROUND: Eldest son of Edward Adderley of Gloucestershire and Mary, dau. of Sir Matthew Hale.
MARRIED: (1) [9 Oct. 1740] Elizabeth (d. 1743), dau. of Francis Bernard (**0124**), wid. of Hon. James Caulfeild, 3rd Viscount Charlemont (**0368**); (2) [1769] Margaretta, o. dau. and co-h. of Edmund Bourke of Urrey, Co. Mayo (she m. (2) Rt Hon. Robert Hobart, 4th Earl of Buckinghamshire (**1026**)).
CHILDREN: (1) Edward Hall; Elizabeth, m. [1768] Maj. David Ross.
(2) George Augustus; Richard Boyle (entered Glasgow University 1794); Maria, m. Robert Ross.
EDUCATION: Entered TCD 17 Nov. 1730, BA 1735, LLD *hon. caus.* 1755.
CAREER/OCCUPATION: *Governor of the Workhouse 1749–68, Foundling Hospital and Workhouse 1769–d.; Freeman of the Corporation of Taylors 9 July 1753; Burgess of Kinsale and was presented with Freedom 1755; Burgess of Bandon Oct. 1756; Commissioner and Overseer of the Barracks and Public Works 1759–69 (patent, 18 May 1759, 29 Sept. 1762, 3 Nov. 1763, 23 Apr. 1765, 26 Sept. 1766); High

Sheriff of Co. Westmeath 1761; Treasurer to the Barrack Board June 1773–82 (at £800 or £900 p.a.); *elected to the Committee of 15 of the Incorporated Society 1756; *elected to the Court of Assistance June 1767–9, 1773; *Director of the Tyrone Collieries 1768–9, 1773; *Commissioner for Paving the Streets of Dublin 1778–80; *Governor of the Charitable Loan Society 1778–90 (f.); *Governor of the Charitable Musical Society 1780.

POLITICAL ACTIVITY: Adderley's origins are obscure, and this has led to some biographical confusion. By his first marriage, in 1740, to Elizabeth (née Bernard), Viscountess Charlemont, Adderley became stepfather and guardian to the 1st Earl of Charlemont. The Bernard connection strengthened his influence in Co. Cork, as did his political alliance with the 1st and 2nd Earls of Shannon (0210, 0213). From 1776 to 1791 he sat for the Shannon borough of Clonakilty.

In 1760 he was reputed to be trying to edge himself into the Duke of Devonshire's borough of Bandon-Bridge. Lord Charlemont wrote to the duke that 'Could I have imagined that Mr Adderley had been guilty of so great an oversight as to propose himself a candidate for the borough of Bandon without previously acquainting your Grace of his intentions, I should by no means have taken the liberty of soliciting you in his favour.' In 1782 he was reputed still to have some influence there.

In politics he had a long connection with the Shannon party, voting for the expulsion of Arthur Jones-Nevill (1125) and against the Money Bill in the 1750s. He remained attached to the Shannon party for the rest of his life. He would probably have considered himself an independent country gentleman with an interest in public affairs, and the breadth of these was reflected in the local and central organisations in which he occupied a prominent position.

In the House of Commons he was an active and frequent attender, nominated for no fewer than 82 committees between 1755 and 1760. The House of Commons designated him to bring in the bill 29 Geo. II, c. 21, 'For the relief of the creditors of the Bank lately kept by William Lennox and George French of the city of Dublin; and of the Bank lately kept by the said William

Lennox'. Lennox & French failed in March 1755. It was one of the earlier bank failures that marked the late 1750s, and the bill set up commissioners to settle claims against the bankers.

In 1769 it was noted that he 'must be spoken to on interesting questions'. He was a friend of the radical MP Charles Lucas (1276) and a supporter of the reform of Dublin Corporation. In 1777 he was described by an anonymous agent of Lord Lieutenant Buckinghamshire as one of the six out of 17 MPs returned by Lord Shannon (0213) who were 'under [his] absolute dominion ... [but] with places and pensions'. As a satellite of the Shannon party he was generally a government supporter, although he followed Shannon's reluctant lead over questions such as the regency. He was little influenced by his stepson's politics.

He was a progressive and, in many ways, a model landlord. He built and owned the town of Innishannon where, in 1747, he established the linen manufacture, bringing over some 60 Huguenot families for the purpose. Later in the century he encouraged cotton weaving, but the weaving industry did not survive him. He also supported boat-building. The town itself was considered neat and tidy, with a single street containing some good houses occupied by the leading citizens. Contemporaries considered that 'Innishannon presented a tidy appearance, undoubtedly due both to its relative prosperity, based on cotton-weaving and boat-building, and to the vigilance of its proprietor, Thomas Adderley, MP, who promoted both industries ... Its single street had some quite superior houses ... which would have been occupied by a master shipwright or other leading townsman.' Adderley had an interest in town planning; in 1757 he was one of the first commissioners appointed to oversee town planning in Dublin.

His public activities, both local and national, were numerous. These interests were reflected in Innishannon, which he planned as a model industrial community. In 1756 he was elected to the Committee of Fifteen which supervised the charter schools, and in 1758 he was chairman of the commission to inquire into the management of the Dublin workhouse. He was appointed in 1765 to the committee to inquire into the public works necessary to the nation. Not surprisingly, he was a member of the Royal Dublin Society; originally elected in 1748, he was among those listed in the election of members after the royal charter was granted in 1750. In 1766 he received the Royal Dublin Society's gold medal for his large plantation of white mulberry trees at Innishannon: presumably he intended to embark on silk weaving, but little more is known of this venture.

Other aspects of his career were less admirable. There was some suspicion about his financial integrity as Lord Charlemont's guardian. In 1759 he was appointed to the patentee office of Overseer of the Barracks and in 1772, with the consent of Lord Lieutenant Townshend, he exchanged his Commissionership with Hugh Henry Mitchell (**1415**), the Barrack Board Treasurer at a salary of £300 p.a.; in 1774 the salary was estimated at £400 p.a. and was subsequently raised to £600 by Lord Lieutenant Buckinghamshire; some estimated its returns as high as £800–900 p.a.

In 1782 Lord Lieutenant Temple (later Buckingham) launched an inquiry into the finances of various government departments. This precipitated the discovery of a financial scandal at the Barrack Board, of which Adderley was still Treasurer. 'I have routed the accounts of the Barrack board,' Temple remarked to his brother and Chief Secretary W. W. Grenville, 'Adderley the Treasurer has failed for above £5,000.' Not surprisingly, Adderley dissented from the address of thanks to Lord Temple. 'Mr Adderley said he would oppose the motion and assign his reason for dissenting from the vote of thanks. A clerk of his at the Barrack Board had embezzled the public money; as soon as it came to his knowledge, he waited on Lord Temple and promised to make good the deficiency in a few months: the clerk also attended and confessed he owed the money. He said Lord Temple lamented his situation – but as soon as he (Mr Adderley) left that nobleman, the crown solicitor was ordered to proceed against him without mercy. Thus was he used with unheard of cruelty. He would be glad to know what good this man had done for Ireland – he insisted he had done nothing meritorious. The addresses presented to him were procured by himself – and that he verily believed he was not a Protestant as

his carriage had been seen at the chapel doors in this city. He had heard of many addresses but he believed they were all solicited and procured by the Earl himself.'

In 1785 he was still thought to owe the government £400–500, but by 1788 he had cleared his debt. Lord Shannon subsequently tried to obtain compensation for him, and eventually he obtained a pension upon liquidating his accounts. Although Adderley considered that he had been treated with undue harshness, in fact he had probably been a victim of the changing political attitudes reflected in the economical reform movement that followed the War of American Independence.

DIVISION LISTS:

1753 (1) voted for the expulsion of Arthur Jones-Nevill (**1125**).

1753 (2) voted against the Money Bill.

1768 (1) voted for army augmentation – Commissioner of the Barracks.

1771 (1) voted against Lord Townshend as Lord Lieutenant.

1771 (2) voted against Sir Lucius O'Brien's (**1558**) motion for retrenchment – 'a placeman'.

1772 (2) voted against a Short Revenue Bill.

1773 (1) voted for the Absentee Tax.

1773 (2) voted against an untaxed press.

1774 (1) voted for the Stamp Bill.

1774 (2) voted against Catholic relief.

1775 (1) voted against the pro-American amendment to the Speech from the Throne.

1777 (1) voted against Grattan's (**0895**) motion for retrenchment.

1778 (2) voted against the Popery Bill.

1779 (1) voted for new taxes.

1779 (2) voted against a six-months Loan Bill.

1780 (1) voted against Grattan's declaration of the Rights of Ireland.

1780 (2) voted against Yelverton's (**2268**) motion to modify Poynings' law.

1780 (3) voted against the Tenantry Bill.

1780 (4) voted for the Perpetual Mutiny Bill.

1784 (1) voted against a committee on the Reform Bill.

1785 (1) voted for the Commercial Propositions.

1789 (1) voted for a regency.

1790 (1) voted for Grattan's motion for
reducing the influence of the Crown.

1790 (2) voted for Ponsonby (**1709**) on the
election of a Speaker.

1791 (1) voted for Curran's (**0560**) resolution against the sale of peerages.

1791 (2) voted for Grattan's motion for the
exercise of Free Trade.

1791 (3) voted for Grattan's motion to
abolish the Dublin police.

ESTATES/RESIDENCE: Innishannon, Co. Cork (main country residence); Granby Row, Dublin (town residence);
in 1785 he was living at 34 Rutland Square, Dublin.

SOURCES: *CJ Ire.* (Bradley ed.) vol. 9 p. 749 (0529); *Par-
liamentary Register* vol. 2 pp. 12–13; PRONI D/302;
NLI MS 13057 Heron Papers; PRONI T/448 pp. 7,
29–30, 39, 41, 54, 76, 89, 94, TSPI 1715–16; PRONI
T/559 vol. 5 p. 22, Burke, extract pedigrees; PRONI
T/618/325 Crossle Papers [says he had another dau.
Elizabeth who married in 1768 Captain David
Rogerson] while T/618/329 [says his dau. Elizabeth m.
Major David Ross s. of Robert Ross (**1814**)]; PRONI
T/993 Abstract of Will; PRONI T/1584 Pinkerton
transcripts p. 451, 3 Jan. 1792; RCBL T34, Extracts
from the Parish Registers of St Andrew's, Dublin [bur.
1 June 1791]; Ellis thesis; McCracken thesis; GEC *P,
Alum. Dub.*; *Coll. Gen.*; Cork MPs; Hughes, *Pat. Offic-
ers; Index to Hibernian Chronicle, 1769–1775* (Society
of Genealogists, 1936) vol. 1 p .1; W. I. Addison (ed.),
*The Matriculation Albums of the University of Glasgow
1728–1858* (Glasgow, 1913); B. De Breffny and R.
Ffolliott, *The Houses of Ireland* (Dublin, 1975), p. 125;
M. Kelleher, *List of Members of the Dublin Society, 1731–
1800* (Dublin, 1982); Berry *RDS* pp. 24–7; *Dublin Hist.
Record* vol. 38 no 1, Dec. 1984, Sean Murphy, 'The
Corporation of Dublin, 1660–1760'; *Cork Hist. Soc.
Jn.* vol. 3 second ser. (1897) pp. 50–58, F. E. Ball, 'Tho-
mas Adderley of Innishannon, MP' [says he is son of
Francis Adderley and his first wife Elizabeth Fowkes
and also says he married first 1730; this latter piece of
information is evidently incorrect as his 1st wife was
not widowed until 1734]; *Ir. Gen.* vol. 5 no 6 (1979),
H. F. Morris, 'Ramsey's Waterford Chronicle, 1786–
91' [says he is the son of Thomas and great grandson of
Edward]; Johnston, *Gt B. & Ire.*, p. 256; *Almanacks;
BNL* 27 Dec. 1765; *DJ* 10 July 1753, 26–30 Oct. 1756;
FJ 25–7 June 1772; Parliamentary Lists, 1769 (1), 1772
(2), 1773 (1), (2), 1774 (1), 1775 (1), 1776 (1), (2),
(3), 1777 (1), 1778 (1), 1780 (1), 1782 (1), 1783 (1),

(2), 1784 (1), (2), (3), 1785 (1), (2), (3), (4), 1787 (1),
1788 (1), 1789 (1), 1790 (1), 1791 (1).

0010 ADDISON, Rt Hon. Joseph

MP for Cavan B. 1709–13; [GB] Lostwithiel
1708–9; Malmesbury 1710–19

> b. 1 May 1672; d. 17 June 1719
> HONOURS: PC appointed 1708, 30 Sept. 1714,
> [GB] 1717.
> FAMILY/BACKGROUND: Son of Lancelot Addison,
> Dean of Lichfield, and Jane, dau. of Nathaniel
> Gulston DD.
> MARRIED: [9 Aug. 1716] Charlotte, dau. and h. of
> Sir Thomas Middleton, 2nd Bt, wid. of Edward
> Rich, 6th Earl of Warwick and 3rd Earl of
> Holland.
> CHILDREN: 1 dau. (b. 30 Jan. 1719 d. unmar.
> 1797).
> EDUCATION: School: Charterhouse; entered
> Oxford (Queen's College) 12 July 1687, aged 15
> years; demy from Magdalen College 1689–97,
> BA 1691, MA 14 Feb. 1694, Fellow 1697–1711;
> Grand Tour 1699–1703.
> CAREER/OCCUPATION: Secretary to the Earl of
> Wharton, Lord Lieutenant 1708–10; Secretary to
> the Lord Justices, 1714; Secretary to the Earl of
> Sunderland, Lord Lieutenant 1714–15; Keeper of
> the Records in the Bermingham Tower 1709–19
> (patent, 2 Dec. 1709, 10 Jan. 1715, 27 Oct.
> 1715); Commissioner of Appeals in Exchequer
> [E.] 1704–8; Under Secretary to Sir Charles
> Hedges, Secretary of State for the Southern
> Department 1705–6, 1717–18; Lord Commis-
> sioner of the Board of Trade 1715; appointed
> Secretary of State for the Northern Department
> in 1717 through the influence of Lord Sunder-
> land, his health declined shortly after. He retired
> on 14 Mar. 1718, and on 19 Mar. he was granted
> a pension of £1,600 p.a. on the Irish Establish-
> ment.

POLITICAL ACTIVITY: Wharton's appointment of
Addison as Chief Secretary in 1708 caused universal surprise that such a sensitive young man
should be attached to such a reprobate. Macaulay
was later to write that Wharton's licentious behaviour and corruption were in 'the strongest contrast to the Secretary's gentleness and delicacy'.
Addison showed a degree of scrupulousness in his
dealings unusual for the age, and seemed to owe

much to the strong Christian ethos reflected in his writings. He was Chief Secretary 1708–10, Secretary to Lords Justices 1714, and Chief Secretary 1714–15.

His career was largely in England, and his particular fame lies in his literary achievements. While in the Irish parliament he was nominated for nine committees during the 1709 and 1710 sessions. As MP for Cavan Addison was not very active. His inherent shyness seems to have made him physically incapable of making a speech, and he suffered from defective eyesight. He did not go to Ireland for his second term as Chief Secretary.

ADDITIONAL INFORMATION: He was a gentle and retiring person quite unsuited to the political positions that he required in order to make a living. He was the principal contributor to Sir Richard Steele's *Tatler* and, with Steele, owned *The Spectator*. Swift described him to Archbishop King as 'a most excellent person ... my most intimate friend ... and a person you will think worth your acquaintance'. He also wrote that Addison was '*le plus honnête homme du monde*', and further reported that Addison loved Wharton as little as Swift did. In reply Addison called Swift 'the most agreeable companion, the truest friend, and the greatest Genius of his age'. Their friendship endured although they were at opposite ends of the political spectrum.

Swift recorded in *The Drapier's Letters* 'that Mr Addison was forced to purchase an old obscure place, called Keeper of the Records of Bermingham's Tower of £10 a year, and to get a salary of £400 annexed to it, though all the records there are not worth half-a-crown either for curiousity or use'. A salary of £500 p.a. was subsequently attached to this post.

As well as being a poet, dramatist and politician, Addison dabbled in the commercial world. His attempt in 1710 to trade in shoes was a complete failure. His love of wine was well known, and it was suggested that it was only by over-indulgence that he overcame his shyness. This habit was encouraged by the wine he was entitled to duty-free as a Privy Counsellor.

ESTATES/RESIDENCE: Dublin Castle; Bilton, Warwickshire; Holland House, Kensington. He had an estate in the West Indies worth £14,000 which he lost in 1710.

SOURCES: *DNB*; *Index to Irish Privy Counsellors, 1711–1910*; Hughes, *Pat. Officers*; *Alum. Oxon.*; *Coll. Gen.*; *HP 1715–54*; King (ed.) *A Great Archbishop of Dublin, William King DD, 1650–1729*, pp. 25, 179; *JRSAI* vol. 34 (1904) pp. 133–158, H. Wood, 'Addison's Connexion with Ireland'; *Proc. RIA* no 77, Sec. C no 1 (1977) p. 17, J. C. Sainty, 'The Secretariat of the Chief Governors of Ireland, 1690–1800'; Parliamentary Lists, 1711 (1), 1713 (1).

♦♦♦ AGAR, Charles [n.d.e.]

MP for Kilkenny City May–July 1778

> b. 28 May 1755; d. 15 May 1789
> FAMILY/BACKGROUND: Son of James Agar (**0015**) and Rebecca, dau. of Rt Hon. William Flower, 1st Baron Castle Durrow (**0767**).
> MARRIED: [ ] dau. of [ ] of Madenhead, Queen's Co.
> CHILDREN: *d.s.p.*
> EDUCATION: School: Eton 1767–8; entered TCD 11 June 1775.
> CAREER/OCCUPATION: Archdeacon of Emly 1782–8.

POLITICAL ACTIVITY: He sat very briefly for Kilkenny City following the death of Ralph Gore (**0873**) early in March 1778. Agar's return was successfully challenged by Gervase Parker Bushe (**0310**).

ESTATES/RESIDENCE: [?]Co. Kilkenny.

SOURCES: PRONI T/559 vol. 5 p. 94, Burke, extract pedigrees; Ellis thesis; Burke *Ext. P* (1883) p. 2; *Alum. Dub.*; R. A. Austen-Leigh (ed.), *The Eton College Register, 1753–90*, 3 vols (Eton, 1921) [confuses his date of birth with that of his brother (**0011**)]; Kilkenny MPs.

0011 AGAR, Rt Hon. George

MP for Callan 1776–83–90

> b. 18 Apr. 1754; d. 9 Oct. 1815
> HONOURS: PC, sworn 12 Sept. 1789.
> PEERAGES: Cr. Baron Callan 4 June 1790, extinct on death; Rep. Peer 1801–15.
> FAMILY/BACKGROUND: Son of James Agar (**0015**) and Rebecca, dau. of Rt Hon. William Flower, 1st Baron Castle Durrow (**0767**).
> MARRIED: Unmarried.

EDUCATION: School: Eton 1767–9; entered Cambridge (Trinity College) 2 Apr. 1770, aged 18 years, did not graduate.
CAREER/OCCUPATION: *Trustee of the Linen Board for Munster 1786–1800 (f.); *Deputy Sovereign of Callan 1795–87; *Magistrate of Callan 1795–7.
MILITARY: Captain in the Callan Infantry, Dec. 1796.

POLITICAL ACTIVITY: He entered parliament in 1776 as a government supporter. His father (0015) was killed in 1769 in a duel with Henry Flood (0762) over the borough of Callan, which both claimed. In 1778 Agar was noted as an 'infrequent attender' in parliament. However, his political interest increased, as by the mid-1780s he had come to an agreement with Henry Flood and established his claim to both seats. In 1783 he returned himself and his friend John Bourke O'Flaherty (1570).

He possessed a large property and had the expectation of another from his aunt, the Countess of Brandon. His ambition was a peerage and preferment in the church for his brother. Although he was on friendly terms with his cousin, Lord Clifden (0016), he wished to be considered independent. In general he was in opposition, as is shown by his voting pattern, but from time to time he anounced his friendship to the government.

When the Duke of Rutland became Lord Lieutenant in 1784, Agar declared his disinterested support along with that of Mr O'Flaherty. However, he wanted to be a Trustee of the Linen Board and by 1788 he had his eyes on the Privy Council. Although he had voted for the regency, in 1790 he was elevated to the House of Lords as Lord Callan. In return he placed his borough at the disposal of government in the 1790 general election, dutifully returning William Meeke (1393), Comptroller of the Lord Lieutenant's Household and subsequently Clerk to the House of Lords, and Alderman Nathaniel Warren (2190), the Chief Commissioner of the Dublin Police. In 1799 his parliamentary followers included Patrick Welch (2199) and James Savage (1888), whom he returned for Callan. He supported the Union and was made a representative peer.

DIVISION LISTS:
1779 (2) voted for a six-months Loan Bill.
1780 (2) voted for Yelverton's (2268) motion to modify Poynings' Law.
1780 (4) voted against the Perpetual Mutiny Bill.
1783 (1) voted against Flood's (0762) motion for parliamentary reform.
1784 (1) voted against a committee on the Reform Bill.
1785 (1) absent.
1786 (2) voted for Forbes' (0778) motion for retrenchment.
1788 (2) voted for Forbes' motion for limiting pensions.
1789 (1) voted for a regency.

ADDITIONAL INFORMATION: *A subscriber to the Public Assembly Rooms from 1787; *a member of the Royal Dublin Society, 1788. As a student at Cambridge he gained a reputation for wild behaviour. It was reported that 'At the County Midsummer Sessions, Mr Agar and Mr O'Meara, Fellow Commoners, who stood indicted for an assault on Thomas Fletcher, printer, at a public coffee house in Cambridge on 18 March 1771, moved by their Counsel to stay proceedings alleging that the University ought to have sole cognisance of the case. The claim was subsequently heard in the Court of King's Bench, but was disallowed.'

ESTATES/RESIDENCE: Ringwood, Co. Kilkenny; Westcourt, Callan, Co. Kilkenny; Merrion Square, Dublin; Cranham Hall, Essex.

SOURCES: Ellis thesis; GEC P; Index to Irish Privy Counsellors, 1711–1910; Alum. Cantab.; R. A. Austen-Leigh (ed.), The Eton College Register, 1753–90, 3 vols (Eton, 1921); Coll. Gen. [says he was born 18 Apr. 1754]; Kilkenny MPs; Almanacks; BNL 17 Oct. 1815 [says he died in his 62nd year]; FJ 21–4 Feb. 1778, 3 Dec. 1796; Parliamentary Lists, 1776 (1), 1778 (1), 1780 (1), 1782 (1), 1783 (1), (2), 1784 (1), (2), (3), 1785 (1), (2), (3), (4), 1787 (1), 1788 (1), 1789 (1), 1790 (1), 1791 (1), 1793 (1), 1794 (2), 1799 (2), (3), 1800 (2).

0012 AGAR, Henry

MP for Gowran 1727–46

b. 1707; d. 28 Oct. 1746
FAMILY/BACKGROUND: Eldest son of James Agar
(**0014**) and his second wife Mary, dau. of Sir
Henry Wemys (**2204**).
MARRIED: [29 May 1733] Anne, only dau. of
Welbore Ellis, Bp of Meath, (she m. (2) [20 Jan.
1753] George Dunbar (**0668**)).
CHILDREN: Rt Hon. James, 1st Viscount Clifden
(**0016**); Welbore-Ellis, m. [21 Oct. 1762]
Gertrude, dau. of Sir Charles Hotham, 5th Bt;
Charles (Abp of Dublin, cr. Earl of Normanton
1806), m. [22 Nov. 1776] Jane, e. dau. of
William Benson; Rev. Henry, m. Mary, dau. of
Benjamin Tyrrell; Diana.
EDUCATION: School: Mr Cashen, Limerick;
entered TCD 1 May 1724.
CAREER/OCCUPATION: *Magistrate 1741; *Portreeve
1741; Sovereign of Thomastown 29 Sept. 1744;
Trustee of the Linen Board for Munster 1745–d.

POLITICAL ACTIVITY: He does not appear to have
been a very active MP, as he is listed as sitting on
only six committees between 1729 and 1745. On
21 November 1741 his excuse for not attending
parliament was not accepted by the House, and
he was ordered into the custody of the Serjeant-
at-Arms. His marriage to Anne Ellis, the sister of
Welbore Ellis, 1st Baron Mendip, brought an
important connection for the political future of
the family, as her children were his heirs.

ESTATES/RESIDENCE: Gowran Castle, Co. Kilkenny (main
country residence).

SOURCES: *CJ Ire.* (Bradley's ed.) vol. 7 p. 292; McCracken
thesis; *Alum. Dub.*; Kilkenny MPs; *Almanacks*; *Pue's
Occurrences* 2 Oct. 1744, 1 Nov. 1746.

0013 AGAR (-ELLIS), Hon. Henry Welbore

MP for Co. Kilkenny 1783–9 [r. Gowran 1783];
[GB] Heytesbury 1793–1802

b. 22 Jan. 1761; d. 13 July 1836
PEERAGES: Suc. as 2nd Viscount Clifden 1789;
2nd Baron Mendip [GB] 1802 (he took the
surname Ellis on 4 Feb. 1804, after inheriting
this peerage from his great-uncle Welbore Ellis,
1st Baron).

FAMILY/BACKGROUND: Eldest son of Rt Hon. James
Agar, 1st Viscount Clifden (**0016**) and Lucia,
dau. of John Martin of Dublin, wid. of Hon.
Henry Boyle-Walsingham (**0216**).
MARRIED: [10 Mar. 1792] Caroline, dau. of Rt
Hon. George Spencer Churchill, 3rd Duke of
Marlborough.
CHILDREN: George James Welbore, 1st Baron
Dover [UK], m. [1822] Georgina, dau. of Rt
Hon. George Howard, 6th Earl of Carlisle;
Caroline Anne (d. unmar).
EDUCATION: School: Westminster 12 June 1770,
K.S. (Captain) 1774, left 1778; entered Oxford
(Christ Church) 19 June 1778, BA 1782.
CAREER/OCCUPATION: Clerk of the PC 1785–1817
(patent, 14 Sept. 1785, 19 Sept. 1800); Recorder
of Gowran, 1783; Trustee of the Linen Board for
Munster 1789 (f.); *Governor of Erasmus Smith's
Schools and other Charities 1788–97.
MILITARY: Commander, Gloucester Horse (Co.
Kilkenny) 1797.

POLITICAL ACTIVITY: He represented Co. Kilkenny
from 1783 to 1789, following the political lead
of his father, Lord Clifden (**0016**). His Irish parliamentary career was low-key. By 1785 he had a
sinecure office, Clerk to the Privy Council, estimated to be worth £1,200 p.a.; by 1788 it was
noted that he was 'often in England'. He succeeded
his father as Lord Clifden in 1789 and then sat in
the British House of Commons representing
Heytesbury, for which he was returned through
the influence of his father-in-law, the Duke of
Marlborough.

He controlled the four members who sat for
Gowran and Thomastown in the Irish House of
Commons: Patrick Welch (**2198**), his step-grand-
father George Dunbar (**0668**), George Bunbury
(**0273**) and George Burdett (**0277**). Dunbar, who
married Anne (née Ellis), widow of Henry Agar
(**0012**), sat in parliament for Clifden boroughs
for nearly 40 years and had a pension of £300
granted during Lord Townshend's administration.
Patrick Welch was Collector of Naas. Bunbury and
Burdett both received Commissionerships worth
£500 p.a. in 1800.

In the (Irish) House of Lords the government
could usually depend on the solid support of the
18 bishops and four archbishops, although many
of them were connected with prominent politicians by family ties. Some of these prelates had
political leanings, like the Archbishop of Cashel,

who was 'very active in business – a good speaker – and very ambitious of being employed by Government in the House of Lords'. Supported by the interest of his brother Lord Clifden (**0016**) and his uncle, Welbore Ellis, by 1790 the archbishop was 'a Political Character of great consideration', and in 1799 Lord Cornwallis noted that 'The Archbishop is looked upon in this country as a wise and able politician and I conceive the acquisition of his support as an object of no small importance.' This political prelate was afterwards Baron Somerton and Earl of Normanton.

Lord Clifden owed his seat at Westminster to his marriage to the Duke of Marlborough's daughter. He supported Pitt's administration in the British parliament, for the most part silently. In his only known speech, on 21 January 1794, he moved the address in favour of the prosecution of war with France; on 24 November 1795 he was a government teller. He returned to Ireland, 18 February 1797, saying that he would be of more service to the British government there than in England. For his Irish services in 1798 his sinecure office was made perpetual, although it was later commuted to £203 1s 14d p.a. and abolished during his lifetime. He was an ardent supporter of the Union, and turned out three of the four MPs then sitting for his two Irish boroughs because they were hostile to it, insisting that his members voted for it. At the Union he received £30,000 in compensation for the disfranchisement of Gowran and Thomastown.

After Pitt's death in 1806 Lord Clifden supported the Whigs and became a prominent advocate of Catholic relief. He lived to see Catholic Emancipation, dying on 13 July 1836 'perhaps the only person to sit consecutively in four different Houses of Parliament – the two houses in Ireland and the two houses in England'.

DIVISION LISTS:
  1783 (1) absent.
  1784 (1) absent? – son to a Commissioner and heir apparent to half a county and 3 boroughs.
  1785 (1) voted for the Commercial Propositions.

ADDITIONAL INFORMATION: Fellow of the Society of Antiquities, 8 December 1803.

ESTATES/RESIDENCE: Bramblestown, Co. Kilkenny.

SOURCES: PRONI D/1901/4/1 Gowran estate correspondence; GEC *P*; Burke *PB* (1906) p. 356 (1903) p. 330; Kilkenny MPs; Johnston, *Gt B. & Ire.*, p. 264; G. F. Russell-Barker and A. H. Stenning (eds), *Record of Old Westminsters: A Biographical List*, 2 vols (London, 1928); *HP 1790–1820*; *Ir. Gen.* vol. 1 no 10 (1941) p. 295, W. Clare, 'Irish Compensations and Pensions'; *Almanacks*; Parliamentary Lists, 1783 (2), 1784 (1), (2), (3), 1785 (1), (2), (3), (4), 1787 (1), 1788 (1), 1790 (1), 1791 (1), 1793 (1), 1794 (2), 1798 (1), 1799 (2), (3), 1800 (2).

0014 AGAR, James

MP for Old Leighlin 1703–13; Gowran 1713–14; Callan 1715–27; St Canice 1727–33 [r. Gowran 1715]

b. 1672; d. 30 Dec. 1733
FAMILY/BACKGROUND: Eldest son of Charles Agar of Yorkshire and his first wife Ellis, dau. of Peter Blanchville of Rathgarvan, Co. Kilkenny.
MARRIED: (1) [10 Jan. 1693] his cousin Susanna, dau. of John Alexander; (2) Mary (b. 1665 d. 1771 aged 106), eldest dau. of Sir Henry Wemys (**2204**).
CHILDREN:(1) James and 2 others (all d. yg). (2) Henry (**0012**); James (**0015**); Ellis (cr. Countess of Brandon 1 Aug. 1758), m. (1) [4 Mar. 1725] Theobald Bourke, 7th Viscount Mayo, (2) [17 Aug. 1745] Francis Bermingham, 14th Baron Athenry; Mary, m. [1742] James Smyth (**1948**).
EDUCATION: School: Kilkenny College 2 Feb. 1686, aged 14 years.
CAREER/OCCUPATION: Alderman and Mayor of Kilkenny.

POLITICAL ACTIVITY: During the reign of Queen Anne he supported the Court party. From 1703 to 1713 he sat for Old Leighlin, a constituency controlled by the Bishop of Ferns; it was noted in the Parliamentary List of 1713 that 'The Bishop will "put in good men".' Although he voted against a Money Bill in 1709, he supported the Court over the Dublin mayoralty issue and the election of Sir Richard Levinge (**1230**) for Speaker.

In 1713 Agar was returned for Gowran, which

adjoined his seat, Gowran Castle. He undoubtedly had Tory inclinations, though probably more 'whimsical' than Jacobite. In 1714–15 he was on the 'black list' of Tories. On 22 October 1715 he was returned for Callan with 96 votes. The other candidates, Francis Flood (**0760**), William Despard (**0625**) and Serjeant Robert FitzGerald received 96, 47 and 39 votes respectively. On 21 November Agar was ordered into the custody of the Serjeant-at-Arms because of the riot at the Callan election.

The Agars were a 'new' family during this period, and James Agar probably saw his real role as consolidating his family's position in Co. Kilkenny and in his locality around Gowran. As Mayor of Kilkenny he was one of the Memorialists in August 1700 seeking to have the port of New Ross – which had been shut to discourage the woollen trade with England – reopened, as its closure was depressing the industry in Leinster. Locally he founded the poorhouse of Gowran as a private charity and continued to endow it during his lifetime.

His activity in parliament appears to have been slight. In 1703–13 he was listed for six committees, in the short-lived 1713 parliament for only one, in 1715–27 for three, and for three between 1727 and his death in 1733. In 1719 he was thought to be a likely opponent of the repeal of the Test Clause against the Dissenters.

DIVISION LISTS:

1709 (1) voted against a Money Bill.
1711 (1) voted for the Court on the Dublin mayoralty issue.
1713 (1) voted for Sir Richard Levinge (**1230**) for Speaker.
1721 (1) voted against a national bank.
1721 (2) voted against a national bank.

ESTATES/RESIDENCE: Gowran Castle, Co. Kilkenny. In 1700 Sir Richard Cox sub-let to James Agar Bramblestown and Ballyshanemore, barony of Gowran, which he had leased for leases/lives (probably renewable) from the Duke of Ormonde in 1699. (Welbore Ellis later lived at/owned Bramblestown, as did his heir, Lord Clifden (**0013**)). In 1703 the Hollow Blades company bought more than 250,000 profitable acres across 22 counties, including the greater part of the estate of Lord Clancarty and Lord Galmoye. James Agar purchased much of the Galmoye estate. In addition he purchased 3,776 acres in Co. Kilkenny from the Commissioners for Sale of Forfeited Estates in 1702–3. Agar's income in 1713 was estimated at £700.

SOURCES: Information from T. Shelby, supplied by J. Kennedy, 'Notes on the election of Callan MPs c. 1870'; PRONI T/3411 Blenheim Papers; PRONI LC 1752; McCracken thesis; Kilkenny MPs; Simms, *Williamite Confiscation*, pp. 152, 155, 182; *JRSAI* vol. 31 (1901) p. 56, P. D. Vigors, 'Extracts from the Old Corporation Books of New Ross, County Wexford'; *JRSAI* vol. 40 (1910) pp. 343–4, A. V. Hogg, 'The Collegiate Church of St Mary, Gowran, County of Kilkenny, and its Monuments' [says he died at age 63 and had 3 other children by his first wife]; *JRSAI* vol. 54 (1924) pp. 55–67, T. U. Sadleir, 'The Register of Kilkenny School (1685–1800)'; *The Dublin Gazette* 1 Jan. 1734; *Pue's Occurrences* 1 Jan. 1734; Record Nos EC 372, 373, 3123, 1035, 1375, 1374, 1551, 1813, 2082, and CDB 3266 cont'd; LC 1752; Parliamentary Lists, 1706 (1), 1711 (3), 1713 (1), (2), 1714–15 (1), 1719 (2).

0015 AGAR, James

MP for Gowran 1747–60; Tulsk 1768–9 [n.d.e. Callan 1761]

b. 7 Sept. 1713; d. 25 Aug. 1769 in a duel with Henry Flood (**0762**).
FAMILY/BACKGROUND: Son of James Agar (**0014**) and his second wife Mary, dau. of Sir Henry Wemys (**2204**).
MARRIED: [6 July 1741] Rebecca, only dau. of Rt Hon. William Flower, 1st Baron Castle Durrow, (**0767**).
CHILDREN: James; Henry Flower (d. yg); Rt Hon. George (**0011**); Charles (♦♦♦); Mary, m. [30 Aug. 1761] Philip Savage of Kilgibbon, Co. Wexford; Ellis-Mayo (d. unmar.).
EDUCATION: School: Rev. Edmund Lewis, Kilkenny; entered TCD 17 Jan. 1730, BA 1733, LLD 1748.
CAREER/OCCUPATION: Trustee of the Linen Board for Ulster 1759–d.

POLITICAL ACTIVITY: The families of Flood and Agar disputed the representation of the borough of Callan for many years, and the quarrel resulted in the death of James Agar in 1769, when he was killed in a duel with the Rt Hon. Henry Flood (**0762**). Agar had been declared not duly elected for Callan in 1761, and was thought to have purchased his seat for Tulsk in 1768. He was acknowledged to be an independent gentleman of large fortune who 'must be spoken to on interesting questions'. This was the government formula for country gentlemen, and his voting pattern indicates a certain independence combined with a predilection towards supporting government: for instance, he supported the government over the Money Bill crisis in 1753. He was moderately active in the House of Commons, being listed for 21 committees between 1753 and 1760.

DIVISION LISTS:

1749 (1) voted for the election of James Digges La Touche (♦♦♦♦).
1753 (1) voted against the expulsion of Arthur Jones-Nevill (**1125**).
1753 (2) voted for the Money Bill.
1757 (1) voted for the resolutions on pensions.

ESTATES/RESIDENCE: Ringwood, Co. Kilkenny.

SOURCES: McCracken thesis; *Alum. Dub.*; Kilkenny MPs; *JRSAI* vol. 76 (1946) p. 133, W. E. J. Dobbs, 'A Supplement to the Entrance Register of Kilkenny School, 1684–1800'; Johnston, *Gt B. & Ire.*, p. 164; *Almanacks*, Parliamentary List, 1769 (1).

0016 AGAR, Rt Hon. James

MP for Gowran 1753–60, 1776; Co. Kilkenny 1761–8–76 [r. Gowran, 1768]

b. 25 Mar. 1735; d. 29 Dec. 1788 at Gowran
HONOURS: PC, sworn 16 Oct. 1784.
PEERAGES: Cr. Baron Clifden 27 July 1776, Viscount Clifden 12 Jan. 1781.
FAMILY/BACKGROUND: Eldest son of Henry Agar (**0012**) and Anne, dau. of Welbore Ellis, Bp of Meath.
MARRIED: [20 Mar. 1760] Lucia, dau. of Henry Martin of Dublin, wid. of Hon. Henry Boyle-Walsingham (**0216**).
CHILDREN: Henry Welbore (**0013**); Rev. John Ellis, m. [11 Mar. 1792] Harriet, dau. of William Flower, 2nd Viscount Ashbrook (she m. (2) Pryse Loveden Pryse); Charles Bagenal, m. [1804] Anne Maria, o. dau. of Thomas Hunt of Cheshire; Anne Emilia (d. unmar.).
EDUCATION: School: Westminster Nov. 1746; entered Oxford (Christ Church) 20 Apr. 1752.
CAREER/OCCUPATION: Commissioner of the Revenue 1772–85 (patent 3 Feb. 1772, 19 Nov. 1772, 16 Dec. 1780, 28 Jan. 1784); *Commissioner for Paving the Streets of Dublin 1778–80; *Director 1784–8; Joint Postmaster General 1784–9 (patent 16 July 1784); Trustee of the Linen Board for Munster, June 1770–d.; *Governor of Erasmus Smith's Schools and other Charities 1779–d.; *Commissioner of the Tillage Act for Munster 1779–84.
MILITARY: Colonel of the Thomastown Battalion, the Kilkenny Independent and the Dublin Revenue Volunteers.

POLITICAL ACTIVITY: His father married on 29 May 1733 and, if his date of birth is correct, he was an MP when 18 years old. Certainly he was returned under age as, on 30 January 1753, Primate Stone wrote to Lord George Sackville (**1835**) that 'The Chief Baron tells me that Mr [Welbore] Ellis intends that his nephew, young Agar, should be chose at his borough of Gowran in the place of Chaigneau. Should you think it worth while to talk with Ellis on that subject? The young man is under age. If a friend could come in there for the present it might be of use, and we have enough that would be glad to pay money. That family of Agar, when it appears, will from their property be considerable. A simple marriage of the mother's throws the management of their affairs upon Ellis, and he may be very instrumental in serving us. I wish he were properly prepared. I would take it upon me to answer for the rights of the family being preserved to them.'

A contemporary assessment was that 'He is a good-humoured man and best of all the Agars, who had not the best of characters.' He was unanimously returned for Co. Kilkenny in 1761. Co. Kilkenny, which he represented for 15 years, was controlled by the Ponsonbys, Butlers, Floods and Agars. In Co. Kilkenny politics he was allied with the Ponsonbys but the alliance was not sufficient to prevent him from being detached, for, when Speaker Ponsonby (**1702**) was dismissed, he became a Commissioner of the Revenue on half-pay in 1772 and the following year on full pay. As a major office-holder he was a government supporter and, apart from substantial patronage to himself and his family, he received the patronage of a number of revenue offices: for example, Lord Lieutenant Harcourt gave him the nomination to a number of boatmen, three tidewaiters, three supernumerary gaugers, four Hearth Money Collectors, two Distributors of Stamps and a Supervisor of Hearth Money. In the sphere of military patronage he had the valuable nomination of two ensigncies. Not surprisingly, he was considered to be 'a great jobber'.

Agar was elevated to the peerage as Baron Clifden in 1776 and promoted to the rank of viscount, on the recommendation of Lord Lieutenant Buckinghamshire, in 1781. Prior to his elevation he had consistently sold his seats, but in the 1780s he began to build up a political party. On 14 January 1779 Lord Buckinghamshire wrote to Lord George Sackville (Germain) that 'It is said that the friends of the Agar family express their dissatisfaction upon the promotion of Dr Fowler (archbishop of Dublin) with a warmth bordering upon resentment. Yet it appears to me that the favours of Government have rather been lavished upon them. The Bishop of Cloyne, discontented as he may be, is morally sure of being recommended to the Archbishoprick of Cashel, Lord Clifden has just been created a peer and is a commissioner of the Revenue. As he sold his seats in parliament he has no influence in the House of Commons, and I should suppose that Mr Ellys [*sic*] holding a Capital Office in England is not intitled to advance claims here. He had however weight sufficient at Westminster to prevent the removal of the Dublin Customs House, which evidently, besides being a great inconvenience to trade, loses many thousands of pounds to the Revenue. In this and in some other instances English Ministers are most amazingly mistaken with respect to the consequences of individuals here.'

The Order of the Knights of St Patrick was founded on 17 March 1783. Explaining its necessity, Lord Lieutenant Temple wrote to Secretary Townshend in November 1782: 'Pray let me have my order of Knighthood as it is necessary for our House of Peers.' A year later his successor, Lord Northington, expressed his 'opinion that this Honour should be bestowed in the channel of great Parliamentary Weight, or to those who shall shew a disposition to support Government by their

Activity and Abilities in Parliament'. He pointed out that the political necessity for such an inducement was shown by the behaviour of Lord Clifden, who was alleged to feel himself under the necessity 'of bringing in no one, who would not implicitly follow him in all political questions either for or against the Castle'.

In 1784, at the beginning of the Rutland administration, it was reported that 'The Duke of Leinster (**0745**) declared himself totally attached to Mr. Fox; Conolly declared the same sentiments [Fox was the cousin of the former and the nephew of the latter], with this reserve, however, that the present times required every man to support Government – that was, in other words, that he would do so until the Reform Bill was rejected; Mr Ponsonby (**1702**) waited for orders for the Duke of Portland; Lord Clifden and the Archbishop had heard from Ellis and did not choose to work for nothing.' In 1784 they got their reward, as Lord Clifden, along with William Brabazon Ponsonby (**1709**), was made Joint Post Master General, with John Lees, one of the efficient Castle apparatchiks, as Secretary.

The Agar brothers were a family combination, backed up by their childless uncle, Welbore Ellis, who was a prominent political figure in England. Charles Agar was successively Bishop of Cloyne, Archbishop of Cashel and Archbishop of Dublin; he was possibly the cleverest and most active of his family. By 1782 it was noted that the Archbishop was 'very active in business – a good speaker – and very ambitious of being employed by the government in the House of Lords'. At the time of the Union, Lord Lieutenant Cornwallis remarked that 'The Archbishop is looked on in this country as a wise and able politician and I conceive the acquisition of his support as an object of no small importance.' In 1806 the political archbishop became Earl of Normanton.

In 1785 it was commented that 'This is the first time Lord Clifden ever pretended to a following in parliament as he constantly sold his five seats and depended upon Mr Welbore Ellis to advance him. His fortune is not equal to such an exertion as he has now made and therefore it is impossible for him to continue it ... The Archbishop of Cashel ... is working Heaven and Earth to raise the consequence of the family in order to advance himself to the Primacy.' In fact the archbishop was never Primate, but possibly a United Kingdom earldom was some compensation, particularly after the Union. In 1794 Welbore Ellis was created Baron Mendip (GB), with remainder to the descendants of his sister, Anne (Ellis) Agar.

Ellis outlived both his brother and his nephew, dying in 1802 at the age of 89, when his much-coveted title duly devolved on James Agar's eldest son Henry Welbore Agar, 2nd Viscount Clifden (**0013**). Agar's voting pattern reflected his political situation and ambitions.

DIVISION LISTS:

1757 (1) voted against the resolutions on pensions.

1768 (1) voted for army augmentation.

1771 (1) voted for Lord Townshend as Lord Lieutenant – expects a Commissioner's place.

1771 (2) voted against Sir Lucius O'Brien's (**1558**) motion for retrenchment – 'a Commissioner to be'.

1772 (2) voted against a Short Revenue Bill.

1773 (1) voted against the Absentee Tax.

1773 (2) voted against an untaxed press.

1774 (1) voted for the Stamp Bill.

1774 (2) voted against Catholic relief.

ADDITIONAL INFORMATION: The Irish Post Office before 1784 ran at a loss; after that year its gross receipts increased from £40,115 10s 1d to £77,473 17s 11d in 1799.

ESTATES/RESIDENCE: Gowran Castle, Co. Kilkenny; Arran Quay, Dublin. According to Wakefield, Lord Clifton [*sic*] owned 20,000 acres including the towns of Graigue and Gowran. He was also fortunate in his inheritance; the *Dublin Journal* noted that: 'Died. On Monday 15 inst. [April 1771] at Ringwood in this County [Kilkenny], Mrs Mary Agar a widow [of **0014**] aged 106 by whose death a jointure of £1,000 per ann. together with a great share of her personal fortune devolves to her grandson James Agar.'

SOURCES: PRONI T/1584 Pinkerton transcripts, p. 54, 28 Mar. 1760, 2 Jan. 1789; PRONI MIC/474 Irish Volunteers; McCracken thesis; Wakefield, *Account of Ire.*, vol. 1 p. 264; *Index to Irish Privy Counsellors, 1711–1910*; Kilkenny MPs; Hughes, *Pat. Officers*; *HMC Lothian* p. 343; Johnston, *Gt B. & Ire.*, p. 286; G. F.

Russell-Barker and A. H. Stenning (eds), *Record of Old Westminsters: A Biographical List* (London, 1928) [says incorrectly that his wife was the dau. of Colonel John Martin of Dublin]; *Ir. Gen.* vol. 4 no 6 (1973) p. 635, H. F. Morris, 'Births, Marriages and Deaths in Ramsey's Waterford Chronicle 1771'; *HMC Sackville I* p. 189; J. T. Gilbert, *History of the City of Dublin*, 3 vols (1861) vol. 3 pp. 137–8; A. P. W. Malcomson, *Archbishop Charles Agar: Churchmanship and Politics in Ireland 1760–1810* (forthcoming, 2002); *Almanacks*; *DJ* 28 Apr. – 2 May 1761, 3–6 Jan. 1789; *FJ* 9–12 June 1770; Parliamentary Lists, 1769 (1), 1772 (2), 1773 (1), (2), 1774 (1), 1775 (1), 1777 (1), 1782 (1), 1783 (1), 1784 (1), (3), 1785 (1), (2), (4), 1787 (1), 1788 (1), 1790 (1).

0017 AGHMOOTY (*alias* AUCHMUTY), John

MP for St Johnstown (Longford) 1695–9, 1703–13

b. *ante* 1640; d. 1726

FAMILY/BACKGROUND: Son of Hector Auchmuty.

MARRIED: Isabella, dau. of Rev. J. Stirling.

CHILDREN: James; Robert (admitted to Middle Temple 5 Apr. 1705, called to the Bar there 23 Nov. 1711); Richard; Forbes; Arthur; Catherine (d. yg 1691).

CAREER/OCCUPATION: High Sheriff of Co. Longford 1702.

MILITARY: Quarter Master, regiment of Foot 1661; Earl of Arran's Regiment of Horse 1655; wounded serving against the Moors in Tangier 1680; Lieutenant in Royal (Scots) Regiment of Foot 1684, Adjutant 2 Jan. 1685; Royal Regiment of Foot (a Williamite regiment) 1685, Captain-Lieutenant 8 Apr. 1687, Captain 1 Mar. 1688, Captain of Grenadiers in the Royal Regiment of Foot 31 Dec. 1688; Captain in Colonel William Wolseley's Regiment of Horse 20 July 1689; half pay 1690–1.

POLITICAL ACTIVITY: He was a professional soldier who probably first came to Ireland during the Cromwellian period, when he acquired lands and settled in Co. Longford. Aghmooty sat on three committees in the 1695 parliament and eight in the 1703–13 parliament; by that time he would have been over 60 years of age and, therefore, excused from committee service. He was returned by Lord Lanesborough in the general elections of 1695 and 1703, but the extent to which he was influenced by him is unknown. In 1696 he signed the Association for the protection of William III in parliament. During Queen Anne's reign he supported the Court party, and in 1711 he was one of the 31 Tories who met at the Fleece Tavern in Dublin. In 1713 it was thought that he would be returned again for St Johnstown 'if Lord Lanesborough thinks fit'. However, he was not returned.

DIVISION LISTS:
1711 (1) voted for the Court on the Dublin mayoralty issue

ESTATES/RESIDENCE: Newtown Flood, Co. Longford. The Ahmuty or Aughmuty family held lands in the barony of Longford, and are mentioned as holding Ballymacbrien in 1675, Ballykenny in 1681 and in Bryanstown in 1766 and 1800.

SOURCES: PRONI D/302; PRONI T/559 vol. 6 p. 342, Burke, extract pedigrees; LC 1994; Hayton thesis; *Cal.SP Dom. 1691–2* pp. 97, 134; *Coll. Gen.* [says died 1722]; C. Dalton (ed.), *English Army Lists and Commission Registers, 1661–1714* (London, 1892) vol. 1 pp. 318, 329, 334 (London, 1894) vol. 2 p. 255 (London, 1896) vol. 3 p. 27 [says he died 1722]; H. F. Berry (ed.), *The Registers of the Church of St Michan, Dublin, 1636–1700* (Parish Register Society of Dublin, 1909) p. 392; *Middle Temple Admissions* vol. 1 p. 257; Simms' cards; *Boulter Letters* vol. 2 p. 97 [one of his sons may have been an army chaplain at Minorca]; EEC Recovery 1800 and rental 1849; Parliamentary Lists, 1696 (1), 1706 (1), 1711 (2), (3), 1713 (1).

0018 ALCOCK, Henry

MP for Clonmines 1761–8 [n.d.e. Waterford B. 1768]

b. 1717; d. 1784
FAMILY/BACKGROUND: Son of William Alcock and Henrietta, dau. of Sir John Mason (**1350**).
MARRIED: [7 Sept. 1748] Jane Shepperd of Waterford.
CHILDREN: Henry Mason (d. yg).
EDUCATION: School: Dr Fell, Waterford; entered TCD 8 July 1734, aged 17 years, BA 29 Sept. 1737; Lincoln's Inn 1739; called to the Irish Bar 1745.
CAREER/OCCUPATION: *Clerk of the House of Lords *c.* 1746; *Commons 1747–79; *Magistrate of Waterford 1757; *Mayor of Waterford 1757, 1766; Sheriff of Co. Waterford, patent, 2 Feb.

1768; ?High Sheriff of Co. Tyrone 1768.

POLITICAL ACTIVITY: Although he was a lawyer, he appears to have started his career in the army, as in 1769 he was described as a 'half-pay Captain'. He became Clerk of the House of Lords about 1746 and of the House of Commons from 1747 to 1779: in 1760 this was worth *c.* £250 (parliament granted £500 for the two clerks) per session.

Clonmines was a Loftus borough under the patronage of the Earl of Ely (**1250**), but in politics Alcock associated with Speaker Ponsonby (**1702**) and in 1768 he voted against the augmentation of the army. He belonged to and married into Waterford families, and was prominent in city and county politics, being Mayor of Waterford in 1757 and again in 1766; in 1768 he was Sheriff of Co. Waterford. Nevertheless, he was opposed, and in 1768 unseated, by the Carew interest in Waterford city.

DIVISION LISTS:
1768 (1) voted against army augmentation – 'half-pay Captain'.

ADDITIONAL INFORMATION: He was a member of the Royal Dublin Society from 1766.

ESTATES/RESIDENCE: Nymph Hall, Co. Waterford (main country residence).

SOURCES: PRONI D/302; NAI MFCI Reel 8, Parish Registers of Kill St Nicholas, Co. Waterford; O'Neill thesis; Burke *LGI* (1904) p. 3; Hughes, *Pat. Officers*; *IMC King's Inns Admissions*; *Alum. Dub.*; *Coll. Gen.*; Vicars, *Prerog. Wills*; Smyth, *State of Waterford*, p. 163; M. Kelleher, *List of Members of the Dublin Society, 1731–1800* (Dublin, 1982); *Lincoln's Inn Records* vol. I p. 419; R. H. Ryland, *The History, Topography and Antiquities of the County and City of Waterford* (London, 1824) pp. 408, 410; *Almanacks*; *Statutes at Large* 1 Geo. III c. 1; *DJ* 5–9 June 1764; Parliamentary List, 1769 (1).

0019 ALCOCK, Henry

MP for Waterford city, 1783–90–7; Fethard (Wexford) 1797–9; [Escheator of Munster, patent, 10 (12) Dec. 1799]

b. 1735–37; d. July 1812
FAMILY/BACKGROUND: Eldest son of William

Alcock (**0020**) and Mary, dau. of Rt Hon. Nicholas Loftus, 1st Viscount Loftus (**1254**).

MARRIED: (1) [5 June 1764] Philippa Melesina, dau. of Richard Chenevix, Bp of Waterford and Lismore; (2) [6 Sept. 1766] Elizabeth Catherine, dau. of Beverley Ussher (**2129**).

CHILDREN: (2) William Henry (d. Paris 1783); Ussher, William Congreve (**0021**); Harry, m. Margaret Elinor, dau. and h. of James Savage (**1888**); Eliza Jane; Mary Anne (insane by 1810); Henrietta, m. [1804] James Wallace of Waterford; a child (d. yg 1797).

CAREER/OCCUPATION: Mayor of Waterford 1777, 1803.

MILITARY: An officer in the 13th Light Dragoons; Captain of the Waterford No.1 Corps, Independent Volunteers.

POLITICAL ACTIVITY: By 1783 the Alcocks and Carews appear to have reached a reconciliation, for Henry Alcock came in for Waterford on his own interest as 'The corporation of this city is pretty nearly in the possession of Mr Alcock, who returns himself and was the means of doing the same by Mr Carew (**0347**).' Politically he was considered 'popular' and against the government. He was a delegate to the Volunteer National Convention for Waterford city.

The Corporation had the power to make freemen at will; in 1785 it was noticed that it had made many Wexford men freemen and they pressurised the MP in the popular interest. To an extent they were counterbalanced by John Beresford (**0115**), the MP for Co. Waterford, and Cornelius Bolton (**0181**), the MP for Waterford city, who supported the government and enjoyed some support from the merchants. Bolton, a local entrepreneur and industrial developer, lost his seat to Alcock in 1783, but his supporters purchased one of the Lanesborough seats for him. In 1790 it was commented that 'The three families of Alcock, Bolton and Carew have, however, for a series of years monopolised its representation, leaving the citizens little other choice than to select two of them, colouring ... the deformity of family combinations against freedom with the vivid tints of personal attachment to the individual ... new combinations may take place at the next general election for connections fluctuate much here but Mr Alcock's re-election appears at present indisputably certain.' Nevertheless, he was described as a 'less than reliable' supporter of the opposition in 1791.

In 1797 he was returned for the Ely (Tottenham-Loftus) (**2088**) borough of Fethard. He was a strong anti-Unionist, a view in which his Waterford city politics certainly played a part, but Lord Ely was pro-Union. On 16 February 1799 Ely wrote to Castlereagh that 'Alcock is entangled by his Waterford interest not to vote for any measure leading to a Union, and Carroll (**0358**) ... thinks he is bound to vote likewise. I shall get rid of each of them as soon as possible' – and he did. Alcock applied for the Escheatorship of Munster in December 1799. Alcock's voting was consistent with his populist opposition politics and his need to keep the support of his constituents.

DIVISION LISTS:
1783 (1) voted for Flood's (**0762**) motion for parliamentary reform.
1784 (1) voted for a committee on the Reform Bill.
1784 (2) voted for protective duties (wool).
1785 (1) voted against the Commercial Propositions.
1786 (2) voted for Forbes' (**0778**) motion for retrenchment.
1787 (1) voted for a Pension Bill.
1788 (1) voted for Hartley's (**0979**) motion against the Dublin police.
1789 (1) voted for a regency.
1790 (2) voted for Ponsonby (**1709**) on the election of a Speaker.
1791 (2) voted for Grattan's (**0895**) motion for the exercise of Free Trade.
1791 (3) voted for Grattan's motion to abolish the Dublin police.
1793 (1) voted for Knox's (**1180**) motion for Catholic Emancipation.

ESTATES/RESIDENCE: Wilton, Co. Wexford (main country residence). In 1791 Henry Alcock was granted fairs at Bree. The lands were partly in Mangan in the barony of Scarawalsh, the lands of Dranagh in the barony of Bantry and Kilgibbon in the barony of Shelmaliere West. According to Wakefield, the rental was £3,500.

SOURCES: Information from H. F. Morris Esq.; PRONI T808, p. 3172; Abstract of Will; PRONI T/1584 Pinkerton transcripts, p. 76, 15 June 1764; PRONI T/3166/1D Hartnell notes; PRONI MIC/474 Irish Volunteers; LC 1798; EC 2511; NAI MFCI Reel 12, Parish Registers of Christchurch, St Olave and St Patrick, Waterford; O'Neill thesis; Burke *LGI* (1904) p. 3; *Coll. Gen.*; Hughes, *Pat. Officers*; Wakefield, *Account of Ire.*, vol. 1 p. 282; Smyth, *State of Waterford*, p. 163; Bolton, *Passing of the Act of Union*, p. 174 n. 2; G. O'Brien, *Anglo-Irish Politics in the Age of Grattan and Pitt* (Dublin, 1987) p. 182; R. H. Ryland, *The History, Topography and Antiquities of the county and city of Waterford* (London, 1824), pp. 410–11; *Ir. Gen.* vol. 6 no 2 (1981) pp. 159, 161, H. F. Morris, 'The Waterford Herald 1792' [says returned for Waterford 1769 (n.d.e.)]; *Ramsey's Waterford Chronicle* 23 July 1812; *DJ* 4–6 Dec. 1783; Parliamentary Lists, 1783 (2), (3), 1784 (1), (2), (3), 1785 (1), (2), (3), (4), 1787 (1), 1788 (1), 1789 (1), 1790 (1), 1791 (1), 1793 (1).

0020 ALCOCK, William

MP for Fethard (Wexford) 1764–8

b. 5 June 1705; d. (bur. 17) Mar. 1779 at Bellelake nr. Waterford

FAMILY/BACKGROUND: Eldest son of William Alcock and Henrietta, dau. of Sir John Mason (**1350**).

MARRIED: [24 May 1734] Mary, dau. of Nicholas Loftus, 1st Viscount Loftus (**1254**).

CHILDREN: (1) Henry (**0019**); Maj. William, m. (1) [ ] Goldfrap, (2) Beata, dau. of Turner; Sir John, m. [7 Apr. 1777] Sarah, dau. of Rev. William Dennis of Waterford; Mary, m. James Kearney of Waterford; Henrietta, m. [Dec. 1785] John Burchall of Waterford; Alexander (d. yg).

CAREER/OCCUPATION: High Sheriff of Co. Wexford 1740; Magistrate of Waterford 1764–?8; Mayor of Waterford 1753, 1764–?8; Free Burgess of New Ross 12 Aug. 1788.

MILITARY: ?Major Commanding Waterford No.1 Corps, Independent Volunteers; Colonel of Waterford Militia.

POLITICAL ACTIVITY: Little is known of his parliamentary activities. His principal objective appears to have been to build up his family's interest in Waterford city. By marriage he allied himself with the powerful Loftus interest, which controlled three parliamentary boroughs (Bannow, Fethard and Clonmines) in nearby Co. Wexford. Most of his children married into Waterford families or families with Waterford connections. At the 1761 election for Waterford city, he was one of the un-

successful candidates along with Robert Snow; they polled 105 and 125 votes respectively. Samuel Barker (**0083**) and Shapland Carew (**0348**) were returned with 142 votes each.

After Alcock failed to secure his return for Waterford city in 1761, he was returned for Fethard in 1764 following the succession of the Hon. Nicholas Loftus-Hume (**1255**) to the peerage. Alcock was sworn on 18 February 1764. He voted against the augmentation of the army on 2 May 1768, as did his brother Henry Alcock (**0018**) and all of Lord Ely's (**1256**) MPs except John Tottenham (**2091**), who was absent. Parliament was dissolved a fortnight later, and he was not returned at the ensuing general election.

DIVISION LISTS:
1768 (1) voted against army augmentation.

ESTATES/RESIDENCE: Wilton, Co. Wexford. In 1724 Patrick Lattin 'a papist' and another appealed to the House of Lords against George Robinson and others, over lands bought by the 'late William Alcock ... in trust ... from Patrick Lattin'. At the beginning of the case it was revealed that William Alcock of Dublin was seized of real estate of the yearly value of £1,000 and also possessed a personal estate of around £50,000, and that on 12 April 1717 he devised part of his real estate worth £300 p.a. to William Alcock of Waterford (this MP).

SOURCES: PRONI D/302; PRONI MIC/474 Irish Volunteers; NAI M5957, Extracts from the Parish Registers of Trinity and St Olave's, Waterford; NAI MFCI Reel 12, Parish Registers of Christchurch, St Olave and St Patrick, Waterford; Brown's Reports of House of Lords Appeals, 1701–1800, NLI reps. vol. 3 pp. 575–81; Burke *LGI* (1904) p. 3, *IFR* (1976) p. 5; *Coll. Gen.*; Wakefield, *Account of Ire.*, vol. 1 p. 282; *JRSAI* vol. 21 (1892) p. 298, P. D. Vigors, 'Alphabetical List of Free Burgesses of New Ross 1658–1839'; R. H. Ryland, *The History, Topography and Antiquities of the county and city of Waterford* (London, 1824) pp. 409–11 [says William Alcock Mayor of Waterford 1724, 1753, 1764]; *DJ* 19–23 May 1761, 18–20 Mar. 1779; *Ir. Gen.* vol. 6 no 3 (1982) p. 278, H. F. Morris, 'The Registers of Waterford Cathedral, 1655/6 – 1706/7' [says that his parents were m. in 1701]; *Dublin Gazette* 19 Feb. 1740; *Almanacks*.

0021 ALCOCK, William Congreve

MP for Waterford City 1797–1800 [r. Enniscorthy 1797]; [UK] 1801 – 7 Dec. 1803 [when declared n.d.e.]; Co. Wexford 1807–12

b. 1771; d. (bur. 9) Oct. 1813
FAMILY/BACKGROUND: Son of Henry Alcock (**0019**) and his second wife Elizabeth Catherine, dau. of Beverley Ussher (**2129**).
MARRIED: Unmarried.
EDUCATION: School: Mr Austin; entered TCD 22 Oct. 1788.
MILITARY: Captain, Co. Wexford Militia 1796.

POLITICAL ACTIVITY: As he was returned only in 1797, his career in the Irish parliament was short. He was strongly against the Union and voted accordingly in both 1799 and 1800. Lord Lieutenant Cornwallis considered that he was the principal instigator of hostility to the Union in Waterford city. Nevertheless, on 9 September 1801 Edward Lee (**1211**) wrote that 'I think I shall also be able to get William Congreve Alcock who is my cousin german, and has uniformly opposed the Irish government, and has not yet taken his seat in the Imperial parliament, to take it this winter, and to support government.'

After the Union Alcock continued to represent Waterford city until 1803, when his election in 1802 was declared void. In 1807 he was returned for Co. Wexford. During the election he quarrelled with another candidate, John Colclough, whom he considered to be poaching his promised voters. In the ensuing duel – which was said to have taken place in front of the County Sheriff, 16 magistrates (most of whom the government removed in the aftermath of the affair) and a large crowd of spectators – he killed Colclough. Although he stood trial and was acquitted, it affected his mind to such an extent that 'He became melancholy; his understanding declined; a dark gloom enveloped his entire intellect; and an excellent young man and a perfect gentleman at length sank into irrecoverable imbecility.' His father (**0019**) put him under Dr Willis's care in 1809, and he was subsequently confined in Thomas Warburton's lunatic asylum. Nevertheless, despite a petition for his removal from his constituents, he continued to represent Co. Wexford until the 1812 general election. The Castle became aware of his state of mind when he demanded the entire patronage of Waterford city even though he was not its representative.

DIVISION LISTS:
1799 (1) voted against the Union – 'Has £4,000 p.a. in landed property or is heir apparent to it'.
1800 (1) voted against the Union.

ESTATES/RESIDENCE: Wilton Castle, Co. Wexford. His property eventually devolved on his brother, Harry Alcock.

SOURCES: PRONI T/3166/1D Hartnell notes; NAI MFCI Reel 12, Parish Registers of Christchurch, St Olave and St Patrick, Waterford; O'Neill thesis; Jupp thesis; J. Kelly, *'That Damn'd thing called Honour': Duelling in Ireland 1570–1860* (Cork, 1995) pp. 236–9, 240, 265; *HP 1790–1820*; *Alum. Dub.*; J. O'Hart, *Irish Pedigrees* (Dublin, 1892), vol. 2 p. 24; *Coll. Gen.*; *Cornwallis Corr.* (London, 1859) vol. 3 p. 124; Parliamentary Lists, 1799 (3), 1800 (3).

ALDBOROUGH, Viscount and Earl of: *see* **STRATFORD**

2025 Stratford, John, 1st Baron Baltinglass, Viscount Aldborough, Viscount Amiens, Earl of Aldborough, MP Baltinglass 1721–7–60, 1761–3
2024 Stratford, Hon. Edward Augustus (styled Viscount Amiens 1775–7), 2nd Earl of Aldborough, MP Baltinglass 1759–60, 1761–8, 1775–7
2026 Stratford, Hon. John, 3rd Earl of Aldborough, MP Baltinglass 1763–8–76, 1790–7–1800, Co. Wicklow 1776–83–90
2022 Stratford, Hon. Benjamin O'Neale, 4th Earl of Aldborough, MP Baltinglass 1777–83, 1790–7–1800

0022 ALDRIDGE (-BUSBY), Robert

MP for Carysfort 1799–1800

b. c. 1768; d. 9 July 1837 near Naples, of cholera
FAMILY/BACKGROUND: Son of John Clater Aldridge
of New Lodge, St Leonard's Forest, Sussex, and
Henrietta Tomlinson, wid. of William Busby of
Stoughton Grange near Leicester. He took the
additional surname and arms of Busby 19 Oct.
1820 as h. to Rev. William Beaumont Busby.
MARRIED: [31 Dec. 1802] Elizabeth, dau. of James
Verner (**2142**).
CHILDREN: Robert, m. [1829] Caroline Anne, e.
dau. of Charles George Beauclerk of St Leonard's
Forest.
CAREER/OCCUPATION: Clerk in the Chief Secre-
tary's Office; Gentleman-at-Large Jan. 1800 at c.
£145 p.a.; Land Waiter at Customs House
Docks, Dublin, 1800 at c. £428 p.a.

POLITICAL ACTIVITY: He was an Englishman and a
clerk in the Chief Secretary's Office without any
known Irish connection. He appears to have been
drafted to vote for the Union and for that purpose returned by Lord Carysfort, when Henry
Osborne (**1610**), Lord Carysfort's brother-in-law,
who was hostile to the Union, accepted the office
of Escheator of Ulster. Osborne was subsequently
returned for Enniskillen and sworn on 3 February 1800 – he voted against the Union.

Aldridge was appointed Gentleman-at-Large in
January 1800, a sinecure worth c. £145 p.a.,
thereby vacating his seat; he was also Landwaiter
at Customs House Docks, Dublin, worth c. £428
p.a. Mark Singleton (**1925**), Lord Cornwallis' son-
in-law, was sworn in his place on 5 February 1800,
just in time for the final Union debate. Lord
Carysfort obtained a British peerage in January
1801.

DIVISION LISTS:
1800 (1) voted for the Union.

ESTATES/RESIDENCE: Dublin Castle.

SOURCES: PRONI T/3166/1D Hartnell notes; O'Neill
thesis; Burke *LG* (1846) p. 73, *LG* (1937) p. 17; *Coll.
Gen.*; *GM* (1837); *The Times* 31 July 1837; Parliamentary Lists, 1799 (2), (3), 1800 (3).

0023 ALDWORTH, Rt Hon. Richard

MP for TCD 1695–9

b. 1646 at Lambeth, Surrey; d. 1707
HONOURS: PC, gazetted 17 July 1695.
FAMILY/BACKGROUND: ?Son of Richard Aldworth
and Anne, dau. and h. of William Gwynn of
Frogmore House, Windsor, Berks.
MARRIED: [30 Apr. 1677] Mary, dau. and h. of
William Crofton of Co. Sligo, wid. of George
Perceval.
CHILDREN: John; Richard; Anne; Jane.
EDUCATION: Entered Oxford (St John's College)
20 Nov. 1661, aged 15 years, BA 1665, (All
Soul's College) MA 11 Feb. 1669; Barrister,
Middle Temple 1672, LLD.
CAREER/OCCUPATION: 2nd Secretary to the Earl of
Essex, 1672–7; Chief Secretary to the Lord
Justices July 1693–May 1695, to Baron Capel 27
May 1695 – 16 May 1696; Chief Remembrancer
of the Exchequer, at £600 for life (patent 3 Mar.
1676) 1676–1707; Craner in Dublin (patent, on
reversion, for life 14 June 1677) 1677–95.

POLITICAL ACTIVITY: In the 1695 session of parliament he sat on six committees, but thereafter he
appears to have run into some conflict. He surrendered his patent of the Cranership of Dublin
on 10 May 1695, and on the following 15 October Stephen Moore (**1473**) informed the Commons 'that he had in his hand articles of high
crimes and misdemeanours against Richard
Aldworth ... which he prayed might be received;
and being demanded that he would take upon
himself the proof of the said articles, he refused to
do so, saying he believed the said articles would
be proved, and that witnesses were ready; whereupon Mr Coghlan (**0432**) ... undertook to prove
one of the said articles, and the question being
put that the said articles be received, the House
divided.' They were rejected, 53 for and 155
against. Coghlan vociferously objected to the decision and was charged with 'disorder'. The House
divided on this charge 104 against and 104 for,
and, using his casting vote, the Speaker found
Coghlan guilty. He demanded, and received, an
apology.

Aldworth voted for the accusations against Lord
Chancellor Porter of favouring Catholics, possi-
bly following Lord Capel's hostile opinion of the
Chancellor. The following year, 1696, he signed

the Association for the protection of William III in parliament. In 1702 Aldworth, as chief Remembrancer, for his 'ancient fee' received £51 19s 2d; by then he was an absentee, as the Committee of Public Accounts that reported on 19 October 1703 was 'humbly of opinion the persons above [including Aldworth] ought to attend to the duty of their several employments'.

ESTATES/RESIDENCE: Newmarket, Co. Cork (main country residence); Stanlakes, Hurst St Nicholas, Wiltshire. The Co. Cork estate comprised lands in the baronies of Duhallow and Fermoy. In 1623 the Manor of Newmarket had been granted to Sir Richard Aldworth (?father). In 1672 Sir Richard Aldworth, under 32 Chas II, received a Chancery grant of lands in the barony of Imokilly, Co. Cork. In 1674 Sir Richard Aldworth was granted a second patent for a fair at Ballyhooly and also at Newmarket. A third patent for Newmarket was granted to Richard Aldworth (this MP) in 1701. Four fairs at Rockhill were granted to Richard Aldworth (0024) in 1731. A market was also granted at Dromagh.

SOURCES: *CJ Ire.* vol. 2 p. 720, vol. 6 pp. 747, 779; PRONI TSPI 1717–19, T/519 p. 87; *HP 1660–90* p. 524 [Richard Aldworth, this is possibly his father]; PRONI T/559, vol. 5 p. 259, Burke, extract pedigrees; EC 2440, 3153, 3440, 4824 and 1866; EC 6450; LC 137; NLI vol. 171, 16 Nov. 1880; *Cal. SP Dom. 1693* p. 238, *1694* pp. 407, 468, 471–2, 490, 501, *1695* pp. 5, 21, 28, 37, 40, 86, *1696* pp. 40, 71, 117–19, 161; Simms' Cards; *Alum. Oxon.*; *Coll. Gen.*; *Index to Irish Privy Counsellors, 1711–1910*; Hughes, *Pat. Officers* [says he was Sir Richard]; *IMC King's Inns Admissions*; J. G. Simms, *William Molyneux of Dublin* (Dublin, 1982) p. 94; *Proc. RIA* no 77 sec. C no. 1 (1977) p. 17, J. C. Sainty, 'The Secretariat of the Chief Governors of Ireland, 1690–1800'; Parliamentary Lists, 1695 (1), 1696 (1).

the only woman ever made a Freemason.)
CHILDREN: Boyle, m. (1) Jane, dau. of Robert Oliver (**1583**), (2) [Oct. 1775] Martha, dau. of Col. Christopher Rogers of Co. Cork; St Leger, 1st Viscount Doneraile (**0026**).
CAREER/OCCUPATION: High Sheriff of Co. Cork 1724.

POLITICAL ACTIVITY: He was a poor attender, as on 10 October 1737 his excuse for non-attendance was rejected by the Commons and he was ordered into custody. On 21 November 1737 the House learnt that indisposition prevented his attendance; it was resolved that the order to take him into custody be discharged. In 1749 the government noted him as 'absent and doubtful'. Certainly he does not appear to have been very energetic in the early part of his political career. He sat on ten committees between 1735 and 1756.

He was more active in the 1750s disputes, when he espoused the Country party, voting for the expulsion of Arthur Jones-Nevill (**1125**) and against the Money Bill. This may have had an element of Cork solidarity with the Speaker (**0210**).

DIVISION LISTS:
1749 (1) absent and doubtful.
1753 (1) voted for the expulsion of Arthur Jones-Nevill (**1125**).
1753 (2) voted against the Money Bill.

ESTATES/RESIDENCE: Newmarket, Co. Cork.

SOURCES: PRONI D/302; PRONI T/559 vol. 5 p. 259, Burke, extract pedigrees; PRONI T/993 Abstract of Will; NAI M2611, Extracts from the Parish Registers of Clonfert and Newmarket, Co. Cork; NAI, Index to Marriage Licence Bonds of Cork and Ross Diocese; McCracken thesis; Burke *LGI* (1904) p. 4, *PB* (1906) p. 511; Lodge *P.*

0024 ALDWORTH, Richard

MP for Lismore 1728–60

b. 1694; d. 25 (bur. 27) Apr. 1776
FAMILY/BACKGROUND: Only son of Boyle Aldworth (drowned on passage to England 12 Mar. 1698) and Elizabeth, dau. of William Cullyford, Commissioner of the Revenue (she m. (2) [July 1700] John Raives, (3) [ ] Butler).
MARRIED: [1713] Elizabeth (d. 1773), o. dau. (whose issue became h.) of Rt Hon. Arthur St Leger, 1st Viscount Doneraile (**1852**). (She was

0025 ALDWORTH, Richard

MP for Doneraile 1768–76

b. (Jan.) 1741; d. 4 Apr. 1824
FAMILY/BACKGROUND: Eldest son of Boyle Aldworth and his first wife Jane, dau. of Robert Oliver (**1583**).
MARRIED: [1 Feb. 1770] Ann, dau. of John Ryder, Abp of Tuam, wid. of Adm. Thomas Cotes.
CHILDREN: *d.s.p.*

CAREER/OCCUPATION: ?Clerk of the Treasury 1786–7.

MILITARY: Colonel of the Blackwater Volunteers 1782; Captain in Newmarket Infantry 1796.

POLITICAL ACTIVITY: Nephew to St Leger (Aldworth) St Leger (0026) and attached to his uncle, who was soliciting the title Baron Doneraile, having inherited the St Leger estates through his mother, Elizabeth St Leger. He was usually in opposition and considered to be a lightweight: 'a trifling sort of little man but will always follow his uncle'. He was also attached to the 2nd Earl of Shannon (0213) and – when he attended, which in the mid-1770s was seldom – he voted with them. His voting pattern reflected his politics.

He only sat in one parliament. He had a marked accent and was obviously something of a 'character', as Lord Shannon remarked to his son in 1798 that 'Like old Aldworth "Agad I left them all togither".'

DIVISION LISTS:
1771 (1) voted against Lord Townshend as Lord Lieutenant.
1771 (2) voted for Sir Lucius O'Brien's (1558) motion for retrenchment.
1773 (1) voted for the Absentee Tax.
1773 (2) voted against an untaxed press.

ADDITIONAL INFORMATION: His mother, Elizabeth St Leger, was the only woman ever to be made a freemason in Ireland; she is buried in St Finbar's Cathedral, Cork.

ESTATES/RESIDENCE: Newmarket and Rock Mill Lodge, Co. Cork. Formerly of Anne's Grove, Co. Cork. According to Wakefield, 'Mr Aldworth possesses the fee of an immense tract but it is leased chiefly forever.'

SOURCES: PRONI T/993 Abstract of father's Will; NAI M2611, Extracts from the Parish Registers of Clonfert and Newmarket, Co. Cork [says he died aged 84 years i.e. in his 84th year]; Coll. Gen.; Burke LGI (1904) p. 4 (1958) p. 6; McNevin, Volunteers; Index to Hibernian Chronicle, 1769–1775 (Society of Genealogists, 1936) vol. I p. 1; C. H. Wilson, A Complete Collection of the Resolutions of the Volunteers, Grand Juries, and Co. of Ireland (Dublin, 1782), p. 177; E. Hewitt (ed.), Lord Shannon's Letters to his Son (PRONI 1982) p. 93; Wakefield, Account of Ire., vol. 1, p. 250; Almanacks; FJ 17 Nov. 1796; Parliamentary Lists, 1769 (1), 1772 (2), 1773 (1), (2), 1774 (1), 1775 (1).

0026 ALDWORTH (ST LEGER), St Leger

MP for Doneraile 1761–8–76, 1776

b. c. 1715; d. 15 May 1787 at Doneraile of a burst blood vessel

PEERAGES: Cr. Baron Doneraile 2 Aug. 1776, Viscount Doneraile 22 June 1785.

FAMILY/BACKGROUND: Son of Richard Aldworth (0024) and Elizabeth, o. dau. of Rt Hon. Arthur St Leger, 1st Viscount Doneraile (1852). He assumed the name of St Leger in lieu of Aldworth 9 May 1767.

MARRIED: [1752] Mary, dau. of Redmond Barry of Ballyclogh, Co. Cork.

CHILDREN: Hon. Hayes, 2nd Viscount Doneraile (1856); Richard, m. [20 July 1779] (1) Anne, e. dau. of Charles Blakeney, (2) [1809] Elizabeth, dau. of Daniel Robert Bullen; Rev. James, m. [1809] Catherine, dau. of Thomas Williams; Maj.-Gen. Arthur (HEICS); Barry Boyle (1854); Henrietta, m. (1) John Godsell, (2) Hon. Joseph Lysaght (1295); Elizabeth, m. William Annesley Baillie; Mary, m. John Watkins of Co. Cork; Louisa Anne, m. [1805] Lieut.-Col. Francis Knyvett Leighton; Caroline Catherine, m. [1802] Col. Thomas Alcock of Surrey; Charlotte Theodosia, m. Rt Hon. William Tonson, 2nd Baron Riversdale; Georgiana, m. [15 Jan. 1798] Pascoe Grenfell of Buckinghamshire.

CAREER/OCCUPATION: *Commissioner of the Tillage Act for Munster 1764–84; Trustee of the Linen Manufacture.

MILITARY: Cornet in Colonel Henry De Grangues's Regiment of Dragoons 1745; Colonel of the Doneraile Rangers, Volunteers 1782.

POLITICAL ACTIVITY: In 1773 he was described as 'a positive muleish man closely connected with Lord Shannon (0213) but totally independent'. As heir to his uncle, Lord Doneraile, he was anxious to revive the title in his own name; for a number of years the government refused his request, so he tended to be in opposition. Along with the two Jephsons of Mallow (1086, 1087) he was usually part of Lord Shannon's Cork contingent. His inheritance included the borough of Doneraile, and Lord Harcourt's conciliatory regime courted him with the recommendation to a supernumerary gauger, a lieutenancy in the army for his son and the promise of a peerage which, with the support of Lord Shannon and after the 1776 election, was fulfilled. In 1785 he was created Viscount Doneraile.

He returned his two sons (**1860**, **1856**) for Doneraile in the 1776–83 parliament (one replacing him on his elevation to the peerage), but in 1783 he sold the second seat to James Chatterton (**0390**) a lawyer who supported government. His voting pattern – against the army augmentation and against Lord Townshend, for the Tontine amendments and stamps but against popery, against an untaxed press and for the Absentee Tax, against the 1774 Catholic Bill and against the pro-American amendment to the Speech from the Throne – was predictable given his attitudes and ambitions.

DIVISION LISTS:

1768 (1) voted against army augmentation – Has asked for the Peerage of Doneraile.

1771 (1) voted against Lord Townshend as Lord Lieutenant.

1771 (2) voted for Sir Lucius O'Brien's (**1558**) motion for retrenchment.

1773 (1) voted for the Absentee Tax.

1773 (2) voted against an untaxed press.

1774 (2) voted against Catholic relief.

1775 (1) voted against the pro-American amendment to the Speech from the Throne.

ESTATES/RESIDENCE: Doneraile Court, Co. Cork (main country residence); Great Britain Street, Dublin (town residence); Kilmeadon, Co. Waterford. He succeeded in 1767 to the estates of his maternal uncle, the 4th Viscount Doneraile – and last of that creation. In 1775 George Ponsonby valued his Waterford estate at £1,800 p.a. In 1777 Lord Doneraile's Ballyhooly estate contained 1,059 acres, including 647 in his own possession, at a rental of £525 for the 412 acres. He (or his father) let an estate forever at £2,000 p.a. and lived to see it re-let at a profit rent of £18,000. In 1785 Lord Doneraile was granted fairs at Tramore.

SOURCES: NLI MS 10933 Oliver Papers, Rental *c.* 1777; NLI reps no. 22; Wakefield, *Account of Ire.*, vol. 1 p. 253; PRONI T/1060/1, TSPI p. 24; PRONI MIC/474 Irish Volunteers; McNevin, *Volunteers*; NAI, Index to the Marriage Licence Bonds of Cloyne Diocese; GEC *P*; Burke *PB* (1906) p. 511 [says incorrectly that as St Leger Aldworth he represented Doneraile in 1749]; T. Bartlett and D. W. Hayton (eds), *Penal Era and Golden Age* (Belfast, 1979) p. 107 f/n. 57, Thomas Bartlett, 'The Townshend Viceroyalty, 1767–72', L. Hewitt (ed.), *Lord Shannon's Letters to his Son* (PRONI 1982) p. liii; *Waterford Arch. Soc. Jn.* vol. 16 (1913) p. 51, T. U. Sadleir (ed.), 'The County of Waterford 1775';

Almanacks; *DJ* 17–20 July 1779; Parliamentary Lists, 1769 (1), 1772 (2), 1773 (1), (2), 1774 (1), 1775 (1), 1776 (2), 1777 (1), 1782 (1), 1783 (2), 1784 (1), 1785 (1), 1787 (1).

0027 ALEXANDER, Hon. Du Pre

MP for Newtown Jan.–Dec. 1800 (elected 29 Jan. 1800)

b. 14 Dec. 1777; d. 8 Apr. 1839
HONOURS: Knight of St Patrick 1821.
PEERAGES: Suc. as 2nd Earl of Caledon 23 Mar. 1802; Rep. Peer 1804.
FAMILY/BACKGROUND: Son of James Alexander, 1st Earl of Caledon (**0029**), and Anne, dau. of James Crawford of Crawfordsburn, Co. Down.
MARRIED: [16 Oct. 1811] Catherine Freeman, dau. and co-h. of Rt Hon. Philip Yorke, 3rd Earl of Hardwicke.
CHILDREN: James Du Pre, 3rd Earl of Caledon, m. [1845] Jane Frederica Harriot Mary Grimston, dau. of James Walter, 1st Earl of Verulam.
EDUCATION: School: Eton 1791–6; entered Oxford (Christ Church) 19 Apr. 1796, aged 18 years, BA 1799.
CAREER/OCCUPATION: First Governor of Cape of Good Hope 1807–11; Sheriff of Co. Armagh 1801; Lord Lieutenant of Co. Tyrone 1831–d.
MILITARY: Colonel of the Co. Tyrone Militia.

POLITICAL ACTIVITY: He was elected on 29 January 1800 for his father's borough of Newtown(ards) on the eve of the great debate on the Union, 5–6 February 1800, which he supported. Parliament was prorogued on 2 August and finally dissolved on 31 December 1800. His career was, therefore, largely post-Union. He succeeded his father as 2nd Earl of Caledon in 1802 and was Governor of the Cape of Good Hope from 1807 to 1811. He was chairman of the London-based Irish Distress Committee, 1831–5, which provided cargoes of food for distressed parts of Counties Galway and Mayo. It dissolved itself in 1835 and handed over its remaining funds to local committees.

ESTATES/RESIDENCE: Caledon House, Co. Tyrone; Old Sarum and various lands in Wiltshire. In 1817 the Caledon estate was valued at £200,000, the Old Sarum estate at £46,583, and the rest of the Wiltshire estate at £27,180. He also had title to several manors in Kent. The second and third earls made extensive improvements to Caledon village, erecting Caledon flour mills, giving financial support to the poor of Caledon and to schools on the estate, and improving their property by draining, liming, etc.

SOURCES: PRONI D/2433/B/4/1/160–2, B/4/2/7 Caledon Papers; PRONI T/3166/1A Hartnell notes, GEC *P*; Burke *PB* (1903) pp. 250–1 (1906) p. 271; *Alum. Oxon.*; R. A. Austen-Leigh (ed.), *The Eton College Register, 1753–90*, 3 vols (Eton, 1921); *BNL* 4 Feb. 1800.

0028 ALEXANDER, Henry

MP for Newtown 1788–90; Askeaton 1790–7; Londonderry City 1797–1800; [UK] 1801–2; Old Sarum 1802–6

  b. 1763; d. 6 May 1818 at the Cape of Good Hope
  FAMILY/BACKGROUND: Son of Robert Alexander of Boom Hall, Co. Londonderry, and Anne, dau. and co-h. of Henry McCullagh of Ballyarton, Co. Londonderry.
  MARRIED: [1807] Dorothy, dau. of Francis Rivers of London.
  CHILDREN: James m. [ ] Harvey of Merlin Hall, Co. Donegal; Gen. Robert (HEIC); Catherine; Mary; Elizabeth; Anne, m. [1839] George Rowlandson.
  EDUCATION: Entered TCD 24 Mar. 1779, BA 1783; entered Cambridge (Emmanuel College) 25 Mar. 1779; Lincoln's Inn 30 Aug. 1779; called to the Irish Bar 1785.
  CAREER/OCCUPATION: *Listed in Judges and Barristers 1789–1800 (f.); Clerk of Deliveries, Ordnance, 1797–9; Chairman of the Committee of Ways and Means Jan. 1798–1800 (received £500 p.a. compensation, equivalent to his salary at the Union); Chairman of Ways and Means [UK] Nov. 1801–6 at £1,200 p.a.; Recorder of Londonderry 1791–2; Secretary to the Governor of Cape of Good Hope 1806–18.

POLITICAL ACTIVITY: He has been described as an 'intelligent Tory'. In 1796 he warned of the dangers of the middle-class radicals who were taking an increasing interest in politics, and the danger of their alienation from active politics. Advising their inclusion in some meaningful way, he wrote that they were: 'men of industry and general good character ... elated by the sudden acquisition of wealth, who with strong but uneducated minds perpetually brood over the artificial distinctions birth and rank create in society ... talk themselves and their auditors into a conviction that landed property supplies the means of oppression and the education of a gentleman the habits of aggravating such.'

A nephew of James Alexander (0029), he succeeded John Ponsonby (1702) as MP for Newtown(ards), which had belonged to the Ponsonbys. In 1778, after the death of John Ponsonby, the Ponsonbys and the Alexanders exchanged Banagher for Newtown(ards). Along with John Richardson (1782), Henry Alexander had unsuccessfully contested the Londonderry city seats in 1790. Alexander was considered to be of the Ponsonby party, but any connection was probably fairly thin and may have dated from the borough exchange. His uncle, now Lord Caledon, purchased the seat at Askeaton for him, and certainly by 1794 he was considered a government supporter.

In 1797 he was returned for Londonderry city where the Alexander family, originally Londonderry merchants, had considerable influence. From 1797 to 1799 he was Clerk of Deliveries in the Ordnance Department, and from 1798 to 1800 Chairman of the Ways and Means Committee with a salary of £500 p.a. In 1802 his brother, Nathaniel, was consecrated Bishop of Clonfert and was rapidly translated to Killaloe, within six months to Down, and finally, in 1823, to Meath. Henry Alexander was said to have been so pro-Union that he enrolled his two infant nephews as Unionists, as well as 'the embryo which his sister was then carrying'. He acted as a contact man for the government during the Union negotiations.

After the Union he sat for Londonderry city, 1801–2, and for Old Sarum, 1802–6. He was Chairman of the Ways and Means Committee of the UK parliament 1801–6 at a salary of £1,200 p.a. The British administration found him an efficient but irritating busybody. He voted against Burdett's censure of Pitt's wartime government, 12 April 1802. He opposed the extension of the bankruptcy laws, 23 February 1802 – he was involved in banking in Londonderry. He also took part in debates about the Irish currency, which had retained its separate status after the Union. He defended Irish militia and legal compensation arrangements on 16 March and 4 May 1803. He defended the prompt suppression of Emmet's rebellion in the debates of 28 July and 11 August 1803. He opposed the exemption of the Irish linen trade from duties in March 1804. In general he supported Pitt's second ministry and the suspension of habeas corpus in Ireland, 8 February 1805. In May 1805 he opposed the Catholic claims. Initially he supported the Grenville ministry, but he disliked the measures on the reform of Irish corporations and on the Poor Law proposed by Sir John Newport.

He accompanied his cousin (0027) to the Cape of Good Hope as Secretary, and acted in a similar capacity to his successor. He died there in 1818. While at the Cape he interested himself in agricultural improvement, to the extent that he impoverished his wife and family. After his death his wife pleaded for some financial provision 'in consideration of the large sums which her late husband spent reclaiming land and improving agriculture at the Cape'.

DIVISION LISTS:

1788 (1) voted for Hartley's (0979) motion against the Dublin police.

1789 (1) voted for a regency.

1790 (2) voted for Foster (0805) on the election of a Speaker.

1798 (1) voted against Sir Laurence Parsons' (1636) motion for an investigation into 'the present discontents'.

1799 (1) voted for the Union – Ordnance, Dublin Castle and since appointed Chairman of Ways and Means.

1800 (1) voted for the Union.

ESTATES/RESIDENCE: Glentogher, Co. Donegal; Sackville Street, Dublin.

SOURCES: PRONI D/345/1 Alexander Family Pedigree; PRONI D/2096/1/19E Maxwell Given notes; PRONI D/2096/1/19E, D/2433/C/11/36 Caledon Papers; PRONI T/3166/1B Hartnell notes; PRONI MIC/315/9/59 Blackwood pedigrees; O'Neill thesis; Jupp thesis; *HP 1790–1820*; *King's Inns Admissions*; *Alum. Cantab.*; *Coll. Gen.*; *Lincoln's Inn Records* vol. 1 p. 494; R. B. McDowell, *Irish Public Opinion, 1750–1800* p. 195; Bolton, *Passing of the Irish Act of Union*, pp. 175–6; *Ir.*

Gen. vol. 1 no 10 (1941) p. 294, W. Clare, 'Irish Compensations and Pensions'; *Almanacks*, Parliamentary Lists, 1789 (1), 1790 (1), 1791 (1), 1793 (1), 1794 (2), 1798 (1), 1799 (2), (3), 1800 (1), (3).

0029 ALEXANDER, James

MP for Londonderry city 1775–6–83–90

b. 1730; d. 23 Mar. 1802

PEERAGES: Cr. Baron Caledon 6 June 1790, Viscount Caledon 23 Nov. 1797, Earl of Caledon 29 Dec. 1800.

FAMILY/BACKGROUND: Son of Nathaniel Alexander of Co. Donegal and Elizabeth, dau. of William McClintock of Dunmore, Co. Londonderry.

MARRIED: [London 25 Oct. 1774] Anne (d. 21 Dec. 1777), dau. of James Crawford of Crawfordsburn, Co. Down.

CHILDREN: Du Pre (b. 14 Dec. 1777), 2nd Earl of Caledon (0027); Mabella (b. 7 Aug. 1775; d. Mar. 1854), m. [5 July 1796] Andrew Thomas Blayney, 11th Baron Blayney; Elizabeth (b. 21 June 1776; d. unmar. 1851).

ILLEGITIMATE: 1 dau., m. [1787] Langford Heyland (Mrs M'Tier wrote to her brother Dr William Drennan that Langford Heyland is to be married 'to a bastard of nabob Alexander's, – young and ugly, with £10,000').

CAREER/OCCUPATION: Sheriff of Co. Tyrone 1780, Co. Armagh 1781; Trustee of the Linen Board for Munster 1783–1800 (f.); *Governor and Guardian for the Lying-in Hospital 1787–1800 (f.).

POLITICAL ACTIVITY: James Alexander came from a Londonderry merchant family and made a fortune while in the service of the East India Company 'with a clear character'. After his return he purchased in 1776 the Caledon estate for the huge sum of £96,400, and settled down to the political and social life of a wealthy country gentleman 'of large property and good character'. He was Sheriff of Co. Tyrone 1780 and Co. Armagh 1781 (his estate lay on the border of the two counties), a colonel in the Volunteers and a delegate to the National Convention for Co. Tyrone.

Shortly after his return he had politically secured his position with the Corporation of Londonderry, stepping into the vacancy for the parliamentary representation created by the death of Provost Andrews (0040) in 1774. He was reputedly friendly with John Kilpatrick (**1148**) – a wealthy Anglo-Indian who brought his agent, Alexander's nephew (**0030**), into parliament – and with the Maunsells, but these may simply have been Indian rather than political connections. In any case, Thomas Maunsell (**1371**) died in 1778 and Kilpatrick in 1779. In general he was attached to government but, given his wealth, independent. As a Volunteer colonel and delegate he was in opposition in the early 1780s, as can be seen from his voting record. However, in 1785 he was considered to be 'against for special reasons' and in 1787 his continued hostility was attributed to his desire for a peerage.

Then, in the late 1780s, he consolidated his political position by purchasing the borough of Banagher, King's County from Peter Holmes (**1033**) for £10,000; almost immediately, in 1787, he exchanged it with the Ponsonbys for Newtown(ards). It was a good bargain as, apart from considerable political advantages, he received £15,000 in compensation for its disfranchisement at the Union. Another Londonderry family, the Stewarts, also based on East India wealth, owned the town of Newtownards but, to their enduring chagrin, not its parliamentary representation. Thus there was a certain irony in Alexander's control of Newtownards, which was not lost on contemporaries. The landlord of the borough was Robert Stewart (**2008**), the father of Lord Castlereagh (**2009**). When a borough changed hands the burgesses resigned and the new owner appointed his nominees, and in the summer of 1787 Mrs Martha M'Tier wrote to her brother, Dr William Drennan that 'We dined at Newtown[ards] the same day Nabob Alexander was entertaining under the nose of the Stewarts, his burgesses for the borough for which he paid £10,000.'

Alexander obviously retained considerable East India interests, as in 1788 the Marquess of Buckingham wrote to his brother, W. W. Grenville: 'As to your Mr Alexander; he has very good reasons for wishing me to court him, for he has offered himself and his borough (for he has one) to me; but his terms are a peerage, which is (even estimating the choice of a Director as you please) rather a dear purchase.' However, East India Company interest was valuable to the government, and

Buckingham continued: 'Can any vote be made by purchasing stock now, and can they vote by proxy? For if they can buy, I will undertake that you shall have some Irishmen, good men and true upon the list … no time may be lost and you will send me over a list of voters, I will see if there is any connexion here which can assist you, for we have many nabobs exclusive of Mr Alexander settled in this kingdom; and you will send me your recommended list.'

In 1790 he was elevated to the peerage as Lord Caledon (along with Robert Stewart, Lord Londonderry) and was reputed to have given his seats for Newtownards to the government in return. Seven years later he was advanced to a viscounty. In 1798 he was reputed to be 'very cautious [but on the question of the Union] not disinclined on fair terms'. In fact Alexander's support for the Union was rewarded with an earldom for himself and a bishopric for his nephew, Nathaniel Alexander. Lord Caledon supported the Union, as did his nephew Henry Alexander (**0028**), Londonderry city. One MP for Newtown was another nephew, Robert Alexander (**0030**), a banker, who voted for the Union in 1799 but accepted the Escheatorship of Ulster, possibly to make way for Alexander's son Du Pre Alexander (**0027**), who was returned on 29 January 1800 on the eve of the decisive vote; the other MP was Sir John Blaquiere (**0162**), who was elevated to the peerage in 1800 as Baron de Blaquiere.

DIVISION LISTS:
    1775 (1) voted for the pro-American amendment to the Speech from the Throne.
    1778 (2) voted against the Popery Bill.
    1779 (2) voted for a six-months Loan Bill.
    1780 (2) voted for Yelverton's (**2268**) motion to modify Poynings' Law.
    1780 (3) voted for the Tenantry Bill.
    1780 (4) voted against the Perpetual Mutiny Bill.
    1783 (1) voted for Flood's (**0762**) motion for parliamentary reform.
    1784 (1) voted for a committee on the Reform Bill.
    1784 (4) voted against the Address to His Grace the Duke of Rutland.

1785 (1) voted against the Commercial Propositions.

1786 (1) voted for the rights of Grand Juries.

1787 (1) voted for a Pension Bill.

1788 (1) voted for Hartley's (**0979**) motion against the Dublin police.

1789 (1) voted for a regency.

ADDITIONAL INFORMATION: *A member of the Royal Dublin Society from 1779; *a subscriber to the Public Assembly Rooms, 1787. The Alexanders, the Fergusons and the Hills were all involved in Derry politics and business. At different times they sent MPs to the Irish parliament to represent the city.

In 1755 James Alexander's father, Alderman Nathaniel Alexander, and other Derry merchants embarked on a sugar-baking enterprise with a capital of £8,000. Nathaniel Alexander died in September 1761 and was succeeded in his local enterprises by his son Robert, who in 1762 leased tenements 31–33 in the Diamond (the city business centre) with 18 acres of land in Shantallow and 120 perches in the island of Derry. In 1762 Robert built the Sugar House in Sugar House Lane. Robert Alexander also began the Inch herring fishery at Downings in 1772, and with a small fleet of ships exported herrings to various places, but in particular to the West Indies.

ESTATES/RESIDENCE: Caledon, Co. Tyrone; 1 Rutland Square, Dublin. Before he bought the estate at Caledon he lived at Londonderry and built Boom Hall, a house overlooking the Foyle and near where the famous boom was placed at the siege of Londonderry (it was afterwards the residence of the Bishop of Derry). He amassed a large fortune in the East Indies. In 1776 he purchased the Caledon estate in Counties Tyrone and Armagh for £96,400 from the 7th Earl of Cork and Orrery, whose father had acquired it, in 1738, by marriage into the Hamilton family of Caledon. James Alexander had already acquired property outside his native Londonderry: the house and demesne of Boom Hall, the Churchland estate of Moville, Co. Donegal (with a rental of £351 p.a.) and a fee simple estate near Ballycastle, Co. Antrim. The Caledon estate was extended by piecemeal purchases of adjoining townlands and by the leasing of other adjoining townlands belonging to the Archbishop of Armagh.

SOURCES: PRONI D/302; PRONI D/345/1 Alexander Family Pedigree; PRONI D/691/244, D/2433 Caledon Papers; PRONI T/1584 Pinkerton transcripts, p. 511, 8 July 1796, 28 Oct. 1774, p. 77, 12 Oct. 1764; PRONI T/3166/1A Hartnell notes; PRONI MIC/315/9/59 Blackwood pedigrees [says (incorrectly) he married 28 Nov. 1774, and (incorrectly) that he resigned his seat in 1784]; GEC *P*; D. A. Chart (ed.), *Drennan Letters*, pp. 43 and MSS; *HMC Fortescue* I pp. 111–12; T. H. Mullins, *Derry/Londonderry* (1986) pp. 80–81; Burke *PB* (1903 ed.) p. 250 (1906 ed.) p. 271; *IHS* 28 (1973) p. 340, Malcomson, 'The Newtown Act of 1748: revision and reconstruction'; R. B. McDowell, *Ireland in the Age of Imperialism and Revolution, 1760–1801* (Oxford, 1979) p. 137; *Almanacks*; Parliamentary Lists, 1775 (1), 1776 (1), (2), (3), 1777 (1), 1778 (1), 1780(1), 1783 (1), (2), (3), 1784 (1), (2), (3), 1785 (1), (2), (4), 1787 (1), 1788 (1), 1789 (1), 1790 (1), 1791 (1), 1793 (1), 1798 (1), 1799 (2), (3), 1800 (2).

0030 ALEXANDER, Robert

MP for Dingle 1777–83; Newtown 1797–1800; [Escheator of Ulster 1800]

b. 1752; d. 14 July 1827

FAMILY/BACKGROUND: Son of Alderman William Alexander of Dublin and Mary, dau. of [ ] Porter of Vicardale, Co. Monaghan.

MARRIED: (1) [May 1785] Henrietta (d. 1839), dau. of Henry Quinn MD of Dublin.

CHILDREN: William James, m. Gertrude, e. dau. of Gustavus Hamilton of Waterstown, Co. Westmeath; Henry Alexander, m. (1) Elizabeth, dau. of Joseph Pringle, Consul General of Madeira, (2) [1843] Salina, e. dau. of Thomas Taylor of Sevenoaks, Kent; Robert; Charles (Rector of Drumcree, Diocese of Armagh), m. Elizabeth, dau. of Edward Smith Godfrey of Newark, Nottinghamshire; Edward; Anne, m. Rev. J. Nussey; Isabella, m. William John Alexander.

CAREER/OCCUPATION: Partner in Sir William Newcomen's Bank and a Governor of the Bank of Ireland; *Governor of the Foundling Hospital and Workhouse 1788; Commissioner for Paving, Cleansing and Lighting the Streets of Dublin 1796; Freeman of the City of Dublin 1797; Sheriff of Co. Dublin 1805.

POLITICAL ACTIVITY: He was a nephew of James Alexander (**0029**). When he was first returned in 1777 he was an agent to John Kilpatrick (**1148**), whose father had made a fortune in India. Kilpatrick, who was a friend of James Alexander, brought Robert Alexander into parliament. Kilpatrick died in 1779 and Alexander subsequently became a partner in Sir William Newcomen's bank. He was a member of the Swords Election Committee, 6 December 1777. In his early parliamentary career he tended to support the opposition in economic and constitutional divisions.

Robert Alexander was a nominee in the life annuities of 1779. Later he became a Governor of the Bank of Ireland and a prominent Dublin citizen. In 1788 he was a Governor of the Foundling Hospital and Workhouse, and in 1796 one of the Commissioners for Paving, Cleansing and Lighting the streets of Dublin. The following year he was elected a freeman of the city of Dublin. He was 6th Captain in the Dublin City Corps (Infantry), Rotunda Division in November 1796. In April 1797 he was appointed a member of a committee for the relief of Dublin manufacturers.

At the 1797 election he was returned by his uncle James Alexander, Lord Caledon, for Newtown(ards). In 1799 he voted for the Union but then accepted the Escheatorship of Ulster to vacate his seat for Lord Caledon's son, Du Pre Alexander (0027). Although he followed Lord Caledon's line over the Union, as a Dublin banker he may not have been sorry to resign his seat before the final vote.

DIVISION LISTS:
1777 (2) voted against the Trade Embargo.
1778 (2) voted against the Popery Bill.
1779 (2) voted for a six-months Loan Bill.
1780 (2) voted for Yelverton's (2268) motion to modify Poynings' Law.
1780 (4) voted against the Perpetual Mutiny Bill.
1799 (1) voted for the Union.

ESTATES/RESIDENCE: Seamount, Co. Dublin; Sackville Street, Dublin.

SOURCES: PRONI D302; PRONI D345/1 Alexander Family Pedigree; PRONI D2433/B/2/5/1-15 Caledon Paper, (gives a Robert Alexander senior, wine merchant of Dublin, then Robert junior, partner in Newcomen's Bank, of Seamount, Co. Dublin – this is the MP and to confuse matters further he had a son called Robert who probably went to India; Burke, PB (1857) pp.153-4); PRONI T1584, p.339, 17 May 1785, Pinkerton

transcripts; PRONI T/3166/1A Hartnell notes; RCBL P80/1/1, Parish Registers of St Thomas, Dublin; O'Neill thesis; Watson's, *The Gentleman's and Citizen's Almanack* (Dublin, 1799); *Coll. Gen.*; *Ir. Gen.* vol. 1 no 8 (1940) p. 237, 'A List of Irish Stockholders, 1779' [says he is aged 27 in 1779]; *Almanacks*; FJ 6–9 Dec. 1777, 18 June; Parliamentary Lists, 1776 (1), 1778 (1), 1780 (1), 1782 (1), 1783 (1), 1799 (2), (3).

0031 ALLAN, Thomas

MP for Killybegs 1768–76; Naas 1777–83

b. 1725; d. 12 June 1798
FAMILY/BACKGROUND: Son of [ ] Allan.
MARRIED: Sarah, dau. and h. of [ ] Greer, a wealthy sugar-baker.
CHILDREN: Allan (at Eton 1763–4; d. 16 Nov. 1764). Illegitimate: a dau., Maria Gordon or Allan, inherited most of his estate.
CAREER/OCCUPATION: Taster of Wines, patent 8 Feb. 1763–70; Surveyor of the Outs and Defects; Commissioner of the Revenue 1772 (patent, 3 Feb. 1772; pension £600, which he exchanged for a seat on the English Customs Board); Customs Commissioner [GB] 1776–85.

POLITICAL ACTIVITY: Allan appears to have arrived in Ireland as the agent of a leading firm of Baltic timber traders. Wood was the universal material for all types of construction and Ireland was largely denuded of usable timber, much of which had to be imported from the Baltic. He was a self-made man, a Scot who, it is said, got his initial break by drawing a lucky number in Moss's lottery. The ticket was reputedly worth £10,000 but he traded it for £9,000 instead of collecting on it, and there is some doubt as to whether the purchaser managed to collect. He then furthered his fortunes by an advantageous marriage to the daughter and heiress of a wealthy sugar-baker called Greer. His only legitimate child, a son, was sent to Eton where he died in 1764.

Allan had excellent contacts in the political and commercial worlds of both London and Dublin. He was a substantial shareholder in the East India Company. In 1769, when the voting qualification was £500, he held stock worth £2,000 and was personally acquainted with Lawrence Sullivan and Warren Hastings. At this time Samuel Touchet, the MP for Shaftesbury in England, remarked to Macartney (1302) that Allan had lately had the thanks of both the Duke of Grafton and Lord North for his support at India House.

He probably entered the Irish political scene under the auspices of Lord Halifax, who appointed him to the then worthless office of Taster of Wines and Surveyor of the Outs and Defects. He attempted to recover the lapsed fees of his office, with the assistance of Samuel Touchet, who wrote to Macartney in 1769 that 'Mr Allan is now in the Irish Parliament and I really think will be of real service to the government.' He also had some connection with Sir Henry Cavendish (0380), as John Beresford (0115) wrote to him in 1778 that 'I will freely own to you (whose connection with the late Sir Harry Cavendish I well know), that this appointment completes the law arrangements of the Revenue' (the new Counsel to the Revenue was reputed to be to be Frederick Flood (0761), whose wife was Frances Cavendish)

Allan's endeavours to make his office profitable soon brought him into conflict with the Dublin merchants, who raised a fund to defray their legal expenses. These did not materialise, and with the money they were able to start to build the Royal Exchange (now the City Hall). Allan then attempted unsuccessfully to have a salary attached to the office or to exchange it for one of real profit. Possibly this was part of the reason for his purchase from Lord Conyngham (0464) of one of the seats for Killybegs in the 1768–76 parliament. He achieved some profitability for his office in 1772 when he relinquished it to John Beresford for £800 and became – for a brief time, after Lord Lieutenant Townshend divided the Revenue Board – a Commissioner of the Irish Custom. When Lord Harcourt reunited the Board he was made redundant, but with a pension of £600 p.a.

He was reputed to have 'accidently bought a black boy who proved to be an African Prince. Our King desired to see him, since when Allan has been taken notice of. He has the true Scotch sense. He was offered a large sum for the black boy. He would not take it but gave him to K[ing] G[eorge].'

Allan was probably introduced to Viscount Townshend by his brother, Charles Townshend.

He was on social terms with the viceroy, who on at least one occasion invited him to shoot at Rainham. When he first entered parliament he was thought to be influenced by Sir Henry Cavendish, the Teller of the Exchequer.

From 1769 to 1772 Allan was Lord Townshend's personal representative in London. His duties included 'giving every information within my knowledge relative to Irish affairs that may be called for by the administration and ... continuing to advise ... regularly what passes'; to this he added 'the chit-chat of the town'. Accurate news was vital to any viceroy, and not always easy to obtain. Allan was in London during the crucial months of 1770 when Lord North established his ministry and Townshend overturned the authority of the Irish undertakers, led by Speaker Ponsonby (1702). Remuneration for his activities appears to have been masked as services to the Linen Board.

Allan's appointment to the Irish Revenue Board was unpopular with the Irish politicians, and neither was he popular with the long-time Castle officials, possibly because it was a major office given to a 'foreigner' and perhaps also for the reason that John Robinson afterwards suggested to George III: that he was 'too much attached to corresponding with English government'. The Under-Secretary, Thomas Waite (2154), on one occasion suggested that the Chief Secretary, Sir George Macartney, should 'solicit the good offices of "that great minister" Thomas Allan'. In 1773 Waite wrote to Macartney that: 'I give you a thousand thanks for your last favour of 14 December and for the very high entertainment which I received from your excellent dialogue betwixt His Majesty and Mr Allan. This gentleman has for some time been distinguished by his particular friends with the appellation of Brass Allan but since this last exhibition of him, Dialogue Allen will very probably efface the other. I assure you that I have read it to many persons with infinite applause and approbation.'

He occasionally served Lord Harcourt in the same capacity between 1773 and 1777, and in 1776 Harcourt wrote to Lord North that 'his services had been uniformly zealous and essential'. Apart from the commissionership, Allan received 'several small favours from Lord Townshend' and the recommendation to two tidewaiters and one coast officer from Lord Harcourt.

In 1775 it was noted that his health was bad, and that if he could avoid it he would not come into parliament again. In fact he did come in, as after the 1776 election he was returned for Naas following John Bourke's (0192) elevation to the peerage as Lord Naas. The return was at the request of the government, and probably for a reduced purchase price.

As a parliamentarian Allan formed one of the silent majority. For the most part his career was uneventful, although in 1773 he was subject to a 'very violent and illiberal attack made by young Chapman (0388) on the debate' (on the supply). Allan's award of £350 for his alleged services to the Linen Board appears to have caused the attack, but the Speaker was able to prevent the threatened duel over what Allan considered were untruths impinging on his honour. From his correspondence he supplied the House with the odd piece of factual information and, in 1776, he introduced the heads of a routine bill to improve the road from Kilcullen, Co. Kildare, through Athy to Timoho in Queen's County. Although he sat in two parliaments, there is little indication of his participating in debates.

Shortly after his return in 1776 Allan negotiated his Irish pension for a seat on the British Customs Board, and, from 1778 until the fall of the North ministry in 1782, he advised North and assisted John Robinson in the conduct of Irish affairs, acting as 'unofficial undersecretary' for Ireland. He was particularly active during the 1779 crisis. For instance, he sounded out Beresford, possibly on behalf of North, as to whether he would be Chief Secretary.

He retired from the British Customs Board in 1785 because of increasingly poor eyesight, possibly caused by cataracts. He was permitted to make terms with his successor, £2,000 down and £400 p.a. for the remainder of his life. He appears to have spent a comfortable retirement at his house of Richmond Hill, where he died on 12 June 1798. His career illustrates some of the openings available to self-made men in the eighteenth century, and the importance of this type of personal link

between London and Dublin.

DIVISION LISTS:

1771 (1) voted for Lord Townshend as Lord Lieutenant.

1771 (2) voted against Sir Lucius O'Brien's (1558) motion for retrenchment – 'a spy and expectant'.

1773 (2) voted against an untaxed press.

1774 (2) voted against Catholic relief.

1775 (1) voted against the pro-American amendment to the Speech from the Throne.

ESTATES/RESIDENCE: From about 1778 he resided permanently in England, where he had considerable property and business interests in addition to his position in the Customs House. At the time of his death in 1798 he resided at Richmond Hill, Surrey. He bequeathed real estate in London, Surrey, Essex and Dublin. In addition he had nearly £30,000 in government stocks, and the unspecified residue of his will included £1,225 East India stock. Lord Kingston (1150) owed him £4,100, and there may have been other outstanding debts.

SOURCES: Will – Somerset House, probate 9 July 1798 at Doctors' Commons; *IHS* vol. 10 (1956–7) pp. 279–334, Johnston, 'The Career and Correspondence of Thomas Allan, 1725–98'; *Beresford Corr.* vol. 1 p. 30 and various; Ellis thesis; Hughes, *Pat. Officers*; Johnston, *Gt B. & Ire.*, pp. 82–5, 192, 250; J. Kelly, 'That Damn'd Thing Called Honour': Duelling in Ireland 1570–1860 (Cork, 1995), p. 129; T. Bartlett, *Macartney in Ireland 1768–72, A Calendar of the Chief Secretaryship Papers of Sir George Macartney* (PRONI 1978) [prints various letters] pp. xxx–xxxi, pp. 228, 230, 237; R. A. Austen-Leigh (ed.), *The Eton College Register, 1753–90*, 3 vols (Eton, 1921); J. T. Gilbert, *History of the city of Dublin*, 3 vols (1861) vol. 2 p. 56; *Almanacks*; Parliamentary Lists, 1769 (1), 1773 (1), (2), 1774 (1), 1775 (1), 1776 (1), 1778 (1), 1780 (1), 1782 (1), 1783 (1).

0032 ALLEN, Francis

MP for Co. Kildare 1725–7

b. *ante* 1682; d. 9 July 1741

FAMILY/BACKGROUND: Eldest son of Maj.-Gen. Patrick Allen of St Wolstans, Co. Kildare, and Mary, dau. of Thomas Brown of Dublin.

MARRIED: [1703, settlement date 4 Sept.] Frances, dau. of Col. Charles Whyte of Leixlip, Co. Kildare.

CHILDREN: John, m. [1730] Frances Walsh; William; George (officer in Austrian service); Thomas; Patrick; Robert; Mary, m. [Aug. 1734] Edward Plunkett, 12th Baron Dunsany; Catherine; Jane; Frances; Margaret.

POLITICAL ACTIVITY: He was originally a Catholic, and conformed to the Established Church on 5 December 1709. Little is known of the political activity of this MP in the two years that he sat for Co. Kildare.

ESTATES/RESIDENCE: St Wolstans, Co. Kildare. After his death the St Wolstans estate became the subject of an Exchequer suit, as a result of which it was sold to Rt Rev. Dr Clayton, Bishop of Clogher, in 1752.

SOURCES: *Coll. Gen.*; Kildare MPs; *The Dublin Gazette* 11 July 1741 [says died 9 July]; IMC *Convert Rolls*; *Kildare Arch. Soc. Jn.* vol. 4 (1903–5) pp. 103–4, H. Lyster Denny, 'An Account of the Family of Alen, of St Wolstans, Co. Kildare' [says he is Francis Alen but that his wife is Mary dau. of John Browne of Castle Browne, Co. Kildare – ? confusion between his wife and mother].

ALLEN, Baron and Viscount: *see* **ALLEN**
0033 Allen Rt Hon. John, 1st Baron and Viscount Allen, MP Co. Dublin 1692–3, 1703–13, 1715–17; Co. Carlow 1695–9; Co. Wicklow 1713–14
0036 Allen, Rt Hon. Joshua, 2nd Viscount Allen, MP Co. Kildare 1709–13–14, 1715–26
0034 Allen, Hon. John, 3rd Viscount Allen, MP Carysfort 1733–42
0035 Allen, John, 4th Viscount Allen, MP Co. Wicklow 1742–5

0033 ALLEN, Rt Hon. John

MP for Co. Dublin 1692–3, 1703–13, 1715–17; Co. Carlow 1695–9; Co. Wicklow 1713–14

b. 13 Feb. 1661; d. 8 Nov. 1726, in London
HONOURS: PC, sworn 9 Oct. 1714.
PEERAGES: Cr. Baron Allen and Viscount Allen 23 Aug. 1717.
FAMILY/BACKGROUND: Son and h. of Sir Joshua Allen and Mary, dau. of John Wybrow of Co.

Kerry. He was one of 15 children of whom only 4 survived.
MARRIED: [1684] Mary, dau. of the Rt Hon. Robert FitzGerald (**0741**).
CHILDREN: Rt Hon. Joshua, 2nd Viscount Allen (**0036**); Hon. Robert (**0039**); Hon. Richard (**0037**).
EDUCATION: School: Mr Ryder; entered TCD 24 Nov. 1677, BA *spec. grat.* 1692, LLD *hon. caus.* 1709.
CAREER/OCCUPATION: Sheriff of Co. Dublin 1691.
MILITARY: Captain in William III's army (on 25 July 1692 he, along with Thomas Browne, obtained a pass to go to Holland); Lieutenant in General Browne's Regiment of Horse 1702, subsequently a Colonel. Finding further promotion closed because of his political activities, he retired from military life.

POLITICAL ACTIVITY: Sheriff of Co. Dublin, 1691. He took a keen interest in local politics, as on 24 September 1700 Sir Richard Cox (**0507**) wrote to Ormonde concerning Allen's lease of Arklow Manor, recommending his appointment as seneschal, and on 16 April 1701 he was one of the gentlemen of Co. Carlow who petitioned against the return and residence of Mark Baggot, 'a violent Papist' in that county of which he had been 'titular High Sheriff' in 1689.

In parliament he supported Lord Chancellor Porter against accusations of favouring Catholics in 1695, and the following year he signed the Association for the protection of William III in parliament. In 1702 he was a lieutenant in General Browne's Regiment of Horse. Subsequently he rose to the rank of colonel but, finding further promotion closed because of his political activities, retired from military life. By 1706 he was considered to be hostile to the government. He opposed the Jacobite tendencies of Queen Anne's ministers, was a strong supporter of the succession of the House of Hanover in Ireland, and one of the principal witnesses against the Rev. Francis Higgins – the 'Irish Sacheveral'. He was a teller for the controversial Money Bill in 1709 and also on the Whig side in July 1711. By this time he was an entrenched member of the opposition, and in the 1713 Parliamentary List noted as a Whig. He was a member of the Commons Committee that reported on the alleged misconduct of Sir Constantine Phipps in 1713.

He used his patronage to secure the return of his sons unopposed in 1715. This provided the unusual occurrence of a father and his three sons (**0036, 0037, 0039**) all sitting in parliament at the same time. He was appointed to the Privy Council through the influence of his brother-in-law, the Earl of Kildare and William King, Archbishop of Dublin (King was the leading Irish churchman for the decade following the death of Queen Anne for, as Primate Lindsay had been appointed for his Tory views in December 1713, he was ineffective from the accession of George I until his death in 1724). An active MP, Allen is known to have been listed for 105 committees, 59 of which were in the years 1715–16.

DIVISION LISTS:
  1709 (1) teller for a Money Bill.

ADDITIONAL INFORMATION: Parliamentary returns for 1719 give four MPs for Lifford: David Creighton (**0518**), who represented the borough until 1729; Michael Sampson (**1862**), who died in 1719 and was replaced by Richard Hamilton (**0942**), who continued to represent the Borough until 1727; and lastly and unaccountably the Rt Hon. John Allen – probably a clerical error.

ESTATES/RESIDENCE: Stillorgan, Co. Dublin; Arklow Manor, Bullock and Dalkey, Co. Wicklow; Punchestown, near Naas, Co. Kildare; Mullinahac, Dublin (family town residence until *c.* 1735); tenements in Capel Street and Jervis Street, Dublin. He left £1,000 p.a. between his second and third sons, Robert and Richard, and the Manor of Arklow instead if the eldest son did not honour the bequest.
  By 1 Jas II (1685), lands in the baronies of Rathdown, Co. Dublin and Naas and Salt, Co. Kildare, were granted to Sir Joshua Allen and John Allen. By 1 Jas II, Sir Joshua Allen and John Allen were granted a fair at Tipper. The Wicklow lands were all in the barony of Arklow. In 1702–3 he purchased 229 acres in Co. Dublin from the Commissioners for Sale of Forfeited Estates.
  In 1705, the Duke of Ormonde's commissioners granted part of the lordship of Arklow, containing 8,528 Irish acres, to John Allen, for £1,215 and a rent of £300. According to Wakefield, by the early nineteenth century the leases were in general for 21 years and one life.
  The Allen family of Stillorgan, Co. Dublin were succeeded by the Proby family, Lords Carysfort.

SOURCES: PRONI D/302; Fuller Coll., London, 32/17 Allen's will 13 Nov. 1726; NLI ref. no. 335; Hayton thesis; GEC *P*; *Cal. SP Dom. 1691–2* (London, 1900)

p. 382; *Index to Irish Privy Counsellors, 1711–1910*; E. Kimber, *The Peerage of Ireland* (London, 1768), vol. 2 p. 81 [says he was born 13 Feb. 1666]; *HMC Ormonde* new ser. vol. 8 p. 242; C. Dalton (ed.), *English Army Lists and Commission Registers, 1661–1714* (London, 1894) p. 244 [says John Allen Captain in Sir John Guise's Regiment of Foot 31 Dec. 1688 – a Williamite Regiment]; *Alum. Dub.*; *Coll Gen.*; Kildare MPs; *JRSAI* vol. 28 (1898) pp. 31–2, F. E. Ball, 'Stillorgan Park and Its History'; *JRSAI* vol. 28 p. 331, F. E. Ball 'Mount Merrion and Its History'; NLI reps no 29; J. T. Gilbert, *History of the City of Dublin*, 3 vols (1861) vol. 1 pp. 351–2 [gives family background]; Wakefield, *Account of Ire.*, vol. 1 p. 284; EC 492; Simms, *Williamite Confiscation*, p. 182; Parliamentary Lists, 1695 (1), 1696 (1), 1706 (1), 1711 (3), 1713 (2), 1713 (3).

0034 ALLEN, Hon. John

MP for Carysfort 1733–42

  b. (bapt. 11 June) 1713; d. 25 May 1745
  PEERAGES: Suc. as 3rd Viscount Allen 1742.
  FAMILY/BACKGROUND: Only surviving son of Rt Hon. Joshua Allen, 2nd Viscount Allen (**0036**), and Margaret, dau. of Samuel Du-Pass of Epsom, Surrey.
  MARRIED: Unmarried.
  CAREER/OCCUPATION: *Governor of the Workhouse 1743–d.; *Commissioner of Oyer and Terminer 1743–d.; Trustee of the Linen Board for Leinster 1743–d.

POLITICAL ACTIVITY: He was a strangely mixed personality. He took a reasonably active part in political life, being listed on 43 committees between 1733 and 1741. Furthermore, he was a Governor of the Workhouse, a Trustee of the Linen Board and *a foundation member of the Dublin Society (1731). However, in 1730 he was satirised along with his uncle Robert Allen (*see* **0039**) by Dean Swift writing under the name of 'Traulus'. But, according to the *Dublin Journal*, 25–28 May 1745: 'The great benevolence, good sense, and public spirit, with other good qualifications that so eminently distinguished this young nobleman has rendered his death a universal loss to the kingdom, and generally as well as deservedly lamented.' Furthermore, 'He gave practical assistance to Lord Mountjoy's efforts to relieve the prevalent distress by employing the poor, during the hard frost of

1739 to clear Stillorgan Park of stones, as is re-corded on an obelisk still to be seen there.'

The manner of his death reflects the other side of his personality. On the night of 26 April 1745 he killed a dragoon in a street brawl. 'His Lord-ship was at a house in Eustace Street. At twelve in the night, three dragoons making a noise in the street, he threw up the window and threatening them, adding as is not unusual with him a great deal of bad language. The dragoons returned it. He went out to them loaded with a pistol. At the first snapping of it, it did not fire. This irritated the dragoon who cut his fingers with his sword, upon which Lord Allen shot him.' However, the wound occasioned a fever which eventually caused Lord Allen's death. His sisters became his heir-esses while the title devolved upon his first cousin John Allen, 4th Viscount Allen (0035).

ADDITIONAL INFORMATION: Foundation member of the Dublin Society. He was a prominent figure in the Masonic Order. In 1733 he was a member of the Dublin Aristocratic Lodge of Freemasons, and in 1744 Grand Master of the Grand Lodge of Irish Freemasons. He was re-elected Grand Master, 15 May 1745, but he did not resume his office as he died on 25 May.

ESTATES/RESIDENCE: Mullinahac House, Dublin; Stillorgan House, Co. Dublin. On his death the Allen estates were separated from the Allen title, which be-came impoverished. Most of the Allen estates went to his sister, Elizabeth, the daughter and heiress of the 2nd Viscount, and through her to her husband and to their descendants, Lords Carysfort. The remainder went to his other sister, Frances, Lady Mayne. In 1799 Lord Carysfort's Irish rental amounted to between £14,000 and £15,000 a year. This divorce of the peerage from the substance that sustained it caused problems to sub-sequent Viscounts Allen; for instance, Lord Lieutenant Northington remarked of the 5th Viscount that 'Lord Allen is certainly a worthy man and I believe very well beloved'; in 1782 a contemporary commented that he had scarcely any property but was a government sup-porter with 'a pension of £600 p.a.'.

SOURCES: PRONI T/3019/618 Wilmot Papers; McCracken thesis; GEC P; Burke *Ext. P* (1883) p. 5; H. Wood (ed), *The Register of St Catherine, Dublin, 1636–1715* (Parish Register Society of Dublin, 1908) p. 214; J. H. Lepper and P. Crossle, *History of the Grand Lodge of Free and Accepted Masons of Ireland* (Dublin, 1925), vol. 1; J. T. Gilbert, A *History of the City of Dub-lin* (Dublin, 1859), vol. 1 p. 353; Berry RDS pp. 24–7; *JRSAI* vol. 28 (1898) pp. 31–2, F. E. Ball 'Stillorgan Park and Its History'; Malcomson, *Pursuit of the Heir-ess* (Belfast, 1982) p. 31; Johnston, *Gt B. & Ire.*, p. 267; *Almanacks*, *The Dublin Gazette* 11 Oct. 1743 [reports him deceased].

0035 ALLEN, John

MP for Co. Wicklow 1742–5

> b. *ante* 1720; d. 10 Nov. 1753
> PEERAGES: Suc. as 4th Viscount Allen 1745.
> FAMILY/BACKGROUND: Son of Hon. Richard Allen (0037) and Dorothy, dau. of Samuel Green (0900).
> MARRIED: Unmarried.
> CHILDREN: John (supposed illeg. son; bur. 27 June 1754).
> MILITARY: Lieutenant in Browne's Regiment of Horse; Captain, Apr. 1742.

POLITICAL ACTIVITY: He was in parliament for only two years. He was a wild character and there is no record of his parliamentary activities except for his hostility to government, as it is recorded that 'His Lordship having taken an active part against government found his military services not likely to be rewarded, he therefore retired from public life.'

ADDITIONAL INFORMATION: In July 1745 'Lord Allen was taken out of a house of ill fame at four in the morning last Friday by a constable who was sent for by the people of the house. He wounded a man in the neck, but slightly.' On 21 July 1750 Under-Secretary Waite (2154) reported to Chief Secretary Weston (2223) that 'This morning I am informed that Lord Allen and Captain Eustace of Irvine's have slit if not cut off a great part of a gentleman's nose in a fray which happened a day or two ago in the road between Dublin and Naas. The occasion of it was very trifling, such as the gentleman returning the salutation of a fellow which they gave him and which they thought proper to deem an affront upon persons of their rank and in red coats. The story is told very dif-ferently in some circumstances, but in every way I think for the disadvantage of the officers. How-ever, they do not keep out of the way, nor have I heard of the gentleman whose name they say is Butler, son to a gentleman of Tipperary, has as yet determined how he will deal with them.'

Waite wrote again, 11 August 1750: 'I am informed that the indictments were found last week at Naas against Lord Allen and Captain Eustace for the assault upon Mr Butler. His Lordship preferred an indictment against Butler which was rejected with great indignation. Mr Commissioner Bourke (0192) was foreman of the Grand Jury and Lord Allen named him for one of his bail, but though his Lordship is Mr Bourke's near neighbour in the county, Mr Bourke told the Court he did not know Lord Allen. The trials will not be brought on until next assizes. It is generally thought that this affair will turn out one of the most unfortunate for his lordship that he has ever engaged in, and that he will have three or four Butlers to fight after they have harassed him by due course of law.' What happened next is unknown, but presumably Lord Allen conveniently died before the affair was finally resolved. The years 1742–5 that he spent in the House of Commons are similarly obscure.

ESTATES/RESIDENCE: Punchestown, Co. Kildare.

SOURCES: PRONI T/3019/654, /6455/241, 243 Wilmot Papers; PRONI T/1584 Pinkerton transcripts, p. 228a, 16 Nov. 1753; NAI M5088, Transcript of Parish Registers of Crumlin, Co. Dublin [bur. 13 Nov. 1753]; McCracken thesis; Lodge *P*; GEC *P*.

0036 ALLEN, Rt Hon. Joshua

MP for Co. Kildare 1709–13–14, 1715–26

b. (bapt. 12 May) 1685; d. 5 Dec. 1742
HONOURS: PC, sworn 12 June, 19 June, 24 Nov. 1727.
PEERAGES: Suc. as 2nd Viscount Allen 1726.
FAMILY/BACKGROUND: Eldest son of Rt Hon. John Allen, 1st Viscount Allen (0033), and Mary, dau. of Rt Hon. Robert FitzGerald (0741).
MARRIED: [18 Nov. 1707] Margaret, dau. of Samuel Du-Pass of Epsom, Surrey.
CHILDREN: John, 3rd Viscount Allen (0034), Elizabeth, m. [1750] John Proby, 1st Baron Carysfort; Frances, m. Rt Hon. Sir William Mayne, 1st Baron Newhaven (1386).

EDUCATION: School: Dr Jones, Dublin; entered TCD 1 July 1701, LLD *hon. caus.* 1718.
CAREER/OCCUPATION: 1st Clerk in Secretary of State's Office 17??; Sheriff of Co. Wicklow 1709; Sheriff of Co. Dublin 1720, 1725; *Commissioner of the Tillage Act for Leinster 1735, 1739; *Commissioner of Oyer and Terminer 1732–d.; *Trustee of the Linen Board for Leinster 1734–d.; *Governor of the Workhouse 1733–d.

POLITICAL ACTIVITY: He was a noted Whig in the latter years of Queen Anne, and the parliamentary list of 1711 marked him as one. In 1713 he was considered likely to be returned again for Co. Kildare, and he was returned. He was again returned for Co. Kildare in 1715, and was instrumental in managing 2 Geo. I, c. 24, 'An Act for changing the site and new Building of the Parish Church of St Werburgh's in the City of Dublin' – this was the parish church of the Castle. On 7 July 1719 he was one of those summoned by the Lord Lieutenant on the eve of parliament to consider how far the relief of Dissenters should be pressed. In 1721 he voted for a national bank.

He was one of the Memorialists who, in February 1723, sought on behalf of the Protestant gentlemen of Ireland either an explanation or revocation of a clause in an act of Queen Anne's reign for naturalising foreign Protestants in which favour was given to the children of natural-born subjects. The Memorialists feared this clause would allow the children of papists who had served James and then fled to Europe to return to Ireland and undermine the post-Revolution settlement in church and state, particularly by reclaiming their lands.

He subscribed to a declaration of sheriffs, justices of the peace, Grand Jury, nobility, clergy, gentlemen and freeholders of Co. Dublin against Wood's Halfpence. An active MP, he was listed for no fewer than 123 committees. He appears to have been at the height of his activity during the 1723–4 session, when he was nominated for 23 committees.

DIVISION LISTS:
  1721 (1) voted for a national bank.
  1721 (2) voted for a national bank.

ADDITIONAL INFORMATION: A contemporary described him as a 'a weak and dissipated man, who was trepanned [tricked] by Lionel Duke of Dorset into a marriage with Margaret ... Du Pass ... whom he subsequently refused to acknowledge as his wife. "But the Lady, after living for some time in close retirement, caused an advertisement to be inserted in the papers, stating the death of a brother in the East Indies, by which Miss Margaret Du Pass had succeeded to a large fortune. Accordingly, she put on mourning, and assumed an equipage conforming to her supposed change of fortune. Lord Allen's affairs being very much deranged, he became now as anxious to prove the marriage ... as he had formerly been to disown the unportioned Damsel; and succeeded after such opposition as the lady judged necessary to give colour to the force. Before the deceit was discovered Lady Allen, by her good sense and talents, had obtained such ascendance over her husband, that they ever afterwards lived in great harmony."'

He first 'caressed and courted and solicited' the friendship of Dean Swift before incurring Swift's wrath by 'rattling him bitterly under various infamous appellations'. He was subsequently satirised in the most virulent manner by the Dean, using the pen-name 'Traulus', in 1730. The following are extracts:

Let me now the vices trace,
From the father's scoundrel race ...
In him tell me which prevail,
Female vices most, or male?
What produced him, can you tell?
Human race, or imps of hell? ...
Positive and overbearing,
Changing still and still adhering,
Spiteful, peevish, rude, untoward,
Fierce in tongue, in heart a coward,
Reputation ever tearing,
Ever dearest friendship swearing,
Judgement weak and passion stony,
Always various, always wrong.

He was a foundation member of the Dublin Society.

ESTATES/RESIDENCE: Mullinahac, Dublin; Stillorgan, Co. Dublin. The Allens lived in their town residence of Mullinahac until about 1735. The estimated income in 1713 was £4,500 (including Dublin and Wicklow). Stillorgan is just outside Dublin; Mrs Delany visited it

in October 1731 and wrote that 'The house is like one made of cards, the gardens laid out in the old fashioned taste, but capable of being made a fine thing; nothing can be prettier than the situation.' In 1750 the Allen estates were centred round Carysfort, Co. Wicklow. Hence the husband of the 2nd Viscount Allen's elder daughter, and his principal coheiress, became Baron Carysfort. However, Proby had interests of his own in Huntingdon, which he looked after to the neglect of the Allen estates.

SOURCES: *CJ Ire.* (Bradley ed.) vol. 4 p. 273 (0173); PRONI T/519 p. 165, T/580 pp. 2–6, TSPI 1717–19, 1723–4; PRONI T/3411 Blenheim Papers; GEC *P*; Burke *Ext. P* (1883) p. 5; *Index to Irish Privy Counsellors, 1711–1910*; *Alum. Dub.*; A. P. W. Malcomson, *The Pursuit of the Heiress* (Belfast, 1982), p. 31; Gilbert, *History of Dublin* vol. I pp. 352–3; H. Wood (ed.), *The Register of St Catherine, Dublin, 1636–1715* (Parish Register Society of Dublin, 1908) pp. 5, 66; Llandover, *Delany Corr.*, vol. I p. 300 n. 1 [gives 18 Nov. 1704 for his marriage, which would have made him only 19 years]; Berry *RDS* pp. 24–7; *JRSAI* vol. 28 (1898) pp. 29–31, F. E. Ball, 'Stillorgan Park and Its History'; J. T. Gilbert, *History of the City of Dublin*, 3 vols (1861) vol. I pp. 352–5 [marriage story]; *Almanacks*; *GM* Dec. 1742 [says he died 4 Dec.]; *The Dublin Courant* 25 Nov. 1719; *The Dublin Gazette* 14 Oct., 29 Nov. 1724; BL Add. MSS 38,716 f. 93; PL (Sayles) p. 281; Parliamentary Lists, 1711 (3), 1713 (1), (2), (3).

0037 ALLEN, Hon. Richard

MP for Athy 1715–27; Co. Kildare 1727–45

b. (bapt. 22 July) 1691; d. 14 Apr. 1745 at Crumlin, Co. Dublin
FAMILY/BACKGROUND: Son of Rt Hon. John Allen, 1st Viscount Allen (**0033**), and Mary, dau. of Rt Hon. Robert FitzGerald (**0741**).
MARRIED: Mary, dau of Maj. Samuel Green (**0900**) of Killaghy, Co. Tipperary.
CHILDREN: John, 4th Viscount Allen (**0035**); Richard; Samuel; Joshua, 5th Viscount Allen, m. [5 Aug. 1781] Frances, dau. of Gaynor Barry of Co. Meath; Richard (**0038**); Mary; Dorothea; Jane; Elizabeth, m. [18 Dec. 1767] Col. John Browne.
MILITARY: Served for a time in the army, becoming a Captain in the 4th Dragoon Guards.

POLITICAL ACTIVITY: He was nominated for ten committees during the 1715–27 parliament and for 14 between 1727 and 1741, when his parliamentary activity ceased, possibly due to infirmity. Charles Delafaye, writing on 31 May 1716, described most probably this MP's bizarre behaviour during a debate on the size of the Establishment: 'Young Allen made the House merry by declaring before they began to tell that he saw so many of his friends on our side that he was ashamed to be told against them and so left his father and brother and came over to us, acting contrary to the speeches he had made, and then to complete the matter made a short one against the vote he had just given.'

In 1719 he was listed as a placeman and in 1721 he voted for a national bank. Probably he matured, as on his death the *Dublin Journal* declared him to have been 'a gentleman of the strictest honour, justice and humanity, and a sincere friend to the interests of true liberty and his country'.

DIVISION LISTS:
1721 (1) voted for a national bank.

ESTATES/RESIDENCE: Punchestown, Co. Kildare; Crumlin, Co. Dublin. In 1713 Sir John and Michael Fleming let lands in the barony of Monaghan to Richard Allen.

SOURCES: PRONI T/519 pp. 304–5, TSPI 1717–19; PRONI T/1584 Pinkerton transcripts, 24 Dec. 1767; NAI M5088, Transcript of Parish Registers of Crumlin, Co. Dublin [bur. 16 Apr. 1745]; McCracken thesis; Burke *Ext. P* (1883) p. 5; Kildare MPs; C. Dalton, *George the First's Army, 1714–27*; *Coll. Gen.*; J. O'Hart, *Irish Pedigrees* (Dublin, 1892) vol. 1 p. 636 [there is a certain confusion between Dorothy and Mary Green, who were sisters]; H. Wood (ed.), *The Register of St Catherine, Dublin, 1636–1715* (Parish Register Society of Dublin, 1908) p. 102; *JRSAI* vol. 28 (1898) p. 28, F. E. Ball, 'Stillorgan Park and Its History'; *GM* Apr. 1745; EC 6734; Parliamentary List, 1719 (1).

0038 ALLEN, Richard

MP for Harristown 1776–83

b. *post* 1728; d. 22 Jan. 1800
FAMILY/BACKGROUND: Son of Richard Allen (0037) and Mary, dau. of Samuel Green (0900).
MARRIED: ?Unmarried.
CHILDREN: *d.s.p.*
CAREER/OCCUPATION: Sheriff of Co. Meath 1775; Burgess of Harristown 8 May 1780; Collector of the Revenue for Armagh 1783–1799.

MILITARY: Lieutenant, Otway's Foot, May 1756; ?Captain-Lieutenant, City of Dublin 1st Regiment of Foot; *Lieutenant-Colonel of the 11th Regiment of Foot 1773; Colonel of the Naas Independent Light Dragoons, Volunteers; Lieutenant-Colonel of the Dublin Volunteers 1782.

POLITICAL ACTIVITY: A brother of Lord Allen (0035), he was returned by the Duke of Leinster (0745), to whom he was a second cousin and who obtained a promise of the first military government for him. The government of Cork became vacant and by a private arrangement this went to Lieutenant-Colonel Pigott (1683), for whom Lord Shannon (0213) was equally anxious, but the profits of the employment, £350 p.a., were to go to Colonel Allen until he should receive an equivalent appointment. In 1783 Lord Lieutenant Temple made him Collector of Armagh, *c.* £300 p.a.

He did not come into parliament at the 1783 general election. He voted with the Duke of Leinster's adherents and supported the policies of Lord Buckinghamshire and Lord Carlisle's administrations.

DIVISION LISTS:
1777 (1) voted against Grattan's (0895) motion for retrenchment.
1779 (2) voted for a six-months Loan Bill.
1780 (1) voted against Grattan's declaration of the Rights of Ireland.
1780 (2) voted against Yelverton's (2268) motion to modify Poynings' Law.
1780 (3) voted for the Tenantry Bill.
1780 (4) voted for the Perpetual Mutiny Bill.

ESTATES/RESIDENCE: Naas, Co. Kildare. By 1777 he had sold his commission and purchased a small annuity which, in the Parliamentary List of 1777, was said to be 'his only support', although as an MP he must technically have had some property. After he was appointed Collector of Armagh, estimated at £300 p.a., he moved to Armagh and spent the last ten years of his life there. He bequeathed his property to his nieces Dorothea and Mary Jane Browne, who appear to have kept house for him.

SOURCES: PRONI D/3078/4 Minute book of the borough of Harristown, county of Kildare, 1714–90; PRONI MIC/474 Irish Volunteers; Ellis thesis; Burke *Ext. P* (1883) p. 5; *Coll. Gen.*; Kildare MPs; *Almanacks*;

DJ 15–18 May 1756, 1–5 Jan. 1760, 15–19 June 1762, 28 Jan. 1800; *FJ* 11 Apr. 1797; Parliamentary Lists, 1776 (1), (2), (3), 1777 (1), 1778 (1), 1780 (1), 1782 (1), 1783 (1).

0039 ALLEN, Hon. Robert

MP for Carysfort 1713–14; Co. Wicklow 1715–27–41

b. (bapt. 12 May) 1687; d. 16 Dec. 1741, in York Street, Dublin
FAMILY/BACKGROUND: Son of Rt Hon. John Allen, 1st Viscount Allen (0033), and Mary, dau. of Rt Hon. Robert FitzGerald (0741).
MARRIED: [16 Jan. 1707] Frances, dau. of Robert Johnson (1101).
CHILDREN: Mary, m. [1732] Robert Boswell of Co. Wicklow; Frances, m. [3 Apr. 1738] William Paul Warren of Co. Kildare.
EDUCATION: School: Dr Jones, Dublin; entered TCD 3 June 1704.
CAREER/OCCUPATION: Secretary to the Revenue Commissioners 17 Sept. 1736–d; Sheriff of Co. Wicklow 1720; Commissioner of the Tillage Act for Leinster 1732; *Governor of the Workhouse 1733–d.

POLITICAL ACTIVITY: Returned for the family borough of Carysfort in 1713, Allen, like the rest of his family, was a Whig and, during Queen Anne's reign, a member of the opposition. On the accession of George I he supported the Hanoverian succession. He reported and carried through the House a number of bills between 1729 and 1735 including the Protestant Indemnity Act, 3 Geo. II, c. 6; administration of local government, 3 Geo. II, c. 9; an act for the punishment of deer stealers, 7 Geo. II, c. 8, and an act allowing the Quakers to make an affirmation instead of an oath, 9 Geo. II, c. 16. In 1721 he voted consistently for a national bank; in 1723 he was a teller for the government candidate in the Co. Westmeath election petition.

He was an active MP, nominated for one committee in the short 1713 parliament, 29 in the 1715–26 parliament and possibly as many as 73 between 1727 and 1739.

DIVISION LISTS:
1721 (1) voted for a national bank.

1721 (2) voted for a national bank.
1723 (1) a teller for the Court candidate on the Westmeath Co. election petition.

ADDITIONAL INFORMATION: He eloped with the daughter of Robert Johnson (1101), as on 16 January 1707 Johnson wrote to Ormonde that Allen 'has stolen a marriage with my daughter; no consent or acquainting of him with me. I fancy they will find they have two very difficult fathers to persuade to part with anything to either of them.' In 1730, he was satirised along with his nephew John Allen (0034) by Dean Swift, writing under the name of 'Traulus':

—— Allens Jack and Bob,
First in every wicked job,
Son and brother to a queer,
Brain-Sick brute, they call a peer,
We must give them better quarter,
For their ancestor trod mortar,
And at Howth, to boast his fame,
On a chimney cut his name.

He was a foundation member of the Dublin Society in 1731.

ESTATES/RESIDENCE: Old Court, Co. Wicklow. In 1713 the income of Robert Allen, MP for Carysfort, was estimated at (?)£500.

SOURCES: *CJ Ire.* (Bradley ed.) vol. 5 pp. 698, 720 (0277, 0280) vol. 6 pp. 371, 539 (0325, 0359); PRONI T/3411; McCracken thesis; Burke *Ext. P* (1883) p .5; *Alum. Dub.*; Gilbert, *Dublin*, vol. 1 p. 353; H. Wood (ed.), *The Register of St Catherine, Dublin, 1636–1715* (Parish Register Society of Dublin, 1908) p. 75; *HMC Ormonde* new ser. vol. 8 p. 277; *JRSAI* vol. 28 (1898) p. 28, F. E. Ball, 'Stillorgan Park and Its History' [says he had two sons who died unmarried and three daus]; *Almanacks*; *GM* Dec. 1741; *Dublin Courant* 25 Nov. 1719; Parliamentary Lists, 1713 (2), (3).

ALTAMONT, Earl of: *see* BROWNE and BROWNE-KELLY

0258 Browne, John, 1st Baron Mounteagle, Viscount Westport, Earl of Altamont, MP Castlebar 1744–60

0262 Browne-Kelly, Hon. Peter, 2nd Earl of Altamont, MP Co. Mayo 1761–8

0260 Browne, Rt Hon. John Denis (styled Lord Westport 1776–80), 3rd Earl of Altamont, 1st Marquess of Sligo, Baron Mounteagle [UK], MP Jamestown 1776–80

AMIENS, Viscount: *see* **STRATFORD**

2024 Stratford, Hon. Edward Augustus (styled Viscount Amiens 1755–7), 2nd Earl of Aldborough, MP Baltinglass 1759–60, 1761–8, 1775–7

0040 ANDREWS, Rt Hon. Francis

MP for Midleton 1759–60; Londonderry city 1761–8–74 [r. Old Leighlin 1761, Ballyshannon 1768]

b. 1718; d. 12 June 1774
HONOURS: PC, sworn 6 Apr. 1761.
FAMILY/BACKGROUND: Son and h. of Alexander Andrews of Co. Antrim.
MARRIED: Unmarried.
EDUCATION: School: Mr Blackall, Londonderry; entered TCD 23 Apr. 1733, BA 1737, MA 1740, Fellow 1740; Middle Temple 19 Nov. 1741–6, LLB 1743, LLD 1745, 1760, 1763–70; called to the Irish Bar 1746; Provost of TCD 28 Oct. 1758–70, 1774, Professor of Modern History 1762.
CAREER/OCCUPATION: *Governor of Dr Steevens' Hospital 1758–d.; *Governor of Erasmus Smith's Schools and other Charities 1758–d., Treasurer 1765, 1767–9; Freedom of Cork, 26 Aug. 1761; Freedom of the Corporation of Weavers, 1 Oct. 1763; Freedom of the City of Dublin, 14 Oct. 1763; *Governor of the Blue-Coat Hospital 1764–73; Trustee of the Linen Board for Leinster May 1765–d.; *Governor of the Workhouse and Foundling Hospital 1766–d.; *elected (June) to the Court of Assistants 1766–69.

POLITICAL ACTIVITY: Obviously a good committee man, he was listed for 27 committees in the year 1759–60. At the 1761 election for Londonderry city he produced enough non-resident freemen to give him a majority of about 20 over his opponent, Mr Stewart (♦♦♦♦). As a result Stewart withdrew without holding a poll although he claimed that he would have had a majority of about 90 resident freemen. In 1768 he was again returned for Londonderry, but by 1773 it was thought that he 'came in by his own interest which was great but is now lessened. He is a Privy Councillor and Trustee of the Linen Manufacture. An excellent politician and is never out of his road. He would sacrifice to his lust or ambition some of the most sacred duties of humanity. His life is defiled with what is generally a very gentleman-like vice. He is arbitrary, supercilious and turbulent yet a most faithful counsellor to Government.'

He ensured the return of his relation, William Gamble (**0839**) for Ballyshannon and acquired for him a position at the Barrack Board worth £400 p.a. In the church he obtained preferment to the Bishopric of Limerick for his uncle, Dr Averill, a living for his friend Dr Leland, a living worth £300 p.a. to Mr Andrews, and the agency of the Archbishopric of Dublin to another relation; various minor places were assigned to his disposal. The 1774 Parliamentary List notes his death and adds: 'As there is no danger of his being re-chosen I drop all animadversions on his past conduct.' He was a convivial companion 'and figures in the pages of *Baratriana* [*sic*] under the name of Don Andrea del Bumperoso'. 'A quick-witted man of affairs as well as a scholar, he distinguished himself in debate and became one of the confidential advisors of the Lord Lieutenant.'

DIVISION LISTS:
    1768 (1) voted for army augmentation – PC and Provost of TCD.
    1771 (1) voted for Lord Townshend as Lord Lieutenant.
    1771 (2) voted against Sir Lucius O'Brien's (**1558**) motion for retrenchment – 'the noted Provost of Dublin'.

ADDITIONAL INFORMATION: He had been a fellow for 18 years before becoming Provost; his predecessor, the celebrated Provost Baldwin, left a large amount of money which enabled Andrews to introduce Professorships of Divinity, Greek and Feudal Law. These were established by statute and liberally endowed out of college funds. In addition he obtained from the governors of the

Erasmus Smith Foundation a grant for the establishment of Chairs of Oriental Language and of Modern History, and for the provision of assistants to those professors. His own 'classical attainments are said to have been so great that he astonished and charmed the professors of Padua and the Roman Cardinals by the fluency and purity of his Latin in which he conversed freely'.

Andrews was frequently absent and sometimes inattentive, but the college flourished during his administration and the numbers increased to 520. 'He was a man of learning and talents, and possessed of every quality to conciliate affection. He was one of the most beloved men of his time, except in his College ... Though this seminary of learning had received from this amiable man such important benefits, he was incessantly persecuted with libels during his life, nor was this virulence appeased at his death.'

He is said to have been born in Londonderry prison while his father was confined for debt. It was thought at the time that his appointment as Provost was due to the backstair influence of the celebrated actress Peg Woffington.

ESTATES/RESIDENCE: Provost's House, Dublin. Estates in Counties Galway and Meath. He built the Provost's House, a nobleman's mansion, for himself and his successors beside the college but detached from it. Built in the classical Italianate style, it is one of the jewels of Georgian Dublin. In his will he bequeathed £3,000 to build an astronomical observatory and to endow a chair, and the sum of £250 p.a. for the professor and his assistants.

SOURCES: PRONI T/1584 Pinkerton transcripts, p. 193, 21 June 1774; PRONI T/2915/6/1, 7, 12 Bedford Papers; PRONI T/3459 C/2/78, 7/1–10 p. 3, Donoughmore Papers; McCracken thesis; *Index to Irish Privy Counsellors, 1711–1910*; Hughes, *Pat. Officers*; IMC *King's Inns Admissions*; *Middle Temple Admissions* vol. l. p. 330; Hickson, *Records of Old Kerry*, pp. 272–3; E. McPartland, *The Buildings of Trinity College Dublin* [reprinted from *Country Life*] pp. 13–20 [there is a portrait of Provost Andrews on p. 20]; R. B. McDowell and D. A. Webb, *Trinity College Dublin, 1592–1952* (1982) pp. 37, 50, 52–3, 56, 58, 64, 385, 521; R. B. McDowell, *Ireland in the Age of Imperialism and Revolution, 1760–1801* (Oxford, 1979) pp. 231–2; *Almanacks*; *BNL* 5 May 1761; *DJ* 4–8 Oct. 1763, 15–18 Oct. 1763; *FJ* 25–9 May 1765; Parliamentary Lists, 1769 (1), 1772 (2), 1773 (1), (2), 1774 (1).

0041 ANKETELL, Oliver

MP for Monaghan B. 1753–60

b. 1676; d. 27 May 1760
FAMILY/BACKGROUND: Son of Matthew Anketell of Anketell's Grove, Co. Monaghan, and Matilda, dau. of Robert Moore of Garvey Castle and Ravella, Co. Tyrone.
MARRIED: (1) [1 Feb. 1716] Sarah, dau. of Rt Hon. William Caulfeild, 2nd Viscount Charlemont; (2) (when aged 80) Anne Stephens (née Tuton).
CHILDREN: (1) William, m. [11 Mar. 1748] Anne, dau. of Charles Coote (0479); Anne, m. Rev. Edward Lill; Rebecca, m. Samuel Coulston MD; Catherine, m. Thomas Singleton.
EDUCATION: School: Dr Jones, Dublin; entered TCD 27 Jan. 1695, BA 1700, MA and LLB 1703.
CAREER/OCCUPATION: Sheriff of Co. Monaghan 1703 and 1713.

POLITICAL ACTIVITY: Anketell had been a leading figure in local politics for many years before he was elected for Monaghan town in 1753. Given Anketell's own age (77) and that of the king (George II was 70), Anketell might be regarded as a suitable 'seat-warmer'. Certainly, with his interest in local politics and agricultural improvement, he was a very typical country gentleman, as was his neighbour and predecessor, Baptist Johnston (1106). As early as 1713 it had been rumoured that Sir Alexander Cairnes (0334) was going to recommend Anketell for the borough; but for the fact that there were only two general elections (1715 and 1727) between then and 1753, he might well have been returned earlier.

On his election he followed the Country party line during the Money Bill dispute, voting against the bill. This obviously pleased his constituents, as in 1754 the Provost, burgesses and freemen of Monaghan Borough gave a 'genteel entertainment' to Oliver Anketell at the White Hart Inn in Monaghan Town, and at the same time 'returned him their thanks for his steadiness this session of Parliament'.

Due to his age on entering parliament, his parliamentary activity appears to have been slight – he sat on one committee in 1753. In any case, as he was over 60 years of age when returned to parliament, he was excused committee service.

DIVISION LISTS:
1753 (2) voted against the Money Bill.

ESTATES/RESIDENCE: Anketell Grove, Co. Monaghan. The estate, advertised for sale in 1860, included the townlands of Ballynabone and Glannan barony, and of Trough near Glasslough: a total of 346 statute acres, but it was possibly larger in the eighteenth century.

SOURCES: PRONI T/1584 Pinkerton transcripts, p. 494, 20 Feb. 1795, p. 56, 3 June 1700; NLI vol. 89, 20 Apr. 1860; McCracken thesis; Burke *LGI* (1904) p. 7; PRONI T/1769/1–9; Anon, *A Short History ... of the Family ... of Anketill or Anketel* (Belfast, 1901) [says b. 1680]; Berry *RDS* pp. 77, 60, 65; *Almanacks*; *The Dublin Gazette* 13 Dec. 1712, 16 Feb. 1754.

ANGLESEY, Earl of: *see* ANNESLEY

0042 Annesley, Rt Hon. Arthur, 6th Viscount Valentia, 5th Earl of Anglesey [E], MP New Ross 1703–10, [E] Cambridge University 1702–10

ANNALY, Baron: *see* GORE

0869 Gore, Rt Hon. John, Baron Annaly (1st creation), MP Jamestown 1747–60, Co. Longford 1761–4

0867 Gore, Henry, Baron Annaly (2nd creation), MP Co. Longford 1758–60, 1768–76–83–9, Lanesborough 1761–8

0042 ANNESLEY, Rt Hon. Arthur

MP for New Ross 1703–10; [E] Cambridge University 1702–10

b. *c.* 1678; d. 1 Apr. 1737
HONOURS: PC, sworn 1711, 6 Aug. 1714, 22 Oct. 1715, 19 June 1727, 22 June 1728, [GB] 1710.
PEERAGES: Suc. as 6th Viscount Valentia, 5th Earl of Anglesey 18 Sept. 1710.
FAMILY/BACKGROUND: Son of James Annesley, 2nd Earl of Anglesey, and Elizabeth, dau. of John Manners, 8th Earl of Rutland.
MARRIED: [July 1702] his cousin Mary (d. 1718), dau. of John Thompson, 1st Baron Haversham.

CHILDREN: *d.s.p.*
EDUCATION: Entered Cambridge (Magdalene College) 4 Feb. 1697, MA 1699; High Steward, Cambridge University 9 Feb. 1722–d., benefactor to Magdalene.
CAREER/OCCUPATION: Joint Vice-Treasurer and Treasurer at War 1710–16; Lord Justice in the period between Queen Anne's death and arrival of George I; Free Burgess of New Ross 31 Oct. 1702; Trustee of the Linen Manufacture for the Province of Leinster 10 Oct. 1711; Governor of Co. Wexford Nov. 1727.

POLITICAL ACTIVITY: He was concurrently an English/British and an Irish MP, and during Queen Anne's reign his interest was mainly in England. The Parliamentary Lists of 1706 and 1707 note him as absent.

After he succeeded to the earldom in 1710 he began to look towards the viceroyalty. He was a Lord Justice between the death of Queen Anne and the arrival of George I, leader of the Hanoverian or 'whimsical' Tories in England and an aggressive and outspoken High Church Tory, driven by a hatred of Dissenters and in particular of Presbyterians. Although frequently absent in England – for instance, he was noted as absent 'in London' in the Parliamentary Lists of both 1706 and 1707 – 'He had been an active member of both the British and Irish Parliaments since the beginning of Anne's reign and in November 1711 had been described as "the darling of the Church party" in Ireland. However, his ambition was the viceroyalty and his Hanoverian support appears to have been primarily a means to this end.' But for all his Hanoverian speeches at Westminster, in Ireland Anglesey was as enthusiastic a Tory as Ormonde or Phipps.

When Shrewsbury was appointed viceroy instead of him, Anglesey was determined to see him fail. In Council he and Phipps opposed any compromise with the Whig-dominated Dublin Corporation. 'Shrewsbury was disgusted and spoke of "persons there ... who had designs of their own in view".' On his return to England in 1714 Anglesey had hoped to see Oxford wholeheartedly adopt a 'thorough' policy against the Irish Whigs through a new Lord Lieutenant, preferably himself. His demeanour was a disappointment to the Hanoverian envoy, Schutz, who reported that

'Those who have seen Lord Anglesey, and are his friends, acknowledge that he is a good deal more cool than he was before he went to Ireland, and he declines to enter into what our friends propose to him.' Oxford's policy of inactivity brought him back towards the Hanoverians, and he and the leader of the 'Whimsicals' in the Commons, Sir Thomas Hamer, agreed to cooperate with the Whigs on the succession. 'On 5 Apr. 1714 Anglesey and other Tory Lords voted that the succession was in danger, Anglesey making a speech in which he "ripped up the peace".' Over the following weeks, when Oxford, Bolingbroke and the Whigs all attempted to woo him he took no definite line, but eventually came down on Bolingbroke's side since his policy coincided most with his objectives: the lord lieutenancy and the defence of the Irish church. He could not go back on the succession issue, but he came to Bolingbroke's aid on more than one occasion.

On 27 July 1714 Oxford was dismissed. Two days earlier Anglesey had been commissioned to remodel the army in Ireland by conducting a purge of the Whigs, but before he landed the queen was dead and the Hanoverian succession proclaimed.

The victorious Whigs in the Irish Commons were determined on revenge. On 21 January 1716 the House recalled a motion of 15 November 1714, that whosoever had advised the late queen to prorogue parliament at a time when a bill to attaint the Pretender was under 'consideration ... was an enemy to the succession as by law established in the illustrious House of Hanover, to the Protestant interest of this Kingdom, and a favourer of the Pretender'. Another resolution was then agreed to, *nemine contradicente*, 'that whosoever advised the irregular breaking of a great part of the army of this Kingdom, immediately after the unseasonable prorogation of the late Parliament ... were enemies to the Protestant Succession, and designed to bring in the Pretender and Popery'. The House then voted 85 to 46 that in its opinion 'Arthur, Earl of Anglesey was one of the principal advisers of her late Majesty to break the army and prorogue the late Parliament.' A committee was appointed to prepare an address for forwarding to the king by the Lords Justices that Anglesey be removed from the king's council and serv-

ice 'for the security of his Government and the Protestant interest of Ireland'.

ESTATES/RESIDENCE: Camolin, Co. Wexford. A 1741 law suit, *Anglesey v. Annesley*, mentions that part of the Anglesey estate was situated in the town of New Ross, and that Arthur, Earl of Anglesey (this MP), 'being seized in county of Wexford ... built a large mansion house and offices, which cost him £5,000 at least'; the woods in the park are also reputed to be worth £6,000 at least.

At the 'exemplification' of his parent's marriage in 1669, the Annesleys held property in Counties Armagh, Wexford, Tyrone, Dublin, Kildare, Meath, Kilkenny, Cork, Queen's County, Tipperary, Clare and Kerry. In 1687, the rental of Lord Anglesey's estate was £3,534.

Under an act of 19 Chas II (1668), Lord Anglesey was granted fairs at Camolin, and at Ballycanew, *alias* Ballycarron; under 32 Chas II, Lord Anglesey was granted a patent erecting the manors of Bantry and Altham, with the right to hold fairs and markets at Ballygobban, *alias* Oldtown. (The Hedges family and the White family inherited the Co. Cork estates of the Lords Altham.) The denominations in the Anglesey lands in Bere and Bantry, including reprises for George Walters Esq., were: Gurteen, Killernane, Garryduffe, Drumleigh, Kouskey, Whiddy Island, Drumclogh, Seskin, Drumoneene, Shandrum, Inchyclogh, Brinny, Kingdisert and Cananemadra and Crissconagh (six ploughlands of Crissconagh are stated to be in the possession of Major Deane). The reserved (quit) rent on all these was £132.

A rental of Clonmines, Co. Wexford, and the rest of the lands let by Lord Anglesey and Peter Wallis for 99 years in 1660, was *c.* 1740 £328 gross, but the 'improved rent' was £660. There were only five tenants and the lands included Dunganstown and Arklow, as well as Clonmines. The Kerry estates, inherited from Arthur, Earl of Anglesey in 1737, probably had rental of £1,200 *c.* 1775.

Lord Anglesey left all his Irish estates to his kinsman, Francis Annesley (0045), while Richard, Lord Altham, succeeded him as 6th Earl of Anglesey and heir at law. The estate of Tankertstown, Cloonpierce, etc., left by Lord Anglesey to the father of the 1st Earl Annesley in 1737, was for the remainder of the century the subject of endless litigation with the Hovenden and Saunders families. It had a rental of £450 in 1774, which had risen to £1,654 in 1851.

SOURCES: McCracken thesis; GEC *P*; *Index to Irish Privy Counsellors, 1711–1910*; *Alum. Oxon.* [says the MP for Cambridge University 1702–10 was Arthur Annesley, 4th Baron Altham; this appears unlikely since Baron Altham was 13 years old in 1702]; Burke *PB* (1921) p. 2184 [says his e. brother was baptised 18 Jan. 1676, hence d. of b. *c.* 1678]; *Alum. Cantab.*; *Coll. Gen.*; Lewis,

Topographical Dictionary (London, 1901) p. 248; *JRSAI* vol. 21 (1892) p. 298, P. D. Vigors, 'Alphabetical List of Free Burgesses of New Ross 1658–1839'; PRONI Cal. 2368 Hewson Papers; PRONI C/2405 [account of Lord Anglesey's quit rent (1660–80s?)]; PRONI D/1503/2/8 Anglesey Papers; NLI Brown's Reports of the Lords Appeals 1701–1800 vol. 1 pp. 289–99 [Angelsey v. (Charles) Annesley]; LC 1090; PRONI T/3350/1; PRONI D/1225/2/3 Martin & Henderson Papers, H. L. Brief in Hovenden v Annesley and Saunders, 15 Nov. 1805; PRONI D/1503/4/10 and /2/8 Annesley Papers; Parliamentary Lists, 1706 (1), 1707 (3), (4).

0043 ANNESLEY, Hon. Francis

MP for Bangor 1692–3

b. 23 Jan. 1628; d. *ante* 1705
FAMILY/BACKGROUND: Eldest son of Rt Hon. Francis Annesley, 1st Viscount Valentia, and his second wife Jane (d. 1683), dau. of Sir John Stanhope of Elvaston, Derby, wid. of Sir Peter Courten, Bt, of Adlington, Worcestershire.
MARRIED: [1662] Deborah (d. 1672), dau. of Henry Jones, Bp of Meath, wid. of John Bowdler of Dublin.
CHILDREN: Francis (**0045**); Arthur (*d.s.p.*); Henry (*d.s.p.*); Jane, m. James Bailie of Inischargie, Co. Down; Deborah, m. Rev. Charles Ward; Mary (d. yg.); Anne, m. Henry Woods; Catherine (d. yg).
EDUCATION: Entered Cambridge (Queen's College) 20 June 1644.
CAREER/OCCUPATION: MILITARY Like many during this period he possibly had a military career.

POLITICAL ACTIVITY: He sat in the very brief parliament of 1692 and was described by Sydney as a gentleman intent on 'mischief', having attended 'several seditious meetings' in reaction to the prorogation of parliament, 3 November 1692. He attached his name to the petition to the king requesting Irish parliamentary representation at Court. Sydney replied that if they should send somebody, let him beg the king's pardon for their 'factious and riotous assemblies'.

ESTATES/RESIDENCE: Castlewellan, Co. Down.

SOURCES: Lodge *P*; GEC *P*; Burke *Ext. P* (1883) p. 6, *PB* (1903) p. 1518 (1906) p. 1630; *Cal. SP Dom. 1695* (London, 1908) p. 219; Vicars, *Prerog. Wills* [gives a Francis (**0044**) of Ballyshannon, Co. Kildare will proved 1709]; *Alum. Cantab.*; *Coll. Gen.*; Simms' cards; C.

Dalton (ed.), *English Army Lists and Commission Registers, 1661–1714* (London, 1892), vol. 1 p. 9 [says a Francis Annesley, Captain in the Tangier Regiment of Foot, Oct. 1661; the Regiment arrived in Tangier 29 Jan. 1662].

0044 ANNESLEY, Francis

MP for New Ross 1695–9

b. *c.* 1653; d. 1707
FAMILY/BACKGROUND: Eldest son of Capt. the Hon. John Annesley (b. 1616) of Ballysonan, Co. Kildare, and Charity, dau. of Henry Warren.
MARRIED: Deborah, dau. of Joshua Paul.
CHILDREN: Charity; Deborah, m. Robert Doyne (**0662**); Elizabeth, m. Thomas Hughes of Co. Tipperary; Hannah, m. Thomas Springe.
EDUCATION: Entered TCD 9 July 1670; entered Lincoln's Inn 25 Nov. 1671.
CAREER/OCCUPATION: Free Burgess of New Ross, 7 Aug. 1693 – 12 July 1707; High Sheriff of Co. Kildare 1701–2.

POLITICAL ACTIVITY: An active politician, he was listed for 46 committees between 1695 and 1699. On 5 October 1695 he presented to the House a paper entitled 'a State of the Case of the Inhabitants of the Province of Ulster, in relation to the demands of their clergy for small tithes and other dues'. The paper argued that Ulster suffered under a table of tithes differing from the rest of the country, and that the clergy there received 9d for every milch cow and calf, where only 1d to 2d was due, and received other payments 'contrary to all law and reason'. In 1695 he voted for the accusation of favouring Catholics against Lord Chancellor Porter, and in 1696 he signed the Association for the protection of William III in the country. He was chairman of a Commons committee in 1697 to 'consider the abuses in coinage, counterfeiting and importing halfpence into this Kingdom'.

However, he was far from popular and on 18 November 1703 the Commons heard a petition from Sir Kildare Dixon Burrowes (**0290**), John Allen (**0033**), Robert Dixon (**0639**), Francis Spring (**1976**), Alexander Gradon (**0890**) and 'other inhabitants of the County of Kildare complaining, that the inhabitants of the said County have been under great oppressions and grievances by the exorbitant power of Maurice (**0047**), John and Francis Annesley, Esqrs, Justices of the Peace'. Shortly before this, the burgesses and freemen of Naas also complained about the activities of the Annesleys. The allegations against Maurice and Francis were found not to be proved, but John was found to have illegally extorted money under cover of warrants and fees and was removed as sheriff.

Annesley unsuccessfully contested the seat for New Ross in July 1707 against Amyas Bushe (**0307**). After the election a number of protests were issued against Bushe's victory, on the grounds that more than 24 burgesses voted, that being the number limited by charter; Bushe was not a legal burgess; 'Freemen' had no right to vote; and Robert Coleman and John Elly were disqualified, being Quakers. Annesley died shortly thereafter.

ESTATES/RESIDENCE: Ballysonan, Co. Kildare.

SOURCES: PRONI D/302; PRONI T/559 vol. 5 p. 328, Burke, extract pedigrees; Burke *PB* (1906) p. 1630; *Alum. Dub.*; *Coll. Gen.*; Simms' cards; *Lincoln's Inn Records* vol. I p. 312; *Numismatic Society of Ireland, Occasional Papers* nos 24–8 (1983) pp. 21–40, Colm Gallagher, 'The Irish Copper Coinage, 1660–1700; Notes towards a history'; *JRSAI* vol. 21 (1892) p. 298, P. D. Vigors, 'Alphabetical List of Free Burgesses of New Ross 1658–1839'; *JRSAI* vol. 31 (1901) p. 59, P. D. Vigors, 'Extracts from the Old Corporation Books of New Ross, County Wexford'; Parliamentary Lists, 1695 (1), 1696 (1).

0045 ANNESLEY, Francis

MP for Downpatrick 1695 – 9 Sept. 1703 [expelled 28 Sept. 1703], 1713–14; [E/GB] Preston 1705–8; [GB] Westbury 1708–15, 28 March – 1 June 1715, 1722–34

b. 14 Oct. 1663; d. 7 Aug. 1750
FAMILY/BACKGROUND: Son of Hon. Francis Annesley (**0043**) and Deborah, dau. of Henry Jones, Bp of Meath.
MARRIED: (1) [5 July 1695] Elizabeth, dau. of Sir Joseph Martin of London; (2) [July 1732] Elizabeth, dau. of John Cropley of Rochester, wid. of William Gomeldon of Summerfield Hall, Kent; (3) [31 Aug. 1737] Sarah, o. dau. of

William Sloane of Portsmouth, wid. of Sir Richard Fowler of Harnage Grange, Salop.
CHILDREN: (1) Rev. Francis of Clough and Bletchington, Oxon., m. Anne, dau. and co-h. of Sir Robert Gayer; Rev. Martin, m. [12 Dec. 1732] Mary, dau. and co-h. of William Hanbury of Hereford; William, 1st Baron Annesley and Viscount Glerawly (**0049**).
(2) Capt. Henry (RN); John; James; Arthur; Elizabeth, m. Richard McGuire (Dublin banker); Deborah.
EDUCATION: School: Dr Wetenhall; entered TCD 5 May 1679, BA 1682; Inner Temple 1684; called to the Bar 1690, Bencher 1713, LLD *hon. caus.* 1725.
CAREER/OCCUPATION: Commissioner for Forfeited Estates 1699; Commissioner to build 50 new churches in London 1711; Commissioner of Public Accounts 1711–14.

POLITICAL ACTIVITY: A prominent politician, he was nominated for 50 committees, 21 of which were in 1695. The first parliament of Queen Anne's reign met on 21 September 1703, and before his expulsion on 28 September he was listed for six committees. In 1696 he signed the Association for the protection of William III in parliament.

He was one of the seven commissioners empowered by an act of the English parliament to investigate Irish forfeitures, and he was expelled from the Irish Commons on 28 September 1703 for his part in *The Report of the Commissioners appointed by Parliament into the Irish Forfeitures*, printed in London, containing the paragraph: 'And indeed it does appear to us, that the Freeholders of this Kingdom, through length of time and by contracting new friendship with the Irish, or by inter-purchasing with one another, but chiefly through a general dislike of the disposition of the forfeitures, are scarce willing to find any person guilty of the late rebellion, even upon full evidence.' The Irish House of Commons found that Annesley had 'scandalously and maliciously misrepresented and traduced the Protestant Freeholders of this Kingdom and thereby endeavoured to create a misunderstanding and jealousy between the people of England and the Protestants of this Kingdom'.

Annesley shared Archbishop King's concern about the possibly unfavourable effects of the Scottish Act of Union on the Irish linen manufacture.

In 1706 he wrote that 'Your thoughts about the linnen of Scotland interfering with that of Ireland are very truly grounded ... I take it that all the produce of Scotland, when part of Great Britain, will infallibly have a preference to anything that relates to Ireland. Can it be doubted that those of the established religion in Scotland will not have all imaginable countenance in Ireland, as well as in England, after the union, have they not now?' In England, towards the end of Queen Anne's reign, he was a prominent member of the ultra-Tory October Club.

In 1713 he was again returned for Downpatrick. In the 1713 Irish Parliamentary List he was stated to be a Tory. He voted with the Court party for Sir Richard Levinge (1230) as Speaker. He did not come in in 1715, and appears to have turned his energies to pursuing his legal career. Interestingly, he was counsel for the ultra-Whig Archbishop King in his case against the Irish Society. Annesley was a friend of both Southwell (1968) and King: the latter wrote that he was pleased to have found somebody on whose 'skill, prudence and integrity' he could rely.

DIVISION LISTS:

1713 (1) voted for Sir Richard Levinge (1230) for Speaker.

ESTATES/RESIDENCE: Castlewellan, Co. Down; Thorganby, Yorkshire. He inherited the Irish estates of his cousin Arthur, 5th Earl of Anglesey (0042). These included the estate of Tankertstown, which was to be the subject of unending litigation with the Hovenden and Saunders families for the remainder of the century.

He purchased 161 acres in Co. Kildare from the Commissioners for Sale of Forfeited Estates in 1702–3. Prior, in his list of absentees, estimated his Irish income at £1,000 p.a.

SOURCES: PRONI T/2506/15 Annesley pedigree notes; PRONI MIC/315/6/27 Blackwood pedigrees; CJ Ire. (Grierson ed.) vol. 11 part 1 p. 321; Burke PB (1903) pp. 1518–19; Alum. Dub.; Simms' cards; W. H. Crawford, Letters from an Ulster Land Agent, 1774–85 (Belfast, 1977) [the Clough estate of the Rev Francis Annesley (of Bletchington, Oxon.) rental £1,450 in 1776 and over £1,800 in 1785; in the following year it was sold to David Ker of Portavo for £33,845]; King, A Great Archbishop of Dublin, William King DD, pp. 117, 118 n. 1; Simms, Williamite Confiscation, pp. 99–100, 182; Parliamentary Lists, 1695 (1), 1696 (1), 1713 (1), (2).

0046 ANNESLEY, Hon. Francis Charles

MP for Downpatrick 1761–8–70

b. 27 Nov. 1740; d. 19 Dec. 1802
PEERAGES: Suc. as 2nd Viscount Glerawly 1770; cr. Earl Annesley 17 Aug. 1789 (with remainder to his brother Richard (0048), should he d. childless).
FAMILY/BACKGROUND: Eldest son of William Annesley, 1st Viscount Glerawly (0049) and Anne, dau. of Marcus Beresford, 1st Earl of Tyrone (0118).
MARRIED: (1) [8 Feb. 1766] Mary (d. 1792), dau. and h. of Richard Grove of Ballyhimmock, Co. Cork; (2) [1797 (bigamously, as she was already m. to at least one husband living)] Sophia Lowry (alias Connor) (b. 1769; d. 1850).
CHILDREN: d.s.p.l., but at least seven illeg. sons: (2) William, styled Lord Glerawly; Francis Charles (d. 1803); George de la Poer Beresford (d. ?1817). He had also by Mrs 'Muckelroy', son (c. 1802, a Lieutenant in the 38th Regiment); Charles (officer in the army in Egypt); son (RN officer); and another son 'presently' (c. 1802) in Edinburgh.
MILITARY: Colonel of Castlewellan Rangers Volunteers; Captain in the Castlewellan Infantry, Dec. 1796; Colonel of the South Down Militia 1 Apr. 1800. (Sir J.S. Blackwood (0147) was Colonel of the North Down Militia.)

POLITICAL ACTIVITY: Although he sat in the House of Commons for nearly ten years, he does not appear to have been a particularly active MP. He was a nephew of Lord Tyrone (0113), who may have exerted some influence over him. However, he voted against the augmentation of the army in 1768. He was anxious to become a Privy Counsellor (which he did not achieve) and to be advanced to an earldom (which, in 1789, he did achieve).

He had potentially a leading interest in Co. Down, but the Annesley estates lay in the south, and largely Catholic, part of the county. In the House of Lords, where most of his parliamentary career was spent, he was violently against electoral reform and 'generally' hostile to the Commercial Propositions.

ADDITIONAL INFORMATION: A member of the Royal Dublin Society from 1768. A prominent Mason, he was Grand Master of the Grand Lodge of Irish Freemasons, 1787–9.

Lord Annesley had a strong anti-Catholic fixation. On 29 June 1794, Major George Matthews, of the Downshire Militia, informed Lord Downshire (**1016**) that Lord Annesley 'is very much displeased about some of the men having gone to Mass last Sunday ... He talks of resigning and of staying at home to defend his property against Papists.' When told that there were no orders forbidding attendance at Mass, he replied: 'Not a man of them should go to ... Mass, and that he would not serve in a Papish regiment. He talks of the Papists being in arms immediately, and seems to doubt the regiment.' On 30 October 1796, he wrote to Downshire of his annoyance at Downshire's decision not to make an example of Sergeant Sharks, but withdrew his resignation as lieutenant-colonel, which he had offered him on 14 September.

In 1800, upon the Marquess of Downshire's dismissal from the command of the Royal Downshire Militia, the regiment was divided into two battalions, one for South and the other for North Down. 'Lord Frank', as he was affectionately named, was appointed colonel in command of the Royal South Downs ('the South Down Militia').

In November 1795, the 1st Earl Annesley, a childless widower of 55, came to dine with his brother (**0048**) and heir presumptive, with whom he was on the most affectionate terms. 'On the way up the drive he was, "much struck by the appearance" of one Sophia Connor, the wife of his brother's gardener.' He talked to her and 'In the short time that such conversation lasted, the said Sophia was so dazzled by the rank and splendour of the said Earl ... that, in violation of her marriage vow, she consented to elope ... with the said Earl on his return to Dublin that evening.' Two years later, on 5 September 1797, Lord Annesley went through a ceremony of marriage with Sophia Connor. She, in the famous Annesley case, is also called Kelly or Lowry. The latter name was given to her by Lord Annesley, after the local minister, because he thought Connor and Kelly too papist. Sophia denied that her marriage to Martin Connor, the gardener, was ever valid although she did admit marrying one Kelly, who, she claimed, was 'pressed' into the Army and later died. Connor

was paid £19 6s 9d per quarter by Lord Annesley to offset 'Sophia's debts'.

Although his brother 'offered ... "to concur in any act that might meet the wishes of Lord Annesley to make a provision for the woman he co-habited with and for any children he might have by her", Sophia said she "would not agree to it, but would take her chance".' After Lord Annesley's death in 1802, Sophia endeavoured to prove the legitimacy of her son by him, and his right to the Annesley earldom and the family estate of nearly £5,500 a year. The ensuing litigation lasted until 1819, when Sophia settled for an annuity of £455. She was then living in Paris and complained that this would not allow her to live in the (very considerable) style to which she had become accustomed.

DIVISION LISTS:
1768 (1) voted against army augmentation.

ESTATES/RESIDENCE: Castlewellan and Mount Panther, Co. Down; Annesley House, Marlborough Street, Dublin. The estates in Co. Down of which the 1st Earl was possessed at the time of his death had a rental of £5,459; it had been £4,654 in 1788. His unsettled property (inherited from his father, Baron Glerawly) had a rental of £3,000 in 1802. This figure includes the value of the town house in Marlborough Street, but the rest derives from land in Co. Down – Walchestown, Ballydonnell and Clonvaraghan. In 1798 the Marlborough Street house and Dublin city property were valued at £11,000 (this value would have declined after the Union), and the Co. Down property at £38,000.

Annesley, in a deed of 2 July 1798, desired that Sophia was to receive a £10,000 lump sum on his death and £1,000 p.a. until all unsettled estates were sold off (which were to include Mount Panther and the Marlborough Street house), and then a further £10,000 from the proceeds of this sale.

Under the terms of the marriage settlement Lord Annesley's (first) wife, who was heiress to the Grove estate, retained the power to dispose of it 'as she should think fit'. Annesley's first marriage, although childless, does not appear to have been unhappy and in 1784 his wife saw fit to devise its use to her husband, during his life; the remainder went to aunts and female cousins, with General Annesley, her husband's nephew, the residual heir. In 1784 this nephew was about to come of age, and provision for him was probably the responsibility of the 1st Earl.

The estate of which the 1st Earl was possessed at the time of his death (in 1802) in Co. Down had a rental of £5,459; this had been £4,654 in 1788; Moyad is mentioned so Banfield seems to be included, as well as Castlewellan and Newcastle.

The 1st Earl's unsettled property (inherited from his father, Lord Glerawly) had a rental of £3,000 in 1802; this figure includes the value of the town house in Marlborough Street, but the rest derives from land in Co. Down – Walchestown, Ballydonnell and Clonvaraghan.

SOURCES: PRONI D/1503/61 and /3/5, Rent book 1788, and rental [copied in 1809 for use in Annesley v. Annesley]; PRONI D/1503/3/8/17, /3/5/20 and 13/6/2 Annesley Papers [comments by John Pollock on Lord Annesley's proposed settlement 10 Mar. 1798, copy deed of trust, 2 July 1798 and draft statement of case (pre-2 Apr. 1803)]; PRONI D/1759/3A/7 [says he died 9 Mar. 1803]; PRONI D/607/C/42, 43, D/168, 266 Downshire Papers; PRONI T/684/8, G. Aynworth Pilson, Obituaries, Downpatrick [says he died 20 Dec. 1802 aged 60 years]; PRONI MIC/474 Irish Volunteers; GEC *P*; Burke *PB* (1906) p. 49; J. H. Lepper and P. Crossle, *History of the Grand Lodge of Free and Accepted Masons of Ireland* (Dublin, 1925), vol. 1; Malcomson, *The Pursuit of the Heiress* (Belfast, 1982) pp. 2, 22; *Almanacks FJ* 6 Dec. 1796; *BNL* 8 Apr. 1800; Parliamentary Lists, 1769 (1), 1777 (1), 1782 (1), 1785 (2), 1787 (1), 1788 (1).

0047 ANNESLEY, Maurice

MP for Clonmines 1695–9

b. *post* 1653; d. 17 Feb. 1718
FAMILY/BACKGROUND: Son of John Annesley of Ballysonan Castle, Co. Kildare, and Charity, dau. of Henry Warren.
MARRIED: Sarah (d. 8 July 1705), dau. of Richard Blayney, 4th Baron Blayney.
CHILDREN: Elizabeth, m. Sir Arthur Gore, 2nd Bt (0857).
CAREER/OCCUPATION: Sheriff of Co. Kildare 1693.

POLITICAL ACTIVITY: He supported Lord Chancellor Porter against accusations of favouring Catholics made against him in 1695, and signed the Association for the protection of William III in parliament in 1696. An active politician, he was nominated for 45 committees between 1695 and 1699. His busiest year was 1697, when he was listed for 19 committees. He may have been a military officer.

A claim that had important repercussions was lodged by Maurice Annesley in respect of the es-

tate of Christopher Sherlock. On 25 May 1705 Eustace Sherlock, gentleman, petitioned the Commons for Relief from 'the great oppressions he lies under, by the undue practices and power of Maurice Annesley, a Justice of the Peace'. The House appointed a committee to consider the petition. Maurice Annesley was the guardian of the Sherlock children and a cousin of Francis Annesley (0045); by a natural piece of patronage the trustees had appointed him receiver for Co. Kildare. The estate, forfeited by Christopher Sherlock, was charged with portions for his sisters Hester and Mary and with legacies to his younger brothers. Maurice Annesley's story was that the widowed mother of these children appealed to him to lease the estate from the forfeiture commissioners, and also persuaded him to act as guardian of the minors. He alleged that he had spent considerable sums for the maintenance and education of the children and had also provided the daughters with their portions. The claim allowed by the trustees for these disbursements came to more than the value of the estate, possession of which was accordingly handed over to Annesley, and the reversion only was sold by the trustees.

The case was complicated. Annesley had bought out some of the estate in part payment of his services. His entitlement to do this was challenged in the Court of the Exchequer and the Court found in his favour. Six years later Hester Sherlock, the widow, appealed this decision to the House of Lords and on 19 June 1716 it reversed the original judgment. The following May Annesley appealed to the British House of Lords, thus opening up the vexed question of ultimate jurisdiction for they ordered he be restored to possession, reversing the decision of the Irish House of Lords.

In July 1719 Lord Lieutenant Bolton, anxious to avoid a clash that would threaten the Supply Bills, organised a compromise whereby Mrs Sherlock received in full the claims that she made on the estate and Annesley's heir received some compensation, but the Irish Lords would not be stopped and began an investigation into the actions of the Irish Barons of the Exchequer. The furore eventually resulted in the passing by the British parliament of the 1720 Declaratory Act known as 6 Geo. I, confirming the British House of Lords as the final Court of Appeal for Irish cases.

ESTATES/RESIDENCE: Little Rath, Co. Kildare. In 1694 Annesley petitioned for confirmation of the forfeited estates rented to him by the Commissioners of Revenue before the 'troubles'. In January 1696 Maurice Annesley petitioned that a wood he owned in Co. Monaghan, consisting of 30,000 oak trees, had been cut down by the king's soldiers camped at Dundalk. In compensation he asked for the grant of title 'to such discoveries as he had already made' and any further concealments, not exceeding £2,000, discovered by him of forfeited leases. In addition he was to retain the quarter part promised him by the Commissioners of Forfeitures in reward for any discovery.

His claims received favourable consideration and he received a grant in fee: 'In consideration of many good and acceptable services by him performed, and of his great sufferings and losses in the late troubles, particularly in a wood of 30,000 oak trees that were cut down and destroyed by his Majesty's camp at Dundalk; and in his diligence and industry in persecuting the "Raparees" in this county, that thereby he did reduce that part of the country where he lives into perfect obedience and still does continue very useful to his country.'

SOURCES: PRONI D/302; GEC *P*; Burke *Ext. P* (1883) p. 602; Burke *PB* (1906 ed.) p. 1630 (1903 ed.) p. 1518; *Cal. SP Dom. 1694–5* (London, 1906) p. 90, *1696* (London, 1913) pp. 28, 73; *Coll. Gen.*; C. Dalton (ed.), *English Army Lists and Commission Registers, 1661–1714* (London, 1892) vol. 1 p. 286 [says a Maurice Annesley, Ensign in the Duke of Monmouth's Regiment of Foot, 12 June 1679 and in 1696 a Capt. Maurice Annesley was given a pass to Hoylake, England]; *Ir. Gen.* vol. 5 no 2 (1975) pp. 186–9, H. F. Morris, 'Announcements in *Impartial Occurrences*, Jan. 1705 – Feb. 1706'; *HMC HL Papers* new ser. vol. 4 p. 36; PRONI T/3365; Simms, *Williamite Confiscation*, p. 145; G. O'Brien (ed.), *Parliament, Politics and People* (1989) pp. 9–29, I. Victory, 'The Making of the 1720 Declaratory Act'; Parliamentary Lists, 1695 (1), 1696 (1).

0048 ANNESLEY, Rt Hon. Richard

MP for Coleraine 1776–83; St Canice 1783–90; Newtown 1790–7; Blessington 1797–1800; Midleton 1800 [r. Fore 1797; n.d.e. Clogher 1800]; [Escheator of Ulster 19 Jan. 1800]

b. 14 Apr. 1745; d. 9 Nov. 1824 at Dublin

HONOURS: PC, sworn 1798.

PEERAGES: Suc. as 2nd Earl Annesley 1802.

FAMILY/BACKGROUND: Son of William Annesley, 1st Viscount Glerawly (0049) and Anne, dau. of Marcus Beresford, 1st Earl of Tyrone (0118).

MARRIED: [25 Sept. 1771] Anne, only dau. and h. of Robert Lambert of Dunlady, Co. Down.

CHILDREN: William Richard, 3rd Earl Annesley, m. (1) [May 1803] Isabella, dau. of William St Lawrence, 2nd Earl of Howth, (2) Priscilla Cecilia, dau. of Hugh Moore of Eglinton, Co. Londonderry; Robert, m. [1 Mar. 1798] Mary Anne, dau. of James Gandon; Lieut.-Gen. Arthur, m. Elizabeth o. ch. of John Mahon of Bessborough, Co. Tipperary; Capt. Francis Charles (RN), m. [31 July 1813] Mary, dau. of William Radcliffe; Catherine, m. [1801] Sir Neale O'Donal Bt; Anna Maria, m. Rev. G.H. McDowell Johnstone.

EDUCATION: School: Mr Dubourdieu; entered TCD 8 July 1761; Inner Temple 1765; called to the Irish Bar 1770.

CAREER/OCCUPATION: Commissioner of the Revenue 30 Dec. 1785–1810 at £1,400 p.a. and pension of £1,000 p.a.; Commissioner of Bankruptcy 1772–7; Customer of Youghal and Dungarvan 9 Mar. 1778; *Commissioner for Paving the Streets of Dublin 1778–80; *Land Waiter of Ross 1779–83; Collector of Co. Dublin Excise 1784–6; Commissioner of the Revenue 1786–99 (f.); *listed in Judges and Barristers 1789–1800 (f.); Sheriff of Co. Down 1783; *Governor of the Foundling Hospital and Workhouse 1795–98; Freeman and Freeholder of Dublin City 1797; Member of Grand Jury for Co. Down 1798; Commissioner of Relief for Suffering Loyalists 1798–1800 (f.).

MILITARY: First Captain in Custom House Cavalry Infantry 1796.

POLITICAL ACTIVITY: Annesley was a lawyer and a 'civil servant' type of placeman, holding a variety of legal and revenue jobs – Commissioner of Bankrupts, 1780; Customer of Youghal, £400 (with an additional salary); in 1783 he was allowed to exchange places with Mr Lambart (1192), the Collector of Dublin (£700–900). Then, in 1785, he was appointed a Commissioner of the Revenue in the reshuffle that followed the election of John Foster (0805) as Speaker (Annesley replaced Sir John Parnell (1633), who succeeded Foster as Chancellor of the Exchequer). The First Commissioner of the Revenue was yet another cousin (and a brother of Lord Tyrone), John Beresford (0115).

Annesley was returned for Coleraine in the 1776 general election through the influence of his cousin, Lord Tyrone, and for St Canice in 1783 through the influence of Lord Tyrone's brother, Dr William Beresford, Bishop of Ossory; he followed his Beresford relations in politics. The probably apocryphal tale is told that on going to St Canice he met his opponent on the road and asked him where the town was.

In 1790 he was returned for Newtownards at the nomination of government on Lord Caledon being made a peer. At the next general election in 1797, Lord Downshire (**1016**), with whom he was on friendly terms, returned him for Blessington, but as Lord Downshire was hostile to the Union and Annesley had supported it since its inception, he followed convention and applied for the Escheatorship of Ulster. He was immediately returned by Lord Midleton for Midleton, Co. Cork.

By 12 December 1798 he was certainly a firm supporter of the Union, considering that opposition to the measure was probably motivated by 'self interest'. Lord Downshire asked him to resign the Blessington seat in January 1800 because of his support for the Union. Their parting was 'free of any personal rancour'. He had written to Downshire on 12 January 1799 on the subject of the Union: 'My sentiments, you know, were always in favour of it, provided it was granted on fair terms ... [as] otherwise it would be injurious to both countries'; and on 30 January: 'My opinion is [a] decided one. This country will never be quiet without a Union of Legislatures, or the empire have that strength which in that case it would, and which in my mind it ought to have; for while the parliaments are distinct, they will be considered as separate countries, jealousies raised, and everything endeavoured to disunite them, and the speeches made in the House of Commons inflame more than anything else ... but though I have said so much in favour of a Union, do not think I approve of the time it is brought forward, or the manner or management. I disapprove of both. But I am not a political man, and as I considered only the object itself, it was not my business to reject what I considered a benefit on account of mismanagement, or what I thought just, who could not be so good a judge as those having in their hand the government of the country and consequently better information than I could have.'

Annesley also feared that 'Rebellion is only smothered. I fear it will break out with greater force – nay, I am satisfied of it, and that those persons who are now confined are going on as usual with their diabolical schemes.' While diplomatically declaring to Downshire that the timing and management were wrong, he stated that 'I am satisfied that the wealth of the country w[oul]d increase, and that *Dublin* from local situation w[oul]d reap great benefit.'

Forces, then imperfectly understood, were militating against this optimistic prediction. Also, this tactful correspondence probably reflected an element of Co. Down politics. The Hills and the Stewarts both had large estates centred in Protestant north Down where, in 1790, they had fought what was probably the most savage electoral campaign in the history of the Irish parliament. The marquess was most unlikely to approve a plan brought forward by a Stewart. Annesley signed a Co. Down petition in favour of discussing the proposed plan of Union early in 1800. After the Union he was one of the three commissioners appointed to assess the sums to be paid in compensation to the patrons of the disfranchised boroughs, from which the Marquess of Downshire was the greatest beneficiary.

In 1789 a less than friendly commentator gave the following description of him as a parliamentarian: 'Mr Annesley is but little befriended by his voice, as it is feeble, indistinct, confined, and unharmonious, with a childishness of tone uncommon and offensive, whilst his management of it is very defective in that art that would conceal its deficiencies and meliorate its harshness ... His language is plain, simple and unadorned, neither copious in terms nor abundant in phrases; as destitute of dignity to command as of elegance to captivate, it serves merely to convey not to embellish his thoughts ... His action much resembles that of the Bar pleader, for the law was his original profession and therefore alike fails in grace and strength. In reasoning he is acute, argumentative and by no means weak. In general adhering closely to the question with more perseverance than abler speakers ... The arrangement of his thoughts possesses merit, as it is clear and regular and methodical, neither involved in obscurity by affected abstruseness, nor confused by muddiness of conception – and his matter is mostly strong and but seldom despicable. As he is a man of information, though certainly not the first in the first class in that respect, when he speaks on subjects with which he is acquainted he is instructive and well worthy of attention, but either the *ignis status* of mistaken ambition or the command of his leader sometimes urges him to the contest when he is totally unprepared for the field and he is exposed unarmed to a combat ... The consequence need not be told. As a Commissioner of the Revenue, the nephew of Lord Tyrone and the friend of Lord Hillsborough, Mr Annesley is an invariable supporter of Administration.'

Annesley described himself as 'not a political man': today he would be a civil servant. He is a representative of the group of nominal politicians who were essentially administrators and emerged to play an important part in the late eighteenth century governments of both Great Britain and Ireland.

DIVISION LISTS:

1777 (1) voted against Grattan's (**0895**) motion for retrenchment.

1778 (2) voted for the Popery Bill.

1779 (1) voted for new taxes.

1779 (2) voted against a six-months Loan Bill.

1780 (1) voted against Grattan's declaration of the Rights of Ireland.

1780 (2) voted against Yelverton's (**2268**) motion to modify Poynings' Law.

1780 (3) a teller against the Tenantry Bill.

1780 (4) voted for the Perpetual Mutiny Bill.

1783 (1) voted against Flood's (**0762**) motion for parliamentary reform.

1784 (1) voted against a committee on the Reform Bill.

1785 (1) voted for the Commercial Propositions.

1789 (1) voted against a regency.

1790 (2) voted for Foster (**0805**) on the election of a Speaker.

1793 (1) voted for Knox's (**1180**) motion

for Catholic Emancipation.

1799 (1) voted for the Union – Commissioner of Revenue.

ESTATES/RESIDENCE: Annesley Lodge, Co. Dublin; Gloucester Street, Dublin; Donard Lodge, Newcastle, Co. Down. He had also property in Dublin, including, after his brother's death, a house in Marlborough Street and estates in Counties Cavan and Wexford, bought prior to 1779. The Cavan estate, inherited from their kinsman, the Earl of Anglesey (**0042**), in 1737, comprised 14,291 acres. In 1769, the rental of the undivided Cavan estate of Lord Glerawley and Arthur Annesley was £3,315. In 1788–9 Richard Annesley owned 1,332 Irish acres in the barony of Castlereagh, Co. Down, including Dunlady (338 acres), Ballyoran, Churchquarter, Cullintraw, Loughmoney, Ballyhenry and Tullycary, at a rental of £1,004. The Dunlady estate came to him through marriage and included the lands of Ballydoran, Castle Espie, Islandreagh and part of Tullynakill. It was reckoned to produce £600–700 p.a.

For almost 20 years, during the course of the famous Annesley case, he contested title and estates of his brother (**0046**) with his brother's 'wife', Sophia Connor (*alias* Kelly and Lowry). The case of the Annesley family concentrated on Sophia's colourful past and dubious matrimonial standing. Finally, in 1819, Richard agreed that Sophia should receive £455 p.a., forgo her other claims and leave for France, where she died in 1850 aged 81 years.

The Grove estate of Ballyhimock, near Castletownroche, Co. Cork came to his son Arthur after the death of Arthur's uncle, the 1st Earl Annesley's (**0046**) (first) wife and the falling in of remaindered life interests in the mid-1840s.

SOURCES: PRONI D/302; PRONI D/1503/6/1B and / 3/10 Annesley Papers; PRONI D/607/D102, /G/16, 41 Downshire Papers; PRONI D/2309/4/4; PRONI D/3030/407 Castlereagh Papers; PRONI T/684/8G, Aynworth Pilson, Obituaries, Downpatrick; PRONI T/ 1584 Pinkerton transcripts, p. 151, 18 Oct. 1771; PRONI T/3166/1C and /1D Hartnell notes; PRONI MIC/315/6/27 Blackwood pedigrees; RCBL P80/1/1, Parish Registers of St Thomas, Dublin; GEC *P*; Burke *PB* (1906) pp. 49–50; *Index to Irish Privy Counsellors, 1711–1910*; Hughes, *Pat. Officers*; IMC *King's Inns Admission Papers, 1607–1867*; *Alum. Dub.*; G. C. Bolton, *The Passing of the Irish Act of Union* (1966), pp. 62, 179–80; A. P. W. Malcomson, *The Pursuit of the Heiress* (Belfast, 1982) p. 22; *Coll. Gen.*; Kilkenny MPs; *Almanacks, Drogheda Newsletter or Ulster Journal* 8–10 Mar. 1800; *FJ* 24 Nov. 1796, 11 Apr. 1797; *DJ* 17 Mar 1798; Parliamentary Lists, 1776 (1), (2), (3), 1777 (1), 1778 (1), 1780 (1), 1782 (1), 1783 (1), (2), 1784 (1),

(2), (3), 1785 (1), (2), (3), 1787 (1), 1788 (1), 1789 (1), (2), 1790 (1), 1791 (1), 1793 (1), 1794 (1), (2), 1798 (1), 1799 (3), 1800 (1).

0049 ANNESLEY, William

MP for Midleton 1741–58

b. 1709; d. 12 Sept. 1770 at Clontarf
PEERAGES: Cr. Baron Annesley 20 Sept. 1758, Viscount Glerawly 14 Nov. 1766.
FAMILY/BACKGROUND: Son of Francis Annesley (0045) and his first wife Elizabeth, dau. of Sir Joseph Martin of London.
MARRIED: [16 Aug. 1738] Anne, e. dau. of Marcus Beresford, 1st Earl of Tyrone (0118).
CHILDREN: Hon. Francis Charles (0046); Rt Hon. Richard (0048); Rev. William, m. Jane dau. of John Digby of Co. Kildare; Marcus; Catherine, m. [14 July 1760] Rt Hon. Arthur Saunders Gore, 2nd Earl of Arran (0861).
EDUCATION: School: Westminster Jan. 1721, aged 12 years; Inner Temple ?1731; called to the Irish Bar 1738. (He was probably the TCD student who in 1724/5 was ring-leader of a faction that came into conflict with the authorities and the new Primate, Dr Hugh Boulter, who felt that his well-placed relatives sought to prevent his expulsion from the College.)
CAREER/OCCUPATION: *Magistrate of Gorey 1739–43, *Sovereign 1739, Deputy Sovereign 1741, Town Clerk 1743; High Sheriff of Co. Down 1751; *Governor of the Workhouse 1749–d.; *Trustee of the Linen Board for Munster 1759–69.

POLITICAL ACTIVITY: A reasonably active MP, he was nominated for some 37 committees between 1743 and 1758. In January 1749/50 he introduced a local government bill 'for the better securing of persons who have served or hereafter shall serve in the office of Sheriff in this Kingdom against the defaults and neglects of their Sub-sheriffs and Attornies'. On 21 November 1751 he complained that Michael and William Carroll, farmers, of Garrynoe, Co. Tipperary, had forcibly entered on to his lands of Earl's Hill, Co. Tipperary with stock, and with armed force pulled down the houses of his cottagers, during time of privilege.

He supported the government over the Money Bill dispute in the early 1750s, and voted the gov-ernment line in support of Arthur Jones-Nevill (1125). Previously he had voted for the election of James Digges La Touche (♦♦♦) On 30 January 1753 Stone wrote to Lord George Sackville (1835) re pensions: 'If, upon application you may think it worth while to spare small sums I should imagine the Annesley affair might go at 150.'

DIVISION LISTS:
1749 (1) voted for the election of James Digges La Touche (♦♦♦).
1753 (1) voted against the expulsion of Arthur Jones-Nevill (1125).
1753 (2) voted for the Money Bill.

ADDITIONAL INFORMATION: A Freemason in 1739. A member of Royal Dublin Society from 1755; a member of the Down Society for Promoting Agriculture, August 1757, August 1759, 1760.

Mrs Delany found his wife, 'daughter to my Lord Tyrone, such another slatternly ignorant hoyden I never saw, and the worst of it is she is very good humoured, but *will be familiar*: her husband ... is well enough'. Some time later she wrote that 'They are very rich and *know it*, and spend their lives in *increasing not enjoying* their good fortune; but he is a very honest man in all his dealings, still would be more agreeable as well as useful if he thought *less* of his possessions. His lady suits him exactly ... but they are very civil neighbours to us in the country.' In 1750 Mrs Delany wrote that 'We dined at our neighbours Mr Annesley; his father is dead, and has left him above £7,000 a year.' In September 1758 Mrs Delany wrote to her sister that recently she had 'spent the day at Castle Wellan, Mr Annesley's and walked two or three miles before dinner, saw all his farming affairs, which are indeed very fine. Three large courts: round the first, which is arched round a kind of piazza, are houses for all his carriages, and over them his granaries; the next court are stables and cow-houses, and over them hay-lofts; the third court two such barns as I never saw, *floored with oak* and finished in a most convenient manner for the purposes of winnowing, &c. and in that court are the stands for hay and corn ... it is so neat, strong, and clever.'

ESTATES/RESIDENCE: Castlewellan – the Mount Panther residence appears to have been built in the 1750s, as in

July 1751 Mrs Delany noted that 'Within four miles of Mount Panther we met Mrs Annesley and Lady Anne Annesley on horseback, going to dine under a tent on cold meat about a mile from that place where they are going to build'; before they may have lived at Clough, Co. Down; Annesley House, Marlborough Street, Dublin. The Castlewellan estate, including his residence of Mount Panther, was bought from the Maguires in 1731, out of his wife's portion. (The Mount Panther house that the Delanys lived in when the Dean visited the diocese was rented from the Rev. Ward. The Mount Panther estate comprised the lands of Backadery, Ballymagreehan (?and Ballymaginahy), Benraw, Castlewellan, Clarkhill (*alias* Clarehill), Legananny, Leitrim, Slievenaboley, Magheramayo (this townland not on 1816 rental, but on earlier documents) and Slievenisky (on the 1816 rental, but not the earlier documents).

In 1750 he bought the Banfield estate from Samuel Close for £13,975, comprising almost 15 townlands in Counties Down and Monaghan. After running into financial difficulties, Close's family contested the sale. In 1760 Annesley acquired land at Knocktopher, Co. Kilkenny, and about the same time he gained a 31-year fishing lease for Ballaghbeg, Co. Down.

In 1769 the undivided estate of Lord Glerawly and Arthur Annesley (possibly the 1737 inheritance from the Earl of Anglesey (**0042**)) had a gross rental of £1,830. The estate included Clonmines, Ballybrassil, Horeswood, Knocknaveagh, Johnstown, etc. There are schedules of the joint estate and Lord Glerawly's income and debts (*c.* 1775) in the PRONI, as well as a statement of William and Arthur Annesley's title to lands in Co. Cork, pre-1760. The Cork estate must have come from the 1st Lord Glerawly's father-in-law, and consisted of the lands of Ballytrasnagh.

SOURCES: *CJ Ire.* (Bradley ed.) vol. 8 pp. 199, 204, 224–5, 340 (0476); PRONI D/302 [described as of Clough]; PRONI D/1503/2/19, 1503/2/8, 1503/2/9 and 1503/2/43 Annesley Papers [Probate of John Grove of Ballyhimock, Co. Cork, 8 June 1750]; PRONI D/1503/2/9 and 2/8, /4/2 and 4/3 and /7/2 Annesley Papers [statement of Lord Glerawly's encumbrances, 1774, and 1851; rentals of the Annesley estate, 1769 (*c.* 1802) 1810]; D/1503/3/2 and /3/1 Annesley Papers; PRONI T/1584 Pinkerton transcripts, p. 56, 22 July 1760; PRONI MIC/315/6/27 Blackwood pedigrees; McCracken thesis; *King's Inns Admissions*; *Index to Hibernian Chronicle, 1769–1775* (Society of Genealogists, 1936) vol. 1 p. 24; G. F. Russell-Barker and A. H. Stenning (eds), *Record of Old Westminsters: A Biographical List* (London, 1928); *Coll. Gen.*; HMC *Sackville I* p. 188; Llandover, *Delany Corr.*, vol. 2 pp. 323, 577, vol. 3 pp. 42, 170, 509; *Almanacks*; *Pue's Occurrences* 11 Dec. 1739; *BNL* 2 Sept. 1757, 25 Sept. 1759, 7 Oct. 1760;

Dublin Weekly Journal 9 Mar. 1751; Boulter, *Letters*, vol. 1 p. 14 [mentions, March 1724/5, an Annesley 'a remote relation of Lord *Anglesey's*' who caused a considerable stir in TCD and was expelled and whose relations, to Boulter's disapproval, interceded for his restoration].

ANTRIM, Earl and Marquess of: *see* **MACDONNELL**
1317 MacDonnell, Rt Hon. William Randall (styled Viscount Dunluce 1749–75), 6th Earl of Antrim, 1st Marquess of Antrim, MP Co. Antrim 1768–75

0050 ARCHDALL, Mervyn

MP for Co. Fermanagh 1761–8–76–83–90–7–1800, [UK] 1801–2

b. 1725; d. 18 June 1813
FAMILY/BACKGROUND: Only son of Nicholas (Montgomery) Archdall (**0051**) of Derrygonnelly, Co. Fermanagh, and his first wife, Angel, dau. and h. of William Archdall of Castle Archdall, Co. Fermanagh.
MARRIED: [15 July 1762] Mary, dau. of William Henry Dawson, 1st Viscount Carlow (**0597**).
CHILDREN: Mervyn, m. [1805] Jane, dau. of Gustavus Hume Rochfort (**1802**); William, m. Martha Hawley, dau. of James Clarke of Somerset; Edward, m. [1809] Matilda, dau. of William Humphrys; Henry, m. [1816] Jane, dau. of Philip Doyne; Mary, m. Rt Hon. Sir John Stewart, 1st Bt (**2006**); Angel, m. [1807] Maj. John Richardson of Rossfad, Co. Fermanagh; Martha Caroline (d. 1784); Anna; Catherine; Elizabeth, m. [1805] Dacre Hamilton of Cornacassa, Co. Monaghan; Sidney, m. [10 May 1800] Robert Hamilton of Dublin; Wilhelmina Henrietta, m. [1820] Augustine MacNamara of Dublin.
EDUCATION: School: Dr Thompson; entered TCD 10 July 1740; Lincoln's Inn 2 July 1745.
CAREER/OCCUPATION: Governor of Co. Fermanagh 1756–63, Joint Governor 1763–1800 (f.); Governor of Co. Armagh 1761–2; High Sheriff of Co. Fermanagh 1773–4; *Listed in Attorneys of the Courts of King's Bench, Common Pleas and Exchequer 1789–1800 (f.).

MILITARY: Colonel of the Fermanagh Militia Dragoons 1756; Captain in Sir Ralph Gore's Regiment of Foot 23 Jan. 1760; signatory to the Dungannon Resolutions 1782; Colonel of the Fermanagh True Blue Legion, Volunteers, 1782; Colonel of a Fencible regiment 1784; noted as a half-pay Colonel in 1799.

POLITICAL ACTIVITY: The dominance of the Archdalls and the Coles in Co. Fermanagh was shown in August 1797, when the election results were: John W. Cole (**0441**), 804; Colonel Mervyn Archdall, 751; Major Henry Brooke (**0249**), 279; Humphrey Butler (**0318**), 97. This was not surprising, as Archdall was the sitting member and the Archdalls and the Coles were popular; Sir Arthur Brooke (**0247**), the former MP, had died in 1785 without a male heir and the estate had passed to his brother, Francis, and his descendants, who were not yet in a position to challenge the more established interests.

In his early years Archdall was reputed to be influenced by the Gore family, Lords Bellisle and Earls of Ross (**0881**), and he was a brother-in-law of Lord Portarlington (**0589**). Nevertheless, his behaviour was consistently that of an independent country gentleman. He represented the county for over 40 years, and throughout that time was, as his voting record shows, generally in opposition. In 1774 he was listed as 'not too constant in his attendance in the House, but when there, is generally in the county interest'. He appears to have had a military enthusiasm, as in the 1780s the Duke of Portland gained his support by recommending him for a regiment of fencibles. This made him unpopular in his county, where the fencibles were correctly considered to be a government attempt to undermine the power of the Volunteers. Nevertheless, Archdall consistently complained about his military rank, although in 1799 he was noted as a colonel on half-pay (he was 74 years old).

In the 1790s Archdall was regarded as an 'enlightened Irishman' who welcomed the relaxation of the penal laws but opposed any further concessions, including Catholic Emancipation. He said during a debate on 21 April 1795 that he would denounce the word emancipation as applicable to Catholics, as: 'Emancipation means that a slave is set free. The Catholics are not slaves. Nothing more absurd has ever been said, since language has been abused for the delusion of mankind.' In October 1796, he criticised one of Henry Grattan's (**0895**) motions on Catholic Emancipation, saying: 'It has come to this. In 1793 Catholics were to be eternally grateful for admission to the franchise; they say now, Admit us to Parliament, and we will not thank you; refuse, and we will rebel.' In January 1791 he had also criticised Grattan, saying 'that the public owed more to the practical motions of honourable gentlemen who usually sat in silence, than to invective and brilliant rhetoric, which died as it flashed and left no mark.' This attitude to Grattan was more widespread among his contemporaries than is often believed by their successors.

He was a pioneer member of the Irish Whig Club, 26 June 1789, and he consistently opposed the Union, supposedly saying when he rejected the offer of a barony that 'He would rather sit at the head of the Commons, than at the tail of the Lords.' By March 1801 he was regarded by the Castle as 'inactive', and not likely to cause much trouble. At the 1802 general election he withdrew in favour of his son, Mervyn. In 1790 it was said of his influence in Co. Fermanagh that he 'always rides the first horse, as well in the political, as in the fox chase. The precedency in both being generally conceded to him, not less for his eagerness in the pursuit, than for his spirited conduct after his acquisition of the game.'

ADDITIONAL INFORMATION: A member of the Royal Irish Academy, 1791. He was chosen to be a member of the Committee of the Ulster Volunteers at the Dungannon Convention on 15 February 1782, his signature appearing second on the list of resolutions passed. This made his acceptance of a fencible regiment all the more unpopular. In 1787 he was one of the original trustees or governors of the Vaughan charter school at Tubrid.

DIVISION LISTS:
    1768 (1) voted against army augmentation.
    1771 (2) voted for Sir Lucius O'Brien's (**1558**) motion for retrenchment.
    1772 (2) voted for a Short Revenue Bill.
    1773 (1) voted against the Absentee Tax.
    1774 (2) voted against Catholic relief.

1775 (1) voted for the pro-American amendment to the speech from the Throne.

1777 (1) voted for Grattan's (0895) motion for retrenchment.

1778 (2) voted against the Popery Bill.

1779 (2) voted for a six-months Loan Bill.

1780 (2) voted for Yelverton's (2268) motion to modify Poynings' Law.

1780 (4) voted against the Perpetual Mutiny Bill.

1780 (5) voted for the duty on imported sugar.

1783 (1) voted for Flood's (0762) motion for parliamentary reform.

1784 (1) voted for a committee on the Reform Bill.

1784 (4) voted against the Address to His Grace the Duke of Rutland.

1785 (1) voted against the Commercial Propositions.

1786 (1) voted for the rights of grand juries.

1787 (1) voted for a Pension Bill.

1789 (1) voted for a regency.

1790 (1) voted for Grattan's motion for reducing the influence of the Crown.

1790 (2) absent.

1791 (3) voted for Grattan's motion to abolish the Dublin police.

1793 (2) voted for the Convention Bill.

1795 (2) voted against Catholic Emancipation.

1795 (3) voted against Sir Laurence Parsons' (1636) resolution against alleged troop removals.

1799 (1) voted against the Union – 'Colonel on half-pay and Governor of the County'.

ESTATES/RESIDENCE: Castle Archdall, Enniskillen, Co. Fermanagh; Trillick, Co. Tyrone; 1 Kildare Place, Dublin. He inherited the family estates on the death of his mother in 1745. In 1753 the annual rental of the Archdall estates was between £3,000 and £4,000 (not including the Mount Eccles, Dublin estate). In the same year he took a lease from Philip Percival, Arthur Cooper and Jane Carleton of the town lands of Drummonaghan and Drummaran adjoining his demesne. There were nine corn mills on his estates, 'as well as several minor sources of income'.

In 1776 he inherited all the Mervyn family estates in Co. Tyrone that had not already been sold under the terms of the will of the late Henry Mervyn (1407). He began building the family seat in 1773, and seemingly had taken up residence by 1777. It was said that the house was built from stone taken from the monastic ruins in the neighbourhood, hence the prediction that no male heir would ever be born within its walls; his son Edward was actually born in the gate lodge. His seat was situated in one of the most beautiful parts of Ireland and the view magnificent, being the 'best view of Lough Erne, you command the whole lower lough and islands, seeing up to Enniskillen nine miles, and down to Castle Caldwell twelve miles ... This, from its elevation is the most conspicuous demesne on the shores of Lower Lough Erne.' He also rented for many years a hunting lodge called the Grove, at Emo in Queen's County.

At the beginning of the nineteenth century Wakefield calculated that Colonel Archdale had an estate of 'the like extent' as Lord Enniskillen (i.e. £13,000 a year).

SOURCES: PRONI D/302; PRONI T/618/329 Crossle Papers [says a Mervyn Archdall married second, 25 Nov. 1782, a Miss Abigail Young]; PRONI T/1584 Pinkerton transcripts, p. 409, 9 June 1789, p. 561, 16 May 1800; PRONI T/1366/1B Hartnell notes; PRONI MIC/474 Irish Volunteers; O'Neill thesis; Jupp thesis; Burke LGI (1958) pp. 27–8; *HP 1790–1820*; Hughes, *Pat. Officers*; McNevin, *Volunteers*; Fermanagh and Tyrone MPs; *Coll. Gen.*; *Lincoln's Inn Records* vol. 1 p. 430; H. B. Archdale, *Memoirs of The Archdales* (Enniskillen, 1925), pp. 27–33; T. Bartlett and D. W. Hayton (eds), *Penal Era and Golden Age* (Belfast, 1979), p. 113 f/n. 1, P. D. H. Smyth, 'The Volunteers and Parliament, 1779–84'; *Ir. Gen.* vol. 6 no 5 (1984) p. 611, H. F. Morris, 'Finn's Leinster Journal 1767'; *Almanacks*; *FJ* 5 Aug. 1797; Wakefield, *Account of Ire.*, vol. 1 p. 259; Parliamentary Lists, 1769 (1), 1772 (2), 1773 (1), (2), 1774 (1), 1775 (1), 1776 (1), 1777 (1), 1778 (1), 1780 (1), 1782 (1), 1783 (1), 1784 (1), (2), 1785 (1), (2), (3), (4), 1787 (1), 1788 (1), 1789 (1), 1790 (1), 1791 (1), 1793 (1), 1799 (3), 1800 (3).

0051 (MONTGOMERY) ARCHDALL, Nicholas

MP for Co. Fermanagh 1731–60

b. *ante* 1702; d. 19 May 1763

FAMILY/BACKGROUND: Eldest son of Hugh Montgomery and Catherine, dau. and h. of Captain Richard Dunbar of Derrygonnelly, Co. Fermanagh. He assumed the name Archdall in lieu of Montgomery in 1728.

MARRIED: (1) [Apr. 1724] Angel, dau. and eventual h. of William Archdall of Castle Archdall, Co. Fermanagh; (2) Sarah, dau. of [ ] Spurling of London.

CHILDREN: (1) Mervyn (0050). (2) Maj. Robert (17th Dragoons); Richard (0052); Nicholas, m. [Aug. 1782] Sarah Arabella Abigail, dau. of Ven. Samuel Meade; Commander Edward (RN); Catherine, m. [26 Sept. 1777] James Byrn of Park, Co. Carlow; Sarah; Augusta, m. [1778] Rev. Jonathan Bruce; Elizabeth.

CAREER/OCCUPATION: *Trustee of the Linen Board for Munster 1744–d.; High Sheriff of Co. Fermanagh 1723; Justice of the Peace 22 Mar. 1746; *Governor of the Workhouse 1745–d.; *Commissioner of the Tillage Act for Ulster 1759–d.

MILITARY: Served as a Major under Colonel Willoughby 24 May 1723; Colonel of a regiment of dragoons in Fermanagh, 17 May 1740.

POLITICAL ACTIVITY: He was a very active MP, listed for 164 committees between 1733 and 1760 and his activities give some idea of the work and interests of a mid-eighteenth century MP. On 10 November 1737 he was excused attendance in the House by a fairly close vote, 86–75. On 13 December 1743 he was named as one of those who were to prepare and bring in the heads of a bill 'for rendering more effectual the several Acts passed in this Kingdom for transporting Felons and Vagabonds'. On 28 January 1743/4, he was appointed to the Committee which was to investigate the numbers of transportees who had actually been transported, escaped or died, how much money had been raised for their transportation, and to whom it had been paid. On the same day he was chosen for a committee 'to inquire into the Causes of the present bad state of the Streets in ... Dublin'.

On 27 November 1745 he was appointed to the committee 'to inquire into the state of the turnpike Road leading from Dublin to Navan'. He appears to have been interested in communications, as in December 1749 he was specifically appointed to introduce the heads of a bill 'for the more effective amending and keeping in repair the several turnpike roads of this Kingdom; and for better securing the creditors of the said roads'.

On 12 December 1747 he was appointed to a committee 'to inspect into the State and Condi-

tion of Parliament-House, and to inquire by proper estimates, what will be necessary to repair the same'. He was one of the Trustees of the Linen industry, and as such was picked as a member of the Committee to investigate the state of that industry. At the same time he was selected as one of the three MPs to bring forward the heads of a bill 'for the further encouragement of the Hempen and Flaxen Manufactures'. Then, on 21 December 1757, he was ordered by the House to attend the Lord Lieutenant with heads of a bill 'to prevent the distilling of spirits from wheat, etc., and desired the same may be transmitted into Great Britain in due form'. Finally, on 29 October 1759 he was appointed to a Committee to investigate 'in what manner and to what uses' the government grants 'for the Encouragement or Advancement of Manufactures, Arts or Sciences, have been put'.

Archdall was an ardent participant in the constitutional debates on Anglo-Irish relations that blew up from time to time. At the beginning of the 1750s the conflict between the British administration and the Irish parliament had encouraged Henry Fox, a brother-in-law of Lord Kildare, to point out the 'eventual necessity' of a union to Henry Pelham. About the same time, in 1751, an anonymous pamphlet (possibly by Lord Hillsborough) appeared advocating a union and enumerating its potential blessings for Ireland. Among the indignant replies that it attracted was one from Archdall: *An Alarm to the people of Great Britain and Ireland: in Answer to a late Proposal for Uniting these Kingdoms*. Archdall took the view that Ireland enjoyed a special status in relation to England, declaring that 'Ireland should be looked on rather as a sister whom England has taken under her protection on condition she complies with the economy of the family, yet with such distinction and deference to show they were originally upon an equality.' He then pointed out that for Ireland a union would be neither practical nor profitable. Ireland would be overtaxed and its positions in church and state filled with Englishmen.

In 1759, for some months there had been renewed rumours of a union, which from the official correspondence appear to have been without foundation although they were fuelled by the usual series of pamphlets. On 26 November of that year Archdall and Mr Morres (**1490**) were instructed to bring in heads of a bill for the 'better ordering' of the county militia forces in Ireland. On the same day he was appointed to a committee 'to find out the names and abodes of the "low and disorderly persons, who have of late asembled in a tumultuous manner, in and about the Avenues leading to this House, and have behaved with the most audacious insolence towards several Members thereof"'. In fact the government was concerned with the state of emergency created by the French war, and to this end on 7 November 1759 Chief Secretary Rigby had been given permission to introduce a bill to enable parliament to be assembled quickly during an adjournment or a prorogation.

Always excitable, the Dublin mob were stirred up whether by their own volition or assisted by French agents, as some suggested – again without real evidence. The underlying causes may have been economic, as the trouble appears to have started in one of the poorest areas of the city and there was considerable economic disruption in the late 1750s. The smouldering unrest finally erupted into the serious anti-union riot of 3 December 1759, in the course of which the mob took over the Parliament House and installed an old woman on the throne in the House of Lords.

Archdall's other enduring political interest was the promotion of Irish trade. In 1753 he wrote a pamphlet entitled *A Letter to His Excellency Henry Boyle, Esqre, Speaker of the House of Commons in Ireland: with Remarks on the Linen Trade and Manufacturers of the Kingdom, and some Hints for promoting the same*. After the outbreak of the Seven Years' War late in 1756, Archdall moved in 1757 for an address to the king for leave to send 30,000 coats of the manufacture of Ireland to the king of Prussia. Robert Wilmot, an Englishman who acted for many years as the Lord Lieutenant's Secretary in England, recorded this suggestion in a letter to Chief Secretary Rigby (**1789**), 24 November 1757, adding: 'Did you ever hear such blockheads? ... If I had any feeling for the honour and credit of this Parliament, I should be assuredly ashamed to write such ridiculous stuff.' The motion was rejected,

90 votes to 32. Notwithstanding Wilmot's dismissiveness, it does indicate a genuine concern for stimulating textile manufactures usually depressed by war.

DIVISION LISTS:

1753 (1) voted for the expulsion of Arthur Jones-Nevill (**1125**).
1753 (2) voted for the Money Bill.
1757 (1) voted for the resolutions on pensions.

ESTATES/RESIDENCE: Mount Eccles, Co. Dublin; Castle Archdall, Derrygonnelly, Co. Fermanagh. By his first marriage the greater part of the Montgomery and Dunbar property in Co. Fermanagh became merged in the Archdall estates. Nicholas inherited the Derrygonnelly lands on his mother's death, and also received from his uncle Robert the church lands of Derrybrusk. In 1748 he purchased Mount Eccles, Co. Dublin, which he estimated as worth *c.* £300 p.a.

SOURCES: *CJ Ire.* (Bradley ed.) vol. 8 p. 187, vol. 10 p. 143 (0479, 0534); PRONI D/302; PRONI T/3019/6457/571 Wilmot Papers; McCracken thesis; *CJ Ire.* (Grierson ed.), 13 Dec. 1743, 28 Jan. 1744, 27 Nov. 1745, 12 Dec. 1747, 13 Oct. 1757; H. B. Archdale, *Memoirs of the Archdales* (Enniskillen, 1925), pp. 22, 25–7; Fermanagh and Tyrone MPs; R. B. McDowell, *Irish Public Opinion, 1750–1800* p. 244; G. O'Brien (ed.), *Parliament, Politics & People* (1989), pp. 49–68, S. Murphy, 'The Dublin Anti-Union Riot of 3 December 1759'; *Almanacks*; *DJ* 17–21 May 1763.

0052 ARCHDALL, Richard

MP for Ardfert 1790–7; Killybegs 1797–1800; [UK] Kilkenny City 1801–2; Dundalk 1802–6

b. *c.* 1750; d. 8 Feb. 1824 at Tours in France
FAMILY/BACKGROUND: Third son of Nicholas Archdall (Montgomery) (**0051**) and his second wife Sarah Spurling.
MARRIED: [by 1787] Anna Maria, illeg. dau. of George Montagu, 5th Earl of Halifax.
CHILDREN: Robert (d. Mar. 1810; a halfpenny, accidentally swallowed when a schoolboy, eventually caused his death); Rev. George, m. [1835] Jemima Elizabeth, e. dau. of Rev. William Kinleside of Angmering, Sussex; Edmund Moulton; Anne, m. [Aug. 1805] Charles Newberry of Mincing Lane, London.
EDUCATION: School: Harrow *c.* 1766; entered

TCD 1 Nov. 1767, Scholar 1770, BA 1772;
Middle Temple 13 Mar. 1772; called to the Irish
Bar 12 Feb. 1779 and later to the English Bar;
elected auditor of TCD Historical Society 1774
and gained a medal for composition, the first ever
awarded by that Society.

CAREER/OCCUPATION: *Listed in Judges and
Barristers 1790–1800 (f.); Keeper of Stores,
Ordnance, 17 Apr. 1792–7; Commissioner and
Overseer of Barracks 1 June 1798.

POLITICAL ACTIVITY: A barrister looking for a 'civil
service' employment. In 1790 he purchased his
seat for Ardfert from Lord Glandore (0534), paying, it was thought, full price. He was a friend of
Sir John Parnell's (1633), and in 1791 already
noted as an able speaker. In 1793 he was Storekeeper to the Ordnance, and the following year
Clerk of the Ordnance in the Military Department. In 1797 he was returned by Lord
Conyngham for Killybegs; the following year he
was a Commissioner and Overseer of the Barracks.
He was said to be 'perfectly well disposed to an
Union upon fair terms', and he voted for the Union in both 1799 and 1800.

Archdall was promised civil employment worth
£500 p.a. for supporting the Union, but waived
engagements on being returned to the Imperial
parliament – it was agreed that this waiver was to
expire with the parliament. There he supported
Addington's administration, defending the continuation of martial law in Ireland, 27 May 1801,
commending Abbot as Irish Secretary and reject-
ing Burdett's criticism of the Irish government. In
1802 government returned him for Lord Roden's
borough of Dundalk after he failed to be returned
for Kilkenny. He was listed as the third most important Irish placeman requiring a seat. He was a
spokesman for ministers on Ireland and the peace,
8 December 1802. On the resumption of hostili-
ties with France, he defended the ministers and
assured the House that Ireland would resist invasion by Bonaparte. He spoke in favour of the defence arrangements for Ireland on 30 June, 28 July,
and 4 and 10 August 1803. In the following session he was a member of the Irish Finance Committee and rejected Wrottesley's censure, 7 March
1804, of the handling of Emmet's rising. He was
teller for the Irish Militia Augmentation Bill on
11 and 28 March, praising the record of the Irish

militia. He supported Pitt's second ministry and,
on 14 May 1805, spoke and voted against Catholic claims.

Archdall, who was 'not in easy circumstances',
did not find a seat in 1806.

DIVISION LISTS:

> 1790 (2) voted for Foster (0805) on the
> election of a Speaker.
> 1791 (1) voted for Curran's (0560) resolu-
> tion against the sale of peerages.
> 1798 (1) voted against Sir Laurence Par-
> sons'(1636) motion for an investigation into
> 'the present discontents'.
> 1799 (1) voted for the Union – Barrack
> Board.
> 1800 (1) voted for the Union.

ADDITIONAL INFORMATION: A member of the Royal
Irish Academy, 1790.

ESTATES/RESIDENCE: Great George's Street, Dublin;
Spondon, Derbyshire.

SOURCES: PRONI T/3166/1A Hartnell notes; O'Neill
thesis; M. MacDonagh, *The Viceroy's Postbag* (1904), p.
50; *HP 1790–1820*; IMC *King's Inns Admissions*; H. A.
C. Sturgess, *Middle Temple Admissions*, p. 374; H. B.
Archdale, *Memoirs of the Archdales* (Enniskillen, 1925),
pp. 58–9; Kilkenny MPs; *Almanacks*; Parliamentary
Lists, 1791 (1) [says he was a natural (?half) brother of
(0050)], 1793 (1), 1794 (1), (2),1798 (1), 1799 (3),
1800 (3).

ARDEE, Baron: *see* BRABAZON

0226 Brabazon, Hon. William (styled Lord Ardee
1789–90), 9th Earl of Meath, MP Co. Dublin
1789–90

0053 ARMITAGE, Timothy

MP for Randalstown 1703–13

> b. 1675; d. (Apr.–21 June) 1717
> FAMILY/BACKGROUND: Eldest son of Timothy
> Armitage and Jane (marriage licence 24 Oct.
> 1672), dau. of [ ] Markham.
> MARRIED: Mary, dau. of Arthur Forbes of

Newstone, Co. Meath.

CHILDREN: Markham; Catherine (under 18 in 1715), m. Richard Chapel Whaley.

EDUCATION: School: Mr Morris, Drogheda; entered TCD 11 Apr. 1692, BA 1697.

CAREER/OCCUPATION: Freeman of Ardee 17 Oct. 1692; Burgess of Ardee, Portreeve 1704–5; Alderman of Drogheda 1715–17.

POLITICAL ACTIVITY: He was returned by Charles O'Neill (**1587**) for Randalstown. In 1706 he was counted a Court supporter and attended the Duke of Ormonde's birthday celebrations. Furthermore, he was one of the 34 Tory MPs who met at the Fleece Tavern to decide on their strategy in the ensuing session. In 1711 he was still a Court supporter, voting for the Court on the Dublin mayoralty issue.

Nevertheless, he does not appear to have been a very energetic MP: he is listed for only six committees between 1705 and 1711. In some of his parliamentary behaviour he acted as a country gentleman and possibly he was more interested in local politics, for in 1705 he presented Ardee with a clock for the Market House. The Parliamentary List of 1713 suggested that Joshua Nutley should use his influence with O'Neill to secure Armitage's return, but this did not eventuate.

DIVISION LISTS:

1709 (1) voted against a Money Bill.

1711 (1) voted for the Court on the Dublin mayoralty issue.

ESTATES/RESIDENCE: Ardee, Cardistown, Coole and Dromin, Co. Louth; Newstone, Co. Meath. The lands of Coole and Drummin, barony of Ardee, granted by patent 18 Chas II were still in Armitage possession in the late nineteenth century.

SOURCES: *Louth Arch. Soc. Jn.* 1988 p. 332, T. Gogarty (ed), 'Council Book of the Corporation of Drogheda' vol. 1 [says on 22 June 1717 Sheriff Gilbert was elected Alderman in the room of Alderman Armitage, deceased]; *Louth Arch. Soc. Jn.* 'Caraher of Cardistown Family Papers' [his genealogy is confused even apart from mixing up generations: information courtesy of Larry Conlon Esq.]; PRONI D/562/1052 Account of Armitage estate *post*-15 Dec. 1743; PRONI T/559 vol. 6 p. 89, Burke, extract pedigrees; PRONI T/808/380–81, /327 Grove MS [says d. 1715 leaving a young widow pregnant]; PRONI T/808/380–81, /366 [says m. Catherine Dixon, Mary Forbes being his grandmother]; PRONI T/2842/2 Ardee Corporation Minutes; Burke

LG (1846) p. 22; *Alum. Dub.*; *Coll. Gen.*; Simms' cards; *Ir. Gen.* vol. 4 no 1 (Oct. 1968) p. 13, D. MacIomhair, 'A Dunleer Election of 1715'; NLI LC 301; Parliamentary Lists, 1706 (1), (2), 1707 (2), 1711 (3), 1713 (1).

0054 ARMSTRONG, Rt Hon. John

MP for Fore 1768–76; Kilmallock 1783–90–1

b. 1732; d. 12 Sept. 1791

HONOURS: PC, sworn 9 Sept. 1789.

FAMILY/BACKGROUND: Only son of William Armstrong and Mary, dau. and co-h of Francis Heaton of Mount Heaton, King's County

MARRIED: [17 July 1770] Letitia, dau. and co-h. of Abraham Greene of Ballymacreese, Co. Limerick.

CHILDREN: William Henry (**0055**); Elizabeth Mary (d. yg).

CAREER/OCCUPATION: *Listed in Judges and Barristers 1789.

MILITARY: Colonel of Shinrone Light Infantry.

POLITICAL ACTIVITY: A lawyer with a large fortune, he purchased his seat for Fore from Lord Westmeath. 'A very good humoured, hearty, jolly fellow', he was a steady supporter of Lord Townshend, who promoted his friend, Captain Lumme, to a company. Among the Macartney papers there is a draft, dated 17 January 1771, of a letter from Macartney (**1302**) to Armstrong, then in Toulouse, requesting the support of himself and Mr Barry (**0094**): 'Our parliament here is appointed to meet on the 26th of February for the dispatch of business. As I believe the great stress will be on the first two or three days of the sessions, you will give me leave to mention how very necessary your support and Mr Barry's would be to the government on that occasion. To have the support of two such respectable and independent gentlemen would do us an infinite deal of honour and could not fail to have great weight with many others. Will you please excuse me on the privilege of an old friend to entreat your earliest attendance if possible?' Macartney submitted this draft for Townshend's approval, and Townshend endorsed it: '*Probatum* – and I wish to God I had learnt to say half so much to a man who says nothing.' Armstrong and Barry were brothers-in-law, having married the coheiresses of Abraham Greene of Ballymacreese, Co. Limerick.

Towards the end of Lord Townshend's viceroyalty Armstrong was abroad for much of the time. The 1775 Parliamentary List considered that he could 'scarcely be considered under the influence of the person to whom he is classed unless to effect some point personal to himself, then he becomes united but not otherwise'. By 1774 he was largely an absentee. He did not come into parliament in 1776, but in 1783 he purchased one of the seats for Kilmallock from Silver Oliver (**1585**). The other member was John Fitzgibbon (**0749**). In the 1780s Armstrong was in opposition, but by the end of the decade he was looking for some mark of honour, preferably a peerage. In 1789 he was made a Privy Counsellor. He again purchased in 1790, and emerged from the election a government supporter. In 1791 he was on the point of being raised to the peerage as Baron Dunamore when he died before the patent passed the Great Seal.

DIVISION LISTS:

1771 (2) voted against Sir Lucius O'Brien's (**1558**) motion for retrenchment.

1783 (1) voted against Flood's (**0762**) motion for parliamentary reform.

1785 (1) voted against the Commercial Propositions.

1790 (2) voted for Foster (**0805**) on the election of a Speaker.

ADDITIONAL INFORMATION: A member of the Royal Dublin Society from 1769.

ESTATES/RESIDENCE: Farney Castle, Co. Tipperary; Mount Heaton, King's County; Leinster Street, Dublin.

SOURCES: PRONI T/1584 p. 446, 16 Sept. 1791, PRONI T/559 Pinkerton transcripts, vol. 6 p. 136; Burke, extract pedigrees; PRONI MIC/474 Irish Volunteers; Burke *LGI* (1904) p. 11; *Index to Irish Privy Counsellors, 1711–1910*; *Coll. Gen.*; *Ir. Gen.* vol. 6 no 1 (1980) p. 30, H. F. Morris, 'The Waterford Herald 1791'; Bartlett (ed.), *Macartney in Ireland 1768–72* (PRONI 1978) p. 286; *Almanacks, GM* Oct. 1791, Parliamentary Lists, 1769 (1), 1772 (2), 1773 (1), (2), 1775 (1), 1777 (4), 1783 (2), 1784 (1), (2), (3), 1785 (1), (2), (3), (4), 1787 (1), 1788 (1), 1789 (1), 1790 (1), 1791 (1).

0055 ARMSTRONG, William Henry

MP for Wicklow B. 1798–1800

b. 21 June 1774; d. 21 Sept. 1835 at Passy, near Paris

FAMILY/BACKGROUND: Son of Rt Hon. John Armstrong (**0054**) and Letitia, dau. of Abraham Greene of Ballymacreese, Co. Limerick. MARRIED: [1809] Bridget, only dau. (and in her issue) co-h. of Charles MacDonnell (**1316**). CHILDREN: John m. [1849] Josephine Therese Mary [ ]; Charles; William Edward Armstrong MacDonnell, m. [1858] Juliana Cecilia, dau. of Lucius O'Brien, 13th Baron Inchiquin; Charles, m. [1856] Georgina Maria, dau. of Richard John Stacpoole; Letitia Mary; Letitia Charlotte, m. [1841] Charles William Hamilton of Hamwood, Co. Meath; Catherine, m. [1839] John Bayly of Co. Tipperary; Bridget, m. [1849] James Dobree of Devon; Mary, m. [1842] Rev. Evans Johnston; Emily Dorothea (d. unmar.); Louisa, m. [1861] Rev. Francis Henry Hall. MILITARY: Captain in Shinrone Cavalry Oct. 1796; Captain in the Farneybridge Cavalry Dec. 1796.

POLITICAL ACTIVITY: Armstrong was 21 years of age in 1795, and in 1798 he secured his return for Wicklow town, one of the two Co. Wicklow boroughs controlled by William Tighe (**2073**). He was joined in January 1800 by Henry Grattan (**0895**). A fervent anti-Unionist, he 'refused *all* terms from the government', presumably including the peerage offered to his father, and voted against the Union in both 1799 and 1800. From 1816 he resided almost entirely on the continent, and thereafter sold his extensive Irish estates.

DIVISION LISTS:

1800 (1) voted against the Union.

ESTATES/RESIDENCE: Mount Heaton, King's County. Estates also in Counties Limerick and Fermanagh and in England covering 135,000 acres. Not intending to return to Ireland, he sold Mount Heaton in 1817 and in 1834 his Fermanagh and nearly all his Limerick, Tipperary and English estates.

SOURCES: PRONI T/3166/1D Hartnell notes; O'Neill thesis; Burke *LGI* (1904) p. 11; *Coll. Gen.*; *Almanacks*; *FJ* 20 Oct. 1796, 8 Dec. 1796; Parliamentary Lists, 1799 (3), 1800 (3).

ARRAN, Earl of: *see* **GORE**

0859 Gore, Rt Hon. Sir Arthur, 1st Baron Saunders, Viscount Sudley, Earl of Arran, MP Donegal B. 1727–58

0861 Gore, Rt Hon. Arthur Saunders (styled Viscount Sudley 1762–73), 2nd Earl of Arran, MP Donegal B. 1759–60, 1768–73, Co. Wexford 1761–8

0862 Gore, Hon. Arthur Saunders (styled Viscount Sudley 1773–1809), 3rd Earl of Arran 1809, MP Baltimore 1783–90, Co. Donegal 1800, [UK] 1801–6

0056 ASGILL, John

MP for Enniscorthy Sept.–Oct. 1703 [expelled 11 Oct. 1703]; [E] Bramber, Sussex, 1 Apr. 1699–1700, 1702–18 Dec. 1707 [expelled]

> b. Mar. 1659; d. 10 Nov. 1738
> FAMILY/BACKGROUND: Son of Edward Asgill of Hanley Castle, Worcestershire and Hester [ ].
> MARRIED: [*c.* 1703] Jane (d. *c.* 1708), dau. of Nicholas Browne, 2nd Viscount Kenmare.
> CHILDREN: *d.s.p.*
> EDUCATION: Middle Temple 1686; called to the Bar 1692.
> CAREER/OCCUPATION: Commissioner for taking subscriptions to the Land Bank 1696; Assistant, Royal Corporation of England; Assistant, Merchant Adventurers Co. 1691; Agent for the Hollow Blades Co.

POLITICAL ACTIVITY: Asgill's parliamentary career was colourful, with strong traces of the interregnum. He was the friend and executor of Dr Barbon (died 1679) a paedobaptist (believed in infant baptism) minister. Barbon was a popular Puritan preacher: he combined his trade of leather-seller with his ministerial duties. He was a strong anti-monarchist and imprisoned but released at the Restoration. As Barbon's heir, Asgill acquired an interest in the borough of Bramber.

Before he arrived in Ireland his views had given him the reputation of dubious sanity. He was expelled from the Irish House on account of a pamphlet published in Dublin in 1698 arguing that man may pass into eternal life without dying: 'al-

though the human nature of Christ himself could not be thus translated, till he had passed through Death'. The pamphlet was burnt by the common hangman. The Commons ordered that 'he be forever hereafter incapable of being chosen, returned, or sitting a Member of any succeeding Parliament in this Kingdom.' While in Ireland he had become involved with a Colonel Rice, who for services at Limerick received £10,000 in debentures on forfeited estates. Rice promised part of this to various people and invested the rest in lands in which Asgill also invested. After complaints from creditors, Rice was called to account for the £10,000. The commissioners' report shows that Asgill, and the guardian of Kenmare's children, conveyed lands and woods to a Mr Matthew and a Mr Wetton for £2,500 worth of Rice's debentures. In a complicated transaction, money went missing and Asgill was blamed.

Asgill returned to England, where he was MP for Bramber, but by 1705 he was a prisoner in the Fleet. On 16 December 1707 the House discharged him from prison. He then appeared in the English House of Commons, but was expelled within two to three days on account of the religious pamphlet. Subsequently he was recommitted to the Fleet. He blamed his fall on land speculation in Ireland rather than his religious convictions. Possibly both played a part, as parliament took a serious view of blasphemy.

Asgill spent the rest of his long life in the Fleet or within the rules of the King's Bench. He continued to produce religious pamphlets and died in 1738, officially in his 80th year but reputedly 100. Given his association with 'Praise God' Barbon, he may well have been older than 80 years when he died.

ESTATES/RESIDENCE: Ross Castle, Co. Kerry. Purchased in 1702–3 from the Commissioners for Sale of Forfeited Estates 6,538 acres in Co. Cork, 2,961 acres in Co. Kildare, 873 acres in Co. Louth, 2,058 acres in Co. Meath, 131 acres in Co. Tipperary, 326 acres in Co. Wexford, 856 acres in Co. Westmeath and 1,269 acres in King's County. He purchased for *c.* £3,000 the forfeited estates of Sir Nicholas Browne, 2nd Viscount Kenmare, 1703. Kenmare had been attainted and was living abroad. After the Treaty of Limerick, the estates of which the life interest only was sold amounted to some 95,000 acres, the greater part of which was represented by the Kenmare estate. Sir Nicholas Browne's son, Valentine, was among the heirs who established claims to reversions on the death of their forfeiting fathers. Apart from the Hollow Blades Company, very few of the purchasers came from England. The most important of those who did was John Asgill, who bought 15,000 acres outright as well as a life interest in the Kenmare and Bagenal estates. Asgill soon got into difficulties over the payment of the various family allowances with which the Kenmare estate was charged. He was obliged to hand over the Hospital estate in Co. Limerick to Melchior Levallin, the brother-in-law of Lady Kenmare. His affairs, which figure prominently in *IMC Kenmare*, became extremely complicated. Other creditors took proceedings against him and he was eventually declared a bankrupt.

SOURCES: Simms, *Williamite Confiscation*, pp. 47, 91–2, 137, 155, 182, *CJ Ire.* vol. 2 pt 1 pp. 333–4; *Cal. SP Dom. 1695* (London, 1908) p. 71; *IMC Kenmare* p. x, pp. 3,328–38, 475–6; *DNB*; *Coll. Gen.*

0057 ASHE, Joseph

MP for Trim 1735–60

b. 1707; d. *post* 1760
FAMILY/BACKGROUND: Eldest son of Richard Ashe (**0058**) and Anne, dau. of [ ] Deane.
MARRIED: [1 Aug. 1730] Susannah, dau. of Capt. Dudley Loftus of Killyan, Co. Meath.
CHILDREN: Richard, m. Anne, dau. of Richard Warren (**2191**), wid. of Thomas Cooper; Sir Thomas, m. [1775] Mary, dau. of Sir David Kinloch, 5th Bt; Dudley (killed in the storming of Mora Castle in Flanders); Joseph (killed storming Mora Castle); Maj. William (23rd Welsh Fusiliers); Alice, m. Damer Edgeworth of Longwood, Co. Westmeath; Anne, m. Dudley Loftus of Clara Castle, Co. Meath.
EDUCATION: School: Mr Garnett, Athy; entered TCD 1 July 1725, aged 18 years.
CAREER/OCCUPATION: High Sheriff of Co. Meath 1729.
MILITARY: Cornet, Queen's Own Regiment of Horse 21 May 1733.

POLITICAL ACTIVITY: He was a fairly typical country gentleman MP and not a very energetic one, as he was listed for only eight committees between his return in 1735 and the dissolution of parliament on 25 November 1760. He presented a petition, 1 December 1735, asking for heads of a

bill to vest part of his deceased father's estate of Ashfield, Co. Cavan, in trustees, to be sold to pay off his father's debts and legacies. He petitioned again on 22 February 1747 for leave to sell part of his deceased father's estate to provide the portions and legacies owed his brothers and other debts amounting to £7,000. He followed the Country party and voted with them for the election of James Digges La Touche (♦♦♦♦), for the expulsion of Arthur Jones-Nevill (**1125**) and, in 1753, against the Money Bill. He was defeated at the Trim election of 1761, receiving only 82 votes; his opponents, Robert Perceval (**1667**) and John Pomeroy (**1695**), received 177 and 167 votes respectively.

DIVISION LISTS:
1749 (1) voted for the election of James Digges La Touche (♦♦♦♦).
1753 (1) voted for the expulsion of Arthur Jones-Nevill (**1125**).
1753 (2) voted against the Money Bill.

ESTATES/RESIDENCE: Ashfield, Co. Meath.

SOURCES: PRONI D/302; McCracken thesis; Burke *LG* (1846) p. 28; *Alum. Dub.*; *Ir. Gen.* vol. 5 no 6 (1979) p. 764, E. J. McAuliffe and J. C. Walton, 'Monumental Inscriptions from Lucan, Co. Dublin'; *DJ* 25–8 Apr. 1761.

0058 ASHE, Richard

MP for Trim 1713–14, 1727–8; Athboy 1721–7 [r. Athboy 1727; on 13 Jan. 1728 the Speaker read a letter from Ashe, who was 'confined by sickness', opting to sit for Trim rather than Athboy]

b. *ante* 1686; d. (20) Jan. 1727/8
FAMILY/BACKGROUND: Son of William Ashe of Summerstown, Co. Meath and his first wife Martha Leigh.
MARRIED: Anne, dau. of [ ] Deane.
CHILDREN: Joseph (**0057**); Dillon; St George; Thomas (bapt. 12 May 1720); Richard; Anne, m. [1734] Hans Bailey; Mary, m. [1740] William Lynden; Elizabeth, m. Benjamin Fish.

POLITICAL ACTIVITY: He was nominated for two committees in each of the 1713, 1723 and 1725 sessions. He was part of the extensive Ashe family and noted as a Tory in 1713, when he voted for the government's candidate for Speaker, Sir Richard Levinge (**1230**). He was on a 'black list' of Tories in 1714–15. He supported the scheme for a national bank. Apart from this little is known of him, and by the time of his return in the general election of 1727 his health was obviously failing.

DIVISION LISTS:

1713 (1) voted for Sir Richard Levinge (**1230**) for Speaker.

1721 (1) voted for a national bank.

ESTATES/RESIDENCE: Ashfield, Co. Meath; Blind Quay, Dublin. He inherited lands in Counties Cavan and Meath. His income was estimated in 1713 at £400. He inherited the estate of his friend and kinsman Thomas Ashe (**0060**) (estimated at *c.* £1,000 p.a.), who died on 28 January 1722. 'In 1748 Samuel Yeates of Colganstown, obtained the lands of Moone from the heirs of Thomas Ashe.' Under 12 Geo. II, Thomas Ash (?son) was granted fairs at Moone.

SOURCES: *CJ Ire.* (Bradley ed.) vol. 3 p. 530; PRONI T/ 1003/1 Welply's Prerog. Will Extracts; PRONI T/3411 Blenheim Papers; RCBL P326/1/1, Parish Register of St Werburgh's, Dublin; Vicars, *Prerog. Wills*; McCracken thesis; Parliamentary Lists, 1713 (2), 1714–15 (1).

0059 ASHE, Thomas

MP for Cavan B. 1692–3, 1695–9, 1703–13

b. *ante* ?1664; d. *ante* 17 Aug. 1721
FAMILY/BACKGROUND: ?Son of Thomas Ashe (?Steward to Primate Marsh) and Susanna, dau. of Richard Warburton of Dublin (she m. (2) Daniel Gahan (*see* **0835**)).
MARRIED: [?7 Aug. 1685] Mary Carr.
CHILDREN: Thomas (d. yg); Thomas (King's Inns admissions, 18 Aug. 1721, states father deceased).

POLITICAL ACTIVITY: As an MP he was fairly active, being listed for four committees in the short 1692 parliament, seven in the 1695 and seven in the 1703 parliaments. He supported Lord Chancellor Porter against the accusations of favouring Catholics made by some MPs in 1695, and in 1696 was among those who signed the Association for the protection of William III in parliament. During Queen Anne's reign he was a listed Court supporter in 1706, and he attended Ormonde's birthday celebrations. In 1711 he was

still adhering to the Court party; he supported the government over the Dublin mayoralty issue. In 1713 it was correctly thought that he would not be returned in the general election.

DIVISION LISTS:

1711 (1) voted for the Court on the Dublin mayoralty issue.

ESTATES/RESIDENCE: Ashfield, Co. Meath. [?]Purchased 298 acres in Co. Kildare from the Commissioners for Sale of Forfeited Estates in 1702–3.

SOURCES: Simms, *Williamite Confiscation*, p. 182; *Alum. Dub.*; IMC *King's Inns Admissions*; *Register of the Parish of St Peter and St Kevin, 1669–1761* (Parish Register Society of Dublin, 1911) pp. 93, 97 [says he had a son Thomas bapt. 12 May 1686]; *Ir. Gen.* vol. 4 no 3 (1970) pp. 83–93, W. G. Skehan, 'Extracts from the Minutes of the Corporation of Fethard, Co. Tipperary'; Parliamentary Lists, 1695 (1), 1696 (1), 1706 (1), (2), 1711 (3), 1713 (1).

0060 ASHE, Thomas

MP for Swords 1695–9; Clogher 1713–14, 1715–22

b. 1656; d. 28 Jan. 1722
FAMILY/BACKGROUND: Eldest son of Thomas Ashe of St John's, Co. Meath, and Mary, dau. of Capt. Richard St George.
MARRIED: ?
CHILDREN: *d.s.p.*
EDUCATION: School: Mr Norris; entered TCD 14 Nov. 1671 aged about 15 years, BA 1686, MA 1692; Grays Inn 30 Jan. 1683.
CAREER/OCCUPATION: Provost of the Corporation of Trim.
MILITARY: A Captain.

POLITICAL ACTIVITY: On 2 August 1705 he unsuccessfully petitioned the Duke of Ormonde for the bishopric of Meath for his brother, St George. In 1713 and 1715 Ashe was returned for Clogher by his brother, the bishop (Dr St George was Bishop of Clogher 1697–1717). In 1717 the bishop was translated to Derry, where he died in the following year.

The Ashes were a large family. Dean Swift was warmly attached to them, and in a *Letter to the Earl of Pembroke* wrote the dying speech, years before he died, of Tom Ashe, the punster. Thomas Ashe was described as 'a facetious pleasant companion, but the most eternal unwearied punster that ever lived. He was thick and short in his person, being not above five feet high at the most, and had something very droll in his appearance ... There is a whimsical story, and a very true one, of Tom Ashe, which is well remembered to this day. It happened that, while he was travelling on horseback, and at a considerable distance from any town, there burst from the clouds such a torrent of rain as wetted him through. He galloped forward; and as soon as he came to an inn, he was met instantly by a drawer; "Here," said he to the fellow, stretching out one of his arms, "take off my coat immediately." "No, sir, I won't," said the drawer. "… confound you," said Ashe, "take off my coat this instant!" "No, Sir," replied the drawer, "I dare not take off your coat, for it is a felony to strip an ash." Ireland in the eighteenth century was almost denuded of trees and this referred to a statute, probably that of 1698, aimed at their preservation. Tom was delighted beyond measure, frequently told the story, and said he would have given fifty guineas to have been the author of that pun.'

He was nominated for six committees in the 1695 parliament and two in that of 1713–14. In 1695 he supported Lord Chancellor Porter against the accusations of favouritism to Catholics made by some MPs; the following year he signed the Association for the protection of William III in parliament. On his return in 1713 he espoused the Tory faction, voting for Sir Richard Levinge (**1230**) as Speaker, and following the death of Queen Anne he was on the 'black list' of Tories. Thereafter his parliamentary activity appears to have been low-key. He voted against the establishment of a national bank in 1721.

DIVISION LISTS:

1713 (1) voted for Sir Richard Levinge (**1230**) for Speaker.

1721 (1) voted against a national bank.

1721 (2) voted against a national bank.

ESTATES/RESIDENCE: St John's, Co. Meath. He left his estate of about £1,000 p.a. to his intimate friend and kinsman, Richard Ashe of Ashfield (**0058**).

SOURCES: PRONI T/559 vol. 6 p. 270, Burke, extract pedigrees; Burke *LG* (1846) p. 1175; *Alum. Dub.*; *HMC Ormonde* new ser. vol.8 pp. 171, 250; King, *A Great Archbishop of Dublin: William King, DD, 1650–1729* pp. 316–17 f. 1; Fermanagh and Tyrone MPs; *Coll. Gen.*; B. De Breffny and R. Ffolliott, *The Houses of Ireland* (Dublin, 1975), p. 132; Parliamentary Lists, 1695 (1), 1696 (1), 1713 (1), (2), 1714–15 (1).

ASHTOWN, Baron: *see* **TRENCH**

2108 Trench, Frederick, 1st Baron Ashtown, MP Maryborough 1785–90, Portarlington 1798–1800, [UK] 1801

0061 ASTON, Tichborne

MP for Ardee 1741–8

b. 1 Nov. 1716; d. 4 Mar. 1748

FAMILY/BACKGROUND: Only surviving son of William Aston (**0062**) and Salisbury, dau. and h. of Rt Hon. Sir Henry Tichborne, 1st Baron Ferrard (**2061**).

MARRIED: [May 1746] Jane, dau. of William Rowan KC (she married (2) [1750] Gawen Hamilton of Killyleagh, Co. Down).

CHILDREN: William (bapt. 8 Apr. 1747; d. 1769).

EDUCATION: Entered TCD 29 Nov. 1732.

CAREER/OCCUPATION: Sheriff of Co. Louth 1742.

POLITICAL ACTIVITY: This MP was the last to represent the once powerful Aston/Tichbourne (**2061**) (Ferrard) interest in Co. Louth, inheriting the Tichbourne interest from his mother, the heiress of the 1st Baron Ferrard. Little is known about him apart from the fact that he was listed for three committees between 1743 and 1744. His sister, Sophia, married Thomas Tipping (**2074**), and what remained of the Ferrard estates along with the Aston passed into that family, apparently by sale (Tichbourne) or guardianship (Aston).

ESTATES/RESIDENCE: Beaulieu, Richardstown, Dunleer, Co. Louth. He left Beaulieu and Richardstown to his brother-in-law Thomas Tipping, possibly as guardian to the young William, who was the last of the Astons and in an 'eccentric will' alienated the Aston property from his aunt Sophia Tipping, née Aston.

SOURCES: PRONI T/559 vol. 1 p. 1, Burke, extract pedigrees; PRONI MIC/338/1 Crossle notes; NAI M5127, Extracts from the Parish Registers of St Peter's, Drogheda [bur. 9 Mar. 1748]; McCracken thesis; *Alum. Dub.*; G. S. Montgomery, *A Family History of the Montgomerys of Ballyleck from whom are descended the Montgomerys of Beaulieu and Convoy* (Belfast, 1887), pp. 82–4; Malcomson, *Foster*, pp. 112, 117, 127.

0062 ASTON, William

MP for Dunleer 1721–7; Co. Louth 1727–44

b. *ante* 1674; d. 23 Aug. 1744 of an apoplexy at Castle Bellingham
FAMILY/BACKGROUND: Eldest son of Thomas Aston and Margaret, dau. of Col. Robert Sandys of Co. Roscommon.
MARRIED: Salisbury, dau. and h. of Rt Hon. Sir Henry Tichborne, 1st Baron Ferrard (**2061**) of Beaulieu (and on the latter's death succeeded to his estates).
CHILDREN: Henry (d. yg); Tichborne (**0061**); Sophia dau. and h., m. 1741 Thomas Tipping (**2074**).
CAREER/OCCUPATION: Sheriff of Co. Louth 1715; Burgess of Ardee, Portreeve 6 Jan.–24 Sept. 1724; *Common Council Corporation for the City of Dublin 1729; Trustee of the Linen Board for Leinster 1743.

POLITICAL ACTIVITY: Aston was returned in a by-election for Dunleer in 1721. He represented one of the major interests in Co. Louth. In the 1727 general election he came in for the county on his own and the Ferrard interest against the Tisdalls. The election was disputed, but the return was confirmed after a House of Commons vote. He was against the establishment of a national bank.
In 1731 he was appointed, by act of parliament (5 Geo. II, c. 15), a trustee for repairing the road from Dublin to Dunleer. On 19 October 1733 he and other trustees, including Arthur Hill (**1015**), William Cooper (**0476**), Faithful Fortescue (**0790**) and Thomas Fortescue (**0793**), petitioned for heads of a bill to increase the toll and widen their powers under the act. Between 1723 and 1725 he was listed for three committees, but between his election for Co. Louth in 1727 and his death in 1744 he was nominated for no fewer than 69.

DIVISION LISTS:
1721 (1) voted against a national bank.
1721 (2) voted against a national bank.

ADDITIONAL INFORMATION: A foundation member of the Dublin Society, 1731.

ESTATES/RESIDENCE: Beaulieu, Richardstown, Dunleer, Co. Louth.

SOURCES: *Statutes at Large* vol. 5; PRONI T/2842/2 Ardee Corporation Minutes; McCracken thesis; Lodge *P*; Malcomson, *Foster*, pp. 112, 117, 127; G. S. Montgomery, *A Family History of the Montgomerys of Ballyleck from whom are descended the Montgomerys of Beaulieu and Convoy* (Belfast, 1887), pp. 82–4; *Louth Arch. Soc. Jn.* vol. 2 p. 180, T. G. F. Paterson, 'The Chamberlaines of Nizelrath'; *Almanacks*; *The Dublin Gazette* 9–12 Oct. 1742 [says he died 10 Oct. 1742, but he was listed for committees until 1744 and the by-election was 1745].

ATHENRY, Baron: *see* BERMINGHAM

0122 Bermingham, Rt Hon. Thomas, 15th Baron Athenry, 1st Earl of Louth, MP Co. Galway 1745–50

0063 ATKINSON, Anthony

MP for St Johnstown (Longford) 1711–13; Belfast 1713–14

b. 12 Apr. 1681; d. Dec. 1743
FAMILY/BACKGROUND: Son and heir of William Atkinson of Cangort, King's County, and Anne, dau. of Sir Francis Hamilton of Killeshandra, Co. Cavan.
MARRIED: (1) [*c.* 1694] Mary Taylor (marriage declared invalid); (2) [1709] Mary, dau. of Adm. John Guy of Greenwich, Kent.
CHILDREN: (2) William (admitted to Middle Temple 8 May 1732); Rev. Guy, m. (1) [1746] Jane, dau. of Charles Maule, (2) Jane, dau. of Jackson Wray of Co. Donegal; Anthony; Charles, m. Mary, dau. of Robert Saunderson of Co. Cavan; Newcomen; Anne, m. Francis Saunderson of Castle Saunderson, Co. Cavan; Mary, m. Newcomen Lestrange; Elizabeth (d. yg); Jane; Frances; Catherine; Harriet (?Henrietta), m. (1) Robert Saunderson of Drumkeen, Co. Cavan, (2)

William Stewart (**2013**).

EDUCATION: School: Mr Kennedy, Dublin; entered TCD 15 Mar. 1697; Middle Temple 1 Jan. 1700; called to the Irish Bar 1708.

POLITICAL ACTIVITY: Although he sat for only four years, he was returned for two parliaments: for St Johnstown (Co. Longford) in a by-election in 1711, and for Belfast at the general election of 1713. Both were close boroughs. He supported the Court party, and in 1713 the Duke of Ormonde was to recommend him to Lord Charlemont for the borough of Charlemont should Lord Lanesborough not 'see fit' to return him for St Johnstown. Obviously Lord Lanesborough did not, as at the 1713 general election he was returned for the Donegall borough of Belfast.

He was a known Tory, voting for the Court candidate, Sir Richard Levinge (**1230**), for Speaker; he was on the 1713–14 'black list' of Tories. He was listed for one committee in each of the two sessions that he was in parliament, namely, 1711 and 1713; otherwise he does not appear to have been a very active MP. He was not a wealthy man, and his Tory predilection probably closed his parliamentary career in 1714.

DIVISION LISTS:

1713 (1) voted for Sir Richard Levinge (**1230**) for Speaker.

ADDITIONAL INFORMATION: In 1707 he was involved in a marriage dispute with his first wife, Mary (*alias* Taylor). She issued a suit against him claiming denial of conjugal rights and lack of support. He replied that he was only 13 years old when he married and that he had been deceived into doing so, therefore the marriage was invalid. His wife claimed that he said he was 17 years old at the time of the marriage so was therefore responsible. The marriage was declared invalid on 14 July 1707.

ESTATES/RESIDENCE: Cangort, King's County. In 1713 his income was estimated at £250 p.a. In 1734 he was granted fairs at Kilcummin in the barony of Kilcoursey.

SOURCES: PRONI T/559 vol. 6 p. 299, Burke, extract pedigrees; PRONI T/1075/29 Canon Leslie's notes; NLI Report on Private Collections no 120; Burke *LGI* (1904) p. 14; Burke *LG* (1846) p. 36; *King's Inns Ad-*

missions; *Coll. Gen.*; *Middle Temple Admissions* vol. 1 pp. 246, 312; Simms' cards; Parliamentary Lists, 1713 (1), (2), 1714–15 (1).

AUCKLAND, Baron: *see* **EDEN**
0681 Eden, Rt Hon. William, 1st Baron Auckland [I and GB], MP Dungannon 1781–3, [GB] New Woodstock 1774–84, Heytesbury 1784–93

0064 AUNGIER, Ambrose

MP for Longford B. 1697–9

b. *c.* 1649; d. 23 Jan. 1705
PEERAGES: Suc. his bro. Dec. 1700 as 4th Baron Aungier, 2nd Viscount Longford 1700 and 2nd Earl of Longford.
FAMILY/BACKGROUND: Son of Rev. the Hon. Ambrose Aungier and Grisel, dau. of Launcelot Bulkeley, Abp of Dublin.
MARRIED: ?
CHILDREN: *d.s.p.*
EDUCATION: Entered Lincoln's Inn 24 Aug. 1666.
CAREER/OCCUPATION: Commissioner of the Revenue.
MILITARY: Cornet to Lieutenant-Colonel Moses Hill 1663; Cornet 1665; Cornet in the Guards Apr. 1672; Lieutenant in Lord Longfield's Troop of Horse Mar. 1675, Captain July 1680; Captain commanding a troop of Horse June 1682; Captain in Earl of Arran's Regiment of Horse 1685 (left army in same year); Duke of Ormonde's Regiment, Captain in the Earl of Donegall's Regiment of Foot 1693; Major 13 June 1696; half-pay 1697; Major in the Earl of Donegall's Regiment 1702.

POLITICAL ACTIVITY: In 1696 he signed the Association for the protection of William III, apparently before he came into parliament. He was a serving officer probably until after the Peace of Ryswick in September 1697, hence there is little record of any parliamentary activity. In 1700 he went to the House of Lords. In May 1702 the War of Spanish Succession broke out and he returned to active service. The first parliament of Queen Anne did not meet until September 1703.

ESTATES/RESIDENCE: Dublin. In 1700 the boundaries of the estate of Francis, 1st Earl of Longford were St Stephen's churchyard and St Stephen Street on the north and Whitefriars' Street, Peter's Row and Redman's Hill on the west. The nucleus of Aungier's estate was the former estate of the Whitefriars. Protestant Row marked the southern boundary. The eastern estate boundary was the western boundary of the properties fronting St Stephen's Green between Great Cuffe Street and Raparee Alley. The estate comprised land acquired from the Crown, the city, the Vicars Choral of St Patrick's Cathedral and the parish of St Peter. It was held by three different types of tenure, namely fee simple, fee farm (fee simple but subjected to a perpetual fixed rent), and terms of years. It was extensively developed with the intention to supply the needs of the greater gentry.

Aungier also had lands in the baronies of Granard and Ardagh, Co. Longford. The estates devolved upon his sister Mrs Ludlow and after her death passed to his nephews, Francis Cuffe (**0549**) (whose grand-daughter married Thomas Pakenham, hence the connection between the Aungier and Pakenham families, successively Lords Longford) and James Macartney (**1304**) by an equal division.

At the beginning of the nineteenth century Wakefield estimated that 'Lord Longford's (Pakenham) estate, which is let much under its value, brings in £4,000 per annum.'

Under 17 Jas I, Sir Francis and Lady Margaret Aungier were granted fairs/markets at Longford and Granard, and Lord Aungier received a further grant of fairs at Longford from Charles II in 1678.

SOURCES: GEC *P*; Burke *Ext. P* (1883) p. 18; *HP 1660–90* (his e. bro. Francis Aungier was an English MP); Simms' cards; C. Dalton (ed.), *English Army Lists and Commission Registers, 1661–1714* (London, 1896), vol. 3 p. 13; C. Dalton (ed.), *Irish Army Lists 1661–85* (London, 1907), pp. 47, 78, 111, 122, 132, 140, 148; J. H. Bernard (ed.), *The Register of St Patrick, Dublin 1677–1800* (Parish Register Society of Dublin, 1907) p. 17 [bur. 26 Jan. 1705]; *Ir. Geography* vol. 6 no 4 (Wexford, 1972) pp. 365–85, N. T. Burke, 'An Early Modern Dublin Suburb: The Estate of Francis Aungier, Earl of Longford'; *Lincoln's Inn Records* vol. 1 p. 298 [does not say that his father was a cleric]; NLI EC 7186, 7557 and 8632; cross-ref to NLI EC 845; Wakefield, *Account of Ire.*, vol. 1 p. 268; Parliamentary List, 1696 (1).

AVONMORE, Baron and Viscount : *see* **YELVERTON**
2268 Yelverton, Rt Hon. Barry, 1st Baron Yelverton, Baron Avonmore, Viscount Avonmore, MP Donegal B. 1774–6, Carrickfergus 1776–83, 1783

0065 AYLMER, Sir FitzGerald

MP for Roscommon B.1761–8; Old Leighlin 1768–76; Kildare B.1776–83; Harristown 1783–90–4

> b. 14 Sept. 1736; d. Feb. 1794
> HONOURS: Suc. as 6th Bt 1737.
> FAMILY/BACKGROUND: Only son of Sir Gerald Aylmer (d. Jan. 1736/7), 5th Bt, and Lucy, dau. of Adm. Sir John Norris of Hampstead, Kent (she m. (2) [Nov. 1737] Robert Fisher).
> MARRIED: [15 Sept. 1764] Elizabeth (d. *c.* 1797), dau. of Fenton Cole of Silver Hill, Co. Fermanagh.
> CHILDREN: Sir Fenton (d. 23 May 1816), 7th Bt, m. [4 June 1795] Jane (d. 31 Dec.1827), dau. of Sir John Freke (Evans) 1st Bt (**0820**); Capt. John (89th Regiment), m. [1801] Grace Jane, dau. of William Evans, wid. of William Speirs; Lieut.-Gen. Arthur, m. [1807] Anne, dau. of John Harrison of Walworth Castle, Durham; Margaret, m. [1789] Sir John Hart, 1st Bt of Hartland, Co. Kildare; Gerald.
> EDUCATION: Dr Sauxay's School, Cheam, Surrey.
> CAREER/OCCUPATION: Sheriff of Co. Kildare 1761; Director of the Grand Canal Company; Committee of Works 1772–4.
> MILITARY: Captain of the Loyal Kilcock Rangers.

POLITICAL ACTIVITY: He succeeded to the baronetcy in infancy and was largely brought up in England by his mother and her family; as a young man he claimed friendship with Edward Gibbon. He had extensive estates in Kildare and belonged to the Duke of Leinster's party, invariably voting with them in opposition. The 1773 Parliamentary List declared that 'Sir Fitzgerald has very little understanding but will do as the Duke of Leinster (**0745**) bids him'; however, a 1774 list considered him to be: 'a true independent gentleman unconnected with any party and generally votes for the service of his country': as the Duke of Leinster was usually considered in this light also, the two lists are not incompatible. But, although Sir FitzGerald may have had a natural Whiggish inclination, this list was unique as he otherwise is invariably listed as part of the duke's political following.

In 1768 he was returned by the Bishop of Ferns on the recommendation of Lord Hillsborough. Dr Young had previously been Bishop of Dromore, near Lord Hillsborough's seat in Co. Down, and was married to an illegitimate daughter of Lord Holland, the Duke of Leinster's (0734) brother-in-law. From 1776 Sir FitzGerald was returned for Leinster (0745) boroughs. He was a member of the Royal Dublin Society from 1764 and was a fairly typical country gentleman. His was one of the letters sent to Lord George Sackville Germain (1835) by Sir James Caldwell on 28 September 1779 pointing out the depressed condition of trade in Ireland and the potential danger from the Volunteers. During the 1780s and 1790s his voting pattern shows that he followed the usual opposition line. His death was announced in the House of Commons on Wednesday, 12 February 1794.

DIVISION LISTS:

1768 (1) voted against army augmentation.
1771 (1) voted against Lord Townshend as Lord Lieutenant.
1771 (2) voted for Sir Lucius O'Brien's (1558) motion for retrenchment.
1772 (2) voted for a Short Revenue Bill.
1773 (1) voted against the Absentee Tax.
1774 (2) voted in favour of Catholic relief.
1775 (1) voted for the pro-American amendment to the Speech from the Throne.
1777 (1) voted against Grattan's (0895) motion for retrenchment.
1778 (2) voted for the Popery Bill.
1779 (2) voted for a six-months Loan Bill.
1780 (1) voted against Grattan's declaration of the Rights of Ireland.
1780 (2) voted against Yelverton's (2268) motion for parliamentary reform.
1783 (1) voted against Flood's (0762) motion for parliamentary reform.
1784 (1) voted against a committee on the Reform Bill.
1785 (1) voted against the Commercial Propositions.
1786 (2) voted for Forbes's (0778) motion for retrenchment.
1787 (1) voted for a Pension Bill.
1788 (1) voted for Hartley's (0979) motion against the Dublin police.
1789 (1) voted for a regency.
1790 (1) voted for Grattan's motion for reducing the influence of the Crown.
1790 (2) voted for Ponsonby (1709) on the election of a Speaker.
1791 (1) voted for Curran's (0560) resolution against the sale of peerages.
1791 (2) voted for Grattan's motion for the exercise of Free Trade.
1791 (3) voted for Grattan's motion to abolish the Dublin police.
1792 (1) voted for the Catholic petition.
1793 (1) voted for Knox's (1180) motion for Catholic Emancipation.
1793 (2) voted against the Convention Bill.

ADDITIONAL INFORMATION: A member of the Royal Dublin Society from 1764.

ESTATES/RESIDENCE: Donadea, Co. Kildare; Grafton Street, Dublin. On 3 April 1764 he mortgaged his lands for a loan of £6,000 which was not repaid until 1784. His marriage settlement charged his lands with a jointure of £500 p.a. (to be increased to £600 on the death of his mother) and with £4,000 for younger children. The trustees were able to raise £13,000 to pay debts, charges and encumbrances. In January 1777 the town and lands of Ovidstown were sold for £2,300. By his will his younger sons Arthur and John got an additional £2,500 and £2,000 respectively. Wakefield described Sir Fenton's estate as 'an immense tract' and implied that the rental exceeded £6,000–£7,000.

SOURCES: PRONI D/302; PRONI MIC/474 Irish Volunteers; RCBL P80/1/1, Parish Registers of St Thomas, Dublin; GEC *B*; Burke *PB* (1906) p. 3; Wakefield, *Account of Ire.*, vol. 1 p. 263; *Coll. Gen.*; Lt Gen. Sir F. J. Aylmer Bt, *The Aylmers in Ireland* (London, 1931), pp. 224–5; HMC *Stopford-Sackville I* p. 258; Kildare MPs; *Almanacks*; *GM* Feb. 1794; *DJ* 11 June 1795; Parliamentary Lists, 1769 (1), 1772 (2), 1773 (1), (2), 1774 (1), 1775 (1), 1776 (1), (2), (3), 1777 (1), 1778 (1), 1780 (1), 1782 (1), 1783 (1), (2), 1784 (1), (2), (3), 1785 (1), (2), (3), (4), 1787 (1), 1788 (1), 1789 (1), 1790 (1), 1791 (1), 1793 (1).

0066 AYLMER, John

MP for Naas 1692–3

b. *c.* 1652; d. 1705
FAMILY/BACKGROUND: Eldest son of John Aylmer.
MARRIED: [1678] Mary, dau. of Thomas Breedon
of Bearecourt, Berkshire (she married (2) George
Aylmer).
CHILDREN: John, m. [1705] Mary, dau. of
Thomas Whyte; Thomas; Charles, m. [ ] dau. of
Gerard Crosbie; Andrew; Matthew; James;
Dorothy; Elizabeth; Cecily; Lydia; Alice; Anne.
CAREER/OCCUPATION: Sheriff of Co. Kildare 1680–
5; Deputy Governor of Co. Kildare 1699;
Sovereign of Naas 1694.
MILITARY: Entered the army of Charles II as a
young man in 1682–4; in 1687 was a Captain
serving in Tangier; described as Colonel in 1690.

POLITICAL ACTIVITY: The first parliament of William
and Mary lasted less than a month before its pre-
mature prorogation and dissolution in June 1693.
There is therefore little to report on the activities
of MPs, particularly military ones. Parliament
quarrelled with Lord Lieutenant Sidney over its
constitutional rights and in particular its financial rights, declaring that 'It was and is the sole
and undoubted right of the Commons to prepare
heads of bills for raising money.' This became a
recurrent quarrel until after the amendment of
Poynings' Law in 1782.

The only definite piece of information about
Aylmer's attitudes is that, in common with most
of his fellow MPs, he was strongly anti-Catholic.
The War of the League of Augsburg was not concluded until 1697, and as a professional soldier
Aylmer was probably more concerned with the
wars of the period than with parliament.

ESTATES/RESIDENCE: Ballykenane, Co. Kildare. When he
died in 1705 he was possessed of an estate of £500 p.a.
He left only 5 shillings to his second son, Thomas, who
had become a Roman Catholic.

SOURCES: PRONI D/302; Burke *LGI* (1904) p. 17, *IFR*
(1976) p. 42 [says his younger brother was born *c.*
1654]; *Coll. Gen.* [will dated 22 Mar. 1705]; Lt Gen.
Sir F. J. Aylmer Bt, *The Aylmers of Ireland* (London,
1931), pp. 122–3; Simms' cards; *JRSAI* vol. 55 (1925)
pp. 38, 47, H. A. S. Upton, 'A List of Governors and
Deputy Governors of Counties in Ireland in 1699' [says
he married in 1678 and that it may have been his father who was Deputy Governor of Co. Kildare in 1699].

0067 AYLWARD, Nicholas

MP for Thomastown 1727–56

b. 1688; d. 5 June 1756
FAMILY/BACKGROUND: Eldest son of Peter Aylward
of Shankhill, Co. Kilkenny, and Elizabeth, dau.
and co-h. of Sir Richard Butler, 2nd Bt of
Paulstown, Co. Kilkenny.
MARRIED: [3 Aug. 1719] Catherine, dau. of
Maurice Keating (**1132**).
CHILDREN: Maurice; Nicholas (admitted to
Middle Temple 8 Sept. 1744), m. (1) [14 July
1756] Mary, dau. of Benjamin Kearney, (2) [8
Apr. 1769] Susanna, dau. of Samuel Mathews of
Bonnetstown and wid. of Edmund Waring of
Kellymount, Co. Kilkenny; Peter; Anne, m. [6
Nov. 1751] John Vigors of Old Leighlin;
Elizabeth, m. [4 Feb. 1749] John Hely of
Foulkscourt, Co. Kilkenny; Catherine (d.
unmar.); Mary (d. unmar).
EDUCATION: School: Kilkenny College 27 Jan.
1703, aged 15 years; Middle Temple 11 Feb.
1706; called to the Irish Bar 1711.
CAREER/OCCUPATION: Sovereign of Athy 1733;
Sheriff of Co. Kilkenny 1742; Magistrate of
Thomastown 1754; Burgess of Thomastown
1743; Recorder of Thomastown, Recorder of
Gowran 1748, 1754.

POLITICAL ACTIVITY: The Aylwards were an old Kilkenny family, and Nicholas Aylward was brought
up a Catholic. His father fought in the Jacobite
army until the end of the war and was outlawed.
However, both father and son conformed to the
Established Church, Nicholas Aylward conforming (enrolled on Convert Roll 11 July – certifi-
cate dated 25 June) in 1711, the same year as he
was called to the Irish Bar.

In November 1731 he introduced a turnpike
act 'for repairing the road leading from the town
of Kilcullen in the county of Kildare to the city of
Kilkenny'. He was an active parliamentarian, and
is listed on 44 committees between 1727 and
1753. By 1753 he would have been 65 and no
longer required to sit on committees. He was absent when the Money Bill dispute began in 1749,
but thereafter appears as a government supporter,
voting in 1753 against the expulsion of Arthur
Jones-Nevill (**1125**) and for the Money Bill.

DIVISION LISTS:

1749 (1) absent.

1753 (1) voted against the expulsion of Arthur Jones-Nevill (**1125**).

1753 (2) voted for the Money Bill.

ESTATES/RESIDENCE: Shankill, Co. Kilkenny (main country residence). Also lands in Counties Carlow and Galway as well as in Dublin city.

His father, who had been outlawed and had fought in the Jacobite army until the end of the war, had married Elizabeth Butler of Paulstown around 1685 and through her (died 1708) had obtained the house and estate of Shankill – the townland alone was in area 1,831 acres – which in extent was more than all the previously held and lost Aylward estates put together. His father conformed, and by 1719 a settlement reveals that he had leased back most of the Aylwardstown estate from Lord Duncannon (**1706**). Peter Aylward rebuilt the old Butler residence at Shankill and also had control of lands in Counties Carlow and Galway. In 1721 Nicholas had a lease of premises in Usher Street, Dublin. In 1726 he mortgaged these premises to Richard Grattan. He had succeeded his father by 1725 and renewed the lease of Aylwardstown from Brabazon Ponsonby, 2nd Viscount Bessborough (**1696**). In 1740 he purchased the townland of Ballygurteen in Shankill parish. In 1741 he mortgaged his estate of Shankill and in 1746 granted his lands in Counties Kilkenny and Galway, in trust, to Thomas Keating, his brother-in-law.

Before the Commonwealth, Paulstown was a lordship possibly containing 7,561 statute acres *c.* 1640–70, including the lands of Shankill, 1880; Paulstown, 1076; and Jordanstown, 147. By 1670 only these lands seem to have been left to the family, and Shankill seems to have passed down a female line. Elizabeth Butler, sister of Sir Walter, 3rd Bt (since 1686) carried it into the family of her husband, Peter (Piers) Aylward of Aylwardstown, Co. Waterford; she died in 1708. Sir Walter mortgaged Paulstown and 'his part of' Jordanstown to James Agar and others in the period 1718–19, and died insane in 1723. The Agars seem to have acquired Paulstown in fee, and then let it in perpetuity to Francis Flood (**0760**).

In 1785–94, the rental from Peter Aylward's Glasnevin estate was £1,416 plus £230 from Dublin city. The Shankill estate itself had a rental of only £286 and comprised 1,153 acres in 1792.

SOURCES: *CJ Ire.* (Bradley ed.) vol. 6 pp. 80, 95 (0312); NLI MS 785 William Prendergast's MS history of Paulstown, 1943, pp. 442–74; PRONI T/1075/32 Canon Leslie's notes [says m. 5 Aug. 1719, and son of Piers Aylward and Sarah dau. of Sir Richard Butler];

NLI rep. no 37; McCracken thesis; *King's Inns Admissions*; E. O'Byrne, *IMC The Convert Rolls*; *Middle Temple Admissions* vol. 1 pp. 258, 334; *JRSAI* vol. 54 (1924) pp. 55–67, T. U. Sadleir, 'The Register of Kilkenny School (1685–1800)'; *Ir. Gen.* vol. 5 no 1 (1974) pp. 61–6, J. C. Walton, 'The Family of Aylward'; *Almanacks*; *GM* June 1756; *Pue's Occurrences* 6 Oct. 1733.

0068 AYLWAY, Robert

MP for Dunleer 1692–3, 1695–9

b. *ante* 1645; d. 1702

FAMILY/BACKGROUND: Son of [ ] Aylway.

MARRIED: ?

CHILDREN: ?

CAREER/OCCUPATION: Auditor-General of Virginia 1677 (life); Commissioner of Stores, Artillery, 1689; Clerk of Ordnance and Deliveries 27 Feb. 1682 – 3 July 1685.

MILITARY: Lord Dartmouth's agent. On 2 Feb. 1692 his petition for the return of his post of Auditor-General of Virginia and his posts of Clerk of the Ordnance and the Deliveries in Ireland, with back-pay, was referred to Baron Ginkel; Commissary of Stores in the artillery train for Ireland, 20 June 1689, at 8 shillings per day.

POLITICAL ACTIVITY: Little is known of this man. He was a government placeman and, in 1696, signed the Association for the protection of William III in parliament. During the period he was in the House of Commons he was nominated for 12 committees, six of which were in 1697.

ESTATES/RESIDENCE: Mount Rawdon, Co. Wicklow; Dublin.

SOURCES: Malcomson thesis; *Cal. SP Dom. 1691–2* (London, 1900) p. 122; C. Dalton (ed.), *English Army Lists and Commission Registers, 1661–1714* (London, 1896), vol. 3 p. 40; Hughes, *Pat. Officers*; Vicars, *Prerog. Wills*; *Coll. Gen.*; Simms' cards; Parliamentary Lists, 1696 (1).

B

0069 BABINGTON, David

MP for Ballyshannon 1797–1800

b. 1753; d. 1836
FAMILY/BACKGROUND: Son of Richard Babington,
Rector of Portglenone, Co. Antrim, and Mary,
dau. of Cornelius Marshal of Caledon, Co.
Tyrone.
MARRIED: (1) Helen, dau. of Bryan McManus; (2)
[14 Jan. 1792] Mary, dau. of George Bannerman.
CHILDREN: ?
CAREER/OCCUPATION: *Listed in Attornies of the
Courts of King's Bench, Common Pleas and
Exchequer 1790–1800 (f.); Attorney in the
Exchequer 1781; Chirographer of the Court of
Common Pleas 12 Mar. 1803.

POLITICAL ACTIVITY: He was the law agent to the
Hon. Irish Society for the Plantation of Ulster.
He was returned by Thomas Conolly (0459) for
Ballyshannon, a borough that Conolly sold shortly
afterwards to the Earl of Belmore (1269).
Babington was strongly against the Union, and
voted accordingly in 1799 and 1800.

DIVISION LISTS:
1799 (1) voted against the Union.
1800 (1) voted against the Union.

ESTATES/RESIDENCE: St Helena, Co. Antrim; Grocers'
Hall, Co. Londonderry. He obtained the remainder of
the lease for the Grocers' portion of Eglington in 1804
from the financially embarrassed heir of the Rt Hon.
Thomas Conolly. After protracted and unsuccessful
negotiations for renewal of the lease by the Hon. Irish
Society, Babington was bought out in 1823 for £7,000
for his improvements and £527 for his furniture.

SOURCES: PRONI T/3166/1A Hartnell notes [says Sher-
iff of Co. Antrim 1769, i.e. at 16!]; RCBL P277/1/3,
Parish Registers of St Mary's, Dublin; O'Neill thesis;
Burke *LGI* (1958) p. 42; Hughes, *Pat. Officers*; *King's
Inns Admissions*; *Coll. Gen.*; Alan Rogers, *A Twice-Born
Village, Muff (Eglinton) Co. Londonderry* (NUU 1984)
pp. 10–14; *Almanacks*; Parliamentary Lists, 1799 (3),
1800 (3).

0070 BADHAM, Brettridge

MP for Charleville 1713–14; Rathcormack 1743–4

b. *c.* 1678; d. (*ante* 18 Feb.) 1743/4
FAMILY/BACKGROUND: Son of Thomas Badham of
Cork and Jane [m.1677], dau. of Roger
Brettridge.
MARRIED: (1) [1709] Elizabeth (d. Feb. 1709/10),
dau. of Hon. Henry Boyle (0207); (2) [8 Apr.
1715] Sophia, dau. of Rt Hon. John King, 3rd
Baron Kingston.
CHILDREN: (2) King (d. yg); James (admitted to
Middle Temple 7 Apr. 1741); Sophia, m. (1)
Richard Thornhill of Co. Cork, (2) [Sept. 1752]
John Cuffe, 2nd Baron Desart.
CAREER/OCCUPATION: Collector of Customs and
Excise for Youghal and Dungarvan.

POLITICAL ACTIVITY: He sat in two parliaments, for
a matter of months in each case. In the last parliament of Queen Anne he was a Tory and a signatory of the County address in favour of Lord
Chancellor Phipps. It was predicted that he would
be returned for Dungarvan at the next election,
but by 1714–15 he was on a 'black list' of Tories,
and his Tory sympathies probably precluded his
return in the general election of 1715. He was
dismissed from his Collectorship in the transfer
of offices following the Hanoverian succession,
despite an attempt by Lord Lieutenant Sunderland to save him. The Revenue Commissioners
considered that he and John Lloyd, the Surveyor-
General, had been 'as obnoxious as any in the revenue of all Ireland by their late behaviour to the
public'.

In 1743 he was returned at a by-election for
Rathcormack, but he died soon after and nothing
is known of his parliamentary activity. A Cork MP,
he was connected by marriage with two of the
county's most prominent families, the Boyles and
the Kings. He was a brother-in-law of Henry Boyle
(0210).

ESTATES/RESIDENCE: Ballyheen, Co. Cork; in 1714 he
leased Blueford and Meenatarriff in the Barony of
Duhallow from Charles (Boyle), Earl of Orrery.

SOURCES: PRONI T/797/43 Welply's Prerog. Will Extracts and Marriage Registers [will pr. 18 Feb. 1744 so he probably died at least a month before]; NAI MFCI Reel 20, Parish Registers of Youghal, Co. Cork [his first wife was bur. 13 Feb. 1709/10]; NAI, Index to Marriage Licence Bonds of Cork and Ross Dioceses [his parent's marriage licence is dated 1677]; McCracken thesis; Hayton thesis; *Coll. Gen.*; *Middle Temple Admissions* (London, 1949) vol. 1 p. 329; Cork MPs; *GM* July 1744 [reports his death]; EC 5239; P. McNally, *Parties, Patriots & Undertakers* (Dublin, 1997) p. 73; Parliamentary Lists, 1713 (1), (2), 1714 (1), 1714–15 (1).

0071 BAGENAL, Beauchamp

MP for Enniscorthy 1761–8; Co. Carlow 1768–76, 1778–83

b. 1741; d. 1 (bur. 4) May 1802
FAMILY/BACKGROUND: Only son of Walter Bagenal of Dunleckny, Co. Carlow, and [m.1740] Eleanor, dau. of John Beauchamp (**0103**).
MARRIED: Maria, wid. of Stannard Ryan of Inch, Co. Tipperary.
CHILDREN: o. s. Walter (Lincoln's Inn 25 Jan. 1775), m. Eliza Jane dau. of John Black of Bordeaux and Belfast and wid. of [ ] Chambers; Emilia, m. Edward Carroll of Co. Wicklow; Catherine, m. Alexander Bissett (in England without 'her father's consent'); Sarah, m. Col. Philip Newton of Co. Carlow; Julian.
EDUCATION: School: Hillsborough, Yorkshire (Mr Thompson); entered Cambridge (Trinity College) 11 June 1753, aged 17 years, did not graduate; Grand Tour.
CAREER/OCCUPATION: High Sheriff of Co. Carlow 1759; *Joint Governor of Co. Carlow 1767–1800 (f.); Freeman of Fethard (Tipperary) 1774; with his son Walter elected a Councilman of Kilkenny Jan. 1782; *Commissioner of the Tillage Act for Leinster 1783–4.
MILITARY: Colonel of the Grange and Dunkealy Union Volunteers, and of the Dunleckny, Kiladmond and Mount Leinster Volunteers; Captain in Bagenalstown and Kiladmond Infantry 1796.

POLITICAL ACTIVITY: One of the most colourful characters in the Irish parliament, and the source of endless stories. By 1785 he was considered 'a wild ungovernable man' – he was reputed to combine 'the eccentricity of the Bagenals, the parsi-

mony of the Beauchamps, and the pride of the Mathews'. By any standards he was eccentric to the point of being unbalanced. Of an ancient Co. Carlow family, he succeeded to his father's large estates in Co. Carlow when he was four years old. His wealth encouraged his personal eccentricity and ensured his political independence.

For a large part of his parliamentary career he was abroad, at first on the Grand Tour and later for pleasure. Sir Jonah Barrington, who seldom failed to embellish a story, gives a report of his activities abroad that resembles that of Mozart's Don Giovanni, viz.: 'He had fought a prince – jilted a princess – intoxicated the Doge of Venice – carried off a Duchess from Madrid – scaled the walls of a convent in Italy – narrowly escaped the inquisition at Lisbon – concluded his exploits by a duel in Paris and returned to Ireland with a sovereign contempt for all continental men and manners; and an inveterate antipathy to all despotic kings and arbitrary governments.'

At home his eccentricity in political and social life continued; for example: 'He used to keep a brace of pistols loaded upon his dinner-table. When the meal was over the claret being produced in an unbroached cask, he would tap the cask with a bullet from one of his pistols, while he kept the other for any of those who failed to do justice to the wine'. He also had a penchant for fighting duels in a churchyard so that he could steady himself by leaning against a tombstone.

He was returned for Enniscorthy in 1761, probably under age, which may explain why he did not stand for Co. Carlow. His parliamentary career was in keeping with his unpredictable personality. He was too wealthy and too eccentric to be anything other than independent. A 1773 Parliamentary List stated that 'He came in here by his own interest and spirit. The Burtons formerly supported the Butlers of this County against him who opposed his agent Thos Gurly being made a Justice of the Peace, but he fought Butler and frightened Burtons who worship him now as the Egyptians do the S[acred] C[ow].' The 1769 Parliamentary List noted that he was 'doubtful' and 'should be spoken to upon interesting questions' – the phrase denoting an independent. It was unrealistically thought that he might be influenced by his fellow county MP, William Henry Burton (**0304**), a nephew of Speaker Ponsonby (**1702**).

Bagenal was reputed to want to be a Privy Counsellor, an ambition that remained unfulfilled. In 1772 he promised Lord Townshend his support if Townshend would sanction the purchase of a majority of dragoons by Bagenal's friend Major Pigott (**1683**). This was agreed, and Bagenal went abroad soon after, but not before he had fought a duel with the new Chief Secretary, Sir John Blaquiere (**0162**). The reason for the duel appears to have been that when Blaquiere was chargé d'affaires in Paris Bagenal was unknown to him, so Blaquiere had refused to introduce him to the King of France until Lord Rochford had vouched for him. It was reported that 'Sir John stood one shot and then allowed him to snap his pistol seven times.' Sir John had a narrow escape, as in that one shot 'the ball went so close to him that it took away a little of his hair and the fur of his hat. The next day he felt his face a little sore.' There is a substantially similar but less dramatic account of this duel in a letter from Robert Waller (**2161**) to the former Chief Secretary Sir George Macartney (**1302**).

After this affair Bagenal demanded the Collectorship of Drogheda for his friend Townley Dawson. The 1773 list also remarks that 'He ran out a great part of his estate, yet has a good one remaining. He never attends; likes amusements more than business. Absent.' Curiously, Bagenal was one of those who indicated that the day of the duellist was over when, in 1788, he indicted his neighbour, a Mr Weld, for sending him a challenge and making an assault on him. The case was tried in the summer assizes in Co. Carlow and the judge, Alexander Crookshank (**0531**), delivered a severe reprimand and sent Weld to jail for a month in addition to a fine of £70.

Probably to the chagrin of the administration, which had thought that he would not return to parliament in 1776, he was returned again for Co. Carlow. He was then either abroad or simply absent from parliament until, in the late 1770s, he became an enthusiastic Volunteer and colonel of the Grange and Dunkealy Union Volunteers. In 1783 he was a delegate to the National Volunteer Convention for Co. Carlow. He opposed Lord

Lieutenant Carlisle for refusing his recommendation in favour of his friend Mr Doyle. However, he supported the Duke of Portland and was then considered 'an honourable but wild man'. He was the MP who in 1782 moved that Henry Grattan (**0895**) should be granted a 'national gift' of £100,000 for 'his eminent and unequalled service to the kingdom'. In the event, this sum was halved by a special committee. In 1783 it was thought that he would support on the promise of an employment for his brother (?son).

As late as 1783, despite his sales, he apparently still had 'the chief property interest' in Co. Carlow. Although he did not stand for re-election in 1783, he continued to participate in county politics, using his influence to ensure the return of Richard Butler (**0327**) against John Rochfort. Rochfort was a substantial Co. Carlow landowner, the father of John Staunton Rochfort (**1804**) and the brother-in-law of John Foster (**0805**).

DIVISION LISTS:

1768 (1) absent, sick.
1778 (2) voted for the Popery Bill.
1779 (2) voted against a six-months Loan Bill.
1780 (2) voted against Yelverton's (**2268**) motion to modify Poynings' Law.

ADDITIONAL INFORMATION: *A member of the Royal Dublin Society from 1779.

ESTATES/RESIDENCE: Moneybeg (*alias* Bagenalstown) and Dunleckny, Co. Carlow. In 1702–3 Dudley Bagenal had 403 acres in Co. Carlow forfeited. The life interest in the manor, town and lands of Dunleckny and other manors and lands in Co. Carlow of Dudley Bagenal, father of Walter Bagenal, were forfeited as a result of his attainder for high treason, but on his death in April 1712 the estate descended to Walter Bagenal. In 1725 a case was brought by Walter Bagenal against Ann Bagenal, widow of another Walter Bagenal, concerning the marriage portions for younger children charged upon it. Beauchamp Bagenal succeeded to these estates in 1745. 'This gentleman came into possession of an immense estate in the County Carlow: in fact all or nearly all, had been granted to his ancestor by James I.' He also had lands, 1,430 acres in the townlands of Kilsleane and Kilmore in Co. Armagh. He, however, commenced selling portions of his estate immediately on his accession to it. By 1762 he was deeply in debt. In 1763 he advertised in the public papers lands to be sold, let at £1,357 p.a. This was insufficient to pay off his debts and he proposed to sell more namely lands of Knockbower, Murney, Toppernathy, Coolnapish, etc., with half the bog of Ballywilliamroe, and the bog of Newton, all in Co. Carlow, at a clear yearly rental, after deduction of quit rents, of £2,019, which at 21 years' purchase amounted to £42,402. Negotiations were entered into with Richard Chapel Whaley (**2225**) but fell through. Because of this Whaley brought an unsuccessful action against Bagenal in 1765. The case turned on whether there was sufficient evidence in writing of Bagenal's intention to sell them to establish that intention under the Irish Statute of Frauds and Perjuries, 7 Will. III, c. 12. The British House of Lords decreed that there was not. Later 'He made two extensive sales of land to the La Touche family, one lot of which has since been sold to Lord Viscount Beresford (the illegitimate son of **0113**). The late Henry Bruen Esq. (**0268**) likewise made a great purchase from him.'

The Bagenal rental was £6,681 in 1760. In 1773 he sold lands in the barony of Idrone East to La Touche. However, in 1779 Young reckoned Mr Bagenal's rental at £7,000. In 1789, Beauchamp Bagenal sold lands to Rt Hon. David La Touche (**1203**), probably including Sliguff and Kilgreany (the subsequent Pack-Beresford estate). On the death of Beauchamp Bagenal in 1802, a partition may have been made among his children; his will of that date mentions the lands of Ballingarrane, Ballywilliamroe Bog, Curracrut, Dunleckny, Killedmond, Knockroe, Moyvally, Rahany, Raheens, Rathendan, Rosdellig and Tomduff. Estate maps of Ballytarsney, barony of Idrone (484 acres in 1761) and Bohermore, Kildreenagh and Ballywilliamroe (667 acres in 1785) survive among the Bruen papers, so these lands were presumably bought by Bruen post-1792.

Wakefield noted in 1812: 'Thirty years ago the Bagenal property, which is now very small, was equal to 32,000 acres.'

In 1642, under 17 Chas I, Walter Bagenal was granted a fair at Killedmond; in 1627, under 2 Chas I, he had been granted a fair at Orchard.

SOURCES: PRONI MIC/474 Irish Volunteers; RCBL P45/2/3, Parish Registers of St Peter's, Dublin; Ellis thesis; *Alum. Cantab.*; Young, *Tour in Ire.*, vol. 2 App. p. 82; Wakefield, *Account of Ire.*, vol. 1 p. 248; *Memorials of the Dead* [says he died 1802 aged 67 years (this must be a mistake for 61 given the 1740 marriage of his parents) and was buried 4 May]; J. Ryan, *The History and Antiquities of the County of Carlow* (Dublin, 1833) pp. 358–9 [says he was born in 1741]; *Lincoln's Inn Records* vol. 1 p. 478; *The Register of the Parish of St Peter and St Kevin, 1669–1761* (Parish Register Society of Dublin, 1911) p. 304; P. H. Bagenal, *Vicissitudes of an Anglo-Irish Family, 1530–1800* (London, 1925) [incorrectly says son of Dudley]; Maxwell, *Country and*

Town, pp. 21–2; Maxwell, *Dublin under the Georges*, pp. 132–3; Simms, *Williamite Confiscation*, p. 177; Gilbert, *History of the City of Dublin*, vol. 3 p. 126; *Coll. Gen.*; *Ir. Gen.* vol. 4 no 4 (1971) p. 314, W. G. Skehan, 'Extracts from the Minutes of the Corporation of Fethard, Co. Tipperary'; *Almanacks*; *FJ* 14–16 Oct. 1783, 15 Nov. 1796; *DJ* 24–6 Jan. 1782; NLI reps nos 20, 64 and 123; LC 444; Brown's Reports of House of Lords Appeals 1701–1800 (NLI) vol. I pp. 345–55, vol. 4 pp. 81–9; J. Kelly, *'That Damn'd Thing Called Honour': Duelling in Ireland 1570–1860* pp. 111–12, 150, 196–7; Parliamentary Lists, 1769 (1), 1772 (2), 1773 (1), (2), 1774 (1), 1775 (1), 1776 (1), 1778 (1), 1780 (1), 1782 (1), 1783 (1), (3), 1785 (2), 1790 (1).

0072 BAGSHAWE, Samuel

MP for Tallow 1761–2

b. 1 Jan. 1689; d. 20 Oct. 1762
FAMILY/BACKGROUND: Son of Samuel Bagshawe of Ford, Derbyshire, and Sarah, dau. and co-h. of Samuel Child.
MARRIED: [25 Mar. 1751] Catherine, dau. of Sir John Caldwell, 3rd Bt.
CHILDREN: Samuel; Richard (d. yg); John; Rev. William, m. Anne, dau. of Samuel Foxlowe; 1 dau.
MILITARY: Colonel of the 8th Regiment, which he raised at his own cost in Ireland in 1760. 'A devoted military man' and spent much of his career in India; he was for a time second in command in the West Indies. He lost an eye and a leg in various actions. *Colonel of a Regiment of Foot 1753, 1756–7, (rank 39) 1759, 1760–1; *Lieutenant-Colonel of a regiment of Foot 1754–5, 1759; Colonel of the 93rd Regiment.

POLITICAL ACTIVITY: He was in parliament for about six months, as the session began on 22 October 1761 and ended on 30 April 1762. Despite the initial opposition of Major Cane and a Mr Croker, Bagshawe was brought in for Tallow, through his Derbyshire connections with the Duke of Devonshire and possibly at the Duke's request rather than his own. Sir Robert Wilmot wrote to Devonshire, 14 September 1758, that 'I will take the first opportunity of communicating to Colonel Bagshawe what your Grace is so kind as to mention'– possibly support for military preferment.

ADDITIONAL INFORMATION: The Bagshawes were

'one of the oldest families in Derbyshire and of very strong religious beliefs'. He met his wife when part of his regiment was stationed at Ballyshannon. Although he was absent much of the time pursuing his military career, the marriage seemed quite happy and they had a family of four boys and a girl. The colonel had been 62 when he married and he died in October 1762, thus the marriage lasted for only 11 years.

'He was buried first in Reading where he died but afterwards in the chancel of Chapel-en-le-Frith Church, Derbyshire ... Unfortunately, Mrs Bagshawe and her eldest son were not on good terms and in later years and she was often in very cramped financial straits as he repeatedly withheld payments due to her, on one occasion even for as long as four years. She eventually had to take him to Chancery Court to get legal redress.'

ESTATES/RESIDENCE: Ford Hall, Derbyshire.

SOURCES: Information supplied by P. G. I. Green Esq., Organist and Choirmaster, Parish Church of St Thomas Becket, Chapel-En-Le-Frith [says he d. 16 or 18 Aug. 1762]; Burke, *Commoners* (1836) p. 29; J. B. Cunningham, *A History of Castle Caldwell and its Families* (Monaghan, 1980) p. 113; *Coll. Gen.*; J. J. Howard (ed.), *Miscellanea Genealogica et Heraldica*, vol. 1 new ser. (1874) p. 171 [says he was buried 22 Sept. 1762]; *Kildare Arch. Soc. Jn.* vol. 8 (1915–17) p. 104, 'Diary of Anne Cooke'; *Almanacks*; *DJ* 23–6 Oct. 1762; PRONI T/3158/1635 Devonshire MSS Rev. Thos Dawson, Tallow, to Devonshire.

0073 BAGWELL, John

MP for Tulsk 1761–8

b. *ante* 1715; d. (*ante* 7) Sept. 1784
FAMILY/BACKGROUND: Eldest son and heir of John Bagwell of Kilmore, banker, and [   ] Shaw, dau. of a Presbyterian clergyman in Dublin.
MARRIED: (1) [1736] Ann Calwell, dau. of a Bristol merchant; (2) [Oct.1757] Fanny, dau. and co-h. of Hamilton Lowe.
CHILDREN: (1) ?*d.s.p.*; ?John, entered Glasgow University 1754.
CAREER/OCCUPATION: Freeman of Fethard (Tipperary) 1732; High Sheriff of Co. Tipperary 1763.
MILITARY: In the 1750s he was Colonel of the

Clonmel Independents; Colonel of the Boyne Society of Volunteers 1782; delegate to the Dungannon convention 1782.

POLITICAL ACTIVITY: In 1756 parliament granted £1,500 to make the River Suir navigable from Carrick-on-Suir to Clonmel. In 1761 Sir William Osborne (**1615**), Bagwell and others were appointed to a select committee to report on progress. Five years later the work was completed. In December 1765 he was appointed to the committee to inquire into the public works necessary to the nation. He voted for the augmentation of the army.

Bagwell stood unsuccessfully, although with the support of Lord Shannon (**0213**), for Cork city in the general elections of 1776 and 1783 and for the by-election of 1784; he withdrew just before the 1784 poll, possibly because of ill health as he died shortly after.

DIVISION LISTS:
1768 (1) voted for army augmentation.

ADDITIONAL INFORMATION: A member of the Royal Dublin Society from 1764.

ESTATES/RESIDENCE: Kilmore, Burgagery and Clonmel, Co. Tipperary. In 1736 John Bagwell, eldest son and heir of John Bagwell of Kilmore, merchant, married Ann Calwell, daughter of a Bristol merchant; portion £4,000, jointure £400. In 1755 his rental income was £2,000 and he was described as John Bagwell of Kilmore, a candidate for the county. He died in 1784 and presumably left his property to his brother, William's (**0076**, died 1756) only son and heir, John (**0074**).

SOURCES: PRONI D/302; NLI reps no 48; Vicars, *Prerog. Wills*; McNevin, *Volunteers*; C. H. Wilson, *A Complete Collection of the Resolutions of the Volunteers, Grand Juries, & c of Ireland* (Dublin, 1782) p. 176; *Coll. Gen.*; *Alum. Glas.*; W. P. Burke, *History of Clonmel* (reprinted Kilkenny 1983) pp. 128–9; *Ir. Gen.* vol. 4 no 4 (1971) p. 315, W. G. Skehan, 'Extracts from the Minutes of the Corporation of Fethard, Co. Tipperary'; E. Hewitt (ed.), *Lord Shannon's Letters to his Son* (PRONI 1982) pp. lv, lxiii, J. Kelly, *'That Damn'd Thing Called Honour': Duelling in Ireland 1570–1860* (Cork, 1995), pp. 143–4, 146; *Almanacks*; *BNL* 27 Dec. 1765; *DJ* 25–9 Oct. 1757 (says late Col. of the Clonmel Independents, but this is probably confusing him with **0074**); Wakefield, *Account of Ire.*, vol. 1 p. 276; *Analecta* no 21.

0074 BAGWELL, John

MP for Co. Tipperary 1792–7–1800 [r. Doneraile 1790], [UK] 1801–6

b. 1752; d. 28 Sept. 1816

FAMILY/BACKGROUND: Only son and heir of William Bagwell (0076) and Jane, dau. and co-h. of John Harper of Belgrove, Co. Cork.

MARRIED: [4 Feb. 1774] Mary, dau. of Richard Hare of Ennismore, Co. Kerry.

CHILDREN: Rt Hon. William (0077); Rev. Richard (0075); John (MP in the United Parliament); Margaret, m. John Kiely Jr of Belgrove, Co. Cork; Jane, m. Sir Eyre Coote (0484); Catherine, m. John Croker; Mary, m. Henry Langley; Benjamin.

EDUCATION: Entered Oxford (Christ Church) 10 Mar. 1768, aged 16 years, MA 22 June 1771.

CAREER/OCCUPATION: Joint Governor of Co. Tipperary 1793–96, 1800 (f.), Governor 1797; High Sheriff of Co. Tipperary 1794.

MILITARY: Colonel of the Clonmel Independent Corps of Volunteers 1782; Colonel of the County Tipperary Militia, which he helped raise in 1793.

POLITICAL ACTIVITY: The Bagwells had strong mercantile and Nonconformist links. Bagwell was raised by his mother's family, the Harpers of Cork, in the Nonconformist tradition, although he subsequently conformed. His wife, Mary Hare, was a member of another Cork family. This background told against him in society, as did nicknames associated with his building of flour mills such as 'the miller', 'Old Bags' and (as colonel of the militia) 'Marshal Sacks'. Curran (0560) is reputed to have described him at the head of the regiment as 'Marshal Saxe with the flour of Tipperary at his back'. He fought at least three duels.

In the 1790 election he stood for Co. Tipperary and safeguarded his return by purchasing a seat for Doneraile. The Co. Tipperary election was disputed, but he was eventually declared the duly elected MP. He did not vote while the election was under dispute. Once his election was confirmed he appears to have taken an independent position. In 1793 he was against the government and the following year a supporter. In the last parliament he returned his sons William for Rathcormack and Richard, who was barely of age, in a late by-election for Cashel.

On 5 February 1800 Cornwallis wrote to Portland that Bagwell had deserted with his two sons as the majority of the freeholders of Tipperary had signed a resolution opposing the Union. Castlereagh wrote to Cornwallis that Bagwell's desertion was unexpected, since 'The objects he solicited were promised.' Castlereagh attributed his behaviour partly to fear and partly to the promises of the opposition should they be elected. This potential family defection, making a difference of six votes, caused considerable concern at the Castle. Bagwell was given half the patronage of Co. Tipperary and his recently elected son Richard, who had just been ordained, was made a dean.

In 1799 he voted against the Union, and in 1800 for. In the course of the Union debates he changed sides twice. He told Castlereagh (2009) that opposition had offered him £9,000 but he would change his mind for £10,000. In the end caution won, and he decided to return to the fold for fear of losing everything.

At Westminster he and his sons were expected to be 'on sale'. He protested against the ban on Irish county governors (he was one) from interfering in elections, 3 February 1801. On 20 February he objected to the prospect of Irish MPs paying taxes in England as well as Ireland; he spoke in favour of an inquiry into the salt tax in Ireland, 14 May 1801. He also spoke for the Irish poor and on 10 June 1802 supported the Irish Election Bill. On 8 February 1803 he called for a levy of poor relief as a remedy for Irish poverty. He supported government on 'all leading national questions' despite rivals for Tipperary patronage, notably Lord Donoughmore (1003), making ground with government. He supported the Irish Militia Augmentation Bill, 16 April 1804, and went on to support Pitt but expected patronage in return – the promised deanery of Clogher for Richard, full-time employment in the army for John and the succession of his colonelcy of the Tipperary Militia for William. He spoke in favour of the suspension of habeas corpus in Ireland, and voted against Catholic relief. He was not thought sufficiently 'proper' for the Irish peerage.

DIVISION LISTS:

1790 (2) absent.

1799 (1) voted against the Union.

1800 (1) voted for the Union.

ESTATES/RESIDENCE: Marlfield and [?]Kilmore, Co. Tipperary. He had lands also in Waterford town and Cork city. In about 1784 he purchased the lease of Marlfield and 'carried out extensive corn milling and biscuit making there'. On 9 August 1800 Bagwell bought from Lords Enniskillen (**0444**) and Desart, as trustees for the Earl of Ormonde (**0333**), 'the lordship, manor or reputed manor of the town of Clonmel and all rights, royalties and franchises appertaining thereto'. The grant was also said to convey 'all the messuages, houses, lands, waste and waste plots, within the walls of the said town of Clonmel and all the Burgagery land and a parcel entitled Duke's Island in the barony of Upperthird and County of Waterford'. With the Manor of Clonmel he obtained the patronage previously enjoyed by the Moores. 'At a meeting [of the Corporation on 31 December 1800] for the purpose of electing five burgesses in the room of the Hon. William Moore (**1485**), the Hon. and Rev. Robert Moore, the Hon. John Moore, William Foulks Moore and John Robertson resigned. Ordered that Colonel John Bagwell of Marlfield Esq., Lieutenant Colonel William Bagwell, Richard Bagwell, Lieutenant Colonel John Bagwell, Benjamin Bousfield, John Keighly jun., Arthur Gething of Lorintoun, Charles Riall of Clonmel, Edward Crocker of Ballinaguard and William Pennefather of Darlinghill, Esq., be and are hereby admitted Freemen of this Corporation.' Canon Burke states that the second party included Bagwell, his three sons, his son-in-law, his cousin german, his wife's brother-in-law, Croker, Croker's cousin german, Pennefather, 'together with Benjamin Bousfield and Arthur Gething – poor relations probably'.

In the first decade of the nineteenth century Wakefield stated that Mr (John) Bagwell of Marlfield 'is proprietor of the whole town of Clonmel, together with an immense estate in the neighbourhood'. It was said to be worth £18,000 p.a. in 1812.

SOURCES: PRONI D/302; PRONI T/3166/1C Hartnell notes; PRONI T/3459 Donoughmore Papers C/1/165 p. 11; NLI EC3693; NLI EC 5651 rental 1910, map and terrier (possibly of Marlfield), 1768; PRONI MIC/465/1; R. Ffolliott, *Biographical Notices, 1756–1827* [*The Cork Advertiser* 30 Sept. 1816 says he died 28 Sept. 1816]; O'Neill thesis; Jupp thesis; Burke *LGI* (1958) p. 46; *HP 1790–1820*; *Alum. Oxon.*; *Cornwallis Corr.*, vol. 3 pp. 180, 182, 266 [says he died 4 Mar. 1806]; W. P. Burke, *History of Clonmel* (reprinted Kilkenny, 1983) pp. 131, 175, 321 [says his son John was MP for Co.

Tipperary 1798–1800; this is unlikely since he was born *c.* 1780); Wakefield, *Account of Ire.*, vol. 1 p. 276; E. Hewitt (ed.), *Lord Shannon's Letters to his Son* (PRONI 1982) p. xxii; Cork MPs; *Coll. Gen.* [says he died 21 Dec. 1816]; *Almanacks*; *DJ* 11 Sept. 1800; Parliamentary Lists, 1783 (1), 1791 (1), 1793 (1), 1794 (2), 1799 (2), (3), 1800 (3).

0075 BAGWELL, Richard

MP for Cashel 1799–1800, [UK] Jan.–Nov. 1801

b. (*ante* 28 Mar.) 1778; d. Apr. 1826

FAMILY/BACKGROUND: Son of John Bagwell (**0074**) and Mary, dau. of Richard Hare.

MARRIED: [1806] Margaret, dau. of Edward Croker.

CHILDREN: John, m. [1838] Frances Eliza, dau. of Henry Sadlier Prittie, 2nd Baron Dunalley (**1743**); Edward Bagwell Purefoy, m. [1854] (1) Isabella Petronella, dau. of Maj. Langley of Brittas Castle, Co. Tipperary, (2) [1861] Charlotte, dau. of John Green Wilkinson; Margaret, m. Joseph Gore of Co. Clare; Mary, m. George Gough of Co. Limerick; Jane, m. Benjamin Friend.

EDUCATION: Entered TCD 5 Aug. 1793, aged 15 years; clergyman ordained 1800.

POLITICAL ACTIVITY: He was in the Irish parliament for under a year. His father brought him in, almost certainly by purchase from the Pennefathers (**1654**), who controlled the returns for Cashel, which retained a seat after the Union. Although, with the rest of his family connection, he opposed the Union, he soon became involved in his father's terms for supporting the measure. In his maiden speech on 15 January 1800 he spoke in favour of the Union. Three weeks later he defected with his father to the opposition.

On 4 September 1801 his father applied to the Castle for church preferment for him. By this time he was ordained and, it was thought, due to be disqualified from sitting under the bill passed on 23 June 1801 to prevent those in holy orders being MPs. However, because he had been ordained before the passing of the bill, his case caused considerable debate. His father requested the deanery of Clogher for him, and he was given Kilmacduagh (October 1804 – February 1806) until Clogher became vacant in 1806. Further pressure for promotion was ineffective, and he remained at Clogher until his death some 20 years later.

DIVISION LISTS:
1800 (1) voted for the Union.

ESTATES/RESIDENCE: Clonmel. His eldest son succeeded to Marlfield.

SOURCES: PRONI T/3166/1C Hartnell notes; O'Neill thesis; Jupp thesis; Burke *LGI* (1904) p. 19, (1958) p. 46; *HP 1790–1820* [says he married 1808]; *Coll. Gen.*; *Cornwallis Corr.* vol. 3 pp. 163, 180 [says he married 1808]; Parliamentary Lists, 1799 (2), (3), 1800 (3)

0076 BAGWELL, William

MP for Clonmel Jan.–July 1756

b. *c.* 1728; d. 26 July 1756
FAMILY/BACKGROUND: Second son of John Bagwell of Clonmel and Burgagery, Co. Tipperary, and [   ] Shaw, dau. of a Presbyterian clergyman in Dublin.
MARRIED: [1749] Jane, dau. and co-h. of John Harper of Belgrove, Co. Cork (head of the private banking firm of Harper and Armistead).
CHILDREN: John (0074); Dorcas, m. [Apr. 1769] Benjamin Bowfield; Jane, m. [June 1769] John Kelly of Lismore, Co. Waterford; Isabella, m. [   ] Creagh.
CAREER/OCCUPATION: A banker; Freeman of Fethard (Tipperary) 1737; Freeman of Clonmel 1748.

POLITICAL ACTIVITY: Parliament was prorogued on 8 May 1756, so he sat for only a few months and there is no record of his activity during that time. However, his election was interesting. His father, along with Matthew Jacob (1080), was a leader in the Presbyterian community in Clonmel. Bagwell was a Dissenter and a banker. The Presbyterian Church in eighteenth-century Clonmel was an active and probably a fairly liberal one – in 1791 Thomas Addis Emmet married Jane Patten, the daughter of the then minister. Bagwell's election in 1756 was, according to Canon Burke, 'the most notable election in the history of the borough ... Bagwell had the united support of the bourgeoisie. He was a dissenter and the dissent-

ing bodies then included the most influential traders in the place. He also stood for the resident freemen against the country party who made up two thirds of [Guy] Moore's (1459) supporters.'

ESTATES/RESIDENCE: Clonmel, Co. Tipperary. His father, who was a draper, merchant and banker, died in 1754, after amassing a fortune chiefly invested in landed estates. His wife's father was head of the bank Harper and Armstead. The marriage settlement, 8–9 April 1749, entailed part of the burgagery lands called Cooleens on him and his male issue, but was charged as security for the portions of any daughters. It is said to have been worth £20,000 p.a.

SOURCES: Michael O'Donnell Esq.; Abstract of Will in W. P. Burke MS, Mount Melleray Abbey, Cappoquin, Co. Waterford; PRONI T/559 Burke, extract pedigrees, vol. 7 p. 48; PRONI MIC/465/1 R. Ffolliott, *Biographical Notices, 1756–1827*; NAI Index to the Marriage Licence Bonds of Cloyne Diocese; McCracken thesis; Burke *LGI* (1958) p. 46; *GM* July 1756; W. P. Burke, *History of Clonmel* (reprinted Kilkenny, 1983) pp. 118, 319; *Ir. Gen.* vol. 4 no 4 (1971) p. 315, W. G. Skehan, 'Extracts from the Minutes of the Corporation of Fethard, Co. Tipperary'.

0077 BAGWELL, Rt Hon. William

MP for Rathcormack 1798–1800; [UK] Clonmel 1801–19; Co. Tipperary 1819–26

b. (*ante* 2) Apr. 1776; d. 4 Nov. 1826
HONOURS: PC, sworn 17 Jan. 1809.
FAMILY/BACKGROUND: Eldest son of John Bagwell (0074) and Mary, dau. of Richard Hare of Ennismore, Co. Kerry.
MARRIED: Unmarried.
EDUCATION: School: Westminster Sept. 1787; also educated in Germany.
CAREER/OCCUPATION: Freeman of Fethard (Tipperary) 1782; Mayor of Clonmel 1804–5; Governor of Co. Tipperary 1807; Trustee of Linen Board 1818–26.
MILITARY: Lieutenant-Colonel of Tipperary Regiment of Militia 17 Nov. 1794, Colonel 1805–d; Muster Master General for Ireland 1807–26 at £4,007 p.a.

POLITICAL ACTIVITY: None of the Bagwells sat for very long in the Irish House of Commons, and William Bagwell was no exception. In 1799 he made a violent speech against the Union and voted accordingly. However, by February 1800 he had joined his father in deserting to the government camp in time for the rewards of his change of mind, namely the Tipperary Regiment. In the United parliament he followed his father in supporting government 'on all leading national questions'. He was active in opposition to the Grenville ministry but rallied to the Portland ministry in March 1807 despite criticising its military arrangements on 28 July 1807. He was made Joint Muster Master General (£4,007 p.a.), partly as a reward to his father. He voted against Catholic Emancipation until 1810 but not thereafter.

DIVISION LISTS:
1799 (1) voted against the Union.
1800 (1) voted for the Union.

ESTATES/RESIDENCE: Marlfield, Co. Tipperary.

SOURCES: PRONI T/3166/1A Hartnell notes; O'Neill thesis; Jupp thesis; Burke *PB* (1903) p. 94; Burke *LGI* (1904) p. 19, *IFR* (1976) p. 51; *HP 1790–1820*; *Index to Irish Privy Counsellors, 1711–1910*; *Cornwallis Corr.* vol. 3 p. 180; G. F. Russell-Barker and A. H. Stenning (eds), *Record of Old Westminsters: A Biographical List* (London, 1928); *Coll. Gen.*; W. P. Burke, *History of Clonmel* (reprinted Kilkenny, 1983) p. 321; *Ir. Gen.* vol. 4 no 4 (1971) p. 315, W. G. Skehan, 'Extracts from the Minutes of the Corporation of Fethard, Co. Tipperary'; Parliamentary Lists, 1799 (2), (3), 1800 (3).

0078 BAILEY, William

MP for Augher 1797–1800

b. *ante* 1765; d. 25 Sept. 1808
FAMILY/BACKGROUND: Son of William Bailey and Eleanor Morris.
MARRIED: [1786] Sarah, dau. of Rev. Hugh Stewart of Tynan, Co. Armagh.
CHILDREN: Ellen; Catherine (d. unmar.); Julia.
CAREER/OCCUPATION: High Sheriff of Co. Tyrone 16 Feb. 1787.
MILITARY: Captain of Tyrone Regiment of Militia.

POLITICAL ACTIVITY: During the 1790s Lord Abercorn was trying, with the help of George Knox (**1180**), to build up a party in the Irish House of Commons. As part of this policy he purchased the borough of Augher, Co. Tyrone. The marquess already had a major interest in Co.

Donegal and was anxious to improve his already substantial interest in Co. Tyrone. Bailey (*alias* Bailie) was a small landowner and in January 1795 John Stewart wrote to Abercorn, following the Catholic enfranchisement of 1793, that 'I had a letter this day from Dungannon, in which Bailie mentions that he had then registered between 50 and 60 (freeholders) and had many more to produce.'

Bailey was a safe and useful choice, and his appointment pleased some of his more far-flung family, as Captain William Bailie of Tarbert, Co. Kerry wrote to Abercorn on 22 August 1797 thanking him for returning Bailie for Augher (and taking the opportunity to ask about a vacant lieutenancy). Following Lord Abercorn's wishes, he voted for the Union in 1799 and in 1800 he was made a Commissioner of the Board of Works.

DIVISION LISTS:
1800 (1) voted for the Union.

ESTATES/RESIDENCE: Tirnaskea, Co. Tyrone. His estate was inherited by his daughter, Catherine Bailey; she left it to Robert Gage, who assumed the name of Bailey.

SOURCES: PRONI D/302; PRONI T/2541/1B3/6/24 Abercorn MSS; PRONI T/618/329 Crossle Papers; PRONI T/808 p. 792; PRONI MIC/338/3 Crossle notes; PRONI T/3166/1C Hartnell notes; NAI Index to the Marriage Licence Bonds of Armagh Diocese [his parents' marriage licence is dated 1753]; O'Neill thesis; Hughes, *Pat. Officers*; Fermanagh and Tyrone MPs; *King's Inns Admissions*; *BNL* 7 Oct. 1808; Parliamentary Lists, 1799 (2), (3), 1800 (3).

0079 BAILIE, James

MP for Hillsborough 1777–83–7

b. 1724; d. 22 Sept. 1787
FAMILY/BACKGROUND: Son of John Bailie and Jane, dau. of Mathew Forde (**0781**).
MARRIED: Anne, dau. of Francis Hall of Strangford, Co. Down.
CHILDREN: *d.s.p.*
CAREER/OCCUPATION: Chief Serjeant-at-Arms House of Commons 1759–68; Sheriff of Co. Down 1767; Land Waiter for Newry 1766 9, Galway 1772–3; Member of the Down Society for promoting agriculture Aug. 1759, 1760.

MILITARY: Major of a Regiment of Dragoons 1754–6.

POLITICAL ACTIVITY: He was returned by Lord Hillsborough and formed part of his parliamentary party. In 1779 Hillsborough wrote to John Reilly (**1773**), then newly elected for the Hillsborough borough of Blessington, that 'I request the favour of you to communicate this letter to Mr Bailie and Mr Montgomery (**1447**), as I should wish that my opinion on this subject should be made known to them.' Hillsborough felt that the administration would need all the support that it could get, and the only reason they were to oppose government was if the Absentee Tax should be reintroduced.

Bailie was a member of the Swords Election Committee, 6 December 1777. Swords was a potwalloping borough and its elections were frequently a scene of chaos and confusion. In fact W. W. Grenville, a former Chief Secretary, wrote to Lord Castlereagh that they were 'the very worst species of Representation'.

Bailie appears to have faithfully followed Hillsborough's instructions for the 11 years he was in parliament. These are reflected in the division lists. In 1782 Hillsborough secured for him a small customs post at Dingle, Co. Kerry worth *c.* £400 p.a. Interestingly, this position had also been sought by the former Lord Lieutenant, Lord Buckingham, for General Sandford. Patronage was the gauge of a political magnate's power. The *Dublin Journal* in his obituary noted the 'remarkable circumstance that his great-grandfather, grandfather, father and himself, died in the 63rd year of their age'.

DIVISION LISTS:
1778 (2) voted against the Popery Bill.
1779 (1) voted for new taxes.
1779 (2) voted against a six-months Loan Bill.
1780 (1) voted against Grattan's (**0895**) declaration of the Rights of Ireland.
1780 (2) voted against Yelverton's (**2268**) motion to modify Poynings' Law.
1780 (3) voted for the Tenantry Bill.
1780 (4) voted for a Perpetual Mutiny Bill.
1783 (1) voted against Flood's (**0762**) motion for parliamentary reform.

1784 (1) voted against a committee on the Reform Bill.
1785 (1) voted for the Commercial Propositions.

ADDITIONAL INFORMATION: A member of the Royal Dublin Society from 1766.

ESTATES/RESIDENCE: Inishargy, Ringdufferin, Co. Down. In 1785 a *BNL* sale advertised part of James Bailie's estate, in the baronies of Ards and Kinelarty, with a rental of £1,691 16s 1¹/₂d. Eventually he sold his estate to the Rev. Charles Ward.

In 1769, 9 Geo. III, James Bailey was granted fairs at Kircubbin, parish of St Andrew, barony of Ards.

SOURCES: PRONI T/1584 Pinkerton transcripts, p. 377, 21 Sept. 1787; PRONI MIC/315/8/44 Blackwood pedigrees; O'Neill thesis; PRONI D/607/B/106 Downshire MSS; J. H. Lepper and P. Crossle, *History of the Grand Lodge of Free and Accepted Masons of Ireland* (Dublin, 1925) vol. 1 [says Alderman Hans Bailie, son of James (?John) Bailie of Inninschargie was Junior Grand Warden of the Grand Lodge 1747–9 and Senior Grand Warden 1759]; *Almanacks; BNL* 25 Sept. 1759, 7 Oct. 1760; *FJ* 6–9 Dec. 1777; *DJ* 27–9 Sept. 1787; Parliamentary Lists, 1776 (1), 1778 (1), 1780 (1), 1782 (1), 1783 (1), (2), 1784 (1), (3), 1785 (1), (2), (3), 1787 (1), 1788 (1).

0080 BALFOUR, William

MP for Carlingford 1705–13; Augher 1713–14, 1715–27–39

> b. *ante* 1684; d. 19 Apr. 1739
> FAMILY/BACKGROUND: Only son of Charles Balfour of Castle Balfour, Co. Fermanagh and Cicely, dau. and h. of Sir Robert Bryan of Colwick, Nottinghamshire.
> MARRIED: ?
> CHILDREN: ?John (Middle Temple 1725, called to Irish Bar 1732) predeceased his father, who *d.s.p.*
> EDUCATION: LLD of TCD *spec. grat.* 1718.
> CAREER/OCCUPATION: Sheriff of Co. Fermanagh 1731 (excused), 1734.
> MILITARY: Army Captain on half-pay 1713.

POLITICAL ACTIVITY: He was a soldier, and appears to have followed the Court line when active service allowed. In 1706 he was recorded as a Court supporter and in 1711 he was one of the 31 Tories who met at the Fleece Tavern to discuss tactics for the next session. In another 1711 list he was again considered a Tory supporter; he supported the government over the Dublin mayoralty question, but by the time the 1713 list was compiled he had become a Whig and, although he voted for Sir Richard Levinge (**1230**), the government's choice of Speaker, was considered to be 'now against us in all things'. Balfour supported a national bank. He was listed for six committees between 1711 and 1731.

DIVISION LISTS:

1711 (1) voted for the Court on the Dublin mayoralty issue.

1713 (1) voted for Sir Richard Levinge (**1230**) for Speaker – 'is now against us in all things'.

1721 (1) voted for a national bank.

1721 (2) voted for a national bank.

ESTATES/RESIDENCE: Castle Balfour, Lisnaskea, Co. Fermanagh. On the Lisnaskea, as opposed to Knockninny, side of Lough Erne was the manor of Carnashee (Castle Balfour). Between 1698 and 1713 the whole Fermanagh estate was under a statute stage for debt, the receiver being one Captain Dobbin. His estimated income in 1713 was £500. His estates, said to be worth £1,200 at his death in 1739, were inherited by Henry Townly Balfour (**2097**). In 1722, the rental of Carnashee was £436, plus £198 for tenements in Lisnaskea. The estate included the Manors of Leggin and Dresternan – lands of Callowhill, Aghyoule (Aghiole), Gartavally, etc. In 1714 the rental was £538.

In 1720, the (?agent), Maguire, advised William Balfour not to sell any part of his estate, but, if Balfour insisted, pointed out land in the manors suitable for sale with a rental of £261 and a valuation of £347; he recommended selling it at 35 years' purchase, calculated on a rental of £334 (this estate was on the barony of Knockninny side of Lough Erne). Leggin and Dresternan, also surveyed in 1723, were estimated to contain 5,583 profitable acres and 2,614 of bog. In 1722 the rental of these townlands was £798. It had been £372 in 1698. By 1726 rental of Leggin and Dresternan had been reduced to £393 by sales, mainly to Colonel Mountgomery and Mr Enery, but there was still an estate in Leggin and Dresternan at the time of the sale by Balfour's heirs to Lord Erne in the 1770s.

Professor Roebuck states that in 1723 the estate comprised 8,197 Irish acres at a rental of £469, in 1770 £1,949, in 1815 5,071 Irish acres, rental of £3,157 (this last figure excludes 22 holdings from acreage – though apparently not from rental – which were let for ever). By 1730 Mr Balfour must have been an absentee, as on 12 September 1730, his 'house in Lisnaskea, for which he paid £100, is inhabited by Hugh Latimer, who keeps an alehouse. The windows are broke, the joyces [*sic*] stolen, the floors spoiled, and no rent paid for it or promised.'

In 5 Chas I, Lord Balfour was granted fairs at Legan, and at Carrowshee, *alias* Castle Balfour, barony of Clynestulcy, later called Lisnaskea.

SOURCES: PRONI T/3411 Blenheim Papers; McCracken thesis; Hayton thesis; Burke *LGI* (1912) p. 24; *Alum. Dub.*; Fermanagh and Tyrone MPs; Prior, *Absentees*; Vicars, *Prerog. Wills*; *The Dublin Gazette* 24 Nov. 1730; *The Dublin Weekly Journal* 28 Nov. 1730; *DJ* 19 Jan. 1734; *Pue's Occurrences* 21 Apr. 1739; *BNL* 24 Apr. 1739; PRONI D/1939/21/2 Erne Papers [rental 1714, valuation 1723 and letter 26 July 1720], PRONI D/1939/17/10/57, 41 and 34 [valuation 1723, and rentals 1698 and 1722]; PRONI D/1939/17/10/22 and 41 [rentals 1703 and 1727]; PRONI D/1939/17/10/61 ['A view of Mr Balfour's affairs', 12 Sept. 1730); NLI reps no 390; NLI MS 9543 [rental calculations 1767–77], NLI 16 H/1/7–8; PRONI D1939/17/10, 41 and 39 Erne Papers [rental 1726–7 and list of arrears, Oct. 1725], D/1939/17/10/57 and 50 and D/1939/2/17 [rental 1723, 1770 and 1815]; Parliamentary Lists, 1706 (1), 1711 (2), (3), 1713 (2).

0081 BALL, Charles

MP for Clogher Mar.–Aug. 1800

b. *c.* 1755; d. 1822

FAMILY/BACKGROUND: Son of Sterne Ball, military chaplain and curate of Drogheda, and Hannah Wardlaw.

MARRIED: Mildred, dau. of Robert Ball of Dublin.

CHILDREN: *d.s.p.*

EDUCATION: Entered TCD 1772; Lincoln's Inn 7 Aug. 1776, BA 1780; called to the Irish Bar 1781.

CAREER/OCCUPATION: *Listed in Judges and Barristers 1789–1800 (f.).

POLITICAL ACTIVITY: A brother of John Ball (**0082**), he was a pro-Catholic pamphleteer and strongly against the Union. He was anxious to be returned to parliament, and in early February 1800 contested Newry against Isaac Corry (**0497**), who was seeking re-election on his appointment as Chancellor of the Irish Exchequer, following the dismissal of Sir John Parnell (**1633**). Parnell had refused to support the government over the Union.

Corry, who was pro-Union and pro-Catholic, had a considerable personal interest in Newry and Ball finally decided that discretion was the better part of valour, as the Roman Catholic priest at Newry replied to Archbishop Troy (who had asked him to mobilise the Catholic vote for Corry) that 'Mr Ball and his partisans after canvassing the town for eight days, declined the poll, and surrendered yesterday.'

In 1800 he succeeded in being returned for Clogher, although the election was disputed and he stood against the government candidates. However, the former Bishop of Clogher was Dr William Foster, the Speaker's (**0805**) brother and, although as a bishop's borough it should have been government-controlled, the Speaker may have influenced the election. In any case, Ball's time in parliament was short.

ESTATES/RESIDENCE: Drogheda, Co. Louth; Dominick Street, Dublin.

SOURCES: Vicars, *Prerog. Wills* 1811–58 [says Charles Ball, Dublin, will pr. 1822]; O'Neill thesis; *Alum. Dub.*; *King's Inns Admissions*; Fermanagh and Tyrone MPs [says he is the son of John Ball (**0082**) of Drogheda and grandson of Sterne Ball]; Malcomson, *Foster*, pp. 171, 270; Bolton, *Ir. Act of Union*, pp. 136–7; Rev W. B. Wright, *Ball Family Records* (York, 1908) pp. 98–102; *Lincoln's Inn Records* vol. 1 p. 485; *Almanacks*; Parliamentary Lists, 1800 (3) [says he voted for the Union in 1799 and 1800].

0082 BALL, John

MP for Drogheda 1796-7–1800

b. 1748; d. 24 Aug. 1813
FAMILY/BACKGROUND: Eldest son of Sterne Ball, military chaplain and curate of Drogheda, and Hannah Wardlaw.
MARRIED: [Sept. 1791] Miss Osborne of Dandestat, a Roman Catholic.
CHILDREN: Nicholas.
EDUCATION: Entered TCD 1771; Lincoln's Inn 7 Aug. 1776; called to the Irish Bar 1778.
CAREER/OCCUPATION: Examiner of Spirit Books 1772–1800 (f.); Sheriff of Drogheda 1790; *listed in Judges and Barristers 1789–1800 (f.); *listed in Attorneys of the Courts of King's Bench, Common Pleas and Exchequer 1789–

1800 (f.); Freeman and Freeholder of Dublin city 1797; 3rd Serjeant-at-Law 1805, 2nd Serjeant 1806.

POLITICAL ACTIVITY: An elder brother of Charles Ball (**0081**), he first came in for Drogheda in the by-election following John Forbes's (**0778**) appointment as Governor of the Bahamas. Although Ball was a native of Drogheda and a freeman since 1786, his election was a surprise as he stood against Edward Hardman (**0963**), the richest Protestant merchant in Drogheda and a former mayor. Ball stood on the popular and independent interest. In 1797 Hardman and Ball came to an agreement and both, Ball leading, were returned on an anti-Union ticket. Ball's attitude was expressed in the following terms: 'Let us not deceive ourselves by a name, but consider the projected union to be what in fact it is ... an absolute subjection to the will and uncontrolled domination of a superior.' He pointed out that it was a step which, if the anti-Unionists' suspicions proved founded, it would be difficult to undo. He voted against it in both 1799 and 1800, claiming with Ponsonby (**1709**), Plunket (**1686**), Curran (**0560**) and other opposition lawyers that the bill was a nullity, void *ab initio*, that the 'transaction, thought fortified by seven-fold form, was radically fraudulent; that all the forms and solemnities of the law were but so many badges of the fraud, and that posterity like a great court of conscience, would pronounce its judgment'.

Drogheda was strongly anti-Unionist, and Ball soon built up a reputation as an 'incorruptible' anti-Unionist. However, despite his Drogheda connections, he was essentially an ambitious Dublin barrister looking for advancement in his profession and hoping (unsuccessfully) to acquire it by linking his interest to that of Speaker Foster (**0805**). Foster was reputed, with dubious accuracy, to dominate the town and Ball was a leading member of the group who raised a subscription, subsequently aborted, to pay Foster's debts. This scheme was partly sponsored by the Ponsonbys, allegedly as a method of bringing the Speaker under their control. At the Union the representation of Drogheda was reduced to one MP, to be decided either by private agreement or public ballot, and Hardman won that contest. Ball returned to his profession and was successively Third and Second Serjeant at law.

DIVISION LISTS:

1797 (1) voted for Ponsonby's (**1709**) motion for parliamentary reform.

1799 (1) voted against the Union.

1800 (1) voted against the Union.

ESTATES/RESIDENCE: Drogheda, Co. Louth.

SOURCES: RCBL MS6 Miscellaneous Gravestone Inscriptions [says he died in his 66th year, this is the date accepted here]; Rev W. B. Wright, *Ball Family Records* (York, 1908) pp. 98–102 [says he was b. 1744; *Alum. Dub.* and *King's Inns Admissions* might suggest a date of birth as late as 1754]; *Lincoln's Inn Records* vol. I p. 485; Ellis thesis; Barrington, *The Rise and Fall of the Irish Nation*; *Cornwallis Corr.* vol. 3 p. 238 [says his wife is Miss Osborn of Dandiston]; Malcomson, *Foster*, pp. 168–73; Bolton, *Ir. Act of Union*, pp. 112, 118; J. T. Gilbert, *History of the City of Dublin*, 3 vols (1861) vol. 3 p. 173; *Coll. Gen.*; Dalton, *Drogheda*; *Almanacks*; *FJ* 13 Apr. 1797; Parliamentary Lists, 1799 (3), 1800 (3).

BALTINGLASS, Baron: *see* **STRATFORD**

2025 Stratford, John, 1st Baron Baltinglass, Viscount Aldborough, Viscount Amiens, Earl of Aldborough, MP Baltinglass 1721–7–60, 1761–3

BANDON, Baron, Viscount and Earl of: *see* **BERNARD**

0126 Bernard, Francis, 1st Baron Bandon, Viscount Bandon, Earl of Bandon, MP Ennis 1778–83, Bandon 1783–90

BANGOR, Baron and Viscount: *see* **WARD**

2176 Ward, Bernard, 1st Baron Bangor, Viscount Bangor, MP Co. Down 1745–60, 1761–8–70

0083 BARKER, Samuel

MP for Waterford B. 1747–60, 1761–8

b. 10 Apr. 1707; d. (bur. 4) Feb. 1769 at Waterford

FAMILY/BACKGROUND: Son of Francis Barker of Waterford and Anne Elmes.

MARRIED: Unmarried.

CAREER/OCCUPATION: A banker; Sheriff of Waterford 1729; Mayor of Waterford 1737, 1741, 1752.

POLITICAL ACTIVITY: A banking controversy (see below) probably restricted Barker's early parliamentary career, but between 1753 and 1755 he is known to have been nominated for eight committees. He was a government supporter, voting against the expulsion of Arthur Jones-Nevill (**1125**) and for the Money Bill.

Barker was returned for Waterford city at the 1761 election: he and Shapland Carew (**0348**), the other member, each polled 142 votes. The unsuccessful candidates were Robert Snow and William Alcock (**0020**), who polled 125 and 105 votes respectively.

ADDITIONAL INFORMATION: Together with Ambrose Congreve (♦♦♦♦) he established a bank in Waterford in 1737. However, on 13 February 1740 William Jones, Eaton Edwards, and other Waterford merchants, who were creditors of Edward and Richard Weeks, petitioned the Commons for relief. They alleged that the Weeks were considerable merchants and bankers in the city but on 28 February 1738 their credit failed and they became bankrupt and absconded. Barker and his partner Congreve were aware of their declining condition, and advanced them money and took an assignment of their ships etc. According to the merchants, Barker and Congreve made more out of the bankrupts than they were owed, consequently the Weeks were still due money that might go towards other creditors, but because of their absence this money was not called in. On 29 February the committee appointed to consider the petition reported that the allegations in it had not been proved. A further resolution that it was false, scandalous and malicious divided the House 65 for and 49 against.

DIVISION LISTS:

1749 (1) absent, in the country.

1753 (1) voted against the expulsion of Arthur Jones-Nevill (**1125**).

1753 (2) voted for the Money Bill.

ESTATES/RESIDENCE: Waterford. He acquired property in the city.

SOURCES: PRONI T/1584 Pinkerton transcripts, p. 127, 14 Feb. 1769; NAI MFCI Reel 12, Parish Registers of Christchurch, St Olave and St Patrick, Waterford; McCracken thesis; R. H. Ryland, *The History, Topography and Antiquities of the county and city of Waterford* (London, 1824), p. 409; *Ir. Gen.* vol. 7 no 3 (1988) p. 408, J. C. Walton, 'The Boltons of County Waterford' [says he died 1773, this is unlikely]; *DJ* 19–23 May 1761, 7–9 Feb. 1769 [reports his death]; Watson, *Gentleman's and Citizen's Almanack* (1744) p. 69.

0084 BARRETT, Dacres

MP for Co. Monaghan 1692–3

b. *ante* 5 Oct. 1671; d. 1 Jan. 1725
FAMILY/BACKGROUND: Son of Richard Barrett-Lennard and Anne, dau. of Sir Robert Loftus.
MARRIED: (1) Jane, dau. of Rt Hon. Arthur Chichester, 2nd Earl of Donegall; (2) Elizabeth, dau. and co-h. of Thomas Moore; (3) Sarah, dau. of Sir Capel Luckyn, Bt, of Essex.
CHILDREN: (1) Richard, m. [15 June 1716] Anne, Baroness Dacre, dau. of Thomas Lennard, 1st Earl of Sussex.
(2) Elizabeth, m. William Sloan of Chelsea.
CAREER/OCCUPATION: Sheriff of Essex 1706.

POLITICAL ACTIVITY: He was an Englishman and sat only for the short session 5 October–3 November 1692, consequently little is known of his activity in parliament.

ESTATES/RESIDENCE: Clones, Co. Monaghan; Bellhouse, Essex.

SOURCES: PRONI MIC/338/9 Crossle notes; Burke *Ext. P* (1883) p. 329; *Coll. Gen.*; Simms' cards.

0085 BARRINGTON, John

MP for Ballynakill 1692–3, 1703–13–14, 1727–56 [n.d.e. 1715]

b. 1666; d. 27 Jan. 1756 (referred to by his great-grandson Sir Jonah Barrington (**0087**) as sitting in parliament at the age of 90)
FAMILY/BACKGROUND: Son of Alexander Barrington and Eileen Cosby of Stradbally, Queen's County (she married (2) Pierce Bryan).
MARRIED: [1693] Dorcas, dau. of Jonah Wheeler, Co. Kilkenny.
CHILDREN: Jonah (**0086**); Wheeler (Captain of Foot); Elinor, m. Maj. Beard; Catherine.
EDUCATION: School: Mr Wall; entered TCD 4 Mar. 1675, BA 1679, MA 1682; incorporated at Oxford 10 July 1683.
CAREER/OCCUPATION: High Sheriff of Queen's County 1697, 1711, and 1728.
MILITARY: Colonel of the Queen's County Militia 1689, but declared for William; captured by the Jacobites and sentenced to death but freed after his step-father appealed to James II. Bryan was granted Barrington's confiscated estate.

POLITICAL ACTIVITY: He was an active parliamentarian, even managing to be nominated for a committee in 1692. He was listed on 22 committees between 1703 and 1711 and one in the 1713 parliament. During the reign of Queen Anne he supported the Court party and was recorded as a Court supporter in 1706; he was one of the 34 Tories who met in 1707 at the Fleecc Tavern to discuss tactics for the ensuing session, and in 1711 he was described as of the Court party.

In 1713 he was thought likely to be returned (he was) with 'another good man but we know him not'. His return in 1715 was contested and he was declared not duly elected. His Tory sympathies had probably not helped, but he was returned again in 1727 and sat in parliament for the remainder of his long life. During this parliament he was listed for 17 committees: the last, in 1755, when he was 89 years of age. He appears to have supported the government of the day regardless of its complexion.

DIVISION LISTS:

1709 (1) voted against a Money Bill.

1711 (1) voted for the Court on the Dublin mayoralty issue.

1713 (1) voted for Sir Richard Levinge (**1230**) for Speaker.
1749 (1) voted against the election of James Digges La Touche (♦♦♦♦).

ESTATES/RESIDENCE: Castlewood and Cullenagh, Queen's County. Ousted from his estates by the Jacobites, he was later reinstated. His estimated income in 1713 was £400.

SOURCES: PRONI D/302; PRONI T/1584 Pinkerton transcripts, p. 34; PRONI T/3411 Blenheim Papers; McCracken thesis [says son of Thomas Barrington]; *Alum. Oxon.*; H. B. Archdale, *Memoirs of the Archdales* (Enniskillen, 1925), p. 74 [says he was b. 1652, and that he died aged 104 years]; Patrick F. Meehan, *The Members for Queen's County and its Boroughs, 1585–1800*; *GM* Jan. 1756 [confirms he died aged 90 years]; *The Dublin Gazette* 12 Dec. 1710; Parliamentary Lists, 1706 (1), 1711 (2), (3), 1713 (1), (2).

0086 BARRINGTON, Jonah

MP for Ballynakill 1747–60

b. *c.* 1698 d. Dec. 1784
FAMILY/BACKGROUND: Son of John Barrington (**0085**) and Dorcas, dau. of Jonah Wheeler of Co. Kilkenny.
MARRIED: Margaret, dau. of Sir Daniel Byrne of Timogue, Queen's County.
CHILDREN: John, m. Sibella, dau. of Patrick French of Peterswell, Co. Galway; other younger children.
CAREER/OCCUPATION: Sheriff of Queen's County 1728; Magistrate and Sovereign of Ballinakill 1756; *Commissioner of the Infirmary 1763; had a Civil Pension worth £200, listed 15 Feb. 1755.
MILITARY: Colonel in the militia; listed in General Officers as Major-General 1762–3.

POLITICAL ACTIVITY: He sat on 17 committees between 1749 and 1758. He was a very typical mid-eighteenth-century minor country gentleman. As a pensioner he was inclined to follow the government's lead. In 1753 he voted against the expulsion of Arthur Jones-Nevill (**1125**) and for the Money Bill, but he voted for the 1757 resolution against improper pensions, i.e. pensions to people not living in, or without real connection to, Ireland. Using Irish sinecures and pensions to reward Englishmen or members and hangers-on of

the royal family was already a considerable drain on the Irish revenue, and the problem was increasing. It was also complex, as Irish MPs were not against Irishmen receiving pensions. Barrington was himself a small pensioner. The preceding year a bill to vacate seats in parliament on receipt of pensions had been defeated by 85 to 59 votes.

DIVISION LISTS:
1749 (1) absent, in the country.
1753 (1) voted against the expulsion of Arthur Jones-Nevill (**1125**).
1753 (2) voted for the Money Bill.
1757 (1) voted for the resolutions on pensions – pensioner.

ADDITIONAL INFORMATION: A member of the Royal Dublin Society from 1753. In 1759 he fought a famous duel with a Mr Gilbert at Maryborough, Queen's County. His grandson (**0087**) related that: 'It was fought on horseback before a great concourse of persons, with holster pistols and broad-bladed swords, both combatants receiving slight wounds, but escaping with life, and agreeing to shake hands as friends.' Early in the eighteenth century this type of duelling was not unknown.

ESTATES/RESIDENCE: Cullenagh, Queen's County.

SOURCES: PRONI T/3019/6456/376 Wilmot Papers; McCracken thesis; H. B. Archdale, *Memoirs of the Archdales* (Enniskillen, 1925), p. 74; J. C. O'Hanlon and E. O'Leary (eds), *History of the Queen's Co.*, vol. I (Dublin, 1907) p. 196; *Almanacks*; *Walker's Hibernian Magazine* (1784) p. 744; J. Kelly, '*That Damn'd Thing Called Honour', Duelling in Ireland 1570–1860*, p. 76; S. J. Conolly, *Religion, Law and Power* (1992) p. 68 [a 1733 duel]; *The Dublin Weekly Journal* 20 Jan. 1728.

0087 BARRINGTON, Sir Jonah

MP for Tuam 1790–7; Clogher 1798–Jan. 1800; [Escheator of Munster 14 Jan. 1800]

b. 1764; d. 8 Apr. 1834 at Versailles
HONOURS: Knight 13 May 1807.
FAMILY/BACKGROUND: Third son of John Barrington and Sibella, dau. of Patrick French of Co. Galway.
MARRIED: [6 June 1789] Catherine, dau. of Edward Grogan, silk merchant, of Dublin.

CHILDREN: Edward (5th Dragoon Guards); Jane Catherine, m. [1815] Thomas de Grenier de Fonblanque; Sybella, m. [1815] William Otway; Patricia, m. Alexander Hunter; Arabella Henrietta, m. [1826] Edward Hughes; Margaret, m. [1829] Capt. R. Worthy.

EDUCATION: School: Mr Crawley; entered TCD 8 July 1773, aged 16 years; Middle Temple 13 June 1783; called to the Irish Bar 1787, LLD *hon. caus.* 1798.

CAREER/OCCUPATION: King's Counsel 1793, 1796– (f.); *Listed in Judges and Barristers 1789–1800 (f.); Judge in the High Court of Admiralty 1797–1829; *listed as Advocate in the Courts of Delegates, Prerogative, Admiralty and Consistory 1800 (f.); Clerk of the Ships Entries of the Port of Dublin 1793–6; Freeman of Dublin City 1797.

MILITARY: Lieutenant 1796. He gained a degree of fame by resigning his commission in the Dublin lawyers' cavalry when he joined the 'patriots'.

POLITICAL ACTIVITY: He purchased a seat for Tuam from John Bingham (0144) in 1790. On his entry to parliament he supported the government: 'I directed my earliest efforts against Grattan (0895) and Curran (0560) and on the first day of my rising, exhibited a specimen of what I may now call true arrogance.' His attitude to the Catholic question was one of cautious and cynical realism. He was aware that the opposition commanded a greater share of ability and that it would be more difficult to make a profitable mark on the political scene from their side, and he acknowledged that it was this that essentially made him a government supporter.

A seat in parliament was the road to personal advancement for him, like many lawyers, and in 1793 he was appointed a KC just before the Place Act, so he did not have to seek re-election. By 1793 he held the sinecure position of Clerk of the Ships Entries of the Port of Dublin, estimated at £400–£1,100 p.a. In 1797 he was a Judge of the Admiralty, a post he retained until 1830, when various and repeated inconsistencies in the accounts of his court came to light and he was dismissed on petition of both Houses of Parliament.

In 1795 he was a member of the Dublin district of the Association for the protection of Property and the Constitution. He was returned for Clogher in a 1798 by-election. Traditionally a government borough, it turned popular under

Bishop Foster, the Speaker's (0805) brother. The 1799 Parliamentary List states that 'Till the Union was proposed, no man was more forward in support of administration; no debate passed in the Commons in which he did not bear a part and out of it, as an officer in the lawyer's corps, he repeatedly risqued his life in the field against the insurgents. He does not rank high either as a lawyer or a speaker, but has great application and consequently some business. As a speaker his manner is bold and daring and to his intrepidity it has been said, he owes his advancement.'

He was one of the witnesses for the defence at the trial for treason of John and Henry Sheares in 1798 (*see* 1909), and he opposed the Martial Law Bill in 1799 – a bill giving stringent emergency powers in face of the continuing unrest following the 1798 rebellion. Despite his position he took a strong anti-Unionist stance, writing an anti-Union pamphlet in December 1798. The pamphlet, published anonymously, was said to be titled *Cease your Funning*. The pamphlet war of which it was a part was described as 'all Bedlam not Parnassus is let out'. Subsequently he claimed that because of his stand he lost not only his Revenue sinecure but further advancement in his profession. He said that Lord Clare (0749) offered him the Solicitor Generalship if he supported. Nevertheless, he was supposedly instrumental in assisting the government to bribe at least one member to vote for the Union. Moreover, on 14 January 1800 he accepted the Escheatorship of Munster, thereby vacating his seat. Parliament reassembled on 15 January, so he resigned before the decisive vote on 6 February 1800. The former Lord Lieutenant, Lord Westmorland, wrote to him pointing out that Clogher was a government seat and therefore if he was against the government's policy he was in honour bound to resign. Speaker Foster had tried to persuade him that this was not the case. But Barrington, with a view to the future, decided to take Westmorland's advice.

In September 1801 he called on Lord Lieutenant Hardwicke to explain his position. Hardwicke reported that 'Mr Barrington seemed desirous of explaining the situation in which he has stood in regard to government before the question of Union and though he was aware that he could not be considered as entitled to early favour, yet he wished not to be looked on as hostile, and claimed some merit for having given up his seat in Parliament after the first session in which the Union was discussed. He does not appear to have any particular object, though I presume that he some time or other will look to the Bench.' He stood, unsuccessfully, for Dublin city in 1803 although Grattan, Curran, Ponsonby (**1708**) and Plunket (**1686**) voted for him.

ADDITIONAL INFORMATION: In 1809 he published, in five parts, the first volume of *The Historic Memoirs* …, and it 'is thought that he was induced to delay the second volume – the Government shrinking from the exposure of their conduct in carrying the Union, and it was understood that to purchase his silence he was permitted to reside in France from about 1815, and act as judge by deputy.' His fame is as the author of *Personal Sketches of His Own Times*, 2 vols (1827), 3rd vol. 1832, *Historic Memoirs of Ireland*, 2 vols (1832), *The Rise and Fall of the Irish Nation* (Paris, 1833). These contain family anecdotes and interesting, if colourful, accounts of Irish life. The *Sketches* in particular were written for the English market, for which a degree of embroidery was expected. For example, he describes an almost incredible scene of Bacchanalian devastation which he met when visiting his brother. He alleged, with generalised examples, that the Irish gentry were divided into three categories: half-mounted gents, every inch gents and gents-to-the-backbone.

He married a silk-merchant's heiress, Catherine Grogan – as one of 16 children, a wealthy marriage was virtually essential. However, with the malice of a small society, a neighbour, Lady Clonmell, put it about that Lady Barrington sat at the window of her house because she was accustomed to being in front of her father's shop. Barrington promptly blocked up the window, subsequently saving himself some window tax.

Like other members of his family he was a noted duellist, and reported to be 'so good a *marksman, that he can repeatedly strike out the mark upon the ace of spades, at twelve paces distance. He has frequently fought and never missed his man.* Among his (non-fatal) victims was John Egan (**0694**) the MP for Ballynakill, who had a reputation for being a bully. In Ireland it is considered –

not fair to fight him.' Possibly this was also a reflection of the increasing accuracy of duelling pistols, which eventually brought the practice to an end.

DIVISION LISTS:

1790 (2) voted for Foster (**0805**) on the election of a Speaker.

1793 (2) voted for the Convention Bill.

1795 (2) voted against Catholic Emancipation.

1795 (3) teller against Sir Laurence Parson's (**1636**) resolution against alleged troop removals.

1799 (1) voted against the Union.

ESTATES/RESIDENCE: Blackrock, Co. Dublin. TCD Library 386.s.40 (this bill made provision for a jointure of £200 p.a. for Alice Edwards the wife of his eldest brother, John; £9,000 was set aside for the ten (named) younger children of John and Sibella (her jointure was £250)).

SOURCES: PRONI T/3166/1C Hartnell notes; O'Neill thesis; Burke Ext. B. (1844) p. 43; J. Barrington, *Personal Sketches of his own Times, Rise and Fall of the Irish Nation*; *DNB*; J. Kelly, *'That Damn'd Thing Called Honour': Duelling in Ireland 1570–1860* (Cork, 1995) pp. 147–9; *Alum. Dub.*; Hughes, *Pat. Officers*; Fermanagh and Tyrone MPs; *King's Inns Admissions, Cornwallis Corr.* vol. 3 p. 67; *Middle Temple Admissions* vol. 2 p. 395 [calls him Jonas]; R. B. McDowell, *Irish Public Opinion, 1750–1800* pp. 28, 185; B. De Breffny and R. Ffolliott, *The Houses of Ireland* (Dublin, 1975), p. 181; *Castlereagh Corr.* vol. 2 pp. 45, 190; MacDonagh, *The Viceroy's Postbag*, p. 87; *JRSAI* vol. 67 (1937) p. 18, K. R. Brady, 'The Brief for the Defence at the Trial of John and Henry Sheares in 1798'; Watson, *The Gentleman's and Citizen's Almanack 1829 and 1830* [the 1829 *Almanack* has Barrington as Admiralty Judge, but in the 1830 volume he has been replaced by Sir Henry Meredyth]; *Almanacks*; *FJ* 17 Oct. 1795, 20 Oct. 1796, 13 Apr. 1797; Parliamentary Lists, 1791 (1), 1793 (1), 1794 (1), (2), 1798 (1), 1799 (1), (3), 1800 (3).

0088 BARRY, Hon. Arthur

MP for Belfast 1757–60

b. 1724; d. 23 Oct. 1770 at his residence in Sackville Street

FAMILY/BACKGROUND: Son of Rt Hon. James Barry, 4th Earl of Barrymore, and his third wife Anne,

dau. of Arthur Chichester, 3rd Earl of Donegall.
MARRIED: Unmarried.
EDUCATION: Entered Oxford (Brasenose College)
3 Feb. 1742; Lincoln's Inn 29 June 1742.
CAREER/OCCUPATION: Burgess of Belfast 31 Oct.
1753.

POLITICAL ACTIVITY: Barry was returned for Belfast
on 6 December 1757 following the death of
George Macartney (**1300**) the previous October.
Belfast was completely under the Donegall interest. In 1761 Barry stood for the more prestigious
county borough of Carrickfergus in the same interest, but here the Donegall interest was less assured and fluctuated from election to election. The
electorate was much larger and the election disputed by two local figures. Barry polled 192 votes
against the elected members, Arthur Upton
(**2125**), 441 votes and Marriot Dalway (**0565**),
341 votes. Thus Barry sat only for the final two
sessions of George II's parliament; there is no information about his political activity apart from
his being listed for a committee in December
1757.

ESTATES/RESIDENCE: Co. Cork; Sackville Street, Dublin.
At his death his 'very considerable' estates devolved to
his brother, the Hon. John Smith Barry.

SOURCES: McCracken thesis; *Alum. Oxon.*; *Lincoln's Inn
Records* vol. 1 p. 424; G. F. Russell-Barker and A. H.
Stenning (eds), *Record of Old Westminsters: A Biographical
List* (London, 1928) [gives an Arthur at Westminster
school June 1733 aged 10 years, left 1740]; *DJ* 5–9
May 1761, 23–5 Oct. 1770.

BARRY, Hon. Barry Maxwell: *see* **MAXWELL**,
Rt Hon. Barry (**1372**)

0089 BARRY, Hon. David John

MP for Belfast 1727–44

b. 1688; d. Oct. 1744
FAMILY/BACKGROUND: Son of Richard Barry, 2nd
Earl of Barrymore, and his third wife Dorothy,
dau. and h. of John Ferrar of Dromore, Co.
Down.

MARRIED: Margaret, dau. of Frederick Crosbie,
wid. of John Blennerhassett (**0166**).
CHILDREN: ?
EDUCATION: School: Mr Molloy of Cork; entered
TCD 26 Mar. 1705.
CAREER/OCCUPATION: Sheriff of Co. Cork 1727.
MILITARY: Styled Captain – possibly the Mr Barry
referred to by Chief Secretary (Horatio) Walpole
in a letter of 14 January 1720/1 when he writes
that: 'My Lord Lieutenant has, in regard to the
Lords Justices' recommendation, as well as on
account of Mr Barry's being a relation of my Lord
Chancellor's [Brodrick], determined to let him
have the captain's commission vacant in Charles
Hotham's regiment by the death of Mr Gill'.

POLITICAL ACTIVITY: His connection with the
Donegall family ensured his return for Belfast.
Little is known of his activities in parliament apart
from the fact that he was listed for one committee
in 1727 and four in 1731.

ESTATES/RESIDENCE: Mahon, Co. Cork. Trustee to the
Donegall estate.

SOURCES: PRONI T/559, Burke, extract pedigrees vol.
7 p. 249; McCracken thesis; Burke *IFR* (1976) p. 73;
Irish Official Papers in Great Britain vol. 1 p. 29.

0090 BARRY, Sir Edward

MP for Charleville 1744–60

b. 1696; d. 25 Mar. 1776 at Bath
HONOURS: Cr. Bt 1 Aug. 1775.
FAMILY/BACKGROUND: Son of Edward Barry MD of
Cork and Jane [   ].
MARRIED: (1) [*c.* 1725] [   ]; (2) [18 Dec. 1746]
Jane, dau. of Anthony Dopping, Bp of Ossory.
CHILDREN: Sir Nathaniel MD, 2nd Bt, m. [Jan.
1758] Catherine, dau. of Walter Jones of
Headfort, Co. Leitrim; Edward (Captain in
Montague's Regiment); Robert (**0097**); Jane, m.
[1767] Robert Jephson (**1091**).
EDUCATION: Entered TCD 1713, scholar 1716,
BA 1717; MD (Leyden) 1719, MB 1740, MD
1740; College of Physicians 1743, Fellow 1746,
1759–60, Honorary Fellow 1762–4, 1769–70,
1774, Vice-Treasurer 1751, 1761, Vice-President
and Censor 1751, Treasurer 1753; MD Oxford
20 Nov. 1759.
CAREER/OCCUPATION: Freeman of Cork 6 July
1731; State Physician 18 Apr. 1745; Professor of
Physics at Dublin University; licensed to practise

medicine in England 30 June 1761; King's Professor of Physics 1759–61; Fellow of the Royal Society 1733; Fellow College of Physicians London 1761; Vice-President of the Physico-Historical Society of Ireland; Physician-General 1745–76 (he was joined in the appointment by his son Nathaniel, 1749–85); *Governor of the Workhouse 1753–68, Foundling Hospital and Workhouse 1769–d.; *Commissioner of the Infirmary in James's Street 1760–73; Governor of St Patrick's Hospital 1769, 1743.

POLITICAL ACTIVITY: He was nominated for 19 committees between 1745 and 1757, which probably indicates a fairly active political life for a professional man. Although he held a government position, his voting pattern indicates a degree of independence and perhaps also of caution, as he was absent for the vote on the 1753 Money Bill. A month earlier he had voted against the administration.

He came from a medical family and at the start of his career he practised in Cork, later moving to Dublin. A prominent member of the College of Physicians in 1728, he was the author of a treatise on that notorious eighteenth-century killer, consumption of the lungs, as well as several other medical tracts and essays. He also published a 'scientific' work on the history of wines. He did not come into parliament in the 1760 election, as in the late 1750s he moved to London. In 1759 Lady Caroline Fox wrote to her sister, Lady Kildare, that 'He is in vast repute here', and after meeting him wrote that 'Dr Barry seems to be a mighty sensible clever man'; thereafter he appears to have been physician to the Holland family. The opinionated Dr Samuel Johnson considered that 'He was a man who acquired a high reputation in Dublin, came over to England and brought his reputation with him, but had not great success.'

DIVISION LISTS:
1749 (1) voted against the election of James Digges La Touche (♦♦♦♦).
1753 (1) voted for the expulsion of Arthur Jones-Nevill (**1125**) – Physician General.
1753 (3) absent.
1757 (1) voted for the resolutions on pensions – State Physician.

ADDITIONAL INFORMATION: Member of the Medico-Philosophical Society (an offshoot of the Physico-Historical Society fl. 1756–84).

ESTATES/RESIDENCE: College Green, Dublin; Dundeady, Co. Cork; Barry House, Donnybrook, Co. Dublin. The estate in 1878 consisted of 672 acres in Co. Cork and seven in Co. Dublin.

SOURCES: McCracken thesis; GEC *B*; *DNB*; Cork MPs; J. F. Fleetwood, *A History of Medicine in Ireland*, pp. 55, 285; J. T. Gilbert, *History of the City of Dublin*, 3 vols (1861) vol. 3 pp. 23–4; *IMC Leinster 1* (Dublin, 1949) p. 199–201, 573; *DJ* Apr. 4–6 1776; *Almanacks*; Simms, *Williamite Confiscation*, p. 177 [in 1702–3 Edmond Barry had 1,681 acres in Co. Cork forfeited]; J. T. Gilbert, *History of the City of Dublin*, 3 vols (1861) vol. 3 pp. 23–4; J. Walton, *'The King's Business': Letters on the Administration of Ireland, 1741–61* (NY, 1996) no 129.

0091 BARRY, James

MP for Rathcormack (1689), 1692–3, 1695–9, 1713–14; Dungarvan 1703–13, 1715–17 [r. Rathcormack 1703, 1715]

b. 1659; d. 1717
FAMILY/BACKGROUND: Eldest son of Redmond Barry and Mary, dau. of John Boyle of Co. Cork.
MARRIED: (1) Mary, dau. of Abraham Anselm of London; (2) Susanna, dau. of John Townsend of Co. Cork.
CHILDREN: (1) James (**0093**); Redmond (**0095**); Mary.
(2) David MD; Patrick MD; Elizabeth, m. Noblett Dunscomb (**0674**); Katherine, m. John Townshend.
EDUCATION: School: Mr Wilson; entered TCD 15 Sept. 1677, aged 18 years.
CAREER/OCCUPATION: Freedom of Cork 16 Dec. 1697; Deputy Governor of Co. Cork 1699.
MILITARY: ?Serving as a Captain in the Regiment of Foot commanded by Sir George St George 1 Jan. 1692; joined Sir Matthew Bridges' Regiment of Foot as a Captain 20 Apr. 1696; Colonel *c.* 1699.

POLITICAL ACTIVITY: He sat in the 'patriot' parliament of 1689, but on 3 March 1692 he was permitted to bring a Writ of Error for the reversal of his outlawry. He was an active parliamentarian, nominated for a committee on 2 November 1692, the day before parliament was suddenly pro-rogued. The previous day, 1 November, the Commons ordered that 'Mrs Jane Barry be taken into the custody of the Serjeant-at-Arms attending this House for a notorious breach of privilege committed on James Barry Esq. a Member of this House'. In the following parliament, 1695–9, he was listed for 21 committees. He gave his vote against Lord Chancellor Porter, who was accused of favouring Catholics, and signed the Association for the protection of William III in the country.

In the first parliament of Queen Anne he was listed for 57 committees between 1703 and 1713. On 2 August 1707 in a committee of the whole House, 'Colonel Barry attacked the Commissioners of the Revenue and charged them with taking the duty of foreign salt contrary to law', and the taking of the duty was voted to be illegal. He was on the Whig side in a Commons debate in August 1707 and a teller on the Whig side the following October. However, either the Parliamentary Lists are wrong or he was having a bet both ways, as he was noted as being for the Court in the Parliamentary List of 1706 and in 1707 he was listed as one of the 34 Tory MPs who met at the Fleece tavern to coordinate strategy for the ensuing session.

He was returned for Dungarvan by the 2nd Earl of Burlington's (died 1704) interest and, as the 3rd Earl was a minor in 1706, he may have followed his guardian's instructions. He was returned for Dungarvan again in 1713, when he managed to be listed for three committees in the very short second parliament of Queen Anne, 25 November to 24 December. In 1715 was again returned for Dungarvan; he was nominated for 27 committees in the first session of that parliament, 12 November 1715 to 20 June 1716. He died in 1717.

DIVISION LISTS:
1709 (1) spoke for a Money Bill.

ESTATES/RESIDENCE: Rathcormack, Co. Cork. Under 14 Chas I, James Barry was granted fairs/markets at Rathcormack. There was a Chancery grant of Barrymore lands to Redmond Barry, 36 Chas II.

SOURCES: NLI LC 137 vol. 171, 16 Nov. 1880; EC 6450; McCracken thesis; Hayton thesis; Burke *LGI* (1904) p. 23; *Commons' jn. Ire.* vol. 2 p. 32; NLI *House of Lords*

Appeals: Brown's Reports, 1701–1800 vol. 2 p. 485; Cork MPs [says he died 1743 possibly confusing him with **0093**]; *Cal. SP Dom. 1691–2* pp. 81, 171, *1693* p. 46, *1696* pp. 136–7; *Alum. Dub.*; C. Dalton (ed.), *English Army Lists and Commission Registers, 1661–1714* (London, 1896) vol. III p. 57; C. Dalton (ed.), *Irish Army Lists 1661–85* (London, 1907) pp. 119, 151 [it is difficult to decide if this is the right officer as the name was not uncommon]; *HMC Ormonde*, new series vol. 8 p. 306; *JRSAI* vol. 55 (1925) pp. 37, 45, H. A. S. Upton, 'A List of Governors and Deputy Governors of Counties in Ireland in 1699' [says (probably incorrectly unless he had 3 wives) that his first wife was a dau. of John Lyons of Castle Lyons]; *The Barry family of Rathcormack*; Parliamentary Lists, 1695 (1), 1696 (1), 1706 (1), 1707 (2), 1713 (1).

0092 BARRY, James

MP for Naas 1695–9, 1711–13; Kildare B. 1715–25 [n.d.e. Naas 1703]

b. (15) Jan. 1661; d. 16 Apr. 1725
FAMILY/BACKGROUND: Eldest son of Redmond Barry and Mary, dau. of John Houghton of Wexford.
MARRIED: (1) Elizabeth, dau. of Sir Thomas Boothby, wid. of Hugh Wood of London; (2) [9 Oct. 1698] Anne, dau. of Charles Meredyth (**1398**).
CHILDREN: Judith, m. [June 1719] John Maxwell 1st Baron Farnham (**1374**).
EDUCATION: School: Mr Ryder; entered TCD 10 July 1678, aged 16 years.
CAREER/OCCUPATION: Clerk of the Pipe for life, patent, 19 Jan. 1693; Joint Prothonotary of the Court of the Common Pleas 2 Dec. 1701; Sheriff of Co. Kildare 1694; Sovereign of Naas 1708.
MILITARY: ?Captain in Colonel Courthope's Regiment of Foot, 1694.

POLITICAL ACTIVITY: He supported Lord Chancellor Porter against accusations of favouring Catholics in 1695, and signed the Association for the protection of William III in parliament in 1696. He was declared not duly elected for Naas in 1703, but was returned at a by-election in 1711. He sat on four committees in the final session of Queen Anne's first parliament, 9 July to 9 September 1711.

As the Parliamentary List of 1711 anticipated, he was not returned for Naas in 1713, but he was returned for Kildare in the general election of

1715. He was listed for ten committees between 1715 and his death in 1725. In 1719 he was noted as 'a Tory' and unlikely to support the repeal of the Test Clause. He was caught in the South Sea Bubble disaster, for Philip Perceval wrote to Lord Perceval on 29 October 1720 that Barry: 'with his son [in-law], Maxwell, are sunk by South Sea from the most plentifull and affluent fortune, to the miserable circumstance of being many thousands worse than nothing. He is now obliged to sell all he has in the world ... his house in Capel Street is going with the rest.'

DIVISION LISTS:

1721 (1) voted against a national bank (may have been **0093**).

1721 (2) voted against a national bank.

1723 (1) voted for the Court candidate on the Westmeath Co. election petition.

ESTATES/RESIDENCE: Newtownbarry, Co. Wexford; Capel Street, Dublin. In 1702 he purchased 330 acres from the Commissioners for Sale of Forfeited Estates for *c.* £686: the castle, town and lands of Great and Little Posseckstown, Co. Meath. It was probably towards the end of his life that he built, or at any rate laid out, the little town of Bunclody, Co. Wexford, to which he gave the name Newtownbarry. In *c.* 1830 (paper-marked 1821) the Newtownbarry estate had a rental of £1,378 (the Carlow part of it £1,732). In 1850 the Wexford acreage was 2,639 (st.) out of a total of 9,568.

SOURCES: With more than one Barry sitting at the time, identification is uncertain. PRONI MIC/338/2 Crossle notes; NLI Farnham MS 3502, MS 3134 Farnham Papers, rental (*c.* 1850); PRONI T/559 vol. 7 p. 240, Burke, extract pedigrees; BL Add. MS 47029 f. 41 Egmont Papers, Philip Perceval to Lord Perceval, 29 Oct. 1720; Hayton thesis; *Cal. SP Dom. 1693* (London, 1903) p. 13, *1694–5* (London, 1906) pp. 111, 128; *Alum. Dub.*; Kildare MPs; *JRSAI* vol. 76 (1946) p. 134 W. E. J. Dobbs, 'A Supplement to the Entrance Register of Kilkenny School, 1684–1800' [says he is the son of Richard Barry]; Simms, *Williamite Confiscation*, p. 183; King, *A Great Archbishop of Dublin*, p. 116; Parliamentary Lists, 1695 (1), 1696 (1), 1711 (1), 1719 (2).

0093 BARRY, James

MP for Dungarvan 1713–14, 1721–7; Rathcormack 1727–43

b. 1689; d. 1743

FAMILY/BACKGROUND: Eldest son of James Barry (**0091**) and his first wife Mary, dau. of Abraham Anselm of London.

MARRIED: Unmarried.

EDUCATION: School: Mr Molloy, Cork; entered TCD 23 May 1706, aged 18 years.

CAREER/OCCUPATION: Clerk of the Pipe in the Court of Exchequer 1729; Sheriff of Co. Cork 1721.

POLITICAL ACTIVITY: In 1713 he was counted a Whig. He was returned at a by-election for Dungarvan in 1721, and was nominated for five committees between then and 1725. In 1727 he was returned for the family borough of Rathcormack, which he represented until his death in 1743. Barry was appointed Clerk of the Pipe in the Court of the Exchequer in 1729, a sinecure office. He was listed for 18 committees between 1727 and 1736.

DIVISION LISTS:

1721 (1) voted against a national bank (may have been **0092**).

1723 (1) voted for the Court candidate on the Westmeath Co. election petition.

ADDITIONAL INFORMATION: Foundation member of the Dublin Society, 1733.

ESTATES/RESIDENCE: Lisnegar and Rathcormack, Co. Cork.

SOURCES: With more than one Barry sitting at the time, identification is uncertain. PRONI T/559 vol. 7 p. 247, Burke, extract pedigrees; Hayton thesis; Burke *LGI* (1904) p. 23; *CJ Ire.* vol. 3 p. 120; *Alum. Dub.*; Berry *RDS* pp. 24–7; *Almanacks*; Parliamentary List, 1713 (2).

0094 BARRY, James

MP for Rathcormack 1768–76

b. 1739; d. 25 Oct. 1793 at Bath

FAMILY/BACKGROUND: Eldest son of Redmond Barry of Ballyclogh, Co. Cork and Henrietta, dau. of William Dunscombe of Mount Desart, Co. Cork.

MARRIED: [Mar. 1765] Elizabeth, dau. and co-h. of Abraham Greene of Co. Limerick.

CHILDREN: Redmond; Gen. Henry Greene, m. [1804] Phoebe, dau. of John Armstrong of

Drought, King's County.
EDUCATION: School: private tutor; Kilkenny
College 25 July 1754, aged 14 years; entered
TCD 20 July 1757, aged 18 years.

POLITICAL ACTIVITY: Macartney (1302) believed
Barry to be influenced by his brother-in-law, John
Armstrong (0054), and wrote to Armstrong asking for his and Barry's support at the opening of
parliament in February 1771: 'To have the support of two such respectable and independent gentlemen would do us an infinite deal of honour
and could not fail to have great weight with many
others.' Armstrong and Barry married the coheiresses of Abraham Greene of Ballymacreese, Co.
Limerick, while Barry's sister Mary married St
Leger Aldworth (St Leger) (0026). Both of these
MPs were supposed to be able to influence him,
as was Lord Shannon (0213). In 1772 he was
noted as 'Lord Shannon's friend' but 'will not come
in again'.

The Barrys had the 'natural' interest in
Rathcormack, but his and his father's negligence
had almost destroyed it. By 1773 he was considered 'too ill ever to attend' and in 1774 he was
'generally absent'. By 1775 he had sold the
Rathcormack estate with its interest in the borough to William Hull (Tonson) (1051). The 1775
list remarked that this type of MP 'can scarcely be
considered under the influence of the person to
whom they are classed unless to effect some point
personal to themselves, then they become united
but not otherwise'. In politics he was against the
recruitment of Roman Catholics into the army,
as he felt that on their demobilisation they would
present an even greater danger to their Protestant
neighbours.

ESTATES/RESIDENCE: Rathcormack and Ballyclogh, Co.
Cork. He succeeded to the estates of his cousin,
Redmond Barry (0095).

SOURCES: Burke *LGI* (1904) p. 23 (1958) p. 57 [says he
died 25 Oct. 1793]; *Alum. Dub.*; Johnston, *Gt B. &
Ire.*, p. 162; *Ir. Gen.* vol. 6 no 2 (1981) p. 177, Bartlett
(ed.), *The Macartney Papers* (PRONI 1978) p. 286; R.
B. McDowell, *Irish Public Opinion, 1750–1800* p. 47;
H. F. Morris, 'The Waterford Chronicle 1792'; *JRSAI*
vol. 54 (1924) pp. 55–67, T. U. Sadleir, 'The Register
of Kilkenny School (1685–1800)'; Parliamentary Lists,
1769 (1), 1772 (1), 1773 (1), (2), 1774 (1), 1775 (1).

BARRY, Rt Hon. John: *see* **MAXWELL**
(**MAXWELL-BARRY**), Rt Hon. John (**1375**)

BARRY, Hon. John James: *see* **MAXWELL**
(**BARRY-MAXWELL**), Hon. John James
(**1376**)

0095 BARRY, Redmond

MP for Dungarvan 1717–27; Tallow 1727–50

b. *ante* 17 Sept. 1696; d. Sept. 1750
FAMILY/BACKGROUND: Son of James Barry (0091)
and Mary, dau. of Abraham Anselm of London.
MARRIED: [11 Aug. 1727] Anne Smyth of
Coolmore, Co. Cork.
CHILDREN: *d.s.p.*
CAREER/OCCUPATION: Sheriff of Co. Cork 1734.

POLITICAL ACTIVITY: His main parliamentary activity appears to have confined to the 1720s: he was
nominated for two committees in 1723, three in
1725 and two in 1729. He voted against a national bank in 1721 and for the Court candidate
in the Co. Westmeath election debate. In 1747
he had a small pension of £150 p.a. Both
Dungarvan and Tallow were Burlington (Boyle)
seats.

DIVISION LISTS:
    1721 (1) voted against a national bank.
    1721 (2) voted against a national bank.
    1723 (1) voted for the Court candidate on
    the Westmeath Co. election petition (0092
    or 0093).[†]
    ([†]With more than one Barry sitting at the
    time, identification is uncertain.)

ESTATES/RESIDENCE: Rathcormack, Co. Cork. The manor
and advowson and 11 ploughlands of Rathcormack.
When he died his sister, Mary Barry, succeeded to the
estate, although her succession was contested by
Henrietta Barry, widow of Redmond Barry of
Ballyclogh, the half-brother of James Barry (0091).
Henrietta Barry took possession of the mansion house
and part of the lands of Rathcormack, on behalf of her
son James, a minor, and remained in possession until
the death of Mary Barry, which appears to have occurred in 1750. The litigation, eventually brought to
the attention of the Lords, concerns the competing

claims to sums of money charged on the estate in favour of various female Barrys of the branch of the family that owned it in 1750. But another issue was the existence or otherwise of an entail under which the estate passed to James Barry, the heir of the half-blood.

SOURCES: PRONI T/3019/844 Wilmot Papers; PRONI T/559 vol. 7 p. 256, Burke, extract pedigrees; RCBL P195/1/1, Carrigaline Parish Register [says Redmond Barry married 11 Aug. 1727, Anne Smyth of Coolmore, Co. Cork]; Burke *LGI* (1904) p. 23 (1958) p. 57; NLI *House of Lords Appeals: Brown's Reports, 1701–1800* vol. 2 p. 485; Cork MPs [possibly confuses two branches of this very complex family – says Sheriff of Co. Cork 1721, son of Redmond Barry and his second wife Jane, dau. of Nicholas Purdon; married 1700 Catherine, dau. of William Taylor of Co. Cork, second [?] dau. of Samuel Crofts; children, Redmond]; *GM* Sept. 1750; *Pue's Occurrences* 19 Jan. 1734.

chequer. In 1695 he voted to censure Lord Chancellor Porter, and the following year he signed the Association for the protection of William III in the country. In 1713 he was considered a Tory.

DIVISION LISTS:
1713 (1) absent – 'in England'.

ESTATES/RESIDENCE: [?]Dromore, Co. Down.

SOURCES: PRONI T/448 p. 7, TSPI 1715–16; Hayton thesis; GEC *P*; Burke *Ext. P* (1883) p. 25; Hughes, *Pat. Officers*; *Alum. Dub.*; *JRSAI* vol. 76 (1946) p. 134, W. E. J. Dobbs, 'A Supplement to the Entrance Register of Kilkenny School, 1684–1800' [says Richard son of Richard Barry, born Dublin, at Kilkenny school, entered TCD 1686 aged 17 years]; *Louth Arch. Soc. Jn* (1912–15) pp. 273–83 H. Tempest (ed.), 'The Roll of the Sovereigns and Burgesses of Carlingford, 1706–1828'; Parliamentary Lists, 1695 (1), 1696 (1), 1713 (2).

0096 BARRY, Hon. Richard

MP for Enniscorthy 1692–3, 1695–9 (Aug.–Nov. 1695 absent in England); Baltimore 1713–14 (There is some confusion in the Returns over this MP.)

b. 1665; d. 1754
FAMILY/BACKGROUND: Son of Richard Barry, 2nd Earl of Barrymore, and his third wife Dorothy, dau. and h. of John Ferrar of Dromore, Co. Down.
MARRIED: ?
CHILDREN: ?
EDUCATION: School: ?Mr Scott; entered TCD 19 Feb. 1681, aged 16 years, BA 1685, MA 1688.
CAREER/OCCUPATION: Joint 2nd Remembrancer of the Court of Exchequer, 26 June 1683; Burgess of Carlingford *c.* 1713.
MILITARY: A Lieutenant-Colonel; on 22 Jan. 1715 he was recommended for a pension of £200 p.a. promised him by the late Queen Anne.

POLITICAL ACTIVITY: Little is known of the parliamentary activity of this MP. He was a serving army officer and the country was at war for most of his period in parliament. His pattern of parliamentary activity more or less follows the periods of war. For instance, he was listed for a committee on 11 October 1692 and then five committees in 1797 and two in 1713. When he was 18, in 1683, he was appointed to a sinecure office in the Ex-

0097 BARRY, Robert

MP for Charleville 1761–8–76

b. 1731; d. 1793
FAMILY/BACKGROUND: Son of Sir Edward Barry 1st Bt (**0090**) and his first wife.
MARRIED: (1) [July 1762] Elizabeth (d. Apr. 4 1779), dau. of Henry Lyons (**1290**); (2) Elizabeth, dau. of James (Jacques) Digges La Touche (♦♦♦♦).
CHILDREN: Edward (went to India); Henrietta; Sophia, m. Edward Hoare of Co. Cork.
EDUCATION: School: Winchester; entered TCD 2 Aug. 1748, aged 17 years; Lincoln's Inn 20 July 1750, BA 1753; called to the Irish Bar 1759.
CAREER/OCCUPATION: Seneschal of the King's Manors at £600 (patents 11 Dec. 1761, 19 Apr. 1763–9); Commissioner of the Revenue Appeals 1764–d (patents renewed 16 Nov. 1764 – 14 Apr. 1790); King's Counsel 1768–d; *Bencher in the Honorable Society of King's Inns 1768–74; *listed in Judges and Barristers 1789–d.

POLITICAL ACTIVITY: Son of the famous physician (**0090**), he was brought into parliament by Lord Shannon (**0213**), with whom he formed a lifelong friendship when they were students at Trinity College. He held various sinecures, viz. Seneschal of the King's Manors, £600 p.a.; Commissioner of Appeals, £300 p.a. He supported both as a placeman and as a friend of Lord Shannon.

His two most interesting votes are in 1773 for the Absentee Tax. The Irish administration was very short of money, and this was a measure to tax the Irish income of absentees. It particularly affected two powerful and vociferous types: the great English magnates such as the Marquess of Rockingham, who had large subsidiary estates in Ireland, and the prominent Irish–British politicians whose main estates were in Ireland, such as Lord Hillsborough. Lord North's government, scared by the storm that the measure had aroused, ordered Lord Lieutenant Harcourt to 'sink it'. Chief Secretary Blaquiere successfully hoodwinked the majority of the Irish parliament – but obviously not Barry – by insinuating that it was the forerunner of a land tax and then offering the Commons a free vote.

The 1774 Catholic Bill essentially concerned an oath of allegiance and a denial of certain alleged Catholic doctrines, and while offering no concessions in itself the measure was obviously the first step to securing subsequent benefits. Barry's vote was probably a simple anti-Catholic one.

DIVISION LISTS:

1768 (1) absent – sick.

1771 (1) voted for Lord Townshend as Lord Lieutenant – 'a placeman and a pensioner'.

1771 (2) voted against Sir Lucius O'Brien's (**1558**) motion for retrenchment – 'a placeman and a pensioner'.

1772 (2) voted against a Short Revenue Bill.

1773 (1) voted for the Absentee Tax.

1773 (2) voted against an untaxed press.

1774 (2) voted against Catholic relief.

ADDITIONAL INFORMATION: *A member of the Royal Dublin Society from 1762.

ESTATES/RESIDENCE: Dalkey, Co. Dublin; Merrion Street and Hume Street, Dublin.

SOURCES: PRONI T/559 vol. 7 p. 277, Burke, extract pedigrees; PRONI MIC/465/1 R. Ffolliott, *Biographical Notices, 1756–1827*; GEC *B*; Burke *IFR* (1976) p. 693; Hughes, *Pat. Officers*; Vicars, *Prerog. Wills*; *Lincoln's Inn Records* vol. 1 p. 438; IMC *King's Inns Admissions*; *Alum. Dub.*; Cork MPs; *Almanacks*; *DJ* 31 July–3 Aug. 1762, Apr. 4–6 1779; Parliamentary Lists, 1769 (1), 1772 (2), 1773 (1), (2), 1774 (1), 1775 (1).

0098 BARTON, Thomas

MP for Fethard (Tipperary) 1783–90–7

b. 26 Jan. 1757; d. 1820

FAMILY/BACKGROUND: Eldest son of William Barton of Fethard, Co. Tipperary, and Grace, dau. of Charles Massy, Dean of Limerick. MARRIED: [1786] Mary, dau. of Chambre Brabazon Ponsonby (**1697**).

CHILDREN: Thomas (entered Kilkenny School 24 Aug. 1797, aged 8 years); William (entered Kilkenny School 24 Aug. 1797, aged 9 years), m. Catherine Perry of Co. Tipperary; Lieut.-Col. Chambre Brabazon; Maj. Charles Robert; Mary, m. George FitzGerald; Grace, m. (1) Lieut.-Col. Kingsmill Pennefather, (2) Maj. Michael Galliazzi; Catherine, m. Edmund Staples. EDUCATION: Middle Temple 12 Nov. 1777.

CAREER/OCCUPATION: Elected Freeman and Burgess of Fethard (Tipperary) June 1 1780, *vice* Mathew Jacob, during the 1774–82 Corporation split; one of the eight Burgesses asked to resign in 1795, but was re-elected Recorder and Town Clerk between 29 June 1801 and 30 June 1806, resigned 26 June 1809; Sovereign of Fethard (Tipperary) 1787–88, 1791–92, 1801–2, 1811–14, Recorder 1801–9 (resigned); Sheriff of Co. Tipperary 1785; *Governor of the Hibernian Marine Society 1775–9.

POLITICAL ACTIVITY: He shared the control of the borough of Fethard with Cornelius O'Callaghan (**1562**), and they both represented it. Although it had a comparatively large electorate (900–1,000 – larger than many counties), the electors were largely absentees: there were only about 20 resident Protestants. The rest 'considered themselves rather as the trustees of the family that introduced them here'. Thus O'Callaghan, later Lord Lismore, possessing 'not a single foot of ground, either in the town or its vicinity', was able to sustain his influence. Barton's father, William Barton, fought a famous duel with Cornelius O'Callaghan over a contest to elect the sovereign of Fethard in 1772. William Barton was wounded in the left thigh but survived. Barton was the proprietor of the town, politically independent and mainly in opposition.

Barton's voting record shows him to be a supporter of the parliamentary reform movement of the early 1780s, and thereafter he followed the usual opposition line against the Commercial Resolutions, for retrenchment and economy, for a regency, against corruption as evinced in the 'sale' of peerages for political favours; in the early 1790s he was a supporter of Grattan (**0895**). In 1789 he was thanked by the Corporation of Fethard for his services in parliament and promised its support at the next general election. The other Patriot, O'Callaghan, was a son-in-law of John Ponsonby (**1702**), and this relationship tended to obscure Barton's real influence. At the Union Fethard was disfranchised and the compensation divided between them. Barton appears to have been an active politician until the early 1790s. He did not seek re-election in the general election of 1797.

DIVISION LISTS:

1783 (1) voted for Flood's (**0762**) motion for parliamentary reform.

1784 (1) voted for a committee on the Reform Bill.

1785 (1) voted against the Commercial Propositions.

1786 (2) voted for Forbes's (**0778**) motion on retrenchment.

1787 (1) absent – had previously voted for a Pension Bill.

1789 (1) voted for a regency.

1790 (1) voted for Grattan's (**0895**) motion for reducing the influence of the Crown.

1790 (2) voted for Ponsonby (**1709**) on the election of a Speaker.

1791 (1) voted for Curran's (**0560**) resolution against the sale of peerages.

1791 (2) voted for Grattan's motion for the exercise of Free Trade.

1791 (3) voted for Grattan's motion to abolish the Dublin police.

ESTATES/RESIDENCE: Clonmel, Co. Tipperary; St Stephen's Green, Dublin. In 1751 the Bartons acquired the Grove estate containing *c.* 2,650 Irish acres at an estimated rental of £1,500 in 1775.

In legal papers before the Lords in 1765, Thomas Barton (probably an uncle) was the appellant and William Barton and others the respondents. Part of Thomas Barton's answer was: 'That in June 1754 and for many years before he was a merchant in France and resided in Bordeaux, where he carried on commerce until 1755, and that he was still a merchant and engaged in a very extensive trade, and that in June 1754 he was seized in fee simple of the town and lands of

Fethard and of the town and lands therein particularly mentioned, worth as he believes £36,000 and of the yearly value of £1,600 and upwards, and upon the expiration of some short leases and the fall of an indifferent life will be worth £2,300 and upwards.'

In 1856 the Barton rental was £4,128 from 225 tenancies.

SOURCES: PRONI MIC/465/1 R. Ffolliott, Biographical Notices, 1756–1827 [says a T. Barton of Grove, Co. Tipperary died 25 Oct. 1818 at Cheltenham]; Draft of an English Act for sale of the Everard estates in Middlethird and statement of the Everard title, *post*-1743; NLI MS 5622 Barton Papers, rental 1856; Burke *LGI* (1904) p. 26; NLI ILB 34.11, *House of Lords Appeals: Printed Case Papers, 1710–1800*; NLI EC Box 5562, 1394, 5304; *Cornwallis Corr.* vol. 3 p. 13; *Middle Temple Admissions* vol. I p. 385; B. F. Barton, *Some Account of the Family of Barton* (Dublin, 1902), pp. 60–62; J. Kelly, *'That Damn'd Thing Called Honour': Duelling in Ireland 1570–1860* (Cork, 1995) p. 140; *Ir. Gen.* vol. 4 no 4 (1971) p. 310, W. G. Skehan, 'Extracts from the Minutes of the Corporation of Fethard, Co. Tipperary'; *JRSAI* vol. 37 (1906) pp. 152–3, T. Laffan, 'Fethard, Tipperary County: Its Charters and Corporation Records, With Some Notice of the Fethard Everards'; *JRSAI* vol. 54 (1924) pp. 55–67, T. U. Sadlier, 'The Register of Kilkenny School (1685–1800)'; *DJ* 3–6 1780; *Almanacks*; *FJ* 1–3 Feb. 1785; Parliamentary Lists, 1783 (2), 1784 (1), (2), 1785 (1), (4), 1787 (1), 1788 (1), 1789 (1), 1790 (1), 1791 (1), 1793 (1).

0099 BARTON, William

MP for Co. Monaghan 1692–3, 1695–9, 1703–13

b. *ante* 1665; d. (Aug.) 1721
FAMILY/BACKGROUND: Son of [   ] Barton, Collector of London under Cromwell.
MARRIED: [   ]
CHILDREN: Margaret, dau. and h., m. (1) Richard Tenison (**2054**), (2) Patrick Delany DD (he married (2) Mary Pendarves née Granville – see *DNB* for both).
CAREER/OCCUPATION: Deputy Governor of Co. Monaghan 1699; High Sheriff of Co. Louth 1701; Burgess of Ardee.
MILITARY: ?Lieutenant in Colonel Thomas Brudenell's Regiment 6 Oct. 1695.

POLITICAL ACTIVITY: In a list of Irish sheriffs in March 1686 the Lord President wrote: 'of his father's principles, Collector of London under Cromwell'. Clarendon replied: 'What his father's principles were, or whether he was Collector in London under Cromwell is not known in Ireland; where he resided not long, having been dead many years since. But this gentleman is known to be a very honest civil gentleman, and has as fair character as any one in the county, and for aught has yet appeared, very loyal. And in truth he has no temptation to be otherwise, for all his concerns in that county are old interest, where he is only tenant to the Lord Weymouth and the Lord Ferrers. And though he is very wealthy has not made purchase of any new interest.'

He took an active part in parliament, nominated to three committees in the short parliament of 1692 and 19 in the two sessions of the 1695 and 1699 parliament. He supported Lord Chancellor Porter against accusations of favouring Catholics in 1695, and in 1696 signed the Association for the protection of William III in parliament. He sat on four committees between 1703 and 1707. In 1706 he was noted as being against the Court, obviously Whig in sympathies; thereafter he appears to have taken a less active role. In 1711 he was counted as in actual opposition.

ESTATES/RESIDENCE: Carrickmacross, Co. Monaghan; Thomastown, Co. Louth. According to tradition, his family occupied the Castle of Carrick at the time that it is said to have been burnt. This appears to have been in 1688–9. He bought extensive lands in the barony of Balruddery, Co. Dublin, 776 acres from the Trustees of Forfeited Estates in 1703 for £2,014, and lands in the barony of Atherdee, Co. Louth, 98 acres (Lord Slane's estate) for £274.

SOURCES: PRONI D/302; PRONI T/559 vol. 8 p. 40, Burke, extract pedigrees; PRONI T/2842/2 Ardee Corporation Minutes; *Cal. SP Dom. 1695* (London, 1908) p. 77; S. W. Singer (ed.), *Clarendon Corr.*, vol. 1 p. 287; B. F. Barton, *Some Account of the Family of Barton* (Dublin, 1902); E. P. Shirley, *The History of the County of Monaghan* (1877–8) p. 273; *JRSAI* vol. 55 (1925) pp. 39, 50. H. A. S. Upton, 'A List of Governors and Deputy Governors of Counties in Ireland in 1699'; Simms, *Williamite Confiscation*, p. 183; Parliamentary Lists, 1695 (1), 1696 (1), 1706 (1), 1711 (3).

0100 BATEMAN, Rowland

MP for Tralee 1761–8; Co. Kerry 1776–83

b. *c.* 1737; d. 1803

FAMILY/BACKGROUND: Son of Rowland Bateman and Elizabeth, dau. of Nicholas Colthurst of Co. Cork.

MARRIED: (1) [1758] Letitia, dau. and co-h. of Sir Thomas Denny Bt; (2) [*ante* 1777] [   ] Staunton of Co. Kerry.

CHILDREN: Rowland, m. Arabella, dau. of Sir Barry Denny, 1st Bt (**0617**); Thomas (d. June 1783); Agnes (d. July 1791), m. [1785] Richard Chute of Chute Hall, Co. Kerry; Elizabeth, m. James Crosbie (**0533**); Letitia, m. Emmanuel Hutchinson.

CAREER/OCCUPATION: High Sheriff of Co. Kerry 1758.

POLITICAL ACTIVITY: Returned for Tralee, a Denny family borough, in 1761 and for Co. Kerry 1776–83. He was thought to have been returned partly through the 'poverty and folly of Barry Denny' (**0617**) and partly through the influence of Lord Shannon (**0213**) and Richard Townshend (**2100**) against the Crosbie (**0540** – Lord Glandore) interest. Estimates of his fortune varied from 'considerable' to 'much embarrassed'. In politics he was independent, with a tendency to follow Lord Shannon and a weak inclination towards government.

By 1782, with the general election looming, he had joined up with the Blennerhassett interest and was a lieutenant-colonel in Arthur Blennerhassett's (**0164**) regiment of Volunteers. It was thought that this connection would work against rather than for his election prospects. Bateman tried to increase his popularity by giving various undertakings (tests) about his behaviour in parliament. None the less, Bateman and Blennerhassett lost to Sir Barry Denny, who had been the MP in the previous parliament, and Richard Townshend Herbert (**1009**). Kerry was a county with a number of competing interests and 'harassed by electioneering divisions'.

He had a reputation for making absurd statements, known as 'bulls', surpassed only by Sir Boyle Roche (**1796**). For instance, on one occasion (when he was complaining against the stinted allowance served to wine drinkers at taverns, and by wine merchants, through the short measure that glass-blowers allowed in their nominal quart bottles) he declared that 'every quart bottle should hold a quart' – this was wrongly attributed to Roche. His son Rowland signed the pro-Union petition for Co. Kerry.

DIVISION LISTS:
 1768 (1) absent, sick.
 1777 (1) voted against Grattan's (0895) motion for retrenchment.
 1778 (2) voted against the Popery Bill.
 1779 (2) voted for a six-months Loan Bill.
 1780 (2) voted for Yelverton's (2268) motion to modify Poynings' Law.

ADDITIONAL INFORMATION: *Member of the Royal Dublin Society from 1766.

ESTATES/RESIDENCE: Oak Park, Killeen, Co. Kerry. 11,442 Irish acres in the barony of Trughennackony and Corkaquinny. In 1851, including Oak Park, a rental of £4,269 and a valuation of £6,169.

SOURCES: PRONI D/302; PRONI D/2021/39; Ellis thesis; *Memorials of the Dead*; Vicars, *Prerog. Wills*; J. J. Howard (ed.), *Miscellanea Genealogica et Heraldica*, vol. I new ser. (1874) p. 281 [Letitia, dau. of Rowland Bateman, married Emanuel Hutchinson, a distinguished genealogist]; *Kerry Magazine* vol. 3 no 36 (Dec. 1856) pp. 185–90, 'Parliamentary Representation of Kerry'; *Almanacks*; *DJ* 5–7 June; 19–21 July 1791; Parliamentary Lists, 1776 (1), (2), (3), 1777 (1), 1778 (1), 1780 (1), 1782 (1), 1783 (1), 1785 (2) [The 1777 (1) parliamentary list says that he was married to a Miss Staunton of Kerry, if so she was his second wife.]

0101 BAYLY, Sir Edward

MP for Newry 1705–13–14

 b. 20 Feb. 1684; d. 28 Sept. 1741
 HONOURS: Cr. Bt [I and GB] 4 July 1730.
 FAMILY/BACKGROUND: Only son and heir of Nicholas Bayly, Governor of Aran Islands, and Dorothy (or Anne), dau. and h. of [   ] Hall.
 MARRIED: [Aug. 1708] Dorothy (d.16 Aug.1745), dau. of Hon. Oliver Lambart.
 CHILDREN: Sir Nicholas, 2nd Bt, m. Caroline, dau. of Brig. Thomas Paget; Rev. Edward, m. [13 Jan. 1738] Catherine, dau. of Capt. James Price, wid. of John Savage of Portaferry, Co. Down;

Lambart, m. Elizabeth, dau. of John Rotton; Capt. Charles (RN), m. Anne dau. of [   ] Graves of Worcester.
 CAREER/OCCUPATION: Burgess of Carlingford c. 1714; Sheriff of Co. Down 1730.
 MILITARY: Dalton (q.v.) gives two relevant entries: (1) Edward Bailey, Lieutenant in Sir Robert Peyton's Regiment of Foot 10 June 1689; (2) Edward Bayly, Lieutenant in the Earl of Danby's (Volunteer) Regiment of Dragoons raised by the City of London, 16 July 1690.

POLITICAL ACTIVITY: He was not a very active MP. The only record of his activity is that he was nominated for a committee on May 1705. He was described in 1707 as having been an opponent of Ormonde's (Tory) administration: on 13 March 1707 Robert Johnson (1101) wrote to Ormonde describing Mr Bayly 'the member for Newry as the nephew of Mr Bagenal whose town it is', adding that 'He has never divided but it was always with them.' In 1711 he was noted as being in opposition (i.e. a Whig), but by 1713 he had become a Tory. However, in 1713 he was discreetly absent for the important division on the Speakership.

DIVISION LISTS:
 1713 (1) absent.

ESTATES/RESIDENCE: Mount Bagnall, Co. Louth; Plas-Newydd, Anglesey. Succeeded on the death in 1712 of his cousin, Nicholas Bagenal, to the estates in Anglesey and in Ireland. In 1779, Young reckoned Sir N. Bayley's rental at £2,000. In 1783, the Irish estate was thus described: 'The nature of the soil in general is by no means good, and an immense proportion so very bad, that, much as the English are improved in agriculture, there is a vast deal that would perplex an ingenious Englishman to know how to treat it.'

SOURCES: PRONI D/619/7/2, 32 and 33, D/619/3/5, 7–9; PRONI MIC/315/10/76 Blackwood pedigrees; Hayton thesis; GEC *B*; Burke *PB* (1903) pp. 42–3; Simms's cards; C. Dalton (ed.), *English Army Lists and Commission Registers, 1661–1714* (London, 1896), vol. 3 pp. 65, 135; *HMC Ormonde* new ser. vol. 8 p. 291; *Louth Arch. Soc. Jn.* (1912–15) pp. 273–83, H. Tempest (ed.), 'The Roll of the Sovereigns and Burgesses of Carlingford, 1706–1828'; PRONI T/1490/1 Anglesey Papers, Thomas Harrison, Newry, to Lord Paget, 25 July 1783; Young, *Tour in Ire.*, vol. 2 App. p. 83; *Delany Corr.* ser.1 vol. 2 pp. 323–5 [visit to Rev. Edward Baylis (*sic*)]; Parliamentary Lists, 1711 (3), 1713 (2).

0102 BEAMISH, Francis Bernard

MP for Rathcormack 1776–83

> b. 1751; d. 1805
> FAMILY/BACKGROUND: Eldest son of Capt. William
> Beamish RN and Alice, dau. of Maj. William
> North Ludlow Bernard of Castle Bernard, Co.
> Cork.
> MARRIED: Unmarried.
> EDUCATION: Middle Temple 1769; called to the
> Irish Bar 1775.
> CAREER/OCCUPATION: *Listed in Judges and
> Barristers 1789–1800 (f.).

POLITICAL ACTIVITY: He was returned for
Rathcormack by its new owner William Hull
Tonson (**1051**), who was trying to re-establish the
authority over the borough of the Lord of the
Manor of Rathcormack, which he had recently
purchased from James Barry (**0094**). In 1773 Hull
Tonson had inherited his father's (**2083**) banking
business in Cork, and he was now pursuing a
political career with a view to a peerage: to do this
he had to secure the borough. Beamish was a relative of Hull Tonson's wife, and the son of a Cork
alderman. He was called to the Irish Bar in 1775.
The 1777 Parliamentary List noted that he was:
'in point of ability I am informed moderate and
taken up this time to exclude Mr Devonshire
(**0627**) in the Borough' (Rathcormack).

He was a member of the Swords Election Committee, 6 December 1777. Swords was a
potwalloping borough and its elections tended to
be scenes of devastation and chaos. He supported
the 1778 Catholic Relief Act, 17 & 18 Geo. III,
c. 49, which *inter alia* allowed Catholics to hold
999-year leases. He obtained a pension of £300
from Lord Lieutenant Buckinghamshire. Beamish
was a firm government supporter until after 1780.
In 1782 the Parliamentary List noted that 'He is
at present out of his senses from the effects of
Mercury'; the 1783 list noted simply that he was
mad. Mercury was the conventional treatment for
venereal disease.

DIVISION LISTS:
> 1778 (2) voted for the Popery Bill.
> 1779 (2) voted for a six-months Loan Bill.
> 1780 (1) voted against Grattan's (**0895**)
> declaration of the Rights of Ireland.

1780 (2) voted against Yelverton's (**2268**)
motion to modify Poynings' Law.

ESTATES/RESIDENCE: Willsgrove, Co. Cork. He sold the
estate to Lord Bandon.

SOURCES: Ellis thesis; *King's Inns Admissions*; Cork MPs;
Almanacks; *FJ* 6–9 Dec. 1777; Fleetwood, *The History
of Medicine in Ireland*, p. 100; Parliamentary Lists, 1776
(1), (2), (3), 1771 (1), 1778 (1), 1780 (1), 1782 (1),
1783 (1).

BEAUCHAMP, Viscount: *see* **SEYMOUR-
CONWAY (INGRAM-SEYMOUR-
CONWAY)**
1896 Seymour-Conway (Ingram-Seymour-
Conway), Rt Hon. Francis (styled Viscount
Beauchamp 1750–93), 1st Earl of Yarmouth, 2nd
Marquess of Hertford, MP Lisburn 1761–8, Co.
Antrim 1768–76, [GB] Lostwithiel 1766–8,
Orford 1768–94

0103 BEAUCHAMP, John

MP for Old Leighlin 1695–9, 1713–14, 1715–
27–45; Thomastown 1703–13

> b. *ante* 1661; d. 1745
> FAMILY/BACKGROUND: Son of John Beauchamp of
> Killeigh, Co. Dublin.
> MARRIED: [1694] Catherine, dau. of Bartholomew
> Vigors, Bp of Ferns and Leighlin.
> CHILDREN: Bartholomew; Rev. Richard, m. [3
> May 1743] Juliana, dau. of Maurice Keating
> (**1133**); Benjamin, m. Anne [   ]; Vigors (d. yg);
> Margaret, m. (1) Caleb Barnes, (2) [1729] Henry
> Colclough; Martha, m. Rev. James Harvey of Co.
> Wexford; Eleanor, m. [1740] Walter Bagenal.
> CAREER/OCCUPATION: High Sheriff of Co. Carlow
> 1683; Free Burgess of New Ross 5 Dec. 1719 –
> 29 June 1731.
> MILITARY: Colonel 7 Oct. 1723.

POLITICAL ACTIVITY: In 1696 he signed the Association for the protection of William III in the
country. He was a professional soldier, which perhaps explains his being listed for only 22 committees during a parliamentary career of 50 years.

On 16 April 1701 he was one of the gentlemen of Co. Carlow who petitioned against the return and residence of Mark Baggot, 'a violent Papist', to that county, of which he had been 'titular High Sheriff' in 1689. In 1711 he was noted as a Court supporter and in general he supported the administration, particularly during the last years of Queen Anne, when he supported the Court over two important issues: the Dublin mayoralty and Sir Richard Levinge's (**1230**) candidature for the Speakership, in opposition to that of Alan Brodrick (**0237**). It was not surprising that in the 1713 election the administration thought the Borough of Thomastown 'well secured' but that it needed 'a good man for Leighlin'. However, Beauchamp had previously been returned for Old Leighlin, and was again returned in the general elections of 1713, 1715 and 1727.

As a soldier he may have followed the tradition of voting with the government, for he signed a County address in favour of the unpopular Chancellor, Sir Constantine Phipps, and was on the 1714–15 'black list of Tories'. However, given his anti-Catholic sentiments and the nature of his estates, he cannot have been anything other than a 'whimsical' Tory. In the financial instability of the early 1720s he was hostile to the idea of a national bank. By 1720 he was probably already 60 years of age and therefore excused committee service.

He brought in the heads of several bills to encourage the discovery of mines and minerals which do not appear to have come to fruition, although individual grants were given to various enterprises, especially those connected with coal. However, in 1727 he introduced 1 Geo. II, c. 8, 'an act to prevent inconveniences that may happen by Privilege of Parliament'. This stated that an MP could not be sued during the fortnight before or following parliament and that he enjoyed freedom from arrest for 40 days on either side of parliament meeting.

DIVISION LISTS:
1709 (1) spoke against a Money Bill.
1711 (1) voted for the Court on the Dublin mayoralty issue.
1713 (1) voted for Sir Richard Levinge (**1230**) for Speaker.

1721 (1) voted against a national bank.
1721 (2) voted against a national bank.

ESTATES/RESIDENCE: Ballyloughan, Co. Carlow. Purchased 379 acres in Co. Carlow from the Commissioners for Sale of Forfeited Estates in 1702–3. This was in addition to lands he had already been granted. In 1684 John Beauchamp was granted the lands of Lorum (232), Donganbegg (143), Ballynegon, etc. (40) Knockrillart (245), Ballyteigelea (163 and 29), Ballyloughan (437 and 157), making a total of 1,446 acres, all in the barony of Idrone. In 1704 John Beauchamp's estate – these lands plus Aghnabeg – contained 2,495 acres. In 1713 his income was calculated to be £350 p.a. but it must have been more.

In 1792 the estate of the then late John Beauchamp, apparently including all these lands plus Aghnabeg, contained 1,775 acres. This estate appears to have been purchased in 1792 by Henry Bruen (**0268**).

SOURCES: *CJ Ire.* (Bradley ed.) vol. 5 p. 525, 737, 744; PRONI T/1075/32 Canon Leslie's notes, McCracken thesis; Kilkenny MPs; J. H. Bernard (ed.), *The Register of St Patrick's, Dublin, 1677–1800* (Parish Register Society of Dublin, 1907) p. 29; *HMC Ormonde* new series vol. 8 p. 39; *JRSAI* vol. 21 (1892) p. 299, P. D. Vigors, 'Alphabetical List of Free Burgesses of New Ross 1658–1839'; NLI reps no 20; PRONI T/3411; Simms, *Williamite Confiscation*, p. 183; Parliamentary Lists, 1696 (1), 1711 (3), 1713 (1), (2), 1714 (1), 1714–15 (1).

BECTIVE, 2nd Earl of: *see* **TAYLOR** and **TAYLOUR**

2046 Taylor (*alias* Taylour), Rt Hon. Thomas, 1st Baron Headfort, Viscount Headfort, Earl of Bective, MP Kells 1747–60

2051 Taylour, Hon. Sir Thomas (styled Viscount Headfort 1766–95), 2nd Earl of Bective, 1st Marquess of Headfort, MP Kells 1776–83–90, Longford B. 1790–4, Co. Meath 1794–5

0104 BEECHER, Michael

MP for Baltimore 1713–14, 1715–26

b. 1673; d. (*post* 8 Mar.) 1726
FAMILY/BACKGROUND: Son of Thomas Beecher (**0105**) and Elizabeth, dau. of Maj. Henry Turner.

MARRIED: Peniel, dau. of [ ] Gates.
CHILDREN: ?Rev. Michael, m. Catherine French.
EDUCATION: School: Mr Robert Gurney; entered
TCD 9 May 1690, aged 17 years, BA 1695.
MILITARY: Honorary Lieutenant-Colonel.

POLITICAL ACTIVITY: Very little is known of this MP.
He inherited his father's (0105) estate of
Aghadown, Co. Cork on the latter's death in 1709,
but did not come in for his father's seat of Baltimore until the next general election. In 1713 he
was classed as a Tory but probably of the 'whimsical' variety. He was listed for a committee on 30
September 1717; little else is known of his activity in parliament.

ESTATES/RESIDENCE: Aghadown, Co. Cork. In 1713
Michael Beecher's income was reckoned to be £600 p.a.

SOURCES: PRONI T/559 vol. 8 p. 216, Burke, extract
pedigrees; PRONI T/3411; Simms' cards; *Alum. Dub.*;
G. F. Russell-Barker and A. H. Stenning (eds), *Record
of Old Westminsters: A Biographical List* (London, 1928);
Cork MPs; Eustace, *Abstracts of Wills*; *GM* Nov. 1759;
Ir. Gen. vol. 6 no 6 (Nov. 1985) pp. 814–23, R. Refausse,
'The Welply Will Abstracts in the Representative Church
Body Library, Dublin'; Parliamentary List, 1713 (2).

0105 BEECHER, Thomas

MP for Baltimore 1692–3, 1695–9, 1703–9

b. 1640; d. 1709
FAMILY/BACKGROUND: Son of Sir Henry Beecher.
MARRIED: Elizabeth, dau. of Maj. Henry Turner.
CHILDREN: Thomas; Edward; Michael (0104);
Henry; John; Lionel; Martha, m. Dillon
Newman of Newbury, Co. Cork; others (at least
7 sons and 2 dau.).
EDUCATION: School: Mr French, Baltimore;
entered TCD 2 June 1658, aged 18 years.
CAREER/OCCUPATION: Governor of the Island of
Inisherkin, near Baltimore, at 10 shillings a day
1 July 1692.
MILITARY: Ensign to Major Richard McGuire
c.1663–5 (left army by 1675); militia officer in
Co. Cork under Lord Orrery 1666; Colonel in
William III's army, said to have served as his aide-
de-camp at the Boyne and to have been presented
with a watch.

POLITICAL ACTIVITY: He was nominated for seven
committees between 1695 and 1698 but only one,

on 5 October 1703, in the 1703–13 parliament.
He voted for the resolutions against Lord Chancellor Porter, but in 1696 he signed the Association for the protection of William III in the country. On 20 April 1704 he petitioned Sir Richard
Cox (0507) to have two ships sent to guard the
Kerry coast, where there were increasing instances
of piracy. By 1706 he is noted as being 'against
the Court'. He died three years later.

ESTATES/RESIDENCE: Aghadown, Sherky and Castle
Mahowne, Co. Cork. In 1689 his estates were estimated
to be worth £898 p.a.
Pre-1686 Colonel Beecher bought the 2,967 acres,
barony of West Carbery, of Cape Clear Island, Monae,
Knocknaculine, Craig, Munnig, etc.

SOURCES: *Alum. Dub.*; Cork MPs; Eustace, *Abstracts of
Wills*; C. Dalton (ed.), *English Army Lists and Commission Registers, 1661–1714* (London, 1896) vol. 3 p. 283;
C. Dalton (ed.), *Irish Army Lists 1661–85* (London,
1907) p. 48; *HMC Ormonde*, new ser. vol. 8 p. 66;
Cork Hist. Soc. Jn. vol. I (1895) p. 387, D. Townshend,
'Notes on the Council Book of Clonakilty'; PRO C/
106/138 Pt 2, 'A brief state of the case as to reprised
land' n.d.; Parliamentary Lists, 1695 (1), 1696 (1), 1706
(1).

BELFAST, Earl of: *see* **CHICHESTER**
0394 Chichester, Rt Hon. George Augustus
(styled Viscount Chichester 1769–91), 1st Earl
of Belfast, 2nd Marquess of Donegall, MP
Carrickfergus 1798–9

BELFIELD, Viscount: *see* **ROCHFORT**
1800 Rochfort, Hon. George (styled Viscount
Belfield 1756–74), 2nd Earl of Belvidere, MP
Philipstown 1759–60, Co. Westmeath 1761–8–75

0106 BELL, Thomas

MP for Antrim B. 1703–13

> b. *ante* 1652; d. 16 Jan. 1718
> FAMILY/BACKGROUND: Son of [   ] Bell.
> MARRIED: [1705] Mary, dau. of William Knox of Co. Mayo.
> CHILDREN: ?
> CAREER/OCCUPATION: Merchant; Alderman of Dublin 1692–6, Mayor 1702.

POLITICAL ACTIVITY: He was a Presbyterian merchant. On 16 November 1692 a letter was intercepted by the Admiralty indicating that Thomas Bell was maintaining trading links with France, and on 26 November the Earl of Nottingham informed the Lord Lieutenant that Bell was to be prosecuted for trading with the enemy. Then on 5 August 1693, Nottingham requested that the Lords Justices approach Bell and offer him terms. His ships trading with St Malo and Brest were to be issued passes giving them free passage, and granting them indemnity on their return, as long as Nottingham was provided with any information on French preparations. His entry into parliament in 1703 may have been to protect his mercantile interests.

He was nominated for 18 committees during the 1703–13 parliament. This parliament met for the last time on 9 November 1711. Bell was definitely a member of the opposition from 1706, when he was noted as 'against the Court', and in 1711 he was still counted among the opposition. The Court correctly conjectured that he would not be returned for Antrim in the 1713 election. In fact he did not come into parliament again. He was probably quite an old man, as he may have been born some years before 1652.

ESTATES/RESIDENCE: Co. Antrim; Newmarket, Co. Dublin.

SOURCES: PRONI T/559 vol. 8 p. 277, Burke, extract pedigrees; Hayton thesis; *Cal. SP Dom. 1691–2* pp. 505, 512, *1693* p. 251, *1694–5* p. 388, *1695* p. 222, *1696* (London, 1913) p. 210; Simms' cards; Burke *LGI* (1904) p. 311; *The Ir. Builder* 1 Apr. 1887, 'St Audoen's Church, Corn Market: Its History from its Foundation to the Present Time' [says Alderman Thomas Bell was buried 17 July (? Jan.) 1718, see *Pue's Occurrences* 18 Jan. 1718]; Parliamentary Lists, 1706 (1), 1711 (3), 1713 (1).

0107 BELLASIS (*alias* BELASYSE or BELLASISE), Sir Henry

MP for Galway B. 1692–3; [GB] Morpeth 1695–8, 1700–1; Durham City 1701–8, 1710–15 Feb. 1712; St Michael 1713–15

> b. 1649; d. 16 Dec. 1717 aged 69 years
> HONOURS: Knight *c.* 1678–81.
> FAMILY/BACKGROUND: Second son of Sir Richard Belasyse of Potto, Yorkshire, and Ludworth, Co. Durham, and Margaret, dau. of William Lambton of Lambton.
> MARRIED: (1) [(lic. 3 Mar.) 1680] Dorothy, dau. of Tobias Jenkins, wid. of Robert Benson of Wrenthorpe, Yorkshire; (2) [(bond 23 Apr.) 1709] Fleetwood, dau. of Nicholas Shuttleworth of Forcett, Yorkshire.
> CHILDREN: (1) 1 s. *d.v.p.*, 2 dau. *d.v.p.* (2) 1 s.
> EDUCATION: School: Houghton; entered Cambridge (Christ's College) 29 Mar. 1666, matriculated 1667; Middle Temple 1 Apr. 1668.
> CAREER/OCCUPATION: Commissioner for inquiry into the state of the forces in Spain, Portugal and Italy 1711–12.
> MILITARY: Raised a company of musketeers for the service of the United Provinces 1674; served at the siege of Grave 1674, Maastricht 1676 and the Battle of St Denis 1678; Colonel of the regiment 1678; Captain, Engineer regiment in Dutch service (later the 6th Foot) 1675–Oct. 1676; Lieutenant-Colonel Oct. 1676–Mar. 1678; Colonel Mar. 1678–88; Colonel 22nd Foot 28 Sept. 1689–June 1701, 2nd Foot June 1701–3; Brigadier-General 1 Apr. 1689; Lieutenant-General 1694; Major 1690, Major-General of Foot 1692, Lieutenant-General 1695; Governor of Galway 1691–2, Berwick 1713–15.

POLITICAL ACTIVITY: A professional soldier of fortune who backed the right side. He sat only for the short parliament of 1692 and, apart from trying to benefit from forfeited estates, there is little evidence of any political activity in Ireland. On 26 January 1692 he was incorporated into the Company of the Royal Fisheries of Ireland; on 30 June 1693 he was incorporated into the Company for Digging and Working Mines in England, where his political and military future obviously lay.

His regiment was stationed at Galway before its intended departure for Flanders, 1694, where he took part in the Battle of Landen.

ADDITIONAL INFORMATION: He was in England with his regiment at the outbreak of the Monmouth rebellion in 1685. In 1687 he is reputed to have incurred the displeasure of the Prince of Orange and was forbidden at the Dutch Court. He had ceased to command one of the Holland Regiments, although not deprived of it until April 1688. It is possible that the story was circulated to protect his Orangeist activities while in England. He was certainly back in favour when he took an active part in the Northern rising under Lord Danby in Yorkshire, forcing Sir John Reresby, a Jacobite, to surrender in December 1688. He also made a loan to the Crown of £7,000 on the security of the 12d aid. He was at Dundalk with the Duke of Schomberg, September 1689, and took part in the siege of Limerick, 1690. Around this time he fought a duel with Colonel Richard Leveson and received 'a large wound' in the thigh.

On 19 August 1691 he successfully negotiated the surrender of the Island and Fort of Boffin, the articles of which were presented by petition before the Lord Lieutenant on 15 March 1692. The warrant for ratification was issued on 20 April 1692. In consideration of his handling of the embarkation of troops, the Commissioners of the Treasury were requested by the queen to pay him £200 on 28 June 1692. On 1 July 1692, he received a pass to go to Portsmouth 'whereupon he was to take charge of several individuals in their Majesties Special Service'. He went to France with the rank of major-general, under the Duke of Leinster in 1692. He succeeded to Tollemache's Regiment in 1694 and carried William III's message of congratulation to the Elector of Bavaria on the birth of his son. However, suspicion followed him. For instance, on 7 August 1695 a Mr Franks, an alehouse keeper, denied before the Irish Lords Justices that Belasyse had ever been to Mass, or taken oaths to King James.

In 1695 he successfully repulsed Marshal Villeroy at Nieuport. He took part in the court martial of the Danish General Ellenberg in which the latter was sentenced to death. His regiment returned from Flanders, early 1696. *En route* they were captured by the French and totally disarmed. In 1702 he took part in a projected landing at Cadiz: 'Belasyse argued that the best place of landing was El Puerto de Santa Maria across the bay, from where they could march round to Cadiz. His secret motive for this plan was reported to have been that he had heard treasure from the Spanish Galleons was hidden there. When he landed with his troops, Belasyse found that bullion had been taken further inland, which so enraged him that, according to eye-witnesses, he led the plunder of the town starting with the churches. His troops broke into cellars "plentifully stored with rich and strong wines" and then proceeded to ransack the town and rape the women, including nuns in local convents. The material damage was "modestly computed at three millions sterling". Directly he heard of what had happened Ormonde, his commanding officer, placed him under arrest. Count Wrotislaw, the Imperial envoy, made the strongest representations regarding these outrages, urging severe punishment for Belasyse. On arrival in England, Belasyse walked off at Deal claiming parliamentary privilege. He could not be tried for his conduct in Spain, so he was tried for breaking his arrest, was dishonourably discharged from the army and lost his regiment. The Queen's Speech on 21 Oct. publicly condemned the great "disorders and abuses committed at St Mary's bay".' However, despite this and Swift's condemnation of him as a 'most covetous cur', Belasyse was sent back to Spain in 1710. It was said that '*Il étoit le plus ancien officier sous le duc d'Ormond au siège de Cadiz. Il fut cassé pour avoir pillé a Port Ste Marie. Il fut rétabli par le dernier ministère, fait gouverneur de Berwick et un des trois commissaires qui allèrent en Italie, en Espagne, et en Portugal pour y examiner nos comptes publics.*'

ESTATES/RESIDENCE: Co. Galway and forfeited estates in Kerry; Brancepeth Castle, Durham; Pottoe, Co. York. He competed unsuccessfully with Colonel Gustavus Hamilton (0924) for the custodiam – a grant by the Exchequer, for three years, of lands in the possession of the Crown – of Roger O'Shaughnessy's estate.

SOURCES: Information from Dr Eveline Cruickshanks and Dr David Hayton of the *History of Parliament*; HP 1715–54 vol. 1 p. 182 n. 42; *Cal. SP Dom. 1691–2* pp. 112, 175, 180, 236, 247, 341, 346, 414, 519, 531, *1693* pp. 33, 166, 207, 298, *1694–5* pp. 33, 72, 88, 234, 249, 252, 342, 388, 399, 402, *1695* pp. 40, 98, 165, 281, 352, *1696* pp. 1, 58, 77, 141, 146, 148, 404, 478; *Alum. Cantab.*; *Middle Temple Admissions* vol. 1 p.

176; Simms' cards; J. L. Chester (ed.), *The Marriage, Baptismal and Burial Registers of the Collegiate Church or Abbey of St Peter, Westminster* (London, 1876) pp. 239, 290 [he was bur. 21 Dec. 1713 (?1717)]; C. Dalton (ed.), *English Army Lists and Commission Registers, 1661–1714* (London, 1892), vol. 1 p. 51 [the entries relating to Sir Henry Belasyse and Dalton's annotations are rather confused in this volume], *ibid.* (London, 1894) vol. 2 p. 228, *ibid.* (London, 1896) vol. 3 pp. 7, 99, 110 (London, 1898) vol. 4 pp. 4, 50, 91, 217, 246; J. J. Howard (ed.), *Miscellanea Genealogica et Heraldica* vol. 1 new ser. (1874) p. 123.

0108 BELLEW, Thomas

MP for Mullingar 1713–14, 1715–27

b. *ante* 1668; d. 12 June 1746
FAMILY/BACKGROUND: Son of [   ] Bellew.
MARRIED: Ann [   ].
CHILDREN: Catherine, m. Henry Whyte of Pitchfordstown, Co. Kildare.
CAREER/OCCUPATION: Military: Captain in Brigadier Stewart's Regiment of Foot *ante* 1693; Captain in Viscount Charlemont's Regiment of Foot 12 June 1696; half-pay 1698; Major in Colonel Meredith's Regiment of Foot 13 Feb. 1702; Lieutenant-Colonel at Blenheim 13 Aug. 1704; was at the siege of Palames, Catalonia, and served on two campaigns at sea; Lieutenant-Colonel in the Dublin Militia Dragoons in 1715, Colonel 1726.

POLITICAL ACTIVITY: The 1713–14 parliament was in session for one month, 25 November to 25 December 1713; during this time he was nominated for six committees. He was a Tory and voted on the Court side for Sir Richard Levinge (**1230**) as Speaker. In 1714–15 he was on the 'black list' of Tories. However, he was again returned for Mullingar in 1715 and was listed for 17 committees in the parliament of George I.

Bellew continued a convinced Tory. In 1719 he was considered a likely opponent to the repeal of the Test Clause. He voted for a national bank in 1721, and in 1724 he subscribed to a declaration of high sheriffs, justices of the peace, Grand Jury, nobility, clergy, gentlemen and freeholders of Co. Dublin against Wood's Halfpence.

He had a reputation as a duellist, and on 24 December 1701 he duelled with Major-General Stewart (**2011**) – both men had had their right hands disabled as a result of war wounds, and Bellew had served under Stewart. On this occasion Stewart fired from two yards and blew Bellew's hat off. Bellew threw his pistol away, saying he did not wish to kill Stewart.

DIVISION LISTS:
1713 (1) voted for Sir Richard Levinge (**1230**) for Speaker.
1721 (1) voted for a national bank.
1721 (2) voted for a national bank.

ESTATES/RESIDENCE: In 1702–3 he had 189 acres of forfeited land in Co. Meath, and he purchased 198 acres in Co. Dublin from the Commissioners for Sale of Forfeited Estates. In 1714–15 his income was estimated at £200 p.a.

SOURCES: *CJ Ire.* (Bradley ed.) vol. 4 p. 319; PRONI T/559 vol. 8 p. 337, Burke, extract pedigrees; RCBL T34, Extracts from the Parish Registers of St Andrew's, Dublin; Hayton thesis; *Cal. SP Dom. 1693* p. 206, *1696* p. 47; Lodge *P;* Simms' cards; Simms, *Williamite Confiscation*, pp. 177, 183; C. Dalton (ed.), *English Army Lists and Commission Registers, 1661–1714* (London, 1898) vol. 4 pp. 77, 156; *The Dublin Gazette* 14 Oct. 1724; Parliamentary Lists, 1713 (2), 1714–15 (1), 1719 (2).

0109 BELLINGHAM, Henry

MP for Dundalk 1703–13–14

b. 1676; d. (15 Mar.) 1740/1
FAMILY/BACKGROUND: Only son of Thomas Bellingham (**0111**) and Abigail, dau. of William Handcock.
MARRIED: Mary, dau. and co-h. of Thomas Moore.
CHILDREN: Henry (**0110**); Alan, m. [1738] Alice, dau. and co-h. of Rev. Hans Montgomery of Grey Abbey, Co. Down; Elizabeth, m. Hon John Fortesque.
EDUCATION: School: Mr Lodge, Preston, Lancashire; entered TCD 16 May 1692, aged 16 years.
CAREER/OCCUPATION: Admitted Freeman of Ardee 1700; Collector of Customs and Excise for Kinsale 1729.

POLITICAL ACTIVITY: He was a Whig and, under Queen Anne, an opponent of the Court. In the Parliamentary Lists of 1706 he was noted as against the Court; in 1711 he was still in opposition and in 1713 classified definitely as a Whig. He was nominated for 12 committees in the first parliament of Queen Anne, 1703–13, and for one in the short parliament of 1713.

On 16 September 1717 the Commons appointed a committee to consider his petition to be brought to the favourable attention of the Lord Lieutenant because of the 'particular services and sufferings of his father, Thomas (0111)' – Castle Bellingham was destroyed by the Jacobite army. The House approved the recommendation on 18 September 1717.

ESTATES/RESIDENCE: Castle Bellingham, Co. Louth.

SOURCES: *CJ Ire.* (Bradley ed.) vol. 4 pp. 317–23; PRONI T2842/2 Ardee Corporation Minutes; Hayton thesis; Burke *PB* (1903) p. 140; J. O'Hart, *Ir. Pedigrees* (Dublin, 1892), vol. 2 p. 43; *Almanacks*; Simms' cards; *DJ* 22 Mar. 1740; NLI reps no 131; Parliamentary Lists 1706 (1), 1711 (3), 1713 (2).

0110 BELLINGHAM, Henry

MP for Co. Louth 1741–55

b. *ante* 1713; d. 18 May 1755
FAMILY/BACKGROUND: Elder son of Henry Bellingham (0109) and Mary, dau. of Thomas Moore.
MARRIED: [2 Mar. 1739] Margaret, dau. of Hugh Henry (1005).
CHILDREN: *d.s.p.*
CAREER/OCCUPATION: Burgess of Ardee, High Sheriff of Co. Louth 1734.

POLITICAL ACTIVITY: He was listed for eight committees between his return in the by-election of 1741 and his death in 1755. He was a government supporter, voting against the expulsion of Arthur Jones-Nevill (1125) and for the controversial 1753 Money Bill. An indication of the problem of law and order in mid-eighteenth-century Ireland is that in company with Charles Coote (0479) he was 'robbed of several valuable things' by 'five persons well armed with pistols' in the vicinity of St Paul's Church, Dublin.

DIVISION LISTS:
1749 (1) absent, sick.
1753 (1) voted against the expulsion of

Arthur Jones-Nevill (1125).
1753 (2) voted for the Money Bill.

ESTATES/RESIDENCE: Castle Bellingham, Co. Louth. Succeeded by his brother Alan.

SOURCES: PRONI D/302; PRONI T/2842/2 Ardee Corporation Minutes; NAI Parish Registers of St Mary's Dublin [says son Hugh Henry (bapt. 10 Sept. 1740)]; McCracken thesis; *Memorials of the Dead* [says (? erroneously) his wife's name is Jane]; *GM* May 1755; *Pue's Occurrences* 19 Jan. 1734; *DJ* 17–20 May 1755; *The Dublin Newsletter* 23 Jan. 1742.

0111 BELLINGHAM, Thomas

MP for Co. Louth 1692–3, 1695–9, 1703–13

b. 1646; d. 15 Sept. 1721
FAMILY/BACKGROUND: Son of Henry Bellingham and Lucy, dau. of William Denning.
MARRIED: [1678] Abigail, dau. of William Handcock of Twyford, Co. Westmeath.
CHILDREN: o. s. Henry (0109).
EDUCATION: School: Dr Bayly, then Mr Golborne, St Patrick's, Dublin; entered TCD 16 Feb. 1661, aged 15 years, BA 1664, MA 1692.
CAREER/OCCUPATION: High Sheriff of Co. Louth 1684, 1691.
MILITARY: A Colonel in the Williamite army and acted as guide and aide-de-camp to William from Dundalk to the Boyne, entertaining him at Castle Bellingham on the eve of the battle – in retaliation James II's army destroyed Castle Bellingham with fire.

POLITICAL ACTIVITY: He kept a diary giving a vivid account of the 1689–90 Williamite campaign in Ireland. It begins in 1688 when he is living in Preston in England. In December he wrote: 'We had a report of the King's death [James II], but, God be praised, it proved false.' Possibly this indicates a revulsion against regicide, as in August the following year he left Preston for Carrickfergus where he joined the Williamite forces under the Duke of Schomberg.

His diary also reveals the continuance of the Puritan tradition and a strongly religious side to his character. He is indignant when prayers are offered incorrectly and has critical notes on preachers and their sermons. However, alongside these religious entries are more secular notes on bowling, shooting, hunting, cockfighting, bull-baiting, horse-racing, card playing and nights of 'hard' drinking, giving a rounded picture of his class and age.

He took an active part in parliament, being listed for ten committees (two of them on 11 October 1695) in the second parliament of William III – 27 August 1695 to 26 January 1699. He voted against the resolutions critical of Lord Chancellor Porter, and signed the Association for the protection of William III in the country. In 1706 he was a supporter of the Court, but by 1711 he had moved over to the opposition. During this parliament he was nominated for 15 committees.

ESTATES/RESIDENCE: Castle Bellingham, Co. Louth. Purchased in 1702–3 from the Commissioners for Sale of Forfeited Estates 55 acres in Co. Louth. In 14 Chas II (1663), Henry Bellingham, his father, was granted a market at Garlandstown; the manors of Athboy and Ratoath, and the lands of Carackstown, were still Sir Richard Bellingham's in 1694. But in 1763 there was House of Lords litigation over them. Bellingham had bought them from Lord Gormanston in 1666, and Gormanston's hopes of getting them back were frustrated by the Williamite war. Athboy and Ratoath had a rental of £521 in 1688.

SOURCES: PRONI D/302; Burke *PB* (1903) p. 140; J. O'Hart, *Ir. Pedigrees* (Dublin, 1892), vol. 2 p. 43 [says his father was married to a Miss Sibthorpe]; Simms' cards; NLI EC 7890; *JRSAI* vol. 38 (1908) p. 307, 'Proceedings'; *JRSAI* vol. 39 (1909) pp. 207, 208, 209, 'Notices of Books' [says he is not called Colonel in any document of the period, only Captain]; Simms, *Williamite Confiscation*, p. 183; Parliamentary Lists, 1695 (1), 1696 (1), 1706 (1), 1711 (3).

BELLISLE, Viscount: *see* **GORE-ST GEORGE**
0881 Gore-St George, Sir Ralph, 1st Baron Gore, Viscount Bellisle, Earl of Ross, MP Co. Donegal 1747–60, 1761–4

BELLOMONT, Earl of: *see* **COOTE**
0480 Coote, Rt Hon. Charles, 5th Baron Coote of Coloony, 1st Earl of Bellomont, MP Co. Cavan 1761–6

BELMORE, Baron, Viscount and Earl: *see* **LOWRY-CORRY**
1269 Lowry-Corry, Armar, 1st Baron Belmore, Viscount Belmore, Earl Belmore, MP Co. Tyrone 1768–76–81
1270 Lowry-Corry, Hon. Somerset, styled Viscount Corry 1797–1802, 2nd Earl of Belmore, MP Co. Tyrone 1797–1800, [UK] 1801–2

BELVIDERE, Earl of: *see* **ROCHFORT**
1807 Rochfort, Rt Hon. Robert, 1st Baron Belfield, Viscount Belfield, Earl of Belvidere, MP Co. Westmeath 1731–8
1800 Rochfort, Hon. George (styled Viscount Belfield 1756–74), 2nd Earl of Belvidere, MP Philipstown 1759–60, Co. Westmeath 1761–8–75

0112 BENNETT, John

MP for Castlemartyr 1775–6, 1783–7 [r. Charleville 1783; n.d.e. Dungarvan 1777]

> b. *c.* 1731; d. 25 Dec. 1791
> FAMILY/BACKGROUND: Eldest son of George Bennett of Cork City and Elizabeth Buchanan.
> MARRIED: [13 Jan. 1776] Jane, dau. of Jonathan Loffet (?Lovett) of Kingswell, Co. Tipperary.
> CHILDREN: John; George (Lincoln's Inn 16 Nov. 1797); Susan; Jane, m. Richard Pennefather.
> EDUCATION: Entered TCD 10 Oct. 1748; Middle Temple 25 July 1753; called to the Irish Bar 17 Nov. 1758.
> CAREER/OCCUPATION: *Commissioner for taking Affidavits for Newport 1760; Fourth Justice of the King's Bench 10 May 1787 (at his death he was Second Justice); *listed in Judges and Barristers 1789–91; Freeman of Fethard (Tipperary) 1782; Justice of Assize for Connaught, Lent 1788, Summer 1789; Leinster Summer 1791.
> MILITARY: Colonel of the Cork Inniskilleners.

POLITICAL ACTIVITY: An ambitious Cork lawyer, he sat for about five years spread over two parliaments, 1775–6 and 1783–5. Originally he was returned by Lord Shannon (**0213**) for Castlemartyr at a by-election in 1775. He supported the government, as did his patron, Lord Shannon. However, there was a general election in 1776 and he stood for Dungarvan. Subsequently he was declared not duly elected. Nevertheless, in 1777, while still sitting for Dungarvan, he voted against Grattan's (**0895**) motion for retrenchment, thereby illustrating the significance of not duly elected MPs whose return was later overturned. Grattan had decided that, given the financial difficulties of the government, retrenchment was a good topic to launch his oratorical career as a (then) potential opposition leader.

In 1783 described as 'a lawyer of eminence', Bennett ensured his return by being returned for both the Shannon boroughs of Castlemartyr and Charleville. He elected to sit for the former. His aim was the Bench, which he achieved in 1787 when he was made a Justice of King's Bench. While in parliament he voted against Flood's (**0762**) motion for parliamentary reform and a motion to set up a committee on a Reform Bill.

DIVISION LISTS:

1777 (1) voted against Grattan's (**0895**) motion for retrenchment.

1783 (1) voted against Flood's (**0762**) motion for parliamentary reform.

1784 (1) voted against a committee on the Reform Bill.

1785 (1) absent.

ESTATES/RESIDENCE: Co. Cork; Merrion Street, Dublin.

SOURCES: PRONI T/559 vol. 9 p. 20, Burke, extract pedigrees; PRONI MIC/465/1 R. Ffolliott, *Biographical Notices, 1756–1827* [his wife may have remarried Cole Maxwell jnr in 1794]; NAI, Index to Marriage Licence Bonds of Cork and Ross Dioceses [his parents' marriage licence is dated 1731]; PRONI MIC/474 Irish Volunteers; Ellis thesis; *Alum. Dub.*; *WHM* (1792), p. 480; *King's Inns Admissions; Lincoln's Inn Records* (Lincoln's Inn, 1896) vol. 1 p. 561; *Middle Temple Admissions* vol. 1 p. 346; Ball, *Judges; Ir. Gen.* vol. 4 no 4 (1971) p. 316, W. G. Skehan, 'Extracts from the Corporation of Fethard, Tipperary Co.'; *Ir. Gen.* vol. 5 no 3 (1976) p. 339, H. F. Morris, 'Ramsey's Waterford Chronicle, 1776' [the *Waterford Herald* reported his death 3 Jan. 1792 but this is corrected in *ibid.* vol. 6 no 2 (1981) p. 154 where H. F. Morris, 'The Waterford Herald 1792' says he died 25 Dec. 1791, but that his

death was reported in the issue of 3 Jan. 1792]; *Almanacks; DJ* 29–31 Dec. 1791 (2nd Justice); *FJ* 9–12 Feb. 1788, 2–4 July 1789, 26–8 July 1791; Parliamentary Lists, 1776 (1), (2), (3), 1777 (1), 1783 (2), 1784 (1), (2), (3), 1785 (1), (2), (3), 1788 (1).

0113 BERESFORD, Rt Hon. George de la Poer

MP for Co. Waterford 1757–60; Coleraine 1761–3

b. 8 Jan. 1735; d. 3 Dec. 1800

HONOURS: PC, sworn 19 Sept. 1763–4; Knight of St Patrick Mar. 1783.

PEERAGES: Suc. as 2nd Earl of Tyrone 1763; cr. Baron Tyrone [GB] 21 Aug. 1786, Marquess of Waterford 16 Aug. 1789.

FAMILY/BACKGROUND: Son of Marcus Beresford, 1st Earl of Tyrone (**0118**), and Catherine, only dau. and h. of James Power, 3rd Earl of Tyrone.

MARRIED: [18 Apr. 1769] Elizabeth, only dau. and h. of Henry Monck (**1430**).

CHILDREN: Marcus (died aged 12); Rt Hon. Henry, 2nd Marquess of Waterford (**0114**); John (Abp of Armagh, Primate of All Ireland); Lieut.-Gen. George Thomas, m. Harriet dau. of [   ] Schiltz; Isabella Anne, m. [1812] Sir John William Head Brydges; Catherine; Anne; Elizabeth Louisa, m. (1) Maj.-Gen. Sir Denis Pack, (2) Lieut.-Gen. Sir Thomas Reynell Bt. Illegitimate: Adm. Sir John Poo (Beresford), Bt (b. 1766; d. 1844); William Carr (Beresford) (b. 1768; d. 1854; cr. Viscount Beresford).

EDUCATION: School: Dr Hewetson, Kilkenny; entered TCD 15 Jan. 1752, BA 1754.

CAREER/OCCUPATION: Freeman of Fethard (Tipperary) 1746; Freeman of Limavady 1760; High Sheriff of Co. Waterford 1762; *Trustee of the Linen Board for Leinster 1763–d.; *Commissioner of the Tillage Act for Munster 1764–84; Governor of Co. Waterford and city 1765–d.; Custos Rot. for Co. Waterford 7 Oct. 1766, *for Co. Tyrone 1769, 1773, 1777; *Governor of the Charitable Loan Society 1778–d.; *Governor of the Charitable Musical Society 1780; Freeholder of Dublin City 1797.

MILITARY: General of Volunteers 1784; Colonel of Co. Waterford Militia 1793; Captain in Upperthird Cavalry 1796.

POLITICAL ACTIVITY: During his time in the House of Commons he was an active parliamentarian, being nominated for 26 committees between 1757 and 1759. A contemporary description of Lord

Tyrone was that 'He was ... a genial, down-to-earth, unintelligent man, so full of the right sort of Irish pride that when he was given a British barony in 1787 he chose the title "Tyrone" and, when told that the territorial designation of the title must at least be British, insisted on being "Lord Tyrone of Haverfordwest", because that was the British town nearest to county Waterford, where his residence and the bulk of his property were situated.'

The Beresfords' opportunity came with the downfall of the Ponsonbys during Lord Townshend's viceroyalty. Townshend required aristocratic parliamentary leaders to replace the long-established Ponsonby connection. Lord Tyrone had been originally against the augmentation of the army in 1768, but 'It was thought prudent to make him alter his Way of thinking by giving his Brother a good Living.' Having come over to the government, Tyrone, or more probably his brothers, realised the potential benefits of the new order. Moreover, as early as 1769, the Earl of Tyrone wished to be elevated to the rank of marquess. Lord Lieutenant Townshend wrote to Lord Weymouth to state his case, enclosing Lord Tyrone's letter which said that 'In consequence of the position he took up re the augmentation the whole artillery of those persons who might think they had a right to assist their friends, or to punish him for the part he had acted had been levelled as he foresaw against his two friends who had been elected for the borough of Swords.'

Although unsuccessful in 1769, from this time Lord Tyrone worked ceaselessly to acquire a marquessate, which he eventually achieved in 1789. In the meantime many personal and family favours came his way from the various administrations that he assiduously supported. By 1775 he was a Privy Counsellor, Governor of Waterford County and a Trustee of the Linen Board for Leinster in addition to various other public and social positions. His clergyman brother had a living of £600 p.a.; he was eventually to become Archbishop of Tuam and Baron Decies. Lord Tyrone had been given the nomination to other church preferments worth £200 p.a. In addition he had been given the nomination to various Revenue posts including the Distributor of Stamps for Co. Waterford and two Hearth Money Collections. Two years later, in 1777, he had received further patronage – his brother had livings valued at £1,400 and he had the nomination to the Revenue position of Surveyor of Killybegs and to an ensigncy in the army. However, he was still looking for his marquessate and a bishopric for his brother.

The real strength of the family lay in his other brother, John (0115), a 'man of business' who was gradually working his way up the Revenue Board. By 1782 things had further improved – his brother had become Bishop of Ossory, worth £2,100 p.a. and, because of the parliamentary borough attached to the see, this bishopric was usually considered as a step to further ecclesiastical preferment. He himself was considered to be a man of sense and judgement, attached to government and even able to exert some influence over his brothers-in-law Cobbe (0426) and Cary (0362), while he returned his brother John, now First Commissioner of the Revenue, for Co. Waterford and his relative Mr Annesley (0048) for a seat that he controlled in Coleraine. After the 1784 election his party was estimated to comprise a possible six members: his brother with a salary of £2,000 p.a. as First Commissioner of the Revenue and a sinecure of £1,000 which he held with one of his sons, Marcus Beresford (0119), Richard Annesley, Collector of Dublin, estimated at £700 p.a., Arthur Wolfe (2243), ambitious for high legal office, and Beresford's more independent brothers-in-law Thomas Cobbe and Edward Cary.

The actual interest of the marquess was probably quite small, but that of his friends and relations was extensive and sustained by a united family, some of whom had administrative ability that no government could afford to ignore. In the 1790s the family group was increased as more of his brothers' sons entered parliament. The marquess was personally popular with George III, and the close friendship between himself and his brother John ensured that he would be listened to by British administrators such as John Robinson, George Rose and William Eden (0681). In 1790 a patriotic opinion declared that 'Considering the humbleness of his means in every point of view, no man has been more successful, in his applications to Government for favours to himself and his brothers than he.' Inevitably the Patriots blamed him for engineering Lord Fitzwilliam's downfall, but probably he did nothing more than present family solidarity with his brother. By 1798 he had openly declared his long-held opinion in favour of the Union, in which he was supported by his family, with the notable exception of his nephew, John Claudius Beresford (**0117**), the MP for Dublin city which, apart from John Claudius' own reservations, was very hostile to the Union.

DIVISION LISTS:
1757 (1) voted against the resolutions on pensions.

ADDITIONAL INFORMATION: *A subscriber to the Public Assembly Rooms, 1787.

ESTATES/RESIDENCE: Curraghmore, Co. Waterford; St Catherine's Grove, Swords, Co. Dublin. In *c.* 1769 he had a rental of some £8,000 p.a., subject to debts of some £40,000. In 1775 George Ponsonby valued Lord Tyrone's Waterford estate at £13,000 p.a., and in 1777 Lord Tyrone's Wicklow rental was stated to be £1,518 and his Co. Londonderry rental was calculated to be £2,964, but it is uncertain whether that included all his Londonderry property, as later calculations refer only to Freemore. His wife, who was heiress-apparent (at least as far as personal estate was concerned) had a portion of £8,000 and expectations, after the death of both her parents, of £32,000 more (only half of it actually guaranteed by previous settlements). In the end, her inheritance, including her original portion, seems to have amounted to little less than £110,000 plus some property of unspecified value. Most of this fortune was earmarked for younger children, although her husband and she seem to have received £24,000 of it in the acceptable form of 'presents'. However, by the time of the 1st Marquess's death the family estates were burdened with a capital debt of £130,000 and annual interest charges of £7,000.
In 1674 Lady Beresford, widow of 1st baronet, purchased lands comprising the greater part of the parishes of Aghanloo, Bovevagh, Balteagh, and parts of Drumachose and Dungiven. These, with the rest of Lord Waterford's Co. Londonderry interests, an aggregate of 40,000 acres, were sold in 1872. In 1789 Lord Waterford paid a quit rent to the Irish Society formerly payable by the Haberdashers' Company, and in 1793 Lord Tyrone (*sic* – Waterford) was a tenant of the Irish Society for various lands. J. C. Beresford (the Irish Society's agent and Waterford's nephew) was asked by the Irish Society to use his influence to get Waterford to take

out a new lease on terms that the Irish Society wanted to make standard among its tenants.
Some idea of the Waterford property in North Ulster is given by the fact that in 1871, the then Lord Waterford advertised 7,533 acres in the barony of Coleraine (all fee simple, except for one perpetuity under the Mercers), 30,647 in the barony of Keenaght (all held in fee farm of 1674 under the Irish Society), and property in and around Coleraine at a rental of *c.* £100 a year. 'The Bovagh estate' comprised most of the rural property in the barony of Coleraine, and was two miles from Kilrea. In 1844, Lord Waterford's estate of the manor of Freemore had a rental of £9,546 (Artikelly etc.), manor of Lizard (Bovagh etc.) £2,434, and manor of Coleraine (presumably part only) £648.
In 35 Chas II, Lord Tyrone (of the Poer family) was granted a market at Donard.

SOURCES: PRONI D/302; PRONI MIC/474 Irish Volunteers; RCBL P45/2/3, Parish Registers of St Peter's, Dublin; RCBL P/80/1/1, Parish Registers of St Thomas, Dublin; McCracken thesis; GEC *P*; Burke *PB* (1903) p. 1555; *Index to Irish Privy Counsellors, 1711–1910*; Johnston, *Gt B. & Ire.*, pp. 163, 245; A. P. W. Malcomson, *The Pursuit of the Heiress*, pp. 16, 21; *Proc. RIA* vol. 88 C no 4 (Dublin, 1988) p. 63, Malcomson, 'A Lost Natural Leader: John James Hamilton, First Marquess of Abercorn (1756–1818)'; *Ir. Gen.* vol. 4 no 4 (1971) p. 317, W. G. Skehan, 'Extracts from the Minutes of the Corporation of Fethard, Co. Tipperary'; *JRSAI* vol. 41 (1911) p. 168, E. M. F.-G. Boyle, 'Records of the Town of Limavady, 1609–1804'; *Waterford Arch. Soc. Jn.* vol. 16 (1913) p. 50, T. Sadleir (ed.), 'The County of Waterford 1775'; *Almanacks, FJ* 25–7 Apr. 1793, 12 Nov. 1796, 11 Apr. 1797; *BNL* 9 Dec. 1800; *DJ* 9 Dec. 1800; NLI vol. 142, 12 Dec. 1871; rentals 1844–55, Waterford Papers, C/2/1–6; D/20 4/13/10/4/5 [Calculations of Lord Tyrone's rental (11 Nov. 1777)]; Co. Londonderry rentals 1844–55, Curraghmore papers, C/2/1–6 and /19 of his income and debts (May 1778); Smith, *Irish Society*, p. 83; Parliamentary Lists, 1775 (1), 1777 (1), 1782 (1), 1783 (2), 1784 (1), (3), 1785 (1), (2), (3), (4), 1787 (1), 1788 (1), 1790 (1), 1791 (1), 1793 (1), 1794 (2), 1798 (1), 1799 (1), (2), (3).

0114 BERESFORD, Rt Hon. Henry de la Poer

MP for Co. Londonderry 1790–7–1800 [r. Coleraine 1797]

b. 23 May 1772; d. 16 July 1826 at Carmarthen
HONOURS: PC, sworn 16 June 1801; Knight of St Patrick 14 Mar. 1806.

PEERAGES: Styled Lord La Poer 1783–9, Earl of Tyrone 1789–1800; suc. as 3rd Earl of Tyrone and 2nd Marquess of Waterford 1800.

FAMILY/BACKGROUND: Son of Rt Hon. George De La Poer Beresford (**0113**), 2nd Earl of Tyrone and 1st Marquess of Waterford, and Elizabeth, dau. and h. of Henry Monck (**1430**).

MARRIED: [1805] Susanna (d. 7 June 1827), only dau. and h. of George Carpenter, 2nd Earl of Tyrconnell.

CHILDREN: George De La Poer (died aged 14 years); Henry (b. 26 Apr. 1811; *d.s.p.* 29 Mar. 1859), 3rd Marquess of Waterford, m. [1842] Louisa (*d.s.p.* 12 May 1891), dau. and co-h. of Rt Hon. Charles Stuart, 1st Baron Stuart de Rothesay; William (1st Life Guards) (b. 2 Dec. 1812; d. 18 Oct. 1850); Rev. John (b. 1814; d. 6 Nov. 1866), 4th Marquess of Waterford, m. [1843] Christiana, dau. of Charles Powell Leslie (**1224**); James (army officer) (b. 16 Oct. 1816; d. 1841); Sarah (d. 13 Oct. 1884), m. [1828] Henry John Talbot, 18th Earl of Shrewsbury, Waterford and Talbot.

EDUCATION: School: Eton 1785–9; entered Oxford (Christ Church) 19 May 1790, aged 18 years, MA 7 Dec. 1792.

CAREER/OCCUPATION: Governor and Custos Rot. Co. Waterford 1801–d.

MILITARY: Colonel of the Wexford Militia. The disarming of Queen's County in 1798 was carried out with the minimum of disturbance. Most of the troops according to Wellesley-Pole (**2216**) acted humanely and with discipline; the exception was a detachment commanded by Beresford, who 'would have been very ready to destroy the whole country indiscriminately had we suffered it'.

POLITICAL ACTIVITY: Although he was returned for Co. Londonderry in 1790, he did not come of age until May 1793 (this is interesting in view of the comments on Lord Castlereagh's (**2009**, born 1769) return for Co. Down in the same election). In parliament he followed the family line. His most prominent appearance in the House of Commons was in January 1799, when he moved the address of thanks in reply to the King's Speech advocating the Union. In a speech, allegedly written in his hat, he carefully tried to defuse the strong anti-Union feeling by pointing out that 'the Address does not pledge the House in its decision upon that great and important question which now so much occupies and interests the public mind. As to the measure of a Union between Great Britain

and Ireland, I at present can give no opinion; it would be to prejudge and anticipate that which is of so much weight, nor can I fairly decide upon it until it shall come regularly in detail before the House.' This attempt at conciliating the already hostile anti-Unionists was unsuccessful. He was immediately and totally opposed by the formidable Sir John Parnell (**1633**), quickly followed by George Ponsonby (**1699**) and Sir Laurence Parsons (**1636**), who moved and seconded a classic Irish parliamentary motion supporting the Empire while maintaining the 'birthright' of the Irish people to a resident and independent legislature. Lord Tyrone voted for the Union in both 1799 and 1800.

DIVISION LISTS:

1790 (2) absent – minor.

1795 (2) voted against Catholic Emancipation.

1799 (1) voted for the Union – a Colonel of Militia.

ADDITIONAL INFORMATION: He was nicknamed 'Tone' by Lord Shannon (**0213**).

ESTATES/RESIDENCE: Curraghmore, Co. Waterford; Tyrone House, Co. Dublin. Through his wife the Waterford family acquired the Ford Castle and Seaton Sluice estate, Northumberland and one seat for the parliamentary borough of Berwick-upon-Tweed.

SOURCES: PRONI T/3166/1B Hartnell Papers; RCBL P90/1/1, Parish Registers of St Thomas, Dublin [bapt. 15 June 1772]; O'Neill thesis; GEC *P*; Burke *PB* (1903) p. 1555; *Index to Irish Privy Counsellors, 1711–1910*; *Alum. Oxon.*; R. A. Austen-Leigh (ed.), *The Eton College Register, 1753–90*, 3 vols (Eton, 1921); E. Hewitt (ed.), *Lord Shannon's Letters to his Son*, p. xxii; Malcomson, *The Pursuit of the Heiress*, p. 35; Bolton, *The Passing of the Ir. Act of Union*, p. 106; Lecky, *Ire.*, vol. 5 p. 220; T. Pakenham, *The Year of Liberty* (London, 1978), p. 76; *BNL* 23 Dec. 1800; Parliamentary Lists, 1791 (1), 1793 (1), 1794 (2), 1799 (2), (3), 1800 (2), (3).

0115 BERESFORD, Rt Hon. John

MP for Co. Waterford 1761–8–76–83–90–7–1800 [r. Coleraine 1768, 1783, and 1790], [UK] 1801–5 Nov. 1805

b. 14 Mar. 1738; d. 5 Nov. 1805 of ?pneumonia complicated by gout

HONOURS: PC, sworn 9 June 1768, [GB] 6 Sept. 1786.

FAMILY/BACKGROUND: Son of Sir Marcus Beresford, 1st Earl of Tyrone (0118), and Catherine, dau. and h. of James Power, 3rd Earl of Tyrone.

MARRIED: (1) [15 Nov. 1760] Annette Constantia (d. 26 Oct.1770), dau. of Gen. Comte de Ligondes; (2) [4 June 1774] Barbara (d. 29 May 1795), dau. of Sir William Montgomery, 1st Bt (1448).

CHILDREN: (1) Marcus (0119); George (b. 19 July 1765; d. 15 Oct. 1841), Bp of Kilmore and Ardagh, m. [1794] Frances, dau. of Gervase Parker Bushe (0310); John Claudius (0117); Rev. Charles Cobbe, m. [22 Nov. 1795] Amelia (d. 14 Mar 1839), dau. of Sir William Montgomery, 1st Bt (1448); Catherine (d. 7 Jan. 1836), m. Rt Hon. Henry Theophilus Clements (0412); Anne Constantia, m. (1) [1790] Robert Uniacke (2122), (2) [1805] Robert Doyne of Wells, Co. Wexford; Jane (d. 1836), m. [1788] Rt Hon. Sir George FitzGerald Hill (1017).

(2) James Hamilton (RN) (b. 18 Feb. 1782; drowned 7 Dec. 1806); Henry Barre (b. 25 Sept. 1784; d. 15 Dec. 1837), m. [1812] Eliza (d. 1831), dau. of John Baily of Gloucestershire; William Hamilton (b. 1788; d. 16 Sept. 1865); Hannah; Frances Honoria, m. [1807] James Whyte of Barnstaple; Elizabeth (d. 17 Jan. 1860); Anna, m. (1) Charles Gardiner, (2) Charles Edward Stuart Comte d'Albanie; Clara (d. 4 Apr. 1862), m. [1813] Rev. James Spencer Knox (d. 1 Mar. 1862); David Jones; Barbara; Ann Marie.

EDUCATION: School: Kilkenny, Rev. Dr Pack; entered TCD 1754; Lincoln's Inn 12 Nov. 1756, BA 1758; Middle Temple 1760; called to the Irish Bar 1761.

CAREER/OCCUPATION: Commissioner of the Revenue May 1770–9 (patent, 1 May 1770, 3 Feb. 1772); 1st Revenue Commissioner 1780–1802; Treasury Commissioner Dec. 1793; *Lord Commissioner of the Treasury 1794; Member of the Board of Trade 1802; Governor of St Patrick's Hospital 4 May 1763–88; Deputy Governor of Co. Waterford 1763; Freeman of Limavady 1763; Freeman of Dublin City 1797; Taster of Wines, Port of Dublin 1772–d.; Trustee for the Linen Board for Connaught 1783–1800 (f.); *Commissioner for Paving the Streets of Dublin 1778–1800 (f.); *Director for Paving, Cleansing and Lighting the Streets of Dublin 1789–1800 (f.); *on Corporation for Preserving and Improving the Port of Dublin 1787–8; *listed in Judges and Barristers 1789–1800 (f.); Freedom of the Guild of Merchants and Freedom of Dublin Jan. 1761.

MILITARY: ?Colonel of the Dungarvan Volunteers.

POLITICAL ACTIVITY: John Beresford came into parliament in 1761. At the same time he embarked on a moderately successful professional practice at the Bar; some of his critics considered that he retained throughout his career 'a good deal of the habits and manners of the Four courts'. Otherwise his parliamentary career appears to have been efficient but low-key. In December 1765 he was appointed to the committee to inquire into the public works necessary to the nation and to distribute £17,000 for the encouragement of certain manufactures. He came to prominence during the Townshend 'revolution in government' which led to the fall of the Ponsonbys and the permanent residence of the viceroy. Beresford then appears to have had a choice: either standing for Speaker, with the government's backing, or becoming a Commissioner of the Revenue. Townshend did not intend to recreate Ponsonby's position by uniting the two offices in the one person. Beresford chose the Revenue Board, and his administrative talents were quickly revealed. He remained loyal to the administration of the day for the rest of his parliamentary career. His elevation resulted in a conflict between the Beresford and Ponsonby families that continued for the remainder of the Irish parliament and was indisputably an element in the Fitzwilliam episode of the mid-1790s.

In 1782 Beresford described himself to his friend Isaac Barré as 'neither a fool nor a scoundrel'. With his legal training and administrative abilities, he was typical of a late eighteenth-century 'man of business' and a forerunner of the modern civil servant. Contemporary English examples – and men with whom he was on friendly terms – were John Robinson, George Rose and William Eden (0681), whom he got to know intimately when he was Chief Secretary in Ireland. In 1783 a contemporary described him as 'very knowing, able and industrious in the duties of his station. Seldom speaks in Parliament but in the line of his office'; and in 1789 a hostile reporter considered that 'As a public Speaker his voice is clear, distinct and sufficiently strong … his management of it is really judicious, as he constantly preserves to it that evenness of tenour adapted to his elocution and never allows it to deviate into any faulty extreme. His language is neither marked by elegance nor ornament … and at times both confused and obscure and his speeches are mostly distinguished by a uniformed flow of unimpassioned declamation that can never arouse, though it may sometimes instruct. Of the character of an orator he, indeed, appears not emulous and … the regulations and details of the customs and excise, admit not … of any elevated strains of eloquence or excursive flights of imagination … his replies to his opponents are constantly tart and acrimonious … he labours in office with indefatigable assiduity. The only character of which he seems ambitious is that of being a man of business and that he undoubtedly is.'

Beresford provided a focus for the administrative meritocracy of late eighteenth-century Ireland. He was influenced by the economic thinking of Adam Smith. After the retirement of John Bourke (0192) in 1779 he was First Commissioner of the Revenue and as such presided over the Revenue Board, the central government department with tentacles throughout the country. Politically he was part of a group that included John Scott (1891) and Arthur Wolfe (2243), both Attorneys General and Chief Justices of the King's Bench, while Lord Chancellor Fitzgibbon's (0749) sister, Elizabeth, was married to his episcopal brother, William Beresford.

In autumn 1770 Lord Lieutenant Townshend and Beresford lost their wives within six weeks of one another. They subsequently married two sisters, Anne and Barbara Montgomery. The families remained close, and in 1787 Townshend asked Beresford to use his good offices with Pitt (whom Beresford probably got to know through Eden and over the commercial negotiations) to expedite his marquessate. His influence, which sprang from this mixed basis of family, ability and friendship, was undoubtedly the cause of much envy and resentment but no one ever questioned his integrity or his capacity for hard work. He was an early exponent of the doctrine of economical reform – efficiency and economy in government departments. He played a leading part in the abortive commercial negotiations.

In 1779 Lord Lieutenant Buckinghamshire

wished to appoint either John Beresford or John Foster (0805) as Chief Secretary. The British government was reluctant to endorse someone with definite Irish connections and Beresford agreed, writing to John Robinson that 'I therefore do freely advise you not to suffer his Excellency to nominate an Irish Secretary; for if you do you will have a man more attentive to Irish popularity than to the interest of the English Government'. During the War of American Independence he headed a party of politicians who were attached to the administration of Great Britain, with which they had an ongoing private correspondence, much to the natural chagrin of the viceroy, Lord Buckinghamshire. The party accepted the 'parliamentary lead of the reigning Chief Secretary, regardless of their private views'. He was among the many who fought a duel with Sir Edward Newenham (1535), who challenged him in 1779 because he disapproved of his political stance at that time.

When the Duke of Portland, the Lord Lieutenant appointed by the Rockingham Whigs, arrived in 1782 he made extensive changes (some of which were subsequently reversed), removing Attorney General Scott, Prime Sergeant Browne (0256, the brother of Lord Altamont), Lees (a prominent behind-the-scenes figure in the secretariat) and Copinger (0491), Counsel to the Revenue Commissioners. However, before Chief Secretary Fitzpatrick (0758) had even arrived in Ireland, Beresford's friend (and Rockingham and Shelburne's friend) Isaac Barré, the new Treasurer to the Navy, had written to him that Beresford 'is one of the most efficient officers of the crown there. His knowledge and integrity have recommended him to many of your predecessors.' On this occasion Beresford wrote to Townshend 'I know not what may be my fate; I do not expect however, that I shall be disturbed … I am not weak in myself and I stand too well in the public opinion to be ill-treated'; he added that since becoming First Commissioner he had saved the public £72,459 in the financial year 1781–2 and, he estimated, a further £90,000 since.

Portland's viceroyalty was short, but in retrospect it provided a preview of Fitzwilliam's much-interpreted viceroyalty in 1795. During Portland and Northington's administrations Beresford kept a low profile. However, after the Pitt administration appointed the Duke of Rutland viceroy, Chief Secretary Orde (**1594**) soon realised that however highly principled Portland and Northington's friends were, they were unreliable supporters of the administration. After Northington's departure many of Portland's dismissals were nullified. For instance, Scott became Chief Justice of the King's Bench, and in April 1784 Beresford wrote to Robinson hoping that Scott had been recommended to a peerage with the Chief Justiceship, 'for they must have him there [in the House of Lords] and they know it'. Subsequently Beresford assisted Orde with the abortive commercial negotiations of 1784–5. Along with Foster he acted as the Dublin administration's envoy to London, and Orde warned Pitt against the 'jealousies' between the two. Their difference in outlook was illustrated by their contradictory interpretations of the 1660 Navigation Act. This statute established the mercantalist system and prohibited non-British merchants from re-exporting colonial produce into Great Britain. Foster took a convoluted interpretation favouring the Irish merchants, while Beresford adhered to the conventional and more straightforward interpretation.

Beresford opened the face-to-face discussions, and in the course of them became friendly with Pitt, Rose and various other English 'men of business'. He had been worried that he might become the scapegoat if the negotiations failed. In fact the reverse happened, and his knowledge and organisation gained him long-term credit. Pitt was convinced that in return for a final settlement of the commercial differences between England and Ireland, Ireland should make a contribution to the common resources used for the defence of their common trade. Despite its history of dissension, Pitt selected the Hereditary Revenue as the most likely fund to provide this contribution. Both Beresford and Foster tried to convince him that this would ensure that the scheme would be stillborn, and so, despite various attempts at compromise, it ultimately proved. Government opposition in both England and Ireland declared that Ireland was being required to barter her newly acquired legislative independence for her commerce. Beresford thought, probably unjustly given Irish sensitivities, that Orde could have managed

parliament to better effect; Scott and Fitzgibbon agreed with him. Given the impasse between British and Irish views, the ultimate result appears to have been inevitable.

Apart from the commercial negotiations Beresford's career in the 1780s was relatively uneventful. Both his brother and his brother-in-law received their marquessates and his eldest son joined him in the House of Commons. Much of his energies was devoted to overseeing the building of the Customs House and planning the wide streets for which Dublin is famous. The increasing tempo of the 1790s brought changes, particularly over the Catholic question, in which he followed the leadership of his friend John Fitzgibbon, from 1790 Lord Chancellor. Meanwhile the country's financial state and the demands upon it gave increasing cause for concern, especially as social unrest required ever larger numbers of troops, who had to be paid.

Beresford was a trusted adviser of Lord Lieutenant Westmorland in the early 1790s. Then, to meet British political exigencies, Earl Fitzwilliam was appointed Lord Lieutenant in 1795. Like his mentor, Portland, Fitzwilliam envisaged a clean sweep of the existing administration in Ireland and a restoration of the Ponsonby family, now represented by the brothers William (**1709**) and George (**1699**) and allied to Henry Grattan (**0895**). The responsibility for the Fitzwilliam débâcle must lie with the Duke of Portland, for he knew Fitzwilliam's personality and his almost complete lack of political experience. Nevertheless, Portland, who had insisted on his appointment as part of the Portland–Pitt coalition, realised too late his unsuitability. The cabinet then attempted to confine him to rigid guidelines. Fitzwilliam appears to have considered that these were advisory only, and that as soon as he set foot in Ireland he could disregard them: probably the Ponsonby brothers persuaded him that a *fait accompli* would be accepted. When the British government realised his intentions it tried to stop him, but the coalition was fragile and Fitzwilliam was Rockingham's nephew and heir. He was married to Lady Charlotte Ponsonby (cousin to William and George Ponsonby). Within a week of his arrival he sent Denis Bowes Daly (**0571**) to tell Beresford to retire or be dismissed. Beresford refused and

Fitzwilliam, without any consultation with London, then attempted to dismiss him. This was beyond his powers, as Beresford was appointed by the Lords of the Treasury in London and could only be dismissed by them.

The Castle Under-Secretaries Sackville Hamilton (0945) and Edward Cooke (0468) were also dismissed. Fitzwilliam then foreshadowed his intention to dismiss the Attorney General, Arthur Wolfe, and the Chancellor, John Fitzgibbon; at the same time he announced his intention to introduce full Catholic Emancipation – possibly the most delicate issue in Irish politics. All this was done virtually immediately he arrived, entirely on the advice of his associates – he did not have time for personal investigation – and without any consultation with London. Beresford promptly appealed to London. Pitt, the First Lord of the Treasury, was dumbfounded and believed that there must be some mistake because, apart from anything else, 'It would be an open breach of a most solemn promise.' The coalition had barely settled down, the war was going badly and the last thing the government needed was an unpredictable viceroy in an already disturbed Ireland. Fitzwilliam was recalled. Portland, who was Home Secretary, wrote that regardless of the outcome of his various actual and intended dismissals, 'The cause of government abstractly considered requires that you should not continue to administer that of Ireland.'

After Fitzwilliam's return to England, Beresford challenged him to a duel for impugning his integrity. Fitzwilliam had written an 'open' letter to Lord Carlisle in which he said that Beresford was 'a person under universal and heavy suspicions, subject to opprobrium and unpopularity attendant on mal-administration and much imputed malversation'. Fitzwilliam had been unable to make any specific charges against any of the people he dismissed, and fell back on vague rumours and hearsay. These unproven accusations were certainly unjust and, given the open nature of Irish society, almost certainly untrue. Beresford's formal challenge to Fitzwilliam is interesting at a time when duelling was beginning to decline. It looks backwards to the code for such encounters: Beresford points out that Fitzwilliam has made these nebulous accusations 'to a gentleman by birth your equal, and ... of reputation as unsullied as

your own ... there is no charge, however monstrous, of which the idea is not here conveyed, and yet there is none to which the paragraph points directly, so as to afford an opportunity for vindication ... you will render to me and to my character that justice which one man of honour has a right to expect from another.' The magistrates were informed and the duel averted.

From his correspondence Beresford emerges as a devoted family man, and he obviously enjoyed domestic life. Both of his wives were noted beauties. In 1760 Mrs Delany wrote to her sister that 'Mlle Le Gondez [sic] ... is engaged to a son of Lord Tyrone's, and they are to be married when he has finished his studies at the Temple. His mother, who has a great estate, settles fifteen hundred a year on him at his marriage. Mlle has no fortune; a near relation of Lady Rawdon's, of a considerable family, bred a Roman Catholic, and was going into a convent sore against her will. When Lord and Lady Rawdon were abroad they rescued her with the consent of her parents, and on their promise not to endeavour to change her religion; and as they had no fortune, they were glad to put her into such good hands; last year Mlle Le Gondez renounced the Romanish religion and came into our church. They say it was the Archbishop of Dublin that made her a convert. Lord and Lady Rawdon were in no way accessory to it.' It is perhaps worth noting that his second wife, of whom he was very fond, died in May 1795. Her health had been failing in the preceding months (which were marked by his altercation with Lord Lieutenant Fitzwilliam), and her death was the reason why the intended duel was not due to be held until the end of June.

Beresford continued in office until his retirement in 1802, when he received a pension of £2,000 p.a., granted for a long life in the public service. After the Union he entered the parliament of the United Kingdom where, as a senior Irish statesman, he remained politically influential until his death in 1805. He is a transitional figure, modern in his approach to the administration and business of government, but he belonged to an older age in his extensive use of the patronage traditionally attached to the Revenue Board. Personal salaries were often augmented by a sinecure (he was Taster of Wines during pleasure with reversion to his sons) and long service then as now merited a pension; this became more established as the century drew to a close. In 1777 it was noted that during Lord Townshend's administration many employments in the Revenue had been given to his friends, while Lord Harcourt had given to his recommendation '1 Coast Surveyor, 1 Deputy Surveyor, 1 Carriage Land Officer, 2 Walking Officers, 1 Gatekeeper, 1 Coast Officer, 10 Supernumerary Gaugers, 23 Tidewaiters, 17 Boatmen and 1 Hearth Money Collection'. However, there is no evidence of his requesting a peerage for himself or his immediate family, although his influence was behind his brother's marquessate and his other brother's archbishopric and peerage.

As a Commissioner for Wide Streets and the guiding influence behind the new Customs House, he is possibly more than any other man responsible for the wide streets and elegant public buildings that came to adorn late eighteenth-century Dublin. He persuaded the architect James Gandon to design the Customs House and subsequently Gandon worked on other public buildings, such as the completion of the Four Courts and pillared portico of the House of Lords, which was added to the Parliament House in the 1780s.

He supported the Union, saying that he loved both his native country and Great Britain. At the same time he was very conscious of the financial bankruptcy of the country and of many of her leading citizens: for instance, on 6 February 1799 he wrote to Auckland explaining the causes of the initial failure of the Union and pointing out that 'As to the boroughs many of the proprietors are very poor, and have lived by the sale of them.' He foresaw the ultimate need for massive financial subsidies (although he could not have foreseen the collapse of land returns and prices following the Napoleonic War). As First Revenue Commissioner he advised government on the fiscal aspects of the Union. In the UK parliament he took little part in debate, although he supported the Dublin Improvement Grant in 1801–2 and the linen trade in 1802, and defended Irish retail duties in 1802. He reverted to his favourite role as adviser behind the scenes. In politics he remained a Pittite, disliking Addington's vacillatory Irish policy.

DIVISION LISTS:

1768 (1) voted for army augmentation.

1771 (1) voted for Lord Townshend as Lord Lieutenant – a placeman and his lady a pensioner.

1771 (2) voted against Sir Lucius O'Brien's (**1558**) motion for retrenchment – 'a Commissioner'.

1772 (2) voted against a Short Revenue Bill.

1773 (1) voted for the Absentee Tax.

1773 (2) voted against an untaxed press.

1774 (1) voted for the Stamp Bill.

1774 (2) voted for Catholic relief.

1775 (1) voted against the pro-American amendment to the Speech from the Throne.

1777 (1) voted against Grattan's (**0895**) motion for retrenchment.

1777 (2) teller for the Trade Embargo.

1778 (2) voted for the Popery Bill.

1779 (1) voted for new taxes.

1779 (2) voted against a six-months Loan Bill.

1780 (1) voted against Grattan's declaration of the Rights of Ireland.

1780 (2) voted against Yelverton's (**2268**) motion to modify Poynings' Law.

1780 (3) voted against the Tenantry Bill.

1780 (4) voted for the Perpetual Mutiny Bill.

1783 (1) voted against Flood's (**0762**) motion for parliamentary reform.

1784 (1) voted against a committee on the Reform Bill – a Commissioner.

1785 (1) voted for the Commercial Propositions.

1789 (1) voted against a regency.

1790 (1) voted against Grattan's motion for reducing the influence of the Crown.

1790 (2) voted for Foster (**0805**) on the election of a Speaker.

1798 (1) voted against Sir Laurence Parsons' (**1636**) motion for an investigation into 'the present discontents'.

1799 (1) voted for the Union – Privy Councillor in both kingdoms, 1st Commissioner of the Revenue and Deputy Governor of Waterford Co.

1800 (1) voted for the Union.

ADDITIONAL INFORMATION: A member of the RDS from 1765. Henry Flood (0762), the husband of Lady Frances Beresford, was Beresford's brother-in-law.

ESTATES/RESIDENCE: Abbeyville, Co. Dublin, built by Gandon; Walworth, Co. Londonderry. On 24 June 1747 the 1st Earl of Tyrone (0118) leased from the Fishmongers the manor of Walworth for 61 years (no lives mentioned), in consideration of the surrender of the previous lease of 1704 to General Frederick Hamilton (0920) deceased (he married Jane Beresford, daughter of Sir Randal Beresford, and died in 1732), a 'fine' of £6,000, and annual rent of £400.

In 1775 George Ponsonby wrote that he had 'no estate in the County [of Waterford], except a small freehold given by his brother'. What probably happened is that the 1st Earl of Tyrone left the Fishmongers lease to John Beresford, not to the 2nd Earl, as in 1806 the Fishmongers' property was held by the heirs of the late Rt Hon. John Beresford. Electorally it undoubtedly produced votes, though, apparently, in combination with the Haberdashers, only 300 at the 1806 general election.

SOURCES: *Beresford Correspondence* (1770–1804) 2 vols esp. vol. II pp. 111–13, 210; PRONI MIC/474 Irish Volunteers; RCBL P80/1/1, Parish Registers of St Thomas, Dublin [says Thomas Cobbe son of Rt Hon. John Beresford and Ann his wife bapt. 18 Jan. 1771]; O'Neill thesis; Burke *PB* (1903) pp. 1554–5; *DNB*; *IMC King's Inns Admissions*; *Index to Irish Privy Counsellors, 1711–1910*; *The Records of the Honourable Society of Lincoln's Inn* (Lincoln's Inn, 1896) vol. I p. 446; *The Register of the Parish of St Peter and St Kevin, 1669–1761* (Parish Register Society of Dublin, 1911) p. 335; J. Kelly, *Prelude to Union* (Cork, 1992), pp. 85–6, 92, 169–70, 195; McDowell, *Ir. public opinion, 1750–1800*, pp. 29, 117, 130; Llandover, *Delany Corr.*, vol. 3 pp. 587–8; B. De Breffny and Rosemary Ffolliott, *The Houses of Ireland* (Dublin, 1975), p. 168; P. and B. Rowan (antiquarian booksellers), *The Eighteenth Century, An Irish Perspective* (Belfast, 1986) no 80; *HP 1794–1820*; Johnston, *Gt B. & Ire.*, pp. 43–4, 71, 82, 236, 265; J. Kelly, *'That Damn'd Thing Called Honour': Duelling in Ireland 1570–1860* (Cork, 1995) pp. 132–3, 206, 208; E. Kelleher, *List of Members of the Dublin Society, 1731–1800* (Dublin, 1982); *JRSAI* vol. 41 (1911) p. 168, E. M. F.-G. Boyle, 'Records of the Town of Limavady, 1609–1804'; *Waterford Arch. Soc. Jn.* vol. 16 (1913) p. 50, T. U. Sadleir (ed.), 'The County of Waterford 1775'; *Almanacks*; *BNL* 27 Dec. 1765; *DJ* 13–17 Jan. 1761, 7–10 May 1763; *FJ* 24–7 Feb. 1787, 11 Apr. 1797; *UJA* xvi p. 56, M. Given, 'Parliamentary Representation of Ulster'; 24 June 1747; PRONI MIC/9B/11 Printed state of the poll, 3–4 Dec. 1806; PRONI D/

1449/8 Lenox-Conyngham Papers; Parliamentary Lists, 1769 (1), 1772 (2), 1773 (1), (2), 1774 (1), 1775 (1), 1776 (1), (2), (3), 1777 (1), 1778 (1), 1780 (1), 1782 (1), 1783 (1), (2), 1784 (1), (2), (3), (4), 1787 (1), 1788 (1), 1789 (1), (2), 1790 (1), 1791 (1), 1793 (1), 1794 (1), (2), 1799 (1), (2), (3), 1800 (1), (3).

0116 (HORSLEY-) BERESFORD, Hon. John

MP for Coleraine 1797–1800

b. 20 Jan. 1774; d. 1 Mar. 1855

PEERAGES: Suc. as 2nd Baron Decies 1819; Rep. Peer 1821.

FAMILY/BACKGROUND: Son of William Beresford, 1st Baron Decies, Abp of Tuam, and Elizabeth, dau. of John FitzGibbon (0748). Assumed additional surname of Horsley on his marriage in 1810.

MARRIED: [1810] Charlotte Philadelphia, only dau. and h. of Robert Horsley of Bolam, Northumberland.

CHILDREN: William Robert John, 3rd Baron Decies, m. [1860] Catherine Anne, dau. of William Dent of Northumberland; Georgina Catherine, m. (1) [1831] William Watson of North Seaton, Northumberland, (2) [1845] Henry Edward Brown; Louisa Elizabeth, m. [1834] Rt Hon. Ernest Augustus Charles Brudenell-Bruce, 3rd Marquess of Ailesbury; Caroline Agnes, m. (1) [1836] Rt Hon. James Graham, 5th Duke of Montrose, (2) [1876] William Stuart Stirling Crawford of Lanark.

EDUCATION: Entered TCD 21 Oct. 1789, aged 15 years; Cambridge (Emmanuel College) 15 Feb. 1791, BA 1795; Lincoln's Inn 29 Jan. 1795; called to the Irish Bar 1797, MA 1809.

CAREER/OCCUPATION: Purse Bearer to Lord Chancellor; took Holy Orders, sometime Rector of Tuam.

POLITICAL ACTIVITY: Known as 'tall Beresford', he was returned by his uncle, the Marquess of Waterford (0113), for Coleraine. Lord Shannon (0213) reported that he behaved with some ferocity in 1797 when he was a member of the Dublin Yeomanry. During the three years he was in parliament he followed the family line and supported the Union. At the Union, he received £91 1s 3d compensation for the loss of his office as Purse Bearer to his uncle, the Lord Chancellor. Lord Shannon appeared to think that he lost £700 p.a. by his uncle, the Chancellor's, death in February 1802 as his purse-bearer, but this may have been gossip or there may have been a fee component. Trained for the law, he subsequently embarked on an ecclesiastical career and finally succeeded his father as 2nd Baron Decies.

DIVISION LISTS:

1799 (1) voted for the Union – Pursebearer to the Chancellor.
1800 (1) voted for the Union.

ESTATES/RESIDENCE: St Stephen's Green, Dublin.

SOURCES: PRONI T/3166/1B Hartnell notes; O'Neill thesis; GEC *P*; Burke *PB* (1903) p. 430 [says he was born 20 Jan. 1773]; *IMC King's Inns Admissions, Alum. Cantab.* [says he was born 1773 and died 1865]; *Lincoln's Inn Records* vol. I p. 553; E. Hewitt (ed.), *Lord Shannon's Letters to his Son* (PRONI 1982) pp. 49, 216; *Ir. Gen.* vol. 1 no 10 (1941) p. 294, W. Clare, 'Irish Compensations and Pensions'; Parliamentary Lists, 1799 (2), (3), 1800 (3).

0117 BERESFORD, John Claudius

MP for Swords 1790–7; Dublin city 1797–1800 [r. Coleraine 1790]; [UK] Dublin city 1801–Mar. 1804; Co. Waterford 6 Jan. 1806 – June 1811

b. 23 Oct. 1766; d. 20 July 1846.
FAMILY/BACKGROUND: Son of Rt Hon. John Beresford (0115) and his first wife Annette Constantia, dau. of Gen. Comte de Ligondes.
MARRIED: [3 Mar. 1795] Elizabeth McKenzie, dau. of Archibald Menzies of Culdares, Perth.
CHILDREN: John Claudius, m. [1836] Catherine, dau. of Lieut. William Cuddy (69th Regiment); Constantia Anne, m. [1819] Thomas Walker of Yorkshire; Catherine Charlotte, m. Henry Moore Cairnes of Dublin; Georgina Frances.
EDUCATION: School: Dr Stokes; entered TCD 1783, BA 1787, MA 1832.
CAREER/OCCUPATION: Banker and partner in a bank with Mr Wood-Mason; Free Merchant of the City of Dublin 1797; Registrar General of Tobacco 1784 – 26 Jan 1799 (resigned); Taster of Wines, Dublin Port, 1798–1800, Inspector General of Exports and Imports 1796 – 25 Jan. 1799 (resigned); Storekeeper for the Inland Department 1783–1802; General Agent of the Irish Society 17 Dec. 1789 –1837; Trustee of the

Linen Board 1802; Governor of the Foundling Hospital and Workhouse; Alderman of Dublin 1808; Lord Mayor of Dublin 1814; Commissioner of Wide Streets; Governor of Steevens' Hospital.
MILITARY: Captain in the County of Dublin Cavalry 1796. He was very unpopular during the 1798 rebellion due to the reported activities of the Corps of Yeomen he had raised: suspect persons were alleged to have been savagely flogged at his Riding House in Marlborough Street, Dublin, in order to extort confessions (the outside of the riding house was daubed with the slogan 'Mangling done here *gratis* by Beresford and Co.'). In response to the excesses of his yeomanry the rebels burned his banknotes in an attempt to ruin him. Certainly he appears to have been unable to control his troops, and probably shared commercial Dublin's dread of civil unrest.

POLITICAL ACTIVITY: As his father (0115) was First Commissioner of the Revenue, it was thought that he owed his return for Swords to the influence of the revenue officials in that notorious potwalloping borough. A Dublin banker, he took a prominent part in the political life of the city. From 1795 he was a member of the Dublin district of the Association for the protection of Property and the Constitution, and in 1797 he received a vote of thanks from the Guild of Merchants for his efforts in securing the withdrawal of the Coal Bill in April 1797. In that year the election results of the Corporation of Skinners and Glovers were: J. C. Beresford, 39 votes; Arthur Wolfe (2243), 36; Colonel H. Gore Sankey, 20; Edward Bradstreet, 3; William Smith 1; Mr Leeson, 0.

Beresford's politics appear to have confused the opposition, which in the 1798 Parliamentary List declared that 'Although the most inveterate enemy of the *United Irishmen*, he with the same inveteracy opposes the Union and it is remarkable that he is the only one of the family adverse to the measure. He is intemperate in his *politics*, though unimpassioned in *manner*. He expressed a wish for the late rebellion, in order to have an opportunity of showing the world that it might be quelled – *in two days*. His opposition to the Union may possibly arise from deference to his constituents, who are known to be hostile to this measure. He represents the city of Dublin.'

In July 1798 he was appointed by ballot to the

House of Commons Secret Committee, receiving 38 votes to his father's 93. Partly from his constituency and partly from inclination, he was not an automatic government supporter. In December 1798 he wrote to Castlereagh that as a result of a meeting of the aldermen of Skinners' Alley and having taken soundings from the Orangemen of Dublin, he believed that the citizens of Dublin were ten to one against the Union. Furthermore he felt himself bound by the opinions of his constituents and his own convictions to oppose the measure. He was, however, content to try to maintain 'good humour between the two countries' while the question was being debated. His father, although disappointed, agreed with his stand and his resignation of government office as Inspector General of Imports and Exports. On the day that he resigned, 25 January 1799, his father wrote to his old friend Lord Auckland that 'My son John has resigned his office; this cannot be pleasant to me, but I think he is right to do so.' This was an indication of the emergence of the idea of political consistency. Beresford felt that not only had he to support his constituents but when he supported government it would not be to save his job. In the same month he seconded motions of William Digges La Touche that were framed as the resolutions of the Bankers and Merchants against the Union.

Prior to his resignation Cornwallis had written to Portland that Beresford 'has been very hostile' to the Union: 'his dismissal seemed desirable'. However, in order not to be seen to force the hand of parliament, Cornwallis drew back, saying that 'There seemed an objection to a very early exercise of Ministerial authority on the inferior servants of the Crown.' Beresford's hostility to the Union, however, did not lead to his joining the Ponsonby faction in declared opposition to the government, and he voted against Sir Lawrence Parsons' (**1636**) motion in 1798. He was General Secretary of Orange Lodges, 1799–1800. Lord Shannon (**0213**) nicknamed him 'Appius'.

On his return to the Imperial parliament he was reckoned a government supporter, and on 12 and 18 March 1801 he defended the Irish Martial Law Bill. In 1802 he spoke on the Dublin Paving Bill and in support of Irish linen, and in 1803 against the repeal of the Irish retail duties. On 2 December 1803 he supported the Irish Martial Law Bill, and five days later spoke exonerating the Irish government from blame for Emmet's rising the previous July. In March 1804, after being placed on the Irish Currency Committee – he was already a member of the Finance Committee – he resigned his seat and did not come in again until he succeeded his late father for Co. Waterford. To him now fell the mantle of the old rivalry between the Beresfords and the Ponsonbys as an Irish scene was transferred to the British House of Commons. Financial difficulties led to the resignation of his seat in June 1811. However, as Lord Mayor of Dublin in 1814 he displayed 'a princely hospitality' and remained 'joyous, frank and entertaining', but withdrew from public life.

DIVISION LISTS:

> 1790 (2) voted for Foster (**0805**) on the election of a Speaker.
> 1798 (1) voted against Sir Laurence Parsons' (**1636**) motion for an investigation into 'the present discontents'.
> 1799 (1) voted against the Union – Keeper of the Stores, Custom House.
> 1800 (1) voted against the Union.

ESTATES/RESIDENCE: Beresford Place, Dublin; Abbeyville, Co. Dublin. He was appointed agent for the Co. Londonderry estates of the Irish Society in 1787, and on his resignation in 1837 received a pension of £320 p.a. In February 1799 Beresford was reported to be in London negotiating a renewal of his father's lease from a London company, presumably the Fishmongers.

SOURCES: PRONI T/3166/B Hartnell notes; Burke *PB* (1903) p. 1554 [says he died 3 July]; Jupp thesis; O'Neill thesis; *Alum. Dub.*; *Cornwallis Corr.* vol. 3 pp. 35, 50–51 [says he died 3 July 1843]; E. Hewitt (ed.), *Lord Shannon's Letters to his Son*, p. xxi; *Castlereagh Corr.* vol. 2 pp. 41–3, 47; *HP 1790–1820*; *A Concise View of … the Irish society* (1822) p. 134, *Almanacks*; *FJ* 17 Oct. 1795, 20 Oct. 1796, 11, 15 Apr., 22 July 1797; PRONI MIC/9A/10 (Irish Society out-letters book, 1789–1826) Robert Slate to J. C. Beresford, 26 Mar. 1793; PRONI D/607/6/75 Robert Johnson to Downshire, 19 Feb.1799; Parliamentary Lists, 1791 (1), 1793 (1), 1794 (1), (2), 1798 (1), 1799 (1), (3), 1800 (1).

0118 BERESFORD, Sir Marcus

MP for Coleraine 1715–20

b. 16 July 1694; d. 4 Apr. 1763
HONOURS: Suc. as 4th Bt 1719.
PEERAGES: Cr. Baron Beresford and Viscount
Tyrone 4 Nov. 1720, Earl of Tyrone 18 July
1746.
FAMILY/BACKGROUND: Only son and heir of Sir
Tristram Beresford, 3rd Bt (0121), and Nichola
Sophia, dau. and co-h. of Hugh Hamilton, 1st
Baron Hamilton of Glerawly.
MARRIED: [16 July 1717] Catherine, only dau. and
h. of James Power, 3rd Earl of Tyrone. (In Nov.
1767 the Irish House of Lords declared her right
to the barony of La Poer *suo iure*, which George
III confirmed a month later.)
CHILDREN: James (d. yg); Marcus (d. yg); Rt Hon.
George De La Poer, 2nd Earl of Tyrone (0113);
Rt Hon. John (0115); Rt Hon. William, 1st
Baron Decies, Abp of Tuam, m. Elizabeth dau. of
John FitzGibbon (0748); Anne, m. William
Annesley, 1st Viscount Glerawly (0049); Jane, m.
Rt Hon. Edward Cary (0362); Catherine, m. (1)
Thomas Christmas (0404), (2) Rt Hon.
Theophilus Jones (1117); Araminta, m. George
Paul Monck (1429); Frances Maria, m. Rt Hon.
Henry Flood (0762); Elizabeth, m. Thomas
Cobbe (0426).
CAREER/OCCUPATION: *Trustee of the Linen Board
for Ulster 1735–d.; *Commissioner of the Tillage
Act for Munster 1735, 1739–d.

POLITICAL ACTIVITY: He was nominated for six committees between 1715 and 1719, and in the Parliamentary List of 1717 he was noted as an office-
holder – the following year he was created Viscount Tyrone and in 1746 Earl of Tyrone. His
wife was the heiress of the 3rd Earl of Tyrone of
an earlier creation, the heirs male of the family
having been attainted for service under James II –
the last of this line died unmarried in Dublin in
1742.

ADDITIONAL INFORMATION: Deputy Grand Master
of the Grand Lodge of Irish Freemasons, 1733;
Grand Master, 1736 and 1737. There is a repro-
duction of a portrait at Curraghmore in Lepper
and Crossle.

ESTATES/RESIDENCE: Curraghmore, Co. Waterford;
Tyrone House, Marlborough Street, Dublin; Coleraine,
Co. Londonderry, these estates were leased on very fa-
vourable terms from the Irish Company. He appears to

have divided them between his sons, George, 1st Marquess of Waterford (0113) and the Rt Hon. John
Beresford (0115). In 1713 Sir Marcus Beresford's income was estimated at £800 p.a. On the death of his
mother-in-law, the Dowager Countess of Tyrone, her
jointure of £1,500 p.a. fell to her son-in-law Lord
Tyrone.

SOURCES: PRONI T/3411; NAI MFCI Reel 13, Parish
Registers of Clonegam, Co. Waterford [bur. 9 Apr.
1763]; RCBL P80/1/1, Parish Registers of St Thomas,
Dublin [bur. 5 Apr. 1763]; RCBL T/34, Extracts from
the Parish Registers of St Andrew's, Dublin; GEC *P*;
Burke *PB* (1900) pp. 1539–41 [d. 4 Apr. 1763]; J. H.
Lepper and P. Crossle, *History of the Grand Lodge of
Free and Accepted Masons of Ireland* (Dublin, 1925), vol.
1; *Almanacks, The Dublin Gazette* 21 Oct. 1729; Par-
liamentary List, 1719 (1).

0119 BERESFORD, Marcus

MP for Dungarvan 1783–90–7, July–Nov. 1797

b. 14 Feb. 1764; d. 16 Nov. 1797 of a mortifica-
tion in the intestines (?appendicitis)
FAMILY/BACKGROUND: Eldest son of Rt Hon. John
Beresford (0115) and his first wife Annette
Constantia, dau. of Gen. Comte de Ligondes.
MARRIED: [25 Feb. 1791] Frances Arabella, dau. of
Rt Hon. Joseph Leeson, 1st Earl of Milltown
(1212).
CHILDREN: John Theophilus (b. 1792; d. in Spain
1812); William (b. 1797; d. 6 Oct. 1883), m.
[1833] Catherine (b. 1808; d. 1895), dau. of
George Robert Heneage of Lincolnshire;
Elizabeth (b. *c.* 1794; d. 1856), m. [1827] Felix
Sadbrooke of Surrey.
EDUCATION: School: Westminster 13 Feb. 1778;
Lincoln's Inn 19 Oct. 1779; entered TCD 1781,
BA 1784; called to the Irish Bar 1786.
CAREER/OCCUPATION: Joint Taster of Wines with
his father (0115) 1773–97; Counsel at Law for
Dublin Port Business 1789–4; King's Counsel
1791; 1st Counsel to the Revenue Commission-
ers 1795–6.

POLITICAL ACTIVITY: Electoral influence in
Dungarvan came to the Devonshire family
through the 4th Duke's marriage with the great
heiress, Lady Charlotte Boyle. The Devonshires
neglected it although it was a manor borough and
the Duke appointed the seneschal, who was the
returning officer. By the 1780s the representation

was divided between the Ponsonbys and the Boyles (Shannon) who at that time handled the Devonshire political interest in Ireland, and the Beresfords, who exerted at least some influence over one seat through the Revenue officers in the port. Marcus Beresford sat for it for the 14 years of his parliamentary career.

In 1787 Baron Hamilton of the Exchequer (**0936**) wrote to John Beresford about Marcus that 'I think he is almost everything you could wish him ... and will, I am persuaded, qualify himself for any bar preferment nearly as soon as you can wish to obtain it for him.' Certainly he appears to have been determined to make his mark in parliament, as the indignant author of the 1789 'opposition' Parliamentary List noted that 'This young orator's first parliamentary exhibition ... was a pointed attack on the most conspicuous member of the House of Commons, on a man whose voice rolls the thunder and whose tongue carries the conviction of a Demosthenes ... so daring have been his outset in this political field his succeeding campaigns have been distinguished by similar deeds of hardihood and have been alike marked by a full confidence in his own superior powers and a supercilious disregard of the eloquent, the dignified and the venerable. As a public speaker his voice is clear, articulate and audible ... His language is plain, level and simple, copiously flowing without let or hinderence ... absolutely unadorned.'

His letter to George Ponsonby (**1699**) on the latter's dismissal and his own appointment in 1789 shows some of the qualities that his contemporaries at the bar, including Wolfe Tone, obviously found attractive: 'Give me leave,' he wrote, 'to assure you that I shall feel pleasure in making way for you to resume your former situation [First Counsel to the Revenue] if ever it should suit you to come into that situation again.' He considered that the opposition's schemes of reform in 1797 were impractical and inopportune and would lead electorally to the worst form of potwalloping boroughs, while the Catholic claim should be attended to in a more tranquil time; meanwhile, he considered that Catholics had a splendid opportunity to prove their loyalty.

He was deeply concerned and involved in the security of the country in the 1790s. Nevertheless, while not condoning Wolfe Tone's behaviour, he was a friend and was, at the risk of considerable unpopularity with the administration, the chief negotiator of Tone's permission to go to America. His father, who was in his confidence, supported him while warning him to protect himself against the Castle's displeasure. In fact, Tone provided him with a statement as to at least some of the plans and intentions of the United Irishmen on the condition that no use be made of it to prejudice those mentioned in it. Beresford kept his promise despite Tone's subsequent behaviour; after his death this document was handed to Lord Clare (**0749**) by Beresford's widow. Clare likewise did not use it to incriminate any specific person, although he knew of its contents at the time of Tone's trial, and it is probable that he destroyed it as his son, who searched for it at the request of Marcus Beresford's son William, could find no trace of it.

DIVISION LISTS:

1783 (1) voted against Flood's (**0762**) motion for parliamentary reform.

1784 (1) voted against a committee on the Reform Bill.

1785 (1) voted for the Commercial Propositions.

1789 (1) voted against a regency.

1790 (2) voted for Foster (**0805**) on the election of a Speaker.

ESTATES/RESIDENCE: Abbeyville, Co. Dublin.

SOURCES: Burke *PB* (1903) p. 1554; O'Neill thesis; PRONI T/1584 Pinkerton transcripts, p. 528, 24 Nov. 1797; *Lincoln's Inn Records* vol. I p. 494; G. F. Russell-Barker and A. H. Stenning (eds), *Record of Old Westminsters: A Biographical List* (London, 1928); *King's Inns Admissions*; Beresford Corr. vol. 1 p. 321, vol. 2 pp. 1, 2, 24–33, 65, 67, 84, 108–110; McDowell, *Ir. public opinion, 1750–1800* p. 235; M. Elliott, *Wolfe Tone* (Yale, 1989), pp. 87, 243–4; F. MacDermot, *Tone and his Times* (1939), pp. 126–7; *Almanacks*; Parliamentary Lists, 1783 (2), 1784 (1), (2), 1784 (3), 1785 (1), (2), (4), 1787 (1), 1788 (1), 1789 (1), (2), 1790 (1), 1791 (1), 1793 (1), 1794 (1), (2).

0120 BERESFORD, Marcus

MP for St Canice 1790–4; [Escheator of Munster 1794]; Swords 1798–1800

b. 1 June 1764; d. 1803 in Barbados, West Indies
FAMILY/BACKGROUND: Eldest son of William Beresford, 1st Baron Decies, Abp of Tuam, and Elizabeth, dau. of John Fitzgibbon (**0748**).
MARRIED: Unmarried.
EDUCATION: School: Dr Smith; Westminster 13 Jan. 1777–80; entered TCD 7 Nov. 1780, aged 16 years; Lincoln's Inn 14 Apr. 1785.
MILITARY: Ensign 9th Foot 26 Oct. 1786, Lieutenant 30 June 1787; Captain 27th Foot 30 Nov. 1789; Major 102nd Foot 31 Oct. 1793; Lieutenant-Colonel 135th Foot 26 Nov. 1794; Brevet Colonel 1 Jan. 1801, Brigadier-General in the Windward, Leeward and Caribbean Islands 27 June 1802; full pay 1795–8, half-pay 1798–1803; Lieutenant-General of the Ordnance, patent 11 Oct. 1800; member of the Faughinvale Volunteers.

POLITICAL ACTIVITY: A soldier and on active service for most of his political career. The eldest son of Archbishop Beresford, who as Bishop of Ossory returned the members for the borough at the 1783 election: government usually decided the returns for this borough but gratified the bishop on this occasion. He resigned from parliament in 1794, taking the Escheatorship of Munster. Subsequently he sat for the notorious potwalloping borough of Swords where his uncle, John Beresford (**0115**), was able to influence the voters through the Revenue officials. He voted for the Union in both 1799 and 1800, and was probably brought into parliament for this purpose.

DIVISION LISTS:
1790 (2) voted for Foster (**0805**) on the election of a Speaker.
1799 (1) voted for the Union – Collector of Excise in Dublin and Colonel, 135th Foot.
1800 (1) voted for the Union.

ESTATES/RESIDENCE: St Stephen's Green, Dublin.

SOURCES: PRONI T/3166/1B Hartnell notes; PRONI MIC/474 Irish Volunteers; O'Neill thesis; *Lincoln's Inn Records* vol. 1 p. 513; G. F. Russell-Barker and A. H. Stenning (eds), *Record of Old Westminsters: A Biographical List* (London, 1928); Kilkenny MPs; Hughes, *Patentee Officers*, p. 10; *Almanacks*; Parliamentary Lists, 1791 (1), 1793 (1), 1799 (2), (3), 1800 (3).

0121 BERESFORD, Sir Tristram

MP for Co. Londonderry 1692–3, 1695–9

b. 1669; d. 16 June 1701
HONOURS: Suc. as 3rd Bt 1681.
FAMILY/BACKGROUND: Only surviving son of Randal Beresford, 2nd Bt, and Catherine, dau. of Rt Hon. Francis Annesley, 1st Viscount Valentia.
MARRIED: [Feb. 1687] Nichola Sophia (b. 23 Feb. 1666; d. 23 Feb. 1713), dau. and co-h. of Hugh Hamilton, 1st Baron Hamilton (she married (2) [1704] Lt.-Gen. Richard Gorges (**0884**)).
CHILDREN: Marcus, 1st Earl of Tyrone (**0118**); Susanna Catherine, m. Hyacinth Richard Nugent, Baron Riverston; Arabella Maria; Jane, m. George Lowther (**1271**); Araminta.

POLITICAL ACTIVITY: He raised and commanded an infantry regiment for William III and sat in the two parliaments of his reign, which lasted a total of only about eight months. During this time he was listed for two committees in the very brief parliament of 1692 and for three in 1695 – the first session of the 1695–9 parliament. In 1695 he supported Lord Chancellor Porter in his impeachment by the House of Commons, but he does not appear to have signed the Association for the protection of William III in 1696. In the course of the second parliament he complained of a breach of privilege, and on 4 August 1696 Sir James Caldwell and Robert Saunderson (**1885**) were ordered into the custody of the Serjeant-at-Arms. 'Some heats' had arisen between Beresford and Robert Saunderson, the other successful candidate for Co. Londonderry. Saunderson was eventually expelled from parliament for refusing to sign the association. Caldwell spent 12 months in the custody of the House before being fined and released.

ADDITIONAL INFORMATION: Of his wife the following story is told. 'Lord Glenawly had a son and two daughters. The eldest was married to Sir John Magill (**1325**) of Gill Hall and the younger to Sir Tristram Beresford of Coleraine. In early youth, the younger Nicola Sophia, had been brought up with John Le Poer Decies, 2nd Earl of Tyrone, elder son of Richard, 1st Earl of Tyrone. Their instructor was a confirmed Deist, and induced both his pupils to adopt his principles; and it appeared they made a mutual promise that whoever died first should appear to the other and confirm or deny the truth of revealed religion. On 14 October 1693, Lady Beresford and her husband were on a visit at Gill Hall with her brother-in-law, Sir John Magill. At this time they had been married for some years, had several daughters but no son. During this visit Lady Beresford came down to breakfast late, in a very agitated state, with a black ribband tied round her wrist. When Sir Tristram spoke to her she implored him to ask no questions; she could tell him nothing but that in the next year he would be father of a son, and that the post would bring tidings of John, Lord Tyrone's death. A Letter with a black seal very shortly arrived saying Lord Tyrone had died in Dublin on the preceding Saturday. In 1694 an only son (0118) was born, and in 1701 Sir Tristram died.'

She subsequently married Richard Gorges (0884), but the marriage was unhappy. In 1713 she asked a party to dine with her at her house in Dublin to celebrate her 48th birthday: 'Among them was an old clergyman who had christened her. He was the first arrival and she told him she was just forty eight that day. "No," he said, "you are only forty seven, you were born in 1666." She grew deadly pale. "Are you sure?" she said. "Certain," he said. "You have then," she replied, "signed my death-warrant. I have only a few hours to live." She retired to her room, sent for her son, Sir Marcus, for her daughter, Lady Riverston, and I believe Henry, Archbishop of Dublin. She then told the story for the first time of Lord Tyrone's appearing to her, telling her of his death; that she would have a son who would marry his [Lord Tyrone's] brother's daughter, and that she would make a most unfortunate [second] marriage, and die on her forty-seventh birthday. He touched her wrist to show his appearance was real and the flesh and sinews shrank, on which she always wore a black ribband ... Such was the story as it was recorded by her granddaughter Lady Betty Cobbe who had it from Lady Riverston her aunt, and perhaps from her father, who was created Earl of Tyrone.'

ESTATES/RESIDENCE: Coleraine, Co. Londonderry. He spent over £400 fortifying Coleraine with timber and iron between 1689 and 1691. However, his estates in Counties Londonderry and Tyrone, including his houses, and the town of Ballygawley were 'burnt and pillaged' by the Irish. He estimated his losses at more than £4,000, and in 1696 petitioned for redress. When his widow married again she took with her as her portion the Ballygawley estate.

SOURCES: PRONI D/2096/1/93A Maxwell Given notes; PRONI T/2531/4/1–2 Hamilton Genealogical notes; PRONI MIC/338/6 Crossle notes; GEC *B*; Burke *PB* (1903) p. 1553 (1906) p. 1667 [says he d. 16 June 1701]; *Cal. SP Dom. 1696* (London, 1913) p. 128; Simms' cards [says he d. 16 June 1703]; *The Register of the Parish of St Peter and St Kevin, 1669–1761* (Parish Register Society of Dublin, 1911) p. 124; *JRSAI* vol. 55 (1925) pp. 38, 49, H. A. S. Upton, 'A List of Governors and Deputy Governors of Counties in Ireland in 1699'; Hill, *Plantation*, pp. 404, 433; Parliamentary Lists, 1695 (1), 1696 (1).

0122 BERMINGHAM, Rt Hon. Thomas

MP for Co. Galway 1745–50

b. 16 Nov. 1717; d. 11 Jan. 1799 at Bermingham, Co. Galway
HONOURS: PC 1754–69, 1782–3 (sworn 21 Apr. 1755, 1 Nov. 1760, 8 July 1761, removed 7 May 1770, gazetted 25 May 1782, resworn 21 Nov. 1783).
PEERAGES: Suc. as 15th Baron Athenry (Premier Baron of Ireland) 4 Mar. 1750; cr. Earl of Louth 23 Apr. 1759.
FAMILY/BACKGROUND: Eldest son of Francis Bermingham, 14th Baron Athenry and his first wife Margaret, eldest dau. of Thomas Nugent, 4th Earl of Westmeath.
MARRIED: (1) [1 Nov. 1745] Jane, eldest dau. of Sir John Bingham, 5th Bt (0141); (2) [2 Jan. 1750 (marriage settlement 30 Dec. 1749)] Margaret, dau. of Peter Daly of Co. Galway.
CHILDREN: (2) Elizabeth, m. Francis Duffield (marriage settlement, 19 June 1779, specified that anything she might subsequently inherit would be for her own use, independent of any contracts entered into by her husband); Mary (d. 30 July 1793), m. [1 June 1777] William (Viscount St Lawrence), 2nd Earl of Howth; Louisa, m. (1) Joseph Henry Blake, 1st Baron Wallscourt (0152) (2) James Daly of Dublin; Matilda [d. unmar. in her father's lifetime].
CAREER/OCCUPATION: *Trustee of the Linen Board for Ulster 1749–59, Munster 1760–d.

POLITICAL ACTIVITY: He does not appear to have been a particularly active member of the House of Commons. He was reported as nominated for only two committees, both in 1746. His main activity, which appears to have been low-key, took place in the House of Lords where he was the premier baron of Ireland and in his patent as earl, he asked that upon failure of male issue his title should descend on his female heiresses. He was dismissed from the Privy Council during Lord Townshend's viceroyalty and when his request to become Constable of the Bermingham Tower, a sinecure, was refused he went into 'strong' opposition.

In 1782 he was noted as being largely absent but during the Duke of Rutland's viceroyalty he became a supporter of the government, probably because of his anxiety to secure the succession to his peerage. He was still an 'expectant' supporter in 1787, and in 1788 was noted as 'always ready to attend'. His interest was sustained by receiving 'a few trifling requests'. At the time of his death in 1799 he had still failed to achieve his ambition to secure the succession to his peerage in the female line, and at his death the title became extinct.

DIVISION LISTS:

1749 (1) voted against the election of James Digges La Touche (♦♦♦).

ADDITIONAL INFORMATION: *A member of the Royal Dublin Society from 1766.

ESTATES/RESIDENCE: Bermingham, Co. Galway – his estates devolved on his daughters Lady Elizabeth Duffield, Mary, Viscountess St Lawrence (she died in 1793, leaving a daughter who inherited), and Lady Louisa Blake.

SOURCES: PRONI T/1584 Pinkerton transcripts, 6 Sept. 1749; PRONI T/2915/5/22 Bedford Papers; McCracken thesis; Burke *Ext. P.* (1883) p. 49 [says he m. secondly 10 Jan. 1750]; Kilkenny MPs; *Index to Irish Privy Counsellors, 1711–1910*; *BNL* 5 Jan. 1749, 9 Mar. 1749, 5 Feb. 1799; *Almanacks*; *DJ* 28–30 May 1782, 15 Aug. 1793, 22 Jan. 1799; TCD Library 186.s.39 Private Member's Bills; Parliamentary Lists, 1775 (1), 1777 (1), 1782 (1), 1784 (2), 1787 (1), 1788 (1).

0123 BERNARD, Arthur

MP for Bandon 1713–14

b. 1666; d. *post* 1714
FAMILY/BACKGROUND: 4th surviving son of Francis Bernard and Elizabeth, dau. of Arthur Freke of Rathbarry Castle, Co. Cork.
MARRIED: [22 Dec. 1695] Anne, dau. of Roger Power of Mount Eglantine, Co. Waterford.
CHILDREN: Anne, m. William Conner (0458); Roger.
CAREER/OCCUPATION: High Sheriff of Co. Cork 1697, 1706.

POLITICAL ACTIVITY: Bernard was connected both with the Boyles, through his mother, and with the Powers, a prominent Waterford family, through his wife. His elder brother (0124) was attainted by James II's parliament in 1689, but, restored by William and Mary, he was Solicitor General in the government of Queen Anne and in the important election of 1713 he was returned for Baltimore, an event that the government had predicted. In parliament he voted for Sir Richard Levinge (1230) as Speaker against Alan Brodrick (0237), although the latter was leader of the Cork 'squadron'. In 1714 he signed a Co. Cork address in favour of the Tory Chancellor, Sir Constantine Phipps, and by the end of Anne's reign he was on a 'black list' of Tories. He did not come into the parliament elected in 1715 following the accession of George I.

DIVISION LISTS:

1713 (1) voted for Sir Richard Levinge (1230) for Speaker.

ESTATES/RESIDENCE: Palace Anne, Co. Cork. In 1713 his income was estimated at £300 p.a., which appears to be an underestimate.

SOURCES: PRONI D/302; PRONI T/3411; Simms' cards; Burke *PB* (1903) p. 98; Cork MPs; *Cork Hist. Soc. Jn.* vol. 1 second ser. (1895) pp. 346–54, D. Townshend, 'Notes on the Council Book of Clonakilty'; Parliamentary Lists, 1713 (1), (2), 1714 (1), 1714–15 (1).

0124 BERNARD, Francis

MP for Clonakilty 1692–3; Bandon 1695–9, 1703–13–14, 1715–27

   b. 1663; d. 30 June 1731

HONOURS: ?Privy Counsellor.

FAMILY/BACKGROUND: Eldest son of Francis Bernard of Castle Mahon, Co. Cork, and Elizabeth, dau. of Arthur Freke of Rathbarry Castle, Co. Cork.

MARRIED: [1697] Alice, dau. of Stephen Ludlow (**1281**).

CHILDREN: Francis (**0125**); Stephen (**0128**); North Ludlow (Major of Dragoons), m. [1728] Rose, dau of John Echlin of Co. Down; Arthur; William; Elizabeth, m. (1) James Caulfeild, 3rd Viscount Charlemont (**0368**), (2) Thomas Adderley (**0009**).

EDUCATION: Entered TCD 20 Apr. 1680, BA 1682; Middle Temple 14 Dec. 1683.

CAREER/OCCUPATION: Solicitor General 3 July 1711; Prime Serjeant 25 Jan. 1724/5; Surveyor General June 1711; Judge of the Common Pleas, patents 20 June 1726, 10 Nov. 1727; Justice of Assize for Munster, Summer 1725, Connaught, Lent 1726, NW Ulster, Summer 1726, Lent 1728, Leinster, Summer 1728, 1730, NW Ulster, Summer 1731; Recorder of Clonakilty 7 Sept. 1692; Recorder of Kinsale 18 Jan. 1693, Burgess 1694; Chief Justice of the Palatinate of Tipperary 1704; ?Seneschal of the Liberty of Tipperary 1704–15; Trustee of the Linen Manufacture for the Province of Munster 10 Oct. 1711.

POLITICAL ACTIVITY: He was attainted by the 'patriot' parliament in 1689, but restored to his estates by William and Mary. Along with Edward Riggs (**1790**), he was appointed by the Commons a trustee to receive the £2,500 levied on Munster for the relief of the inhabitants of Bandon. They had disarmed the garrison in 1688 and had been heavily punished and fined for it by Colonel Macarthy.

His committee service gives the picture of a busy political life. He was nominated for two committees in the short parliament of 1692, then 26 in 1695–8, 87 in the first parliament of Anne's reign and 58 between 1715 and 1726, when he was elevated to the Bench. In 1695 he voted in support of Lord Chancellor Porter, one of the signatories to the Treaty of Limerick, whom the House of Commons suspected of being unduly lenient to

Catholics; the following year he signed the Association for the protection of William III in the country.

By 1706 he was a noted Tory; he was present on all the leading Tory political occasions of Queen Anne's reign. For instance, he attended Lord Lieutenant Ormonde's birthday celebrations in 1706; he was one of the 34 MPs who met at the Fleece Tavern in Dublin in 1707 to concert Tory strategy for the forthcoming parliamentary session, and one of the 31 members who met there for the same purpose in 1711. In 1709 he was one of those responsible for introducing 8 Anne, c. 10, an important 'Act for the public registering of all Deeds, Conveyances and Wills that shall be made of any Honors, Manors, Lands Tenements or Hereditaments'. In 1711, when he was appointed Solicitor General, he was obviously a leading Tory. In the 1713 election he was a confirmed Tory, and his return was said to be supported by his relation Lord Burlington's extensive interest in Co. Cork. At the time of the queen's death he was firmly on a 'black list' of Tories.

However, he survived the Hanoverian succession, although with the loss of the office of Solicitor General (estimated to be worth £2,000 p.a.) to his brother-in-law John Rogerson (**1812**) (their wives were sisters). He retained his Tory sympathies and in 1719 he was thought likely to be hostile to the repeal of the Test Act, which excluded Protestant Dissenters from office. By the end of the decade he was one of the proposed managers of the 'intended' national bank proposed in 1719. Finally, he was able to resume his legal career under Lord Lieutenant Carteret's rehabilitation of the Tories and in January 1725 he became Prime Serjeant. Some 18 months later, in June 1726, he became a Justice of Common Pleas. This appointment (for Irish judges still held during the king's pleasure) was renewed in 1727 on the accession of George II. He died four years later.

DIVISION LISTS:

   1709 (1) spoke against a Money Bill.

   1711 (1) voted for the court on the Dublin mayoralty issue.

   1713 (1) voted for Sir Richard Levinge (**1230**) for Speaker.

1721 (1) voted for a national bank.

1721 (2) voted for a national bank.

ADDITIONAL INFORMATION: In 1716 his wife was reputed to be a 'furious Tory if not a degree beyond it'. He was admitted as a Freemason at the Yellow Lyon, Werburgh Street, Dublin, 6 March 1731.

ESTATES/RESIDENCE: Castle Bernard, Co. Cork. According to Burke (1900 edition) the Bernards came to Ireland about the reign of Queen Elizabeth. Francis Bernard's estate appears to have been partly inherited pre-1688, and greatly increased by additions afterwards; thereby illustrating the piecemeal manner whereby many estates were amassed. There are extant deeds of conveyance dated 22 January 1661 by Ralph Fuller of Bandonbridge to Francis Bernard of Castle Mahon, both in Co. Cork, lands that he purchased from John Coker of Kilbrogan parish by deed dated 30 January 1655 and from William Abbott and Garrett FitzGerald by deed dated 17 May 1656, all of which said lands are situated in the barony of Carbery, Co. Cork. Deed of conveyance dated 17 October 1670 by Henry and Charles Allen of Co. Leitrim, sons of Edward Allen deceased to Francis Bernard of Castle Mahon, Co. Cork of lands in the barony of Carbery, Co. Cork, which had been granted by letters patent to Elizabeth Allen, widow of said Edward, Thomas Allen and said Henry and Charles Allen, dated 15 April, 22 Charles II. Another deed of conveyance is dated 13 May 1672 by Theophilus Cary of Ballyburdenmore, barony of Barretts and William Cary of Derry Castle, barony of Carbery East to Francis Bernard of Castle Mahon, all in Co. Cork, the lands of Derry and Lisbehogy, together with the castle of Derry, Co. Cork. A further deed of conveyance dated 19 September 1696 by Richard Goodman of Bandonbridge to Francis Bernard of Castle Mahon, both in Co. Cork, of the lands of Ballahanure and Adrinall, barony of Carbery East, Co. Cork and finally a deed of conveyance dated 13 April 1678 by Delivoranne Barrow of Cork city to Francis Bernard of Castle Mahon, Co. Cork of the lands in the barony of Carbery, Co. Cork which they had both purchased in 1674.

Then in 1702–3 Francis Bernard purchased from the Commissioners for Sale of Forfeited Estates 3,195 acres in Co. Cork, part of the Clancarty estate. There are three deeds of grant by the Trustees of Forfeited Estates to Francis Bernard of Dublin City of lands in the barony of Muskerry, Co. Cork; the first is dated 19 March 1702 and the other two are also in the barony of Muskerry, Co. Cork, both dated 23 June 1703. There are also two deeds of grant by the Governor and Company for making Hollow Sword Blades to Francis Bernard of Dublin

city of the lands of Ballymohill and Curra and Kilnerobanagh, all in the barony of Muskerry, Co. Cork, dated 6 March 1705 and 16 September 1709, and, interestingly, there is extant a deed of release dated 7 June 1711 by William Penn, Proprietary Governor of the Province of Pennsylvania in America, Hannah his wife, William Penn his son and Mary his wife to Francis Bernard, Dublin city, Solicitor General, of lands in the barony of Ibane and Barryroe, Co. Cork.

In the period 1681–1707 the Bernards were of Castle Mahon and at this time they leased the lands of Dunowen from Lord Barrymore, and later sub-let them to the Hungerford family of Dunowen, Clonakilty. On 3 and 4 October 1704 there were conveyances and a deed of grant by Yelverton Dennis of Rathmore, Co. Cork, son and heir of Thomas Dennis of Cork city, merchant, to Francis Bernard of Castlemahon, Co. Cork, of lands of East Coppeen, Lackanashinnagh and Slinoge, formerly the estate of William Wright of Bandon, deceased, and in the barony of Carbery East, Co. Cork.

In 1712 Francis Bernard was granted a market at Macroom.

SOURCES: *CJ Ire.* (Bradley ed.) vol. 3 pp. 674–5 (0216); PRONI T/3411; NLI EC 4237; PRONI T/3315/2/f. 33 Egmont Papers; McCracken thesis; Hayton thesis; GEC *P*; Burke *PB* (1903) p. 98 [1900 ed. says he d. 1726 but this is incorrect]; *King's Inns Admissions*; Smyth, *Law Officers*; Ball, *Judges*; *Middle Temple Admissions* vol. 1 p. 212; Simms' cards; *Boulter Letters* vol. 2 p. 13 & n.; *Cork MPs*; *Cork Hist. Soc. Jn.* vol. 1 (1895) p. 399, D. Townshend, 'Notes on the Council Book of Clonakilty' [says he was born 1663]; *Ir. Gen.* vol. 3 no 3 (July 1958) pp. 114–15, T. Blake Butler, 'Seneschals of the Liberty of Tipperary'; P. McNally, *Parties, Patriots & Undertakers* (Dublin, 1997) pp. 63, 83; Simms, *Williamite Confiscation*, p. 183; *Almanacks*; *Dublin Weekly Journal* 26 June 1725, 24 Feb. 1728, *DJ* 13 Mar. 1730; *The Dublin Intelligence* 19 Feb. 1726, 9 July 1726; *The Dublin Gazette* 20 June 1730, 16 Feb. 1731, 3 July 1731; *Pue's Occurrences* 3 July 1731; Parliamentary Lists, 1695 (1), 1696 (1), 1706 (1), (2), 1707 (2), 1711 (2), (3), 1713 (1), (2), 1714–15 (1), 1719 (2).

0125 BERNARD, Francis

MP for Clonakilty 1725–7–60; Bandon 1766–8–76

b. 28 Sept. 1698; d. (bur. 21) Mar. 1783

FAMILY/BACKGROUND: Eldest son of Francis Bernard (0124) and Alice, dau. of Stephen

Ludlow (**1281**).
MARRIED: [26 Mar. 1722] Anne, o. dau. of Rt
Hon. Henry Petty, 1st Earl of Shelburne (**1672**).
CHILDREN: *d.s.p.*, suc. by his nephew James
Bernard (**0127**).
EDUCATION: Entered Oxford (Christ Church) 13
Dec. 1716; member of King's Inns 1724.
CAREER/OCCUPATION: Freedom of Cork 8 Nov.
1731; Commissioner of Excise Feb. 1772.

POLITICAL ACTIVITY: In February 1723 he was one
of the Memorialists on behalf of the Protestant
gentlemen of Ireland seeking either an explanation or revocation of a clause in an act of Queen
Anne's reign for naturalising foreign Protestants
in which favour was given to the children of natural-born subjects. The Memorialists feared that this
clause would allow the children of papists who
had served James and then fled to Europe and
converted to Protestantism to return to Ireland to
undermine the church and state, as well as reclaiming their lands.

During his period in parliament he was listed
for 11 committees, all between 1727 and 1735.
He had considerable influence in the parliamentary borough of Bandon, which was divided between the Bernards and the Earl of Cork and
Burlington, whose heiress married the 4th Duke
of Devonshire.

DIVISION LISTS:
1749 (1) absent, in England.
1768 (1) absent, in England.

ADDITIONAL INFORMATION: In 1735 he went to live
in England and never after returned to Ireland.
From 1756 he was noted as being absent and probably a doubtful supporter of government even if
he was present. It was repeatedly stated that he
had a 'very large fortune' but 'some years ago
[1772] he took it in his head that he should die
for want, so retired from the world and took lodgings at an apothecary's house in the Hay-market,
London and never stirs from thence.'

ESTATES/RESIDENCE: Castle Bernard, Co. Cork;
Bassingbourne Hall, Essex. Pre-1740, Francis Bernard
let his Hollow Blade lands, the castle, town and lands
of Macroom, to Richard Hedges in perpetuity at £255.
Richard Eyre (married 1747) was Hedges' grandson and
heir. In 1768, the gross rental of the lands was over
£735.

In 1814 *Robert William Meade v. the Earl of Bandon*
referred to Lord Bandon's mortgage for £1,121 on the
lands of Kippagh and Killany, Co. Cork. In the evidence it was mentioned that 'Francis Bernard died in
1731, and that his whole interest in said mortgaged
premises vested in Francis Bernard of Bassinburnhall
in England, his son, heir-at-law and sole executor, and
that in the year 1735 he went to live in Great Britain
and never after returned to Ireland, but died in Great
Britain in March 1783, leaving respondent's father, the
third James Bernard, his nephew and heir-at-law, to
whom letters of administration of his personal estate
and effects were duly granted by the ecclesiastical court.'

SOURCES: PRONI T/580 pp. 2–6, TSPI 1723–4; RCBL
P45/2/3, Parish Registers of St Peter's, Dublin;
McCracken thesis [says he died 19 Mar. 1783]; Burke
PB (1903) p. 98; *King's Inns Admissions*; NLI Brown's
Reports of House of Lords Appeals 1710–1800, ILB 340
pt 5 pp. cciii–cciii; NAI M.1027–8 Hedges Eyre Papers; EC 5613; *FJ* 6–8 Feb. 1772; Parliamentary Lists,
1756 (1), 1769 (1), 1772 (2), 1773 (1), (2), 1774 (1),
1775 (1).

0126 BERNARD, Francis

MP for Ennis 1778–83; Bandon 1783–90

b. 26 Nov. 1755; d. 30 Nov. 1830
PEERAGES: Cr. Baron Bandon 26 Nov. 1793,
Viscount Bandon 4 Oct. 1795, Earl of Bandon
29 Aug. 1800; Rep. Peer 1801–30.
FAMILY/BACKGROUND: Only son and heir of James
Bernard (**0127**) and Esther, dau. of Percy Smith,
wid. of Robert Gookin.
MARRIED: [12 Feb. 1784] Catherine Henrietta (d.
8 July 1815), only dau. of Rt Hon. Richard
Boyle, 2nd Earl of Shannon (**0213**).
CHILDREN: James, 2nd Earl of Bandon, m. [1809]
Mary Susan Albinia, dau of the Hon. Charles
Brodrick, Abp of Cashel; Rev. Richard Boyle,
Dean of Leighlin; Lieut. Francis (9th Light
Dragoons); Lieut.-Col. William Smyth, m.
[1831] Elizabeth o. dau. of Lieut.-Col. Gilman of
Co. Cork; Henry Boyle; Charles Ludlow;
Catherine Henrietta; Charlotte Esther, m. [1816]
Hayes St Leger, 3rd Viscount Doneraile; Louisa
Ann.
CAREER/OCCUPATION: Colonel of the Bandon
Independent Company, Volunteers 1782;
Captain of Bandon Cavalry 1796.

POLITICAL ACTIVITY: He entered parliament by purchasing the seat for Ennis left vacant when Sir Lucius O'Brien (**1558**) successfully contested the disputed election for Co. Clare. It was thought that he might be influenced by Sir Lucius and Francis Pierpoint Burton (**0299**). In 1780 he was considered a 'doubtful' supporter of government and it emerged that he was dominated by his father, James Bernard (**0127**), who was returned for Co. Cork in the 1781 by-election created by the elevation of Sir Robert Tilson Deane (**0609**) to the peerage. Before the arrival of Lord Lieutenant Portland, both father and son opposed.

In 1783 he was returned for Bandon-Bridge – the Bernards and the Duke of Devonshire had agreed to return one member each, the borough being divided between their estates. He was a delegate to the Volunteer National Convention for Co. Cork, where he declared that he would relinquish his patronage of rotten boroughs for the public good. This self-denial appears to have been short-lived, although he followed the 'patriotic' line until 1786. However, in 1784 he married Lord Shannon's (**0213**) only daughter and it was thought that the marriage was partly to consolidate the Shannon interest in the county, which had been badly shaken by the 1783 election. His politics, though, veered from the independent to popular opposition, yet it was noted in 1788 that he probably wanted a peerage; in fact he was already trying to persuade Lord Shannon to support him in this ambition, but Shannon considered that the time was inopportune.

In the late 1780s Bernard, reversing his father's position of neutrality verging on hostility to the Shannon interest, joined his father-in-law's political following and, as a result of Lord Shannon's reluctant stand over the Regency Crisis, 'lost two very good employments'. By 1793 his rift with the government was healed and he was elevated to the peerage as Baron Bandon. In June 1798 Lord Shannon wrote to his son (**0211**): 'I have got an earldom for Feugle. That is, his Excellency has recommended it.' However, this promise was not redeemed until the Union, when Bandon was created an earl and made a representative peer. His considerable possessions and political connections were not matched by his personal gifts.

DIVISION LISTS:
1780 (2) voted for Yelverton's (**2268**) motion to modify Poynings' Law.
1783 (1) voted for Flood's (**0762**) motion for parliamentary reform.
1784 (1) voted for a committee on the Reform Bill.
1785 (1) absent.
1786 (2) voted for Forbes's (**0778**) motion for retrenchment.

ADDITIONAL INFORMATION: He was nicknamed 'Feugle' by his father-in-law, Lord Shannon. Lord Shannon was very fond of his daughter but his personal relationship with his son-in-law was decidedly diplomatic; for example he wrote to his son in 1799 following a visit from his daughter, her husband and son that 'Feugle ... really out-Feugled Feugle. I never saw such a very offensive countenance or conduct.' He considered that Bernard made his wife's life 'dismal' and that 'few would submit to it'. On one occasion he wrote how thankful he was that he and Lady Shannon had concluded their visit to Castle Bernard, although they were deeply concerned for their daughter.
*A subscriber to the Public Assembly Rooms, 1787.

ESTATES/RESIDENCE: Castle Bernard, Co. Cork. Next to the Ponsonbys, the Bernards were the second largest purchasers of Burlington lands. Young estimated the rental in 1779 at £8,000, and in 1791 the estates produced £18,000 p.a. According to Wakefield, in the first decade of the nineteenth century the rental was over £30,000.

SOURCES: Ellis thesis; GEC *P*; Wakefield, *Account of Ire.*, vol. 1 p. 250; Young, *Tour in Ire.*, vol. 2, App. p. 82; Burke *PB* (1903) p. 99 [says he was born 26 Nov. 1755]; McNevin, *Volunteers*; *Cornwallis Corr.* vol. 3 p. 245 [says he was b. 30 Nov. 1755]; E. Hewitt (ed.), *Lord Shannon's Letters to his Son* (PRONI 1982) pp. xxi, lviii, lix, 21, 188; *Almanacks*; *FJ* 20 Oct. 1796; *DJ* 9–11 Apr. 1778; Parliamentary Lists, 1776 (1), 1778 (1), 1780 (1), 1782 (1), 1783 (1), (2), (3), 1784 (1), (2), (3), 1785 (1), (2), (3), (4), 1787 (1), 1788 (1), 1789 (1), 1790 (1), 1800 (2).

0127 BERNARD, James

MP for Co. Cork 1781–3–90, June–July 1790

b. 8 Dec. 1729; d. 9 July 1790
FAMILY/BACKGROUND: Son of North Ludlow
Bernard and Rose, dau. of John Echlin of
Echlinville, Co. Down.
MARRIED: (1) [1752] Esther (d. 1780), dau. of
Percy Smyth, wid. of Robert Gookin; (2) [5 Sept.
1789] [   ], dau. of Rev. John O'Sullivan of
Clonakilty.
CHILDREN: (1) Francis, 1st Earl of Bandon (0126);
Rose, m. (1) William Hull (Tonson), 1st Baron
Riversdale (1051), (2) James Millard; Esther, m.
[1775] Sampson Stawell; Charlotte, m. Hon.
Hayes St Leger, 2nd Viscount Doneraile (1856);
Mary, m. Sir Augustus Louis Carre Warren, 2nd
Bt (2187); Charlotte, m. Roger Acklom of
Wiseton Hall, Nottinghamshire.

POLITICAL ACTIVITY: He was elected unopposed for
Co. Cork in 1781 *vice* Lord Muskerry (0609). It
was thought that his unopposed election was by
agreement with Lord Shannon (0213), but he
acted independently of him. Bernard's attitude to
Shannon was at best ambivalent; a contemporary
noted that he was 'elected by the popular interest,
but there is an understanding between him and
Lord Shannon'. His enthusiastic Volunteering gave
him a popular image and he valued his independence, but, at the same time he was careful not to
provoke an open breach with Lord Shannon, to
whose only daughter he married his son and heir
in 1784.

In fact Bernard was in opposition prior to the
arrival of Lord Lieutenant Portland in 1782, and
he remained doubtful thereafter. This is reflected
in his consistent opposition support in the division lists. Furthermore, his vote for Foster (0805)
against Brabazon Ponsonby (1709) was in direct
opposition to Lord Shannon's desire to support
his brother-in-law. In 1785 he voted against the
Commercial Propositions, which were very unpopular with the Cork merchants; he was reputed
to have lost money in the Cork banking crisis of
1784. However, he still had a large fortune and
by 1785 he was looking for a peerage to match
his wealth and political influence: the Bernard
family had been gradually taking over the Devonshire borough of Bandon (part of the Burlington
inheritance). In 1767 Lord Shannon, who supervised the Boyle interest in Co. Waterford, brokered
an agreement with James Bernard whereby the
Dukes of Devonshire and the Bernards would
share the borough and its representation between
them. This agreement remained in force until after the Union.

Before the 1790 election he appears to have
suffered a stroke, and Lord Shannon wrote to his
son about 'the indecent use made of Bernard, who,
under his present deplorable state of human infirmity, is practiced upon for the private views of
those who surround him ... He has not the use of
legs or arms, nor can he at times speak to be understood; yet his young wife, to whom Lord
Kingsborough (1167) had promised a living for
her brother, makes him advertise' for the county
nomination: despite his condition, he was elected.
Furthermore, he took his seat by the side of the
Speaker: 'a dismal spectacle, totally disabled in
limbs, and in the last stages of weakness of mind'.
He died a few weeks later.

DIVISION LISTS:
> 1783 (1) voted for Flood's (0762) motion
> for parliamentary reform.
> 1784 (1) voted for a committee on the
> Reform Bill.
> 1785 (1) voted against the Commercial
> Propositions.
> 1787 (1) absent – had previously voted for a
> Pension Bill.
> 1790 (2) voted for Foster (0805) on the
> election of a Speaker.

ADDITIONAL INFORMATION: In April 1790 the *Gentleman's Magazine* reported that 'Though he had
an immense fortune, he did not live at the rate of
£300 a year. His taylor's bill never amounted to
£61 per annum. He did not absolutely starve himself to death, as he lately showed himself a mere
voluptuary, having a few months since married a
fortunate girl of tender years, to whose tender
embraces, it is feared, he fell a sacrifice.'

ESTATES/RESIDENCE: Castle Bernard, Co. Cork; Dame
Street, Dublin. Succeeded his uncle, Francis Bernard
(0125).

SOURCES: PRONI MIC/465/1 R. Ffolliott, *Biographical Notices, 1756–1827* [*Hibernian Chronicle* says he
died 7 July 1790]; NLI EC 372; Ellis thesis; Burke *PB*

(1903) p. 98 (1906) p. 106; *GM* Apr. 1790 [reports his death in Apr. 1790, but he was returned in the 1790 election!]; *Cork Hist. Soc. Jn.* vol. 14 (1908), R. Day (ed.), 'Minutes from the Council Book of the Borough of Bandon' pp. 122–7 [says he d. 7 July 1790]; The *DJ* notes his death twice, 13–15 Apr. 1790 [at Castle Bernard] – this report was incorrect – 8–10 July 1790 [at his lodgings in Dame Street]; E. Hewitt (ed.), *Lord Shannon's Letters to his Son* (PRONI 1982) pp. lxiv, 1–2, 6; Parliamentary Lists 1776 (1), 1782 (1), 1783 (1), 1784 (1), (2), (3), 1785 (1), (2), (3), (4), 1787 (1), 1788 (1), 1789 (1), 1790 (1).

0128 BERNARD, Stephen

MP for Bandon 1727–60

b. 17 July 1701; d. 6 Sept. 1761, at Barriers, France

FAMILY/BACKGROUND: Second son of Francis Bernard (**0124**) and Alice, dau. of Stephen Ludlow (**1281**).

MARRIED: Unmarried.

EDUCATION: School: Mr Sheridan, Dublin; entered TCD 27 May 1718, BA 1721; Middle Temple 20 Dec. 1721; called to the Irish Bar 1727.

CAREER/OCCUPATION: A Six Clerk in Chancery; *Sovereign of Kinsale 1750, 1752, Recorder 10 Oct. 1732, 1755–6, *Magistrate 1732, 1750, 1752, 1755–6; *Commissioner of the Tillage Act for Munster 1735, 1739–59.

POLITICAL ACTIVITY: Nothing much is known of this MP. He was a younger son and had a small legal sinecure. He sat on 12 committees between 1727 and 1740. In the 1750s his support for government was considered doubtful, but he was probably absent – as he was in 1749 on the one division list available for him.

DIVISION LISTS:
1749 (1) absent, in the country.

ESTATES/RESIDENCE: Prospect Hall, Co. Waterford; St Stephen's Green, Dublin.

SOURCES: PRONI T/1584 Pinkerton transcripts, p. 63; McCracken thesis [says he d. Oct. 1757 at Tarbes in France]; Burke *PB* (1903) p. 98 [says he died Oct. 1757, but he was still sitting in parliament in 1759]; *King's Inns Admissions; Middle Temple Admissions* vol. 1 p. 290; Cork MPs; *Almanacks; DJ* 3–7 Nov. 1761 [obit.]; Parliamentary List, 1756 (1).

0129 BERRY, William

MP for Enniscorthy 1703–13, 1715–27–39; Duleek 1713–14

b. *c.* 1668; d. Dec. 1739

FAMILY/BACKGROUND: Son of [ ] Berry.

MARRIED: [ ].

CHILDREN: Mary, m. Rt Hon. Humphrey Butler, 1st Earl of Lanesborough (**0317**).

EDUCATION: Entered TCD, ?BA *spec. grat.* 1687, LLD *spec. grat.* 1718.

CAREER/OCCUPATION: High Sheriff of Co. Cavan 1724; Freedom of Drogheda.

MILITARY: Lieutenant, Kirke's Regiment at Tangier, 3 Feb. 1681; Captain-Lieutenant, 1st Tangier Regiment (second Queen's) 25 Dec. 1681; Lieutenant of an independent troop of horse 20 June 1685; Lieutenant, Inniskilling Horse Mar. 1689; Lieutenant-Colonel, Inniskilling Horse 20 July 1689; half-pay 1690–1; ?Lieutenant in Sir Henry Bellasise's Regiment 9 Nov. 1695. On 20 Apr. 1696 a Captain William Berry was commissioned into Sir George St George's Regiment of Foot from Sir Mathew Bridges' Regiment of Foot. Lieutenant-Colonel in Marquess de Montandre's Regiment of Foot. A Lieutenant-Colonel William Berry was in Brigadier Wolseley's Regiment of Horse and included on a list of half-pay 'Reformed Officers' serving in 1704; *Lieutenant-Colonel of Foot 1729.

POLITICAL ACTIVITY: Essentially a soldier, he was a Whig during the reign of Queen Anne and so described in 1710. As such he displeased Lord Lieutenant Ormonde. On 6 February 1716 Charles Delafaye (**0611**) wrote: 'We send you a list for our new levies, pray do what you can for poor Colonel Will. Berry for whom my Lord Sunderland has an inclination and who has the Lords Justices best wishes.' The Lord Lieutenant's wishes appear to have been granted, as by 1719 he was in employment and considered a placeman. Berry had been forced to sell his lieutenant-colonelcy for £1,000 by the Duke of Ormonde because he had not voted as the latter had pleased or, more probably, because he changed his allegiance as the queen's death drew near: he was noted on the Parliamentary Lists as a government supporter in 1706, when he attended Ormonde's birthday celebrations. As late as 1711 he was counted as a Tory supporter and he voted for the Court over the Dublin mayoralty dispute, but by 1713 he had become a Whig; possibly he was an Irish example of a 'whimsical Tory'.

DIVISION LISTS:

1711 (1) voted for the Court on the Dublin mayoralty issue.

1721 (2) voted against a national bank.

ESTATES/RESIDENCE: Wardenstown, Co. Meath. His daughter and heir Mary, who married Humphrey Butler (**0317**), later 1st Earl of Lanesborough, in 1726 was 'reputed to have £800 p.a. in land' (probably the estimated income of the Wardenstown estate) and £12,000 in cash.

SOURCES: PRONI D/302; *Commons' jn. Ire.* (Bradley ed.) vol. 4 p. 552 [says that a Lt Col. Berry d. after 1717 – there may have been more than one, certainly this one was alive over twenty years later]; PRONI T/448 pp. 228–9, TSPI 1715–16; PRONI T/559 vol. 9 p. 82, Burke, extract pedigrees; McCracken thesis; Hayton thesis; King, *State of the Protestants*; *Cal. SP Dom. 1695* p. 98, *1696* pp. 136, 137; C. Dalton (ed.), *English Army Lists and Commission Registers, 1661–1714* (London, 1892) vol. 1 pp. 282, 302, 320 (London, 1896) vol. 3 p. 27 (London, 1898) vol. 4 p. 154; *Almanacks*; *The Dublin Gazette* 30 Nov. 1723; *Ir. Sword* vol. 1 (1949–53) pp. 133–5, R. Wyse Jackson, 'Queen Anne's Irish Army Establishment in 1704'; NLI Mahon of Castlegar Papers, Knightly Chetwood to Dr John Ussher, 11 Apr. and 14 May 1726; Parliamentary Lists, 1706 (1), (2), 1711 (3), 1713 (2), 1719 (1).

BESSBOROUGH, Earl: *see* PONSONBY

1696 Ponsonby, Brabazon, 2nd Viscount Duncannon, 1st Earl of Bessborough, [GB] Baron Ponsonby, MP Newton(ards) 1705–13–14, Co. Kildare 1715–24

1707 Ponsonby, Rt Hon. William (styled Viscount Duncannon 1739–58), 2nd Earl of Bessborough, MP Newton(ards) 1725–7, Co. Kilkenny 1727–58, [GB] Derby 1741–2, 1747–54, Saltash 1754–5, Harwich 1756–8

0130 BETTESWORTH, Richard

MP for Thomastown 1721–7; Midleton 1727–41

b. 1689; d. 31 Mar. 1741

FAMILY/BACKGROUND: Son of Richard Bettesworth and Catherine Foulke.

MARRIED: [   ] (she d. July 1779).

CHILDREN: ?

EDUCATION: School: Mr Gifford, Drogheda; entered TCD 9 July 1705; Middle Temple 24 Nov. 1710; called to the Irish Bar, 1716, LLD *hon. caus.* 1725.

CAREER/OCCUPATION: 2nd Serjeant-at-Law 29 Apr. 1732–4; Freedom of Fethard (Tipperary) 1725, of Cork 22 Nov. 1728; *Commissioner of Oyer and Terminer 1733–40; *Council to the Barracks 1733–d.; *Commissioner of the Tillage Act for Munster 1735, 1739.

POLITICAL ACTIVITY: He took a prominent part in parliament in procuring the passing of an act by which the clergy were deprived of a portion of their tithes, and he supported the repeal of the Test in 1733. He thus gained the enmity of Swift, and later claimed that Swift's lampoons made him so unpopular and ridiculous that his professional income declined by £1,200 a year. He appears to have considered that he was a government servant first and his votes on the national bank, if correct, were certainly curious. He was a prominent and busy MP, especially in the decade 1729–39. He was listed for 138 committees during his parliamentary career.

In 1729 he introduced 3 Geo. II, c. 19, 'an act for repairing the Road leading from the City of Dublin to the town of Navan in the County of Meath', setting the tolls etc. for the road; in 1733 he introduced a similar act, 7 Geo. II, c. 20, improving the road from Cork to the Kilworth mountains. In 1735, with Sir Richard Cox (**0508**), he introduced 9 Geo. II, c. 7, 'An Act for encouraging the planting of Timber Trees' – Ireland was very short of wood throughout the eighteenth century. In 1737 he presented 11 Geo. II, c. 10, 'An Act to prevent malicious maiming and wounding and to prevent carrying secret arms'. His busiest year was 1737, when he was nominated for 20 committees. In that year he introduced the recurrent Indemnity Act including a clause to modify the treatment of Dissenters' marriages, and brought in the heads of a bill to give effect to a large number of resolutions agreed by the House to encourage fisheries. Finally, in 1739 he introduced a bill for repairing the road from Timahoe to Ballynakill and thence to Cashel.

ADDITIONAL INFORMATION: Dean Swift, always a passionate supporter of the Established Church and a dangerous enemy, wrote:

Thus at the bar the booby Bettesworth,
Though half-a-crown o'er pays his sweat's worth,
Who knows in law nor text nor margent,
Calls Singleton his brother Serjeant.

DIVISION LISTS:
1721 (1) voted for a national bank.
1721 (2) voted against a national bank.

ESTATES/RESIDENCE: Dublin.

SOURCES: *Commons' jn. Ire* (Bradley ed.) vol. 5 pp. 742, 760, vol. 6 p. 367, 437, 545, 610, 785, 842, 857, vol. 7 p. 149 (0290, 0337, 0350, 0378, 0380, 0384, 0403); McCracken thesis; Kilkenny MPs; *Alum. Dub.*; *IMC King's Inns Admissions*; *Ir. Gen.* vol. 4 no 4 (1971) p. 317, W. G. Skehan, 'Extracts from the Minutes of the Corporation of Fethard, Co. Tipperary'; *Almanacks*.

0131 BINDON, David

MP for Ennis 1715–27 [n.d.e. 1713]

b. *c.* 1650; d. 1733
FAMILY/BACKGROUND: Son of David Bindon and [   ].
MARRIED: Dorothy, dau. of Samuel Burton ?of Buncranny, Co. Clare.
CHILDREN: Thomas, Fellow of TCD, Dean of Limerick; Francis (portrait painter); David (0132); Samuel (0133); Henry (entered TCD 1711, aged 17 years).
CAREER/OCCUPATION: High Sheriff of Co. Clare 1694.

POLITICAL ACTIVITY: He was a Limerick merchant and a Whig. In 1713, although he was subsequently declared not duly elected, he sat long enough to vote for Alan Brodrick (0237) in the Speakership election. Brodrick declared that he was 'well meaning' but wholly under the direction of a great man of the County of Clare (Lord Inchiquin), and 'hath too great a deference (some

people think) to a son of his [Bindon's] that is a fellow of the College'.

He stood again in 1715 and was duly elected; he was nominated for seven committees between 1715 and 1725. On 13 May 1729 Primate Boulter (Lord Justice) wrote to Lord Lieutenant that there had been a great storm over the currency and that 'The merchants who appeared were persons concerned in the remittances and one *Bindon* a broken merchant of Limerick.' This statement is footnoted (*c.* 1770) by an indignant editor – '*David Bindon* esq.; a very eminent merchant, of exceeding good family, of great knowledge in trade, suffered much in the South Sea Scheme in 1720, and was a member of parliament in the reign of George II.' The last part of this statement may be a confusion with his sons (0132, 0133), as this Bindon did not sit in the parliament of George II.

By 1719 he was considered a placeman and in some government employment, but at the same time he was listed as a Tory and considered likely to oppose the repeal of the Test Act.

DIVISION LISTS:
1721 (1) voted for a national bank.
1723 (1) voted for the Court candidate on the Westmeath Co. election petition.

ESTATES/RESIDENCE: Cloney, Co. Clare. He received the grant in fee of Cloney from his father-in-law Samuel Burton in October 1670 (if this is correct he was married by 1670, hence he must have been born *c.* or *ante* 1650). He held lands leased from Lord Thomond in 1712.

About the middle of the century the Bindons had 962 Irish acres, mostly in the barony of Bunratty, including the mansion house of Cloney, at a valuation of £1,025 a year. Rossrawley was sold to Francis Bindon by Lord Inchiquin's trustees in 1750.

SOURCES: PRONI D/302; Hayton thesis; *Alum. Dub.*; Vicars, *Prerog. Wills*; *Boulter Letters* pp. 243–4; J. Frost, *The History and Topography of the County of Clare, from the Earliest Times to the Beginning of the 18th Century, With Map and Illustrations*, pp. 624–7; *JRSAI* vol. 21 (1892) p. 78, P. D. Vigors, 'Alphabetical List of Free Burgesses of New Ross 1658–1839'; B. Ó Dálaigh, *Ennis in the 18th Century: Portrait of an Urban Community* (Maynooth Studies in Local History, 1995), pp. 40–41; NLI vol. 34, 7 June 1853; NLI EC 5584; Parliamentary Lists, 1719 (1), (2).

0132 BINDON, David

MP for Ennis 1731–60

b. *c.* 1687; d. 13 July 1760
FAMILY/BACKGROUND: Third son of David Bindon
(**0131**) of Co. Clare and Dorothy, dau. of Samuel
Burton.
MARRIED: Frances, dau. of Capt. Richard Pope of
Co. Limerick.
CHILDREN: ?
EDUCATION: Inner Temple 18 Sept. 1725; Middle
Temple 4 Aug. 1731; LLD of TCD *hon. caus.* 9
July 1734.
CAREER/OCCUPATION: A merchant of Limerick;
Sheriff of Co. Limerick 1716; *Magistrate and
Provost of Ennis 1745.

POLITICAL ACTIVITY: A consistent government supporter, as his voting record confirms, he was nominated for 90 committees between 1731 and 1758.
On 30 January 1753 Primate Stone wrote to Lord
George Sackville (**1835**) about the Pension List,
stating that 'one hundred was asked for Bindon',
and in February 1755 Bindon was listed as having a civil pension of £100 in the augmentation.

DIVISION LISTS:
1749 (1) voted against the election of James
Digges La Touche (♦♦♦♦).
1753 (1) voted against the expulsion of
Arthur Jones-Nevill (**1125**).
1753 (2) voted for the Money Bill – a
pensioner.
1753 (3) a placeman.

ADDITIONAL INFORMATION: A foundation member
of the Dublin Society, 1731. He translated several treatises on trade, manufactures and ex-
changes. In January 1724/5 Philip Perceval wrote
to Lord Perceval: 'As to the authors of the pamphlets: the Draper's Letters are agreed to be Dean
Swift. The reasons showing the necessity &c. was
written by one Mr Bindon, a gentleman who has
the misfortune of being confined to the Marshalsea
for debt.'
    He was a brother of the famous portrait painter
Francis Bindon, whose portrait of Primate Boulter
hangs in the Provost's House, TCD; and his most
famous portrait of Dean Swift, whom he painted
four times between 1735 and 1740, is at Howth
Castle. Dean Swift was a friend of the painter and
probably knew the family well.

ESTATES/RESIDENCE: Ennis, Co. Clare; Limerick city.

SOURCES: PRONI T/559 vol. 9 p. 217, Burke, extract
pedigrees; PRONI T/3019/6456/376 Wilmot Papers;
BL Add. MSS 47030 f. 129, Perceval to Perceval, 12
Jan. 1724/5; McCracken thesis; *Middle Temple Admis-
sions* vol. 1 p. 311; Berry *RDS* pp. 24–7; *HMC Sackville
I* p. 188; *Almanacks*; *DJ* 15–19 July 1760; *Pue's Occur-
rences* 13 July 1734; B. Ó Dálaigh, *Ennis in the 18th
Century: Portrait of an Urban Community* (Maynooth
Studies in Local History, 1995) pp. 40–41; A.
Crookshank & the Knight of Glin, *The Painters of Ire-
land, c. 1660–1920* (1978), p. 21.

0133 BINDON, Samuel

MP for Ennis 1715–27–60

b. 1680; d. 12 Aug. 1760
FAMILY/BACKGROUND: Son of David Bindon
(**0131**) of Co. Clare and Dorothy, dau. of Samuel
Burton.
MARRIED: [9 Nov. 1716] Anne, dau. of Thomas
Coote of Cootehill, Co. Cavan.
CHILDREN: Henry William (admitted to Middle
Temple 22 Jan. 1742/3), m. Anne dau. of
Thomas Bluet of Co. Limerick; Burton; Ann, m.
1760 Walter Widenham, merchant in Limerick.
EDUCATION: School: Mr Ellis Walker, Drogheda;
entered TCD 14 Dec. 1698.
CAREER/OCCUPATION: Provost of Ennis *ante* 1715–
d.; High Sheriff of Co. Clare 1719. He was in
receipt of a yearly stipend, usually about £7 16s
2d for keeping in repair the infirmary at
Limerick.

POLITICAL ACTIVITY: Like the rest of his family he
appears to have been a solid government supporter,
particularly in the crucial 1750s. He was a fairly
active House of Commons man, listed for service
in eight committees between 1715 and 1725 and
for 30 between 1727 and 1756, by which time he
would have been an old man, well over 60 (MPs
were exempted from committee service after reaching that age). He was interested in the commercial
side of the fishery industry and in 1733 he introduced 7 Geo. II, c. 11, 'An Act for the further Encouragement of the Fishery of this Kingdom', which
attempted to regulate the size of nets, forbid dredg-
ing for oysters from May to August, inspect fish
barrelled for export, and regulate partnerships.
Anxious to assist the faltering woollen industry, he

brought in 'An Act to encourage the Home consumption of wool by burying in wool only'.

He was also interested in communications, especially in the south-west, and in 1733 he brought in an act to repair and organise the turnpike from Kinnegad to Athlone followed by another to repair and establish the turnpike from Tubber to Ennis and from there to Limerick city. Finally he brought in a bill to refurbish and establish street lighting in Dublin, Cork and Limerick. He also assisted in the final stages of a bill to regulate parliamentary elections.

Apart from these successful bills he made a number of interesting suggestions, for instance in 1732 he prepared a scheme for granting licences to retailers of spirits, which the Commissioners of the Revenue submitted to the House of Commons. Perhaps most interesting of all was the heads of a bill, which was favourably received by the House and taken to the Lord Lieutenant (what happened to it thereafter is uncertain), to supply industrious men with money to carry on their trades and better providing for the poor of this kingdom – an early form of venture capital.

DIVISION LISTS:

1721 (1) voted for a national bank.

1723 (1) voted for the Court candidate on the Westmeath Co. election petition.

1749 (1) absent, in the country.

1753 (1) voted against the expulsion of Arthur Jones-Nevill (1125).

1753 (2) voted for the Money Bill.

ESTATES/RESIDENCE: Rockmount, Co. Clare; Temple Montgret, Limerick.

SOURCES: *CJ Ire.* (Bradley ed.) vol. 5 pp. 741, 762 , vol. 6 pp. 361, 373, 379, 390, 417, 435–6, vol. 7 pp. 300, 306, 338, 837 (0328, 0330, 0336, 0342, 0416); PRONI T/559 vol. 9 p. 217, Burke, extract pedigrees; PRONI MIC/465/1 R. Ffolliott, *Biographical Notices, 1756–1827*; McCracken thesis; *Alum. Dub.*; *Middle Temple Admissions* vol. 1 p. 332 [says of Temple Montgret, Co. Limerick]; *King's Inns Admissions* p. 36; B. Ó Dálaigh, *Ennis in the 18th Century: Portrait of an Urban Community* (Maynooth Studies in Local History, 1995) pp. 40–41; J. Frost, *The History and Topography of the County of Clare, from the Earliest Times to the Beginning of the 18th Century, With Map and Illustrations*, pp. 624–7; *DJ* 19–23 Aug. 1760, 2–6 Sept. 1760; *Pue's Occurrences* 20 Dec. 1718.

0134 BINGHAM, Sir Charles

MP for Co. Mayo 1761–8–76 [r. Castlebar 1761]; [GB] Northampton 1782–4

b. 22 Sept. 1735; d. 29 Mar. 1799 at his house in Charles Street, Berkeley Square, London
HONOURS: Suc. as 7th Bt [S.] 1749.
PEERAGES: Cr. Baron Lucan 24 July 1776, Earl of Lucan 1 Oct. 1795.
FAMILY/BACKGROUND: Son of Sir John Bingham, 5th Bt (0141), and Anne, dau. of Agmondisham Vesey (2144) of Lucan, Co. Dublin.
MARRIED: [25 Aug. 1760] Margaret, dau. and co-h. of James Smith of Cannons Leigh, Devon, and St Aundries, Somerset.
CHILDREN: Richard, 2nd Earl of Lucan, m. [26 May 1794] Elizabeth (d. 1819), dau. and co-h. of Henry Belasyse, 3rd Earl of Fauconberg, divorced w. of Bernard Edward Howard, 17th Duke of Norfolk; Lavinia (d. 8 June 1831), m. [1781] Rt Hon. George John Spencer, 2nd Earl of Spencer; Margaret (d. 27 May 1839), m. Thomas Lindsay, Hollymount House, Co. Mayo (1240); Anne (d. 6 Mar. 1840).
CAREER/OCCUPATION: High Sheriff of Co. Mayo 1756; *Governor of Co. Mayo 1756–63, Joint Governor 1766–98; *Trustee of the Linen Board for Ulster 1762–d.
MILITARY: Colonel of the Mayo Legion, Volunteers; Second Lieutenant in the Longford (Clanricarde) Cavalry 1796.

POLITICAL ACTIVITY: He was first returned in a contested election for Co. Mayo in 1761, after having secured his return for his own borough of Castlebar. In the Parliamentary List for 1775 he was described as 'in private life a respectable amiable man. Independent from fortune.' His fortune made him independent and he adopted an opposition line in politics, being described in another list as 'a true patriot'. However, in 1769 he was anxious to be a member of the Privy Council but was in opposition to both Lord Lieutenant Townshend and Lord Lieutenant Harcourt. He appears to have formed a friendship with Chief Secretary Blaquiere (0162), whom he assisted in some negotiations with Charles James Fox in the mid-1770s. Towards the end of Harcourt's viceroyalty he appears to have changed his mind, and warmly supported the viceroy during his final parliamentary session, when he voted against the pro-American amendment to the Speech from the

Throne. He was rewarded with some Revenue patronage (one supernumerary gauger and two hearth money collectors) and also, in 1776, with a peerage. In the ensuing election he returned Thomas Coghlan (0433) for one seat 'at Lord Harcourt's insistance' (this was the conventional return for a peerage), and for the other the notorious confidence man, Stephen Popham (1712), who 'gulled him out of' it.

He was an enthusiastic Volunteer. His friendship with the opposition in Great Britain was confirmed in 1781 when he married his daughter Lavinia to Earl Spencer's heir, Lord Althorp. He was returned on the Spencer interest for Northampton in 1781, probably as a seat warmer, for he was not returned at the 1784 election. In 1785 he came over to Ireland to support the Whig alliance in the Irish House of Lords, but normally he resided in England and he sold the two seats for Castlebar. He was created Earl of Lucan in 1795. He died in 1799, having promised his support for the Union.

DIVISION LISTS:

1768 (1) voted against army augmentation.
1771 (1) voted against Lord Townshend as Lord Lieutenant.
1771 (2) voted for Sir Lucius O'Brien's (1558) motion for retrenchment.
1773 (1) voted against Absentee Tax.
1775 (1) voted against the pro-American amendment to the Speech from the Throne.

ADDITIONAL INFORMATION: His wife's fortune was £20,000. His great-grandfather, William Sarsfield, was the elder brother of Patrick Sarsfield, the Jacobite Earl of Lucan; his great-grandmother was Mary Crofts, a sister of the Duke of Monmouth and an illegitimate daughter of Charles II.

He wrote *An Essay on the Use and Necessity of Establishing a Militia in Ireland* (Dublin, 1767). In it he advocated raising a militia of 6,400 men, 200 from each county, officers and men to be chosen by ballot. A tax was to be laid on absentees to finance this force. A militia, as opposed to augmenting the regular taxes, was a feature of many 'Patriot' programmes. Bingham's ideas were drawn from the example of Switzerland, and were later to be implemented by the Volunteers.

A subscriber to the Marine Society, March 1759; *a member of the Royal Dublin Society from 1764.

ESTATES/RESIDENCE: Castlebar, Co. Mayo. In the first decade of the nineteenth century Wakefield estimated that Lord Lucan had a rental of £10,000.

SOURCES: PRONI D/302; PRONI MIC/474 Irish Volunteers; RCBL P80/1/1, Parish Registers of St Thomas, Dublin; Burke *PB* (1903) p. 973; GEC *P*, *HP 1754–90*; G. F. Russell-Barker and A. H. Stenning (eds), *Record of Old Westminsters: A Biographical List* (London, 1928); Johnston, *Gt B. & Ire.*, p. 193; J. Kelly, *Prelude to Union* (Cork, 1992), p. 165; G. O'Brien (ed.), *Parliament, Politics and People* (1989) pp. 40–1, J. O'Donovan, 'The Militia in Munster'; Wakefield, *Account of Ire.*, pp. i, 271; *Almanacks*; BNL 30 Mar. 1759; DJ 29 Jan. – 2 Feb. 1760, 30 Dec. 1760 – 3 Jan. 1761, 16–19 May 1761, 10–13 Mar. 1781; FJ 24 Nov. 1796; Parliamentary Lists, 1769 (1), 1772 (2), 1773 (1), 1774 (1), 1775 (1), 1777 (1), 1782 (1), 1783 (2), 1787 (1), 1788 (1), 1790 (1), 1791 (1), 1793 (1), 1798 (1), 1799 (2), (3), 1800 (2).

0135 BINGHAM, Sir Henry

MP for Co. Mayo 1692–3, 1695–9, 1703–13–14

b. 1654; d. 5 July 1714
HONOURS: Suc. as 3rd Bt [S].
FAMILY/BACKGROUND: Eldest son of Sir George Bingham, 2nd Bt, and his first wife [   ] Palmer.
MARRIED: (1) [4 Sept 1677] Jane, dau. of Sir James Cuffe of Ballinrobe, Co. Mayo; (2) Letitia, dau. of Charles Bingham of Newbrook, Co. Mayo.
CHILDREN: *d.s.p.m.*
EDUCATION: Middle Temple 1673.
CAREER/OCCUPATION: High Sheriff of Co. Mayo 1684–5, 1694; Governor of Co. Mayo, 1699.

POLITICAL ACTIVITY: He was a Tory and in 1695 voted for the impeachment of Lord Chancellor Porter, a signatory to the Treaty of Limerick, who was considered unduly sympathetic to the Catholics. The following year he signed the Association for the protection of William III in parliament. During Queen Anne's reign he was a consistent Tory, including his 1709 hostility to one of the Money Bills.

In 1713 his return for Co. Mayo was correctly

predicted, and in 1714 he signed a County address in favour of the Tory Chancellor, Sir Constantine Phipps. Not surprisingly, he was on the 1714–15 'black list' of Tories. He was listed for one committee in the short 1692 parliament, 23 between 1695 and 1699, and 21 during the 1703–13 parliament of Queen Anne.

DIVISION LISTS:

1709 (1) spoke against a Money Bill.

1711 (1) voted for the Court on the Dublin mayoralty issue.

1713 (1) voted for Sir Richard Levinge (1230) for Speaker.

ESTATES/RESIDENCE: Castlebar, Co. Mayo. Sir Richard Bingham, an army commander, came to Ireland in the reign of Queen Elizabeth to quell the various rebellions. The family fortunes were considerably augmented in 1702–3 by the purchase, from the Commissioners for Sale of Forfeited Estates, of 3,043 acres in Co. Mayo. His income in 1713 was estimated at £600.

SOURCES: PRONI D/302 [calls him Sir 1684–5, 1694, Bart 1684, 1694]; PRONI T/3411; Rev. Henry Gilmore from Memorial Tablet, Castlebar Parish Church, says he died aged 60 years; GEC B; Burke PB (1906) p. 1047; *Middle Temple Admissions* vol. 1 p. 187; *Proc. RIA* Sept. 1924; Burke PB (1903) p. 973 [does not mention a second marriage unlike the 1900 ed.]; Simms' cards; Simms, *Williamite Confiscation*, p. 183; *The Register of the Parish of St Peter and St Kevin, 1669–1761* (Parish Register Society of Dublin, 1911) p. 60; *JRSAI* vol. 55 (1925) pp. 39, 42, H. A. S. Upton, 'A List of Governors and Deputy Governors of Counties in Ireland in 1699' [says he m. Jane dau. of James Cuffe of Ballinrobe, Co. Mayo]; Parliamentary Lists, 1695 (1), 1696 (1), 1706 (1), 1711 (3), 1713 (1), (2), 1714 (1), 1714–15 (1).

0136 BINGHAM, Rt Hon. Henry

MP for Co. Mayo 1707–13–14; Castlebar 1715–27–43

b. 1688; d. 5 Dec. 1743

HONOURS: PC, sworn 15 Nov. 1735.

FAMILY/BACKGROUND: Only son of Maj. Charles Bingham of Newbrook and Foxford, Co. Mayo, and Mary, dau. of Henry Blennerhassett of Enniskillen, Co. Fermanagh.

MARRIED: Anne, dau. of John Vesey, Abp of Tuam

(a Lord Justice, 1714).

CHILDREN: John (0142); Henry (0137); Susanna; Catherine; Rebecca; Dorothy; Mary, m. Joshua Cooper (0473).

EDUCATION: School: Mr Price, Galway; entered TCD 4 Mar. 1705.

CAREER/OCCUPATION: Lord Justice; High Sheriff of Co. Mayo 1712; *Governor of the Workhouse 1733–d.; *Commissioner of the Tillage Act for Connaught 1736, 1739–d.; *Trustee of the Linen Board for Ulster 1739–d.

POLITICAL ACTIVITY: Like the rest of his family, he was a Tory and a supporter of the Court party during the reign of Queen Anne. He was on the 1714–15 'black list' of Tories. As predicted, he was returned for Co. Mayo in 1713 but in subsequent parliaments he sat for Castlebar, where the family had considerable influence. He appears to have come to terms with the Hanoverian succession, although he continued to be Tory in outlook and, in 1719, was considered unlikely to support the repeal of the Test Act. He was nominated for some 54 committees during his political career and was made a Privy Counsellor in 1735.

DIVISION LISTS:

1709 (1) voted against a Money Bill.

1711 (1) voted for the court on the Dublin mayoralty issue.

1721 (1) voted for a national bank.

1721 (2) voted for a national bank.

ADDITIONAL INFORMATION: In 1715 his income was estimated at £1,500 p.a. Mrs Pendavers (Delany) visited them in 1732 and recorded that 'Mr Bingham and his lady are very agreeable people; he has been a great beau, and has seen a good deal of the world, is now turned perfect country gentleman, and affects bluntness and humour, which he manages so as to be very entertaining; Mrs Bingham is very civil, and a smart woman.' She also commented that Mr Bingham lived in a house near Castlebar: 'The house is a good old house, and Mr Bingham is improving it.'

ESTATES/RESIDENCE: Foxford and later Newbrook, Co. Mayo. In 1743 Rt Hon. Henry Bingham let Carrowneden etc. in perpetuity to Andrew Rutledge; this contained at least 1,648 statute acres, and probably far more.

SOURCES: PRONI D/302; PRONI T/559 vol. 9 p. 208, Burke, extract pedigrees; PRONI T/3411; NLI vol. 125, 12 Feb. 1867; McCracken thesis; *GM* Dec. 1743; Burke *LGI* (1904) p. 37; *Index to Irish Privy Counsellors, 1711–1910*; Llandover, *Delany Corr.*, vol. 1 p. 352; *Almanacks*; *The Dublin Gazette* 25 Dec. 1711, 6 Dec. 1743; Parliamentary Lists, 1711 (3), 1713 (1), (2), 1714–15 (1), 1719 (2).

0137 BINGHAM, Henry

MP for Tuam 1750–60, 1761–8

b. 1715; d. 15 Apr. 1769
FAMILY/BACKGROUND: Second son of Rt Hon. Henry Bingham (0136) and Anne, dau. of John Vesey, Abp of Tuam.
MARRIED: Cornelia Tighe.
CHILDREN: *d.s.p.*
EDUCATION: School: Dr McMullin; entered TCD 28 Feb. 1733, BA 1738; Middle Temple 9 July 1739; called to the Irish Bar 1744; LLD *hon. caus.* 1762.
CAREER/OCCUPATION: Portreeve of Castlebar 1757; Recorder of Tuam 1756–61; *Magistrate 1752, 1756, of Tuam 1755–60.

POLITICAL ACTIVITY: He was nominated for 31 committees between 1751 and 1760. He was a government supporter, as is shown by his voting pattern, and a pensioner. On 21 February 1755 he was granted a (further) pension of £200 p.a. This appears to have been a reward for his support during the Money Bill dispute.

DIVISION LISTS:
1753 (1) voted against the expulsion of Arthur Jones-Nevill (1125).
1753 (2) voted for the Money Bill – a pensioner.
1757 (1) voted against the resolutions on pensions – pensioner.
1768 (1) voted for army augmentation – a pensioner.

ESTATES/RESIDENCE: Castle Burke, Co. Mayo.

SOURCES: McCracken thesis; R. E. McAlmont, *Memoirs of the Binghams* (London, 1915), p. 136; *King's Inns Admissions*; *Middle Temple Admissions* vol. 1 p. 326; *Almanacks*; *BNL* 20 Feb. 1767; *Pue's Occurrences* 5 Oct. 1751.

0138 BINGHAM, Henry

MP for Tuam 1761–8

b. (bapt. 7 Nov.) 1739; d. Dec. 1789
FAMILY/BACKGROUND: Son of John Bingham (0142) and Frances, eldest dau. of Sir Arthur Shaen, 2nd Bt (1900).
MARRIED: [28 Oct. 1761] Letitia, dau. of Denis Daly of Raford, Co. Galway.
CHILDREN: John, 1st Baron Clanmorris (0144); Henry; Denis; 6 dau. (one m. [1778] Christopher St George of Tyrone, Co. Galway).
EDUCATION: School: ?Eton 30 Apr. 1756–7.

POLITICAL ACTIVITY: Very little is known of his parliamentary activities. The opposition press suggested that he preferred to sell the seats for Tuam rather than serve in parliament: 'He rather chooses to be a wholesale manufacturer of Members of Parliament than to go into the House himself.' Certainly he had to provide for a very large family, and he may not have enjoyed very good health.

DIVISION LISTS:
1768 (1) absent, sick.

ESTATES/RESIDENCE: Newbrook, Co. Mayo. In 29 Geo. III (1789) Henry Bingham was granted fairs at Carraghreagh, *alias* Melcombe Regis.

SOURCES: RCBL P277/1/1, Parish Register of St Mary's, Dublin; Burke *PB* (1906) p. 341 [says he died 1790]; *Memorials of the Dead* [says he died Dec. 1789 in his – 3rd (*sic*) year]; R. A. Austen-Leigh (ed.), *The Eton College Register 1753–90*, 3 vols (Eton, 1921); *DJ* 29–31 Dec. 1778; 31 Oct. – 3 Nov. 1761; Parliamentary List, 1790 (1).

0139 BINGHAM, John

MP for Castlebar 1692–3; Co. Mayo 1695–9, 1703–6

b. *c.* 1655; d. (*ante* 25 Mar.) 1706/7
FAMILY/BACKGROUND: Son and heir of John Bingham of Bellanaloobe, Co. Mayo.
MARRIED: [30 June 1684] Mary, dau. of Rt Hon. George Lane, 1st Viscount Lanesborough.
CHILDREN: *d.s.p.*
EDUCATION: Middle Temple 19 July 1682.
CAREER/OCCUPATION: High Sheriff of Co. Mayo 1686, 1691–2; Deputy Governor of Co. Mayo 1699.

MILITARY: Captain in the Duke of Ormonde's Regiment of Foot 1685.

POLITICAL ACTIVITY: In 1695 he voted for the impeachment of Lord Chancellor Porter, who was considered by some MPs to be unduly favourable to the Catholics in the aftermath of the Treaty of Limerick, to which Porter had been a signatory. In 1696 he signed the Association for the protection of William III in the country. He was nominated for three committees in 1692 and one in 1695. In the first parliament of Queen Anne he was nominated for nine committees between 1703 and 1705. He died in 1706/7.

ESTATES/RESIDENCE: Newbrook, Co. Mayo. Lands in Kilmaine. Grant to John Bingham, 1685, of lands in Carra and Clanmorris. In 35 Chas II (1684), John Bingham was granted fairs at Foxford, and in 13 Will. III (1701) at Bunfinglass.

SOURCES: PRONI D/302 (calls him senr in 1686, which presupposes he was born *c.* 1650s); R. E. Altamont, *Memoirs of the Binghams* (London, 1915); C. Dalton (ed.), *English Army Lists and Commission Registers, 1661–1714* (London, 1896), vol. 3 p. 12 [on 22 March 1689 John Bingham appears on a list of Protestant Officers lately in the army of Ireland but now unemployed and in England seeking employment in His Majesty's service; notes he was lately a Captain in Colonel Justin Macarthy's Regiment of Foot, 1686]; C. Dalton (ed.), *Irish Army Lists 1661–85* (London, 1907), p. 150 [may be (0140)]; HMC *Ormonde* new ser. vol. 8 pp. 227, 229 [Robert Johnson (1101) reports his death on 25 Mar. 1706/7]; H. F. Berry (ed.), *The Registers of the Church of St Michan, Dublin, 1636–1700* (Parish Register Society of Dublin, 1909) p. 170; *Middle Temple Admissions* vol. 1 p. 207; *JRSAI* vol. 55 (1925) pp. 39, 49, H. A. S. Upton, 'A List of Governors and Deputy Governors of Counties in Ireland in 1699'; EC 1642; Parliamentary Lists, 1695 (1), 1696 (1), 1707 (1).

0140 BINGHAM, John

MP for Castlebar 1715–27

b. *ante* 12 Nov. 1694; d. 1728
FAMILY/BACKGROUND: ?Son of Charles Bingham and Mary, dau. of Henry Blennerhassett of Enniskillen, Co. Fermanagh.
MARRIED: ?
CHILDREN: ?

POLITICAL ACTIVITY: Virtually nothing is known of this MP, except that he was part of the Bingham of Newbrook family and probably a brother of the Rt Hon. Henry Bingham. He came into parliament for Castlebar, which belonged to the other branch of the Bingham family. He was a Tory by inclination and, in 1719, thought to be hostile to the repeal of the Test Act. He had a reasonably active parliamentary life, being nominated for nine committees between 1715 and 1728.

DIVISION LISTS:
1721 (2) voted against a national bank.

ESTATES/RESIDENCE: Newbrook, Co. Mayo.

SOURCES: Vicars, *Prerog. Wills*; Parliamentary Lists, 1719 (2).

0141 BINGHAM, Sir John

MP for Co. Mayo 1727–49

b. 1690; d. 21 Sept. 1749
HONOURS: Suc. as 5th Bt [S] *c.* 1730.
FAMILY/BACKGROUND: Eldest son of Sir George Bingham, 4th Bt, of Castlebar, Co. Mayo, and his first wife Mary Scott.
MARRIED: [*c.* 1730] Anne, dau. of Agmondisham Vesey (2144).
CHILDREN: Sir John Bingham, 6th Bt (0143); Sir Charles, 1st Earl of Lucan (0134); Jane, m. Rt Hon. Thomas Bermingham, 1st Earl of Louth, (0122); Mary, m. (1) Hugh Montgomery, (2) Sir Vesey Colclough (0436); Charlotte; Henrietta; Anna, m. Croasdaile Miller.
EDUCATION: School: Mr Price, Galway; entered TCD 26 Nov. 1713; Middle Temple 27 July 1717.
CAREER/OCCUPATION: High Sheriff of Co. Mayo 1721; Governor of Co. Mayo 1727; *Trustee of the Linen Board for Munster 1732–d.; *Governor of the Workhouse 1733–d.; *Commissioner of the Tillage Act for Connaught 1735, 1739–d.

POLITICAL ACTIVITY: He was nominated for 34 committees between 1727 and 1744, when he would have been 54. In May 1728 he was the leading member of the group entrusted with a penal act 'for further strengthening the Protestant interest in this kingdom' which placed restrictions on Catholic lawyers, solicitors and other legal officials except those protected by the Treaties of Limerick and Galway.

In 1736 his parliamentary behaviour elicited the following description:

There observe the tribe of Bingham,
For he never fails to bring 'em;
While he sleeps the whole debate,
They submissive round him waite;
Yet would gladly see the hunks,
In his grave and search his trunks;
See they gently twitch his coat,
Just to yawn and give his vote;
Always firm in this vocation,
For the court against the nation.

ADDITIONAL INFORMATION: His wife had some artistic talent and left a portrait of her great-uncle Patrick Sarsfield, the Jacobite Earl of Lucan.

ESTATES/RESIDENCE: Castlebar, Foxford, Co. Mayo.

SOURCES: *CJ Ire.* (Bradley ed.) vol. 5 p. 627 (0264); PRONI D/302 [Calls him Sir and Bart 1721]; PRONI T/559 vol. 9 p. 207, Burke, extract pedigrees; McCracken thesis; GEC *B*; Burke *PB* (1903) p. 973; Gilbert, *Dublin*, vol. 3 pp. 262–3; *Middle Temple Admission* (London, 1949) vol. 1 p. 280; *Almanacks*; GM July 1749.

0142 BINGHAM, John

MP for Tuam 1739–60

b. 1714; d. (*ante* 24) Oct. 1780
FAMILY/BACKGROUND: Eldest son of Rt Hon. Henry Bingham (**0136**) and Anne, dau. of John Vesey, Abp of Tuam.
MARRIED: [1 June 1738] Frances, dau. of Sir Arthur Shaen, 2nd Bt (**1900**).
CHILDREN: Henry (**0138**).
EDUCATION: School: Mr McMullin, Dublin; entered TCD 1 Feb. 1732, aged 18 years, LLD *hon. caus.* 1744.
CAREER/OCCUPATION: *Governor of Co. Mayo (in the absence of Lord Tyrawley 1746–53), 1754–9; High Sheriff of Co. Mayo 1753; *Commissioner of the Tillage Act for Connaught 1733–d.

POLITICAL ACTIVITY: He was nominated for 19 committees during his parliamentary career. He avoided, through absence, the vote on the very

controversial return for Dublin city in 1749. Unlike most of his family, he appears to have supported the Country party in the 1750s. He controlled the returns for Tuam, which the family acquired from his grandfather, Archbishop Vesey.

DIVISION LISTS:
1749 (1) absent, in town.
1753 (1) voted for the expulsion of Arthur Jones-Nevill (**1125**).
1753 (2) voted against the Money Bill.

ESTATES/RESIDENCE: Newbrook, Co. Mayo.

SOURCES: PRONI D/302; McCracken thesis; Burke *PB* (1903) p. 316; *Almanacks*; *Pue's Occurrences* 13 Jan. 1753; *DJ* Oct. 24–6 1780.

0143 BINGHAM, Sir John

MP for Co. Mayo 1749–50

b. (*ante* 29) Nov. 1728; d. 27 Nov. 1750 of a fever in his Grafton Street lodgings, bur. at Castlebar
HONOURS: Suc. as 6th Bt [S] 1749.
FAMILY/BACKGROUND: Eldest son of Sir John Bingham, 5th Bt (**0141**), and Anne, dau. of Agmondisham Vesey (**2144**).
MARRIED: Unmarried.

POLITICAL ACTIVITY: He was nominated for one committee during his short parliamentary career. In voting for the return of James Digges La Touche (♦♦♦♦) in the highly controversial 1749 Dublin City election, he appears to have been inclining to the Country or opposition party.

DIVISION LISTS:
1749 (1) voted for the election of James Digges La Touche (♦♦♦♦).

ADDITIONAL INFORMATION: 'He set apart the great share of his [fortune] to pay off large debts he was no way liable to', out of regard for his parents.

ESTATES/RESIDENCE: Castlebar, Co. Mayo. Succeeded by his brother Charles, 1st Earl of Lucan (**0134**). In 7 Jas I (1610) Sir James (also described as Sir John) Bingham was granted a market at Castlebar.

SOURCES: PRONI D/1201/54 EEC rental, 1854; PRONI T/1584 Pinkerton transcripts, 4 Dec. 1750;

McCracken thesis; *GM* Nov. 1750; Burke *PB* (1900, 1903) pp. 969, 973 [says (incorrectly) he died 1752]; *BNL* 4 Dec. 1750 [says he died in his 22nd year].

0144 BINGHAM, John

MP for Tuam 1797–Feb. 1800; [Escheator of Munster 1800]

> b. 1762; d. 18 May 1821
> PEERAGES: Cr. Baron Clanmorris of Newbrook 31 July 1800.
> FAMILY/BACKGROUND: Son of Henry Bingham (**0138**) and Letitia, dau. of Denis Daly of Co. Galway.
> MARRIED: [21 May 1791] Anne Maria, only dau. of Rt Hon. Barry Yelverton, 1st Viscount Avonmore (**2268**).
> CHILDREN: Charles Barry, 2nd Baron of Clanmorris, m. [1816] Sarah, dau. of Walter Lambert of Castle Lambert, Co. Galway; Denis Arthur, 3rd Baron Clanmorris, m. [1825] Martha Helena, dau. of Robert Persse of Co. Galway; Letitia Maria, m. Robert French of Co. Galway; Anna Maria, m. [1829] Bentinck Walter Yelverton of Co. Tipperary; Louisa Catherine, m. [1838] Rev. Benjamin Chapman Frederick Yelverton; Caroline Harriet.
> CAREER/OCCUPATION: Captain in the Carra Cavalry Dec. 1796.

POLITICAL ACTIVITY: He was returned for the last Irish parliament and appears to have tried to sell his interest to the highest bidder. The 1800 (opposition) black list declares that 'The Author of this work was deputed to learn from Mr Bingham what his expectations from Government for his seats were; he proposed to take from the Opposition £8,000 for his two seats for Tuam and oppose the Union. Government afterwards added a Peerage and £15,000 for the Borough.' Lord Lieutenant Cornwallis perhaps put it more elegantly; in recommending him for the peerage he wrote that he: 'has the borough of Tuam, for the seat of which two friends of Government are returned. Mr Bingham has a large fortune.' He actually received £14,000 for the disfranchisement of the borough, as the Commissioners required him to pay £1,000 to Walter Yelverton (**2269**), the other sitting MP, in compensation.

One of Lord Downshire's correspondents wrote to him on 19 February 1999 that 'I hear a Mr Bingham (Yelverton's son-in-law) is to be made a peer. Bingham is a ruffian in his manners, so I wish your Lordships joy of him.' He supported the Union and was created Lord Clanmorris. The crucial divisions on the Union were no sooner over than Bingham asked for the Escheatorship of Munster and his relative George Vesey, who, government may have felt, was more predictable, was returned as a Unionist in his place.

DIVISION LISTS:
> 1799 (1) voted for the Union.
> 1800 (1) voted for the Union.

ADDITIONAL INFORMATION: He stood unsuccessfully for Co. Mayo in 1790 and fought a duel with Denis Browne (**0253**) of Westport, whom he accused of being a 'Castle hack'. Neither was injured because Browne 'fired his last shot in the air, perceiving from Mr Bingham's position at the time, had he done otherwise, he must have mortally wounded his antagonist'.

ESTATES/RESIDENCE: Newbrook, Co. Mayo. Lands in the barony of Tyrawley. Lands were leased in 1759 from Henry Ormsby. Wakefield calculated that Lord Clanmorris's rental was £10,000 at the beginning of the nineteenth century.

SOURCES: O'Neill thesis; Burke *PB* (1903) p. 316; GEC *P*, *Memoirs of the Binghams*, *Memorials of the Dead* [says he died 10 May 1821 aged 56 years]; Bolton, *The Passing of the Irish Act of Union* (1966), p. 103 & n.; J. Kelly, *'That Damn'd Thing Called Honour': Duelling in Ireland 1570–1860* (Cork, 1995), p. 146; *Cornwallis Corr.* vol. 3 pp. 255–6; *FJ* 6 Dec. 1796; CDB 9988; Wakefield, *Account of Ire.*, vol. 1 p. 271; Parliamentary Lists, 1783 (1), 1793 (1), 1799 (1), 1800 (1).

0145 BIRCH, Robert

MP for Belturbet 1771–6–83

> b. *ante* 1741; d. *post* 1800
> FAMILY/BACKGROUND: Son of [   ] Birch.
> MARRIED: ?(1) Isabella Sarah [   ]; ?(2) Catherine [   ].
> CHILDREN: (1) Charles (b. 1762; Royal School, Armagh; entered TCD 1778, aged 16 years);

William Reeves (b. 1768); Robert Henry (bapt. 6 Mar. 1772).

(2) Mary (bapt. 30 July 1775).

CAREER/OCCUPATION: Assistant Clerk of Quit-Rents 1779–8, for the Port Business 1800 (f.).

POLITICAL ACTIVITY: He was a political adventurer and financial speculator. On the death of George Glover (0854), he purchased (for £2,200) his seat for Belturbet from the Earl of Lanesborough (0313), who was in financial difficulties. Given Birch's rather dubious financial affairs, this may have been an insurance against arrest. He was involved in the failure of Wilcock and Dawson's bank in 1763 and the settling of its affairs by parliament, 3 Geo. III, c. 10, and there was 'a strong resolution of the House against him about the banking business'. He was alleged to have obliterated 'the accounts of a public bank, making a false defence on oath and kindly assisting to prevent just creditors from getting their due'.

His mercenary characteristics were well known to the government. However, government needed votes and he was a steady supporter even if in return he expected certain benefits – 'He has all his life been a money-making man. He certainly intends to make the best bargain he can' – including social favours, such as 'a dinner at the Castle and a nod from the Secretary'. He was particularly anxious to obtain 'eight or nine perpetual advowsons' that belonged to an estate he had purchased from Lord Kingsland. He does not appear to have obtained these, but his brother-in-law was allowed to resign his place to his nephew and he was given the appointment of a hearth money collector and a coast officer. His support for Lord Harcourt was similarly rewarded with the patronage of a clerkship worth £60 p.a., a surveyorship valued at £70 p.a., a supernumerary gauger, a tidewaiter and two coast officers – this list probably includes his previous patronage.

The government's financial crisis of 1778 was increased by the failure of three bankers, namely Birch, Hugh Henry Mitchell (1415) and Richard Underwood (2120). Lord Buckinghamshire made Birch, now a broken merchant, Clerk of the Quit Rents at £150 p.a. It is uncertain whether he bargained with the 2nd Earl of Lanesborough in 1776 for the 1783 parliament or whether he 'sold on'

his seat, but he was not returned again.

ADDITIONAL INFORMATION: He is described as 'the very quintessence of effrontery' and 'a Man of bad Character in private Life a sort of Merchant banker traffics much in the purchase of pensions and Reversions of Estates, by which it is supposed he has acquired a large property'. In 1778 he went bankrupt and 1782 one of his contemporaries gave the following outline of his career: he '... was originally a grocer, afterwards a dealer in money, purchased several pensions, but at last became a bankrupt. Lord Buckingham[shire] made him Clerk of the Quit Rent, £150 a year; he will support any Government and take any thing he can get.'

DIVISION LISTS:

1771 (1) voted against the amendment to the Revenue Bill.

1771 (2) voted against Sir Lucius O'Brien's (1558) motion for retrenchment – 'formerly a grocer'.

1772 (1) voted against the separation of the Revenue Board.

1772 (2) voted against a Short Revenue Bill.

1773 (1) voted for Absentee Tax.

1773 (2) voted against an untaxed press.

1774 (1) voted for the Stamp Bill.

1774 (2) voted for Catholic relief.

1775 (1) voted against the pro-American amendment to the Speech from the Throne.

1777 (1) voted against Grattan's (0895) motion for retrenchment.

1778 (2) voted for the Popery Bill.

1779 (1) voted for the new taxes.

1779 (2) voted against a six-months Loan Bill.

1780 (1) voted against Grattan's declaration of the Rights of Ireland.

1780 (2) voted against Yelverton's (2268) motion to modify Poynings' Law.

1780 (4) voted for a Perpetual Mutiny Bill.

ESTATES/RESIDENCE: Turvey, Co. Dublin; Birchgrove, Co. Wexford. In 1763 Robert Birch was granted fairs at Birchgrove.

SOURCES: *Ir. Statutes*, 3 George III cap. 10 [Willcocks & Dawson Bank] (0597); NAI, Parish Registers of St Mary's Dublin [says Robert Henry, son of Robert Birch and Catherine his wife bapt. 6 Mar. 1772]; RCBL P80/

1/1, Parish Registers of St Thomas, Dublin [gives entries regarding Robert Birch: (1) Catherine, dau. of Robert and Isabella Sarah Birch bapt. 10 Nov. 1773 (2) Mary, dau. of Robert and Catherine Birch bapt. 30 July 1775]; Ellis thesis; *Alum. Dub.*; M. L. Farrar, *Register of the Royal School: Armagh* (1933); Johnston, *Gt B. & Ire.*, pp. 228, 254–5; *Ir. Gen.* vol. 1 no 8 (1940) p. 237, 'A List of Irish Stockholders, 1779' [says William Ryves Birch, aged 11 years, second son of Robert Birch and his wife Catherine, of Donnabate, Co. Dublin]; *Almanacks*; Parliamentary Lists, 1771 (1), 1772 (1), (2), 1773 (1), (2), 1774 (1), 1775 (1), 1776 (1), (2), 1777 (1), 1778 (1), 1780 (1), 1782 (1), 1783 (1).

0146 BLACKWOOD, Hon. Hans

MP for Killyleagh 1799–Jan. 1800; [Escheator of Munster 7 Jan. 1800]

> b. Oct. 1758; d. 18 Nov. 1839 at Dublin
> HONOURS: Suc. as 4th Bt.
> PEERAGES: 3rd Baron Dufferin and Claneboye 1836.
> FAMILY/BACKGROUND: Son of Sir John Blackwood, 2nd Bt (0148), and Dorcas, Baroness Dufferin and Claneboye, dau. of James Stevenson (1997).
> MARRIED: (1) [19 June 1784] Mehetabel Hester, dau. and co-h. of Robert Temple of Ten Hills, Boston, USA; (2) [8 July 1801] Elizabeth, dau. and co-h. of William Henry Finlay, of Co. Meath.
> CHILDREN: (1) Capt. Robert Temple (69th S. Lincolnshire Regiment, killed at Waterloo); Hans; Price, 4th Baron Dufferin and Claneboye, m. [4 July 1825] Helen Selina, dau. of Thomas Sheridan (she later married George, Earl Gifford); Henrietta, m. [Apr. 1807] William Stewart Hamilton of Brown Hall, Co. Donegal. (2) Rev. William Stear, m. [24 Mar. 1832] Elizabeth, dau. of Robert Hamilton of Clonsilla, Co. Dublin; Capt. Henry Stevenson (17th Lancers), m. [25 Apr. 1857] Amelia Katherine, dau. of Hon. John Thomas Capel; Marianne, m. [15 Oct. 1831] Walter Mant, Archdeacon of Co. Down; Elizabeth Dorcas, m. [26 July 1839] Rear Adm. James Hamilton Ward; Sophia Louisa, m. (1) [5 Jan. 1832] Hans Hamilton of Gardiner Place, Dublin, (2) [15 June 1837] Capt. Alexander Grant (HEICS, 5th Madras Cavalry); Henrietta Catherine, m. (1) [20 Feb. 1841] the Hon. and Rev. Thomas Clotworthy Skeffington, s. of Thomas Henry, 2nd Viscount Ferrard (0809), (2) [18 Mar. 1869] Edwin Arnold of

Yiewsley, Middlesex; Anne Dorothea, m. [1 Mar. 1842] David Stewart Ker of Montalto, Co. Down.
> CAREER/OCCUPATION: Director General of Inland Navigation, 1800 at £500 p.a.; Commissioner of Audit 1813–32 at £800 p.a.
> MILITARY: *Major of Brigade to the Yeomanry Forces of Co. Meath 1799 (f.).

POLITICAL ACTIVITY: He came into parliament on the death of his father (0148) and was returned by his brother, Sir James Blackwood (0147). He was a Dublin businessman and probably a reluctant politician. He sat for approximately nine months before he accepted the office of Escheator of Munster, before the crucial vote of 6 February 1800.

ADDITIONAL INFORMATION: He was a partner in a firm of wine merchants in Dublin – Blackwood, Sneyd and Benton – one of the other partners being Nathaniel Sneyd (1955). The firm had its offices in Harcourt Street, and Hans Blackwood valued Lord Chancellor Clare's (0749) wine cellar at £2,100 at his death in January 1802.

ESTATES/RESIDENCE: Ballyleidy, Claneboye, Co. Down. In 1874 his descendant, the Marquess of Dufferin and Ava, possessed Claneboye, 5,476 statute acres, Ballyholme 844, Ards 3,926 and four estates between Killyleagh, Crossgar, Comber and Saintfield collectively known as Dufferin estates. The total acreage was 18,539.

SOURCES: PRONI D/1071A/G/2 Map; PRONI T/684/7 G, Aynworth Pilson, Obituaries, Downpatrick [says he died 19 Nov. 1839 aged 84 years], see also T684/9, Pilson, Marriages; PRONI T/3166/1A Hartnell notes; PRONI MIC/315/8/35, /9/51 Blackwood Pedigrees [says married 19 June 1783]; O'Neill thesis; GEC *P*; Burke *PB* (1903) p. 497; T. K. Lowry (ed.), *The Hamilton Manuscripts* (Belfast, 1867), pp. lxvii, 64 [says his first wife is a dau. of Sir Robert Temple, Baronet]; E. Hewitt (ed.), *Lord Shannon's Letters to his Son*, p. 219; *Almanacks*; *FJ* 30 Jan. 1798; Parliamentary Lists, 1799 (2), (3).

0147 BLACKWOOD, Hon. James Stevenson

MP for Killyleagh 1788–90–7–1800; [UK] Helston 1807–12; Aldeburgh 1812–18

> b. 8 July 1755; d. 8 Aug. 1836

HONOURS: Suc. as 3rd Bt 1799.

PEERAGES: Suc. his mother as 2nd Baron Dufferin and Claneboye 8 Feb. 1808; Rep. Peer 1820–36.

FAMILY/BACKGROUND: Son of Sir John Blackwood, 2nd Bt (**0148**) and Dorcas, *suo iure* Baroness Dufferin and Claneboye, dau. of James Stevenson (**1997**).

MARRIED: [15 Nov. 1801] Anne Dorothea (d. 1865, aged 93), o. dau. of Rt Hon. John Foster, 1st Baron Oriel (**0805**).

CHILDREN: *d.s.p.*

CAREER/OCCUPATION: Secretary to Rt Hon. Robert Stewart, Lord Castlereagh (**2009**); Governor of Co. Down 1808–31; High Sheriff of Co. Down 1804; Trustee of the Linen Board 1805.

MILITARY: Lieutenant 13th Dragoons 1778; Captain 8th Dragoons 1781 (ret. 1787); Lieutenant-Colonel Commanding 33rd Dragoons 1794–6; Lieutenant-Colonel 1796–1802; aide-de-camp to Earl of Kilmorey 1798; Captain of the Loyal Ballyleidy, Killyleagh and Killinchy Infantry 1798; appointed Col. of the North Battalion of the Downshire Militia Apr. 1800; militia aide-de-camp to William IV 1830–6.

POLITICAL ACTIVITY: Although his eldest brother Robert Blackwood (**0149**), whom he succeeded in the representation of Killyleagh, died as the result of an accident in June 1786, James Blackwood was not sworn until February 1789. He had been destined for a military career. When he first entered parliament he followed his father's (**0148**) lead in opposition and remained so until about 1795. He supported Catholic Emancipation in the early 1790s but, like his father, he was never a good attender and this probably made him an unreliable member of any party. Unlike his father, he became a firm supporter of the Union, which he voted for in both 1799 and 1800. Indeed, as Lord Castlereagh's (**2009**) secretary he could scarcely do anything else. He refused to accept a peerage for his support, but it was conferred upon his mother, Dorcas Blackwood née Stevenson. The borough of Killyleagh had been part of her inheritance and, declared a contemporary in 1790: 'Sometimes it is sold and sometimes two of the Blackwood family are returned for it. Contingencies must determine what will be its fate at the next general election.'

In the event, James Blackwood was returned along with Robert Ward (**2184**), the third son of one of the local magnates, Bernard Ward, 1st Vis-count Bangor (**2177**). He was a member of the Grand Jury for Co. Down, 1797, and in March 1800 he signed a Co. Down petition in favour of discussing the proposed plan of Union. In a list of MPs recommended for the peerage by Cornwallis in June 1800, it was stated that he had a fortune of £10,000 a year. Blackwood received £15,000 for the disfranchisement of Killyleagh at the Union.

After the Union he remained an influential figure in Down politics. Government found him a seat at Helston through the Duke of Leeds' interest. 'He was inconspicuous at Westminster, his chief wish being to obtain favours for his family.' Government thought he asked too much: 'Lord Dufferin wanted his brother a bankrupt to have a situation. He wants another brother a wine merchant to another situation and a clergyman to keep his living ... and have a valuable deanery. All this for one silent vote.' In the Imperial parliament he was ambivalent on the Catholic question, voting against Catholic relief in 1812 but for it in the following year; he remained a supporter of Catholic relief in the divisions of 1815 and 1817. Otherwise he expressed approval of Peel's Irish policy. In 1820 he became a representative peer. As a landlord he had 'a reputation of much intelligence and liberality, building schools, encouraging manufactures and when necessary providing employment for the poor at his own expense'.

DIVISION LISTS:

1790 (2) voted for Ponsonby (**1709**) on the election of a Speaker.

1793 (1) voted for Knox's (**1190**) motion for Catholic Emancipation.

1795 (2) voted for Catholic Emancipation.

1800 (1) voted for the Union.

ADDITIONAL INFORMATION: His political ambivalence was also shown in his offer (refused) to be Grattan's (**0895**) second in the latter's duel with Isaac Corry (**0497**) in 1800.

ESTATES/RESIDENCE: Ballyleidy, Claneboye, Co. Down. In 1800 his income was estimated at £10,000 p.a. At the beginning of the nineteenth century, Wakefield estimated Lord Dufferin's rental at £15,000.

A notebook kept by his nephew, 4th Lord Dufferin, *c.* 1850, entitled *Irish Statistics (Miscellaneous)*, states that the estate comprised 17,296 statute acres in 1847–8.

SOURCES: PRONI D/302; PRONI D/607/E/3/9
Downshire Papers; PRONI T/3166/1A Hartnell notes;
PRONI MIC/315/8/35, /9/51 Blackwood Pedigrees
[says born 4 Sept. 1754]; O'Neill thesis; GEC *P*; *HP
1790–1820*; Sir A. Lyall, *The Life of the Marquis of
Dufferin and Ava*, vol. I (London, 1905) pp. 5, 6;
Cornwallis Corr. vol. 3 pp. 215, 254; T. K. Lowry (ed.),
The Hamilton Manuscripts (Belfast, 1867), p. lxvii; J. T.
Gilbert, *History of the City of Dublin*, 3 vols (1861) vol.
3 p. 165; *The Drogheda Newsletter or Ulster Journal* 8–
10 Mar. 1800; *BNL* 8 Apr.1800; Wakefield, *Account of
Ire.*, vol. 1 p. 255; PRONI D/107H/T/30; Parliamentary Lists, 1783 (2), 1789 (1), 1790 (1), 1791 (1), 1793
(1), 1794 (2), 1799 (2), (3), 1800 (3).

0148 BLACKWOOD, Sir John

MP for Killyleagh 1761–8, 1776–83–90, 1798–
9; Bangor 1768–76, 1790–7

b. 1722; d. 26 Feb. 1799
HONOURS: Suc. as 2nd Bt 1774.
FAMILY/BACKGROUND: Son of Sir Robert
Blackwood, 1st Bt, and Joyce (sister of the 1st
Earl of Milltown), dau. of Joseph Leeson of
Dublin.
MARRIED: [licence 22 May 1751] Dorcas (b. 1726;
d. 8 Feb. 1807), dau. of James Stevenson (**1997**);
at the request of her son, for his political services,
she was cr. 31 July 1800 Baroness Dufferin and
Claneboye.
CHILDREN: Robert (**0149**); Sir James Stevenson,
2nd Baron Dufferin and Claneboye (**0147**); Rev.
John, m. (1) [1778] Sophia, dau. of Rev. Trevor
Hill Benson, (2) [4 June 1803] Eliza, e. dau. of
Josias Dupre of Wilton Park, Buckinghamshire,
wid. of Col. Arthur Brice; Hans, 3rd Baron
Dufferin and Claneboye (**0146**); Price, m. (1) [29
Aug. 1787] Louisa, dau. and co-h. of William
Southwell, (2) [21 Jan. 1804] Anne, dau. of
Richard Cox (**0509**); Capt. Leeson (28th
Regiment); Vice-Adm. Sir Henry, m. (1) [12 Jan.
1795] Jane Mary, dau. of Launcelot Crosbie, (2)
[3 June 1799] Eliza, dau. of Martin Waghorn
RN, (3) [9 May 1803] Harriet, dau. of Francis
Gore; Anne, m.(1) [Feb. 1777] John Ryder, Dean
of Lismore, (2) [1 Oct. 1796] James Jones,
Rector of Urney, s. of Rt Hon. Theophilus Jones
(**1117**); Sophia, m. [26 Nov. 1800] James Green
of Yorkshire; Dorcas, m. [25 July 1799] Col.
Peter Francis Venault de Charmilly; Catherine,
m. (as a minor) [12 June 1788] Sir George Dallas
Bt; Charlotte (d. in infancy).

EDUCATION: He belonged to a Presbyterian family
and matriculated at Glasgow University in 1739,
MA 1741. Prof. Hutcheson wrote, 'the wretched
turn their [the students'] minds take is to the silly
manliness of taverns. Jack Blackwood was a bad
sight this way to lads of smaller fortunes, tho'
otherways of a fine temper'. Much of his later
independence may have derived from his
educational background.
CAREER/OCCUPATION: A member of the Grand
Jury for Co. Down 1796.

POLITICAL ACTIVITY: His political career was marked
by a determined independence. However, he was
not a particularly good parliamentary attender and
probably this as well as his temperament made
him an unlikely party man. He had a reputation
as a 'decent respectable country gentleman'. He
adopted an opposition position prior to the arrival of the Duke of Portland in 1782, after which
he appears to have softened his approach; he was
not hostile to the Duke of Rutland's administration. In 1768 and 1790 he was returned for Bangor by a complicated arrangement, as in 1768 Lord
Ikerrin (**0316**), the heir to Lord Carrick, who controlled one of the seats for Bangor, was returned
for Killyleagh and in 1790 Robert Ward (**2184**),
the son of Lord Bangor (**2177**), who controlled
the other, was likewise returned for Killyleagh. The
reason why the families swapped seats is unclear.

He was consistently hostile to parliamentary
reform, but appears to have changed his views on
the Catholic question between the 1770s and
1790s. At the time of his death he was a firm opponent of the Union then being proposed, and
on 15 January 1799 he wrote to Castlereagh
(**2009**) expressing his indignation at being summoned to attend the House 'in the style as to one
of the vassals of Administration', although that
letter came from the office over which his son presided as secretary to the Chief Secretary. He wrote
that 'The only authority I acknowledge is that of
our Speaker, as directed by the call of our House.
I wish to inform the Lord Lieutenant that I have
a pride of feeling my own independence … a pride
I would not barter for any honour, station, place
or pension in his power to grant … Your Lordship knows I had intended to attend my duty; let
it not be said that I attended by the persuasion of
his Excellency's summons.' This pride in his inde-

pendence was particularly strong over the question of the Union, on which he declared: 'I shall not be finally determined till I shall have heard and digested the best information on the subject in the House.'

The following anecdote relates to an episode leading up to the Union: 'On one occasion an emissary from the Castle was dining with him, and after dinner, taking up one of the spoons observed, "Sir John, I greatly admire your crest, don't you think it would be a great improvement if it were surmounted with balls?" "Perhaps it might," replied Sir John, "but do me the favour to bestow part of your admiration to the motto, *per vias rectas.*"' The story is handed down that Sir John was just starting out for Dublin to vote against the Union when he died suddenly in the act of putting his boots on for the journey.

DIVISION LISTS:

1768 (1) voted against army augmentation.

1771 (1) voted against Lord Townshend as Lord Lieutenant.

1771 (2) voted for Sir Lucius O'Brien's (**1558**) motion for retrenchment.

1772 (2) voted for a Short Revenue Bill.

1773 (1) voted against Absentee Tax.

1773 (2) voted for an untaxed press.

1774 (2) voted in favour of Catholic relief.

1777 (2) voted against the Trade Embargo.

1778 (1) voted for Grattan's (**0895**) motion for retrenchment.

1778 (2) voted against the Popery Bill.

1779 (2) voted for a six-months Loan Bill.

1780 (2) voted for Yelverton's (**2268**) motion to modify Poynings' Law.

1780 (4) voted against the Perpetual Mutiny Bill.

1783 (1) voted for Flood's (**0762**) motion for parliamentary reform.

1785 (1) voted against the Commercial Propositions.

1787 (1) absent – had previously voted for a Pension Bill.

1788 (1) voted for Hartley's (**0979**) motion against the Dublin police.

1790 (2) voted for Ponsonby (**1709**) on the election of a Speaker.

1793 (1) voted for Knox's (**1180**) motion for Catholic Emancipation.

ADDITIONAL INFORMATION: *A member of the Royal Dublin Society from 1764; a member of the Down Society for Promoting Agriculture, and Treasurer of the society, 24 August 1757.

A member of the Whig Club of Down County, which actively and energetically supported the candidature of Robert Stewart (**2009**) and Edward Ward (**2179**) in the 1790 election.

ESTATES/RESIDENCE: Ballyleidy, Co. Down: he and his wife, Dorcas, inherited most of her father, James Stevenson's (**1997**) estates in and around Killyleagh; Grafton Street, Dublin.

SOURCES: PRONI D/607/D/102 Downshire Papers; PRONI T/1584 Pinkerton transcripts, p. 545, 1 Mar. 1799; PRONI T/684/8, G. Aynworth Pilson, Obituaries, Downpatrick; PRONI T/3166/1A Hartnell notes; PRONI MIC/315/9/51 Blackwood Pedigrees [says born 1721]; RCBL P80/1/1, Parish Registers of St Thomas, Dublin; O'Neill thesis; Burke *PB* (1903) pp. 152, 497; *Castlereagh Corr.* vol. 2 pp. 113–14; Johnston, *Gt B. & Ire.*, pp. 220–25; T. K. Lowry (ed.), *The Hamilton Manuscripts* (Belfast, 1867), pp. 64, lxvi, lxvii; Sir A. Lyall, *The Life of the Marquis of Dufferin and Ava* (London, 1905), vol. 1 pp. 3, 4; W. I. Addison, *The Matriculation Albums of Glasgow University, 1728–1858* (Glasgow, 1913); *Almanacks*, BNL 2 Sept. 1757, 25 Sept. 1759, 7 Oct. 1760, 1 Mar. 1799; Parliamentary Lists, 1769 (1), 1773 (1), (2), 1774 (1), 1775 (1), 1776 (1), (2), (3), 1777 (1), 1778 (1), 1780 (1), 1782 (1), 1783 (1), (2), (3), 1785 (1), (2), (3), (4), 1787 (1), 1788 (1), 1789 (1), 1790 (1), 1791 (1), 1793 (1), 1794 (2).

0149 BLACKWOOD, Robert

MP for Killyleagh 1776–83–6

b. (Apr.) 1752; d. 30 June 1786 'by a fall from his horse [at Comber] near Belfast'

FAMILY/BACKGROUND: Eldest son of Sir John Blackwood, 2nd Bt (**0148**), and Dorcas, Baroness Dufferin and Claneboye, dau. of James Stevenson (**1997**).

MARRIED: Unmarried.

EDUCATION: Matriculated Glasgow 1767.

CAREER/OCCUPATION: A Volunteer while an MP – Captain of the Killyleagh Volunteers.

POLITICAL ACTIVITY: The son and heir of Sir John Blackwood, he came into parliament at the first available opportunity and represented the family borough of Killyleagh until his untimely death in a riding accident in 1786. He followed his father's essentially opposition lead in parliament.

DIVISION LISTS:

1778 (2) voted against the Popery Bill.
1779 (2) voted for a six-months Loan Bill.
1780 (2) voted for Yelverton's (**2268**) motion to modify Poynings' Law.
1785 (1) voted against the Commercial Propositions

ESTATES/RESIDENCE: Ballyleidy, Co. Down. On 2 January 1760 he leased for lives (renewable for ever) the townland of Rathgill and other lands and premises in Co. Down for £97 p.a. to John Moor.

SOURCES: PRONI D/1071A/H2/45 Dufferin and Ava Papers; PRONI T/1584 Pinkerton transcripts, p. 349, 27 Jan. 1786; PRONI MIC/315/9/51 Blackwood pedigrees; PRONI MIC/474 Irish Volunteers; GEC *P* [says he died 31 Jan. 1785]; Burke *PB* (1903) p. 497 [says 1786]; T. K. Lowry (ed.), *The Hamilton Manuscripts* (Belfast, 1867), p. lxvii [says he died 29 June 1786]; W. I. Addison, *The Matriculation Albums of Glasgow University, 1728–1850* (Glasgow, 1913); T. Bartlett and D. W. Hayton (eds), *Penal Era and Golden Age* (Belfast, 1979), p. 113 f. 1, P. D. H. Smyth, 'The Volunteers and Parliament, 1779–84'; *Walker's Hibernian Magazine* (1786), p. 111; Parliamentary Lists, 1776 (1), (2), (3), 1771 (1), 1778 (1), 1780(1), 1782 (1), 1783 (1), (2), (3), 1785 (1), (2), (3).

0150 BLADEN, Rt Hon. Martin

MP for Bandon 1715–27; [GB] Stockbridge 1715–34; Maldon 1734–41; Portsmouth 1741–6

b. 1682; d. 15 Feb. 1745/6
HONOURS: PC, sworn 1 Nov. 1715, 1733–7, 1739–42, 1745.
FAMILY/BACKGROUND: Son of Nathaniel Bladen of Bolton Percy, Yorkshire, and Isabella, dau. of Sir William Fairfax of Steeton, Yorkshire.
MARRIED: (1) Mary, dau. of Colonel Gibbs; (2) [29 Mar. 1728] Frances, wid. of John Foche, niece and co-h. of Col. Joseph Jory of Essex, a West India merchant from whom she inherited a large sugar plantation in Nevis.

CHILDREN: (1) 2 dau.
EDUCATION: School: Westminster 1695–7; entered Cambridge (St John's College) 17 Apr. 1697, aged 16 years; Inner Temple 23 Mar. 1697.
CAREER/OCCUPATION: Comptroller of the Mint [GB] 17 Dec. 1714–28; Secretary to the Lord Justices 1715–17; one of the Lords of Trade and Plantations [GB] July 1717–d.; Director of the Royal African Company 1717–26; Commissioner to the Court of France 1719–20; Commissioner for settling commerce at Antwerp June 1732–Feb. 1742.
MILITARY: Ensign in Colonel T. Fairfax's Regiment of Foot, 12 Dec. 1697; Ensign to a Company added to this Regiment in Ireland, 1 Mar. 1702; Captain in Sir Charles Hotham's new Regiment of Foot, 25 Mar. 1705. He served in the Low Countries and Spain, becoming aide-de-camp to Henri de Massue de Ruvigny, Earl of Galway; Brevet Colonel; Colonel of a British Regiment raised in Spain 26 Oct. 1709 (sold out 26 June 1710); in 1717 declined the office of Envoy Extraordinary to the Court of Spain.

POLITICAL ACTIVITY: He was a soldier and brought to Ireland as Secretary to the Lords Justices. He proved an efficient civil servant both in Ireland and later in England, where his real career was made.

Bladen represented an evolution in the office of Chief Secretary. During the 1715–16 session he had a public altercation with the recently appointed Chancellor's son, St John Brodrick (**0242**), in the House of Commons where Brodrick insinuated that it was inappropriate for a man who had no property in Ireland to be taking such a leading part in her affairs. Bladen's period in Ireland appears to have been 1715–16, and at this time he was nominated to 16 committees. On 13 December 1715 Henry Maxwell (**1373**), reporting on a Committee of Supply, wrote that 'Mr Bladen is a servant that by his integrity and candour brings credit to those who employ him.' On 5 March 1715/6 Bladen was given leave in the British House of Commons to bring in a bill to continue the privilege of exporting Irish linen cloth to British plantations. He wrote to Delafaye on 19 March that the bill was facing problems from those who believed that Ireland should pay the same export duty on linen as England and Scotland. The bill was debated and had passed its first reading by 26 March, despite some strong opposition. On 30 March 1716 Bladen complained that the opponents of the bill were trying to delay it in its committee stage. Eventually the bill passed.

On 19 March 1715 he wrote to Charles Delafaye asking his advice about amending the Mutiny Bill with regard to Ireland to prevent Irish soldiers from deserting owing to a particular clause in the bill. On 28 March he wrote again regretting his failure to have the Irish amendments inserted in the Mutiny Bill. Given the Mutiny Bill issue in the latter part of the century, Bladen's ideas showed considerable foresight. By 1719 he was noted as an absentee.

ADDITIONAL INFORMATION: He was one of Sir Robert Walpole's steadiest supporters in the House of Commons. After his Secretaryship to the Lords Justices, 1715–17, his career was in England. In 1717 he was reputed to have been offered and declined the position of Envoy Extraordinary to the Court of Spain. For the remainder of his life he was one of the Lords of Trade. Here his efficiency led to the comment that he was Trade and his colleagues the Board. He was part of the West Indian lobby and a strong supporter of the 1733 Molasses Act. Through his second wife he owned a West Indian sugar plantation. In 1744 he was a strong opponent of Henry Pelham's proposal for an additional duty on sugar amounting to a farthing per pound (weight) for the consumer.

Pope described him as a gamester, and noted that he lived in the 'utmost magnificence in Paris, and kept open table, frequented by persons of the first quality in England, and even by Princes of the blood in France'. His nephew, the poet William Collins, said that Bladen was the inspiration for the account of Camoens in the *Essay of the Epic Poets of all Nations by Voltaire*, as previous to this Voltaire was completely ignorant of the said poet. He translated and published *Caesar's Commentaries* (1712) and was the author of the tragi-comedy *Solon* (1705). Another nephew was Admiral Lord Hawke, whose early career benefited from the connection.

ESTATES/RESIDENCE: Aldborough Hatch, Essex. He left an estate to his nephew, the poet William Collins, who by then was unable to take possession on account of a deranged mind.

SOURCES: PRONI TSPI 1715–16, T/448 p. 172, 1717–19, T/519 pp. 16–19, 24, 29, 33, 34, 36–8; *DNB*; *HP 1715–54*; *Index to Irish Privy Counsellors, 1711–1910*; *Alum. Cantab.* [says of Albery Hatch]; C. Dalton (ed.), *English Army Lists and Commission Registers, 1661–1714* (London, 1898), vol. iv p. 175; G. F. Russell-Barker and A. H. Stenning (eds), *Record of Old Westminsters: A Biographical List* (London, 1928) [says he was Comptroller of the Mint 23 Dec. 1714–27, a Commissioner for Trade and Plantations 1715–17 and first Commissioner from 1720; it also says his wife's uncle was Colonel Jory]; P. McNally, *Parties, Patriots & Undertakers* (Dublin, 1997) pp. 120–21, 137; F. W. Pitman, *The Development of the British West Indies, 1700–68* (Yale, 1917), p. 187 n. 67; Cork MPs; J. T. Gilbert, *A History of the City of Dublin* (Dublin, 1859), vol. 1 pp. 12–13 [says that his ancestor was William Bladen, Lord Mayor of Dublin in 1647 and State Printer during the Commonwealth]; *Almanacks*; Parliamentary List 1719 (1).

0151 BLAIR, William

MP for Monaghan B. 1747–60

b. *ante* 1726; d. [1 Mar.] 1782
FAMILY/BACKGROUND: Son of [   ] Blair.
MARRIED: ?
CHILDREN: ?
CAREER/OCCUPATION: 2nd Secretary (Harrington) Nov. 1746–Dec.1750; Private Secretary to Harrington as Secretary of State [GB] 1730–42, 1744–6; Clerk to the PC [GB] (extra.) 1731–56, (ord.) 1756–79; Commissioner of Stamps [GB] 1737–61, 1765–81; Clerk of Signet [GB] 1746–82; Commissioner of Taxes [GB] 1761–5.

POLITICAL ACTIVITY: He was part of the Castle secretariat brought over by Lord Harrington when the latter became Lord Lieutenant, and probably returned to England with him. He was brought into parliament for Monaghan town by Lady Blaney. The two committees to which he was nominated were both in 1749. He was a friend and, when he returned to England, a correspondent of Nathaniel Clements (**0414**).

In 1755 Lord Lieutenant Hartington sent for him to attend, and Lord Duncannon was anxious for him to give support over the Wexford election petition – but not if he would support the Rams (**1760**). Lord George Sackville (**1835**) wrote to Under-Secretary Wilmot that he certainly could not communicate with Blair on the subject. In England he was considered a 'minor politician'.

DIVISION LISTS:

1749 (1) voted against the election of James Digges La Touche (♦♦♦♦).

ESTATES/RESIDENCE: Dublin Castle.

SOURCES: McCracken thesis; *Proc. RIA* vol. 77 C no 1 (1977), J. C. Sainty, 'The Secretariat of the Chief Governors of Ireland, 1690–1800'; Walton, *'The King's Business': Letters on the Administration of Ireland, 1741–61* (NY, 1996) nos 222, 231, 313; Magennis thesis (Belfast, 1996) p. 128 n. 9.

0152 BLAKE, Joseph Henry

MP for Co. Galway 1792–7–1800 [n.d.e. 1790]

b. 5 Oct. 1765; d. 28 Mar. 1803
PEERAGES: Cr. Baron Wallscourt 30 July 1800.
FAMILY/BACKGROUND: Son of Joseph Blake of Ardfry, Co. Galway, and Honoria, dau. of Dermot Daly.
MARRIED: [18 Aug. 1784] Lady Louisa Mary Catherine, dau. and co-h. of Rt Hon. Thomas Bermingham, 1st Earl of Louth (0122) (she married (2) James Daly).
CHILDREN: Anastasia, m. [1803] Luke Dillon, 2nd Baron Clonbrock.
CAREER/OCCUPATION: Joint Governor of Co. Galway 1792–1800, Governor *post* 1800; *Trustee of the Linen Board 1798–1800.
MILITARY: Colonel of Galway Militia.

POLITICAL ACTIVITY: The Blake family were one of the leading interests in Co. Galway, and until this MP they were Catholic. There had been a longstanding feud between the Blakes and the Dalys over the control of Galway town, which in the mid-1770s erupted into a famous duel between Patrick Blake of Drum and Denis Daly of Dunsandle (0570). Daly emerged triumphant. However, when Denis Daly decided not to stand for the county in 1790 he was said to have placed his influence behind Blake, who was returned although, later petitioned against by Anthony Daly, he was forced to seek re-election. He was basically a government supporter, except on the Catholic question. Blake, who had married one of the co-heiresses of the Earl of Louth, voted for the Un-

ion and was ennobled as Lord Wallscourt.

DIVISION LISTS:

1790 (2) voted for Foster (0805) on the election of a Speaker.
1792 (1) voted for the Catholic petition.
1793 (1) voted for Knox's (1180) motion for Catholic Emancipation.
1798 (1) voted against Sir Laurence Parsons' (1636) motion for an investigation into 'the present discontents'.
1799 (1) voted for the Union – Colonel, Militia.
1800 (1) voted for the Union.

ADDITIONAL INFORMATION: *A subscriber to the Public Assembly Rooms, 1787. His father was a Roman Catholic. In December 1798 he wrote to Castlereagh that if a Union was proposed he would take the sense of the county. He signed a Co. Galway petition in favour of the Union, March 1799.

ESTATES/RESIDENCE: Ardfry, Co. Galway; North Great George's Street, Dublin. The rental was £4,502 in 1790. Blake took out a mortgage of £20,000 with the Earl of Caledon (0029) in 1794, which the Earl foreclosed on in 1800. In 1791, Joseph Blake described the estate to a potential mortgagee (0029) as follows: 'There are no long leases cases and almost the whole estate is underlet. It is in the best and most open parts of the county, near the towns of Galway, Loughrea and Ballinasloe.' His wife, Lady Louisa, was the coheiress of Thomas Bermingham, Earl of Louth (0122), who died in January 1799.

SOURCES: NLI EC 4786; PRONI D/2433/B/2/2/1 Caledon Papers, Hamilton McClure to Lord Caledon, 22 July 1790; PRONI D/2433/B/2/4/1, Blake to Lord Caledon, 7 July 1791; PRONI T/3166/1B Hartnell notes; O'Neill thesis; Burke *PB* (1903) p. 1543; GEC *P*; J. Kelly, *'That Damn'd Thing Called Honour': Duelling in Ireland 1570–1860* (Cork, 1995) pp. 140–41; *Castlereagh Corr.* vol. 2 p. 47; C. Ross (ed.), *Cornwallis Corr.*, vol. 3 p. 255 [says he died 8 (*sic*) Mar. 1803]; *Almanacks*; *BNL* 22 Mar. 1799; *FJ* 17 Nov. 1796; *DJ* 22 Jan. 1799; Parliamentary Lists, 1785 (2), 1790 (1), 1791 (1), 1793 (1), 1794 (2), 1799 (3), 1800 (3).

0153 BLAKENEY, John

MP for Athenry 1727–47

b. *c.* 1703; d. 21 Aug. 1747
FAMILY/BACKGROUND: Eldest son of Robert
Blakeney (**0156**) and Sarah, dau. of Gilbert
Ormsby.
MARRIED: Grace, dau. of Henry Persse.
CHILDREN: Robert (**0157**); John (**0154**);
Theophilus (**0158**); William (**0160**); Sarah, m.
[1750] William Persse; Mary, m. [1759] Thomas
Taylor.
CAREER/OCCUPATION: Sheriff of Co. Galway 1727
and 1738.
MILITARY: Colonel of Galway Militia Dragoons.

POLITICAL ACTIVITY: He was not a very active member of parliament. He was nominated for six committees between 1727 and 1739. In 1741 his excuse for non-attendance at parliament was not
accepted, and he was ordered into the custody of
the Serjeant-at-Arms on 21 November. He died
in 1747 and his greatest claim to fame appears to
have been his purchase of the Abbert estate, gaining with it control of the borough and establishing the family's popularity in the locality.

ADDITIONAL INFORMATION: On 20 September 1731
his bay mare Sweetest When She is Naked won
the £20 plate at the Gort races.

ESTATES/RESIDENCE: Abbert, Co. Galway. The Abbert
estate was bought 14 May 1734. Lands in barony of
Tiaquin and Dunkellin.

SOURCES: *CJ Ire.* (Bradley ed.) vol. 7 p. 292; NLI EC
7706 Box no 3630; McCracken thesis; Burke *LGI*
(1904) p. 44; *IFR* (1976) p. 127; *Pue's Occurrences* 9
Oct. 1731.

0154 BLAKENEY, John

MP for Athenry 1763–8–76–83–9

b. *c.* 1729; d. 25 July 1789
FAMILY/BACKGROUND: Son of John Blakeney
(**0153**) and Grace, dau. of Henry Persse.
MARRIED: Unmarried; (mistress) Bridget Kelly.
CHILDREN: (*d.s.p.l.*). Illeg.: William; Robert; John;
Sarah.
CAREER/OCCUPATION: *Portreeve of Athenry 1766–
7; *Magistrate 1766–7; High Sheriff of Co.

Galway 1768.
MILITARY: Captain 27th Foot; present at the
battles of Culloden 16 Apr. 1746, Ticonderoga 8
July 1758, Crown Point, Montreal, 8 Sept. 1760,
Martinique and Havana 5 June 1762; mentioned
in despatches 1763, wounded at Las Navira);
Colonel in Galway Militia (Dragoons).

POLITICAL ACTIVITY: John Blakeney, who was a
younger son, came into parliament in 1763 on
the death of his older brother, Robert (**0157**).
Robert Blakeney's heir was a minor, and John
Blakeney was reputed to have persuaded some of
the freemen of Athenry to tell his nephew's guardians that they would not consent to the seats being sold but that the borough was to be represented by the heir's two uncles, John and
Theophilus (**0158**). The guardians may have been
influenced by the fact that the Blakeney control
of the borough was disputed by Mr Trench of
Monevey.

By 1783 there were no resident freemen and
the population of the town was calculated as comprising 65 Protestants and 890 Catholics. The
Blakeneys were a military family, and John
Blakeney had fought in most of the wars of the
mid-eighteenth century. In 1769 he was a half-
pay officer, his personal fortune was small and Lord
Townshend secured for him a pension of £200
and, although he had not purchased it, leave to
sell his company, beyond the regulated price.

In parliament the Blakeneys were usually government supporters, and Blakeney gave unwaver-
ing support to both Lord Lieutenants Townshend
and Harcourt. Lord Townshend procured him a
pension of £200; under Lord Harcourt it was increased to £450 and he was also allowed to recommend a supernumerary gauger. In the 1776
election he was returned along with his nephew
(**0155**), but the nephew died in 1781 and probably left a son, who may have died young, as little
is known of him. By 1785 the borough was in the
hands of the Blakeney brothers John and
Theophilus, and on John's death his seat and
claims appear to have gone to another brother,
William (**0160**). By the time of his death he was
Collector of Excise for Dublin county but, as he
voted for the regency, he would probably have lost
his position had he not died in July 1789.

DIVISION LISTS:

1768 (1) absent, sick.

1771 (1) voted for Lord Townshend as Lord Lieutenant.

1771 (2) voted against Sir Lucius O'Brien's (1558) motion for retrenchment – an officer in the army.

1772 (2) voted against a Short Revenue Bill.

1773 (1) voted for Absentee Tax.

1773 (2) voted against an untaxed press.

1774 (2) voted against Catholic relief.

1775 (1) voted against the pro-American amendment to the Speech from the Throne.

1779 (2) voted against a six-months Loan Bill.

1780 (1) voted against Grattan's (0895) declaration of the Rights of Ireland.

1780 (2) voted against Yelverton's (2268) motion to modify Poynings' Law.

1783 (1) voted for Flood's (0762) motion for parliamentary reform.

1785 (1) absent.

1789 (1) voted for a regency.

ESTATES/RESIDENCE: Ashfield and Mulpit, Loughrea, Co. Galway; St Stephen's Green, Dublin.

SOURCES: PRONI D/302; Ellis thesis; Burke LGI (1904) pp. 44–5; IFR (1976) p. 127; Alum. Dub.; WHM (1789) p. 504; Almanacks, DJ 30 July – 1 Aug. 1789; Parliamentary Lists, 1769 (1), 1772 (1), 1773 (1), (2), 1774 (1), 1775 (1), 1776 (1), (2), (3), 1777 (1), 1778 (1), 1780 (1), 1782 (1), 1783 (1), (2), 1784 (1), (2), (3), 1785 (1), (2), (3), 1787 (1), 1788 (1), 1789 (1).

0155 BLAKENEY, John

MP for Athenry 1776–81

b. 12 Sept. 1756; d. 23 Aug. 1781 at Abbert

FAMILY/BACKGROUND: Son of Robert Blakeney (0157) and Gertrude, dau. of Maj. Robert Blakeney.

MARRIED: ? [   ].

CHILDREN: ?Son (d. yg).

EDUCATION: School: Mr Ford; entered TCD 1 July 1772.

CAREER/OCCUPATION: Cornet of Dragoons.

POLITICAL ACTIVITY: His father was the eldest of the four Blakeney brothers and as such controlled the borough of Athenry, which he and this MP's uncle (0154) represented. He was under age at his return, but, as parliament was prorogued until 14 October 1777, he would have been of age by the time it met. He was said by one contemporary to have 'no fortune' and by another to have a 'reasonable fortune'; probably, as he represented the senior line, the latter is correct. John Ponsonby (1702) was his godfather, but his uncle John Blakeney appears to have been the dominant political influence with him, although he was considered an independent and by 1780 a member of the opposition. He was in parliament for only five years.

DIVISION LISTS:

1780 (1) voted against Grattan's (0895) declaration of the Rights of Ireland.

1780 (2) voted for Yelverton's (2268) motion to modify Poynings' Law

ESTATES/RESIDENCE: Abbert, Co. Galway.

SOURCES: NLI EC 7706; Alum. Dub.; The Register of the Parish of St Peter and St Kevin, 1669–1761 (Parish Register Society of Dublin, 1911) p. 297 [bapt. 6 Nov. 1756]; DJ 21–3 Aug. 1781; NAI Will and Grant 1781, Prerog. (office copy); Parliamentary Lists, 1776 (1), (2), (3), 1771 (1), 1778 (1), 1780 (1).

0156 BLAKENEY, Robert

MP for Athenry 1721–7–33

b. 1679; d. 1 May 1733

FAMILY/BACKGROUND: Eldest son of John Blakeney and Sara, dau. of Dudley Persse, Dean of Kilmacduagh.

MARRIED: [?1600] Sarah, dau. of Gilbert Ormsby.

CHILDREN: John (0153); George; Gilbert; Margaret; Dorothy; Lettice.

EDUCATION: Kilkenny School 12 Oct. 1693, aged 14 years.

CAREER/OCCUPATION: Portreeve of Limerick; High Sheriff of Co. Galway 1709 and 1729.

POLITICAL ACTIVITY: This MP had a very low-key political career; virtually nothing is known about him except that he voted against a national bank shortly after he came into parliament in 1721. He was nominated for seven committees between 1723 and 1725 and ten between 1727 and 1731.

DIVISION LISTS:

1721 (2) voted against a national bank.

ESTATES/RESIDENCE: Abbert, Castle Blakeney, Co. Galway.

SOURCES: PRONI D/302; PRONI T/559 vol. 9, p. 356, Burke, extract pedigrees; McCracken thesis; Burke *LGI* (1904) p. 44; *JRSAI* vol. 54 (1924) pp. 55–67, T. U. Sadleir, 'The Register of Kilkenny School (1685–1800)'; *The Dublin Evening Post* 15 July 1732; *Pue's Occurrences* 5 May 1733.

0157 BLAKENEY, Robert

MP for Athenry 1747–60, 1761–2

b. *c.* 1724; d. 30 Dec. 1762
FAMILY/BACKGROUND: Eldest son of John Blakeney (**0153**) and Grace, dau. of Henry Persse.
MARRIED: [28 May 1752] Gertrude, dau. of Maj. Robert Blakeney of Mount Blakeney, Co. Limerick.
CHILDREN: John (**0155**); Grace, m. [1786] Thomas Lyon.
EDUCATION: Entered TCD 12 July 1741.
CAREER/OCCUPATION: *Portreeve of Athenry 1739–60; *Magistrate 1739–59; *Coroner of Ireland for Co. Galway 1747–52; High Sheriff of Co. Galway 1754.
MILITARY: Colonel of Galway Militia.

POLITICAL ACTIVITY: He was listed for two committees, on 5 October 1755 and 11 October 1757. He was a solid government supporter during the Money Bill crisis and thereafter, as in May 1760 Speaker Ponsonby (**1702**) thought it necessary to remind Lord Bedford's Secretary, Richard Rigby (**1789**), of the promises that had been made to his 'friends'. Robert Blakeney had been promised a pension of £200 p.a. and Speaker Ponsonby was godfather to his son (**0155**), born in 1756.

DIVISION LISTS:

1749 (1) voted against the election of James Digges La Touche (♦♦♦).
1753 (1) voted against the expulsion of Arthur Jones-Nevill (**1125**).
1753 (2) voted for the Money Bill.

ESTATES/RESIDENCE: Abbert, Co. Galway.

SOURCES: PRONI D/302; PRONI T/2915/9/47 Bed-

ford Papers; McCracken thesis; *Alum. Dub.*; Burke *LGI* (1904) p. 44; *IFR* (1976) p. 127; *The Register of the Parish of St Peter and St Kevin, 1669–1761* (Parish Register Society of Dublin, 1911) p. 328; *Pue's Occurrences* 30 May 1752, 22 Jan. 1754; *Almanacks.*

0158 BLAKENEY, Theophilus

MP for Athenry 1768–76, 1783–90–7–1800; [Escheator of Ulster 12 Apr. 1800]; Carlingford 1776–83

b. *c.* 1730–4; d. 22 Sept. 1813
FAMILY/BACKGROUND: Son of John Blakeney (**0153**) and Grace, dau. of Henry Persse.
MARRIED: [Dec. 1782] Margaret, dau. of John Stafford of Gillstown, Co. Roscommon, and St Stephen's Green, Dublin.
CHILDREN: John Henry (at Cambridge (St John's College) 5 Oct. 1808), m. Charlotte dau. of Sir Ross Mahon, 1st Bt (**1332**); Bridget, m. Sir Richard Bligh St George, 2nd Bt (**1848**); Margaret, m. John O'Dwyer; Elizabeth, m. Capt. de Hugo (French National Guard); Harriet, m. Arthur St George.
CAREER/OCCUPATION: High Sheriff of Co. Galway 1773; County Treasurer of ?Co Galway; Surveyor General of Connaught 20 June 1772–82; Collector of the City of Dublin Excise 1782–1800 (f.) at *c.* £600–700 p.a. and had a pension of £674 p.a.
MILITARY: A Lieutenant in Otway's Regiment of Foot, May 1756; Captain of the Royal Sussex Regiment; served at Quebec 1759–60 and Staten Island.

POLITICAL ACTIVITY: He came in in the 1768 election for the family borough of Athenry, which officially belonged to his nephew (**0155**), who was a minor. But the Blakeney control of Athenry was not entirely secure – even at the time of the Union claims were made against it, so the guardians may have felt that the uncles (*see* **0154**) were its best protectors. Theophilus Blakeney had leave to sell his captaincy in the 31st Regiment of Foot, which he had not purchased, in order to qualify himself to be Surveyor General of Connaught, estimated at £500 p.a. During Lord Townshend's viceroyalty he and his brother attended constantly and consistently supported government, although this assiduity appears to have wavered towards the end of Lord Harcourt's administration, as their absence on some critical occasions was noted. He petitioned the House to increase his salary as county Treasurer, which was granted.

In 1776 his nephew was almost of age and Theophilus was looking for a seat, but, he explained, his assets amounted to only £800 and unless the government assisted him he could not hope to be returned again. A seat was found for him at Carlingford but whether by his own purchase or an assisted one is uncertain. Both uncles and nephew supported the re-election of Pery (**1671**) to the Chair, although Ponsonby (**1702**) was godfather to the nephew. Lord Harcourt gave a small employment of £40 p.a. to his recommendation.

By 1778 his and his brother's attendance was 'bad'. However, by 1782 he had exchanged his Surveyorship of Connaught for the more lucrative one of Collector of the Dublin Excise, estimated at £600–700 p.a. His nephew died in 1781 and he was again returned for Athenry in 1783. He and his brother (**0154**) shared the representation of the borough until the latter died in 1789. Thereafter Theophilus Blakeney appears to have been in sole control and, despite counter-claims, he was awarded the £15,000 compensation for the borough in 1800.

On John Blakeney's death a fourth brother, Lieutenant-Colonel William Blakeney (**0160**) was returned. Both brothers vacated their seats in April 1800. The Blakeneys appear to have been popular with their tenants and the citizens of Athenry, for the Parliamentary List for 1790 recorded that 'Such attention to the wishes of the inhabitants all of whom are their tenants, is seldom to be met with in boroughs of this description. If their Members at any time prove venal, and such accidents are at least within the compass of possibility, the veil of affection is kindly drawn by the townsmen over the lapses of their friends and parents.' Although the borough appears to have been 'close', the populace probably appreciated the fact that the family sat for it themselves and did not sell it.

DIVISION LISTS:
    1771 (1) voted for Lord Townshend as Lord Lieutenant.
    1771 (2) voted against Sir Lucius O'Brien's

(**1558**) motion for retrenchment – an officer in the army.
1773 (1) voted for Absentee Tax.
1773 (2) voted against an untaxed press.
1774 (2) voted against Catholic relief.
1775 (1) voted against the pro-American amendment to the Speech from the Throne.
1779 (2) voted against a six-months Loan Bill.
1780 (1) voted against Grattan's (**0895**) declaration of the Rights of Ireland.
1780 (2) voted against Yelverton's (**2268**) motion to modify Poynings' Law.
1780 (3) voted for the Tenantry Bill.
1783 (1) voted against Flood's (**0762**) motion for parliamentary reform.
1785 (1) absent.
1790 (2) voted for Foster (**0805**) on the election of a Speaker.

ADDITIONAL INFORMATION: It was said that he had 'not more than £800 in the world which he [would] apply towards the purchase of a seat, but unless he [was] assisted by Government he [would] not be able to accomplish it'. The date of his marriage suggests that his prospects improved following the death of his nephew in 1781, and the fact that his older brother (**0154**) had a mistress and an illegitimate family may have encouraged him to marry.

ESTATES/RESIDENCE: Abbert, Co. Galway, St Stephen's Green, Dublin.

SOURCES: PRONI D/302; PRONI T/3166/1B Hartnell notes; Ellis thesis; O'Neill thesis; Burke *LGI* (1904) p. 44, *IFR* (1976) pp. 127–8; *Alum. Cantab.*; Cork MPs; Johnston, *Gt B. & Ire.*, p. 198n.; EC 7706; *Almanacks*; *DJ* 15–18 May 1756, 30 Nov. – 3 Dec. 1782; NAI Will and Grant 1813, Prerog. (office copy); Parliamentary Lists, 1769 (1), 1772 (2), 1773 (1), (2), 1774 (1), 1775 (1), 1776 (1), (3), 1777 (1), 1778 (1), 1780 (1), 1782 (1), 1783 (1), (2), (3), (4), 1787 (1), 1788 (1), 1790 (1), 1791 (1), 1793 (1), 1794 (1), (2), 1799 (2), (3).

0159 BLAKENEY, Sir William

MP for Kilmallock 1725–7–56

    b. 1670; d. 20 Sept. 1761 (bur. Westminster Abbey)

HONOURS: Knight of the Bath 27 Nov. 1756.

PEERAGES: Cr. Baron Blakeney 18 Dec. 1756.

FAMILY/BACKGROUND: Son and heir of William Blakeney of Thomastown, Co. Limerick, and Elizabeth, dau. of Henry Boreman (**0186**).

MARRIED: Unmarried.

CAREER/OCCUPATION: Freedom of Drogheda 18 Aug. 1725, of Cork 24 Dec. 1756; *Magistrate for Drogheda 1755; *Coroner of Ireland for Drogheda Town 1756.

MILITARY: Joined the army in Flanders as a Volunteer; Ensign in Royal Regiment of Foot of Ireland 4 Sept. 1695, Lieutenant and Adjutant 19 Jan. 1699, Ensign in additional company of the Royal Regiment 31 May 1701, Lieutenant 1 Aug. 1701, Captain 25 Aug. 1704, served at Blenheim, Brevet Major 1 Jan. 1707; transferred to 1st Foot Guards as Lieutenant and Captain 9 Mar. 1708, Lieutenant-Colonel 22 Dec. 1712; Lieutenant-Colonel of Lord John Kerr's Regiment 3 Apr. 1718; Lieutenant-Colonel of Foot 1729, ?1732, ?1738; *Lieutenant-Colonel of Dragoons 1733–6; Colonel of the 27th Inniskilling Foot 27 June 1737; Brigadier-General at the Cartagena Expedition 1741; Lieutenant-General 11 Sept. 1745; Lieutenant Governor of Stirling 1745; Lieutenant Governor of Plymouth 1746–8; Lieutenant Governor of Minorca 1748–56, *Foot 1750, Colonel Lieutenant-General 1753–6. He successfully defended Stirling against the forces of the Young Pretender in 1745; in Minorca he was less successful and was forced to surrender to the French in 1756.

POLITICAL ACTIVITY: He was listed for one committee in 1725 and for 12 between 1727 and 1737, all during the period when Britain was at peace. In any case, after 1730 he would have been 60 years of age and not required to sit on committees. He was a distinguished soldier and thereafter for much of his parliamentary career was probably absent on active service. He was particularly famous for his defence of Minorca, where his courage and tenacity were considered to reflect unfavourably on Admiral Byng, who had been sent to relieve the island. Defending Minorca was virtually a lost cause from the start, as regardless of its proximity to France its defences had suffered from years of neglect. As the *de facto* governor, Blakeney had made frequent representations to the home government about the island's defencelessness, a fact that he stated in his evidence at Byng's court martial.

ADDITIONAL INFORMATION: Grand President of the Laudible Order of the Antigallicans, 23 April 1757. On St Patrick's Day 1759 the Friendly Brothers of St Patrick (an anti-duelling club) erected a statue of him in Sackville Street, Dublin.

ESTATES/RESIDENCE: Castle Blakeney, Co. Galway.

SOURCES: McCracken thesis; GEC *P*; *DNB*; J. L. Chester (ed.), *The Marriage, Baptismal and Burial Registers of the Collegiate Church or Abbey of St Peter, Westminster* (London, 1876), p. 398 [bur. 9 Oct. 1761]; C. Dalton (ed.), *English Army Lists and Commission Registers, 1661–1714* (London, 1898), vol. 4 p. 227 [says Lieutenant-General Sept. 1747]; J. Kelly, 'That Damn'd Thing Called Honour': Duelling in Ireland, 1570–1800* (Cork, 1995), pp. 65, 164–5; A. Webb, *A Compendium of Irish Biography* (Dublin, 1878); *Almanacks*; *BNL* 10 May 1757, 20 Mar. 1759; *DJ* 26–9 Sept. 1761 [says he died aged 91 years].

0160 BLAKENEY, William

MP for Athenry 1781–3, Jan.–Apr. 1790, 1790–7–Apr. 1800; [Escheator of Munster Apr. 1800]

b. 1735; d. 2 Nov. 1804

FAMILY/BACKGROUND: Son of John Blakeney (**0153**) and Grace, dau. of Henry Persse.

MARRIED: [6 Sept. 1770] Sarah, dau. and h. of Samuel Shields of Ouseburn, Newcastle-upon-Tyne.

CHILDREN: Rt Hon. Sir Edward, m. [1814] Maria dau. of Col. Gardiner (HEICS); John Theophilus (at Cambridge (St John's College) 18 Nov. 1790).

MILITARY: Served throughout the Seven Years' War (1756–63) and was wounded at Minden and Rhynberg; Major Royal Welsh Fusiliers, 1775; in the American War of Independence he was severely wounded at Bunker Hill, 17 June 1775; Colonel.

POLITICAL ACTIVITY: He came in on the death of his nephew (**0155**) in 1781, and again on the death of his brother (**0154**) in 1789. He sat, with his brother Theophilus (**0158**), for the family borough of Athenry. He was a lieutenant-colonel in the army and a career soldier. When he came in to parliament he supported Lord Carlisle and was recommended for a military pension. He did not come in in 1783, and the pension does not appear to have been conferred until after the next election, when he was returned and a pension of £350 was granted. On 14 March 1793 it was increased to £450 and granted for his and his wife's lifetime.

He appears to have voted for the Union in 1799 and against it in 1800 – one list gives him voting against in both 1799 and 1800 – his pension was for life, and if better terms were not forthcoming he probably felt that he could follow his own inclination.

DIVISION LISTS:
1790 (2) voted for Foster (**0805**) on the election of a Speaker.
1799 (1) voted for the Union – pensioner.
1800 (1) voted against the Union.

ESTATES/RESIDENCE: Castle Blakeney, Co. Galway; Newcastle-upon-Tyne.

SOURCES: PRONI T/3166/1B Hartnell notes; McCracken thesis; Ellis thesis; O'Neill thesis; Burke *LGI* (1904) p. 44, *IFR* (1976) p. 127; *Alum. Cantab.*; Parliamentary Lists, 1782 (1), 1783 (1), 17 (1), 1790 (1), 1791 (1), 1793 (1), 1794 (2), 1799 (2), (3), 1800 (1), (3).

0161 BLAQUIERE, James

MP for Carlingford 1790–7

b. 1722; d. 6 Feb. 1802
FAMILY/BACKGROUND: Son of John Blaquiere and Marie Elizabeth, dau. of Pierre de Varennes.
MARRIED: (1) Mary Robinson; (2) Bridget Menton.
CHILDREN: (1) Henry, m. Jane [   ]; George. (2) Samuel; John (Lincoln's Inn 24 Nov. 1791).
CAREER/OCCUPATION: Surveyor General of the Province of Leinster 1776–93, of Ireland 1795–6; *Governor of the Foundling Hospital and Workhouse 1795–8; *Governor of the Hibernian Society 1799 (f.); Member of the 1797 Committee to investigate the Foundling Hospital – his brother (**0162**) was Chairman.
MILITARY: Lieutenant-Colonel in the 13th Regiment of Heavy Dragoons ('he was bred up in an Irish Regiment of Cavalry, like his brother'); Major, Douglass' Regiment of Dragoons Feb.

1764, Lieutenant-Colonel 1765, of the 5th Dragoons 1766–8, 1773.

POLITICAL ACTIVITY: His seat for Carlingford in 1790 was purchased either by or for him. His main claim to political recognition was that he was the brother of Sir John Blaquiere (**0162**), Chief Secretary to Lord Lieutenant Harcourt. He was appointed Surveyor General of the Revenue, £500 p.a. As might be expected, he was a government supporter. He was a Governor of the Foundling Hospital and the Dublin Workhouse, and part of the parliamentary inquiry into the Foundling Hospital which revealed conditions that shocked Dublin society. He was also a Governor of the Hibernian Hospital. This was a school for the education of the children of soldiers who belonged, or had belonged, to regiments on the Irish Establishment. The school had a distinctly military organisation, but the boys (it was co-educational) did not seem inclined to embark on military careers, preferring to be apprenticed to a trade.

DIVISION LISTS:
1790 (2) voted for Foster (**0805**) on the election of a Speaker.
1795 (3) voted against Sir Laurence Parsons' (**1636**) resolution against alleged troop removals.

ADDITIONAL INFORMATION: A member of the Royal Dublin Society, 1793f; a member of the Royal Irish Academy, 1796; treasurer, 1797–8; council, 1799–1800.

ESTATES/RESIDENCE: Gort, Co. Galway.

SOURCES: Vicars, *Prerog. Wills*; Burke *PB* (1903) p. 429; *Memorials of the Dead*; Lincoln's Inn Records vol. I p. 541; *Ir. Gen.* vol. 1 no 8 (1940) pp. 237–8 'A List of Irish Stockholders, 1779'; J. Carr, *A Stranger in Ireland* (1805) p. 498; Hugh Howard, *Parliamentary History of Ireland* (n.d.); *Almanacks*; DJ 25–8 Feb. 1764; FJ 22 Apr. 1797; Parliamentary Lists, 1791 (1), 1793 (1), 1794 (1), (2).

0162 BLAQUIERE, Rt Hon. Sir John

MP for Old Leighlin 1773–6–83; Carlingford 1783–90; Charleville 1790–7; Newtown 1797–

1800 [r. Enniskillen 1783]; [UK] Rye 1801– 02; Downton 1803–6

b. 15 May 1732; d. 27 Aug. 1812
HONOURS: PC, sworn 30 Nov. 1772, 1774; Knight of the Bath 3 Aug. 1774; cr. Bt 16 July 1784.
PEERAGES: Cr. Baron de Blaquiere, 30 July 1800.
FAMILY/BACKGROUND: Son of John Blaquiere [Huguenot refugee settled in London 1685], a London merchant, and Marie Elizabeth, dau. of Pierre de Varennes.
MARRIED: [3 Dec. 1775] Eleanor, dau. and h. of Robert Dobson of Ann's Grove, Co. Cork (0644).
CHILDREN: John, 2nd Baron de Blaquiere; William, 3rd Baron de Blaquiere, m. [1811] Lady Harriet Townshend, dau. of Rt Hon. George Townshend, 1st Marquess Townshend; George; Peter Boyle, m. (1) [1804] Eliza, dau. of Denis O'Brien of Co. Limerick, (2) [1818] Eliza, dau. of William Roper of Co. Dublin; Anna Maria, m. John Kirkwall; Elizabeth, m. [1807] John Bernard Hankey of Surrey; Eleanor, m. [1822] Joseph Knight.
EDUCATION: LLD *hon. caus.* TCD 1773.
CAREER/OCCUPATION: Secretary to the British Ambassador in Paris, 1771–2, Chief Secretary 30 Nov. 1772 – 6 Dec. 1776; Alnager 1775–1812 (1797 renewed until 1845 to him and his assigns, abolished 1817); Bailiff of Phoenix Park 14 Jan. 1775–89; Trustee of the Linen Board for Connaught 1781; *Governor of the Hibernian Society 1782; *Company of Undertakers of the Grand Canal 1783–4; *Director for Paving, Cleansing and Lighting the Streets of Dublin 1784; Commissioner of Dublin Paving Board 1786; *Governor of the Foundling Hospital and Workhouse 1784–96; *Governor of Erasmus Smith's Schools and other Charities 1796–8; Freeman at Large of the City of Dublin 1797.
MILITARY: Major 18th Dragoons 1759, Brevet Lieutenant-Colonel 1762; Lieutenant-Colonel 17th Dragoons 1763; *Lieutenant-Colonel of Dragoons 1765–6, *7th Dragoons 1767–70; ret. 1777; Second Lieutenant in Collon Cavalry 1796.

POLITICAL ACTIVITY: He was unique among late eighteenth-century Chief Secretaries in that he settled in Ireland and continued to be an Irish MP after he had been Chief Secretary. He was reputed to be 'the most popular Secretary that ever held office'. One reason for this may have been his famous duel with Beauchamp Bagenal (0071),

which took place shortly after his arrival. The cause was Blaquiere's failure to have Bagenal presented to the French king when he was secretary to Lord Harcourt, at that time Ambassador to France. Bagenal fired repeatedly, but Blaquiere fired only once and missed.

He attributed his partial deafness to his ready ear for business while sitting in the Irish Commons. As Chief Secretary he proved a competent manipulator and leader of the House of Commons. He was nicknamed 'Swiss' by Lord Shannon (0213). In 1773 the Solicitor General said that if Sir John 'splits upon any rock it will be that of parliamentary speaking', and, later in the year, that 'Contrary to my Expectation Blaquiere is growing a good speaker in debate.' This was important, as the Chief Secretary was the leader for the government in the House of Commons and it was possibly the major rock on which his successor, Sir Richard Heron (1010), foundered.

Blaquiere's skill was probably best demonstrated over the Absentee Tax in 1773. In the latter part of the eighteenth century the Irish government ran a continually escalating deficit budget; consequently there was an ever-increasing search for new taxes that would not be unduly distasteful to parliament and the people. In 1773 a tax on the rents of absentee landlords was introduced into the Irish parliament. This caused a furore among the absentee landlords led by the Whig leader, the Marquess of Rockingham. The British government was taken aback by the storm and requested the Lord Lieutenant to quash the tax, but it had already been introduced and could only be stopped by a rejection by the Irish parliament. Blaquiere managed to achieve this by employing two tactics: he insinuated firstly that the Absentee Tax might be the forerunner of a general land tax, which Ireland did not have; and secondly that government would allow an open vote on the question: 'If Administration should take any part in it,' he told the House, 'it will be to follow and not to lead the wishes of this House' and, as a Castle observer commented on another occasion, 'Neutrality on any question produces relaxation of discipline.' The MPs thought that they smelt the proverbial rat and rejected the measure, although the division lists were barely closed before they realised their mistake. By then it was too late, and government firmly refused further debate on the subject.

In 1775 he married an Irish heiress, Eleanor Dobson, and decided to make his career in Ireland. Blaquiere ensured his return for the government borough of Old Leighlin in 1776. Shortly after Lord Harcourt retired, and a year later met an accidental death. His successor, Lord Lieutenant Buckinghamshire, was confronted with the problems of the War of American Independence and his Chief Secretary, Sir Richard Heron, was weak and ineffective. Blaquiere condemned Lord Buckinghamshire's viceroyalty as 'the most scandalous dereliction of the power of government'. Apart from Lord Temple (Buckingham), whom he described as 'an imperious, reserved , supercilious man ... haughty to the humble and humble to the stout', Blaquiere appears to have got on reasonably well with succeeding administrations and blended into the Irish political scene. In 1782 he was noted as: 'very hospitable. Has a good cook and good wines and knows their influence.'

In 1784 he introduced a Wide Streets Bill, 23 & 24 Geo. III, c. 31, which was part of the town planning of the capital begun in 1757 by the Wide Streets Commission. These acts, which have given Dublin its elegant and distinctive character, aroused a certain amount of resentment at a perceived erosion of the charter rights of Dublin Corporation, while the financial implications of the compulsory purchases involved in widening the streets gave the opposition ammunition for debate.

Blaquiere also took a genuine interest in various social problems. In the mid-1780s, with the viceregal support of the Duke of Rutland, he founded the Free Fountain Association to supply water to the Dublin poor because of the 'want of a supply of free water, a necessary of life, which most of them could only obtain in miserable quantity, by buying it at the huxter's pipe'. He succeeded in establishing free conduits and fountains throughout the city. In 1797 he was chairman of the committee to investigate the notorious abuses in the Foundling Hospital.

Blaquiere appears to have been responsible for quartering troops during the 1798 rebellion, and in December 1798 Cornwallis wrote to the Duke of Portland that the government was much indebted to Blaquiere for his aid. At the time of the Union Blaquiere's social and political skills were much in evidence; in recommending him for the peerage in June 1800 Cornwallis wrote that he: '... has exerted himself through the whole contest of the Union question both in and out of Parliament with great zeal, has expressed himself personally in the warmest moments of debate with great spirit, and repeatedly been an object of the fury of the populace, who twice attacked his house. He has also kept the friends of the measure together by his constant conviviality ... Having filled offices of considerable trust under His Majesty, and faithfully served him for a long series of years, and having married an heiress of considerable fortune in the county of Derry, he trusts His Majesty will raise him to the dignity of the peerage, and confer on him the title of De Blaquiere, which his ancestry enjoyed in France.'

In January 1799 Blaquiere sought an Irish peerage for his wife; in this he was unsuccessful, as was his ambition to become a representative peer. Portland replied that making Blaquiere a representative peer would be 'impudent'. However, he did acquire an Irish peerage in the Union honours. Horace Walpole had earlier considered 'Col. Blaquiere a frank, good humoured but weak and conceited man'. Lord Camden considered his elevation to the peerage as 'almost intolerable'. In an age of social climbers, Blaquiere was certainly among the most ambitious, and he had the advantage of knowing the system from the inside. With great difficulty Cornwallis persuaded him to drop his representative peerage claim for 'more substantial objects', namely a pension of £1,000 to add to his £3,200 compensation p.a. for lost sinecures. Blaquiere then decided on a Westminster seat.

Among the perquisites that had fallen to Blaquiere as Chief Secretary had been the office of Alnager for Ireland, and this created a difficulty over his possible disqualification under the Irish Place Act of that session. He had been granted this office for 31 years in 1775 but had resigned the fees from new drapery by 1782 for a pension of £2,000 p.a. He kept the old drapery fees, c.

£400 p.a., and tried unsuccessfully to convert this into a pension in 1794. He then resigned the office to be given a new lease for 38 years, and in 1797 this was extended to 48 years. He was prepared to assign the Alnagership to his son, but wanted a seat in the parliament of the United Kingdom for himself. This he achieved, as he was returned for Rye in 1801 and for Downton in the following parliament. He considered Pitt's resignation a calamity but made himself useful to Addington's administration by defending the Irish measures, 16 March 1801, particularly martial law, stating that in July 1800 his house had been burnt down by Irish malcontents. He was also a spokesman in March and April 1801 for the Dublin Paving Board, against charges of jobbery. In the British parliament he remained hostile to Catholic Emancipation.

DIVISION LISTS:

1773 (1) voted for the Absentee Tax.

1774 (1) voted for the Stamp Bill.

1775 (1) voted against the pro-American amendment to the Speech from the Throne.

1779 (2) voted against a six-months Loan Bill.

1780 (4) voted for the Perpetual Mutiny Bill.

1783 (1) voted against Flood's (0762) motion for parliamentary reform.

1784 (1) voted against a committee on the Reform Bill.

1784 (2) voted for protective duties (wool).

1785 (1) voted for the Commercial Propositions.

1789 (1) voted for a regency.

1790 (2) voted for Foster (0805) on the election of a Speaker.

1793 (2) voted for the Convention Bill.

1795 (2) voted against Catholic Emancipation.

1795 (3) teller against Sir Laurence Parsons' (1636) resolution against alleged troop removals.

1798 (1) voted against Sir Laurence Parsons' motion for an investigation into 'the present discontents'.

1799 (1) voted for the Union – Privy Counsellor, Alnager of Ireland and First Director of Paving Board and pensioner.

1800 (1) voted for the Union.

ADDITIONAL INFORMATION: A member of the Royal Dublin Society from 1780. Fellow of the Society of Antiquities, 13 January 1803. He was employed in a counting house in London before entering the army in an Irish regiment. Lord Harcourt, colonel of his brother James's regiment, the 13th Dragoons, took him as his secretary to Paris and to Dublin.

ESTATES/RESIDENCE: Ardkill, Co. Londonderry, in right of his wife; Port Loman, Co. Westmeath. The Port Loman estate, baronies of Corkaree and Moygoish (in a bloc), near Mullingar; 1,228 statute acres in 1866, at a rental of £1,182. The house was situated on Lough Owell. In 1800 BNL reported the burning of a house belonging to Sir John Blaquiere at Kilnahard, Co. Cavan and a reward of £100 was offered for each of the culprits.

'The Chief Secretary's income,' Blaquiere informed Harcourt in 1772, 'may amount to from £3,500 to £4,000 a year ... and generally four hundred, at his starting, is voted in council for his advantage.' In 1783 this salary was increased by £2,000, and Lord Castlereagh (2009) received £450 from the Civil List and £250 from fees when he was appointed in 1798. The Chief Secretary was also entitled to a major sinecure falling vacant during his tenure of office as a type of pension. Blaquiere was made Alnager for 31 years and also Bailiff of the Phoenix Park – £1,200. In 1782 he resigned the new drapery side of the Alnager for a pension of £200 p.a. for the remainder of his 31-year term and sold the office of Bailiff to the government for £7,000; the latter sale appears dubious both from its amount and the fact that the Parliamentary Lists continued to attribute the office to him. It had been vainly hoped that the 1783 increase in salary would obviate the necessity of making additional provision for the Chief Secretary.

SOURCES: *Ir. Statutes*, 23 & 24 G. III c. 31 (1011); NLI reps vol. 118, 22 June 1816; NLI LC 2137; PRONI MIC/465/1 R. Ffolliott, *Biographical Notices, 1756–1827* [Hibernian Chronicle says he married Elinor Dobson on 30 Dec. 1775]; RCBL P277/1/3, Parish Registers of St Mary's, Dublin; O'Neill thesis; *Proc. RIA*, vol. 77 C no 1, J. C. Sainty, 'The Secretariat of the Chief Governors of Ireland, 1690–1800' (1977); *HP 1794–1820* [see for his UK career]; Fermanagh and Tyrone MPs; Burke *PB* (1903) p. 429 [says he married 24 Dec. 1775]; *DNB*; *Index to Irish Privy Counsellors, 1711–1910*; Hughes, *Pat. Officers*; McDowell, *Ir. public opinion, 1750–1800*, p. 132 n. 1; J. Kelly, *'That*

Damn'd Thing Called Honour': Duelling in Ireland 1570–1860 (Cork, 1995) pp. 111–12; J. Smyth, *Men of no Property* (Dublin, 1992), p. 136; *Cornwallis Corr.* vol. 3 pp. 4, 30, 253, 269, 276–8, 286; E. Hewitt (ed.), *Lord Shannon's Letters to his Son* (PRONI 1982) p. xxii; Johnston, *Gt B. & Ire.*, pp. 40, 42, 280; *Ir. Gen.* vol. 5 no 3 (1976), H. F. Morris, 'Ramsey's Waterford Chronicle, 1776' p. 336 [his wife was third dau. and co-h. of Alexander Timpkins of Ardess, Co. Londonderry (*sic*)]; *JRSAI* vol. 27 (1897) p. 180, T. Drew, 'The Stolen Fountain and Rutland Monument of Merrion-Square, Dublin'; *FJ* 12 Nov. 1796, 11, 22 Apr. 1797; McDowell, *Ire. in Age of Imp. & Rev.*, p. 55 and various; *Almanacks*; Parliamentary Lists, 1773 (1), 1774 (1), 1775 (1), 1776 (1), (2), (3), 1777 (1), 1778 (1), 1780 (1), 1782 (1), 1783 (1), (2), 1784 (1), (2), (3), 1785 (1), (2), (3), 1787 (1), 1788 (1), 1789 (1), (2), 1790 (1), 1791 (1), 1793 (1), 1794 (1), (2), 1798 (1), 1799 (1), (3), 1800 (1), (3).

0163 BLENNERHASSETT, Arthur

MP for Tralee 1727–43

b. 1687; d. 3 Jan. 1758
FAMILY/BACKGROUND: Eldest son of Robert Blennerhassett (0170) and Alice, dau. of Sir William Osborne, 4th Bt.
MARRIED: Mary, dau. and co-h. of Capt. Richard Pope of Derryknockhane, Co. Limerick.
CHILDREN: ?
EDUCATION: School: Dr Jones, Dublin; entered TCD 15 May 1704, BA 1708; Middle Temple 22 May 1708; called to the Irish Bar 1714; LLD *hon. caus.* 1734.
CAREER/OCCUPATION: King's Counsel 1728; Prime Serjeant 14 Jan. 1742–3; Third Justice of the King's Bench 5 May 1743–58; Freedom of Cork, High Sheriff of Co. Kerry 1720; *Co. Limerick 1739; *Magistrate of Kinsale 1732, ?Limerick 1736, 1739–2; *Mayor of Co. Limerick 1736, 1739, 1742; *Recorder of Co. Limerick 1741–2; *Commissioner of the Tillage Act for Munster 1735, 1739–57; *Commissioner of Oyer and Terminer 1742–53; Justice of Assize for Munster Lent 1742, Summer 1742, Lent 1743, NW Ulster Summer 1743, Leinster Lent 1744, Munster Summer 1744, Leinster Lent 1745, Munster Summer 1745, Lent and Summer 1746, NW Ulster Lent 1747, NW Ulster Lent 1748, Connaught Summer 1748, Munster Summer 1749, NE Ulster Lent 1750, Munster Lent 1751, Leinster Summer 1751, Munster Lent 1753,

Leinster Summer 1753, Munster Lent 1754, Leinster Summer 1755.

POLITICAL ACTIVITY: The Blennerhassetts were an old Co. Kerry family with a number of branches. This MP was a lawyer, King's Counsel, Prime Serjeant and a Justice of King's Bench. Otherwise very little is known about him. He was a man of business around the House, and was nominated for 43 parliamentary committees during his career. His father (0170) was Prime Serjeant in 1711.

ESTATES/RESIDENCE: Riddleston, Lincolnshire; Shanid and [?]Ballyseedy, Co. Kerry; Dawson Street, Dublin.

SOURCES: PRONI D/302; EC 3997; RCBL P273/1/3, Parish Registers of St Paul's, Dublin [bur. 9 Jan. 1758]; McCracken thesis; T. Barnard, *The Abduction of a Limerick Heiress: Social and Political Relations in Mid-eighteenth Century Ireland* (Maynooth Studies in Local History, 1998) [portrait p. 25] *IMC King's Inn Admissions*; Smyth, *Law Officers*; Ball, *Judges* [says m. Mary dau. of Edward Rice and widow of William Degge]; H. A. C. Sturgess, *Middle Temple Admissions*, vol. 1 p. 263; *Ir. Gen.* vol. 4, no 4 [Nov. 1971] p. 308, W. G. Skehan, 'Extracts from the Minutes of the Corporation of Fethard, Co. Tipperary'; *Almanacks*; *The Dublin Courant* 25 Nov. 1719; *Pue's Occurrences* 20 Feb. 1742, 17 July 1742, 15 Feb., 21 June, 28 June 1746, 21 Feb., 24 Feb. 1747, 19 Feb., 9 July 1751, 17 Feb., 28 July 1753, 1 July 1755; *DJ* 14 Feb., 19 June 1744, 26 Feb., 13 July 1745; *The Dublin Gazette* 26 Feb., 9 July 1743; *The Dublin Weekly Journal* 5 Mar., 16 July 1748, 1 July 1749, 10 Mar. 1750.

0164 BLENNERHASSETT, Arthur

MP for Tralee 1743–60; Co. Kerry 1775–6–83

b. 1719; d. (*ante* 13) June 1799 at Bath
FAMILY/BACKGROUND: Son of John Blennerhassett (0167) and Jane, dau. of Edward Denny (0619).
MARRIED: Jane, dau. of [   ] Giradot, wid. of Col. Hamilton.
CHILDREN: Jane, m. [24 June 1784] George Winn, 1st Baron Headley; Juliana, m. Michael Tisdall.
CAREER/OCCUPATION: Deputy Governor of Co. Kerry 6 Aug. 1779.
MILITARY: Colonel of the Ballymacelligot Volunteers; Colonel of the Kerry Legion, 1782.

POLITICAL ACTIVITY: In 1743 he was returned for

Tralee in place of his relative Arthur Blennerhassett (**0163**), who was elevated to the King's Bench as Third Justice. He was an independent but considered to be a 'moderate fair man' – his first two votes could be interpreted as supporting the administration, but after 1753 he was inclined to vote with the opposition. He was nominated to seven committees between 1746 and 1753. In the later 1750s he was possibly an absentee.

He was a strong supporter of the Protestant interest and in the 1770s, while still an independent, he inclined towards Lord Shannon (**0213**); this connection may well have told against him in the 1783 election, when he was defeated by Sir Barry Denny (**0617**) and Richard Townsend Herbert (**1009**): the latter was associated with Shannon's opponent in Co. Cork, Richard Longfield (**1263**). Another factor against him was the fact that he was colonel of a fencible regiment – the creation of such regiments was an attempt on the part of the government to control the Volunteers. Blennerhassett was nominated for the regiment by Lord Shelburne, one of the leading interests in Co. Kerry.

DIVISION LISTS:

1749 (1) voted against the election of James Digges La Touche (♦♦♦♦).
1753 (1) voted against the expulsion of Arthur Jones-Nevill (**1125**).
1753 (2) voted against the Money Bill.
1777 (1) voted against Grattan's (**0895**) motion for retrenchment.
1778 (2) voted against the Popery Bill.
1779 (2) voted for a six-months Loan Bill.
1780 (2) voted for Yelverton's (**2268**) motion to modify Poynings' Law.

ADDITIONAL INFORMATION: In December 1782 he wrote to Grenville requesting that, as the Duke of Portland had accepted his recommendation of someone to succeed Mr Mahoney as Sheriff of Co. Kerry, Lord Temple would honour him with the same indulgence. This was important, as the sheriff was the returning officer in county elections and an election was imminent. Kerry was a complex county with a number of conflicting interests.

ESTATES/RESIDENCE: Ballyseedy, Co. Kerry. There are abstracts of the wills of Arthur Blenerhassett of Ballyseedy, 1799, and Jane, Dowager Lady Headley, of Aghadoe House, 1827. He was succeeded by his son-in-law, Lord Headley, and Wakefield reckoned Lord Headley's rental at £4,000.

SOURCES: NLI EC 7344; PRONI MIC/474 Irish Volunteers; Ellis thesis; McCracken thesis; Hughes, *Pat. Officers*; Burke *LGI* (1904) p. 46 [says b. 1709]; *Proc. RIA* vol. 77 C no 1 (1977); Johnston, *Gt B. & Ire.*, pp. 223–4; *WHM* (1799) p. 72; NLI EC 7344; McNevin, *Volunteers*; *DJ* 13 June 1799; Parliamentary Lists, 1756 (1), 1776 (1), (2), (3), 1777 (1), 1778 (1), 1780 (1), 1782 (1), 1783 (1), 1785 (2).

0165 BLENNERHASSETT, Conway

MP for Tralee 1723–4

b. 3 Oct. 1693; d. 7 June 1724
FAMILY/BACKGROUND: Eldest son of John Blennerhassett of Kilorglin, Co. Kerry, and Elizabeth, dau. of Benjamin Cross, Rector of Christ Church, Cork.
MARRIED: Elizabeth, only dau. of Wentworth Harman (**0970**).
CHILDREN: Conway, m. Elizabeth, dau. of Thomas Lacy; a son (married and had issue); Alice (b. 10 June 1718); Margaret (b. 27 Oct. 1721), m. (1) William Gun, (2) John Henry FitzGerald.
EDUCATION: Middle Temple 30 Nov. 1710; called to the Irish Bar 17 July 1714.
CAREER/OCCUPATION: King's Counsel 1722.
MILITARY: Captain of Battle-Axe Guards.

POLITICAL ACTIVITY: He was a lawyer and obviously hoped for a legal career as, during the short time that he sat in parliament, he was listed for 12 committees – although, as a member was often listed simply as 'Mr _____', some of these may refer to John Blennerhassett (**0167**).

ESTATES/RESIDENCE: Castle Conway, Kilorglin, Co. Kerry.

SOURCES: PRONI MIC/338/2 Crossle notes; Burke *IFR* (1976) p. 137; Hickson, *Selections from Old Kerry Records*, first ser. p. 163; Hughes, *Pat. Officers*; IMC *King's Inns Admissions*; G. F. Russell-Barker and A. H. Stenning (eds), *Record of Old Westminsters: A Biographical List*, 2 vols (London, 1928); *Middle Temple Admissions* vol. 1 p. 268; J. Foster, *The Royal Lineage of our Noble and Gentle Families* (London, 1886), pp. 586, 593; *Kerry Magazine* vol. 3 no 36 [Dec. 1856] pp. 185–90, 'Parliamentary Representation of Kerry'.

0166 BLENNERHASSETT, John

MP for Tralee 1692–3; Dingle 1695–9; Co. Kerry 1703–9

b. 1665; d. 1709
FAMILY/BACKGROUND: Son of John Blennerhassett and Elizabeth, dau. of Sir Edward Denny.
MARRIED: Margaret, dau. of Patrick Crosbie of Tubrid (she married (2) Hon. David Barry (**0089**)).
CHILDREN: John (**0167**); Arthur; Thomas, m. Avice Spring; Pierce; William, m. Mary, dau. of Alderman John Morley; Robert; Agnes, m. Robert Rogers.
EDUCATION: School: Mr Richards; entered TCD 26 June 1683, aged 18 years, BA 1685.
CAREER/OCCUPATION: Sheriff of Co. Kerry 1696, 1702; Deputy Governor of Co. Kerry 1699.

POLITICAL ACTIVITY: He appears to have been a fairly typical country gentleman. In 1695 he was hostile to Lord Chancellor Porter, who was accused by some MPs of favouring Catholics, and in 1696 he signed the Association for the protection of William III in the country. During Queen Anne's reign he was in opposition, and listed as 'against the Court' in 1706. In 1705 he introduced the heads of a bill that became 4 Anne, c. 5, 'for the Relief of Creditors against Fraudulent Devises', which was largely concerned with inheritance frauds. He died four years later.

ESTATES/RESIDENCE: Ballyseedy, Co. Kerry. In 1671, John Blennerhassett (same family) was granted fairs at Currans.

SOURCES: *CJ Ire.* (Bradley ed.) vol. 3 p. 299 (**0086**); PRONI D/302; Burke *LGI* (1904) p. 46; Lodge *P*; *Cal. SP Dom. 1694–5* p. 341; Simms' cards; *Alum. Dub.* [says he is MP for Tralee 1709]; Eustace, *Abstracts of Wills*; *JRSAI* vol. 55 (1925) pp. 38, 47, H.A.S. Upton, 'A List of Governors and Deputy Governors of Counties in Ireland in 1699' [says he is Sir John and died 1708]; Parliamentary Lists, 1695 (1), 1696 (1), 1706 (1). The Blennerhassetts were a complex family with many branches and there is sometimes confusion between them; the following two references are probably incorrect for this reason: PRONI MIC/338/2 Crossle Notes [says his mother was Martha, dau. of George Lynne of Southwick Hall]; J. Foster, *The Royal Lineage of our Noble and Gentle Families* (London, 1886) [says he is the son of John Blennerhassett and Martha Lynne, and that he married Elizabeth Denny].

0167 BLENNERHASSETT, John

MP for Co. Kerry 1709–13, 1715–27, 1761–8–75; Tralee 1713–14, 1727–60

b. 1691; d. 5 May 1775 at Oak Park, Co. Kerry, aged 84 years
FAMILY/BACKGROUND: Eldest son of John Blennerhassett (**0166**) and Margaret, dau. of Patrick Crosbie of Tubrid, Co. Kerry.
MARRIED: [marriage settlement 1713] Jane, dau. of Edward Denny (**0619**).
CHILDREN: John (**0168**); Arthur (**0164**); Agnes, m. Sir Thomas Denny; Arabella, m. (1) Richard Ponsonby (**1704**), (2) Arthur Blennerhassett; Letitia; Mary, m. Lancelot Crosbie (**0536**).
CAREER/OCCUPATION: High Sheriff of Co. Kerry 1717; Governor of Co. Kerry 1747–53; Provost of Tralee 25 June 1757; *Commissioner of the Tillage Act for Munster 1767–74.

POLITICAL ACTIVITY: He was returned for Co. Kerry on the death of his father in 1709. His electoral background gives some indication of the complexity of Co. Kerry electoral politics as well as the uncertainty of national politics during the final years of Queen Anne. During his election campaign he was supported by a Tory interest in Kerry against Thomas Crosbie (**0538**), who was aided by the Whigs. He was listed on 14 committees between 1709 and 1711. This alignment seems to have continued in 1710, but by 1712 there had been a regrouping of the families in the county and Blennerhassett was seen working with the Whigs. He was reported as having divided on the Whig side in October 1711 in a vote concerning the activities of the Irish Privy Council. Thereafter he appears to have been in opposition. He was listed for only one committee in 1713.

He sat in the House of Commons for 66 years – from 1709, when he was returned under age, until his death in 1775. During that time he represented either Co. Kerry or the borough of Tralee. Apart from supporting the national bank his political activities appear to have been relatively low-key during the reign of George I, although he was nominated for 11 committees in the latter part of George I's reign: these nominations, or some of them, possibly referred to Conway Blennerhassett (**0165**) as there was a custom of listing Mr _____ in the Journals with only an occasional indication of the Christian name.

In 1727 he signed the family compact with Sir Maurice Crosbie (**0537**) of Ardfert and Arthur Denny (**0615**) of Tralee partitioning the county representation among the three families. 'It is true that, as will appear, this obligation became "null and void" in the very next generation, that the high contracting parties broke through their engagements as if they were pie-crust, and that the natural course of events must have rendered such an engagement null and void in course of time and events, still the intention to make the bond of union perpetual is evident.' During the parliament of George II he was listed for 54 committees between 1729 and 1760. He was interested in communications, and in 1731 he introduced the heads of a bill to improve the road from Naas to Maryborough, 5 Geo. II, c. 21, then in 1735 the road from Maryborough to Tomivanah, 9 Geo. II, c. 22 and, two years later, 11 Geo. II, c. 18, a continuation of this road through Nenagh and Tullo to Limerick city. Although he was consistently in opposition, on 14 February 1758 he was granted a pension of £200 p.a.

He was returned again for Co. Kerry in 1761 and, despite being a pensioner, voted against the army augmentation. By 1769 he was the Father of the House and reputedly influenced by Speaker Ponsonby (**0702**) and Lord Shannon (**0213**), but although favouring the opposition he was probably an absentee from about 1772; he was noted in the Parliamentary List of that year as 'old never attends'.

DIVISION LISTS:

1711 (1) voted for the Court on the Dublin mayoralty issue.
1721 (2) voted against a national bank.
1749 (1) voted against the election of James Digges La Touche (♦♦♦♦).
1753 (1) voted for the expulsion of Arthur Jones-Nevill (**1125**).
1753 (2) voted against the Money Bill.
1768 (1) voted against army augmentation – a pensioner.

ADDITIONAL INFORMATION: *A member of the Royal Dublin Society from 1767.

ESTATES/RESIDENCE: Ballyseedy and Conway Castle, Killorglin, Co. Kerry; Little Cuffe Street, Dublin. In

1713 John Blennerhasset's income was estimated to be £600.

SOURCES: *CJ Ire.* (Bradley ed.) vol. 6 pp. 570–72, 823, 836 (0315, 0365, 0338); PRONI D/302; PRONI T/1584 Pinkerton transcripts, p. 227, 30 May 1775; PRONI T/3411; Hayton thesis; McCracken thesis; Burke *IFR* (1976) p. 141; *Alum. Dub.* [says the MP for Tralee, 1709, entered TCD 1683 aged 18 years]; *Index to Hibernian Chronicle, 1769–75* (Society of Genealogists, 1936) vol. 2 p. 73 [says he died 22 May 1775 aged 83 years]; *WHM* 1776, p. 438; *The Kerry Magazine* vol. 3 no 36 [Dec. 1856] pp. 185–90, 'Parliamentary Representation of Kerry'; *Almanacks*; *BNL* 20 Feb. 1767, 30 May – 2 June 1775; *DJ* 25–8 June 1757; Parliamentary Lists, 1711 (3), 1713 (2), 1756 (1), 1769 (1), 1772 (1), 1773 (1), 1774 (1).

0168 BLENNERHASSETT, John

MP for Co. Kerry 1751–60, 1762–3

b. 1715; d. (May) 1763
FAMILY/BACKGROUND: Eldest son of John Blennerhassett (**0167**) and Jane, dau. of Edward Denny (**0619**).
MARRIED: (1) Anne, dau. of William Crosbie (**0539**); (2) [Apr. 1753] Frances, dau. of Edward Herbert.
CHILDREN: John; Arthur; Frances, m. [1782] Rev. Jemmett Browne of Co. Cork.
EDUCATION: Entered TCD 22 June 1732; Middle Temple 18 Dec. 1733.
CAREER/OCCUPATION: High Sheriff of Co. Kerry 1740 [John Blennerhassett, the younger of Ballyseedy].

POLITICAL ACTIVITY: He was the son of John Blennerhassett (**0167**), and both of his wives and his mother were from leading Co. Kerry families. He came into parliament at the height of the Money Bill crisis and supported the opposition in two key votes – the expulsion of Arthur Jones-Nevill (**1125**) and against the Money Bill. Between his election in 1751 and 1756 he was listed for 13 committees. In 1756 he was recorded as being probably in the opposition but absent.

DIVISION LISTS:

1753 (1) voted for the expulsion of Arthur Jones-Nevill (**1125**).
1753 (2) voted against the Money Bill.

ESTATES/RESIDENCE: Ballyseedy, Co. Kerry.

SOURCES: PRONI D/302; PRONI MIC/465/1 R. Ffolliott, *Biographical Notices, 1756–1827*; McCracken thesis; Burke *LGI* (1904) p. 46; *Alum. Dub.*; H.A.C. Sturgess, *Register of Admissions to the Honourable Society of the Middle Temple* (London, 1949), vol. 1 p. 316; Parliamentary List, 1756 (1).

0169 BLENNERHASSETT, John

MP for Co. Kerry 1790–4

b. 1769; d. 6 July 1794 at Mallow
FAMILY/BACKGROUND: Eldest son of William Blennerhassett of Ballyseedy, Co. Kerry, and Catherine, eldest dau. of Noble Johnson.
MARRIED: Unmarried.
EDUCATION: School: Mr Martin; entered TCD 30 June 1784, aged 15 years, BA 1790; Middle Temple 31 Aug. 1788; MA 1792.

POLITICAL ACTIVITY: He was in parliament for only a brief time, but during it he appears to have adopted a moderate opposition position, very much that of a county MP. The government was hopeful of winning him over 'with management'. He voted for Foster (**0805**), pre-eminently a country gentleman's Speaker, but otherwise followed the opposition lead (see Division Lists). The free trade issue had been brought up in 1784–5, and Grattan (**0895**) had strongly disagreed with the proposed settlement of that occasion. The sale of peerages as a means of government influence over the legislature had become notorious by 1790. The Dublin Police Bill that had been introduced in 1786 in an attempt to bring law and order to the city was manifestly desirable but, as it transferred power from the city to the government, was open to the charge of being a 'patronage bill' and of violating the charter of the city of Dublin and interfering with the rights of the corporation – Grattan was one of the MPs for Dublin city.

Fitzgibbon (**0749**) declared that the 1793 Convention Act (33 Geo. III, c. 29) 'in ten lines did no more than declare that there should only be one parliament in Ireland'. It was aimed at preventing a repetition of the quasi-parliament held by the Catholics in 1792 by declaring unlawful assemblies brought together 'for the purpose of

procuring an alteration of matters established by law in Church and state'. Kerry was a county with an overwhelming Catholic majority, and Blennerhassett's attitude to this would have squared with his support for Knox's (**1180**) motion on Catholic Emancipation.

DIVISION LISTS:
    1790 (2) voted for Foster (**0805**) on the election of a Speaker.
    1791 (1) voted for Curran's (**0560**) resolution against the sale of peerages.
    1791 (2) voted for Grattan's (**0895**) motion for the exercise of Free Trade.
    1791 (3) voted for Grattan's motion to abolish the Dublin police.
    1793 (1) voted for Knox's (**1180**) motion for Catholic Emancipation.
    1793 (2) voted against the Convention Bill.

ESTATES/RESIDENCE: Elmgrove, Tralee, Co. Kerry.

SOURCES: PRONI (transcript) Landsdowne papers, 6 Apr. 1790; Burke *LGI* (1904) p. 46, *IFR* (1976) p. 140; *Alum. Dub.*; *Middle Temple Admissions* vol. 2 p. 404; *Walker's Hibernian Magazine* Aug. 1794 p. 192; *Kerry Magazine* vol. 3 no 36 (Dec. 1856) pp. 185–90 'Parliamentary Representation of Kerry' [says he died aged 24 years]; Mc Dowell, *Ire. in the age of Imp. & Rev.*, p. 436; *Proc. RIA* vol. 71 sect. C no. 5, Johnston, 'Members of the Irish Parliament 1784–7', pp. 146–56; *DJ* 12 July 1794; *Watson's Almanack* (1791 and 1795); Parliamentary Lists, 1791 (1), 1793 (1).

0170 BLENNERHASSETT, Robert

MP for Clonmel 1692–3, 1695–9; Limerick B. 1703–12

b. 1652; d. [Oct.] 1712
FAMILY/BACKGROUND: Second son of Arthur Blennerhassett of Tralee, Co. Kerry, and Mary, dau. of Garrett FitzGerald of Ballynard, Co. Limerick, Archdeacon of Emly.
MARRIED: Alice, dau. of Sir William Osborne, 4th Bt.
CHILDREN: Arthur (**0163**); 4 dau.
EDUCATION: School: Mr Wall; entered TCD 22 May 1667, aged 15 years; Middle Temple 21 Nov. 1673.
CAREER/OCCUPATION: Prime Serjeant 11 Apr. 1711; Recorder of the Corporation of Cashel 17

Apr. 1680–7, retained in office and named as one of the 24 Burgesses by Charter of James II 1687, re-appointed by William III 5 Aug. 1690; Deputy Seneschal of the Liberties of the County Palatine of Tipperary 22 June 1705, and 2nd Justice, Master of the Rolls and Prothonotary of the Liberties and Regalities of Tipperary; Justice of Assize for NW Ulster Summer 1711, Munster Lent and Summer 1712.

POLITICAL ACTIVITY: He was a lawyer and fairly active, as he was listed on two committees on 11 October 1792 during William and Mary's brief parliament, and 18 during William III's second parliament, 1695–9. In 1695 he supported Lord Chancellor Porter against the parliamentary accusations brought against him of favouring Catholics, and he signed the 1696 Association for the protection of William III in parliament. His connection with the Duke of Ormonde, who held the Palatinate of Tipperary, ensured that he would be a government supporter during the reign of Queen Anne: he was noted as a Court supporter in 1706 and 1711 and, not surprisingly, he attended the Duke of Ormonde's birthday celebrations in 1706. Blennerhassett was nominated to 35 committees between 1703 and 1711. He was correctly thought unlikely to be returned for Limerick city in 1713, as he had in fact died some months before the election.

DIVISION LISTS:
1711 (1) voted for the Court on the Dublin mayoralty issue.

ESTATES/RESIDENCE: Clonmel, Co. Tipperary; Dublin.

SOURCES: PRONI T/559 vol. 10 p. 24, Burke, extract pedigrees; Hayton thesis; *Alum. Dub.*; Simms' cards; Vicars, *Prerog. Wills*; Smyth, *Law Officers*; *Middle Temple Admissions* vol. 1 p. 188; W. P. Burke, *History of Clonmel* (reprinted Kilkenny, 1983), p. 317; *Ir. Gen.* vol. 3 no 3 (1958) pp. 114–15, T. Blake Butler, 'Seneschals of the Liberty of Tipperary'; *Ir. Gen.* vol. 4, no 4 (Nov. 1971) p. 308, W. G. Skehan, 'Extracts from the Minutes of the Corporation of Fethard, Co. Tipperary'; *The Dublin Intelligence* 11 Aug. 1711; *The Dublin Gazette* 26 Feb., 12 July 1712; Parliamentary Lists, 1695 (1), 1696 (1), 1706 (1), (2), 1711 (3), 1713 (1).

BLESSINGTON, Viscount: *see* **BOYLE**
0202 Boyle, Hon. Charles, 2nd Viscount Blessington, MP Blessington 1711–13–14, 1715–18

0171 BLIGH, Hon. Edward

MP for Athboy Jan.–Aug. 1800

b. 19 Sept. 1769; d. 2 Nov. 1840 at Ditton House, Kingston
FAMILY/BACKGROUND: Son of John Bligh, 3rd Earl of Darnley (**0173**), and Mary, dau. and h. of John Stoyte (**2021**).
MARRIED: Unmarried.
EDUCATION: School: Eton 1778–87; barrister.
CAREER/OCCUPATION: Military: Lieutenant-Colonel on half-pay of the 107th Regiment of Foot 1794; Colonel 1798; Major-General 1805; Lieutenant-General 1811; General 1825.

POLITICAL ACTIVITY: A professional soldier drafted in to vote for the Union.

ADDITIONAL INFORMATION: Signed a Co. Meath petition in favour of the Union, March 1800.

ESTATES/RESIDENCE: Brittas, Kells, Co. Meath. He also appears to have inherited his mother's estate in Co. Westmeath.

SOURCES: PRONI T/3166/1C Hartnell notes; O'Neill thesis; Burke *PB* (1903) p. 420; R.A. Austen-Leigh (ed.), *The Eton College Register, 1753–90*, 3 vols (Eton, 1921); A. P. W. Malcomson, *The Pursuit of the Heiress* (Belfast, 1982) p. 23; *The Drogheda News-Letter or Ulster Journal*, 8–10 Mar. 1800.

0172 BLIGH, John

MP for Trim 1709–13; Athboy 1713–14, 1715–21

b. 28 Dec. 1687; d. 12 Sept. 1728
PEERAGES: Cr. Baron Clifton 14 Sept. 1721, Viscount Darnley 7 Mar. 1723, Earl of Darnley 29 June 1725.
FAMILY/BACKGROUND: Son and heir of Rt Hon. Thomas Bligh (**0174**) and Elizabeth, dau. of James Naper of Co. Meath.

MARRIED: [24 Aug. 1713] Theodosia, Baroness Clifton, dau. of Edward Hyde, 3rd Earl of Clarendon and Catherine, Baroness Clifton.
CHILDREN: George; Edward, 2nd Earl of Darnley; John, 3rd Earl of Darnley (**0173**); Mary, m. William Tighe (**2071**); Anne, m. (1) Robert Magill (Hawkins) (**1327**), (2) Bernard Ward, 1st Viscount Bangor (**2177**); Theodosia, m. Rt Hon. William Crosbie, 1st Earl of Glandore (**0540**).

POLITICAL ACTIVITY: He entered parliament in 1709 and, although he started his career by voting against a Money Bill, thereafter he was a government supporter, voting on the administration's side in particular over the 1709 Money Bill and the Dublin mayoralty issue in 1711. In 1713 and 1715 he was returned for Athboy, which he controlled. He was thought to be a Tory and given his wife's connections he was probably sympathetic to the Tory cause, but he was discreetly absent in England in 1713. His opposition to the repeal of the Test Act was anticipated in 1719 but, in 1721, he supported the formation of a national bank.

DIVISION LISTS:
    1709 (1) voted against a Money Bill.
    1711 (1) voted for the Court on the Dublin mayoralty issue.
    1713 (1) absent, in England.
    1721 (2) voted for a national bank.

ESTATES/RESIDENCE: Rathmore, Co. Meath. Through his marriage he inherited large but financially encumbered Kentish estates including Cobham Hall. He cleared the debts with the income from the Irish estates. In 1729 Lord Darnley had an estimated income of £5,000 p.a. In the first decade of the nineteenth century Wakefield estimated his income at £12,000.

SOURCES: PRONI T/3411 Blenheim Papers; Burke *PB* (1903) p. 420 (1906) p. 360 [says he was b. 28 Dec. 1687]; GEC *P*; J. L. Chester (ed.), *The Marriage, Baptismal and Burial Registers of the Collegiate Church or Abbey of St Peter, Westminster* (London, 1876), p. 323 [bur. 25 Sept. 1728; says he died in his 41st year]; Prior, *Absentees*, p. 2; Parliamentary Lists, 1711 (3), 1713 (1), (2), 1719 (2).

0173 BLIGH, Hon. John

MP for Athboy 1739–47; [GB] Maidstone 1741–7

b. 2 Oct. 1719; d. 31 July 1781
PEERAGES: Suc. as 3rd Earl of Darnley 1747.
FAMILY/BACKGROUND: Son of John Bligh, 1st Earl of Darnley (**0172**), and Theodosia, Baroness Clifton, dau. of Edward Hyde, 3rd Earl of Clarendon.
MARRIED: [11 Sept. 1766] Mary (d. 1803), dau. and h. of John Stoyte (**2021**).
CHILDREN: John, 4th Earl of Darnley, m. [26 Aug. 1791] Elizabeth, dau. of Rt Hon. William Brownlow (**0265**); Edward (**0171**); Col. William, m. [1806] Georgina Charlotte Sophia, dau. of John Stewart, 7th Earl of Galloway; Mary, m. [7 Aug. 1789] Sir Lawrence Palk, 2nd Bt; Theodosia, m. Thomas Cherburgh Bligh (**0176**); Sarah; Catherine, m. Rt Hon. Charles William Stewart, 3rd Marquess of Londonderry (**2001**).
EDUCATION: School: Westminster Jan. 1727–9; entered Oxford (Merton College) 13 May 1735, aged 15 years, MA 13 July 1738.

POLITICAL ACTIVITY: He was returned for the family borough of Athboy. His career was mainly in England where, following the example of his brother, he attached himself to the circle of Frederick, Prince of Wales.

ADDITIONAL INFORMATION: Always eccentric, in later life he suffered from the delusion that he was a teapot. 'In 1766 when he was nearly fifty and had held the family title and estates for nearly twenty years, Lord Darnley suddenly and unexpectedly married; and between 1766 and his death in 1781, he fathered at least seven children, in spite of his initial alarm that his spout would come off in the night.'

ESTATES/RESIDENCE: Rathmore, Co. Meath; Cobham Hall, near Gravesend, Kent. This estate was heavily encumbered but he and his sons managed to clear its encumbrances by using the income of their Irish estates. By 33 Chas II (1682), Thomas Bligh was granted fairs at Athboy. In 1767 a survey showed that 976 acres were in Co. Westmeath (Clonkeen, the Barradrums). This appears to have been the estate of the Stoyte family of Street, whose heiress the 3rd Earl married on 11 September 1766. The estate was well situated to form an adjunct to his own Meath/Westmeath estate. Her property, however, appears to have passed to their second son. In 1776 the rental from Cobham Hall was £2,931 net including £338 from the London estate. In his will he left his wife £2,200 p.a., William £20,000, Edward £4,000 and £1,500 p.a., and the new Lord Darnley £6,000 p.a. In 1784 the Irish estate was worth £8,000 p.a.

SOURCES: PRONI T/2851/2 Darnley Papers; *HP 1715–54*; NLI reps no 12; McCracken thesis; Burke *PB* (1903) p. 420; *HP 1715–54*; GEC *P*; *Alum. Oxon.*; G. F. Russell-Barker and A. H. Stenning (eds), *Record of Old Westminsters: A Biographical List*, 2 vols (London, 1928); A. P. W. Malcomson, *The Pursuit of the Heiress* (Belfast, 1982), pp. 3 [Lord Darnley's delusion], 23; *Ir. Gen.* vol. 6 no 1 (1980) p. 29, H. F. Morris, 'The Waterford Herald 1791'.

0174 BLIGH, Rt Hon. Thomas

MP for Athboy 1692–3; Co. Meath 1695–9, 1703–10

   b. 1654; d. 28 Aug. 1710 at Bath
   HONOURS: PC Nov./Dec. 1706–1711.
   FAMILY/BACKGROUND: Son of John (?Robert) Bligh of Rathmore and London and Catherine, sister of William Fuller of Lincoln.
   MARRIED: [9 Dec. 1682] Elizabeth, dau. of Col. James Naper of Loughcrew, Co. Meath.
   CHILDREN: John, 1st Earl of Darnley (**0172**); Thomas (**0175**); Robert, Dean of Elphin (d. Apr.1778), m.(1) [July 1742] Catherine Elliot, wid. of Charles Boyle, (2) [18 Mar. 1759] Frances, dau. of [   ] Winthorp of London; Hannah, m. Maurice Cuffe (**0555**); Sarah, m. [1 Apr. 1733] William Gore (**0877**).
   CAREER/OCCUPATION: Portreeve of Trim; Deputy Governor of Counties Meath and Louth 1699.

POLITICAL ACTIVITY: He was returned first for the family borough of Athboy and then for Co. Meath. He was nominated to four committees in the short parliament of 1692 and seven between 1695 and 1699. In 1695 he was hostile to Lord Chancellor Porter, who was accused of favouring Catholics; in 1696 he signed the Association for the protection of William III in parliament. Early in 1706 he was noted as an absentee whose support was hoped for, and later in the year he attended Ormonde's birthday celebrations. In the same year he was made a Privy Counsellor and another MP, Robert Johnson (**1101**), wrote to Benjamin Portlock (**1715**) that 'The malicious envious part ... of this town, have in this case lost many of

their usual ready and favourite topics upon the occasion of any man's being advanced. They do not say with their usual spiteful air he is not a man of fortune, he has not an estate fit for such a post, he is a Jacobite, he is a high flyer, he is a great favourer of them, he is an enemy to the succession in the Protestant line, he is disaffected to the Government; none of this artillery is made use of, for none of it with probability can be brought to bear upon him.'

He had the reputation of being something of a rough diamond, lacking many of the social graces, but time was said to improve him in this respect. In 1707 he was one of the 34 MPs at the Fleece Tavern meeting called to concert government strategy. He was listed for 18 committees between 1703 and his death in 1710. The government numbers man was obviously behind the times when, in 1713 (his death is reported in the *Journals* for 1711), he noted that he is 'supposed good' and that he would be again returned for Co. Meath: the reason for the supposition was that he may have been a 'whimsical Tory'; certainly the Whigs were thought to have him in their sights.

DIVISION LISTS:
   1709 (1) voted against a Money Bill.

ADDITIONAL INFORMATION: Patron of Trim and supposedly brought over to the Whig side. Interestingly, he was succeeded by Garret Wesley (**2211**) and the Wesleys and their heirs were subsequently the patrons of Trim.

ESTATES/RESIDENCE: Brittas and Nobber, Co. Meath. In 1694 he received a patent erecting his lands into the Manor of Rathmore, in the barony of Lune, Co. Meath.
   He purchased 2,993 acres in Co. Meath from the Commissioners for Sale of Forfeited Estates in 1702–3.

SOURCES: PRONI T/1075/33 Canon Leslie's notes [says his dau. Catherine married as second wife 1748 Thomas Le Hunt (**1216**)]; PRONI T/3166/1C Hartnell notes; Hayton thesis; Burke *LGI* (1904) p. 47 [says he was of Rathmore]; *Cal. SP Dom. 1694–5* (London, 1906) p. 6; *Memorials of the Dead*; HMC *Ormonde* new ser. vol. 8 pp. 271–12; Simms' cards; Simms, *Williamite Confiscation*, p. 183; G. F. Russell-Barker and A. H. Stenning (eds), *Record of Old Westminsters: A Biographical List*, 2 vols (London, 1928); *JRSAI* vol. 55 (1925) pp. 39, 50, H. A. S. Upton, 'A List of Governors and Deputy Governors of Counties in Ireland in 1699'; J. T. Gilbert,

History of the City of Dublin, 3 vols (1861) vol. 2 p. 268 [says his father was Robert Bligh MP for Athboy in 1661 Commissioner of Customs (1663) & Excise (1665) d. 1666]; Parliamentary Lists, 1695 (1), 1696 (1), 1706 (1), (2), 1707 (2), 1713 (1).

0175 BLIGH, Hon. Thomas

MP for Athboy 1715–27–60, 1761–8–75

b. 14 Aug. 1693; d. 17 Aug. 1775
FAMILY/BACKGROUND: Son of Rt Hon. Thomas Bligh (0174) and Elizabeth, dau. of James Naper. MARRIED: (1) [19 Aug. 1737] Elizabeth, sister of William Bury of Shannon Grove, Co. Limerick; (2) [Oct. 1760] Frances, dau. of Walter Jones of Dublin.
CHILDREN: *d.s.p.*
EDUCATION: School: Mr Chamberlain, Co. Meath; entered TCD 17 Nov. 1709.
CAREER/OCCUPATION: *Governor of the Royal Hospital (Kilmainham) 1755–74.
MILITARY: Captain 27 Dec. 1717; Major 5th Dragoons 11 Jan. 1719; *Colonel 1729, Lieutenant-Colonel of Horse 1733–7, 1739, 1740–1, Lieutenant-Colonel 2 Oct. 1739, Colonel of 20th Regiment of Foot 26 Dec. 1740; Colonel of 12th Dragoons 3 Feb. 1741; Colonel of Foot 1742–3; Colonel 12th Dragoons Apr. 1746; Major-General 15 Sept. 1747; Brigadier-General 5th Dragoon Guards 22 Dec. 1747; *Major-General (as Brigadier-General) 1750; *Colonel of Horse 1750–7; *Major-General 1752–3; Lieutenant-General 23 Mar. 1754; Lieutenant-General (as Major-General) 1755–8; Captain of the Troop of Horse Guards (Lieutenant-General) 1755–74. He saw service at Dettingen, Val, Melle, Fontenoy and Cherbourg.

POLITICAL ACTIVITY: He was a professional soldier and his parliamentary career is bisected by the wars of the mid-eighteenth century, when he was on active service. By 1719 he was noted as a placeman and in 1721 he gave consistent support to the formation of a national bank. He nominated for 30 committees between 1731 and 1760. In August 1758 he was appointed Commander-in-Chief of an expedition to the French coast. This proved to be one of the early disasters of the Seven Years' War. The expedition landed at Cherbourg and met no resistance, the town being deserted. The troops re-embarked and were landed at St Lunar on the coast of Brittany. The plan was to attempt St Malo, but French troops appeared at St Cas in very superior numbers and Bligh re-embarked once again. This was effected only with the loss of nearly 1,000 men of the rearguard. The fleet under Admiral Howe then returned home. 'The feeling in England was so strong at this disaster that General Bligh resigned his Regiment and retired into private life.'

In politics he followed the military line and almost invariably voted for the government. After the arrival of Lord Townshend in 1767 he was considered to have behaved 'very honourably' towards government, particularly over the augmentation of the army, originally the principal task of Townshend's administration. Lord Lieutenant Townshend gave to his brother a deanery (Elphin), and later to his recommendation an ensigncy. By 1773 he was 'a very old grave steady man' and by 1774 he 'seldom attends' but when he does joins Black Phil (?Philip Tisdall (2078)). In fact he did not attend on any 'material' issue during Lord Harcourt's viceroyalty.

DIVISION LISTS:
1721 (1) voted for a national bank.
1721 (2) voted for a national bank.
1749 (1) voted against the election of James Digges La Touche (♦♦♦♦).
1753 (1) voted against the expulsion of Arthur Jones-Nevill (1125) – Major-General on Establishment and Colonel of Horse.
1753 (2) voted for the Money Bill.
1757 (1) voted against the resolution on pensions.
1768 (1) voted for army augmentation – late General.
1771 (1) voted for Lord Townshend as Lord Lieutenant.
1771 (2) voted against Sir Lucius O'Brien's (1558) motion for retrenchment.
1772 (2) voted against a Short Revenue Bill.

ESTATES/RESIDENCE: Brittas and Nobber, Co. Meath; [?]Ballyhorsey, Co. Wicklow. Left his fortune of £100,000 to his brother, the Dean of Elphin.

SOURCES: McCracken thesis; Burke *LGI* (1904) p. 77; C. Dalton, *George the First's Army, 1714–27*; *Memorials of the Dead* [a monument to him at Brittas says he was born 1695 and died 17 Aug. 1775 aged 80 years; this article also says he married Elizabeth, dau. of Colonel James Napier]; *JRSAI* vol. 63 (1933) p. 164, H.G. Leask, 'Rathmore Church, Co. Meath' [says he was born 1695]; *Almanacks*; Parliamentary Lists, 1719 (1), 1769 (1), 1772 (2), 1773 (1), (2), 1774 (1), 1775 (1).

0176 BLIGH, Thomas Cherburgh

MP for Athboy 1783–90–7–1800; [UK] Co. Meath 1802–12

b. 1761; d. 17 Sept. 1830
FAMILY/BACKGROUND: Son of Robert Bligh, Dean of Elphin, and his second wife Frances Winthorp of London.
MARRIED: Theodosia, dau. of John Bligh, 3rd Earl of Darnley (**0173**).
CHILDREN: Capt. Thomas (Coldstream Guards), m. Helena dau. of Col. Thomas Paterson; Edward; Charles, m. [1837] Fanny Catherine, dau. of Sir William George Parker, Bt; Frances, m. [1830] George Vicessimus Wigram; Sarah; Elizabeth, m. (1) [1828] John Cuming, (2) [1838] John Fountain Elwin.
EDUCATION: School: Armagh; entered Cambridge (St John's College) 1 June 1780, aged 19 years.
CAREER/OCCUPATION: Military: Colonel of the Meath Militia, Lieutenant-Colonel in Royal Meath Regiment 1796.

POLITICAL ACTIVITY: He represented Athboy on the interest of his kinsman and brother-in-law, John, 4th Earl of Darnley. When he attended he was in opposition and reputedly influenced by Edward Tighe (**2064**) and possibly Henry Grattan (**0895**). Neither he nor his patron voted on the Union, although he signed a Co. Meath petition in its favour in March 1800.

Lord Darnley promoted his candidature for Co. Meath. He acted in the Imperial parliament with Darnley, who was in opposition, and on 14 May 1806 he voted for Catholic relief. He was said never to have spoken in the United Kingdom parliament, and there is no record of his verbosity in the Irish parliament either. He appears to have been a bad attender, although in 1790 he 'tied' with another MP of opposing views. Possibly he inherited some of the eccentricity of his family.

DIVISION LISTS:
1783 (1) voted against Flood's (**0762**) motion for parliamentary reform.
1785 (1) absent.
1787 (1) voted for a Pension Bill.
1790 (2) absent (tied).

ADDITIONAL INFORMATION: *A subscriber to the Public Assembly Rooms, 1787; *a member of the Royal Dublin Society from 1787.

'As a result of either mental instability or a genuine sense of grievance on some personal matter, Bligh had first tried to call out his brother-in-law in 1806 and then again in 1812; on both occasions he was brought to trial at the King's Bench and bound over on heavy sureties to keep the peace. By 1820, however, Bligh was annoying the Earl and his family again and was bound over for another four years. The quarrel was never subsequently patched up and Bligh died in his apartment in the King's Bench prison.'

ESTATES/RESIDENCE: Brittas, Co. Meath; Dawson Street, Dublin.

SOURCES: PRONI T/3166/1C Hartnell notes; Jupp thesis; O'Neill thesis; Burke *LGI* (1904) p. 47; *HP 1790–1820*; *Alum. Cantab.*; *Almanacks*; *The Drogheda Newsletter or Ulster Journal* 8–10 Mar. 1800; *FJ* 12 Nov. 1796; Parliamentary Lists, 1783 (2), 1784 (1), (2), (3), 1785 (1), (2), (3), 1785 (4), 1787 (1), 1788 (1), 1789 (1), 1790 (1), 1791 (1), 1793 (1), 1799 (2), (3).

0177 BLUNDELL, Sir Francis

MP for King's County 1692–3, 1695–9, 1703–7

b. 30 Jan. 1643; d. (*ante* 29 July) 1707
HONOURS: Suc. as 3rd Bt *c.* 1665.
FAMILY/BACKGROUND: Son and heir of Sir George Blundell, 2nd Bt, and Sarah, dau. of Sir William Colley of Edenderry, King's County.
MARRIED: (1) [29 Dec. 1670] Ursula (*d.s.p.* May 1673), dau. of Sir Paul Davys, sometime Secretary of State for Ireland; (2) Dec. 1675 Anne (d. 14 July 1705), o. dau. of Rt Hon. Sir Henry Ingoldsby, 1st Bt (**1065**).
CHILDREN: (2) Montague (b. 1689), 1st Viscount Blundell, m. [Sept. 1709] Mary, dau. of John Chetwynd of Warwick; Anne, m. Robert Echlin (**0680**); William; George; Charles.

EDUCATION: Entered Lincoln's Inn, 13 May 1662.
CAREER/OCCUPATION: Deputy Governor of King's Co. 1699.

POLITICAL ACTIVITY: He was essentially a government man, supporting Lord Chancellor Porter against accusations of favouring Catholics in 1695, signing the Association for the protection of William III in 1696, and being noted as a member of the Court party in 1706. In parliament he was obviously a man of business, being listed for four committees on 11 October 1692 and for 55 in the following parliament. The Irish administration had been corrupt, inefficient and generally chaotic since 1690, and in 1693 he was among those who gave evidence to the House of Lords during the English parliament's inquiry into the state of Ireland. The inquiry led to the censure of the Irish government and the recall of the Lord Lieutenant, Lord Sydney.

In Queen Anne's first parliament he was nominated for 28 committees between 1703 and 1705. In 1703 he was the leading sponsor of 2 Anne, c. 13, 'Act for continuing two acts against Tories, Robbers and Raparees', which reflected the continuing lawlessness in the country, and of 2 Anne, c. 17, 'an Act for better regulating weights and measures throughout this Kingdom' – weights and measures were not standardised. He died in 1707.

ADDITIONAL INFORMATION: Acquitted 1674 of the murder of the 3rd Viscount Tara. On his way to England in June 1706 his ship was seized by a privateer and he was forced to pay a ransom of £60.

By his will he left *c.* £4,000 to poor of the parish in which he lived.

ESTATES/RESIDENCE: Blundell Manor, Edenderry, King's County. This estate eventually came to the Hill family through the marriage of the 2nd Marquess of Downshire with Mary Sandys in 1786: at this time the Edenderry estate amounted to *c.* 14,000 acres.

SOURCES: *CJ Ire.* (Bradley ed.) vol. 3 pp. 35, 196 (0075, 0079); Simms' cards; Burke *Ext. P* (1883) p. 56; GEC *B*; Vicars, *Prerog. Wills; The Register of the Parish of St Peter and St Kevin, 1669–1761* (Parish Register Society of Dublin, 1911) pp. 55, 78, 85; *HMC Ormonde*, new ser. v. 8 pp. 239–40, 302 [he died [*ante* 29 July] 1707]; *Lincoln's Inn Records* vol. 1 p. 287; T. Bartlett and D. W. Hayton (eds), *Penal Era and Golden Age* (Belfast,

1979) p. 25, James I. McGuire, 'The Irish Parliament of 1692'; *JRSAI* vol. 55 (1925) pp. 38, 47, 48, H.A.S. Upton, 'A List of Governors and Deputy Governors of Counties in Ireland in 1699'; W.A. Maguire, *The Downshire Estates* (Oxford, 1972) p. 6; Parliamentary Lists, 1695 (1), 1696 (1), 1706 (1).

0178 BLUNDEN, John

MP for Kilkenny City 1727–52

> b. *ante* 1685; d. 8 Jan. 1752
> FAMILY/BACKGROUND: Son of John Blunden of Castle Blunden, Co. Kilkenny and [ ].
> MARRIED: (1) Martha, dau. of Agmondisham Cuffe (0547) and sis. of John, 1st Baron Desart (0554); (2) [1733] Charlotte, dau. of [ ] Mead.
> CHILDREN: (1) 5 sons, sole survivor, Sir John, 1st Bt (0179); dau. [ ], m. Samuel Waring of Springfield, Co. Kilkenny.
> EDUCATION: Probably the John Blundell admitted to Kilkenny College 24 April 1699, aged 14 years.
> CAREER/OCCUPATION: Sheriff of Kilkenny 1716, Alderman 1717, Mayor 1719–20, 1728–30.

POLITICAL ACTIVITY: He does not appear to have been a very energetic MP: he was ordered into the custody of the Serjeant-at-Arms, 21 November 1741, when his excuse for not attending parliament was not accepted. He was named for four committees during his sojourn in parliament: one in 1727, two in 1728 and one in 1737.

ESTATES/RESIDENCE: Castle Blunden, Co. Kilkenny. At the Restoration, holdings totalled 254 statute acres; in 1878 the 3rd Baronet was the proprietor of 1,846 statute acres in Kilkenny.

SOURCES: *CJ Ire.* (Bradley ed.) vol. 7 p. 292, McCracken thesis; GEC *B*; Burke *PB* (1903) p. 163; Kilkenny MPs; *JRSAI* vol. 54 (1924) pp. 55–67, T.U. Sadleir, 'The Register of Kilkenny School (1685–1800)' [gives a John Blundell admitted to Kilkenny College 24 Apr. 1699 aged 14 years, this variation in spelling is not unknown]; M. A. Brennan, 'The making of an Ascendancy Family: The Blundens of Kilkenny' [unpublished paper read at the Conference of the American Committee for Irish Studies, Dublin 1987]; *GM* Jan. 1751.

0179 BLUNDEN, Sir John

MP for Kilkenny City 1761–8–76

b. *c.* 1718; d. Jan. 1783 at Castle Blunden
HONOURS: Cr. Bt 12 Mar. 1766.
FAMILY/BACKGROUND: Eldest son of John Blunden
(**0178**) and Martha, dau. of Agmondisham Cuffe
(**0547**).
MARRIED: [lic. 25 Feb. 1755/6] his first cousin
Lucy Susanna (d. 1812), dau. of John Cuffe, 1st
Baron Desart (**0554**).
CHILDREN: Sir John, 2nd Bt, m.(1) Miss
Hewitson, (2) [1812] Hester, dau. of John
Helsham of Co. Kilkenny; William Pitt, m.
[1813] Harriet, o. dau. of Thomas Pope of
Popefield, Queen's County; Gen. Ovington
(1767–1838); Martha, m. James Wemys of
Danesfort (**2207**); Araminta, m. (?cousin)
Samuel Waring of Springfield; Sophia, m.
Abraham White Baker of Ballytobin; Charlotte,
m. Samuel Matthews of Bennettstown;
Dorothea, m. [Oct. 1780] William Bolton of The
Island, Co. Wexford.
EDUCATION: Entered TCD 21 Aug. 1735; Middle
Temple 16 Nov. 1739; called to the Irish Bar
1744.
CAREER/OCCUPATION: Alderman of Kilkenny, May
1753–Jan. 1783; Mayor of Kilkenny 1753–4;
Recorder of Kilkenny.

POLITICAL ACTIVITY: 'A droll kind of man, he makes
no great figure. Is entirely independent', but he
was anxious to be noticed and was inclined to be
influenced by John Ponsonby (**1702**) and to follow the powerful Ponsonby interest in Kilkenny
city and county, where he had 'a good estate'. He
wanted a pension and had some claim on the government, but Lord Townshend 'lost [the] vouch-
ers of it'. He once had a half interest in Kilkenny
city, but by 1773 it had declined. By 1774 he seldom attended and in 1775 he was reputed to be
influenced by Lord Tyrone. He was said to have
'supported and opposed alternately. Always, to use
his own expression to Lord North, in the Wrong
Box.'

DIVISION LISTS:
1768 (1) voted against army augmentation.
1771 (1) voted against Lord Townshend as
Lord Lieutenant.

ADDITIONAL INFORMATION: In 1780 he and the
newly raised Volunteers had a disagreement and

the Volunteers burned him in effigy. Sir John, to
show his contempt, warmed himself at the fire.
He was described as 'the greatest Oddity of his
time ... He kept my Aunt Blunden [his wife]
whom he called Joany entirely at home ... he would
let none of his Sons go to a public School: and
kept his Daughters a set of beautiful Girls shut up
in a Nursery making lace under an old Governess
and their Mammy nurse till they were 15 or 16.'

In his will he expressed the macabre wish 'that
he may not be buried till his body begins to be
putrified or his head severed from his body, and
laid without ceremony in the round part of the
wood where the laurel is planted and the ditch of
water surrounds it'.

ESTATES/RESIDENCE: Castle Blunden, Co. Kilkenny. He
took great pride in his fruit orchard and delighted in
raising exotic fruits and vegetables in his extensive hot-
houses. It is not known how much property Martha
Cuffe (his mother) or Lucinda Cuffe brought into the
family, but the wife of his son, the 2nd Baronet, brought
with her 'a delightful Estate in the Co. Kilkenny and
several other articles amounting to a clear £8,000 a year'.
Birchfield appears to have been added to the family
property in the Liberties of Kilkenny sometime before
1789. According to Wakefield, Sir John Blundel [*sic*]
had a rental of £5,000.

SOURCES: PRONI T/559, Burke, extract pedigrees, vol.
10 p. 61; Kilkenny MPs; *Alum. Dub.*; *WHM* (1783) p.
56; Burke *PB* (1903) p. 163; GEC *B*; *King's Inns Admissions*; *Middle Temple Admissions* (London, 1949) vol.
1 p. 327; Johnston, *Gt B. & Ire.*, p. 153; M. A. Brennan,
'The Making of an Ascendancy Family: The Blundens
of Kilkenny' [unpublished paper read at the Conference of the American Committee for Irish Studies,
Dublin 1987]; *DJ* Jan. 9–11, 1783; Wakefield, *Account
of Ire.*, vol. 1 p. 266; Parliamentary Lists, 1769 (1), 1772
(2), 1773 (1), (2), 1774 (1), 1775 (1).

BOLTON, Baron: *see* ORDE (ORDE-POWLETT)

1594 Orde (Orde-Powlett), Rt Hon. Thomas,
1st Baron Bolton [GB], MP Rathcormack
1784–90, [GB] Aylesbury 1780–4, Harwich
1784–96

0180 BOLTON, Cornelius

MP for Waterford city 1768–76

b. c. 1714; d. 16 Sept. 1779

FAMILY/BACKGROUND: Son of Henry Bolton and Elizabeth, dau. of Benjamin Alcock of Kilkenny.

MARRIED: [Oct. 1738] Elizabeth, dau. of Francis Barker of Co. Waterford.

CHILDREN: Mary, m. [July 1761] Phineas Riall of Clonmell [marriage dissolved by parliament in 1768; he married again]; Cornelius (**0181**); Henry; Harriet, m. [June 1780] Richard Irwin of Co. Leitrim; dau. (?Samuela), m. [Sept. 1775] John Stone of Faithlegg, Co. Waterford; Elizabeth, m. [June 1767] Capt. John Hassard (Haggard) of Cara, Co. Fermanagh (he m. (2) Samuella Barker of Co. Waterford); Sophia, m. [19 Sept. 1775] James Barclay Stone of Jamaica; Frances, m. [6 Oct. 1772] Robert Dobbyn, Recorder of Waterford.

CAREER/OCCUPATION: Freeman of Waterford 1737; Sheriff of Waterford 1738, 1743, Mayor 1743–4, 1761; *Magistrate of Co. Waterford 1743; High Sheriff of Co. Waterford 1743, 1778.

MILITARY: ?Colonel of the Waterford Royal Oak Volunteers.

POLITICAL ACTIVITY: In 1773 he was described as 'a gentlemanlike man. Came in by his own interest. Neither good nor harm in him. He constantly resides among the people and spends his money in Waterford which will always secure him a seat. Against.' He was 'very independent' and generally against. Reputed to be friend of John Ponsonby (**1702**), and it was thought that Lord Tyrone (**0113**) might have some influence with him. In 1774, he and Shapland Carew (**0348**), the other MP for Waterford city, were both opposed to concessions being granted to the Catholics.

DIVISION LISTS:

1771 (1) voted against Lord Townshend as Lord Lieutenant.

1771 (2) voted for Sir Lucius O'Brien's (**1558**) motion for retrenchment.

1772 (2) voted for a Short Revenue Bill.

1774 (2) voted against Catholic relief.

ADDITIONAL INFORMATION: He strengthened his interest by living in Waterford, and in 1760–61 he declared himself a candidate for one of the two Waterford seats but withdrew before polling day.

ESTATES/RESIDENCE: Faithlegg, Co. Waterford. The estate and castle were confiscated from the Aylward family. The original Cromwellian grant comprised the townlands of Killure, Faithlegg, Kilmacomb, Ballynamoyntragh, Ballyvelly and Carrowgarriff, all in the barony of Gaultier and computed at 1,750 plantation acres (2,334 statute acres). The heart of the estate was Faithlegg, six miles east of Waterford. In 1709–10 his father was forced to sue his grandmother, uncle and aunt to obtain the ratification of his parents' marriage settlement. He succeeded but in 1712 abruptly sold his interest in the estate to his cousin William for £200 'and disappeared'. Cornelius's claim to the estate was pressed with vigour by the Alcocks and determinedly contested by his uncle, who claimed he was not Henry's son but the child of Mary Alcock, Elizabeth's sister. However, this was not accepted and c. 1729 agreement was reached whereby William was to remain at Faithlegg, holding it on lease from Cornelius, in return for a cash settlement. The court decree awarded Cornelius £1,021 with interest and £329 costs.

In October 1738 he married Elizabeth Barker, who had a dowry of about £1,500. His brother-in-law Samuel Barker (**0083**) died in 1769, leaving his estate to Cornelius Bolton in trust for his three nieces, Mary, Samuella and Elizabeth.

In 1747 he leased a part of the River Shure (Suir) for 99 years for a rent of one peppercorn. In 1758 and 1765 he rented two parts of the townland of Ballycanvan, which adjoined his Faithlegg estate. He was a progressive landlord.

SOURCES: PRONI T/1075/36 Canon Leslie's notes; PRONI MIC/474 Irish Volunteers; NAI MFCI Reel 8, Parish Registers of Kill St Nicholas, Co. Waterford [says children, Hugh, Elizabeth, Penelope and Sophia all d. yg]; NAI MFCI Reel 12, Parish Registers of Christchurch, St Olave and St Patrick, Waterford; C. K. Bolton, *Bolton Families in Ireland* (Boston, 1937); Johnston, *Gt B. & Ire.*, p. 153; R. H. Ryland, *The History, Topography and Antiquities of the county and city of Waterford* (London, 1824), pp. 409–10; *Irish Genealogy* vol. 4 no 2 (1987) pp. 186–200, vol. 7 no 3 (1988) pp. 405–20, J. C. Walton, 'The Boltons of County Waterford'; *Almanacks*; *DJ* 4 Jan. 1743; Parliamentary Lists, 1769 (1), 1772 (2), 1773 (1), (2), 1774 (1), 1775 (1).

0181 BOLTON, Cornelius

MP for Waterford city 1776–83; Lanesborough 1783–90

b. 1 Oct. 1751; d. 11 Mar. 1829

FAMILY/BACKGROUND: Son of Cornelius Bolton (**0180**) and Elizabeth, dau. of Francis Barker of Co. Waterford.

MARRIED: [23 May 1789] Eliza, dau. of Charles MacDonnell (**1315**).

CHILDREN: Cornelius Henry, m. [1816] Alicia, dau. of Rev. W. Saltoun of Co. Wexford; Charles (killed at the battle of Vitoria 1813); Henry, m. [1830] Anne, dau. of William Kearney; Edward, m. Mary, dau. of S. Daly of Co. Cork; Elizabeth Mary, m. [1832] Samuel Crossthwaite of Co. Carlow.

EDUCATION: School: Rev. William Jessop, Lismore; entered TCD 10 Oct. 1769, aged 17 years; Middle Temple 21 Jan. 1772, BA 1773.

CAREER/OCCUPATION: High Sheriff of Co. Waterford 1778; *Trustee of the Linen Board for Connaught 1795; Mayor of Waterford 1810, 1816; Sheriff of Co. Waterford 1815.

MILITARY: Captain of the No. 4 Waterford Independent Volunteers.

POLITICAL ACTIVITY: He was elected in 1776 and reputed to be a 'young man of good fortune' and 'a sensible intelligent little man'. He was an independent and generally in opposition. When he first came into parliament Lord Shannon (**0213**), Lord Tyrone (**0113**) and John Ponsonby (**1702**) were all reputed to have some influence with him, and by 1782 he was 'inclined to Mr Foster' (**0805**). He was an enthusiastic Volunteer and a delegate to the Volunteer Convention at Mallow in May 1782. He was also a delegate at the Volunteer Convention at the Royal Exchange, Dublin. The Waterford Volunteers had endorsed the resolutions of the Dungannon Convention in March 1782, and urged Bolton to demand their constitutional privileges. His written reply assured them that he would 'pay particular attention to the great constitutional questions you have pointed out'. In 1783 he was a captain in the Volunteers and a delegate to the Volunteer National Convention for the County of the City of Waterford.

Nevertheless, in the 1783 election for Waterford city he was unsuccessful, reputedly because the successful candidates, Henry Alcock (**0019**) and Robert Shapland Carew (**0347**), had introduced a number of freemen from Wexford. However, 'The merchants of Waterford subscribed to purchase him a seat, and [he] will be elected for Mr Dillon's (**0637**) Borough of Lanesborough'; this duly happened. Both Alcock and Carew were

in opposition, and by 1784 Bolton was 'much attached to Mr Beresford (**0115**) and to Mr Foster and inclined to support government'. By 1788 he was 'much connected with the Speaker' (Foster) and an applicant for government favour: in particular he was anxious to purchase, at a fair valuation, the lands assigned to the aborted colony at New Geneva. Bolton had been a key figure in plans to build New Geneva, a project to settle Swiss refugees, at Passage East in Waterford but the immediate necessity for this fell through when affairs in Switzerland resolved themselves acceptably to the potential refugees.

In 1789 an opposition source commenting on his 'irreproachable integrity and strict propriety of conduct' and the respect and affection he enjoyed among the citizens of Waterford, over whose welfare he continued to watch, described him as follows: 'Mr Bolton is a remarkable instance, [of one] whose approved honesty and undeviating rectitude of public life claimed every return of attachment from the citizens of Waterford; but, though defeated at the last election there, he soon amply experienced that a most respectable part of its inhabitants entertained a due sense of his merits and a just esteem for his worth. As a public speaker his voice, though not strong, is distinct and well toned and without much extent not deficient in harmony; scarcely powerful enough for a large assembly, it is more adapted to the key of private conversation than to the pitch of parliamentary debate: but he manages it with judgement and skill, by which it is highly aided. His language is plain, pure, and correct, simple with neatness and spirited without elevation, never affecting any ornament, but never carelessly neglecting due selection, and his delivery is judicious, neither precipitate nor languid, but temperate. His manner, in general calm and sedate, free from all violence and impetuosity, is at times warm and animated and forcible, properly varied with the occasion and his action, which is indeed very sparingly used, is when used easy and expressive, devoid of awkwardness, tho' not strongly marked by grace or force. In argument he is remarkably able, being close, severe, accurate and acute, keen without severity and profound without dullness ... adhering rigorously to the subject and reasoning with justice and energy and his arrangement is exact, clear, and methodical, for he has not forgotten that acquaintance which logic afforded him by his excellent education. The matter of his speeches is uniformly good, for he is a man of real knowledge ... He delivers not to the House the random observations of presuming pertness, nor the slight productions of (what is called) summer reading, but arguments solid, apposite and momentous, well selected and homely applied, clearly convincing the understanding without, perhaps, much amusing the fancy. In Parliament, Mr Bolton has laudably endeavoured, particularly in the corn business, to serve the community and has mostly supported the character of an independent country gentleman, too candid to oppose from prejudice and too honest to comply from venality: but of late, and that on some questions that really surprised us, he seemed decidedly inclined to comply with the desires of the minister ... Though deprived of the representation of such a man as we have mentioned he forfeits not their affections.'

In commercial matters he supported the Waterford merchants; otherwise his parliamentary behaviour, as is shown by his voting, was very much that of a moderate independent. He was a member of the committee appointed by the Commons to distribute £17,000 for the encouragement of certain manufactures. Interestingly, he was among the MPs who were anxious to develop the country's infrastructure and bring to Ireland industry of the type being developed in England. To this end he improved the village of Cheekpoint on the Faithlegg estate, where he established a cotton mill and stocking factory and tried to make it a packet station for the Milford Haven steamer. He also built the adjoining new town of Bolton.

None of his ventures prospered. Cheekpoint proved to be a poor site and the industries and other enterprises fared badly; for instance, at Cheekpoint he built a hotel whose imposing structure was surpassed only by its notoriety. So difficult was the day-to-day running of the hotel that one of the managers threw himself off the pier and drowned.

At his marriage in 1789 his debts were £27,176 13s 4d, and by 1800 they had increased by a fur-

ther £12,560. In April 1818 his finances finally collapsed, and the Faithlegg estate was sold to Nicholas Power of Ballinakill. He did not sit in parliament after 1790.

DIVISION LISTS:
    1777 (1) voted for Grattan's (0895) motion for retrenchment.
    1777 (2) voted against the Trade Embargo.
    1778 (1) voted for Grattan's motion for retrenchment.
    1779 (2) voted for a six-months Loan Bill.
    1780 (2) voted for Yelverton's (2268) motion to modify Poynings' Law.
    1780 (3) voted for the Tenantry Bill.
    1780 (4) voted against a Perpetual Mutiny Bill.
    1780 (5) voted for the duty on imported sugar.
    1783 (1) voted for Flood's (0762) motion for parliamentary reform.
    1785 (1) voted for the Commercial Propositions.
    1786 (2) voted for Forbes's (0778) motion for retrenchment.
    1787 (1) voted for a Pension Bill.

ADDITIONAL INFORMATION: *A member of the Royal Dublin Society from 1778; *a member of the Royal Irish Academy from 1790.

ESTATES/RESIDENCE: Ballycanvan and Faithlegg, Co. Waterford. In 1775 George Ponsonby valued his Waterford estate at £1,200 p.a. In 1784 Cornelius Bolton was granted fairs at Farthleg [sic].
    In 1800, beset by debt, he obtained a private act of the Irish parliament vesting his lands in trustees Edward Lee and Charles Osborne, empowering them to demise, mortgage or sell any part of his estate to pay off his debts.

SOURCES: PRONI D/302; NLI EC 3638 [there are maps of the estate in 1769 and 1780]; PRONI MIC 474 Irish Volunteers; Lodge P; Hughes, Pat. Officers; Smith, State of Waterford, p. 166; R. H. Ryland, The History, Topography and Antiquities of the county and city of Waterford (London, 1824), p. 411; Middle Temple Admissions vol. 1 p. 374; C. K. Bolton, Bolton Families in Ireland (Boston, 1937); Ir. Gen. vol. 7 no 3 (1988) pp. 405–20, J. C. Walton, 'The Boltons of County Waterford' [says he married 13 May 1789, and had issue – four sons and two daus – one of whom married Pierse Barron; he died 11 Mar. 1829 not May 1830 as stated on his tombstone]; *County Waterford Arch. Soc. Jn.* vol. 16 (1913) p. 54, T. U. Sadleir (ed.), 'The County of Waterford 1775'; *Almanacks*; *FJ* 24–7 Feb. 1787; Parliamentary Lists, 1776 (1), (3), 1771 (1), 1778 (1), 1780 (1), 1782 (1), 1783 (1), (2), (3), 1784 (1), (2), (3), 1785 (1), (2), (3), (4), 1787 (1), 1788 (1), 1789 (1), (2), 1790 (1).

0182 BOLTON, Edward

MP for Swords 1727–58

b. 1696; d. 5 Aug. 1758
FAMILY/BACKGROUND: Eldest son of Richard Bolton and Anne Catherine, dau. of Stein Bill of Copenhagen.
MARRIED: [*ante* Dec. 1719] Letitia, dau. of Robert Molesworth, 1st Viscount Molesworth (**1419**).
CHILDREN: Richard (d. yg); Robert; Edward; Theophilus; Letitia, m. [1749] Rev. Gustavus Hamilton; Anna Catherine; Anna Marcia, m. Capt. Archibald Grant; Elizabeth; Charlotte; Isabella Charlotte Emilia.
EDUCATION: School: Mr Sheridan, Dublin; entered TCD 24 Feb. 1715, aged 19 years.
CAREER/OCCUPATION: Alderman of Dublin 1711; Sheriff of Co. Dublin 1722, 1723; *Commissioner for Oyer and Terminer 1732–53.

POLITICAL ACTIVITY: A Dublin alderman and businessman, he was nominated to eight committees between 1729 and 1757. He was taken into custody of the Serjeant-at-Arms for giving false information to a committee of the House. After expressing sorrow for his offences and praying to be released, he was discharged. Having voted solidly against the administration, he was thought to have changed his mind in 1756 but he absented himself, so this could not be tested.

DIVISION LISTS:
1749 (1) voted for the election of James Digges La Touche (♦♦♦♦).
1753 (1) voted against the expulsion of Arthur Jones-Nevill (**1125**).
1753 (2) voted against the Money Bill.
1757 (1) voted for the resolutions on pensions.

ADDITIONAL INFORMATION: A foundation member of the Dublin Society, 1731.

ESTATES/RESIDENCE: Brazil, Co. Dublin. His uncle, Edward Bolton of Brazil, died in 1705 leaving his estate 'being £1,500 per ann. to his brother Richard Bolton Esq. who took possession of it yesterday' (19 October 1705). Edward Bolton presented a petition to the House on 27 December 1735 for heads of a bill to enable him to more effectively secure a mortgage of £1,500 on his deceased father's estate for the benefit of his three younger brothers. Another Edward Bolton of Brazil (a son or probably a grandson) claimed he had 200 acres in the borough of Swords and hoped he would receive compensation for its devaluation because of the disfranchisement of the borough at the Union.

SOURCES: *CJ Ire.* (Bradley ed.) vol. 4 p. 609; PRONI T/ 559 vol. 10 p. 142, Burke, extract pedigrees; McCracken thesis; *Further Proceedings of the Commissioners under the Union Compensation Act of Ireland* (1805); *The Register of the Parish of St Peter and St Kevin, 1669–1761* (Parish Register Society of Dublin, 1911) p. 261; C. K. Bolton, *Bolton Families in Ireland* (Boston, 1937); *Ir. Gen.* vol. 5 no 2 (1975) pp. 186–9, H. F. Morris, 'Announcements in Impartial Occurences, Jan. 1705–Feb. 1706'; Berry *RDS* pp. 24–7; *Almanacks*; *GM* Aug. 1758; *The Dublin Courant* 16 Dec. 1721, 17 Nov. 1722; *The Dublin Intelligence* 15 Nov. 1729; Parliamentary List, 1756 (1).

0183 BOLTON, Thomas

MP for Athenry 1733–41

b. 1706; d. 17 Mar. 1740/1
FAMILY/BACKGROUND: Son of Thomas Bolton of Knock, Co. Louth, and Sidney, eldest dau. of Chichester Fortescue.
MARRIED: [1734] Alice, dau. of John Foster.
CHILDREN: Theophilus (admitted to Middle Temple 6 Jan. 1757); Sidney, m. [1 June 1763] George Clive.
EDUCATION: School: the Cathedral School, Dublin, under Dr Floyd 1720; entered TCD 15 Feb. 1722, aged 16 years, BA 1726; Middle Temple 13 Feb. 1728; MD 1733.
CAREER/OCCUPATION: A physician; Alderman of Dublin 1730.

POLITICAL ACTIVITY: Very little is known of this man's political activities apart from the fact that he was nominated to six committees between 1733 and 1739. He was a brother-in-law of Anthony Foster (**0804**), later Chief Baron of the Exchequer and father of Speaker Foster (**0805**). He was the nephew and heir of Archbishop Bolton of Cashel. Like Anthony Foster, the archbishop was interested in economic questions such as the wool trade, coinage, the utility of premiums and the national debt, and his nephew may well have shared his interests. This speculation is based not only on his connections but on the fact that, in 1731, he was a foundation member of the Dublin Society.

ESTATES/RESIDENCE: Knock, Co. Louth.

SOURCES: RCBL P328/1/3, Parish Registers of St John's, Dublin; McCracken thesis; Burke *LGI* (1904) p. 51; *IMC King's Inns Admissions*; *Alum. Dub.*; Malcomson, *Foster* (1978) p. 10; Berry *RDS* pp. 24–7; J. H. Bernard (ed.), *The Register of St Patrick, Dublin, 1677–1800* (Parish Register Society of Dublin, 1907) p. 27; *Middle Temple Admissions* (London, 1949) vol. 1 pp. 303, 351; C. K. Bolton, *Bolton Families in Ireland* (Boston, 1937); *Almanacks*, *The Dublin Intelligence* 3 Nov. 1711.

0184 BOND, Sir James

MP for Naas 1791–7; [Escheator of Munster 1797]

b. 11 June 1744; d. 2 June 1820
HONOURS: Cr. Bt 21 Jan. 1794.
FAMILY/BACKGROUND: Second son of James Bond (d. 1762), Presbyterian minister (ordained Corboy, Co. Longford), of Comber, Co. Down, and Catherine, dau. of Rev. Thomas Wensley of Lifford, Co. Donegal.
MARRIED: [27 July 1770] Anne (d. 3 July 1809), dau. of William Hornby (Governor of Bombay) and wid. of Richard Eyre (HEICS).
CHILDREN: 1 s. (d. yg); Sir Thomas, 2nd Bt (b. Bombay 27 Oct. 1776; *d.s.p.* 3 Mar. 1822), m. [Mar. 1803] Louisa Sarah, dau. of John Read of Porchester, Hants; Anne (b. 24 Jan. 1774; d. 30 Mar. 1796), m. [24 Dec. 1792] Christopher Hely-Hutchinson (**0999**); Louisa (b. 13 Apr. 1778; d. May 1835), m. (1) John Miller of Russell Square, London, (2) Holwell Walshe of Dublin.
CAREER/OCCUPATION: *Listed in Judges and Barristers 1792–f.

POLITICAL ACTIVITY: He purchased his seat, presumably on his return from India. He was in India certainly in 1776 and probably for some years before, and was considered a 'nabob'. He sup-

ported in the hope of being made a baronet, which he achieved in 1794; in 1797 he resigned his seat and did not come into parliament again.

ADDITIONAL INFORMATION: A member of the Royal Dublin Society from 1789.

ESTATES/RESIDENCE: Colamber, Co. Longford; Mountjoy Square, Dublin.

SOURCES: GEC *B*; Rev. J. and S. G. McConnell, *Fasti of the Irish Presbyterian Church, 1613–1840* (Belfast, 1951) p. 407; *Almanacks*; Parliamentary Lists, 1791 (1), 1793 (1), 1794 (2).

0185 BOOTH, Samuel

MP for Callan 1692–3, 1695–9

b. ? 1641; d. (*c.* Sept.) 1701
FAMILY/BACKGROUND: Son of [   ] Booth.
MARRIED: Hannah, dau. of Col. William Warden.
CHILDREN: Samuel; Henry (on whom Burnchurch was entailed by his uncle, John Warden); Anne; Hannah, m. [Oct. 1696] Richard Downing of Cork; Catherine.
CAREER/OCCUPATION: Sheriff of Co. Kilkenny 1678, 1679; Sheriff of Cork 1679, 1680; Burgess of Callan by James II's Charter; Commissioner for levying the taxes imposed upon the county; Seneschal of the Duke of Ormonde's manor.
MILITARY: Major, Lieutenant in Company of Foot May 1662, Lieutenant in Lord Power's Regiment of Foot 1672 (left army by 1678).

POLITICAL ACTIVITY: Little is known of this MP. He was a military officer and probably on active service for most of the period. He was listed for one committee on 11 October 1692 and another in the following parliament on 19 October 1695. He supported Lord Chancellor Porter in 1695 when he was under attack by the House of Commons for allegedly favouring Catholics, and signed the Association for the protection of William III in the country in 1696. He was seneschal or steward of the Duke of Ormonde's estates.

ESTATES/RESIDENCE: [?]The Poodle, Co. Kilkenny.

SOURCES: Simms' cards; Kilkenny MPs; Hughes, *Pat. Officers*; *The Register of the Parish of St Peter and St Kevin, 1669–1761* (Parish Register Society of Dublin, 1911) p. 166 [records the burial of Samuel Booth of the Poddle in 1701]; C. Dalton (ed.), *Irish Army Lists 1661–85* (London, 1907) pp. 25, 32, 81 [no mention of him as Major]; *HMC Ormonde*, new ser. vol. 8 p. 42 [a letter of 10 Sept. 1701 says Mr Booth seneschal of the Duke of Ormonde's manor is dead]; Parliamentary Lists, 1695 (1), 1696 (1).

0186 BOREMAN (*alias* BOWERMAN), Henry

MP for Charleville 1692–3

b. *ante* 1662; d. 1701
FAMILY/BACKGROUND: Son of ?Henry Bowerman of Cooleen, Co. Cork.
MARRIED: Catherine [   ].
CHILDREN: Henry; Edward; Elizabeth, m. William Blakeney; another dau. (?Sarah), m. Barry Moore; ?Penelope, m. Henry Purdon (**1747**).
CAREER/OCCUPATION: Military: Colonel in William III's army.

POLITICAL ACTIVITY: Nothing is known of the parliamentary career of this MP. The parliament to which he was elected sat for less than a month, and he may have been on active service during this period.

ESTATES/RESIDENCE: Cooleen, Co. Cork.

SOURCES: NAI, Index to the Marriage Licence Bonds of Cloyne Diocese; Burke *LG* (1846) p. 285; Simms' cards; Cork MPs [says married Elizabeth Gibbings]. His will was proved in Jan. 1701 and there may be some confusion between him and his father or son, also Henry Boreman; PRONI T/581 vol. 3 pp. 1–2 [gives the will of Henry Bowerman the elder, proved Jan. 1701; his wife's name is Catherine and his sons are Henry (?d.1718) and Edward; his dau. Elizabeth married William Blakeney and another dau., probably Sarah, m. Barry Moore].

BORROWES, Kildare: *see* **BURROWS** (*alias* **BORROWES** or **BURROWES**), Sir Kildare (**0290**)

0187 BORROWES (*alias* BURROWES), Sir Kildare Dixon

MP for Co. Kildare 1745–60, 1761–8–76 [r. Randalstown 1761]

b. (bapt. 20 Jan.) 1721/2; d. 22 June 1790
HONOURS: Suc. as 5th Bt 1741.
FAMILY/BACKGROUND: Eldest son of Sir Walter Dixon Borrowes, 4th Bt (**0188**), and Mary, dau. of Edward Pottinger.
MARRIED: (1) [17 Feb. 1759] Elizabeth (d. 23 Aug. 1766), dau. and h. of John Short of Grange, Queen's County; (2) [10 May 1769] Jane (d. Sept. 1793), dau. of Joseph Higginson of Mount Ophaley, Co. Kildare.
CHILDREN: (1) Eramus, m. [1783] Henrietta, dau. of Arthur Champagne de Robillard, Dean of Clonmacnoise; Walter; Rev. Kildare; Jane Mary. (2) William, m. Angeline, o. dau. of Rt Hon. Sir Michael Smith, 1st Bt (**1938**); Rev. Joseph, m. Anne, dau. of Frederick Trench of Co. Galway; Robert, m. Charlotte, dau. of S. Madden; Richard (d. yg); Emily, m. [Apr. 1797] Ven. Thomas Kingsbury.
EDUCATION: School: Dr Thompson; entered TCD 12 Aug. 1738.
CAREER/OCCUPATION: High Sheriff of Co. Kildare 1751; Burgess of Harristown 12 July 1754; Commissioner of the Tillage Act for Leinster 1756–84; *Trustee of the Linen Board for Ulster 1756–d.; *Clerk to the Trustees 1759; Freedom of the Guild of Merchants, 29 Apr. 1754; admitted a free brother of the Holy Trinity Guild of Merchants of Dublin by grace especial 4 Aug. 1754.

POLITICAL ACTIVITY: He sat for Co. Kildare, where the Duke of Leinster's interest was paramount, and he was a constant part of the 1st (**0734**) and 2nd (**0745**) Dukes of Leinster's political entourage. Between 1745 and 1760 he was nominated for 19 committees. The 1773 Parliamentary List declares indignantly that 'So far from having an interest in this County that he is universally hated. A mere lickspittle of the Duke of Leinster's (**0745**) and brought in by him. The Duke is a man who wishes to have despotic power and would Jehu-like drive furiously on until he overturned Ireland or governed it and indeed from him all our tumults and factions have sprung. His pampered Ambition leads his way, Hatred and Malice, Rancour and Revenge follow him. All the poisonous qualities in nature like an army of destroying angels attend his motions and try to execute his designs. In short, the Baronet is nothing. Against.'

Both dukes were essentially well-meaning country gentlemen very conscious of their rank and status as Ireland's only dukes. Borrowes appears to have followed them fairly blindly and taken an opposition line on most matters. His vote for the election of James La Touche (♦♦♦♦) probably reflects the Leinster (Kildare) involvement with Dublin city politics. He voted against the removal of the Customs House, which was essential to the development of the trade of the capital and the country's principal port.

DIVISION LISTS:

1749 (1) voted for the election of James Digges La Touche (♦♦♦♦).
1753 (1) voted for the expulsion of Arthur Jones-Nevill (**1125**).
1753 (2) voted against the Money Bill.
1757 (1) voted against the resolutions on pensions.
1768 (1) voted against army augmentation.
1771 (2) voted for Sir Lucius O'Brien's (**1558**) motion for retrenchment.
1772 (2) voted for a Short Revenue Bill.
1773 (1) voted against Absentee Tax.
1773 (2) voted for an untaxed press.
1774 (2) voted in favour of Catholic relief.
1775 (1) voted for the pro-American amendment to the Speech from the Throne.

ADDITIONAL INFORMATION: He was a member of the Kildare knot of the Friendly Brothers of St Patrick, a society formed to regulate duelling.

ESTATES/RESIDENCE: Gilltown, Grayabbey and Calverstown, Co. Kildare; [?]Kildare Street, Dublin. On 26 October 1747 he petitioned for heads of a bill to sell part of the estate of Robert Dixon (**0640**) of Calverstown, Co. Kildare for payment of debts and other legacies.

SOURCES: PRONI D/302; PRONI D/3078/4 Minute book of the borough of Harristown, county of Kildare, 1714–90; NLI EC 2935; RCBL P45/2/3, Parish Registers of St Peter's, Dublin [says Mary, dau. of Sir Kildare and Elizabeth Borrowes, bapt. 18 Nov. 1764; RCBL P251/1/1 Dunlavin Parish Register; McCracken thesis; *CJ Ire.* (Bradley ed.) vol. 7 p. 917; Burke *PB* (1903) pp. 176–7; J. T. Gilbert, *History of the City of*

Dublin, vol. 3 p. 292; J. Kelly, '*That Damn'd Thing Called Honour*': *Duelling in Ireland 1570–1860* (Cork, 1995), pp. 65–6; *Almanacks*; *BNL* 30 Apr. 1754, 23 Feb. 1759; *DJ* 6 Apr. 1797; Parliamentary Lists, 1769 (1), 1772 (2), 1773 (1), (2), 1774 (1), 1775 (1).

0188 BORROWES (*alias* BORROWES), Sir Walter Dixon

MP for Harristown 1721–7; Athy 1727–41

b. 1691; d. 9 June 1741 at Colverstown, Co. Kildare
HONOURS: Suc. as 4th Bt 1709.
FAMILY/BACKGROUND: Eldest son of Sir Kildare Burrowes, 3rd Bt (**0290**), and Elizabeth, dau. of Sir Richard Dixon of Co. Kildare.
MARRIED: [18 Mar. 1720] Mary, dau. of Capt. Edward Pottinger.
CHILDREN: Sir Kildare Dixon, 5th Bt (**0187**); Rev. Robert; Walter.
EDUCATION: School: Dr Jones, Dublin; entered TCD 6 Sept. 1708, aged 17 years.
CAREER/OCCUPATION: High Sheriff of Co. Kildare 1716, Queen's County 1723; Free Burgess of New Ross 27 Nov. 1711 – 29 June 1731.

POLITICAL ACTIVITY: Burrowes was listed for 17 committees between 1728 and 1737. He sat for (Leinster) Kildare boroughs and almost certainly followed the FitzGerald line in parliament. Apart from this very little is known or can be deduced about his politics, except that he supported the establishment of a national bank.

DIVISION LISTS:

1721 (1) voted for a national bank.

ESTATES/RESIDENCE: Gilltown and Calverstown, Co. Kildare. In 1725 John Putland and others sued Sir Walter Burrows [*sic*] over the Burrows family's failure to pay punctually the interest on the mortgage of £3,000 charged on their manor, town and lands of Castletown Omy, Queen's County, and the town and lands of Grangemellon and Gilltown, Co. Kildare, in spite of the fact that the interest, at 8 per cent, was 2 per cent lower than the current rate of interest in Ireland in 1700, when the mortgage was granted.

SOURCES: PRONI D/302; RCBL P251/1/1 Dunlavin Parish Register [bur. 14 June 1741]; McCracken thesis; Burke *PB* (1903) p. 176; *JRSAI* vol. 21 (1892) p. 299, P. D. Vigors, 'Alphabetical List of Free Burgesses of New

Ross 1658–1839'; *Pue's Occurrences* 16 June 1741; NLI *Brown's Report of House of Lords Appeals 1701–1800* vol. 5 pp. 236–44.

0189 BOTET, Anthony

MP for Tulsk 1797–Jan. 1800

b. 1741; d. 11 May 1811
FAMILY/BACKGROUND: Son of [ ] Botet.
MARRIED: ?unmarried.
CHILDREN: ?
MILITARY: Major in the 10th Regiment of Foot for 24 years, served in America; Comptroller of Barracks at £500 p.a.; *Barrack Master 1785, 1788–91, 1793; *Comptroller of the Works 1795–96; Barrack Officer (Tulsk) 1797–1800; Constable of Castlemaine 23 February 1784 – 28 Nov. 1803; Gentleman-at-Large 1800 at *c*. £145 p.a.; *Commissioner and Overseer of Barracks 1799.

POLITICAL ACTIVITY: Very little is known of this MP. He was a soldier and voted for the government. He probably was brought in or purchased his seat. He was part of Lord Tyrawley's political following. Tyrawley was First Commissioner of the Barrack Board and a firm supporter of the Union. Botet voted for the Union in both 1799 and 1800.

DIVISION LISTS:
1799 (1) voted for the Union – Barrack Board and Constable of Castlemaine.
1800 (1) voted for the Union.

ESTATES/RESIDENCE: Owned a valuable estate in Co. Kerry which was inherited by his relative, John Dowdall.

SOURCES: PRONI T/3166/1C Hartnell notes; O'Neill thesis; Burke *LG* (1846) p. 105; *Memorials of the Dead*; Hughes, *Pat. Officers*; *Almanacks*; John Watson Stewart, *The Gentleman's and Citizen's Almanack* (1822–3) [Botet may have been succeeded as Constable of Castlemaine by a relative as there is an Anthony Botet Constable of Castlemaine in the 1822 but not in the 1823 edition]; Parliamentary Lists, 1799 (2), (3), 1800 (3).

0190 BOURCHIER, Charles

MP for Dungarvan 1692–3, 1695–9; Armagh B. 1715–16

b. 1665; d. 18 May 1716
FAMILY/BACKGROUND: Son and heir of Abraham Bourchier of London.
MARRIED: Barbara, eldest dau. of Richard Harrison of Balls Park, Hertfordshire (MP for Lancaster 1669–79).
CHILDREN: Charles (d. yg); Francis (d. yg); Richard (Governor of Bombay), m. Sarah, dau. of George Hawkins of Clay Hill, Epsom, Surrey; Edward, Vicar of All Saints and St John's, Hertford, m. Elizabeth, dau. of Rev. Edward ?Gattacre; Mary; Barbara, m. Richard Prittie of Dunally, Co. Tipperary; Anne-Marie, m. John Ward, Viscount Dudley; Catherine, m. William Yarner; Arabella (unmar.).
EDUCATION: Gray's Inn 12 Jan. 1682.
MILITARY: An officer in the Regiment of Horse commanded by Lord Windsor.

POLITICAL ACTIVITY: He was a soldier and probably on active service for at least part of the time he sat in parliament. He was a government supporter, voting in support of Lord Chancellor Porter, who was accused of favouring Catholics, in 1695. In 1696 he signed the Association for the protection of William III in parliament. He was nominated to three committees during the second parliament of William III, on 17 October 1695, 31 July 1697 and 15 October 1698. As a regimental agent he obviously caused some dissatisfaction, for on 21 December 1715 the Commons heard a petition from the corporals, trumpets and private horsemen of the regiment first commanded by the Duke of Ormonde and then by Lord Ashburnham, complaining that they had not received their proper clothing allowance and that Mr Bourchier, the regiment's agent, had received payment for providing such clothing. The Commons immediately named a committee to inquire into this allegation. What happened to this petition is uncertain, and Bouchier may have died before it was resolved.

ESTATES/RESIDENCE: [?]London.

SOURCES: PRONI T/559, Burke, extract pedigrees, vol. 11 p. 28; *Memorials of the Dead* [says he died in his 52nd year]; J. Foster, *The Royal Lineage of our Noble and Gentle Families* (London, 1886) pp. 604–5; Simms' cards; J. Foster, *Gray's Inn Admissions* p. 331; Parliamentary Lists, 1695 (1), 1696 (1).

0191 BOURKE (*alias* BURKE), Dominick

MP for Galway B. 1735–47

> b. *ante* 1703; d. 8 Dec. 1747
> FAMILY/BACKGROUND: Son of [ ] Bourke.
> MARRIED: [ ].
> CHILDREN: Dominick, m. Margaret, dau. of
> Edward Eyre (**0710**) and wid. of Francis Annesley
> of Co. Kildare; Bingham.
> CAREER/OCCUPATION: Attorney 11 June 1724;
> Master (took apprentices); Sheriff of Co. Mayo
> 1724; Mayor of Galway 20 Sept. 1737; Recorder
> of Galway 1740–8; *Magistrate of Galway 1741,
> 1746.

POLITICAL ACTIVITY: Little is known of this MP except that he was listed for nine committees between 1735 and 1745.

ESTATES/RESIDENCE: Fartimore, Co. Galway.

SOURCES: McCracken thesis; Burke *LG* (1846) p. 389;
IMC King's Inns Admissions pp. xi, 61; *Almanacks*; *The
Dublin Gazette* 30 Nov. 1723; *GM* Dec. 1747; *Pue's
Occurrences* 24 Sept. 1737.

♦♦♦ BOURKE (*alias* BURKE), Gerald/Garrett [n.d.e.]

MP for Maryborough Oct.–Dec. 1713

> b. *c.* 1679–81; d. 23 Apr. 1740
> FAMILY/BACKGROUND: Third son of Thomas
> Bourke (*alias* Burke) of Tiaquin, Co. Galway.
> MARRIED: Mary [ ].
> CHILDREN: Thomas; Hercules.
> EDUCATION: Middle Temple 17 June 1699; called
> to the Bar 1703.
> CAREER/OCCUPATION: Queen's Counsel 1711–14.

POLITICAL ACTIVITY: One of the nine 'converts' (ex-
Catholics) elected to the 1713 parliament in the
Tory interest and complained of by the Whigs. In
the three months between his return and his being declared not duly elected he was established
as a Tory; in the following year he confirmed this
by signing a County address in favour of the unpopular Tory Chancellor, Sir Constantine Phipps.

ESTATES/RESIDENCE: Dysert, Co. Galway. In 1702–3
Thomas Burke had forfeited 138 acres in Co. Galway
and 938 acres in Co. Mayo.

SOURCES: RCBL P328/1/2, Parish Registers of St John's,
Dublin; *Historical Studies*, iv (1963) pp. 84, 91 f. 5;
IMC King's Inns Admission Papers, 1607–1867; H. A.
C. Sturgess, *Register of Admissions to the Honourable So-
ciety of the Middle Temple* (London, 1949) vol. 1 p. 245;
Simms, *Williamite Confiscation*, p. 177; Parliamentary
Lists, 1713 (2), 1714 (1).

0192 BOURKE, Rt Hon. John

MP for Naas 1727–60, 1768–76, May–Aug.
1776; Old Leighlin 1761–8

> b. 1700; d. 3 Dec. 1790 at Palmerston, Co.
> Kildare, 'in the 90th year of his age'
> HONOURS: PC.
> PEERAGES: Cr. Baron Naas 1 Aug. 1776, Viscount
> Mayo 13 Jan. 1781, Earl of Mayo 24 June 1785.
> FAMILY/BACKGROUND: Only son of Richard Bourke
> of Dublin and Catherine, dau. of Charles
> Minchin of Co. Tipperary.
> MARRIED: [May 1725] Mary (d. 1774), dau. and
> co-h. of Rt Hon. Joseph Deane, Chief Baron of
> the Exchequer (**0603**).
> CHILDREN: John, 2nd Earl of Mayo (**0193**), m.
> Lady Mary Leeson; Joseph Deane (Abp of Tuam
> and 3rd Earl of Mayo), m. [1760] Elizabeth, o.
> dau. of Sir Richard Meade 3rd Bt (**1389**);
> Richard; Thomas; Catherine; Elizabeth;
> Margaret, m. Sir Thomas Newcomen, 8th Bt
> (**1534**); Eleanor.
> EDUCATION: School: Mr Campbell, Dublin; entered
> TCD 4 Aug. 1718, LLD *hon. caus.* Sept. 1730.
> CAREER/OCCUPATION: Commissioner of Excise 25
> Mar. 1749 (patent, 6 Apr. 1749); 1st Commis-
> sioner of the Revenue; Commissioner of the
> Revenue and Excise 6 Apr. 1749–Dec. 1780
> (patent, 21 Apr. 1761, 3 Feb. 1772; on resigning
> received pension of £1,000 p.a. as reward for long
> and faithful service); Receiver General of the
> Stamp Office 1776–82, 1784–6; Burgess of Naas
> 29 Sept. 1725; Sheriff of Co. Kildare 1736,
> 1737; Trustee of the Linen Board for Connaught
> 1738–d.; Commissioner of Tillage Act for
> Province of Connaught 1739–63; *Magistrate of
> Naas 1739, 1741; Sovereign of Naas 1739, 1741;
> *Governor of Erasmus Smith's Schools and other
> Charities 1741–73, Freedom of Cork 27 July
> 1752; *Governor of the Workhouse 1768,
> Foundling Hospital and Workhouse 1769–d.;
> *elected to the Court of Assistants June 1773;
> Commissioner for Paving the Streets of Dublin
> 1778–80.

POLITICAL ACTIVITY: He sat in parliament for 64 years, and in the House of Commons for nearly 50 of these. A government supporter and a 'man of business', he sat on the Revenue Board for 31 years and on his retirement received the, by then, customary pension. His career opened colourfully, as on 7 October 1731 a complaint was made to the Commons 'that Mr Anthony Tenison did, in a violent and notorious manner, assault John Bourke, Esq., a Member of this House, by presenting a pistol to his breast, and threatening to shoot him, on the thirtieth of December last' (during time of privilege).

Things settled down, and by 1737 his career as a man of business in the House was well under way. In that year he introduced the heads of a bill that afterwards became 11 Geo. II, c. 7, 'an act for the more effectual preventing the enlisting of His Majesty's Subjects to serve as soldiers in Foreign Service without His Majesty's Licence', and in 1739 he introduced the Linen Bill, 13 Geo. II, c. 11, which endeavoured to encourage, regulate and control this important manufacture – the linen web was to be 22 inches wide, lapped and stamped. At the time of the 1745 rebellion he introduced what became 19 Geo. II, c. 1, 'An act for making it High Treason to hold Correspondence with the Sons of the Pretender to His Majesty's Crown ...', reflecting the panic caused by the Scottish rebellion. A fortnight earlier, on 7 November 1745, he had introduced 19 Geo. II, c. 18, the recurrent Quaker Bill to allow Quakers to make an affirmation instead of an oath. In 1749 he introduced a Revenue Bill, 23 Geo. II, c. 5, earmarked for the improvement of tillage and building canals, and in the same year an 'act for the further encouragement of finding and working mines and minerals within this kingdom', which protected the rights of finders and discoverers and encouraged the development of coal mines by granting a 41-year lease.

On 21 January 1755 Primate Stone wrote to Lord George Sackville (1835) about Bourke as a possible replacement for Nathaniel Clements (0414), the Teller of the Exchequer and Stone's great *bête noire* – if he could get rid of him. But: 'Mr Bourke I think would not change his situation without great reluctance; as it must occasion

his leaving his country-house, and entire new settlement of his family, and a total alteration in all the habits of his life.' He was the eighteenth-century equivalent of a very senior civil servant, and as such he invariably voted for the government. He was nominated for 306 committees between 1727 and 1760.

In 1773 a government list declared that he was: 'a man who is immovable and unalterable to his purpose. He stands firm as a rock to his friend though all the world be in an uproar round about him, neither solicitations nor threatenings can disturb him, but whatever attempts are made upon him, he scorns to show the least compliance that shall either stain his honour, or discompose the regular, the equal, the uniform honour of his life. He is a Commissioner of the Revenue [and a] Trustee of the Linen Manufacture.' In 1774 it was said by the opposition that he was: 'not often in the house, but when there always votes on the side of administration, be the question what it will. Whenever this gentleman appears in the House, it is a signal that something bad is intended.' He had the additional advantage of controlling the borough of Naas, for which in 1776 he returned his son and, at Lord Harcourt's request, Thomas Allan (0031), the confidential agent of Lord Lieutenants Townshend and Harcourt.

Such virtues had their reward in 1772. The bishopric of Ferns was vacant, and Lord Townshend wrote, on making his recommendation that 'The Rev. Mr Bourke, Dean of Dromore, whom he has recommended for the vacant bishoprick of Ferns is son to Mr Bourke, the First Commissioner of the Customs in Ireland, who ... [has] always been a faithful, zealous, and steady friend to Government ... He has two seats in parliament, filled by himself and his eldest son. The borough of Old Leighlin, sending two members to Parliament is absolutely in the disposal of the Bishop of Ferns. By the enclosed copy of a letter from the Rev. Mr Bourke, it will be seen it has been secured for the use of government during his incumbency ... The services of his father and brother ... very justly entitle them to this mark of favour.' For himself there was a peerage and eventually an earldom, and he enjoyed the disposal of considerable Revenue patronage. By 1782 he was

Viscount Bourke of Mayo, in the House of Lords and an almost permanent absentee: 'a very old man, tormented with the stone'. His son was now the Archbishop of Tuam. By 1788 he was 'so old and infirm, that he cannot attend'. He died in 1790 aged 90 years.

DIVISION LISTS:

1749 (1) voted against the election of James Digges La Touche (♦♦♦♦).

1753 (1) voted against the expulsion of Arthur Jones-Nevill (**1125**) – Commissioner of Revenue.

1753 (2) voted for the Money Bill.

1753 (3) a placeman.

1757 (1) voted for the resolutions on pensions.

1768 (1) voted for army augmentation – Commissioner of the Revenue.

1771 (1) voted for Lord Townshend as Lord Lieutenant.

1771 (2) against Sir Lucius O'Brien's (**1558**) motion for retrenchment.

1773 (1) voted for Absentee Tax.

1773 (2) voted against an untaxed press.

ADDITIONAL INFORMATION: A foundation member of the Dublin Society, 1731.

Until about the mid or late 1770s the Bourkes' control over Naas was not secure. At the election for Naas on 12 July 1768, John Bourke the elder received 36 votes, John Bourke the younger (**0193**) 31 votes, Walter Hussey (**1059**) of Donore 15 votes, and William Burgh (**0286**) of Bert 2 votes. The Bourkes were declared duly elected. About 1780 Bourke appears to have come to an agreement with William Burgh whereby Burgh controlled one seat, at least during the lifetime of Lord Mayo and possibly his son.

In 1750 he was with difficulty prevented from fighting a duel with Colonel Butler over (linen) spinning wheels.

ESTATES/RESIDENCE: Kill and Palmerstown, Co. Kildare; Moneycrower, Co. Mayo. In 1751 he succeeded to family estates in Co. Mayo on the death of his cousin, Theobald Bourke of Moneycrower. In November 1782 a map of the estate of Viscount Mayo, surveyor John Hamilton, gives the following particulars: lands in the townlands of Cloonkeeghan Commons, Lecarrow,

Ballina, parish of Kilmainemore; Lishenmanus, parish of Kilcommon; Moylish; Barony of Kilmaine.

Grants of James I and George III had given the Corporation of Naas the right to hold a market, and in 1815 the 4th Earl of Mayo was given a grant to hold an additional market.

SOURCES: *CJ Ire.* (Bradley ed.) vol. 6 pp. 821, 833, 856, vol. 7 p. 153, 723, 727–8, 708, 722, 828, vol. 8 pp. 186, 224, 226 (0377, 0400, 0430, 0447, 0468, 0472); NLI MS 21 f. 72; TCD, S.3, 1–4, Naas corporation books, 1665–1840, 4 vols; McCracken thesis; *CJ Ire.* (Bradley ed.) vol. 4 p. 20; Burke *PB* (1903) p. 1033; GEC *P*; Berry *RDS* pp. 24–7; *EHR* (Oct. 1905) pp. 756–7, C. L. Falkiner, 'Correspondence of Archbishop Stone and the Duke of Newcastle'; PRO SP63/467 f. 45; Johnston, *Gt B. & Ire.*, p. 244; J. Kelly, *'That Damn'd Thing Called Honour': Duelling in Ireland 1570–1860* (Cork, 1995), p. 62; *Almanacks*; *DJ* Dec. 14–16, 1790; Parliamentary Lists, 1769 (1), 1772 (2), 1773 (1), (2), 1774 (1), 1775 (1), 1776 (1).

0193 BOURKE, Hon. John

MP for Naas 1763–8–76–83–90

b. 1729; d. 21 Apr. 1792 at Blackrock, Co. Dublin, 'of dropsy in which he underwent much agony before he died'

PEERAGES: Styled Lord Naas 1785–90; suc. as 2nd Earl of Mayo 1790.

FAMILY/BACKGROUND: Son of Rt Hon. John Bourke, 1st Earl of Mayo (**0192**), and Mary, dau. of Rt Hon. Joseph Deane (**0603**).

MARRIED: [10 Feb. 1764] Mary, dau. of Rt Hon. Joseph Leeson, 1st Earl of Milltown (**1212**).

CHILDREN: *d.s.p.*

EDUCATION: School: Mr Young, Dublin; entered TCD 29 Oct. 1747, BA 1751, LLD *hon. caus.* 1769.

CAREER/OCCUPATION: *Surveyor and Comptroller in the Store 1764–73; Sovereign of Naas Sept. 1764; *Commissioner of the Tillage Act for Connaught 1764–84; *Governor of the Foundling Hospital and Workhouse 1790.

MILITARY: ?Volunteer Captain, Naas Light Infantry.

POLITICAL ACTIVITY: The 1773 Parliamentary List described him as follows: 'he will serve him truly that will put him in trust, loves him that is honest, converses with him that is wise, says little, and when known an heart-approved friend. In short he is sensible but not assuming, humble but not mean, familiar but not loquacious, religious but not gloomy', adding that although 'brought in by his father. He has also a good interest himself', and that he had a Revenue employment. An opposition list of the following year stated that he was: 'Surveyor and Comptroller in the Stamp Office. He is famous for his loud voice and horse laugh, also for the length of his chin, and the shortness of his head. He voted for amending the Tontine Act, for the Stamp Act, and every other ministerial measure. Yet to do him justice, he was a spirited and strenuous opposer of the bills in favour of Popery, and a firm friend to the Foundling Hospital.' He probably was 'a useful member of parliament'. Both he and his father voted for the Absentee Tax and both were against concessions to the Catholics.

He held a number of Revenue posts including the Receiver General of Stamps, originally worth £400 p.a. but increased to £600 by Lord Carlisle. He was also given the disposal of several small Revenue positions and his friend Mr Ormsby was given a pension of £200 p.a. He appears to have been under his father's shadow, and the whole family operated as a clan. Dying without surviving issue, he was succeeded by his brother, the Archbishop of Tuam.

DIVISION LISTS:

1768 (1) voted for army augmentation – Surveyor of stores.

1771 (1) voted for Lord Townshend as Lord Lieutenant.

1771 (2) voted against Sir Lucius O'Brien's (1558) motion for retrenchment.

1772 (2) voted against a Short Revenue Bill.

1773 (1) voted for an Absentee Tax.

1773 (2) voted against an untaxed press.

1774 (1) voted for the Stamp Bill.

1774 (2) voted against Catholic relief.

1775 (1) voted against the pro-American amendment to the Speech from the Throne.

1777 (1) voted against Grattan's (0895) motion for retrenchment.

1778 (2) voted against the Popery Bill.

1779 (1) voted for new taxes.

1779 (2) voted against a six-months Loan Bill.

1780 (1) voted against Grattan's declaration of the Rights of Ireland.

1780 (2) voted against Yelverton's (2268) motion to modify Poynings' Law.

1783 (1) voted against Flood's (0762) motion for parliamentary reform.

1785 (1) absent.

1790 (2) voted for Foster (0805) on the election of a Speaker.

ADDITIONAL INFORMATION: A member of the Royal Dublin Society from 1766; a member of the Royal Irish Academy, 1790.

At the election for Naas on 12 July 1768, John Bourke the elder (0192) received 36 votes, John Bourke the younger 31 votes, Walter Hussey (1059) of Donore 15 votes, and William Burgh (0286) of Bert 2 votes. The Bourkes were declared duly elected.

He was found guilty of obtaining goods belonging to Richard Maxwell, merchant, after duties being paid and fined c. £1,422.

ESTATES/RESIDENCE: Palmerstown, Naas, Co. Kildare.

SOURCES: TCD, S.3, 1–4, Naas corporation books, 1665–1840, 4 vols; PRONI T/1584, Pinkerton transcripts, p. 74, 17 Feb. 1764; PRONI MIC/474 Irish Volunteers; RCBL P45/2/3, Parish Registers of St Peter's, Dublin; Ellis thesis; GEC P; Ir. Gen. vol. 6 no 2 (1981) p. 165, H. F. Morris, 'The Waterford Herald 1792'; Almanacks; FJ 2–6 Oct. 1764, 1–5 Jan. 1765; DJ 14–16 Dec. 1790; BNL 17–27 Apr. 1792; DJ 24–6 Apr. 1792; Parliamentary Lists, 1769 (1), 1772 (2), 1773 (1), (2), 1774 (1), 1775 (1), 1776 (2), 1777 (1), 1778 (1), 1780 (1), 1782 (1), 1783 (1), (2), (3), 1785 (1), (2), (3), (4), 1787 (1), 1788 (1), 1789 (1), 1790 (1), 1791 (1).

0194 BOURKE, Rt Hon. John

MP for Naas 1790–4

b. 18 June 1766; d. 23 May 1849
HONOURS: PC, sworn 20 Feb. 1810; GCH.
PEERAGES: Styled Lord Naas 1792–4; suc. as 4th Earl of Mayo Aug. 1794; Rep. Peer 1816–49.
FAMILY/BACKGROUND: Son of Joseph Deane Bourke, 3rd Earl of Mayo, Abp of Tuam, and Elizabeth (d. 1807), dau. of Sir Richard Meade, 3rd Bt (1389), and sis. of 1st Earl of Clanwilliam (1388).

MARRIED: [24 Apr. 1792] Arabella (d. 1843), dau. of William Mackworth Praed.

CHILDREN: *d.s.p.*

EDUCATION: Entered Oxford (Christ Church) 12 Jan 1784; DCL 13 July 1793.

CAREER/OCCUPATION: *Listed in Judges and Barristers 1780 (f.) and Attorneys of the Court's of King's Bench, Common Pleas and Exchequer 1789 (f.); *Inspector General of Dublin City Excise and Licenses 1795–6.

MILITARY: Lieutenant in the Naas Cavalry 1796.

POLITICAL ACTIVITY: Unlike the rest of his family he was in opposition, and he voted for W. B. Ponsonby (**1709**) for Speaker after the 1790 election. He sat in parliament for only four years before succeeding his father as 4th Earl of Mayo. In 1799 both members for Naas voted for the Union. Although Lord Mayo was supposed to control the borough, he shared the compensation with his brother Richard (the father of the 5th earl) and the sovereign and burgesses of Naas.

DIVISION LISTS:

1790 (2) voted for Ponsonby (**1709**) on the election of a Speaker.

ESTATES/RESIDENCE: Tuam, Co. Galway. Succeeded by his nephew Robert, 5th Earl of Mayo. Lands in the barony of Kilmaine. There is an abstract beginning with a 1793 deed of trust from Archbishop Bourke/Mayo to Lord Naas. The owner in *c.* 1900 was Lord Mayo.

SOURCES: NLI CDB 9810; NLI EC 657 and 6055; GEC *P*; Burke *PB* (1903) pp. 1033–4; *Index to Irish Privy Counsellors, 1711–1910*; *Almanacks*; *FJ* 20 Oct. 1796; Parliamentary Lists, 1783 (2), 1791 (1), 1793 (1), 1794 (2), 1799 (3).

0195 BOURKE, Theobald

MP for Naas 1713–14, 1715–26

b. *c.* 1683–5; d. June 1726

FAMILY/BACKGROUND: Son of John Bourke and Catherine, dau. of Meyler Fay.

MARRIED: [c. May 1725] Mary Deane.

CHILDREN: *d.s.p.*

CAREER/OCCUPATION: Sheriff of Co. Kildare 1700.

POLITICAL ACTIVITY: As one of the group of recent converts from Roman Catholicism, he was complained of by the Whigs during the 1713 elec-

tion. He voted for the Tory candidate, Sir Richard Levinge (**1230**), as Speaker in 1713. He was a Tory and on the 1714–15 'black list' of Tories. He appears to have been a low-key MP, being listed for only two committees, on 7 August 1719 and 20 September 1723. He voted against the establishment of a national bank in 1721.

DIVISION LISTS:

1713 (1) voted for Sir Richard Levinge (**1230**) for Speaker.

1721 (1) voted against a national bank.

ESTATES/RESIDENCE: Palmerstown, Co. Kildare. In 1713 Theobald 'Burke's' income was estimated at £300.

His estate comprised lands in the baronies of Salt South and Naas South. An abstract begins with lease and release from George Aylmer of Lyons to Theobald Bourke of Palmerstown, 1697.

SOURCES: NLI EC 657; T/3411; PRONI T/559 vol. 10 p. 308, Burke, extract pedigrees; Burke *PB* (1903) p. 1033 (1906) p. 1111; Simms' cards; Kildare MPs; *IHS* (1980–81) vol. 22 p. 203 f. 6, D. Hayton, 'The crisis in Ireland and the disintegration of Queen Anne's last ministry'; Parliamentary Lists, 1713 (2), 1714–15 (1).

♦♦♦♦ BOWEN, John [n.d.e.]

MP for Mullingar Nov. 1727–Jan. 1727/8

b. *c.* 1697; d. *c.* 1776

FAMILY/BACKGROUND: Son of [ ] Bowen.

MARRIED: Frances, dau. of Edward Drury.

CHILDREN: Hugh; Robert; Frances, m. Cabell Powell; Elinor; Elizabeth; Anne Margaret, m. [7 Dec. 1776] Edmond Beasley.

POLITICAL ACTIVITY: He sat for about three months before being declared not duly elected; nothing is known of his political activities during this time.

ESTATES/RESIDENCE: Fanvilly, Mullingar, Co. Westmeath.

SOURCES: PRONI T/559 vol. 11 p. 59, Burke, extract pedigrees; Vicars, *Prerog. Wills*; *Alum. Dub.*; *DJ* 7–10 Dec. 1776.

BOWERMAN, Henry: *see* BOREMAN (*alias* BOWERMAN*), Henry (**0186**)

0196 BOWES, Rt Hon. John

MP for Taghmon 1731–42

b. 1691; d. 22 July 1767 at his house in Drumcondra (bur. Christ Church Cathedral, 25 July)
HONOURS: PC, sworn 23 Jan. 1742, 1745, 1 Nov. 1760, 8 July 1761.
PEERAGES: Cr. Baron Bowes (of Clonlyon) 15 Aug. 1758.
FAMILY/BACKGROUND: Son of Thomas Bowes of London and [   ], dau. of [   ] North.
MARRIED: Unmarried.
EDUCATION: Admitted Inner Temple 6 Dec. 1712; called to the Bar 1718; called to the Irish Bar 29 Sept. 1725.
CAREER/OCCUPATION: 3rd Serjeant 1727, 18 Jan. 1728–30; Solicitor General 1730–39; Attorney General 11 Sept. 1739–41; Chief Baron of the Exchequer 15 Jan. 1742–56 (renewed 10 Mar. 1752); Clerk of the Paper Office 7 May 1748, 1751–66 (renewed 6 Feb. 1761); Commissioner of Accounts 1747–65 (worth £200 p.a. and perquisites); Lord Chancellor 22 Mar. 1757–66 (renewed 6 Feb. 1761); Speaker of the House of Lords 1757–8, 1759–60, 1761–6; Lord Justice 22 Feb. 1765, 9 June 1766; Judge in the Court of Exchequer Chamber 1757–67; Bencher of the Hon. Society of King's Inns 1766; Justice of Assize for Leinster Lent 1730, NW Ulster Summer 1731, Leinster Lent 1732, Connaught Lent 1733, 1740, Munster Lent 1741, Leinster Summer 1741, Leinster Lent 1742, Munster Summer 1742, Leinster Lent 1743, NW Ulster Summer 1743, NE Ulster Lent 1744, NW Ulster Summer 1744, Munster Lent 1745, 1746, NW Ulster Lent 1747, Munster Summer 1747, Connaught Summer 1748, NE Ulster Lent 1748, Leinster Lent 1749, NE Ulster Summer 1749, NE Ulster Lent 1750, NW Ulster Summer 1750, NW Ulster Lent 1751, NE Ulster Lent 1752, Leinster Lent 1753, NE Ulster Lent 1754, Munster Summer 1754, Leinster Lent 1755, NW Ulster Summer 1755; *Trustee of the Linen Manufacture for Leinster 1732–d.; *Commissioner of Oyer and Terminer 1732–54; *Governor of the Workhouse 1732–d.; *Governor of the Royal Hospital 1742–d.; *Governor of Erasmus Smith's Schools and other Charities 1742–56; *Governor of Dr Steevens' Hospital 1742–d.; *Commissioner of the Tillage Act 1756–d.; *Governor of the Lying-in Hospital 1757–65 (Vice-Principal 1766); *Governor of St Patrick's Hospital 1758–64; Governor of the Blue-Coat Hospital 1763–6; Treasurer to the Hon. Society

of King's Inns 1749–66; In 1747 he was voted a Freeman of the Guild of Merchant Tailors.

POLITICAL ACTIVITY: He arrived in Ireland *c.* 1725 with Lord Chancellor West. As Solicitor General in October 1737 he took a leading part in the debates over the Cork petitions against the realignment of the gold currency. On 27 October 1737 Lord George Sackville (**1835**) wrote to his father, the recently recalled Lord Lieutenant Dorset, that the petitions against the lowering of the gold were considered the previous day in the House. They first proposed a committee and, when that was negatived by 108 to 55, Stannard (**1981**) moved for a resolution that the lowering was prejudicial to the trade of the country. This was rejected by 11 to 40, and Carter (**0360**) proposed that the further consideration of the petitions should be postponed to 1 October 1738, which was carried by 118 to 30. 'The chief speakers on the side of the minority were Stannard, Sir Richard Cox (**0508**) (who abus'd the Privy Council very grossly) Mr Morgan (**1487**), Mr Maloun [*sic*] (**1336**). On the other side the Solicitor General (**0196**), Mr Cope (**0489**), Mr Coote, Mr Cuff [*sic*] (**0557**) and Mr Hill (**1015**).'

He was essentially a lawyer: Dr Thomas Rundle, Bishop of Derry, described Solicitor General Bowes' performance in the Santry murder case in 1739 as 'so perfect a piece of eloquence. Its beauty arose from true simplicity and unaffected ornaments; from the strength and light of his reason, the fairness and candour and good nature of his heart; from the order and disposition of what he said, the elegance and fulness of his expressions, the shortness and propriety of his reflections, the music of his voice, and the gracefulness of his elocution.' In the 1745 crisis, Bowes, then Chief Baron, wrote that 'We are largely over-numbered by Papists …': a thought that obviously gave him some concern at this time. Like most lawyers in the House he was in demand for committee service, and he was nominated for 88 committees between 1731 and 1741.

On the death of Lord Chancellor Jocelyn, Bowes was promised the vacant Chancellorship by Lord Lieutenant Hartington (Devonshire), but the Lord Lieutenant left office before the appointment was made, leaving the fulfilment of his promise to his successor, the Duke of Bedford. Not surprisingly, the hiatus caused Bowes some concern. However, the appointment was eventually made and, on 23 June 1758, Bedford confirmed that the king intended to increase Bowes' salary by £500 p.a. as well as make him a baron. Jealous of the powers of his office, in 1759 Bowes proposed that the Lord Chancellor of Ireland should have the same power to administer the affairs of lunatics as that of the Lord Chancellor of England.

He was mobbed going to the House of Lords during the anti-Union riots of 1760. It was said that 'He performed every part of his important duty with great ability and dispatch, under the complicated infirmities of old age, bad health, the weakest and lowest state of spirits.' He appears to have felt that he was being forced out of office by those who looked to fill his shoes; nevertheless, he died in office in 1767. After his death there was a considerable clamour for his office, which, it was felt, should be filled by an Irishman. In his obituary the *Dublin Journal* described him as 'an indulgent and bountiful master, a steady and affectionate friend, easy of access ... great dignity united to perfect good breeding. No man ever filled the high office of Lord Chancellor with more distinguished abilities; his judgment was solid, his expression clear, his style nervous and elegant, and his discernment extremely quick; and, what is very remarkable, his talents in the opinion of some of the ablest judges, seemed rather to improve, than to be impaired, by his age.'

ADDITIONAL INFORMATION: There is a curious idea that Lifford, who succeeded Bowes, hounded him into retirement. This is incorrect. Bowes died in office on 22 July 1767; Lifford, who does not appear to have been thought of previously, was not sworn until 9 January 1768, and that after considerable discussion with the Pitt–Grafton administration.

When Bowes arrived he found that the society in which he moved 'have no notion of the pleasures of conversation. Drinking is the business of their leisure hours', and that without drinking sessions 'people wondered how I preserved my rank in business'.

ESTATES/RESIDENCE: Islandbridge, Co. Dublin; Henrietta Street, Dublin. He resided in Werburgh Street, Dublin

from 1730 to 1742 and he had a house in Drumcondra, where he died. At his death £60,000 devolved on his relatives.

SOURCES: PRONI T/2915/4/52/, 7/8 Bedford Papers; PRONI T/3459/C/2/48, 52 Donoughmore Papers; PRONI T/3019/1001 Wilmot Papers; PRONI T/3228/1/17 Bowes to Ryder 5 Oct. 1745; J. Walton, '*The King's Business': Letters on the Administration of Ireland, 1741–61* (NY, 1996) no 296; S. J. Conolly, *Religion, Law and Power* (1992) pp. 66–7, 257–8; McCracken thesis; GEC P; Ball, *Judges; King's Inns Admissions; Index to Irish Privy Counsellors, 1711–1910; DNB*; Johnston, *Gt B. & Ire.*, pp. 17, 236–7; W. R. Anson (ed.), *Autobiography and Political Correspondence of Augustus Henry, 3rd Duke of Grafton* (1898), p. 157; Gilbert, *History of the City of Dublin* (Dublin, 1859), vol. 1 p. 42, vol. 3 p. 94; HMC *Sackville I* p. 167; *JRSAI* vol. 48 (1918) p. 57, H. F. Berry, 'The Merchant Tailors' Gild – That of St John the Baptist, Dublin, 1418–1841'; *Almanacks; BNL* 25 Aug. 1767; *The Dublin Gazette* 21 Feb. 1730, 13 July 1731, 22 Feb. 1732, 13 Feb. 1733, 23 Feb. 1740, 26 Feb., 9 July 1743; *Pue's Occurrences* 7 Feb., 27 June 1741, 20 Feb., 17 July 1742, 21 June, 28 June 1746, 10 Feb., 21 Feb., 24 Feb., 1747, 19 Feb. 1751, 17 Feb. 1753, 23 Feb., 13 July 1754, 15 Feb., 1 July 1755; *DJ* 14 Feb., 19 June 1744, 26 Feb., 13 July 1745, 21 July 1747, 21–5, 25–8 July 1767; *The Dublin Weekly Journal* 5 Mar., 16 July 1748, 18 Feb., 1 July 1749, 10 Mar., 14 July 1750, 29 Feb. 1752.

0197 BOYD, Hugh

MP for Co. Antrim 1794–5

b. 1765; d. 26 Nov. 1795 while on a visit at Goagh, Co. Tyrone
FAMILY/BACKGROUND: Son of Ezekiel Davys Boyd (and great grandson of Col. Hugh Boyd).
MARRIED: Rose, dau of Alexander Boyd (his cousin).
CHILDREN: Hugh (d. 1862); Alexander (*d.s.p.*); Amy (*d.s.p.*), m. [   ] Keats; Harriet, m. Sir John Boyd of Dawson Hall, Kent.
EDUCATION: School: Mr Sterick; entered TCD 27 Nov. 1782, aged 17 years.
CAREER/OCCUPATION: High Sheriff of Co. Antrim 1792.

POLITICAL ACTIVITY: He was in opposition and a supporter of Catholic Emancipation, but had been only a year in parliament when he died, aged 30 years.

DIVISION LISTS:

1795 (1) voted for a Short Money Bill.

1795 (2) voted for Catholic Emancipation.

ADDITIONAL INFORMATION: A member of the Northern Whig Club.

ESTATES/RESIDENCE: Ballycastle, Co. Antrim. The bulk of the property of Colonel Hugh Boyd (died 15 June 1765), the entrepreneur who established Ballycastle, the harbour, coalmines and a number of industries, eventually came to his great-grandchildren, Rose and Hugh, the MP. When Hugh died in 1795 his eldest son Hugh was still a minor. He grew up a lunatic and the estate was in the hands of Chancery until his death in 1862. As the court was unable to grant leases for more than seven years, this deterred anyone wishing to set up new industries in the town. After the death of Hugh the estate passed to his brother Alexander, and from him to his two sisters.

SOURCES: PRONI D/302; PRONI T/559 vol. 11 p. 108, Burke, extract pedigrees; PRONI T/618/328 Crossle Papers; PRONI T/1584, Pinkerton transcripts, p. 504, 23 Nov. 1795; Burke *PB* (1903) p. 777; J. E. Mullin, *The Causeway Coast* (Belfast, 1974), pp. 67, 161–72; *Charlemont MSS*, second ser. vol. 6-3 A. Halliday to Charlemont 19 Jan. 1792, *c.* 22 Jan. 1796; S. J. Conolly, *Religion, Law and Power* (1992) p. 57; *Alum. Dub.*; Kilkenny MPs; *Memorials of the Dead* [says incorrectly that he died 23 Feb. 1795]; *DJ* 23–7 Nov. 1795; *FJ* 3–6 Mar. 1792.

0198 BOYD, James

MP for Wexford B. 1797–9–1800 (re-elected 1799 on appointment to a place of profit)

b. 1764; d. 29 June 1808

FAMILY/BACKGROUND: Eldest son of Higatt Boyd of Rosslare, Co. Wexford, and Amy Phillips.

MARRIED: Elizabeth, dau. of Col. Walter Hore (**1037**).

CHILDREN: James, m. [1813] Georgina, dau. and co-h. of Hon. George Jocelyn (**1096**); Lieut. Higatt (4th Foot); Charles (HEICS officer); Anne; Amy; Lucy.

EDUCATION: Entered Glasgow University 1780.

CAREER/OCCUPATION: Freeman of Wexford *ante* 1776; Sheriff of Co. Wexford 17 Feb. 1797, 12 Feb. 1802; Collector of Port of Wexford at £1,337 in Jan. 1799.

MILITARY: Captain in the Wexford Cavalry 1796; Captain of the Yeomanry Corps of Wexford Cavalry 1798.

POLITICAL ACTIVITY: He was in parliament for three years, returned probably under the pro-Union Lord Ely's (**2088**) influence, as although the franchise in Wexford was vested in the freemen and freeholders it was seldom contested, and it was considered under the influence of Ely and Richard Nevill (**1527**). Although listed as doubtful in 1799, he was made Port Surveyor of Wexford and this possibly changed his mind. In any case he voted for the Union.

DIVISION LISTS:

1799 (1) voted for the Union – Port Surveyor.

ADDITIONAL INFORMATION: The central committee of the Wexford Republic, 9 June 1798, proclaimed that 'Whereas it stands manifestly notorious that James Boyd, Hawtney White, Hunter Gowan and Archibald Hamilton Jacob, late magistrates of this county, have committed the most horrid acts of cruelty, violence and oppression against our peaceable and well-disposed countrymen: now we the people associated and united ... do call on our countrymen at large to use every exertion in their power to apprehend the bodies of the aforesaid James Boyd, Hawtney White ... and to secure and convey them to the jail of Wexford, to be brought before the tribunal of the people.' Boyd's brother was the only casualty. He paid the price for his magisterial zeal by being piked to death on Wexford Bridge on the first day of the rebel occupation of Wexford. Following the suppression of the rising, Boyd, with George Ogle (**1573**) and other Co. Wexford gentlemen, set up a court of inquiry into the rebellion in the county.

ESTATES/RESIDENCE: Rosslare House, Co. Wexford; he had lands in the barony of Forth.

SOURCES: PRONI 3863 [Pedigree, 1700–1912]; PRONI T/3166/1D Hartnell notes; PRONI MIC/338/2 Crossle notes; O'Neill thesis; Burke *LG* (1846) pp. 130, 593; Hughes, *Pat. Officers*; W. I. Addison (ed.), *Alum. Glas.*; *Ir. Gen.* vol. 5 no 1 (1974) pp. 103–21, D. Goodall, 'The Freemen of Wexford in 1776'; *BNL* 1 July 1808; *FJ* 20 Oct. 1796, 16 Feb. 1797, 8 Jan. 1799; T. Pakenham, *The Year of Liberty* (1978), p. 214; E. Hay, *History of the Insurrection of 1798* (Dublin, 1898), p. xxxix; Parliamentary Lists, 1799 (2), (3).

0199 BOYD, Robert

MP for Boyle 1783–90

b. 1740; d. 1814

FAMILY/BACKGROUND: Second son of John Boyd of Letterkenny, Co. Donegal.

MARRIED: ?

CHILDREN: ?

EDUCATION: School: Mr Torrens, Londonderry; entered TCD 19 Apr. 1758, aged 18 years, BA 1762; Middle Temple 2 May 1763; called to the Irish Bar 1767.

CAREER/OCCUPATION: King's Counsel 1782; Justice of the King's Bench 27 June 1791; Second Justice 1793 (resigned 28 Feb. 1798); 2nd Counsel to the Revenue (resigned 1791); Commissioner of Appeals 1795–7; Bencher of the Honorable Society of King's Inns 1799 (f.); *Coroner of Ireland for Co. Donegal 1747–52, 1760–4; Recorder of Londonderry 22 Apr. 1776; *Council at Law for the Port Business 1789–90; *listed in Judges and Barristers 1789–94 (f.); *Recorder and Magistrate of Londonderry 1789–90; Justice of Assize for Connaught Summer 1791, Connaught Summer 1792, Connaught Lent 1794, Connaught Circuit, Summer Assizes, Home Circuit 1797.

MILITARY: First Lieutenant, Volunteers; elected Honorary member of the Lawyers Corps in 1796.

POLITICAL ACTIVITY: A Donegal lawyer, he had a considerable practice in the north and was connected with the Co. Donegal MP, Alexander Montgomery (**1437**). He purchased his seat for Boyle, Co. Roscommon from Lord Kingston (**1167**). When he first came into parliament it was thought that 'He will probably be forward in opposition, though still subject to be influenced by his friend the Attorney General' (Fitzgibbon, **0749**), and that his ambition might be to be Recorder (?of Dublin) on the popular interest. Since 1776 he had been Recorder of Londonderry, and he became a King's Counsel in 1782.

An ambitious lawyer, he was at first in opposition and then, having made his mark, a government supporter. An opposition list in 1789 expressed the opinion that 'The avowed defender of every measure of Government, is often exposed to situations from which, if not possessed of great prudence, it is not easy to come off with credit, and where not to be exposed is in some degree to be victorious. Of the truth of this observation Mr Boyd is a remarkable instance, for, as cautious and prudential considerations seem to have little influence on his parliamentary conduct, he has sometimes been subjected to the sarcasms of wit and often been refuted by the powers of reasoning. Neither his voice nor action recommend him to notice as a public speaker, as the former, though strong, is disagreeably toned, when loud harsh, when low indistinct and the latter has more of the pedantic stiffness of the bar, than of the graces of elegance or the force of energy. His language is plain, unadorned and tolerably correct ... and his elocution is pompous and sonorous, rather suited to magnificence of terms than to his simplicity of expression. His manner is sufficiently warm and spirited, perhaps sometimes too much so and in debating, he displays with subtlety and acuteness, no small portion of legal sophistry and some powers of legal reasoning, cautiously avoiding the weak parts of the question, however forcibly attacked, dwelling with visible satisfaction on those that are strong, if any such it should chance to have and seizing on with avidity, the mistakes or misapprehensions of his opponents and exposing them forcibly. The arrangement of his arguments is very censurable and the more so, as it could easily be remedied by attention ... His matter is sometimes good, sometimes bad and sometimes indifferent for he takes it [?the subject] as he finds it, without a laborious investigation of its weight, or an anxious scrutiny of its solidity. If it answers the purposes of debate, it is sufficiently strong; if it enables him to harangue with fluency, it is sufficiently cogent. As the determined friend, indeed, follower of the Attorney General (**0749**) and through his interest aspiring to a judge's seat, he uniformly votes with the minister of the day'. He was rewarded with a number of legal offices; finally in 1791 he became a Justice of the King's Bench and in 1793 Second Justice. He resigned in 1798 with a pension of £1,600 p.a.

DIVISION LISTS:

1784 (1) voted against a committee on the Reform Bill.

1784 (3) teller against Foster's (**0805**) Bill to regulate the press.

1785 (1) voted for the Commercial Propositions.

1789 (1) voted against a regency.

ADDITIONAL INFORMATION: He was alleged to have received £1,600 compensation at the Union, but this may have been a judicial pension.

ESTATES/RESIDENCE: Letterkenny. Resided in Dublin successively at Castle Street, Ely Place and Merrion Square.

SOURCES: Hughes, *Pat. Officers*, *Alum. Dub.*; Smyth, *Law Officers*; Ball, *Judges*; *King's Inns Admissions*, *Middle Temple Admissions* vol. 1 p. 360; *Ir. Gen.* vol. 1 no 10 (1941) p. 294, W. Clare, 'Irish Compensations and Pensions'; *Almanacks*, *FJ* 26–8 July 1791, 19–21 July 1792, 8 Mar. 1794, 19, 24 Nov. 1796, 7 Mar., 5 Aug. 1797; *BNL* 6 Mar. 1798; Parliamentary Lists, 1783 (2), 1784 (1), (2), (3), 1785 (1), (2), (3), (4), 1787 (1), 1788 (1), 1789 (1), (2), 1790 (1).

0200 BOYLE, Bellingham

MP for Bandon 1731–60; Youghal 1761–8

b. 1690; d. 13 May 1771

FAMILY/BACKGROUND: Son of Richard Boyle and [   ], dau. of Capt. John Hoyte and wid. of Henry Chalenor.

MARRIED: [27 Nov. 1740] Sarah, o. dau. of John Hoadley, Abp of Armagh and Primate of all Ireland.

CHILDREN: Anne, m. [Mar. 1782] Robert Langrishe, 2nd Bt (**1201**); John (of London); Rev. William (d. 1777).

EDUCATION: School: Mr Wilson, Dublin and Kilkenny School; entered TCD 9 July 1703, BA 1708, LLD 14 July 1741.

CAREER/OCCUPATION: Revenue Commissioner 1768–70 (patent, 3 Dec. 1767); Registrar of the Prerogative Court 1745– dismissed Jan. 1754; Governor of Dublin Workhouse June 1741–68; Trustee of the Linen Board for Munster 1743–71; *Governor of Erasmus Smith's Schools and other Charities 1743–71; Collector of Cork Port 1746–7; Freedom of Cork 10 Sept. 1747; *Commissioner of the Tillage Act for Munster 1747–71.

POLITICAL ACTIVITY: He gives the impression of having been an ambitious political gadfly of limited ability and considerable pretensions. Financially he was unable to sustain his pretensions and assiduously looked for some means of doing so. He married Primate Hoadley's only daughter, but it is unlikely that her dowry matched his expectations, as Speaker Boyle (**0210**) wrote to suggest that Boyle, who was related to him, should get the pension of the recently deceased Sir Richard Levinge (**1231**), saying that Boyle's wife: 'the dau. of the late Primate, whose merit so justly entitled him to the general love and esteem of this country ... (he died in circumstances so low it is hardly to be believed) ... likewise deserves a pension'. Primate Hoadley, the brother of Benjamin Hoadley, was a friend of the deist Thomas Chubb and Lord Chesterfield was far from agreeing with the Speaker as to his merits. Subsequently Boyle got a pension of £400 p.a., later increased to £800 p.a.; both the Speaker and Archbishop Stone supported the recommendation.

However, at the time of the Money Bill crisis Bellingham Boyle had to choose between the Speaker and the administration. He chose the Speaker, and on 27 September 1753 the Chief Secretary, Lord George Sackville (**1835**) wrote to Sir Robert Wilmot, the Lord Lieutenant's Secretary in England, that 'The Prime Serjeant [Anthony Malone, **1336**] is still in the country; all the violence of the party is thought to proceed from that man and Bell Boyle.' Throughout the crisis Boyle voted consistently with the Speaker's party. A few months later he was among those to feel the wrath of the administration. On 28 December 1753 Lord Holdernesse wrote to Dorset that as a mark of His Majesty's displeasure Bellingham Boyle was to lose his pension of £800 p.a. This was obviously foreshadowed, as on 29 December 1753 Waite (**2154**) welcomed his dismissal along with that of the Master of the Rolls, Thomas Carter (**0360**): 'The Friends of Government are highly pleased. Indeed there would not only have been an end of our party, but I think an end of the English Government here if these steps had not been taken.'

In May 1755 it was reported to Under-Secretary Wilmot that at a party given by Bellingham Boyle the toast was 'confusion and disappointment to all those who quit their party till they have full satisfaction and compensation for the injuries they have received and full restitution made'. Nevertheless, in the general armistice he was forgiven and on 16 September 1758 he was granted a pen-

sion of £800 p.a. for 21 years. Thereafter he supported the government unequivocally.

Bellingham Boyle had influential friends, and
on the death of Sir Richard Cox (**0508**) in 1766
the then Lord Lieutenant, Lord Bristol, wrote to
the Marquess of Rockingham recommending
Boyle for his seat at the Revenue Board: he was
made a Commissioner of the Revenue in December 1767. He supported Lord Lieutenant
Townshend over the augmentation of the army in
1769.

He died in 1771; the newspapers reported that
his death 'was very much hastened by the benefit
of burning bricks in the neighbourhood by an
officer of the Revenue'. Eighteenth-century Dublin was a brick-built city, and brick manufacture
proved such an environmental hazard that parliamentary legislation was passed to curb it. In 1772,
11 Geo. III, c. 6 was 'An act to prevent the pernicious practice of burning within the city of Dublin or the neighbourhood thereof'. His death may
have assisted the statute's passage.

DIVISION LISTS:

1749 (1) voted against the election of James
Digges La Touche (♦♦♦♦).

1753 (1) voted for the expulsion of Arthur
Jones-Nevill (**1125**) – Registrar of the
Prerogative Court and a pensioner.

1753 (2) voted against the Money Bill – a
pensioner, £800 p.a.

1757 (1) voted against the resolutions on
pensions.

1768 (1) voted for army augmentation –
Commissioner of the Revenue.

ADDITIONAL INFORMATION: It was reported in April
1751 that his seat at Rathfarnham had been broken into and a great quantity of 'rich wearing cloth'
stolen.

A member of the Royal Dublin Society, 1763
to his death.

ESTATES/RESIDENCE: Glenfield, Co. Cork; Rathfarnham,
Co. Dublin. In 1767 he sold Rathfarnham Castle and
demesne for £17,500. On 6 December 1731 he petitioned for heads of a bill to make leases and to settle a
jointure on any wife he should marry. Eight years later,
3 December 1739, he petitioned to turn the jointure –
he was still not married – into a £3,500 mortgage to
pay debts.

SOURCES: *CJ Ire.* (Bradley ed.) vol. 7 p. 113; PRONI T/
3019/1027, /6456/315, 341, /6459/750 Wilmot Papers; PRONI T/559 vol. 11 p. 132, Burke, extract pedigrees; McCracken thesis [says son of Charles Boyle,
Captain RN]; Burke *PB* (1903) p. 1370; *Alum. Dub.*;
Vicars, *Prerog. Wills*; *Ir. Gen.* vol. 5 no 4 (1977) p. 479,
H. F. Morris, 'Ramsey's Waterford Chronicle, 1777';
O. MacDonagh, W. F. Mandle and Paudric Travers
(eds), *Irish Culture and Nationalism, 1750–1950* (Can-
berra, 1983), p. 25, Johnston, 'Problems common to
both Protestant and Catholic churches in eighteenth-
century Ireland'; *JRSAI* vol. 29 (1899) p. 108, F. E.
Ball 'Descriptive Sketches of Clondalkin, Tallaght and
Other Places in West County Dublin'; *Irish Official
Papers in Great Britain* vol. 1 p. 43; J. Walton, '*The
King's Business': Letters on the Administration of Ireland,
1741–61* (NY, 1996), nos 21, 25, 129, 152, 197, 202,
297–9, 309; *Almanacks*; *BNL* 13 Jan., 22 Jan. 1754, 20
Feb. 1767, 17 May 1771; *DJ* 29 Nov 1740, 11–14 May
1771; *The Dublin Courant* 5 May 1747; *Pue's Occurrences* 30 June, 18 July 1741, 13 Apr. 1751.

0201 BOYLE, Hon. Charles

MP for Charleville 1695–9; [E] Huntingdon
1701–5

b. 28 July 1674 at Chelsea, Middlesex; d. 28 Aug.
1731

HONOURS: Knight of the Thistle 30 Oct. 1705.

PEERAGES: Suc. as 4th Earl of Orrery 1703; cr.
Baron Boyle [GB] 5 Sept. 1711.

FAMILY/BACKGROUND: Son of Roger Boyle, 2nd
Earl of Orrery, and Mary, dau. of Richard
Sackville, 5th Earl of Dorset.

MARRIED: [30 Mar. 1706] Elizabeth, dau. of John
Cecil, 5th Earl of Exeter.

CHILDREN: o. s. John, 5th Earl of Orrery.

EDUCATION: School: St Paul's; entered Oxford
(Christ Church) 5 June 1690, aged 15 years, BA
1694.

CAREER/OCCUPATION: Receiver General in
Alienation Office 1699; Lord of the Bedchamber
[GB] 1714–16; appointed Envoy to Flanders
1710–11 and as Envoy (extra.) and Plenipotenti-
ary took part in the Treaty of Utrecht (1713);
Lord Lieutenant of Somerset 1714–15.

MILITARY: He served under Marlborough in
Flanders and fought at Malplaquet 11 Sept.
1709. Colonel of a Regiment of Foot 1704–10;
Brigadier-General 1708–9; Major-General 17
Aug. 1710; Colonel of the North British Fusiliers
(21st Foot) 8 Dec. 1710–July 1716.

POLITICAL ACTIVITY: He sat for the second parliament of William III and was nominated for three committees in September–October 1695, but his career was mainly in England, where he was a soldier and a diplomat. In 1696 he signed the Association for the protection of William III in the country.

ADDITIONAL INFORMATION: Fellow of the Royal Society, 3 April 1706. Celebrated for his literary contest with Bentley and gave his name, although he did not invent it, to the astronomical instrument known as an orrery. He was imprisoned in the Tower on suspicion of treason for 6 months, 1722. He was one of the descendants of the 'great' Earl of Cork.

ESTATES/RESIDENCE: Marston, Somerset; lands in the barony of Duhallow, Co. Cork; the great Blasket Island barony of Corkaguiny, Co. Kerry. According to Wakefield at the beginning of the nineteenth century, the Cork and Orrery estates had a rental of £20,000. In 1674 the Earl of Orrery had been granted a market at Castlemartyr.

SOURCES: Wakefield, *Account of Ire.*, vol. 1 p. 250; NLI EC 5239; *DNB*; GEC *P*, Cork MPs; Burke *PB* (1903) p. 366; *Alum. Oxon.*; C. Dalton, *George the First's Army, 1714–27*; G. Bruce (ed.), *Harbottle's Dictionary of Battles* (London, 1979) p. 156; Parliamentary List, 1696 (1).

0202 BOYLE, Hon. Charles

MP for Blessington 1711–13–14, 1715–18

b. *post* 1673; d. 2 June 1732 at Paris
PEERAGES: Suc. as 2nd Viscount Blessington 26 Apr. 1718.
FAMILY/BACKGROUND: Son and heir of Rt Hon. Murrough Boyle, 1st Viscount Blessington, and his second wife Anne, dau. of Charles Coote, 2nd Earl of Mountrath.
MARRIED: (1) Rose, dau. and co-h. of the Hon. Charles Coote; (2) [11 July 1709] Martha, dau. of Samuel Matthews of Co. Kilkenny.
CHILDREN: Murrough (d. yg).

POLITICAL ACTIVITY: He sat for the borough of Blessington during the eventful latter years of Queen Anne and the early years of George I. This borough was already firmly under the control of the Boyles (Blessington) by the beginning of the century, as it was reported that Lord Blessington 'puts in who he thinks fit'. During Queen Anne's reign he was considered a Tory and supported the administration, especially on such contentious issues as the Dublin mayoralty. He was nominated for two committees in 1711, three in 1713 and 16 between 1716 and 1725. Anderson Saunders (**1878**) was the defeated Court candidate for the chairmanship of the key Committee on Elections and Privileges. In 1714–15 Boyle was on the 'black list' of Tories. However, he weathered the Whig victory in 1715 and probably kept a fairly low profile during the early years of George I. It was considered that he would probably be hostile to any relaxation of the Test Clause in 1719. He was elevated to the peerage in 1718.

DIVISION LISTS:

1711 (1) voted for the Court on the Dublin mayoralty issue.

1713 (1) absent, 'sick'.

1713 (2) voted for Anderson Saunders (**1878**) for Chairman of the Committee of Elections and Privileges.

ESTATES/RESIDENCE: Blessington, Co. Wicklow. Lord Blessington purchased 737 acres in Co. Kildare from the Commissioners for Sale of Forfeited Estates in 1702–3. On his death the estates devolved on his sister Anne, Viscountess Mountjoy. The Blessington estate descended successively to the Stewart, Dunbar and Hill (Hillsborough/Downshire) families. It contained 15,578 statute acres in Wicklow and 1,308 in Kildare. (W. A. Maguire, in *The Downshire Estates*, reckons the Kildare acreage of the Blessington estate at 1,308 statute acres.) The estate comprised Butterhill, Crosscoole Harbour, Hempstown, Old Court, etc., as well as land in the barony of Talbotstown Lower. In 1779 Young cited Mr Dunbar as an absentee with a rental of £6,000. (As the Blessington estate produced only £4,000 as late as 1810, the bulk of the £6,000 must have come from property in Dublin city and county.) In 1813 the rental for the composite Blessington estate of the Marquess of Downshire was £6,500.

In 1669, Michael Boyle, Archbishop of Dublin (later Archbishop of Armagh and Primate), was granted a market at Blessington.

SOURCES: PRONI D/671/R2/1 Downshire Papers [rental 1810]; W. A. Maguire, *The Downshire Estates* (1972) p. 32; NLI EC 3667; PRONI T/559, Burke, extract pedigrees, vol. 11 p. 121; GEC *P*, Burke *Ext. P*

(1883) p. 70; *JRSAI* vol. 58 (1928) p. 130, T. U. Sadleir, 'The Manor of Blessington' [says his estates devolved upon William Stewart, Viscount Mountjoy, whose mother was Anne Boyle, sister of Charles]; Simms, *Williamite Confiscation*, p. 183; Parliamentary Lists, 1711 (3), 1713 (1), 1714–15 (1), 1719 (2).

0203 BOYLE, Hon. Charles

MP for Co. Cork 1756–9

b. 27 Jan. 1729; d. 16 Sept. 1759
PEERAGES: Styled Lord Boyle 1731–53, Viscount Dungarvan 1753–9.
FAMILY/BACKGROUND: Son of John Boyle, 5th Earl of Cork and Orrery, and his first wife Henrietta, dau. of Rt Hon. George Hamilton, 1st Earl of Orkney.
MARRIED: [18 May 1753] Susanna, dau. of Henry Hoare of Wiltshire.
CHILDREN: *d.s.p.m.*: Henry (d. yg); Henrietta, dau. and h., m. John O'Neill, 1st Viscount O'Neill (**1592**).
EDUCATION: School: Westminster Apr. 1738–44; entered Oxford (St Mary Hall) 23 May 1745, aged 16 years.
CAREER/OCCUPATION: *Trustee of the Linen Manufacture for Munster 1756–61; *Commissioner of the Tillage Act for Munster 1756–59.

POLITICAL ACTIVITY: He represented the great Boyle interest in Co. Cork but sat for only three years and, apart from his vote against the resolutions on pensions, little is known of his career. He was nominated for no fewer than 52 committees between 1757 and 1759.

DIVISION LISTS:
1757 (1) voted against the resolutions on pensions.

ADDITIONAL INFORMATION: Elected a member of the Royal Dublin Society following the charter of 1750.

ESTATES/RESIDENCE: Marston, Somerset; Co. Cork (*see* **0201**).

SOURCES: RCBL T34, Extracts from the Parish Registers of St Andrew's, Dublin; McCracken thesis; GEC *P*; *Alum. Oxon.*; G. F. Russell-Barker and A. H. Stenning (eds), *Record of Old Westminsters: A Biographical List*, 2 vols (London, 1928).

0204 BOYLE, Hon. Charles

MP for Lismore May–June 1758

b. May 1734; d. 6 June 1758
FAMILY/BACKGROUND: Fourth son of Rt Hon. Henry Boyle, 1st Earl of Shannon (**0210**), and his second wife Henrietta, dau. of Charles Boyle, 3rd Earl of Cork and 2nd Earl of Burlington.
MARRIED: [1755] Henrietta, only dau. of James Price.
CHILDREN: John, m. [1799] Eleanor, dau. of the Hon. R. Taylour.
CAREER/OCCUPATION: Military: Cornet of Horse; aide-de-camp to his father as Lord Justice.

POLITICAL ACTIVITY: He sat for barely a month for the Boyle borough of Lismore, which was controlled by his father. Parliament, having been prorogued on 29 April 1758, was not in session during this time and little is known about this MP, except that he would almost certainly have followed his father's lead – at this time his father was a Lord Justice.

ESTATES/RESIDENCE: Castlemartyr, Co. Cork.

SOURCES: McCracken thesis; Burke *PB* (1903) p. 1370.

0205 BOYLE, Hon. Charles

MP for Charleville 1797–1800; [Escheator of Munster 25 Jan. 1800]

b. 1774; d. 26 Nov. 1800
FAMILY/BACKGROUND: Son of Edmund Boyle, 7th Earl of Cork and Orrery, and his first wife Anne, dau. and co-h. of Kelland Courtenay of Devon.
MARRIED: Unmarried.
EDUCATION: Entered Oxford (Christ Church) 19 Jan. 1792, aged 18 years.

POLITICAL ACTIVITY: He was a government supporter and influenced by the 2nd Earl of Shannon (**0213**), who largely controlled the dominant Boyle/Cavendish influence in Co. Cork. Charleville was a 'close' borough controlled by the Earls of Cork and of Shannon, both descendants of the seventeenth-century 'great' Earl of Cork. He was for the Union but he resigned, accepting the office of Escheator of Munster on 25 January 1800, before the decisive vote of 5–6 February 1800.

DIVISION LISTS:

1798 (1) voted against Sir Laurence Parsons' (**1636**) motion for an investigation into 'the present discontents'.

ESTATES/RESIDENCE: Castlemartyr, Co. Cork; Henrietta Street, Dublin.

SOURCES: PRONI T/3166/1A Hartnell notes; PRONI MIC/465/1 R. Ffolliott, *Biographical Notices, 1756–1827* [*Cork Advertiser* says he died in his 27th year]; O'Neill thesis; GEC *P*; Burke *PB* (1903) p. 366; *Alum. Oxon.*; Hughes, *Pat. Officers*; Cork MPs [says Escheator of Munster]; Parliamentary Lists 1799 (2), (3).

0206 BOYLE, Hon. Hamilton

MP for Charleville 1759–60; [GB] Warwick 1761–2

> b. 3 Feb. 1730; d. 17 Jan. 1764
> PEERAGES: Styled Viscount Dungarvan 1759–62; suc. as 6th Earl of Corke and Orrery 26 Nov. 1762.
> FAMILY/BACKGROUND: Son of John Boyle, 5th Earl of Corke and 6th of Orrery, and his first wife Henrietta, dau. of Rt Hon. George Hamilton, 1st Earl of Orkney.
> MARRIED: Unmarried.
> EDUCATION: School: Westminster July 1741, Captain of the school 1747; entered Oxford (Christ Church) 14 June 1748, aged 18 years, LLB 1753, BCL 15 May 1755; High Steward of Oxford University 1762–d.; Doctor of Civil Law 6 July 1763.
> CAREER/OCCUPATION: Trustee of the Linen Manufacture for Ulster 1752–d.

POLITICAL ACTIVITY: Hamilton Boyle appears to have been a man of unfulfilled promise, who made little impression on either the British or the Irish parliament, perhaps because his period in each was so short. In 1761 he was thought of as a possible ambassador to Turin but Lord Shelburne, who knew him very well from their student days at Oxford, had reservations and therefore did not endorse the suggested appointment.

ADDITIONAL INFORMATION: A member of the Royal Dublin Society, 1751 to his death. He joined in the eighteenth-century vogue for theatricals, and at Westminster School 'played the part of "Ignoramus" in the play of 1747 with great success'.

ESTATES/RESIDENCE: He was succeeded by his half-brother Edmund, son of his father's second wife, Margaret (died 1758), daughter and heiress of John Hamilton (**0938**) of Caledon, Co. Tyrone. She was said to be worth £80,000 in 1738, but this was probably a guess at the value of the Caledon estate, which when sold in 1776 realised £96,400.

Their father, the 5th Earl (died 23 November 1762) was an improvident man much given to borrowing. In 1751 he borrowed £20,000 in one transaction.

SOURCES: McCracken thesis; *Alum. Oxon.*; G. F. Russell-Barker and A. H. Stenning (eds), *Record of Old Westminsters: A Biographical List*, 2 vols (London, 1928) [says died 17 Jan.]; *HP 1754–90*; A. P. W. Malcomson, *The Pursuit of the Heiress* (Belfast, 1982) p. 20; *Almanacks*.

0207 BOYLE, Hon. Henry

MP for Youghal 1692–3

> b. *c.* 1648; d. 1693 in Flanders
> FAMILY/BACKGROUND: Son of Rt Hon. Roger Boyle, 1st Earl of Orrery, and Margaret, dau. of Rt Hon. Theophilus Howard, 2nd Earl of Suffolk.
> MARRIED: Mary, dau. of Murrough O'Brien, 1st Earl of Inchiquin (she married (2) Sir Thomas Dilkes (**0633**)).
> CHILDREN: Roger (d. unmar.1705); Rt Hon. Henry, 1st Earl of Shannon (**0210**); Capt. Charles RN; William (**0215**); Elizabeth, m. Brettridge Badham (**0070**); ?Margaret, m. Rt Hon. Joseph Deane (**0603**).
> CAREER/OCCUPATION: Military: Lieutenant in Earl of Orrery's Regiment of Horse Apr. 1672; Captain commanding Troop of Horse Aug. 1677; Captain in the Duke of Ormonde's Regiment of Horse *c.* 1685; removed from the army in 1686; Major in Lord Cavendish's Regiment of Horse 24 Mar. 1689; Lieutenant-Colonel 17 Nov. 1689; Lieutenant-Colonel of Schomberg's Horse at the Battle of the Boyne 1 July 1690.

POLITICAL ACTIVITY: At the time of the Revolution he was 'an active asserter of the Protestant interest in the province of Munster, he was very obnoxious to the Irish Government, so that, 26 February 1688, he was besieged in his house of Castlemartyr, by General MacCarthy with a strong body of horse, and two field pieces. Being determined to defend the castle, he had collected about

140 gentlemen and servants, but being persuaded to use no resistance, he surrendered on the general's promise, that neither their persons nor estates should be molested; without the least regard to which promise the next morning the General caused the house to be plundered, and conveyed in a disgraceful manner, Captain Boyle and his family to Cork. After some confinement he was removed with his family in May 1689 to England, to avoid the troubles then increasing in this kingdom.' He was probably on active service for most if not all of this brief parliament. He was the father of Speaker Boyle (0210), the descendant of the great Earl of Cork and the ancestor of the Earls of Shannon.

ESTATES/RESIDENCE: Castlemartyr, Co. Cork.

SOURCES: PRONI T/559 vol. 2 p. 123, Burke, extract pedigrees; Lodge *P*; GEC *P* [His elder brother Roger was born in 1646 and both he and Roger obtained permission to go abroad for 4 years in 1662]; Burke *PB* (1903) p. 1370 [says he died in Flanders during Marlborough's campaigns] (1906) p. 1474; *Cal. SP Dom. 1693* (London, 1903) p. 412; Cork MPs [says MP Youghal 1695–9 and gives no date of death]; C. Dalton (ed.), *English Army Lists and Commission Registers, 1661–1714* (London, 1896), vol. 3 pp. 13, 24 [says he was out of Cavendish's Regiment 3 Jan. 1694 and died the same year]; C. Dalton (ed.), *Irish Army Lists 1661–85* (London, 1907), pp. 78, 111; E. Hewitt (ed.), *Lord Shannon's Letters to his Son* (PRONI 1982) p. xxiv; Vicars, *Prerog. Wills*; Simms' cards; *The Ir. Gen.* vol. 6 no 6 (Nov. 1985) pp. 814–23, R. Refausse, 'The Welply Will Abstracts in the Representative Church Body Library'.

0208 BOYLE, Rt Hon. Henry

MP for Co. Cork 1692–3; [E] Tamworth 1689–90; Aldborough Feb.–May 1690; Cambridge University 1692–1705; Westminster 1705–10

b. *c.* 1668; d. 14 Mar. 1725 (bur. at Lanesborough)

HONOURS: PC ?1692, appointed 27 Mar. 1701, May 1704, reappointed 30 Sept. 1714 but not sworn.

PEERAGES: Cr. Baron Carleton [GB] 19 Oct. 1714.

FAMILY/BACKGROUND: Son of Charles Boyle, Baron Clifford, and his first wife Jane, dau. of William Seymour, 2nd Duke of Somerset.

MARRIED: Unmarried.

EDUCATION: School: Westminster, under Busby (a Busby trustee 5 Feb. 1724); entered Cambridge (Trinity College) 9 Nov. 1692, MA 1693; DCL *hon. caus.* Oxford 6 July 1720.

CAREER/OCCUPATION: Commissioner for Public Accounts 1695–7; Lord of the Treasury [E] 1 June 1699–Mar. 1701, [I] 5 May 1704–Aug. 1710; Chancellor of the Exchequer [E] 29 Mar. 1701–Feb. 1708; Lord President of the Council [GB] 25 June 1721–5; Secretary of State for the North [GB] 15 Feb. 1708–Sept. 1710; Commissioner for the Union [S] 1706; Commissioner for Assessment, Staffordshire 1690; Vice Adm. Yorkshire 1704–15; Custos Rot. (North and West Ridings) 1704–15; Lord Lieutenant of the West Riding 1704–15.

MILITARY: Cornet, Queen's Horse (later 1st Dragoon Guards) 1685–Nov. 1688; Major 2nd Life Guards by 1691.

POLITICAL ACTIVITY: He was a serving officer at the time of the Revolution, and on 24 November 1688 went over to William of Orange with Prince George of Denmark (Princess Anne's husband) and the 2nd Duke of Ormonde. His political career was in England, and he sat only in the first short parliament (it lasted less than a month) of William III and Mary II. He was a Whig, but 'without any party violence and never engaged in mean things'. He refused office in 1710 and was raised to the peerage as Lord Carleton at the coronation of George I.

ADDITIONAL INFORMATION: One of the managers of Sacheverell's trial, 1710. The third volume of the *Spectator* was dedicated to him by Addison (0010). Known for his attractive manners and his diplomacy, he persuaded Addison to write an ode celebrating Blenheim and its victor.

ESTATES/RESIDENCE: Yorkshire; Pall Mall, Westminster; he left his house, Carleton House, to the Prince of Wales (later George II) and it was used by successive Princes of Wales until the reign of Queen Victoria.

SOURCES: *DNB*; GEC *P*; Burke *Ext. P* (1883) p. 70; Lodge *P* [says his eldest brother died 1675 aged 9 years; since Henry was the third son he was possibly born *c.* 1668]; *HP 1660–90*; Simms' cards; *Cal. SP Dom. 1691–2* (London, 1900) p. 420; *Index to Irish Privy Counsellors, 1711–1910*; *Alum. Oxon.*; C. Dalton (ed.), *Eng-*

lish *Army Lists and Commission Registers, 1661–1714* (London, 1896), vol. 3 p. 175; G. F. Russell-Barker and A. H. Stenning (eds), *Record of Old Westminsters: A Biographical List*, 2 vols (London, 1928).

0209 BOYLE, Henry

MP for Youghal 1695–9

> b. (*ante* 21 Sept.) 1674; d. 1713
> FAMILY/BACKGROUND: Son of [   ] Boyle. Married Mary [   ].
> CHILDREN: ?

POLITICAL ACTIVITY: Very little is definitely known about this man; nevertheless, he was the only Henry Boyle sitting in this parliament, and Lord Deputy Capel wrote to Shrewsbury in August 1695 in reply to his warning of the possible appearance of Mr Harry Boyle as a candidate for the Speakership that he would have a cold reception, as the two leading contenders, Attorney General Rochfort (**1806**) and Thomas Brodrick (**0243**), would join forces against him: 'the people being generally persuaded that he is under the management of my Lord Rochfort and my Lord Ranelagh, neither of which have a credit here in reference to the good of this country on the King's service'.

Youghal was a borough in which the Boyle family had influence, and he is probably a connection. He was nominated for three committees in 1695, on 28 September, 7 and 16 October. In 1695 he was considered a probable but not certain supporter of Lord Chancellor Porter, who was accused of favouring Catholics. He may have left the country thereafter, as he did not sign the Association for the protection of William III in 1696.

ESTATES/RESIDENCE: [?]Co. Cork.

SOURCES: PRONI T/559 vol. 2 p. 123, Burke, extract pedigrees; *Irish Official Papers in Great Britain*, vol. 1 p. 14; Parliamentary Lists, 1695 (1), 1696 (1).

0210 BOYLE, Rt Hon. Henry

MP for Midleton 1707–13, Kilmallock 1713–14; Co. Cork 1715–27–56

> b. 1682; d. 28 Dec. 1764
> HONOURS: PC, sworn 13 Apr. 1733.
> PEERAGES: Cr. Baron Boyle, Viscount Boyle, Earl of Shannon 17 Apr. 1756.
> FAMILY/BACKGROUND: Son of Henry Boyle (**0207**) and Mary, dau. of Rt Hon. Murrough O'Brien, 1st Earl of Inichiquin.
> MARRIED: (1) [1715] Catherine (*d.s.p.*), dau. of Chidley Coote (**0482**); (2) [Sept. 1726] Henrietta, dau. of Rt Hon. Charles Boyle, 3rd Earl of Cork and 2nd Earl of Burlington.
> CHILDREN: (2) Rt Hon. Richard, 2nd Earl of Shannon (**0213**); Henry (**0216**); William; Charles (**0204**); Robert (**0217**); Juliana, m. [18 May 1745] Rt Hon. Somerset Hamilton Butler, 1st Earl of Carrick; Mary; s. (d. 1740, aged 9); dau. (d. 1740, aged 6); Jane (d. 1748, aged 11).
> EDUCATION: School: Westminster 1702; entered Oxford (Christ Church) 5 Mar. 1706, aged 18 years.
> CAREER/OCCUPATION: Speaker of the House of Commons 1733–56; Chancellor of the Exchequer, 1733–5 (patent, 19 Nov. 1733), 1734–54 (11 Apr. 1739), 1755–7 (3 Nov. 1755); Revenue Commissioner 1735–9 (6 Oct. 1735); Commissioner of Public Accompts in the Court of Exchequer 1744–57; Lord Justice (patents, 3 May 1734, 19 May 1736, 28 Mar. 1738, 18 Apr. 1740, 18 Feb. 1741/2, 4 June 1742, 3 Dec. 1742, 12 Apr. 1744, 25 Apr. 1746, 10 Apr. 1747, 20 Apr. 1748, 31 Jan. 1749, 31 July 1749, 20 Apr. 1750, 27 May 1752, 29 Apr. 1758, 2 May 1760, 15 May 1761, 20 Apr. 1762, 11 May 1764); *Trustee of the Linen Board for Leinster 1733–d.; *Governor of Dr Steevens' Hospital 1733–57; *Governor of the Workhouse 1735–56; *Governor of the Blue-Coat Hospital 1735–d.; Freeman of the Guild of Merchant Tailors 1737; *Governor of Erasmus Smith's Schools and other Charities 1739–d.; Governor of Midleton School, Co. Cork; *Commissioner of the Tillage Act 1739–57; *Commissioner of Oyer and Terminer 1742–53; *Governor of the Royal Hospital 1744; *Governor of Co. Cork (in the absence of the Earl of Burlington 1746–53, in the absence of the Duke of Devonshire 1756–60?); *Governor of the Lying-in Hospital 1758–d. (Vice-Principal 1761, 1763).
> MILITARY: Lieutenant-Colonel, Cork Militia Dragoons; Colonel 1729.

POLITICAL ACTIVITY: Interestingly, the two boroughs for which he was originally returned – Midleton in 1707 and Kilmallock in 1713 – were not Boyle boroughs. Midleton was controlled by the Brodricks and Kilmallock by the Oliver family, one of whom (1583) was returned for Castlemartyr (which was a Boyle borough) in 1713. He came to political prominence when he was elected Speaker of the House of Commons, an office he held from 4 October 1733 to April 1756, making him the longest serving Speaker in the eighteenth-century Irish parliament. Before his election to the Chair he appears to have been moderately, but increasingly, active in committees. As a Whig he was not popular during the later part of Queen Anne's reign – he was nominated to only seven committees between 1701 and 1714 – but with the accession of George I his activity increased, and he was listed in 25 committees from 1716 to 1725. After 1727 his political activity increased further; he was busy in the years 1727–33, and thereafter as Speaker. He was nominated for 45 committees between 1727 and 1756.

His appointment, following the unexpected death of Sir Ralph Gore (0872), led a contemporary to declare him to be 'very unfit for that station by reason of his natural modesty ... He is a country gentleman of great good nature and probity, well-beloved, but not of extraordinary abilities.' Furthermore, he did not have oratorical talents; in fact he spoke seldom and usually from a written script. Yet he obviously had very considerable managerial abilities: these are shown in his letters to his supporters, which are both skilful and diplomatic. In the end he achieved everything that he could legitimately desire. In the narrow, envious world in which he operated, did he encourage his contemporaries to underestimate him?

On 15 March 1733 Primate Boulter wrote to Lord Lieutenant Dorset about the vacant Speakership, giving a full review of the situation: 'In our last we represented to your Grace our thoughts concerning the several candidates, and that Mr Boyle appeared to us to have by much the best personal interest, and such as could not without difficulty be opposed, if he persisted in his pretensions (if this is not the case then maybe His Majesty should "wait for such accidents as time may throw in the way") but as it is a thing hardly to be expected that any number of persons should keep themselves disengaged for so long a time as six months, and as there may not be wanting those who may endeavour to persuade Mr *Boyle* that he has not been kindly used by the government's taking no favourable notice of his applications, we are very apprehensive that such delay may give room to the forming some party, which may raise a dangerous opposition to so late a recommendation as your Grace proposes. We should be very unwilling to disoblige either of the candidates, as being persons for whom we have a great regard, but we beg leave to observe, that since such declaration must be made before the election, the effects of any resentment on that account may be worn out the sooner it is made especially if it be in favour of one, who it is generally thought cannot fail of success. It may be proper to take notice that it is almost a general notion, that if Mr Boyle was once recommended by the government, all other opposition would be at an end. People have not been wanting to surmise here that Mr *Boyle's* standing was only in order to transfer his interest at a proper time to some other. The effect of this had been, that Mr *Boyle* has by his friends, discountenanced any such suggestion, and many of his friends have declared against any such transfer ... Your Grace must be sensible that £500 a session cannot be a sufficient provision for the expence of a Speaker, and therefore he will be apt to expect some other support from government. Whether the Chancellorship of the Exchequer be a post proper for a Speaker not otherwise provided for, is a matter we shall not presume to meddle with; but we cannot help taking notice, that from the nature and duties of that office, it may be for his Majesty's service that it should be given to some person of weight, who usually resides here.'

Speaker Boyle was duly appointed to a Revenue position commensurate with his managerial role in the House of Commons. Eventually he succeeded to the role of Speaker Conolly (0460) as chief 'undertaker', and Walpole called him 'the King of the Irish Commons'.

One example of the Speaker's skill was his handling of the devaluation of the currency in 1737.

The Irish currency was overvalued through its dependence on Portuguese gold moidores, but any move to devaluation alarmed the merchant class, and nowhere more than in Cork city. On 20 October 1737 Lord George Sackville (**1835**) wrote to his father – the recent Lord Lieutenant, the Duke of Dorset – that 'The Cork petition was presented to the House last Tuesday and the consideration of it deferr'd till next Wednesday. Mr Cary's friends and all those that think the lowering of the gold absolutely necessary complain terribly that the petition was not at once rejected, for they say giving it a day is doing it a great deal too much honor. They are certainly in the right, and a great majority of the House thought so, but the Speaker was in an ugly situation between the Castle and his Cork interest, so that he artfully made the Duke [of Devonshire] believe that the favourers of the petition were much stronger than they really were, and promised that if a little time was given him, that he would so soften and bring people to a more moderate way of thinking that he should be able to have it dropt. On the other hand he may well tell his friends in Cork that if he had not stood between them and the Castle, that their petition would not have been received, but rejected with scorn and indignation. So that by this means he thinks to oblige both sides.'

In December 1746 Bishop Stone (shortly afterwards Primate) briefing the new Chief Secretary Edward Weston (**2223**), thought that 'The Speaker has undoubtably the largest (though not the sole) influence here, and he is, of course, on some occasions driven to make Requests for Favours which cannot and ought not to be granted. But he is an honest, good-natured, and in his natural Temper not untractable Man: and will, I am persuaded, do everything in his power that may contribute to the ease and honour of my Lord Harrington's Government. And, I think, that, as the Interests and Parties stand at present here, it is for the service of the higher Government, that he should be principally (though as I said before) not solely considered.' Stone also pointed out that the Speaker and the Lord Chancellor (**1098**) were rivals, but their rivalry 'will occasion no real trouble; and I now only mention it as a general map of the Country'. On 22 May 1747 he again wrote:

'I am extremely well satisfied with Mr Bristow's (**0236**) being appointed one of our Commissioners. My situation here laid me under an obligation of forwarding recommendations without a thought of making myself answerable for the propriety … of them. The truth is that the Speaker's friends think that he has received a blow; and his enemies (of which there are a number though not a majority) are pleased at it.'

The Rt Hon. William Bristow was Second or Ulster Secretary in the Castle and was returned for the Cork borough of Lismore, almost certainly with the Speaker's approval. However, this was a major appointment and affected the Speaker's Cork interests, so he may well have felt excluded. Boyle's views were important, as the Speaker was the principal link between parliament and the administration.

Bad relations between the Speaker and the Castle were brewing before the Money Bill crisis. For instance, in October 1750 the Speaker nominated his son to the Lord Lieutenant for appointment to the Privy Council. The Lord Lieutenant at first gave a favourable answer to this request and then reneged on the grounds that his son was too young and would be considered so in England. Boyle pointed out that his services and those of his son should be taken into consideration, moreover there were Irish precedents. The Speaker obviously felt strongly about the rejection of his recommendation and considered it a slur on himself and his son.

It was against this background that the real weakness in the essential connection between the administration and parliament came about in the early 1750s over the king's right to dispose of a surplus in the permanently granted part of the revenue, known as the Hereditary Revenue. King and parliament were agreed that it should be applied to the reduction of the national debt: the question was, should it be done by king or parliament? The House of Commons had always been jealous over Money Bills, and now this inherently confrontational problem got out of hand and created a full-blown constitutional crisis. In December 1753 Stone wrote to Newcastle that 'The constitutional dependency upon England is the object upon which the prime sergeant's [Anthony

Malone, **1336**] eye is constantly fixed. The Speaker is dragged unwillingly by him; but the Speaker is a hardened man, and will do many things contrary to his inclinations and principles, rather than suffer any abatement of power while he can by any means preserve it.'

The Speaker was now over 70 and not averse to retirement should the terms be right, for Boyle was not a wealthy man and he was conscious of the need to make provision for his family. Personalities played a considerable part, as the Primate wished to play a dominant political role in national affairs, and so did Ireland's premier peer, the Earl of Kildare (**0734**), encouraged by his beautiful, clever and well-connected wife. Both the Primate and Kildare were backward-looking: the Primate thought that position, and Kildare thought that birth, should guarantee political influence. Peripheral to these central issues were the desires and ambitions of other politicians, but the Speaker was the central focus. In August 1753 Primate Stone wrote to Newcastle that the Speaker had spent the whole summer in the country. He had been given the king's response to Kildare's memorial and received it with neutral courtesy: 'I believe, he considers that transaction as material either for opposition or accommodation, and is considering to which of the two it will be most advisable to apply it.' The ever-intriguing Primate tried to use Luke Gardiner (**0841**) as a go-between, but Boyle told Gardiner that he required none, to Gardiner's discomfort. On 17 December 1753 the House of Commons rejected the Money Bill.

In January 1754 the first wave of dismissals among Boyle's followers occurred, and, after he had failed to respond, in April 1754 the Speaker was dismissed as Chancellor of the Exchequer. He was replaced by Arthur Hill (**1015**). On 13 May 1754, following the departure of Lord Lieutenant Dorset in April 1754, Speaker Boyle was presented with an address by Sir Samuel Cooke (**0470**) (the MP for Dublin city) accompanied by seven or eight gentlemen, 30 or 40 merchants and 200–300 mob. This address was versified in the doggerel so popular in the eighteenth century; the following is an extract.

I, who was taught to hate the Speaker.
And drink his Downfall o'er each Sneaker.

Was taught to curse the Name of Boyle,
As the Betrayer of our Isle;
And in his Guts would push my Fork,
For meddling with our City, CORKE;
And find how much I was deceiv'd,
And of my Reason quite bereav'd,
For all his Conduct from his Youth,
Demonstrates Honesty and Truth.
In Anna's worst, and latest, Days,
He well deserv'd and had our Praise;
And now our Liberty and Coin
Has sav'd from Them who would purloin.
I think it cannot be deny'd;
That Horace of Him prophecy'd;
When He writ 'Justem et tenacem'
Boyle's very Features! there I trace 'em,
Tho' some among us would deface 'em.

On 25 October 1754 the Primate wrote a long letter to Newcastle setting out his version of the crisis and trying to exculpate himself: 'I had always been on good terms with the Speaker. I used all the observance towards him that is due to a superior, as I did not think that my sudden elevation ought to put me upon a level with a person of his age and dignity I cultivated no friends but those who were, or were willing to be, his, and was cool to those who were not ... [endeavoured to avoid arousing Boyle's jealousy] ... It was in October 1748 that Mr Carter (**0360**) came to me with a very unexpected and abrupt proposal for my assisting in procuring his majesty's appointment of his son (**0361**), at that time a very young man and little known, to succeed him as Master of the Rolls. I declined engaging in it, as thinking it an improper request to be made and improbable to be granted, principally on account of the nature and dignity of the office, which would hardly be allowed to be transferred and handed about as places that are merely lucrative are, without regard being had to the qualifications and experience of the persons who fill them. The Master broke out into the bitterest resentments and set himself from that moment to contrive and execute mischief. I found the Speaker ... by no means dissatisfied with the part I had taken, as it relieved him from some distress; for it was not secret that Mr Malone was destined by him to succeed in that office, it being his favourite object and particularly spoken of in the preceding winter when Mr Carter was dangerously ill. I told the Speaker my apprehensions that Mr Carter would endeavour to destroy the good understanding that subsisted between us. He told me that he was not blind to Mr Carter's faults …'

At this point Stone went to England, and on his return he 'found that the poison was beginning to work … I lost no time in doing all that was in my power to prevent it. I had frequent and free conferences with the Speaker … His manner of talking with other people did not correspond with his professions to me.' This was the state of affairs when Dorset arrived. Stone then describes the Cork election (see 0380), and the mischief of Sir Richard Cox (0508) and his attempts to create trouble between the Speaker and the Ponsonbys (1696, 1702). Anything affecting Cork county or city could be construed as an attack on the Speaker's power base, and this, in fact, was a veiled attack by the Ponsonbys, as Stone well knew, but he continued: 'My Lord Lieutenant, in hopes of preventing differences among the King's servants and with marks of high regard for the Speaker, prevailed upon Mr Cavendish to give up the election before the poll, by which the Speaker's reputation of power was much enlarged and his following increased. The [1751] parliament had not sat many days when a report sprang up at the same moment in all quarters of the town that the Speaker was immediately to retire from business, and everything was settled such as a peerage, a large pension &c. &c.'

In 1755 the Marquess of Hartington (through his dead wife the head of the Boyle family and through the double marriages of his sisters to Lord Duncannon and John Ponsonby, brother-in-law to the two Ponsonby brothers), a great English grandee and soon to be the Duke of Devonshire, was sent over to resolve the crisis; to do so he remained in Ireland from May 1755 to May 1756. Boyle was able to retire from the Chair satisfactorily. He accepted an earldom and a pension of £2,000 for 31 years – similar terms to those offered to the retiring British Speaker. Devonshire wrote to Lady Burlington on 6 March 1756: 'This man's quitting the chair has given a surprising turn to the affairs of this country, and will I think make

my administration very easy and restore the public tranquillity.'

Initially Boyle's resignation was not well received, as it was considered that he had left his friends and the country in the lurch and the mob reaction shows something of the violence of mid-eighteenth-century Irish politics. Anne Ward, in a letter to her husband Michael (2180), relates how on St Patrick's Day 1756 an effigy of the Speaker was placed in a cart and painted black: 'A paper on his breast was wrote in large letters – "He betrayed the city in 1749!" They followed the cart saying he must die … carrying him to the gallows – and when they had hanged him, designed to take Sir Arthur Gore (0859) and put him in the Speaker's chair in the House of Commons. They were forced to have the army to disperse them. The Lord Mayor was in great danger.'

John Ponsonby succeeded him as Speaker and various provisions, not always to their liking, were eventually made for the other *dramatis personae*. On 17 February 1757, Boyle, concerned about his friends, wrote to the Duke of Devonshire: 'Your grace cannot but be sensible that I have been as little troublesome to you in the situation you found me as might have been expected considering my long service in it … my having discharged the trust reposed in me with a proper regard both to his majesty's and the public interest. I am sorry, however … to remind your grace of some of the particular terms upon which I was persuaded to resign the chair.' His friends, Anthony Malone (1336), Charles Gardiner (0840), William Crosbie (0540), Sir Maurice Crosbie (0537) and John Gore (0869), had not received the preferments promised as part of his agreement, and Boyle continued: 'Upon it being, however, represented to me as your grace's earnest desire to have the thing [his resignation] effected, the honour I had for your grace obliged me the more readily to submit to it, upon the repeated and strongest assurances, however, given to me that such of my particular friends as I should recommend to your grace's favour should be served agreeably to that recommendation.'

In 1758 Boyle, now Earl of Shannon, was once again a Lord Justice and he continued to enjoy a prominent position in Irish politics until his death in December 1764, within days of that of his arch-enemy Primate Stone. On his death his eldest son (**0213**) succeeded to the remaining term of his pension and title. Boyle was probably the most successful of the undertakers, for Conolly always had Brodrick (**0237**) at his shoulder. Boyle's power, especially in the 1750s, gives an indication of the degree of self-government that the local Irish politicians had come to exert in the face of the British administration.

DIVISION LISTS:

1713 (2) voted for Anderson Saunders (**1878**) for Chairman of the Committee of Elections and Privileges.
1721 (2) voted against a national bank.
1749 (1) voted against the election of James Digges La Touche (♦♦♦).
1753 (1) voted for the expulsion of Arthur Jones-Nevill (**1125**).
1753 (2) voted against the Money Bill.

ADDITIONAL INFORMATION: In 1710 he gave the site for the established church at Clonakilty. Foundation member of the Dublin Society, 1731, and named in the 1750 charter.

On 14 November 1759 he thanked Lord Lieutenant Bedford for transmitting to the king an address of loyalty from the Catholics of Cork city.

Stone, on 26 April 1748, wrote to Weston giving this picture of Boyle as a father: 'The Speaker has had the misfortune to lose a favourite child by a short and unforeseen illness: and is so much affected by it, that he is not yet able to meet at the places of business.'

ESTATES/RESIDENCE: Castlemartyr, Co. Cork; Henrietta Street, Dublin. He succeeded to the family estates on the death of his elder brother, Roger, in 1707. In 1713 Henry Boyle, MP for Kilmallock's, income was estimated at £1,200. He was entrusted by his brother-in-law, the 3rd Earl of Burlington, with his estates in Counties Cork and Waterford and also acted as head agent to these estates. In 1737 Boyle became patron of Clonakilty by buying the estate on which it stood from Lord Burlington for £17,500 – the estate was worth £1,000 p.a. The daughter and heiress of the 2nd Viscount Shannon, the Countess of Middlesex, died childless in 1763 (in 1729, Richard Boyle, Viscount Shannon had an estimated rental of £2,500). She left her

Co. Cork estate of Shannon Park, Carrigaline, near Cork city, to Shannon, subject only to a life interest that most likely expired *c.* 1778. In 1740 the rental of these lands was £2,300 and by 1820 it had risen to £4,800. In 1674, the Earl of Orrery had been granted a market at Castlemartyr.

SOURCES: NLI LC 747; Wakefield, *Account of Ire.*, vol. 1 p. 250; PRONI T/3411; PRONI D/2707 Shannon Papers; PRONI T/2851/1/9 Darnley Papers; PRONI T/2915/8/39 Bedford Papers; PRONI T/3019/823, 874, 1011 Wilmot Papers; PRONI T/3158/1134, /1149, /1515 Chatsworth Papers; PRONI MIC/465/1 R. Ffolliott, *Biographical Notices, 1756–1827* [*DJ* 29 Dec. 1764 says he was 82 years old when he died]; RCBL T34, Extracts from the Parish Registers of St Andrew's, Dublin; McCracken thesis; GEC *P* [says he was born *c.* 1686]; Burke *PB* (1903) p. 1370; *IMC King's Inns Admissions; Alum. Oxon.* [says died 27 Sept. – error for Dec.]; J. H. Bernard (ed.), *The Register of St Patrick, Dublin, 1677–1800* (Parish Register Society of Dublin, 1907) pp. 50, 52, 73 [says bur. 31 Nov. (?Dec.) 1764]; G. F. Russell-Barker and A. H. Stenning (eds), *Record of Old Westminsters: A Biographical List*, 2 vols (London, 1928); *Boulter Letters* vol. 2 pp. 76–8; *HMC Sackville I* pp. 167, 209, 239–43; R. E. Burns, *Irish Parliamentary Politics in the Eighteenth Century*, 2 vols (Washington, 1989) vol. 1 pp. 238–9; P. McNally, *Parties, Patriots & Undertakers* (Dublin, 1997), p. 107; S. J. Conolly, *Religion, Law and Power* (1992), pp. 93, 96–7, 109; *The Universal Advertiser*, 20 Jan. 1754; *IHS* vol. 18 (1973), A. P. W. Malcomson, 'The Newtown Act: Revision and Reconstruction'; T. Bartlett and D. W. Hayton (eds), *Penal Era and Golden Age* (Belfast, 1979), pp.48–54, D. W. Hayton, 'The Beginnings of the Undertaker System', and also pp. 55–87 esp. p. 55, D. O'Donovan, 'The Money Bill Dispute'; *EHR* (July 1905) pp. 516, 530, C. L. Falkiner (ed.), 'Correspondence of Archbishop Stone and the Duke of Newcastle'; Irish Official Papers in Great Britain vol. 1 pp. 45, 50 et seq.; J. T. Gilbert, *Dublin* (Dublin, 1859), vol. 3 pp. 99, 103; E. Hewitt (ed.), *Lord Shannon's Letters to his Son* (PRONI 1982), p. xxiii; *JRSAI* vol. 48 (1918) p. 57, H. F. Berry, 'The Merchant Tailors' Gild – That of St John the Baptist, Dublin, 1418–1841'; *JRSAI* vol. 82 (1952) p. 15, M. Quane, 'Midleton School: Co. Cork'; Berry *RDS* pp. 24–7, 76–7; *Almanacks; The Dublin Gazette* 25 Mar. 1729, 15 Apr. 1740 [reported that his son aged 9 and dau. aged 6 had died in Henrietta Street of smallpox]; *BNL* 29 Jan. 1754; Parliamentary Lists, 1713 (1), 1713 (2).

0211 BOYLE, Rt Hon. Henry

MP for Clonakilty 1793–7; Co. Cork 1797–1800 [r. Rathcormack 1797]; [UK] Co. Cork 1801–7 [r. Bandon and Youghal 1807]

b. 8 Aug 1771; d. 22 Apr. 1842
HONOURS: Knight of St Patrick 29 June 1809; PC, sworn 19 Sept. 1809.
PEERAGES: Styled Viscount Boyle 1771–1807; suc. as 3rd Earl of Shannon, 2nd Baron Carleton [GB] 1807.
FAMILY/BACKGROUND: Son and heir of Rt Hon. Richard Boyle, 2nd Earl of Shannon (0213), and Catherine, dau. of Rt Hon. John Ponsonby (1702).
MARRIED: [7 June 1798] Sarah (d. 6 Sept. 1820), 4th dau. of John Hyde of Castle Hyde, Co. Cork (1064).
CHILDREN: Richard, 4th Earl of Shannon, m. [1832] Emily Henrietta, dau. of Lord George Seymour; Henry Charles, m. [1841] Catherine Sophronia Jane, dau. of James Ede of Hampshire; Capt. Robert Francis RN, m. [1858] Elizabeth, o. dau. of Capt. W. Hole RN; Catherine (d. 8 Jan. 1767); Sarah (d. unmar. 15 May 1885); Louisa Grace (d. 1852); Jane (d. Mar.1876); Elizabeth (b. 1813; d. 19 Jan. 1886); Charlotte Anne (b. 1819; d. 31 Oct. 1894).
EDUCATION: School: Winchester 1785–8; continental tour.
CAREER/OCCUPATION: One of the Lords Commissioners of the Treasury in the Court of Exchequer 1795; Clerk of the Pells 1806–22; Custos Rot. Co. Cork 1807–42.
MILITARY: Aide-de-camp Extraordinary to the Lord Lieutenant 1796–7; Captain of Yeomanry 1796; Captain in Timokilly Cavalry 1796.

POLITICAL ACTIVITY: He sat in the Irish parliament as a young man and was very much under the kindly guidance of his father, Richard, 2nd Earl of Shannon (0213). He was a government supporter and voted for the Union in 1799 and 1800. Like his father he was a pillar of the Established Church and against Catholic Emancipation.

DIVISION LISTS:
1799 (1) voted for the Union.
1800 (1) voted for the Union.

ADDITIONAL INFORMATION: A member of Daly's Club, Dublin.

Before the Union he was one of his father's 11 MPs who supported government. *Lord Shannon's*

Letters to His Son is, as its title suggests, only one side of the correspondence, but the letters give a very pleasant picture of mutual affection and confidence as well as a political commentary over the period covering the 1798 rebellion. There is a rather charming vignette of family life in when his father warns him that 'If a post is missed your mother will think something horrid has happened', and on the eve of his marriage in 1798 he wrote: 'I hope you will escape the chicken-pox but don't hold out if you find any symptom of the attack.'

The 3rd Earl continued to support government in the Imperial parliament, but was not a good attender, although he sat on the Irish Finance Committees of 1805 and 1806. He voted, on 14 May 1805, against Catholic relief. His father's support of government was generous, and Boyle often complained of too little in return. As a reward, after his father's death Boyle was made Knight of St Patrick and an Irish Privy Counsellor. However, in 1817 he quarrelled with government over Cork politics and forfeited extensive patronage by going over to opposition.

ESTATES/RESIDENCE: Castlemartyr, Co. Cork.

SOURCES: PRONI D/2707 Shannon Papers; PRONI D/607/E/142 Downshire Papers; Jupp thesis; GEC *P*; Burke *PB* (1903) p. 1370 (1906) p. 1474; *HP 1790–1820*; *Index to Irish Privy Counsellors, 1711–1910*; E. Hewitt (ed.), *Lord Shannon's Letters to his Son* (PRONI 1982); Cork MPs; *Almanacks*, *FJ* 20 Oct. 1796, 26 Aug. 1798, 9 Mar. 1799; *DJ* 21 June 1798; Parliamentary Lists, 1794 (2), 1799 (2), (3), 1800 (3).

0212 BOYLE, Richard

MP for Old Leighlin 1695–9

b. 1655; d. (bur. 24) Nov. 1711
FAMILY/BACKGROUND: Son of Richard Boyle, Bp of Leighlin and Ferns, and Abigail, dau. of [ ] Worth.
MARRIED: (1) Anne, dau. of Valentine Savage; (2) Rebecca, dau. of Sir Daniel Bellingham, 1st Bt.
CHILDREN: (1) Mary, m. Richard Tisdall (2079). (2) Bellingham; Richard.
EDUCATION: School: Mr Jones, Kilkenny; entered TCD 17 Dec. 1672, aged 17 years.

CAREER/OCCUPATION: Military: Entered Regiment of Foot Guards Mar. 1674; Ensign to Captain John Boteter in the Irish Foot Guards April 1678 (left army as an Ensign before 1685); ?Major of Horse (and Cornet of Troop) in the Duke of Ormonde's Troop of Guards, 1 Feb. 1696.

POLITICAL ACTIVITY: A soldier, he sat in the second parliament of William III. He supported Lord Chancellor Porter against accusations of favouring Catholics in 1695, and signed the Association for the protection of William III in the country in 1696. In 1697–8 he was nominated one of the Commissioners for Co. Carlow for raising a tax of £12,000.

ESTATES/RESIDENCE: Co. Kilkenny.

SOURCES: PRONI T/559 Burke, extract pedigrees, vol. 2 p. 132; Burke *Ext. P* (1844) p. 600; *Cal. SP Dom. 1696* (London, 1913) p. 33; Carlow MPs; *Alum. Dub.*; Simms' cards; Vicars, *Prerog. Wills*; C. Dalton (ed.), *English Army Lists and Commission Registers, 1661–1714* (London, 1896), vol. 3 p. 132 [says Richard Boyle, Captain in Colonel Robert Byerley's Regiment of Horse 1 Mar. 1690, Captain 10 Mar. 1692, Major 1 Aug. 1697]; C. Dalton (ed.), *Irish Army Lists 1661–85* (London, 1907), pp. 109, 117; *Ir. Gen.* vol.6 no 6 (Nov. 1985) pp. 814–23, R. Refausse, 'The Welply Will Abstracts in the Representative Church Body Library, Dublin'; *JRSAI* vol. 76 (1946) p. 134, W. E. J. Dobbs, 'A Supplement to the Entrance Register of Kilkenny School: 1684–1800'; *Kildare Arch. Soc. Jn.* vol. 13 (1946–63) p. 199, A. Mac Lochlainn, 'Rex v. Crossly'; Parliamentary Lists, 1695 (1), 1696 (1).

0213 BOYLE, Rt Hon. Richard

MP for Dungarvan 1749–60; Co. Cork 1761–4 [r. Clonakilty 1761]

b. 30 Jan. 1728; d. 20 May 1807
HONOURS: PC, sworn 19 Sept. 1763–70, removed 7 May 1770, resworn 19 Dec. 1774–89, 1793–1807, [GB] 9 Jan. 1782; Knight of St Patrick Mar. 1783.
PEERAGES: Suc. as 2nd Earl of Shannon 1764; cr. Baron Carleton [GB] 6 Aug. 1786.
FAMILY/BACKGROUND: Eldest son of Rt Hon. Henry Boyle, 1st Earl of Shannon (0210), and his second wife Henrietta, dau. of Rt Hon. Charles Boyle, 3rd Earl of Cork and 2nd Earl of Burlington.

MARRIED: [15 Dec. 1763] Catherine, dau. of Rt Hon. John Ponsonby (1702).
CHILDREN: Son (b. 6 Feb. 1767; d. Mar. 1767); Rt Hon. Henry, 3rd Earl of Shannon (0211); Catherine Henrietta, m. Francis Bernard, 1st Earl of Bandon (0126).
EDUCATION: School: Mr Johnson; entered TCD 13 Oct. 1744, BA 1748.
CAREER/OCCUPATION: Vice Treasurer 1781–9 at £3,600 p.a., 1793–1804; Lord Commissioner of the Treasury, patent 25 Dec. 1793–1800 (f); *Trustee of the Linen Board 1749–1800 (f.); *Commissioner of the Tillage Act for Munster 1752–85; Deputy Governor of Co. Cork *c*. 1763, Governor 1765–89, Joint Governor 1790–1, Custos Rot. 1760–1807 (patent, 10 Nov. 1760, 11 Dec. 1760); Freedom of Cork and Kinsale; *Governor of Erasmus Smith's Schools and other Charities 1764–97; *Governor of the Royal Hospital, Kilmainham 1764–81; *Governor of the Hibernian Society 1770–1800 (f.); *Governor of the Charitable Loan Society 1778–1800 (f.); *Governor of the Charitable Musical Society 1780; *Governor of the Foundling Hospital and Workhouse 1785–97.
MILITARY: Colonel Commandant of the Royal Irish Regiment of Artillery; *Colonel-in-Chief of the Artillery Regiment 1766–70; Muster Master General 1766–70, (patent 15 Dec. 1774–81); Clerk of the Cheque of the Armies, Nov. 1774–81; Colonel of the True Blue Legion (Cork Co. and City) Volunteers *c*. 1778.

POLITICAL ACTIVITY: Boyle sat in parliament for 15 years, and was listed for no fewer than 62 committees between 1749 and 1757. During the Money Bill crisis of the early 1750s he gave his father, the Speaker (0210), a solid support from the floor of the House. In 1752 he moved the resolution that Arthur Jones-Nevill (1125) had not complied with the resolutions of the House and had acted in manifest contempt of its authority. Until his father's death in 1764 he was guided by him, and it was as 2nd Earl of Shannon that Boyle's real political significance emerged. From 1764 to the Union he was a dominant force in Irish politics.

In 1768 he, along with John Ponsonby (1702) and John Hely-Hutchinson (1001), opposed the augmentation of the army. In January 1770, in an analysis of the House of Commons, Richard Jackson (1076) wrote to Robert Wilmot that Lord Shannon was one of the 'present great powers!'.

Securing a majority for government usually required an alliance with Lord Shannon or other main interests. In 1782, for instance, Lord Lieutenant Temple (Buckingham) wrote to Lord Shannon asking for his support for his administration. After 1771, although the government was the chief business manager, it could only operate with the support of sufficient great borough proprietors to secure its majority.

He had a reputation for being a correct and honourable patron and, probably for these reasons, he kept his party together. Lord Shannon's power encouraged many MPs to seek his protection and patronage. When James Dennis (0613) wished to succeed Chief Baron Foster as Chief Baron of the Exchequer, Lord Lieutenant Buckingham(shire) wrote to Lord Weymouth that 'His also being a most particular friend of Lord Shannon's adds weight to his pretensions.' Dennis was appointed in July 1777. In February 1789 Lord Lieutenant Buckingham told Grenville that a complaint was made to the Castle by Lord Shannon of 'the want of sufficient power and patronage. He declared that he thought well of Mr Pitt, but that he did not care who was Lord Lieutenant unless the principles were admitted upon which alone he could support government, namely that he should always have the nomination of one bishop, one judge, and one commissioner of the Revenue, besides office for himself, inferior office for his dependents, and the whole patronage of the county and city of Cork.'

Shannon's parliamentary power was multifaceted. In 1777 a contemporary observer divided Lord Shannon's party into three, five MPs being 'under his absolute domination', a further six the same but in receipt of government places and pensions, and six 'quite independent but followed him anyway'. The rest of his interest was shored up by a plethora of small, and not so small, positions. In 1782 his following was said to comprise himself as 'Vice Treasurer [£3,600] and has a pension [from his father] of £2,000 p.a. His Members and influence as follows: Lord Lisle (1294); Lord Carrick (0316); Lord Doneraile (0026) – in the House of Peers. Richard Townsend (2100); Hon. Jas Lysaght (1292); Thos Adderley (0009); Sir Riggs Falkiner (0719); Attiwell Wood (2250);

James Uniacke (2121); Robert Uniacke (2122); the two Mr Jephsons (1087, 1091) and Colonel Pigott (1683); Colonel Southwell (1967); Mr Evans (0708); Mr Hunt (1055). Mr Townsend Jr (2101) and the two Mr St Legers (1856, 1860) are attached to his Lordship and he brings in his nephew Captain Boyle (0214) for Tallow, one of the Duke of Devonshire's Boroughs. A sensible and firm man. Married to a daughter of Mr Ponsonby (1702) but they do not consult or act together politically. Mr Pierce Butler (0325), Lord Carrick's brother, generally votes with his Lordship, and Mr Butler (0322) of the Castle of Kilkenny is inclined to him.'

At the time of Boyle's marriage to Catherine Ponsonby, the Chief Secretary, W. G. Hamilton (0948) wrote on 10 November 1763 to Sir Robert Wilmot that 'The state of the parties in this county is much changed by the marriage of Ponsonby's daughter with Lord Boyle. Their intention is to engross the whole county to themselves, and to annihilate the Primate. The county has taken the alarm at the union of these two powers.' The Boyle–Ponsonby rivalry had come to a head in the Money Bill dispute of 1753; the marriage took place a decade later and a further decade after that Speaker Ponsonby had lost his position and much of his influence. Dr Malcomson points out that 'The most that Lord Shannon's marriage achieved, and could reasonably have been expected to achieve, was to make for greater harmony between the Irish representatives of Lord Burlington in their enforced co-existence on the Burlington power base.' The Ponsonbys never succeeded in wresting control of that power base from Lord Shannon and their influence with the Devonshires, the ultimate heirs of the Burlington inheritance, declined politically after the death of the 4th Duke. His heir was a minor and does not appear to have been particularly interested in his Irish inheritance and, as John Ponsonby and his sons were more indignant at their loss of power than energetic to regain it, Lord Shannon continued to control the delegated Burlington/Devonshire influence in Co. Cork.

Shannon was independent as, although connected with the Ponsonbys, he tended to support government unless it would cause too much family discord, as at the time of the Regency Crisis in 1789 and at the election of the Speaker in 1785 and 1790, when his wife wanted him to support her brother. 'I always dread his wife's influence,' wrote Lord Lieutenant Buckingham to his brother in 1788, 'which in the struggle for the Chair [1785], turned him against Government.' Certainly Lord Shannon placed a high value on his domestic tranquillity, as in consequence of his stand over the Regency Crisis he lost his lucrative office of Vice-Treasurer, £3,600 p.a. However, when he reverted to his usual government support he became a Lord of the Treasury in 1793. On his retirement from the Treasury in 1804 he received a pension of £3,000 p.a.

Lord Shannon's political influence was largely exercised as a great borough proprietor, but while this borough control was the actual basis of his power he exerted considerable personal power and influence, both intrinsic to himself and as the resident representative of the Boyle family in Co. Cork. At the Union he received £37,500 in compensation for Clonakilty, Castlemartyr and half of Charleville; apart from this there was his influence in Cork city and county. The great borough proprietors held their parties together by the patronage they could manage to obtain for their followers from the government, and Lord Shannon was no exception.

Despite the preponderance of the Boyle interest, Cork, a large and prosperous county, contained a multiplicity of interests great and small. In 1785 it was reported that 'The leading interests are those of Lord Shannon; Lord Doneraile; Lord Riversdale (**1051**); Lord Kingsborough (**1167**); Mr Bernard (**0126**); Mr Townsend (**2099**); Mr Longfield (**1263**) [and] Sir J. Freke (**0821**).' Although the Ponsonbys' political interest was mainly in Co. Kilkenny, John Ponsonby had a large estate in Co. Cork and there were a number of minor interests such as Mrs Jeffreyes of Blarney Castle, Sir John Conway Colthurst (one of the unsuccessful candidates for Co Cork in 1783), the Jephsons of Mallow, the Uniackes of Mount Uniacke and the Hydes of Castle Hyde. In 1783 there was a revolt against Lord Shannon's interest, with the result that 'Mr Bernard and Lord Kingsborough who have both very large properties are the Members

and oppose.' The election, which was fought in very unsettled political times, was a particularly violent one and noted for the number of duels it provoked among the supporters of the various parties.

In 1784 Lord Shannon married his only daughter to Francis Bernard, a marriage he may later have regretted as Bernard was far from being a considerate husband. In 1798 he furthered his Cork connections by marrying his eldest son to Sarah Hyde. In fact this network of Co. Cork alliances – Lord Shannon's mother was Henrietta Boyle, a daughter of Lord Burlington; his wife a daughter of John Ponsonby; his son-in-law a Bernard; and his daughter-in-law a Hyde – was indicative of the family alliances that occurred in many counties. Shortly after the Bernard marriage it was noted that 'The county is growing quiet.' Eventually Lord Shannon was instrumental in obtaining a peerage for his son-in-law. Lord Shannon also had interest in Cork city, the constituency of the Provost, John Hely-Hutchinson (**1001**), and it is thought that a mutual interest in Freemasonry may have cemented an alliance. Cork city too was divided by factions: in 1783 Richard Longfield was elected on the popular and independent interest only to be declared not duly elected and his place was taken by the banker, Augustus Warren (**2187**), whose wife, Mary, was a sister of Francis Bernard.

Lord Shannon had a rigid concept of what his honour and his position required of him. Despite his financial problems, particularly after 1787 when he failed to get his father's £2,000 p.a. pension extended, he never sold his seats and was apparently punctilious in his discharge of the trust he enjoyed as the representative of the Burlington/Devonshire interest. He spent much of his time at Castlemartyr, which was not rebuilt after the extravagant fashion of many Irish landowners. Lord Shannon is a good example of how the patronage system worked even after the Castle resumed its control of patronage. He was probably the most Irish-oriented of the great borough proprietors: most of the others, such as the Duke of Leinster (**0745**), Conolly (**0459**) and the Ponsonbys (**1699, 1709**), were clearly attached to British 'parties' but, in 1791, the Marquess of

Abercorn was advised that if the English opposition should prevail over the present administration and any schism arise in the new government, then 'Lord Shannon would not know whom to resort, and would be jealous of his coadjutors.'

DIVISION LISTS:

1749 (1) voted against the election of James Digges La Touche (♦♦♦♦).
1753 (1) voted for the expulsion of Arthur Jones-Nevill (**1125**).
1753 (2) voted against the Money Bill – eldest son of the Speaker.

ADDITIONAL INFORMATION: A member of the Royal Dublin Society, incorporated in 1750, from 1753. A lifelong member and leading light of the Hanover Society of Youghal. *A subscriber to the Public Assembly Rooms, 1788.

ESTATES/RESIDENCE: Castlemartyr, Co. Cork. He inherited the remaining term of his father's pension of £2,000, granted in 1756 for 31 years, and John Ponsonby estimated that this would give him an income of near £7,000 p.a. However, Speaker Boyle's peerage etc. had probably outstripped his family's means to support it. The pension finished in 1787 and was not renewed, although Shannon had other lucrative offices. The only major planned addition to his patrimony, the purchase of Clonakilty in c. 1738, was not paid for until 1800 – out of the compensation paid to Shannon for the disfranchisement of Clonakilty and other boroughs at the Union. In 1791 Shannon's total landed income (Shannon Park included) was just over £6,000. However, Wakefield estimated, probably inaccurately, that in the first decade of the nineteenth century Lord Shannon had a rental of more than £20,000. Young praised Lord Shannon as an improving landlord and Wakefield deplored the state of the Shannon estates.

SOURCES: PRONI T/3019/6459/735, /745, /775, /809 Wilmot Papers; NLI MS 13057 Heron Papers; PRONI D/2707, D/2707/B (provisional) Shannon Papers [rentals 1740 and 1820]; Wakefield, *Account of Ire.*, vol. 1 p. 278; Young, *Tour in Ire.*, vol. 1 p. 320–31; McCracken thesis; GEC *P*; Burke *PB* (1903) p. 1370; *Index to Irish Privy Counsellors, 1711–1910*; Hughes: *Patentee Officers*; McNevin, *Volunteers*; HMC Fortescue *I* p. 383, 421; E. Hewitt (ed.), *Lord Shannon's Letters to his Son* (PRONI 1982) esp. p. xxxvii; J. T. Gilbert, *History of the City of Dublin*, 3 vols (1861) vol. 3 p. 101; Johnston, *Gt B. & Ire.*, pp. 20, 260–62, 281, 288–9; *Ir. Gen.* vol. 6 no 5 (1984) pp. 608, 613, H. F. Morris, 'Finn's Leinster Journal 1676'; *Ir. Sword* vol. 11 no 42

(summer 1973), pp. 32–8; Forde, 'The Royal Irish Artillery, 1755–1801'; *Almanacks*; *BNL* 8 June 1753; *DJ* Jan. 12–16 1782; Parliamentary Lists, 1775 (1), 1776 (1), 1777 (1), 1780 (1), 1782 (1), 1783 (2), 1784 (1), (3), 1785 (1), (2), (4), 1787 (1), 1788 (1), 1790 (1), 1791 (1), 1793 (1), 1794 (2), 1798 (1), 1799 (1), (2), 1800 (2).

0214 BOYLE, Richard O'Brien

MP for Tallow 1782–3 (elected unanimously *vice* Nicholas Lysaght (**1296**) dec'd)

b. 1762; d. 13 Oct. 1788
FAMILY/BACKGROUND: Only son and heir of Hon. Robert Boyle (Boyle-Walsingham) (**0217**) and Charlotte, dau. and co-h. of Sir Charles Hanbury-Williams.
MARRIED: Unmarried.
CAREER/OCCUPATION: Military: Cornet in the 10th Dragoons 1779; appointed aide-de-camp (extraordinary) to Lord Lieutenant 1780; Lieutenant in 13th Dragoons.

POLITICAL ACTIVITY: He was aide-de-camp to Lord Carlisle, the Duke of Portland and Lord Temple and a nephew of Lord Shannon who brought him in for Tallow, without a contest on the Duke of Devonshire's interest, following the death of Nicholas Lysaght (**1296**) on 27 February 1782. Lord Shannon did not bring him in again in 1783 He was an improvident young man (he ran up very considerable gaming debts) with a not very robust constitution. He spent the winter of 1785–6 in France for his health, accompanied by Captain John Colpoys, a friend of his late father.

ADDITIONAL INFORMATION: He was a nominee in the life annuities of 1779.

ESTATES/RESIDENCE: Castlemartyr, Co. Cork.

SOURCES: PRONI D/2707 Shannon Papers; Ellis thesis; Burke *PB* (1906) p. 1474; *GM* Oct. 1788; E. Hewitt (ed.), *Lord Shannon's Letters to his Son* (PRONI 1982), p. xvi; *Ir. Gen.* vol. 1 no 8 (1940) p. 238, 'A List of Irish Stockholders, 1770'; *DJ* 21–3 Oct. 1788; Parliamentary Lists, 1776 (1), 1782 (1), 1783 (1).

0215 BOYLE, William

MP for Charleville 1715–25

> b. *c.* 1678; d. [Oct.] 1725
> FAMILY/BACKGROUND: Son of Henry Boyle (**0207**) and Mary, dau. of Rt Hon. Murrough O'Brien, 1st Earl of Inchiquin.
> MARRIED: Martha Beaufoy, dau. and h. of Sir Samuel Garth.
> CHILDREN: Henry; Robert; Beaufoy, m. [11 June 1736] John Wilder of Berkshire; Henrietta, m. [9 Dec. 1736] William Nichols of Buckinghamshire; Elizabeth, m. [9 Oct. 1736] Matthew Graves.
> CAREER/OCCUPATION: Revenue Appeals Commissioner 14 July 1716.
> MILITARY: Cornet of Duke of Schomberg's Regiment of Horse 1 May 1694; Lieutenant 24 Feb. 1708; Brevet Captain 6 Apr. 1708; fought at Oudenarde (1708) and Malplaquet (1709); Lieutenant-Colonel of Dormer's Dragoons 21 Dec. 1717; out of the Regiment 1 Dec. 1720.

POLITICAL ACTIVITY: A professional soldier and a younger brother of Speaker Boyle, he was a government supporter and a placeman. Boyle was nominated to 20 committees between 1716 and 1725.

DIVISION LISTS:

> 1721 (1) voted for a national bank.
> 1721 (2) voted for/against a national bank (in both 'for' and 'against' columns).

ESTATES/RESIDENCE: Castlemartyr, Co. Cork.

SOURCES: NLI Private Collections no 393, Shannon Papers; Burke *PB* (1903) p. 1370 (1906) p. 1473; Hughes *Pat. Officers*; C. Dalton (ed.), *English Army Lists and Commission Registers, 1661–1714* (London, 1898), vol. 4 p. 12; C. Dalton, *George the First's Army, 1714–27*; Parliamentary List, 1719 (1).

0216 BOYLE-WALSINGHAM, Hon. Henry

MP for Tallow 1751–6

> b. *c.* 1729–30; d. 27 Mar. 1756
> FAMILY/BACKGROUND: Son of Rt Hon. Henry Boyle, 1st Earl of Shannon (**0210**), and his second wife Henrietta, dau. of Rt Hon. Charles Boyle, 3rd Earl of Cork and 2nd Earl of Burlington; he assumed the additional name of Walsingham.
> MARRIED: Lucia, dau. of John Martin of Dublin (she married (2) Rt Hon. James Agar, 1st Viscount Clifden (**0016**)).
> CHILDREN: Henry.
> CAREER/OCCUPATION: Freedom of Cork 14 July 1752.
> MILITARY: Captain in Lord George Sackville's Regiment of Horse 3 June 1752; aide-de-camp to the Lord Lieutenant (Hartington/Devonshire) 1753–5.

POLITICAL ACTIVITY: He was a professional soldier and followed his father's politics in parliament. He was nominated to 11 committees between 1751 and 1755.

DIVISION LISTS:

> 1753 (1) voted for the expulsion of Arthur Jones-Nevill (**1125**).
> 1753 (2) against the Money Bill – second son of the Speaker, Captain of a Troop of Horse and aide-de-camp to the Lord Lieutenant.
> 1753 (3) Captain in Bligh's horse [1753 (2)].

ESTATES/RESIDENCE: Dublin. Estates in Norfolk.

SOURCES: PRONI D/2707 Shannon Papers; McCracken thesis; *GM* Apr. 1756 [says he died on 3 Apr.]; E. Hewitt (ed.), *Lord Shannon's Letters to his Son* (PRONI 1982), p. xviii; *Almanacks*; *BNL* 22 June 1753 [his son was born June 1753].

0217 BOYLE-WALSINGHAM, Hon. Robert

MP for Dungarvan 1758–60, 1761–8; [GB] Knaresborough 1758–61, 1768–79; Fowey 1761–8

> b. Mar. 1736; d. Oct. 1779
> FAMILY/BACKGROUND: Fifth son of Rt Hon. Henry Boyle, 1st Earl of Shannon (**0210**), and his second wife Henrietta, dau. of Rt Hon. Charles Boyle, 3rd Earl of Cork and 2nd Earl of Burlington; he assumed the additional name of Walsingham in 1756, on the death of his brother.
> MARRIED: [17 July 1759] Charlotte, o. surviving dau. and co-h. of Sir Charles Hanbury-Williams.
> CHILDREN: Richard O'Brien (**0214**); Charlotte, Baroness de Ros, m. Lord Henry FitzGerald (**0733**).

CAREER/OCCUPATION: Military: Lieutenant RN 1756; Commander Feb. 1757; Captain June 1757; aide-de-camp to the Lords Justices, May 1758; Commander of HMS *Thunderer* in West Indies 1779, where he perished in a hurricane with all his crew.

POLITICAL ACTIVITY: A professional sailor. Returned without a contest for Dungarvan in 1761. He followed his father's political lead in Ireland, where he was nominated for one committee in 1760. He was also an English MP and his wife's connections ensured that his main political career would be in England, where he followed the lead of the Cavendish family – Knaresborough was part of the inheritance of Lady Charlotte Boyle, Marchioness of Hartington.

DIVISION LISTS:
1768 (1) absent, in England.

ADDITIONAL INFORMATION: He was the person to whom Lord Sandwich turned when his mistress had been murdered, writing: 'My dear Walsingham, For God's sake come to me immediately, in this moment I have much want of the comfort of a real friend. Poor Miss Ray was inhumanly murdered last night as she was stepping into her coach at the playhouse door. I am ever yours, Sandwich.' For some months after his ship was lost, it was hoped that Boyle-Walsingham had somehow escaped shipwreck.

ESTATES/RESIDENCE: Castlemartyr, Co. Cork; Gainsborough, Lincolnshire.

SOURCES: PRONI D/2707 Shannon Papers; McCracken thesis; *HP 1715–54*; Burke *P* (1939) p. 2217; *Ir. Gen.* vol. 6 no 1 (1980) p. 27, H. F. Morris, 'The Waterford Herald 1791'; *BNL* 19 May 1758; *DJ* 25–8 Apr. 1761.

BOYNE, Viscount: *see* **HAMILTON**
0924 Hamilton, Rt Hon. Gustavus, 1st Baron Hamilton, Viscount Boyne, MP Co. Donegal 1692–3, 1695–9, 1703–13, Strabane 1713–14

0218 BOYSE, James

MP for Bannow 1715–24

b. ?*c.* 1660; d. (May) 1724
FAMILY/BACKGROUND: Son of Nathaniel Boyse of Saint Johns, Co. Wexford, and Magdalen [   ].
MARRIED: ?
CHILDREN: ?*d.s.p.*
CAREER/OCCUPATION: Sheriff of Co. Wexford 1720.
MILITARY: Captain in Lord Mountjoy's Regiment; apparently still in the army in 1717.

POLITICAL ACTIVITY: A professional soldier. Very little is known about this man: he was nominated for only two committees, in December 1717 and September 1723.

DIVISION LISTS:
1721 (1) voted against a national bank.

ESTATES/RESIDENCE: Dublin; Ballydusker, Polrain, Talbotstown, Ballyraine, Graige, Grange, Ballydurry, Little Assilly and Ballough Island, Co. Wexford. He willed his property to his sister Patience Vicary and three nephews, Samuel, James (Jacob) and Nathaniel Boyse.

SOURCES: PRONI T.559 v.2 p.145, Burke, extract pedigrees; Burke, *LGI* (1904) p.59; Simms' cards; Eustace, *Abstract of Wills* v.1 no. 305.

0219 BOYSE, Nathaniel

MP for Bannow 1692–3, 1695–9, 1703–13–14

b. *c.* 1656; d. 1714
FAMILY/BACKGROUND: Son of Nathaniel Boyse of Saint Johns, Co. Wexford, and Magdalen [   ].
MARRIED: Frances, dau. of Samuel Helsham of Kilkenny.
CHILDREN: Nathaniel, m. Elizabeth, dau. of Richard Rowe of Co. Wexford; Samuel (**0220**); Jacob; Frances, m. [1736] Nathaniel Radford of Co. Wexford; Anne, m. Thomas Cooke.
EDUCATION: Entered Oxford, BA 1673, MA 1676.

POLITICAL ACTIVITY: Probably an older brother of James Boyse (**0218**), but again very little is known of him despite the fact that he had a much more active parliamentary career, although he appears to have been listed for only two committees, in January 1699 and October 1703. In 1695 he supported Lord Chancellor Porter against accusations of favouring Catholics, and in 1696 he signed the Association for the protection of William III in parliament. In Queen Anne's reign he attended Ormonde's birthday celebrations in 1706, but was noted as being in opposition, as he continued to be in 1711. In 1713 he was marked as definitely a Whig and 'likely to be returned again for Bannow', which he was. He voted for Alan Brodrick (**0237**) as Speaker against the Court candidate, Sir Richard Levinge (**1230**). He died in 1714 and his brother James was returned for Bannow at the next election.

DIVISION LISTS:
     1713 (1) voted against Sir Richard Levinge (**1230**) for Speaker.

ESTATES/RESIDENCE: Cullenstown, Bannow, Co. Wexford. Purchased 245 acres in Co. Wexford and 581 acres in King's County from the Commissioners for sale of Forfeited Estates in 1702–3.

SOURCES: PRONI T/559 vol. 2 p. 145, Burke, extract pedigrees; Burke *LGI* (1904) p. 59; Simms' cards; Simms, *Williamite Confiscation*, p. 183; Parliamentary Lists, 1695 (1), 1696 (1), 1706 (1), (2), 1711 (3), 1713 (1), (2).

0220 BOYSE, Samuel

MP for Bannow 1725–7–30

     b. (bapt. 2 Feb.) 1697; d. 1 Apr. 1730 as a result of a duel
FAMILY/BACKGROUND: Son of Nathaniel Boyse (**0219**) and Frances, dau. of Samuel Helsham of Kilkenny.
MARRIED: Anne, dau. of Thomas Cooke.
CHILDREN: Thomas, m. Margaret, dau. of Edmund Jackson of Co. Kilkenny; Frances; Elizabeth; Anne.
EDUCATION: School: Dr Drury, Dublin; entered TCD 18 Oct. 1711.

POLITICAL ACTIVITY: He succeeded his uncle as MP for Bannow but was in parliament for a very short time. The cause of the duel that led to his untimely demise is unknown.

ADDITIONAL INFORMATION: *The Dublin Gazette*, 4 April 1730, reported that 'We hear from Water-

ford that Samuel Boyse ... was lately wounded in a duel and lies dangerously ill.'

ESTATES/RESIDENCE: Cullenstown, Co. Wexford. The family obtained a grant of Bannow under the Act of Settlement.

SOURCES: PRONI T/559, Burke, extract pedigrees, vol. 2 p. 145; McCracken thesis; *Ir. Gen.* vol. 7 no 2 (1987) p. 219, A. Dusek, 'Baptisms in St Bride's, Dublin, 1633–1713'; *The Dublin Gazette*, 20 Sept. 1729, 4 Apr. 1730; J. Kelly *'That Damn'd Thing Called Honour': Duelling in Ireland 1570–1860* (Cork, 1995) pp. 51–2.

0221 BRABAZON, Hon. Anthony

MP for Co. Wicklow 1745–60; Co. Dublin 1761–8–72

     b. Feb. 1722; d. 4 Jan. 1790 at Kilrothery, Co. Wicklow
PEERAGES: Styled Lord [Brabazon] Ardee 1763–72; suc. as 8th Earl of Meath 1772.
FAMILY/BACKGROUND: Eldest son of Hon. Edward Brabazon, 7th Earl of Meath (**0224**), and Martha, dau. of Rev. Samuel Collins of Warwickshire.
MARRIED: [20 May 1758] Grace, dau. of John Leigh of Rosegarland, Co. Wexford (**1220**).
CHILDREN: e. son (d. Jan. 1780 at Bath, bur. in family vault, St Catherine's, Dublin, 29 Jan. 1780); William, 9th Earl of Meath (**0226**); Rt Hon. John Chambre, 10th Earl of Meath, m. Melosina Adelaide, dau. of John Meade, 1st Earl of Clanwilliam (**1388**); Mary (d. 1851), m. [23 June 1781] Arthur Knox of Co. Mayo; Martha, m. Maurice Bagenal St Leger Keating (**1135**); Juliana (b. 1848); Cecilia (d. 1849); Catherine (d. 24 Dec. 1847), m. [6 Aug. 1799] Rev. Francis Brownlow; Arabella Barbara, m. [1803] Rev. John Scott; Grace.
EDUCATION: School: Dr Fullen; entered TCD 12 Nov. 1740, BA 1744.
CAREER/OCCUPATION: Revenue Commissioner 1747; *Trustee of the Linen Board for Leinster 1756–89; Freeman of Fethard (Tipperary) 1764; Custos Rot. Co. Dublin and Co. Wicklow 1772–d.

POLITICAL ACTIVITY: When he first came into parliament in 1745 it was as MP for Co. Wicklow, and during the rest of this parliament he supported the government. He was nominated to 14 committees between 1752 and 1760. However, in 1761 he was returned for Co. Dublin and thereafter he was in opposition. He supported Speaker Ponsonby (**1702**) during the augmentation crisis although his father, the Earl of Meath, lost his pension of £500 in consequence of his son's opposition. In addition the earl was struck off the Privy Council. The Dublin Liberty of the Earl of Meath was part of the Meath estates, 'and yet he must study to please these people as the Domvils will be ever on the watch to out him, who have a great interest in this Co. These are the mob of Dublin and their representative must please them. Always oppose Government. Against.'

In 1772 Lord Brabazon succeeded his father as 8th Earl of Meath, but opposed Lord Harcourt because he refused to make him Governor of both Co. Dublin and Co. Wicklow. He had also a 'good estate' in Co. Wicklow for which his brother (**0225**) was returned. He and his brother, who was attached to Mr Ponsonby, went into violent opposition. In 1782 he was described as 'a plain, honest, country nobleman [who] has generally opposed'. It was inevitable that he would be 'much influenced by popular interests', as many of his voters were in the Liberty which had a reputation for violence and mob rule. Nevertheless, even the opposition press referred to 'the honest and incorruptible Earl of Meath', suggesting that for this reason on the elevation of Luke Gardiner (**0842**) to the peerage in 1789 Lord Meath's heir, Lord Ardee (**0226**), would be elected unopposed; however, Ardee's time in parliament was short as his father died within the year. Despite its surprisingly small electorate, many interests competed for Dublin county. In 1785 the chief interests were listed as: 'the archbishop of Dublin, Lord Meath, Lord Howth, Colonel Talbot, Lord Carhampton, Mr Domvile (**0647**), Mr Gardiner (**0842**), Sir Edward Newenham (**1535**), Sir Stratford Tynte and Mr Deane (**0605**)'. At this time the chief interests elected Luke Gardiner and the popular party the noted duellist, Sir Edward Newenham.

DIVISION LISTS:
1749 (1) voted against the election of James Digges La Touche (♦♦♦♦).
1753 (1) voted against the expulsion of Arthur Jones-Nevill (**1125**).

1753 (2) voted for the Money Bill.
1768 (1) voted against army augmentation.
1771 (1) voted against Lord Townshend as Lord Lieutenant.
1771 (2) voted for Sir Lucius O'Brien's (**1558**) motion.
1772 (2) voted for a Short Revenue Bill.

ADDITIONAL INFORMATION: *A member of the Royal Dublin Society from 1766; *a subscriber to the Public Assembly Rooms, 1788. According to his obituary: 'In an age when Libertinism and infidelity but too often mark the manners of the great, he was not ashamed to confess himself a Christian.'

ESTATES/RESIDENCE: Tara, Co. Meath; Kilrothery, Co. Wicklow.

SOURCES: RCBL P45/2/3, Parish Registers of St Peter's, Dublin; McCracken thesis; Burke *PB* (1903) p. 1036; GEC *P*; *GM* (Jan. 1790); *Ir. Gen.* vol. 4, no 4 (1971) p. 318, W. G. Skehan, 'Extracts from the Minutes of the Corporation of Fethard, Co. Tipperary'; *The Dublin Courant*, 5 May 1747; *DJ* 23–6 Aug. 1760, 5–7 Jan 1790; Parliamentary Lists, 1769 (1), 1772 (2), 1773 (1), 1775 (1), 1777 (1), 1782 (1), 1785 (2), 1787 (1), 1788 (1), 1790 (1).

0222 BRABAZON, Rt Hon. Chambre

MP for Co. Dublin 1692–3

b. *c.* 1645; d. 1 Apr. 1715
HONOURS: PC appointed 1710, re-appointed 30 Sept. 1714 but not sworn before his death.
PEERAGES: Suc. as 5th Earl of Meath 1708.
FAMILY/BACKGROUND: Son of Rt Hon. Edward Brabazon, 2nd Earl of Meath, and Mary, dau. of Calcot Chambre of Denbigh, Wales, and Co. Wicklow.
MARRIED: [c. 1682] Juliana, o. dau. and h. of Patrick Chaworth, 3rd Viscount Chaworth.
CHILDREN: Rt Hon. Chaworth, 6th Earl of Meath (**0223**); Edward, 7th Earl of Meath (**0224**); Juliana; Mary, m. Rev. William Tisdall; Catherine, m. T. Hallowes of Bethick Hall, Derbyshire; Frances, m. Brig.-Gen. Henry Ponsonby (**1701**).
EDUCATION: Entered TCD 10 Oct. 1667.
CAREER/OCCUPATION: Paymaster 1675; Custos Rot. Dublin 1709.

MILITARY: Captain of the Horse, Aug. 1677; on 22 Mar. 1689 he appears on a list of Protestant officers lately in the army of Ireland but now unemployed and in England seeking employment in His Majesty's service.

POLITICAL ACTIVITY: The 5th, 6th, 7th, 8th and 9th Earls of Meath all represented Co. Dublin during the century. Occasionally the family also represented Co. Wicklow. The 5th Earl was a professional soldier. There is no evidence of his activity in the House of Commons, and he was probably on active service during the very short duration of this parliament.

ESTATES/RESIDENCE: Tara, Co. Meath; Kilrothery, Co. Wicklow. In 1671 the then Lord Meath was granted a market 'within liberties of Thomas Court or Donore', Dublin and in 1674 he was granted a market at Bray.

SOURCES: GEC *P*; Burke *PB* (1903) p. 1036; *Index to Irish Privy Counsellors, 1711–1910*; H. Wood (ed.), *The Register of St Catherine, Dublin, 1636–1715* (Parish Register Society of Dublin, 1908) p. 5 [says his dau. is called Maria]; C. Dalton (ed.), *English Army Lists and Commission Registers, 1661–1714* (London, 1896), vol. 3 p. 13; C. Dalton (ed.), *Irish Army Lists 1661–1685* (London, 1907), pp. 114, 116 [says (incorrectly) he is the second son of the 3rd Earl of Meath, suc. as 5th Earl in 1707 – three sons, William, Edward and Chambre succeeded the 2nd Earl].

for Munster 1739–d.; *Commissioner of the Tillage Act for Leinster 1739–d.; Governors of Counties Dublin and Wicklow 1747–d.

POLITICAL ACTIVITY: He was MP for Co. Dublin in the last parliament of Queen Anne, which was called on 25 November 1713 and dissolved by the queen's death on 1 August 1714. Its only session, which was stormy, lasted less than a month, from 25 November to 24 December 1713. During this time he was listed for five committees. Before the next parliament had met he had succeeded his father as 6th Earl of Meath.

ADDITIONAL INFORMATION: According to Mrs Delany he was 'a man of good sense and great fortune': about a month after the death of his first wife he 'married Miss Prendergrass, sister to Sir Thos Prendergrass: he has been in love with her for several years; she has little or no fortune, and is far from handsome'.

ESTATES/RESIDENCE: Tara, Co. Meath; Dublin city; Bray, Co. Wicklow. In 1738 Lord Meath mortgaged the manors of Donore and Thomas Court for £8,000.

Lord Brabazon, MP for Co. Dublin's, income was calculated in 1713 at £6,000 – the largest amount mentioned in that source. Succeeded by his only brother, Edward (**0224**).

SOURCES: PRONI T/3411; GEC *P*; Burke *PB* (1903) p. 1036; *Index to Irish Privy Counsellors, 1711–1910*; Llandover, *Delany Corr.*, vol. 1 p. 330; *Almanacks*.

0223 BRABAZON, Rt Hon. Chaworth

MP for Co. Dublin 1713–14

b. 1686; d. 14 May 1763
HONOURS: PC (sworn 23 Jan. 1716, 19 June 1727), 1733–64 (sworn 24 June 1761).
PEERAGES: Styled Lord Brabazon 1707–15; suc. as 6th Earl of Meath 1715.
FAMILY/BACKGROUND: Son of Rt Hon. Chambre Brabazon, 5th Earl of Meath (**0222**), and Juliana, dau. and h. of Patrick Chaworth, 3rd Viscount Chaworth.
MARRIED: (1) [when quite young] his aunt's chambermaid (with whom he never lived); (2) [13 Dec. 1731] Juliana, dau. of Sir Thomas Prendergast, 1st Bt (**1724**).
CHILDREN: *d.s.p.*
CAREER/OCCUPATION: *Governor of the Workhouse 1733–6; Commissioner of Oyer and Terminer 1733–53; *Trustee of the Linen Board

0224 BRABAZON, Hon. Edward

MP for Co. Dublin 1715–27–60

b. (bapt. 24 Nov.) 1691; d. 24 Nov. 1772
PEERAGES: Suc. as 7th Earl of Meath 1763.
FAMILY/BACKGROUND: Son of Rt Hon. Chambre Brabazon, 5th Earl of Meath (**0222**), and Juliana, o. dau. and h. of Patrick Chaworth, 3rd Viscount Chaworth.
MARRIED: [1720] Martha (d. 24 Apr. 1762), dau. of Rev. Samuel Collins of Warwickshire.
CHILDREN: Anthony, 8th Earl of Meath (**0221**); William (**0225**).
CAREER/OCCUPATION: *Commissioner of Oyer and Terminer 1732–53; *Governor of the Foundling Hospital and Workhouse 1743–d.; elected to the Court of Assistants June 1766–9; *Governor of

Cos Dublin and Wicklow 1764–d.; Custos Rot. *Co. Meath 1764–7, Co. Dublin 1765–71, Co. Wicklow 1763–d.; Free Burgess of New Ross 30 Sept. 1732.

POLITICAL ACTIVITY: He was not a particularly active parliamentarian, being listed for two committees in the 1715–27 parliament of George I and only nine in the 1727–60 parliament of George II. In the early 1720s he was an opponent of the national bank and subscribed to the declaration of the high sheriffs, justices of the peace, Grand Jury, nobility, clergy, gentlemen and freeholders of Co. Dublin against Wood's Halfpence. By 1738 his brother, Lord Meath (0223), appears to have been in some financial difficulties as he mortgaged his manors of Donore and Thomas Court, and on 26 July 1742 Edward Brabazon was given a pension of £300 p.a. This ensured his support for the government during the 1749 Dublin election, the Arthur Jones-Nevill (1125) affair and the Money Bill crisis of the early 1750s.

DIVISION LISTS:

1721 (1) voted against a national bank.
1721 (2) voted against a national bank.
1749 (1) voted against the election of James Digges La Touche (♦♦♦♦).
1753 (1) voted against the expulsion of Arthur Jones-Nevill (1125) – pensioner.
1753 (2) voted for the Money Bill.
1753 (3) a placeman [1753 (2)].

ESTATES/RESIDENCE: Tara, Co. Meath.

SOURCES: NLI reps no 319; PRONI T/3019/844 Wilmot Papers; F. G. James, *Lords of the Ascendency* (1995), n. 20; McCracken thesis; GEC *P*; Burke *PB* (1903) p. 1036; *Index to Hibernian Chronicle, 1769–75* (Society of Genealogists, 1936) vol. I p. 61; *JRSAI* vol. 21 (1892) p. 299, P. D. Vigors, 'Alphabetical List of Free Burgesses of New Ross, 1658–1839'; *Almanacks*; *BNL* 20 Feb. 1767; *The Dublin Gazette* 14 Oct. 1724.

0225 BRABAZON, Hon. William

MP for Co. Wicklow 1765–8–76–83

b. Aug. 1723; d. (*ante* 9) Dec. 1790 at Bath, bur. 3 Jan. 1791 in St Catherine's Church, Dublin
FAMILY/BACKGROUND: Second son of Hon. Edward Brabazon, 7th Earl of Meath (0224), and Martha, dau. of Rev. William Collins of Warwickshire.
MARRIED: [10 May 1764] Catherine (d. 11 Feb. 1833), dau. and h. of Arthur Gifford of Aghern, Co. Cork (her dowry was £20,000).
CHILDREN: Edward, m. [ ] Tuke (*d.s.p.*); Arthur Gifford (b. 16 June 1768; *d.s.p.*1817), m. [20 Jan. 1788] Margaret, e. dau. of John Haig MD; Martha (d. yg); Barbara, m. [24 May 1788] John Moore of New Lodge, Hertfordshire.
EDUCATION: School: Dr Fullen; entered TCD 12 Nov. 1740, aged 15 years, BA 1744; Lincoln's Inn 7 Aug. 1745.
CAREER/OCCUPATION: High Sheriff of Co. Louth 1751; Freeman of Fethard (Tipperary) 1764; *Governor of the Workhouse 1764–68; Foundling Hospital and Workhouse 1769–d.

POLITICAL ACTIVITY: Returned on the family's interest for Co. Wicklow. The family acted together, and the 1773 Parliamentary List declared that 'He will always go with Lord Brabazon (0221) his elder brother who, to secure the votes of the weavers of the liberty, always is in opposition to Government.' Their position in Co. Dublin virtually compelled them to vote with the opposition, and his voting pattern bears this out. They supported Speaker Ponsonby over the augmentation crisis and their father, Lord Meath (0224), lost his pension because of it. However, his friendship with Ponsonby was personal and he 'can scarcely be considered under the influence of the person to whom he is classed unless to effect some point personal to himself, then he becomes united but not otherwise'. He was hostile to the removal of the Customs House, which had long outgrown its position. He was thought to be influenced by the Marquess of Rockingham and Lord Aldborough, two other Wicklow interests, but his politics appear to have been entirely family-oriented. Although his re-election was considered probable, he declined to stand in 1783.

DIVISION LISTS:

1768 (1) voted against army augmentation.
1771 (1) voted against Lord Townshend as Lord Lieutenant.
1771 (2) voted for Sir Lucius O'Brien's (1558) motion for retrenchment.
1772 (2) voted for a Short Revenue Bill.
1773 (1) voted against Absentee Tax.

1774 (2) voted against Catholic relief.

1775 (1) voted for the pro-American amendment to the Speech from the Throne.

1777 (2) voted against the Trade Embargo.

1778 (1) voted for Grattan's (**0895**) motion for retrenchment.

1780 (2) voted for Yelverton's (**2268**) motion to modify Poynings' Law.

1780 (3) voted for the Tenantry Bill.

1780 (4) voted against the Perpetual Mutiny Bill.

1780 (5) voted for the duty on imported sugar.

ADDITIONAL INFORMATION: A member of the Royal Dublin Society from 1767.

ESTATES/RESIDENCE: Tara House, Co. Meath; Dublin city; Bray, Co. Wicklow; [?]Willville, Co. Louth.

SOURCES: PRONI D/302; PRONI MIC/465/1 R. Ffolliott, Biographical Notices, 1756–1827; RCBL P45/2/3, Parish Registers of St Peter's, Dublin; Ellis thesis; *WHM* (1790) p. 568; GEC *P*; *Lincoln's Inn Records* vol. 1 p. 430; Johnston, *Gt B. & Ire.*, p. 151; *Ir. Gen.* vol. 4, no 4 (1971) p. 318, W. G. Skehan, 'Extracts from the Minutes of the Corporation of Fethard, Co. Tipperary'; *Almanacks*; *The Dublin Weekly Journal* 9 Mar. 1751; *FJ* 8–13 May 1764; *DJ* 9–11 Dec. 1790; *BNL* 7–11 Jan. 1791; Parliamentary Lists, 1769 (1), 1772 (2), 1773 (1), (2), 1774 (1), 1775 (1), 1776 (1), (2), 1777 (1), 1778 (1), 1780 (1), 1782 (1), 1783 (1).

0226 BRABAZON, Hon. William

MP for Co. Dublin 1789–90

b. 6 July 1769; d. 26 May 1797 of a wound received in a duel with Mr Gore

PEERAGES: Styled Lord Ardee 1789–90; suc. as 9th Earl of Meath 4 Jan.1790.

FAMILY/BACKGROUND: Son and h. of Hon. Anthony Brabazon, 8th Earl of Meath (**0221**), and Grace, dau. of John Leigh (**1220**).

MARRIED: Unmarried.

CAREER/OCCUPATION: Custos Rot. Co. Wicklow 1793–7.

POLITICAL ACTIVITY: Parliament was in recession for the brief period that he was an MP. He was killed in 1797 as a result of one of the more spectacular duels of the century.

ADDITIONAL INFORMATION: Succeeded by his brother, John Chambre Brabazon.

ESTATES/RESIDENCE: Tara, Co. Meath; Dublin city; Bray, Co. Wicklow. According to Wakefield, Lord Meath's leases were 'in general' for 21 years and 1 life. Lord Meath said that land near Bray, and nearer to Dublin, let for 'enormous rents', probably because of its seaside proximity to Dublin.

SOURCES: Wakefield, *Account of Ire.*, pp. i, 284; RCBL P45/2/3, Parish Registers of St Peter's, Dublin [bapt. 6 July 1769]; GEC *P*; Burke *PB* (1903) p. 1036; *GM* (1797); J. Kelly, *'That Damn'd Thing Called Honour': Duelling in Ireland 1570–1860*, pp. 209, 239–40; Parliamentary List, 1790 (1).

0227 BRADSTREET, Sir Samuel

MP for Dublin B. 1776–83–4

b. Oct. 1738; d. 2 May 1791 (suddenly) at Booterstown, bur. 6 May

HONOURS: Suc. bro. as 3rd Bt 1773.

FAMILY/BACKGROUND: Son of Sir Simon Bradstreet, 1st Bt, and Anne, dau. of Sir Henry Cavendish (**0380**).

MARRIED: [19 Jan. 1771] Elizabeth (d. 25 Dec. 1799), o. dau. and h. of James Tully MD of Dublin.

CHILDREN: Simon (b. 25 Nov.1772; d. 25 Oct.1853), 4th Bt, m. [1808] Clare Margaret, dau. of John Murphy of Dublin; Samuel James; Edmond; John (d. Dec.1831); Eleanor, m. William Wynne (**2267**).

EDUCATION: School: Mr Ball, Dublin; entered TCD 1752; Middle Temple 1753; called to the Irish Bar 1758.

CAREER/OCCUPATION: Recorder of Dublin City 14 July 1766–84; King's Council 1767; Commissioner of the Great Seal; 4th Justice of the King's Bench 13 Jan. 1784–8; 3rd Justice of the King's Bench 1790–1; Justice of Assize for Leinster Lent and Summer 1784, Connaught Lent 1785, Leinster Summer 1785, Munster and Connaught Lent 1786, Munster Lent 1787, Leinster Lent 1788, Connaught Summer 1788, Leinster Lent 1789, Connaught Summer 1789, Leinster Lent 1790, Munster Summer 1790; *listed in Judges and Barristers 1789–90; *Governor of the Foundling Hospital and Workhouse 1766–8, 1769–83; elected to the Court of Assistants June 1766–9; *Governor of the Blue-Coat Hospital 1766–d.; *Governor of Erasmus Smith's Schools and other Charities 1766–83; *Governor and Guardian of the Lying-in Hospital 1767–84; *Governor of the Hibernian Society 1769–83; *Hibernian Marine Society 1775–81; *Commissioner for Paving the Streets of Dublin 1778–80; *Governor of the Charitable Loan Society 1778–83; *Governor of the Charitable Musical Society 1780; *Company of Undertakers of the Grand Canal 1783.

POLITICAL ACTIVITY: In the 1776 election, Sir Samuel, Recorder of Dublin, was returned for Dublin without opposition. In 1777 he was described in a government list as 'Independent and a Patriot. Against.' In 1783 he was listed as 'an able lawyer. His object is the Bench. Was much privately connected with Mr Eden (0681), whom he supported as much as was in his power and opposed the Duke of Portland, dividing with Mr Flood (0762). Will probably be re-elected. Is re-elected.' The Attorney General, John Fitzgibbon (0749), in his correspondence with Orde (1594), referred to him as 'slippery Sam'. His political behaviour was motivated by the necessity of keeping his electors satisfied (the Dublin electorate was one of the largest in the country, estimated at 4,000) and his personal ambition to be elevated to the bench – this he achieved in 1784. He was described as 'in character decisive and firm, in manner rough and in stature enormous'.

DIVISION LISTS:

1777 (1) voted for Grattan's (0895) motion for retrenchment.
1777 (2) voted against the Trade Embargo.
1778 (1) voted for Grattan's motion for retrenchment.
1778 (2) voted for the Popery Bill.
1779 (2) voted for a six-months Loan Bill.
1780 (2) voted for Yelverton's (2268) motion to modify Poynings' Law.
1780 (3) voted for the Tenantry Bill.
1784 (3) teller against Foster's (0805) Bill to regulate the press.

ADDITIONAL INFORMATION: Freedom of the Guild of Merchants, October 1766.

ESTATES/RESIDENCE: Stacumny, Co. Kildare; Merrion Street, Dublin; Booterstown, Co. Dublin. He may also have had lands in Co. Longford.

SOURCES: RCBLP45/2/3, Parish Registers of St Peter's, Dublin; Ellis thesis; GEC B; Burke PB (1903) p. 190; DNB; Ball, Judges; Keane, Phair and Sadleir, King's Inns Admissions; Ir. Gen. vol. 5 no 6 (1979) p. 752, H. F. Morris, 'Ramsey's Waterford Chronicle, 1786–1791' [calls him Broadstreet]; PRONI Devonshire MSS, 18 Aug. 1758, Bessborough to Devonshire; Almanacks; BNL 21 Oct. 1766; FJ 6–9 Mar., 8–10 July 1784, 10–12 Feb., 12–14 July 1785, 9–11 Mar. 1786, 3–6 Mar. 1787, 9–12 Feb. 1788, 12–14 June 1788, 26–8 Feb. 1789, 2–4 July 1789, 2–4 Mar. 1790, 1–3 July 1790, 10–12 Mar. 1791; DJ 26–8 Oct. 1779, 3–6 May 1791; GM May 1791; Parliamentary Lists, 1776 (1), (2), (3), 1777 (1), 1778 (1), 1780 (1), 1783 (1), (2).

0228 BRAGG, Philip

MP for Armagh B. 1749–59

b. 1684; d. 6 June 1759
FAMILY/BACKGROUND: Son of [   ] Bragg.
MARRIED: ?Unmarried.
CHILDREN: d.s.p.
CAREER/OCCUPATION: Ranger Phoenix Park; Freedom of Drogheda 24 Mar. 1732, of Cork 11 Mar. 1744; *Governor of the Workhouse 1734–5; *Alderman of Dublin 1733; *Governor of the Royal Hospital, Kilmainham 1733, 1743–d.
MILITARY: Ensign in 1st Foot Guards 10 Nov. 1702; Captain in Primrose's Regiment; Lieutenant-Colonel of Colonel Robert Hargreave's Regiment (31st Foot); aide-de-camp to Duke of Dorset 1731, 1734–5, Lord Cornwallis 1733, 1736–7; Master of Kilmainham hospital 12 June 1732; suc. Major-General Price as Colonel of 28th Foot 10 Oct. 1734; Lieutenant-Colonel 1735; Colonel of a Regiment of Foot 1737–56; Lieutenant-Colonel of a Regiment of Guards 1744–60; Major-General 1744–7; Brigadier-General 1747; Lieutenant-General 1748–60; Lieutenant-General as Brigadier-General 1751, as Major General 1753–9; appointed to the staff in Ireland 1751. Bragg had fought in Europe during the War of the Austrian Succession, but after Fontenoy was ordered home to assist in putting down the 1745 Jacobite rebellion. He was a Lieutenant-General at the time of his death.

POLITICAL ACTIVITY: He was a friend and drinking companion of Primate Stone, who returned him for the borough of Armagh. He helped Stone taste the wines for Lord Lieutenant Dorset in May 1751. As a member of the Castle inner circle he voted for the administration. He was listed for 24 committees between 1749 and his death in 1759.

DIVISION LISTS:

1749 (1) voted against the election of James Digges La Touche (♦♦♦♦).
1753 (1) voted against the expulsion of Arthur Jones-Nevill (**1125**) – Major-General on the Establishment and Colonel of a Regiment of Foot.
1753 (2) voted for the Money Bill.
1753 (3) a placeman.

ADDITIONAL INFORMATION: He left the bulk of his fortune, estimated at about £4,000, to Lord George Sackville (**1835**), who had served under him as lieutenant-colonel of the 28th Foot, Dublin.

ESTATES/RESIDENCE: Dublin, [?]Henry Street.

SOURCES: PRONI T/1584 Pinkerton Transcripts, p. 51, 15 June 1759; McCracken thesis; *Irish Official Papers in Great Britain*, vol. 1 p. 45; *HMC Stopford-Sackville* p. 171; *BNL* 15 June 1759; *GM* June 1759; L. Marlow, *Sackville of Drayton* (1948), pp. 39, 64, 83, 87; *Almanacks*.

BRANDEN, Baron: *see* **CROSBIE**

0537 Crosbie, Sir Maurice, 1st Baron Branden, MP Co. Kerry 1713–14, 1715–27–58
0540 Crosbie, Rt Hon. William, 2nd Baron Branden, 1st Viscount Crosbie, Earl of Glandore, MP Ardfert 1735–60, 1761–2
0534 Crosbie, Rt Hon. John, styled Viscount Crosbie 1776–81, 2nd Earl of Glandore, MP Athboy 1775–6, Ardfert 1776–81

0229 BRASIER, Kilner

MP for Dundalk 1695–9; St Johnstown (Donegal) 1703–13; Kilmallock 1715–25

b. *c.* 1659–64; d. 1725
FAMILY/BACKGROUND: Son of Paul Brasier of Coleraine, Co. Londonderry, and Sarah, dau. of Sir Tristram Beresford, 1st Bt (she married (2)

Edward Cary).
MARRIED: Anne, dau. of Sir Henry Brooke (**0248**).
CHILDREN: Kilner, m. (1) Anne, dau. of Henry Vaughan, (2) Elizabeth dau. of Very Rev. Charles Massey; Lieut. (of Foot) Henry; Anne.
EDUCATION: LLD *hon. caus.* TCD 1709.
CAREER/OCCUPATION: Military: Captain in Viscount Mountjoy's Regiment of Foot 1685; Major in Sir Robert Peyton's Regiment of Foot 10 June 1689, present at siege of Londonderry, Apr.–July 1689; Lieutenant-Colonel 16 Feb. 1694; Colonel in Gustavus Hamilton's Regiment 1708.

POLITICAL ACTIVITY: A professional soldier, he was listed for two committees in 1697 and three between 1703 and 1707 when he was probably on active service, as between 1715 and 1721 he was nominated for 12. His political attitude was more that of a country gentleman than that of a soldier. In 1695 he voted for the accusations against Lord Chancellor Porter of leniency to Catholics, and the following year signed the Association for the protection of William III in the country. During Queen Anne's reign he was noted as in opposition in both 1706 and 1711. He supported government after the accession of George I.

On 12 October 1719 he complained of a breach of privilege by John Knox, William O'Sheridan and Turlough MacAllister, who, he alleged, had disturbed his tenants on the lands of Oghterlin, Co. Donegal. On 9 November 1723 he complained of being disturbed in possession of his lands at Creeve-Oghter, Co. Donegal, during time of privilege. He voted for the Court candidate in the Westmeath election petition of 1723, although in 1721 he had been firmly against the establishment of a national bank.

DIVISION LISTS:

1721 (1) voted against a national bank.
1721 (2) voted against a national bank.
1723 (1) voted for the Court candidate on the Westmeath Co. election petition.

ESTATES/RESIDENCE: Ray, Co. Donegal; Rivers, Co. Limerick. On 10 July 1719 Kilner Brasier, senior and junior, petitioned the Commons to be allowed to sell lands in Co. Donegal and settle others, of greater value, in Co. Limerick more contiguous to their estate. In 1719, a private act was passed empowering Kilner Brasier to sell his Donegal estate of Ray, including the lands of

Ballyconnelly, Drumharry, etc., worth £276 a year, because of their remoteness from his Limerick/Tipperary estate. By 1709, Kilner Brasier owned the mansion, demesne and lands of Lissard, *alias* Lissard Connell, 300 acres, and also Knockballynallow, Co. Tipperary, 200 acres nearly; between 1709 and 1719 he acquired the lands of Castletray etc. in the county of the city of Limerick, worth £493 a year.

SOURCES: PRONI D/79 [Draft act, 1719]; PRONI T/559 Burke, extract pedigrees, vol. 2 p. 270; Hayton thesis; *CJ Ire.* (Bradley ed.) vol. 4 pp. 511, 648, vol. 5 p. 166; *Cal. SP Dom.* 1694–5 (London, 1906) pp. 30, 119; Burke *LGI* (1904) p. 60; Simms' cards; *Alum. Dub.*; C. Dalton (ed.), *English Army Lists and Commission Registers, 1661–1714* (London, 1896), vol. 3 pp. 65, 371; C. Dalton (ed.), *Irish Army Lists 1661–85* (London, 1907) p. 151; T. H. Mullin, *Coleraine in by-gone centuries* (Belfast, 1976) p. 150; Parliamentary Lists, 1695 (1), 1696 (1), 1706 (1), 1711 (3).

0230 BRAY, Robert

MP for Lanesborough 1715–27 [n.d.e.1727]

b. 1675; d. 1747
FAMILY/BACKGROUND: Son of Edmund Bray of Dublin.
MARRIED: [23 Aug. 1698] Jane Parker of Dublin.
CHILDREN: Zechariah.
EDUCATION: School: Mr Gordon, Dublin; entered TCD 9 July 1688, aged 13 years, LLB 1693; called to the Irish Bar 1703; LLD 1719.

POLITICAL ACTIVITY: Virtually nothing is known about this MP, who was listed for 12 committees between 1715 and 1723. He was declared not duly elected for Lanesborough in 1727.

DIVISION LISTS:
1721 [1] voted against a national bank.

ESTATES/RESIDENCE: Portanure, Longford, Co. Limerick.

SOURCES: PRONI T/559 Burke, extract pedigrees, vol. 2 p. 266; *Alum. Dub.*; Vicars, *Prerog. Wills*; *IMC King's Inns Admissions*; Eustace, *Abstracts of Wills*, *The Register of the Parish of St Peter and St Kevin, 1669–1761* (Parish Register Society of Dublin, 1911) p. 234; *Ir. Gen.* vol. 7 no 2 (1987) p. 223, A. Dusek, 'Baptisms in St Bride's, Dublin, 1633–1713'.

0231 BREWSTER, Sir Francis

MP for Tuam 1692–3, 1695–9; Doneraile 1703–5

b. *ante* 1642; d. 1705
HONOURS: Knighted by Charles II 8 July 1670.
FAMILY/BACKGROUND: Son of [ ] Brewster.
MARRIED: (1) [lic. dated 1663] Jane Lane; (2) [lic. dated 1665 and 1667] Ann Cramer; (3) [ ] Fownes (this marriage is uncertain); (4) Hester [ ].
CHILDREN: Lucy; Ann, m. Capt. Longlish; Francis (0232); William, m. Anne [ ]; Lucy, m. Rev. Bland.
CAREER/OCCUPATION: Commissioner for Forfeited Estates appointed by the English parliament in 1698 to investigate the disposal of Irish forfeitures; Alderman of Dublin 1670, 1695, Mayor of Dublin 1674.

POLITICAL ACTIVITY: The borough of Tuam was in the hands of the archbishop at this time, and he returned Brewster for both parliaments of William III. Brewster was a Dublin city politician and merchant/manufacturer. From the outset of the 1692 parliament he was one of the main opposition leaders against Sydney and Court policy. An 'English troublemaker' sent from 'England purposely to obstruct everything', he gave evidence before both English Lords and Commons during their investigation into the state of Ireland, February 1693. He was greatly disliked by the Earl of Nottingham.

He voted against Lord Chancellor Porter, who was accused of favouring Catholics, in 1695; in 1698 he complained of those who 'under the subterfuge of Limerick and Galway etc. have sheltered themselves from common justice and live splendidly and securely on the spoils of ruined Protestants', and as late as 1704 he wrote from Killarney that 'The daily rescues, the insolence of the old proprietors, this whole side of the country sheltering and siding with the Tories at one time by whom they are protected at another.' Brewster had estates in Co. Kerry. Like many MPs of his generation, he was probably of humble origins; some of his contemporaries referred to him as 'the barber's son of Tralee'.

In 1696 he signed the Association for the protection of William III in the country. By 1697 he was obviously trusted by the government, as Lord Chancellor Methuen recommended him to Lord Somers on 6 October 1697 as 'a man who has been very serviceable to the King's government in Ireland' and who could give Somers a clear account of the proceedings in the Irish House of Commons and elsewhere. He was listed for eight committees in 1692 and for 32 in 1695–7.

ADDITIONAL INFORMATION: He was a Master of the Dublin Guild of Merchants, 1670–72, and one of the overseers appointed in 1680 by the parish of St John, Dublin to supervise the rebuilding of the church. In July 1693 he asked to be incorporated into the Company for Improving Iron Works. At the same time he claimed that his iron works and estate in Co. Kerry had been devastated to the cost of £30,000. In 1695 he was still petitioning for forfeited lands as compensation for his losses.

ESTATES/RESIDENCE: Brewsterfield, Co. Kerry; Lower Blind Quay, Dublin. In 1676 the lands of Lassaboy and Ross and other lands in the parish of Killigarrilandes, barony of Trughanacmy, were leased by Sir Francis Brewster to Francis Drew and the owner in the late nineteenth century was a Drew. The lands of Gullada, barony of Glanerought, were let by Francis Brewster, 1699.

SOURCES: NLI CBD 9512 and 9622; NLI EC 817 and 1957; PRONI T/559 Burke, extract pedigrees, vol. 12 p. 4 [says will proved 1740]; PRONI T/618/323 Crossle Papers; *Cal. SP Dom. 1691–2* p. 480, *1693* p. 221, *1694–5* pp. 12, 388, *1695* pp. 136, 209, 215, *1696* pp. 221, 240; *DNB*; *Irish Official Papers in Great Britain* vol. 1 p. 19; J. J. Howard (ed.), *Miscellanea Genealogica et Heraldica*, vol. 2 (1876) p. 130 [says his wife is Ann Cramer]; Simms, *Williamite Confiscation*, pp. 97–100; Simms' cards; S. J. Conolly, *Religion, Law and Power* (1992), pp. 65, 208, 265; *Memorials of the Dead*; Cork MPs; T. Bartlett and D. W. Hayton (eds), *Penal Era and Golden Age* (Belfast, 1979), pp. 11, 14, 25, James I. McGuire, 'The Irish Parliament of 1692'; *JRSAI* vol. 30 (1900) p. 67, H. F. Barry 'The Records of the Dublin Gild of Merchants, Known as the Gild of the Holy Trinity, 1438–1671'; *Cork Hist. Soc. Jn.* vol. 6 second ser. (1900) p. 116, 'Notes and Queries'; Parliamentary Lists, 1695 (1), 1696 (1), 1706 (1).

0232 BREWSTER, Francis

MP for Midleton 1695–9; Dingle 1703–13

b. 1667; d. *post* 1713
FAMILY/BACKGROUND: Son of Sir Francis Brewster (**0231**) and Ann Cramer.
MARRIED: Arabella, dau. of Edward Herbert of Muckross, Co. Kerry.
CHILDREN: Dau., m. Alexander Anderson (she was co-h. with her sis.); Lucy, m. Arthur Herbert of Co. Kerry; Elizabeth, m. Ralph Dore (?Drew).
EDUCATION: School: Mr Torway; entered TCD 13 Aug. 1683, aged 16 years; Middle Temple 13 Nov. 1685.

POLITICAL ACTIVITY: Like his father he was hostile to Lord Chancellor Porter, who was accused of favouring Catholics, in 1695, but for some reason (possibly illness or absence) he did not sign the Association for the protection of William III. In 1706 he was considered a probable supporter of the Court. He was nominated for nine committees between 1695 and 1697 and nine between 1705 and 1710.

ESTATES/RESIDENCE: Brewsterfield, Co. Kerry.

SOURCES: PRONI T/559 Burke, extract pedigrees, vol. 11 p. 4; McCracken thesis; Burke *LG* (1846) p. 5 (S); *Alum. Dub.*; Simms' cards; *Middle Temple Admissions* vol. 1 p. 216; J. J. Howard (ed.), *Miscellanea Genealogica et Heraldica*, vol. 2 (1876) p. 130 [suggests his mother was Ann Cramer]; Parliamentary Lists, 1695 (1), 1696 (1), 1706 (1).

0233 BRICE, Edward

MP for Dungannon 1703–13

b. 1659; d. 11 Aug. 1742
FAMILY/BACKGROUND: Son of Robert Brice JP (b. 1599/1603, d. 1676; a merchant who offered trade tokens in 1671, acquired a fortune and d. in Dublin) of Islandmagee, Co. Antrim, and Elizabeth Stewart (b. 1616, d. 1704) of Ballintoy.
MARRIED: (1) Dorothy (b. 1667), 4th dau. of Arthur Upton (**2124**), and Dorothy Beresford; (2) [1718] Jane, dau. of Richard Dobbs of Castle Dobbs, Co. Antrim, and Mary, dau. of Archibald Stewart of Ballintoy.
CHILDREN: (1) Dorothy, m. [1713] Rt Hon. Henry Maxwell (**1373**).

(2) Edward, m. (1) [1752] Rose, dau. of Alexander Stewart of Co. Armagh, (2) Jane Adair; Mary Elizabeth (d. aged 2).

CAREER/OCCUPATION: Merchant of Belfast from the 1680s; Freeman of Belfast 1680, admitted after serving apprenticeship; Burgess of Belfast 23 Dec. 1697.

MILITARY: Lieutenant-Colonel, and Captain of Upton's Horse raised Co. Antrim 1715; he fled to Scotland during the Jacobite rising and raised a company there.

POLITICAL ACTIVITY: He was a Belfast merchant and listed for 22 committees between 1703 and 1710. In 1706 he was reported to be 'against the Court'. Brice was removed, 29 November 1707, from Belfast Corporation in consequence of the 1704 Test Clause in the 'Act to prevent the further growth of popery'. Furthermore, he was Sovereign of Belfast in 1707 and on 24 June 1707 he was removed from that office as he declined to qualify himself under the Test Act.

A Presbyterian elder of first Rosemary Street congregation, he was one of the trustees of the Lisburn brief in 1710. His sister Mary married Thomas Knox (**1185**), who in 1692 purchased the Dungannon estate 'worth near £1,000 p.a.', and this may explain Brice's return for Dungannon, which in the eighteenth century was a Knox borough. In 1703 Knox was sitting for the other seat.

ADDITIONAL INFORMATION: He gave a set of silver communion cups with Dublin hallmark of 1680 to the congregation at Ballycarry, Co. Antrim, and left money to the Belfast (Rosemary Street) congregation. [?]His son Edward was High Sheriff of Co. Antrim, 1748.

ESTATES/RESIDENCE: Belfast, Kilroot, Co. Antrim; 200-acre farm in Co. Down. There was land in Dunboe leased by (Arthur) Upton held in trust by Brice, *c.* 1696. He was involved with James Anderson and Richard Caddell of Downpatrick in the purchase of lands from the Forfeiture Commissioners 1703, his share being land at Portlaghan, Tullyhermon and Conney Island, Ardglass and Ballynarry, Co. Down. In 1718 he purchased Kilroot, including the mansion house and lands in the baronies of Dunluce and Cary, Co. Antrim, and in the barony of Ards, Co. Down, for consideration of £325 and annuity of £280 from his nephew, Randal Brice, in order to settle them on children of his second marriage.

SOURCES: PRONI D/302; Information from Dr Jean Agnew, UHF [says his grandfather Edward Brice entered Edinburgh University in 1593 and that his father was from Castle Chichester]; PRONI D/501 p. 54; PRONI D/1556/16/7; PRONI T/559 Burke, extract pedigrees, vol. 12 p. 14; PRONI T/3374/1/3 Antiquarian Compilations [confused genealogy, says Colonel Edward Brice died 28 June 1728 (*sic*) at an old age; he lived in Belfast and had a 200-acre farm in Co. Down]; Hayton thesis; Burke *LG* (1846) p. 152; Fermanagh and Tyrone MPs; J. Agnew, *Belfast Merchant Families in the Seventeenth Century* (1996), pp. 212–4 [death, will & family details], 227; McSkimin, *Carrickfergus*; Rev J. and S. G. McConnell, *Fasti of the Irish Presbyterian Church, 1613–1840* (Belfast, 1951), p. 5; Parliamentary List, 1706 (1).

0234 BRICE, Randolph (Randal)

MP for Lisburn 1692–3, 1695–7

b. 1646; d. (*ante* 15) Sept. 1697 aged 51 at Dublin

FAMILY/BACKGROUND: Son of Robert Brice and Elizabeth Stewart of Ballintoy.

MARRIED: [Mar. 1676] Penelope, dau. of Peter Beaghan Sr of Dublin (and sis. and co-h. of Peter Beaghan Jr).

CHILDREN: Edmond (d. yg); Randal (School: Lisburn; entered Cambridge (Trinity College) 16 Oct. 1707, aged 16 years; Middle Temple 10 Mar. 1710 and Inner Temple, London); Thomas; John; William; Penelope, m. [29 Jan. 1699] Charles Ryves; Elizabeth, m. Joshua Wilkins of Bangor, Co. Down.

CAREER/OCCUPATION: High Sheriff of Co. Antrim 21 Jan. 1675, Co. Down 25 Nov. 1675; Freeman of Carrickfergus.

POLITICAL ACTIVITY: A Presbyterian. He was nominated for a committee in 1692 and for 45 committees between 1695 and 1697. In 1695 he voted against Lord Chancellor Porter, who was accused of favouring Catholics, and in the following year he signed the Association for the protection of William III in parliament.

ESTATES/RESIDENCE: Castle Chichester, Islandmagee, Kilcoole, Kilroot, Hillhall and Lisburn, Co. Antrim; Bangor, Co. Down. He claimed a loss of £300 from his estate post-1689.

SOURCES: PRONI D/302; Information from Dr Jean

Agnew, UHF; PRONI T/559 Burke, extract pedigrees, vol. 12 p. 11; PRONI T/932/ 1; PRONI T/3374/1/3 Antiquarian Compilations; Burke *LG* (1846) pp. 151–2; Hughes, *Pat. Officers*; *Alum. Cantab.*; *Memorials of the Dead* [says he died 8 Sept. 1697 aged 51 years]; *Middle Temple Admissions* vol. 1 p. 266; Rev J. and S. G. McConnell, *Fasti of the Irish Presbyterian Church, 1613–1840* (Belfast, 1951), p. 5; *JRSAI* vol. 55 (1925) pp. 37, 43, H. A. S. Upton, 'A List of Governors and Deputy Governors of Counties in Ireland in 1699' [lists him as Deputy Governor of Co. Antrim, but Hughes' *Pat. Officers* does not, and says his wife is sister and co-h. of Peter Beaghan of Dublin]; J. Agnew, *Belfast Merchant Families in the Seventeenth Century* (1996), pp. 213–14; *UJA* vol. 5, p. 232; Parliamentary Lists, 1695 (1), 1696 (1).

0235 BRIDGES, Sir Matthew

MP for Strabane 1692–3

b. 1651; d. 1703, buried at St Matthew's Church, Flanders
HONOURS: Knighted 18 June 1688.
FAMILY/BACKGROUND: Son of Col. Robert Bridges and his wife Mary.
MARRIED: ?Unmarried.
CHILDREN: *d.s.p.*
CAREER/OCCUPATION: High Sheriff of Co. and City of Londonderry 1679.
MILITARY: Constable Culmore Castle 13 Sept. 1684; Captain in Viscount Mountjoy's Regiment of Foot 1685; Lieutenant-Colonel of Colonel Richards' Regiment of Foot 1688; Lieutenant-Colonel commissioned as a Captain in Sir George St George's Regiment of Foot, 1692; Colonel of Regiment of Foot (had been Courthope's, formerly St George's) 1695, present at Namur 1695.

POLITICAL ACTIVITY: He brought the news to Ireland of the birth of James II's son, and was knighted by Tyrconnell in Dublin Castle 'but went immediately after to England without paying any fees at all' (on his knighthood). He must have gone over to King William, as in 1691 he produced 'His Majesty's Commission to him as Governor of Londonderry [?Culmore] and Coleraine and required the usual salary of £200 a year payable to the Governor of Culmore Fort and the acres belonging thereto, respecting which the Society [the Irish Society] determined to consult counsel'.

There is no information about his brief parliamentary appearance. As he was a professional soldier, he may not have been in Ireland throughout the few weeks of the parliament's duration. He appears to have had a knack of keeping out of trouble.

ADDITIONAL INFORMATION: On 14 August 1681 he was godfather to Matthew, the son of Alexander Forester, Clerk of Derry Cathedral. The boy died on 24 November 1681.

ESTATES/RESIDENCE: Finglass, Co. Dublin.

SOURCES: PRONI D/302; PRONI T/618/319(a) Crossle Papers; *Cal. SP Dom., 1691–2* p. 490, *1693* (London, 1903) pp. 6, 52, *1695* p. 135, *1696* pp. 82, 95, 105, 107, 137, 146, 478; Simms' cards; *Memorials of the Dead*; Fermanagh and Tyrone MPs; C. Dalton (ed.), *English Army Lists and Commission Registers, 1661–1714* (London, 1898), vol. 4 p. 84 [says he was knighted by James II in honour of the Prince of Wales' birth as he happened to be at Windsor at that time]; Hughes, *Pat. Officers*; *The Register of Derry Cathedral (S. Columb's), Parish of Templemore, Londonderry, 1642–1703* (Parish Register Society of Dublin, 1910) pp. 251, 371–12; C. Dalton (ed.), *English Army Lists and Commission Registers, 1661–1714* (London, 1894), vol. 2 p. 257; C. Dalton (ed.), *Irish Army Lists 1661–85* (London, 1907), p. 151.

0236 BRISTOW, Rt Hon. William

MP for Lismore 1745–58

b. *c.* 1697–9; d. 18 Mar. 1758
HONOURS: PC, sworn 21 Apr. 1755–d.
FAMILY/BACKGROUND: Son of Robert Bristow of London and Catherine, dau. of Robert Woolley of London.
MARRIED: Unmarried.
EDUCATION: Entered Middle Temple 21 June 1717, LLD *hon. caus.* TCD 11 Feb. 1746.
CAREER/OCCUPATION: 2nd Secretary to Lord Lieutenant Jan. 1745–Nov. 1746; Chief Revenue Commissioner 1747–58 (patent, 3 June 1747); Freedom of Cork 1 Jan. 1746; Freedom of Limerick city and Galway town June 1757.

POLITICAL ACTIVITY: He came over as Second Secretary to Lord Lieutenant Chesterfield and was returned for one of the Burlington/Devonshire boroughs which were usually controlled by

Speaker Boyle (**0210**). However, in 1749 the Bishop of Down referred to Bristow as one of the 'particular friends' of the Primate. His appointment as a Revenue Commissioner was obviously contrary to the Speaker's wishes, as Archbishop Stone wrote to Chief Secretary Weston (**2223**) on 22 May 1747 that 'I am extremely well satisfied with Mr Bristow's being appointed one of our Commissioners. My situation here laid me under an obligation of forwarding recommendations as they were given to me, which I did without a thought of making myself answerable for the propriety ... of them. The truth is that the Speaker's (**0210**) friends think that he has received a blow; and his enemies (of which there are a number though not a majority) are pleased at it.' Stone had just been appointed Primate, and this was possibly one of the opening plays in the Boyle–Stone duel. Bristow was absent, although in town, when the vote was taken on the election of James Digges La Touche (♦♦♦), but on the expulsion of Arthur Jones-Nevill (**1125**) and the Money Bill he voted the straight government line.

In 1750 he and his fellow Commissioners had got caught up in a dispute between the Speaker and the British government over the appointment of the lucrative Collectorship of Cork. The British administration appointed an Englishman, John Love, while the Lords Justices under the influence of Boyle (**0210**) appointed Hugh Dixon (*alias* Dickson) (**0638**), MP for Cork city. At the Speaker's insistence Dixon was reinstated, and Love given a pension of £400, but the dispute appears to have been ongoing when Dixon – who proved a disastrous appointment – died on 14 October 1738. Love was then appointed, but Boyle still resented what he considered to be the infringement of his right to the patronage of the city of Cork, while Sir Richard Cox (**0508**), who had supported the government against Lucas (**1276**) coveted the Collectorship. However, Bristow, and his fellow English (but not the Irish) Commissioners, Frankland and Cavendish (**0380**), supported Love, and pointed out to Lord Lieutenant Harrington that 'We cannot find any precedent in our books for the dismissal of any officer of the revenue under our management except for misbehaviour, or upon his voluntary resignation. As to Mr Love's behaviour, we are so far from having any exception against him that we esteem him to be one of the ablest and best officers in the service, and are of the opinion that it will be hazardous if not hurtful to remove him. As to his voluntary resignation, we ... had, some time ago, the honour of laying before your Excellency a letter from him, earnestly desiring to be continued in the collection of Cork ... we do not apprehend ourselves to be sufficiently authorised to comply with your Excellency's desire [to remove him], having received neither his Majesty's commands nor the direction of the Lords of the Treasury on this occasion ...' Love had turned down a pension of £500 for his compliance.

Bristow was listed for 35 committees between his election in 1745 and his death in 1758. He appears to have been interested in town planning, as in 1757 he advanced the money to widen several of the streets around the Parliament House and elsewhere in Dublin. Parliament later reimbursed this, and under 21 Geo. II, c. 19 (1757) he received £240 for property 'lately added' to Essex Street together with the lawful interest from the time he advanced the same. By the same act he was appointed a Commissioner for Wide Streets.

DIVISION LISTS:

> 1749 (1) absent, in town.
> 1753 (1) voted against the expulsion of Arthur Jones-Nevill (**1125**) – Revenue Commissioner.
> 1753 (2) voted for the Money Bill.

ADDITIONAL INFORMATION: Elected a member of the Royal Dublin Society following the charter, 1750.

ESTATES/RESIDENCE: Dublin.

SOURCES: PRONI T/3019/874 Wilmot Papers; J. Walton, *'The King's Business': Letters on the Administration of Ireland, 1741–61* (NY, 1996) no 76; *Statutes at Large*, 31 Geo. II cap. 19; A. P. W. Malcomson (ed.), *Eighteenth Century Irish Official Papers in Great Britain* (PRONI 1990) pp. 22, 32; McCracken thesis; Hughes, *Pat. Officers*; Gilbert, *History of the City of Dublin*, 3 vols (1861) vol. 2, p. 24–5; *Proc. RIA* vol. 77 C no 1 (1977), J. C. Sainty, 'The Secretariat of the Chief Governors of Ireland, 1690–1800'; R. E. Burns, *Irish Parliamentary Politics in the Eighteenth Century*, 2 vols

(Washington, 1989); *Almanacks*; *Pue's Occurrences* 15 Feb. 1746; *DJ* 4–7 June 1757.

0237 BRODRICK, Rt Hon. Alan

MP for Cork B. 1692–3, 1695–9, 1703–10; Co. Cork 1713–14; [GB] Midhurst 1717–28

b. 1656; d. (bur. 29) Aug. 1728

HONOURS: PC appointed ?1695, 1703, removed 17 July 1711, resworn 14 Oct. 1714, 6 July 1727, 24 Nov. 1727; cr. Bt 1709.

PEERAGES: Cr. Baron Brodrick 13 Apr. 1715, Viscount Midleton 15 Aug. 1717.

FAMILY/BACKGROUND: Second son of Sir St John Brodrick (0240) and Alice, dau. of Randal Clayton, of Co. Cork.

MARRIED: (1) Catherine, dau. of Redmond Barry, of Rathcormack, Co. Cork; (2) [1695] Alice (d. 1703), dau. of Sir Peter Courthorpe Kt of Little Island, Co. Cork; (3) [1 Dec. 1716] Anne (d. 5 Jan. 1747), dau. and h. of Rt Hon. Sir John Trevor (2113), wid. of the Rt Hon. Michael Hill (1019).

CHILDREN: (1) Rt Hon. St John (0242).
(2) Alan, 2nd Viscount Midleton (Cambridge (Clare College) 19 Feb. 1718; Middle Temple 1 Nov. 1721), m. [7 May 1729] Mary, dau. of Algernon Capel, 2nd Earl of Essex; Courthorpe (b. and d. 1700/1); Alice, m. [1736] Rev. John Castleman.

EDUCATION: Inner Temple 7 Jan. 1670; entered Oxford (Magdalen College) 3 May 1672, aged 16 years; Middle Temple; called to the English Bar 1678, to the Irish Bar 10 May 1678.

CAREER/OCCUPATION: 3rd Serjeant 19 Feb. 1690 – c. 9 Nov. 1692; Solicitor General 1695–1704; Speaker of the House of Commons 21 Sept. 1703 – 19 May 1710, 25 Nov. 1713 – 12 Nov. 1715; Attorney General 1707–9; Chief Justice of the Queen's Bench 1709–11; Lord Chancellor 1 Oct. 1714–25 (patent, 11 Oct. 1714); Lord Justice 22 Feb and 26 Nov.1717, 8 Oct.1719, 30 Dec. 1722, 7 Apr. 1724; Recorder of Cork Nov. 1690; Deputy Governor of Co. Cork 1699; Freedom of Dublin 1702; Justice of Assize for NE Ulster Summer 1710, Munster Lent 1711, 1722.

POLITICAL ACTIVITY: Alan Brodrick was one of the most outstanding Irish politicians of the eighteenth century. He was Speaker of the House of Commons in various parliamentary sessions of William III and Anne, and Lord Chancellor for most of the reign of George I. He was also a Lord Justice on five occasions between 1715 and 1724. His power base was in Co. Cork, the most politically represented county in Ireland. It was said that in the early eighteenth century he could influence the return of the entire representation of the county – 26 MPs. During the reign of Queen Anne, Charles Delafaye (0611) from the Castle secretariat referred to his followers as 'Mr Brodrick's party whom we call the Cork Squadron'. He was a convinced Whig and Hanoverian and, following his election as Speaker in 1703, on 5 December 1704 Lord Coningsby wrote to Lord Lieutenant Ormonde that he thought it inexpedient to continue parliament while Brodrick was Speaker. Much of his influence was that exerted by a powerful and charismatic personality.

Brodrick emerged as leader of the opposition to Lord Sydney in 1692. His opposition was grounded in the (subsequently recurring) question of the 'sole right' of the House of Commons to inaugurate Money Bills. This argument was not new in 1692. It had been preceded by such documents as *An Argument delivered by Patrick Darcy Esquire by express order of the Parliament of Ireland, 9 June 1641*, which declared that no statute law was valid in Ireland until it had been enacted by the Irish parliament: a view that was immediately contested by the English parliament (1742 Adventurer's Act, 16 Chas I, c. 33 (Eng.)). The issue was taken up again at the Restoration by the Attorney General, Sir William Domvile. Domvile wrote a disquisition on the subject, and was subsequently the father-in-law of William Molyneux (1425), who in 1698 'reduced the thesis into form and now at last brought it forth into the world' in *The Case of Ireland's Being Bound by Acts of Parliament in England Stated*. The argument was given a legal expression by Brodrick in 1692, by Malone (1336) in 1753 and 1761 and by Flood (0762) in 1783, reaching its climax in the Renunciation Act (23 George III, c. 28 (Gt B.)). Meanwhile Molyneux, Swift and other writers kept the thesis before the public mind.

Brodrick had a genuine fear that if the House of Commons did not retain this right, especially as regarded Money Bills, the way would be open to the exercise of executive power entirely through the Privy Council. This in turn brought back fears of Strafford, Charles I and 'arbitrary' government and the circumvention of parliament through the executive powers of the Privy Council. For instance, in June 1793 Brodrick wrote to his brother, Thomas Brodrick (0243), that he had been told by an Irish PC that 'We should be governed by the Council Board and that they would give us the law … [and] render the meeting of future Parliaments inadvisable.'

Brodrick was generally in tune with many of the country gentlemen, who were at least partly aware that parliament was their security and were hostile to Lord Chancellor Porter for his suspected leniency to the Catholics. Brodrick shared their suspicions, and voted against the Chancellor when this accusation was made in parliament in 1695. A true Whig, like all of his family, the following year he signed the Association for the protection of William III in open parliament. His hostility to the defeated Catholics was reflected in a letter of 17 December 1695 to his brother St John Brodrick (0241) in which he referred to the penal legislation of the 1695 parliament (affecting the hierarchy and the regular clergy, Catholic education, intermarriage between Catholics and Protestants and the prohibition to Catholics of the acknowledged accoutrements of a gentleman – owning a good horse and carrying arms): 'The country hath had such laws passed as they have long wanted and wished for.' He is said to have had strong dissenting religious opinions, and he supported the Dissenters in their efforts to obtain the repeal of the Sacramental Test imposed on them by the penal laws of 1704 and 1709. Indeed, on one occasion, in a session of parliament early in Queen Anne's reign, he 'had insolently shaken one of the Irish Prelates, Dr Lindsay, at the time Bishop of Killaloe by his lawn sleeve, and told him in a menacing manner "that he hoped to live to see the day when there should not be one of his order left in Ireland".' Dr Lindsay was a noted Tory and subsequently Bishop of Raphoe; he was appointed Lord Primate in the concluding months of Queen Anne's reign, much to the annoyance of the Whigs.

Certainly Brodrick made life exceedingly diffi-

cult for successive administrations. He was an early opponent of Lord Lieutenant Ormonde, possibly fearing the Jacobite leanings of the Butler family. On 29 July 1707 Richard Stewart (2007) wrote to Ormonde concerning the passing of supply: 'Interest is more Mr Brodrick's God than his country, nor ought they [the opposition] to be surprised that the same man should now betray them for an Attorney's gown, who before had done it for a Solicitor's.' Brodrick was a professional lawyer and always anxious for advancement in his profession. However, although appointed Attorney General in 1707, he remained Speaker until May 1710. The Whig Lord Lieutenant Wharton appointed him Chief Justice of the Queen's Bench on 4 January 1709/10 and, as judges held their position at the pleasure of the sovereign (*durante bene placito regis*), he was dismissed by the Tory Ormonde in 1711. This was perhaps inadvisable, as it left him free to stand for Co. Cork in the election of 1713, and when the new parliament met he was again elected Speaker after a very stormy contest with the government's nominee, Sir Richard Levinge (1230). He was listed on 136 committees during the reign of William III, a further 69 in 1703–11 and 16 in 1713.

After the Hanoverian succession in 1715 Brodrick was appointed Chancellor, in succession to the now disgraced Tory Chancellor, Sir Constantine Phipps. He was created Lord Brodrick and two years later raised to a viscounty as Viscount Midleton. At this time he had a personal following estimated at about 30 MPs. A struggle for dominance now emerged between the two former Whig allies, Lord Chancellor Brodrick and Speaker William Conolly (0460). To successive Lords Lieutenant between 1715 and 1725 Midleton emphasised how difficult he could be if he was ignored, while Conolly showed how pleasantly indispensable he could become if given adequate support. Midleton and his elder brother Thomas (0243) had long supported the family interest in England and Ireland respectively. However, from 1717 Midleton shored up his position by getting himself and from 1721 his son (0242) also returned to the British parliament. Here he at first supported Sunderland but fell out with him over his opposition to the 1719 Peerage Bill; this pushed him into the Townshend–Walpole camp.

For Brodrick, like Walpole, Jacobitism was a real threat and in 1719, when there was a short-lived invasion by the Earl of Lucan, he considered that 'The Protestants seem to be a little too secure, and not to apprehend so much danger as there certainly was and I doubt still is from their enemies.' In Ireland Midleton was known to have fomented unrest over Wood's Halfpence, writing to his brother in 1725: 'I always was and always shall be against Wood's patent'; nevertheless, Lord-Lieutenant Grafton was unable to persuade Walpole, whom Midleton had supported in the British House of Commons, that he might be removed from office without causing unrest in both countries. However, Lord Lieutenant Carteret, when forced to choose between Conolly and Brodrick, chose the former, and in 1725 Midleton, now nearly 70 years of age, was forced to resign.

Brodrick's period as Chancellor was marked by recurrent distrust between him and the British government and by feuding with Conolly and, to a lesser degree, with Archbishop King. He was the last eighteenth-century Irish Chancellor until the appointment of John Fitzgibbon (**0749**) in 1789. Brodrick and Fitzgibbon were both outstandingly able, and shared the same capacity for attracting friends and enemies. Neither did Brodrick suffer fools gladly; he once told his son that, when dealing with a long-winded barrister: 'I love to humble him particularly if he is pert and saucy which is sometimes the case.' He had a similar pride in his independence, declaring that he would never support a knave because he was born great nor court a villain because he had an interest at Court. He died in August 1728; Conolly died on 30 October 1729.

ADDITIONAL INFORMATION: As Chancellor he presided over the House of Lords, and it is recorded that on 17 May 1718 he received £500 'being the usual allowance, a Speaker (Chairman) of the House of Lords, for the session of parliament'. On his appointment as Chancellor he received £1,000 for equipage. He was a founder member of the Dublin Guild of Brewers and Maltsters, 20 April 1696. His uncle Alan (Allen) Brodrick was MP for Dungarvan 1661–6 and also sat in the English parliament for Orford in 1660 and 1661.

In 1718 he told Alan, the son of his second marriage, that he wished him to be 'bred up virtuously according to my best wishes'. He even took him to Newmarket to 'make you hate gaming, cockfighting and its attendant vices ... and that you see that horse racing is an introduction to cheating, sharping, hypocrisy, and lying, and ends in the ruin of men's estates as well as the loss of their characters gradually'.

ESTATES/RESIDENCE: Ballyannan, Co. Cork. In October 1696 Elizabeth Villiers conveyed to him a portion of her estates at Midleton, Co. Cork for the endowment of the school there of which he was a governor. His father, Sir St John Brodrick, had received substantial grants of land under the Protectorate and also for his part in the Restoration, when he received large grants of land in Co. Cork, including the parliamentary borough of Midleton. About 1689, Sir St John Brodrick held under the crown 1,958 Irish acres (Ballytrasney, Mallfastown, Disert, etc. in the barony of Barrymore). Brodrick purchased 340 acres in Co. Cork from the Commissioners for Sale of Forfeited Estates in 1702–3. In 1754, Viscount Midleton was granted additional fairs at Glanworth. In 1713 Alan Brodrick's income was reckoned to be £2,000. According to Wakefield c. 1805–10, Lord Midleton had a rental of £8,000.

SOURCES: NLI reps no 172; Guildford Muniment Room, Guildford, Surrey, Midleton MSS, Corr. of Alan & Thomas Brodrick; PRONI T/3411; BL Add MS 4755 [Crown rental c. 1683]; *CJ Ire.* (Bradley ed.) vol. 2 pp. 750–51, vol. 4 p. 542; vol. 5 pp. 304–45; PRONI T/488 p. 210, TSPI 1715–16; PRONI T/2825 Conolly–Castletown Papers, p. 12; PRONI MIC/315/9/52 Blackwood pedigrees; GEC *P*; *HP 1715–54*; Burke *PB* (1903) p. 109 [says his mother was dau. of Sir Randal Clayton]; *Cal. SP Dom. 1694–5* pp. 372, 469, 482, *1695* pp. 219, 339, *1696* (London, 1913) pp. 140, 145, 184, 304; *Index to Irish Privy Councillors, 1711–1910*; *Alum. Oxon.*; *Alum. Cantab.*; Ball, *Judges*; *Middle Temple Admissions* vol. 1 p. 180, 289 [says admitted to the Middle Temple 7 Jan. 1670]; *Hist. Stud.* vol. 4 (1963) p. 87; Johnston, *Gt B. & Ire.*, p. 236; T. Bartlett and D. W. Hayton (eds), *Penal Era and Golden Age* (Belfast, 1979), D. W. Hayton, 'The Beginings of the Undertaker System'; D. Dickson, *New Foundations: Ireland 1660–1800* (Dublin, 1987), p. 42; J. J. Howard (ed.), *Miscellanea Genealogica et Heraldica*, vol. 2 (1876) p. 366 [says his mother's name is Lucy]; *HMC Ormonde* new series vol. 8 pp. 122, 303; W. King, *A Great Archbishop of Dublin, William King DD 1650–1729* (London, 1906) p. 35; S. J. Conolly, *Religion, Law and Power* (1992), pp. 70, 75, 89–93, 255; P. McNally, *Parties, Patriots & Undertakers* (Dublin, 1997), pp. 126–7;

JRSAI vol. 55 (1925) pp. 37, 44, H. A. S. Upton, 'A List of Governors and Deputy Governors of Counties in Ireland in 1699' [says his mother was the dau. of Sir Ronald Clayton, also says his second wife's name was Lucy]; *ibid.*, vol. 82 (1952) pp. 5, 13, M. Quane, 'Midleton School: Co. Cork'; *The Dublin Intelligence* 27 June 1710, 17 Feb. 1711; *Harding's Imperial Newsletter* 20 Feb. 1722; Simms, *Williamite Confiscation*, p. 183; R. E. Burns, *Irish Parliamentary Politics in the Eighteenth Century*, 2 vols (Washington, 1989) vol. 1 pp. 7, 29–31; Wakefield, *Account of Ire.*, vol. 1 p. 250; Parliamentary Lists, 1695 (1), 1696 (1), 1706 (1), 1713 (1), (2).

0238 BRODRICK, Edward

MP for Midleton 1768–76

b. (bapt. 25 Mar.) 1743/4; d. *post* 1776
FAMILY/BACKGROUND: Only son of Vice-Adm. Thomas Brodrick (0244) and Mary, dau. of Benjamin Robins; great-grandson of Sir St John Brodrick (0240) and great-nephew of Alan Brodrick (0237).
MARRIED: Unmarried.
CAREER/OCCUPATION: Military: He was a soldier and at the time of his election held a commission in the Guards.

POLITICAL ACTIVITY: He was brought in by and 'influenced entirely by Lady Midleton' (widow of 3rd Viscount), who ensured his return for the Brodrick borough of Midleton. At the time of his election it was reported that he 'has never yet been in Ireland'. His support for Lord Lieutenant Townshend, whom 'he sometimes assisted and as often opposed', appears to have been at best uncertain. However, in 1772 and 1773 he came over from England to support the government, and in 1774 'on purpose to vote for the Board of Accounts'. By 1775 it was noted that he 'seldom attends' and 'not at all during the last session'. He did not come in again at the 1776 election. He was a soldier, and was possibly posted to America. It is also possible that Lady Midleton decided to return her own son, Henry (0239), although he was under age.

DIVISION LISTS:
1771 (2) voted against Sir Lucius O'Brien's (1558) motion for retrenchment.

1771 (3) voted against the amendment to the Revenue Bill.

ESTATES/RESIDENCE: Co. Cork.

SOURCES: Cork MPs; J. J. Howard (ed.), *Miscellanea Genealogica et Heraldica*, vol. 2 (1876) p. 365; Parliamentary Lists, 1769 (1), 1771 (1), 1772 (2), 1773 (1), (2), 1774 (1), 1775 (1).

0239 BRODRICK, Hon. Henry

MP for Midleton 1776–83 [elected under age]

b. 12 Dec. 1758; d. 16 June 1785 at Lisbon
FAMILY/BACKGROUND: Son of George Brodrick, 3rd Viscount Midleton, and Albinia, dau. of the Hon. Thomas Townshend.
MARRIED: Unmarried.
EDUCATION: School: Eton 1769–74.
CAREER/OCCUPATION: Military: Ensign in 33rd Foot 23 Mar. 1775; Lieutenant 8 Aug. 1776; Captain 55th Foot 12 June 1777, 1782 Major; eventually a Colonel in the Coldstream Guards.

POLITICAL ACTIVITY: In 1776 Lord Midleton returned two of his younger brothers, Thomas Brodrick (0245) and Henry. Thomas was not quite of age and Henry definitely under age, but the list adds 'they are seldom here'. They were thought to be guided by their brother and 'possibly follow the conduct of their uncle in England, Mr T[homas] Townshend' (later Lord Sydney). Under these influences they would vote against. Henry's brother, Viscount Midleton, sat in the British House of Commons for Whitechurch, 1774–80. As this was the period of the War of American Independence, Henry may well have been absent on military service.

ESTATES/RESIDENCE: Midleton, Co. Cork; London.

SOURCES: Ellis thesis; R. A. Austen-Leigh (ed.), *The Eton College Register, 1753–90*, 3 vols (Eton, 1921); J. J. Howard (ed.), *Miscellanea Genealogica et Heraldica*, vol. 2 (1876) p. 368; Johnston, *Gt B. & Ire.*, p. 287; Parliamentary Lists, 1776 (1), (2), (3), 1777 (1), 1778 (1), 1780 (1), 1782 (1), 1783 (1).

0240 BRODRICK, Sir St John

MP for Kinsale (1661–6); Co. Cork 1692–3, 1695–9

b. 3 Dec. 1627; d. (bur. 23) Jan. 1710/11 at
Wandsworth, London

HONOURS: Knighted 20 Mar. 1660.

FAMILY/BACKGROUND: Fourth son of Sir Thomas
Brodrick, of Wandsworth, Surrey, and Catherine,
dau. of Robert Nicholas of Manningford Brice,
Wiltshire.

MARRIED: Alice (d. Apr. 1696), dau. of Sir Randal
Clayton Kt of Thelwall, Cheshire, and ?Co.
Cork.

CHILDREN: Rt Hon. Thomas (**0243**); Rt Hon.
Alan, 1st Viscount Midleton (**0237**); St John
(**0241**); Randal (d. unmar.); William (**0246**);
Laurence (Chaplain to the House of Commons
[GB] in 1708), m. [27 Apr. 1710] Anne
Humphreys; Catherine, m. Dr William
Whitfield.

CAREER/OCCUPATION: High Sheriff of Co. Cork
1662; Deputy Governor of Co. Cork 1699.
He was a governor of Midleton School.

MILITARY: Came to Ireland as a Captain of Foot
and took part in the suppression of disorders in
Munster 1641; considered one of Cromwell's
spies in Ireland. Provost Marshal of Munster
1661 for life; Commander of Troop of Horse and
Company of Foot 1661 (left army c. 1679).

POLITICAL ACTIVITY: Although he could have
claimed immunity on grounds of age, he was listed
for two committees in November 1692 and 76
between 1695 and 1698. In 1696 he signed the
Association for the protection of William III in
the country. He sat with three of his sons (**0237**,
0241, **0243**) in the second parliament of William
III. He died, aged 83, in 1711.

ADDITIONAL INFORMATION: His grandfather, a Yorkshire man, was embroiderer to James I, but the
family's Irish fortunes appear to have been
Cromwellian in origin. His eldest brother, Alan
Brodrick (1623–80) of Wandsworth, Surrey, sat
in the English House of Commons for Orford in
1660 and 1661 and in the Irish House of Commons for Dungarvan, 1661–5.

ESTATES/RESIDENCE: Midleton and Barrymore, Co. Cork.
He obtained a large grant of land in 1753 and the grants
were confirmed, 1654 and 1669. [?]Built the town and
church of Midleton.

SOURCES: PRONI D/302; Burke *PB* (1906) p. 1128 [says

he died 1731]; GEC *P*; Cork MPs; C. Dalton (ed.),
Irish Army Lists 1661–1685 (London, 1907), p. 4; *HP
1660–90* [this entry gives some general family back-
ground]; *JRSAI* vol. 55 (1925) pp. 37, 44, H. A. S.
Upton, 'A List of Governors and Deputy Governors of
Counties in Ireland in 1699' [says he married Alice,
dau. of Sir Ronald Clayton of Thelwall, Chester]; M.
Quane, 'Midleton School: Co. Cork' in *ibid.* vol. 82
(1952) pp. 4, 15; J. J. Howard (ed.), *Miscellanea
Genealogica et Heraldica*, vol. 2 (1876) p. 364; Parliamentary List, 1696 (1).

0241 BRODRICK, St John

MP for Midleton Aug.–Sept.1695 (excused from
attendance on account of bodily infirmity),1703–7

b. 1659; d. 12 June 1707 bur. at Wandsworth,
London

FAMILY/BACKGROUND: Third son of Sir St John
Brodrick (**0240**) and Alice, dau. of Sir Randal
Clayton Kt of Thelwall, Cheshire, and ?Co.
Cork.

MARRIED: Unmarried.

CAREER/OCCUPATION: Serjeant-at-Law 1705.

EDUCATION: Entered Oxford (Magdalen College)
14 June 1672, aged 13 years; Middle Temple 7
Nov. 1672; barrister Middle Temple 30 May
1679.

POLITICAL ACTIVITY: Nothing much is known about
the political conduct of this MP: when he was
present, he doubtless followed the family line. He
appears to have had bad health, but recovered sufficiently to be named for 49 committees between
1703 and 1707, when he died.

ESTATES/RESIDENCE: Lamb's Buildings, Middle Temple,
London; Wandsworth, Surrey.

SOURCES: GEC *P*; Burke *PB* (1906) p. 1128; *Alum.
Oxon.*; *Middle Temple Admissions* (London, 1949) vol.
1 p. 186; Guildford Muniment Room, Guildford, Surrey, Midleton MSS; Cork MPs.

0242 BRODRICK, Rt Hon. St John

MP for Castlemartyr 1709–13; Cork city 1713–
14; Co. Cork 1715–27–8; [GB] Bere Alston
1721–7

b. *c.* 1685; d. 21 Feb. 1728

HONOURS: PC, sworn 9 June 1724, 19 June 1727.

FAMILY/BACKGROUND: Eldest son of Rt Hon. Alan Brodrick, 1st Viscount Midleton (**0237**), and his first wife Catherine, dau. of Redmond Barry of Rathcormack, Co. Cork.

MARRIED: [20 Apr. 1710] Anne, dau. of Rt Hon. Michael Hill (**1019**).

CHILDREN: *d.s.p.m.* Catherine (d. yg 1713); Anne, m. James Jeffreyes (**1082**); Alice, m. Charles O'Neill (**1588**); Jane, m. Rev. Lawrence Brodrick; Mary, m. Sir John Redmond Freke (**0822**).

EDUCATION: School: Eton 1698; entered Cambridge (King's College) 1700; Middle Temple 17 June 1700; called to the Irish Bar 1707.

CAREER/OCCUPATION: Recorder of Cork 28 Sept. 1708, 1721

POLITICAL ACTIVITY: He came into parliament in 1709, returned for Castlemartyr on the Boyle interest. He was a teller on the Whig side in a division, June 1710, and by that time an active member of the Whig opposition. He was nominated for 50 committees between 1709 and 1711, 14 in 1714 and 110 between 1715 and 1726. He was the principal manager of 11 Anne, c. 5, 'an act for the better preventing of excessive and deceitful gaming'. But in 1712 information was given on oath to Lord Chief Justice Cox (**0507**), who had recently replaced Brodrick's father, that Brodrick spoke words 'highly reflecting' on Her Majesty, and he was summonsed before the Queen's Bench. His father, who 'made as much mischief as possible ... in the House of Commons ... with [his son's] ... assistance', claimed that he 'was a wild young man beyond parental control'. In 1713 after he was returned for Cork city it was thought that government would make some compact with him, although this appears to have been unlikely in view of his father's election as Speaker against the wishes of government. Certainly, in the same year he was noted as a Whig and either he or, more probably, his father was a member of the Commons Committee to inquire into the conduct of the unpopular Tory Chancellor, Sir Constantine Phipps.

When the new parliament met, the Whig majority, while very substantial, was not complete. Conflict between the various sections of the victorious Whigs was not long in emerging. In his ensuing feud with Conolly (**0460**), Brodrick used his son to conduct a covert opposition in the

House of Commons. In 1715 the Chief Secretary complained that he had spent each day of the session 'running about to solicit the members and keep our forces together, whom Brodrick with as much diligence endeavoured to debauch'. In 1716 he joined the Tory rump in opposing a bill to abolish the Test Clause as it related to militia commissions and for ten years for army commissions; this was not the only occasion that he allied with them. In 1717 he was the principal organiser of 4 Geo. I, c. 10, 'an act for limiting certain times within which Writs of Error shall be brought for the reversing Fines and common Recoveries' – the time was limited to ten years.

In 1719 St John Brodrick was listed as 'a placeman' and presumably held some legal office. On 7 July 1719 he was one of those summoned by the Lord Lieutenant on the eve of parliament to consider how far the relief of Dissenters should be pressed. On 2 June 1720 he attached his name to a petition of the proposed managers of the 'intended' national bank to 'help forward their obtaining a charter' and was a teller for it on the first vote, which was lost by 102 to 95 votes. But by November the Brodricks had changed their minds, Lord Chancellor Midleton declaring it to be 'of a pernicious nature'. A variety of motives probably lay behind his voting against a national bank on the second occasion that it came before parliament: the South Sea Bubble débâcle and the ensuing financial instability, the financial demands of the British politicians in return for the bank's charter, suspicions of the possible constitutional misapplication of the charter, and possibly its growing unpopularity.

In February 1723 he was one of the Memorialists on behalf of the Protestant gentlemen of Ireland seeking either an explanation or revocation of a clause in an act of Queen Anne's reign for naturalising foreign Protestants in which favour was given to the children of natural-born subjects. The Memorialists feared this clause would allow the children of papists who had served James and then fled to Europe to return to Ireland and undermine the church and state as well as reclaiming their lands.

On 22 March 1725/6 Primate Boulter wrote to the Duke of Newcastle about the Brodricks, father (**0237**), brother (**0243**) and son (a difference of six on the division list), that 'I would hope that the disobliging two or three members of the House of Commons in *England*, will not be thought of greater consequence than the keeping things quiet here, by shewing a just displeasure to those who could embroil this kingdom.' Following the resignation of Lord Chancellor Midleton Boulter wrote that 'The influence of the first of them must everyday decrease, as the father is now out of post, and upon retiring to England; and as the son himself is far from being beloved here.' However, he was perhaps over-optimistic, as on 29 June 1727 when he wrote to Lord Lieutenant Carteret on the various renewals consequent on the accession of George II, he added that a general election was to be called as soon as possible and: 'I find Mr *Brodrick* has declared he will stand for Speaker against Mr *Conolly*, and uses his utmost efforts to secure as many as he can among the new members. The whole kingdom is in the utmost ferment about the coming elections; but I hope this will have no worse consequences than are usual on such occasions.' In the event Brodrick thought better of opposing Conolly, who was elected unopposed.

Both the Brodricks, father and son, appear to have looked at the British House of Commons through Irish eyes. Lord Carteret had opposed St John Brodrick's election to the British parliament for Bere Alston in 1721 and initially Brodrick was defeated, but he succeeded in having the return overturned on petition. Subsequently the quarrel was patched up, and Brodrick welcomed Carteret's appointment as Lord Lieutenant because he thought that he was hostile to Wood's Halfpence and 'perfectly free from all suspicion of being concerned in, or wishing well to, that vile project'. When he discovered his mistake he went into violent opposition in the Irish House of Commons, although he usually supported government in England.

DIVISION LISTS:
1709 (1) spoke for a Money Bill.
1721 (1) teller for a national bank.
1721 (2) voted against a national bank.

ESTATES/RESIDENCE: Midleton, Co. Cork. St John's income was estimated at £1,000 in 1713.

SOURCES: *CJ Ire* (Bradley ed.) vol. 3 p. 911, vol. 4 p. 20 (0147, 0183); PRONI T/3411; PRONI T/519 p. 165, T/580 pp. 2–6, TSPI 1717–19, 1723–4; PRONI T/2825 Conolly/Castletown Papers, p. 13; PRONI T/3315/2/f. 33 Egmont Papers; RCBL P273/1/1, Parish Registers of St Paul's, Dublin [dau. Catherine bapt. 17 Feb. 1713]; McCracken thesis; Hayton thesis; Burke *PB* (1903) p. 1049; *Index to Irish Privy Counsellors, 1711–1910*; *Alum. Cantab.*; R. A. Austen-Leigh (ed.), *The Eton College Register, 1698–1752*, 3 vols (Eton, 1927); J. J. Howard (ed.), *Miscellanea Genealogica et Heraldica*, vol. 2 (1876) p. 366; *Middle Temple Admissions* vol. 1 p. 247; *IMC King's Inns Admission Papers, 1607–1867*; *HP 1715–54*; *Boulter Letters* vol. 1 pp. 44, 55, 139–40; *Dublin Gazette* 29 Jan. 1712; R. E. Burns, *Irish Parliamentary Politics in the Eighteenth Century* (Washington, 1989), vol. 1 pp. 125 et seq.; Parliamentary Lists, 1711 (3), 1713 (1), (2), (3), 1719 (1).

0243 BRODRICK, Rt Hon. Thomas

MP for Midleton 1692–3, 1715–27; Co. Cork 1695–9, 1703–13; [GB] Stockbridge 1713–22; Guildford 1722–7

b. 4 Aug. 1654; d. 3 Oct. 1730
HONOURS: PC, 10 May 1695, *ante* Apr. 1711, removed 17 July 1711, reappointed 30 Sept. 1714; [GB] sworn 9 Oct. 1714.
FAMILY/BACKGROUND: Eldest son of Sir St John Brodrick (**0240**), and Alice, dau. of Sir Randal Clayton Kt of Thelwall, Cheshire, and ?Co. Cork.
MARRIED: Anne (b. 1657; d. 3 May 1731), dau. of Alexander Pigott of Innishannon, Co. Cork.
CHILDREN: *d.s.p.* Lawrence (d. yg).
EDUCATION: Entered Cambridge (Trinity College) Easter 1670, LLB. 1677; Oxford (Magdalen Hall) 15 Nov. 1671, aged 17 years; Middle Temple 7 Jan. 1670.
CAREER/OCCUPATION: Proctor in the Arches Court; Judge for the Common Pleas for Munster 1695; Comptroller of the Salt Duties 1706; Joint Comptroller of Army Accounts 1708–11; he was one of the governors of Midleton School.

POLITICAL ACTIVITY: The older brother of Lord Chancellor Brodrick (**0237**). The brothers were allies, and eventually Thomas looked after the family interest in London and Alan in Ireland. He signed the Association for the protection of William III in parliament. He went to London with Brigadier Wolseley (**2249**) about August 1696 and stayed until December, when he was replaced by other Irish parliamentary representatives. Brodrick was listed for ten committees in 1692 and 94 in the following parliament, 1692–5, 88 between 1703 and 1711 and one in 1713. In a letter to Vernon, 9 December 1696, he asked that the replacement for Lord Chancellor Capel be anything but a Tory and definitely not Sir John Meade (**1387**).

He was a staunch Whig and listed as 'against the Court' in 1705. He was absent in London in 1707 and was in opposition, not surprisingly in view of his brother's (**0237**) hostile relations with Ormonde, which culminated in his dismissal as Lord Chief Justice of the Queen's Bench in 1711. Before the 1713 election it was thought that he would be again returned for Co. Cork. However, he transferred his activities to the British parliament, where he was returned for Stockbridge and Guildford successively, and in so doing safeguarded the interests of the family as he and his brother Alan, Lord Chancellor Midleton, worked in combination. For example, he supported the appointment of Josiah Hort against William Gore as chaplain to the House of Commons as Gore, although Irish, was Conolly's candidate.

At Westminster he involved himself in the affair of the South Sea Company, which put forward a plan to 'privatise the national debt'. Initially this stunned the House of Commons until Brodrick suggested that the government should 'make the best bargain' by taking offers from all interested parties. When the South Sea Company collapsed Brodrick headed the ballot for the secret committee established to investigate the affair, and became its chairman. His nephew, St John Brodrick (**0242**), wrote that 'My uncle ... is the most popular, best regarded man in the House.' Certainly he was one of its watchdogs. He outlived both his brother and his nephew, who sat in the British parliament with him. The Rt Hon. Thomas Brodrick died in 1730.

DIVISION LISTS:
1709 (1) spoke for a Money Bill.

ADDITIONAL INFORMATION: He was a horse-racing enthusiast; his brother Alan was afraid that he might corrupt his son.

ESTATES/RESIDENCE: Midleton, Co. Cork; Wandsworth, Surrey. He held the estates of Elizabeth Villiers at Midleton in Cork on her behalf.

SOURCES: Hayton thesis; *Cal. SP Dom. 1694–5* pp. 327, 372, 390, 469, 500, *1696* (London, 1913) pp. 305, 455, 459; Burke *PB* (1900, 1906); *HP 1715–54*; *Alum. Cantab.* [says died 22 Oct. 1730 aged 77 years]; *Alum. Oxon.* [says MP for Cork Co. 1715–27]; *Index to Irish Privy Counsellors, 1711–1910*; J. J. Howard (ed.), *Miscellanea Genealogica et Heraldica*, vol. 2 (1876) p. 365 [says *d.s.p.*]; *Middle Temple Admissions* vol. 1 p. 180; Cork MPs; *Historical Studies* vol. 4 (1963); P. McNally, *Parties, Patriots & Undertakers* (Dublin, 1997), p. 90; S. J. Conolly, *Religion, Law and Power* (1992), pp. 70, 111; *JRSAI* vol. 82 (1952) pp. 4, 13, M. Quane, 'Midleton School: Co. Cork'; Parliamentary Lists, 1696 (1), 1706 (1), 1707 (1), (4), 1711 (3), 1713 (1), (3).

0244 BRODRICK, Thomas

MP for Midleton 1761–8

b. 1705; d. 1 Jan. 1769
FAMILY/BACKGROUND: Son of William Brodrick (**0246**) and Alice, dau. of Laurence Clayton of Mallow, Co. Cork.
MARRIED: Mary (b. 1710; d. 1760), dau. of Benjamin Robins.
CHILDREN: Edward (**0238**); Althia (d. unmar.); Mary Elizabeth (b. 1739; d. unmar. 1761); Anne and Charlotte (twins b. and d. Apr. 1745).
CAREER/OCCUPATION: Naval: Entered Navy *c.* 1723, Lieutenant of the *Burford* 1739, commanded landing party that stormed the Castillo de Fierro; promoted to command *Cumberland* fireship in which he took part in Admiral Vernon's Cartagena expedition 1741, posted into *Shoreham* 25 Mar. and took part in the expedition to Cuba; returned England 1743; appointed to *Exeter* (60 guns) 1744, to *Dreadnought* Mar. 1745; in the Leeward Islands 1744–8; in the Mediterranean May 1756 in command of reinforcements for Admiral Byng, whom he joined at Gibraltar; promoted Rear Admiral of the Red 1756 and served under Sir Edward Hawke; member of Byng's court martial January 1757; 3rd in command of expedition against Rochefort 1757; 2nd in command in Mediterranean in *Prince George* (90 guns) 1758 ('Going to the Mediterranean in the *Prince George* of ninety guns, she took fire and was burnt, and most of

the crew were drowned; Admiral Brodrick was taken up (stark naked, after swimming for over an hour) by a merchant ship's boat'); in Gibraltar, raised his flag in St George; promoted Vice-Admiral of the Red 1759; commanded under Admiral Boscawen at the blockade of Toulon and in the action which culminated in the burning and capture of the French ships in Lagos Bay, and blockaded the French ships at Cadiz on Boscawen's departure 1759.

POLITICAL ACTIVITY: Along with James St John Jeffreys (**1082**), he was returned for Midleton in 1761 without opposition. He was an admiral and mainly absent.

DIVISION LISTS:
1768 (1) absent – Admiral, England.

ESTATES/RESIDENCE: Peper Harrow, Surrey.

SOURCES: Burke *PB* (1903) p. 1048; *DNB*; J. J. Howard (ed.), *Miscellanea Genealogica et Heraldica*, vol. 2 (1876) p. 365; *BNL* 24 Apr. 1761.

0245 BRODRICK, Hon. Thomas

MP for Midleton 1776–83

b. 17 Apr. 1756; d. 13 Jan. 1795 at Chislehurst, Kent
FAMILY/BACKGROUND: Second son of George Brodrick, 3rd Viscount Midleton, and Albinia, dau. of Hon. Thomas Townshend.
MARRIED: Unmarried.
EDUCATION: School: Eton 1766–72; entered Cambridge (St John's College) 29 Apr. 1773; Middle Temple 1 Jan. 1773; called to the Bar 12 Nov. 1779.
CAREER/OCCUPATION: Counsel to the Admiralty 1792–4; Under Secretary of State for the Home Department 1794–5; King's Counsel for the Duchy of Lancaster, 1786.

POLITICAL ACTIVITY: He was barely of age when elected along with his under-age brother, Henry (**0239**), for the family borough of Midleton; it seems probable that he was mainly an absentee. Certainly he is listed as 'always absent'.

The Brodrick family's careers were by now almost entirely in England, and in 1783 it was said that 'Lord Midleton has offered his seats, one to Mr Ponsonby (**1702**), the other to Lord Shannon

(**0213**). The voters wished to transfer the Borough [Midleton] into Lord Shannon's hands, but his Lordship declined the offer. Lieutenant Colonel Pigott (**1683**), Governor of Cork £365 p.a. has been elected, as Lord Shannon's friend.' Actually the Pigotts, an eminent Cork family, were connected with the Brodricks (*see* **0243**).

ADDITIONAL INFORMATION: Thomas's brother, Viscount Midleton, sat in the British parliament of 1774–80 for the borough of Whitechurch.

ESTATES/RESIDENCE: Midleton, Co. Cork; London.

SOURCES: Ellis thesis; *Alum. Cantab.*; R. A. Austen-Leigh (ed.), *The Eton College Register, 1753–90*, 3 vols (Eton, 1921); *Middle Temple Admissions* vol. I p. 376; Johnston, *Gt B. & Ire.*, p. 287; Parliamentary Lists, 1776 (1), (2), (3), 1777 (1), 1778 (1), 1780 (1), 1782 (1), 1783 (1).

0246 BRODRICK, William

MP for Mallow 1716–27

b. *c.* 1666; d. *post* 1733
FAMILY/BACKGROUND: Son of Sir St John Brodrick (**0240**), and Alice, dau. of Randal Clayton of Mallow, Co. Cork.
MARRIED: [   ].
CHILDREN: Thomas (**0244**).
EDUCATION: Entered Cambridge (Emmanuel College) 3 Nov. 1683; Inner Temple 1696; LLD *spec. grat.* of TCD 1709.
CAREER/OCCUPATION: Attorney General for the Island of Jamaica Oct. 1692, Apr. 1696, 1710, 1715; Speaker of the House of Assembly, Jamaica, 1711–13; 2nd Serjeant at Law 23 Dec. 1718.

POLITICAL ACTIVITY: He was already 50 years of age when he entered the Irish parliament, having previously held office in Jamaica as Attorney General and Speaker of the Jamaican assembly. This last office may have had an interesting consequence, as in the eighteenth century the British government was anxious to get the Jamaican assembly to agree to an equivalent of Poynings' Law, and the assembly was always adamant in its refusal. His voting for and against a national bank may be explained by the financial instability created by the South Sea Bubble, as well as suspicions about the motives of the administration. His elder brother (0243) was greatly interested in this issue. He was appointed Second Serjeant at Law in 1718 and in the 1719 list was noted as being 'a Placeman'. He was nominated for 58 committees between 1717 and 1721.

DIVISION LISTS:
1721 (1) voted for a national bank.
1721 (2) voted against a national bank.

ADDITIONAL INFORMATION: He had a taste for playing cards, much to the disapproval of his older brother Alan (0237), who considered that he should spend less time gossiping and more at his legal studies.

ESTATES/RESIDENCE: Surrey, England; St Jago de la Vega (Spanish Town), Jamaica.

SOURCES: Burke *PB* (1903) p. 1048 (1906) p. 1128; *Cal. SP Dom. 1696* p. 138; Hughes, *Pat. Officers*; *Alum. Cantab.*; Cork MPs; J. J. Howard (ed.), *Miscellanea Genealogica et Heraldica*, vol. 2 (1876) p. 365; Parliamentary List, 1719 (1).

0247 BROOKE, Rt Hon. Sir Arthur

MP for Co. Fermanagh 1761–8–76–83; Maryborough 1783–5

b. 1726; d. 7 Mar. 1785 at his house in Sackville Street after a short illness
HONOURS: Cr. Bt Jan. 1764; PC, sworn 15 May 1770.
FAMILY/BACKGROUND: Son of Henry Brooke (0248), and Letitia, dau. of Benjamin Burton (0292).
MARRIED: (1) [6 Aug. 1751] Margaret (b. 27 Mar. 1728; d. 22 Sept. 1756 at Bath), o. dau. of Thomas Fortescue of Randalstown (?Reynold's), Co. Louth (0793) and sis. of 1st Earl of Clermont; (2) [21 Sept. 1775] Elizabeth, dau. of [   ] Foorde.
CHILDREN: *d.s.p.m.* (1) Henry (d. yg); Arthur (d. yg); Selina, m. [24 Apr. 1769] Thomas Vesey, 1st Viscount de Vesci; Letitia (d. 1783), m. [19 July 1774] Rt Hon. Sir John Parnell (1633).
EDUCATION: Entered TCD 1743, BA 1746.
CAREER/OCCUPATION: High Sheriff for Co. Fermanagh 1752; Distributor of Stamps for Co. Fermanagh; *Governor of Co. Fermanagh 1752–

d.; *Commissioner of the Tillage Act for Ulster 1763–d.; *Trustee of the Linen Board for Connaught 1763–d.
MILITARY: Colonel of the Brookborough Volunteers, while an MP.

POLITICAL ACTIVITY: Like most county representatives, he was independent. He had a good estate although it was reputed to be 'involved'. In 1764 Brooke was created a baronet and he represented Co. Fermanagh for nearly 25 years. He was politically ambivalent, being 'against government in his heart'. However, Lord Townshend had him made a Privy Counsellor and obtained a majority of dragoons for his brother without purchase. During the latter part of Townshend's viceroyalty he acted with the Tyrone faction and with his relatives, the Fortescues.

He was supposed to have tricked Lord Lieutenant Harcourt out of the Distributorship of Stamps for the county 'at the very moment he was opposing the duty in the House', and when Chief Secretary Blaquiere (0162) objected he lost no opportunity of publicly maligning him. However, 'In private life he is generally esteemed – in public very insincere and ungrateful to the crown, and never to be depended upon.' Brooke voted for Catholic relief in 1774, and in 1775 he published a pamphlet arguing that Catholics who acquired property and became gentlemen would want official positions and so would turn Protestant. He opposed Lord Buckinghamshire but supported Lord Carlisle and was thought to be looking for a peerage, as he was afraid of losing his county, although he was a Volunteer colonel and a Co. Fermanagh delegate to the National Convention. Co. Fermanagh was said to be 'divided by electioneering contests and thence has been of late forward on popular questions'.

Brooke was defeated in 1783 but returned by his son-in-law, Sir John Parnell (1633) for Maryborough. In 1783, the principal interests in Co. Fermanagh were said to be Lord Enniskillen (0444), Lord Belmore (1269), Lord Loftus (2088), Sir A. Brooke and Colonel Archdall (0050). Mervyn Archdall and Arthur Cole-Hamilton were returned in 1783. Sir Arthur Brooke died in 1785.

DIVISION LISTS:

1763 (1) voted against an inquiry into the pension list.

1768 (1) voted against army augmentation.

1771 (1) voted for Lord Townshend as Lord Lieutenant.

1771 (2) voted for Sir Lucius O'Brien's (1558) motion for retrenchment.

1771 (3) voted against the amendment to the Revenue Bill.

1772 (1) voted against the separation of the Revenue Board.

1772 (2) voted for a Short Revenue Bill.

1773 (1) voted for the Absentee Tax.

1773 (2) voted for an untaxed press.

1774 (2) voted for Catholic relief.

1777 (1) voted against Grattan's (0895) motion for retrenchment.

1777 (2) voted against the Trade Embargo.

1779 (2) voted for a six-months Loan Bill.

1780 (2) voted against Yelverton's (2268) motion to modify Poynings' Law.

1780 (3) voted for the Tenantry Bill.

1780 (4) voted for the Perpetual Mutiny Bill.

1783 (1) voted against Flood's (0762) motion for parliamentary reform.

ADDITIONAL INFORMATION: One of the ten MPs fined by Justice Robinson for failing to attend Petty Juries, but a committee of inquiry found that Robinson had violated the House's privileges. A member of the Royal Dublin Society from 1757.

ESTATES/RESIDENCE: Colebrook, Co. Fermanagh; Sackville Street, Dublin. Lands in the barony of Ormond Upper, Co. Tipperary. Patent of lands there and in Fermanagh to Sir John Cole, 18 Chas II. Tipperary lands were still in Brooke ownership in 1793. In 1775, Francis Brooke, brother (and residuary heir) of Sir Arthur, had a rental of £800. In the first decade of the nineteenth century Wakefield considered that 'Mr Brooke of Brookeborough' had an estate 'of the like extent' to Lord Enniskillen (£13,000 a year).

SOURCES: PRONI D/302; Wakefield, *Account of Ire.*, vol. 1 p. 259; NLI LC 1138 and 1260; *Analecta* no 21; PRONI MIC/474 Irish Volunteers; Ellis thesis; GEC *B*; Burke *PB* (1903) p. 205; *GM* Apr. 1785; R. B. McDowell, *Irish Public Opinion, 1750–1800*, pp. 11–12; T. Bartlett and D. W. Hayton (eds), *Penal Era and Golden Age* (Belfast, 1979) p. 113 n. 1, P. D. H. Smyth,

'The Volunteers and Parliament, 1779–84'; *Almanacks*; *FJ* 5–7 Mar. 1772; *DJ* 8–10 Mar. 1785; Parliamentary Lists, 1769 (1), 1771 (1), 1772 (1), (2), 1773 (1), (2), 1774 (1), 1775 (1), 1776 (1), (2), (3), 1777 (1), 1778 (1), 1780 (1), 1782 (1), 1784 (1), (2), (3), 1785 (2).

0248 BROOKE, Henry

MP for Dundalk 1713–14, 1715–27; Co. Fermanagh 1727–60

b. (bapt. 22 Jan.) 1670/1; d. 14 July 1761
FAMILY/BACKGROUND: Eldest son of Thomas Brooke (0250), and Catherine, e. dau. of Sir John Cole, 1st Bt of Newland, Co. Dublin, and sis. and co-h. of 1st Lord Ranelagh.
MARRIED: [29 Mar. 1711] Letitia (d. 1763), dau. of Benjamin Burton (0292).
CHILDREN: Rt Hon. Arthur, 1st Bt (0247); Francis, m. [24 June 1765] Hannah, dau. of Henry Prittie of Co. Tipperary; Anne, m. Kilner Brasier (0229); Letitia, m. Robert Gore; Grace, m. [30 Jan. 1756] John Bateman of Callow, Co. Limerick.
CAREER/OCCUPATION: High Sheriff of Co. Fermanagh 1709; Custos Rot. of Co. Fermanagh; *Trustee of the Linen Manufacture for Connaught 1732–d.; *Commissioner of the Tillage Act for Ulster 1735, 1739–d.; Governor of Co. Fermanagh 1747–52; *Barracks Master 1750, of Philipstown 1752–5.

POLITICAL ACTIVITY: He came into parliament in 1713 as a Whig. He was nominated to 57 committees during his political career. Little is known of his parliamentary career.

ADDITIONAL INFORMATION: His father-in-law was the famous banker Ben Burton.

A foundation member of the Dublin Society, 1731. On a list of money borrowed from the government through Sir Henry Cavendish (0380), Henry Brooke is noted as having borrowed on 8 March 1756 a mortgage of £5,300.

ESTATES/RESIDENCE: William Street, Dublin (1751); Colebrook, Co. Fermanagh. In 1706, Henry Brooke had been granted fairs at Brookborough, *alias* Aghalum. Henry Brooke, MP for Dundalk's income in 1713 was estimated to be £1,000.

SOURCES: PRONI D/302; PRONI T/3411; PRONI T/3019/6457/464 Wilmot Papers; J. Walton, *'The King's*

Business': Letters on the Administration of Ireland, 1741–61 (NY, 1996) no 267; McCracken thesis; Burke PB (1903), p. 205; Alum. Dub.; Ir. Gen. vol. 7 no 1 (1986) p. 18A; J. T. Gilbert, History of the City of Dublin, 3 vols (1861) vol. 3 pp. 332–6 [there is some confusion here and possibly two Brookes are mixed up, e.g. or he cannot be sitting in Parliament in 1713 if, as Gilbert suggests, he was b. 1708]; Berry RDS pp. 24–7; A. Dusek, 'Baptisms in St Bride's, Dublin, 1633–1713'; R. B. McDowell, Irish Public Opinion, 1750–1800 (London, 1944) pp. 11, 23; Almanacks, BNL 8 June 1739; T. Bartlett, The Fall and Rise of the Irish Nation (Dublin, 1992), p. 54; DJ, 14–18 July 1761 [says he died 15 July 1761]; Parliamentary List, 1713 (2).

0249 BROOKE, Henry Vaughan

MP for Donegal B. 1777–83; Co. Donegal 1783–90–7–1800 [r. Augher 1783]; [UK] 1801–2, 1806 – 27 Nov. 1807

> b. 1743; d. 27 Nov. 1807 at his house in Spring Gardens, London.
> FAMILY/BACKGROUND: Eldest son of Basil Brooke of Co. Donegal and Jane, daughter of Henry Wray of Co. Donegal.
> MARRIED: [?1806] Elizabeth dau. of the Rev. Travers Hume (?unmarried).
> CHILDREN: d.s.p.
> EDUCATION: School: Mr McClean; entered TCD 7 July 1761.
> CAREER/OCCUPATION: Sheriff of Co. Donegal 1786–7.
> MILITARY: Colonel of the Leck Volunteers; Colonel, Donegal Militia 1798.

POLITICAL ACTIVITY: A local landowner with an independent fortune, on first coming into parliament he purchased his seat from Lord Arran. He was considered a sensible young man who generally supported government. 'It is believed he will stand for the County. A moderate and well inclined man. Is anxious to have a relation preferred in the Church.' From 1783 until the Union he represented Co. Donegal. He was supported by Alexander Montgomery (1437) and the popular interest in the county against William Burton Conyngham (0303), who, along with Lord Donegall, Lord Leitrim (0418) and Thomas Conolly (0459), had the 'real' interest in the county. Brooke was probably supported by Robert Stewart (2008).

Not surprisingly, in 1785 Brooke was 'sometimes in support but in all material matters is in opposition (obliged from the nature of his election)' – he was particularly anxious to obtain a church living for his brother-in-law. In 1789 an opposition list declared that 'To be chosen by a spirited and independent County to represent them in Parliament, is a distinction that Mr Brooke in a great measure owes to the general opinion of his integrity and honour entertained by his constituents; for the powerful interests of the County were combined against him and he possessed not the ideal merit of a brother fallen in the imagined cause of liberty [which Montgomery had] ... the public conduct of Mr Brooke ... has been firm, temperate and manly and as distant from the mulish obstinacy of an indiscriminate opposition, as from the slightest suspicion of venality or corruption. He neither is nor affects to be an orator, as he possesses not the natural abilities, or the acquired habits requisite to sustain that eminent character, but he delivers the opinions of an honest man with firmness and decision ... If his language is at any time feeble, it is supported by the strength of his thoughts and the energy of his sentiments in some measure compensates for the coldness of his manner. He never long engages the attention of the House, but satisfies himself with some pertinent and pointed observations, concisely expressed and forcibly applied and therefore in argument he has more of the condensed closeness of Thucydides than of the majestic abundance of Livy. His matter is in general very good, nervous, masculine and instructive. As he is not ambitious of speaking on every question, it is as well digested as selected and, as he enjoyed the advantage of a liberal education, he is possessed of stores not readily exhausted and very different from those displayed by the gleaners of pamphlets and the retailers of the fungous productions of the press. It were, indeed, to be wished that such a man would exert himself more; that he would call forth his latent powers and rouse his torpid energies, nor suffer dissipation or play to repress his faculties. He would find a reward in the very spirit of the effort but, to a person of his liberal mind one much more flattering in the increased power which he would thus acquire of serving the community.' A list in the following year, 1790, praises his 'propriety, integrity and moderation'.

In 1797 he also stood for Co. Fermanagh but was substantially defeated by John Willoughby Cole (**0441**) (Enniskillen) and Mervyn Archdall (**0050**). His voting pattern shows that he almost invariably – the Convention Bill and Catholic Emancipation being the principal exceptions – voted for the opposition. As he had voted for Knox's (**1180**) motion for Catholic Emancipation, his volte-face in 1795 was surprising, and possibly the product of the unusual circumstances of that time. He was a consistent opponent of the Union. He continued to sit for Co. Donegal after the Union in the parliament of the UK, where government viewed him as a country gentleman, 'well meaning but not a party man'. He gave Grenville and Portland a moderate support.

DIVISION LISTS:

1778 (2) voted for the Popery Bill.

1779 (2) voted for a six-months Loan Bill.

1780 (2) voted for Yelverton's (**2268**) motion to modify Poynings' Law.

1783 (1) voted for Flood's (**0762**) motion for parliamentary reform.

1784 (1) voted for a committee on the Reform Bill.

1785 (1) voted against the Commercial Propositions.

1786 (1) voted for the rights of the Grand Juries.

1787 (1) voted for a Pension Bill.

1788 (2) voted for Forbes's (**0778**) motion for limiting pensions.

1789 (1) voted for a regency.

1790 (1) voted for Grattan's (**0895**) motion for reducing the influence of the Crown.

1790 (2) voted for Ponsonby (**1709**) on the election of a Speaker.

1791 (1) voted for Curran's (**0560**) resolution against the sale of peerages.

1791 (2) voted for Grattan's motion for the exercise of Free Trade.

1791 (3) voted for Grattan's motion to abolish the Dublin police.

1793 (1) voted for Knox's (**1180**) motion for Catholic Emancipation.

1793 (2) voted for the Convention Bill.

1795 (2) voted against Catholic Emancipation.

1800 (1) voted against the Union.

ADDITIONAL INFORMATION: A member of the Royal Dublin Society from 1780. Declared himself against the Union, January 1799. In his obituary in the *Belfast News Letter* he was described as a 'benevolent and amiable man'.

ESTATES/RESIDENCE: Brooke Hall, Co. Donegal (Rockville, Letterkenny); Duke Street, Dublin; Spring Gardens, London. Left property amounting to £5,000 p.a. to his next of kin, Henry Brooke.

SOURCES: PRONI T/3166/1A Hartnell notes; PRONI MIC/474 Irish Volunteers; O'Neill thesis; *Alum. Dub.*; Jupp thesis [says he was unmarried]; Hughes, *Pat. Officers*; Ellis thesis [says married 1806 Elizabeth, dau. of Rev Travers Hume]; *BNL* 8 Dec. 1807; *FJ* 5 Aug. 1797, 31 Jan. 1799; Parliamentary Lists, 1776 (1), 1778 (1), 1780 (1), 1782 (1), 1783 (1), 1784 (1), 1785 (1), (2), (3), (4), 1787 (1), 1788 (1), 1789 (1), (2), 1790 (1), 1791 (1), 1793 (1), 1799 (3), 1800 (3).

0250 BROOKE, Thomas

MP for Antrim B. 1695–6

b. *ante* 1650; d. 1696

FAMILY/BACKGROUND: Son of Sir Henry Brooke and his second wife Anne, dau. of Sir George St George Kt.

MARRIED: Catherine, dau. of Sir John Cole, 1st Bt, of Newland, Co. Dublin, and sis. and co-h. of 1st Lord Ranelagh.

CHILDREN: Arthur; Henry (**0248**); Mary; Anne; Catherine.

POLITICAL ACTIVITY: He was only very briefly in parliament, but appears to have followed the usual country gentleman's opposition to Lord Chancellor Porter's supposed favouritism to the Catholics, and in 1695 voted against him.

ESTATES/RESIDENCE: Colebrook, Co. Fermanagh.

SOURCES: PRONI T/559, Burke, extract pedigrees, vol. 12 p. 84; Simms' cards; Burke *PB* (1903) p. 205; C. Dalton (ed.), *English Army Lists and Commission Registers, 1661–1714* (London, 1892), vol. 1 p. 210 [says Thomas Brookes, Ensign, Villier's Regiment of Foot

15 Feb. 1678]; S. W. Singer (ed.), *Clarendon Corr.*, vol. 1 (London, 1828) pp. 436–7 [says a Captain Brooke paid £1,600 for his commission in Lord Ardglasse's Regiment and was deprived of it when James succeeded to the throne; in June 1686 he was petitioning the King concerning it]; Parliamentary List, 1695 (1).

0251 BROWNE, Hon. Arthur

MP for Gowran 1769–76; Co. Mayo 1776–9

b. 1732; d. 21 (bur. 26) July 1779
FAMILY/BACKGROUND: Son of John Browne, 1st Earl of Altamont (0258), and Anne, dau. of Sir Arthur Gore, 2nd Bt (0857).
MARRIED: [1766] Anne (d. July 1807), dau. of Sir John Gardiner MD of Boston, New England.
CHILDREN: Maj. John (67th Regiment) (b. 1756; d. 1814), m. [1784] Rosa Mary, dau. of Adm. Sir Richard Hughes Bt; George Townshend (b. 1760; d. 4 June 1856), m. Miss Fleetwood; Anne, m. [Apr. 1784] Maj. Thomas Bucknall Lindsey of Co. Mayo; Augusta Louisa (d. 1850), m. [1803] Lieut.-Col. Dominick Browne of Co. Mayo; Henry; Lucinda.
CAREER/OCCUPATION: *Town Major of Galway 1749–52.
MILITARY: Lieutenant-Colonel 28th Foot (by purchase, Lord Townshend's regiment); *Lieutenant-Colonel of the 5th Regiment of Foot 1767, 6th Regiment of Foot 1769, 7th Regiment of Dragoons 1770, 9th Regiment of Dragoons 1774; Constable of Carrickfergus 15 Dec. 1774, 1776–9, Insp. of Recruiting.

POLITICAL ACTIVITY: A professional soldier, he was one of those who supported General Wolfe when he was mortally wounded at Quebec in 1759. He 'purchased from Mr James Agar (0016) for £2,000 who has this Borough [Gowran] entirely. Lieutenant Colonel of the 28th Foot, Lord Townshend's Regiment. A bustling, swaggering man of no great abilities but very friendly – For.' Lord Lieutenant Townshend gave him 'a Cornetcy for his son, a Surveyor Generalship to one of his brothers, £500 p.a. and a Collection of [Foxford, Co. Mayo] £270–300 to another'. In addition his father was made a viscount and then advanced to an earldom. Not surprisingly, 'He and his family [are] very strongly attached to Lord Townshend.' In 1774 he was described by an opposition list as

'Lieutenant Colonel of the 28th [Lord Townshend's] Regiment of Foot. A staunch friend and supporter of this as well as the last administration. The white-washer of Lord Townshend's black character, the bitter enemy of Aldermen's claret and custard, retailer of Horace, by bits and scraps; and the nice distinguisher between a cat and a merchant ship. Voted for Tontines, Stamps, Popery, and removal of the Custom house, etc. but in private life an amiable and steady friend.'

Lord Harcourt found him 'a most zealous friend of Government. Although a bad speaker a most useful and necessary Member for the Castle and much beloved. He has supported Lord Harcourt with great steadiness and very ably. His Excellency obtained for him the Constableship of Carrickfergus with a salary of £365. It is said the lands belonging to it are worth £200 more, and his Excellency has given to his recommendation 1 Boatman, 1 Gauger, 1 Hearth Money Collector.'

He was a prominent defender of the government over the 1776 embargo, and replied effectively to opposition claims that it was destroying the provision trade: 'Besides troops already sailed for America, there are at least 24,000 men more to embark for that country; the transports are all to be victualled at Cork, the fleet likewise must be victualled there, and provisions must be bought there to victual the whole army and navy during the campaign in America. Sir the very demand for provisions to this armament, is, in my opinion, more than sufficient for all the provisions now on sale in Ireland, and it is reasonable that Great Britain should have the pre-emption of them; but, say gentlemen, this embargo will lower the price; I say no, if notwithstanding the embargo, there is an ample demand the merchant will take care to have the full value of his goods, when he knows the buyer cannot supply himself at all events.' After the outbreak of the War of American Independence, in addition to being Inspector of Recruits he was 'Superintendent of the Recruiting Service in Ireland'.

DIVISION LISTS:
1771 (1) voted for Lord Townshend as Lord Lieutenant.
1771 (2) voted against Sir Lucius O'Brien's (1558) motion for retrenchment – an officer

in the army.

1772 (2) a teller against a Short Revenue Bill.

1773 (1) voted for Absentee Tax.

1773 (2) voted against an untaxed press.

1774 (1) voted for the Stamp Bill.

1774 (2) voted for Catholic relief.

1775 (1) voted against the pro-American amendment to the Speech from the Throne.

1777 (1) voted against Grattan's (0895) motion for retrenchment.

1778 (2) voted for the Popery Bill.

ESTATES/RESIDENCE: Gloucester Street, Dublin.

SOURCES: *IHS* vol. 2 (1940–41) pp. 3–11, T. M. O'Connor, 'The more immediate effects of the American Revolution in Ireland 1775–85'; RCBL P80/1/1, Parish Registers of St Thomas, Dublin; Burke *PB* (1903) pp. 1396–7 (1906) p. 1501; Kilkenny MPs; Hughes, *Pat. Officers*; PRONI T/1584 Pinkerton transcripts, p. 285, 21 July 1778 [calls him Charles]; *Almanacks*; Parliamentary Lists, 1772 (2), 1773 (1), (2), 1774 (1), 1775 (1), 1776 (2), 1776 (3), 1777 (1), 1778 (1).

0252 BROWNE, Arthur

MP for TCD 1783–90–7–1800 (re-elected after appointment to place of profit 1795)

b. 1756; d. 8 June 1805

FAMILY/BACKGROUND: Son of Marmaduke Browne, Rector of Trinity Church, Newport, Rhode Island.

MARRIED: (1) [   ]; (2) Bridget [   ].

CHILDREN: (1) dau.

(2) 5 children.

EDUCATION: Entered TCD, BA 1776, Fellow 1777; Middle Temple 1777; called to the Irish Bar 1779, MA of TCD 1779, LLB 1780, LLD 1784, Professor of Laws 1785, Regius Professor of Greek 1797–9, 1801–6.

CAREER/OCCUPATION: *Commissioner of Bankruptcy 1787–8; *King's Counsel 1795; *listed in Judges and Barristers 1789–1, 1793, 1795–1800 (f.); *Advocate in the Courts of Delegates, Prerogative, Admiralty and Consistory 1799 (f.); Commissioner of Accounts Apr. 1801–Jan. 1802 at £800 p.a.; Prime Serjeant 29 Dec. 1802 and 1803 (last to hold this office); *Governor of Erasmus Smith's Schools and other Charities 1795–7.

MILITARY: Commandant of the Trinity College Volunteers.

POLITICAL ACTIVITY: Browne was born in America, but came to Ireland and was educated at Trinity College. Apart from some of his father's clerical friends, who were more worthy than influential, he had little support except his own personal and intellectual merits. He was a Fellow of the College and a lawyer. Returned for Dublin University in the turbulent election of 1783, when his American background probably helped him. The college electorate comprised 70 scholars and 22 Fellows, in all 92, 'who,' it was declared, 'cannot be corrupted, even by the present Provost' (Hely-Hutchinson, **1001**), and it was said that he was returned by 'the young men against the Provost' – they also chose Sir Laurence Parsons (**1636**), the other member. Both MPs were able and almost permanently in opposition.

In 1787, responding to Chief Secretary Orde's (**1594**) education proposals, he complained that the college had not been consulted: 'a fresh instance of that disrespect which coxcombs from Eton and Westminster were apt to show them'. This was also a veiled criticism of the Provost, who wished the college to produce elegant and finished young gentlemen and had sent at least two of his sons to Eton. Nevertheless, he was concerned with the gap between the rich and the poor and with the social problems created by high rents and low wages. Like Orde, he felt that there was a connection between crime and poverty and lack of education.

A contemporary description of Browne in 1790 declared that: 'Educated in Trinity College his distinguished learning and excellent conduct procured his election to a fellowship there and, when an attempt was made to convert the university into a family Borough [by the Provost], the independent part of the body fixed on him as the fittest person to support their rights and succeeded in electing him unanimously representative for the seat of learning, at the commencement of the present parliament. Mr Browne's voice is clear and distinct, but not commanding; always audible, generally well toned and but sometimes a little too shrill. His language is uncommonly good, choice, correct and flowing, the effect of study without smelling of the lamp and duly tempered between the extremes of a glowing poetical phraseology and the cold lifelessness of creeping prose. His action, though at times somewhat marked by professional manner, is mostly well considered, never transgressing the bounds of decorum and uniting with force a due portion of grace and elegance. His manner is warm, not violent spirited, not impetuous and the rapidity of his elocution corresponds to the quickness of his conceptions. In argument he is acute, strong and forcible, seeing at once the strong points of the question, seizing them with avidity and enforcing them with energy and possessing all the accuracy of logical reasoning, without the pedantic affectation of its use. From a mind well stored with the richest products of ancient and modern learning, he invariably draws matter apposite, copious, and weighty; well selected, well arranged and adapted to compel conviction; forcing its way against the obstinacy of prejudice and the predetermination of party. Representing the seat of science, his conduct has done honour to her choice, being liberal, manly and spirited; equally adverse to the strides of authority and to the struggles of licentiousness and equally friendly to the due equipoise of the constitution in church and state. In the late debates on tithes, so much talked of and so little understood, he eminently distinguished himself, standing forth the supporter of the just rights of the clergy, with a spirit that captivated the young and with a knowledge that astonished the old and that too against the first orator in the House of Commons [Grattan, **0895**], whom few dare to encounter and fewer still encounter with success. Mr Browne had that rare felicity and has by that, as well as by the whole of his public conduct, ensured the affections of his learned and respectable constituents.'

Browne was one of the few parliamentary speakers who could hold his own against Grattan. In 1790 he was again returned, this time with the Provost's son, Francis Hely-Hutchinson (**1000**). In 1793 His Excellency was pleased 'to promote eight young gentlemen to the rank of King's counsel. Three of them, Messrs Browne, Hoare (**1022**) and Fletcher (**0759**), forgot that by accepting office they vacated their seats in Parliament, and

seem now not a little surprised to find that they must take their chance for a fresh election, which they are not sure of.' This was one of the unanticipated boomerangs of the 1793 Place Act, which had been so ardently and so long desired by the reformers.

Browne's support for the March 1794 Reform Bill came at the height of the French Revolution, and he thought that this fairly moderate measure would counterbalance the current demand for universal male suffrage and the wilder theories that the revolution had unleashed. He was concerned that in these circumstances society should not become polarised. To the same end he was an advocate of friendly societies, which would help the poor in sickness and distress. He had an enviable reputation as an essayist. However, on 17 January 1799 he wrote to Castlereagh (**2009**) claiming that the majority of his constituents had urged him to vote against the Union, and possibly angling for some professional advancement before the door finally closed on such ambitions. In any case, in 1800 he '*changed sides and principles*, and was appointed [Prime] Serjeant. In 1799 opposed the Union, and supported it in 1800.' He was the last Prime Serjeant.

DIVISION LISTS:

1783 (1) voted for Flood's (**0762**) motion for parliamentary reform.

1784 (1) voted for a committee on the Reform Bill.

1784 (4) voted against the Address to His Grace the Duke of Rutland.

1785 (1) voted against the Commercial Propositions.

1786 (2) voted for Forbes's (**0778**) motion for retrenchment.

1787 (1) voted for a Pension Bill.

1788 (1) voted for Hartley's (**0979**) motion against the Dublin police.

1788 (2) voted for Forbes' motion for limiting pensions.

1789 (1) voted for a regency.

1790 (1) voted for Grattan's (**0895**) motion for reducing the influence of the Crown.

1790 (2) voted for Ponsonby (**1709**) on the election of a Speaker.

1791 (1) voted for Curran's (**0560**) resolution against the sale of peerages.

1791 (3) voted for Grattan's motion to abolish the Dublin police.

1792 (1) voted for the Catholic petition.

1793 (2) a teller against the Convention Bill.

1795 (1) voted for a Short Money Bill.

1796 (1) voted for parity of trade with Great Britain.

1797 (1) voted for Ponsonby's motion for parliamentary reform.

1798 (1) voted for Sir Laurence Parsons' (**1636**) motion for an investigation into 'the present discontents'.

1799 (1) voted against the Union.

1800 (1) voted for the Union.

ADDITIONAL INFORMATION: A member of the Whig Club, 1790; a member of the Royal Irish Academy from 1797.

ESTATES/RESIDENCE: Trinity College, Dublin.

SOURCES: PRONI D/3030/505 Castlereagh Papers; PRONI T/3459 Donoughmore Papers, p. 5; PRONI T/3166/1B Hartnell notes; O'Neill thesis; Hughes, *Pat. Officers*; *King's Inns Admissions*; R. B. McDowell and D. A. Webb, *Trinity College Dublin, 1592–1952: An Academic History* (Cambridge, 1982) p. 81; McDowell, *Ir. public opinion*, pp. 124, 192, 232; Johnston, *Gt B. & Ire.*, p. 239; R. B. McDowell, *Ireland in the Age of Imperialism and Revolution, 1760–1801* (Oxford, 1979), pp. 93–5; *Almanacks*; *BNL* 22–6 Jan. 1790; *FJ* 31 Dec. 1796; Parliamentary Lists, 1783 (2), 1784 (1), (2), (3), 1785 (1), (2), (3), (4), 1787 (1), 1788 (1), 1789 (1), (2), 1791 (1), 1793 (1), 1799 (1), (3), 1800 (3).

0253 BROWNE, Rt Hon. Denis

MP for Co. Mayo 1782-3-90-7-1800 [r. Castlebar 1797]; [UK] 1801-18; Kilkenny B. 1820-6

b. 1763; d. 14 Aug. 1828

HONOURS: PC 20 Jan. 1794.

FAMILY/BACKGROUND: Son of Peter Browne-Kelly, 2nd Earl of Altamont (**0262**), and Elizabeth, o. dau. and h. of Dennis Kelly (**1139**).

MARRIED: [1790] Anne, dau. of Ross Mahon.

CHILDREN: James, m. (1) [1820] Eleanor

Catherine, dau. of John Wells of Bickley, Kent, (2) [1825] Elizabeth, dau. of John Puget of Hertfordshire; Peter, m. [1822] Catherine Esther, dau. of John Puget; Rev. Denis, m. [1824] Anne Alicia, dau. of Thomas William Filgate of Co. Louth; John Denis, m. [1832] Esther, e. dau. of John Wells of Kent; Rev. George, m. [1828] Elizabeth Anne, dau. of Rev. Edward Day of Co. Kerry; Anne Louisa; Elizabeth, m. [1832] George Harrison; Charlotte, m. [1824] Rev. William Purdon; Harriet Mary, m. [1829] Rev. Robert Pakenham.

CAREER/OCCUPATION: High Sheriff of Co. Mayo 30 Jan. 1786; *Coroner for Co. Down 1789–96; Member of Linen Board 1814.

MILITARY: Cornet 5th Royal Irish Dragoons 1779–84; Ashford Art Volunteers; Colonel of Co. Mayo Militia, 1793; Captain in Murish or Murrisk Cavalry 1796–9, Claremorris Infantry 1822.

POLITICAL ACTIVITY: When first elected for Co. Mayo in 1782, he was in the army. He followed the political lead of his brother, Lord Altamont (**0260**), who had gone into opposition when Lord Lieutenant Portland dismissed his uncle (**0256**) from the office of Prime Serjeant. However, his approach to reform appears to have been lukewarm, and more related to Co. Mayo politics than conviction: he 'has given up his inclination to reform as his opponents in the County have taken it up'. The family supported the Duke of Rutland, and a pension was found for his uncle.

The county and Grand Jury were against the Commercial Resolutions, but both Browne and Cuffe (**0552**), the other MP, were absent for the debate. He was a frequent parliamentary speaker; an unfriendly contemporary, recollecting his early military career, wrote in 1789 that: 'His voice is strong, full, distinct and mellow, by no means ill-toned and though not remarkable for great harmony or melody, deep yet clear and high without any offensive shrillness and his management of it, certainly neither artful nor scientific, is yet not injudicious; in general showing all its advantages, unless when some uncommon impulse hurries him beyond the bounds of propriety. His language, neither elegant nor animated, is little adapted to command the attention, conciliate the regards, or invigorate the minds of his hearers, as alike deficient in philosophical clearness and grammatical precision, it is mostly expressed in a peremptory and magisterial tone and is abundant without selection and flowing without energy. His delivery, very far from all sleepy languor, is at times so rapid as to embarrass his pronunciation and frequently destroys all propriety of emphasis and his manner, totally averse from diffidence or soothing address, is vehement, impetuous, and overbearing; more suited to soldierly command than oratorical insinuation and more fitted to offend than delight. His action, entirely diverse of grace, has not much force, for it is violent not spirited, he belabouring the air at a most unconscionable rate.'

Despite these strictures, the writer concludes that his view is: 'indeed advanced with peculiar courage and without any shadow of timidity or fear of contradiction and is obviously the unborrowed property of the speaker; heavy if not solid, and occasionally sparkling if not brilliant. His parliamentary conduct is not easily to be described by any one specific term ... What it will be hereafter no time past enables us to prognosticate.' A year later another commentator wrote that 'Mr Browne has at various times in the House of Commons veered about to every point of the political compass.' However, despite a serious challenge from the Binghams, emphasised by three duels before the polling started, Browne sat for the county until the Union, which he supported, and lobbied administration for a marquessate for his brother, which was granted.

In 1801 'the great Leviathan' of Mayo was returned unopposed after eliminating one of his opponents in a duel. His family had been supported for 50 years by the Catholic interest in the very Catholic county of Mayo and he had, since the 1790s, felt obliged to favour their claims. This he continued to do in the parliament of the United Kingdom.

DIVISION LISTS:
1783 (1) voted for Flood's (0762) motion for parliamentary reform.
1784 (1) voted for a committee on the Reform Bill.
1785 (1) absent.
1788 (1) voted for Hartley's (0979) motion against the Dublin police.
1789 (1) voted against a regency.
1790 (1) voted against Grattan's (0895)

motion for reducing the influence of the Crown.
1790 (2) voted for Foster (0805) on the election of a Speaker.
1791 (3) teller against Grattan's motion to abolish the Dublin police.
1792 (1) voted for the Catholic petition.
1793 (2) voted for the Convention Bill.
1798 (1) voted against Sir Laurence Parsons' (1636) motion for an investigation into 'the present discontents'.
1799 (1) voted for the Union – a Privy Councillor and Captain in the County Militia.
1800 (1) voted for the Union.

ADDITIONAL INFORMATION: A subscriber to the Public Assembly Rooms, 1787; *a member of the Royal Irish Academy, 1795.

In his petition to the Commissioners of Union Compensation he claimed to be seised of a real estate within the Borough of Swords producing a yearly rental of £11 7s 6d.

ESTATES/RESIDENCE: Claremont House, Co. Mayo; Claremorris, in the barony of Clanmorris.

SOURCES: D/302; PRONI D/1201/55 EEC rental 1854; Wakefield, *Account of Ire.*, vol. 1 p. 271; PRONI T/3166/1C Hartnell notes; PRONI MIC/454; O'Neill thesis [says he died 1826]; Jupp thesis; Burke *PB* (1903) p. 1397 (1906) p. 1502; *HP 1790–1820*; Hughes, *Pat. Officers*; *Index to Irish Privy Counsellors, 1711–1910*; J. Kelly, *'That Damn'd thing Called Honour': Duelling in Ireland 1570–1860* (Cork, 1995), pp. 146, 156; *Further Proceedings of the Commissioners under the Union Compensation Act of Ireland* (1805); *Almanacks*; *FJ* 25–7 Apr. 1793, 20 Oct. 1796; Parliamentary Lists, 1782 (1), 1783 (1), 1784 (1), (2), (3), 1785 (1), (2), (3), (4), 1787 (1), 1788 (1), 1789 (1), (2), 1790 (1), 1791 (1), 1793 (1), 1794 (2), 1798 (1), 1799 (2), (3), 1800 (3).

0254 BROWNE, (Sir) George

MP for Castlebar 1713–14

b. *c.* 1680–8; d. 8 May 1737
HONOURS: Suc. as 4th Bt [S] *c.* 1712 (but never assumed the baronetcy).
FAMILY/BACKGROUND: Son and h. of (Sir) John Browne, 3rd Bt (but never assumed), a Captain

in the Irish army of James II who was taken prisoner at Londonderry, and his second wife Julia, dau. of Sir Patrick Bellew, 1st Bt.
MARRIED: [1709] his cousin Bridget, dau. of Edward Bellingham, Lord Athenry.
CHILDREN: *d.s.p.*
CAREER/OCCUPATION: High Sheriff of Co. Mayo 1690.

POLITICAL ACTIVITY: He sat only in the brief single session of the last parliament of Queen Anne. He was certified as a Protestant on 22 March 1711 and was enrolled accordingly, 24 March 1711. This was probably to keep the estate intact, as his father's will (dated 1700) was proved 21 November 1712. The penal law of 1704 (2 Anne, c. 6; 8 Anne, c. 3), 'an act to prevent the further growth of Popery', was confirmed in 1709 and contained a gavelling clause that divided Catholic property among all the deceased's sons. He was one of the nine 'converts' (ex-Catholics) elected to the 1713 parliament in the Tory interest and complained of by the Whigs.

ADDITIONAL INFORMATION: The Irish act of 1697 (9 Will. III, c. 2), 'an act for the confirmation of the articles made at the surrender of the city of Limerick'), deprived the king of the power to pardon persons who had actually been outlawed and were not the subject of a saving clause. Pardons, however, could still be given to persons who had not been outlawed, and the list includes a certain number of pardons of this class which were given after 1697. Thus George Browne of the Neale and his son John were pardoned in June 1698. Neither had been indicted or outlawed, although George had been Sheriff of Mayo and John had been taken prisoner at Derry.

ESTATES/RESIDENCE: The Neale, Co. Mayo.

SOURCES: GEC *B*; *IMC The Convert Rolls* p. 23; Historical Studies vol. 4 (1963) pp. 84, 91 f. 5; Simms, *Williamite Confiscation*, p. 81; Parliamentary Lists, 1713 (2), 1714 (1), 1714–15 (1).

0255 BROWNE, Hon. George

MP for Co. Mayo 1779–82

b. *c.* 1735–7; d. 22 July 1782

FAMILY/BACKGROUND: Third son of John Browne, 1st Earl of Altamont (**0258**) and Anne, e. dau. of Sir Arthur Gore, 2nd Bt (**0857**).
MARRIED: Dorcas, dau. and h. of James Moore of Newport, Co. Mayo.
CHILDREN: Margaret, m. [1785] Dominick Geoffrey Browne of Castle MacGarret.
CAREER/OCCUPATION: *Collector of the Revenue for Foxford and Newport 1756–69; *Surveyor General for Connaught 1773.

POLITICAL ACTIVITY: Returned by his brother, Lord Altamont (**0262**), on the death of their brother Lieutenant-Colonel Arthur Browne (**0251**). Lord Altamont was at that time a government supporter. George Browne was a placeman, but by 1780 his support was considered doubtful, probably in the face of the Buckinghamshire débâcle, as he appears to have supported government during the viceroyalty of Lord Carlisle.

DIVISION LISTS:
1779 (2) voted against a six-months Loan Bill.
1780 (1) voted against Grattan's (**0895**) declaration of the Rights of Ireland.
1780 (2) voted against Yelverton's (**2268**) motion to modify Poynings' Law.

ESTATES/RESIDENCE: Westport, Co. Mayo.

SOURCES: Ellis thesis; Burke *PB* (1903) p. 1397; *Alum. Dub.*; *Almanacks*; Parliamentary Lists, 1776 (1), 1780 (1).

0256 BROWNE, Hon. James

MP for Jamestown 1768–76; Tuam 1776–83; Castlebar 1783–90

b. *c.* 1736–8; d. 22 Oct. 1790
FAMILY/BACKGROUND: Fourth son of John Browne, 1st Earl of Altamont (**0258**) and Anne, e. dau. of Sir Arthur Gore, 2nd Bt (**0857**).
MARRIED: Unmarried.
EDUCATION: Middle Temple 7 May 1755; called to the Irish Bar 1760.
CAREER/OCCUPATION: Prime Serjeant 14 June 1780–2 (appointed by the Earl of Buckinghamshire *vice* Hussey-Burgh, resigned, removed by the Duke of Portland 1782, restored by the Duke of Rutland 1784), 1783–7; *listed in Judges and

Barristers 1789; Freeman of Fethard (Tipperary) 1774, Governor of the Hibernian Society 1779–86; *Governor of the Foundling Hospital and Workhouse 1780–6.

MILITARY: Colonel of the Brown Hall Volunteers and of the Mayo Legion Volunteers.

POLITICAL ACTIVITY: He was a lawyer and one of the men of business in the House of Commons. In March 1778 he spoke in support of an address to the king on the present critical situation. This was a big set debate and the address, despite some of the opposition MPs, passed *nem. con.* On 29 November 1779 Lord Lieutenant Buckinghamshire wrote to Lord George Germain (Sackville, **1835**) about 'Mr Brown, brother to Lord Altamont, tho' his abilities are not brilliant, is esteemed as a man of business with a sound useful understanding. He is much esteemed, and has a brother and nephew whose political conduct will be determined by his.' In his speeches he was said to be 'a great dealer in circumbendibuses'. In fact the picture from the Parliamentary Lists is that he was solid, weighty, worthy and rather dull.

On 31 December 1779 Lord Buckinghamshire wrote to Lord North on the resignation of the Prime Serjeant, Walter Hussey-Burgh (**1059**), and the need to fill that office speedily, that: 'The two persons, one of which it is in my contemplation to recommend to His Majesty for the office of Prime Serjeant are Mr Fitz Gibbon and Mr Browne, brother to the Earl of Altamont. The Parliamentary abilities of the first would clearly decide the preference in his favour, if he had not lately, contrary to assurances given, taken a warm part in Opposition ... the Attorney General interests himself in his favour. Mr Browne is a man of business, but is deficient in that readiness and activity in parliamentary debate which times like these hourly call for ... My own preference would rather incline to Mr Fitz Gibbon.' Buckinghamshire thought that the next seat at the Revenue Board might satisfy Browne. The Brownes operated as a political family in parliament. To please one was to please all and, as the Duke of Portland learnt when he dismissed James Browne in 1782, to offend one was to offend all.

On his arrival in 1782 the Duke of Portland decided on dismissing as many of the established office-holders as he could in order to make room for his friends and supporters. The Attorney General John Scott (**1891**) was replaced by Barry Yelverton (**2268**), and James Browne was replaced as Prime Serjeant by Walter Hussey-Burgh. On this occasion Browne wrote to Buckinghamshire that 'I (amongst others) without any kind of previous notice received an official letter acquainting me that my office was granted to another and that his Majesty had no further occasion for my service ... my nephew, Lord Altamont (**0260**), making my cause his own, directly wrote to his Grace and requested to know what offence or fault could have given cause for this treatment of his nearest relation. The Duke was pleased to answer that he knew not of any offence given by or fault alleged against me ... and it was not at all meant thereby to throw any slight on me on him or on his family. Lord Altamont replied that ... [it was] ... so evident an injury as he could not be insensitive of or patient under and therefore he must beg leave to resign his Government of the county of Mayo.' Browne continued that for one vote: 'any little weight my family [has] in parliament there has been very uncommon pains taken to lose. It consists only of one vote in the Lords and at present only two in the Commons, but at the next election to rise to its usual number of three in that House; whence one might compute that this change might on any division make the difference of seven voices in the Commons and two in the House of Lords against the Government.'

Over the Renunciation affair in 1783, he argued that the problem was that although the English Privy Council would still have the power of stopping Irish bills, the essential limitation to Yelverton's Act was that it admitted the right of the English cabinet to advise in the case of Irish legislation regarding whether it received the Royal Assent. Parsons (**1636**) probably came closest to the truth when he said that 'The great seal is the bond of connection between the two kingdoms ... [it gives the British parliament a veto] by such a remote and severe action that there is no reason to apprehend that it will be abused.'

He was restored to the office of Prime Serjeant by Lord Lieutenant Rutland in 1784 and retired the following year; his health appears to have deteriorated, and he was granted a pension.

DIVISION LISTS:

1771 (1) voted for Lord Townshend as Lord Lieutenant.

1771 (2) voted against Sir Lucius O'Brien's (**1558**) motion for retrenchment.

1772 (2) a teller against a Short Revenue Bill.

1773 (1) voted for Absentee Tax.

1773 (2) voted against an untaxed press.

1774 (1) voted for the Stamp Bill.

1774 (2) voted for Catholic relief.

1775 (1) voted against the pro-American amendment to the Speech from the Throne.

1777 (1) voted for Grattan's (**0895**) motion for retrenchment.

1777 (2) voted against the Trade Embargo.

1778 (1) voted for Grattan's motion for retrenchment.

1778 (2) voted for the Popery Bill.

1779 (2) voted against a six-months Loan Bill.

1780 (1) voted against Grattan's declaration of the Rights of Ireland.

1780 (2) a teller against Yelverton's (**2268**) motion to modify Poynings' Law.

1780 (4) voted for a Perpetual Mutiny Bill.

1783 (1) voted for Flood's (**0762**) motion for parliamentary reform.

1785 (1) voted for the Commercial Propositions.

1788 (1) voted for Hartley's (**0979**) motion against the Dublin police.

ADDITIONAL INFORMATION: A member of the Royal Dublin Society, 1765 to his death. There is a portrait of him at Westport House, Co. Mayo.

ESTATES/RESIDENCE: Castlebar, Co. Mayo; Earl Street, Sackville Street, Dublin.

SOURCES: PRONI MIC/474 Irish Volunteers; Ellis thesis; *IMC King's Inns Admission Papers*; *Middle Temple Admissions* vol. 1 p. 349; Smyth, *Law Officers*; *HMC Stopford-Sackville I* p. 262; *Beresford Corr.* vol. 1 pp. 26, 124, 184; McDowell, *Ir. public opinion*, p. 76; *Alum. Dub.*; *Ir. Gen.* vol. 4 no 4 (1971) p. 319, W. G. Skehan, 'Extracts from the Minutes of the Corporation of Fethard, Co. Tipperary'; *Almanacks*; *GM* Nov. 1790; *DJ* 9–11 May 1780, 2–4 Nov. 1790; Parliamentary Lists, 1769 (1), 1772 (2), 1773 (1), (2), 1774 (1), 1775 (1), 1776 (1), (2), (3), 1777 (1), 1778 (1), 1780 (1), 1782 (1), 1783 (1), (2), 1784 (1), (2), (3), 1785 (1), (2), (3), (4), 1787 (1), 1788 (1), 1789 (1), 1790 (1).

0257 BROWNE, Hon. James Caulfeild

MP for Carlow B. 21 Jan.–9 Apr. 1790

b. 16 Mar. 1765; d. 22 May 1825

PEERAGES: Suc. as 2nd Baron Kilmaine 1794.

FAMILY/BACKGROUND: Son of Sir John Browne, 1st Baron Kilmaine (**0259**), and Alicia, dau. of James Caulfeild, 3rd Viscount Charlemont (**0368**).

MARRIED: [25 July 1793] Anne, dau. of Rt Hon. Sir Henry Cavendish, 2nd Bt (**0381**).

CHILDREN: John Cavendish, 3rd Baron Kilmaine, m. (1) [1822] Eliza, dau. of David Lyon, (2) [1839] Mary, dau. of Hon. Charles Ewan Law; Henry Montague (b. 3 Oct. 1799; d. 22 Nov.1884), Dean of Lismore, m. [1822] Catherine Penelope (d. 24 June 1858), e. dau. of Rt Hon. Lodge Evans Morres, 1st Viscount Frankfort de Montmorency (**1491**); Maj. George Augustus (b. 18 Feb. 1801; d. 1878), m. (1) [1845] Anne Hammond, o. ch. of Sir Charles Morgan, wid. of Sir John Blacker, (2) [1853] Frances Mary, e. dau. of Charles Prideaux Brune of Prideaux Place, Cornwall; Augustus Caulfeild James (b. 15 Nov. 1803; drowned 9 Aug 1831); Capt. Richard Howe (b. 1 Oct. 1811; d. 1 Apr. 1888), m. (1) [1833] Elizabeth (d. 28 Oct. 1876), dau. of Colonel Hon. John Browne, (2) Elsie dau. of Col. H. L. Watkins (Bombay Army); Frederick Longworth (b. 1 Oct 1811; d. 6 Jan 1864); Sarah Louisa (d. 22 June 1881), m. [1825] Lieut.-Col. George Disbrowe.

CAREER/OCCUPATION: *Trustee of the Linen Board for Munster 1789–92; *Joint Governor of Co. Mayo 1795–1800 (f.).

POLITICAL ACTIVITY: He succeeded his father when the latter became a peer in 1789, but he sat only for the short session, 21 January to 5 April 1790. He, or his father, purchased his seat for Carlow from Mr William Burton (**0304**), as 'In this Borough the Burton interest is not only predominant, but omnipotent.'

ESTATES/RESIDENCE: The Neale, Co. Mayo.

SOURCES: Ellis thesis; Burke *PB* (1903) pp. 851–2 (1906) p. 918; GEC *P*; *Almanacks*; Parliamentary Lists 1789 (1), 1790 (1).

0258 BROWNE, John

MP for Castlebar 1744–60

b. 1709; d. 4 July 1776
PEERAGES: Cr. Baron Mounteagle 10 Sept. 1760,
Viscount Westport 24 Aug. 1768, Earl of
Altamont 4 Dec. 1771.
FAMILY/BACKGROUND: Son of Peter Browne (d.
1722) of Co. Mayo and Mary, dau. of Denis
Daly of Carrownakelly (Justice CP).
MARRIED: [Dec. 1729] Anne, dau. of Sir Arthur
Gore, 2nd Bt (**0857**).
CHILDREN: Peter, 2nd Earl of Altamont (**0262**);
Arthur (**0251**); George (**0255**); James (**0256**);
Henry (*d.s.p.* Mar. 1812), m. [ ], dau. of Sir
Henry Lynch, Bt; John, m. (1) Mary Cocks, (2)
Rosalinda (d. 30 Apr. 1812), dau. of Eneas
Gilker; Anne, m. [1762] Ross Mahon of
Castlegar, Co. Galway.
EDUCATION: Entered Oxford (Christ Church) 17
July 1725.
CAREER/OCCUPATION: Sheriff of Co. Mayo 1731;
Governor Co. Mayo in the absence of Lord
Tyrawley 1752–3, of Lord Westport 1752–61,
Governor 1765–75; *Governor of the Blue-Coat
Hospital 1757; Member of Trinity Guild 1755–
6, Senior Master 1758.

POLITICAL ACTIVITY: His grandfather was a colonel
in the army of James II and was one of the parties
to the Treaty of Limerick. One of the great political strengths of the Brownes was that in this overwhelmingly Catholic county they carried the
Catholic support.

As an MP he does not appear to have been personally very active, and on 1 December 1757 he
was ordered into the custody of the Serjeant-at-
Arms for defaulting on a call of the House, without offering an excuse for non-attendance. He was
probably a bad attender anyway, as he was nominated for only seven committees between 1746
and 1760. However, on 13 December the Speaker
informed the House that Browne had fallen from
his horse and so had been unable to attend, and
the order for his arrest was discharged.

He supported government on the vital issues of
the early 1750s, and was created Baron
Mounteagle in 1760. Four of his sons (**0251**,
0255, 0256, 0262) were sitting in parliament between 1768 and 1783, and the family should be
considered as a political unit. His son Colonel
Arthur Browne's (**0251**) connection with Lord

Townshend proved valuable; in 1768 this MP became Viscount Westport and finally, in 1771, Earl
of Altamont.

In the 1768 general election Viscount Westport
(**0262**) returned two of his younger sons, and in
the 1776 election the same MP, now Lord
Altamont, returned three sons, including his heir,
Lord Westport (**0260**).

At the Union, this MP's grandson (**0260**) was
created Marquess of Sligo.

DIVISION LISTS:
1749 (1) voted against the election of James
Digges La Touche (♦♦♦).
1753 (1) voted against the expulsion of
Arthur Jones-Nevill (**1125**).
1753 (2) voted for the Money Bill.

ESTATES/RESIDENCE: Westport, Co. Mayo.

SOURCES: NLI reps nos 204 and 176; *CJ Ire.* (Bradley
ed.) vol. 10 pp. 363, 403–4; PRONI T/1584 Pinkerton
transcripts, p. 254, 26 July 1776; McCracken thesis;
Burke *PB* (1903) p. 1397; GEC *P*; Johnston, *Gt B. &
Ire.*, p. 217; *Almanacks*; Parliamentary List, 1775 (1).

0259 BROWNE, Sir John

MP for Newtown 1776–83; Carlow B. 1783–9

b. 1730; d. 7 June 1794
HONOURS: Suc. as 7th Bt [S] 1765.
PEERAGES: Cr. Baron Kilmaine 21 Sept. 1789.
FAMILY/BACKGROUND: Son of Sir John Browne, 5th
Bt, and Margaret, dau. and co-h. of Henry
Dodwell of Athlone, Co. Westmeath.
MARRIED: [23 Apr. 1764] Alice, 2nd dau. of James
Caulfeild, 3rd Viscount Charlemont (**0368**).
CHILDREN: James Caulfeild, 2nd Baron Kilmaine
(**0257**); Lieut.-Col, John (b. 28 Aug. 1770, d. 8
Feb. 1855; at Cambridge (Corpus Christi) 1 Jan.
1790), m. [20 Sept. 1797] Anne (d. 23 Apr.
1751), dau. of John White of Jamaica; George (b.
2 Mar. 1774), m. [12 Oct. 1801] Mary, dau. of
Rev. Alexander Colston; Alicia Margaret (d.
1826), m. [9 Nov. 1787] John Longworth of
Cregan Castle, Co. Westmeath; Maria Sarah, m.
[3 Sept. 1795] Francis Longworth; Emily Juliana,
m. [3 Sept. 1795] Rev. John Cromie (bro. of
0530); Letitia (d. 1809), m. [30 Apr. 1798]
Lieut.-Col. John Ross.

EDUCATION: Entered TCD.

CAREER/OCCUPATION: High Sheriff of Co. Mayo 1778, 1788; Trustee of the Linen Board *vice* Viscount Southwell dec'd. Sept. 1780–2, 1784–8; Commissioner of Tillage and Navigation for the Province of Connaught 7 Feb. 1782–5,

POLITICAL ACTIVITY: He purchased his seat for Newtown(ards) from John Ponsonby (**1702**) in 1776. He belonged to the senior branch of the Browne family of Westport, Co. Mayo. He appears to have made no secret of his ambition to acquire a peerage, as this was suspected as early as 1776, when it was also noted that he had a good estate, if encumbered. Although he was married to a sister of Lord Charlemont, 'it is presumed he will not follow him in his opposition', despite the doubts about his conduct that his independence aroused. In 1782 the list declared that 'His object is the Peerage and he has supported Government uniformly.' The following year his chances improved, as his wife inherited 'a fortune of near £60,000, upon the death of Mr Bernard (**0125**) of Essex' (her uncle). He was now anxious to extend his political influence in Co. Mayo, but he was defeated in the 1783 election and bought a seat for Carlow from William Burton (**0304**), who represented Co. Carlow himself and sold both the seats for Carlow Borough, which he controlled absolutely. Browne's pro-Catholic vote in 1778 reflected his Co. Mayo politics.

Throughout the 1780s he continued to support the government and press his claims for a peerage. Finally, in 1789, he was successful and created Baron Kilmaine. In return, in 1790 he purchased the representation of Donegal town from Lord Arran (**0861**). In 1791 it was reported that 'The seats were sold by him [Lord Arran] to Sir J. Browne now Lord Kilmaine, who gave them to Government for his Peerage and as the story goes, betrayed the transaction to the opposition, hence the clamour *upon the Sale of Peerages*.' This activity was actually fairly well known, as in 1762 Chief Secretary W. G. Hamilton (**0948**) stated that 'Whenever a judgeship or a peerage was asked for any person in Parliament an offer was constantly made to government of the seat which should be vacated.' Promotions, therefore, were usually made at the beginning of a parliament. Lord Kilmaine was elevated at the end of a parliament – it had only about three months to run – hence the seats for the new parliament. Lord Kilmaine's crime was not to state what was generally known but to make it public. Grattan (**0895**) moved in the House of Commons on whether the government had: 'entered into any corrupt Agreement with any Person or Persons to recommend such Person ... to be ... made Peers of this Realm in consideration of such Person or Persons giving certain Sums of Money to be laid out in procuring the Return of Members to serve in Parliament.' The motion was rejected by 144 to 88 votes.

DIVISION LISTS:

1777 (1) voted against Grattan's (**0895**) motion for retrenchment.

1778 (2) voted for the Popery Bill.

1779 (1) a teller for new taxes.

1779 (2) voted against a six-months Loan Bill.

1780 (1) voted against Grattan's declaration of the Rights of Ireland.

1780 (2) voted against Yelverton's (**2268**) motion to modify Poynings' Law.

1780 (3) voted against the Tenantry Bill.

1780 (4) voted for the Perpetual Mutiny Bill.

1783 (1) voted against Flood's (**0762**) motion for parliamentary reform.

1784 (1) voted against a committee on the Reform Bill.

1784 (2) voted for the amendment on the woollen manufacture (?).

1785 (1) voted for the Commercial Propositions.

1787 (1) voted for a Pension Bill.

1788 (1) voted for Hartley's (**0979**) motion against the Dublin police (**0256**).

1789 (1) voted against a regency.

ADDITIONAL INFORMATION: His children were listed as nominees in the life annuities of 1779.

ESTATES/RESIDENCE: Henry Street, Dublin; the Neale Park, Co. Mayo; Gaulston Park, Co. Westmeath, purchased from the Earl of Belvidere; lands in Co. Wexford, including 2,161 statute acres in the barony of Ballaghkeen at a rental of £1,059, 323 in Scarawalsh at £162, an urban property in Wexford town at nearly

£200. Also, 4,300 acres in Scarawalsh at a minute fee-farm rent. It is unknown when the fee farm/perpetuity was originally granted. Lands in the baronies of Kilmaine, Clanmorris and Carra; also Athlone South, Co. Roscommon, and Brawny, Co. Westmeath. In 10 Jas I, Josiah Browne was granted fairs at Neale.

SOURCES: PRONI D/302; NLI LC 415; NLI EC 812, 1145, 2014, 2044; NLI CBD 2014 and 3055; PRONI MIC/315/9/52 Blackwood pedigrees; Ellis thesis; GEC *P*; Burke *PB*. (1903) pp. 851–2; *Alum. Cantab.*; Johnston, *Gt B. & Ire.*, p. 193–4; *Ir. Gen.* vol. 1 no 8 (1940) p. 238, 'A List of Irish Stockholders, 1779'; *Almanacks*; *DJ* 3–7 Apr. 1764, 11–14 Apr. 1779, 12 June 1794, 10 Apr. 1798; *FJ* 4–6 Mar. 1788; Parliamentary Lists 1776 (1), (2), (3), 1777 (1), 1778 (1), 1780 (1), 1782 (1), 1783 (1), (2), 1784 (1), (2), (3), (4), 1787 (1), 1788 (1), 1791 (1).

0260 BROWNE, Rt Hon. John Denis

MP for Jamestown 1776–80

b. 11 June 1756; d. 2 Jan. 1809 in Grafton Street, Piccadilly
HONOURS: PC, sworn 28 Nov. 1785; Knight of St Patrick 5 Aug. 1800.
PEERAGES: Styled Lord Westport 1776–80; suc. as 3rd Earl of Altamont 28 Dec. 1780; cr. Marquess of Sligo 29 Dec. 1800, Baron Mounteagle [UK] 20 Feb. 1806; Rep. Peer 1801.
FAMILY/BACKGROUND: Son and h. of Peter Browne-Kelly, 2nd Earl of Altamont (0262) and Elizabeth, dau. and h. of Dennis Kelly of Jamaica (1139).
MARRIED: [21 May 1787] Louisa Catherine (d. 1817), yst dau. and co-h. of Adm. Richard Howe, 1st Earl Howe (she m. (2) Lord Stowell).
CHILDREN: Rt Hon. Howe Peter (b. 18 May 1788), 2nd Marquess of Sligo, m. [1816] Hester Catherine, e. dau. of Rt Hon. John Thomas De Burgh, 13th Earl of Clanricarde.
EDUCATION: School: Eton 1768–71.
CAREER/OCCUPATION: High Sheriff of Co. Mayo 1779; Governor of Co. Mayo 1781, Joint Governor 1797–1800 (f.), *Governor of the Foundling Hospital and Workhouse 1798–1800 (f.); *Governor of the Hibernian Society 1799 (f.).
MILITARY: 3rd Major in the Mayo Legion Volunteers.

POLITICAL ACTIVITY: He was returned in the 1776 election, purchasing his seat at Jamestown from Gilbert King (1155). In 1777 a Parliamentary List noted that 'The family [were] much united and attached to each other.' Political unity was their strength: they usually returned one member for the county and purchased two seats for other members of the family. At the dismissal of Lord Altamont's uncle in 1782 the whole family, which had hitherto supported the government, went into opposition and Lord Altamont resigned his government of Co. Mayo (*see* 0256); the 1782 Parliamentary List comments that 'Upon the late Prime Serjeant Browne's (0256) being removed from office by the Duke of Portland, his lordship took up Mr Flood's (0762) principles, which have given him a little popularity. He is a weak, vain, stingy young man.' In 1783 he was a Volunteer major and a delegate to the National Convention for Galway town. After the restoration of James Browne (0256), the family reverted to the government.

After the death of his uncle (0255) in 1782, Lord Altamont returned his brother, Denis Browne (0253), for Co. Mayo and he sat for the county for the rest of the Irish parliament. However, they had to be mindful of their popularity in the county, for instance over the 1778 Catholic Relief Bill and the 1785 Commercial Propositions, when: 'The County and Grand Jury have been stirring against the Propositions, but their measures might be kept down were the Members [the other Member was James Cuffe (0552)] to co-operate and exert themselves. They were absent at the debate on Mr Orde's (1594) bill.'

Not surprisingly, neither he nor his brother Denis was popular with the opposition press, which in 1790 gave the following description of him: 'Nothing, except an over-weening opinion of superior parts, joined to the insolence of new rank, can produce ... an opinion seldom justified by the event and which even when most successful, displays more vanity than judgement. He has a full, strong and distinct voice; his language is neither elegant nor animated, little adapted to command the attention, conciliate the regard, or invigorate the minds of his hearers and is alike deficient in philosophical clearness and grammatical precision. He, for the most part, expresses himself in a peremptory magisterial tone and is abundant without selection and flowing without energy. His delivery is at times so rapid as to embarrass his pronunciation and destroy all propriety of emphasis. His manner is vehement and overbearing and his action ungraceful, belabouring the air without mercy. In argument he is dilated and diffuse and his arrangement ill calculated to reflect light upon his reasoning. It has no claims to regularity or order. What he advances, he does with apparent peculiar courage, or fear of contradiction and is obviously the unborrowed property of the speaker; heavy, if not solid and occasionally sparkling, if not brilliant. His parliamentary conduct is not easily described by any one specific term, for it has proceeded from its outset, undulating from the Court party to opposition, in a course not unlike Hogarth's line of beauty, but without any marked consistency or plan.' The brothers' (0253) oratorical style had certain similarities.

In 1799 Ross Mahon (1332), MP for Granard, and Altamont's brother Denis were numbered as his political following. He sought and achieved a marquessate at the Union.

DIVISION LISTS:

1777 (1) voted against Grattan's (0895) motion for retrenchment.
1777 (2) voted against the Trade Embargo.
1778 (1) voted for Grattan's motion for retrenchment.
1778 (2) voted for the Popery Bill.
1779 (1) a teller against new taxes.
1779 (2) voted against a six-months Loan Bill.
1780 (1) voted against Grattan's declaration of the Rights of Ireland.
1780 (2) voted against Yelverton's (2268) motion to modify Poynings' Law.

ADDITIONAL INFORMATION: In March 1787 he is recorded as possessing £10,000 worth of bank stock. A member of the Royal Dublin Society 1799(f.).

ESTATES/RESIDENCE: Westport, Co. Mayo; 18 Sackville Street, Dublin. In 21 (1781) & 36 (1796) George III, Lord Altamont was granted fairs at Westport and Louisburgh respectively. In 1796 Lord Altamont's rental was £11,389, of which £11,181 had been received.

SOURCES: PRONI D/302; PRONI T/618/329 Crossle Papers; PRONI MIC/474 Irish Volunteers; Ellis thesis; GEC *P*; Burke *PB* (1903) p. 1397; *Index to Irish Privy Counsellors, 1711–1910*; R. A. Austen-Leigh (ed.), *The Eton College Register, 1753–90*, 3 vols; *Almanacks*; *DJ* 6–8 Mar. 1781; Parliamentary Lists 1776 (2), (3), 1777 (1), 1778 (1), 1780 (1), 1782 (1), 1783 (3), 1785 (2), 1787 (1), 1788 (1), 1799 (1), (2), 1800 (2).

0261 BROWNE, William

MP for Portarlington 1790–7

b. 3 Jan. 1763; d. 1 Apr. 1840
FAMILY/BACKGROUND: Son of Robert Browne of Dublin and Eleanor, dau. of Redmond Morres (1492).
MARRIED: (1) [27 July 1793] Charlotte, dau. of Joseph Deane Bourke, 3rd Earl of Mayo and Abp of Tuam; (2) [1813] Letitia, dau. of Rt Hon. John Toler, 1st Earl of Norbury (2081).
CHILDREN: ?
EDUCATION: Entered Oxford (Christ Church) 31 Jan. 1781, aged 18 years.
CAREER/OCCUPATION: *Listed in Attornies of the Courts of King's Bench, Common Pleas and Exchequer 1789–1800 (f.); Distributor of Votes (House of Commons); High Sheriff of Co. Carlow 1794, Custos Rot. 1818.

POLITICAL ACTIVITY: He bought his seat for Portarlington from Lord Portarlington (0589). When he first came in it was thought that he might be under the influence of his uncle Lodge Morres (1491), a close friend of the Ponsonbys, but apparently by 1794 he had joined the ranks of the government supporters.

DIVISION LISTS:

1790 (2) voted for Ponsonby (1709) on the election of a Speaker.
1791 (1) voted for Curran's (0560) resolution against the sale of peerages.
1791 (2) voted for Grattan's motion for the exercise of Free Trade.
1791 (3) voted for Grattan's motion to abolish the Dublin police.

ADDITIONAL INFORMATION: He received £130 compensation at the Union for the loss of his office of Distributor of Votes.

ESTATES/RESIDENCE: Brownshill, Co. Carlow. Contained at least 125 acres in 1773. By 1767 Robert Browne was head tenant (effective owner) of 945 acres and urban property in Carlow.

A Robert Browne, possibly an ancestor, purchased 266 acres in Co. Kildare from the Commissioners for Sale of Forfeited Estates in 1702–3.

SOURCES: PRONI D/302; PRONI D/623/A/133/28 Abercorn Papers; RCBL P45/2/3, Parish Registers of St Peter's, Dublin [bapt. 29 Jan. 1763]; NLI reps no 42; Burke *PB* (1906) p. 664; *Alum. Oxon.*; Hughes, *Pat. Officers*; J. Ryan, *The History and Antiquities of the County of Carlow* (Dublin, 1833), p. 359; *Memorials of the Dead*; *Ir. Gen.* vol. 1 no 10 (1941) p. 294, W. Clare, 'Irish Compensations and Pensions'; Simms, *Williamite Confiscation*, p. 183; *Almanacks*; Parliamentary Lists, 1791 (1), 1793 (1), 1794 (2).

0262 BROWNE-KELLY, Hon. Peter

MP for Co. Mayo 1761–8

b. 1731; d. 28 Dec. 1780
PEERAGES: Suc. as 2nd Earl of Altamont 4 July 1776.
FAMILY/BACKGROUND: Son and h. of John Browne, 1st Earl of Altamont (0258), and Anne, dau. of Sir Arthur Gore, 2nd Bt (0857).
MARRIED: [16 Apr. 1752] Elizabeth, dau. and h. of Dennis Kelly of Jamaica (1139).
CHILDREN: John Denis, 3rd Earl of Altamont (0260); Denis (0253); Anne (d. 1814), m. [18 Aug. 1785] Otway Cuffe, 1st Earl of Desart; Elizabeth (d. 1795), m. [Aug. 1786] Sir Ross Mahon, Bt; Jane (d. unmar.); Charlotte (d. 1851), m. John Mahon.
EDUCATION: Entered Oxford (Christ Church, 26 Oct. 1748), aged 17 years.
CAREER/OCCUPATION: Sheriff of Galway 11 Dec. 1766; High Sheriff of Co. Galway 1767.
MILITARY: Colonel of the Castlebar Volunteers.

POLITICAL ACTIVITY: He sat for Co. Mayo, 1761–8, along with Sir Charles Bingham (0134). The figures for the return are interesting, as they show the balance and nature of interests in the county. 'The votes were as follows: Peter Browne-Kelly, 454 votes (237 £10 freehold, 217 40s freehold); Sir Charles Bingham, 444 votes (231 £10 free-hold, 213 40s freehold); Hon. Richard Gore (0874), 364 votes (117 £10 freehold, 247 40s free-

hold); James Cuffe (0551), 333 votes (120 £10 freehold, 213 40s freehold). Browne-Kelly and Bingham were declared duly elected.'

He succeeded his father as Earl of Altamont in 1776. Lord Altamont was a firm supporter of government, as were all his family. His brother (*see* 0251) had served with Lord Lieutenant Townshend in Canada. The family operated as a political unit.

DIVISION LISTS:
1768 (1) voted for army augmentation.

ADDITIONAL INFORMATION: 'John Browne, his father had a small fortune in the County of Mayo, which he improved by *commerce* and the 2nd Earl by a marriage with Miss Kelly, the dau. and h. of an opulent planter in Jamaica, from whom he assumed the name of *Kelly*' (Dennis Kelly (1139), Chief Justice of Jamaica). Subscriber to the Marine Society, March 1759.

ESTATES/RESIDENCE: Mount Browne and Westport, Co. Mayo; [?]Lisduff, Co. Galway.

SOURCES: PRONI D/302; PRONI MIC/474 Irish Volunteers; GEC *P*; Burke *PB* (1903) p. 1397; *Alum. Oxon*; Hughes, *Pat. Officers*; BNL 30 Mar. 1759; *DJ* 30 Dec. 1760–63 Jan. 1761, 16–19 May 1761; Parliamentary List, 1777 (1).

0263 (CHAMBERLAIN) BROWNLOW, Arthur

MP for Co. Armagh (1689), 1692–3, 1695–9, 1703–11

b. 20 Mar. 1645; d. (27) Mar. 1711
FAMILY/BACKGROUND: Son of Patrick Chamberlain of Nizelrath, Co. Louth, and Lettice, dau. of William Brownlow (she survived four husbands). He was heir to his maternal grandfather and assumed the name Brownlow in lieu of that of Chamberlain.
MARRIED: [*c.* 1677] Jane, dau. of Sir Standish Hartstonge, 1st Bt.
CHILDREN: William (0264); Standish; John; Philemon; Anne, m. [1698] Mathew Forde (0781); Lettice, m. Robert Cope (0489).
EDUCATION: School: Mr Jones; entered TCD 20 Sept. 1660, aged 15 years, BA 1664.

CAREER/OCCUPATION: Sheriff of Co. Louth 1667, of Co. Armagh 9 January 1679.

POLITICAL ACTIVITY: In March 1686 Brownlow was described to Lord Clarendon as 'a loyal honest gentleman' and to this recommendation Clarendon responded: 'This needs no answer.' He was one of the few sheriffs appointed by Clarendon whom Tyrconnell allowed to retain their posts, and he was one of the half-dozen MPs who had sat in the 1689 parliament of James II, although he 'withdrew before the end of the session'. During the reign of Charles II he acted as an agent for disarming Catholic Irish when there were fears of an uprising in 1673 and 1678. Nevertheless, he was tolerant in matters of religion: having conformed to the Established Church, he allowed the Presbyterians to establish a church in Lurgan and gave tenancy to the Quakers on his lands, including the right to build a meeting-house in Lurgan. He developed the town of Lurgan, encouraging the linen trade and founding the linen market there.

In the 1695 parliament he supported Lord Chancellor Porter, who was accused of favouring Catholics; he signed the 1696 Association for the protection of William III in the country, and in 1706 he was noted as a supporter of the Court. He was nominated for three committees in 1692, for 28 in 1695–9 and for 24 in 1703–9. He died in 1711.

ADDITIONAL INFORMATION: He was an Irish scholar, a collector, transcriber and translator of Gaelic manuscripts, his prize possession being the Book of Armagh, now in the library of Trinity College. He carried out experiments on fossilised wood from Lough Neagh.

ESTATES/RESIDENCE: Lurgan, Co. Armagh. His maternal grandfather and great-grandfather, Sir William and John Brownlow respectively, arrived in Ireland in 1610 from the Isle of Epworth in Lincolnshire and together obtained grants of land totalling 3,500 acres at Doughcorn in O'Neill barony, Co. Armagh, later known as the manor of Brownlows Derry and later still as Lurgan. He also had lands in Counties Monaghan and Louth.

SOURCES: PRONI T/581 vol. 3 pp. 254–5, Society of Genealogists, London; Burke PB (1903) p. 975 (1906) p. 1051; Hughes, Pat. Officers; Alum. Dub.; R. G. Gillespie (ed.), Settlement and Survival on an Ulster Estate (PRONI 1988) pp. xi–xiii; D. Hayton and G. O'Brien (eds), War and Politics in Ireland 1649–1730, J. G. Simms, Williamite Confiscation (London, 1956) p. 68; Clarendon Corr. vol. 1 p. 287; Upper Ards Historical Society Journal no 11 (1987) pp. 8–9, W. S. Brownlow, 'The Brownlows' [says born 1647]; The Dublin Intelligence 27 Mar. 1711; Parliamentary Lists, 1695 (1), 1696 (1), 1706 (1).

0264 BROWNLOW, William

MP for Co. Armagh 1711–13–14, 1715–27–39

b. (bapt. 31 Dec.) 1683; d. 27 Aug. 1739
FAMILY/BACKGROUND: Eldest son of Arthur (Chamberlain) Brownlow (0263) and Jane, dau. of Sir Standish Hartstonge, 1st Bt.
MARRIED: [2 Jan. 1712] Elizabeth, dau. of Rt Hon. James Hamilton, 6th Earl of Abercorn (0933).
CHILDREN: William (0265); Elizabeth, m. Sir John Denny Vesey, 1st Baron Knapton (2148); Isabella, m. George Matthew of Thomastown; Mary, m. John Pigott (1681).
EDUCATION: School: Dr Walker, Drogheda; entered TCD 8 July 1699, BA 1702.
CAREER/OCCUPATION: High Sheriff of Co. Armagh 1711; Trustee of the Linen Manufacture for Ulster 10 Oct. 1711; *Governor of the Workhouse 1734–d.

POLITICAL ACTIVITY: He was returned for Co. Armagh on the death of his father in 1711. He supported the Court party, and backed it over the Dublin mayoralty and the unsuccessful proposal of Sir Richard Levinge (1230) as Speaker. In 1713 he was classified as a Tory, and consolidated this view by signing a county address in favour of Sir Constantine Phipps. He was on the Whig 'black list' of Tories in 1714–15.

He continued to represent Co. Armagh after the accession of George I, and was thought to have Tory sympathies that, in 1719, would make him hostile to the repeal of the Test Clause against the Dissenters. In 1721 he favoured the establishment of a national bank. He was listed for two committees in 1711 and for three in the very short 1713 parliament. Possibly he kept a low profile after the accession of George I, as he was nominated on only five committees between 1716 and 1723;

however, in the ten years following the accession of George II he was listed on 18 committees.

DIVISION LISTS:

1711 (1) voted for the Court on the Dublin mayoralty issue.

1713 (1) voted for Sir Richard Levinge (**1230**) for Speaker.

1721 (1) voted for a national bank.

ESTATES/RESIDENCE: Lurgan, Co. Armagh.

SOURCES: PRONI D/302; McCracken thesis [says born 1681]; Burke *PB* (1903) p. 975 [says born 1683, married 1711]; *Upper Ards Historical Society Journal* no 11 (1987) pp. 8–9, W. S. Brownlow, 'The Brownlows' [says born 1683]; *Louth Arch. Soc. Jn.* vol. 2 pp. 184–5, T. G. F. Paterson, 'The Chamberlaines of Nizelrath'; Llandover, *Delany Correspondence*, vol. 3 p. 467 n. 1; *Almanacks*, *The Dublin Gazette* 12 Dec. 1710; Parliamentary Lists, 1711 (3), 1713 (2), 1714 (1), 1714–15 (1), 1719 (2).

0265 BROWNLOW, Rt Hon. William

MP for Co. Armagh 1753–60, 1761–8–76–83–90–4 [r. Strabane, 1768]

b. 10 Apr. 1726; d. 28 Oct. 1794 at Lurgan
HONOURS: PC 1765 (sworn 11 Mar. 1766).
FAMILY/BACKGROUND: Son of William Brownlow (**0264**) and Elizabeth, dau. of Rt Hon. James Hamilton, 6th Earl of Abercorn (**0933**).
MARRIED: (1) [18 May 1754] Judith Letitia, dau. of Charles Meredyth, Dean of Ardfert; (2) [23 Nov. 1765] Catherine, dau. of Roger Hall (**0908**).
CHILDREN: (1) William (**0266**); Charles, m. [1785] Caroline, dau. and co-h. of Benjamin Ashe of Bath.
(2) James; Rev. Francis, m. Catherine dau. of Anthony Brabazon, 8th Earl of Meath (**0221**); Catherine, m. [1783] Matthew Forde; Isabella, m. [9 Feb. 1796] Richard Wingfield, 4th Viscount Powerscourt; Elizabeth, m. [26 Aug. 1791] John Bligh, 4th Earl of Darnley; Mary Anne; Frances Letitia, m. [25 Aug. 1800] John Vesey, 2nd Viscount De Vesci (**2147**); Silvia (b. 1782; d. Nov. 1799 at Exmouth, aged 17).
CAREER/OCCUPATION: High Sheriff of Co. Armagh 1750; *Trustee of the Linen Board for Ulster 1752–93; *Commissioner of the Tillage Act for Ulster 1759–84; *Governor of the Foundling Hospital and Workhouse 1781; *Governor of the Charitable Loan Society 1762; presented with the freedom of Dublin in a silver box 18 July 1760; sworn Freeman of the Guild of Merchants and granted Freedom of the City of Dublin 30 Oct. 1760.
MILITARY: Lieutenant-Colonel of the Ulster First Regiment, Volunteers, 1782 and of the Lurgan Volunteers.

POLITICAL ACTIVITY: He entered parliament in 1753 as a result of one of the most famous by-elections of the century, caused by the death of Robert Cope (**0489**) in March 1753. It was bitterly fought between Brownlow and Francis Caulfeild (**0366**), Lord Charlemont's brother, who, if he was born in 1735, was under age. Not only was the election a contest between the political interests in Armagh – which were evenly divided – but Primate Stone, who envisaged himself as the leading servant of the government was, as Archbishop of Armagh, *ex officio* one of them. Brownlow was returned.

Brownlow was first elected to parliament at the height of the Money Bill dispute, and was seen as a government man. The election had turned into a contest between the Primate and the Speaker. On 16 November 1753 Sackville (**1835**) wrote to Sir Robert Wilmot: 'Brownlow takes his seat this day, and I am told the Speaker's (Boyle, **0210**) son (**0213**) moves a petition against him. Brownlow will be well supported, and I verily believe for the first time that the Speaker will lose an election point in the house of Commons; if that should happen it would more effectually hurt his interests than ten other questions.' Newcastle wrote to Dorset expressing his satisfaction with the result, and saying that the king had remarked that 'Mr Brownlow must now be supported.' This, wrote Newcastle, was 'as great an indication of what we wish as could be given'.

The election return was contested by the defeated candidate, Caulfeild. The election, which had cost Lord Charlemont £1,000, had been managed on behalf of his brother by Thomas Adderley (**0009**), his guardian. Lord Charlemont supported the opposition both from inclination and from an old family friendship with Speaker Boyle. When the election petition came before the House it was decided in Brownlow's favour in an exceptionally large House, by one vote: 120–119. Every vote had counted. Thomas Adderley wrote to Lord Charlemont that: 'Mr Hamilton (0921) arrived here the 7th [December] from London, on purpose to serve his nephew Mr [William] Brownlow this gentleman has been a member since 1727, but did not take his seat before this session.' This was the beginning of a long and illustrious parliamentary career.

On 6 December 1753 Waite (2154) wrote, probably to Sir Robert Wilmot, outlining the importance of this petition and the issues involved: 'The Armagh election is this day before the House of Commons, and I hear it said everywhere that if the patriots, as they are called, have anything of a majority against Brownlow they are to vote the Primate an enemy to the country and address the King to remove him from the government and from His Majesty's councils. If they carry this election no doubt is made of their carrying the other of Galway, and the next consideration will be what is to become of the Money Bill that is altered …' In 1758 Brownlow and Edmond Pery (1671) moved, successfully, that the Chief Secretary and his principal officials should be paid a salary and not depend on fees levied on the services provided by their office (the Chief Secretary £2,500 p.a., Under-Secretary (Waite) £1,000 p.a., and his chief clerk (Meredyth, 1400) £500 p.a.).

Brownlow was nominated for 113 committees between 1753 and 1760. He had a particular interest in the thriving linen trade around his estate at Lurgan, Co. Armagh, and in October 1757 he introduced 31 Geo. II, c. 19, 'an act to prevent Frauds in Lappers and others; and to prevent Abuses in the Manufacture of Kelp; and to prevent unlawful Combinations in Weavers and others'. There was a strong streak of independence throughout the linen manufacture, and abuses could creep in if it was not watched carefully. It was the leading Irish manufacture and quality control was essential to its prosperity.

Brownlow's economic interests were reflected in his appointment, in December 1765, to the committee to inquire into the public works necessary to the nation. He was in many ways a country gentleman *par excellence*, and in March 1771 he missed being elected Speaker by only four votes.

He was made a Privy Counsellor in 1766. His wife was a relation of the Duke of Leinster (0745), and it was thought that this might incline him to that party, although his wealth made him independent and he was 'of the Northern Clan'. In 1774 an opposition list pointed out that while he had voted for 'Popery and Stamps', he 'has often spoke and voted for the real good of the nation'.

He was an able and much respected parliamentarian: 'independent. Inclined against Government but not always' and 'much attended to by the House … upon almost every matter of importance he gave Lord Harcourt a very effectual support and was of the utmost service in carrying through the new taxes'. In return government gave to his recommendation the nomination to some important ecclesiastical (a living of £300 p.a.), Revenue ('an employment in the Stamps worth near £300' as well as considerable lesser employments) and military ('a company to his son, a boy, in the 57th – a favour of very great magnitude') patronage. In 1782 it was again emphasised that he was: 'an able and experienced Member of Parliament and much attended to as a speaker. Elected by the popular party, which he has ever served. Opposed Lord Buckingham and Lord Carlisle. Supported the Duke of Portland and was chosen out to second Mr Grattan's (0895) amendment' to George Ponsonby's (1699) motion on the address stating the still outstanding claims of Ireland, in particular the perpetual nature of the Mutiny Bill.

He was a lieutenant-colonel in the Volunteers and a delegate to the Volunteer National Convention for Co. Armagh. In this he resembled that other prototype of a country gentleman, Thomas Conolly (0459), but they took opposite sides over the question of a 'more equal representation of the people in parliament'. Conolly moved the Address to the King expressing 'perfect satisfaction' with the *status quo*, while Brownlow supported Flood (0762). In the mid-1780s he was 'much attached to the popular side but not naturally inclined to go great lengths. He supports Reform of Parliament [and] Protecting Duties.' In fact he was prepared to go to considerable lengths for both. He was a teller for Flood's motion in 1783 and again in 1784, and in 1785 he and John O'Neill (**1592**) were the first to require the sheriffs of their respective counties (Armagh and Antrim) to call a meeting to oppose the Commercial Resolutions. He made a stinging criticism (describing Ireland as a 'tributary Nation') of the contribution element of the Commercial Negotiations, based on what he afterwards agreed was a mistaken belief that it was intended to place the Hereditary Revenue under British control. At the same time he added that it was a tribute to Ireland's civilised state that Chief Secretary Orde (**1594**) had not been lynched. On learning of his mistake he apologised.

His independence sometimes laid him open to the charge of inconsistency. Unlike most MPs in his position, he does not appear to have been interested in a peerage: possibly his main concern was the establishment of his children. For instance, in 1777 Brownlow was said to be 'disobliged' because the newly arrived Lord Lieutenant Buckinghamshire refused to recommend 'his second son a cornet of about 13 months standing ... to the King over every Lieutenant in the army for a company'. The government kept a tight hand on military and ecclesiastical patronage, although most MPs felt that they had an *ex officio* claim to it. In 1780 the Earl of Buckinghamshire, now more acquainted with Irish politics, wrote to the Secretary of State for the Southern Department as follows: 'In stating my recommendation of Lieutenant Brownlow to his Majesty you will please observe that the commander-in-chief has expressed his wish that a preference should be given to Lieutenant Urqhuart of the 66th but when Mr Brownlow's Consequence in this Kingdom is considered ...' In 1784 Brownlow wanted 'a living for his son'.

The opposition press in 1789 referred to him, probably quite correctly, as an 'honest and upright senator ... never thought on without reverence nor remembered without regard'. Despite his reputation as an orator, 'his voice is thin, sharp and disagreeably toned' yet 'His language, though sparingly ornamented ... possesses a degree of easy and unstudied elegance ... but what gives an irresistible weight to every word he utters is the acknowledged independence of his mind and the undeviating rectitude of his parliamentary con-

duct.' He died on 28 October 1794.

DIVISION LISTS:

1753 (1) voted against the expulsion of Arthur Jones-Nevill (**1125**).

1753 (2) voted for the Money Bill.

1757 (1) voted for the resolutions on pensions.

1768 (1) voted against army augmentation – a PC.

1771 (1) voted against Lord Townshend as Lord Lieutenant.

1771 (2) voted for Sir Lucius O'Brien's (**1558**) motion for retrenchment.

1772 (2) voted for a Short Revenue Bill.

1773 (1) voted for the Absentee Tax.

1773 (2) voted for an untaxed press.

1774 (1) voted for the Stamp Bill.

1774 (2) voted for Catholic relief.

1777 (1) voted for Grattan's (**0895**) motion for retrenchment.

1777 (2) voted against the Trade Embargo.

1778 (1) voted for Grattan's motion for retrenchment.

1779 (2) voted for a six-months Loan Bill.

1780 (2) voted for Yelverton's (**2268**) motion to modify Poynings' Law.

1780 (4) spoke and voted against a Perpetual Mutiny Bill.

1783 (1) teller for Flood's (**0762**) motion for parliamentary reform.

1784 (1) teller for a committee on the Reform Bill.

1784 (3) voted against Foster's (**0805**) Bill to regulate the Press.

1784 (4) voted against the Address to His Grace the Duke of Rutland.

1785 (1) voted against the Commercial Propositions.

1786 (1) voted for the rights of grand juries.

1786 (2) voted for Forbes's (**0778**) motion for retrenchment.

1787 (1) absent, indisposed. Had previously voted for a Pension Bill.

1788 (1) voted for Hartley's (**0979**) motion against the Dublin police.

1788 (2) voted for Forbes' motion for limiting pensions.

1789 (1) voted for a regency.

1790 (1) voted for Grattan's motion for reducing the influence of the Crown.

1790 (2) absent.

1791 (3) voted for Grattan's motion to abolish the Dublin police.

ADDITIONAL INFORMATION: A member of the Royal Dublin Society from 1758. A member of the Committee of Fifteen on the Charter (Schools) Society of Dublin, 1760.

ESTATES/RESIDENCE: Lurgan, Co. Armagh; Co. Monaghan; 12 Merrion Square, Dublin. In 1790–94 the Co. Monaghan rental was £1,030, having been only £504 in 1778. The estate occupied the small part of the barony of Farney, on the Louth–Monaghan border, which was not part of the Essex grant. The Brownlow estate, Co. Armagh, had 300 freeholders in 1789. Its rental was popularly reckoned at £6,000 in 1794, but rents actually received averaged £7,490 over the period 1791–4, and had averaged £4,074 in 1761–5. In 1879 its acreage was 15,166 statute acres, when it was valued at £20,424 a year. It may have been larger earlier, as in the 1790s it was calculated to contain at least 22,720 acres.

SOURCES: *CJ Ire.* (Bradley ed.) vol. 10 p. 119 (0549); PRONI D/302; PRONI D/1606/1/139 Gosford Papers, and /165 [election calculations (June 1789)], J. Turner to Lord Gosford, 5 Nov. 1794, calculations on the Brownlow rental, 1761–5 and 1791–4, were made by W. H. Crawford [from papers in the office of Messrs Watson & Neill, Lurgan]; PRONI D/2667/5/10; D/1606/1/165 W. Brownlow's a/c book, 1778–94; PRONI T/1584 Pinkerton transcripts, p. 25, 31 Mar. 1754, p. 489, 27 Oct. 1794, p. 445, 6 Aug. 1791; PRONI T/3019/6456/326 Wilmot Papers; PRONI MIC/315/8/44 Blackwood pedigrees [says married second, 25 Nov. 1765]; PRONI MIC/474 Irish Volunteers; RCBL P45/2/3, Parish Registers of St Peter's, Dublin; Ellis thesis [says born 1727]; McCracken thesis; GEC *P*; Burke *PB* (1903) pp. 975–6; Calculations made by Dr W. H. Crawford on the Brownlow rentals, 1761–5 and 1791–4, in the office of Messrs Watson and Neill, Lurgan; R. E. Burns, *Irish Parliamentary Politics in the Eighteenth Century*, 2 vols (Washington, 1989) vol. 2 pp. 144–5, 168–9; J. Walton, 'The King's Business': Letters on the Administration of Ireland, 1741–61 (NY, 1996) nos 135, 141, 335, 340–41; *EHR* (July 1905) p. 520, C. L. Falkiner (ed.), 'Correspondence of Archbishop Stone and the Duke of Newcastle'; *HMC Charlemont I* pp. 5–6, 189; T. Bartlett and D. W. Hayton (eds), *Penal Era and Golden Age* (Belfast, 1979) p. 60, 113 f. 1, P. D. H. Smyth, 'The Volunteers and Parliament, 1779–84'; McNevin, *Volunteers, Index to*

Irish Privy Counsellors, 1711–1910; McDowell, *Ir. public opinion*, p. 83; J. Kelly, *Prelude to Union* (Cork, 1992) pp. 106, 167; W. H. Crawford, *Domestic Industry in Ireland* (Dublin, 1973) [linen industry]; Johnston, *Gt B. & Ire.*, pp. 54, 219, 221–3; J. T. Gilbert, *History of the City of Dublin*, 3 vols (1861) vol. 3 p. 125; *Ir. Gen.* vol. 6 no 1 (1980) p. 29, H. F. Morris, 'The Waterford Herald 1791'; *Upper Ards Historical Society Journal* no 11 (1987) pp. 8–9, W. S. Brownlow, 'The Brownlows'; *Louth Arch. Soc. Jn.* vol. 2 pp. 184–5, T. G. F. Paterson, 'The Chamberlaines of Nizelrath' [states he was bapt. 25 Apr. 1726]; *Almanacks*; *BNL* 22 July 1760, 4 Nov. 1760, 27 Dec. 1765; *The Dublin Courant* 6 Mar. 1750; *DJ* 28 May 1754, 28 Oct. – 1 Nov. 1760, 13 Feb 1796, 30 Nov. 1799, 4 Sept. 1800; Parliamentary Lists, 1769 (1), 1772 (2), 1773 (1), (2), 1774 (1), 1775 (1), 1776 (1), (2), (3), 1777 (1), 1778 (1), 1780 (1), 1782 (1), 1783 (1), 1784 (1), (2), (3), 1785 (1), (2), (3), (4), 1788 (1), 1789 (1), (2), 1790 (1), 1791 (1), 1793 (1).

0266 BROWNLOW, William

MP for Co. Armagh 1795–7; [UK] 13 Mar. 1807 – 10 July 1815

b. 1755; d. 10 July 1815

FAMILY/BACKGROUND: Eldest son of Rt Hon. William Brownlow (0265) and Judith Letitia, e. dau. of Charles Meredyth, Dean of Ardfert.

MARRIED: [1795] Charity, dau. of Mathew Forde (0783).

CHILDREN: *d.s.p.*

CAREER/OCCUPATION: High Sheriff of Co. Armagh 13 Feb. 1787; Trustee of Linen Board 1808. A banker, 'evidently discovering that Lisburn was not an advantageous locality for the gratification of his banking proclivities, he transferred his bank, founded 1804 (William Brownlow Esq. and Co.) to Lurgan, where his social influence was paramount. The house was opened there about 1806, and the partners were William Brownlow, Joseph Malcomson, Henry MacVeagh, John Cuppage and John Waite – a goodly and heterogeneous company. The bank did what must now be regarded as a wild business. Within a twelve month it had put its notes, to the face value of £170,000 into circulation. These were issued payable at Wilcock's and John Phelps', Capel St, Dublin, and there alone were redeemable. Brownlow died in 1815 but prior to this date he and Cuppage and Waite had retired from the business.'

MILITARY: Captain of Lurgan Yeomanry 1797.

POLITICAL ACTIVITY: He was returned on the death of his father and served out the remaining term of the 1790–7 parliament. Little is known of his activities, except that he voted against Catholic Emancipation. For social reasons Armagh had become a bitterly divided county, especially following the 'Battle of the Diamond' in 1795 and the foundation of the Orange Order. From 1807 to 1810 Brownlow sat for Co. Armagh in the United Kingdom parliament, where he voted against Catholic relief on 2 March and 24 May 1813.

DIVISION LISTS:
1795 (2) voted against Catholic Emancipation.

ADDITIONAL INFORMATION: A member of the Dublin Society 1777–1815.

ESTATES/RESIDENCE: Lurgan, Co. Armagh. In the 1790s the Brownlows possessed an estate of at least 2,720 acres and a total rent roll of £9,000. Succeeded by his brother, Lieutenant-Colonel Charles Brownlow.

SOURCES: PRONI D/302; Burke *PB* (1903) pp. 975–6 (1906) pp. 1051–2; Hughes, *Pat. Officers*; Jupp thesis; *HP 1790–1820*; M. Kelleher, *A List of the Members of the Dublin Society 1713–1800* (Dublin, 1982); S. Clark & J. S. Donnelly Jr (eds), *Irish Peasants: Violence and Political Unrest* (1983), pp. 155–91 esp. pp. 180–81, D. W. Miller, 'The Armagh Troubles, 1784–95'.

0267 BRUCE, Sir Stewart

MP for Lisburn 1798–1800

b. *c.* 1764–7; d. 19 Mar. 1841
HONOURS: Cr. Bt 24 Dec. 1812.
FAMILY/BACKGROUND: Son of James Bruce of Killyleagh of Co. Down and Henrietta, dau. of the Hon. and Rev. H. Hervey Aston.
MARRIED: [1838] Emma, dau. of James Ramsbottom of Windsor.
CHILDREN: *d.s.p.*
CAREER/OCCUPATION: Gentleman Usher of the Black Rod and Master of the Ceremonies 19 Feb. 1800; at the Union received £237 compensation for the loss of the Gentleman Usher's office.
MILITARY: A Captain and Major in the army. Served in the Royal Navy.

POLITICAL ACTIVITY: Brought in by Lord Hertford to assist the Union. Lisburn was a potwalloping borough and elections could be strongly contested, but, in 1798, the country was disturbed by the rebellion. Bruce was a Castle official and by that fact alone a Union supporter, voting for the Union in both 1799 and 1800. He was created a baronet and compensated for his loss of employment.

DIVISION LISTS:
1799 (1) voted for the Union – Major in the Army and aide-de-camp to the Lord Lieutenant.
1800 (1) voted for the Union.

ADDITIONAL INFORMATION: Genealogist of the Order of St Patrick, 18 December 1804.

ESTATES/RESIDENCE: Dublin Castle.

SOURCES: PRONI T/3166/1A Hartnell notes; O'Neill thesis; GEC *B*; *Ir. Gen.* vol. 1 no 10 (1941) p. 294, W. Clare, 'Irish Compensations and Pensions'; *The Annual Register* 1841; Parliamentary Lists, 1799 (2), (3), 1800 (3).

0268 BRUEN, Henry

MP for Jamestown 1783–90; Co. Carlow 1790–5

b. 1741; d. 14 Dec. 1795
FAMILY/BACKGROUND: Younger son of Moses Bruen and [   ].
MARRIED: [16 Oct. 1787] Dorothea Henrietta, dau. of Francis Knox of Co. Mayo.
CHILDREN: Col. Henry, m. Miss Kavanagh; John Francis, m. Catherine, dau. of Rt Hon. George Frederick Nugent, 7th Earl of Westmeath (**1547**); Maria, m. Richard Longfield of Longueville, Co. Cork; Margaret, m. Rev. Francis Ruttledge of Co. Mayo; Harriet, m. Rev. George Vernon.
CAREER/OCCUPATION: Sheriff of Co. Carlow 14 Feb. 1785; Governor of Co. Carlow, Custos Rot.; *Governor and Guardian of the Hospital for the relief of Lying-in Women 1786–d.; *Portreeve of Duleek 1790–d.; *Magistrate of Duleek 1790–d.
MILITARY: Colonel in the Army; Deputy Quarter Master General in America during the War of Independence (amassing a fortune of £400,000; it was alleged that he 'subsequently acquired large estates and considerable political influence in Ireland as an insurance against prosecution in Great Britain'); Colonel of Co. Carlow Militia 1793.

POLITICAL ACTIVITY: He purchased his seat for Jamestown, and another for his brother-in-law Henry Cope (**0488**) from Lord Belvidere (**1800**) for Philipstown. Jamestown was controlled by the King family (**1155**), and 'It is not men, but money they represent.' In 1784 it was noted that he had 'made a very large fortune as Commissary in America. Is constantly in opposition.' However, by the following year he and his brother-in-law were 'generally in support'. In 1788 it was reported that he 'opposes, but difficult to guess the reason'. In 1790 he was returned for Co. Carlow, which he represented until his death in 1795. It was admitted in 1790 that 'He is not indeed a speaker in the House ... but on his steadiness of decision dependence may be placed and full confidence in his honesty of mind. Of a man who aspires to no other character than that of an independent country gentleman, much more could not be said and the strictness of truth would not warrant less.'

On his purchase of Duleek for £10,000 from the Ram family (**1760**), the opposition press wrote that 'We trust that in this case good will spring out of evil and that this Borough, long noted for weak or worthless representatives, the time-serving sycophants of the hour, may at length obtain, through the influence of its new-owner, two able and honest Members, as Mr Bruen's liberality of mind and generous public spirit are known and acknowledged. He is too rich to sell and we believe of too worthy a nature to prostitute his interest.' In 1791 there was some speculation that he might be attracted to a peerage, and it was noted that he 'made an *immense* fortune in America, from nothing, in the Quarter Master Generals department'. He was reputed to be a member of the Ponsonby party, and in 1790 voted for W. B. Ponsonby (**1709**) for Speaker, but by 1793 he was again noted as in support along with his MPs. This was probably wishful thinking, as his voting pattern is entirely opposition. On 14 December 1795 he died, leaving a young family.

DIVISION LISTS:

1784 (1) voted for a committee on the Reform Bill.
1784 (2) voted for protective duties (wool).
1785 (1) voted against the Commercial Propositions.

1787 (1) voted for a Pension Bill.
1789 (1) voted for a regency.
1790 (1) voted for Grattan's (**0895**) motion for reducing the influence of the Crown.
1790 (2) voted for Ponsonby (**1709**) on the election of a Speaker.
1791 (1) voted for Curran's (**0560**) resolution against the sale of peerages.
1791 (2) voted for Grattan's motion for the exercise of Free Trade.
1791 (3) voted for Grattan's motion to abolish the Dublin police.

ADDITIONAL INFORMATION: Bruen controlled the parliamentary boroughs of Taghmon, Co. Wexford ('purchased from the Hore family in the early 1790s'), and Duleek, Co. Meath ('purchased from the Rams about 1789'). A member of the Royal Dublin Society from 1785; *a subscriber to the Public Assembly Rooms, 1787.

ESTATES/RESIDENCE: Oak Park, Co. Carlow; George's Street, Dublin. Also lands in Co. Wexford (bequeathed 8,948 acres held under various tenures to his son Francis for life in 1795). The Oak Park estate, his principal residence, was purchased *c.* 1775. It included the lands of Ballycarnen, Park and Quinagh, barony of Carlow, apparently leased in fee farm by Henry, Earl of Thomond, to Katherine Dunbar in 1712. According to Wakefield, 'Mr Brewen' had one of the three largest estates in the county. In 1879 these amounted to 16,477 statute acres valued at £14,097 p.a.

SOURCES: NLI EC 2847, EC 5319, EC 5832; PRONI T/3166/1D Hartnell notes; PRONI MIC/315/9/56 Blackwood pedigrees [says John and Francis were separate sons]; Jupp thesis; Burke *LGI* (1904) p. 69, *IFR* (1976) p. 177; Carlow MPs; *Memorials of the Dead* [says he married Harriet Dorothea]; Hughes, *Pat. Officers*; Wakefield, *Account of Ire.*, vol. 1 p. 248; J. Ryan, *The History and Antiquaries of the County Carlow* (Dublin, 1833), p. 351 [his headstone is in Nurney graveyard and says he died in his 55th year]; A. P. W. Malcomson, 'The Treaty of Paris and Ireland' [unpublished paper 1983] p. 12; *Almanacks*; *FJ* 25–7 Apr. 1793; *DJ* 19 Dec. 1795; Parliamentary Lists 1783 (2), 1784 (1), (2), (3), 1785 (1), (2), (3), (4), 1787 (1), 1788 (1), 1789 (1), 1790 (1), 1791 (1), 1793 (1), 1794 (2), 1799 (2), (3).

BUCKINGHAMSHIRE, Earl of: *see* **HOBART**

1026 Hobart, Rt Hon. Robert (styled Lord Hobart 1793–8), Baron Hobart [GB], 4th Earl of Buckinghamshire [GB], MP Portarlington 1784–90, Armagh B. 1790–7, [GB] Bramber 1788–90, Lincoln 1790–6

0269 BUCKNER, William

MP for Dungarvan 1692–3, 1695–9

b. [*ante* 5 Oct.] 1671; d. 1700
FAMILY/BACKGROUND: Son of [   ] Buckner.
MARRIED: ?
CHILDREN: ?

POLITICAL ACTIVITY: Virtually nothing is known about this MP. In 1695 he supported Lord Chancellor Porter against accusations of favouring Catholics, and the following year he signed the Association for the protection of William III in the country.

ESTATES/RESIDENCE: Coolfinn, Co. Waterford.

SOURCES: Vicars, *Prerog. Wills*; PRONI T/559; Burke, extract pedigrees, vol. 13 p. 38; Parliamentary Lists, 1695 (1), 1696 (1).

0270 BUCKWORTH, Richard

MP for Cashel 1715–27–38

b. (bapt. 18 Apr.) 1675; d. Sept. 1738
FAMILY/BACKGROUND: Son of John Buckworth of Ballycormick, Co. Tipperary, and his first wife Elizabeth, dau. of Richard Le Hunte.
MARRIED: Anne, dau. and h. of William Carr.
CHILDREN: John; William (Carr) (**0357**); Anne; Elizabeth.
CAREER/OCCUPATION: Sheriff of Co. Tipperary 1704; Free Burgess of New Ross 22 Feb. 1731.
MILITARY: Captain, Colonel in the army.

POLITICAL ACTIVITY: He was returned for two parliaments, but very little is known about this MP. He was a professional soldier and, although these years were a period of peace, he may have been posted elsewhere. He voted against the establish-

ment of a national bank in 1721, and was nominated for a committee on 29 November 1727.

DIVISION LISTS:
1721 (1) voted against a national bank.

ADDITIONAL INFORMATION: A foundation member of the Dublin Society, 1731.

ESTATES/RESIDENCE: Lisheen (Keadragh), Co. Tipperary.

SOURCES: PRONI T/559, Burke, extract pedigrees, vol. 13 p. 40; NAI MFCI Reel 7, Parish Registers of St John's, Cashel, Co. Tipperary; McCracken thesis; *JRSAI* vol. 21 (1892) p. 299, P. D. Vigors, 'Alphabetical List of Free Burgesses of New Ross, 1658–1839'; *Ir. Gen.* vol. 3 no 5 (1960) p. 160, T. Blake Butler, 'The Sheriffs of the Liberty of the County Tipperary'; Berry *RDS* pp. 24–7; *Pue's Occurrences* 5 Sept. 1738.

BUCKWORTH, William: *see* **CARR** (**BUCKWORTH**), William (**0357**)

0271 BUDGELL, Eustace

MP for Mullingar 1715–27

b. 19 Aug. 1686; d. May 1737 (suicide; he 'threw himself into the Thames off London bridge and was drowned')
FAMILY/BACKGROUND: Son of Gilbert Budgell DD of Symondsbury, Dorset, and his first wife Mary, o. dau. of Rev. Gulston, Bishop of Bristol.
MARRIED: [   ].
CHILDREN: Anne.
EDUCATION: Entered Oxford (Trinity College) 31 Mar. 1705, aged 18 years; Inner Temple 1705; called to the Bar.
CAREER/OCCUPATION: Under Secretary to Chief Secretary Oct. 1714–Apr. 1718; Accountant General of the Revenue 1717–18.

POLITICAL ACTIVITY: Budgell appears to have been one of those unfortunate people who have a gift for rubbing people up the wrong way. He came from England under his relative, Addison's (**0010**), patronage and he was in his secretariat. Lord Granard, a Tory peer seeking rehabilitation, was responsible for his return. His duties included the administration of the secret service money under the supervision of the Chief Secretary, and his predecessor, the long-serving Joshua Dawson (**0591**), did not make life easy for him. On 12 March 1715 Addison wrote to Archbishop King that 'I shall leave Mr Budgell to lay before your Grace what has been usual as to the secret service money & take care to put it to the proper use. I am forced often to advance money here [in England] to take out warrants for gentlemen in Ireland, to pay messengers, & sometimes to relieve such indigent petitioners as are not able to carry on a just pretension, not to mention the article of stationary ware &c. and as I do not follow my predecessors in taking fees for recommendatory letters or any business done in England the usual allowances on this head will be an ease to me', and on 4 August 1715 King authorised Budgell to send Addison a bill for £200: Addison gratefully acknowledged this and assured King that it would be put to a proper use. Budgell was nominated to 12 committees between 1715 and 1717.

On 28 January 1717/8 the Speaker, William Conolly (**0460**), wrote to Charles Delafaye (**0611**), Joint Chief Secretary 1715–7: 'By all I can find here [Budgell] makes few friends and to my knowledge he has by his late Conduct lost those that could have served him. He is in ye right to pray for Mr Adison's life for when anything happens to him, Mr Budgell (if I am not greatly mistaken) will fall as fast as he rose.' Budgell was seeking six weeks' leave of absence to go to London, and Conolly believed he was looking for the office of Keeper of the Records of Bermingham Tower in reversion after Addison's death. Conolly concluded that it would be 'a shamefull thing to heape more favours upon soe worthless a fellow'.

Even allowing for Irish Anglophobia, Budgell appears to have been incautious and tactless. On 25 April 1747 Charles Delafaye, long after Budgell's suicide, wrote to advise Chief Secretary Weston (**2223**) about the best method of handling revenue business in parliament: 'I always thought (perhaps because I had no talents that way) that it is best to leave it to the Gentlemen of the Country; and if, upon a debate a thought comes into one's head, to put it into the mouth of some friend of their number: the ingenious Mr

Budgell would be displaying his oratory and often so injudiciously that, to prevent his hurting us we were obliged to take care to have it understood that what he said was of his own head and ... not ... the sentiments of ... the Government.'

ADDITIONAL INFORMATION: He was 'x' of the *Spectator*.

ESTATES/RESIDENCE: Dublin Castle. On 15 April 1718 Conolly wrote to Delafaye saying that he believed Budgell to be worth £2,000 a year.

SOURCES: PRONI T/519, TSPI 1717–19, pp. 112, 116; PRONI T/3019/861 Wilmot Papers; King, *A Great Archbishop of Dublin, William King DD*, p. 185 n. 1; P. McNally, *Parties, Patriots & Undertakers* (Dublin, 1997), pp. 70, 78; *DNB*; Hughes, *Pat. Officers*; *Alum. Oxon.*; *Proc. RIA* vol. 77 C no 1 (1977), J. C. Sainty, 'The Secretariat of the Chief Governors of Ireland, 1690–1800'.

0272 BULKELEY, Sir Richard

MP for Fethard (Wexford) 1692–3, 1695–9, 1703–10

> b. 17 Aug. 1660; d. 7 Apr. 1710 at Ewell, Surrey
> HONOURS: Suc. as 2nd Bt 1685.
> FAMILY/BACKGROUND: Eldest son of Sir Richard Bulkeley (d. 17 Mar. 1684/5), 1st Bt, of Dunlavin, Co. Wicklow, and his first wife Catherine (d. 8 Feb. 1661/2), dau. and co-h. of John Bysse.
> MARRIED: [16 Feb. 1686] Lucy (b. 1663; d. Oct. 1710), dau. of Sir George Downing, 1st Bt (she m. (2) the Hon. William Worth (b. 1646; d. 23 Dec 1721), Bulkeley's stepfather.
> CHILDREN: *d.s.p.*
> EDUCATION: School: Mr Ryder, Dublin; entered TCD 4 Sept. 1676, aged 15 years, BA. 1680, Fellow 1681, MA 1681; BA Oxford (Christ Church), 21 May 1680.
> CAREER/OCCUPATION: Appointed by the king as a Commissioner of the Peace for Westminster and Middlesex, 7 Apr. 1692.

POLITICAL ACTIVITY: He was attainted by the 1689 parliament of James II. In 1695 he voted for the accusations of favouring Catholics against Lord Chancellor Porter, and in 1696 he signed the Association for the protection of William III in parliament. He was nominated for 36 committees between 1695 and 1698.

In 1705 he introduced 4 Anne, c. 6, 'an act to Prevent the illegal raising of Money by Grand Juries and the misapplying of Money legally raised; and for the better Execution of an Act for the mending the Highways by Six Days Labour; and for the appointing Oversears of the Highways by the Justices at their Sessions in Default of Naming them by the respective Parishes'. In the same session he introduced 4 Anne, c. 9, 'an Act for explaining and putting into Execution an Act for Planting and Preserving Timber Trees and Woods; and for explaining and putting into Execution an Act to avoid and prevent divers Misdemeanours in idle and Lewd Persons in Barking of Trees' and, also in the same session, 'an Act for Regulating the weights used in this Kingdom; and that salt and meal shall be sold by weight'. This was an attempt to coordinate weights throughout Ireland, and the statute lists towns where standard weights were available.

He was a strange man, and thereafter he appears to have been mainly absent in London for most of Queen Anne's reign, although always threatening to attend. Eventually he did, shortly before his death in 1710 – with the idea of establishing a university on his estate, Dunlavin, Co. Wicklow.

ADDITIONAL INFORMATION: A member of the Royal Society and of the Dublin Philosophical Society; a Fellow of the Royal Society *ante* 1685.

On 28 October 1685 he reported to the Royal Society an extraordinary invention. John Evelyn, one of his contemporaries, recorded it in his diary – it was a chariot that Bulkeley claimed was impossible to overturn. There were, however, a number of inconveniences yet to be remedied: it could hold only one person, it was ready 'to take fire every ten miles', and running on ten rollers 'it made a most prodigious noise, almost intolerable'.

According to Lynch's *Life of St Patrick* he vandalised the wall paintings and decorations in the little building at St Doulough's Well while returning with his troops from the Battle of the Boyne. In later life he became involved with some prophetic enthusiasts called 'French Prophets', and he wrote a number of pamphlets in their defence. They persuaded him to sell his estates and give

the proceeds to the poor, but death intervened. They also promised him supernatural protection if he would burn his house and walk through the flames.

ESTATES/RESIDENCE: Oldbawn House, near Tallaght, Co. Dublin; Dunlavin, Co. Wicklow. Under 14 Chas II (1663) Richard Bulkeley was granted a market at Dunlavin, and this was confirmed on 20 April 1692 when he was granted a patent for a market there. He petitioned the Commons, 1 September 1697, to bring in heads of a bill enabling him to raise £2,000 on his estate 'for payment of debts'. On his death his estates passed to his stepfather, the Hon. William Worth (born 1646, died 23 December 1721), whom Sir Richard's widow married (i.e. Worth married both Bulkeley's stepmother and his widow).

SOURCES: *CJ Ire.* (Bradley ed.) vol. 2 p. 886, vol. 3 pp. 77, 99, 143, 161; *John Evelyn's Diary* (28 Oct 1685); *Cal SP Dom. 1691–2* (London, 1900) pp. 36, 165, 220, 247; GEC *B*; *DNB*; *Alum. Dub.*; *Alum. Oxon.*; J. G. Simms, *William Molyneux of Dublin* (Dublin, 1982) p. 56; S. J. Conolly, *Religion, Law and Power* (1992) p. 195; J. T. Gilbert, *History of the City of Dublin*, 3 vols (1861) vol. 2 p. 174; *JRSAI* vol. 43 (1913) p. 316, H. G. Leask, 'House of Oldbawn, Co. Dublin'; Parliamentary Lists, 1695 (1), 1696 (1), 1706 (1), 1707 (1), (4).

0273 BUNBURY, George

MP for Thomastown 1786–90–7; Gowran 1797–1800; [Escheator of Munster 1800]

b. *c.* 1750–2; d. 17 May 1820
FAMILY/BACKGROUND: Second son of Thomas Bunbury of Kill, Co. Carlow, and his first wife Catherine, dau. of Josias Campbell.
MARRIED: Unmarried.
EDUCATION: School: Mr Hobert; entered TCD 28 June 1768; Middle Temple 6 Sept. 1770; BA 1772.
CAREER/OCCUPATION: High Sheriff of Co. Carlow 1777; Commissioner of a Public Board £500 p.a.

POLITICAL ACTIVITY: Thomastown was a 'close' borough, and its MPs followed the political instructions of Lord Clifden (**0016, 0013**). Their obedience increased Lord Clifden's political power and they could hope to be rewarded by their patron's influence with government: in this case with a position valued at £500 p.a. In 1790 it was declared, probably truthfully, that such MPs were: 'the confidential depositaries of his Lordship's power, not the honest dischargers of a constitutional trust. Its fate is similar to that of the Borough of Gowran, both being the property of the same person. Its representatives either accelerate, by their pliant parliamentary votes, the creation of Peers and Archbishops, or the purchase of their stations swells the coffers of the noble Lord who appoints them.' Furthermore, regarding the electors who returned them: 'Between these worthy wights and the place of which they are electors, there is not the slightest connexion, Lord Clifden not possessing a single foot of property in the town: the whole of that being vested in Eland Mossom (**1501**), Esq. in right of his wife.' The reference to peers is to Lord Clifden's (**0013**) father (**0016**), who was created a baron in 1776 and a viscount in 1781, while Lord Clifden inherited his great-uncle, Welbore Ellis, Lord Mendip's British peerage in 1802.

Lord Clifden was a government supporter, and his members voted for the Union in both 1799 and 1800. The vote for the regency is a surprise, but Lord Clifden may have thought it prudent to vote for the powers apparently to be. Clifden's uncle became Archbishop of Dublin and successively Baron and Viscount Somerton and finally, in 1806, Earl of Normanton.

DIVISION LISTS:
1789 (1) voted for a regency.
1790 (2) voted for Foster (**0805**) on the election of a Speaker.
1800 (1) voted for the Union.

ESTATES/RESIDENCE: Moyle, Co. Carlow.

SOURCES: PRONI D/302; PRONI T/3166/1B Hartnell notes; O'Neill thesis; *Alum. Dub.*; *Middle Temple Admissions* vol. 1 p. 371; Kilkenny MPs; A. P. W. Malcomson, *Archbishop Charles Agar: Churchmen and Politics in Ireland 1760–1800* (forthcoming, 2002); Parliamentary Lists, 1783 (2), 1785 (4), 1787 (1), 1788 (1), 1789 (1), 1790 (1), 1791 (1), 1793 (1), 1794 (2), 1799 (2), (3), 1800 (3).

0274 BUNBURY, Walter

MP for Clonmines 1703–13

b. 1664; d. July 1749
FAMILY/BACKGROUND: Son of [ ] Bunbury.
MARRIED: ?
CHILDREN: ?
EDUCATION: LLD *hon. caus.* TCD 1709.
CAREER/OCCUPATION: Clerk in Court of the Chancery; Solicitor, Court of the Chancery *c.* 1734.

POLITICAL ACTIVITY: He was MP for Clonmines in the first parliament of Queen Anne, and certainly in the early part of it a government supporter, but by 1711 it was thought that he was unlikely to be returned for Clonmines 'but there will be a "good man" [i.e. a Tory] in his stead'. He appears to have led a fairly active parliamentary life, as he was listed for 28 committees between 1703 and 1709.

DIVISION LISTS:
1709 (1) voted against a Money Bill.

ESTATES/RESIDENCE: [?]Moyle, Co. Carlow.

SOURCES: *Alum. Dub.*; *GM* July 1749; *IMC King's Inns Admissions, DJ* 22 July 1749; Parliamentary Lists, 1706 (2), 1711 (1), 1713 (1).

0275 BUNBURY, William

MP for Co. Carlow 1776–8

b. [*post* 2 Mar.] 1736; d. 18 Apr. 1778, having been thrown from his horse
FAMILY/BACKGROUND: Eldest son of Thomas Bunbury and his first wife Catherine, dau. of Josias Campbell of Drumsna, Co. Leitrim.
MARRIED: [1773] Catherine, dau. of Redmond Kane.
CHILDREN: Thomas; Kane; Jane, m. John McClintock.
CAREER/OCCUPATION: ?High Sheriff of Co. Carlow 1769.

POLITICAL ACTIVITY: He had been only a short time in parliament when he was killed, and little is known about his potential parliamentary conduct. He came in for Co. Carlow on the influence of Beauchamp Bagenal (**0071**). He had an independent fortune but was connected with the other MP for Co. Carlow, William Henry Burton (0304), who in turn was connected with the Ponsonbys. Bunbury's parliamentary connections would most likely have inclined him to opposition, as his voting record indicates.

DIVISION LISTS:
1777 (2) voted against the Trade Embargo.
1778 (1) voted for Grattan's (0895) motion for retrenchment.

ESTATES/RESIDENCE: Lisnevagh, Co. Carlow. His wife, who long survived him, retired to Bath and from there petitioned the Commissioners of Union Compensation, claiming that her father Redmond Kane had bought leases of houses and lands in the area of Swords, Co. Dublin in order to create and maintain an electoral interest. He died in 1778 and Catherine, his only child, 'still holds part of these leases – another part is held by the representatives of the Hon. Edward Molesworth, for a term of 41 years. The gross yearly rents amount to £266 and upwards. She feels she is entitled to £3,000 compensation, at least.'

SOURCES: PRONI D/302 [says he is of Kill]; Ellis thesis; *Memorials of the Dead* [says his parents married 2 Mar. 1736]; *Further Proceedings of the Commissioners Under the Union Compensation Act of Ireland* (1805); *Walker's Hibernian Magazine* 1778, p. 248; Parliamentary Lists, 1776 (2), (3), 1777 (1).

0276 BURDETT, Arthur

MP for Harristown 1790–6

b. *c.* 1726–8; d. Dec. 1796
FAMILY/BACKGROUND: Eldest son of Arthur Burdett of Co. Tipperary and Grace, dau. of John Head of Derry Castle, Co. Tipperary.
MARRIED: Unmarried.
CAREER/OCCUPATION: *Listed in Judges and Barristers 1789–1800 (f.); Sheriff of Co. Kildare 4 Feb. 1791.

POLITICAL ACTIVITY: He was a member of the Duke of Leinster's (0745) party and returned for his borough of Harristown, which had the distinction of being inhabited by a single tree. In 1793 the Duke sold it to John La Touche (1205) for £14,000. The Duke of Leinster was in opposition and a supporter of the Catholics – he gave the land for Maynooth College. Mr Burdett followed

the party line exactly; he died in December 1796, just before the end of the 1790 parliament.

DIVISION LISTS:
1790 (2) voted for Ponsonby (1709) on the election of a Speaker.
1791 (1) voted for Curran's (0560) resolution against the sale of peerages.
1791 (2) voted for Grattan's (0895) motion for the exercise of Free Trade.
1791 (3) voted for Grattan's motion to abolish the Dublin police.
1792 (1) voted for the Catholic petition.
1793 (1) voted for Knox's (1180) motion for Catholic Emancipation.
1793 (2) voted against the Convention Bill.
1795 (1) voted for a Short Money Bill.

ADDITIONAL INFORMATION: A member of the Royal Dublin Society from 1759.

ESTATES/RESIDENCE: Bellavilla, Co. Kildare; 4 Gardiner's Row, Dublin.

SOURCES: RCBL T34, Extracts from the Parish Registers of St Andrew's, Dublin [says ? Burdett esq. of Co. Kildare, bur. Dec. 1796]; GEC *P* [his younger sister Grace b. 1735 married Hon. Barry Maxwell (Barry), 1st Earl of Farnham (1372) as his second wife]; Burke *IFR* (1976) p. 181 [says his father married in 1725 and his mother was of Waterford and he was the eldest of four children]; Kildare MPs; *Alum. Dub.*; *WHM* 1797 p. 96; Hughes, *Pat. Officers*; *Almanacks*; Parliamentary Lists, 1791 (1), 1793 (1).

0277 BURDETT, George

MP for Gowran 1783–90, 1797–1800; Thomastown 1790–7

b. *c.* 1730–3; d. 2 Feb. 1818
FAMILY/BACKGROUND: Son of Arthur Burdett of Co. Tipperary and Grace, dau. of John Head of Co. Tipperary.
MARRIED: [1766] Jane, dau. of John Frend of Co. Limerick.
CHILDREN: Arthur (Lincoln's Inn 20 Nov. 1789), m. [1810] Anna, o. dau. of William Ripley of Liverpool; Capt. George RN, m. (1) Jane, dau. of Lieut.-Gen. Whitelock, (2) [1806] Catherine Dorothea, o. dau. and h. of Col. William Brown; Rev. John, m. [1803] Margaret Anne, dau. of

Michael Head of Co. Tipperary; Grace, m. Henry Peisley L'Estrange of King's County; Jane, m. Lieut.-Col. Francis Brooke.

EDUCATION: School Mr Dubourdieu; entered TCD 1 Dec. 1753.

CAREER/OCCUPATION: Commissioner of Appeals May 1798 at £200 p.a. and fees; High Sheriff of Queen's County 30 Jan. 1781; *Bailiff of Maryborough 1789–96; *Magistrate of Maryborough 1789–96.

POLITICAL ACTIVITY: A younger brother of Arthur Burdett (0276), he was returned by Lord Clifden (0016) and followed his political line. In 1790 it was commented that 'Whilst the late Lord was soliciting a Peerage, two of his devoted followers were returned for it, who regularly thickened the ministerial phalanx in the House of Commons. What will be the present Lord's conduct in that respect, we will not venture to affirm but as he is known to entertain a marked dislike to this country which he has too openly and incautiously expressed, he will most probably become an absentee and then the Borough will of course go to market to enlarge the supplies for foreign expenditure.' In fact Lord Clifden continued to support, and had considerable reason for doing so (see 0273).

Burdett was returned for Gowran in 1797 and was made a Commissioner of Appeals in May 1798 at £200 p.a. and fees, the whole estimated at c. £500 p.a. Lord Clifden and his followers supported the Union.

DIVISION LISTS:

1785 (1) voted for the Commercial Propositions.

1789 (1) voted for a regency.

1790 (2) voted for Foster (0805) on the election of a Speaker.

1799 (1) voted for the Union.

1800 (1) voted for the Union.

ESTATES/RESIDENCE: Heath House, Maryborough, Queen's County; Gt George's Street, Dublin.

SOURCES: PRONI D/302; PRONI T/3166/1B Hartnell notes; RCBL P277/1/4, Parish Registers of St Mary's, Dublin [says a George Burdett (bur. 5 Feb.) 1819]; O'Neill thesis; Burke *LGI* (1904) p. 73 [says he died 1817]; Kilkenny MPs; *Alum. Dub.*; Hughes, *Pat. Officers*; *Lincoln's Inn Records* vol. I p. 533; *Almanacks*; Parliamentary Lists, 1783 (2), 1784 (1), (2), (3), 1785 (1),

(2), (3), (4), 1787 (1), 1788 (1), 1789 (1), 1790 (1), 1791 (1), 1793 (1), 1794 (2), 1799 (2), (3), 1800 (3).

0278 BURDETT, Sir Thomas

MP for Co. Carlow 1704–13, 1715–27; Carlow B. 1713–14

b. 14 Sept. 1668; d. 14 Apr. 1727

HONOURS: Cr. Bt 11 July 1723.

FAMILY/BACKGROUND: Second son and h. of Thomas Burdett and Catherine, dau. of Sir Robert Kennedy, 1st Bt.

MARRIED: (1) [c. 1700] Honora (d. Nov. 1710), Dowager Countess of Ardglass, dau. of Michael Boyle, Abp of Armagh, wid. of Francis Cuffe (0548) and of Thomas Cromwell, 3rd Earl of Ardglass; (2) [1715] Martha, dau. of Bartholomew Vigors, Bp of Ferns and Leighlin.

CHILDREN: (2) Sir William Vigors, 2nd Bt, m. (1) [c. Aug. 1739] [ ] niece of Robert Jones, (2) Henrietta (d. c. 1778), dau. of the Hon. James O'Brien (1556), niece of the Dowager Countess of Kildare) and wid. of Terence O'Loghlin.

EDUCATION: School: Kilkenny; entered TCD 29 Sept. 1685, aged 18 years.

CAREER/OCCUPATION: High Sheriff of Co. Carlow 1701; Governor of Co. Carlow 1699, 1725–7.

MILITARY: ?Major in the army, volunteered to raise a Regiment of Foot at his own expense 1715.

POLITICAL ACTIVITY: Before he entered parliament he was one of the gentlemen of Co. Carlow who on 16 April 1701 petitioned against the return and residence of Mark Baggot, 'a violent Papist', in that county, of which he had been 'titular High Sheriff' in 1689. Burdett entered parliament in 1704 as a staunch Tory and as such supported the administration during the reign of Queen Anne. He supported the Court over the Dublin mayoralty dispute, and in October 1713 it was claimed that 'he did not give one vote to the Whigs in the last session'. At the death of Queen Anne he was indisputably a Tory and on the 'black list'. However, his offer to raise a regiment for George I may have mollified the authorities, although they still considered him a Tory in 1719 and for that reason likely to be opposed to the repeal of the Test Clause. He voted for a national bank.

He was listed for five committees between 1705

and 1711 and, after the accession of George I, for two in 1720. On 25 October 1723 he alleged in parliament that he had been disturbed in possession of his lands at Kilmaglish Bolybreen, Rahinkillane, Co. Carlow by under-sheriffs during time of privilege. This type of complaint was quite frequent, and gives some idea of the unsettled nature of the country for at least a generation after the Treaty of Limerick.

DIVISION LISTS:
1711 (1) voted for the Court on the Dublin mayoralty issue.
1721 (1) voted for a national bank.

ESTATES/RESIDENCE: Garahill, Co. Carlow. In 1714–5 his income was estimated at £1,000, which was substantial. However, the family appears to have fallen on hard times, as in March 1779 the Dowager Countess of Kildare wrote on behalf of her niece (the MP's daughter-in-law) who had died, and with her a small pension which was the family's chief support. She wrote that Sir William and their children were now living on the charity of their relations. Lady Kildare begged for something not unbecoming to a gentleman. In 1789 Sir William Burdett, 2nd Bt was described by his brother-in-law as having scarcely a guinea.

SOURCES: PRONI D/302; *CJ Ire.* (Bradley ed.) vol. 5 p. 137; GEC *B*; Carlow MPs; Burke *PB* (1903) p. 1567; NLI MS 39/70 Joly Papers, Lord Inchiquin to Lord Buckingham, 7 June 1789; Hayton thesis; *HMC Ormonde* new ser. vol. 8 pp. 39, 322 [in Nov. 1710 Robert Johnson (**1101**) writes that Major Burdett of Co. Carlow is recovering after accidentally drinking some rat poison]; *JRSAI* vol. 55 (1925) pp. 37, 43, H. A. S. Upton, 'A List of Governors and Deputy Governors of Counties in Ireland in 1699'; *JRSAI* vol. 76 (1946) p. 135, W. E. J. Dobbs, 'A Supplement to the Entrance Register of Kilkenny School: 1684–1800'; *HMC Lothian* p. 348; Parliamentary Lists, 1706 (1), 1711 (3), 1713 (1), (2), 1714–15 (1), 1719 (2).

0279 BURGH, Richard

MP for Naas 1759–60, 1761–2

b. 1725; d. (bur. 21 Sept.) 1762 at Ashlow, Co. Kildare
FAMILY/BACKGROUND: Son and heir of Thomas Burgh of Dromkeen, Co. Limerick, and Mary, dau. of Thomas Burgh (**0280**).

MARRIED: ?
CHILDREN: *d.s.p.*
EDUCATION: School: private tutor; entered TCD 11 July 1744, BA 1748; incorporated Cambridge 1751, Fellow, Cambridge (Trinity College) 21 July 1749, aged 22 years, BA 1751; Middle Temple 19 Oct. 1751; called to the Irish Bar 1755 – described as a Counsellor at Law.

POLITICAL ACTIVITY: Although elected to the last parliament of George II and the first of George III, he was barely a year in each and nothing is known of his parliamentary career. He was listed for seven committees between 1759 and 1760.

ESTATES/RESIDENCE: Dromkeen, Co. Limerick.

SOURCES: PRONI T/1584 Pinkerton transcripts, p. 67, 29 Oct. 1762 [says he died aged 37 years]; RCBL P45/2/3, Parish Registers of St Peter's, Dublin; McCracken thesis; Burke *LG* (1846) p. 162; *King's Inns Admission Papers*; *Middle Temple Admissions* vol. 1 p. 344; *Alum. Cantab.*; *DJ* 23–6 Oct. 1762 [says he died aged 37 years]; *BNL* 29 Oct. 1762 [declares that he died 'a few days ago'].

0280 BURGH, Thomas

MP for Naas 1713–14, 1715–27–30

b. 1670; d. 18 Dec. 1730
FAMILY/BACKGROUND: Son of Ulysses Burgh of Co. Limerick, Bp of Ardagh, and Mary, dau. of Col. William Kingsmill of Co. Tipperary.
MARRIED: [10 July 1700] Mary, dau. of William Smith, Bp of Kilmore.
CHILDREN: Thomas (**0282**); Ulysses (admitted to Middle Temple 19 Dec. 1732); Elizabeth, m. Ignatius Hussey of Co. Kildare; Dorothea, m. [29 July 1749] Rt Hon. Anthony Foster (**0804**); Mary, m. Richard Burgh.
EDUCATION: School: Mr Delany, Dublin; entered TCD 22 Nov. 1685.
CAREER/OCCUPATION: Freeman of Dublin 1704; Freeman of Naas 29 Sept. 1709, 23 June 1726; Trustee of the Linen Manufacture for the Province of Leinster 10 Oct. 1711; Sheriff of Co. Kildare 1711; High Sheriff of Co. Kildare 1712; Sovereign of Naas 15 times before 30 Sept. 1726; Governor of the Royal Hospital, Kilmainham.
MILITARY: First commissioned in Irish Engineers 27 Feb. 1691 at the siege of Namur; Captain Royal Regiment of Foot 1 Aug. 1692, served at Steenkerk 1692, Landen 1693 and at the siege of

Namur; engineer in King William's Own Company Oct. 1696; 3rd Engineer of Ireland; Director General, Engineer and Surveyor General of Fortifications for life 10 July 1700 at £300 p.a. (received £525 4s 1¹/₂d for 21 months to 31 Mar. 1720), Barracks Overseer in Ireland 12 Feb. 1701 (final renewal 14 Feb. 1728); Lieutenant-Colonel 11 Apr. 1706; Brasier's Regiment of Foot 1707–14; Lieutenant of the Ordnance 1714.

POLITICAL ACTIVITY: A professional soldier who served in European campaigns of the War of the League of Augsburg and possibly also in the War of Spanish Succession, as he did not enter parliament until 1713, although he reported to parliament in 1704 recommending the construction of a number of lighthouses around the coast. His last public act, in 1730, was to assist in examining the maps and soundings of Dublin harbour. As a military engineer he would have had experience in various types of construction, and he was responsible for the designing of a large number of buildings in Dublin: the Royal Barracks 1701–4, the old Custom House 1707, the infirmary of the Royal Hospital 1711, Old St Werburgh's 1715, Dr Steevens' Hospital 1719; he also designed the great library of Trinity College, started in 1712 but not finished until 1732, and Marsh's Library. At Dublin Castle he added to and repaired Sir William Robinson's (**1795**) buildings.

He was also interested in the economic development of the country: on 12 February 1722 he and Richard Stewart (**2007**) received the first £2,000 of £8,000 from the Irish parliament for operating their colliery at Ballycastle. The second £2,000 was granted on 31 July 1724. A man of his qualifications and experience was valuable, and the Parliamentary List of 1713 noted that he was 'likely to be returned for Naas and to be given Government help'. He was classed as a Tory in 1713 and voted for Sir Richard Levinge (**1230**) as Speaker. He was on the 'black list' of Tories the following year.

In 1719 he was still classed as a Tory and thought likely to vote against the repeal of the Test. He voted for a national bank on the first division and against it in the second. Many MPs did this: it probably reflected the unsettled financial times, and suspicion of the government's intentions. For his work on a more convenient and accurate method of calculating the results of land surveys he was granted £1,000 by the Irish parliament. He was listed for 41 committees, including seven in the short parliament of 1713.

By the end of the 1720s the construction of a new Parliament House was imminent as, never well built, Chichester House was collapsing beyond further repair. As Surveyor General Burgh could hope to be its architect and designer. However, the young Edward Lovett Pearce (**1646**) looked to this position with the support of the influential Dr Marmaduke Coghill (**0431**), who tried to negotiate the sale of Burgh's position to his protégé. Coghill's endeavours were frustrated by Thomas Carter (**0360**). The reasons for Carter's hostility are unknown; they may have reflected his general hostility to Lord Lieutenant Carteret or his association with the Boyle and therefore Burlington interest. Burgh held the triple office of Engineer, Designer of Fortifications and Surveyor General. There was already a movement to link the first two of these offices to the Ordnance Department and place them under the supervision of the Master of the Ordnance. Burgh objected on the grounds that he was an independent officer of the Crown, holding his office *for life* and as such not even responsible to parliament; moreover, he would not 'be slurred, & the dignity of his office taken from him & be put in a station lower than either of his predecessors had been'.

Pearce's main objective was to design the Parliament House, and despite Burgh's prior claim he managed to get his plans submitted to the Commons building committee: it is assumed that this was the plan approved by the House of Commons on 30 April 1728. Pearce was not only well connected but had the support of Speaker Conolly (**0460**), not surprisingly in view of the design of Castletown, on which Pearce had worked. The plan approved by the Commons was forwarded to the Lord Lieutenant. On the same day, 30 April, Surveyor General Burgh was invited to forward his plan directly to the Lord Lieutenant. The House of Lords asked the Lord Lieutenant to lay the several plans before them prior to seeking royal approval for any of them, and invited their committee to solicit further designs. Parliament was prorogued and the Lord Lieutenant, Burgh and Pearce all went to England. The final decision was given for Pearce, which must have been a bitter disappointment for Burgh, who had designed all the major buildings erected in Dublin since his appointment in 1700. The Irish parliamentarians were becoming more aware of the wider world, and probably felt that they wanted something in a more modern design.

Burgh died on 18 December 1730. His memorial is the great library of Dublin University.

DIVISION LISTS:

1713 (1) voted for Sir Richard Levinge (**1230**) for Speaker.
1721 (1) voted for a national bank.
1721 (2) voted against a national bank.

ADDITIONAL INFORMATION: He built his own house at Oldtown as well as being associated with Stackallan, Co. Meath (1717), Santry Court, Co. Dublin and Saunders Grove, Co. Wicklow.

As a member of the Dublin Philosophical Society, Burgh took an active interest in science, and in 1724 he published *A Method to Determine the Areas of Right-Lined Figures Universally. Very Useful for Ascertaining the Contents of Any Survey.*

ESTATES/RESIDENCE: Naas and Oldtown, Co. Kildare. Thomas Burgh's income in 1713 was reputed to be £500.

SOURCES: I am greatly indebted to Dr McParland for information from his new book which is to be published in 2001 by Yale University Press; PRONI D/302; *CJ Ire.* (Bradley ed.) vol. 4 p. 759, vol. 5 pp. 49, 304–45; TCD, S.3 1–4, Naas corporation books, 1665–1840, 4 vols; PRONI T/1203/20; PRONI T/3411; RCBL T34, Extracts from the Parish Registers of St Andrew's, Dublin; McCracken thesis; Hayton thesis; Burke *LG* (1846) p. 162; *King's Inns Admission Papers*; *Middle Temple Admissions* vol. 1 p. 314; J. T. Gilbert, *Dublin*, vol. 3 p. 74; C. Dalton, *George the First's Army, 1714–27*; *HMC Ormonde* new ser. vol. 8 p. 408; P. and B. Rowan (antiquarian booksellers), *The Eighteenth Century: An Irish Perspective* (Belfast, 1986), no 50; *JRSAI* vol. 40 (1910) p. 327, W. P. Pakenham-Walsh, 'Roll of the Corps of Royal Engineers of Ireland, 1251–1801'; *Irish Sword* vol. 13 (1977–9) pp. 110–18, R. Loeber, 'Biographical Dictionary of Engineers in Ireland, 1600–1730'; *The Dublin Gazette* 19 Dec. 1730; *DJ* 22 Dec. 1730; Parliamentary Lists, 1713 (1), (2), 1714–15 (1), 1719 (2).

0281 BURGH, Thomas

MP for Lanesborough 1727–58

b. 1696; d. 20 Sept. 1758
FAMILY/BACKGROUND: Son and h. of William Burgh (**0285**) and Margaret, dau. of Thomas Parnell of Cheshire.
MARRIED: Anne, o. dau. of Dive Downes, Bp of Cork and Ross.
CHILDREN: William (**0286**); Thomas (**0284**); Anne, m. Rt Hon. Walter Hussey (Hussey-Burgh) (**1059**); Margaret Amelia, m. Rt Hon. John Foster, 1st Baron Oriel (**0805**); Anne Marie m. Michael Keating (**1136**).
EDUCATION: School: Mr Scott, Dublin; entered TCD 24 Feb. 1711, BA 1714; Middle Temple 27 Feb. 1714.
CAREER/OCCUPATION: *Governor of Dr Steevens' Hospital 1733–d.; *Recorder of Cashel 1747, 1755–d., *Mayor 1752, 1754, 1758; *Magistrate, *Cashel 1747, 1752, 1754–d.

POLITICAL ACTIVITY: He was a lawyer but does not appear to have been ambitious for national office, preferring local appointments, for example as a Recorder for Cashel and as a magistrate. Although it is not always clear which Thomas Burgh the *Journal* refers to, he was probably nominated for 46 committees between 1727 and 1755, when he would have been approaching 60.

In 1735 he introduced an act for repairing and establishing a turnpike road from Mullingar to Lanesborough through Rathconra and Ballymahon. He voted against the election of James Digges La Touche (♦♦♦♦) for Dublin city in 1749, but with the Country or Speaker's party during the Money Bill crisis in the early 1750s.

DIVISION LISTS:

1749 (1) voted against the election of James Digges La Touche (♦♦♦♦).
1753 (1) voted for the expulsion of Arthur Jones-Nevill (**1125**).
1753 (2) voted against the Money Bill.

ADDITIONAL INFORMATION: A foundation member of the Dublin Society, 1731.

ESTATES/RESIDENCE: Bert, Co. Kildare.

SOURCES: *CJ Ire.* (Bradley ed.) vol. 6 pp. 556, 571 (0357); McCracken thesis; *Middle Temple Admissions* vol. 1 p. 273; Berry *RDS* pp. 24–7; *Almanacks*; *GM* Sept. 1758.

0282 BURGH, Thomas

MP for Naas 1731–59

b. (bapt. 4 Nov.) 1707; d. 23 June 1759
FAMILY/BACKGROUND: Eldest son of Thomas Burgh
(0280) and Mary, dau. of William Smith, Bp of
Kilmore.
MARRIED: (1) [21 Dec. 1734] Margaret, dau. of
William Sprigge (1975); (2) [June 1752]
Catherine, dau. of Sir Richard Wolseley, 1st Bt
(2247) (she m. (2) Caulfeild Byrne Caulfeild,
Archdeacon of Clogher).
CHILDREN: Thomas (0283); Catherine, m. Dixie
Coddington (0427).
EDUCATION: School: Mr Sheridan, Dublin;
entered TCD 9 Feb. 1722, BA 1726; Middle
Temple 10 Apr. 1728.
CAREER/OCCUPATION: Sheriff of Co. Kildare 1723,
?1733; ?High Sheriff of Naas 1732; Sovereign of
Naas 11 times, 1736, 1740, *1741, 1742;
*Recorder of Naas 1740, 1742; *Magistrate of
Naas 1736, 1740, 1742; Burgess of Harristown
1 Nov. 1752, *Athy 1757.

POLITICAL ACTIVITY: This member voted for the
administration over the James Digges La Touche
(♦♦♦♦) election petition. Unlike his namesake
(0281), he also voted for the administration over
Jones-Nevill (1125), and for the Money Bill. The
Journal does not always make clear which Thomas Burgh it is referring to, but he was apparently nominated for 31 committees between 1731
and 1755.

DIVISION LISTS:
  1749 (1) voted against the election of James
  Digges La Touche (♦♦♦♦).
  1753 (1) voted against the expulsion of
  Arthur Jones-Nevill (1125).
  1753 (2) voted for the Money Bill.

ESTATES/RESIDENCE: Naas and Oldtown, Co. Kildare.

SOURCES: PRONI D/3078/4, Minute book of the borough of Harristown, county of Kildare, 1714–90;
PRONI T/1203/20; RCBL T34, Extracts from the Parish Registers of St Andrew's, Dublin; McCracken thesis [says b. 1706]; *Middle Temple Admissions* vol. 1 p.
303; *Almanacks*; *GM* June 1759; *The Dublin Gazette*
28 Nov. 1732; *Pue's Occurrences* 24 Dec. 1734.

0283 BURGH, Thomas

MP for Harristown 1775–6, 1783–90; Athy
1776–83

b. 23 Jan. 1754; d. 1832
FAMILY/BACKGROUND: Eldest son of Thomas Burgh
(0282) and his second wife Catherine, dau. of Sir
Richard Wolseley, 1st Bt (2247).
MARRIED: [10 Aug. 1784] Florinda, dau. of Rt
Hon. Charles Gardiner (0840).
CHILDREN: Rev. Thomas John, m. [1811] Anne,
dau. of Hon. Francis Hely Hutchinson (1000);
Charles (d. yg); Rev. Walter, m. [1839] Elizabeth,
dau. of James Langrishe, Dean of Anchonry;
Luke (RN); Arthur (RN); Maj. Charles (23rd
Highlanders); John, m. Emma Maria Hunt; Rev.
William, m. (1) [1827] Anne, dau. of Rev. John
Coppinger, (2) [1851] Janet Macartney; Florinda;
Dorothea, m. [1819] Capt. Thomas Monck
Mason RN; Maria; Anna Maria, m. Ernest
Augustus Belford.
EDUCATION: Entered TCD 1770, BA 1772;
Middle Temple 30 Oct. 1776; called to the Irish
Bar 1779.
CAREER/OCCUPATION: Burgess of Harristown 9
Oct. 1775; *Commissioner of the Tillage Act for
Leinster 1784–5; *Company of Undertakers of
the Grand Canal 1783–4.
MILITARY: Lieutenant Oct. 1775.

POLITICAL ACTIVITY: He was returned by the Duke
of Leinster and one of the duke's party. He was
known as Thomas Burgh of Old Town to distinguish him from the Thomas Burgh (0284) who
was from 1776 to 1790 also returned by the Duke
of Leinster and was a brother-in law of John Foster (0805). The Parliamentary Lists appear to have
some uncertainty as to whether this Thomas Burgh
was a soldier or a lawyer. He appears to have been
both. In 1777 he was a lieutenant in artillery, and
the following year a captain.

By 1782 the War of American Independence
was drawing to its close and he was 'a young lawyer. Returned by and attached to the Duke. Useful as a Chairman in Committees. Much in confidence with Mr Foster.' In 1783 he was returned
for Harristown as the duke wished to bring in for
Athy one of his younger brothers, Lord Edward
FitzGerald (0730), who had returned from the
American war. Meanwhile the duke was anxious
to find a legal position worth £300–400 p.a. for
Burgh, who was 'naturally disposed to govern-

ment', probably because of his relationship to Foster and Foster's brother-in-law, Luke Gardiner (**0842**), in 1789 created Lord Mountjoy.

In 1789 he was assessed as follows: 'Parliamentary knowledge has become of late years, from the multiplicity of its objects, so complicated a science that an acquaintance with it is not to be attained without serious and severe study ... Mr Burgh, in whose character sound sense and not exterior glitter forms a constituent part, has visibly taken pains to make himself master of it and his success, as might be expected, has corresponded to the ardour of his application. Mr Burgh's voice is not such as an orator would wish for, as, though clear, articulate and possessed of a great variety of tones, it is weak, hollow and sometimes scarcely audible ... His delivery has much dignity and [is] exceedingly well tempered between the faulty extremes ... and his language is copious, nervous and brilliant, uniting purity and correctness with precision and elegance. It is not studiously adorned with the flowers of rhetoric, nor affectedly elevated by the splendour of figures ... His manner is earnest, warm and animated, but perhaps, at times with too strong a tendency to vehemence and his action combines in a pleasing degree grace with force ... In reasoning he is strict, acute and argumentative, in general confining himself to the immediate subject of discussion without any excursive flights or devious wanderings ... In Parliament Mr Burgh has been ever a friend of liberty and constant in his support of the general interests of the people and on some important questions has taken a decided and manly part, alike honourable to himself and beneficial to his country.' By some arrangement, before 1790, he acquired one seat at Naas which he sold to James Bond (**0184**), an Indian nabob in search of a baronetcy.

DIVISION LISTS:

1775 (1) voted for the pro-American amendment to the Speech from the Throne.
1777 (1) voted against Grattan's (**0895**) motion for retrenchment.
1777 (2) voted against the Trade Embargo.
1779 (2) voted for a six-months Loan Bill.
1780 (1) voted against Grattan's declaration of the Rights of Law (?Ireland).

1780 (3) a teller for the Tenantry Bill.
1780 (4) spoke and voted for a Perpetual Mutiny Bill.
1783 (1) voted against Flood's (**0762**) motion for parliamentary reform.
1784 (1) voted against a committee on the Reform Bill.
1785 (2) voted against the Commercial Propositions.
1786 (1) voted for the rights of grand juries.
1787 (1) voted for a Pension Bill.
1789 (1) voted for a regency.
1790 (1) voted for Grattan's motion for reducing the influence of the Crown.
1790 (2) voted for Foster (**0805**) on the election of a Speaker.

ADDITIONAL INFORMATION: A member of the committee appointed by the Commons to distribute £17,000 for the encouragement of certain manufactures. *A member of the Royal Dublin Society from 1783; *a subscriber to the Public Assembly Rooms, 1787; *a member of the Royal Irish Academy, 1790–1800.

ESTATES/RESIDENCE: Oldtown, Naas, Co. Kildare; Kildare Street, Dublin.

SOURCES: PRONI D/3078/4, Minute book of the borough of Harristown, county of Kildare, 1714–90; O'Neill thesis; Ellis thesis; *IMC King's Inns Admissions; Middle Temple Admissions* vol. 1 p. 383; *Almanacks*; J. Kelly, *Prelude to Union* (Cork, 1992), p. 152; *FJ* 24–7 Feb. 1787; Parliamentary Lists, 1776 (1), (2), (3), 1777 (1), 1778 (1), 1780 (1), 1782 (1), 1783 (1), (2), 1784 (1), (2), (3), 1785 (1), (3), (4), 1787 (1), 1788 (1), 1789 (1), (2), 1790 (1), 1791 (1), 1793 (1).

0284 BURGH, Thomas

MP for Athy 1776–83–90; Kilbeggan 1790–7; Clogher 1797–Jan. 1800; Fore Feb.–Aug. 1800

b. May 1744; d. (bur. 17) June 1810
FAMILY/BACKGROUND: Son of Thomas Burgh (**0281**) and Anne, dau. of Dive Downes, Bp of Cork and Ross.
MARRIED: [20 Mar. 1775] Anne, dau. and h. of David Aigoin of Dublin.
CHILDREN: Ulysses Bagenal, 2nd Baron Downes, m. (1) [1815] Mary, dau. and h. of Walter

Bagenal, (2) [1848] Christopheria, dau. of James Buchanan, wid. of John Willis Fleming; Anne, m. Nathaniel Sneyd (**1955**); Mary, m. [1814] Col. John Staunton Rochfort (**1804**); Charlotte, m. [1815] Rev. Zachariah Cornock; Catherine, m. [Mar. 1796] Alexander Hamilton (**0913**).

EDUCATION: School: Dr Norris; entered TCD 1 Feb. 1768, BA 1773.

CAREER/OCCUPATION: Comptroller and Accountant General 1784–93; Commissioner of Education 10 May 1788; Secretary to the Commissioners of the Court of Exchequer 1796, to Lords of Treasury 1796–9; Joint Weigh Master of Cork 1799; Commissioner of Paving 1799; Accounts Commissioner 23 June 1799–1804; Revenue Commissioner 1807.

MILITARY: For some years a military officer; Treasurer of the Ordnance and Comptroller General 23 Jan. 1779; Treasurer of the Ordnance Civil Branch 1788–91 (f.); at the Union he received £500 compensation for the loss of the Treasurer- and Paymastership of the Ordnance and £1,112 16s for the loss of the Agency to the Royal Artillery Regiment in Ireland.

POLITICAL ACTIVITY: A soldier and a man of good connections and some abilities, but of small fortune. He was a brother-in-law to Walter Hussey-Burgh (**1059**) and John Foster (**0805**), both of whom married his sisters. Hussey-Burgh had the reversion, but Burgh performed the duties of the office of Accomptant General – remitting the profits of the office to Agmondisham Vesey (**2145**) until alternative provision could be found for Vesey. The value of the office was variously quoted in the Parliamentary Lists as between £950 and £1,380. In the meantime he was also Treasurer of the Ordnance, £100, but as late as 1783 they were still waiting for Vesey to be given a pension, although this appears to have been granted shortly after. However, Hussey-Burgh died unexpectedly in September 1783 and Burgh was appointed Accomptant General.

In 1782 he was noted as 'an active and useful man who understands telling the House', and in 1784 'He is a very useful man as an observer in the House and keeps the Friends of Government together.' In this capacity he may well have provided some of the information contained in the Parliamentary Lists. Burgh was essentially a man of business and well disposed to the government. He was also related to the Duke of Leinster (**0745**)

and much in his confidence, possibly when the duke was looking for patronage and peerages for his friends. The duke allowed him, as an office holder, to vote with the government and in 1784 it was remarked that 'He wishes to attach the Duke of L[einster] to Government, but has not so much influence over him as he had.'

In 1793, as Accountant General he was perhaps scared by the rising national debt, as when Thomas Conolly (**0459**), MP for Co. Londonderry, and James Stewart (**2004**) for Co. Tyrone advocated that the poor be assisted by abolishing the Hearth Money Tax, Burgh insisted that it was the landlord that actually paid, and would doubtless increase his demands if the tax were abolished, and that even if it was the labourers that paid the tax, the solution was for them to keep fewer holidays – four saints' days would pay the tax. The act, 33 Geo. III, c. 14 (1793), exempted the very poor – those with only one hearth and a holding worth less than £5 p.a.

Even the hostile 1789 list credits him with the 'spirit of a soldier, which he once was and the character of a gentleman, which he surely supports with credit ... As a parliamentary speaker Mr Burgh's voice is strong and deep, without much compass or melody and at particular times it has a vulgarity of tone surprising in a man of his rank ... Of the strength of his reasoning and the method of his arrangement we should wish to speak with approbation were that in our power, but the former is as loose, desultory and inconclusive, as the latter is destitute of regularity or clearness. As on certain subjects he is very well informed, when he confines himself to them, the matter of his speeches is replete with instruction and justly merits regard, but as his general knowledge is not very extensive, nor appears to have been laboriously sought after, when he ventures beyond those limited bounds we may admire the boldness of the attempt, yet cannot say that it is justified by the success of its execution. Holding two employments under Government and connecting himself solely with the Speaker (**0805**), though brought into Parliament by his relation the Duke of Leinster, he has for many years been a determined supporter of Administration.'

In 1790 he was returned by either his own or

government-assisted purchase for Kilbeggan, but in 1797 he was returned for the government borough of Clogher, Co. Tyrone. Clogher was controlled ostensibly on behalf of the government by the Bishop of Clogher, who at this time was Speaker Foster's brother, and both of the members returned were Foster supporters. Shortly after the election the bishop died.

Cornwallis found Burgh's support for the Union less than enthusiastic, and so moved him from the Treasury to the Board of Accounts; this change required him to seek re-election and vacate his seat for the normally government-controlled borough of Clogher. However, because he had voted for the Union Cornwallis agreed to make his new income, said to be £800, equal with that of his former post. His removal from his post as Secretary to the Lords of Treasury, to become Accounts Commissioner, had meant a drop in income of about £200 p.a. Charles Broderick, Bishop of Cashel, in a letter to Lord Midleton, 11 July 1799, said the reason for his removal was that 'Though he voted for the Union, he was too free in talking against it.' Apart from his own views Burgh was, after all, Speaker Foster's brother-in-law and this may explain Cornwallis' change in Burgh's office that forced him to seek re-election. Burgh was not re-elected for Clogher, but instead sat for the Marquess of Devonshire's recently acquired borough of Fore from February to August 1800. He was sworn on 19 February 1800; the address in favour of the Union had passed on 5–6 February 1800.

DIVISION LISTS:

1777 (1) voted against Grattan's (0895) motion for retrenchment.
1778 (2) voted for the Popery Bill.
1780 (1) voted against Grattan's declaration of the Rights of Ireland.
1780 (2) voted against Yelverton's (2268) motion to modify Poynings' Law.
1780 (4) voted for the Perpetual Mutiny Bill.
1783 (1) voted against Flood's (0762) motion for parliamentary reform.
1784 (1) voted against a committee on the Reform Bill.
1784 (2) voted for the amendment on the

woollen manufacture.
1785 (1) voted for the Commercial Propositions.
1787 (1) voted for a Pension Bill.
1789 (1) voted against a regency.
1799 (1) voted for the Union – Secretary to the Lords of the Treasury, Weighmaster of Cork, Treasurer of the Ordnance and Commissioner of Paving.

ADDITIONAL INFORMATION: *A member of the Royal Irish Academy, 1795.

ESTATES/RESIDENCE: Clogher, Co. Down; Sackville Street and Chapelizod, Dublin.

SOURCES: PRONI Midleton Papers, p. 17, f. 107; PRONI T/3166/1C Hartnell notes; PRONI T/1584 Pinkerton Transcripts, pp. 222, 224, Mar. 1775; RCBL P277/1/3, Parish Registers of St Mary's, Dublin; Ellis thesis; O'Neill thesis; Fermanagh and Tyrone MPs; Kildare MPs [says born 1744]; Hughes, *Pat. Officers*; *Cornwallis Corr.* vol. 3 p. 107 [says he was born May 1744]; *Irish Genealogy* vol. 1 no. 10 (1941) p. 294, W. Clare, 'Irish Compensations and Pensions'; Malcomson, *Foster*, pp. 269–70; McDowell, *Ir. public opinion*, pp. 125–6; *BNL* 23 July 1799; *Almanacks*; *DJ* 15 Mar. 1796 [reports marriage of Alexander Hamilton to Miss Catherine Burgh second dau. of the late (*sic*) Robert]; Parliamentary Lists, 1776 (1), (2), (3), 1785 (1), (2), (3), (4), 1787 (1), 1788 (1), 1789 (1), (2), 1790 (1), 1791 (1), 1793 (1), 1794 (1), (2), 1799 (1), (3), 1800 (1).

BURGH, Walter: *see* **HUSSEY (HUSSEY-BURGH)**, Rt Hon. Walter (**1059**)

0285 BURGH, William

MP for Lanesborough 1713–14 [n.d.e. 1715]

b. 1667; d. (bur. 23 Oct.) 1744
FAMILY/BACKGROUND: Son of Ulysses Burgh, Bp of Ardagh, and Mary, dau. of Col. William Kingsmill of Co. Tipperary.
MARRIED: [1 June 1693] Margaret, dau. of Thomas Parnell of Congleton, Cheshire.
CHILDREN: Thomas (**0281**); William; Richard; Dorothea; Elizabeth, m. Anthony Foster (**0804**).

CAREER/OCCUPATION: Comptroller and Accountant General 8 Feb. 1695, 8 Aug. 1702, 31 Dec. 1714 (on 28 Apr. 1710 he received £300 'for stating and balancing the public accounts' and £600 on 10 Apr. 1712; on 19 Oct. the Public Accounts Committee requested the House to establish a Committee to solemnly examine Burgh and Capt. John Pratt (**1721**) 'touching an article of five hundred and thirty pounds and such other particulars in the accompts as shall be demanded of them'); *Engineer and Surveyor 1729; Freeman of Naas 29 Sept. 1709; Trustee of the Linen Board of Munster 10 Oct. 1711, 1732–43.
MILITARY: Captain in Sir Richard Atkins' Regiment of Foot 1 May 1695; half-pay 1698.

POLITICAL ACTIVITY: Returned as a Tory in the 1713 election, he sat in parliament for only a few weeks. He supported the Court over the Speakership, and was on the 'black list' of Tories when the queen died on 1 August 1714.

DIVISION LISTS:
1713 (1) voted for Sir Richard Levinge (**1230**) for Speaker.

ESTATES/RESIDENCE: Co. Tipperary. In 1714 his estimated income was £600 p.a. Richard Burgh purchased 795 acres in Co. Tipperary from the Commissioners for Sale of Forfeited Estates in 1702–3.

SOURCES: *CJ Ire.* (Bradley ed.) vol. 5 pp. 281, 304–45; TCD, S.3, 1–4, Naas corporation books, 1665–1840, 4 vols; PRONI T/559, Burke, extract pedigrees, vol. 13 p. 114; RCBL P277/1/2, Parish Registers of St Mary's, Dublin; McCracken thesis; Hayton thesis; Burke *Ext. P* (1883) p. 92; Simms' cards; Simms, *Williamite Confiscation*, p. 183; Hughes, *Pat. Officers*; H. F. Berry (ed.), *The Registers of the Church of St Michan, Dublin, 1636–1700* (Parish Register Society of Dublin, 1909) pp. 323, 328, 340, 349; C. Dalton (ed.), *English Army Lists and Commission Registers, 1661–1714* (London, 1898), vol. 4 p. 109; *Almanacks*; *GM* Oct. 1744; *HMC Ormonde* new ser. vol. 8 p. 88; *Kildare Arch. Soc. Jn.* vol. 4 (1903–5) p. 471; J. J. de Burgh, 'The de Burghs of Oldtown'; Parliamentary Lists, 1713 (2), 1714–15 (1).

0286 BURGH, William

MP for Athy 1768–76

b. 1741; d. 20 Dec. 1808 at York

FAMILY/BACKGROUND: Eldest son of Thomas Burgh (**0281**) and Anne, dau. of Dive Downs, Bp of Cork and Ross.
MARRIED: [1768] Mary, dau. and co-h. of George Warburton (**2170**).
CHILDREN: *d.s.p.*
EDUCATION: Middle Temple 13 Oct. 1761; Doctor of Civil Law of Oxford, by Diploma, 9 Apr. 1778.
CAREER/OCCUPATION: High Sheriff of Co. Kildare 1767; *Magistrate and Sovereign of Athy 1769; *Coroner for Dublin 1799 (f.).

POLITICAL ACTIVITY: This MP appears to have been far from popular, at least with the government, which considered him not only hostile and 'a violent young man' but 'a man of flippant pertness and dissolute insolence. Delights in saying an ill-natured thing.' However, in 1774 the opposition press declared that when present – which he was not in the 1773–4 parliamentary session – he 'showed himself a worthy friend to Ireland'. He was a distant relative of the Duke of Leinster, who returned him for Athy 1768–76. By 1775 he is described as: 'a mere Spit Fire. A pert peevish boy. His fortune is much involved, and he now lives in England. Has commenced author.' He did not come in again.

DIVISION LISTS:
1771 (1) voted against Lord Townshend as Lord Lieutenant.
1771 (2) voted for Sir Lucius O'Brien's (**1558**) motion for retrenchment.
1772 (2) voted for a Short Revenue Bill.

ADDITIONAL INFORMATION: A member of the Royal Dublin Society from 1767. At the election for Naas Borough on 12 July 1768, John Bourke the elder (**0192**) received 36 votes, John Bourke the younger (**0193**) 31 votes, Walter Hussey (**1059**) of Donore 15 votes, and William Burgh of Bert 2 votes. The Bourkes were declared duly elected.

ESTATES/RESIDENCE: Bert, Co. Kildare. He was succeeded in his estates by his brother, Thomas Burgh (**0284**).

SOURCES: PRONI D/302; TCD, S.3, 1–4, Naas corporation books, 1665–1840, 4 vols; Burke *Ext. P* (1883) p. 91; *DNB*; *Alum. Oxon.* [says died 26 Dec.]; Hughes, *Pat. Officers*; *Middle Temple Admissions* vol. 1 p. 357; Kilkenny MPs; *Almanacks*; Parliamentary Lists, 1769 (1), 1772 (2), 1773 (1), (2), 1774 (1), 1775 (1).

BURKE, Dominick: *see* **BOURKE** (*alias* **BURKE**), Dominick (**0191**)

0287 BURKE, Michael

MP for Athenry 1800

b. 1760; d. 29 Aug. 1838
FAMILY/BACKGROUND: Son of William Burke and Mabel, dau. of Malachy Donnellan of Co. Galway.
MARRIED: [c. 1783] Sarah, o. child of John Monksfield of Co. Galway.
CHILDREN: William Malachy, m. Anna Maria, o. dau. of John Blake; Rev. John, m. Mary, sis. of Arthur Guinness; Michael; Thomas, m. Louisa, dau. of Dominick Daly, wid. of Thomas Burke of Co. Galway; Henry, m. Frances Julie, o. dau. of Valentine Blake of Co. Galway; Denis, m. Maria, dau. of Maj. Graham; Sarah; Mabel, m. [1832] Rev. James Temple Nansel.
CAREER/OCCUPATION: Surveyor General of Ireland, Director of Inland Navigation; Sheriff of Co. Galway 11 Jan. 1786, Galway 1796.

POLITICAL ACTIVITY: On 2 March 1799 he wrote to Castlereagh (**2009**) informing him that the wealthy Catholics of Galway were in favour of the Union. He was sworn on 8 May 1800 – the Union had effectively passed on 5–6 February 1800 – in place of Theophilus Blakeney (**0158**), who had accepted the office of Escheator of Ulster. The borough belonged to the Blakeneys, who duly received the compensation for its disfranchisement.

ESTATES/RESIDENCE: Ballydugan, Co. Galway.

SOURCES: PRONI D/3030/638 Castlereagh Papers; PRONI T/3166/1B Hartnell notes; O'Neill thesis; Burke *LGI* (1904) p. 74; BL SPO 515/85/7; C. Ross (ed.), *Cornwallis Corr.* vol. 3 p. 215 [says his wife is Sarah, dau. of John Morgan of Monksfield].

◆◆◆ **BURROUGHS**, Thomas [n.d.e.]

MP for Carysfort Aug.–Oct. 1703

b. *ante* 1663; d. *post* 1727
FAMILY/BACKGROUND: Son of Francis Burroughs and [ ], dau. of [ ] Musket.

MARRIED: (1) [ ] Rainford; (2) [ ] Nugent.
CHILDREN: Thomas, m. Catherine, dau. of Sir Henry Cavendish, 1st Bt (**0380**); another son.
MILITARY: ?Major in Colonel Edward Lloyd's Regiment of Foot 1693; Major-General Sibourg's Regiment of Foot; Captain in Major-General Owen Wynne's (**2262**) Regiment of Dragoons (9th Lancers) 23 May 1719; left the Army by June 1727.

POLITICAL ACTIVITY: He was a professional soldier and sat for about three months before he was declared not duly elected. Very little is definitely known about him.

SOURCES: *Ext. B.* (1844) p. 92; Burke *LG* (1843) p. 167; *CJ Ire.* vol. 2 pp. 319, 338; *Cal. SP Dom.* 1693 p. 387; C. Dalton, *George the First's Army, 1714–1727*.

0288 BURROWES, Peter

MP for Enniscorthy 1800

b. 1753; d. 1841 in London (bur. Kensal Green cemetery)
FAMILY/BACKGROUND: Eldest son of Thomas Burrowes of Portarlington, Queen's County.
MARRIED: ?
CHILDREN: ?
EDUCATION: School: Mr Ball; entered TCD 8 July 1772; Middle Temple 16 Mar. 1781; called to the Irish Bar 1785.
CAREER/OCCUPATION: *Listed in Judges and Barristers 1789–1800 (f.); King's Counsel 1797; Commissioner of the Insolvent Debtors Court.

POLITICAL ACTIVITY: He was brought into parliament by Lord Lismore specifically to use his powers of oratory in opposition to the Union, which he voted against. He was one of the MPs who were rushed in – he was sworn on 3 February to make a last-minute opposition to the Union.

Long before his election, Burrowes was an eminent figure. He was a barrister and a King's Counsel with a large practice, who had made his way without government favour, and he was noted for his independence of mind and compassion. For instance, he endeavoured to provide John Beresford (**0115**) with evidence, which he had discovered in Waterford, of Beresford's brother-in-law, Henry Flood's (**0762**), legitimacy. He was a friend of Wolfe Tone's and acted as his go-between with Marcus Beresford (**0119**) in Tone's negotiations to secure his safe passage into exile. Later he arranged for Curran (**0560**) to defend Tone, and provided for Tone's mother in her old age. At the same time he deplored revolution, and was no supporter of the Jacobins. His brother, the Rector of Kilmuckbridge, Co. Wexford, was piked to death in 1798. Yet in 1803 he acted as counsel for Robert Emmet.

Burrowes had been marked as a prominent figure from his days in Trinity College. At college he was remarkable for the possession of great genius and application, and at the time he was keeping his commons at the Temple, he was very punctual in his attendances on the debating societies, where he was a constant and always a very superior speaker. He supported parliamentary reform in a pamphlet, written in 1784, entitled *Plain Arguments in Defence of the People's Absolute Dominion over the Constitution*. In the 1790s he supported Catholic enfranchisement, considering that in an enlightened age Roman Catholicism was a backward and superstitious creed which had entered irrevocably into decline and was now alien to the spirit of the times; earlier he had supported the pro-Catholic movement in the Volunteers.

On 9 December 1798 he and 13 other King's Counsel protested against proposals for a Union, to which he was passionately opposed, declaring that 'A loud and universal outcry issues from every quarter of Ireland against this detested measure ... all ranks and all religions are united in one grand and irresistible confederacy against it ... These are solemn moral manifestations of the active sentiment of a Nation; these are awful warnings, which the benignity of Providence interposes between the rash projects of Ministers and the irretrievable mischief. May God avert the storm, and save the Nation.' Like Saurin (**1886**), Ponsonby (**1699**), Curran and other opposition lawyers, he considered that the Act of Union 'was a nullity, void *ab initio* ... [and] was radically fraudulent; that all forms and solemnities of law were but so many badges of fraud, and that posterity, like a great court of conscience, would pronounce its judgment.'

ADDITIONAL INFORMATION: *A member of the Royal Irish Academy, 1790–1800(f.).

In 1790, along with Wolfe Tone and others, he founded a society in Dublin for the discussion of literary and political subjects. Tone referred to him in correspondence as 'the Czar'.

In a duel that he fought at Kilkenny in 1794 with the Hon. Somerset Butler, over an alleged insult to the latter's father, Lord Mountgarrett, at the Kilkenny assizes, his life was said to have been saved by the ball striking some pennies he had in his waistcoat pocket.

Out of Court he was famous for his absent-mindedness, and once while on circuit he was reputedly found with an egg in his hand while his watch was boiling merrily.

ESTATES/RESIDENCE: Dublin, [?]Wexford.

SOURCES: PRONI T/3030/13/5, TSPI; O'Neill thesis; *DNB*; *Alum. Dub.*; *King's Inns Admissions*; Burrowes, *Memoir* (1850); *Cornwallis Corr.* vol. 3 pp. 170, 174 [says he was born 1750]; F. MacDermott, *Tone and his Times* (Dublin, 1969 ed.), pp. 47, 273; M. Elliot, *Wolfe Tone* (1989) pp. 35, 84, 391; *Middle Temple Admissions* vol. 1 p. 390; McDowell, *Ir. public opinion*, p. 96; J. T. Gilbert, *Dublin*, vol. 3 p. 151; J. Kelly, 'That Damn'd Thing Called Honour': Duelling in Ireland 1570–1860 (Cork, 1995), p. 208; A. Webb, *Compendium of Irish Biography* (1878); *Beres. Corr.* vol. 2 pp. 5 & n.(a), 11–12, 27–8; J. T. Gilbert, *History of the City of Dublin*, 3 vols (1861) vol. 3 p. 173; *Almanacks*; Parliamentary Lists, 1799 (1), 1800 (3).

0289 BURROWES, Thomas

MP for Longford B. 1800 (May–August 1800)

b. *c*. 1741; d. 1830

FAMILY/BACKGROUND: Second son of Thomas Burrowes of Stradone, Co. Cavan, and Jane, dau. of Thomas Nesbitt (?**1524**) of Lismore.

MARRIED: (1) [2 Apr. 1777] Mary Dawkes; (2) [1787] Sarah (d. at Tanjore, India 1789), dau. of Capt. Greenland; (3) [1797] Frances, dau. of William Beresford, 1st Baron Decies, Abp of Tuam.

CHILDREN: (1) Arnold.

(2) Arnold Robinson; Col. Brantford, m. [1816] Harriet, o. ch. of Col. Richard Beresford of Fenny Bentley, Ashbourne, Derbyshire.

(3) Lieut.-Col. William Nesbitt, m. his cousin Susanna Henrietta Bermingham; Elizabeth

Catherine, m. [1831] Auguste, Baron de Cetto.
EDUCATION: Middle Temple 1757.
CAREER/OCCUPATION: *Commissioner of Appeals
1795–7; High Sheriff of Co. Cavan 1773, 1803.
MILITARY: Colonel in the East India Company.

POLITICAL ACTIVITY: He was sworn on 12 May 1800
in place of Thomas Pakenham (**1623**), who accepted the place of Gentleman at Large to the Lord
Lieutenant and thereby vacated his seat. Nothing
is known of this gentleman's parliamentary conduct, as the Union was already agreed by the time
he entered parliament.

ESTATES/RESIDENCE: [?]Co. Meath; 20 Rutland Square,
Dublin (1785); Benarth, Conway, Caernarvonshire; 3
Hill Street, Berkeley Square, London. The Benarth es-
tate was sued for in 1834.

SOURCES: PRONI T/282 Swanzy MSS p. 23 [gives the
will, proved 24 Feb. 1812, of a Thomas Burrowes of
Cavan, the MP's father; the testator's father (i.e. MP's
grandfather) was Alexander, his uncle Samuel, and his
sister Henrietta Edwards, who is to get Tullyco after
uncle Samuel's death; the plaintiff declared that: 'my
marriage settlement covering the Lismore Estate, also
the sum of £400 settled by the marriage settlement of
the late Rev. William Wade and Anne his wife or said
Mr Wade's estate in Co. Tyrone, which is payable to me
by my marriage settlement']; PRONI T/1075/29 Canon
Leslie's notes; *Prerog. Wills* 1811–58; O'Neill thesis;
Burke *LGI* (1904) p. 75; *IFR* (1976) pp. 185–6; *Alum.
Dub.*; W. T. J. Gun, *The Harrow School Register, 1571–
1800* (London, 1934); *Middle Temple Admissions* (London, 1949) vol. 1 p. 342; *IMC King's Inns Admissions*;
FJ 24 Jan. 1797.

0290 BURROWS (*alias* BORROWES or BURROWES), Sir Kildare

MP for Co. Kildare 1703–9

b. *c.* 1660; d. (bur. 26) Sept. 1709
HONOURS: Suc. as 3rd Bt 1685.
FAMILY/BACKGROUND: Son and heir of Sir Walter
Borrowes, 2nd Bt, and his first wife Eleanor, dau.
of George FitzGerald, 16th Earl of Kildare.
MARRIED: Elizabeth (d. 11 Mar. 1745), dau. of Sir
Richard Dixon of Colverstown, Co. Kildare
(sister and co-h. of Robert Dixon).
CHILDREN: Sir Walter Dixon, 4th Bt (**0188**);
Robert, m. Mary, dau. of John O'Neill of Co.
Antrim; Eleanor; Elizabeth, m. John Short

(?**1918**); Charity (d. yg); Mary (d. yg); Anne (d.
yg).
CAREER/OCCUPATION: High Sheriff of Co. Kildare
1697, 1707.

POLITICAL ACTIVITY: In 1706 he was noted as a Tory
and a supporter of the Court party. He was nominated to 39 committees between 1703 and 1709.
He died after six years in parliament in 1709, before the troubled end of Queen Anne's reign.

ESTATES/RESIDENCE: Gilltown, Co. Kildare. Lands in the
baronies of Maryborough West, Clandouagh and
Upperlands. There is an abstract that begins with a deed
from the Hollow Blades to John Shortt, 1709 and also
a rental of 1865. The owner in 1909 was Sir Kildare
Borrowes.

SOURCES: PRONI D/302; EC 2935; RCBL P251/1/1,
Dunlavin Parish Register; RCBL T34, Extracts from
the Parish Registers of St Andrew's, Dublin; GEC *B*;
Burke *PB* (1903) p. 176; Kildare MPs; J. T. Gilbert,
History of the City of Dublin, 3 vols (1861) vol. 1 pp.
176–7 [Dixon inheritance, Sir Robert Dixon was Mayor
of Dublin in 1634]; Parliamentary List, 1706 (1).

0291 BURT, John

MP for Tallow 1695–9

b. *c.* 1662–4; d. *post* 1699
FAMILY/BACKGROUND: Son of John Burt of Tallow,
Co. Waterford.
MARRIED: Mary [·].
CHILDREN: ?
EDUCATION: Middle Temple 12 May 1682.

POLITICAL ACTIVITY: In 1695 he voted in support
of Lord Chancellor Porter, who was accused of
favouring Catholics, and the following year he
signed the Association for the protection of
William III in the country. He was obviously in
both personal and financial trouble during his
period in parliament, and in addition he over-
stepped the rules governing privilege (see below).

ADDITIONAL INFORMATION: On 11 October 1695
Richard Burt, merchant of Tallow, along with
Abraham Morris, a Cork merchant, petitioned the
House to secure Morris's title to lands bought of
Burt. Then on 21 August 1697 he was involved
in an accusation of misuse of privilege. He ap-

peared in his place to hear a complaint against him 'that he had protected several persons, as his servants, contrary to the resolutions of this House'. He admitted the charge, begging pardon, but, nevertheless was taken into the custody of the Serjeant-at-Arms.

The third case involving him was matrimonial. He had obviously separated from his wife and she was demanding maintenance. On Thursday 24 November 1698 the House heard a petition from Mrs Mary Burt asking that her husband John should waive privilege 'that she may sue him for alimony', and Burt was summoned for the following morning but then was given time to appear, first on Saturday 26 November then on Monday 28 November. He failed to attend, and the House waived privilege on his behalf.

ESTATES/RESIDENCE: Tallow, Co. Waterford.

SOURCES: *CJ Ire.* (Bradley ed.) vol. 2 pp. 714, 871; *Middle Temple Admissions* vol. 1 p. 206; R. Refausse, 'The Welply Will Abstracts in the Representative Church Body Library, Dublin'; *Ir. Gen.* vol. 6 no 6 (Nov. 1985) pp. 814–23 [gives a John Burt of Dublin will proved 1689]; Parliamentary Lists, 1695 (1), 1696 (1).

0292 BURTON, Benjamin

MP for Dublin city 1703–13–14, 1715–27

b. *ante* 1665; d. 13 May 1728
FAMILY/BACKGROUND: Third son of Samuel Burton and Margery Harris; brother of **0296**.
MARRIED: [22 May 1686] Grace, dau. of Robert Stratford of Belan, Co. Kildare (**2027**).
CHILDREN: Samuel (**0301**); Sir Charles, 1st Bt (**0295**); Robert (**0300**); Francis (Major of Horse); Abigail, m. John Walsh of Dollardstown; Jane, m. John Carlton; Letitia, m. [1711] Henry Brooke (**0248**); Grace, m. [1703] Edward Hoare (**1023**); Elizabeth, m. Richard Hoare; Mary, m. [1704] Philip Doyne (**0660**).
CAREER/OCCUPATION: Sheriff 1694, Alderman of Dublin 1694, Lord Mayor 1706–7; Burgess of Sligo (probably a dissenter as he was disfranchised in 1710 for refusing to take the oath in the 1709 Act (8 Anne c. 3)); Trustee of the Linen Manufacture for the Province of Connaught 10 Oct. 1711; incorporated in the Company of the Royal Fishery of Ireland 26 Jan. 1692.

MILITARY: Was to have been Colonel of the proposed Dublin City Regiment of Foot Militia 1708.

POLITICAL ACTIVITY: A zealous Whig, he had been attainted by the Jacobites in 1689. Between 1698 and 1700 he, along with Francis Harrison (**0973**), established a bank at 4 Castle Street, Dublin. He entered parliament in 1703 and during the 1707 session he introduced 6 Anne, c. 20, 'an act for cleansing the Port Harbour and river of Dublin and for erecting a ballast Office in the said City'. In 1706 he was reputed to be a government supporter but by 1711 he was in opposition: possibly because of the Test Clause, as he was disfranchised from Dublin Corporation in 1710 for refusing to take the oath in the 1709 penal statute, 8 Anne, c. 3, which excluded Dissenters from municipal corporations but not from sitting in parliament.

He was one of the Whig aldermen of Dublin who defied the government over the election of a lord mayor, 1711–14. In 1712–13 he had a newspaper published, *The Anti-Tory Monitor*, to support his candidacy for the Dublin seat. By 1713 he was definitely a Whig. He was nominated for 48 committees between 1703 and 1713. In 1713, Burton and Harrison were appointed Commissioners for carrying out the rebuilding of St Werburgh's Church in Dublin which had been destroyed by fire, and to which they had contributed £150. He was again returned for Dublin city in 1715, and in 1717 he introduced an act, 4 Geo. I, c. 11, to cleanse the streets of Dublin, control the drivers of carts, drays or cars and regulate the selling of hay in the city of Dublin and the adjoining Liberties.

Burton's bank survived the panic of 1720. He voted against the establishment of a national bank in 1721, and in 1724 he subscribed to the declaration of Dublin bankers refusing to handle Wood's Halfpence. Initially his name was synonymous with solvency, and gave rise to the Dublin saying 'as safe as Ben Burton'; after 1733 this saying became a sarcasm for insecurity. His partner Harrison died on 27 June 1725, revealing liabilities of over £65,000 in the accounts. The taking into partnership of his son Samuel (**0301**), and five months later Daniel Falkiner (**0717**), secured these liabilities.

The bank was closely connected with the government – one of its activities was to equalise the pay and allowances of regiments transferred from the British to the Irish establishments in accordance with the exchange rates between the two countries, for the pound sterling was at a premium against all currencies in Britain's dependencies. For instance, on 19 July 1719 they received £267 10s 6d for the 'exchange of two thousand, four hundred and seventy pounds ten shillings, remitted to the Earl of Lincoln for three regiments'. The difference in exchange rates continued to be good business. On 1 April 1727 he received £2,205 for making up the differences of regiments abroad; on 24 November 1727 Samuel Burton and Hugh Henry (1005) received £3,393 for these services. The bank continued until 25 June 1733, when it closed owing 8,000–9,000 creditors upwards of £90,000 and other debts.

On 25 February 1734 Primate Boulter wrote to the Duke of Newcastle that 'Among other bills sent over for passing the Privy Council in *England* is one for the relief of the creditors of *Ben Burton* and *Francis Harrison* &c. which I must beg leave to recommend particularly to your Grace's care, that it may be returned to us. The several bankers mentioned in the title of the bill, continued the same bank without interruption with great credit; but as it appears at last, had drawn off unreasonable dividends, and *Ben Burton* and *Francis Harrison* had bought great estates, so that the bank was worth nothing at the time of *Harrison's* death, but the succeeding banks paid off the former bank with the money of the new creditors, till at last payment was stopped. The equity of the bill is founded on the first bankers having had their debts of the bank paid with the later creditors monies; and an act 8 *Georg.* I by which the unsettled estate of any banker is liable at the time of his death to all the bank debts; so that when *Harrison* died his estate was liable to pay all the debts of the bank as well as *Burton's* since they were answerable jointly and severally. His estate is since gone into the hands of strangers, from whence it could by long and expensive suits be fetched out by 8 *Georg.* I but as this would be very tedious and expensive, and no creditor could have any benefit that way, this act vests the estates of the several bankers in trustees, who are to determine claims in a summary way, and to sell as much as will pay the debts of the several banks; but as to Harrison they are not to sell more than will answer the debts of the bank at the time of his death; and if by such sale he has paid more than his share of those debts, it is to be made good out of the unsold estates of the other bankers, or the remaining debts and securities belonging to the bank; since that is not an affair between the creditors and the bankers, but between the bankers themselves to adjust their several proportions. When this bank stopped payment last *June*, it had very nigh overturned all our paper credit here, and if this bill miscarries, it is not doubted but our bankers will all be blown up. And at the same time we have so little specie here, probably at the most not above £500,000 that without paper credit, our trade cannot be carried on, nor out rents paid'. Eventually the bank failed by the huge sum of £180,000 and 900 customers had been faced with losing their deposits.

Boulter supported the petition but he had only £200 in the bank, so 'It is not any regard to my own concern in the bank ... but a regard to the publick credit of this kingdom, which is in danger of being sunk if this bill should miscarry.' Boulter wrote to Walpole on 28 March 1734 regarding 'Burton's Bill' and some reports of objections to it being sent over from Ireland. 'That Lord Chief Justice *Rogerson* (1812) should have written against that bill is not strange, since whatever is taken from *Harrison's* estate towards paying the debts of the bank is taken from Mr *Creighton* (0515) who married the Lord Chief Justice's daughter; so that the Chief Justice's letter is not from an indifferent hand. But the truth of our case, and what every man of sense here knows, is, that if this bill miscarries, it must put an end to our paper credit here, by an immediate run upon the bankers, or gradual forbearing to lodge money there: and it is certain we have not cash enough in the nation to carry on our common trade or pay our rents or taxes: and I very much question whether if our paper credit fails, it would not be with the utmost difficulty that our army could be subsisted.'

This was the most spectacular, though far from

the only, Irish bank failure in the eighteenth century. By 1757, four acts of parliament had been passed over this closure and in an attempt to regulate banking. In addition to 48 committees during Queen Anne's reign, Burton was listed for 75 in the parliament of George I.

DIVISION LISTS:
1721 (1) voted against a national bank.
1721 (2) voted against a national bank.

ESTATES/RESIDENCE: Burton Hall, Co. Carlow. Purchased with other lands in that county from the Trustees for the Sale of Forfeited Estates, 26 September 1712. The estate was all in the barony of Rathrilly, 15 miles from Carlow town, and included most of the town of Hacketstown. Much of it was granted away in perpetuity or fee farm, the former by Francis Harrison in 1714–15 and Benjamin Burton in 1723–5 (Burton seems to have owned the whole 'lordship of Clonmore'). The income of Benjamin Burton of Dublin, MP for Sligo Borough (this was a mistake for his son Samuel, but the figure may be correct) in 1713 was estimated at £1,000. By September 1733 all the contents of Burton Hall and all their other goods and chattels were put on sale by public auction to meet their debts. Also purchased 1,627 acres in Co. Limerick from the Commissioners for Sale of Forfeited Estates in 1702–3.

SOURCES: PRONI T/3411; NLI reps vol. 149, 22 May 1874; *CJ Ire.* (Bradley ed.) vol. 3 p. 516, vol. 4 pp. 542, 457, vol. 5 pp. 304–45, pp. 681–2 (0115, 0184); PRONI D/3000/27/1, 2 Falkiner Genealogical notes [says died 13 May 1728 as does *Ir. Statutes* vol. 7, p. 31, George II c. 12]; Hayton thesis; GEC *B*; Burke *LGI* (1904) p. 77; *IFR* (1976) p. 187; *Cal. SP Dom. 1691–2* (London, 1900) pp. 113; *Boulter Letters* vol. 2 pp. 93–5; R. E. Burns, *Irish Parliamentary Politics in the Eighteenth Century*, 2 vols (Washington, 1989), vol. 2 pp. 23–4; J. Ryan, *The History and Antiquities of the County Carlow* (Dublin, 1833) p. 360; Gilbert, *Dublin*, vol. 1 p. 17; Simms, *Williamite Confiscation*, p. 183; W. G. Wood-Martin, *History of Sligo*, vol. 3 p. 439; *The Flying Post* 7 Apr. 1708; *The Dublin Courant* 17 Aug. 1724; Parliamentary Lists, 1706 (1), 1711 (3), 1713 (2).

0293 BURTON, Rt Hon. Benjamin

MP for Knocktopher 1741–60; Co. Carlow 1761–7

b. 12 Jan. 1709; d. 1 Oct. 1767
HONOURS: PC, sworn 19 Sept. 1760, 21 Nov.

1760, 8 July 1761–d.
FAMILY/BACKGROUND: Eldest son of Samuel Burton (0301) and his first wife Anne, dau. of Charles Campbell (0339).
MARRIED: [9 Dec. 1734] Anne, dau. of Rt Hon. Brabazon Ponsonby, 1st Earl of Bessborough (1696).
CHILDREN: Benjamin (0294); William Henry (0304); Campbell (d. yg); Sarah, m. John Hyde (1064); Anne; Ponsonby (d. yg).
EDUCATION: School: Eton 1725–8; entered TCD 11 Mar. 1729, aged 16 years.
CAREER/OCCUPATION: Revenue Commissioner 7 Nov. 1755 – 20 Nov. 1767 (patent 7 Nov. 1755, 21 Apr. 1761); Deputy Governor of Co. Carlow 1733; High Sheriff of Co. Carlow 1736; *Governor of Co. Carlow 1746–d.; Free Burgess of Newtownards Oct. 1745; *Trustee of the Linen Board for Ulster 1744–d.; *Commissioner of the Tillage Act for Leinster 1749–d.; Freedom of Fethard (Tipperary) 1754, of Cork 21 Nov. 1759.

POLITICAL ACTIVITY: He was part of Archbishop Stone's alliance with the Ponsonbys against the Boyles. Benjamin Burton was the son-in law of Brabazon Ponsonby, 1st Earl of Bessborough (1696), and on 10 February 1753 Stone wrote to the Chief Secretary, Lord George Sackville (1835) about the ever-increasing merits of Ben Burton – 'every day some fresh merit'. This was part of his vendetta against Nathaniel Clements (0414), who was allied to Anthony Malone (1336) and the Speaker's (0210) party. On 21 January 1755 Stone wrote to Sackville: 'I shall next offer my notions about succession, in case the removal [of Clements] takes place.' He then reviewed the various possibilities: Richard Dawson (0592), John Bourke (0192), William Richardson (1786), Benjamin Burton (this MP, married to a sister of John Ponsonby – which Stone realised was an obstacle). 'I am more and more convinced of the expediency ... of putting that business into the hands of more than one person ... Several manifest conveniences I think appear. And particularly one. The whole stock of the nation (as it may be called) is now in the hands of one person: and where or how vested is known to him only. The sudden death of that person would at any time occasion great confusion: and an uninformed executor might never be able to unravel the intricacies of such accounts. Whereas a surviving partner in office, of equal trust and equally answerable, obviates this inconvenience ... The Chancellor of the Exchequer [Hill, **1015**] in the last conversation I had with him himself started and insisted much upon this point' – for this plan, Stone would recommend Richardson and Burton. 'If circumstances, unknown and unapprehended by me, should make the execution of this or any other clear measure at this time inconvenient or inadvisable, the necessity must be submitted to. But even in that case I do not suppose that his Majesty's faithful servants, and the friends of his government will be left utterly defenceless: to which condition they are inevitably reduced, if Mr Clements keeps the possession he now enjoys. Upon the supposition, therefore, that what is advised in the preceding parts of this letter is not thought proper to be executed, I shall ... propose the last expedient, and mark out the smallest portion of ground on which we can possibly subsist: which is, the adding of Mr Burton as a colleague to Mr Clements. This would certainly be attended by some good effects. It would in the first place abate the triumph on the one side, and relieve the disappointment on the other.' Clements, however, was a friend of the king's mistress, the Countess of Yarmouth, and Stone's schemes were frustrated.

However, on 16 March 1755 Stone and Bessborough wrote to Newcastle that 'We find ourselves under an absolute necessity of renewing and enforcing our application to your grace concerning a proper settlement of the treasury ... all that we can say will be rejected, unless the alteration now to be made in the government is marked with a measure the meaning of which cannot be misunderstood, not rendered equivocal by any possible construction, nor the force of it anyway eluded. There is no way of effecting this but by weakening at least the influence of Mr Clements: his entire removal would without all doubt be the soundest and best means of procuring full security to the future administration here: for we must insist upon it from repeated experience, that while any share of the power of this country remains in that person's hands, so far as that goes our system will be rotten; and no assurance of his can in any degree alter this opinion. Nevertheless, if there lies any strong objection against dismissing him from

the post in which he has almost openly distressed instead of serving the government we think it will be practicable to carry on his majesty's service with sufficient security if a colleague be given him ... The person whom we recommend is Mr Richardson ... We must also entreat your grace to take Mr Burton's services and merits into your consideration. It is absolutely necessary upon many counts that he should *now* be distinguished by some considerable mark of favour; and we desire with repeated earnestness that the plan already proposed of promoting him to a seat at the board of commissioners of the revenue may by your Grace's favour be carried into execution. And we humbly apprehend that if the present vacancy cannot be so disposed, Mr Trevor (**1015**) might receive an equivalent upon the establishment here, without any dissatisfaction to him, or inconvenience to the public. These two points would effectually put a stop to the triumphs which must be expected among the followers of those who are, or pretend to be, elated with having obliged the government of England to remove a lord lieutenant' (Dorset).

Stone and Bessborough say that among the tricks of the opposition was that of implying that they were quarrelling, but they take this opportunity to assure Newcastle jointly that this calumny is baseless. 'We are, in all events, determined reciprocally to protect and support each other: and are not in the least apprehensive that it is possible anything can arise which should shake, much less destroy, this mutual confidence, which is cemented by the most important motives of public consideration, and at the same time fortified by the strongest ties of private friendship.' In effect Stone and Bessborough sought to manipulate each other for their mutual advantage.

On 29 January 1755 Stone told Sackville that since he last wrote he had spoken to Bessborough, who said that Stone's plan 'met with his full approbation. He said he concluded Mr Clements would be removed, but that it would be done in a manner very distressing to us; that we should be charged with the odium, and envy, as well as the consequences of the measure; which consideration would tend to the disappointing of the good effects that were hoped for and almost depended upon, had it been executed with more appearance of resolution. He seemed more than commonly affected with the apprehension that he should be considered as having insisted upon this sacrifice, in order to make way for one of his own relations ... and added with great emotion that he would rather lose Mr Burton's friendship than live under the load of so much public clamour, and possibly of cooler and more deliberate censure, that he was likely to be exposed to. In the course of our conversation it occurred to me that a seat at the board of commissioners of the revenue was still vacant ... that the person for whom it was intended might be better pleased and more conveniently provided for by such a pension as should be judged equivalent, upon this establishment: and that if his majesty should condescend to that proposal the revenue here could well afford it: and in that case Mr Burton to be appointed commissioner, and Mr Richardson joined with Mr Clements in the treasury. Lord Bessborough was exceedingly delighted with this disposition [Chancellor also in agreement] ... I think this would do the business, and that if Mr Clements has any influence you would by these means secure it, without losing any of your present strength ... If it [this scheme] is rejected we must take down our standard, and everything must take a new turn. If it is received (which I believe will be the case) you will find us all less reserved, and less diffident than we have been. The whole now turns on this single point, and I am happy that it is at last brought to a crisis. And Clements by this will be little hurt; all the apprehension of shaking public credit vanish ...'

As Teller of the Exchequer Clements was the government cashier, and, as was the custom in the eighteenth century, he had large balances on hand of which he could make use before he was required to disburse them. Clements used these to make loans and thereby cement his influence. What ultimately happened was that in 1755, Luke Gardiner (**0841**), the Deputy Vice-Treasurer died and Clements succeeded him, thereby gathering together a considerable fortune. The incompetent Sir Henry Cavendish (**0380**) succeeded him as Teller and Benjamin Burton became a Commissioner of the Revenue; the Revenue Board was

presided over by Speaker Ponsonby (**1702**), his brother-in-law. In politics Burton followed the government line and was a useful man about the House: he was nominated for 102 committees in 1741–60.

DIVISION LISTS:
> 1749 (1) voted against the election of James Digges La Touche (♦♦♦♦).
> 1753 (2) voted against the expulsion of Arthur Jones-Nevill (**1125**) – son-in-law to Lord Bessborough.
> 1753 (2) voted for the Money Bill.

ADDITIONAL INFORMATION: A member of the Royal Dublin Society from 1764.

ESTATES/RESIDENCE: Burton Hall, Co. Carlow. Benjamin Burton was granted fairs at Bunnanadden in 32 Geo. II (1759), and in 1761 a fair at Palatine-town. On 3 March 1756 Benjamin Burton Esq. borrowed a mortgage of £10,000 from the government through Sir Henry Cavendish. He was the residuary heir of his grandfather, Charles Campbell (**0339**).

SOURCES: PRONI D/302; BL Add. MSS 19997, Newtownards Borough Book, 1741–75; PRONI T/3019/6547/464 Wilmot Papers; J. Walton, 'The King's Business': Letters on the Administration of Ireland, 1741–61 (NY, 1996) nos 267, 324; PRONI T/3411 Blenheim Papers; RCBL P80/1/1, Parish Registers of St Thomas, Dublin; McCracken thesis; Burke LGI (1904) p. 77; Hughes, Pat. Officers, Cork Corporation Book, p. 727; R. A. Austen-Leigh (ed.), The Eton College Register, 1698–1752, 3 vols (Eton, 1927); HMC Sackville I p. 192; EHR (Oct. 1905) pp. 755–62, C. L. Falkiner, 'Correspondence of Archbishop Stone and the Duke of Newcastle'; Ir. Gen. vol. 4 no 4 (1971) p. 317, W. G. Skehan, 'Extracts from the Minutes of the Corporation of Fethard, Co. Tipperary'; JRSAI vol. 21 (1892) p. 299, P. D. Vigors, 'Alphabetical List of Free Burgesses of New Ross, 1658–1839' [says a Benjamin Burton was a Free Burgess of New Ross, Co. Wexford 12 Aug. 1738]; Almanacks; Pue's Occurrences 1 May 1733, 11 Jan. 1735 [says married 10 Jan. 1734/5].

0294 BURTON, Benjamin

MP for Co. Sligo 1757–60; Boyle 1761–3

b. 12 Mar. 1736; d. (31 May – 4 June) 1763 at Bristol
FAMILY/BACKGROUND: Eldest son of Rt Hon.

Benjamin Burton (**0293**) and Anne, dau. of Rt Hon. Brabazon Ponsonby, 1st Earl of Bessborough (**1696**).
MARRIED: Unmarried.
EDUCATION: School: Kilkenny College 17 Oct. 1746, aged 9 years; entered TCD 18 Feb. 1755.
CAREER/OCCUPATION: High Sheriff of Co. Carlow 1760, Co. Sligo 1761.

POLITICAL ACTIVITY: Apart from the fact that he belonged to the Burton family and was a nephew of John Ponsonby (**1702**), little is known of this MP. He sat in parliament for about five years, broken by the death of George II. He was nominated for eight committees 1757–60.

ADDITIONAL INFORMATION: A subscriber to the Marine Society, March 1759.

ESTATES/RESIDENCE: Burton Hall, Co. Carlow.

SOURCES: PRONI D/302; PRONI D/3000/27/1 Falkiner Genealogical notes; PRONI T/1584 Pinkerton transcripts, p. 70, 7 June 1763; McCracken thesis; NLI vol. 43 (7 May 1854); *JRSAI* vol. 54 (1924) pp. 55–67, T. U. Sadleir, 'The Register of Kilkenny School (1685–1800)'; *BNL* 30 Mar. 1759.

0295 BURTON, Sir Charles

MP for Dublin city 1749–60

b. 1702; d. 6 June 1775
HONOURS: Knighted 9 Jan. 1750; cr. Bt 2 Oct. 1758.
FAMILY/BACKGROUND: Son of Benjamin Burton (**0292**) and Grace, dau. of Robert Stratford (**2027**).
MARRIED: [lic. 9 Sept. 1731] Margaret (b. 1699; d. Jan 1788), eldest dau. of (Sir) Richard Meredyth, of Shrowland, Co. Kildare (**1401**).
CHILDREN: Sir Charles, 2nd Bt, m. [11 Aug. 1778] Catherine, dau. and co-h. of John Cuffe, 2nd Baron Desart; Catherine, m. John Bowes-Benson; Grace, m. Sir Edward Newenham (**1535**); Jane, m. [Mar. 1781] Robert Hutchinson of Grange, Co. Louth.
EDUCATION: School: Kilkenny College 16 Aug. 1710, aged 8 years.
CAREER/OCCUPATION: (First) President of Court of Conscience, Dublin, on its establishment 29 Sept. 1760; Sheriff of Dublin 1733–4; *Governor of the Blue-Coat Hospital 1740–d.; Alderman 3

Nov. 1748, of Dublin 1741–75; served as Lord Mayor 1752, 1764–9, 1773; *Sheriffs Peer 1744–5; Mayor 1751–2; *Governor of the Workhouse 1750–68, Foundling Hospital and Workhouse 1769–5; *Governor of Erasmus Smith's Schools and other Charities 1753–75; Rep. of Trinity Guild Dublin Corporation 1732; *Justice of the Peace 1764–75; elected to the Court of Assistants June 1765–70. He was voted a Freeman of the Guild of Merchant Tailors. Under 3 Geo. III c.16 he was appointed, along with James Dunn (**0671**), a receiver of the rates of £1,500 for the lighting of Dublin (for which he was entitled to 6d per £1 collected).

POLITICAL ACTIVITY: He came in on the bitterly contested Dublin by-election of 1749, when he successfully challenged the return of James Digges La Touche (◆◆◆), in support of the government, and voted for the Money Bill in 1753. He was in receipt of a pension. He was nominated to 57 committees during his 11 years in parliament. On 27 February 1760 he presented heads of a bill to regulate and reform Dublin Corporation; it received the royal assent on 17 May.

He stood for re-election in 1761. After 13 days' polling, James Grattan (**0896**), the Recorder (and father of Henry Grattan (**0895**)), and Charles Lucas (**1276**) were returned for Dublin city. On the final day of polling Grattan had received 1,569 votes, Lucas 1,302, Sir Charles Burton 1,210, Alderman P. Hunt 673, and James Digges La Touche 77. James Dunn (**0671**) dropped out of the poll on the tenth day, having polled *c.* 990 votes. The successful candidates were chaired through the streets to Parliament House at the end of the election.

DIVISION LISTS:
1753 (2) voted for the Money Bill – a pensioner.

ADDITIONAL INFORMATION: Subscriber to the Marine Society, March 1759. When he died in 1775 he was the senior alderman and 'Father of the City'.

ESTATES/RESIDENCE: Dublin.

SOURCES: PRONI D/3000/27/1 Falkiner Genealogical notes; McCracken thesis; GEC *B*; *Index to Hibernian Chronicle, 1769–1775* (Society of Genealogists, 1936) vol. 2 p. 75 [says he died 2 June 1775]; *Dublin Hist.*

Record 38 no 1, Dec. 1984, Sean Murphy, 'The Corporation of Dublin 1660–1760'; R. E. Burns, *Irish Parliamentary Politics in the Eighteenth Century*, 2 vols (Washington, 1989), vol. 2 p. 110; *JRSAI* vol. 48 (1918) p. 57, H. F. Berry, 'The Merchant Tailors' Gild – That of St John the Baptist, Dublin, 1418–1841'; *JRSAI* vol. 55 (1924) pp. 55–67, T. U. Sadleir, 'The Register of Kilkenny School (1685–1800)'; *Almanacks*; *BNL* 16 Jan. 1750, 30 Mar. 1759; *DJ* 28 Apr. – 2 May, 2–5 May, 5–9 May 1761, 13–15 Aug. 1778, 29–31 Mar. 1781.

0296 BURTON, Francis

MP for Ennis 1692–3, 1695–9, 1703–13–14

b. 1659; d. 1 July 1714
FAMILY/BACKGROUND: Eldest son of Samuel Burton and Margery Harris; brother of **0292**.
MARRIED: Alice, dau. of Thomas Tilson, Clerk of the House of Commons.
CHILDREN: Rt Hon. Francis (**0297**); Elizabeth, m. Theophilus Clements (**0419**).
EDUCATION: School: Mr Ryder; entered TCD 22 Aug. 1676, aged 17 years.
CAREER/OCCUPATION: Usher of Chancery 2 Mar. 1690; High Sheriff of Co. Clare 1691–2; Deputy Governor of Co. Clare *c.* 1690.

POLITICAL ACTIVITY: He sat for the parliaments of William and Anne, and was listed for committees in October 1692, August 1697 and September 1698, and possibly for a further 24 in the parliaments of Queen Anne. He supported Lord Chancellor Porter against accusations of favouring Catholics, and signed the Association for the protection of William III in parliament. In February 1701 his name appeared as one of the petitioners to the Lord Lieutenant for securing the remainder of the purchase money for forfeited estates.

In the reign of Queen Anne he appears to have joined the opposition, although he attended Ormonde's birthday celebrations in 1706, and by 1713 he was listed as a Whig. It was incorrectly thought that he would be replaced for the borough of Ennis by Henry O'Brien in the 1713 election.

ESTATES/RESIDENCE: Buncraggy, Co. Clare. He purchased the fee of Buncraggy and other lands in Counties Clare and Limerick from the 8th Earl of Thomond, and he purchased 30,180 acres in Co. Clare from the Commissioners for Sale of Forfeited Estates in 1702–3. In 1702 the lands of Molougha, barony of Moyarta, were sold by the Forfeiture Trustees to Francis Burton, Nicholas Westby and James McDonnell.

His estimated income in 1713 was £2,500.

SOURCES: PRONI D/302; NLI LC 2283; Simms, *Williamite Confiscation*, pp. 155, 183; PRONI T/3411 Blenheim Papers; Burke *LGI* (1904) p. 77, *PB* (1903) p. 354 (1906) p. 382, *IFR* (1976) p. 187; *Alum. Dub.*; Simms' cards; Hughes, *Pat. Officers*; J. Frost, *The History and Topography of the County of Clare, from the Earliest Times to the Beginning of the 18th Century, With Map and Illustrations*, pp. 624–7; S. W. Singer (ed.), *Clarendon Corr.*, vol. 2 (London, 1828) pp. 348–9; *N. Munster Antiq. Jn.* vol. 23 (1981) pp. 25–65, Leo F. McNamara, 'The Diary of an Eighteenth Century Clare Gentleman'; *JRSAI* vol. 21 (1892) p. 77, P. D. Vigors, 'Alphabetical List of Free Burgesses of New Ross, 1659–1839' [says born 1669 and his wife was called Anne], *JRSAI* vol. 55 (1925) pp. 37, 44, H. A. S. Upton, 'A List of Governors and Deputy Governors of Counties in Ireland in 1699'; Parliamentary Lists, 1695 (1), 1696 (1), 1706 (1), (2), 1711 (3), 1713 (1), (2).

0297 BURTON, Rt Hon. Francis

MP for Coleraine 1721–7; Co. Clare 1727–44

b. 1 Dec. 1696; d. 20 Mar. 1744
HONOURS: PC, sworn 20 Nov. 1733–d.
FAMILY/BACKGROUND: Eldest surviving son of Francis Burton (**0296**) and Alice, dau. of Thomas Tilson.
MARRIED: [1720] Mary, dau. of Henry Conyngham (**0463**).
CHILDREN: Francis Pierpoint (Conyngham), 2nd Baron Conyngham (**0299**); Rt Hon. William (Conyngham) (**0303**); Mary; Alice, m. [22 Sept. 1743] Sir George Gore, 5th Bt.
CAREER/OCCUPATION: *Trustee of the Linen Board for Leinster 1732; *Commissioner of the Tillage Act for Connaught 1735.

POLITICAL ACTIVITY: In 1724 he was one of the Memorialists seeking to revive attempts to explain or revoke the clause in the act of Queen Anne's reign for naturalising foreign Protestants in which favour was given to the children of natural-born subjects. It was felt that this could undermine Protestant interests in Ireland by allowing the return of the children of Jacobites who had served James in Ireland before fleeing to Europe. He was nominated for 29 committees between 1727 and 1744.

ADDITIONAL INFORMATION: On his marriage, his wife's uncle William Conolly (0460) settled £5,000 on the couple and they received further sums from his will, 18 October 1729.

A foundation member of the Dublin Society, 1731.

ESTATES/RESIDENCE: Buncraggy, Co. Clare; Harcourt Place, Dublin. His income was estimated to be c. £1,000 p.a.

SOURCES: PRONI T/580 pp. 176g, 176h, TSPI 1723–4; PRONI T/2825 Conolly/Castletown Papers, p. 14; McCracken thesis; *Index to Irish Privy Counsellors, 1711–1910*; Berry RDS pp. 24–7; *Almanacks*; *GM* Mar. 1744.

0298 BURTON, Hon. Sir Francis Nathaniel

MP for Co. Clare 1790–7–1800 [r. Killybegs 1790, 1797]; [UK] Co. Clare 1801–4 July 1808

> b. 26 Dec. 1766; d. 27 Jan. 1832
> HONOURS: KCB 1822, GCB 1824.
> FAMILY/BACKGROUND: Son of Francis Pierpoint Burton (Conyngham), 2nd Baron Conyngham (0299), and Elizabeth (d. 1814), dau. of Rt Hon. Nathaniel Clements (0414); he was the twin of 1st Marquess Conyngham.
> MARRIED: [1801] Valentina Letitia (d. 1844), dau. of Nicholas Lawless, 1st Baron Cloncurry (1209).
> CHILDREN: Henry Stuart Burton, m. [1836] Alicia Mary, o. dau. of Rev. Viscount Simpson; William Conyngham.
> CAREER/OCCUPATION: Foreman of the Clare Grand Jury 1792; Governor of Co. Clare 1805; Lieutenant Governor of Lower Canada 29 Nov. 1808–32.
> MILITARY: Colonel of the Clare Militia, 1797–d.

POLITICAL ACTIVITY: A nephew of Colonel Burton-Conyngham (0303), he sat for Co. Clare for the decade before the Union and thereafter in the parliament of the United Kingdom. He was a soldier and wanted office, so he was in support. He voted for Foster (0805) in the 1790 election for Speaker. By 1800 he was a colonel. In March 1800 he signed a Co. Meath petition in favour of the Union, and he voted for the Union in both 1799 and 1800.

In the United Kingdom parliament he supported government but wanted attention in return. He voted in support of the Catholic claims in May 1805. After failing to obtain a seat at one of the Irish Revenue Boards, in 1808 he was appointed to the lucrative sinecure of Lieutenant-Governor of Lower Canada, which he held until his death in 1832.

DIVISION LISTS:
> 1790 (2) voted for Foster (0805) on the election of a Speaker.
> 1799 (1) voted for the Union – Colonel, Clare Regiment of Militia.

ADDITIONAL INFORMATION: *A member of the Royal Irish Academy, 1798–1800(f.).

ESTATES/RESIDENCE: Buncraggy, Co. Clare.

SOURCES: O'Neill thesis; Jupp thesis; PRONI T/3166/1A Hartnell notes; *HP 1790–1820*; *FJ* 22–5 Sept. 1792; *The Drogheda News-Letter or Ulster Journal* 8–10 Mar. 1800; Parliamentary Lists, 1791 (1), 1793 (1), 1799 (3), 1800 (3).

0299 BURTON (CONYNGHAM), Francis Pierpoint

MP for Killybegs 1753–60; Co. Clare 1761–8–76

> b. c. 1721–9; d. 22 May 1787 'of a burst blood vessel' 'at the Hot Wells, Bristol'
> PEERAGE: Suc. his uncle as 2nd Baron Conyngham 4 Apr. 1781.
> FAMILY/BACKGROUND: Eldest son of Rt Hon. Francis Burton (0297) and Mary, dau. of Henry Conyngham (0463). Assumed name of Conyngham in lieu of Burton 3 May 1781.
> MARRIED: [19 Mar. 1750] Elizabeth, e. dau. of Rt Hon. Nathaniel Clements (0414).
> CHILDREN: Henry, 1st Marquess Conyngham, m. [5 July 1794] Elizabeth, dau. of Joseph Denison; Francis Nathaniel (0298); Catherine, m. [1785] Rev. J. S. Fermor; Helen, m. Stewart Weldon (2200); Henrietta.
> CAREER/OCCUPATION: Freedom of Ennis 1751; Freeman and Burgess of Limavady 22 Apr. 1757; Provost of Ennis 13 Dec. 1760; Freeman of Galway Corporation Sept. 1761; *Commissioner of the Tillage Act for Munster 1763.

POLITICAL ACTIVITY: On 21 January 1755 Primate Stone wrote to Lord George Sackville (**1835**), still carrying on his vendetta against Nathaniel Clements (**0414**), whom he accused of being in office but not supporting government (actually Clements gave just enough support to refute this allegation), that 'We are to see next what Mr Clements offers in contre-ballance. Macarrell (**1298**), Mitchell (**1414**), and his son-in-law Mr Burton. Macarrell, as Mr Gardiner (**0841**) tells me, will do right; but he is not to be put to Mr Clements' account. Mitchell will go with his hundred and twenty thousand pounds, the sum now deposited, and with the remitance to the regiments in foreign service. The return of son-in-law from France is uncertain: his health is bad and his fortune in disorder.'

By 1769, although he attended that session, he 'usually resides in England'. He was acknowledged to have the principal interest in Co. Clare: 'where he is very well liked and very deservedly'. He was totally independent, although it was thought that Nathaniel Clements might have some influence over him. Lord Townshend obtained for his wife a pension of £600 p.a. and for his friend Mr Finucane a quartermaster's commission. Lord Harcourt allowed him to nominate a coast officer. Despite these favours he was considered independent.

Lord Lieutenant Buckinghamshire secured a special remainder for him under which, in April 1781, he inherited his childless uncle's peerage. His brother, Colonel Burton-Conyngham (**0303**), was Teller of the Exchequer, £2,500 p.a., and responsible for the most ambitious fisheries programme in Co. Donegal. Lord Conyngham's party in the House of Commons included his brother, Mr Colvill (**0454**), Agent to the Widows of Officers, £150 p.a., and Mr Weldon (**2202**). They all supported government.

DIVISION LISTS:
    1757 (1) voted against the resolutions on pensions.
    1768 (1) voted for army augmentation.
    1773 (2) voted against an untaxed press.

ADDITIONAL INFORMATION: Elizabeth Clements' dowry was £5,000 and a further £2,000 from Mrs Conolly, £7,000 in all. His marriage settlement (1750) provided for a jointure of £600 p.a. for his wife and £7,000 for two or £10,000 for three or more younger children (his daughter, Helen Weldon's, dowry was £3,000); the remaining £7,000 was divided between the other three children – the sum set aside for the younger children did not have to be divided evenly among them.

A private member's bill vesting in trustees the settled estate in Co. Limerick of his son and heir, Henry, was passed to ensure the MP's wife's jointure of £600 and £10,000 for portions for his younger children in accordance with his (1750) marriage settlement. For this purpose these estates were to be sold or mortgaged to raise £12,000 sterling and 'a competent part' of the unsettled part of his estate in Co. Clare to be settled on his son Henry (later 1st Marquess Conyngham) in lieu of these. Later a further act was passed to tidy up these provisions and switch the security for them to the unsettled part of the Co. Clare estates, as his heir wished to use the proceeds (sale or mortgage) of the Co. Limerick estates for other purposes.

A subscriber to the Marine Society, March 1759.

ESTATES/RESIDENCE: Buncraggy, Co. Clare; Shanagolden, Co. Limerick; Dublin. Several of the purchasers of forfeited lands were members of families prominent in the Irish life of the eighteenth century. Major General Henry Conyngham (**0463**), who bought Slane Castle, was the father of the first Lord Conyngham. The title then passed to Francis Pierpoint Burton, Henry Conyngham's grandson, who was also grandson of Francis Burton (**0296**), who had bought a large part of Lord Clare's estate. The Conyngham family was thus doubly endowed with Williamite forfeitures.

SOURCES: McCracken thesis; GEC *P*; Burke *PB* (1903) p. 354; *HMC Charlemont I* p. 183 (dowry); J. Frost, *The History and Topography of the County of Clare, from the Earliest Times to the Beginning of the 18th Century, With Map and Illustrations*, pp. 606–7; *JRSAI* vol. 41 (1911) pp. 86–8, 168, E. M. F.-G. Boyle, 'Records of the Town of Limavady, 1609–1804'; *Almanacks*; *EHR* (Oct. 1905) p. 755, C. L. Falkiner, 'Correspondence of Archbishop Stone and the Duke of Newcastle'; *BNL* 30 Mar. 1759; *DJ* 20–23 Dec. 1760, 6–10 Oct. 1761, 11–15 May 1762; *GM* 1787; TCD Library 186.s.38, 186.s.40 (Private Member's Acts); Parliamentary Lists, 1769 (1), 1772 (2), 1773 (1), 1774 (1), 1775 (1), 1782 (1), 1784 (1), 1785 (2), (4), 1787 (1).

0300 BURTON, Robert

MP for Co. Carlow 1727–60; Carlow B. 1761–5

b. 1695; d. Jan. 1765
FAMILY/BACKGROUND: Son of Benjamin Burton
(**0292**) and Grace, dau. of Robert Stratford
(**2027**).
MARRIED: Catherine, dau. of Thomas Byres of
Rathsallagh, Co. Wicklow.
CHILDREN: *d.s.p.*
EDUCATION: School: Kilkenny College 11 June
1705, aged 10 years.
CAREER/OCCUPATION: High Sheriff of Co. Carlow
1730; *Governor of the Royal Hospital,
Kilmainham 1736–64.
MILITARY: Captain 4th Dragoon Guards 17 May
1717; Captain of the Battle-Axe Guards 1 Dec.
1725, Sept. 1727 (with rank of Colonel of Foot),
on 9 Jan. 1731 Colonel Burton was granted £740
by King's Letter for reclothing the Battle-Axe
Guards; *Captain of the Yeoman of the Guard
1737, 1741–8, 1750–62; Colonel 1763–4;
*Colonel of a Company of Battle-Axe Guards
1734–54; *Captain as Colonel 1755–8; *Colonel
as Captain 1759–60.

POLITICAL ACTIVITY: A professional soldier and a
placeman, he supported the government. Burton
sat for the entire parliament of George II and was
nominated for 25 committees between 1727 and
1757. He voted against the election of James
Digges La Touche (♦♦♦), against the expulsion
of Arthur Jones-Nevill (**1125**) and for the Money
Bill.

DIVISION LISTS:
    1749 (1) voted against the election of James
    Digges La Touche (♦♦♦).
    1753 (1) voted against the expulsion of
    Arthur Jones-Nevill (**1125**) – Colonel of the
    Battle-Axe Guards.
    1753 (2) voted for the Money Bill.
    1753 (3) a placeman [1753 (2)].

ESTATES/RESIDENCE: Harristown, Co. Kildare;
Hacketstown, Co. Carlow.

SOURCES: PRONI D/302; *CJ Ire.* (Bradley ed.) vol. 6 p.
227; PRONI T/559 vol. 13 p. 198, Burke, extract pedigrees; McCracken thesis; Burke *IFR* (1976) p. 187; C.
Dalton, *George the First's Army, 1714–27*; *JRSAI* vol.
54 (1924) pp. 55–67, T. U. Sadleir, 'The Register of
Kilkenny School (1685–1800)'; *Ir. Gen.* vol. 4 no 4
(1971) p. 320, W. G. Skehan, 'Extracts from the Minutes of the Corporation of Fethard, Co. Tipperary' [says
he died 1763]; *Almanacks*; *FJ* 5–8 Jan. 1765.

0301 BURTON, Samuel

MP for Sligo B. 1713–14, 1715–27; Dublin B.
1727–33

b. 1687; d. 8 July 1733
FAMILY/BACKGROUND: Eldest son of Benjamin
Burton (**0292**) and Grace, dau. of Robert
Stratford (**2027**).
MARRIED: (1) [17 June 1708] Anne (d. 1714), o.
ch. of Charles Campbell (**0339**); (2) Mary
Hindle.
CHILDREN: (1) Rt Hon. Benjamin (**0293**);
Hughes; Samuel; Catherine, m. [28 Feb. 1732]
Nicholas Netterville, 5th Viscount Netterville
(dowry £9,000).
(2) Mary.
EDUCATION: School: Eton 1706–7; Middle
Temple 10 June 1706.
CAREER/OCCUPATION: A banker; High Sheriff of
Co. Carlow 1724; Alderman of Dublin 18 June
1728–32; *Commissioner of Oyer and Terminer
1732.

POLITICAL ACTIVITY: He came into parliament in
1713; he was, like his father (**0292**), a Whig, and
like him he voted against the formation of a national bank in 1721. It appears probable that both
were concerned about how this might affect their
banking business. He was nominated to six committees in 1713, 19 between 1715 and 1723, and
24 between 1727 and 1731. In 1727 he introduced 1 Geo. II, c. 16, 'an Act for regulating the
Price and Asize of Bread and the Markets'. This
act regulated the Dublin market and included a
schedule for the assize of bread in the city.
    His father, Benjamin Burton, founded Burton
and Harrison's bank along with Francis Harrison
(**0973**) *c.* 1700. Samuel Burton became a partner
after Harrison's death in June 1725. At the time
the bank's liabilities outstretched reserves by some
£65,173. On 17 November 1725 Daniel Falkiner
(**0717**) joined the partnership, on the condition
that both Samuel and his father separately signed
a bond for £100,000 and promised to pay the
£65,000 sum back to the bank within six months.
No part of it was ever paid, and when his father

died in May 1728 the bank became Samuel Burton and Daniel Falkiner's. From 14 December 1730 to 18 January 1731 he shared with Hugh Henry (**1005**) £9,513 – the exchange and fees on £77,220 sterling. With the failure of the bank, the contents of Burton Hall and all other goods and chattels owned by the Burtons were put up for public auction in September 1733. The family was probably saved by his father-in-law, Charles Campbell (**0339**).

DIVISION LISTS:
> 1721 (1) voted against a national bank.
> 1721 (2) voted against a national bank.

ADDITIONAL INFORMATION: His wife, Anne Campbell, was the only child of Charles Campbell who left his grand-daughter, Catherine, £6,000 (in addition to the provision made in her mother's marriage settlement) should she marry with her father's consent. If Catherine married without consent, the £6,000 was to be divided among Campbell's nephews and nieces. Catherine married Nicholas, 5th Viscount Netterville, but the £6,000 was not forthcoming. The case brought before the Lords in 1737 concerned the question of Burton's consent and how far it had been affected by his inability to meet the terms of Campbell's will because of his impending bankruptcy. The rest of Campbell's property went to his grandson Benjamin (**0293**). Lord Netterville was represented as having an estate of more than £2,000 a year, clear of encumbrances. On 11 March 1732 Mrs Pendavers (Delany) wrote to her sister Ann Granville: 'Miss Burton … is since married to Lord Netterville – a fop and a fool but a lord with a tolerable estate, who always wears fine clothes; she has £9,000 for her portion, with a pretty person much in vogue.'

ESTATES/RESIDENCE: Burton Hall, Co. Carlow (and his son resided there in 1757); Capel Street, Dublin. Anne (Campbell) Burton's marriage settlement of 11 June 1708 settled on her a cash dowry of £3,500 and a large portion of land in Counties Meath, Cavan and Louth, see 31 Geo. II, c. 12 (1758). In addition, Burton's land was subject to an IOU to Campbell for £1,232 10s 8d.

SOURCES: PRONI D/302; *CJ Ire.* (Bradley ed.) vol. 4 p. 257; 31 Geo. II c. 12 [says d. on or about 8 July 1733]; PRONI D/3000/27/2 Falkiner Genealogical notes [says

he died the night of Sunday 8 July 1733 and that his second wife was called Mary Hinde]; McCracken thesis; Burke *LGI* (1904) p. 77; TCD House of Lords Appeals: Printed Case Papers, 1711-39, 202r. pp. 135, 142–3; R.A. Austen-Leigh (ed.), *The Eton College Register, 1698–1752*, 3 vols (Eton, 1927); *Middle Temple Admissions* vol. I p. 259; *JRSAI* vol. 48 (1918) p. 57, H. F. Berry, 'The Merchant Tailors' Gild – That of St John the Baptist, Dublin, 1418–1841'; Llandover, *Delany Corr.*, vol. I p. 341; *Almanacks*; *The Dublin Weekly Journal* 22 June 1728; Parliamentary Lists, 1713 (2).

0302 BURTON, Thomas

MP for Ennis 1761–8

> b. 1706; d. (*ante* 6) May 1773, probably in a carriage accident
> FAMILY/BACKGROUND: Son of [ ] Burton.
> MARRIED: [ ].
> CHILDREN: Alice, m. Crofton Vandeleur (**2135**); Anne Catherine, m. [Sept. 1778] Edward FitzGerald (**0729**).
> EDUCATION: School: Kilkenny College 26 Jan. 1715, aged 9 years.
> CAREER/OCCUPATION: High Sheriff of Co. Clare 1756; Provost of Ennis 1 Sept. 1760, resigned 13 Dec. 1760.
> MILITARY: *Major of a Regiment of Dragoons 1750, 1752.

POLITICAL ACTIVITY: He was unanimously returned on the family interest for Ennis in 1761. He was a professional soldier and appears to have been abroad for some if not all of this parliamentary session. He was not returned in 1768.

ADDITIONAL INFORMATION: *Dublin Journal*, 4–6 May 1773 reported that 'It was Col. [*sic*] Thomas Burton, NOT Col. Wm Burton, that met with the melancholy accident of being overturned in his chaise, by which he was killed on the spot, in his return home, in company with a gentleman who was to have been married to his daughter the following day.' When his daughter Anne Catherine was married in early September 1778 she was described as 'daughter of the late Major Burton'.

DIVISION LISTS:
> 1768 (1) absent, abroad.

ESTATES/RESIDENCE: Carrigaholt, Co. Clare.

SOURCES: Burke, *PB* (1903) p. 596; *Index to Hibernian Chronicle, 1769–75* (Society of Genealogists, 1936) vol. 2 p. 5 [says Major Thomas Burton killed in a carriage accident May 1773]; J. Frost, *The History and Topography of the County of Clare, from the Earliest Times to the Beginning of the 18th Century, With Map and Illustrations*, pp. 624–7; *JRSAI* vol. 21 (1892) p. 79, P. D. Vigors, 'Alphabetical List of Free Burgesses of New Ross, 1658–1839'; *JRSAI* vol. 54 (1924) pp. 55–67, T. U. Sadleir, 'The Register of Kilkenny School (1685–1800)'; *Almanacks*; *DJ* 2–6 Sept. 1760, 28 Apr. – 2 May 1761, 4–6 May 1773; 8–10 Sept. 1778; *FJ* 2–6 Apr. 1765.

0303 BURTON (CONYNGHAM), Rt Hon. William

MP for Newtown Limavady 1761–8–76; Ennis 1776–83, 1790–6; Killybegs 1783–90 [r. Killybegs and Newtown Limavady 1776]

b. 1733; d. 31 May 1796 at his house in Harcourt Street after a few days' illness
HONOURS: PC, sworn 4 June 1777.
FAMILY/BACKGROUND: Second son of Rt Hon. Francis Burton (0297) and Mary, e. dau. of Henry Conyngham (0463).
MARRIED: Unmarried. Assumed the name and arms of Conyngham in lieu of that of Burton 3 May 1781.
EDUCATION: Entered Cambridge [Queen's College] 4 June 1750; Lincoln's Inn 13 Jan. 1753.
CAREER/OCCUPATION: Teller of the Exchequer 1778–93; Lord Commissioner of the Treasury 25 Dec. 1793, 27 Oct. 1795–6; Trustee of the Linen Board for Leinster 1781–94; Deputy Governor of Co. Londonderry and City and Coleraine 17 May 1765; Freeman of Limavady 29 Sept. 1724, Freeman and Burgess 22 Apr. 1757, 7 Apr. 1764 (resigned 14 Dec. 1781); *Commissioner of the Tillage Act for Munster 1764–84, for Leinster 1769–79; *Governor of the Hibernian Society 1769–d.; *Court of Directors of the Grand Canal Company, Committee of Works 1772–5, Company of Undertakers of the Grand Canal 1783–4; Commissioner of Wide Streets; *Commissioner for Paving the Streets of Dublin 1778–80; *Governor of the Charitable Loan Society 1780–9; *Governor of the Charitable Musical Society 1780; Governor of Foundling Hospital and Dublin Workhouse; Governor of

Co. Donegal 19 Apr. 1781–3, 1785–94, Joint Governor 1785–6; *Vice Admiral of Ulster 1783–6; *Governor of Erasmus Smith's Schools and other Charities 1785–94; Foreman of the Grand Jury of Co. Donegal 1792.
MILITARY: Captain in army 1759; Major in the 16th Regiment of Foot 1762; Lieutenant-Colonel 12th Dragoons 1763; *Major of a Regiment of Foot 1762–3; Lieutenant-Colonel 64th Regiment of Foot 1764; *aide-de-camp to the Lord Lieutenant 1765–74; *Lieutenant-Colonel of 4th Dragoons 1765–70, *of a Regiment of Foot 1765–6; Lieutenant-Colonel 12th Dragoons 1766 (restructured this regiment under royal assent, to be known as the 12th or Prince of Wales Regiment of Light Dragoons, 1767); retired 1774. Barracks Commissioner 1775–7, Supervisor of Barrack Accounts 1775–7; *Agent to Regiments serving abroad 1788. Col. of Donegal Militia.

POLITICAL ACTIVITY: Rt Hon. William Burton Conyngham was one of the most prominent figures in the Irish parliament. He was a professional soldier, with an excellent reputation as an engineer, but later played a leading role in trying to encourage the development of Irish commerce. He was brought into parliament by his uncle, Rt Hon. Henry Conyngham, 1st Earl Conyngham (0464), 'who has this Borough [Newtown Limavady] entirely. It is thought Lord Conyngham will make him his heir', and he inherited on the death, 4 April 1781, of his uncle the family estates in Co. Donegal and Slane, Co. Meath, part of which was the inheritance from Speaker Conolly (0460).

By 1772 he was anxious to sell out and acquire a civil employment. Not being able to do this, in 1773 he was noted as being 'nettled'. However, in 1774 he was 'Aide de camp to the Lord Lieutenant consequently a courtier. Voted for amending the Tontine, and in favour of Popery. For Stamps. A strong advocate for new Bridge and Custom house.' He was also considered 'a sensible man', and at that time practical expertise was often found in the army.

In 1775 his position was summed up as follows: 'Nephew and entirely dependent on Lord Conyngham. Lord Townshend gave his uncle the Linen Board, and a living of £400 to his friend Dr Nesbitt. Mr Burton is very able in Parliament, of strict honour, and never opposed Lord Townshend but when obliged by express directions from his uncle. He has been permitted and supported Lord Harcourt with great zeal and ability. He is Aide-de-camp to his Excellency although of the Army and was lately appointed a Commissioner and Comptroller of the Barrack Board worth £600. His Excellency has given to his recommendation the following employments in the Revenue: 1 Examiner, 2 Tidewaiters, 2 Gaugers, 1 Hearth Money and another Hearth Money Collection and Coxwain of a Barge. Supervisor of Stamps to Mr Fisher £70.'

In 1776 he was Teller of the Exchequer, probably appointed to sort out the debt and confusion left by Sir Henry Cavendish (0380). However, Burton had to give a bond of £40,000. In 1776 he was returned for Ennis by his brother, Pierpoint Burton-Conyngham. On 5 May 1780 he wrote to Lord Lieutenant Buckinghamshire expressing his desire to assist (as did H. T. Clements (0412)), and saying that 'From the time that question of a Mutiny Bill has been agitated I have had but one opinion, that of the necessity of passing it, from this very obvious reason, that the execution of every part of the British Act subjects those concerned to the prosecution and trial by jury.'

Both brothers changed their name to Conyngham following the death of their uncle. A Parliamentary List in 1783 assessed his position as follows: 'He was Teller of the Exchequer, £2,500 p.a., made by Lord Harcourt, to whom he was Aide-de-camp. Lately came to a large fortune and the Killybegs Borough by the death of his uncle, Earl Conyngham. A well-disposed, sensible man, a great promoter of public improvements and much concerned in the north-west fisheries. Has a seat in the Killybegs Borough open' (i.e. available). It was thought that he might stand for the county, where his success was thought virtually certain, but he was defeated by Alexander Montgomery (1437), who stood on the popular interest in that very popular election. Instead Conyngham was returned for his borough of Killybegs.

In 1784 his interest in developing the Co. Donegal fisheries was commented on 'as giving an opening to provide for many friends upon a place

totally independent of Government. Mr Conyngham is a very respectable man much esteemed in Ireland, and may be very useful to Government.' The next year he had a private member's bill passed 'raising the sum of twenty thousand pounds upon the Manor of Port Dungloe in the County of Donegal ... to be expended together with another sum of twenty thousand pounds granted by Parliament, in promoting fisheries on the western coast of the County of Donegal'. The money was for building quays, stores etc. and completing the road from Letterkenny. Conyngham had already spent considerable sums in developing the industry and an estate in which he had only a life interest, and the other interested parties in the entail felt that he should receive some benefit from his developments. The trustees were Rt Hon. Sexton Pery (1671) (Speaker); Rt Hon. John Foster (0805) (Chancellor of the Exchequer); Rt Hon. John Beresford (0115) (Senior Commissioner of HM Revenue), Rt Hon. Thomas Conolly (0459) and Rt Hon. Luke Gardiner (0842) and the survivors or survivor of them.

In the 1780s Burton-Conyngham was behind much of the Irish parliament's interest in the fishing industry. Since 1763 parliament had been anxious to encourage this industry, partly as a policy of import substitution, by a subsidy on small fishing vessels and a small export bounty on Irish fish, but Burton was behind an extensive legislative overhaul in 1781 and 1785. In 1785 he secured £20,000 from parliament towards the development of the Donegal herring fishery 'specifically for the new island fishing town of Rutland on which he expended a further £30,000 and he also persuaded parliament to impose much higher duties on herring imports'. By the late 1780s herring catches were falling, and Rutland was a disaster before 'Sand overwhelmed the town itself.' He was a member of the committee appointed by the Commons to distribute £17,000 for the encouragement of certain manufactures. In 1788 he was noted as a 'respectable gentleman and has a following. For.'

The critical commentator of 1789 was less so than usual, stating that 'To the advantage of a voice good, though not excellent, being clear, distinct, and thoroughly audible, but, with some tendency to a lisp, he adds a pronunciation perfectly accurate and a delivery very well tempered between vehemence and languor, but more inclining to rapidity than slowness. His language has always the merit of precision and unites with much force some elegance, sparing, though not destitute of ornament ... and his manner is warm and spirited, but certainly too strongly marked with the remains of soldierly importance and military insolence ... Being a man of considerable information in all parts of elegant learning and well versed in the principles of trade and policy, though not of profound erudition, the matter of his speeches possesses real merit ... it is obviously the effect of studious care and attentive investigation ... In his political capacity he has ever been a steady supporter of Administration, enforcing its measures and palliating its misconduct and has always deserved the thanks of the minister, although but sometimes those of his country.' In 1790 he sold both seats for Killybegs, perhaps hoping to recoup some of his losses on the fisheries, and was returned for Newtown Limavady, which at that time belonged to Thomas Conolly (0459). When the Irish Revenue was reorganised in 1793 he became a Lord of the Treasury.

Despite his good sense and capabilities, he was very much a man of his age and class. For instance: 'He had great care and elegance united with a sort of personal courage which was apt to boil over. This led him into many quarrels and not a few duels, one of which was fought across a table of no great length from end to end, and not strange to tell of in Ireland several of the party stood near enjoying the sport.'

DIVISION LISTS:
1768 (1) voted for army augmentation – Lieutenant-Colonel 12th Dragoons.
1771 (1) voted for Lord Townshend as Lord Lieutenant.
1771 (1) voted against the amendment to the Revenue Bill.
1771 (2) voted against Sir Lucius O'Brien's (1558) motion for retrenchment – 'Col. in the Army'.
1772 (2) voted against a Short Revenue Bill.
1773 (1) voted for the Absentee Tax.
1774 (2) voted for Catholic relief.

1775 (1) voted for the Pro-American amendment to the Speech from the Throne.
1777 (1) voted against Grattan's (0895) motion for retrenchment.
1778 (2) voted for the Popery Bill.
1779 (2) voted against a six-months Loan Bill.
1780 (1) voted against Grattan's declaration of the Rights of Ireland.
1780 (2) voted against Yelverton's (2268) motion to modify Poynings' Law.
1780 (3) voted for the Tenantry Bill.
1780 (4) voted for a Perpetual Mutiny Bill.
1785 (1) voted for the Commercial Propositions.
1787 (1) absent – had previously voted for a Pension Bill.
1789 (1) voted against the regency.
1790 (1) voted for Grattan's motion for reducing the influence of the Crown.
1790 (2) voted for Foster (0805) on the election of a Speaker.
1791 (3) voted for Grattan's motion to abolish the Dublin police.
1793 (1) a teller against Knox's (1180) motion for Catholic Emancipation.

ADDITIONAL INFORMATION: Fellow of the Royal Society; Fellow of the Society of Antiquities; Vice-President and Treasurer, 1791, of the Royal Irish Academy; *a member of the Royal Dublin Society, 1769; *a subscriber to the Public Assembly Rooms, 1788.

He travelled widely in the Iberian peninsula. He presented to Dublin University the Irish harp that is displayed in the great library.

ESTATES/RESIDENCE: Mount Charles, Co. Donegal; Slane Castle, near Drogheda, Co. Meath; Harcourt Place, Dublin. William Burton-Conyngham (who had no issue) was a tenant for life under the terms of the will of Henry, Earl of Conyngham with remainder to his children and failing them to those of his elder brother Francis Pierpoint, Lord Conyngham (0299) in tail-male etc. On his death in 1796 these estates went to his nephew, Henry, 3rd Baron and (1816) 1st Marquess Conyngham (0464).

SOURCES: G.E.C. P; Burke PB (1906) p. 382; Hughes, Pat. Officers; Index to Irish Privy Counsellors, 1711–1910; Alum. Cantab.; Lincoln's Inn Records vol. 1 p. 441; C. E.

F. Trench, 'William Burton Conyngham 1733–96' [un-published paper presented to the Meath Arch. Hist. Soc. in Slane Castle, 13 Mar. 1985, later published in *JRSAI* vol. 115 (1985) pp. 40–63]; *HMC Lothian* p. 365; *JRSAI* vol. 41 (1911) pp. 86–8, 168, E. M. F.-G. Boyle, 'Records of the Town of Limavady, 1609–1804'; *Ir. Sword* vol. 16 (1984–6) pp. 216–20, C. E. F. Trench, 'Lieutenant Colonel The Right Hon. William Burton Conyngham, 1733–96' [says he d. 27 May 1796]; *Almanacks; GM* Apr. 1794, p. 169; *DJ* 2 June 1796; *FJ* 24–7 Feb. 1787, 22–5 Sept. 1792; D. Dickson, *New Foundations: Ireland 1660–1800* (Dublin, 1987), p. 167; Parliamentary Lists, 1769 (1), 1771 (1), 1772 (1), (2), 1773 (1), 1774 (1), 1775 (1), 1776 (1), (2), (3), 1777 (1), 1778 (1), 1780 (1), 1782 (1), 1783 (2), 1784 (1), (3), 1785 (1), (2), (3), (4), 1787 (1), 1788 (1), 1789 (1), (2), 1790 (1), 1791 (1), 1794 (1), (2).

0304 BURTON, William Henry

MP for Gowran 1761–8; Co. Carlow 1768–76–83–90–7–1800 [r. Ballynakill 1776]; [UK] 1801–2

b. 16 July 1739; d. 7 Jan. 1818

FAMILY/BACKGROUND: Son of Rt Hon. Benjamin Burton (0293) and Anne, dau. of Rt Hon. Brabazon Ponsonby, 1st Earl of Bessborough (1696).

MARRIED: [12 Dec. 1765] Mary, dau. of Henry Aston of Co. Wicklow.

CHILDREN: Benjamin (fractured his skull falling from a horse while hunting, but, having apparently recovered, went out again with the hounds, which brought on an attack of brain fever from which he died, 26 Apr. 1808), m. [15 Dec. 1794] Anne, dau. of Thomas Mainwaring of Lincolnshire; William Henry (at Cambridge (St John's College), 10 Nov. 1785); Martha.

EDUCATION: School: Kilkenny College 17 Oct. 1746, aged 7 years; entered TCD 12 June 1755, BA 1759.

CAREER/OCCUPATION: Paymaster of Foreign Troops 1784; Commissioner of Treasury 15 Apr. 1806–7; Governor of Co. Carlow 6 Oct. 1767, Joint Governor 1767–1800 (f.); Freeman of Fethard (Tipperary) 1774; *Commissioner of the Tillage Act for Leinster 1779–84; Trustee of the Linen Board for Connaught 1779–1800 (f.); *Governor of the Hibernian Society 1795.

MILITARY: Captain 13th Dragoons 1766–70; Colonel of Carlow Volunteers *c.* 1783.

POLITICAL ACTIVITY: He was unanimously returned for Gowran at the 1761 election. In the 1768 election he joined his interest for the county with that of Beauchamp Bagenal (0071), and was returned. He controlled the borough of Carlow and was returned for the county. A nephew of Speaker Ponsonby (1702) and, although in point of fortune independent, attached to the Ponsonby party.

As a young man he was a professional soldier, a 'Captain of the 13th Dragoons which he threw up in a passion upon being ordered into Quarters'. This was sometime before 1773. During Lord Harcourt's viceroyalty he was definitely in opposition, and voted against both Catholic relief and stamp duties. In 1776 he was again returned for Co. Carlow and also for Ballynakill on Lord Drogheda's interest, thereby creating a valuable 'double return'. He supported Lord Carlisle and the Duke of Portland.

In general he was a systematic Ponsonby supporter, as is very clear from the division lists where he voted solidly in opposition for the last 30 years of the Irish parliament, but whether the personal tie with the Ponsonbys was so strong after the death of his uncle in 1787 is less certain. Lord Lieutenant Rutland tried to attach the Ponsonbys to the government and Burton was made Paymaster of the Troops on the Irish Establishment employed abroad, £1,000 or £1,200 p.a. However, he voted against the Commercial Negotiations in 1785 and for a regency in 1789.

He appears to have been absent actually or diplomatically throughout the mid-1790s as there is no record of his vote on the Catholic question. On 17 December 1798 he wrote to Edward Cooke (0468) that he would give the Union Bill his dispassionate consideration; in the end he voted solidly against the Union. He is reputed to have sold the seats for Carlow Borough in 1783 and 1790 and in 1795 he sold the borough to Charles Bury for £13,000 (Bury was created Lord Tullamore in 1797, Viscount Charleville in 1899 and Earl of Charleville in 1806); Carlow was not disfranchised by the Act of Union. By 25 March 1801 he had not taken his seat for Co. Carlow at Westminster. He made no mark there, and was defeated in the 1802 election.

DIVISION LISTS:

1768 (1) voted against army augmentation – Captain, 13th Dragoons.

1771 (1) voted against Lord Townshend as Lord Lieutenant.

1771 (2) voted for Sir Lucius O'Brien's (**1558**) motion for retrenchment.

1772 (2) voted for a Short Revenue Bill.

1773 (1) voted against the Absentee Tax.

1774 (2) voted against Catholic relief.

1775 (1) voted against the pro-American amendment to the Speech from the Throne.

1777 (1) voted for Grattan's (**0895**) motion for retrenchment.

1777 (2) voted against the Trade Embargo.

1778 (1) voted for Grattan's motion for retrenchment.

1778 (2) voted against the Popery Bill.

1779 (2) voted for a six-months Loan Bill.

1780 (2) voted for Yelverton's (**2268**) motion to modify Poynings' Law.

1780 (3) voted against Tenantry Bill.

1780 (4) voted for a Perpetual Mutiny Bill.

1783 (1) voted for Flood's (**0762**) motion for parliamentary reform.

1784 (1) voted for a committee on the Reform Bill.

1785 (1) voted against the Commercial Propositions.

1789 (1) voted for regency.

1790 (1) voted for Grattan's motion for reducing the influence of the Crown.

1790 (2) voted for Ponsonby (**1709**) on the election of a Speaker.

1791 (1) voted for Curran's (**0560**) resolution against the sale of peerages.

1791 (2) voted for Grattan's motion for the exercise of Free Trade.

1799 (1) voted against the Union – Governor of the County. 'Has £4,000 p.a. in landed property or is heir apparent to it.'

1800 (1) voted against the Union.

ADDITIONAL INFORMATION: A member of the Royal Dublin Society, 1768–1800(f.).

ESTATES/RESIDENCE: Burton Hall, Co. Carlow; Sackville Street, Dublin.

SOURCES: PRONI D/3030/415 Castlereagh Papers; PRONI T/3166/1A Hartnell notes; PRONI MIC/474 Irish Volunteers; RCBL P80/1/1, Parish Registers of St Thomas, Dublin; O'Neill thesis; Ellis thesis; Jupp thesis; Burke *LGI* (1904) p. 77; *HP 1790–1820*; Hughes, *Pat. Officers*; *Alum. Dub.*; *Alum. Cantab.*; W. T. J. Gun, *The Harrow School Register, 1571–1800* (London, 1934); Kilkenny MPs; Carlow MPs; J. Frost, *The History and Topography of the County of Clare, from the Earliest Times to the Beginning of the 18th Century, With Map and Illustrations*, pp. 624–7 [says a William Burton of Clifden, High Sheriff of Co. Clare 1800]; *JRSAI* vol. 52 (1922) p. 176, W. G. Strickland, 'Miscellanea'; *JRSAI* vol. 54 (1924) pp. 55–67, T. U. Sadleir, 'The Register of Kilkenny School (1685–1800)'; *Almanacks*; *DJ* 28 Apr. – 2 May 1761; *FJ* 3 Dec. 1796; Parliamentary Lists, 1769 (1), 1772 (2), 1773 (1), (2), 1774 (1), 1775 (1), 1776 (1), (2), (3), 1777 (1), 1778 (1), 1780 (1), 1782 (1), 1783 (1), (2), 1784 (1), (2), (3), 1785 (1), (2), (3), (4), 1787 (1), 1788 (1), 1789 (1), 1790 (1).

0305 BURY, Charles William

MP for Kilmallock Jan.–Apr. 1790, 1792–7

b. 30 June 1764; d. 3l Oct. 1835

PEERAGES: Cr. Baron Tullamore 26 Nov. 1797, Viscount Charleville 29 Dec. 1800, Earl of Charleville 16 Feb. 1806: Rep. Peer 1801–35.

FAMILY/BACKGROUND: Only son and h. of John Bury (d. 1764, 'unfortunately drowned near Dublin') of King's County and Catherine, dau. and co-h. of Francis Sadleir of Co. Tipperary (she m. (2) Henry Prittie (**1742**)).

MARRIED: [4 June 1798] Catherine Maria, dau. and h. of Thomas Townley Dawson of Co. Dublin, wid. of James Tisdall of Bawn, Co. Louth.

CHILDREN: Only s. Charles William, 2nd Earl of Charleville, m. [1821] Harriet Charlotte Beaujolois, 3rd dau. of Col. John Campbell of Shawfield and granddau. of 5th Duke of Argyll.

EDUCATION: School Mr Turpin; entered TCD 11 Oct. 1781, BA 1785.

CAREER/OCCUPATION: High Sheriff of King's County 1825; *Governor and Guardian of the Hospital for the relief of Lying-in Women 1781–96; *Governor of the Charitable Loan Society 1781, 1783–8, 1792, 1794–6; *Governor of the Hibernian Society 1783–6.

MILITARY: ?Captain of the Tullamore True Blue Rangers, Volunteers 1782; Colonel of Tullamore Cavalry 1796.

POLITICAL ACTIVITY: He came in on the by-election following the appointment of John Fitzgibbon (**0749**) as Lord Chancellor and his elevation to the House of Lords as Lord Fitzgibbon. Bury was reputed to have been an enthusiastic Volunteer and a delegate to the Volunteer National Convention for King's County, although he would have been only 19 years old at the time and he may have been confused with his stepfather, Colonel Prittie. Bury was sworn on 26 January 1790, in the dying months of the 1783–90 parliament. He was returned for Kilmallock, not at the 1790 general election but in the by-election following the death of John Armstrong (**0054**) on 12 September 1791; he was sworn 25 January 1792. It was thought that he might stand for King's County as he had considerable property there, being through his mother the heir-general of an earlier Charleville title.

A 1790 Parliamentary List indignantly declared that 'If the right to represent them [freeholders of King's County] is demanded as a species of family inheritance, arising not from attachment to superior worth and eminent abilities, but from subjugation to the possessor of extensive property; if it is sought for by youths just returned from rambling through Europe, whose principles are unknown, whose integrity is untried; if it is evidently an object of ambition, in order to the attainment of honours. Honours, Peerages, which the representative of a considerable County might seem in some sort entitled to, had they ever been in a branch of his family: in all such cases the Freeholders are called upon to prove their spirit and to mark their independence, not by empty words, but by decisive actions. For in all such cases, their dignity is attacked.' The other contestant was Denis Bowes Daly (**0571**), the brother-in-law of W. B. (**1709**) and George (**1699**) Ponsonby, and he was duly returned.

Bury appears to have single-mindedly pursued his quest for the resumption of his family's former honours. He was created Lord Tullamore in 1797, Viscount Charleville in 1800 and Earl of Charleville in 1806. In 1795 he purchased the borough of Carlow from William Burton (**0304**) and, as Carlow was not disfranchised, he controlled a seat in the United Kingdom parliament. He supported the Union.

DIVISION LISTS:

1790 (1) voted for Grattan's (**0895**) motion for reducing the influence of the Crown.

ADDITIONAL INFORMATION: *A member of the Royal Dublin Society from 1779; *a subscriber to the Public Assembly Rooms, 1787; Fellow of the Royal Society, 31 March 1803; a member of the Royal Irish Academy, 1791–1800, President 1812–22; Fellow of the Royal Society of Antiquities, 28 April 1814.

The family were prominent Freemasons. His father was Junior Grand Warden of the Grand Lodge of Irish Freemasons, 1753–6; Senior Grand Warden, 1757; Deputy Grand Master, 1757; and Deputy Grand Warden, 1758. His uncle William was also a Freemason and his grandmother, Jane Moore, was sister of Charles Moore, 2nd Lord Tullamore, who was Grand Master in 1741.

ESTATES/RESIDENCE: Charleville Forest, King's County; Dunleary, Co. Dublin. According to Wakefield he had a rental of £5,000.

SOURCES: PRONI D/302; GEC *P*; Burke *Ext. P.* (1883) p. 603; McNevin, *Volunteers*; *King's Inns Admissions*; Wakefield, *Account of Ire.*, vol. 1 p. 267; J. H. Lepper and P. Crossle, *History of the Grand Lodge of Free and Accepted Masons of Ireland* (Dublin, 1925), vol. 1; *JRSAI* vol. 29 (1899) p. 240, F. E. Ball 'Some Residents of Monkstown in the Eighteenth Century'; *Almanacks*; *DJ* 3–7 July 1764 [says he was born 2 July 1764]; *FJ* 17 Nov. 1796; *BNL* 15 June 1798; Parliamentary Lists, 1783 (2), (3), 1789 (1), 1790 (1), 1793 (1), 1794 (2), 1799 (3), 1800 (2).

0306 BURY, John

MP for Askeaton 1715–22

b. ?1650; d. 14 Sept. 1722
FAMILY/BACKGROUND: Son of Phineas Bury of Co. Limerick.
MARRIED: Jane, only dau. of William Palliser, Abp of Cashel.
CHILDREN: William, m. [27 Jan. 1723] Jane, o. dau. of Rt Hon. John Moore, 1st Baron Moore (**1461**); John (entered TCD 7 Feb. 1722, aged 16 years; assumed name of Palliser); Richard, m. Anne, dau. of Mountiford Westropp of Co. Limerick; Thomas; Phineas, m. [1734] Hester, dau. of Thomas Moland; Elizabeth, m.

Mountiford Westropp.

CAREER/OCCUPATION: Sheriff of Limerick 9 Dec. 1672, 1693.

POLITICAL ACTIVITY: Nothing is known of his political career, except that he voted against a national bank. He was probably an old man when he entered parliament.

DIVISION LISTS:

1721 (1) voted against a national bank.
1721 (2) voted against a national bank.

ESTATES/RESIDENCE: Shannon Grove, Co. Limerick. He purchased 453 acres in Co. Limerick from the Commissioners for Sale of Forfeited Estates in 1702–3.

SOURCES: PRONI D/302; Burke *LGI* (1904) p. 77; Burke *Ext. P.* (1883) p. 603, *IFR* (1976) p. 190; *Memorials of the Dead*; Hughes, *Pat. Officers*; *JRSAI* vol. 42 (1912) p. 37, W. O. Cavenagh, 'Castletown Carne and its Owners'; Simms, *Williamite Confiscation*, p. 183.[A suggested date of birth was 1666 but this is unrealistic if he is Sheriff of Limerick in 1672, also as he is not nominated for any committees he was possibly over 60 when he entered parliament in 1715].

0307 BUSHE, Amyas

MP for New Ross 1707–13; Thomastown 1713–14

b. *c.* 1657; d. [29] Aug. 1724

FAMILY/BACKGROUND: Son of Col. John Bushe and Mary, dau. and co-h. of Col. John Gray.

MARRIED: (1) Eleanor, dau. of Sir Christopher Wandesforde, 1st Bt; (2) [　], wid. of [　] Drysdale.

CHILDREN: (1) Christopher, m. Margaret [　]; Arthur, m. Mary, dau. of Rev. Thomas Marten; Amyas (entered TCD 14 June 1722, aged 15 years); Elinor, m. Christopher Hewetson (**1011**); Elizabeth m. Edward Deane (**0600**).

CAREER/OCCUPATION: Sovereign of Thomastown 1695; Customs and Excise Collector of New Ross and Kilkenny; Customer of Waterford; Free Burgess of New Ross 21 Sept. 1705 – 29 Sept. 1711; Sheriff of Wexford 1706.

MILITARY: Captain in Company of Foot June 1682 (left the Irish army by Mar. 1686).

POLITICAL ACTIVITY: As a gentleman of Kilkenny he was one of the Memorialists in August 1700 seeking the reopening of the port of New Ross, which had been shut to discourage the woollen trade with England. This was depressing the industry in Leinster.

He contested the seat for New Ross in July 1707 with Francis Annesley (**0044**). The election was interesting as it indicated a number of fairly typical election misdemeanours but, more importantly, the boroughs were trying to discover what their actual powers were; these solidified only during the long parliament of George II. On Bushe's election a number of protests were entered: firstly, that more than 24 burgesses voted, that being the number limited by charter; secondly, that he was not a legal burgess; thirdly, that freemen had no right to vote; and fourthly, that Robert Coleman and John Elly were disqualified, being Quakers. Francis Annesley petitioned against his return alleging unfair practices, threats and the exercise of influence *via* alehouse keepers. The petition was heard on 9 October 1707 and David Horgane told the Committee that he had never been threatened by Bushe but that the latter had once told him: 'Do not concern yourself any further for Mr Annesley, for if you do I will lay you where you shall not see your hand.' The petition was rejected.

He was nominated for 18 committees between 1707 and 1711 and five in 1713. He was a Court supporter and attended Ormonde's birthday celebrations in 1706, although as a resident in Kilkenny he would probably have done so anyway. Nevertheless, he was counted a government supporter in 1711 when he gave them his vote on the Dublin mayoralty issue. In 1713 he was thought likely to be returned for New Ross, but instead he was returned for Thomastown. In the new parliament he supported the government's candidate, Sir Richard Levinge (**1230**) for Speaker and in 1713 and 1714 he was definitely on the 'black' list of Tories. He did not come into parliament in 1715.

DIVISION LISTS:

1711 (1) voted for the Court on the Dublin mayoralty issue.
1713 (1) voted for Sir Richard Levinge (**1230**) for Speaker.

ESTATES/RESIDENCE: Kilfane, Co. Kilkenny. In 1702–3 he purchased 14 acres in Queen's County from the Commissioners for Sale of Forfeited Estates.

SOURCES: Hayton thesis; Burke *LGI* (1904) p. 78; Kilkenny MPs; Hughes, *Pat. Officers*; *Alum. Dub.*; C. Dalton (ed.), *Irish Army Lists 1661–85* (London, 1907), p. 140; *Kilkenny Arch. Soc. Jn.* vol. 1 series 2 (1856–7) p. 90, J. Graves, 'The Records of the Ancient Borough Towns of the County of Kilkenny'; *JRSAI* vol. 21 (1892) p. 300, P. D. Vigors, 'Alphabetical List of Free Burgesses of New Ross, 1658–1839'; *JRSAI* vol. 31 (1901) pp. 56, 59, P. D. Vigors, 'Extracts from the Old Corporation Books of New Ross, County Wexford'; Simms, *Williamite Confiscation*, p. 183; Parliamentary Lists, 1706 (2), 1711 (3), 1713 (1), (2), 1714–15 (1).

0308 BUSHE, Arthur

MP for Thomastown 1695–9, 1703–13–14

b. *ante* 1670; d. 1731
FAMILY/BACKGROUND: Son of Col. John Bushe and Mary, dau. and co-h. of Col. John Gray.
MARRIED: (1) Anne, dau. of Sir Thomas Worsop; (2) [17 Oct. 1695] Mary, dau. of John Forth.
CHILDREN: (1) Worsop; Elizabeth, m. [1707] Joseph Harries.
(2) William, m. [1723] Hannah, e. dau. of Edmund Donnellan of Co. Westmeath; John, (entered TCD, 1735, aged 17 years); Mary; Letitia.
EDUCATION: LLD of TCD 1701.
CAREER/OCCUPATION: Secretary to the Revenue Commissioners; Judge Advocate General 9 Oct. 1702–12; Collector of Cork Port 1693–8 (at a salary of £150 p.a.); Free Burgess of New Ross 2 Sept. 1709; Joint Customer of Dublin *ante* 1711; Trustee of the Linen Manufacture for the Province of Munster 10 Oct. 1711.

POLITICAL ACTIVITY: In 1686 a Mr Bush, Clerk to the Commissioners of the Revenue, was proposed to be the Accountant General: a post for which Clarendon thought him too inexperienced. In July 1695 he voluntarily discharged the Corporation of Thomastown of any salary or allowance while serving it in parliament. He supported Lord Chancellor Porter against accusations of favouring Catholics, and signed the Association for the protection of William III in the country. During the reign of Queen Anne he supported Court, at-

tended Ormonde's birthday celebrations and, in 1711, was one of the 31 Tories who met at the Fleece Tavern to arrange the business for the ensuing session. He voted for the government over the Dublin mayoralty dispute. He was nominated for 37 committees between 1703 and 1711, and in 1711 he introduced 11 Anne, c. 3, 'an Act to enable Guardians and others to renew leases for lives': this was a problem confronting those managing the estates of minors.

In the 1713 election he was again returned for Thomastown: 'this borough being well secured for government'. When parliament assembled he supported Sir Richard Levinge (**1230**), the government's candidate for Speaker. He was listed for seven committees in that very brief parliament. Not surprisingly, he was a marked Tory in 1713 and on the 'black list' of Tories at the time of the queen's death in 1714. He did not come in again in 1715.

DIVISION LISTS:
1711 (1) voted for the Court on the Dublin mayoralty issue.
1713 (1) voted for Sir Richard Levinge (**1230**) for Speaker.

ESTATES/RESIDENCE: Dangan, Co. Kilkenny. Purchased 1,646 acres in Co. Kilkenny from the Commissioners for Sale of Forfeited Estates in 1702–3.

SOURCES: *CJ Ire.* (Bradley ed.) vol. 3 p. 920 (0144); McCracken thesis; Burke *LGI* (1904) p. 78; Hughes, *Pat. Officers*; Eustace, *Abstracts of Wills*; Kilkenny MPs; H. F. Berry (ed.), *The Registers of the Church of St Michan, Dublin, 1636–1700* (Parish Register Society of Dublin, 1909) p. 350; *Clarendon Corr.* vol. 2 p. 11; *Kilkenny Arch. Soc. Jn.* vol. I second ser. (1856–7) p. 90, J. Graves, 'The Records of the Ancient Borough Towns of the County of Kilkenny'; *JRSAI* vol. 21 (1892) p. 300, P. D. Vigors, 'Alphabetical List of Free Burgesses of New Ross, 1658–1839'; *JRSAI* vol. 76 (1946) p. 135, W. E. J. Dobbs, 'A Supplement to the Entrance Register of Kilkenny School: 1684–1800'; Simms, *Williamite Confiscation*, p. 183; Parliamentary Lists, 1695 (1), 1696 (1),1706 (1), (2), 1711 (2), (3), 1713 (1), (2), 1714–15 (1).

0309 BUSHE, Rt Hon. Charles Kendal

MP for Callan 1796–7–9; [Escheator of Munster 7 Feb. 1799]; Donegal B. 1799–1800

b. 1767; d. 10 July 1843
HONOURS: PC, sworn 5 Mar. 1822.
FAMILY/BACKGROUND: Son of Thomas Bushe, Rector of Gowran, and Catherine, dau. of Charles Doyle of Co. Kilkenny.
MARRIED: [Dec. 1793] Anne, dau. of John Crampton of Dublin.
CHILDREN: John, m. [1817] Louisa, dau. of William Hare, 1st Earl of Listowel (0966); Rev. Charles m. (1) [1829] Fanny Elizabeth, dau. of James Bury of Essex, (2) [1839] Emmeline Catherine Egerton, dau. of Vice Adm. Sir Josiah Coghill, 3rd Bt; Thomas, m. [1824] Alicia Jane, dau. of John Phillips; Arthur, m. (1) Mary Anne Christian, (2) Marian, dau. of Robert Martin of Ross, Co. Galway; Anna Maria, m. [1819] Adm. Sir Josiah Coghill, 3rd Bt; Catherine, m. [1818] Charles Michael Fox; Charlotte, m. [1824] John Plunket, 3rd Baron Plunket; Elizabeth; Maria, m. [1836] Rev. John Harris; Henrietta, m. [1833] Robert Franks of Kilkenny.
EDUCATION: School: Dublin; entered TCD July 1782, scholar 1785; Lincoln's Inn 19 June 1786; BA 1787, MA 1791; called to the Irish Bar 1793; LLD 1796.
CAREER/OCCUPATION: Freedom of Dublin 1800; 3rd Serjeant-at-Law July 1805; Solicitor General 1805–22; Chief Justice of the King's/Queen's Bench 20 Feb. 1822–41.

POLITICAL ACTIVITY: His career was really post-Union, when he became one of the great legal figures of the nineteenth century. He was returned by Lord Clifden for Callan at a by-election in 1796 and again at the general election in 1797. In December 1798 he wrote a pamphlet arguing against the Union. However, Lord Clifden supported the Union and Bushe accepted the Escheatorship of Munster on 7 February 1799, thereby vacating his seat. Although he had a numerous family and was heavily in debt, he refused to support the Union. Almost a year later he was returned for Donegal town following the death of Hugh O'Donnell (1569). He was actually returned for Donegal Borough in 1799 before the writ had been issued, but he was sworn on 15 January 1800, just in time for the famous last-ditch stand against the Union.

He was one of the great orators of the Irish House of Commons and utterly incorruptible. Grattan considered that 'He spoke with the lips of an angel', and in a speech that was almost the obituary of the Irish parliament he declared: 'Will you give up your country? For centuries has the British nation and Parliament kept you down, shackled your commerce, paralysed your exertions, despised your character, and ridiculed your pretensions to any privileges, commercial or constitutional. She never conceded a point ... she could avoid, or granted a favour ... not reluctantly distilled. They have all been wrung from her, like drops of her heart's blood ... What covered a country of pasture with tillage? ... intersected an impassable country with roads? ... nearly connected by inland navigation the eastern channel with the western ocean? A resident Parliament. This is not theory ... nothing can supply a resident Parliament watching over national improvement, seizing opportunities, encouraging manufacture, commerce, science, education, and agriculture; applying instant remedy to instant mischief, mixing with the constituent body, catching the sentiment of the public mind, reflecting public opinion, acting upon its impulse, and regulating its excess.'

DIVISION LISTS:
1800 (1) voted against the Union.

ESTATES/RESIDENCE: Kilmurry, Co. Kilkenny; Holles Street, Dublin.

SOURCES: PRONI T/3166/1A and 1/B Hartnell notes; PRONI T/1075/32 Canon Leslie's notes; PRONI MIC/338/3 Crossle notes; O'Neill thesis; Burke *LGI* (1904) p. 78; *DNB*; Hughes, *Pat. Officers, Index to Irish Privy Counsellors, 1711–1910*; *King's Inns Admissions*; *Alum. Dub.*; Ball, *Judges*; *Lincoln's Inn Records* (Lincoln's Inn, 1896) vol. 1 p. 518; Gilbert, Dublin, vol. 3 pp. 152–3; *Castlereagh Corr.* vol. 2 pp. 44, 45; Kilkenny MPs; *Cork Hist. Soc. Jn.* vol. 4 second ser. (1898) p. 110, C. Moore, 'Some Account of Kingston College, Michelstown, Co. Cork'; *FJ* 22 Oct. 1799; Parliamentary Lists, 1798 (1), 1799 (3), 1800 (3).

0310 BUSHE, Gervase Parker

MP for Granard 1767–8–76; Kilkenny city 1778–83; Fore 1783–90; Lanesborough 1790–3

b. (bapt. 22 Dec.) 1744; d. 13 Aug. 1793, at Kilfane, Co. Kilkenny
FAMILY/BACKGROUND: Only son of Amyas Bushe and Elizabeth, dau. and h. of Rt Hon. Gervase Parker (♦♦♦).
MARRIED: [Feb. 1768] Mary, dau. of James Grattan (0896) of Dublin.
CHILDREN: Henry Amyas, m. Lavinia, e. dau. of Richard Gumbleton; Rev. William, m. Letitia e. dau. of Frederick Geale; Gervase Parker, m. [1806] Eliza, dau. of John Latham, wid. of [   ] Hackett; Richard; Robert; Charlotte, m. Rev. John, Viscount Scott; Frances, m. Rev. George de la Poer Beresford; Harriet, m. Sir John Power 1st Bt; Maria.
EDUCATION: School: Kilkenny College 6 Aug. 1759, aged 14 years; entered Glasgow University 1761.
CAREER/OCCUPATION: Accompts Commissioner 13 Dec. 1771, 17 July 1773–6; Stamps Commissioner 11 Feb. 1774–6; Revenue Commissioner 1784–93; High Sheriff of Co. Kilkenny 21 Jan. 1768.
MILITARY: Colonel of the Thomastown Battalion, Volunteers, and the Kilkenny Independent Volunteers.

POLITICAL ACTIVITY: He entered parliament at a by-election for Granard in 1767 caused by the elevation of Edmond Malone (1338) to the bench. He purchased his seat in both this (1761–8) and the succeeding (1768–76) parliament. In 1768 he voted against the augmentation of the army, but his stance appears to have softened, as in 1769 he was recorded as being doubtful/against. He was a follower of Henry Flood (0762) and his second in the duel with James Agar (0015), in which the latter was killed.

He was a Kilkenny man, and also reputedly influenced by Sir Hercules Langrishe (1200), while his wife was a sister of Henry Grattan (0895). In 1769 it was thought that 'His father wants either a peerage for himself or something for his son', and in 1771 he was made 'a Commissioner of Accounts £500 p.a.'. The golden gag of office appears to have kept him quiet as, in 1772, it was said that 'He was once an ingenious speaker against Government, now seldom opens his mouth'; this

silence continued in 1773 and had its reward in 1774, as he was made a 'Commissioner of Imprest Accounts, and Commissioner of the Stamp Duty', 'having voted for every Court measure' and, lamented the compiler of the opposition list of that year, 'for eighteen months he appeared honest and people were beginning to forget the Kilkenny remarks of a Bush, an Agar, and a Flood.' In 1775 another list declared that 'He seldom opens his mouth, and when he does the recollection of his former Patriotism chokes him.' Nevertheless, he was from his position very independent and 'His conduct during the last session [1773–4] was at best equivocal, and in one or two instances hostile to Government'; in 1776 he was removed from office.

Ralph Gore (0873) was returned for Kilkenny city in the election of 1776 but died in 1778. At the disputed by-election Charles Agar (♦♦♦) was declared not duly elected and Bushe was returned in his place. He supported Lord Carlisle and looked for office. In the 1783 election he purchased one of the seats for Fore, a borough composed of 13 non-resident burgesses under Lord Westmeath's control. He tried to calm the Renunciation question by saying that the British Great Seal was used merely to certify the act, and that the royal assent was that given in the Irish parliament. He absented himself during the Commercial Negotiations, but in 1784 was appointed a Commissioner of the Revenue, £1,000 p.a. He was a good speaker – 'lively and useful in debate'. Although much attached to Henry Grattan, his brother-in-law, he was 'not entirely guided by him'. For instance, by 1784 he was strongly against protecting duties, reform and the Volunteers.

The 1789 character sketches of the Irish MPs declared that 'Most of the eminent persons that adorn the Irish Parliament, have marked the beginning of their public life by a vigorous opposition to the measures of the Court and have acquired distinction and celebrity, by fighting what are called the battles of the people. Without any imputation on their sincerity, this conduct may be fairly attributed to the generous ardour of youth and to that warm patriotic flame with which every worthy mind, at that period, invariably burns. Experience, indeed, at length evinces the unproductiveness of their labour and the political adventurer converts into a mercantable commodity the character which he has procured and the fame which he has earned ... Mr Bushe, who early trod with reputation the paths of opposition, has since his enrolment among the servants of the Crown observed a temperature of conduct hardly to be expected from a man of his apparent warmth of disposition. If he has not been assiduous to bring forward popular measures, he has been far from laborious in the support of pernicious schemes; if he has not been loud, as formerly, in the defence of liberty, he has not, like some of his ancient associates, been diligent to enforce by perverted reasoning treacherous plans of policy or delusive phantoms of commerce. There has been a decency in his prostitution and a decorum in his mercenary engagements. In his capacity of a parliamentary speaker, his voice is strong, distinct and mellow, but when unduly raised ... strikingly offensive to the ear. His language is singularly well chosen, pure, correct and animated ... His arrangement is just, clear and regular, reflecting light on the whole series of his thoughts and strongly illustrating them ... Possessed of a good understanding carefully cultivated and well acquainted with the stores of ancient and modern learning, the matter of his speeches is never weak, or slight, or flimsy, but abounding with information and marked with solid sense ... Enjoying a considerable employment under Government, Mr Bushe is a firm adherent to the minister of the day, but the fervour of his attachment, though steady, is not blazing and his zeal in the service, though sincere, is not furious. Others are more impetuous, he is content to be useful.'

In the late 1770s he was member of the reforming 'Society of Granby Row' and he always retained a tincture of liberal views, as is reflected in the pattern his voting and absenteeism.

DIVISION LISTS:

1768 (1) voted against army augmentation.
1771 (1) voted for Lord Townshend as Lord Lieutenant – expects a place directly.
1771 (2) voted against Sir Lucius O'Brien's (1558) motion for retrenchment – [one of] the new Commissioners.
1772 (2) voted against a Short Revenue Bill.

1773 (1) voted for Absentee Tax.
1773 (2) voted against an untaxed press.
1774 (1) voted for the Stamp Bill.
1774 (2) voted for Catholic relief.
1775 (1) voted for the pro-American amendment to the Speech from the Throne.
1778 (2) voted for the Popery Bill.
1779 (2) voted for a six-months Loan Bill.
1780 (1) voted against Grattan's (0895) declaration of the Rights of Ireland.
1780 (2) a teller for Yelverton's (2268) motion to modify Poynings' Law.
1780 (3) voted for the Tenantry Bill.
1780 (5) voted for the duty on imported sugar.
1783 (1) voted against Flood's (0762) motion for parliamentary reform.
1784 (1) voted against a committee on the Reform Bill.
1785 (1) absent.
1789 (1) voted for a regency.
1790 (2) voted for Foster (0805) on the election of a Speaker.

ADDITIONAL INFORMATION: *A member of the Royal Dublin Society from 1766; *a member of the Royal Irish Academy, 1790.

ESTATES/RESIDENCE: Kilfane, Thomastown, Co. Kilkenny; Sackville Street, Dublin.

SOURCES: PRONI D/302; PRONI T/1584 Pinkerton transcripts, p. 473, 20 Aug. 1793; PRONI MIC/315/8/38 Blackwood pedigrees; PRONI MIC/474 Irish Volunteers; RCBL P80/1/1, Parish Registers of St Thomas, Dublin; RCBL T34, Extracts from the Parish Registers of St Andrew's, Dublin; Ellis thesis; Lammey thesis; Burke LGI (1904) p. 78; W. I. Addison (ed.), *Alum. Oxon.* [says he entered Oxford University in 1763 aged 19 years]; GM Aug. 1793; Hughes, *Pat. Officers, Ir. Gen.* vol. 6 no 3 (1982) p. 345, H. F. Morris, 'Extracts from The Waterford Herald 1793, 1794, 1796', *Ir. Gen.* vol. 7 no 2 (1987) p. 254, H. F. Morris, 'Finn's Leinster Journal 1768'; *JRSAI* vol. 54 (1924) pp. 55–67, T. U. Sadleir, 'The Register of Kilkenny School (1685–1800)'; McDowell, *Ir. public opinion,* p. 76; J. Kelly, *'That Damn'd Thing Called Honour': Duelling in Ireland 1570–1860* (Cork, 1995), pp. 100–4; *Almanacks; FJ* 16–18 June 1774; *DJ* 15 Aug. 1793; Parliamentary Lists, 1769 (1), 1772 (2), 1773 (1), (2), 1774 (1), 1775 (1), 1778 (1), 1780 (1), 1782 (1), 1783 (1), (2), 1784 (1), (2), (3), 1785 (1), (2), (3), (4), 1787 (1), 1788 (1), 1789 (1), (2), 1790 (1), 1791 (1), 1793 (1).

0311 BUSTEED, Jephson

MP for Midleton 1713–14; Rathcormack 1715–27 [n.d.e. Doneraile 1727]

b. 1678; d. *post* 1730
FAMILY/BACKGROUND: Son of William Busteed.
MARRIED: [   ], dau. of Redmond Barry of Ballyclough, Co. Cork.
CHILDREN: ?son.
EDUCATION: School: Mr Jones, Dublin; entered TCD 16 July 1694, aged 16 years, BA 1700, MA 1701; called to the Irish Bar 1709.
CAREER/OCCUPATION: King's Counsel 1715; Recorder of Kinsale 1730.

POLITICAL ACTIVITY: On his election in the 1713 election he was classed as a Whig; he was nominated to one committee, on 17 December, during that short parliament. However, in the next parliament, that of George I, his name was listed for 72 committees between 1715 and 1725. His votes both for and against the national bank probably reflect the instability caused by the South Sea Bubble and growing suspicions as to the motivation of government. In the same year, on 6 December 1721, he complained of being disturbed in his possession of lands at Kilvocry during time of privilege, thereby reflecting the insecurity that still existed in many parts of the country and was only gradually diminishing.

DIVISION LISTS:
1721 (1) voted for a national bank.
1721 (2) voted against a national bank.

ESTATES/RESIDENCE: Kilvocry, Co. Cork.

SOURCES: *CJ Ire.* (Bradley ed.) vol. 4 p. 830; McCracken thesis; Hughes, *Pat. Officers*; *IMC King's Inns Admissions*; Parliamentary List, 1713 (2).

0312 BUTLER, Rt Hon. Brinsley

MP for Kells 1703–13; Belturbet 1713–14, 1715–24

b. 1670; d. 6 Mar. 1736
HONOURS: PC, sworn 5 June 1726, 19 June 1727, 9 May 1728, 1733–d.
PEERAGES: Suc. as 2nd Baron Newtown-Butler 11 Mar. 1724; cr. Viscount Lanesborough 12 Aug. 1728.

FAMILY/BACKGROUND: Son of Francis Butler (**0315**) and Judith, dau. of the Rt Hon. Sir Theophilus Jones of Co. Meath.
MARRIED: [1700] Catherine, dau. and co-h. of Neville Pooley of Dublin.
CHILDREN: 23 children, 5 surviving infancy: Rt Hon. Humphrey, 1st Earl of Lanesborough (**0317**); Thomas (**0331**); Robert (**0328**); John (**0321**); Judith, m. [23 Apr. 1724] Balthazar John Cramer. (Francis, James, Stephen, Brinsley, Frances, Katherine, Elizabeth, Mary, Amelia, Catherine all d. yg.)
EDUCATION: School: Mr Price, Dublin; entered TCD 27 Sept. 1686, aged 16 years, LLD *hon. caus.* 1718.
CAREER/OCCUPATION: Gentleman Usher of the Black Rod 1711; High Sheriff of Co. Cavan 1703; *Commissioner of Oyer and Terminer 1732–d.; Governor of the Workhouse 1733–d.; *Trustee of the Linen Board for Leinster 1735–d.; *Commissioner of the Tillage Act for Ulster 1735.
MILITARY: Lieutenant and subsequently Colonel (May–Aug. 1714) of the Battle-Axe Guards.

POLITICAL ACTIVITY: He entered parliament in 1703 and was a supporter of the Court during the reign of Queen Anne. On 16 May 1704 he wrote to Ormonde asking that his employment in the Battle-Axe Guards would not lead to him being discharged from the Duke's bedchamber, which he considered the greatest honour of his life. In 1706 he attended Ormonde's birthday celebrations, and in both 1707 and 1711 he was among the select group of Tories who attended a meeting at the Fleece Tavern to discuss and co-ordinate government policy during the ensuing sessions of parliament. He continued to support the Tories for the remainder of Queen Anne's reign, supporting the government over the Dublin mayoralty dispute in 1711. Between 1703 and 1711 he was listed for 28 committees. As forecast, he replaced the Rt Hon. Richard Tighe (**2066**) as MP for Belturbet in the 1713 general election, and he subsequently voted for Sir Richard Levinge (**1230**) as Speaker. At the time of the queen's death he was on the 'black list' of Tories.

He was dismissed from the Battle-Axe Guards in 1715 despite the support of both Archbishop King and Brodrick (**0237**), and the fact that his brother Theophilus (**0329**) was a leading Whig and a Privy Counsellor. King argued that he had no option, Butler being a younger son with (then) nine surviving children. However, he was later compensated for the loss of his post with a pension.

Again returned for Belturbet in 1715, he was considered a Tory and therefore, in 1719, likely to be an opponent to the repeal of the Test Clause in the 1709 penal law. Nevertheless, between 1716 and 1723 he was nominated for 41 committees. He was a supporter of a national bank. In 1724 he succeeded his brother (**0329**) as 2nd Lord Newtown-Butler with special remainder to the heirs male of his father, Francis Butler (**0315**), and in 1728 he was created Viscount Lanesborough.

DIVISION LISTS:

1711 (1) voted for the Court on the Dublin mayoralty issue.

1713 (1) voted for Sir Richard Levinge (**1230**) for Speaker.

1721 (1) voted for a national bank.

1721 (2) voted for a national bank.

ESTATES/RESIDENCE: Belturbet, Co. Cavan. Purchased 316 acres in Co. Meath from the Commissioners for Sale of Forfeited Estates in 1702–3.

SOURCES: PRONI D/302; RCBL T34, Extracts from the Parish Registers of St Andrew's, Dublin; GEC *P*; Burke *PB* (1903) p. 884; *Index to Irish Privy Counsellors, 1711–1910*; *Alum. Dub.*; *HMC Ormonde*, new ser. vol. 8 p. 76; P. McNally, *Parties, Patriots & Undertakers* (Dublin, 1997) p. 74; *Almanacks*; Simms, *Williamite Confiscation*, p. 183; Parliamentary Lists, 1706 (1), (2), 1707 (2), 1711 (2), (3), 1713 (1), 1714–15 (1), 1719 (2).

0313 BUTLER, Rt Hon. Brinsley

MP for Co. Cavan 1751–60, 1761–8

b. 4 Mar. 1728; d. 15 Jan. 1779
HONOURS: PC, sworn 24 May 1765, removed 7 May 1770, resworn 19 Dec. 1774.
PEERAGES: Styled Lord Newtown-Butler 1756–68; suc. as 2nd Earl of Lanesborough Apr. 1768.
FAMILY/BACKGROUND: Only son of Rt Hon. Humphrey Butler, 1st Earl of Lanesborough (**0317**) and Mary, dau. of William Berry (**0129**).
MARRIED: [26 June 1754] Jane Isabella, o. dau. of

Rt Hon. Robert Rochfort, 1st Earl of Belvidere (**1807**).
CHILDREN: Robert Herbert, 3rd Earl of Lanesborough, m. [1781] Elizabeth, e. dau. of Rt Hon. David La Touche (**1203**); Augustus Richard, m. (1) [8 Mar. 1792] Mary, dau. and h. of Sir John Danvers Bt, (2) [1802] Eliza Bizarre, dau. of Humphrey Sturt of Dorset; Mary, m. [1781] Rt Hon. George Ponsonby (**1699**); Catherine m. George Marley; Charlotte, m. [1806] George Debbieg; Caroline; Sophia, m. [11 Aug. 1787] the Marquis Lewis Marescotti.
EDUCATION: School: private tutor; entered TCD 30 Nov. 1745, BA 1748, MA 1750, LLB and LLD 1754.
CAREER/OCCUPATION: Revenue Commissioner 1761–3 Apr. 1770 (patent, 21 Apr. 1761, 8 Apr. 1765, 3 Dec. 1767); *Clerk of the Pipe 1749–54, 1756, 1758–9, 1762–3; *Deputy Clerk 1755, Joint Clerk 26 Dec. 1749–79; High Sheriff of Co. Cavan 1755, Co. Westmeath 26 Jan. 1763; Governor of the Workhouse 1751–68, Foundling Hospital and Workhouse 1769–78; Trustee of the Linen Board for Leinster Feb. 1754–d.; *Commissioner of the Tillage Act for Ulster 1758–d.; *Governor of Erasmus Smith's Schools and other Charities 1760–d.; *Governor of Co. Cavan 1761–d.; Custos Rot. Co. Cavan 24 Sept. 1761–78; elected to the Court of Assistants June 1766–8; *Vice-President of the Hibernian Marine Society 1775–d.; *Vice-President of the Charitable Loan Society 1778.

POLITICAL ACTIVITY: He was returned for Co. Cavan in 1751 at the height of the Money Bill dispute. The by-election was caused by the death of Charles Coote (**0479**). His return gave the administration a much-needed vote, and in June 1754 the Primate personally celebrated his marriage to Lord Belvidere's only daughter, Jane. He held the Revenue post of Clerk of the Pipe and was a solid government supporter, voting against the expulsion of Arthur Jones-Nevill (**1125**) and for the Money Bill. He was listed for 114 committees between 1751 and 1760.

In the 1761 election he stood again, and was returned, for the county. However, the election was hard fought. At the end of polling on 19 May 1761 the poll for Co. Cavan stood as follows: Lord Newtown-Butler, 506 votes; Hon. Barry Maxwell (**1372**), 467; Charles Coote (**0480**), 466; George Montgomery (**1438**), 436. It was then urged that the sheriff, Sir Archibald Acheson (**0001**), should declare Butler and Maxwell duly elected. Acheson said he was of the opinion that his power did not expire with the return of the writ, and that he would continue to take the suffrage of each freeholder that should offer himself. As a result the poll did not close until 23 May, when it stood as follows: Lord Newtown-Butler, 612; Charles Coote, 600; George Montgomery, 549; Hon. Barry Maxwell, 477. Butler and Coote were declared duly elected.

In 1761 he was made a Commissioner of the Revenue, then under the control of Speaker Ponsonby (1702), whom he supported over the augmentation crisis; in 1770 he was dismissed from the Revenue Board and struck off the Privy Council. Two years earlier he had succeeded his father as 2nd Earl of Lanesborough. Nevertheless, he had two boroughs and he was restored to the Privy Council by Lord Harcourt, who also obtained for him a pension of £1,200 in place of his seat on the Revenue Board. In 1775 he was described as 'an amiable unfortunate man, strongly attached to Lord Harcourt ... [who] ... has given to his recommendation the Distributor of Stamps for Cavan' and other patronage. He supported government, and his connections and followers were John Cramer (Coghill) (0512) and Charles Stewart (2000). The family were poor, and his two boroughs were both disposed of for the 1776 election.

In 1777 he was described as 'a most amiable and universally esteemed man, unfortunate in his domestic situation and though possessed of a good family property very embarrassed in his circumstances. His Excellency has given to his recommendation the Free School of Cavan worth £500 p.a., a living of £400 to Mr Coghill's brother, obtained for him 2 Ensigncies, gave him 2 Supernumerary Tidewaiters, 4 Gaugers, 2 Hearth Money Collections and 1 Walking Officer' – very substantial patronage which must have owed something to his attractive personality.

The family fortunes looked up in 1781 when his son and heir married the beautiful and wealthy Elizabeth La Touche, the daughter of the banker David La Touche (1203): as part of her dowry she restored to the family the borough of Belturbet which they had sold and were to sell again.

DIVISION LISTS:
1753 (1) voted against the expulsion of Arthur Jones-Nevill (1125) – Joint Clerk of the Pipe.
1753 (2) voted for the Money Bill.
1757 (1) voted for the resolutions on pensions.

ADDITIONAL INFORMATION: Junior Grand Warden of the Grand Lodge of Irish Freemasons, 1751–3; Deputy Grand Master, 1753–6; Grand Master, 1757. His brother-in-law George Rochfort, 2nd Earl of Belvidere (1800), was Grand Master in 1774.

Freedom of Dublin, 3 April 1761. *A member of the Royal Dublin Society from 1762.

ESTATES/RESIDENCE: Lanesborough, Co. Longford; Sans Souci House (between the Stillorgan Road and Booterstown), Co. Dublin.

SOURCES: PRONI D/302; PRONI D/3000/99 Robinson Genealogical notes [says he married 26 Jan. 1754]; PRONI T/618/328 Crossle Papers; HMC Stopford-Sackville I p. 214; McCracken thesis; GEC P; Index to Irish Privy Counsellors, 1711–1910; Hughes, Pat. Officers; J. H. Lepper and P. Crossle, History of the Grand Lodge of Free and Accepted Masons of Ireland (Dublin, 1925), vol. 1, p. 235; Ir. Gen. vol. 7 no 2 (1987) p. 262, H. F. Morris, 'Finn's Leinster Journal 1768'; Almanacks; Esdall's Newsletter 1 Apr. 1752; DJ 16 Feb. 1754, 4–7 Apr., 19–23, 23–6 May 1761; Parliamentary Lists 1775 (1), 1777 (1).

0314 BUTLER, Hon. Edmund

MP for Co. Kilkenny 1776–9

b. 17 July 1745; d. 15 July 1793 at his house in St Stephen's Green after 3 days' illness (allegedly brought on by eating strawberries and drinking cider)
PEERAGES: Suc. as 11th Viscount Mountgarret 1779.
FAMILY/BACKGROUND: Eldest son of Rt Hon. Edmund Butler, 10th Viscount Mountgarret, and Charlotte, dau. of Sir Simon Bradstreet.
MARRIED: [7 Oct. 1768] Henrietta (d. 1785), 2nd dau. of Somerset Hamilton Butler, 1st Earl of Carrick.
CHILDREN: Edmund (b. 6 Jan. 1771; d.s.p. 16 July 1846), 12th Viscount Mountgarret and 1st Earl

of Kilkenny, m. [8 June 1793] Mildred, dau. of Robert Fowler, Abp of Dublin; Somerset Richard (b. Dec. 1771; *d.s.p.* 1826), m. Jane, e. dau. of Arthur French, wid. of Daniel Kelly; Henry (b. 16 Feb. 1773; d. 6 Dec. 1842), m. [1811] Anne (d. 1857), yst dau. and co-h. of John Harrison of Yorkshire; Pierce (b. 6 May 1774; d. 1846), m. [1800] Anne (d. 1872), dau. of Thomas March of Lisburn, Co. Antrim; Charlotte Juliana (b. 6 Aug 1778), m. [7 Aug. 1799] Col. John Carrington Smith.

EDUCATION: School: Westminster 1754 (in Mrs Hawkins' boarding house in 1757); Middle Temple 21 Apr. 1763.

POLITICAL ACTIVITY: When he came into parliament he was described as 'a gloomy, determined, young man and strongly opposed personally and politically to Mr Flood (**0762**) the Vice Treasurer', and also as 'very embarrassed in his circumstances'. Nevertheless, he was 'independent' and 'always in opposition'. He was considered an excellent scholar, especially regarding the law and the constitution, and was listened to as a good and logical speaker. He was only three years in the House of Commons before, in 1779, he succeeded his father as 11th Viscount Mountgarret, and in the House of Lords he continued to be in opposition to the government. During his brief time in the House of Commons he was 'an infrequent attender'.

DIVISION LISTS:

1777 (1) voted for Grattan's (**0895**) motion for retrenchment.
1777 (2) voted against the Trade Embargo.
1778 (1) voted for Grattan's motion for retrenchment.
1778 (2) voted against the Popery Bill.

ADDITIONAL INFORMATION: 'On 6 June 1790 a duel took place between Lord Mountgarret and Counsellor Bu[s]he. Lord Mountgarret obtained the right of discharging the first shot. Counsellor B[ushe] received the fire and the ball went in a straight direction along his right hand which held the pistol, the butt of which, most unfortunately broke its direction, as the ball rebounded from the butt of the pistol against the immediate vital part of Counsellor B[ushe]'s stomach, penetrated his waistcoat and shirt and so severely hurt him as to drive him in a staggering position several paces

back; the seconds immediately ran to his aid and in about seven or eight minutes returned with him to the ground but in so feeble and weak a situation from the hurt he had received as to be allowed by the seconds not to be able to fire.' Lord Moungarret remained on the ground until the seconds had made this declaration and 'expressed great uneasiness that Counsellor B[ushe] was so dangerously hurt'. The alleged cause of the duel was claims made by Counsellor B[ushe] that Lord Mountgarret prevented witnesses from attending to give evidence at a trial by bribing them to keep away.

ESTATES/RESIDENCE: Ballyconra, Co. Kilkenny; St Stephen's Green, Dublin. In 1698 the Mountgarret estates included 11,492 acres; Mountgarret itself consists of 195 acres in Co. Wexford. In 1883 they consisted of 14,073 acres in Co. Kilkenny, 505 in Co. Wexford, and 120 in the West Riding of Yorkshire. Total 14,698 acres, worth £9,606 p.a.

Lord Mountgarret granted a 999-year lease of Seskin Mountgarret (460 statute acres) in 1786, and a perpetuity of Sheeptown (102 Irish acres) in 1790. In 1787 he let Tennislattery, barony of Galmoy, to Edward Butler of Tennislattery Lodge. Just after the Union Wakefield estimated that the Mountgarret (Kilkenny) rental was £8,000.

SOURCES: RCBL, Parish Register of St Werburgh's, Dublin [bapt. 16 July 1745]; Ellis thesis; GEC *P*; Kilkenny MPs; G. F. Russell-Barker and A .H. Stenning (eds), *Record of Old Westminsters: A Biographical List*, 2 vols (London, 1928); *Middle Temple Admissions* vol. I p. 360; *FJ* 21–4 Feb. 1778, 5–8 June 1790; J. Kelly, '*That Damn'd Thing Called Honour': Duelling in Ireland 1570–1860* (Cork, 1995), p. 201; *DJ* 11, 18 June, 18 July 1793; NLI reps no 168; PRONI D/1201/42 and 43, Landed Estates Court 1860, and Encumbered Estates rental 1854; NLI EC 5088, EC 6568 [Abstract begins with marriage settlement of Edmond and Henrietta dau. of Somerset Butler, Lord Carrick in 1768]; Wakefield, *Account of Ire.*, vol. 1 p. 264; Parliamentary Lists, 1776 (1), (2), (3), 1777 (1), 1778 (1), 1782 (1), 1787 (1), 1788 (1).

0315 BUTLER, Francis

MP for Belturbet (1662–6), 1692–3, 1695–9

b. 1634; d. 15 Aug. 1702
FAMILY/BACKGROUND: Son of Sir Stephen Butler Kt

of Co. Cavan and Mary, dau. and co-h. of Gervais Brinsley of Nottinghamshire.

MARRIED: Judith, dau. of Rt Hon. Sir Theophilus Jones of Co. Meath.

CHILDREN: 5 s. and 5 dau.: Rt Hon. Theophilus, 1st Baron Newton-Butler (0329); Rt Hon. Brinsley, 1st Viscount Lanesborough (0312); James (0319); Mary Judith.

CAREER/OCCUPATION: Usher of Chancery 2 Mar. 1691.

MILITARY: Fought on the Royalist side in the Civil War.

POLITICAL ACTIVITY: He sat in the 1662 parliament of Charles II, thus in 1692 he was one of the very few MPs with previous parliamentary experience. During the brief 1692 parliament he was nominated for a committee that sat on 11 and 12 October. In the 1695–9 parliament he supported Lord Chancellor Porter against accusations of favouring Catholics, and in 1696 he signed the Association for the protection of William III in parliament. He was nominated for 15 committees. He was the ancestor of the Butlers, Earls of Lanesborough.

ESTATES/RESIDENCE: Belturbet, Co. Cavan.

SOURCES: PRONI T/559, Burke, extract pedigrees, vol. 13 p. 312; Burke *PB* (1906) p. 953; GEC *P*; Cavan MPs; Lodge *P* [says he died 15 Aug. 1702 aged 68 years; Lodge says he fought for Charles I during the rebellion, he would have been young as a contemporary deposition was made by his stepfather, Mr Philpot, of how as a child along with his mother, brothers and sisters, he has been forced off the land during the 1641 rebellion]; C. Dalton (ed.), *Irish Army Lists 1661–85* (London, 1907) pp. 20, 22 [says Francis Butler, probable son of Sir Francis Butler, who fought on the Royalist side during the Civil War, was a Cornet in the Duke of Ormonde's Regiment 1661, a Lieutenant in the Life Guards 1663, and Lieutenant Colonel of the same in 1685]; Hughes, *Pat. Officers*; Parliamentary Lists, 1695 (1), 1696 (1).

0316 BUTLER, Hon. Henry Thomas

MP for Killyleagh 1768–74

b. 19 May 1746; d. 20 July 1813

PEERAGES: Suc. 2nd Earl of Carrick 1774.

FAMILY/BACKGROUND: Eldest son of Somerset Hamilton Butler, 1st Earl of Carrick, and Juliana,

dau. of Henry Boyle, 1st Earl of Shannon (0210).

MARRIED: [7 Aug. 1774] Sarah, dau. and co-h. of Edward Taylor (2040).

CHILDREN: Somerset Richard (b. 28 Sept. 1779; d. 4 Feb. 1838), 3rd Earl of Carrick, m. [1811] Anne, e. dau. of Owen Wynne (2265), (2) Lucy, dau. of Arthur French; Gen. Henry Edward (b. 3 Dec. 1780; d. 7 Dec.1856), m. (1) [1812] Jane (d. 30 Aug. 1834), dau. of Clotworthy Gowan, (2) [1836] Frances Mauleverer (d. 27 June 1844), 2nd dau. of John Parker Toulson; Rev. Pierce (b. 1782; d. 30 June 1866), m. [1806] Mary Sophia, dau. of John Vernon; Rev. James (b. 26 Apr. 1791; d. unmar. 1834); Anne (d. 29 May 1831), m. [5 Sept. 1798] Rev. Henry Maxwell, 6th Baron Farnham; Juliana (d. 1861), m. Somerset Lowry-Corry, 2nd Earl of Belmore (1270); Harriet (d. 25 July 1865), m. Francis Savage (1887) of Holywood, Co. Down; Sarah (d. 1839), m. Hon. Charles Harward Butler Clarke Southwell Wandesford.

CAREER/OCCUPATION: He and his brother (0325) were elected Common Councilmen of Kilkenny 15 Apr. 1780.

MILITARY: Captain in Thomastown Cavalry 1796.

POLITICAL ACTIVITY: He was returned for Killyleagh, Co. Down in 1768 because Sir John Blackwood (0148), who controlled the borough, was sovereign and returning officer. As such he could not return himself. Lord Carrick controlled one seat for the borough of Bangor and either he or Lord Bangor, who had the other seat, returned Blackwood for that borough. He was a government supporter – Lord Townshend had obtained a pension of £1,000 for his father, a company for his brother and a living of £200 for his friend. He was considered to be 'a young man of spirit and honour. A warm supporter, has one pension now, and will have 2 Members in the next Parliament, asks for a pension of £200 for an old gentleman of 76.' He voted against Catholic relief in 1774. His father was a noted anti-Catholic and an implacable enemy of the Whiteboys; he was also energetic in securing the prosecution and execution at Clonmel, 15 March 1766, of Father Sheehy, a Roman Catholic priest accused of murder and Whiteboyism and finally convicted on dubious evidence.

He succeeded his father as 2nd Earl of Carrick in 1774. He controlled two seats in parliament: one for the borough of Askeaton, through his wife, and the other for the borough of Bangor. Lord Harcourt gave to his recommendation a Hearth Money collection, Distributor of Stamps, and in 1777 he obtained a pension of £200 for his friend Mr Maul. In politics he was attached to his cousin, Lord Shannon. By the 1790s he sold his parliamentary seats, 'not aspiring to more political influence than what is attached to his Peerage'.

DIVISION LISTS:

1771 (1) voted for Lord Townshend as Lord Lieutenant.

1771 (2) voted against Sir Lucius O'Brien's (**1558**) motion for retrenchment.

1772 (2) voted against a Short Revenue Bill.

1773 (1) voted against Absentee Tax.

1773 (2) voted against an untaxed press.

1774 (1) voted for the Stamp Bill.

1774 (2) voted against Catholic relief.

ESTATES/RESIDENCE: Mount Juliet, Ballylinch; Co. Kilkenny. According to Wakefield, Lord Carrick had a rental of £5,000–£6,000.

SOURCES: NLI EEC rentals 1855 and 1851; PRONI D/1201/30 and 68; NLI vol. 7, 6 Dec. 1850; Wakefield, *Account of Ire.*, vol. 1 p. 264; RCBL P45/2/3, Parish Registers of St Peter's, Dublin; GEC *P*, Burke *PB* (1903) p. 277 (1906) p. 299; W. P. Burke, *History of Clonmel* (reprinted Kilkenny, 1983), pp. 367, 397; Hughes, *Pat. Officers*; B. De Breffny and Rosemary Ffolliott, *The Houses of Ireland* (Dublin, 1975), p. 155; *DJ* 15–18 Apr. 1780; *FJ* 15 Nov. 1796; Parliamentary Lists, 1769 (1), 1772 (2), 1773 (1), (2), 1775 (1), 1777 (1), 1782 (1), 1783 (2), 1787 (1), 1788 (1), 1790 (1), 1791 (1), 1793 (1), 1799 (3).

0317 BUTLER, Rt Hon. Humphrey

MP for Belturbet 1725–7–36

b. *c.* 1700; d. 11 Apr. 1768 at Stephen's Green, Dublin
HONOURS: PC 1755–d. (sworn 15 Nov. 1759).
PEERAGES: Suc. as 2nd Viscount Lanesborough 1735/6; cr. Earl of Lanesborough 20 July 1756.
FAMILY/BACKGROUND: Eldest son of Brinsley Butler, 1st Viscount Lanesborough (**0312**), and Catherine, dau. of Neville Pooley of Dublin.
MARRIED: [14 May 1726] Mary [d. 19 Dec. 1761], dau. and h. of William Berry (**0129**).
CHILDREN: Rt Hon. Brinsley, 2nd Earl of

Lanesborough (**0313**).
EDUCATION: LLD *hon. caus.* TCD 1730; Bencher King's Inns 1756.
CAREER/OCCUPATION: Governor of Co. Cavan 1746–60; High Sheriff of Co. Cavan 1727, Co. Westmeath 1728, 1763; Attorney of the Exchequer *c.* 1734; Commissioner and Keeper of the Great Seal 1760–8; *Trustee of the Linen Board for Connaught 1734–68; *Governor of the Workhouse 1733–63; *Commissioner of the Tillage Act for Ulster 1735, 1740–d.; *Governor of the Blue-Coat Hospital 1747–67 (Vice-Principal 1756–8); *Governor of Erasmus Smith's Schools and other Charities 1743–67; *Commissioner of Oyer and Terminer 1743–9; *member of the Committee of Fifteen in the Incorporated Society (Charter Schools) of Dublin 1756–60; *Governor of Dr Steeven's Hospital 1759–d.; Speaker of the House of Lords in 1760 during the Lord Chancellor's illness.
MILITARY: Captain of the Battle-Axe Guards.

POLITICAL ACTIVITY: He was listed for 20 committees between 1729 and 1735. In 1736 he succeeded as 2nd Viscount Lanesborough and his career thereafter was in the House of Lords. He was a leading participant in local and central government as well as in the various social activities of the capital. He was a leading Freemason. In 1756 he was created Earl of Lanesborough.

ADDITIONAL INFORMATION: Deputy Grand Master of the Grand Lodge of Irish Freemasons, 1725.

A foundation member of the Royal Dublin Society, 1731; Vice-President, 1750–58, 1760–68; President, 1759; named in the Charter of 1750.

Chairman of the Incorporate Society of Dublin, for promoting English Protestant schools in Ireland, April 1757.

ESTATES/RESIDENCE: Lanesborough, Co. Longford; St Stephen's Green, Dublin.

In 1726, at the time of his marriage to Miss Berry she was supposed to have £800 a year in land and £12,000 in cash. [Wardenstown estate?]

SOURCES: PRONI D/302; NLI Mahon of Castlegar Papers, Knightly Chetwood to Dr John Ussher, 11 Apr. and 14 May 1726; McCracken thesis; Burke *PB* (1903) p. 884; *Index to Irish Privy Counsellors, 1711–1910*; *King's Inns Admissions*; J. H. Lepper and P. Crossle, *History of the Grand Lodge of Free and Accepted Masons of Ireland* (Dublin, 1925), vol. 1; *Ir. Gen.* vol. 7 no 2 (1987) p. 262, H. F. Morris, 'Finn's Leinster Journal 1768' [says incorrectly he was cr. Earl of Lanesborough 3 July 1756];

Berry RDS pp. 24–7, 76–7; *Almanacks*; *BNL* 10 May 1757.

0318 BUTLER, Humphrey

MP for Donegal B. 1790–7

b. 7 Aug. 1767; d. [Oct.] 1837
FAMILY/BACKGROUND: Only son of Hon. John Butler (**0321**) and Anne, wid. of March Harrison of Co. Kildare.
MARRIED: Alicia, dau. of Michael White, Governor of Montserrat.
CHILDREN: Maj. Theophilus (4th Dragoon Guards); Rev. Robert, m. Miss Hamilton; Humphrey, m. [1852] Eliza Margaret, e. dau. of William Tewart of Northumberland; Maria Frances; Sophia Maria, m. Frederick Montgomerie of Norfolk.
EDUCATION: Entered TCD 14 Oct. 1785, aged 18 years; Cambridge (St John's College) 3 Apr. 1787; Middle Temple, 3 Feb. 1786; King's Inns 1786.
CAREER/OCCUPATION: Clerk of the Pipe, Exchequer 6 Dec. 1780–8; *Governor of the Hibernian Marine Society 1799 (f.); he was in the Revenue side of the Exchequer 1800 (f.).

POLITICAL ACTIVITY: He was returned for Donegal town, a close borough belonging to Lord Arran (**0861**), in the 1790 election. 'The seats were sold by Lord Arran to Sir J. Browne now Lord Kilmaine (**0259**), who gave them to Government for his Peerage and as the story goes, betrayed the transaction to the opposition, hence the clamour *upon the Sale of Peerages*. Mr Downes (**0658**) [the other MP] is an eminent lawyer and countenanced very deservedly by the Chancellor (**0749**) and Attorney General (**2243**). He was brought in I believe without paying. Mr Butler having an office was made to pay. He is Clerk of the Pipe', a legal office in the Court of Exchequer. As an office-holder he supported the government.

He stood unsuccessfully for Co. Fermanagh in 1797; the result of the poll was: John W. Cole (**0441**), 804 votes; Colonel Mervyn Archdall (**0050**), 751; Henry Brooke (**0249**), 279; Humphrey Butler, 97. Cole and Archdall were returned, and Butler did not come into parliament again.

DIVISION LISTS:
1790 (2) absent (tied).

ESTATES/RESIDENCE: Clermont, Co. Dublin; Gloucester Place, Marylebone, Middlesex.

SOURCES: Burke *PB* (1903) p. 885 (1906) p. 954; Hughes, *Pat. Officers*; IMC *King's Inns Admission Papers, 1607–1867*; *Alum. Cantab.*; H. A. C. Sturgess, *Register of Admissions to the Honourable Society of the Middle Temple* (London, 1949), vol. 2 p. 399; *Ir. Gen.* vol. 6 no 6 (Nov. 1985) pp. 757–70, H. F. Morris, 'Finn's Leinster Journal, 1767, Births, Marriages and Deaths' [says his mother gave birth to a son, 7 Aug. 1767]; *Almanacks*; *FJ* 5 Aug. 1797; Parliamentary Lists, 1791 (1), 1793 (1), 1794 (1), (2).

0319 BUTLER, James

MP for Clonmines 1703–13; Newcastle 1735–42

b. 1681; d. 19 Nov. 1742
FAMILY/BACKGROUND: Son of Francis Butler (**0315**) and Judith, dau. of Rt Hon. Sir Theophilus Jones.
MARRIED: Anne, dau. of Joseph Stopford, Bp of Cloyne.
CHILDREN: *d.s.p.*
EDUCATION: School: Kilkenny College 18 Oct. 1694, aged 13 years; Middle Temple 22 Sept. 1700.
CAREER/OCCUPATION: Governor of the Royal Hospital, Kilmainham 1732, 1736–41; *at the College of Physicians 1739.
MILITARY: Captain in Ormonde's Regiment; Adjutant General 29 Sept. 1722, 1729–41; Captain of a Troop of Horse Guards 1739–40; Quarter Master General and Barrack Master General 1741–2; *Lieutenant General 1742; *Provost Martial 1754–5.

POLITICAL ACTIVITY: Despite his legal education he appears to have been a professional soldier and, as such, a supporter of the administration. On 25 September 1704 Captain James Butler wrote to Ormonde asking for a company in the new Regiment of Guards and a lieutenancy for his son. In 1706 he was noted as an administration supporter, and the following year he was possibly one of the 34 Tory MPs who met at the Fleece Tavern to coordinate government tactics for the ensuing session. In 1711 he supported the government over the Dublin mayoralty dispute, and was recorded as a government supporter. The administration correctly forecast that he would not be returned for Clonmines in 1713, but hoped for 'a good man in his stead'. He was listed for 19 committees during the 1703–11 parliament.

There was then a gap in his service, which may be on account of his military service or, as Newcastle was a family borough, due to the fact that his return was as a 'seat warmer' for his nephew, John (0321), who succeeded him. He was returned for the Newcastle by-election following the death, in September 1734, of James Coghill (0430), and was listed for five committees between 1735 and his death in 1742.

DIVISION LISTS:
1711 (1) voted for the Court on the Dublin mayoralty issue.

ADDITIONAL INFORMATION: A foundation member of the Dublin Society, 1731.

ESTATES/RESIDENCE: Newtown and Creevyquin, Co. Roscommon; Jackson Upper, Clara, Mustard Garden and the tithes of Killaghy and Lackanny, Kilkenny. Also estates in Co. Longford; Chequer Lane, New Street and St Stephen's Green, Dublin.

SOURCES: PRONI T/559, Burke, extract pedigrees, vol. 14 p. 14; McCracken thesis; Hayton thesis; *HMC Ormonde* new ser. vol. 8 pp. 116, 326; C. Dalton, *George the First's Army, 1714–27*; Eustace, *Abstracts of Wills*; *Middle Temple Admissions* vol. 1 p. 248; *JRSAI* vol. 54 (1924) pp. 55–67. T. U. Sadleir, 'The Register of Kilkenny School (1685–1800)'; Berry *RDS* pp. 24–7; *Almanacks*; Parliamentary Lists, 1706 (1), 1707 (2), 1711 (3), 1713 (1).

0320 BUTLER (-WANDESFORD), Hon. James

MP for Kilkenny city Mar.–June 1796 (never took his seat); [Escheator of Ulster 28 May 1796]; Co. Kilkenny 1796–7–1800; [UK] 1801–20

b. 15 July 1774; d. 18 May 1838
HONOURS: Knight of St Patrick 20 Aug. 1821; Knight 16 July 1826.
PEERAGES: Suc. as 19th Earl of Ormonde, 12th Earl of Ossory, 1820; cr. Baron Ormonde [UK] 17 July

1821, Marquess of Ormonde 5 Oct. 1825.
FAMILY/BACKGROUND: Son of John Butler, 17th Earl of Ormonde and 10th Earl of Ossory (0322), and Frances Susan Elizabeth, dau. and sole h. of John Wandesford, 1st Earl of Wandesford.
MARRIED: [12 Oct. 1807] Grace Louisa, dau. of Rt Hon. John Staples (1985).
CHILDREN: John (b. 24 Aug. 1808; d. 25 Sept. 1854) 2nd Marquess of Ormonde, m. [19 Sept. 1843] Frances Jane, e. dau. of Gen. the Hon. Sir Edward Paget; Walter Wandesford (b. 14 Jan. 1814; d. 18 July 1861); James Wandesford (b. 18 May 1815; d. 13 Dec. 1893), m. [3 Apr. 1856] Rachel Evelyn [21 Feb. 1898], dau. of John Russell, 6th Duke of Bedford; Richard Molesworth Wandesford (b. 13 Jan. 1818; d. 3 Feb. 1838); Charles Wandesford (b. 7 Feb. 1820; d. unmar. 30 Oct. 1857); Harriet Eleanor (d. 28 Sept 1885), m. [1831] Robert Fowler, Bp of Ossory; Anne (d. 28 Nov. 1849), m. [1838] Rt Hon. John Wynne; Louisa Grace (d. 8 Nov. 1896), m. [26 Sept. 1840] Thomas Fortescue, 1st Baron Clermont; Elizabeth (d. 1 Oct. 1892); Mary Charlotte (d. 10 Oct. 1840).
EDUCATION: School: Eton 1783–90.
CAREER/OCCUPATION: Vice Admiral of Leinster; *Joint Governor of Co. Leitrim 1795; *Sovereign of Carlow 1799 (f.); Magistrate of Carlow 1799 (f.); Trustee of the Linen Board 1802; Alderman of Kilkenny, Mayor 1808–9, 1814–15; Lord Lieutenant and Custos Rot. Co. Kilkenny 1831–8.
MILITARY: Cornet 31 Oct. 1790; Lieutenant 31 Mar. 1792; Captain 14th Dragoons Guards 1 Mar. 1793; First Lieutenant in Killenaule Cavalry 1796; Major 19 Feb. 1799; retired 1802; Lieutenant Colonel of Kilkenny Militia 4 Feb. 1806; Colonel 1820–d.; Militia aide-de-camp (extra.) to the King 1832–7, to the Queen 1837–8, Hereditary Chief Butler.

POLITICAL ACTIVITY: Some indication of the influence of the Ormonde family in Kilkenny is given by the changes in the political representation for Co. Kilkenny and Kilkenny city in the first half of 1796. In December 1795 the MP's father John, 17th Earl of Ormonde (0322), died and was succeeded by his eldest son Walter (0333), then MP for Co. Kilkenny. His next brother, John Butler-Wandesford (0323), then sitting for Kilkenny city, accepted the Escheatorship of Munster in order to be returned for Co. Kilkenny. This MP, the third brother, was elected for Kilkenny city in March 1796. Parliament went into recess on 15

April and he never took his seat. Then in April his brother, John, died in London after a few hours' illness and James accepted the Escheatorship of Ulster in order to be returned for Co. Kilkenny in his place, although a general election was pending in 1797 at which he was again duly returned for the county. Both Kilkenny city and Co. Kilkenny were among the most open constituencies in the Irish parliament.

He was in lukewarm opposition, voting against Parsons' (**1636**) motion in 1798, for the Union in 1799 and against the Union in 1800, although he supported the government in 1799 over Lord Corry's (**0497**) motion for a 'Committee to inquire into the state of the Nation' – a holding motion by the anti-Unionists, which was defeated by 123 votes to 103, indicating that despite their initial defeat the Unionists were gaining ground.

At Westminster Butler was expected to support government, but he and his brother were friends of the Prince of Wales. Not surprisingly, he consistently supported the Catholic claims. In general he was considered to support the administration, 'but not warmly'.

DIVISION LISTS:

1798 (1) voted against Sir Laurence Parsons' (**1636**) motion for an investigation into 'the present discontents'.
1799 (1) voted for the Union.
1800 (1) voted against the Union.

ADDITIONAL INFORMATION: His eldest brother, the 18th Earl of Ormonde, controlled one seat for Co. Kilkenny and, in conjunction with Lord Desart, one for Kilkenny city.

ESTATES/RESIDENCE: Castlecomer and Kilkenny Castle, Co. Kilkenny. His eldest brother, the 18th Earl of Ormonde, whom he succeeded in 1820, possessed estates worth £22,000 p.a. in 1799.

SOURCES: Burke, *PB* (1903); PRONI T/3166/1B Hartnell notes; PRONI MIC/315/8/40 Blackwood pedigrees; RCBL P277/1/5, Parish Registers of St Mary's, Dublin [bur. 25 May 1838]; O'Neill thesis; Jupp thesis; GEC *P*; *HP 1790–1820*; Hughes *Pat. Officers*; R. A. Austen-Leigh (ed.), *The Eton College Register, 1753–90*, 3 vols (Eton, 1921); Kilkenny MPs; G. C. Bolton, *The Passing of the Irish Act of Union*, pp. 120–21, 170 and n. 1; *Almanacks*; *FJ* 12 Nov. 1796; Parliamentary Lists, 1799 (2), (3), 1800 (3).

0321 BUTLER, Hon. John

MP for Newcastle 1743–60, 1761–8–76–83 [r. Belturbet 1761]

b. 1703; d. 14 Dec. 1789 at Primrose Hill, Co. Dublin
FAMILY/BACKGROUND: Son of Rt Hon. Brinsley Butler, 1st Viscount Lanesborough (**0312**), and Catherine, dau. of Neville Pooley of Dublin.
MARRIED: Anne, wid. of March Harrison of Co. Kildare.
CHILDREN: Humphrey (**0318**); Catherine, m. Thomas Carter of Co. Kildare; Harriet, m. Henry Brooke of Co. Fermanagh; Mary.
CAREER/OCCUPATION: Joint Clerk of the Pipe 7 June 1735–78; Clerk of the Pipe 1779–88; Proctor of the High Court of Admiralty 1755; *Magistrate of Belturbet 1742, Newcastle 1752; Governor of the Workhouse 1750–68, Foundling Hospital and Workhouse 1771–88; *Sovereign of Newcastle 1754, *Portreeve 1755; *elected to the Court of Assistants 1766–9, 1773; *Governor of the Hibernian Marine Society 1775–81; Committee of Fifteen 1784–89, *Commissioner for Paving the Streets of Dublin 1778–80; Freedom of the Guild of Merchants, 12 Oct. 1761.

POLITICAL ACTIVITY: He was elected on the death of his uncle (**0319**) for the family borough of Newcastle. Subsequently, he was brought in successively by his nephew (**0313**) 'who has entire possession of this borough which my Lord will soon sell as [he] is greatly in debt and very poor' and great-nephew. He was Clerk of the Pipe, an Exchequer office worth £1,200 p.a., for life. Having an office for life made him independent, and by the late 1770s he apparently possessed the office for two lives with £150 p.a. addition during pleasure. When he first came into parliament he followed the administration, voting for the expulsion of James Digges la Touche (♦♦♦), against the expulsion of Arthur Jones-Nevill (**1125**) and for the Money Bill.

He was a friend of Sir Henry Cavendish (**0380**). On 12 March 1756 on a list of money borrowed from the government through the newly appointed Teller of the Exchequer, Cavendish, he is noted as having mortgaged £1,000. He followed his nephew, Lord Lanesborough, in politics and was against Lord Townshend's administration but for Lord Harcourt's; the latter gave the recommendation of an ensigncy to his relation, Mr Harris. In 1777 he attempted to fight a duel with Henry Flood, who had challenged the return of Edmund Butler (**0314**) for Co. Kilkenny in the recent election, but was prevented by the Speaker.

Lord Buckinghamshire joined his son's name to his in the patent. Apparently he tried to buy the borough from his great-great nephew, Lord Lanesborough, but at the last moment Lord Lanesborough sold it to Lord Belmore (**1269**). In 1783 he was 'an old man, but very hale and active'. Although he was 80 years of age, it was felt that as he had such a good employment he ought to find himself a seat: this he did not do.

DIVISION LISTS:

1749 (1) voted against the election of James Digges La Touche (♦♦♦♦).
1753 (1) voted against the expulsion of Arthur Jones-Nevill (**1125**) – Joint Clerk of the Pipe.
1753 (2) voted for the Money Bill.
1757 (1) voted for the resolutions on pensions.
1768 (1) voted against army augmentation – Clerk of the Pipe for life.
1771 (2) voted for Sir Lucius O'Brien's (**1558**) motion for retrenchment.
1773 (1) voted for Absentee Tax.
1774 (1) voted for the Stamp Bill.
1774 (2) voted against Catholic relief.
1775 (1) voted against the pro-American amendment to the Speech from the Throne.
1779 (2) voted against a six-months Loan Bill.
1780 (3) voted for the Tenantry Bill.

ADDITIONAL INFORMATION: One of ten MPs fined by Justice Robinson for failing to attend petty juries. A committee of inquiry found that Robinson had violated the House's privileges.

ESTATES/RESIDENCE: Molesworth Street, Dublin.

SOURCES: PRONI T/3019/6457/464 Wilmot Papers; RCBL T34, Extracts from the Parish Registers of St Andrew's, Dublin; McCracken thesis; Ellis thesis; Burke *PR* (1903) p. 884; J. Walton, 'The King's Business'. Letters on the Administration of Ireland, 1741–61 (NY, 1996) no 267; J. Kelly, 'That Damn'd Thing Called Honour': Duelling in Ireland 1570–1860 (Cork, 1995),

pp. 142–3; *Almanacks*; *Pue's Occurrences* 1 Jan. 1751; *DJ* 25 Feb. – 1 Mar. 1755 , 13–17 Oct. 1761, 22–4 Dec. 1789; *FJ* 5–7 Mar. 1772; Parliamentary Lists, 1769 (1), 1772 (2), 1773 (1), (2), 1774 (1), 1775 (1), 1776 (1), (2), (3), 1777 (1), 1778 (1), 1780 (1), 1782 (1), 1783 (1).

0322 BUTLER, John

MP for Gowran 1776–83; Kilkenny city 1783–90–1

b. 10 Dec. 1740; d. 30 Dec. 1795 at Kilkenny Castle

PEERAGES: Suc. as 17th Earl of Ormonde and 10th Earl of Ossory 1791.

FAMILY/BACKGROUND: Only son of Walter Butler, 16th Earl of Ormonde, and Eleanor, e. dau. of Nicholas Morris of Co. Dublin.

MARRIED: [14 Feb. 1769] Frances Susan Elizabeth, o. ch. and h. of John Wandesford, 1st Earl of Wandesford.

CHILDREN: Hon. Walter (b. 1770), 18th Earl of Ormonde (**0333**); John (**0323**); James, 1st Marquess of Ormonde (**0320**); Charles Harward Butler Clarke Southwell Wandesford (b. 1781; d. 7 Nov. 1860), m. (1) [12 Oct.1812] Sarah (d. 7 July 1838), dau. of Henry Thomas Butler, 2nd Earl of Carrick (**0316**), (2) [1842] Lucy (b. 1800; d. 1884), Countess Dowager of Carrick; Elizabeth, m. Thomas Kavanagh of Borris (**1127**); Eleanor (d. Oct. 1859), m. [11 Aug. 1808; div. 1826] Cornelius O'Callaghan, 1st Viscount Lismore.

CAREER/OCCUPATION: *Deputy Clerk of Outlawries 1758; Freeman of Fethard (Tipperary) 1765; *Land Waiter, Aston's Quay 1783–4; *Governor of the Foundling Hospital and Workhouse 1790; Custos Rot. Co. Kilkenny 1793–5.

MILITARY: Colonel of the Kilkenny Rangers, Volunteers.

POLITICAL ACTIVITY: The arrival of John Butler on the political scene marked the revival of the Ormonde interest. He was returned in 1776 by purchase from Lord Clifden for the Agar borough of Gowran, and it was thought that there was an arrangement about county politics as part of the purchase. He was the only son of Walter Butler of Kilkenny Castle who, as the heir male of the senior Butler line, wanted the restoration of the

Ormonde title; the ducal title belonged to another line that was extinct. He had inherited part of the great Butler estates, which had been bought back after the attainder of the 2nd Duke, and was 'of a great fortune'. His father and mother were both Catholics but he had conformed in 1764 and married Lord Wandesford's only daughter, a great Kilkenny heiress. Lord Harcourt gave 'livings of about £200 each to his father's nominations'. He was independent, apart from his desire for the restoration of at least some of the family honours. By 1780 he was noted as inclined to Lord Shannon (**0213**) and not a good attender.

The Duke of Portland strongly supported his claims to a peerage, which regarding his Irish honours were valid anyway, although he does not appear to have realised this at this time. He 'has great influence in the town of Kilkenny and will possibly name both Members', and in fact he returned himself from 1783 until his peerage was acknowledged in 1791. In 1784 he was described as 'a very weak unsteady man and easily led by different people. Has been at times under the guidance of Mr Flood (**0762**). Has great weight with the Catholics in his Country and keeps up a Corps (chiefly Catholics) at Kilkenny, who are very lawless people. Probably a favourer of Reform. Doubtful.' In 1785 it was noted that 'Mr Butler never attended but is in opposition.' He was considered 'odd' and 'capricious', and was probably annoyed at the length of time it took him to establish his claims.

DIVISION LISTS:
    1785 (1) absent.
    1790 (2) voted for Ponsonby (**1709**) on the election of a Speaker.

ADDITIONAL INFORMATION: *A member of the Royal Dublin Society from 1768.

'He is also premier Earl of the kingdom. This title has lain dormant since the beginning of the reign of George I till within these few years, when it was claimed by John, the late Earl, before the Irish House of Lords, which decided in his favour. James, 2nd Duke of Ormonde, was suspected of having entered into a cabal with the Lords *Oxford*, *Bolingbroke*, etc. to restore the excluded family of Stuart. On the accession of George I his

Grace was attacked by the whole power of an irritated Government and fearing to abide the event, fled to France, where he shortly [1745!] after died. In the mean time, the English parliament passed an Act of attainder, which deprived him of his Dukedom and numerous other Honours in England and Ireland, and forfeited to the Crown his princely domains in both kingdoms.

'As this act was passed in the English parliament *only*, Mr John Butler, representative of the house of Ormonde, taking advantage of the declaration of its independence by the *Irish* Parliament, conformed to the Church of Ireland, and preferred his claim to the Irish Honours of his family, which was allowed.

'An idea may be formed of the magnitude of the property forfeited by the Duke of *Ormonde* from this circumstance. The portion of their ancient inheritance, now preserved to the family, would let for near £50,000 per annum and this was not more than the *jointure* of the last Duchess, who being of a mild and irreproachable character, was suffered, notwithstanding the attainder of the Duke her husband, to retain it till her death; which, having taken place many years afterwards, when party-heat had subsided, either the grandfather or great grandfather of the present Earl took possession of it without the smallest opposition on the part of Government.'

ESTATES/RESIDENCE: Kilkenny Castle, Co. Kilkenny; 11 Rutland Square, Dublin. Was heir to Wandesford estates and on the death of his father succeeded to the estates of the Earl of Arran. In 1795 there was a private member's act 'for the sale of competent parts of the real estates of the Rt Hon. John, Earl of Ormonde, and the Hon. Walter Butler, commonly called Lord Viscount Thurles, his eldest son and heir apparent, for the payment of debts charges and incumbrances, affecting the same: and for settling such part and parts thereof, as shall not be sold for the purposes aforesaid and for other purposes'. The background to this act was the will of Charles, Earl of Arran who left his estates to his sister, Lady Emilia Butler (she died unmar. at Gloucester on 30 March 1760, two months short of her 100th birthday) with remainder in tail-male to John Butler of Kilcash (conformed 16 July 1739) who died on or about 20 June 1766 with remainder in tail-male to Walter Butler of Garryricken, who married Eleanor Morris; their son John, Earl of Ormonde married, 1769 (marriage settlement on or about 13 February 1769) Lady

Anne Wandesford (aged 23), eldest daughter of John, Earl of Wandesford. Her jointure, £1,000 p.a., was charged on the former estates of Charles, Earl of Arran as was the £10,000 set aside as provision for any younger children. Three years earlier, on 25 January 1792, an earlier settlement had been made to allow the sale or mortgage of land so as to reduce the incumbrances on the remaining estate.

The Butler family of Castlecrine: in 1720, the rental was over £1,000 but the true value £1,400–1,500; 73 denominations. Unlike the other Butler estates of Clare (Ballyline, Doon, Bunnahow and Creg), this one did not derive from Act of Settlement grant, but was assembled by purchase by William Butler of Rossroe, high sheriff, 1704 and 1712. Vendors included Burtons, Westbys, MacDonnells, O'Briens, Macnamaras, Vandeleurs, Hartes, O'Dwyers, Butlers of Derryclooney (Tipperary), Drews, Purefoys, Bloods and Lysaghts (there were lawsuits with the last two). Purchase offer made via mortgage.

SOURCES: PRONI MIC/474 Irish Volunteers; Ellis thesis; GEC *P*; Burke *PB* (1903) pp. 1173–4; *Ir. Gen.* vol. 4 no 4 (1971) p. 320, W. G. Skehan, 'Extracts from the Minutes of the Corporation of Fethard, Co. Tipperary'; *DJ* 2 Jan. 1796; *Almanacks*, TCD Library 386.s.40; Parliamentary Lists, 1776 (1), (2), (3), 1777 (1), 1778 (1), 1780 (1), 1782 (1), 1783 (1), (2), 1784 (1), (2), (3), 1785 (1), (2), (3), (4), 1787 (1), 1788 (1), 1789 (1), 1790 (1), 1791 (1).

0323 BUTLER (-WANDESFORD), Hon. John

MP for Kilkenny city 1792–6, Co. Kilkenny Feb.–Apr. 1796; [Escheator of Munster 16 Feb. 1796]

b. 1772; d. (*c.* 30) Apr. 1796 in London (after a few hours' illness)
FAMILY/BACKGROUND: Son of John Butler, 17th Earl of Ormonde and 10th Earl of Ossory (0322), and Frances Susan Elizabeth, o. child and h. of John Wandesford, 1st Earl of Wandesford.
MARRIED: Unmarried.
EDUCATION: School: Eton 1783–9.
CAREER/OCCUPATION: Military: Cornet 14 Dragoons 30 June 1788; Lieutenant 31 Aug. 1790; Captain of Dragoons 31 Mar. 1792.

POLITICAL ACTIVITY: He was a professional soldier and in 1794 he was said to be in the Military Department. He supported and followed the political line laid down by his father, the Earl of Ormonde (0322). In 1794 he was in support of

government both from office and because it was his father's policy.

ADDITIONAL INFORMATION: He inherited the name of Wandesford from his parents in addition to Butler.

ESTATES/RESIDENCE: Kilkenny Castle, Co. Kilkenny.

SOURCES: Burke, *PB* (1903); NLI reps no. 270; PRONI T/1584, Pinkerton transcripts p. 510, 2 May 1796; Burke *PB* (1903) p. 1173 (1906) p. 1261; R. A. Austen-Leigh (ed.), *Eton College Register, 1753–90*, 3 vols (Eton, 1921); *FJ* 3 May 1796; *DJ* 5 May 1796; Parliamentary Lists 1793 (1), 1794 (1), (2).

0324 BUTLER, Rt Hon. Sir Pierce

MP for Co. Carlow 1703–13–14

b. 1670; d. (17) Apr. 1732
HONOURS: PC, sworn 7 June 1712, resworn 23 Aug. 1714, suc. as 4th Bt 1704.
FAMILY/BACKGROUND: Eldest son of Sir Thomas Butler, 3rd Bt (0330) and his first wife Jane, dau. of Richard Boyle, Bp of Ferns and Leighlin.
MARRIED: [Dec. 1697] Anne, dau. of Joshua Gilliard of Edmonton, Middlesex.
CHILDREN: *d.s.p.*
EDUCATION: Entered TCD 27 Feb. 1688, aged 18 years; Lincoln's Inn 14 Jan. 1692.
CAREER/OCCUPATION: Trustee of the Linen Board for Leinster 10 Oct. 1711.

POLITICAL ACTIVITY: He came into parliament in 1703 and was a Court supporter, possibly one of the MPs who met in 1707 at the Fleece Tavern to co-ordinate parliamentary strategy for the ensuing session. He was listed for 20 committees between 1703 and 1711. In 1709 he opposed the Money Bill, a key issue in the Whig Lord Wharton's administration. He stood successfully, despite some doubts, for Co. Carlow in 1713. He was a noted Tory, signing a County address in favour of Sir Constantine Phipps, the unpopular Tory Chancellor, and on the 'black list' of Tories at the time of the queen's death in 1714. He did not come into parliament in 1715.

DIVISION LISTS:
1709 (1) voted against a Money Bill.
1713 (1) voted for Sir Richard Levinge

(**1230**) for Speaker.

ADDITIONAL INFORMATION: As one of the gentlemen of Carlow he was a signatory in August 1700
to a Memorial for the reopening of the port of
New Ross. The shutting of the port to discourage
the woollen trade with England was depressing
industry in Leinster.

On 16 April 1701 he was one of the gentlemen
of Co. Carlow who petitioned against the return
and residence of Mark Baggot, 'a violent Papist',
in that county, of which he had been 'titular High
Sheriff' in 1689.

He signed the Co. Carlow address in support
of Sir Constantine Phipps in defiance of the Commons' address for his removal, and was sufficiently
unrepentant when called before the House, 5
December 1715, to have his excuse declared unsatisfactory and his person placed in the custody
of the Serjeant-at-Arms.

ESTATES/RESIDENCE: Garryhundon, Co. Carlow;
Bridgefoot Street, Dublin. In 1704 'A map of
Ballaghmore, Bwolincrea, Upper Ullard, Lower Ullard
... part of the estate of, and surveyed for, the Hon. Sir
Piers Butler, Bt', came to a total of 1,562 Irish acres. In
1713 Sir Pierce Butler's income was estimated at £1,200.
On 2 November 1725 he, with his nephew Rich-
ard, petitioned for heads of a bill limiting his estate to Richard after his and his wife's death and for leave to sell
part of it to pay off encumbrances. He was succeeded
by his nephew, Sir Richard, 5th Bt (**0326**).

SOURCES: PRONI T/3411; NLI 15 B/6/17; *CJ Ire.*
(Bradley ed.) vol. 4 p. 127, vol. 5 p. 274; GEC *B*; *Alum.
Dub.*; Burke *PB* (1903) p. 241; *Index to Irish Privy Counsellors, 1711–1910*; Vicars, *Prerog. Wills*; *Lincoln's Inn
Records* vol. 1 p. 344; *HMC Ormonde* new ser. vol. 8 p.
39; *JRSAI* vol. 31 (1901) p. 56, P. D. Vigors, 'Extracts
from the Old Corporation Books of New Ross, County
Wexford'; *Pue's Occurrences* 18 Apr. 1732; Parliamentary Lists, 1706 (1), 1707 (2), 1711 (1), 1713 (1), (2),
1714 (1), 1714–15 (1).

0325 BUTLER (-COOPER), Hon. Pierce

MP for Killyleagh 1774–6; Callan 1776–83 [r.
Bangor 1776]

b. 11 Aug. 1750; d. 5 May. 1826
FAMILY/BACKGROUND: Son of Somerset Hamilton

Butler, 8th Viscount Ikerrin and 1st Earl of
Carrick, and Juliana, e. dau. of Rt Hon. Henry
Boyle, 1st Earl of Shannon (**0210**). He assumed
the additional name of Cooper. His twin sister
Harriet, Viscountess Mountgarret d. June 1785.
MARRIED: [24 Dec. 1774] Catherine, dau. of
Richard Roth.
CHILDREN: *d.s.p.*
CAREER/OCCUPATION: *Listed in Judges and
Barristers 1789; he and his brother the Earl of
Carrick (**0316**) were elected Common
Councilmen of Kilkenny 15 Apr. 1780.
MILITARY: Cornet in Johnston's Regiment 1767;
Captain, 45th Regiment 1772.

POLITICAL ACTIVITY: He came into parliament in
1774 on the family interest. He followed the political lead of his brother, Lord Carrick (**0316**),
and was a supporter of government. He was connected with the Agars and, in 1776, was returned
for their borough of Callan, 'famous for the contest between Mr Agar (**0015**) and Mr Flood
(**0762**) and will again be contested, but [1783]
Mr Agar is said to be secure'.

In 1777 he had 'a good property' which gave
him a degree of independence, although by 1783
he was 'much distressed in his circumstances'. By
1778 he was an infrequent attender and, in 1782,
he was voting with his cousin, Lord Shannon
(**0213**), to whom his brother, Lord Carrick, was
attached. In the 1783 election he stood unsuccessfully for Co. Kilkenny on the Butler and
against the Agar and Ponsonby interest.

DIVISION LISTS:
> 1775 (1) voted against the pro-American
> amendment to the Speech from the Throne.
> 1779 (2) voted for a six-months Loan Bill.
> 1780 (2) voted against Yelverton's (**2268**)
> motion to modify Poynings' Law.

ESTATES/RESIDENCE: Co. Londonderry; Co. Kilkenny;
Merrion Square, Dublin.

SOURCES: GEC *B* vol. 5 p. 362 [Cooper] n.(e); Ellis thesis; Kilkenny MPs; *Almanacks*; *FJ* 21–4 Feb. 1778; *DJ*
15–18 Apr. 1780, 18–21 June 1785; Parliamentary
Lists, 1775 (1), 1776 (1), (2), (3), 1777 (1), 1778 (1),
1780 (1), 1782 (1), 1783 (1).

0326 BUTLER, Sir Richard

MP for Co. Carlow 1730–60

b. 1699; d. 25 Nov. 1771
HONOURS: Suc. as 5th Bt 1732.
FAMILY/BACKGROUND: Son of James Butler of Co.
Longford and his first wife Frances, dau. of Sir
Edward Abney, wid. of Sir John Parker of Co.
Longford.
MARRIED: [1728] Henrietta (d. 14 Jan. 1794),
dau. and co-h. of Henry Percy (1669) of Seskin,
Co. Wicklow.
CHILDREN: Sir Thomas, 6th Bt (0332); Capt.
James (1st Regt. of Horse; d. unmar. May 1771);
Maj. Pierce; William Paul, m. Henrietta, dau. of
Abraham Nixon of Munny, Co. Wicklow; Anne,
m. William Stewart of Stewart Lodge, Co.
Carlow; Henrietta, m. Nicholas Gordon; Eleanor,
m. Edward Eustace; Jane, m. N. P. Trench.
EDUCATION: Entered Oxford (Christ Church) 1
Dec. 1719, aged 18 years.
CAREER/OCCUPATION: Sheriff of Co. Carlow 1727.

POLITICAL ACTIVITY: In parliament he appears to
have been independent, voting against the election of James Digges La Touche (♦♦♦♦) and also
against the expulsion of Arthur Jones-Nevill
(1125) but against the Money Bill. He was listed
for 31 committees between 1731 and 1759.

DIVISION LISTS:
   1749 (1) voted against the election of James
   Digges La Touche (♦♦♦♦).
   1753 (1) voted against the expulsion of
   Arthur Jones-Nevill (1125).
   1753 (2) voted against the Money Bill.
   1757 (1) voted against the resolutions on
   pensions.

ADDITIONAL INFORMATION: *In a list of present baronets of Ireland, not being peers, 1749.

ESTATES/RESIDENCE: Cloughcregan, Co. Carlow;
Garryhundon, Co. Carlow, inherited from his uncle,
Rt Hon. Sir Pierce, 4th Bt (0324). In 1747 Sir Richard
Butler let lands of Cranlusky, Tomard, etc. (held under
a fee-farm grant from Ormonde to William Keating of
Dublin, 1702), barony of Idrone W, to Edward
Chamney. These appear to have been owned by John
Latouche of Harristown, 1809.

SOURCES: NLI EC 4917; Burke *PB* (1900) [b. 1699];
McCracken thesis; GEC *B*; *Alum. Oxon.*; *Ir. Gen.* (1974)
no 1 pp. 87–98, H. F. Morris, 'Births, Marriages and

Deaths in Ramsey's Waterford Chronicle, 1771' [b.
1699]; *Almanacks*; *Pue's Occurrences* 18 Apr. 1732, 30
Nov. 1736; *DJ* 28–30 May, 26–8 Nov. 1771.

0327 BUTLER, Sir Richard

MP for Co. Carlow 1783–90, 1796–7–1800;
[UK] 1801–2

b. 14 July 1761; d. 16 Jan. 1817
HONOURS: Suc. as 7th Bt 1772.
FAMILY/BACKGROUND: Son and heir of Sir Thomas
Butler, 6th Bt (0332), and Dorothea, o. ch. of
Edward Bayly DD.
MARRIED: [23 Aug. 1782] Sarah Maria, o. dau. of
Thomas Newenham (1537), Coolmore, Co.
Cork.
CHILDREN: Thomas, m. [1812] Frances, dau. of
John Graham Clarke of Co. York; Richard Pierce
(b. 4 Nov. 1784; d. 10 Sept. 1855), m. [13 June
1822] Charlotte, 3rd dau. of John Graham
Clarke; Col. William Arthur (b. 22 Aug. 1786),
m. [1827] Emma (*d.s.p.* 19 Nov. 1872), dau. of
James Heseltine; James (b. 9 Nov. 1788; d.
1 Mar. 1865), m. Eliza, dau. of Beauchamp Hill;
Capt. Charles George RN (b. 15 Oct. 1793; d.
1 Mar. 1867), m. [1830] Emily (d. 1876), dau.
of John Heseltine Bayford; Maj. Walter (27th
Regt.; b. 19 Nov. 1803, *d.s.p.* 14 Dec. 1878), m.
[9 July 1846] Maria, o. dau. of Col. Jackson of
Carramore, Co. Mayo; Louisa, m. Peter Low;
Henrietta, m. Hugh Faulkner.
EDUCATION: School: private tutor; entered TCD 3
Oct. 1778.
CAREER/OCCUPATION: Sheriff of Co. Carlow 1784.
MILITARY: Captain in Carlow Cavalry; Second
Lieutenant in Cavalry First Troop 1796.

POLITICAL ACTIVITY: He was returned in 1783 as 'a
very young man of fortune. Undetermined but
generally against Government. Yet might be
obliged by a provision for his brother.' A year later
he was still looking for this provision, and by 1785
was definitely in opposition. His canditature for
the county had been espoused by the famous duellist, the 'wild ungovernable' Beauchamp Bagenal
(0071), who had 'the chief property and influence' and was reputed to have set him up 'and
returned him against Mr Rochfort, Mr Foster's
(0805) brother-in-law'. He might be won over to
government but he would always be uncertain.

Before the final vote on the Union he systematically voted with the opposition. Castlereagh (**2009**), writing to Portland in February 1800, said that Butler was 'taken off by a County Cabal' because he favoured the Union and, according to the Parliamentary List of 1799 he changed sides and supported the Union in February 1800. There is a note to the 1800 list implying that his change of opinion had been bought for cash. He had not taken his seat at Westminster by 25 March 1801. In the Chief Secretary's list of Irish members in 1801, 'Tony Lump[in]' appears against his name.

DIVISION LISTS:

1783 (1) voted for Flood's (**0762**) motion for parliamentary reform.

1784 (1) voted for a committee on the Reform Bill.

1785 (1) voted against the Commercial Propositions.

1786 (1) voted for the rights of grand juries.

1786 (2) voted for Forbes's (**0778**) motion for retrenchment.

1787 (1) voted for a Pension Bill.

1790 (1) voted for Grattan's (**0895**) motion for reducing the influence of the Crown.

1800 (1) voted for the Union.

ADDITIONAL INFORMATION: *A subscriber to the Public Assembly Rooms, 1787.

ESTATES/RESIDENCE: Garryhundon, Co. Carlow; Clougrenan, Co. Carlow.

SOURCES: PRONI T/3166/1A Hartnell notes; GEC *B*; Burke *PB* (1903) pp. 241–2; Jupp thesis; O'Neill thesis; *HP 1790–1820*; C. Ross (ed.), *Cornwallis Corr.* vol. 3 p. 182; G. C. Bolton, *The Passing of the Irish Act of Union*, p. 190; *Almanacks*; *FJ* 20 Oct., 17 Nov. 1796; *DJ* 24–7 Aug. 1782; Parliamentary Lists, 1784 (1), (2), (3), 1785 (1), (2), (3), (4), 1787 (1), 1788 (1), 1789 (1), 1790 (1), 1799 (3), 1800 (3).

0328 BUTLER, Hon. Robert

MP for Belturbet 1736–60, 1761–3

b. (bapt. 24 Mar.) 1705; d. Sept. 1763

FAMILY/BACKGROUND: Son of Rt Hon. Brinsley Butler, 1st Viscount Lanesborough (**0312**), and Catherine, dau. of Neville Pooley of Dublin.

MARRIED: [20 Aug. 1753] Mary, dau. of Robert Howard, Bp of Elphin, and sis. of 1st Viscount Wicklow (**1044**), wid. of John Stoyte (*see* **2020**) of Rossana, Co. Wicklow and Street, Co. Westmeath.

CHILDREN: ?

CAREER/OCCUPATION: *Governor of the Workhouse 1739–d.; *Commissioner of the Tillage Act for Ulster 1747–d.; *Magistrate of Newcastle 1750; *Sovereign of Newcastle 1750.

MILITARY: Lieutenant of Battle-Axe Guards 29 Nov. 1726 (to rank as Captain of Foot); *Colonel of Battle-Axe Guards 1729, *Captain 1734–54, *Lieutenant as Captain 1755–8, *Captain as Lieutenant 1759–61.

POLITICAL ACTIVITY: He was returned for the family borough of Belturbet. A professional soldier, he had a pension of £150 p.a. in 1747. As such he was expected to support, and he duly did so. He voted against the election of James Digges La Touche (♦♦♦), against the expulsion of Arthur Jones-Nevill (**1125**) and for the Money Bill. Although he was noted as a Court supporter, he was absent in 1756.

DIVISION LISTS:

1749 (1) voted against the election of James Digges La Touche (♦♦♦).

1753 (1) voted against the expulsion of Arthur Jones-Nevill (**1125**) – Captain of Battle-Axe Guards and pensioner.

1753 (2) voted for the Money Bill.

1753 (3) a placeman.

ADDITIONAL INFORMATION: A member of the Royal Dublin Society from 1752.

ESTATES/RESIDENCE: Rossana, Co. Wicklow. On the death of Rt Hon. Robert Naper (**1513**), Butler came into possession of Heritage, Esker, Co. Dublin.

In 5 Geo. III, Robert Butler was granted fairs at Churchland, *alias* Farrintemple.

SOURCES: PRONI T/3019/844 Wilmot Papers; RCBL T34, Extracts from the Parish Registers of St Andrew's, Dublin; McCracken thesis; Burke *PB* (1900) p. 885 [says he m. 20 Aug. 1753]; C. Dalton, *George the First's Army, 1714–27*; Cavan MPs [says he married 30 Aug. 1753]; *Almanacks*; *DJ* 6–10 Sept. 1763; Parliamentary List, 1756 (1).

0329 BUTLER, Rt Hon. Theophilus

MP for Co. Cavan 1703–13; Belturbet 1713–14

b. 1669; d. 11 Mar. 1724
HONOURS: PC appointed 1710, sworn *ante* Apr. 1711, 17 Aug. 1714, 19 Oct. 1714.
PEERAGES: Cr. Baron Newtown-Butler 21 Oct. 1715.
FAMILY/BACKGROUND: Son and heir of Francis Butler (0315) and Judith, dau. of Rt Hon. Sir Theophilus Jones of Co. Meath.
MARRIED: [Apr. 1702] Emily, dau. of James Stopford of Co. Meath.
CHILDREN: Only s. James *d.v.p.*
EDUCATION: Entered TCD 27 Sept. 1686, aged 17 years; Middle Temple 6 July 1694.
CAREER/OCCUPATION: Joint Clerk of the Pells 28 Oct. 1678 (life).

POLITICAL ACTIVITY: He was returned for Co. Cavan in 1703, but appears to have been abroad in either Italy or London for most of the parliament. He was spoken of in 1707 as likely to support Ormonde's administration. In 1713 he was declared definitely a Whig, and in that election he returned himself for the family borough of Belturbet. He was created Lord Newtown-Butler in 1715.

ADDITIONAL INFORMATION: In a letter of 5 April 1707, Robert Johnson (1101) referred to him as 'Theodore' and, as he calculated absentees at the opening of parliament, he added: 'They say [he] is to be made a lord.' This was some eight years before he was elevated to the peerage.

ESTATES/RESIDENCE: Belturbet, Co. Cavan; St Stephen's Green, Dublin.

SOURCES: Hayton thesis; GEC *P*; Burke *PB* (1903) p. 884; Hughes, *Pat. Officers, Index to Irish Privy Counsellors, 1711–1910*; P. McNally, *Parties, Patriots & Undertakers* (Dublin, 1997), p. 74; Smyth, *Cavan MPs*; *Middle Temple Admissions* vol. 1 p. 235; *HMC Ormonde* new ser. vol. 8 p. 296; Parliamentary Lists, 1706 (1), 1707 (1), (2), (3), (4), 1711 (1), 1712 (1), (2).

0330 BUTLER, Sir Thomas

MP for Co. Carlow 1692–3, 1695–9, 1703–4

b. *ante* 1649; d. Feb. 1704

HONOURS: Suc. as 3rd Bt 1650.
FAMILY/BACKGROUND: Son and h. of Sir Edmund Butler, 2nd Bt, and Juliana, dau. of Bernard Hyde of Shinfield, Berkshire.
MARRIED: (1) Jane, dau. of Richard Boyle, Bp of Ferns and Leighlin; (2) [July 1700] Jane, dau. of Capt. Edward Pottinger, wid. of John Reynolds (1777) (she married (3) Agmondisham Vesey (2144)).
CHILDREN: (1) Rt Hon. Pierce (0324); James, m. [1696] Frances, dau. of Sir Edward Abney, wid. of John Parker of Co. Longford; Boyle; Edmund; Juliana, m. John Kennedy of Mullagh, Co. Longford; Ellen, m. John Mahon of Strokestown, Co. Roscommon (1329).
CAREER/OCCUPATION: High Sheriff of Co. Carlow 1670 and 1691; Governor of Co. Carlow 1699.

POLITICAL ACTIVITY: He was listed on three committees in 1692, ten in 1695–9 and three 1703–4. In 1696 he signed the Association for the protection of William III in parliament. As Governor of Carlow he was one of the signatories in August 1700 to a Memorial for the reopening of the port of New Ross: the shutting of the port to discourage the woollen trade with England was depressing industry in Leinster. On 16 August 1701 he was one of the gentlemen of Co. Carlow who petitioned against the return and residence of Mark Baggot, 'a violent Papist', in that county, of which he had been 'titular High Sheriff' in 1689.

ESTATES/RESIDENCE: Garryhundon, Co. Carlow.

SOURCES: PRONI D/302; GEC *B*; Burke *PB* (1903) p. 241; *Cal. SP Dom. 1691–92* (London, 1900) pp. 110, 165, 220; J. Ryan, *The History and Antiquities of the County of Carlow* (Dublin, 1833) p. 361; *HMC Ormonde* new ser. vol. 8 p. 39; *JRSAI* vol. 31 (1901) p. 54, P. D. Vigors, 'Extracts from the Old Corporation Books of New Ross, County Wexford', also *JRSAI* vol. 55 (1925) pp. 37, 40, H. A. S. Upton, 'A List of Governors and Deputy Governors of Counties in Ireland in 1699'; Parliamentary List, 1696 (1).

0331 BUTLER, Hon. Thomas

MP for Belturbet 1727–53

b. *c.* 1703; d. 9 Dec. 1753
FAMILY/BACKGROUND: Son of Rt Hon. Brinsley

Butler, 1st Viscount Lanesborough (0312), and Catherine, dau. of Neville Pooley.

MARRIED: [11 June 1730] Mary, dau. and co-h. of Duncan Cummin MD of Dublin, wid. of John Ormsby.

CHILDREN: Only ch. Mary, m. [1754] John St Leger (1859).

CAREER/OCCUPATION: *Governor of the Workhouse 1734–d.; Governor of Limerick 1743; *Trustee of the Linen Manufacture for Munster 1743–d.; *Governor of the Royal Hospital 1749–d.

MILITARY: Lieutenant in Colonel Murray's Regiment of Foot Feb. 1734; Captain in Colonel Ponsonby's Regiment 23 Sept. 1735; *Captain 1735–6; Major 26 Aug. 1737, 1739–40, 1744–5; Lieutenant-Colonel; Colonel; Adjutant General May 1744–6, 1751, 1753.

POLITICAL ACTIVITY: Returned by his father for the family borough of Belturbet at the general election of 1727. In October 1735 he complained of breach of privilege by Robert Uniake FitzGerald and his servants, who allegedly forcibly entered into his lands of Corkbeg, Co. Cork and beat some of his servants during time of privilege.

He was a professional soldier and, as such, a government supporter. He voted against the election of James Digges La Touche (♦♦♦) in 1749 and the expulsion of Arthur Jones-Nevill (1125) in 1753. He died just after the 1753 Money Bill crisis. He was nominated to 40 committees between 1729 and 1753.

DIVISION LISTS:
1749 (1) voted against the election of James Digges La Touche (♦♦♦).
1753 (1) voted against the expulsion of Arthur Jones-Nevill (1125).

ADDITIONAL INFORMATION: *A member of the Dublin Society from 1739.

ESTATES/RESIDENCE: Pickardstown, Co. Dublin; St Stephen's Green, Dublin. His wife's fortune was reputed to be £50,000. She was the widow of John Ormsby of Athlacca, Co. Limerick 'who is represented as a very weak man' and who left her not only a jointure of £500 a year charged on his Ballyvenoge, Co. Limerick estate, but also the Athlacca estate in fee, which was worth more than £600 p.a. However, Ormsby's niece, Elizabeth Ormsby Upton, who was married to the Rt Hon. Hercules Langford Rowley (1821), and her sister, claimed the Ballyvenoge estate under the will of their maternal grandfather, John Ormsby the elder (1601). The case came before the Lords in 1739.

SOURCES: *CJ Ire.* (Bradley ed.) vol. 6 p. 478; McCracken thesis; TCD House of Lords Appeals: Printed Case Papers, 1711–39, 202 r. 35, 239–40; Cavan MPs [says he died 16 Dec. 1753]; *Almanacks; GM* Dec. 1753; *The Dublin Gazette* 13 June 1730; *DJ* 18 Dec. 1753.

0332 BUTLER, Sir Thomas

MP for Co. Carlow 1761–8; Portarlington 1771–2

b. 1735; d. 7 Oct. 1772
HONOURS: Suc. as 6th Bt 1771.
FAMILY/BACKGROUND: Son and h. of Sir Richard Butler, 5th Bt (0326), and Henrietta, dau. and co-h. of Henry Percy (1669).
MARRIED: [13 June 1759] Dorothea (d. 1824 at Bath), o. ch. of Edward Bayly, Archdeacon of Ardfert and Dean of St Patrick's.
CHILDREN: Richard, 7th Bt (0327); 3 other s.; Dorothea, m. Charles Lionel FitzGerald of Turlough Park, Co. Mayo; Catherine; Henrietta; Jean.
EDUCATION: School: Dr Hewetson; Kilkenny College 24 Nov. 1743, aged 10 years; entered TCD 14 Apr. 1752, aged 17 years, BA 1755.
CAREER/OCCUPATION: Governor of Co. Carlow 1768, Joint Governor 1768–70; *Governor of the Workhouse 1768, Foundling Hospital and Workhouse 1769–70.

POLITICAL ACTIVITY: He was returned for Co. Carlow on his family interest in 1761, but in 1768 the Bagenal and the Burton interests triumphed. Butler was hostile to the Burtons, who were closely related to and part of the Ponsonby connection: William Henry Burton (0304), the new MP, was a nephew of Speaker Ponsonby (1702). This hostility brought Butler into favour with the government, under whose auspices he was returned for Portarlington in 1771 when the sitting member for Portarlington, William Henry Dawson (0597), was elevated to the House of Lords. Lord Dawson asked government for a recommendation for the seat he was vacating; the government recommended Sir Thomas. He died in the following year, 1772. He obtained the living of Kells for Mr Webb.

DIVISION LISTS:

1768 (1) voted for army augmentation.

1771 (2) voted against Sir Lucius O'Brien's (**1558**) motion for retrenchment.

1771 (3) teller for the Revenue Bill.

1772 (1) teller for the separation of the Revenue Board.

1772 (2) voted against a Short Revenue Bill.

ADDITIONAL INFORMATION: At the time of his marriage in 1759 Mrs Delany considered him 'a young gentleman of a very good character, well enough in his person, genteel and civil in his behaviour'. His bride's dowry was £7,000.

ESTATES/RESIDENCE: Garryhundon, Co. Carlow. In 1759, at the time of his marriage, Thomas Butler had an income of £1,000 p.a.

SOURCES: PRONI MIC/315/10/76 Blackwood pedigrees; RCBL P80/1/1, Parish Registers of St Thomas, Dublin; GEC *B*; Burke *PB* (1903) p. 241; Carlow MPs; *Alum. Dub.*; *Index to Hibernian Chronicle, 1769–75* (Society of Genealogists, 1936) vol. 1 p. 62; *JRSAI* vol. 54 (1924) pp. 55–67, T. U. Sadleir, 'The Register of Kilkenny School (1685–1800)'; *Ir. Gen.* vol. 5 no 1 (1974) pp. 87–98, H. F. Morris, 'Births, Marriages and Deaths in Ramsey's Waterford Chronicle, 1771'; Llandover, *Delany Corr.*, vol. 3 p. 543; *Almanacks*; *BNL* 10 May 1768; Parliamentary Lists, 1772 (2), 1773 (1), (2).

0333 BUTLER, Rt Hon. Walter

MP for Co. Kilkenny 1789–90–5

b. 4 Feb. 1770; d. 10 Aug. 1820

HONOURS: PC, sworn 11 July 1797; Knight of St Patrick 19 Mar. 1798.

PEERAGES: Styled Viscount Thurles 1791–5, 18th Earl of Ormonde, 11th Earl of Ossory 1795; cr. Marquess of Ormonde 1816, Baron Butler [UK] 20 Jan. 1801.

FAMILY/BACKGROUND: Eldest son of John Butler, 17th Earl of Ormonde and 10th Earl of Ossory (**0322**), and Frances Susan Elizabeth, o. dau. and h. of John Wandesford, 1st Earl of Wandesford.

MARRIED: [1805] Anna Maria Catherine, o. ch. and h. of Joseph Hart Price Clarke of Sutton Hall, Derbyshire, and Aldershot, Hampshire.

CHILDREN: *d.s.p.*

EDUCATION: School: Eton 1783–5; entered Oxford (Magdalen College) 24 Jan. 1788, aged 17 years.

CAREER/OCCUPATION: Lord of the Bedchamber 1812–13 [UK]; Hereditary Chief Butler; Alderman of Kilkenny; Governor of Co. Kilkenny 1796–1820, Mayor 1806–7; Custos Rot.

MILITARY: Colonel of Co. Kilkenny Militia, 1793.

POLITICAL ACTIVITY: He was returned for Co. Kilkenny first in a by-election in 1789, when Henry Welbore (Ellis) Agar (**0013**) succeeded his father as 2nd Viscount Clifden, and again at the general election in 1790. He succeeded his father as 18th Earl of Ormonde in 1795. In 1790 it was considered that owing to the prevalence of the popish religion, 'the number of electors is far from numerous, scarcely amounting to a thousand and they are in general rather the devoted adherents of some leading families, than the sturdy yeomanry of an uninfluenced district. The Ponsonby interest in the County is all powerful, partly from personal attachment, but much more from extensive property and a continued attention to making of Freeholders.' Butler voted for W. B. Ponsonby (**1709**) as Speaker in 1790.

In general Lord Thurles supported government while the other MP, W. B. Ponsonby, opposed. The Ormonde family controlled at least one seat for Kilkenny city and, from when the family became politically active, one for the county. Catholic enfranchisement in 1793 would have helped the Butlers, and thereafter they commanded at least one seat for the county. Lord Ormonde supported the Union and received an English peerage. In 1816 he was created Marquess of Ormonde.

DIVISION LISTS:

1790 (2) voted for Ponsonby (**1709**) on the election of a Speaker.

ADDITIONAL INFORMATION: In 1799 it was recorded that 'Walter, the present Earl, is son of the Earl John by the only child of the late Earl of Wandesford. He is a young man of an aspiring disposition and is believed, from his uniform support of Government in a legislative Union and its other measures, to have in view a new creation, if not a *restoration* of the old title of Duke of Ormonde. A jealousy of some centuries has subsisted between this and the *Leinster* family and we should not be surprised, if his lordship should make very great sacrifices to obtain a restoration of his ancient Ducal honours, which would give him precedence over the ancient rivals of his house. Be this as it may, his great influence in the County of Kilkenny has undoubtedly been very service-able to Government.'

In 1811 he sold to the Crown, for the sum of £216,000, the grant of the Prizage of Wines in Ireland.

ESTATES/RESIDENCE: Kilkenny Castle, Co. Kilkenny.

SOURCES: GEC *P*, Burke *PB* (1903) p. 1174; *Index to Irish Privy Counsellors, 1711–1910*; *Alum. Oxon.*; R. A. Austen-Leigh (ed.), *The Eton College Register, 1753–90*, 3 vols (Eton, 1921); Kilkenny MPs; J. Kelly, *'That Damn'd Thing Called Honour': Duelling in Ireland 1570–1860* (Cork, 1995), p. 208; *Almanacks*, *FJ* 25–7 Apr. 1793; Parliamentary Lists, 1789 (1), 1790 (1), 1791 (1), 1793 (1), 1794 (2), 1799 (1), (2), (3), 1800 (2).

C

0334 CAIRNES, Sir Alexander

MP for Monaghan B. 1710–13, 1715–27, Co. Monaghan 1713–14, 1727–32 [r. Co. Monaghan 1727]. Failed in his petition against the return of Samuel Ogle for Belfast in 1707

> b. 1665; d. 30 Oct. 1732
> HONOURS: Cr. Baronet [GB and I] 6 May 1708.
> FAMILY/BACKGROUND: Eldest son of John Cairnes of Co. Donegal and Jane, dau. of James Miller MD of Lanarkshire.
> MARRIED: [1698 or 1702] Elizabeth, dau. of Sir Samuel Gould of Middlesex.
> CHILDREN: Mary (d. 1790), dau. and h., m. (1) [Sept. 1724], as his 2nd wife, Cadwallader Blayney (d. 1732), 7th Baron Blayney; (2) John Murray (1507).
> EDUCATION: School: educated in the household of the Duke of Marlborough.
> CAREER/OCCUPATION: Keeper of the Phoenix Park 1712–28.

POLITICAL ACTIVITY: Cairnes was a Presbyterian and, as such, under the special opprobrium of the establishment. The Cairnes brothers (this MP, 0336, 0337) were bankers in London and Dublin, whose business included maritime insurance, transferring rents, etc., but their roots were in Belfast. Belfast was and remained a very Presbyterian town and, while the Corporation was partly conformist, its sympathies were largely non-conformist. Many of its merchants were recent immigrants, largely from Scotland.

Alexander Cairnes was proposed as a successor to his brother William (0337), who died in August 1707, as MP for Belfast. The Countess of Donegall probably thought that he would not rock the religious boat – he had offered to contribute to Ormonde's reception in 1705 – and that he would be acceptable to Belfast Corporation, dominated by the Macartneys and still smarting from the 1704 Penal Act which barred Dissenters from the Corporation. However, the Corporation favoured Samuel Ogle (1574), an English Presbyterian with Irish connections, who, it felt, would

espouse the Presbyterian cause with more vigour.

The Presbyterians on the Corporation did not vote, and the remaining burgesses present voted 3–3. Ogle was returned by the casting vote of the sovereign, George Macartney (1300), who in any case claimed that one of Cairnes' voters was of dubious legality as he had never been sworn. Cairnes contested the election, but the House of Commons decided in favour of Ogle.

In his *Journal to Stella*, Swift describes Cairnes as 'scrupulous puppy' and a 'shuffling scoundrel', adding 'What can one expect from a Scot and a fanatic.' Swift may have had some justification. Certainly he was a very seventeenth-century character: in 1688 he wrote a long document which begins 'O most dreaded God, for the passion of Thy Son, I beseech Thee, accept thy poor prodigal son, prostrating himself at Thy door. I have fallen from thee by mine own iniquity, the child of hell by my wicked practices.'

Cairnes had the leading interest in Co. Monaghan, and in 1713 it was thought that Ormonde might persuade him to support Francis Lucas (1278) against Alexander Montgomery (1434), who was considered 'hostile'. Lucas was 'a good man' in the eyes of the Castle, which thought that with Cairnes' support it might carry the county and exclude Montgomery. Cairnes was himself returned for the county but, if he was not successful in supporting the case of Lucas for the county, he returned him for Monaghan Borough, whose Corporation he controlled. In 1715 he was petitioning for a horse barracks there.

He retained an interest in his banking business, and was to lose a considerable fortune in the South Sea Bubble. In the unstable financial climate of 1721 he was like most bankers, who, for a variety of reasons, were against a national bank. He was listed for nine committees in 1721 and five in 1727–8.

DIVISION LISTS:
  1713 (1) absent.

1721 (1) voted against a national bank.

1721 (2) voted against a national bank.

ESTATES/RESIDENCE: Co. Monaghan; his brother Henry Cairnes (0336), Blackheath, London, inherited the Co. Monaghan estate. Alexander had succeeded to extensive estates in Ireland on the death of his brother, William. In 1711 he was granted several forfeited estates in Counties Tipperary, Kilkenny and Wexford. In 1713 Sir Alexander Cairnes' income was estimated at £2,000. His daughter Mary, Lady Blayney, was the ultimate residual heir and she had a jointure of £200 against the Blaney estates from 1732 until her death, 58 years later, in 1790.

SOURCES: PRONI T/3411; PRONI T/448 p. 8, TSPI 1715–1716, McCracken thesis; Hughes, *Pat. Officers*; GEC *P*; Burke *Ext. B* (1844) p. 95; A. P. W. Malcomson, *The Earl of Clermont*, p. 48; Ethel M. Richardson, *Long-forgotten Days* (London, 1928), pp. 244–6; J. Agnew, *Belfast Merchant Families in the Seventeenth Century* (1996), pp. 39, 97–101, 135, 137, 158, 174–5; Tenison, *Dublin Bankers* [says his father is of Donoughmore and his father-in-law is Sir Nathaniel Gould]; *Ir. Georgian Soc. Bull.* vol. 9 no. 4 p. 3, L. Boylan, 'The Conollys of Castletown'; *Pue's Occurrences* 7 Nov. 1732 [says died 6 Nov.]; Parliamentary List, 1713 (1).

0335 CAIRNES, David

MP for Londonderry city 1692–3, 1695–9

b. 15 Nov. 1645; d. May 1722

FAMILY/BACKGROUND: Fourth son of David Cairnes of Knockmany, Co. Tyrone.

MARRIED: (1) [c. 1676] Margaret (d. Mar. 1683), dau. of Hugh Edwards of Hastings, Co. Tyrone. (2) [23 Mar. 1684] Mary, dau. of [   ] Barnes.

CHILDREN: (1) Robert (d. May 1681); Mary (d. Jan. 1682); Jane, m. her cousin Thomas Edwards of Castlegrove, Co. Donegal; Elizabeth (d. yg); Margaret (d. yg).

(2) John (d. 1719 in a duel at Newcastle, England); Mary, m. Rev. Richard Choppin (minister of Wood St Presbyterian Church, Dublin).

EDUCATION: Middle Temple 20 Feb. 1668; called to the Irish Bar 29 June 1673.

CAREER/OCCUPATION: Appointed a commissioner with Robert Rochfort (1806) to adopt the best measures for rebuilding Londonderry and granting leases by the Irish Society 9 June 1692; General Agent to the Irish Society; Burgess of

Londonderry 1680; Recorder of Londonderry 1691, 1705.

MILITARY: Lieutenant-Colonel of Murray's Dragoons.

POLITICAL ACTIVITY: He played a prominent part in the defence of Londonderry, April–July 1689, making 'several hazardous journeys' contributing to its relief and his own 'heavy ... losses'. During the English parliament's inquiry into the state of Ireland, February 1693, he gave evidence to the Commons. In 1695 the city petitioned the Irish Commons for relief, and on 5 December the committee appointed to consider the petition reported recommending royal favour and singling out Cairnes, who 'was remarkably instrumental in the first securing of the said city against the Irish, and afterwards underwent several hazardous journeys for preserving the same'.

On 7 October 1695 he petitioned the Commons, on behalf of himself and other Protestant creditors of James Hewetson of Springtown, Co. Longford, for the House's protection while Hewetson prosecuted a bill to enable him to pay off debts. He did not sign the Association for the protection of William III, probably for some acceptable reason, as he would have been a natural supporter of William.

ESTATES/RESIDENCE: Knockmany, Co. Tyrone; Raveagh, Co. Londonderry. He owned considerable property in the city and suburbs of Londonderry.

SOURCES: *CJ Ire.* (Bradley edition) vol. 2 pp. 708, 790; D/3000/114 Edwards Genealogical Table [says son John who died in a duel 28 Mar. 1719 was son of first wife]; *Cal. SP Dom. 1695* (London, 1908) p. 139, *1696* (London, 1913) p. 128; *DNB*; Fermanagh and Tyrone MPs; H. C. Lawlor, *A History of the Family of Cairnes or Cairns* (London, 1906); H. A. C. Sturgess, *Register of Admissions to the Honourable Society of the Middle Temple* (London, 1949), vol. 1 p. 176; Rev J. and S. G. McConnell, *Fasti of the Irish Presbyterian Church, 1613–1840* (Belfast, 1951), p. 407; *The Register of Derry Cathedral, Parish of Templemore, Londonderry, 1642–1703* (Parish Register Society of Dublin, 1910) pp. 249, 255, 266; *A Concise View of the Irish Society* (1822) p. 77; T. H. Mullin, *Coleraine in Georgian Times* (Belfast, 1977), p. 30; T. Bartlett and D. W. Hayton (eds), *Penal Era and Golden Age* (Belfast, 1979), p. 25, James I. McGuire, 'The Irish Parliament of 1692'; *Ir. Gen.* vol. 1 no. 11 (1941) p. 344; Parliamentary Lists, 1696 (1).

0336 CAIRNES, Sir Henry

MP for Monaghan B. 1733–43

b. 1673; d. 16 June 1743
HONOURS: Suc. as 2nd Bt 1732.
FAMILY/BACKGROUND: Second son of John Cairnes
and Jane, dau. of James Miller MD of Lanark-
shire.
MARRIED: [10 July 1711] Frances, dau. of John
Gould of Hackney, Middlesex.
CHILDREN: d.s.p.
EDUCATION: Lincoln's Inn 29 Jan. 1755.
CAREER/OCCUPATION: A merchant and banker in
London; director of the East India Company.

POLITICAL ACTIVITY: Very little is known about him
apart from the fact that he was the brother of Sir
Alexander (0334) and William (0337) Cairnes.
There is no evidence of committee service, and
he probably spent most of his time looking after
his business interests in London.

ESTATES/RESIDENCE: Donaghmore, Co. Donegal. He inherited the estates of his brother Alexander. In turn his
niece Mary, Lady Blayney, Alexander's daughter, appears
to have inherited all his Irish estates, although Gentleman's Magazine claimed he was succeeded by Mr Cairnes
of Berry Street, Westminster (perhaps he was the residuary legatee or this refers to his English property).

SOURCES: McCracken thesis; Burke Ext. B (1844) p. 95;
Memorials of the Dead [says he died 5 June 1743 aged
70 years]; The Records of the Honourable Society of Lincoln's Inn (Lincoln's Inn, 1896) vol. 1 p. 443; J. Agnew,
Belfast Merchant Families in the Seventeenth Century
(1996), p. 174 (see also 0334, 0337); Ethel M.
Richardson, Long-forgotten Days (London, 1928) pp.
244–6; GM June 1743.

0337 CAIRNES, William

MP for Belfast 1703–7 [r. Newtown Limavady
1703]

b. c. 1666–72; d. (bur. 9) Aug. 1707
FAMILY/BACKGROUND: Son of John Cairnes of Co.
Donegal and Jane, dau. of James Miller MD of
Lanarkshire
MARRIED: ?
CHILDREN: d.s.p.

POLITICAL ACTIVITY: He settled in Dublin in 1695
and became a land speculator. He was a Presbyterian and an occasional conformist (which was fairly
rare), but as a Presbyterian he had been struck off
the franchise of the city by the Lord Mayor. He
was reinstated on appeal to parliament. In 1706
he was considered an opposition supporter, which
was hardly surprising in view of the test clause in
the 1703 act to prevent the further growth of popery. He was in parliament for less than four years.
During this time he was nominated to five committees.

ESTATES/RESIDENCE: Dublin; Co. Monaghan. Purchased
lands in Counties Dublin (132 acres), Meath (473
acres), Roscommon (1,549 acres) and Wexford (790
acres) from the Commissioners for Sale of Forfeited
Estates in 1702–3.

SOURCES: PRONI T/559 vol. 15 p. 14, Burke, extract
pedigrees; Will and Grant, 1707 Prerog. (Original.)
Cairnes, William of Dublin City; McCracken thesis;
Fermanagh and Tyrone MPs; Memorials of the Dead [says
he died 1707]; H. C. Lawlor, History of the Family of
Cairnes or Cairns (1906), pp. 82–3; The Register of Derry
Cathedral, Parish of Templemore, Londonderry, 1642–
1703 (Parish Register Society of Dublin, 1910) p. 165
[gives a William son of James Kearns baptised 25 Feb.
1667]; Simms' cards; Simms, Williamite Confiscation,
p. 183; JRSAI vol. 31 (1911) p. 171, E. M. F.-G. Boyle,
'Records of the Town of Limavady, 1609–1804' [says
he is a merchant of Belfast]; Ir. Gen. vol. 1 no. 2 (1941)
p. 344, 'Testamentary Records' [says he was bur. 9 Aug.
1707]; Parliamentary Lists, 1706 (1).

0338 CALDWELL, Andrew

MP for Knocktopher 1776–83; Downpatrick
1783–90

b. 19 Dec. 1733; d. 2 July 1808
FAMILY/BACKGROUND: Second son of Charles
Caldwell and Elizabeth, dau. of Benjamin
Heywood of Drogheda.
MARRIED: ?
CHILDREN: ?
EDUCATION: Entered Glasgow University 1751;
London, Middle Temple 11 Dec. 1752; called to
the Irish Bar 1760.
CAREER/OCCUPATION: *Listed in Judges and
Barristers 1789–1800 (f.); *Commissioner for
Paving the Streets of Dublin 1778–80; Governor
of the Foundling Hospital and Workhouse 1798–
1800 (f.).

MILITARY: Member of the Lawyer Corps of Volunteers.

POLITICAL ACTIVITY: He was a man of 'independent property, left him by his father' returned by purchase in the 1776 general election, paying only £500 (a later list says £1,000), through the influence of John Ponsonby (**1702**) and his brother Lord Bessborough (**1707**). John Ponsonby had some residual personal interest in Knocktopher, which he shared with Sir Hercules Langrishe (**1200**), certainly until 1783 and possibly until his death in 1787, when the entire borough reverted to Langrishe, who received the compensation for it in 1800. Caldwell's father was Lord Bessborough's agent and receiver and, for many years, solicitor to the Commissioners of the Revenue. He was described as: 'attached to Speaker Ponsonby and a barrister worth £1,000 p.a. estate. A man of taste, no business. A quiet respectable man. Against.' He appears to have succeeded his father as agent to Lord Bessborough.

In 1783 he was returned for Downpatrick, again through John Ponsonby's influence as in 1785 it was said that 'This Borough belongs to Southwell, Lord de Clifford, whose guardian gave the return of this half of the Borough to Lord James Cavendish, who gave it to Mr Ponsonby, by whom Mr Caldwell was returned. He goes with Mr Ponsonby in support.' This may have been a method of protecting the borough from predators while Lord de Clifford was a minor – it was said to be under threat from Cromwell Price (**1734**), one of the local gentry. The Ponsonby party supported government in the mid-1780s and up to the Regency Crisis in 1789.

Downpatrick was a potwalloping borough with about 250 voters but the town, which was said to have 3,000 inhabitants, was owned by Lord de Clifford. It was thought that Caldwell did pay something, possibly a reduced price, for the seat. After the Ponsonbys went over to government Caldwell was thought not to be as 'steady' a supporter of their party as previously. The author of one of the 1785 lists admits that 'He is a very honest man, a particular friend of mine, and will vote as he thinks right.' In fact he voted fairly solidly in opposition to the government, and he did not come in again in 1790.

DIVISION LISTS:

1777 (1) voted for Grattan's (**0895**) motion for retrenchment.

1778 (1) voted for Grattan's motion for retrenchment.

1778 (2) voted for the Popery Bill.

1779 (2) voted for a six-months Loan Bill.

1780 (2) voted for Yelverton's (**2268**) motion to modify Poynings' Law.

1783 (1) voted for Flood's (**0762**) motion for parliamentary reform.

1784 (1) voted for a committee on the Reform Bill.

1785 (1) voted against the Commercial Propositions.

1789 (1) voted for a Regency.

1790 (1) voted for Grattan's motion for reducing the influence of the Crown.

ADDITIONAL INFORMATION: *A member of the RDS from 1767; *a member of the Royal Irish Academy, 1790–1800(f.) (Council 1798). An author: in 1770 he published *Observations on the Public Buildings of Dublin* and in 1804 an adventure story, *Account of the Extraordinary Escape of James Stewart from the Turks*.

ESTATES/RESIDENCE: Granby Row, Dublin.

SOURCES: PRONI MIC/474 Irish Volunteers; Ellis thesis; Burke *LGI* (1904) p. 81; *DNB*; IMC *King's Inns Admission Papers, 1607–1867*; W. I. Addison (ed.), *The Matriculation Albums of the University of Glasgow 1728–1858* (Glasgow, 1913); H. A. C. Sturgess, *Register of Admissions to the Honourable Society of the Middle Temple* (London, 1949), vol. 1 p. 345; Kilkenny MPs; *Almanacks*; Parliamentary Lists, 1776 (1), (2), (3), 1777 (1), 1778 (1), 1780 (1), 1782 (1), 1783 (1), (2), 1784 (1), (2), (3), 1785 (1), (2), (3), (4), 1787 (1), 1788 (1), 1789 (1), 1790 (1).

CALEDON, Baron, Viscount, and Earl of: *see* **ALEXANDER**

0029 Alexander, James, 1st Baron Caledon, Earl of Caledon, MP Londonderry city 1775–6–83–90

0027 Alexander, Hon. Du Pre, 2nd Earl of Caledon, MP Newton(ards) 1800

CALLAGHAN: *see* O'CALLAGHAN (1560–1564)

CALLAN, Baron: *see* AGAR

0011 Agar, Rt Hon. George, 1st Baron Callan, MP Callan 1776–83–90

0339 CAMPBELL, Charles

MP for Newtown (?1661–6), 1695–9, 1703–13–14, 1715–25

b. *ante* ?1640; d. 28 Oct. 1725
FAMILY/BACKGROUND: Son of [   ] Campbell of Dovecoathall, Scotland, and Marian, dau. of John Shaw of Greenock.
MARRIED: Catherine [   ].
CHILDREN: Anne, m. Samuel Burton (0301).
CAREER/OCCUPATION: Trustee of the Linen Manufacture for the Province of Ulster 10 Oct. 1711; Controller of Strangford.
MILITARY: Captain in the army.

POLITICAL ACTIVITY: He possibly sat in the parliament of Charles II, 1661–6. Certainly after 1692 he had a fairly active parliamentary life, as he was nominated for 16 committees 1695–9, 47 in 1703–11, four in 1713 and 48 in 1715–23. He was returned on the Colvill–Ponsonby influence in Newtownards. In 1695 he supported Lord Chancellor Porter against the accusations of favouring Catholics made against him by some MPs, and in 1696 signed the Association for the protection of William III in parliament. His name appears as one of the petitioners to the Lord Lieutenant in February 1701 for securing the remainder of the purchase money for the forfeited estates.

During the reign of Queen Anne he appears to have adopted an ambivalent political position, being against the government in 1706 but a supporter in 1711, supporting the government over the Dublin mayoralty affair. In that year he may have been influenced by his appointment to the Linen Board, for by 1713 he was declared a Whig.

His daughter and heiress married Samuel Burton (0301) and in 1721 along with the Burtons he voted solidly against the formation of a national bank. In 1715 he introduced 2 Geo. I, c. 17 'an Act to empower Justices of the Peace to Determine disputes about Servants, Artificers, Day Labourers Wages and other small Demands and to oblige Masters to pay the same and to punish idle and disorderly Servants'.

DIVISION LISTS:
1711 (1) voted for the Court on the Dublin mayoralty issue.
1721 (1) voted against a national bank.
1721 (2) voted against a national bank

ADDITIONAL INFORMATION: Acted as one of Sir Hans Hamilton's (0927) trustees *c.* 1708, and was Sir James Hamilton's (0931) trustee in 1716.

ESTATES/RESIDENCE: Donaghadee, Co. Down; Capel Street, Dublin. Purchased in 1702–3 from the Commissioners for sale of Forfeited Estates lands amounting to 824 acres in Co. Antrim, 1,236 acres in Co. Cavan, 59 acres in Co. Dublin, 41 acres in Co. Louth and 966 acres in Co. Meath.

Anne, his only child, married into the Burtons, the leading Dublin bankers of that period. Before his death he had left £6,000 to his grand-daughter, Catherine, the daughter of Anne, provided she married with her father's consent; this was over and above the £3,000 provided for by the Burtons' marriage settlement. The rest of Campbell's property went to Catherine's brother Benjamin (0293). If Catherine married without consent, the £6,000 was to be divided among Campbell's nephews and nieces. Catherine married Nicholas, 5th Viscount Netterville but the £6,000 was not forthcoming. The case brought before the Lords in 1737 concerned the question of Burton's consent and how far it had been affected by his inability to meet the terms of Campbell's will and his impending bankruptcy.

SOURCES: *CJ Ire.* (Bradley ed.) vol. 4 p. 276 (0166); PRONI D/778/38/54 Dungannon Papers; PRONI MIC/315/9/60 Blackwood pedigrees; RCBL P277/1/1, Parish Registers of St Mary's, Dublin [bur. 2 Nov. 1725]; Hayton thesis; NLI House of Lords Appeals: Printed Case Papers, 1711–39; TCD Library 202r. 35, 142–3 Private Members' Bills; Simms' cards; Simms, *Williamite Confiscation*, p. 183; H. F. Berry (ed.), *The Registers of the Church of St Michan, Dublin, 1636–1700* (Parish Register Society of Dublin, 1909), p. 302; S. W. Singer (ed.), *Clarendon Corr.* (London, 1828), vol. 2 pp. 348–9; *Dublin Weekly Journal* 30 Oct. 1725; Parliamentary Lists, 1695 (1), 1696 (1), 1706 (1), 1711 (3), 1713 (1), 1713 (2).

0340 CAMPBELL, David

MP for Bangor 1692–3, 1695–8

b. 1648; d. (*ante* 27 Sept.) 1698
FAMILY/BACKGROUND: Son of Archibald Campbell of Westminster and Dublin.
MARRIED: ?
CHILDREN: ?
EDUCATION: School: Dr Hill, Dublin; entered TCD 26 Mar. 1664, aged 16 years, scholar 1664; Middle Temple 20 Apr. 1670.
CAREER/OCCUPATION: Military: Officer in King William's army, retired after the siege of Limerick.

POLITICAL ACTIVITY: He was nominated to 25 committees 1695–9. He supported Lord Chancellor Porter against the accusations of favouring Catholics made against him by some MPs in 1695, and signed the Association for the protection of William III in the country in 1696.

ESTATES/RESIDENCE: Comber, Co. Down.

SOURCES: Simms' cards; Vicars, *Prerog. Wills*; *Alum. Dub.*; H. A. C. Sturgess, *Register of Admissions to the Honourable Society of the Middle Temple* (London, 1949), vol. 1 p. 181; T. K. Lowry (ed.), *The Hamilton Manuscripts* (Belfast, 1867), p. lxxviii; Parliamentary Lists, 1695 (1), 1696 (1).

0341 CAMPBELL, Rt Hon. Lord Frederick

MP for Thomastown 1767–8; St Canice 1768–76; [GB] Glasgow burghs 1761–80; Argyllshire 1780–99

b. 20 June 1729; d. 8 June 1816
HONOURS: PC [GB] 29 May 1765, [I] sworn 14 Oct. 1767.
FAMILY/BACKGROUND: Son of John Campbell, 4th Duke of Argyll, and Mary, dau. of John Kerr, 2nd Baron Bellenden.
MARRIED: [28 Mar. 1769] Mary (d. 1807 in fire at Coombe Bank, Kent), dau. of Amos Meredith, wid. of Laurence Shirley, 4th Earl Ferrers.
CHILDREN: *d.s.p.m.*, 2 dau.
EDUCATION: School: St Paul's, Westminster;

entered Oxford (Christ Church) 31 May 1747, aged 17 years; Middle Temple 1751, BCL 1753, called to the Bar 1754, Bencher Middle Temple 1789, Reader 1796, Treasurer 1803; Rector Glasgow University 1772–3.
CAREER/OCCUPATION: Keeper of Privy Seal [S] 29 May–July 1765; Chief Secretary 19 Aug. 1767 – 31 Dec. 1768; Lord Clerk Register [S] 1768–d., £1,200 p.a.; Member of the committee of the PC for Trade and Plantations 1784–6; Board of Trade 1786–1801; Vice-Treasurer [I] 20 July 1787–93; Indian Board of Control 1790–June 1793.

POLITICAL ACTIVITY: Chief Secretary to Lord Townshend, he was unanimously elected MP for Thomastown at the by-election following the death of Alexander McAuley (**1307**) in 1766, and in 1768 for the government borough of St Canice in place of the Under-Secretary, Thomas Waite (**2154**). On 8 November 1767 Waite wrote to Sir Robert Wilmot declaring that Lord Frederick was 'the most agreeable man I ever met with. Sensible, mild, courteous, free from pride; I think myself very happy under him; but *entre nous*, he is sick of my Lord Lieutenant's [George Townshend, the 4th Viscount, later 1st Marquess Townshend] irregularity and most heartily wishes he had not engaged. His Excellency's good nature and jovial spirit lead him into most desperate drinkings; and at such time, it is whispered, he reveals everything he knows. Very generous, lives nobly, is rather a favourite with the people, he walks about the streets of Dublin in his boots, and called at Bell Boyle's (**0200**) this day on foot to see him and afterwards took a hacking coach to go elsewhere. Surely never were such a Lord and Lady Lieutenant; they seem to detest all formality and parade.'

Waite's opinion of Lord Frederick appears to have been widely held: in 1785 Wraxall wrote in his diary that 'He still retained all the graces he had inherited from his mother. His figure united symmetry with elegance and his manners ... conciliated all who approached him. Devoid of shining talents he nevertheless wanted not either ability or eloquence in a certain degree, both which were under the control of reason and temper.' He had accepted the Chief Secretaryship with reluctance, but was poor and 'Finding it handsomely and heartily offered, I thought I owed it to myself not to decline service.' In 1768 he was appointed Lord Clerk Register for Scotland, a position worth £1,200 p.a. It was said in 1774 that he refused a pension of the Irish establishment, but from 1787 to 1793 he held the lucrative sinecure of Vice-Treasurer for Ireland. He was an absentee for virtually all of the 1768–76 parliament.

DIVISION LISTS:

1768 (1) voted for army augmentation – Chief Secretary to the Lord Lieutenant.

ADDITIONAL INFORMATION: When Lord Frederick was appointed Chief Secretary, William Markham, the radical leader Flood's (0762) tutor at Oxford, thought that this was a man with whom Flood could do business, writing: 'I advise you therefore to be confidential with him. If he thinks your plan practicable, you will have his assistance: if not, you will have a plain answer and secrecy.' Flood, however, considered that he was treated badly by both Lord Frederick Campbell and, in the succeeding viceroyalty, Sir John Blaquiere (0162).

A close friend of Pitt, Lord Frederick chaired a committee of the whole House on relief for Scottish Catholics, 23 April 1793, and condemned Fox's motion for an inquiry into the state of Ireland, 23 March 1797.

His wife was the widow of Lawrence Shirley, 4th Earl Ferrers, who was hanged at Tyburn in 1760, after trial by his peers, for murdering his servant.

ESTATES/RESIDENCE: Ardencaple (purchased for him by his father), Scotland; Coombe Bank estate, Seven Oaks, Kent, inherited from his father in 1770. He sold Coombe Bank in 1813 for £40,000; his wife had died as a result of a fire there in 1807.

SOURCES: PRONI T/3019/6459/761 Wilmot Papers; Burke *PB* (1903) p. 61, (1906) p. 63; *Alum. Oxon.*; *HP 1754–90*; Kilkenny MPs; J. Kelly, *Henry Flood* ... (Dublin, 1998), pp. 116, 203–4; Johnston, *Gt B. & Ire.*, p. 154; *Proc. R.I.A.* vol. 77 C no. 1 (1977), J. C. Sainty, 'The Secretariat of the Chief Governors of Ireland, 1690–1800'; *Almanacks*; *BNL* 6 Nov. 1767; Parliamentary Lists, 1769 (1), 1772 (2), 1773 (1), 1774 (1), 1775 (1), 1775 (1).

0342 CANE, Hugh

MP for Tallow 1768–76–83–90–3

b. 1719; d. 19 Jan. 1793 from a fall downstairs
FAMILY/BACKGROUND: Son of William Cane and Alice, dau. of John Stowell of Dublin.
MARRIED: (1) [(settlement 13 July) 1741] Louisa, dau. of Edward Riggs (**1791**); (2) Annabella, Lady Blakiston, wid. of Sir Mathew Blakiston, Lord Mayor of London in 1761.
CHILDREN: (1) John (d. yg); Louisa, m. Col. Robert Anstey; Anne, m. Sir Edward Leslie (**1225**).
CAREER/OCCUPATION: *Governor of the Foundling Hospital and Workhouse 1772–d.; *Governor of the Hibernian Society 1778.
MILITARY: Captain in Otway's Regiment 1763; Colonel of the Carton Union Volunteers 1782 and of the Maynooth Rangers Volunteers; *Major of the Dragoons 1761–4, *1st Dragoons 1764–7, *Colonel 1768–73; Late Lieutenant-Colonel 5th Royal Dragoons.

POLITICAL ACTIVITY: Cane had been in the household of various Lords Lieutenant, including the Dukes of Devonshire and Dorset, as Chamberlain at the Castle. He first sought election for Tallow in 1763, when he was opposed by James Gisborne (**0851**). Sir Henry Cavendish (**0380**) made it clear to him 'that he had no chance of sitting in the House, and that he must forever disoblige the Duke of Devonshire if he persisted in his election'. He eventually stood down when Gisborne agreed to give him compensation of 'two hundred guineas to dispose of as he thought proper'.

The Duke of Devonshire died in 1764, and in 1769 Colonel Cane was returned for Tallow at a disputed election which was decided in his favour; he sat for that borough for the rest of his life. His interest in the borough dated from when he was stationed there in the army, and he gradually built it up until he secured his own return during his lifetime.

Tallow was one of the neglected Devonshire boroughs. The returning officer was the seneschal of the duke's manor, and Lord Shannon (**0213**) exercised a supervisory role in it. In 1790 it was said that both parties were satisfied with the arrangement. At first he was a doubtful government supporter but he subsequently became a steady friend to successive administrations until towards the end of his life: he voted for a Regency in 1789 and for W. B. Ponsonby (**1709**) as Speaker in 1790. In general he followed Lord Shannon's leadership, and these votes probably reflect this. His support of successive administrations was reflected in small items of ecclesiastical and revenue patronage and a pension of £300 p.a. In 1788 he was considered a 'very old and faithful fr[ien]d of government' and, as such, eligible for an addition to his pension. Whether he got it or not is uncertain, as his behaviour over the Regency may have forfeited his claims.

DIVISION LISTS:

1771 (1) voted for Lord Townshend as Lord Lieutenant.

1771 (2) voted against Sir Lucius O'Brien's (**1558**) motion for retrenchment.

1772 (2) voted against a Short Revenue Bill.

1773 (1) voted against the Absentee Tax.

1773 (2) voted against an untaxed press.

1774 (1) voted for the Stamp Bill.

1774 (2) voted against Catholic relief.

1775 (1) voted against the pro-American amendment to the Speech from the Throne.

1778 (2) voted for the Popery Bill.

1779 (1) voted for new taxes.

1779 (2) voted against a six-months Loan Bill.

1780 (1) voted against Grattan's (**0895**) declaration of the rights of Ireland.

1780 (2) voted against Yelverton's (**2268**) motion to modify Poynings' Law.

1780 (3) voted for the Tenantry Bill.

1783 (1) voted against Flood's (**0762**) motion for parliamentary reform.

1784 (1) voted against a committee on the Reform Bill.

1785 (1) voted for the Commercial Propositions.

1789 (1) voted for a Regency.

1790 (2) voted for Ponsonby (**1709**) on the Election of a Speaker.

ESTATES/RESIDENCE: Dowdstown, Maynooth, Co. Kildare; Kildare Street, Dublin.

SOURCES: PRONI T/559 vol. 19 p. 269, Burke, extract pedigrees; PRONI T/3019/6459/733 Wilmot Papers;

PRONI MIC/474 Irish Volunteers; RCBL GS 2/7/3/44, Prerogative Marriage Licences [gives first marriage licence dated 1746]; O'Neill thesis; J. O'Hart, *Irish Pedigrees* (Dublin,1892), vol. 1 p. 626; *GM* 1793 (Exshaw's edition); McNevin, *Volunteers*; Musgrave *Obits*; *Almanacks*; *DJ* 22 Jan. 1792; Parliamentary Lists, 1769 (1), 1772 (2), 1773 (1), (2), 1774 (1), 1775 (1), 1776 (1), (2), (3), 1777 (1), 1778 (1), 1780 (1), 1782 (1), 1783 (1), (2), 1784 (1), (2), (3), 1785 (1), (2), (3), (4), 1787 (1), 1788 (1), 1789 (1), 1790 (1), 1791 (1), 1793 (1).

0343 CANE, James

MP for Ratoath 1798–1800

b. 1762; d. 1806

FAMILY/BACKGROUND: ?Son of Thomas Cane, merchant.

MARRIED: Jane, 3rd dau. of William Roe of Roe's Green, Co. Tipperary.

CHILDREN: William; Jane, m. Capt. Andrew Walsh (12th Dragoons) of Oatlands, Co. Meath.

EDUCATION: School: Dr Browne; entered TCD 11 Oct. 1779, aged 17 years.

CAREER/OCCUPATION: *Seneschal of Ratoath 1799 (f.); Magistrate of Ratoath 1799 (f.); *Governor of the Hibernian Society 1789–95.

MILITARY: Captain and Major in the army, 1789–95.

POLITICAL ACTIVITY: He was a professional soldier and returned in 1798 for Ratoath. He voted against the Union in 1799 but was persuaded, by a pension, to change his mind in 1800. He was a governor of the Hibernian School, which was to educate and, if they opted for a civilian career, apprentice the children of soldiers.

DIVISION LISTS:

1799 (1) voted against the Union.

1800 (1) voted for the Union.

ESTATES/RESIDENCE: Ratoath, Co. Meath; St Stephen's Green, Dublin.

SOURCES: PRONI T/3166/1C Hartnell notes; O'Neill thesis; *Alum. Dub.*; J. O'Hart, *Irish Pedigrees* (Dublin, 1892), vol. 1 p. 626 [gives family details]; *Almanacks*; Parliamentary Lists 1799 (3), 1800 (3).

CARADOC, Sir John Francis: *see* **CRADOCK** (*alias* **CARADOC**), Sir John Francis (**0510**)

CARBERY, Baron: *see* **EVANS**
0704 Evans, Rt Hon. George, 1st Baron Carbery, MP Co. Limerick 1707–13–14, [GB] Westbury 1715–22, 1724–7
0821 Freke, Sir John, 6th Baron Carbery, MP Donegal B. 1783–90, Baltimore 1790–7–1800

0344 CAREW, Robert

MP for Dungarvan 1713–14, 1715–21

b. 1681; d. Sept. 1721
FAMILY/BACKGROUND: Son of Robert Carew of Co. Wexford and Anne, dau. of Andrew Lynn of Co. Waterford.
MARRIED: [1710] Elizabeth, dau. and co-h. of John Shapland, merchant, of Co. Wexford.
CHILDREN: Robert (**0345**); Shapland (**0348**); Thomas (**0349**); Ellen, m. Christmas Paul (**1641**).
EDUCATION: School: Mr France, Co. Waterford; entered TCD 5 Feb. 1698, aged 17 years.
CAREER/OCCUPATION: High Sheriff of Co. Waterford 1711.

POLITICAL ACTIVITY: He was a member of an old Waterford family and married into another. He does not appear to have been an active parliamentarian, as he was nominated for only one committee, on 18 July 1719.

ESTATES/RESIDENCE: Castleboro, Co. Wexford.

SOURCES: PRONI D/302; McCracken thesis; Burke *PB* (1906) pp. 289–90; Simms' cards; Burke *LGI* (1904) p. 83.

0345 CAREW, Robert

MP for Waterford City 1739–40

b. *c.* 1715; d. 18 Aug. 1740
FAMILY/BACKGROUND: Eldest son of Robert Carew

(**0344**) and Elizabeth, dau. and co-h. of John Shapland, merchant, of Co. Wexford.
MARRIED: ?
CHILDREN: *d.s.p.*
EDUCATION: Entered TCD 8 July 1734.

POLITICAL ACTIVITY: Very little is known about this MP, apart from his family background. He was in parliament for only a year, in the course of which he was nominated to two committees, in November 1739 and February 1740.

ESTATES/RESIDENCE: Castleboro, Co. Wexford.

SOURCES: McCracken thesis; Burke *PB* (1906) p. 290; *Alum. Dub.*; *Dublin Newsletter* 16 June 1741.

0346 CAREW, Robert

MP for Dungarvan 1768–76

b. 22 May 1747; d. 11 Apr. 1834
FAMILY/BACKGROUND: Eldest son of Thomas Carew (**0349**) and Eliza, dau. of James May (**1382**).
MARRIED: [4 July 1771] Frances, dau. of Thomas Boyse of Bishop's Hall, Co. Kilkenny.
CHILDREN: Thomas, m. [1807] Jane, e. dau. and co-h. of Sir John Alcock; Capt. Robert Shapland (18th Hussars; killed 1813 at Vitoria); Margaret, m. [7 Aug. 1798] Robert Hunt of Sidbury Manor, Devon.
CAREER/OCCUPATION: Freeman of Fethard (Tipperary) 1774; High Sheriff of Co. Waterford 1779.

POLITICAL ACTIVITY: When he first came into parliament in 1769, it was thought that he was hostile but might be influenced by Lord Shannon (**0213**), Speaker Ponsonby (**1702**) or Lord Tyrone (**0113**). However, he adopted a stance of unrelenting hostility to both Lords Lieutenant Townshend and Harcourt. He may have been influenced by the fact that his relative Sir James May (**1383**) was 'cousin germain to Mr Ponsonby by whom he was recommended to the Duke of Devonshire but as he has some interest himself here [in Dungarvan] it was thought best to keep things quiet to return him'.
In 1774 he was 'generally absent', but in 1775 he was declared to have 'been constantly in opposition. Much connected with Mr Ponsonby. A little with Lord Shannon. Lord Tyrone may perhaps

have some influence with him.' Apart from the former Speaker Ponsonby, probably no one actually had much influence with him; Ponsonby's may have declined when he ceased to be Chief Commissioner of the Revenue. He did not come in again in 1776.

DIVISION LISTS:
>   1771 (1) voted against Lord Townshend as Lord Lieutenant.
>   1771 (2) voted for Sir Lucius O'Brien's (**1558**) motion for retrenchment.
>   1774 (2) voted against Catholic relief.

ESTATES/RESIDENCE: Ballinamona Park, Co. Waterford. In 1775 George Ponsonby valued his Waterford estate at £300 p.a. but he would have £1,000 p.a. on the death of his father.

SOURCES: PRONI D/302; Burke *LGI* (1904) p. 83, *IFR* (1976) p. 211; *Ir. Gen.* vol. 4 no. 6 (1973) pp. 616–24, W. G. Skehan, 'Freemen of the Corporation of Fethard, Co. Tipperary'; *ibid.* p. 641; H. F. Morris, 'Births, Marriages and Deaths in Ramseys Waterford Chronicle, 1771'; *Waterford Arch. Soc. Jn.* vol. 16 (1913) p. 50; T. U. Sadleir (ed.), 'The County of Waterford 1775'; Parliamentary Lists, 1769 (1), 1772 (2), 1773 (1), (2), 1774 (1), 1775 (1).

0347 CAREW, Robert Shapland

MP for Waterford city 1776–83–90–7–1800; [UK] Co. Wexford 1806–7

b. 20 (bap. 23) June 1752; d. 29 Mar. 1829
FAMILY/BACKGROUND: Eldest son of Shapland Carew (**0348**) and Dorothy, dau. and co-h. of Isaac Dobson.
MARRIED: [13 May 1783] Anne, dau. and co-h. of Rev. Richard Pigott of Dysart, Queen's County
CHILDREN: Robert Shapland (b. 9 Mar. 1767; d. 2 June 1856), 1st Baron Carew, m. [1816] Jane Catherine, dau. of Maj. A. Cliffe; Dorothea (d. 3 Jan. 1865), m. Richard Power of Clashmore; Elizabeth Anne, m. William Blacker of Woodbrook, Co. Wexford; Ellen (d. unm. 13 Nov. 1867).
CAREER/OCCUPATION: High Sheriff of Co. Waterford 1777.
EDUCATION: School: Eton 1765–7; entered TCD 4 July 1769; Middle Temple 24 Nov. 1772; BA 1773.

MILITARY: Captain of the Waterford Royal Battalion Volunteers 1782.

POLITICAL ACTIVITY: Elected for Waterford city in the general election of 1776 on the popular interest. He was independent by disposition and fortune, but inclined to the Shannon–Ponsonby (**0213**, **1702**) connection, particularly the latter. It was also thought that Lord Tyrone (**0113**) might have some influence with him, but if so it did not prevent his constant opposition.

Waterford was a county borough with a comparatively large electorate. In 1783 he joined his interest with Henry Alcock (**0019**) against that of Cornelius Bolton (**0181**), the sitting member, and Bolton was defeated. Alcock was reputed to have the dominant interest in the Corporation, while Bolton and John Beresford (**0115**) had considerable influence over the merchants, but Alcock and Carew were inclined to use their influence with the Corporation to make 'many Wexford men freemen', thereby increasing their electoral power.

Carew was a captain in the Volunteers and a delegate to the Volunteer National Convention. In the mid-1780s both members were said to be in support of the Duke of Rutland's administration, but their support was always dubious and short-lived. Carew appears to have been absent at the time of the Regency vote. In 1790 he voted for Ponsonby (**1709**) as Speaker against Foster (**0805**), and then solidly in opposition, voting in support of Knox's (**1180**) motion for Catholic Emancipation. He voted against the Union in both 1799 and 1800. Waterford city returned only one member after the Union, decided by ballot between the sitting members, and Carew lost. He sat briefly for Co. Wexford in 1806–7, returned with government approval, and gave the Grenville ministry a silent support, in and out of office. Because of bad health, he did not seek re-election in 1807.

DIVISION LISTS:
>   1777 (1) voted for Grattan's (**0895**) motion for retrenchment.
>   1777 (2) voted against the Trade Embargo.
>   1778 (1) voted for Grattan's motion for retrenchment.
>   1779 (2) voted for a six-months Loan Bill.

1780 (2) voted for Yelverton's (**2268**) motion to modify Poynings' Law.

1780 (3) voted for the Tenantry Bill.

1780 (4) voted against the Perpetual Mutiny Bill.

1780 (5) voted for the duty on imported sugar.

1783 (1) voted for Flood's (**0762**) motion for parliamentary reform.

1784 (1) voted for a committee on the Reform Bill.

1785 (1) voted against the Commercial Propositions.

1787 (1) voted for a Pension Bill.

1788 (2) voted for Forbes's (**0778**) motion for limiting pensions.

1790 (2) voted for Ponsonby (**1709**) on the Election of a Speaker.

1791 (1) voted for Curran's (**0560**) resolution against the sale of peerages.

1791 (2) voted for Grattan's motion for the exercise of free trade.

1791 (3) voted for Grattan's motion to abolish the Dublin police.

1793 (1) voted for Knox's (**1180**) motion for Catholic emancipation.

1799 (1) voted against the Union.

1800 (1) voted against the Union.

ADDITIONAL INFORMATION: Brother-in-law to Sir (Simon) John Newport.

ESTATES/RESIDENCE: Castleboro, Enniscorthy, Co. Wexford. According to Wakefield, at the beginning of the nineteenth century the rental was £6,000. In 1842–7 the estate comprised 17,479 statute acres at a valuation of £9,226. In addition there was 1,099 acres in Queen's County at £661 and 1,539 in Co. Waterford, not valued. Estate papers include an abstract of the 1783 marriage settlement between Robert Shapland Carew and Anne Pigott.

SOURCES: PRONI D/302; PRONI MIC/465/1 R. Ffolliott, Biographical Notices, 1756–1827; NLI reps no. 192; Ellis thesis; O'Neill thesis; Jupp thesis; Burke *PB* (1906) p. 290; *HP 1794–1820*; Wakefield, *Account of Ire.*, vol. 1 p. 282; McNevin, *Volunteers; Alum. Dub.*; R. A. Austen-Leigh (ed.), *The Eton College Register, 1753–90* (Eton, 1921), 3 vols; B. Cantwell, *Memorials of the Dead*, vol. 9 [says he died aged 79 years]; H. A. C. Sturgess, *Register of Admissions to the Honourable Society of the Middle Temple*, vol. 1 (London, 1949) p.

375; Parliamentary Lists, 1776 (1), (3), 1777 (1), 1778 (1), 1780 (1), 1782 (1), 1783 (1), (2), (3), 1784 (1), (2), (3), 1785 (1), (2), (3), (4), 1787 (1), 1788 (1), 1789 (1), 1790 (1), 1791 (1), 1793 (1), 1799 (3), 1800 (3).

0348 CAREW, Shapland

MP for Waterford city 1748–60, 1761–8, 1769–76

b. 1716; d. (*ante* 14) Oct. 1780

FAMILY/BACKGROUND: Second son of Robert Carew (**0344**) and Elizabeth, dau. and co-h. of John Shapland, merchant, of Co. Wexford.

MARRIED: [18 Feb. 1744] Dorothy, dau. and co-h. of Isaac Dobson.

CHILDREN: Robert Shapland (**0347**); Elizabeth, m. Richard Power of Clashmore (**1718**); Eleanor, m. Rt Hon. Sir John Newport, 1st Baronet; Dorothea, m. Samuel Boyse of Bannow, Co. Wexford; Mary, m. William Morris of Waterford; Dobson, m. Michael Creagh of Laurentinum, Co. Cork.

EDUCATION: School: Dr Fell, Waterford; entered TCD 7 Mar. 1732; Middle Temple 27 Oct. 1735; King's Inns 1740.

CAREER/OCCUPATION: Clerk of the House of Commons 6 Sept. 1745, 47–79, House of Lords 1747; Recorder of Waterford Aug. 1755.

POLITICAL ACTIVITY: He was Clerk to the House of Commons for four years before he was returned in the 1748 by-election for Waterford city following the death, in March 1748, of Christmas Paul (**1641**). He was nominated for 39 committees between 1749 and 1760. He appears to have been independent, inclining towards opposition from the beginning of his parliamentary career. He supported the election of James Digges La Touche (♦♦♦♦) in 1749, and in 1753 voted for the expulsion of Arthur Jones-Nevill (**1125**) and against the Money Bill. In 1758 he introduced a bill that was part of the long-running saga of winding-up the closure of Burton's Bank (**1733**). Creditors were to be paid 15s in the pound and no claims could be made against Benjamin Burton (**0293**) of Burton Hall, who was the heir of his grandfather, Charles Campbell (**0339**).

In the general election of 1761 Carew was again

returned for Waterford city, having polled 142 votes, along with Samuel Barker (**0083**), who polled the same number of votes. The unsuccessful candidates were Robert Snow and William Alcock (**0020**), who polled 125 and 105 votes respectively. Waterford city was a very insecure constituency, and he strengthened his interest by living in Waterford and knowing his constituents.

In December 1765 he was appointed to the committee to inquire into the public works necessary to the nation. He was in opposition under Lords Lieutenant Townshend and Harcourt. In 1773 it was said that he was 'bred a Lawyer but does not practise. He has a good estate here and recommends himself to the people by asserting the right of freedom for many persons here and having mandamus issued out of the King's bench for that purpose. He also ingratiated himself into their favour by giving £100 towards building a market-house for their wool. He is a cunning, spirited man.' Both he and the other MP, Cornelius Bolton (**0180**), opposed the 1774 Catholic Relief Bill. He did not come in in 1776, but was succeeded by his son (**0347**).

DIVISION LISTS:
   1749 (1) voted for the election of James Digges La Touche (♦♦♦♦).
   1753 (1) voted for the expulsion of Arthur Jones-Nevill (**1125**).
   1753 (2) voted against the Money Bill.
   1757 (1) voted against the resolutions on pensions.
   1768 (1) voted against army augmentation.
   1771 (1) voted against Lord Townshend as Lord Lieutenant.
   1771 (2) voted for Sir Lucius O'Brien's (**1558**) motion for retrenchment.
   1772 (2) voted for a Short Revenue Bill.
   1773 (1) voted for an untaxed press.
   1773 (1) voted against the Absentee Tax.
   1774 (2) voted against Catholic relief.

ADDITIONAL INFORMATION: *A member of the RDS from 1750.

ESTATES/RESIDENCE: Castleboro, Co. Wexford.

SOURCES: *CJ Ire.* (Bradley ed.) vol. 10 p. 571 (0544); McCracken thesis; Burke *PB* (1903) p. 268; Hughes, *Pat. Officers; Alum. Dub.; IMC King's Inns Admission Papers, 1607–1867;* H. A. C. Sturgess, *Register of Admissions to the Honourable Society of the Middle Temple* (London, 1949) vol. 1 p. 318; Johnston, *Gt B. & Ire.,* p. 153; *Almanacks; BNL* 27 Dec. 1765; *DJ* 16–19 Aug. 1755, 19–23 May 1761, 18–21 Mar. 1780 [Dolly m. Samuel Boyle of Waterford City in Mar. 1780]; Parliamentary Lists, 1772 (2), 1773 (1), (2), 1774 (1), 1775 (1).

0349 CAREW, Thomas

MP for Dungarvan 1761–8

   b. 11 Aug. 1718; d. 5 June 1793
   FAMILY/BACKGROUND: Third son of Robert Carew (**0344**) and Elizabeth, dau. and co-h. of John Shapland.
   MARRIED: [1 Nov. 1745] Eliza, dau. of James May (**1382**).
   CHILDREN: Robert (**0346**); James May; John and Peter (twins, d. yg); Ponsonby May, m. [ ] Giles; John Mutlow, m. [ ] Jones; Letitia (d. yg); Elizabeth, m. Richard Charters; Letitia, m. Rev. John Kennedy of Fethard Castle, Co. Wexford.
   CAREER/OCCUPATION: High Sheriff of Co. Waterford 1742.

POLITICAL ACTIVITY: He was unanimously returned for Dungarvan Borough in 1761, along with Robert Boyle-Walsingham (**0217**). The family were well known, but he sat for only one parliament and was absent at the crucial vote on the augmentation of the army. Little is known about him personally.

DIVISION LISTS:
   1768 (1) absent, in the country.

ESTATES/RESIDENCE: Ballinamona Park, Co. Waterford.

SOURCES: PRONI D/302; Burke *LGI* (1904) p. 83 (1958) p. 141; Vicars, *Prerog. Wills; Ir. Gen.* vol. 6 no. 3 (1982) p. 341, H. F. Morris, 'Extracts from The Waterford Herald 1793, 1794, 1796'; *DJ* 25–8 Apr. 1761.

0350 CAREY, Rt Hon. Walter

MP for Clogher 1731–57; [GB] Helston 1722–7; Dartmouth 1727

   b. 17 Oct. 1685; d. 27 Apr. 1757
   HONOURS: PC, sworn 15 Sept. 1731.

FAMILY/BACKGROUND: Son of Walter Carey (d. 1714) of Everton, Bedfordshire and Annabella, dau. of Sir William Halford.
MARRIED: (1) [c. 1716] Elizabeth, dau. of Anthony Sturt of London; (2) [18 May 1738] Elizabeth, dau. and co-h. of Anthony Collins of Essex.
CHILDREN: *d.s.p.*
EDUCATION: Entered Oxford (New College) 14 Dec. 1704, aged 18 years; BA 1708; MA 15 Sept. 1730.
CAREER/OCCUPATION: Clerk of the Council [GB] (extra.) 1717–29, (ord.) 1727–d.; Surveyor General to the Prince of Wales [GB] 1723–5; Warden of the Mint [GB] 1725–7; Lord of Trade [GB] 1727–30; Chief Secretary 23 June 1730 – 8 Apr. 1737; Clerk Comptroller of the Household [GB] 1738–d; Freedom of Drogheda 24 Mar. 1732.

POLITICAL ACTIVITY: He came over as Chief Secretary to the Duke of Dorset during his first viceroyalty. In the British House of Commons in 1731 he carried a proviso that excluded Ireland from a bill naturalising children born abroad, which the Irish MPs feared would naturalise the children of Irish Jacobite exiles and thereby endanger the land settlement. Also during this session of the British parliament he was one of a group of 'lords and gentlemen of Ireland' who met 'to consider the matters before the Parliament relating to Ireland'; he chaired a committee of the House which drafted a bill removing the import duty on Irish yarn and another bill allowing unenumerated articles from the colonies to be imported directly into Ireland. In 1733 he unsuccessfully opposed a clause in the Mollasses Bill which prevented the importation of sugar into Ireland except through Great Britain.

He was unpopular in Ireland, where his behaviour was considered to increase the Lord Lieutenant's difficulties in controlling the House of Commons; for example, he reprimanded the Speaker (0210) for allowing his friends to oppose the repeal of the Test Act in 1733; furthermore, the Irish gentry considered that he put on 'airs'. After Dorset's recall Carey continued his English career as a placeman and minor politician. He appears to have resided in England thereafter, and did not come over even for such important occasions as the Money Bill crisis of the early 1750s, when every vote counted.

DIVISION LISTS:
    1749 (1) absent, in England.

ESTATES/RESIDENCE: West Sheen, Surrey.

SOURCES: McCracken thesis; *Alum. Oxon.*; HP 1715–54; Fermanagh and Tyrone MPs; *Index to Irish Privy Counsellors, 1711–1910*.

CARHAMPTON, Earl of: *see* **LUTTRELL**
1285 Luttrell, Rt Hon. Henry Lawes (styled Viscount Luttrell 1785–7), 2nd Earl of Carhampton, MP Old Leighlin 1783–7, [GB] Bossiney 1768–9, 1774–84, Middlesex 1769–74, Plympton Erle 1790–94, [UK] Ludgershall 1817–21

0351 CARIQUE-PONSONBY, James

MP for Tulsk 1776–83; Tralee 1783–90

b. 1738; d. Dec. 1796
FAMILY/BACKGROUND: Son of William Carique and Anne, dau. of Thomas Crosbie (0538); assumed name of Ponsonby 1762.
MARRIED: (1) [   ] dau. of John Cookson MD of Yorkshire; (2) ?Mary, dau. of Charles O'Hara (1575).
CHILDREN: William Carique (at Eton College 1783–6); Richard.
EDUCATION: School: Mr Connolly; entered TCD Nov. 1754, aged 16 years.
CAREER/OCCUPATION: High Sheriff of Co. Kerry 1781.

POLITICAL ACTIVITY: He was returned for the first time in the 1776 election, when he purchased his seat from St George Caulfeild (0371). He was reputed to be in difficult financial circumstances, although he had a good property in Co. Kerry. He belonged to a branch of the family of Speaker Ponsonby (1702), but the link was sufficiently tenuous for him to be independent. He was considered a 'quiet respectable country gentleman and very much disposed to Government'.

Almost as soon as he entered parliament he received a small pension, *c.* £400 p.a., from Lord Lieutenant Buckinghamshire. In 1783 he secured his return for Tralee by giving Sir Barry Denny

(0617) his interest in Co. Kerry and £500. In 1786 the Rutland administration secured him an addition of £200 to his existing pension of £400. In 1785 he had voted for the Commercial Resolutions, and he was anxious to obtain office and to be a Trustee of the Linen Board. He voted solidly for the government but he did not achieve either ambition, although he did get a substantial pension. He did not come in again in 1790.

DIVISION LISTS:

1778 (2) voted against the Popery Bill.
1780 (1) voted against Grattan's **(0895)** declaration of the rights of Ireland.
1780 (2) voted against Yelverton's **(2268)** motion to modify Poynings' Law.
1780 (3) voted against the Tenantry Bill.
1780 (4) voted for the Perpetual Mutiny Bill.
1783 (1) voted against Flood's **(0762)** motion for parliamentary reform.
1784 (1) voted against a committee on the Reform Bill.
1785 (1) voted for the Commercial Propositions.

ADDITIONAL INFORMATION: In 1782 his wife was said to have run away with Lord Bellomont **(0480)**, who was married to Lady Emily FitzGerald, a sister of the Duke of Leinster **(0745)**.

ESTATES/RESIDENCE: Crotto, Co. Kerry; [?]Carique, Co. Clare; Dawson Street, Dublin. Bequeathed to his father by his maternal uncle, Richard Ponsonby **(1704)**, by will dated February 1762. In 10 Geo. III (1770), James Ponsonby was granted fairs at Kilflinn, barony of Clanmorris (Clanmaurice).

SOURCES: PRONI D/302; Ellis thesis; *Alum. Dub.*; R. A. Austen-Leigh (ed.), *The Eton College Register, 1753–90* (Eton, 1921) 3 vols; J. Kelly, *Prelude to Union* (Cork, 1992) p. 219; *WHM* (1797) p. 96; *FJ* 10 Dec. 1796; Parliamentary Lists, 1776 (1), (2), (3), 1771 (1), 1778 (1), 1780 (1), 1782 (1), 1783 (1), (2), 1784 (1), 1785 (1), (2), (3), (4), 1787 (1), 1788 (1), 1789 (1), 1790 (1).

CARLETON, Baron: *see* **BOYLE** and **CARLETON**

0208 Boyle, Rt Hon. Henry, 1st Baron Carleton [GB], MP Co. Cork 1692–3, [E] Tamworth 1689–90, Aldborough 1690, Cambridge University 1692–1705, Westminster 1705–10

0353 Carleton, Rt Hon. Hugh, 1st Baron Carleton [I], MP Tuam 1772–6, Philipstown 1776–83, Naas 1783–7

0352 CARLETON, Christopher

MP for Wicklow B. 1696–9, 1703–4

b. ?1640; d. 2 Jan. 1703/4
FAMILY/BACKGROUND: Son of [ ] Carleton.
MARRIED: Isabella [ ].
CHILDREN: Christopher; Rev. Robert, m. Elizabeth Pomeroy *alias* Donnellan; John; Anne, m. [ ] Barry; Mary Anne, m. Robert Carron.
CAREER/OCCUPATION: Joint Chief Commissioner of Revenue, patent 29 July 1692, May 1696; Revenue Commissioner 13 Aug. 1692, 9 July 1702, 27 Nov. 1702; Commissioner of Forfeited Estates (draft patent Dec. 1693, no salary) Feb. 1696; Collector of Belfast 1689–90, 1693, Cork 1690–93 (at a salary of £150 p.a.); Barracks Trustee 12 Feb. 1701.

POLITICAL ACTIVITY: He was a major office-holder from the days of Charles II, when he worked in the customs office, but he was in parliament for only about four years. In 1696 he signed the Association for the protection of William III in the country. He was nominated for three committees, all in 1697–8. In Queen Anne's parliament he would have been over 60, possibly considerably so, and therefore would have been excused from committee service. In any case, he died shortly after the 1703 general election.

ADDITIONAL INFORMATION: Although he was named on a draft warrant of December 1693 as a Commissioner of Forfeited Estates, Carleton's name did not appear on the new warrant of January 1694. He was to receive no salary, as he was already salaried in a Revenue post.

ESTATES/RESIDENCE: Dublin. Purchased 468 acres in Co.

Dublin from the Commissioners of Forfeited Estates in 1702–3.

SOURCES: PRONI T/559 vol. 15 p. 15, Burke, extract pedigrees; Hayton thesis; *Cal. SP Dom. 1691–1692* (London, 1900) pp. 245, 278, 389, *1693* (London, 1903) pp. 174, 442, *1696* (London, 1913) pp. 161, 305, 423; Hughes, *Pat. Officers*; Benn, *Belfast*, p. 323; Simms' cards; *HMC Ormonde* (1920) new ser. vol. 8 p. 53; Simms, *Williamite Confiscation*, p. 184; Parliamentary List, 1696 (1).

0353 CARLETON, Rt Hon. Hugh

MP for Tuam 1772–6; Philipstown 1776–83; Naas 1783–7

b. 11 Sept. 1739; d. 25 Feb. 1826
HONOURS: PC, sworn 11 May 1787.
PEERAGES: Rep. Peer 1800–26; cr. Baron Carleton 17 Sept. 1787; Viscount Carleton 21 Nov. 1797.
FAMILY/BACKGROUND: Eldest son of Francis Carleton of Cork, merchant, and Rebecca, dau. of Hugh Lawton of Co. Cork.
MARRIED: (1) [2 Aug. 1766] Elizabeth, o. dau. of Maj. Richard Mercer; (2) [15 July 1795] Mary, dau. of Abednego Mathew of Dorset ('a lady of great accomplishments and considerable fortune').
CHILDREN: *d.s.p.*
EDUCATION: School: Kilkenny College 25 June 1752, aged 13 years; entered TCD 7 Apr. 1755; Middle Temple 28 Feb. 1758; called to the Irish Bar 1764; Doctor of Civil Law *hon. caus.* Oxford 1810.
CAREER/OCCUPATION: *Bencher of the Honourable Society of King's Inns 1769–d.; King's Counsel 1768, 1770–6; 3rd Serjeant-at-law 1776; 2nd Serjeant-at-law 1777–8; Solicitor General 1779–86; Chief Justice of the Common Pleas 1787 – resigned 20 Dec. 1800; *listed in Judges and Barristers 1790–1800 (f.); *Assistant Judge in the Court of Exchequer Chamber 1797–1800 (f.); *Commissioner of Appeals 1795–7; a Justice of Assize for Connaught, Lent 1784; Leinster, Lent 1787; NW Ulster, Lent 1788; NE Ulster, Summer 1788; Munster, Lent 1789; Connaught, Summer 1790; NW Ulster, Lent 1791; NE Ulster, Summer 1791; Lent Assizes, Connaught Circuit 1797; Summer Assizes, Leinster Circuit 1797; Lent Assizes, Connaught Circuit 1798; Lent Assizes, Home Circuit 1800; Recorder of Cork City 1769–1800 (f.); *Magistrate of Cork City 1769–75. *Mayor of Cork City 1775;

*Governor of the Hibernian Society 1779–1800 (f.); *Governor of the Foundling Hospital and Workhouse 1779–97; *Governor of the Royal Hospital 1786–1800 (f.); *Governor of Dr Steevens' Hospital 1787–1800 (f.); *Governor of Erasmus Smith's Schools and other Charities 1789–8 (f.).

POLITICAL ACTIVITY: A lawyer with considerable influence in Cork city; indeed, in 1790, it was recollected that 'Such was the ascendancy his father had in the Corporation and in the mercantile interest of the town, that he was called the "*king of Cork*". Such, however, is the uncertainty of all human affairs, that he ultimately failed and was even reduced to extreme poverty.' Lord Lieutenant Townshend may have seen him as a counterbalance to the influence of the then Prime Serjeant and later Provost, John Hely-Hutchinson (**1001**), for in 1775 it was reported that 'There is a shyness between him and the Provost from his family influence in Cork.'

The story is told that Carleton 'contracted an intimacy with Mr Scott, afterwards Lord Clonmell (**1891**), at the college of Dublin, and they studied *together* at the *Temple*, where Mr Carleton's father, in the days of his prosperity, supported them both. Mr Scott was, at the time, so poor, that it is supposed his subsequent call to the Bar could not have been effected without much difficulty. Mr Scott never forgot this debt of gratitude and obligation. When Mr Carleton's difficulties came upon him, he largely contributed to his relief and proved himself a sincere friend to his son.' Ultimately this was to bring Carleton into the powerful Scott/Beresford (**0115**)/Fitzgibbon (**0749**) circle of the late eighteenth century, where he might not otherwise have been.

Towards the end of his career he was characterised as follows: 'As a lawyer he holds the middle rank, not having ever been considered as a first-rate man; persevering industry and methodical arrangement being the leading traits of his professional character. As a professional speaker, he was neat and argumentative, but of no great consideration in Parliament.' He was already a KC when Townshend, to whom he had been a gentleman usher, brought him into parliament in 1772 on the appointment of Richard Power (**1717**) as 3rd Baron of the Exchequer.

Reports varied as to his parliamentary abilities. One government list considered that he was 'able in parliament and a man of honour'; another, three years later, declared him to be 'an able sensible man, of strict honour ... A tolerable speaker. Much esteemed by the Chancellor as a good lawyer and a man of great integrity and application. He supported last session steadily and ably ... His object is the Bench.' In the meantime: 'He is to have a civil employment of not less than £400 for himself, or for a time will be satisfied if Serjeant Hamilton (0922) is made a judge, to be made second or third Serjeant. On the late failure of his father at Cork Lord Harcourt gave his brother Francis the Collection of Athlone worth £300 and appointed the father agent for conducting the embarkation of the 8 regiments lately sent to America. He has given to his recommendation 2 Boatmen.' In addition he was 'much respected by Mr Waite (2154)', the influential long-serving Under-Secretary at the Castle.

He was 3rd Serjeant-at-Law in 1776, 2nd Serjeant-at-Law in 1778 and Solicitor General in 1780. In 1776 he purchased his seat for Philipstown from Lord Belvidere (1800) through an arrangement made by Lord Lieutenant Harcourt. However, Lord Lieutenant Buckinghamshire complained that he 'is exceedingly well qualified for his office as a Lawyer, but can give little Assistance in Parliament' – that first duty of legal MPs. This opinion was supported in 1782 when he was said to be 'a good lawyer but no use as a speaker'. In 1783 he purchased his seat for Naas from Lord Mayo (0192), and his ambition was declared to be either a Chief Justice or a puisne judge with a pension for his wife. In 1784 his reputation remained that of 'a good lawyer and a worthy but nervous man. Very strongly attached to Government. His brother lately made Collector of Newry on the recommendation of Lord Hillsborough as he did not succeed for Mr Reilly (1773).' He was among those whom Orde (1594) consulted in 1785 over the Commercial Resolutions; Orde asked him to canvass the MPs then at Spa.

Finally in 1787 he got his reward: he was appointed Chief Justice of Common Pleas and created Baron Carleton; ten years later, in 1797, he was elevated to the rank of viscount. In December 1798 Carleton declared to Lord Lieutenant Cornwallis his opposition to the Union, but by January 1799 he had become a supporter of the measure, although he felt the timing to be inopportune. When Cornwallis proposed him as a representative peer, Portland objected that this would impair his judicial function. But Carleton, not to be done out of this final accolade, resigned from the Bench and was duly made a representative peer. He received £2,700 compensation at the Union for loss of offices.

DIVISION LISTS:
    1773 (1) voted for an Absentee Tax.
    1773 (2) voted against an untaxed press.
    1774 (1) voted for the Stamp Bill.
    1775 (1) voted against the pro-American amendment to the Speech from the Throne.
    1777 (1) voted against Grattan's (0895) motion for retrenchment.
    1778 (2) voted for the Popery Bill.
    1779 (1) voted for new taxes.
    1779 (2) voted against a six-months Loan Bill.
    1780 (1) voted against Grattan's declaration of the rights of Ireland.
    1780 (2) voted against Yelverton's (2268) motion to modify Poynings' Law.
    1783 (1) voted against Flood's (0762) motion for parliamentary reform.
    1784 (1) voted against a committee on the Reform Bill.
    1785 (1) absent.

ESTATES/RESIDENCE: Willow Park, Co. Dublin.

SOURCES: PRONI T/618/329 Crossle Papers [says appointed Recorder of Cork 24 Aug. 1767]; Ellis thesis; Burke *Ext. P* (1883) p. 104; GEC *P; DNB; Alum. Oxon.*; IMC *King's Inns Admission Papers, 1607–1867*; Smyth, *Law Officers*; Ball, *Judges*; *Index to Irish Privy Counsellors, 1711–1910*; C. Ross (ed.), *Cornwallis Corr.* (London, 1859), vol. 3 pp. 4, 31, 260, 265, 274, 286; H. A. C. Sturgess, *Register of Admissions to the Honourable Society of the Middle Temple* (London, 1949), vol. 1 p. 352; Johnston, *Gt B. & Ire.*, p. 231; J. Kelly, *Prelude to Union* (Cork, 1992), p. 145, 205, 226; J. Kelly, *'That Damn'd thing called Honour': Duelling in Ireland 1570–1860* (Cork, 1995), p. 197; *JRSAI* vol. 30 (1900) p. 310, F. E. Ball, 'The Antiquities from Blackrock to Dublin'; *ibid.* vol. 54 (1924) pp. 55–67, T. U. Sadleir,

'The Register of Kilkenny School (1685–1800)'; *Ir. Gen.* vol. 1 no. 10 (1941) p. 295, W. Clare, 'Irish Compensations and Pensions'; *Almanacks*; *FJ* 6–9 Mar. 1784, 3–6 Mar. 1787, 9–12 Feb. 1788, 12–14 June 1788, 26–28 Feb. 1789, 1–3 July 1790, 10–12 Mar. 1791, 26–28 Mar. 1791, 7 Mar., 5 Aug. 1797, 1 Mar. 1798, 4 Jan. 1800; *DJ* 23 July 1795; Parliamentary Lists, 1772 (2), 1773 (1), (2), 1774 (1), 1775 (1), 1776 (1), (2), (3), 1777 (1), 1778 (1), 1780 (1), 1782 (1), 1783 (1), (2), 1784 (1), (2), 1785 (1), 1799 (1).

DIVISION LISTS:
1796 (1) voted for parity of trade with Great Britain.
1797 (1) voted for Ponsonby's (**1709**) motion for parliamentary reform.

ADDITIONAL INFORMATION: Member of the Friendly Brothers of St Patrick, a society for controlling duelling.

SOURCES: *FJ* 21 May 1799.

CARLOW, Viscount: *see* DAWSON

0597 Dawson, William Henry, 1st Baron Dawson, Viscount Carlow, MP Portarlington 1733–60, 1769–70, Queen's County 1761–8
0589 Dawson, Rt Hon. John, 2nd Viscount Carlow, 1st Earl of Portarlington, MP Portarlington 1766–8, Queen's County 1768–76–9

0354 CARNCROSS, Hugh

MP for Newtown Limavady 1795–7

b. ?1743; d. May 1799
FAMILY/BACKGROUND: Son of [   ] Carncross.
MARRIED: ?
CHILDREN: ?
MILITARY: Major in the army during the War of American Independence.

POLITICAL ACTIVITY: He was returned in the by-election for Newtown Limavady following the retirement of John Richardson, who accepted the office of Escheator of Munster. He was sworn on 24 March 1795. The borough had been sold by Thomas Conolly (**0459**) to Lord Londonderry in 1792 for an undisclosed sum. Carncross, whose political inclinations obviously favoured the opposition, was an unusual choice for Lord Londonderry, whose brother-in-law was Lord Lieutenant Camden. However, he may have been chosen during the previous (brief) viceroyalty of Earl Fitzwilliam. He was not returned in 1797, and very little is known of him.

0355 CARPENTER, George

MP for Newtown 1703–5 (absent on the Queen's service in England); [GB] Whitchurch 1715–22; Westminster 1722–7

b. 10 Feb. 1657; d. 10 Feb. 1732
PEERAGES: Cr. Baron Carpenter 29 May 1719.
FAMILY/BACKGROUND: Son of Warncombe Carpenter and Eleanor, dau. of William Taylor of Herefordshire, wid. of John Hill.
MARRIED: [23 Jan. 1694] Alice, dau. of William Caulfeild, 1st Viscount Charlemont, wid. of James Margetson.
CHILDREN: George, 2nd Baron Carpenter, m. Elizabeth dau. of David Petty of Essex.
CAREER/OCCUPATION: Page (aged 14 years) to 1st Duke of Montagu in his Embassy to France; Envoy to Court of Vienna 1715; Governor of Minorca 5 July 1716–18. *Magistrate of Kilkenny 1743, 1756, *Sheriff of Kilkenny 1743, *Mayor of Kilkenny 1756.
MILITARY: He joined the 3rd Troop of Life Guards as a Gentleman Private; Quartermaster to the Earl of Manchester's Troop in the Earl of Peterborough's newly raised Regiment of Horse 27 June 1685; Cornet 1 June 1687; Captain 1689; Major 18 May 1691; Lieutenant-Colonel of Peterborough's Regiment of Horse 1 Jan. 1692, commanded by Colonel Edward Villiers; Colonel of 3rd (King's Own) Dragoons 1703–d., Brigadier-General 25 Dec. 1705; Major-General 10 Sept. 1708; commanded cavalry brigade at Almanza, 25 Apr. 1707; Lieutenant-General 1 Jan. 1710; wounded at Battle of Almenara July 1710; severely wounded and taken prisoner at Brihuega Dec. 1710 when defending the breach; actively employed in Scotland and England during the 1715 rebellion and was senior General at the taking of Preston 13 Nov. 1715; Commander-in-Chief [S] 1718–19.

POLITICAL ACTIVITY: He was a professional soldier, who ended his career as commander-in-chief in Scotland during and following the 1715 rebellion. He was, unusually, permitted to resign from his seat in parliament because of his military duties which kept him absent in England and elsewhere in Europe during the War of Spanish Succession: on 14 February 1705 the Commons received a letter from Colonel Carpenter saying 'that her Majesty's service required his Attendance in England, and that he cannot attend the Service of the House and desiring that a new Writ may issue ... for ... Newtown.' The House then ordered the writ to be issued.

He appears to have come to Ireland to build up an estate, as he made various land purchases in Co. Kilkenny with money from his wife's dowry, £1,800, part of which he also used to purchase a colonelcy.

ADDITIONAL INFORMATION: On 15 December 1703 he wrote to Ormonde outlining his services to him in parliament and asking the duke's favour if a regiment of horse was raised in or for Ireland. He said he was the eldest lieutenant-colonel in the horse and the joint-eldest brevet of colonel in the army. He had served in Ireland and Flanders. He claimed that he had the interest, money and knowledge in soldiery to make as good a regiment as any man.

ESTATES/RESIDENCE: Longwood, Hampshire; Co. Kilkenny. He purchased from the Commissioners for Sale of Forfeited Estates 1,068 acres in 1702–3 and, on 23 June 1703, Barrowmount, part of the estate of Piers, Viscount Galmoy, attainted, for £1,080, and Killahy, part of the estate of John Grace, also attainted, for £1,585. All these lands were in Co. Kilkenny.

SOURCES: GEC *P*; Burke *Ext. P* (1883) p. 106; *CJ Ire.* vol. 2 part 1 p. 426; *Cal. SP Dom. 1691–1692* (London, 1900) pp. 80, 442; *DNB*; C. Dalton, *George the First's Army, 1714–1727*; *HP 1715–54*; *HMC Ormonde*, (1920) new ser. vol. 8 pp. 50, 324; *Almanacks*; Simms, *Williamite Confiscation*, p. 184; Parliamentary Lists, 1706 (1), 1707 (1), (4).

0356 CARR, Thomas

MP for Newtown Limavady 1703–13

b. 1667; d. 1720
FAMILY/BACKGROUND: Son of Thomas Carr.
MARRIED: ?Jane [   ].
CHILDREN: ?Thomas; ?Jane.
EDUCATION: School: Mr Torway, Dublin; entered TCD 24 Apr. 1685, aged 18 years; BA 1690; MA 1692.
CAREER/OCCUPATION: Joint Cursitor in Chancery (life); on 26 Apr. 1710 received £800 'in consideration of the loss he sustained in the profits of his office as Cursitor'.
MILITARY: He may have had a military career before entering parliament. There was a Thomas Carr (or Kerr), Ensign in Royal Regiment of Foot 1 Oct. 1689; Lieutenant 1 July 1696; wounded at Namur 8 July 1695; commission renewed 1702 (i.e. on the outbreak of war).

POLITICAL ACTIVITY: He was listed for 17 committees between 1705 and 1711, and appears to have been solidly in opposition to the government during that period. He did not come into parliament in 1713.

ESTATES/RESIDENCE: Donore, Co. Kildare.

SOURCES: *CJ Ire.* (Bradley ed.) vol. 5 pp. 304–45; Magherafelt, PRONI MIC/1/1 Church of Ireland Parish Church Register [says Thomas son of Thomas Carr bapt. 1718, a possible son or grandson]; Hayton thesis; Simms' cards; *Alum. Dub.*; C. Dalton (ed.), *English Army Lists and Commission Registers, 1661–1714* (London, 1896), vol. 3 p. 47; Vicars, *Prerog. Wills*; *The Registers of St John the Evangelist Dublin, 1619–1699* (Parish Register Society of Dublin, 1906) p. 229; Parliamentary Lists, 1706 (1), 1711 (3).

0357 (BUCKWORTH) CARR, William

MP for Cashel 1739–53

b. 1705; d. 30 July 1753
FAMILY/BACKGROUND: Son and heir of Richard Buckworth (**0270**) and Anne, dau. of William Carr.
MARRIED: ?
CHILDREN: ?
EDUCATION: School: Mr McDonnell, Cashel; entered TCD 5 Apr. 1721; Middle Temple 28 July 1724; BA 1725; called to the Irish Bar 1731.

CAREER/OCCUPATION: Freeman of Fethard
(Tipperary) 1745.

POLITICAL ACTIVITY: Buckworth *alias* Carr was returned for Cashel in 1739 following the death of
his father, Richard Buckworth (0270), in September 1738. At the time of the Money Bill crisis, he
appears to have wanted to please both sides. Primate Stone wrote on 30 January 1753 to Lord
George Sackville (1835) that 'Bucknall [*sic*] was
with me this morning full of grievances of his being doubted, and protesting fidelity. I hope he
speaks truth. He certainly desires to be thought
faithful. I told him you never gave me the least
hint of any suspicion ... I believe he was willing
to keep fair on all sides and that I take to be the
worst. He has been thoroughly frightened.' He
voted for the election of James Digges La Touche
(♦♦♦♦), against the administration. He was dead
before the vital vote on the Money Bill on 17
December 1753.

DIVISION LISTS:
1749 (1) voted for the election of James
Digges La Touche (♦♦♦♦).

ESTATES/RESIDENCE: Lisheen, Co. Tipperary.

SOURCES: PRONI T/559 vol. 13 p. 40, Burke, extract
pedigrees; McCracken thesis; *IMC King's Inns Admission Papers, 1607–1867*; *Alum. Dub.*; *Register of Admissions to the Honourable Society of the Middle Temple* (London, 1949) vol. 1 p. 295; *Ir. Gen.* vol. 4, no. 4 (1971)
p. 319, W. G. Skehan, 'Extracts from the Minutes of
the Corporation of Fethard, Co. Tipperary'; *HMC
Sackville I* p. 189; *Pue's Occurrences* 4 Aug. 1753.

CARRICK, Earl of: *see* BUTLER
0316 Butler, Hon. Henry Thomas, 2nd Earl of
Carrick, MP Killyleagh 1768–74

0358 CARROLL, Ephraim

MP for Fethard (Wexford) 1783–90; Bannow
1790–7–9; [Escheator of Munster 7 Mar. 1799]

b. (bapt. 10 Mar.) 1753; d. 1824
FAMILY/BACKGROUND: Son of Ephraim Carroll (d.

7 Apr. 1773), a Proctor of the Court of Preroga-
tive, and Barbara, dau. of Charles Tottenham
(2086).
MARRIED: [Sept. 1789] Elizabeth Doherty, wid. of
John Doherty of Dublin.
CHILDREN: John.
EDUCATION: School: private tutor; entered TCD 2
Nov. 1771, aged 16 (?18) years; BA 1776;
Middle Temple 23 Jan. 1777; called to the Irish
Bar 1780.
CAREER/OCCUPATION: *Listed in Judges and
Barristers 1789–1800 (f.).

POLITICAL ACTIVITY: He was returned in 1783 for
Fethard, a borough that had the distinction of representing a corporation, composed of non-resident
burgesses, identical to that of Bannow (for which
he was returned in 1790 and 1797) and
Clonmines. This common corporation was controlled by Charles Tottenham (2088), later Earl
and Marquess of Ely. As part of Lord Ely's party,
Carroll supported. Even after the 1790 election
his two anti-government votes, for a Regency and
for Ponsonby (1709) as Speaker, were in accordance with his patron's policy. On the occasion of
the Regency vote Lord Lieutenant Buckingham
stated that 'These four great rats, Lords Shannon
(0213), Loftus (1252), Ponsonby and the Duke
of Leinster (0745), carry 42 and therefore make a
difference of 84 on the division', indicating how
absolutely they controlled their followers. In the
case of Loftus: 'They are in fact, the agents of the
noble Viscount's power and the means of his political consequence.'

Much to the annoyance of Lord (Loftus) Ely,
who had his eye on an Irish marquessate and a
British peerage, Carroll refused to support the
Union: according to Ely he was 'a mule' and influenced by the attitude of his colleagues at the
bar; Alcock (0021), another Ely MP, was prevented from opposing the Union because of his
involvement in Waterford city politics. Ely wrote,
quite ruthlessly, to Castlereagh (2009) that 'Neither of them shall appear against us. I shall get rid
of each of them as soon as possible. My other
friends in town will attend you.' Carroll duly accepted the office of Escheator of Munster and
thereby vacated his seat. Ironically, his replacement, Robert Shaw (1906), was also an anti-
Unionist and Ely had to go through the whole
process again.

DIVISION LISTS:
> 1783 (1) voted against Flood's (0762) motion for parliamentary reform.
> 1784 (1) voted against a committee on the Reform Bill.
> 1785 (1) voted for (?against) the Commercial Propositions.
> 1789 (1) voted for a Regency.
> 1790 (2) voted for Ponsonby (1709) on the Election of a Speaker.

ESTATES/RESIDENCE: Rockfield, Co. Wexford; Peter Street and St Stephen's Green, Dublin. He lived in Peter Street until 1804, when he acquired the lease of 41 St Stephen's Green.

SOURCES: PRONI T/559 vol. 15 p. 72, Burke, extract pedigrees [says wife's father (sic) is called Doherty]; PRONI T/3166/10 Hartnell notes; O'Neill thesis; Burke LG (1846) p. 1413; *Alum. Dub.*; Hughes, *Pat. Officers*, IMC King's Inns Admission Papers, 1607–1867; J. H. Bernard (ed.), *The Register of St Patrick, Dublin, 1677–1800* (Parish Register Society of Dublin, 1907), p. 62; H. A. C. Sturgess, *Register of Admissions to the Honourable Society of the Middle Temple*, vol. 1 (London, 1949) p. 384 [calls him William Ephraim]; HMC *Fortescue I* p. 418 et seq.; J. Kelly, *Prelude to Union* (Cork, 1992), p. 193 [says he voted against the Commercial Propositions]; Bolton, *The Passing of the Irish Act of Union*, p. 174 and n. 2; *Almanacks*, DJ 8–10 Apr. 1773 [mentions Eph. Carroll (father), a Proctor of the Court of Prerogative who d. 7 Apr. 'at his seat in Co. Carlow']; Parliamentary Lists, 1783 (2), 1784 (1), (2), (3), 1785 (1), (2), (3), (4), 1787 (1), 1789 (1), 1790 (1), 1791 (1), 1793 (1), 1794 (2).

0359 CARTER, Thomas

MP for Fethard (Tipperary) 1695–9; Portarlington 1703–13. On 13 Aug. 1695 Col. Thomas Clere unsuccessfully petitioned against his return for Fethard

> b. *c.* 1650; d. 19 Aug 1726
> FAMILY/BACKGROUND: Son of William Carter of Dinton, Bucks, and his wife Margaret Thorpe.
> MARRIED: (1) [marriage bond 13 Dec. 1681] Margaret Houghton; (2) [2 Aug. 1702] Isabella, dau. of Matthew Boynton of Yorkshire and granddau. of Sir Matthew Boyton MP [E], wid. of the poet Dillon Wentworth, 4th Earl of Roscommon (d. 1684).

> CHILDREN: (1) Thomas (0360); Mary; Joanna.
> EDUCATION: LLD *hon. caus.* 1709.
> CAREER/OCCUPATION: Clerk of the Rules of the King's Bench; Clerk of Errors Court of Exchequer; 2nd Serjeant-at-Arms to the House of Commons 29 Oct. 1692–1723; Black Rod, House of Lords 1692.
> MILITARY: Fought at the Battle of the Boyne.

POLITICAL ACTIVITY: This, as opposed to the Welsh, branch of the family probably came to Ireland in the second half of the seventeenth century. Carter fought at the Battle of the Boyne and afterwards captured 'divers useful books and writings belonging to King James and his secretaries' which had been deposited in the vaults of Christ Church Cathedral. He petitioned for the office of 2nd Serjeant-at-Arms, 3 September 1692, in consideration of his services at Londonderry and after the the Boyne, 1 July 1690. A warrant granting a patent on reversion was issued, 10 October 1692.

He was returned for Fethard, Co. Tipperary in 1695: his return was contested unsuccessfully by Colonel Thomas Clere (0422), who had been returned for this borough in 1692. He was nominated for three committees in 1795–8 and for 20 in 1703–10. He supported Lord Chancellor Porter against the accusations of favouring Catholics made against him by some MPs in 1695, and signed the Association for the protection of William III in parliament in 1696. During Anne's reign he was recorded as opposed to the administration in 1706 and 1711. He was not returned at the general elections of 1713 or 1715.

In 1719 he was electioneering (unsuccessfully) for a seat belonging to Lord Burlington, and on 25 June he wrote to Lord Carleton that: 'I am in principle a Whig, and will ever act upon those principles, let the event be what it may. Nay, so much, that I would not upon any consideration have people mistake me in that affair. As to any disputes between K[ing] and p[eople], I never thought about them. For what may happen here and the people who pretend to be the chiefs, I have no obligations to any of them. I have never asked for nor am I desirous of receiving a favour from any of them.'

ADDITIONAL INFORMATION: The Carters appear to have been a London merchant family who were embroiled in the parliamentary side during the

Civil War. Towards the end of the interregnum they 'trimmed'. During the social upheaval of the Cromwellian period one branch of the family went to Wales and another to Ireland. On 8 November 1692 the Ulster King of Arms granted the request of Thomas Carter 'and to his brother William Carter Gent. [died September 1698], such Armes, Crest and Motto, as may be a distinction from others of their name and family in Wales, they being now resident in Ireland'. The grant points out the various offices that Carter had or held.

ESTATES/RESIDENCE: Robertstown, Co. Meath; Hollybrook, Co. Dublin; Henrietta Street, Dublin. He purchased 12 acres in Co. Dublin, 5 acres in Co. Limerick and 2,157 acres in Co. Meath from the Commissioners for Sale of Forfeited Estates in 1702–3. He purchased from Henry, Viscount Sydney a forfeited estate in Co. Meath for £3,735. In 1702 he purchased from the Commissioners for Sale of Forfeited Estates the Robertstown estate, nr Ashbourne, Co. Meath; at one time this estate produced £4,000 p.a. (by 1850 this had dwindled to £2,500). The Countess of Roscommon was receiving a pension of £100 p.a. in 1675. She and her then husband, Lord Roscommon, were granted, 20 January 1676, the lodgings within St James's Park, London at a rent of 13s 4d p.a. Later Charles II granted her a 'small tenement' for her life. She died in 1721. The family history states that through her the Roscommon estates at Rathnally, Co. Meath came to Thomas Carter and he resided there towards the end of his life.

In 1688 Thomas Carter, with his wife and two children, fled to Wales: at that time he had personal estate valued at £60 and an estate in England worth £200 p.a.

On 17 July 1719 Thomas Carter, Sr and Jr, petitioned the Commons to sell off part of their Robertstown estate in order to pay debts, and for other purposes.

SOURCES: P. Aronsson Esq., who has made a study of the Carter family suggested the above parentage [William Carter was m. in 1641 and alive in 1650 and date of Thomas Carter's second marriage comes from a family tree. His grant of arms from the Ulster King of Arms in 1692 refers to him being an Irish MP]; other information was supplied by P. F. Meehan Esq.; PRONI T/3158/2 (146/0) Chatsworth Papers; *CJ Ire.* (Bradley ed.), vol. 2 (1696) pp. 47, 145–6, 687, 996, 1006; *GEC P*; Burke *LGI* (1904) p. 85, *IFR* (1976) p. 215; *Cal SP Dom. 1691–2* (London, 1900) pp. 433, 477, *1694–5* (London, 1906) p. 470; Gilbert, *Dublin*, vol. 1 p. 125; Simms' cards; *Alum. Dub.*; Hughes, *Pat. Officers*; *Dublin Marriage Bonds Index GO 473*; H. F. Berry (ed.), *The Registers of the Church of St Michan, Dublin, 1636–1700* (Parish Register Society of Dublin, 1909), p. 38

[says Thomas son of Thomas and Ellinor Carter baptised 20 Aug. 1663, this is almost certainly not this Thomas Carter; his brother William Carter and his children were bur. in St Bride's]; *Almanacks*; Simms, *Williamite Confiscation*; Parliamentary Lists, 1695 (1), 1696 (1), 1706 (1), 1711 (3).

0360 CARTER, Rt Hon. Thomas

MP for Trim 1719–26; Hillsborough 1727–60 [r. Dungarvan and Lismore 1727]

b. *c.* 1682; d. 2 Sept. 1763
HONOURS: PC, sworn 23 June 1732, 1734–51, removed 3 May 1754, resworn 31 Oct. 1755–63.
FAMILY/BACKGROUND: Eldest son of Thomas Carter (**0359**) and Margaret Houghton.
MARRIED: [1719] Mary, dau. and co-h. of Thomas Claxton of Dublin.
CHILDREN: Thomas (**0361**); Henry Boyle, m. [23 Feb. 1750] Susanna, dau. and co-h. of Sir Arthur Shaen, 2nd Baronet (**1900**), wid. of James Wynne (**2259**); Frances, m. (1) [27 Feb. 1746] Philip Twysden (b. 1713; d. 1752), Bp of Raphoe, chaplain to Lord Lieutenant Chesterfield, (2) Gen. James Johnstone; Susan, m. [21 Apr. 1743] Stephen Trotter (**2114**) of Duleek, Co. Louth; Mary (d. unm.).
EDUCATION: School: Mr Walls, Dublin; entered TCD 9 Jan. 1707; Middle Temple 28 Apr. 1708; BA 1710.
CAREER/OCCUPATION: Second Serjeant-at-Arms to the House of Commons, patent 13 July 1723, *1732–52; Deputy Master of the Rolls, patent 11 May 1725; Examiner in Chancery, patent 6 May 1727; Clerk of the Crown, Protonotory, Keeper of Writs, Philizer, Clerk of the Entries and Clerk of the Errors 1729–63 (patents 2 Oct. 1733, 1 July 1748); Master of the Rolls 29 Dec. 1731–53, patent, 29 Dec. 1731; *Treasurer to the Honorable Society of King's Inns 1738–41; Principal Secretary of State 1755–60; Joint Secretary of State 1760–3. Burgess of Carlingford *c.* Sept. 1725; Free Burgess of New Ross, 10 Jan. 1727; *Commissioner of Oyer and Terminer 1732–53; *Governor of the Workhouse 1733–62; *Trustee of the Linen Board for Leinster 1733–d.; *Commissioner of the Tillage Act for Munster 1735, 1739–d.; *Judge and the Ranger of the Course of the Curragh 1736; *Ranger of the Curragh of Kildare 1738–52; *Ranger of Dublin Castle 1742; *Governor of the Royal Hospital 1755–d.

POLITICAL ACTIVITY: Thomas Carter was a major political figure in the mid-eighteenth century. In 1724 he subscribed to a declaration of High Sheriffs, Justices of the Peace, Grand Jury, nobility, clergy, gentlemen and freeholders of Co. Dublin against Wood's Halfpence. He was originally a protégé of Alan Brodrick (0237) and joined with St John Brodrick (0242) in persuading country gentry to oppose government on the grounds that they had strong support in England. Carter was able, ambitious and a good parliamentary speaker, with an extraordinary gift for vituperation. A problem, noted by his contemporaries, was an inability to take or seek advice.

On 29 April 1725 Primate Boulter wrote to Lord Townshend that 'We hear that the mastership of the Rolls (which as it is for life, is one of the greatest places in the law here) is permitted to be sold to a native of this place.' Boulter felt that the only way to secure British interest and policy in Ireland was to appoint only Englishmen to the highest positions in the Irish civil and ecclesiastical administration. On 22 March 1725 Boulter had written to the Duke of Newcastle that 'I have formerly wrote about Mr Carter, and I hope when the judges return from their circuits, to be able to point out such a way of dealing with him, as will make his opposition in future sessions of little weight: I am sure the rudeness with which he has, in his speeches in parliament, threated the *English* ministry, not to say the whole nation, as well as those of us who are settled here, deserve that he should be made an example of.'

Despite Boulter's opposition, Thomas Carter purchased the reversion of the Mastership of the Rolls from the Earl of Berkely. He was appointed Deputy Master of the Rolls in 1725 and succeeded to the Mastership of the Rolls in 1731. He had also a King's Bench office, and was made a PC when he became Master of the Rolls. Although he had purchased the office he agreed to hold it 'during pleasure', and for this concession Lord Lieutenant Dorset felt that he should be rewarded, particularly as 'Mr Carter's abilities may be of use in carrying on his Majesty's service.'

In 1729 he was a leading figure in one of the early road acts, 3 Geo. II, c. 18, 'an Act for repairing the road leading from the city of Dublin to Kilcullen Bridge in the County of Kildare', and in 1737 he brought in the heads of a bill to make perpetual 'an Act for preserving all such Ships and Goods thereof which shall happen to be forced on Shore or stranded upon the Coasts of this Kingdom and also for inflicting the Punishment of Death on all such as shall wilfully burn, sink or destroy Ships.' Wrecking was a problem in certain parts of the country.

In the early 1730s, when Speaker Gore unexpectedly died, Marmaduke Coghill (0431) considered Carter as a possible candidate for Speaker. Although Carter was probably the ablest man in the House, he was too intelligent not to realise that abilities could not compensate for the lack of a solid power base, and he supported Henry Boyle (0210), over whom he came to exert a degree of influence. Carter was not without friends, and on 10 January 1734 Lord Lieutenant Dorset wrote to George Dodington that 'Your friend Tom Carter was in the front of the battle, but was strongly supported by men of a very different complexion; Cope (0489), Agm. Vesey (2144) and the Prime Serjeant (1924) distinguished themselves very much.'

In 1737, at the time of the currency crisis, Carter was still very much a government man. On 27 October 1737 Lord George Sackville (1835) wrote to his father, the Duke of Dorset, that 'The [Cork] petitions against the lowering of the gold were considered yesterday in the House. They first proposed a Committee, and when that was negatived by 108 to 55, Stannard (1981) moved for a resolution that the lowering was prejudicial to the trade of the country. This was rejected by 11 to 40, and Carter proposed that the further consideration of the petitions should be postponed to the 1st of October [1738] which was carried by 118 to 30' – this was equivalent to letting it lie on the table. 'The chief speakers on the side of the minority were Stannard, Sir Richard Cox (0508) (who abus'd the Privy Council very grossly) Mr Morgan (1487), Mr Maloun [sic] (1336). On the other side the Solicitor General (0196), Mr Cope (0489), Mr Coote (0479), Mr Cuff [sic] (0557) and Mr Hill (1015).'

By the 1740s Carter's influence was such that Lord Lieutenant Chesterfield wrote that his 'most earnest request' was to promote Carter's son from cornet to captain and give him a company in General Irwin's regiment, because 'Mr Carter, Master of the Rolls in Ireland, who is the leading person in the parliament there, has great influence over the Speaker, whose party constitutes the great majority in that House.' But Carter's relationship with the government soured shortly after when some of his requests were turned down in favour of those of the English Lord Chancellor. Carter showed how awkward he could become when he made a violent speech against a navigation bill that had originated in the Privy Council. This led to a direct confrontation between him and Chesterfield, in which he was told that his duty was to do the king's business or face loss of office. Then, on 16 February 1749, he wrote to Lord Chesterfield's successor, Lord Lieutenant Harrington, asking that his son should succeed him as Master of the Rolls. The office had cost him above £11,000: 'that I might have the honour of being employed in such a station in His Majesty's affairs, a thing which has not been done by many, but where my heart was, there I was resolved to venture my fortunes'.

Primate Stone dated Carter's enmity to Chesterfield's viceroyalty, writing that 'Lord Chesterfield had left this country in very ill temper with the Master of the Rolls, Mr Carter, upon account of the rejection of a bill in the House of Commons with some circumstances of disrespect towards his lordship which he thought it incumbent upon him as chief governor to resent ... His Lordship's sentiments were declared without much reserve ... [the bill was unimportant and] ... the rejection of it drew no attention; but those who were less clear-sighted than Lord Chesterfield considered that proceeding as a specimen of future opposition ... the appointment of a new Lord Lieutenant opened another scene ... as the government fell into the hands of a person who was supposed to have lost the share of his Majesty's favour and confidence which he had once possessed and would consequently become dependent upon them ... My Lord Harrington had not been a week in Dublin before his treaty was completed ... [his position made his course inevitable] ... And it was plain enough at the time, and still plainer from the pangs which the execution of this treaty cost

him, that it was not the measure which his judgment would have dictated ... It was in October 1748 that Mr Carter came to me with a very unexpected and abrupt proposal for my assisting in procuring his Majesty's appointment of his son (0361), at that time a very young man and little known, to succeed him as Master of the Rolls. I declined engaging in it, as thinking it an improper request to be made and improbable to be granted, principally on account of the nature and dignity of the office, which would hardly be allowed to be transferred and handed about as places that are merely lucrative are, without regard being had to the qualifications and experience of the persons who fill them. The Master broke out into the bitterest resentments and set himself from that moment to contrive and execute mischief. I found the Speaker ... by no means dissatisfied with the part I had taken, as it relieved him from some distress; for it was not secret that Mr Malone was destined by him to succeed in that office, it being his favourite object and particularly spoken of in the preceding winter when Mr Carter was dangerously ill. I told the Speaker my apprehensions that Mr Carter would endeavour to destroy the good understanding that subsisted between us. He told me that he was not blind to Mr Carter's faults ... [At this point Stone went to England and on his return he] found that the poison was beginning to work; so that it became my whole employment to remove the strange and unaccountable suspicions and jealousies which were daily infused into his [the Speaker's] mind ...

'The appointment of the Duke of Dorset ... afford[ed] Mr Carter a larger field to exercise himself than he had possessed before. A Lord Lieutenant from former knowledge acquainted with the country and having many personal friends in it, expected to come from his Majesty's presence with a great share of his royal favour and confidence; his son, who was to act as secretary ... capable of supporting any part he undertook with spirit and ability; one of the Lords Justices [Stone] whose age and early settlement in this country were apt for forming connections; the other from the general tenour of his conduct presumed incapable of entering into intrigues ... and personally well disposed [to the new Lord Lieutenant]

...When this was well coloured over it exhibited an assemblage of persons that have not usually appeared together upon this stage, and when frequently presented to view might stir the jealousies and suspicions that become habitual in the minds of persons who are used to live by contraband trade.' When reporting events, Primate Stone had a tendency to selective, retrospective tunnel vision and, as the British administration eventually discovered, it was difficult to know how much reliance to place on his analysis and interpretation of situations and motivation. From shortly after his appointment Stone was hostile to Carter, who responded by circulating the most scurrilous libels about the Primate.

In the early 1750s there was a surplus in the Revenue and a storm had blown up over the constitutional implications of the method of its disposal. There was general agreement that it should be put to the reduction of the national debt, but the question was whether this should be decided by the king or left to the House of Commons. In 1753 Carter was Chairman of the Committee of Supply and as such responsible for introducing the Money Bill into the House of Commons. Lord Lieutenant Dorset stated that he 'absolutely refused to insert the words used in the preamble in the last bill' (i.e. signifying the king's 'previous consent'). Boyle, Carter and Malone were all immovable on this point, and on 17 December 1753 the Money Bill was rejected. Carter and Malone were dismissed in January 1754 and as Speaker Boyle continued to be intractable he was dismissed, in April, from his lucrative position as Chancellor of the Exchequer. Thomas Waite (2154) wrote to Wilmot, 29 December 1753 that 'The Friends of Government are highly pleased. Indeed there would not only have been an end of our party, but I think an end of the English Government here if these steps had not been taken.' Henry Singleton (1924), now old and feeble, was appointed Master of the Rolls.

The letter indicating Carter's dismissal from the Privy Council and the Mastership of the Rolls, and the loss of his pension, was sent by Secretary Holdernesse to Lord Lieutenant Dorset on 28 December 1753, but as late as 20 April 1754 Waite wrote to Wilmot: 'but pray how happens it that no king's letter is yet sent for determining ... the pension of £500 per ann. that Mr Carter [has] during the King's pleasure?'; apparently this letter was not sent until 23 May 1754. On 20 January 1754, Lord George Sackville wrote to Lord Holdernesse: 'As to Mr Carter, he sent an excuse that he could not wait upon my Lord Lieutenant that morning as he was seized with the gout in his hand. Upon that I was sent to his house, but before I saw him the Speaker had acquainted him with the business I went upon. He said he was concerned at being dismissed his Majesty's service, but that he could not have acted otherwise than he did without quitting those friends to whom he had been attached for thirty years past. He desired me to assure my Lord Lieutenant that his being out of employment would not alter his conduct in the least, and if any business was to come into parliament in which he could, before his dismission, have assisted Government, he should be equally ready to do so in his present situation. In the course of his conversation it was very plain that this measure had been first undertaken and afterwards pursued in complyance with the opinion of Prime Serjeant Malone.' On 1 August 1754 Stone reported to Lord George Sackville that the late Master of the Rolls was nominated as a magistrate at Navan, all the force of the party was used, the Speaker wrote urgent letters on his behalf, money was employed; but on Monday he was beaten by ten or twelve voices.

However, the Duke of Dorset was replaced by the Marquess of Hartington, who in the course of his viceroyalty succeeded his father as 4th Duke of Devonshire. Hartington was connected through his late wife, Lady Charlotte Boyle, to both Speaker Boyle and his successor, Speaker Ponsonby (1702), as two of Hartington's sisters had married two sons of the Earl of Bessborough. Hartington was an experienced politician and managed to resolve the conflict, at least temporarily, in view of the impending Seven Years' War. Carter was made Principal Secretary of State for life and the other members of the opposition were accommodated to varying degrees of their satisfaction. About 14 June 1757 Carter had a stroke, which deprived him of speech and movement. After this he was confirmed as Joint Secretary of State at the accession of George III, an office he held until his death in 1763.

DIVISION LISTS:
1721 (1) teller against a national bank.
1721 (2) voted against a national bank.
1749 (1) absent, sick.
1753 (1) voted for the expulsion of Arthur Jones-Nevill (**1125**).
1753 (2) voted against the Money Bill.

ADDITIONAL INFORMATION: There is a problem as to whether he or his father (**0359**) was returned for Trim in 1719. In the Devonshire MSS, PRONI T3158/2, the editor says that his father was MP for Trim in 1719, but this is doubtful as Boulter refers to this MP as in parliament in the 1720s. Apparently his father had been trying to be returned for the Boyle borough – also vacant – of Lismore, and in the Devonshire MSS another candidate says that 'Our friend Carter is as good as chosen for Trim.' Carter senior would have been approaching 60 and his son, 20 years younger, would appear to be a more probable candidate. There were not two Thomas Carters in parliament in the 1720s. Finally, would government have consented to the sale of the reversion of the Mastership of the Rolls in 1725 had Carter not been in parliament?

A foundation member of the Dublin Society, 1731. He was interested in agrarian development; at his death in 1763 the *Dublin Journal* reported that 'He built some very useful mills for grinding corn and he also imported cattle.'

Both his sons, Thomas (**0361**) and Henry Boyle Carter, were placed on the patent of the office of Protonotary of the King's Bench. He was noted for his vivacity and wit, and was reputedly the author of a satirical toast that was used with great effect at the time of the Money Bill crisis. He had a toe cut off 'on account of mortification' in 1739. There is a mezzotint of him in the National Gallery of Ireland.

ESTATES/RESIDENCE: Robertstown and Rathnally, Co. Meath. He leased Castlemartin, Co. Kildare and 9 Henrietta Street, Dublin, where, towards the end of his life, he lived with his widowed daughter, Mrs Twisden, to whom he left all his personal property. His son-in-law, Philip Twisden, Bishop of Raphoe, had died bankrupt on 2 November 1752. He was shot allegedly mas-

querading as a highwayman. The Robertstown estate was left to Mrs Twisden for her life and then to her daughter Frances (Lady Jersey) for seven years. Thereafter it passed to his second son, Henry Boyle Carter, who left the reversion of it to his three sons with remainder to the survivor, who sold it to his nephew *c.* 1830.

SOURCES: A family pedigree in the possession of P. Aronsson Esq. says he was b. 1682; P. Aronsson Esq. also supplied a copy of C. C. H. Moriarty, 'Record of the Shaen Carter Family' (MS 1924); *CJ Ire.* (Bradley ed.) vol. 5 pp. 731, 753, vol. 7 pp. 815, 832, 857 (0289,0379); PRONI D/1201/81; Hughes, *Pat. Officers; Boulter Letters* vol. 1 pp. 17–18, 56; PRONI T/3158/2, 3 Devonshire Papers; PRONI T/3019/0360, 6455/173, /6456/631, 6457/493 Wilmot Papers; J. Walton, 'The King's Business': Letters on the Administration of Ireland, 1741–61…(N.Y., 1996), nos 33, 42, 50, 55, 128, 143, 152, 168, 175; R. E. Burns, *Irish Parliamentary Politics in the Eighteenth Century,* 2 vols (Washington, 1989) vol. 1 pp. 198, 202, 210–1, 214–15, 230, 238, vol. 2 pp. 14, 33, 63, 74–5, 78, 100–1, 130–1, 154, 161–3, 170, 209, 228; P. McNally, *Parties, Patriots & Undertakers…* (Dublin, 1997), pp. 96, 131–2, 142–3, 193; EEC rental (1854); McCracken thesis; Burke *LGI* (1904) p. 85; *Index to Irish Privy Counsellors, 1711–1910;* H. A. C. Sturgess, *Register of Admissions to the Honourable Society of the Middle Temple* (London 1949), vol. 1 p. 263; *JRSAI* vol. 21 (1892) p. 300, P. D Vigors, 'Alphabetical List of Free Burgesses of New Ross…1658–1839…'; *JRSAI* vol. 34 (1904) pp. 7, 8, F. E. Ball, 'Some Notes on the Judges of Ireland in the Year 1739' [says the Earl of Berkeley sold him the Mastership of the Rolls a reversion in 1725]; *Louth Arch. Soc. Jn.* (1912–15) pp. 273–83, H. Tempest (ed.), 'The Roll of the Sovereigns and Burgesses of Carlingford, 1706–1828'; *The Dublin Gazette* 14 Oct. 1724; *Pue's Occurrences* 11 Aug. 1739; *EHR* (1905) p. 522, C. L. Falkiner (ed.), 'Correspondence of Archbishop Stone and the Duke of Newcastle'; *Irish Official Papers in Great Britain* vol. 1 pp. 43, 45, 49–52; *HMC Stopford-Sackville I* pp. 149, 200–1, 206; McDowell, *Irish Public Opinion, 1750–1800* p. 30; J. R. Twisden, *The Family of Twysden and Twisden* (1939), pp. 303–5; Berry *RDS* pp. 24–7; T. Bartlett and D. Hayton (eds) *Penal Era and Golden Age,* pp. 55–87, D. O'Donovan, 'The Money Bill Dispute'; *Almanacks; DJ* 6 Sept. 1763.

0361 CARTER, Thomas

MP for Old Leighlin 1745–60

> b. 1720; d. 10 Sept. 1765
> FAMILY/BACKGROUND: Eldest son of Rt Hon.
> Thomas Carter (0360) and Mary, dau. of
> Thomas Claxton.
> MARRIED: Anna Maria, dau. of Sir Samuel
> Armytage, 1st Baronet (she m. (2) [18 Sept.
> 1766] John Nicholson of Co. Meath).
> CHILDREN: Anna Maria, m. Skeffington
> Thompson.
> EDUCATION: Tutor Rev. Hanover Sterling (whom
> Primate Boulter recommended for the vicarage of
> Carlingford); entered TCD 12 Jan. 1737.
> CAREER/OCCUPATION: *2nd Serjeant-at-Arms
> 1732–52; Clerk of the Crown, Protonotary,
> Keeper of the Writs, Philizer, Clerk of the
> Entries, and Clerk of the Errors 1734–64
> (patents 1 July 1748, 23 Oct. 1755); *Commis-
> sioner of the Tillage Act for Leinster 1755–d.
> MILITARY: Cornet in Viscount Molesworth's
> Regiment of dragoons 21 June 1739; Captain in
> Irwin's Regiment, 1745 (the recently appointed
> Lord Lieutenant, the Earl of Chesterfield, who
> was on a diplomatic mission to The Hague,
> promoted him because he was the son of: 'Mr
> Carter, Master of the Rolls in Ireland, who is the
> leading person in the Parliament there, has great
> influence over the Speaker, whose party consti-
> tutes the great majority in that House'.)

POLITICAL ACTIVITY: His earlier career was as a professional soldier. He was returned for Old Leighlin,
a government borough, in the by-election that
followed the death of Thomas Trotter (2115) in
October 1745, on the direct recommendation of
Lord Lieutenant Chesterfield. Notwithstanding
his father's (0360) ambition for him to succeed
him as Master of the Rolls, he does not appear to
have had any legal training.

In parliament he was very much under the
shadow of his father. He voted against the election of James Digges La Touche (♦♦♦), which
could be considered a pro-government vote, but
thereafter he voted with the Country party. The
1757 pensions fracas was provoked by George II's
desire to place a pension of £6,000 on the Irish
establishment for the support of his daughter
Mary, Langravine of Hesse and her children. This
provoked a series of strongly worded resolutions
against pensions and other recurrent grievances

culminating in a threat to delay the Money Bill:
possibly Carter was anxious to avoid the fate of
his father earlier in the decade.

DIVISION LISTS:
> 1749 (1) voted against the election of James
> Digges La Touche (♦♦♦♦)
> 1753 (1) voted for the expulsion of Arthur
> Jones-Nevill (1125).
> 1753 (2) voted against the Money Bill.
> 1757 (1) a teller against the resolutions on
> pensions.

ESTATES/RESIDENCE: Robertstown and Rathnally, Co.
Meath.

SOURCES: Hughes, *Pat. Officers* [says Thomas, son of
Thomas Junior was included in the patent of 2nd
Serjeant-at-Arms, 13 July 1723 – he would have been
aged 3 years!]; PRONI T/559 vol. 15 p. 92, Burke, extract pedigrees; PRONI T/3019/6457/493 Wilmot Pa-
pers; J. Walton, *'The King's Business': Letters on the Ad-
ministration of Ireland, 1741–61*...(N.Y., 1996), nos 33,
51, 55; McCracken thesis; Burke *LGI* (1904) p. 85;
Musgrave, *Obits* (1899) p. 354; R. E. Burns, *Irish Par-
liamentary Politics in the Eighteenth Century, 1730–1760*
(Washington, 1990), vol. 2 pp. 75, 78, 229–33; *Boulter
Letters* vol. 2 p. 180; Moody & Vaughan (eds), *A New
History of Ireland*, pp. 121–2, J. L. McCracken, 'The
Rise of Colonial Nationalism'; *Almanacks.*

0362 CARY, Rt Hon. Edward

MP for Co. Londonderry 1742–1760, 1761–8–
76–83–90

> b. *c.* 1716–21; d. 16 July 1797
> HONOURS: PC, sworn 7 May 1770.
> FAMILY/BACKGROUND: Eldest son of Henry Cary
> (0363) and Anne, dau. of George Hamilton of
> Co. Londonderry.
> MARRIED: (1) [10 Aug. 1743] Jane, dau. of Sir
> Marcus Beresford, 1st Earl of Tyrone (0118); (2)
> [July 1793] Mary Gore (of Bath).
> CHILDREN: *d.s.p.*
> CAREER/OCCUPATION: *Governor of the Work-
> house 1757–68; Foundling Hospital and
> Workhouse 1769–d.; *elected to the Court of
> Assistants June 1766–9; *Magistrate and Mayor
> of Londonderry 1746, *of Coleraine 1761;
> Trustee of Linen Board for Ulster 1762–d.; *Joint
> Governor of Londonderry city and Co. and town
> of Coleraine 1789–4.

MILITARY: Captain of a company of Battle-Axe Guards 1741–2; a volunteer while an MP; Colonel of the Dungiven Battalion, Volunteers.

POLITICAL ACTIVITY: MP for Co. Londonderry, which had one of the larger and more independent electorates, in successive parliaments, being unanimously returned at the 1761 election. Between 1749 and 1760 he was nominated for 25 committees. He had a large estate and corresponding influence in Co. Londonderry, which he had consolidated by marrying Lord Tyrone's sister. He was made a Trustee of the Linen Board in 1763. In December 1765 he was appointed to the committee to inquire into the public works necessary to the nation. Londonderry was a manufacturing and commercial county, so these appointments were important to him. An independent country gentleman, he was described in 1773 as 'a very good sort of man and easy gentlemanlike'.

As brother-in-law of Lord Tyrone and John Beresford (0115), he supported Lord Townshend's administration, particularly over the augmentation of the army. At this time he was anxious to become a Privy Counsellor, which he became in 1770. As a county MP and a relation of the Beresfords he was in general well disposed to government but on popular questions, like most county MPs, he frequently followed the popular line and was anxious to be thought independent. For example, in 1774 he voted for the Stamp Act but against the Catholic Relief Act.

Lord Harcourt gave to his recommendation two supernumerary gaugers, a Hearth Money Collector and a Scale Porter. He was a colonel in the Volunteers and a delegate for Co. Londonderry to the Volunteer convention. In 1790 a usually critical commentator declared that 'The Rt Hon. Edward Cary, the other Member for the County, has grown grey in its service, having been uniformly chosen its representative from his early youth. Of respectable family and wide-spread connections, who look up to him as their head, he will continue to fill that office as long as life endures. Though brother-in-law to the Marquess of Waterford, he seems to be little subject to the Beresford influence but acts in Parliament with the fairness and firmness of a steady and honest country gentleman.' However, he did not stand

in the 1790 election and he died on 16 July 1797, probably in his 80s.

DIVISION LISTS:

1749 (1) voted for the election of James Digges La Touche (♦♦♦♦).
1753 (1) voted for the expulsion of Arthur Jones-Nevill (**1125**).
1753 (2) voted against the Money Bill.
1768 (1) voted for army augmentation.
1771 (1) voted for Lord Townshend as Lord Lieutenant.
1771 (2) voted against Sir Lucius O'Brien's (**1558**) motion for retrenchment.
1772 (1) voted against the separation of the Revenue Board.
1772 (2) voted for a Short Revenue Bill.
1773 (1) voted for Absentee Tax.
1773 (2) voted against an untaxed press.
1774 (1) voted for the Stamp Bill.
1774 (2) voted against Catholic relief.
1777 (1) voted against Grattan's (**0895**) motion for retrenchment.
1778 (2) voted for the Popery Bill.
1779 (2) voted for a six-months Loan Bill.
1780 (2) voted for Yelverton's (**2268**) motion to modify Poynings' Law.
1780 (4) voted for the Perpetual Mutiny Bill.
1783 (1) voted for Flood's (**0762**) motion for parliamentary reform.
1784 (1) voted for a committee on the Reform Bill.
1785 (1) absent.
1790 (1) voted against Grattan's motion for reducing the influence of the crown.

ADDITIONAL INFORMATION: *A member of the RDS from 1768.

ESTATES/RESIDENCE: Millburn, Dungiven, Newtown Limavady, Co. Londonderry; Mount Kennedy, Co. Wicklow; Marlborough Street, Dublin. In 1742 his father had renewed the lease of Pellipar manor (in Millburn estate) for 61 years, and at the expiration of this lease in 1803 the property was leased by Robert Ogilby, a linen merchant. In 1793, Coolfinny (*see* **0363**), together with 2,600 Irish acres in the manor of Pellipar, constituted part of the terms of the Rt Hon. Edward Cary's (second) marriage to Mary Gore of Bath. He left Millburn to his nephew, Henry Blacker.

In 1728, Edward (?Henry) Cary owned or held, as 'part of' his estate, the lands of Bovedy etc., barony of Loughinsholin, valued at £152 a year. The original Edward Cary of Dungiven (died 1668) was third son of George Cary, Charter Recorder of Derry. His son, Rt Hon. Edward Cary, died at Dungiven, 1714, and was succeeded by his son, Henry, who was succeeded in 1756 by his son, Rt Hon. Edward Cary (this MP) who died childless.

SOURCES: PRONI D/1725/3 [says he is the son of Edward and brother of Henry (0363)]; PRONI T/559 vol. 15 p. 53, Burke, extract pedigrees; PRONI MIC/465/1 R. Ffolliott, Biographical Notices, 1756–1827; PRONI MIC/474, Irish Volunteers; NAI MFCI Reel 13, Parish Registers of Clonegam, Co. Waterford; McCracken thesis; Burke LG (1846) p. 59; Johnston, Gt B. & Ire., p. 132; T. Bartlett and D. W. Hayton (eds), Penal Era and Golden Age (Belfast, 1979) p. 113 f.1, P. D. H. Smyth, 'The Volunteers and Parliament, 1779–84'; Johnson, Drapers, iv, 600–6. Crown rentals 1706 vol. 11 f. 3; T. H. Mullin, Coleraine in By-gone Centuries (Belfast, 1976), p. 141; Index to Irish Privy Counsellors, 1711–1910; UJA vol. 16 p. 56, M. Given, 'Parliamentary Representation of Ulster'; PRONI T/1138/911 Lord Caledon to Henry [Alexander], 20 July 1797, Montgomery Papers; PRONI T/1113/2, 25 Mar. 1697, County valuation; PRONI, D/3067/1 Stewart Survey, 1740; Almanacks, BNL 27 Dec. 1765; DJ 28 Apr.–2 May 1761; Parliamentary Lists, 1769 (1), 1771 (1), 1772 (1), 1773 (1), (2), 1774 (1), 1775 (1), 1776 (1), (2), (3), 1777 (1), 1778 (1), 1780 (1), 1782 (1), 1783 (1), (3), 1784 (1), (2), (3), 1785 (1), (2), (3), (4), 1787 (1), 1788 (1), 1789 (1), 1790 (1).

0363 CARY, Henry

MP for Coleraine 1727–56

b. 1695; d. 14 Oct. 1756
FAMILY/BACKGROUND: Only son of Edward Cary and Martha, dau. of Henry Mervyn (1406).
MARRIED: Anne (d. Feb. 1779), o. dau. of Col. George Hamilton of Co. Londonderry.
CHILDREN: Rt Hon. Edward (0362); Frederick [Cary-Hamilton] (0364); William (admitted to the Middle Temple 17 Aug. 1752); George; Lettice, m. William Blacker; Martha; Anne, m. Jeremiah Coghlan.
CAREER/OCCUPATION: Mayor of Londonderry 2 Nov. 1742–3, 1743, ?1747; *Magistrate of Londonderry city 1743; Deputy Governor of Co. Londonderry.

POLITICAL ACTIVITY: He was not a good attender, and on 10 November 1737 the House rejected his excuse for non-attendance. He was ordered into the custody of the Serjeant-at-Arms. Cary was a member of the Country party, voting for the expulsion of Arthur Jones-Nevill (1125) and against the Money Bill. He was nominated for 14 committees between 1735 and 1760.

DIVISION LISTS:
1749 (1) absent, in the country.
1753 (1) voted for the expulsion of Arthur Jones-Nevill (1125).
1753 (2) voted against the Money Bill.

ESTATES/RESIDENCE: Pellipar Manor, Millburn estate, Dungiven, Co. Londonderry. (The family are buried at Dungiven.) In 1742 he renewed the lease of Pellipar for 61 years and at the expiration of this lease the property was leased by Robert Ogilby, a linen merchant. At his death his estate was worth £4,000 p.a., which demised on his son Edward. The Carys leased land from the Skinners' Guild. In 1697 the Skinners' proportion, valued at £700, came equal second out of 25, and out of a total county valuation of £11,850 p.a. In 1714, Archibald Stewart surveyed the Skinners' proportion at 22,507 Irish acres: 4,354 in Loughinsholin, 6,595 in Tirkeeran, and 11,556 in Keenaght. The Skinners' proportion lay in these three baronies, and the Skinners' Hall was at Dungiven, where 'Capt. Edward Cary [d. 1714] has built an house for an inn at Dungivan (beyond the ordinary size of such in this country) and finished it just before these fatal times [1688–9] at near £400 cost. This, with very fair stables, barns, kills and other office houses, two mills and the town of Dungiven, his ... quicksets about the house and town burnt or prostrated. The houses of tenants in the neighbourhood escaped, but all (except four townlands, whereon are a few tenants, and two townlands, where some of his brother's tenants live by loan of the houses till spring) waste. This is the most mountainous of all the Proportions, and most waste.'

On 3 September 1714, (?David) Jenkins mentioned Mr Cary's renewal in a letter to Joshua Dawson. In 1734, Henry Cary of Dungiven bought in fee the townland of Coolfinny, parish of Faughanvale, barony of Tirkeeran – part of the manor of Grocers – for £1,610 from John Ash of Londonderry. (Since Coolfinny itself contained only 167 statute acres, this appears a high price.)

SOURCES: CJ Ire. (Bradley ed.) vol. 6 p. 747; PRONI D/2096/1/84, Maxwell Given notes; PRONI T/559 vol. 15 p. 50, Burke, extract pedigrees; McCracken thesis; Burke LG (1848) p. 59; Memorials of the Dead vol. 7 p. 264 [says he died 12 Oct. 1756 in his 62nd year]; Register of Admissions to the Honourable Society of the Middle Temple vol. 1 p. 344; T. H. Mullin, *Coleraine in Bygone Centuries* (Belfast, 1976) p. 141; *Almanacks; GM* (Exshaw's edition) Oct. 1757; *Pue's Occurrences* 9 Nov. 1742; *DJ* 16–19 Oct. 1756, 4–6 Feb. 1779; PRONI D/2649/5/11, Alex. Stewart survey, 1728; PRONI D/1393/3, Caldwell and Robinson papers, Deed of sale of Coolfinny, 30 Apr. 1734, and marriage settlement, 16 July 1793.

0364 CARY-HAMILTON, Frederick

MP for Londonderry B. 1743–6

b. *c.* 1719; d. 20 Nov. 1746
FAMILY/BACKGROUND: Second son of Henry Cary (0363) and Anne, dau. of Col. George Hamilton.
MARRIED: [6 Apr. 1743] Elizabeth, dau. of Rt Hon. Sir Ralph Gore, 4th Baronet (0872).
CHILDREN: *d.s.p.*
EDUCATION: BA, TCD 1739.

POLITICAL ACTIVITY: He was only three years in parliament and does not appear to have been very active during that time. Virtually nothing is known about him.

ESTATES/RESIDENCE: Newgrange, Co. Meath. Inherited Lieutenant-General Frederick Hamilton's estates in Co. Londonderry.

SOURCES: McCracken thesis; Burke *LG* (1846) p. 59; Burke *Ext. P* (1883) p. 236; *Alum. Dub.*; *Notes and Queries* (25 Apr. 1925) p. 292, H. B. Swanzy, 'Militia of County Cavan' [says he married Mary, daughter of William Newburgh of Co. Cavan, she m. (2) Sir William Richardson, 1st Baronet (1788); Burke *PB* (1903) p. 658 contradicts this and gives Elizabeth Gore]; *DJ* 25 Nov. 1746.

0365 CASEY, Thomas

MP for Kilmallock 1800

b. 1765; d. 7 Apr. 1840
FAMILY/BACKGROUND: Only son of Thomas Casey of Limerick city.
MARRIED: Wilhemlna, dau. of [   ] Forth.
CHILDREN: Edmund Henry, m. Mary H. S. Tomn.
EDUCATION: Middle Temple 14 June 1784; called to the Irish Bar 1788.

CAREER/OCCUPATION: *Listed in Judges and Barristers 1789–1800 (f.); Commissioner of Bankrupts 1797–1802.

POLITICAL ACTIVITY: He was returned for Kilmallock in 1799 by Silver Oliver (1586). Oliver and his brother Charles had reluctantly returned themselves for their family borough. They had abstained from voting in January 1799. Through Lord Camden's good offices they accepted the Escheatorships of Ulster and Munster and sold both seats to Sir Valentine Richard Quin (1753), who was anxious to obtain a peerage. Quin returned himself and Thomas Casey – both were sworn on 15 January 1800. For providing two votes for the Union, Quin was created Lord Adare in 1800. Casey was made a Commissioner of Bankrupts in the Lord Chancellor's Department and a Dublin magistrate. Meanwhile, the Silvers got both the proceeds of the sale and the compensation for the disfranchisement of Kilmallock.

DIVISION LISTS:
1800 (1) voted for the Union.

ADDITIONAL INFORMATION: He was one of the witnesses for the defence at the trial for treason of John and Henry Sheares in 1798.

ESTATES/RESIDENCE: Ely Place, Dublin.

SOURCES: PRONI T/808 p. 9869 Grove MS [will of Thomas Casey, proved 16 July 1840]; PRONI T/3166/1B, Hartnell notes; O'Neill thesis; *HMC King's Inns Admission Paper, 1607–1867*; Barrington, *Rise and Fall*, p. 295; *Memorials of the Dead*; *Register of Admissions to the Honourable Society of the Middle Temple* vol. 2 p. 397; G. C. Bolton, *The Passing of the Irish Act of Union*, p. 167; *JRSAI* vol. 67 (1937) p. 18, K. R. Brady, 'The Brief for the Defence at the Trial of John and Henry Sheares in 1798'; *Almanacks*; Parliamentary Lists, 1800 (1).

CASTLE COOTE, Baron: *see* **COOTE**
0481 Coote, Rt Hon. Charles Henry, 2nd Baron Castle Coote, MP Queen's County 1776–83, 1797–1800, Maryborough 1783–90–7, [UK] Queen's County 1801–2

CASTLECOMER, Baron and Viscount: *see*
WANDESFORD

2166 Wandesford, Rt Hon. Sir Christopher, 1st
Baron Wandesford and Viscount Castlecomer,
MP St Canice 1692–3, 1695–9, 1703–7, [E]
Ripon 1679–80-1

2167 Wandesford, Rt Hon. Christopher, 2nd
Viscount Castlecomer, MP St Canice 1707,
[GB] Morpeth 1710–13, Ripon 1715–19

CASTLE DURROW, Baron: *see* **FLOWER**

0767 Flower, Rt Hon. William, 1st Baron Castle
Durrow, MP Co. Kilkenny 1715–27,
Portarlington 1727–33

CASTLEMAINE, Baron and Viscount: *see*
HANDCOCK

0960 Handcock, Rt Hon. William, 1st Baron
Castlemaine, Viscount Castlemaine, MP Athlone
1783–90–7–1800, [UK] 1801–3

CASTLEREAGH, Viscount: *see* **STEWART**

2008 Stewart, Rt Hon. Robert, 1st Baron Londonderry, Viscount Castlereagh, Earl of Londonderry, Marquess of Londonderry, MP Co. Down
1771–6–83

2009 Stewart, Rt Hon. Robert (styled Viscount
Castlereagh 1796–1821), 2nd Marquess of Lon-
donderry, MP Co. Down 1790–7–1800, [GB]
Tregony 1794–6, Orford 1796–7, [UK] Co.
Down 1801–5, 1812–21, Boroughbridge 1806,
Plympton Erle 1806–12, Orford 1821–2

0366 CAULFEILD, Hon. Francis

MP for Co. Armagh 1758–60; Charlemont 1761–
8–75

> b. *c.* 1730; d. 20 Oct. 1775 (lost at sea)
> FAMILY/BACKGROUND: Son of Hon. James
> Caulfeild, 3rd Viscount Charlemont (**0368**) and
> Elizabeth, o. dau. of Francis Bernard (**0124**).
> MARRIED: [11 Oct. 1760] Mary, o. dau. of John
> Eyre, 1st Baron Eyre (**0714**).
> CHILDREN: Col. James Eyre (b. 1765 *d.s.p.*);
> Eleanor (d. 1807), m. [31 Mar. 1787] Rt Hon.
> William Forward-Howard, 3rd Earl of Wicklow
> (**0803**),
> EDUCATION: School: Mr Quintin; entered TCD
> 29 Mar. 1751; BA 1754.
> CAREER/OCCUPATION: Freedom of Galway Town,
> 24 Nov. 1760; High Sheriff of Co. Galway 1764;
> *Magistrate and Portreeve of Charlemont 1768.
> MILITARY: Ensign 27th (Inniskilling) Foot 25 Feb.
> 1746; appointed Major of Horse 1755; Cornet,
> Lord George Sackville's Regiment of Horse, Jan.
> 1756; *Major of Light Dragoons 1768.

POLITICAL ACTIVITY: He was the unsuccessful candidate in the famous Co. Armagh election of 1753
when he lost to William Brownlow (**0265**). The
by-election was caused by the death of Robert
Cope (**0489**) in March 1753. The election, which
had cost Lord Charlemont £1,000, had been managed on behalf of his brother, Francis Caulfeild,
by Thomas Adderley (**0009**), Charlemont's stepfather and guardian. Lord Charlemont supported
the opposition both from inclination and from
an old family friendship with Speaker Boyle
(**0210**).

The election was bitterly fought and Caulfeild,
if he was born in 1735, was actually under age.
Not only was it a contest between the political
interests in Armagh, which were evenly divided;
it involved Primate Stone – who saw himself as
the leading servant of the government – as, *ex officio*, one of those interests. It also gave an insight
into the working of the electoral system, as on 4
November 1753 Chief Secretary Sackville (**1835**)
wrote to Wilmot that 'We shall hear tomorrow
something certain about the Armagh elections; it
is thought the Sheriff will not admit any of the
new registered Freeholders to vote, because the
law requires they should be registered six months
before the election, and it seems the lawyers here

are of opinion the election means the day upon which the poll begins. If it were otherwise, the Sheriff by protracting, might be at liberty to create a right in several voters which would not have existed had he acted with all proper expedition. This case does not come within that supposition, but Mr Caulfeild's friends have used every method to create delay and have by riots and trifling objections continued the poll to this time, when the new registered votes may be offered as having a right.'

Brownlow was returned, but Caulfeild contested the return in the House of Commons, where it became an open issue between the Speaker (0210) and the Primate. On 16 November Sackville wrote to Wilmot: 'Brownlow takes his seat this day, and I am told the Speaker's son (0213) moves a petition against him. Brownlow will be well supported, and I verily believe for the first that the Speaker will lose an election point in the house of Commons; if that should happen it would more effectually hurt his interests than ten other questions.' When the election petition came before the Commons it was decided in Brownlow's favour in an exceptionally large House, by only one vote: 120–119. Every vote had counted. Thomas Adderley wrote to Lord Charlemont on 29 December 1753 that 'Mr [Hon. George] Hamilton (0921) arrived here the 7th from London, on purpose to serve his nephew Mr [William] Brownlow this gentleman has been a member since 1727, but did not take his seat before this session.'

Following the death of William Richardson (1786) on 22 February 1758, Caulfeild was returned for Co. Armagh, taking his seat on 3 April. However, confronted with competition from the Brownlows and the Achesons, he sat for the family borough of Charlemont from 1761 until his untimely death in 1775. He was nominated to four committees 1758–60.

Armagh was a 'manufacturing county' dominated by the linen industry, and in December 1765 both Brownlow and Caulfeild were appointed to the committee to inquire into the public works necessary to the nation. Caulfeild followed his brother's lead and voted with the opposition during Lord Townshend's administration. Under Lord Harcourt he was more inclined to support gov-

ernment, particularly as 'He is very poor and greatly embarrassed in his circumstances.' He voted for the major issues of Stamps, Catholic relief and the Tontine, as well as for an Absentee Tax on which the government gave a free vote. He was a major in the army.

DIVISION LISTS:

> 1768 (1) voted against army augmentation.
> 1771 (1) voted against Lord Townshend as Lord Lieutenant.
> 1771 (2) voted for Sir Lucius O'Brien's (**1558**) motion for retrenchment.
> 1772 (2) voted for a Short Revenue Bill.
> 1773 (1) voted for Absentee Tax.
> 1773 (2) voted for an untaxed press.
> 1774 (1) voted for the Stamp Bill.
> 1774 (2) voted for Catholic relief.

ADDITIONAL INFORMATION: His date of birth is sometimes given as January 1735, but this cannot be correct for not only did his father die on 21 April 1734, but he fought the Co. Armagh election in 1753, and in a bitterly contested election there was no mention of his being under age. Therefore he was unlikely to have been born later than 1732. Furthermore, his stepfather Thomas Adderley wrote on 29 December 1753 that 'He is preparing to answer for his degree this next examination, and will, I believe take it with credit': this would suggest an age of 21–22. His older brother, the famous Earl of Charlemont, was born 18 August 1728, and he had two sisters – the younger married Sir John Browne (0259), later Lord Kilmaine, in 1764.

Crossing the Irish Sea always involved some risk, and in 1775 Francis Caulfeild was lost in a storm, with his wife and infant child, on his way to Ireland: 'On Thursday the 19th instant the brig *Trevor*, Totty master, and the brig *Nonpareil*, Davies master, sailed from Parkgate for Dublin. About eight o'clock that evening, these vessels being then near Holyhead, the wind came about from SSW to the westward, and so violent a hurricane arose that they could not carry any sail, but were obliged to lie down and drive before the wind. In this situation Totty's ship drove upon the banks near the Lancashire shore and is totally lost. Every person on board perished except one Samuel Fairclough, a mariner, who miraculously saved his life by leaping on board another vessel, called the *Charming Molly*, Hollyway master, which by accident ran foul of the *Trevor*, and at the instant the two vessels struck together Fairclough made his leap. The *Nonpareil* it is supposed stranded upon Hoylesands and is lost. Not one person is saved … The *Trevor* and the *Nonpareil* had on board near 200 passengers, among whom were the Hon. Major Caulfeild, his lady and daughters … [and] the two Mr Frenches, one of them Member for the County of Roscommon (**0831**) … We are informed that there were on board the two last mentioned vessels £6,000 in specie, besides silks, woollen cloths, jewels and other things to the amount of between £30 and £40,000.' The report concludes that 'As few were more amiable than Mr and Mrs Caulfeild few could be more beloved; all who had any knowledge of them are concerned for their fate, but those who are more particularly intimate feel beyond expression the irreparable loss! They left London in health and spirits, had made every preparation for the gaiety of the Parliament winter, but are lost for ever. They have left an only son at an academy near London and an only daughter who resides with her Grandfather and Grandmother, Lord and Lady Eyre in Ireland.'

ESTATES/RESIDENCE: Dublin. The *Belfast Newsletter* declared that Major Caulfeild had with him on his fatal voyage 22,000 guineas, a legacy lately recovered and to be divided between members of the Caulfeild family.

SOURCES: PRONI D/302; PRONI T/3019/6456/322 Wilmot Papers; McCracken thesis; GEC *P*; Burke *PB* (1903) p. 298; *HMC Charlemont I* pp. 5, 188–91; J. Walton, *'The King's Business': Letters on the Administration of Ireland, 1741–61*…(N.Y., 1996), nos 64, 70; R. E. Burns, *Irish Parliamentary Politics in the Eighteenth Century*, 2 vols (Washington, 1989) vol. 2 pp. 144–5, 168; L. M. Cullen, *Merchants, ships and trade, 1660–1830* (1971), p. 50; Ida Gantz, *Signpost to Eyrecourt, Portrait of the Eyre Family Triumphant in the cause of Liberty, Derbyshire, Wiltshire, Galway c. 1415–1856* (Kingsmead, Bath, 1975), p. 163; Johnston, *Gt B. & Ire.*, p. 233; *Almanacks*; *BNL* 27 Dec. 1765, 22–26 Dec. 1775; *DJ* 3–6 Jan. 1756, 13–16 Dec. 1760; Parliamentary Lists, 1769 (1), 1772 (2), 1773 (2), 1774 (1), 1775 (1).

0367 CAULFEILD, Rt Hon. Francis William

MP for Co. Armagh 1797–9 [r. Charlemont 1797]

b. 3 Jan. 1775; d. 26 Dec. 1863
HONOURS: PC, sworn 13 Feb. 1832; Knight of St Patrick 19 Oct. 1831.
PEERAGES: Suc. as 2nd Earl of Charlemont 1799; cr. Baron Charlemont [UK] 13 Feb. 1837 (with special remainder to his brother); Rep. Peer 1806–63.
FAMILY/BACKGROUND: Eldest son of James Caulfeild (b. 18 Aug. 1728; d. 4 Aug. 1799), 1st Earl of Charlemont, and Mary (d. 1807), dau. of Thomas Hickman of Brickhill, Co. Clare.
MARRIED: [9 Feb. 1802] Anne, yst dau. and co-h. of William Bermingham of Ross Hill, Co. Galway.
CHILDREN: James William (b. Aug. 1803; d. 13 Jan. 1823); William Francis (b. 1805; d. 1807); Maria Melosina (b. Jan. 1807; d. unm. 4 Mar. 1727); Emily Charlotte (b. 1808; d. unm. 1827).
EDUCATION: BA, TCD 1794.
CAREER/OCCUPATION: Freedom of the City of Dublin 19 Oct. 1800; *Governor and Guardian of the Hospital for the relief of Lying-in Women 1798; Lord Lieutenant Co. Tyrone 1839, Custos Rot. Co. Tyrone 1841–d.
MILITARY: Captain in Keady Cavalry Oct. 1796; 1st Captain in the Armagh Cavalry May 1800, *vice* his dec. father.

POLITICAL ACTIVITY: He was returned for Co. Armagh in 1797, but, as he was born in 1775, he was only eligible to sit in the last parliament of Ireland. His return probably owed much to the popularity of his father as the leader of the Volunteers and a lifelong adherent to an independent opposition. He voted for Sir Laurence Parsons' (**1636**) holding motion and in 1799 against the Union. By 1800 he had succeeded his father as Earl of Charlemont. He received £15,000 in compensation for the disfranchisement of Charlemont. In 1806 he became a representative peer.

DIVISION LISTS:
    1798 (1) teller for Parsons' (**1636**) motion for an investigation into 'the present discontents'.
    1799 (1) voted against the Union.

ADDITIONAL INFORMATION: *A member of the Royal Irish Academy, 1799.

ESTATES/RESIDENCE: Castle Caulfeild, Co. Tyrone;

Charlemont House, Rutland Square, Dublin; Clontarf, Co. Dublin. In 1764, Lord Charlemont sold to Acheson Moore of Ravella, *alias* Aughnacloy, two townlands near Ballygawley, in the manor of Castle Caufeild, for £6,604. The Charlemont estate had 250 freeholders in 1789, out of a total of 1,100 tenants in 1793; the rental was £3,043 in 1760, and £7,685 in 1798. Charlemont was not rich, and the £15,000 compensation from the disfranchisement of Charlemont must have been useful.

SOURCES: PRONI T/3166/1A Hartnell notes; GEC *P*; Burke *PB* (1903) p. 298; *Index to Irish Privy Counsellors, 1711–1910*; *Almanacks*; *FJ* 20 Oct. 1796; *BNL* 27 May, 21 Oct. 1800; Malcomson, *Foster*, p. 300; PRONI D/2644/1 statement of accounts, 1759–61 [figures provided by Professor P. A. Roebuck], rental and account book, 1798–1803; NLI Charlemont Papers, MS 2702; PRONI T/1176/3 Charlemont Papers and schedule of leases, 1750–1817, *c*. 1821 [figures again provided by Professor P. A. Roebuck]; PRONI T/458/12 [notes on Registry of Deeds material relating to Dungannon]; Parliamentary Lists, 1783 (2), 1799 (3), 1800 (3).

0368 CAULFEILD, Hon. James

MP for Charlemont 1703–5 (obliged to travel abroad), 1713–14, 1715–26

    b. July 1682; d. 21 Apr. 1734
    PEERAGES: Suc. as 3rd Viscount Charlemont 1726.
    FAMILY/BACKGROUND: Son of William Caulfeild, 2nd Viscount Charlemont, and Anne, dau. of James Margetson, Abp of Armagh.
    MARRIED: Elizabeth (d. 30 May 1742), o. dau. of Francis Bernard (0124); (she m. (2) [1740] Thomas Adderley (0009)).
    CHILDREN: James, 1st Earl of Charlemont m. [2 July 1768] Mary dau. of Thomas Hickman of Brickhill, Co. Clare; Francis (0366); dau. (d. unm.); Alicia (d. 7 June 1794), m. [23 Apr. 1763] John Browne, 1st Baron Kilmaine (0259).
    EDUCATION: Entered TCD, BA 1702, MA 1704.
    CAREER/OCCUPATION: *Trustee of the Linen Board for Ulster 1732–d.

POLITICAL ACTIVITY: He was one of the few people allowed to resign his seat, which he did in 1705; he had been nominated to seven committees in 1703. In 1703 'Mr Speaker informed the House, that he had received a letter from Mr James Caulfeild, a member of this House, dated the 17th of February instant, desiring he may be excused from attending the Service of this House, by rea-

son he is obliged to travel beyond seas, and that a Writ might issue … for the Borough of Charlemont.' This was agreed.

When he was returned for the last parliament of Queen Anne he was considered a Tory and voted for Sir Richard Levinge (1230), the Castle candidate for the Speakership. He was listed on nine committees in 1713, but only four in the parliament of George I, all between 1719 and 1723. He was still considered a Tory in 1719, when it was thought that he would not support any leniency towards the repeal of the Test Clause. He also voted against a national bank.

DIVISION LISTS:
    1713 (1) voted for Sir Richard Levinge (1230) as Speaker.
    1721 (1) voted against a national bank.
    1721 (2) voted against a national bank.

ESTATES/RESIDENCE: Castle Caulfeild, Co. Tyrone. In 1714 his income was estimated at £1,000 p.a. About 1721 the acreage of the estate was 20,186 (statute); the estate was made up of the manors of Charlemont, Castle Caulfeild and Clady More, and lay in the baronies of Lower Fews, Armagh, Oneilland West and Turany.

SOURCES: GEC *P*; Burke, *PB* (1903) p. 298; *CJ Ire.* vol. ii part i p. 436; *Almanacks*; Parliamentary Lists, 1714–15 (1), 1719 (1).

0369 CAULFEILD, Hon. John

MP for Charlemont 1703–7

    b. 1661; d. 1707
    FAMILY/BACKGROUND: Son of William Caulfeild, 1st Viscount Charlemont, and Sarah (bur. 3 Dec. 1672), dau. of Charles Moore, 2nd Viscount Drogheda.
    MARRIED: Sidney, dau. and h. of James Somerville of Co. Fermanagh.
    CHILDREN: 1 son; 1 dau.
    EDUCATION: School Mr Edward Jones; entered TCD 11 July 1678, aged 17 years.
    MILITARY: Colonel in Rev. George Walker's Londonderry Regiment of Foot 19 Apr. 1689; Lieutenant-Colonel Caulfeild replaced Major Smith (removed by court martial April 1691) in Colonel Tiffan's Regiment 22 April 1691; ?Lieutenant-Colonel in Sir George St George's Regiment.

POLITICAL ACTIVITY: He sat in parliament for four years and was listed for 27 committees between 1703 and 1707. He appears to have had a military career, and he would have fought at the Boyne in 1690 – where Walker was killed.

ESTATES/RESIDENCE: Tullydowey, Co. Tyrone.

SOURCES: *Cal. SP Dom. 1693* (London, 1903) p. 352, *1696* (London, 1913) pp. 405, 470; GEC *P,* Simms' cards; Lodge, *P,* C. Dalton (ed.), *English Army Lists and Commission Registers, 1661–1714* (London, 1896), vol. 3 p. 7; *JRSAI* vol. 76 (1946) p. 135, W. E. J. Dobbs, 'A Supplement to the Entrance Register of Kilkenny School: 1684–1800'.

0370 CAULFEILD, Hon. John

MP for Charlemont 1723–7–60

b. *c.* 1690; d. 19 Oct. 1764 at his Jervis Street residence
FAMILY/BACKGROUND: Son of William Caulfeild, 2nd Viscount Charlemont, and Anne (m. 11 July 1678; d. 1729), o. dau. of Primate James Margetson.
MARRIED: ?Unmarried.
CHILDREN: ?*d.s.p.*
CAREER/OCCUPATION: Chancery Clerk in Lord Privy Seal's Office; *A Member of Committee of Fifteen in the Incorporated Society of Dublin (Charter Schools) 1756–7.

POLITICAL ACTIVITY: He had a small sinecure in the Lord Privy Seal's office. In 1753 he voted with the Speaker over the expulsion of Arthur Jones-Nevill (**1125**) and against the Money Bill.

DIVISION LISTS:
1749 (1) absent, in England.
1753 (1) voted for the expulsion of Arthur Jones-Nevill (**1125**).
1753 (2) voted against the Money Bill.
1757 (1) voted for the resolutions on pensions.

ESTATES/RESIDENCE: Jervis Street, Dublin; London.

SOURCES: McCracken thesis; Burke *PB* (1903) p. 298 [he was the 4th of seven sons (and five dau.); his e. bro. was born in 1682]; *Almanacks.*

0371 CAULFEILD, Rt Hon. St George

MP for Tulsk 1727–51

b. 16 Sept. 1697; d. 17 May 1778 at his Aungier Street house
HONOURS: PC, sworn 14 Oct. 1751, 1753–d. (resworn 3 Aug. 1761).
FAMILY/BACKGROUND: Son of William Caulfeild (**0375**) and Lettice, dau. of Sir Arthur Gore, 1st Baronet.
MARRIED: Unmarried.
EDUCATION: Middle Temple 20 Nov. 1716; called to the Irish Bar 1722; LLD 1734.
CAREER/OCCUPATION: Counsel to Revenue Board 1735–8; Solicitor General 6 Oct. 1739–41; Attorney General 15 Jan. 1742–50; Chief Justice of the King's Bench 1 Oct. 1751–60; *Assistant Judge in the Court of Exchequer Chamber 1751–9. A Justice of Assize for Leinster, Summer 1740; NW Ulster, Lent 1741; Leinster, Summer 1741; NW Ulster, Lent 1742; Connaught, Summer 1742; NW Ulster, Lent 1743; Connaught, Summer 1743, Lent 1744; Leinster, Summer 1744, Lent 1745; NW Ulster, Summer 1745; Leinster, Lent 1746; Connaught, Summer 1746; NW Ulster, Summer 1747; Munster, Lent 1748; Connaught, Lent 1749, Summer 1749; Munster, Summer 1750; Connaught, Lent and Summer 1751; NE Ulster, Summer 1752; NW Ulster, Lent 1753; Munster, Summer 1753, Lent 1754; NE Ulster, Summer 1754, Lent 1755; Munster, Summer 1755, Summer 1757; NE Ulster, Lent 1758; Munster, Summer 1758; NE Ulster, Lent 1760; *Governor of the Workhouse 1739–59; *Governor of the Royal Hospital (Kilmainham) 1751–9; *Governor of Erasmus Smith's Schools and other Charities 1751–59; *Commissioner of Oyer and Terminer 1753.

POLITICAL ACTIVITY: A successful lawyer, he was appointed Solicitor General on the appointment of John Bowes to the Chancellorship in 1739, Attorney General in 1742, and finally Chief Justice of the King's Bench in 1751. He was listed for 64 committees between 1728 and 1749. In 1733 he introduced 7 Geo. II, c. 14, 'an Act for the relief of Mortgagees ... and also for better regulating the Payment of the Fees of Attornies and Solicitors', which dealt with mortgagors who absconded and refused to appear in Court, and other problems of the Courts of Equity in this area. Acts tended to be passed for limited periods and therefore came up for review and renewal, and in December 1735 Caulfeild introduced the heads of a bill for this purpose, 9 Geo. II, c. 6. The acts to be renewed were always very varied and in this case included statutes against terrorism and Dublin vagrants and for regulating the merchant navy. In 1747 he introduced 21 Geo. II, c. 3, the tax on hawkers and pedlars which supported the charter schools.

His absence over the Dublin election petition in 1749 may have been diplomatic. In the absence of the Lord Chancellor he was Speaker of the House of Lords 1755–6, and again in 1758. He was hostile to Lord Clanbrassill's bill for the registration of Catholic priests, which was rejected in Council by 14 to 12, despite a long speech to the Council in its favour by Lord Lieutenant Bedford, who considered that the experience of half a century had demonstrated the inefficacy of the current system. In 1759 he was driving with Lord Chancellor Bowes (0196) in the latter's carriage when they were stopped by the anti-Union mob, who demanded that he and the Chancellor alight and swear that they were for the country and against the Union. After his retirement from the bench in 1760 he was granted a pension of £1,000 for life on 5 March 1761; as he did not die until 1778, he had a long retirement to enjoy it.

DIVISION LISTS:

1749 (1) absent, in town.

ADDITIONAL INFORMATION: Elected post-charter to the RDS, 1750.

ESTATES/RESIDENCE: Tulsk, Donamon and Ardmore, Co. Roscommon. Lands in the baronies of Ballymore, Ballintoher and Roscommon. Bridge Street and later Aungier Street, Dublin.

SOURCES: *CJ Ire.* (Bradley ed.) vol. 6 p. 433, 567, 644, vol. 7 p. 947 (0331, 0349, 0453); PRONI T/2915/4/4, 9/53 Bedford Papers; McCracken thesis; Lodge *P* [says he died 19 June 1778]; *IMC King's Inns Admission Papers, 1607–1867*; *Index to Irish Privy Counsellors, 1711–1910*; Ball, *Judges; Ir. Gen.* vol. 2 no. 5 (1947) pp. 141–2, L. E. O'Hanlon, 'Testamentary Records' [says his will pr. 27 May 1778]; H. A. C. Sturgess, *Register of Admissions to the Honourable Society of the Middle Temple* (London, 1949), vol. 1 p. 278; R. E. Burns, *Irish Parliamentary Politics in the Eighteenth Century*, 2 vols (Washington, 1989) vol. 2 pp. 44, 249, 270; J. Kelly, *Henry Flood …* (Dublin, 1998) p. 73; J. Kelly,

'*That Damn'd thing called Honour*': *Duelling in Ireland 1570–1860* (Cork, 1995), p. 59; Berry *RDS* pp. 76–7; *Almanacks*; *BNL* 7 Feb., 9 June 1758, 20 Feb. 1767; *The Dublin Gazette* 1 July 1740, 26 Feb., 9 July 1743; *Pue's Occurrences* 7 Feb., 27 June 1741, 20 Feb., 17 July 1742, 15 Feb., 21 June, 28 June 1746, 10 Feb., 21 Feb., 24 Feb. 1747, 19 Feb. 1751, 17 Feb. 1753, 23 Feb., 13 July 1754, 15 Feb., 1 July 1755; *DJ* 14 Feb., 19 June 1744, 26 Feb., 13 July 1745, 21 July 1747, 14 July 1750, 21–23 June 1757, 29 Jan.–2 Feb. 1760, 19–21 May 1778; *The Dublin Weekly Journal* 5 Mar. 1748, 18 Feb., 1 July 1749.

0372 CAULFEILD, Thomas

MP for Tulsk 1715–27, 1741–7

> b. 1688; d. 23 Oct. 1747
> FAMILY/BACKGROUND: Eldest son of William Caulfeild (0375) and Lettice, dau. of Sir Arthur Gore, 1st Baronet.
> MARRIED: Unmarried.
> CHILDREN: Jane (?illegitimate), m. [5 May 1752] Rt Hon. Sir Edward King, 5th Baronet (1150).
> EDUCATION: Middle Temple 10 Nov. 1710; entered Cambridge (Trinity Hall) 15 Jan. 1711.

POLITICAL ACTIVITY: He does not appear to have been a very active MP, as he was listed for only two committees, both in 1719. He was consistently against a national bank. Very little is known about him; when he came in 1741 he may have been a 'seat warmer'. He was succeeded by a cousin on his mother's side, General Frederick Gore (0864).

DIVISION LISTS:

1721 (1) voted against a national bank.
1721 (2) voted against a national bank.

ESTATES/RESIDENCE: Donamon, Co. Galway. The Donamon estate comprised lands in the baronies of Ballymore, Ballintober and Roscommon.

SOURCES: McCracken thesis; *Alum. Cantab.*; *Memorials of the Dead*; H. A. C. Sturgess, *Register of Admissions to the Honourable Society of the Middle Temple* (London, 1949), vol. 1 p. 267; *GM* (Exshaw's edition) Oct. 1747.

0373 CAULFEILD, Toby

MP for Tulsk 1727–40

b. 1694; d. May 1740
FAMILY/BACKGROUND: Second son of William
Caulfeild (0375) and Lettice, dau. of Sir Arthur
Gore, 1st Baronet.
MARRIED: Unmarried.
EDUCATION: School: Mr Conterine, Donamon;
entered TCD 16 May 1712.

POLITICAL ACTIVITY: He is listed on 12 committees
between 1728 and 1735. Very little is known about
this MP. He was part of a family that successively
represented this borough for most of the century.

ESTATES/RESIDENCE: Donamon, Co. Galway.

SOURCES: McCracken thesis; *GM* (Exshaw's edition)
Sept. 1746; *Memorials of the Dead* [says he died 1742
aged 47 years, but see *CJ Ire.*]; *JRSAI* vol. 54 (1924)
pp. 55–67, T. U. Sadleir, 'The Register of Kilkenny
School (1685–1800)' [gives a Tobias Caulfeild entered
Kilkenny College 17 May 1707 aged 13 years]; *Pue's
Occurrences* 7 June 1740.

0374 CAULFEILD, Toby

MP for Tulsk 1771–2

b. 1750; d. 11 Mar. 1772
FAMILY/BACKGROUND: Son of Rev. Robert
Caulfeild and Mary, dau. of [ ] Brown of Castle
Hill, Co. Down.
MARRIED: Unmarried.
EDUCATION: School: Mr Goldsmith; entered TCD
12 Apr. 1768.
MILITARY: Lieutenant of Dragoons.

POLITICAL ACTIVITY: He was returned by the former
Chief Justice of King's Bench, Lord St George
Caulfeild (0371), and followed his political lead.
He had been in parliament for only about a year
when he died in March 1772, aged 22. He appears not to have had a spectacular career in the
army and to have been disappointed by lack of
promotion; possibly he hoped that a seat in parliament might improve his chances of promotion.

DIVISION LISTS:
1771 (3) voted against the amendment to
the Revenue Bill.

ESTATES/RESIDENCE: Dublin; Donamon, Co. Galway.

SOURCES: *Alum. Dub.*; Lodge *P*; Parliamentary Lists,
1771 (1), 1772 (2), 1773 (1).

0375 CAULFEILD, William

MP for Tulsk 1692–3, 1695–9, 1703–13–14

b. 1665; d. 24 Aug. 1737
FAMILY/BACKGROUND: Eldest son of Capt. Thomas
Caulfeild and Anne, dau. of Rt Hon. Charles
Moore, 2nd Viscount Drogheda.
MARRIED: Lettice, dau. of Sir Arthur Gore, 1st
Baronet.
CHILDREN: Thomas (0372); Toby (0373);
William, m. Frances Gunter; Rt Hon. St George
(0371); Rev. Robert, m. Mary dau. of [ ] Brown
of Castle Hill, Co. Down; Eleanor; Alice, m.
William Walcott; Lettice, m. Blayney Browne of
Co. Limerick.
EDUCATION: Middle Temple 16 Sept. 1700; called
to the Irish Bar 1704.
CAREER/OCCUPATION: 2nd Serjeant 1 Dec. 1708–
11; Prime Serjeant 8 Dec. 1714; 2nd Justice of
the King's Bench 3 June 1715–34; High Sheriff
of Co. Galway 1695; Justice of the Assize for
Connaught, Lent 1715, Summer 1715, Lent
1718; NE Ulster, Summer 1718; Munster,
Summer 1719, Lent 1720; NW Ulster, Lent
1722; Connaught, Summer 1722, Lent 1723,
Summer 1725; NW Ulster, Lent 1726; Connaught, Summer 1726, Lent 1727, Summer
1727, Summer 1728, Lent 1729, Summer 1729
(he received an allowance of £100 for the Lent
circuit of 1729–30); *Commissioner of Oyer and
Terminer 1732–3, *Trustee of the Linen Board
for Leinster 1733, for Connaught 1735–d.

POLITICAL ACTIVITY: A lawyer and the father of Lord
Chief Justice Caulfeild (0371). In 1695 he supported Lord Chancellor Porter against the accusations of favouring Catholics made against him
by some MPs, and in 1696 he signed the Association for the protection of William III in the country. He was listed for one committee during the
short 1692 parliament, 16 in 1695–9 and 66 in
1703–11. In 1707, during the debate on the (unsuccessful) election petition of Sir Alexander
Cairnes (0334) against the return of Samuel Ogle
(1574) for Belfast, the gallery was ordered to be
cleared at the end of the debate. A number of la-

dies were unwilling to leave the gallery. At this, Caulfeild stood up and called out 'Put out the candles, put out the candles!' The ladies left, resenting such an open affront.

Throughout the reign of Queen Anne he was in opposition and a noted Whig. He was appointed Second Serjeant in 1708 and introduced the confirmation of the 1704 penal law in 1709, 8 Anne, c. 3. He remained a prominent Whig in the 1710 session, when he introduced 9 Anne, c. 11, the anti-terrorist 'act to prevent the maiming of cattle'.

His reward came with the Hanoverian succession as he was appointed, on the dismissal of Morley Saunders (**1880**), Prime Serjeant in December 1714 and, in June 1715, 2nd Justice of King's Bench, an office from which he retired in 1734, aged almost 70 years. He had a pension of £237 2s 3¼d. During his tenure of office, the following incident was reported in the state papers. In 1721, during a 'trial [in the court of King's Bench] a neighbouring chimney took fire, blew the smoke into the court and gave a panick to all the people who crowded to get out. Many were actually killed on the spot, and many desperately wounded. Among the first Mr John Ormsby (**1602**), Member of Parliament and a wealthy man of above £1,800 p.ann., was killed. Judge Caulfeild got half in and half out of a window, but could not pass through, lost his wig and at last was forced back. Lord Chief Justice Whitshed (**2233**) kept his place and temper till at last the truth was known.'

DIVISION LISTS:
1709 (1) spoke for a Money Bill.

ESTATES/RESIDENCE: Donamon, Co. Galway. Lands in the baronies of Ballymore, Ballintober S. and Roscommon. William Caulfeild, MP for Tulsk's, income in 1713 was estimated to be £500.

SOURCES: *CJ Ire.* (Bradley ed.) vol. 3 pp. 677, 789, vol. 6 pp. 32–3, vol. 7 pp. 50–1 [pension]; PRONI D/302; PRONI T/3411; CDB 6905; EC 4992; BL Add. MS 34, 778, f. 51; Hayton thesis; Lodge *P*; Hughes, *Pat. Officers*, IMC *King's Inns Admission Papers, 1607 1867*; Ball, *Judges*; *Memorials of the Dead* [says he died in his 73rd year]; PRO SP63/; *HMC Ormonde*, (1920) new ser. vol. 8 p. 313; *Register of Admissions to the Honourable Society of the Middle Temple*, vol. 1 p. 248;

Almanacks; *The Dublin Gazette* 26 Feb. 1715, 28 June 1729, 20 June 1730; *Whalley's Newsletter* 16 July 1715, 1 Mar. 1720, 7 July 1722; *Harding's Dublin Impartial Newsletter* 11 July 1719; *Harding's Impartial Newsletter* 20 Feb. 1722; *Harding's Weekly Impartial Newsletter* 9 July 1723; *The Dublin Intelligence* 19 Feb., 27 June 1724, 19 Feb., 9 July 1726, 11 Feb., 4 July 1728, 22 Feb. 1729; *The Dublin Weekly Journal* 26 June 1725, 24 Feb. 1728; *The Dublin Mercury* 19 Feb. 1773; Parliamentary Lists, 1695 (1), 1696 (1), 1706 (1), 1711 (3), 1713 (2).

0376 CAULFEILD, William

MP for Tulsk 1761–8–71

b. 1698; d. 1771
FAMILY/BACKGROUND: Son of Toby Caulfeild, Archdeacon of Killala.
MARRIED: ?
CHILDREN: ?
EDUCATION: School: Mr Lewis; Kilkenny College 30 Apr. 1707, aged 9 years; entered TCD 28 Jan. 1717, aged 19 years.
CAREER/OCCUPATION: Military: Captain 38th Regiment of Foot.

POLITICAL ACTIVITY: Very little is known about this MP, apart from the fact that he belonged to a well-known parliamentary family, was a professional soldier and voted for the augmentation of the army in 1768.

ESTATES/RESIDENCE: Finglas, Co. Dublin.

DIVISION LISTS:
1768 (1) voted for army augmentation – 38th Regiment of Foot.

SOURCES: *CJ Ire.* vol. 8 p. 365; *Alum. Dub.*; *JRSAI* vol. 54 (1924) pp. 55–67, T. U. Sadleir, 'The Register of Kilkenny School (1685–1800)' [says Lieutenant Governor of Fort George].

0377 CAULFEILD, William

MP for Tulsk 1769–76 83 6

b. 1741; d. (Feb.) 1786
FAMILY/BACKGROUND: Son of William Caulfeild and Frances, dau. of [ ] Gunter.

MARRIED: ?

CHILDREN: ?

EDUCATION: ?School: Mr Hemmings; entered TCD 3 July 1757, aged 16 years.

CAREER/OCCUPATION: Gentleman of the Bedchamber; Collector of the Revenue for Donaghadee 1772–80, £200 p.a.

POLITICAL ACTIVITY: An army officer brought into parliament by his uncle Chief Justice Caulfeild (0371), whose political line he followed. In 1772 he was noted as 'a very steady attender' and in 1775 as 'a steady and certain vote for Government upon all occasions. Lord Harcourt gave to his recommendation a Hearth Money Collection [Collector, who was] since dismissed, and ought to have been hanged.' Apart from this dubious recommendation he was given the appointment of one supernumerary gauger and one supernumerary tidewaiter. By 1780 he had in addition to his collectorship a pension of £200.

DIVISION LISTS:

1771 (1) voted for Lord Townshend as Lord Lieutenant.

1771 (2) voted against Sir Lucius O'Brien's (1558) motion for retrenchment.

1772 (2) voted against a Short Revenue Bill.

1774 (2) voted not in favour of Catholic relief.

1775 (1) voted against the pro-American amendment to the Speech from the Throne.

1777 (1) voted against Grattan's (0895) motion for retrenchment.

1778 (2) voted for the Popery Bill.

1779 (1) voted for new taxes.

1779 (2) voted against a six-months Loan Bill.

1780 (1) voted against Grattan's declaration of the rights of Ireland.

1780 (2) voted against Yelverton's (2268) motion to modify Poynings' Law.

1780 (3) voted for the Tenantry Bill.

1783 (1) voted against Flood's (0762) motion for parliamentary reform.

1785 (1) voted for the Commercial Propositions.

ESTATES/RESIDENCE: He was the residuary heir of Lord Chief Justice Caulfeild (0371) whose estate was valued at £12,000 p.a. in addition to the borough of Tulsk. In

1782 his pension was stated to be £500 p.a. – the pension and the estate were variously stated as £200–500 and £10,000–12,000. However, Mrs Walcott, Lord Chief Justice Caulfeild's sister, who had a life interest in the estate and the borough of Tulsk, outlived him. The estate and borough ultimately descended to St George Caulfeild, who was a minor in 1800 and under the guardianship of James Caulfeild.

SOURCES: *Alum. Dub.*; *Almanacks*; *Walker's Hibernian Magazine*, p. 111; *GM* (Exshaw's edition) Feb. 1786; Parliamentary Lists, 1769 (1), 1772 (2), 1773 (1), (2), 1774 (1), 1775 (1), 1776 (1), (2), (3), 1777 (1), 1778 (1), 1780 (1), 1782 (1), 1783 (1), (2), 1784 (1), (2), (3), 1785 (1), (2), (3).

0378 CAUSABON, William

MP for Doneraile 1715–27

b. *c.* 1688–94; d. *post* 1744

FAMILY/BACKGROUND: Son of William Causabon and Sarah, dau. of Arthur Hyde of Castle Hyde, Co. Cork.

MARRIED: [1743] Arabella, dau. of Rt Hon. John Rogerson (1812); (she m. (2) 1746 Sir James Cotter, 1st Baronet (0503)).

CHILDREN: Arabella, m. George Purdon (1746); Catherine, m. Richmond Newman; William.

CAREER/OCCUPATION: High Sheriff of Co. Cork 1723.

MILITARY: Lieutenant-Colonel, Cork Militia, foot 27 Feb. 1744.

POLITICAL ACTIVITY: Virtually nothing is known of this man's activities in parliament. Probably he was not a very active MP. He was descended from Isaac Causabon, the Swiss scholar and historian, who came to England in 1603 at the request of James I. The first record of Causabons in Ireland is during the reign of Charles I, when they settled near Youghal.

ESTATES/RESIDENCE: Carrig, Co. Cork. Co-trustee for the estate of Captain William Jephson (1093). In 1703 his father obtained the forfeited estate of Carryguidgaed.

SOURCES: PRONI D3/02; NAI MFCI Reel 20, Parish Registers of Youghal, Co. Cork [says William son of Thomas Causabon bapt. 26 Apr. 1666. It appears very likely that this William is his father which would mean he was born *c.* 1688–94]; RCBL GS 2/7/3/44, Kilmore Marriage Licence Books; Jephson, *An Anglo-Irish Mis-*

cellany (Dublin, 1964), p. 67; Burke *LG* (1846) p. 630; G. L. Lee, *The Huguenot Settlements in Ireland* (London, 1936), p. 70; Lodge *P*; Cork MPs; *The Dublin Courant* 17 Nov. 1722; *JRSAI* vol. 23 (1893) pp. 83–4, 429, M. Pattison and R. G. FitzGerald-Uniacke, 'Miscellanea'.

0379 CAVENDISH, Hon. George

MP for St Johnstown (Longford) 1790–7; Cavan B. 1798–1800

b. 26 Aug. 1766; d. 13 Feb. 1849
FAMILY/BACKGROUND: Son of Rt Hon. Sir Henry Cavendish, 2nd Baronet (**0381**) and Sarah (d. 1807), 1st Baroness Waterpark, o. dau. and h. of Richard Bradshaw of Cork.
MARRIED: (1) [26 Feb. 1803] Letitia Catherine (d. 3 Aug. 1805), dau. of James Caulfeild; (2) [15 Nov.1807] Catherine, dau. of Ralph Smyth.
CHILDREN: ?*d.s.p.*
EDUCATION: Lincoln's Inn 26 Jan. 1786; called to the Irish Bar Apr. 1792.
CAREER/OCCUPATION: *Listed in Judges and Barristers 1798–1800 (f.); Commissioner of Inland Navigation 1800 at £500 p.a.; Secretary to Treasury Commissioners 29 Aug. 1801 at £1,000 p.a.
MILITARY: Royal Irish Dragoons.

POLITICAL ACTIVITY: He was returned by purchase through his father (**0381**), who wanted a peerage for his wife. He, his father and his two brothers (**0383, 0384**) all sat in the 1790–7 parliament. The vote for Ponsonby (**1709**) in the 1790 Speakership election was probably personal, reflecting the connection between the Cavendishes and the Ponsonbys. They all supported the administration, and in 1792 his mother was created Baroness Waterford *suo iure*.

In 1798 he was returned for Cavan Borough, probably by purchase from Lord Leitrim (**0418**), whose heir, Lord Clements (**0415**), had made a double return for Cavan Borough and Cavan county in the 1797 general election. Cavan Borough had been divided by a written agreement between the Clements and Nesbitt families as early as March 1722. The Cavendishes voted for the Union in both 1799 and 1800, and George Cavendish was made Secretary to the Treasury

during pleasure with a salary of £1,000 p.a.

DIVISION LISTS:
1790 (2) voted for Ponsonby (**1709**) on the Election of a Speaker.
1799 (1) voted for the Union – employment under his father.
1800 (1) voted for the Union.

ADDITIONAL INFORMATION: An annuity of £1,000 p.a. 28 Mar. 1817.

ESTATES/RESIDENCE: Kilcullen, Co. Cavan.

SOURCES: PRONI T/3166/1A Hartnell notes; Burke *PB* (1906) p. 1671; Hughes, *Pat. Officers*; O'Neill thesis; *King's Inns Admission Papers, 1607–1867*; *The Records of the Honourable Society of Lincoln's Inn* (Lincoln's Inn, 1896) vol. 1 p. 516; *Almanacks*; Parliamentary Lists, 1791 (1), 1793 (1), 1794 (2), 1799 (2), (3), 1800 (3).

0380 CAVENDISH, Rt Hon. Sir Henry

MP for Tallow 1756–60; Lismore 1761–8–76

b. 15 Apr. 1707; d. 31 Dec. 1776
HONOURS: PC, sworn 9 June 1768; cr. Baronet [GB] 7 May 1755.
FAMILY/BACKGROUND: Eldest son of William Cavendish of Derbyshire and Mary, dau. of Sir Thomas Tyrell of Oxford.
MARRIED: (1) [9 June 1730] Anne, dau. and co-h. of Henry Pyne (**1752**) of Waterpark, Co. Cork; (2) [4 Oct. 1748] Catherine (d. 14 Mar. 1779), dau. of Henry Prittie of Dunally, Co. Tipperary, wid. of Sir Richard Meade, 3rd Baronet (**1389**).
CHILDREN: (1) Rt Hon. Sir Henry, 2nd Baronet (**0381**); George; Pyne, m. [1768] Hon. Rev. Maurice Crosby, Dean of Limerick; Mary, m. George Quin; Frances, m. Sir Frederick Flood, 1st Baronet (**0761**); Anne, m. [1759] Sir Simon Bradstreet, 1st Baronet; Catherine, m. Thomas Burroughs.
(2) James (**0382**).
EDUCATION: Entered Oxford (University College) 17 Aug. 1724, aged 17 years.
CAREER/OCCUPATION: Revenue Commissioner 1747 – 1 Oct. 1755 (patent 3 Aug. 1747); Teller of the Exchequer 1755–76; *Gentleman Usher of the Black Rod 1755–6; Sheriff of Derbyshire 1741; Collector of the Revenue for Cork Excise 1743–46; Freedom of Cork 13 July 1743; *Clerk to the Ship Entries 1752–5; *Trustee of the Linen

Board for Munster 1766–d.; *Governor of the Hibernian Society 1769–d.

MILITARY: Colonel of the True Blue of Cork, an independent company, 1747, said to be a hundred gentlemen, well disciplined 'who performed the manual exercises and evolutions with the greatest exactness' (such companies were the forerunners of the Volunteers). Lieutenant in the Slane Volunteers.

POLITICAL ACTIVITY: Henry Cavendish was the descendant of an illegitimate son of the 1st Duke of Devonshire. He was a lightweight with no great abilities, and he owed his success to this rather tenuous connection with the 3rd and 4th Dukes of Devonshire, Lords Lieutenant at various times in the 1730s, 1740s and 1750s. When the 3rd Duke came over as Lord Lieutenant in 1737, Cavendish came with him. He had married an Irishwoman, Anne Pyne, whose grandfather, Sir Richard Pyne, was – along with Sir Richard Ryves and Robert Rochfort – appointed Keeper of the Seals by William III in 1690. In 1690 Sir Richard was Chief Justice of Common Pleas, and in 1695 Chief Justice King's Bench and later of Queen's Bench.

Sir Henry, in November 1746, wrote to Sir Robert Wilmot, the Lord Lieutenant's English Secretary for Ireland from 1740 to 1772, that he was doubtful about accepting a post in Ireland. He was sure of the Duke of Devonshire's interest and Lord Gower's help, but was fearful that the Lord Lieutenant's [Chesterfield] opposition would hinder his success, writing that 'If I thought I had no chance to rise I would ask leave to sell out.' However, he had overcome his anxieties by February 1747, deciding that 'As it is not impossible but some of the Irish Commissioners resident in England and Members of that House may be under some difficulty on account of the act which disqualifies them from sitting in the House of Commons after the next sessions. I beg leave to consult you whether you think it practicable to get one of them to resign to me for a valuable consideration if a bargain of that kind could be made, I dare say the Duke of Devonshire would recommend me to the minister as a proper person to attend the business here [Ireland], which would set Mr Ponsonby (1702) entirely at liberty. If this could be done I do not apprehend any dif-

ficulty in getting leave from the Commissioners here to dispose of my Collection.'

In 1751 there was a vacancy for Cork city following the death of Sir Matthew Deane (0607). The ensuing dispute was not as straightforward as it appeared, for some years previously Cavendish had been one of the Revenue Commissioners who had endeavoured to thwart Sir Richard Cox's (0508) plans for acquiring the Collectorship of Cork, thereby creating a direct conflict between the British administration, who had nominated John Love, and the Irish Lords Justices, who had supported Cox. Primate Stone wrote to Newcastle in October 1754 a long self-justifying letter in which he commented on the Cork election of 1751, the mischief of Cox and his attempts to create trouble between the Speaker and the Ponsonbys: 'Mr Cavendish was a candidate for the city of Cork and would have been chosen without difficulty. Sir Richard Cox stirred up an opposition to him and prevailed upon the Speaker to think his figure concerned in patronising it. It was carried out with the utmost indecency to Mr Cavendish and with great disrespect to the family to which he has the honour of being related. Sir Richard Cox's motive at all events was to bring it to a petition and to draw the Speaker into a measure in which Mr Ponsonby and his friends would be under a necessity of differing from him. The Speaker mentioned this to me with concern ... he gave me the most solemn assurances that if Mr Cavendish should have a majority in the city and there should be a petition, he would himself oppose it ... [Lord Duncannon] ... received the same assurances from the Speaker, which he desired might be understood as a mark of his respect to the Duke of Devonshire. Soon after Lord Duncannon was gone to England, the Speaker altered his mind, saying that some custom house officers had been busy in soliciting votes, and this was contrary to some resolutions of the House of Commons and the case being now altered he must fight it through. The truth was that the family of Gores would then be offered to him for that service, and he chose to break his then subsisting engagements that he might form new ones with people who he knew would go further with him if there should be occasion. My Lord Lieutenant, in hopes of preventing differences among the King's servants and with marks of high regard for the Speaker, prevailed upon Mr Cavendish to give up the election before the poll, by which the Speaker's reputation of power was much enlarged and his following increased.'

Cavendish was made a baronet in 1755, but his good fortune reached its zenith in 1756 when Lord Lieutenant Hartington (Devonshire) appointed him Teller of the Exchequer for Ireland following the death of the Deputy Vice-Treasurer, Luke Gardiner (0841) and the promotion of Nathaniel Clements (0414), the former Teller, to his office. In some quarters it was felt that the efficient and talented Clements had used his powers to establish an unduly strong position, for 'As a perquisite of that office, he was allowed to retain the profit made from the use of balances of public moneys in his hands until such sums exceeded £30,000 when the interest was applied to the discharge of debt' and he could use this in various profitable ways as well as to make diplomatic loans. Sir Henry was probably considered a safe and – with his Devonshire connections – irreproachable repository for such a trust. But his abilities were limited, and this new power went to his head. At his death he owed Government 'near £50,000'; probably the correct figure was £67,305 7s 2d. However, his abler son, Sir Henry Cavendish Jr (0381), duly paid 'a great part ... after much delay'. Henry Seymour-Conway (1897), writing to the Duke of Devonshire on 5 August 1756, was already expressing doubt about Cavendish's handling of the Exchequer: 'I am particularly sorry to see Sir H. goes on lending money out, as it really makes that evil worse every day, and cramps the public service by rendering it more impracticable for the public to avail itself of that surplus nominally in the treasury on any emergency ... There is much danger to themselves in this practice, much discredit to the government if they are supported in it, and much detriment to the public and to the public service in many lights. Sir H. says they could not now make any large remittance to England if demanded ... Mr Clements says he must keep back the public payments as much as possible. The artillery service is checked, the magazines are insufficient, the fortifications and several other mili-

tary preparations must go on slowly – all for the want of ready cash, while the public money is distributed to favour particulars and to enrich the gentlemen of the treasury.' Two days later he wrote: 'I am glad Sir Harry talks of calling in ... about £15,000 or £16,000, but on the whole he has put out about £70,000 now besides that. I am sorry that Sir H. just at this critical time, enters into a traffic of that sort, which is dangerous to himself ... and makes him a sharer in any blame or censure that may follow enquiries into this matter.'

Sir Robert Wilmot, in a letter to the Duke of Devonshire on 19 August 1756, said that the 'great profit which Sir H. says Mr Clements made ... [apparently arose] from the lucky circumstance of buying into stocks low and selling out high. I am afraid a little encouragement would induce Sir H. to risk something in the funds even in these times, but surely it would be the kindest advice to dissuade him from putting into that dangerous lottery. If he had no family, no estate, no honour at stake, the temptation to make a fortune speedily might be strong ... but ... I should recommend it to him to be content with the certain considerable profit ... that must always accrue to him from safe and private securities in Ireland, which instead of raising up enemies would strengthen him with friends in that Kingdom.'

On 10 November 1763, Cavendish wrote to Sir Robert Wilmot about the Tallow by-election (see 0342), giving an interesting insight: 'I thought it material to prevent a poll, and that no man might have it in his power to say that the Seneschal favoured Colonel Gisborne (0851) in his return. Stronger language upon these occasions is frequently made use of, and I therefore endeavour to prevail upon Major Cane (0342) to desist, by making it clearly appear to him that he had no chance of sitting in the House, and that he must forever disoblige the Duke of Devonshire if he persisted in his election. After two days conference upon this subject, I gained my point, upon condition from which I could not prevail upon the Major to depart, that the Colonel should give him two hundred guineas to dispose of as he thought proper.'

In 1773 Cavendish was described as 'a man of affable deportment and a complacency of behaviour'. As a major government office-holder he was invariably a government supporter, and it was remarked that 'In asking favours he seems to use all the delicacy and tenderness of a friend. A Privy Councillor, Cashier or Teller of the Exchequer. A Trustee of the Linen Board.' In 1775 he was considered 'a respectable amiable man, much afflicted with the gout, and on that account his attendance is very uncertain. His great object is to get his son James joined with him in the office of Teller of the Exchequer. He purchased a seat for son in the last session. Lord Harcourt gave him the Collection of Dundalk worth £200.' Fortunately he did not succeed in making his son Teller of the Exchequer as James, the son of Cavendish's second marriage, appears to have been a paler version of his father. Apparently Sir Henry was considering going into opposition (or at least the compiler of a 1776 list thought so), presumably over this, when he died and the chaos that he left behind him was discovered.

DIVISION LISTS:

> 1757 (1) voted against the resolutions on pensions.
> 1768 (1) voted for army augmentation – Teller of the Exchequer.
> 1771 (1) voted for Lord Townshend as Lord Lieutenant.
> 1771 (2) voted against Sir Lucius O'Brien's (**1558**) motion for retrenchment – a placeman.
> 1774 (2) voted against Catholic relief.
> 1793 (1) voted for Knox's (**1180**) motion for Catholic emancipation.

ADDITIONAL INFORMATION: In addition to his career prospects he consulted Wilmot, 16 February 1748, about his private affairs. This is interesting for the insight it gives into eighteenth-century attitudes to marriage: 'Perhaps you may think me drunk or mad or both when I freely ask you and expect as free an answer, if you would give me leave to marry a most agreeable widow with jointure of £600 p.a., of same age with myself, she has a son not four years old, heir to £5,000 p.a. to whom she is guardian with an allowance of £500 p.a. for his present maintenance and a daughter who has a considerable fortune; your advise is

asked in proper time, for at present there are no engagements of either side.' Wilmot's reply was cautious; he feared that marriage might worsen Cavendish's financial difficulties rather than cure them. Cavendish, however, was not to be put off, and replied that 'In the situation I am in it is impossible I should marry to advantage; my only option is to live, therefore, unmarried or to risk the consequences of a married state. The former I grant you is the more prudent choice, the latter to me the more eligible on many accounts exclusive of the passion you hint at. My family greatly wants new regulation; my sister, to you only I write, has not prudence enough to be at the head of it and I intend to take advantage of the report. The report now too current in town that I am going to be married, and to send her back to England with Mrs Dance; this will be a friendly way of parting and though I should not choose to encourage the report I can't well part with her on any other footing without an open breech ... I ought to have told you, the lady in question is the late Sir Richard Meade's (**1389**) widow, that she has £2,000 in money and a very good house in Molesworth Street and I think I should do her so much justice to say that she is not without her difficulties which together with my own are not likely to be removed in haste, so that we are both in the prudent way of reflection which seldom produces bad consequences ... I must say that if I was sure to have no children I should not hesitate a moment for she is indisputably in all respects a most desirable woman in person least so inclined to fat and I think not likely to breed.' Of course he married her, and the result was James Cavendish (**0382**). He must also have been a most unsuitable stepfather to the headstrong future Lord Clanwilliam (**1388**).

ESTATES/RESIDENCE: Pickardstown, Co. Dublin: in 1750 Mrs Delany found it 'flat, but pretty enough'; his second wife's house in Molesworth Street, Dublin; Doveridge, Derbyshire. Sir Henry built two houses on a plot of ground 'demised' to him by James, Earl of Kildare in Kildare Street, Dublin. In November 1782, his son conveyed one of these houses to David La Touche (**1203**) 'in trust and for the use of the gentlemen of the Kildare-street Club', which was founded in 1782. In 1786 the second Cavendish house was also acquired by the club.

SOURCES: PRONI T/3158/1309, /1313, Devonshire MSS; PRONI T/3019/805, /835, /975, /981, /6459, /733, Wilmot Papers; PRONI MIC/465/1 R. Ffolliott, Biographical Notices, 1756–1827; *The Dublin Hibernian Journal* reports his death on 21 Dec. 1776, *DJ* [gives his death with background details 31 Dec. 1776]; Burke *PB* (1906) p. 1671 [says incorrectly that he died 31 May 1776]; PRONI MIC/474 Irish Volunteers; Ellis thesis; McCracken thesis; *Index to Irish Privy Counsellors, 1711–1910*; Hughes, *Pat. Officers*; *Alum. Oxon.* [says died 31 Mar.]; *Irish Official Papers in Great Britain* vol. 1 p. 52–3; Llandover, *Delany Corr.*, vol. 2 pp. 554–5, 557; Johnston, *Gt B. & Ire.*, p. 255–6; J. T. Gilbert, *A History of the City of Dublin* (Dublin, 1859), vol. 3 p. 289; *The Register of the Parish of St Peter and St Kevin, 1669–1761* (Parish Register Society of Dublin, 1911) p. 262; *Ir. Gen.* vol. 5 no. 4 (1977) p. 471, H. F. Morris, 'Ramsey's Waterford Chronicle, 1777'; *Waterford Arch. Soc. Jn.* vol. 16 (1913) p. 51, T. U. Sadleir (ed.), 'The County of Waterford 1775'; J. Walton, *'The King's Business': Letters on the Administration of Ireland, 1741–61...* (N.Y., 1996) nos 71, 73, 267, 317; J. Kelly, *Henry Flood...*(Dublin, 1998), pp. 237, 262–3; R. E. Burns, *Irish Parliamentary Politics in the Eighteenth Century*, 2 vols (Washington, 1989) vol. 2 pp. 114, 121–2; G. O'Brien (ed.) *Parliament, Politics and the People* (1989), p. 36, J. O'Donovan, 'The Militia in Munster'; *Almanacks*; *Pue's Occurrences* 1 Nov. 1755; Parliamentary Lists, 1769 (1), 1772 (2), 1773 (1), (2), 1774 (1), 1775 (1), 1776 (1).

0381 CAVENDISH, Rt Hon. Sir Henry

MP for Lismore 1766–8, 1776–83–90, 1798–1800; Killybegs 1790–7 [n.d.e. Lismore 1791], [GB] Lostwithiel 1768–74

b. 29 Sept. 1732; d. 3 Aug. 1804
HONOURS: PC 1769–d. (sworn 1 July 1779); suc. as 2nd Baronet [GB] 1776.
FAMILY/BACKGROUND: Eldest son of Rt Hon. Sir Henry Cavendish, 1st Baronet (0380) and his 1st wife Anne, dau. and co-h. of Henry Pyne (1752).
MARRIED: [12 Aug. 1757] Sarah, o. dau. and h. of Richard Bradshaw of Cork; she was cr. Baroness Waterpark, 15 June 1792.
CHILDREN: Hon. Sir Richard (0383); Hon. George (0379); Hon. Augustus Cavendish-Bradshaw (0384); Frederick (b. 1777), m. [1801] (1) Eleanor (d. 25 Mar. 1812), dau. of Rt Hon. Arthur Saunders Gore, 2nd Earl of Arran (0861), (2) [5 Oct. 1817] Agnes Catherine e. dau. of Alexander Macdonnell; Catherine (d. 1800), m.

Baron de Ville; Deborah, m. Sir Richard Musgrave, 1st Baronet (1509); Sarah (d. 2 Jan. 1849), m. Arthur Annesley, 1st Earl of Mountnorris; Anne (6 July 1863) m. [1793] James Caulfeild Browne, 2nd Baron Kilmaine (0257).
EDUCATION: School: Eton 1747–8 (he was a Captain in the school rebellion), entered TCD 11 July 1750.
CAREER/OCCUPATION: Receiver General 1779, 29 Sept. 1795–1800 (f.); Vice-Treasurer and Treasury Commissioner 25 Dec. 1793; Lord Commissioner of the Treasury 1795; Receiver, Paymaster General of all Revenues 1795–9; Clerk of the Invoice, port of Dublin Sept. 1751, resigned Mar. 1754.

POLITICAL ACTIVITY: This MP's chief claim to fame was his mastery of Gurney shorthand, which enabled him to take down verbatim debates in both the English and the Irish Houses of Commons at a time when public reporting of debates was still considered a breach of privilege. He never edited his notes, apart from a few corrections, and, of course, he only reported debates when he was present. Nevertheless, they give a vivid, if verbose, picture of the Irish House of Commons in session and the very difficult task of the Speaker in controlling the House and preventing it from erupting into free-ranging discussion instead of keeping to the subject. In this he differed from the *Parliamentary Register*, which précised debates.

He was returned for the Devonshire borough of Lismore in the 1766 by-election, when the Hon. Stephen Moore (1478) succeeded his father (1476) as 2nd Viscount Mountcashell. In 1768 he was returned to the British parliament for the borough of Lostwithiel through the influence of his cousin Lord Edgecumbe. In the British House he was classed as a member of the opposition. Here Horace Walpole, never very charitable, thought that he was 'hot-headed and odd'. He took a considerable interest in Irish affairs and, replying to a taunt from an English member about his Irish birth, he declared that: 'I speak for the good of the community. I hope no distinctions will prevail as to English or Irish members.'

In 1770, when Robert Boyle-Walsingham (0217) moved for papers relative to the sudden prorogation of the Irish parliament, Cavendish opposed him, arguing that bringing Irish affairs of this nature before the British House of Commons risked a censure from the Irish House for interfering in its affairs. Cavendish was a stickler for precedent and points of order: in one of the 1783 Irish Parliamentary Lists he is considered to be 'a frequent and tedious speaker, but knowing in the forms and orders of the House', which were very important to the Irish parliamentarians. Nevertheless, on at least one occasion he was hissed from the gallery. The gallery usually expected to be entertained or to hear a weighty matter discussed, and preferably both. The 'vein of dry sarcastic humour' which 'often pervades his arguments' was not always appreciated. It was said that 'He is fond of his own opinions, adheres to them in general pertinaciously and resigns them reluctantly'; nevertheless, he occupied an almost unique position because 'being an admirable short-hand writer, he enjoys the accumulated knowledge of the ablest speakers in various parliaments and independent of every other source he can draw from the fund largely and always instructively.'

In 1776 he was again returned to the Irish parliament for the Devonshire borough of Lismore and he spent the rest of his political career in Ireland. At first it was thought that he would be non-resident but this soon changed, possibly assisted by the discovery of his father's mismanagement as Teller of the Exchequer. In 1779 he said he hoped that the people would not believe that the commercial concessions given by English government had been extorted by fear. He objected strongly to the Volunteers' attempts to influence MPs, demanding 'Were they all slaves or freemen that sat in parliament, were they men of passive obedience and non-resistance who wanted to be pushed forward by the crowd.' The Duke of Devonshire placed no stipulations on his parliamentary conduct, and he generally supported government in the expectation of office or a peerage for his wife – although he wavered over the Commercial Resolutions and during the Regency Crisis, perhaps drawn by the Ponsonby connection and a desire to save his expectations. In 1780 he had threatened the retiring Lord Lieutenant, the Earl of Buckinghamshire, with a duel for not providing adequately for him.

The Duke of Devonshire was negligent in his control of his Irish borough property, and in 1790 Sir Henry was unseated by Robert Paul (**1644**), a local man connected to Lord Grandison and the Ponsonbys. Cavendish then purchased one of the seats for Killybegs from Colonel Burton Conyngham (**0303**). In 1790 Sir Henry and his three sons all purchased seats, and in 1792 Lady Cavendish was created Baroness Waterpark with remainder to her sons by Sir Henry. In 1794 he was appointed a Commissioner of the Treasury. He supported the government throughout the 1790s and signed a Co. Cork petition in favour of the Union, April 1799. He voted consistently for the Union, and was made Receiver General during pleasure with a salary of £1,500 p.a. Not surprisingly, he was considered to be 'deeply indebted to the crown'.

DIVISION LISTS:
1777 (1) voted against Grattan's (**0895**) motion for retrenchment.
1778 (2) voted for the Popery Bill.
1779 (1) voted for new taxes.
1779 (2) voted against a six-months Loan Bill.
1780 (2) voted for Yelverton's (**2268**) motion to modify Poynings' Law.
1780 (3) voted against the Tenantry Bill.
1782 (1) voted for the Dublin Corporation.
1784 (1) voted against a committee on the Reform Bill.
1785 (1) voted against the Commercial Propositions.
1789 (1) voted for a Regency.
1793 (2) voted for the Convention Bill.
1795 (3) voted against Parsons' (**1636**) resolutions against alleged troop removals.
1799 (1) voted for the Union – Privy Counsellor and Receiver General.
1800 (1) voted for the Union.

ADDITIONAL INFORMATION: He was nicknamed 'Mat o' the Mint' because if an Irish mint had been established he was anxious to be head of it. In addition to his shorthand skills he was a noted billiard player and shooter. *A member of the RDS from 1767.

ESTATES/RESIDENCE: Phoenix Park and Grafton Street, Dublin; Doveridge Hall, Derbyshire. A letter sent by his father to Sir Robert Wilmot, 14 October 1756, recounts how Henry met Miss Bradshaw, the well-connected daughter of a Cork merchant 'by whom he got a large property', while visiting his father's sister Cossart. He had just proposed marriage and his father noted that a dowry of £10,000 would be given, with a further £10,000 at his father-in-law's death. Ultimately, his marriage settlement was reputedly worth £20,000. His father-in-law was supposed to be worth £50,000.

SOURCES: PRONI Cavendish Debates; PRONI T/3019/6457/470 Wilmot Papers; PRONI MIC/465/1 R. Ffolliott, Biographical Notices, 1756–1827 [says Hon. J. Cavendish son of (0381) married Rt Hon. Lady A. Gore, third daughter of Earl of Arran, 28 May 1801]; O'Neill thesis; GEC *P*; *HP 1754–90*; *Index to Irish Privy Counsellors, 1711–1910*; Hughes, *Pat. Officers*; R. A. Austen-Leigh (ed.), *The Eton College Register, 1698–1752* (Eton, 1927). 3 vols; Llandover, Delany Corr., vol. 2 p. 595; McDowell, *Irish Public Opinion, 1750–1800* p. 64, 83; J. Kelly, *'That Damn'd Thing Called Honour': Duelling in Ireland 1570–1860*, p. 134; J. Kelly, *Henry Flood ...* (Dublin, 1998), p. 350; J. Kelly, *Prelude to Union* (Cork, 1992), pp. 166, 189; *Almanacks*; *GM* (Exshaw's edition) Sept. 1751; *Ir. Builder* 1 May 1887, 'St Audoen's Church, Corn Market: Its History from its Foundation to the Present Time' [bapt. 29 Sept. 1732]; *BNL* 26 Mar. 1754; *The Cork Advertiser* 30 Apr. 1799; *DJ* 16–20 Aug. 1757, 1–3 July 1779; Parliamentary Lists, 1774 (1), 1776 (2), (3), 1777 (1), 1778 (1), 1780 (1), 1782 (1), 1783 (1), (2), 1784 (1), (2), (3), 1785 (1), (2), (3), (4), 1787 (1), 1788 (1), 1789 (1), 1790 (1), 1791 (1), 1793 (1), 1794 (1), (2), 1798 (1), 1799 (1), (2), (3), 1800 (1), (3).

0382 CAVENDISH, James

MP for Lifford 1773–6; Banagher 1776–83

b. *c.* 1749; d. Jan. 1808
FAMILY/BACKGROUND: Son of Rt Hon. Sir Henry Cavendish, 1st Baronet (0380) and his 2nd wife, Catherine, dau. of Henry Prittie of Onnally, Co. Tipperary, and wid. of Sir Richard Meade, 3rd Bt (1389).
MARRIED: [July 1773] Harriet, dau. of Guy Moore (Moore-Coote) (1459).
CHILDREN: Henry, m. Elizabeth dau. of Woodhouse Johnston, Thomas; James (d. 1799, of fatigue after the capture of Seringapatam); Catherine, m. John Eschin [Echlin]; Theodosia, m. James Caulfeild Donovan; Maria, m. Henry Bambrick.

CAREER/OCCUPATION: *Collector of the Revenue for Dundalk 1776.
MILITARY: Barracks Commissioner 10 July 1776 – 6 Oct. 1787, at £400 p.a.; Lieutenant in the Slane Volunteers.

POLITICAL ACTIVITY: The government brought him in for Lifford when John Creighton (0519) succeeded his father (0515) as 2nd Lord Erne on 10 June 1772. At the next election, in 1776, his father purchased a seat for Banagher for him from Peter Holmes (1033) on an assurance from Lord Harcourt that he would be appointed a Commissioner of the Barrack Board, £400 p.a. He was already Collector of Dundalk, £150–200 p.a. In 1778 he was already noted as 'an infrequent attender', and he did not improve, as by 1782 he was described as 'extremely involved in his circumstances and owes Government a large balance, having failed when Collector of Dundalk. A bad attendant.' In 1783, although still Commissioner of the Barrack Board, it was said that he 'never attends his duty' and that he would be unable to purchase a seat at the forthcoming election. This proved correct. As expected from an office-holder he voted for the government during the ten years he was in parliament.

DIVISION LISTS:
1773 (2) voted against an untaxed press.
1774 (2) voted against Catholic relief.
1777 (1) voted against Grattan's (0895) motion for retrenchment.
1778 (2) voted for the Popery Bill.
1779 (2) voted against a six-months Loan Bill.
1780 (1) voted against Grattan's declaration of the rights of Ireland.
1780 (2) voted against Yelverton's (2268) motion to modify Poynings' Law.
1780 (4) voted for the Perpetual Mutiny Bill.

ADDITIONAL INFORMATION: He was made Collector of Dundalk by Lord Harcourt. He ceased to hold any substantial Irish office after 1788. In 1800 he received £21 5d for the loss of the office of Messenger to the House of Lords at the Union.

ESTATES/RESIDENCE: Dublin; [?]Co. Meath.

SOURCES: Information from P. F. Meehan Esq.; PRONI T/559 vol. 28, p. 395, Burke, extract pedigrees; PRONI MIC/465/1 R. Ffolliott, Biographical Notices, 1756–1827; PRONI MIC/474, Irish Volunteers; Burke *PB* (1906); Hughes, *Pat. Officers*; Johnston, *Gt B. & Ire.*, p. 256; *Ir. Gen.* vol. 1 no. 10 (1941) p. 295, W. Clare, 'Irish Compensations and Pensions'; *The Gentleman's and Citizen's Almanack* (1788–1800); *Almanacks*; *FJ* 21–24 Feb. 1778; Parliamentary Lists, 1772 (2), 1774 (1), 1775 (1), 1776 (1), (2), (3), 1777 (1), 1778 (1), 1780 (1), 1782 (1), 1783 (1).

0383 CAVENDISH, Hon. Sir Richard

MP for Portarlington 1790–7

b. 13 July 1765; d. 1 June 1830
HONOURS: Suc. as 3rd Baronet [GB] 1804.
PEERAGES: Suc. 2nd Baron Waterpark 1807.
FAMILY/BACKGROUND: Son of Rt Hon. Sir Henry Cavendish, 2nd Baronet (0381) and Sarah, 1st Baroness Waterpark.
MARRIED: [6 Aug. 1789] Juliana, dau. and co-h. of Thomas Cooper of Cooper's Hill and Mullimast Castle, Co. Kildare.
CHILDREN: Henry Manners (b. 8 Nov. 1793; d. June 1 1830), 3rd Baron Waterpark, m. [1837] Elizabeth Jane, dau. of Thomas Anson, 1st Viscount Anson; Richard (b. 1794; d. 18 Mar. 1876), m. [22 July 1841] Elizabeth Maria Margaret (d. 4 June 1858) o. dau. and h. of Thomas Hart; Admiral George John (b. 1796; d. 23 Oct. 1865) m. [1838] Caroline (d. 13 July 1785), dau. of Rev. Charles Prideaux Brune; Rev. Augustus (d. May 9 1863), m. [Dec. 1830] Mary Anne, e. dau. of Thomas Leigh of Cheshire; Capt. Frederick (b. 1800; d. 24 May 1877); Rev. Thomas (d. 25 Mar. 1859), m. [4 May 1835] Sophia (d. 13 July 1891), dau. of Rev. Sir John Robinson, 1st Baronet; Sarah Georgina (d. 19 Sept. 1874), m. [1819] Sir George Richard Philips, Baronet; Anne Emma (b. 1791; d. 9 July 1881); Juliana (d. 19 Jan. 1865), m. [28 Dec. 1816] Frederick Farmer Taylor of Chyknell House, Salop; Catherine (d. 16 May 1863), m. [1839] Thomas Musgrave, Abp of York.
MILITARY: First Lieutenant in Rotunda Division cavalry 1796.

POLITICAL ACTIVITY: The eldest son of Sir Henry Cavendish (0381), he was one of the four MPs for whom Sir Henry purchased seats in 1790 in order to acquire a peerage for his wife. His sons followed their father's lead and, during the 1790s, supported the administration. The vote for Ponsonby (1709) as Speaker was probably a vote for the Devonshire (Cavendish) interest.

DIVISION LISTS:
1790 (2) voted for Ponsonby (1709) on the election of a Speaker.

ESTATES/RESIDENCE: Family estates in 1883 consisted of 6,587 acres in Co. Tipperary, worth £3,705 p.a., besides 1,613 acres in Derbyshire and 91 in Staffordshire, worth £1,319 p.a.

SOURCES: Burke *PB* (1906) p. 1672; GEC *P*; *FJ* 15 Nov. 1796; Parliamentary Lists, 1791 (1), 1793 (1), 1794 (2).

0384 CAVENDISH-BRADSHAW, Hon. Augustus

MP for Carlow B. 1790–6; (UK) Honiton 1805–12; Castle Rising 1812–Feb. 1817

b. 17 Feb. 1768; d. 11 Nov. 1832
FAMILY/BACKGROUND: Son of Rt Hon. Sir Henry Cavendish, 2nd Baronet (0381) and Sarah, 1st Baroness Waterpark. Assumed the name and arms of his maternal grandfather Richard Bradshaw 2 Jan. 1790.
MARRIED: [15 Nov. 1796, at Putney Church, London] Maryanne, e. dau. of James St John Jeffereyes (1082), div. wife of Rt Hon. George Frederick Nugent, 7th Earl of Westmeath (1547).
CHILDREN: *d.s.p.*
EDUCATION: School: Repton; entered Cambridge (Trinity College) 21 Apr. 1788, aged 19 years.
CAREER/OCCUPATION: Teller of the Court of the Exchequer [UK] 9 June 1806; Groom of the King's Bedchamber Aug. 1812.
MILITARY: Ensign Royal Cornwall and Devon Miners 1806; 2nd Lieutenant 1811.

POLITICAL ACTIVITY: His seat was purchased by his father from William Henry Burton (0304), the MP for Co. Carlow. Burton had thought that Cavendish-Bradshaw would support the Ponsonby interest, presumably from the family connection. However, Sir Henry had other plans for his family group, and Cavendish-Bradshaw supported the administration. His career in the Irish parliament was cut short by his involvement in the Westmeath divorce case. He afterwards sat in the British parliament.

DIVISION LISTS:
1790 (2) voted for Ponsonby (**1709**) on the election of a Speaker.

ADDITIONAL INFORMATION: Lord Westmeath was awarded £10,000 damages against him. In 1799 he was elected to Brooks's, sponsored by his distant kinsman, the 5th Duke of Devonshire. His father wanted him to have the reversion of the office of Receiver but Hardwicke, the Lord Lieutenant and Wickham, the Chief Secretary doubted his character 'and habits of life, which to the public opinion, would not point him out to be the fittest person to be the receiver and depository of the public revenue': a view that reflected the growing influence of public opinion. Government urged Sir Henry, his father, to hold on but Cavendish-Bradshaw foolishly took this as a promise and purchased the reversion from the then holder, Sir George Shee (**1910**), for £9,500. Cavendish-Bradshaw's case for reparation was not helped by his devotion to the Prince of Wales's friends in Ireland.

He bought his way into Honiton and, having supported the ministry of All Talents and voted for the repeal of Pitt's Additional Force Act, 30 April 1806, he got in reward the Tellership of the Exchequer in Ireland. His re-election for Honiton was contested and expensive and, although he attempted to hold on to his office under the Portland ministry, he was unsuccessful. Apart from his support for Catholic relief he followed the government line, but was continually dogged by financial difficulties.

ESTATES/RESIDENCE: Hume Street, Dublin; Putney, Surrey; High Elms, near Watford, Hertfordshire.

SOURCES: GEC *P*; *HP 1794–1820*; Burke *PB* (1906) p. 1672; Hughes, *Pat. Officers*; *Alum. Cantab.*; Carlow MPs; *DJ* 29 Nov. 1796; L. Stone, *Uncertain Unions and Broken Lives* (Oxford, 1995), pp. 38, 40, 566–8; L. Stone, *Road to Divorce* (Oxford, 1992) pp. 264–5; Parliamentary Lists, 1791 (1), 1793 (1), 1794 (2).

0385 CHAIGNEAU, David

MP for Gowran 1715–27–53

b. *c.* 1689; d. 20 Jan. 1753
FAMILY/BACKGROUND: Only son of Louis Chaigneau and Elizabeth du Coudre (married 1688).
MARRIED: [26 June 1710] Elizabeth, dau. of Robert Macquarrel and his wife Marie.
CHILDREN: Louis; (Rev.) Peter, m. [29 May 1731] Marie Malet; Josias; Theophilus; Louis David; Marie (d. yg); Elizabeth, m. [Apr. 1733] James Digges La Touche (♦♦♦); Henrietta, m. [ ] Hassard; Mary Anne (d. 1779) m. Rev. Jeremiah Pratt; Charlotte.
EDUCATION: TCD, LLD *spec. grat.* 1719.
CAREER/OCCUPATION: High Sheriff of Co. Dublin 1717; admitted Freeman of Dublin 1711; *Sheriff's Peer 1729, 1738–9, 1742, 1745–6, 1749, 1752; *Commissioner of Oyer and Terminer 1732–50; *Alderman of Dublin 1733, 1740; *Governor of the Workhouse 1733–6, 1738–47, 1749–d.; *Governor of the Blue-Coat Hospital 1739–d.
MILITARY: Agent for 4th Regiment of Horse 1755, 13th Dragoons, 27th Foot (Inniskilling) and 28th Foot.

POLITICAL ACTIVITY: He was a descendant of the Huguenots who came over at the end of the seventeenth century, and one of a group of Huguenot Dublin merchants. He was apprenticed to Ludovic Chaigneau, perhaps his uncle. In parliament he was an active MP, being nominated for 24 committees between 1716 and 1723 and 73 between 1727 and 1746. He introduced about eight heads of bills that subsequently became bills, as well as assisting with others. In 1729 he introduced the heads of a bill that became 3 Geo. II, c. 17, 'an Act for the better enabling the Governors of the Workhouse of the City of Dublin to provide for and employ the Poor therein and for the more effectual Punishment of Vagabonds and also the better securing of and providing for Lunaticks and Foundling Children', and in 1731 he introduced a similar act, 5 Geo. II, c. 14. He was also interested in the plight of insolvent debtors, and in 1735 brought in the heads of a bill for the relief of insolvent debtors, 9 Geo. II, c. 20.

He was interested in economic as well as social issues. He was responsible for two Acts regulating the market and the assize of bread, 11 Geo. II, c.

11 and 19 Geo. II, c. 19, and introduced measures aimed at combating fraud and theft, 7 Geo. II, c. 9 to prevent frauds in the export of bay-yarn to Great Britain, and 17 Geo. II, c. 11, an act 'in relation to Forgery and the Salvage of Ships and Goods stranded': wrecking was a fairly common practice in certain parts of Ireland. His Huguenot ancestry came out in 7 Geo. II, c. 5, 'An Act for the ammendment of the Law in relation to Popish Solicitors and for remedying other Mischiefs in Relation to the Practitioners in the several Courts of Equity'.

He voted for the establishment of a national bank in 1721 and subsequently subscribed to a declaration of High Sheriffs, justices of the peace, Grand Jury, nobility, clergy, gentlemen and freeholders of Co. Dublin against Wood's Halfpence. In 1749 he was absent for the vote on the disputed election of another Huguenot descendant, his son-in-law, James Digges La Touche (♦♦♦♦). His father purchased part of Gowran borough in 1715, and Chaigneau's death in 1753 diminished the influence of the Floods in the borough. James Agar (0016) was elected in Chaigneau's place, and the Agars now felt sufficiently strong to dispense with their former alliance with the Floods. At the time of his death he had a small pension, presumably the pension of £300 p.a. that he had in 1747. 'I return your paper of pensions,' wrote Primate Stone to the Chief Secretary, Lord George Sackville (1835), on 30 January 1753, 'Mr Chaigneau is dead.'

DIVISION LISTS:
     1721 (1) voted for a national bank.
     1721 (2) voted for a national bank.
     1749 (1) absent, in the country.

ADDITIONAL INFORMATION: *A member of the Dublin Society from 1738. His son, Rev. Dr Peter Chaigneau was Assistant Secretary to the Royal Dublin Society, 1762–74 and Registrar, 1798–1808. In December 1770 General Vallency wrote to Sir Lucius O'Brien (1558) urging the formation of a 'Physico-historical and Antiquarian Society ... [the first meeting to be held] at Mr Chaigneau's room in the Dublin Society's House [before Christmas] ... the season approaching fast when gentlemen usually retire to their country seats.'

ESTATES/RESIDENCE: Corkagh, Co. Dublin. Lewis Chaigneau purchased 213 acres in Co. Dublin from the Commissioners for Sale of Forfeited Estates in 1702–3.

SOURCES: *CJ Ire.* (Bradley ed.) vol. 5 p. 761, vol. 6 pp. 368, 373, 385, 394–5, 422, 425, 426–7, 608, 613, 856, 859, vol. 7 482, 489, 547, 817, 858 (0288, 0308, 0322, 0326, 0363, 0381, 0427, 0446); PRONI D/302; *The Huguenot Settlements in Ireland,* G. L. Lee, 'The Huguenots in Cork County' [says his children were Rev. Peter and two other sons all unm.]; PRONI T/3019/844 Wilmot Papers; NAI MFCI Reel 20, Parish Registers of Youghal, Co. Cork [bur. 21 Jan. 1753]; RCBL GS 2/7/3/44 Kilmore Marriage Licence Books [his parents' marriage licence is dated 1688]; McCracken thesis; Kilkenny MPs [says his wife is Elizabeth, daughter of Colonel Renouard, – his sister is Elizabeth who married David Renouard. Also says his children are Rev. Peter, Josias, Theophilus, Henrietta, Mary Anne, Charlotte]; J. Kelly, *Henry Flood ...* (Dublin, 1998), pp. 42–3; Simms, *Williamite Confiscation,* p. 184; *Alum. Dub.;* J. J. Digges La Touche (ed.), *Registers of the French Conformed Churches of St Patrick and St Mary, Dublin* (Dublin, 1893), pp. 16, 20, 29, 112–13, 216; *HMC Sackville I* p. 188; *IMC Inchiquin* p. 211; H. F. Berry, *A History of the Royal Dublin Society,* pp. 384, 421; *Almanacks; The Dublin Gazette* 14 Oct. 1724; *DJ* 1–3 July 1779.

CHAMBERLAIN, Arthur: *see* **BROWNLOW (CHAMBERLAIN)**, Arthur (0263)

0386 CHAMBERLAYNE, (William) Tankerville

MP for Clonmines 1791–3

     b. (bapt. 25 June) 1752; d. 12 May 1802
FAMILY/BACKGROUND: Eldest son of Michael Tankerville Chamberlayne and Deborah, dau. of Robert Roberts (1794).
MARRIED: Lucy, eldest dau. of Higatt Boyd of Co. Wexford.
CHILDREN: Higatt (d. yg); Michael (Major, 84th Regiment), m. [1809] Anna Maria dau. of Hall Plumer of Yorkshire; Tankerville; Charles (b. 1795); Lucy (d. yg); Amy, m. [1807] Rev. Crinus Irwin; Lucy; Margaret; Dorothea; Sophia, m. Henry Benjamin Archer.
EDUCATION: School: St Bees; entered TCD 11 July 1769, aged 17 years, BA 1774; Middle Temple

19 Jan. 1775; called to the Irish Bar 1779.
CAREER/OCCUPATION: *Listed in Judges and
Barristers 1789–1800 (f.); Justice of the Com-
mon Pleas 6 Dec. 1793; Justice of the King's
Bench 20 June 1794; *Fourth Justice of the
King's Bench 1794–7; *Third Justice 1798–1800
(f.); *Commissioner of Appeals 1796–7;
*Bencher of the Honorable Society of King's Inns
1789–1800 (f.); Justice of Assize for NE Ulster,
Lent 1794; Munster, Lent 1797; NE Ulster,
Summer 1797; Munster, Lent 1798; NW Ulster,
Summer 1798; Connaught, Lent 1799; NE
Ulster, Summer 1800.

POLITICAL ACTIVITY: A lawyer and a member of the
Monks of the Screw – a reforming club of the late
1770s. He was in parliament for only a little over
a year before being appointed a Justice of the Court
of Common Pleas. He was third Justice of King's
Bench at the time of his death in 1802.

ESTATES/RESIDENCE: Chamberlainstown, Co. Meath;
Churchtown, Co. Dublin. In 1702–3 Michael Cham-
berlain had 112 acres in Co. Dublin and 278 acres in
Co. Meath forfeited.

SOURCES: RCBL P344/11/8 Registry of Monuments,
St Anne's Parish, Dublin [says he died aged 51 years];
Burke *LGI* (1958) pp. 150–1; Hughes, *Pat. Officers*;
Alum. Dub.; M. L. Ferrar, *Register of the Royal School:
Armagh* (1933); Ball, *Judges*, *The Register of the Parish of
St Peter and St Kevin, 1669–1761* (Parish Register Society of Dublin, 1911) p. 284; *Register of Admissions to
the Honourable Society of the Middle Temple* vol. 1 (London, 1949) p. 379; Simms, *Williamite Confiscation*, p.
178; *Almanacks*; *BNL* 18 May 1802; *FJ* 8 Mar. 1794,
28 Feb., 5 Aug. 1797, 1 Mar., 26 Aug. 1798, 9 Mar.
1799, 10 July 1800; Parliamentary List 1793 (1).

0387 CHAMBRE, Robert

MP for Ardee 1703–13

b. *c.* ?1640; d. *post* 1713
FAMILY/BACKGROUND: Son of Robert Chambre and
Mary.
MARRIED: [?]
CHILDREN: Maria, m. [24 July 1676] Robert
Curtis (0562).
CAREER/OCCUPATION: Burgess of Ardee 1700.

POLITICAL ACTIVITY: He sat in parliament for the
first parliament of Queen Anne; very little is
known of him except that he was a Whig and

counted as in opposition to the administration in
both 1706 and 1711. He was nominated for a
committee in October 1703 and for 22 committees 1707–11.

ESTATES/RESIDENCE: [?]Hermanstown, Co. Louth (as he
was returned for Ardee and was a burgess of the town
he probably had property in the vicinity).

SOURCES: PRONI T/559 vol. 15 p. 146, Burke, extract
pedigrees; PRONI T/2842/2, Ardee Corporation Minutes; Parliamentary Lists 1706 (1), 1711 (3).

0388 CHAPMAN, Sir Benjamin

MP for Fore 1772–6; Co. Westmeath 1776–83

b. 1745; d. July 1810 'at an advanced age' at his
seat at St. Lucy's
HONOURS: Cr. Baronet 11 Mar. 1782 (with
remainder to male descendants of his father
Thomas).
FAMILY/BACKGROUND: Son of Benjamin Chapman
and Anne, dau. of Robert Clements of
Rathkenny, Co. Cavan (sis. of Nathaniel
Clements (0414)).
MARRIED: [lic. 20 Feb. 1776] Anne (?d. 1801), o.
dau. of John Lowther of Staffordstown, Co.
Meath.
CHILDREN: *d.s.p.*
EDUCATION: School: Mr Meares; entered TCD 11
Nov. 1761; Middle Temple 22 June 1764; called
to the Irish Bar 1768; LLD *hon. caus.* 1772.
CAREER/OCCUPATION: *Listed in Judges and
Barristers 1789–1800 (f.); *Advocate in the
Courts of Delegates, Prerogative, Admiralty and
Consistory 1799 (f.); Sheriff of Co. Waterford
1751; Freedom of Dublin Apr. 1776; *Governor
of Dr Steeven's Hospital 1776–1800 (f.);
*Governor of the Royal Hospital (Kilmainham)
1799 (f.).

POLITICAL ACTIVITY: He was returned in a by-election for Fore in 1772 following the death of Thomas Eyre (0716). He opened his political career
by attacking first John Scott (1891), the newly
appointed Counsel to the Revenue Board (and
later, 1784, Chief Justice of King's Bench), and
then Thomas Allan (0031), the Revenue Commissioner and viceregal agent (and later Commissioner of Customs in England). Allan, who was
pensioned when Lord Harcourt reunited the Revenue Board in 1773, was granted £350 for his

expenses in attending the Lords of the Treasury in London. This grant was masked as services to the Linen Board, and caused considerable comment. Another Revenue Commissioner, Robert Waller (**2161**), reported the incident to Sir George Macartney (**1302**) as follows: 'There was an attack on Allan the same night [as the 1773 committee of supply] very violent and illiberal made by young Chapman in the debate. Allan ... gave Chapman the lie direct. They both got out of the House, but the Speaker sent for the Sheriffs and they have since been bound over. This is the second scrape Chapman has been in within a fortnight his former was with Scott.'

He was said to be a good scholar but would be in opposition until he received legal preferment. In 1774 he appears to have been tempering his 'very violent' opposition with discretion and an eye to his advancement. In return Lord Harcourt made his brother (**0389**) Clerk of the Crown for the Province of Connaught, £200 p.a., and gave him the recommendation to a supernumerary gauger. The opposition did not consider that he was wholeheartedly against the Stamp Act, and 'lukewarmness is a crime. We hope he will never be so again.' Another list declared that he 'speaks very often, and is pretty well heard. He is nephew to Mr Clements (**0414**) but in his politics totally unconnected with him.' In 1776, by combining with the Malone (**1336**) interest, he got returned for Co. Westmeath and 'By management he gets his brother returned against the interests of Lord Darnley (**0173**) for Athboy.' Lord Darnley was the established patron of Athboy. A 1782 list considered that he was 'unsteady' and 'an unpleasing speaker'. There was, however, general agreement about his political activity and independence, and Lord Carlisle, whom he supported, successfully recommended him for a baronetcy with limitation to his younger brother should he continue to be childless. Despite petitioning against the 1783 elections in both Co. Westmeath and Athboy, neither he nor his brother was returned in 1783.

DIVISION LISTS:
1773 (1) voted for Absentee Tax.
1773 (2) a teller for an untaxed press.
1774 (1) a teller against the Stamp Bill.
1774 (2) voted for Catholic relief.

1775 (1) a teller for the pro-American amendment to the Speech from the Throne.
1779 (2) voted against a six-months Loan Bill.
1780 (?) voted against Yelverton's (**2268**) motion to modify Poynings' Law.
1780 (3) voted for the Tenantry Bill.
1780 (4) voted for the Perpetual Mutiny Bill.

ADDITIONAL INFORMATION: Some authorities give his mother as Anne, daughter of Robert Tighe, Mitchelstown, Co. Westmeath, but the parliamentary lists repeatedly declare that his mother was a sister of Nathaniel Clements (**0414**). *A member of the RDS from 1770.

ESTATES/RESIDENCE: Killua Castle, St Lucy's, Co. Westmeath; it was part of a large estate granted by Cromwell to Sir Benjamin's great-grandfather, Captain Benjamin Chapman, and Sir Benjamin 'has a good estate. Married a farmer's daughter of great fortune.' The estate comprised lands in Moygoish, Corkaree, Moyashel and Magheradernon, Fore and Moycashel. There is an abstract that begins with conveyance from Simon Isaac and Robert Longfield to Sir Benjamin Chapman, 1786. Rental, £1,910. In 1800 lands in the barony of Delvin were leased from Sir Francis Hopkins to Sir Benjamin Chapman. In 1776, Benjamin Chapman was granted a market at Clonmellon.

SOURCES: PRONI DOD/572/4/57; EC 8003; EC 6720; EC 6987 [will of Sir B. Chapman, 1809]; J. Kelly, 'That Damn'd thing Called Honour': Duelling in Ireland 1570–1860, p. 129; Ellis thesis; GEC B; Alum. Dub.; IMC King's Inns Admission Papers, 1607–1867; H. A. C. Sturgess, Register of Admissions to the Honourable Society of the Middle Temple (London, 1949), vol. 1 p. 361; Almanacks; DJ 5 Mar. 1751; FJ 25–27 Apr. 1776; Parliamentary Lists 1773 (1), (2), 1774 (1), 1775 (1), 1776 (1), (2), (3), 1777 (1), 1778 (1), 1780 (1), 1782 (1), 1783 (1), 1785 (2).

0389 CHAPMAN, William

MP for Athboy 1776–83

b. c. 1750; d. ?1796
FAMILY/BACKGROUND: Son of Benjamin Chapman of St Lucy's, Co. Westmeath, and Anne, dau. of Robert Clements of Rathkenny, Co. Cavan.
MARRIED: [11 Mar. 1786] Martha Roe.
CHILDREN: ?d.s.p.m.; dau., m. [1810] Henry Robert Battersby.

CAREER/OCCUPATION: Clerk of the Crown and Peace for Connaught 13 July 1776–96; Collector of the Revenue for Drogheda 1783–95.

POLITICAL ACTIVITY: He was very much under his brother's (0388) influence, and at the 1776 election was 'got by surprise into Lord Darnley's (0173) Borough'. He held two small places: the Clerkship of the Peace for Connaught, £200, and, from 1783, Collector of the Revenue for Donaghadee, £350. As a placeman he was expected to be a government supporter. In 1783 he stood for Athboy, but Lord Darnley had reasserted his influence and he was defeated.

DIVISION LISTS:
1777 (1) voted for Grattan's (0895) motion for retrenchment.
1779 (2) voted against a six-months Loan Bill.
1780 (1) voted against Grattan's declaration of the rights of Ireland.
1780 (2) voted against Yelverton's (2268) motion to modify Poynings' Law.
1780 (3) voted for the Tenantry Bill.
1780 (4) voted for the Perpetual Mutiny Bill.

ADDITIONAL INFORMATION: *A member of the Royal Irish Academy, 1798–1800 (f.). His name disappears from the list of subscribers to the Royal Irish Academy after 1812, although its records may not have been precise. In fact there is a problem with his dates of birth and death. Under the terms of the baronetcy he must have predeceased his brother (0388), who died July 1810, and his date of death is estimated from his office holding, although this contradicts his apparent membership of the Royal Irish Academy. His approximate date of birth is estimated from both the date of his entry into parliament and the fact that his younger brother was born in 1756, while his older brother was born a decade earlier.

ESTATES/RESIDENCE: Co. Westmeath; Gloucester Street, Dublin.

SOURCES: PRONI T/559 vol. 15 p. 155, Burke, extract pedigrees; Ellis thesis; GEC B [his elder bro. was born c. 1745 and his younger brother in 1756]; Burke LG (1846) p. 71; Alum. Dub.; Memorials of the Dead [says a William Chapman m. 11 Mar. 1786 Martha Roe];

Hughes, Pat. Officers; Almanacks; The Treble Almanack (1812, 1814); Printed Records of the Parliament of Ireland (NY) reel 46 pt. 4 [gives the minutes of the 1783 Athboy election petition]; Parliamentary Lists, 1776 (1), (2), (3), 1778 (1), 1780 (1), 1783 (1).

CHARLEMONT, Baron, Viscount and Earl: see **CAULFEILD**
0368 Caulfeild, Hon. James, 3rd Viscount Charlemont, MP Charlemont 1703–5, 1713–14, 1715–26
0367 Caulfeild, Rt Hon. Francis William, 2nd Earl of Charlemont, Baron Charlemont [UK], MP Co. Armagh 1797–9

CHARLEVILLE, Viscount and Earl of : see **BURY**
0305 Bury, Charles William, 1st Baron Tullamore, Viscount Charleville, Earl of Charleville, MP Kilmallock 1790, 1792–7

0390 CHATTERTON, Sir James

MP for Baltimore 1781–3; Doneraile 1783–90–7

b. c. 1750–2; d. 9 Apr. 1806
HONOURS: Cr. Baronet [UK] 3 Aug. 1801.
FAMILY/BACKGROUND: Only son of Abraham Chatterton of Cork City and Martha, dau. of Edmund Roche.
MARRIED: [8 Jan. 1785] Rebecca, dau. of Abraham Lane of Cork (her dowry reputed to be £10,000).
CHILDREN: Sir William Abraham, 2nd Baronet, m. [1824] Henrietta Georgiana, o. dau. of Rev. Lascelles Iremonger; Sir James Charles, 3rd Baronet, m. [5 Sept. 1821] Annetta, dau. of James Atkinson; Anne, m. [29 Dec. 1806] Rev. Richard Dickson; Martha, m. Abraham Edward Orpen MD; Rebecca, m. [13 Dec. 1822] C. Wedderburn Webster.
EDUCATION: Middle Temple 11 June 1770; called to the Irish Bar 1774; LLD hon. caus. 1781.
CAREER/OCCUPATION: King's Counsel 1780; *listed in Judges and Barristers 1789–1800 (f.); *Clerk of the Paper Office 12 Dec. 1789–98; 3rd Serjeant-at-Law 30 July 1791, 1793; 2nd Serjeant

10 Dec. 1793, 1794, 1796–1800 (f.); *Commissioner of Appeals 1795–7; *Bencher of the Honorable Society of King's Inns 1798–d; *Clerk of the Crown and Peace for Co. Cork and the Co. and City of Waterford 1779–1800 (f.); Justice for Assize for Leinster, Lent 1794.

POLITICAL ACTIVITY: The son of a Cork brewer, he was returned for Baltimore on the death of Jocelyn Deane (0602) on 19 November 1780. He was said to owe his return to the influence of James Dennis (0613), Lord Tracton and Chief Baron of the Exchequer, who died on 15 June 1782, to whom he was both attached and related. This brought him into Lord Shannon's (0213) sphere of political interest. In the 1783 election he purchased his seat for Doneraile from Lord Doneraile. He was a lawyer and, it was said: 'of a very penurious character and will endeavour to turn his seat into the most advantage. He has never spoken, nor do I hear that he has the abilities.'

However, his connections brought him a considerable and profitable legal practice. In 1784 it was said that he had bought his seat 'upon speculation, hoping for professional advancement but is not an object of necessary attention, as perfectly unconnected and of low education and very moderate talents. He will probably continue with Government for the ensuing session.' His ambition was to be a judge, and to this end he supported government assiduously and attached himself to Lord Lifford, the Lord Chancellor, who died in 1789, and to Lord Chief Justice Carleton (0353). He purchased again in 1790 and in 1797. In 1791 he was appointed Third Serjeant, and in December 1793 Second Serjeant. Lord Carleton was a firm upholder of the Union; Chatterton did likewise and was created a baronet in 1801.

DIVISION LISTS:
1783 (1) voted against Flood's (0762) motion for parliamentary reform.
1784 (1) voted against a committee on the Reform Bill.
1785 (1) voted for the Commercial Propositions.
1789 (1) voted against a Regency.
1790 (2) voted for Foster (0805) on the Election of a Speaker.

ESTATES/RESIDENCE: Cork city; 15 Aungier Street, Dublin.

SOURCES: PRONI MIC/465/1 R. Ffolliott, Biographical Notices, 1756–1827; Ellis thesis; Burke *PB* (1857) pp. 186–7; Hughes, *Pat. Officers, IMC King's Inns Admission Papers, 1607–1867*; *Alum. Dub.*; *Register of Admissions to the Honourable Society of the Middle Temple* (London, 1949) vol. 1 p. 371; *Almanacks*; *FJ* 8 Mar. 1794; Parliamentary Lists, 1776 (1), 1782 (1), 1783 (1), (2), 1784 (1), (2), (3), 1785 (1), (2), (3), (4), 1787 (1), 1788 (1), 1789 (1), 1790 (1), 1791 (1), 1793 (1), 1794 (1), (2), 1799 (1).

0391 CHETWOOD, Benjamin

MP for Harristown 1713–14

b. *c.* 1655; d. 1728
FAMILY/BACKGROUND: Son of Valentine Chetwood and Mary, dau. of Francis Shute.
MARRIED: (1) [25 Nov. 1694] Catherine, eldest dau. of Nicholas Jones (1114); (2) [1703] Anne, eldest dau. and co-h. of Sir Maurice Eustace (0701).
CHILDREN: (1) Elizabeth m. [22 Feb. 1715] Christopher Ussher of Co. Wicklow.
(2) Eustace (assumed add. surname of Eustace), m. Susanna, dau. of Aaron Crossley; Hill, m. [1749] Hannah Symes, dau. of George Higgins of Co. Dublin; Benjamin; Anne; Penelope; Henrietta; Harriet; Charlotte.
CAREER/OCCUPATION: Attorney to the Commissioners of Forfeited Estates; Clerk of the Casual Revenue and First Fruits; Solicitor to the Revenue Commissioners; Joint Escheator of Ulster.

POLITICAL ACTIVITY: He sat in the short 1713–4 parliament. He was a Tory and considered by the administration to be a 'good' man – likely to be returned for Harristown. In 1714–15 he was on the 'black list' of Tories, and he did not come in again in 1715.

ADDITIONAL INFORMATION: On 30 November 1715 a committee was appointed to consider the petition of Mary Sherlock, a minor, by Patrick Sherlock and John O'Neill and other creditors of Sir Maurice Eustace, deceased. They complained that Sir Maurice had, by his will, appointed trustees to sell part of his estates to pay debts but that payment was being delayed by Chetwood, 'who married one of the said Sir Maurice's daughters'. The committee eventually found in favour of the petitioners. Sir Maurice's widow, Clotilda and his daughter of the same name petitioned against Chetwood again, on 9 July 1719, declaring that he was preventing them from claiming their respective jointure and portion, by deliberately mismanaging the Eustace estate. On 11 July 1719 the House found proved the allegations against him and leave was given to bring in heads of a bill to sell off sufficient of the Eustace estate to clear debts and encumbrances.

ESTATES/RESIDENCE: Harristown, Co. Kildare. In 1695, a Benjamin Chetwood appeared on a list of proprietors that owed arrears of rent for forfeited lands in Co. Dublin (specifically, part of Captain Nicholas Cusack's forfeited estate). In 1713 it was estimated that Benjamin 'Chettwood' had an income of £1,200.

SOURCES: PRONI T/3411; *CJ Ire.* (Bradley edition) vol. 4 pp. 45, 507, 513; RCBL GS 2/7/3/44, Kilmore Marriage Licence Books; Hayton thesis; *Cal. SP Dom. 1695* (London, 1908) p. 142, *1696* (London, 1913) p. 63; Kildare MPs; *Ir. Gen.* vol. 7 no. 3 (1988) pp 360–1, 363, 365, 367, 369, A. Dusek, 'Baptisms in St Bride's, Dublin 1633–1716'; J. J. Howard (ed.), *Miscellanea Genealogica et Heraldica*, vol. 1 2nd ser. (1886) p. 86 [says he is aged *c.* 58 years in 1713. This is based upon the dates of birth and death of his three elder brothers. Also says dau. Anne Penelope (gives as one dau. not two)]; *Kildare Arch. Soc. Jn.* vol. 9 (1920) pp. 207–8, W. G. Strickland, 'The Chetwoods of Woodbrook in the Queen's County'; Parliamentary Lists, 1713 (1), (2), 1714–15.

0392 CHETWOOD, Jonathan

MP for Downpatrick 1790–7

b. 31 May 1757; d. 11 May 1839
FAMILY/BACKGROUND: Son and h. of Valentine Knightley Chetwood and Henrietta Maria, dau. of Jonathan Cope of Oxfordshire.
MARRIED: Margaret, dau. and co-h. of Laurence Clutterbuck of Co. Tipperary.
CHILDREN: *d.s.p.*
CAREER/OCCUPATION: High Sheriff of Queen's County 1781.
MILITARY: ?Cornet in the Arlington Light Cavalry.

POLITICAL ACTIVITY: He was returned for Downpatrick, a potwalloping borough belonging to Lord de Clifford. An opposition to him was set on foot by Lord Downshire, which failed.

Chetwood followed the direction of Lord de Clifford, who was against until 1794 and then for the government. Very little is known about this MP.

DIVISION LISTS:
1790 (2) absent.
1791 (1) voted for Curran's (**0560**) resolution against the sale of peerages.
1791 (2) voted for Grattan's (**0895**) motion for the exercise of free trade.
1791 (3) voted for Grattan's motion to abolish the Dublin police.

ESTATES/RESIDENCE: Woodbrook, Portarlington, Queen's County. The estates devolved on Edward Wilmot, who assumed the surname and arms of Chetwood.

SOURCES: PRONI D/302; Burke *LG* (1906) p. 213; PRONI MIC/474 Irish Volunteers; Parliamentary Lists 1791 (1), 1793 (1), 1794 (2).

CHICHESTER, Earl of: *see* PELHAM

1650 Pelham, Rt Hon. Thomas, Baron Pelham [GB], 2nd Earl of Chichester, MP Carrick 1783–90, Clogher 1795–7, Armagh B. 1797–9, [GB] Sussex 1780–1801

0393 CHICHESTER, Hon. Charles

MP for Belfast 1695–9

b. *c.* 1665; d. *post* 1699
FAMILY/BACKGROUND: Son of Rt Hon. Arthur Chichester, 2nd Earl of Donegall, and Jane, dau. of John Itchingham of Co. Wexford; (she m. (2) Richard Rooth).
MARRIED: [?1684] Martha Hatton.
CHILDREN: *d.s.p.*
MILITARY: Captain in Earl of Donegall's Regiment 1 Jan. 1694.

POLITICAL ACTIVITY: He was returned for the family borough of Belfast in 1695. He supported Lord Chancellor Porter against the accusations of favouring Catholics made against him by some MPs in 1695, and signed the Association for the protection of William III in the country in 1696. He was nominated for a committee on 27 September 1698, otherwise nothing is known about him.

ADDITIONAL INFORMATION: His date of birth is estimated from his parents' marriage in March 1660. He was said to be the fourth son and his eldest brother (who, although said to have been born in 1666 was a widower by 1682) was probably born in 1660/1.

ESTATES/RESIDENCE: [?]Belfast and Co. Antrim.

SOURCES: PRONI T/3302/2/2; *Cal. SP Dom. 1694–1695* (London, 1906) p. 1; Burke *PB* (1901, 1906) p. 510; Simms' cards; Lodge *P*; C. Dalton (ed.), *English Army Lists and Commission Registers, 1661–1714* (London, 1896), vol. 3 p. 378; *The Register of the Parish of St Peter and St Kevin, 1669–1761* (Parish Register Society of Dublin, 1911) p. 53; Parliamentary Lists, 1695 (1), 1696 (1).

0394 CHICHESTER, Rt Hon. George Augustus

MP for Carrickfergus 1798–9

b. 14 Aug. 1769; d. 5 Oct. 1844
HONOURS: PC, sworn 22 Feb. 1803; Knight of St Patrick 20 Aug. 1821.
PEERAGES: styled Viscount Chichester 1769–91; Earl of Belfast 1791–9; 2nd Marquess of Donegall 1799.
FAMILY/BACKGROUND: Son and heir of Rt Hon. Arthur Chichester, 1st Marquess of Donegall, and his 1st wife Anne, dau. of James Hamilton, 5th Duke of Hamilton.
MARRIED: [8 Aug. 1795] Anna May (b. 1775; d. 6 Feb. 1849), illegitimate dau. of Sir Edward May, 2nd Baronet (**1380**).
CHILDREN: Rt Hon. George Hamilton (b. 10 Feb. 1797; d. Oct. 1883), 3rd Marquess of Donegall, m. (1) [8 Dec. 1822] Harriet Anne (d. 14 Sept. 1860), dau. of Richard Butler, 1st Earl of Glengall, (2) [26 Feb. 1862] Harriet (d. 6 Mar. 1884), dau. of Sir Bellingham Reginald Graham, 7th Baronet, wid. of Lieut.-Gen. Sir Fredrick Ashworth KCB; Rev. Edward (b. 11 June 1799; d. 20 Jan. 1889), Dean of Raphoe, 4th Marquess of Donegall, m. 1821 Amelia Spread (d. 1891), 3rd dau. of Henry Dean Grady (**0891**); Spencer Augustus (b. 27 Nov. 1805; d. 27 May 1825); Arthur (b. 30 Sept. 1808; d. 25 June 1840); Hamilton Francis (b. 9 Mar. 1810; d. 1 Jan. 1854), m. [7 Dec. 1837] Honoria Anastatia (d. 8

Feb. 1878), dau. of Col. Henry James Blake of Ardfry, Co. Galway; John Ludford (b. 1811; d. 22 Apr. 1873), m. [27 July 1844] Caroline, dau. of Henry Bevan; Stephen Algernon (b. 1814; d. 14 Jan. 1890), m. [30 Dec. 1843] Alphonsine Louise Laura de Narbonne (d. 5 July 1881).
CAREER/OCCUPATION: *Trustee of the Linen Board for Leinster 1798–1800 (f.); Governor of Co. Antrim 1799–Dec. 1800; Lord Lieutenant of Co. Donegal 1831–44.

POLITICAL ACTIVITY: He was in parliament for barely a year before succeeding his father as 2nd Marquess of Donegall. He was one of the most notorious rakes of his day. His marriage to Anna May, whose father was a high-class moneylender, obtained his release from a debtor's prison – interestingly, the marriage appears to have been happy. Lord Donegall was a political cipher and much of his life was spent in trying to evade his debtors. He had political influence in Co. Antrim, one seat for Carrickfergus and the borough of Belfast, of which he owned much of the soil. Both Belfast and Carrickfergus were hostile to the Union.

ESTATES/RESIDENCE: Castle Chichester, Co. Antrim; Ormeau, Belfast. In 1719, the rental of the town and manor of Belfast was £791, 'Fall[s], Malone and Dunmurry' £906, 'Cinamont, Cave and Carmony' £622, Ballylinny and Islandmagee £305, Carrickfergus £382, Moylinny £208: total £3,214. In 1730, the rental was £3,572. These figures were sworn to by Thomas Banks of Belfast before Thomas Carter (**0360**), 1732. In 1787 Lord Donegall bought Yelverton's (**2268**) estate of Ballymacarrett.

In 1787 Lord Donegall was granted a fair/market at Parkgate, and in 1789 a fair at Ballyclare.

In the first decade of the nineteenth century, Wakefield thought the Co. Antrim estate of the Donegalls (including Carrickfergus) was worth over £100,000 a year. However, he noted that Lord Donegall 'lets his land for 61 years and a life, but renews at the end of a few years for a fine, which prevents his ever having much power over this immense property'. Perhaps because of this 'fining down' policy, other estimates give a rental of £1,700 in 1706, and over £20,000 in 1800. Hence 'Mr Stewart's proposal, received 20 May 1816' for disentangling the Donegall financial mess, reckoned the Belfast and Carrickfergus rental at £23,000.

The real question with this and other estates is what is included and what is excluded from any given calculation. In 1799, the 2nd Marquess succeeded to real estates 'of the annual value of £30,000 and upwards, situated principally in the counties of Antrim and Donegall'. This statement was made in Lord Donegall's printed response to an appeal case in *Houlditch and others v. Donegall, post* 1832. However, in an MS response of 3 January 1838 in a Chancery suit between the same parties, Lord Donegall stated that his then (1838) rental was £30,000. Elsewhere in this box of case papers there is probably a statement that Lord Donegall's part of Inishowen constituted £8,000 of the £30,000 in 1799, but the case paper concerned has not so far been found.

SOURCES: PRONI T/3076/2/63 Hertford Papers; PRONI MIC/315/9/53 Blackwood pedigrees; O'Neill thesis; GEC *P*; Burke *PB* (1900, 1903) p. 478; *Index to Irish Privy Counsellors, 1711–1910*; A. P. W. Malcomson, *The Pursuit of the Heiress* (Belfast, 1982), p. 33; W. A. Maguire, *Living like a Lord: the second Marquis of Donegall 1769–1844* (Belfast, 1984); additional information from Dr W. A. Maguire; *Almanacks*; PRONI D/2249/61 Hamilton Papers, Rent-book, 1719–30; Wakefield, *Account of Ire.*, vol. 1 p. 24; PRONI D/572/1/18/40 Macartney Papers, Rev George Macartney to Lord Macartney, 4 Dec. 1800; William Salt Library, Stafford, M/521/4 (courtesy of Professor P. A. Roebuck); PRONI D/1255/7/2 Martin & Henderson Papers; PRO C 101/4968 pt 1, Chancery Masters' accounts during the minority of Arthur Chichester [John Ludford the next friend and Thomas Ludford the guardian], 1752–8; *BNL* 9 Dec. 1800; Parliamentary Lists, 1790 (1), 1799 (3), 1800 (2).

0395 CHICHESTER, Hon. John Itchingham

MP for Gorey 1692–3, 1695–9, 1703–13; Belfast 1715–21

b. *post* 1660; d. 1721

FAMILY/BACKGROUND: Son of Rt Hon. Arthur Chichester, 2nd Earl of Donegall, and Jane, dau. and h. of John Itchingham of Dunbrody Park, Co. Wexford.

MARRIED: Unmarried.

CAREER/OCCUPATION: Joint Escheator of Ulster.

MILITARY: Ensign in Sir John Edgeworth's Regiment of Foot 1 May 1689; (?a Lieut. John Chichester refused to go to the West Indies as part of Colonel Hale's Regiment, 31 Aug. 1692); Major in Colonel Richard Keane's Regiment of Foot 16 Feb. 1716; appears on a list of half-pay officers, dead or otherwise, provided for between June 1710 and Sept. 1721 – as a half-pay major he was receiving £123 3s 9d p.a.

POLITICAL ACTIVITY: He sat for the Co. Wexford borough of Gorey until 1714 and then for the family borough of Belfast from 1715 until his death in 1721. In 1695 he supported Lord Chancellor Porter against the accusations of favouring Catholics made against him by some MPs, and in 1696 he signed the Association in favour of William III in the country. During Queen Anne's reign he supported the administration, voting for the Court over the Dublin mayoralty issue, and in 1719 he was noted as 'a placeman'.

He does not appear to have been a very active MP: he is listed for one committee on 27 September 1698 and one on 21 May 1709. However, he did take an interest in local affairs, for as a gentleman of Wexford he was one of the signatories in August 1700 to a 'Memorial for Re-Opening the Port of Ross for Exportation of Wool'. The shutting of the port to discourage the trade of woollen goods with England was depressing the industry in Leinster.

DIVISION LISTS:

1711 (1) voted for the Court on the Dublin mayoralty issue.

ESTATES/RESIDENCE: Dunbrody Park, Co. Wexford. The Dunbrody estate came into the Donegall family with the marriage of his father to his mother, the Itchingham heiress, in 1660. Lands in the barony of Shelburne were granted to John Itchingham in 16 Chas II (1665). It became by family tradition a younger son's endowment (0398). In 1715 the Dunbrody rental was £500, and the agents John and Anthony Cliffe. (In 1702–3 John Etchingham had 919 acres in Co. Wexford forfeited.) In 1755, the rental was £1,466 and the lands included Dunbrody, Coleman, Haggart, Killbride, Duncannon, Monckehee, etc.

By 9 Jas I (1612), John Ichingham was granted fairs at Ballyhack.

SOURCES: PRONI T/3302/2/2; PRONI T/3425/3/8 Chancery a/cs for Donegall estate, 1706–15; *Cal. SP Dom. 1691–1692* (London, 1900) p. 428; Burke *PB* (1906) p. 510; Hayton thesis; C. Dalton (ed.), *English Army Lists and Commission Registers, 1661–1714* (London, 1896), vol. 3 p. 58; C. Dalton, *George the First's Army, 1714–1727*; A. P. W. Malcomson, *The Pursuit of the Heiress* (Belfast, 1982) pp. 22–3; Simms, *Williamite Confiscation*, p. 178; *JRSAI* vol. 31 (1901) p. 55, P. D. Vigors, 'Extracts from the Old Corporation Books of New Ross, County Wexford'; EEC Conveyance and rental, 1861, rental, 1889–90; LC 1063;

Parliamentary Lists, 1695 (1), 1696 (1), 1706 (1), 1711 (3), 1713 (1), 1719 (1).

ESTATES/RESIDENCE: Abinger, Surrey. Owned about 8,000 acres of land near Waterford and Ross, which he let. In 1729 the Hon. John Chichester had an estimated rental of £1,000.

SOURCES: Information from Dr Jean Agnew of The Ulster Historical Foundation; McCracken thesis; GEC *P*, Burke *PB* (1900) p. 473 [d. 1 June 1746]; *GM* (Exshaw's edition) July 1746 [says he died 21 June 1746]; Prior, *Absentees*, p. 3.

0396 CHICHESTER, Hon. John

MP for Belfast 1725–7, 1745–6

b. 1700; d. 1 June 1746
FAMILY/BACKGROUND: Son of Arthur Chichester, 3rd Earl of Donegall, and his 2nd wife (m. 1685) Catherine, o. dau. of Rt Hon. Arthur Forbes, 1st Earl of Granard.
MARRIED: [13 Sept. 1726] Elizabeth, e. dau. of Sir Richard Newdigate, 3rd Baronet of Warwickshire.
CHILDREN: Rt Hon. Arthur (b. 13 June 1739; d. 5 Jan. 1799) 1st Marquess of Donegall, m. (1) [16 Nov. 1761] Anne (d. 1780), o. dau. of James Hamilton, 5th Duke of Hamilton, (2) [24 Oct. 1788] Charlotte, dau. of Conway Spencer of Co. Down, wid. of Thomas Moore (1482), (3) [12 Oct. 1790] Barbara, dau. of Rev. Luke Godfrey, Rector of Middleton, Co. Cork; John (0397).
CAREER/OCCUPATION: Burgess of Belfast 11 Aug. 1724.

POLITICAL ACTIVITY: He was the effective manager of the Donegall interest political and otherwise, since the earl, as described by his estate manager, William Macartney (1306), was: 'neither lunatic or idiot … [but] … proved extremely weak and though he was taught the Latin, Greek and French languages, yet could never by any possible means be taught the use of figures, even common addition, though the utmost endeavours have been used for that purpose.' On 28 October 1723 his mother petitioned for heads of a bill to enable him to settle a jointure on his wife (the earl, who *d.s.p.*, had married Lacy, daughter and heir of Robert Ridgway, 4th Earl of Londonderry, in October 1716). The petition was not considered as a committee was immediately appointed to bring in heads of a bill to settle Dunroby, Co. Wexford on Chichester, with powers to make a jointure and provision for younger children. The Chichesters at this time were largely absentees and John Chichester appears to have lived mostly in England, while keeping a foothold in the family interest in Ireland.

0397 CHICHESTER, John

MP for Belfast 1761–8; Carrickfergus 1768–76

b. 26 Dec. 1740; d. 1783
FAMILY/BACKGROUND: Son of Hon. John Chichester (0396) and Elizabeth, dau. of Sir Richard Newdigate.
MARRIED: Unmarried.
EDUCATION: School: Westminster June 1751–5; entered Oxford (Trinity College) 7 July 1759, aged 18 years.
CAREER/OCCUPATION: *Magistrate and Mayor of Carrickfergus 1767.

POLITICAL ACTIVITY: He was returned for Carrickfergus in the 1768 general election. Carrickfergus was a county borough with a large and independently minded electorate, so it was probably felt desirable to assert the family presence there, as: 'This Corporation would readily give up one seat to Lord Donegall but if he attempts to recommend both in all probability they will give him neither. There are a number of voters as it is more a County than a Corporation. Both Freemen and Freeholders vote for Members of Parliament.' It was also thought that Lord Hertford was trying to exert an influence in the borough.
    Nevertheless, once elected, apart from a visit in June–July 1768, when he was lavishly and deferentially entertained by his supporters, he appears to have returned to England and remained there for most of the parliament, one Parliamentary List stating that he 'never has attended' and another the 'he never comes but for a job'.

DIVISION LISTS:
    1768 (1) absent, in England.

ADDITIONAL INFORMATION: At the general election for Carrickfergus in 1768 he received 392 votes and was returned with Conway Richard Dobbs (**0642**), who received 371 votes. The unsuccessful candidates were Marriot Dalway (**0565**) and Edward Smyth (**1946**), who received 333 and 71 votes respectively. Lord Donegall was proprietor of the soil for the borough of Carrickfergus and thus could command the return of one of his seats, but the other was independent. For the sure seat he nominated John Chichester along with Dalway, while the independent interest supported Dobbs and Smyth.

ESTATES/RESIDENCE: Abinger, Surrey. In 1779, Young reckoned Mr Chichester's rental as £1,000.

SOURCES: Burke *PB* (1906) p. 510; *Alum. Oxon.*; Johnston, *Gt B. & Ire.*, pp. 180–1; G. F. Russell-Barker and A. H. Stenning (eds), *Record of old Westminsters: A Biographical List* (London, 1928), 2 vols; *BNL* 5 July 1768; Young, *A Tour in Ire.* vol. 2 app. p. 83; *Almanacks*, Parliamentary Lists, 1769 (1), 1772 (2), 1773 (1), (2), 1774 (1), 1775 (1).

0398 CHICHESTER, Lord Spencer Stanley

MP for Belfast 1797–8 [r. Carrickfergus 1797]; [Escheator of Munster 6 Mar. 1798]; [UK] Carrickfergus 1802 – 5 Mar. 1807

b. 20 Apr. 1775; d. 22 Feb. 1819
FAMILY/BACKGROUND: Son of Rt Hon. Arthur Chichester, 1st Marquess of Donegall, and his 1st wife Anne, dau. of James Hamilton, 5th Duke of Hamilton.
MARRIED: [8 Aug. 1795] Harriet (b. 1770; d. 30 Jan. 1850), dau. of John Stewart, 7th Earl of Galloway.
CHILDREN: Arthur (b. 8 Jan. 1797; d. 15 Feb. 1885), 1st Baron Templemore m. [27 July 1820] Augusta (d. 6 June 1872), dau. of Rt Hon. Henry William Paget, 1st Marquess of Anglesey; Rev. George Augustus Frederick (d. unm. 8 June 1829); Anne (d. unm.); Elizabeth (d. 19 Sept. 1882), m. 1822 William Hanbury, 1st Baron Bateman; Harriet (d. unm. 1820).
EDUCATION: Entered Glasgow University 1791.

POLITICAL ACTIVITY: He avoided the Union, to which Belfast was hostile, by accepting the Escheatorship of Munster in 1798, and thereby making way for Alexander Hamilton (**0913**), who voted against the Union. After the Union he was returned by his brother (**0394**), the 2nd Marquess for Carrickfergus.

ADDITIONAL INFORMATION: Carrickfergus was considered a family borough, but it was a county borough with a large electorate and very independent. In 1802, despite the support of his brother, the 2nd Marquess of Donegall, Lord Spencer Stanley Chichester faced a contest for Carrickfergus. He made no mark at Westminster. In 1804 he was listed first as a friend of the Prince of Wales and then 'doubtful', which he remained until he vacated the seat in 1807.

ESTATES/RESIDENCE: Dunbrody Park, Co. Wexford. He was the favourite of his father, on whose death in 1799 he received 'every square inch of property within his [father's] disposable power'. The father, who had little in common with his heir, was alarmed by his reckless expenditure, which had landed him in a debtor's prison. Following the family tradition and inheritance pattern Lord Spencer also received Dunbrody, as the portion of a younger son, on marriage. The estate had first come into the Donegall family through marriage with the heiress of its then owners, the Itchinghams, back in 1660. Wakefield estimated that Lord Spencer Chichester's rental was £5,000.

SOURCES: Burke *PB* (1906) p. 510 and 1588; Hughes, *Pat. Officers*; Jupp thesis; *HP 1794–1820*; W. I. Addison (ed.), *The Matriculation Albums of the University of Glasgow 1728–1858* (Glasgow, 1913); A. P. W. Malcomson, *The Pursuit of the Heiress* (Belfast, 1982) pp. 22–3; W. A. Maguire, *Living like a Lord: the second Marquis of Donegall, 1769–1844* (Belfast, 1984) [gives the family background]; *DJ* 15 Aug. 1795; Wakefield, *Account of Ire.* vol. 1 p. 281.

0399 CHINNERY, Sir Brodrick

MP for Castlemartyr 1783–90; Bandon 1790–7–1800; [UK] 1801–6

b. (13) Feb. 1742; d. May 1808
HONOURS: Cr. Baronet 29 Aug. 1799.
FAMILY/BACKGROUND: Fourth son of Rev. George Chinnery (d. *c.* 1755) and Eleanor, dau. of Dr William Whitfield and his wife Katherine Brodrick (sis. of Alan Brodrick, 1st Viscount Midleton (**0237**)).

MARRIED: (1) [Feb. 1768] his cousin Margaret, dau. and h. of Nicholas Chinnery; (2) [2 July 1789] Alice, dau. of Robert Ball of Youghal, Co. Cork.

CHILDREN: (1) Nicholas (b. 1769; d. unm. in Lisbon 1790); George (b. 1774; d. 1797); Sir Brodrick (b. 29 May 1779; d. 19 Jan. 1840), 2nd Baronet, m. [1803] Diane Elizabeth (d. 16 June 1824), dau. of George Vernon; Margaret; Eliza; Eleanor, m. Joseph Folingsby.
(2) St John; Richard Boyle; Maria; Louisa.

EDUCATION: Inner Temple 1763; Barrister, Dublin, 1763.

CAREER/OCCUPATION: Sheriff of Co. Cork 1786; *Governor of the Hibernian Marine Society 1780–1.

MILITARY: Colonel in the Duhallow Volunteers.

POLITICAL ACTIVITY: A lawyer, brought into parliament for Castlemartyr by Lord Shannon (0213), and part of his political party. In 1790 he was returned for Bandon Bridge – one seat for this borough belonged to the Duke of Devonshire and the other to Lord Shannon's son-in-law, Lord Bandon (0126). Lord Shannon managed the Devonshire interest, and it is thought that he made this return.

He voted for W. B. Ponsonby (1709), Lord Shannon's brother-in-law, for Speaker in 1790 against John Foster (0805). After the débâcle of Lord Fitzwilliam's viceroyalty, Lord Shannon had an interview with the new viceroy, Lord Camden, and reported to his son that the viceroy 'talked with a great deal of firmness, is not afraid of mobs or newspapers, sees how much the question involves the interests of both England and Ireland, considers the Protestant establishment as being at stake, and ... if supported is ready to stand the brunt ... I hope all our friends will be good enough to attend [parliament] ... Our friends Chinnery and Cotter (0504) I know will come.'

Chinnery signed a Co. Cork petition in favour of the Union in April 1799, and voted for the Union in 1799 and 1800. He heard and greatly admired Pitt's speech on the Union. He was rewarded with a baronetcy in 1799, and office after the Union. He was essentially a country gentleman and enjoyed rural pursuits: in 1790 he nearly killed himself while shooting rooks on his estate.

DIVISION LISTS:
1783 (1) voted against Flood's (0762)

motion for parliamentary reform.
1784 (1) voted against a committee on the Reform Bill.
1785 (1) voted for the Commercial Propositions.
1790 (1) voted for Grattan's (0895) motion for reducing the influence of the Crown.
1790 (2) voted for Ponsonby (0709) on the Election of a Speaker.
1791 (1) voted for Curran's (0560) resolution against the sale of peerages.
1791 (2) voted for Grattan's motion for the exercise of free trade.
1791 (3) voted for Grattan's motion to abolish the Dublin police.
1799 (1) voted for the Union – Lord Shannon's Borough.
1800 (1) voted for the Union.

ADDITIONAL INFORMATION: Throughout his 23 years in parliament he was always Lord Shannon's member, and Shannon considered him a family friend. At Westminster he was reckoned a supporter of successive governments, with some doubts about his attendance. He voted against Catholic claims in May 1803. 'His principal objective seems to be to get his claims admitted as the representative of his brother to compensation for lands in America surrendered at the peace to the Spaniards.' Failing this, he wanted the reversion of an office for his son or membership, for himself, of the Privy Council. He gave up his seat at the dissolution in 1806, as it was the turn of the Duke of Devonshire to nominate.

He appears to have been something of a gourmet, as Lord Shannon sent a message to 'tell Chinnery that I have tried the recipe he was so good as to send me, with much success', and Shannon continues discussing a projected dinner party of 'all the bigwigs'.

ESTATES/RESIDENCE: Ann's Grove, Flintfield and Midleton, Co. Cork; Castlemore, St Andrew Street, Dublin. Flintfield was inherited through the marriage of Sir Brodrick, 1st Bt, to his cousin, Margaret Chinnery. Between 1770 and 1786 he purchased lands from Lord Muskerry. In 1796, Sir Brodrick Chinnery let for 999 years Raduane, Gortavehy, Knockagillane, etc., barony of West Muskerry – 4,966 statute acres – for £500 a year; in 1875 this land was worth £1,077.

SOURCES: PRONI D/302; PRONI T/3166/1A Hartnell notes; PRONI MIC/465/1 R. Ffolliott, *Biographical Notices, 1756–1827* [says he married 1 July 1789 Alice Ball]; PRONI MIC/474 Irish Volunteers; O'Neill thesis; Jupp thesis; GEC *B*; *HP 1790–1820*; Burke *PB* (1857) p. 194; *IMC, King's Inns Admission Papers, 1607–1867*; E. Hewitt (ed.), *Lord Shannon's Letters to his Son* (PRONI 1982) pp. 1, 34, 213; *Ir. Gen.* vol. 6 no. 2 (1981) p. 182, H. F. Morris, 'The Waterford Herald 1792' [reports the death of his only dau. 13 Dec. 1792]; *Almanacks*; *The Cork Advertiser* 30 Apr. 1799; *DJ* 27 July 1797 [announces the d. of George Chinery, eldest (surviving) son]; NLI MS 18955/1, Pembroke Estate, Chinnery Papers, scrapbook containing misc. fragments; NLI MS 19312; NLI reps vol. 151, 26 Aug. 1874; Parliamentary Lists, 1783 (2), 1784 (1), (2), (3), 1785 (1), (2), (3), (4), 1787 (1), 1788 (1), 1789 (1), 1790 (1), 1791 (1), 1793 (1), 1794 (2), 1799 (2), (3), 1800 (3).

0400 CHOPPIN, Robert

MP for Co. Longford 1692–3

b. ?1638; d. 1695
FAMILY/BACKGROUND: Son of Anthony Choppin of Newcastle, Co. Longford.
MARRIED: Frances, dau. of Lieut.-Col. Henry Gore, wid. of Sir Robert King, 1st Baronet (**1164**).
CHILDREN: ?
CAREER/OCCUPATION: High Sheriff of Co. Longford 3 Feb. 1678.

POLITICAL ACTIVITY: He sat only in the very short parliament of 1692, and little is known about him. As a justice of the peace in 1686 he was one of those responsible for the suppression of rumours sweeping Counties Longford and Westmeath of imminent risings by either Catholics or Protestants to slaughter the other.

ESTATES/RESIDENCE: Newcastle, Co. Longford.

SOURCES: PRONI D/302; Burke *PB* (1906) p. 69; Simms' cards; Hughes, *Pat. Officers*; *Alum. Cantab.* [gives a Robert Choppin, entered Cambridge (Corpus Christi College) 1654, born 1638, but although the dates are plausible, it says son of Tolmash of Goddenham, Suffolk]; King, *State of the Protestants*; S. W. Singer (ed.), *Clarendon Corr.*, vol. 2 (London, 1828) pp. 73–5, 81.

0401 CHRISTIAN, Maynard

MP for Waterford city 1703–13–14

b. 13 Aug. 1668; d. (bur. 9) Aug. 1714
FAMILY/BACKGROUND: Son of Frederick Christian of Waterford and Mary [   ].
MARRIED: Unmarried.
EDUCATION: School: Mr Coulter, Waterford; entered TCD 18 May 1685, aged 17 years, BA 1691.
CAREER/OCCUPATION: ?Recorder of Waterford.

POLITICAL ACTIVITY: He sat for Waterford city throughout the reign of Queen Anne. He was a Tory and a firm supporter of the Court party. He attended Ormonde's birthday celebrations in 1706 and later supported the Court on such major issues as the Dublin mayoralty and the unsuccessful candidature of Sir Richard Levinge (**1230**) for Speaker; he voted against Anderson Saunders (**1878**) for chairman of the important Committee of Privileges and Elections.

He was listed for 12 committees between 1707 and 1711. He died early in August 1714 – a few days after Queen Anne.

DIVISION LISTS:
1711 (1) voted for the Court on the Dublin mayoralty issue.
1713 (1) voted for Sir Richard Levinge (**1230**) for Speaker.
1713 (2) voted against Anderson Saunders (**1878**) for chairman of the Committee of Elections and Privileges.

ESTATES/RESIDENCE: Estimated income in 1713 was £500 p.a.

SOURCES: PRONI T/3411 Hartnell notes [calls him Christmas]; NAI MFCI Reel 12, Parish Registers of Christchurch, St Olave and St Patrick, Waterford; *Alum. Dub.*; Simms' cards; Parliamentary Lists, 1706 (1), (2), 1711 (3), 1713 (1), 1713 (2).

0402 CHRISTMAS, Richard

MP for Waterford city 1695–9, 1703–13

b. 19 Apr. 1661; d. 5 June 1723 aged 62 years
FAMILY/BACKGROUND: Eldest son of Thomas Christmas of Guildford, Surrey, and Elizabeth

Gammon of Barnstaple, Devon.
MARRIED: [settlement 28 Sept. 1683] Susanna (b. c. 1665; d. 10 Feb. 1707), dau. of Henry Aland.
CHILDREN: Thomas (**0403**); Richard (d. in infancy); William (d. 25 Aug. 1720, aged c. 20 years); Elizabeth m. [1709] Jeffrey Paul (**1643**); Sarah (d. in infancy); Susanna [d. aged c. 22 years].
CAREER/OCCUPATION: Mayor of Waterford 29 Sept. 1695 – 29 Sept. 1696; Sheriff of Co. Waterford 1685 (in 1686 the Earl of Clarendon answered a list of criticisms directed against appointed sheriffs); Alderman of Waterford, appointed by King William 26 July 1690.

POLITICAL ACTIVITY: In 1695 he supported Lord Chancellor Porter against the accusations of favouring Catholics made against him by some MPs; in 1696 he signed the Association for the protection of William III in the country. In Queen Anne's reign he supported the Court and was thought likely to be returned again in 1713, but this did not happen. He was elected to a committee on 23 July 1711.

ESTATES/RESIDENCE: Whitfield, Co. Waterford. Lands in barony of Middlethird, Co. Waterford and part of the lands of Ballincrea, barony of Ida, Co. Kilkenny and Toberaheena, barony of Iffa and Offa East, Co. Tipperary. His marriage settlement mentions various lands: 373 acres in Adamstown, 190 acres in Goolderragh, 88 acres part of Raheen, 128 acres in Boghill, 73 acres in Lisnakill, 102 acres in Whitfieldstown, 230 acres in Stonehouse. The will of his father, Thomas Christmas, mentions 260 acres in the barony of Middlethird and Killotteran, 200 acres in the County & City of Waterford.

SOURCES: Brian Christmas Esq.; PRONI T/559 vol. 15 p. 190, Burke, extract pedigrees; EC 8496 Box No. 4192; Burke *PB* (1903) p. 1188; Simms' cards; R. H. Ryland, *The History, Topography and Antiquities of the county and city of Waterford* (London, 1824), p. 408 [says Tho. Christmas Mayor of Waterford 1715]; *Clarendon Corr.* vol. 1 p. 287; Parliamentary Lists, 1695 (1), 1696 (1), 1706 (1), 1713 (1).

Aland.
MARRIED: [21 Apr. 1713] Elizabeth (d. c. 1770), o. dau. of John Marshall of Clonmel, Co. Tipperary.
CHILDREN: Richard (d. yg); Thomas (**0404**); William (**0405**); Elizabeth, m. Rt Hon. Sir William Osborne, 8th Baronet (**1615**); Catherine, m. [17 Apr. 1755] Richard Gorges Jr of Kilbrew, Co. Meath.
EDUCATION: School: Mr France, Waterford; entered TCD 21 Jan. 1703, aged 16 years, BA 1706.
CAREER/OCCUPATION: High Sheriff of Co. Waterford 1715; Mayor of Waterford 1715 and 1725; Freeman of Fethard (Tipperary), 1725
MILITARY: A Colonel, 10 Nov. 1739.

POLITICAL ACTIVITY: Returned for parliament in 1713, he was a Whig. He was listed for two committees in 1715 and 17 between 1727 and 1745. He voted against a national bank, and in the 1720s signed a declaration of Waterford merchants refusing to deal in Wood's Halfpence.

DIVISION LISTS:
1721 (1) voted against a national bank.
1721 (2) voted against a national bank.

ESTATES/RESIDENCE: Whitfield, Co. Waterford. His estimated income in 1713 was £1,200 p.a. His wife's portion was £3,000 and her jointure £300 (10 per cent was fairly usual). In his will he left his wife £1,000 and also his coach and four best horses as well as 'the furniture of all kinds, except the pictures of the best apartment in his house at Whitfield'. She survived him for many years, for her will was proved in 1770.

SOURCES: PRONI D/302; EC 8496 Box No. 4192; Brian Christmas Esq.; NAI MFCI Reel 12, Parish Registers of Christchurch, St Olave and St Patrick, Waterford; PRONI T/559 vol. 15 p. 190, Burke, extract pedigrees; PRONI T/3411 Hartnell notes; McCracken thesis; *Alum. Dub.*; *Memorials of the Dead*; R. H. Ryland, *The History, Topography and Antiquities of the county and city of Waterford* (London, 1824), pp. 408–9; *GM* (Exshaw's edition) Nov. 1747; *The Dublin Gazette* 23 Nov. 1714, 1 Sept. 1724; Parliamentary Lists, 1713 (1).

0403 CHRISTMAS, Thomas

MP for Waterford B. 1713–14, 1715–27–47

b. 22 May 1687; d. (bur. 5) Dec. 1747
FAMILY/BACKGROUND: Eldest son of Richard Christmas (**0402**) and Susanna, dau. of Henry

0404 CHRISTMAS, Thomas

MP for Co. Waterford 1743–9

b. 3 July 1721; d. 28 Mar. 1749
FAMILY/BACKGROUND: Eldest son of Thomas

Christmas (**0403**) and Elizabeth, dau. of John Marshall.
MARRIED: [8 Dec. 1748] Catherine, dau. of Marcus Beresford, 1st Earl of Tyrone (**0118**).
CHILDREN: Alicia, m. her cousin Charles Osborne (**1608**).
CAREER/OCCUPATION: Mayor of Waterford 1748.
MILITARY: Colonel of Militia 1746.

POLITICAL ACTIVITY: Very little is known of this MP. He was listed for a committee in 1743 and another in 1745.

ESTATES/RESIDENCE: Whitfield, Co. Waterford.

SOURCES: Brian Christmas Esq.; NAI MFCI Reel 12, Parish Registers of Christchurch, St Olave and St Patrick, Waterford [bur. 2 Apr. 1749]; NAI MFCI Reel 13, Parish Registers of Clonegam, Co. Waterford; PRONI T/559 vol. 15 p. 190, Burke, extract pedigrees [says Alicia was dau. of William Christmas (**0405**)]; McCracken thesis; Burke *PB* (1903) p. 1175; Smyth, *State of Waterford*; R. H. Ryland, *The History, Topography and Antiquities of the county and city of Waterford* (London, 1824), p. 409; *GM* (Exshaw's edition) Mar. 1749; *Ir. Gen.* vol. 4 no. 6 (1973) pp. 616–24, Rev W. G. Skehan, 'Freemen of the Corporation of Fethard, Co. Tipperary'.

0405 CHRISTMAS, William

MP for Kilmallock 1776–83

b. 24 Sept. 1734; d. (bur. 26) Jan. 1803
FAMILY/BACKGROUND: Son of Thomas Christmas (**0403**) and Elizabeth, dau. of John Marshall.
MARRIED: Catherine, dau. of William Ludlow.
CHILDREN: Thomas; William (captain, 14th Dragoons); Robert, m. (2) [   ] Thompson.
EDUCATION: School: Dr Hewetson; Kilkenny College 16 June 1745, aged 11 years; entered TCD 17 December 1751, aged 16 years.
CAREER/OCCUPATION: High Sheriff of Co. Waterford 1756.
MILITARY: A Colonel.

POLITICAL ACTIVITY: Christmas, who was reputed to have a large fortune in Counties Wexford and Waterford, purchased his seat for Kilmallock from Silver Oliver (**1585**). He was in opposition until the arrival of the Duke of Portland, and did not seek re-election in 1783.

DIVISION LISTS:
1779 (2) voted for a six-months Loan Bill.
1780 (2) voted for Yelverton's (**2268**) motion to modify Poynings' Law.

ADDITIONAL INFORMATION: A member of the RDS from 1766.

ESTATES/RESIDENCE: Dominick Street, Dublin; Whitfield, Co. Waterford. Owned extensive lands in Counties Waterford, Kilkenny, Tipperary and Limerick as well as a wool-combing mill on Clonmel bridge, Co. Tipperary.

SOURCES: Brian Christmas Esq.; PRONI D/302; NAI MFCI Reel 12, Parish Registers of Christchurch, St Olave and St Patrick, Waterford; PRONI T/559 vol. 15 p. 190, Burke, extract pedigrees; Ellis thesis; Vicars, *Prerog. Wills*; *Ir. Gen.* vol. 5 no. 6 p. 735, H. F. Morris, 'Ramsey's Waterford Chronicle, 1786–1791' [gives a William Christmas of Whitfield Co. Waterford died 6 Feb. 1786 leaving a widow Bridget]; *JRSAI* vol. 54 (1924) pp. 55–67; T. U. Sadlier, 'The Register of Kilkenny School (1685–1800)'; Parliamentary Lists, 1776 (1), 1778 (1), 1780 (1), 1782 (1), 1783 (1).

CLANBRASSILL, Earl of: *see* HAMILTON

0934 Hamilton, Rt Hon. James, 1st Baron Claneboye, Viscount of the City of Limerick, Earl of Clanbrassill, MP Dundalk 1715–19, [GB] Wendover 1727–34, 1735–41, Tavistock 1742–7, Morpeth 1747–54
0936 Hamilton, Rt Hon. James, styled Viscount Limerick 1756–8, 2nd Earl of Clanbrassill, MP Midleton 1755–8, [GB] Helston 1768–74

CLANCARTY, Earl and Viscount: *see* TRENCH

2111 Trench, William Power Keating, 1st Baron Kilconnell, Viscount Dunlo, Earl of Clancarty, MP Co. Galway 1768–76–83–90–7
2110 Trench (Le Poer Trench), Rt Hon. Richard (styled Viscount Dunlo 1803–5), 2nd Earl of Clancarty, Baron Trench [UK], Marquess of Heusden [Netherlands], Viscount Clancarty [UK], MP Newtown Limavady 1796–7, Co. Galway 1797–1800, [UK] 1801–5, Rye 1807

CLANMAURICE, Viscount: *see*
FITZMAURICE
0753 Fitzmaurice, Rt Hon. Thomas, 20th Baron
Kerry and Lixnaw, 1st Viscount Clanmaurice, Earl
of Kerry, MP Co. Kerry 1692–3, 1695–7

CLANMORRIS, Baron: *see* **BINGHAM**
0144 Bingham, John, 1st Baron Clanmorris of
Newbrook, MP Tuam 1797–1800

CLANRICARDE, Earl and Marquess of: *see*
DE BURGH
◆◆◆◆ De Burgh, Rt Hon. Henry (styled Lord
Dunkellin 1743–82), 12th Earl of Clanricarde,
1st Marquess of Clanricarde, MP Co. Galway
1768 (n.d.e.)

CLANWILLIAM, Viscount and Earl of: *see*
MEADE
1388 Meade, Sir John, 1st Baron Gilford, Viscount Clanwilliam, Earl of Clanwilliam, MP
Banagher 1764–6

CLARE, Earl of: *see* **FITZGIBBON**
0749 Fitzgibbon, Rt Hon. John, 1st Baron
Fitzgibbon, Viscount Fitzgibbon, Earl of Clare,
Baron Fitzgibbon [GB], MP TCD 1778–83,
Kilmallock 1783–9

CLARINA, Baron: *see* **MASSY**
1354 Massy, Eyre, 1st Baron Clarina, MP Swords
1790–7

0406 CLARKE, Michael

MP for Ballyshannon 1754–60, 1761–8–74

> b. 1712; d. 30 June 1774
> FAMILY/BACKGROUND: Son of Darby Clarke and
> Anne, dau. of William Smyth, Bp of Kilmore.
> MARRIED: (1) Alice Harris; (2) [22 June 1761]
> Anne, dau. of Capt. Berkeley.
> CHILDREN: (2) Michael (at Eton 1779, aged 12
> years); William (d. yg).
> CAREER/OCCUPATION: Examinator of Excise 1742–
> 74; Governor of the Workhouse 1753–68;
> Governor of the Foundling Hospital and
> Workhouse 1769–d.; *elected June to the Court
> of Assistants June 1766–9; *Surveyor of Excise
> for Moyallow 1757–8, Naas 1759.
> MILITARY: Agent to half-pay officers on the Irish
> establishment 1754–75 (in reversion 17 Apr.
> 1758).

POLITICAL ACTIVITY: Agent to Thomas Conolly
(**0459**), who returned him for his borough of
Ballyshannon from 1754 until his death in 1774.
He was 'a very near' relation to Conolly and attached to him. He was listed on 29 committees
between 1755 and 1760. From 1742 until his
death in 1774 he was Examinator of the Excise,
with a salary of £300 p.a. The opposition list of
1774 declared that he was 'Examinator of the
Excise, and a courtier, but – rest his soul, he is
dead'.

DIVISION LISTS:
> 1757 (1) voted against the resolutions on
> pensions.
> 1768 (1) voted for army augmentation –
> Paymaster to half-pay officers.
> 1771 (1) voted for Lord Townshend as Lord
> Lieutenant.
> 1771 (1) voted against Sir Lucius O'Brien's
> (**1558**) motion for retrenchment – a
> placeman.
> 1773 (1) voted for Absentee Tax.
> 1774 (2) voted against Catholic relief.

ADDITIONAL INFORMATION: His son Michael was
listed as a nominee in the life annuities, 1779.

ESTATES/RESIDENCE: Dominick Street, Dublin.

SOURCES: PRONI T/559 vol. 15 p. 224a, Burke, extract
pedigrees; PRONI T/618/329 Crossle Papers;
McCracken thesis; *Ir. Gen.* vol. 1 no. 8 (1940) p. 239;

Memorials of the Dead, 'A List of Irish Stockholders, 1779'; *Almanacks*; *BNL* 21 Apr. 1758; *DJ* 23–27 June 1761, 19–21 Oct. 1773 [states that the MP is not Examinator of Excise, while no fewer than four Parliamentary Lists state that he is!]; Parliamentary Lists, 1769 (1), 1772 (2), 1773 (1), (2), 1774 (1).

0407 CLAYTON, Sir Courthorpe

MP for Mallow 1727–60; [GB] Eye, Suffolk 1749–61

b. *c.* 1706; d. 22 Mar. 1762
HONOURS: KB 17 June 1725.
FAMILY/BACKGROUND: Son of Laurence Clayton (0408) and Anne, dau. and co-h. of Sir Peter Courthorpe of Co. Cork.
MARRIED: [6 Aug. 1745] Theodosia, dau. of Edward Buckworth.
CHILDREN: Ann, m. Arthur Gethin.
CAREER/OCCUPATION: Page to the Prince of Wales 1716–Nov. 1726, Equerry 1726–7; Equerry to the King 1727–60; Averner and Clerk Marshall Oct. 1732–May 1734, Dec. 1757–Nov. 1760; Freedom of Cork 12 Aug. 1730.
MILITARY: Ensign, Coldstream Guards 16 Feb. 1725; Cornet, Royal Regiment of Horse Guards 17 Nov. 1727; Lieutenant, 2nd Troop Horse Grenadier Guards 2 Oct. 1731; Captain and Guidon of same 10 May 1740; Major 1st Troop Horse Grenadier Guards 26 Apr. 1751; Lieutenant-Colonel of same 23 Mar. 1756–d.; Captain and Lieutenant-Colonel 1st Foot Guards 27 Mar 1757; Brevet Colonel Feb. 1762.

POLITICAL ACTIVITY: A professional soldier and not a very high-profile MP, although he came from a prominent Co. Cork family. He was named for a committee on 5 October 1755; nothing else is known about his parliamentary career. However, given his appointment in the Royal Household, he was probably in England most of the time.

DIVISION LISTS:
1749 (1) absent and doubtful.

ESTATES/RESIDENCE: Mallow, Co. Cork; Shepherd's Bush, Middlesex.

SOURCES: PRONI T/559 vol. 15 p. 331, Burke, extract pedigrees; McCracken thesis; *HP 1715–54*; C. Dalton, *George the First's Army, 1714–1727*; *Cork Hist. Soc. Jn.* vol. 5 2nd ser. (1899) pp. 195–6, 'Notes and Queries'.

0408 CLAYTON, Laurence

MP for Mallow 1692–3, 1695–9, 1703–12

b. 1655; d. 1712 (will proved 2 Feb. 1713)
FAMILY/BACKGROUND: Son of Randolph Clayton and Judith, dau. of Sir John Percival, 3rd Baronet.
MARRIED: (1) Catherine, dau. of Sir Henry Tynte; (2) [1698] Anne, dau. of Sir Peter Courthorpe.
CHILDREN: (1) o. son d. yg.
(2) Sir Courthorpe (0407); Randall; John.
EDUCATION: Entered Oxford [Trinity College] 31 July 1671, aged 16 years; Lincoln's Inn 30 May 1671.
CAREER/OCCUPATION: King's Serjeant, High Sheriff of Co. Cork 1679, 1686, 1701; Deputy Governor of Co. Cork 1699.
MILITARY: Captain in Sir James Lesley's Regiment of Foot 1 Oct. 1689; exchanged to Sir George St George's Regiment of Foot 15 Oct. 1689; transferred to Queen's Regiment of Foot 1 Feb. 1690, out of regiment by 1691; a Captain in Colonel Henry Trelawny's Queen's Regiment of Foot *ante* 1692.

POLITICAL ACTIVITY: In a list of Irish Sheriffs in March 1686, the Lord President described him as 'a caballing Whig!'. In reply Clarendon wrote that 'It is not reasonable to conclude this gentleman a Whig, his father being a very old Cavalier and sufferer for the crown, and was condemned to die in Cromwell's time: at the King's Restoration, in reward of his services, he was made a trustee and register for the officers who served in Ireland before 1649; and out of the lands set apart for these old Cavaliers made his fortune, which is since descended to his son, who has not yet by any public actions discovered any inclinations to caballing against the Government, or Whiggism.'

In his youth he had a military career, but appears to have retired after the Battle of the Boyne. He entered parliament in 1692 and sat in successive parliaments until his death in 1712. He was named on 38 committees between 1695 and 1698 and 46 between 1703 and 1710. Major Clayton and nine others, including the Solicitor General, Alan Brodrick (0237), undertook to prove the articles against Lord Chancellor Porter (alleging that he favoured Catholics) when they came before the House, 25 October 1695, even after they had heard him speak in his own defence. The

House rejected the articles but Clayton was, not surprisingly, among those who voted for them. He signed the Association for the protection of William III in the country in 1696.

In the reign of Queen Anne he was considered hostile in 1706. In 1703 he introduced the heads of a bill that became 2 Anne, c. 5, 'An Act to make it High Treason in this kingdom to impeach the Succession of the Crown as limited by several Acts of Parliament'. In the same session he introduced 2 Anne, c. 12, 'An Act for reviving an Act for taking away the Benefit of Clergy in some Cases and for transporting Felons', and in 1707 he continued his strong line on law and order by an act endorsing 'two several Acts against Tories, Robbers and Raparees'. On 14 October 1703 as chairman of the Committee to Inspect the Public Accounts, he received the thanks of the House for his committee's 'faithful and diligent discharge of the trust reposed in them, whereby they have saved the kingdom the sum of £103,368 8s 4d which by misrepresentation was charged as a debt on the nation'. The accusation was made, not very successfully, against Sir William Robinson (**1795**), the deputy Receiver General.

Along with the Whig leader and Cork politician, Alan Brodrick, he sought to secure the choice of MP for Co. Limerick in 1706 at the election caused by the death of Mr Oliver (**1579**). He appears to have given the impression of being a Whig, or at least a fellow traveller, but this may have been out of concern for his lands, and the same concern may have motivated his attack on Porter, who was considered too lenient to the defeated Catholics in the still unstable land situation and the insecurity of the succession.

DIVISION LISTS:
 1709 (1) spoke for a Money Bill.

ESTATES/RESIDENCE: Mallow, Co. Cork. Had a yearly estate of £590 in 1688. In October 1696 Elizabeth Villiers conveyed to him a portion of her estates at Midleton, Co. Cork for the endowment of the school there, of which he was a governor.

SOURCES: *CJ Ire.* (Bradley edition) vol. 3 pp. 23–4, 170, 174, 519 (**0067, 0074, 0106**); PRONI D/302; *CJ Ire.* (Bradley ed.) vol. 2 pp. 750–1, vol. 3 p. 54; PRONI T/559 vol. 15 p. 331, Burke, extract pedigrees; Hayton thesis; *Cal. SP Dom. 1691–1692* (London, 1900) p.

536; *Alum. Oxon.*; Cork MPs; Simms' cards; C. Dalton (ed.), *English Army Lists and Commission Registers, 1661–1714* (London, 1896), vol. 3 p. 55; S. W. Singer (ed.), *Clarendon Corr.*, vol. 1 (London, 1828) p. 288; *The Records of the Honourable Society of Lincoln's Inn* (Lincoln's Inn, 1896) vol. 1 p. 310; *HMC Ormonde* (1920) new ser. vol. 8 p. 126; *Cork Hist. Soc. Jn.* vol. 5 2nd ser. (1899) pp. 195–6, 'Notes and Queries' [says his will pr. 2 Feb. 1713]; *JRSAI* vol. 55 (1925) pp. 37, 45, H. A. S. Upton, 'A List of Governors and Deputy Governors of Counties in Ireland in 1699' [says his will was proved 1710 but *CJ Ire.* give him as still sitting in 1711]; *JRSAI* vol. 82 (1952) pp. 5, 13, M. Quane, 'Midleton School, Co. Cork'; Parliamentary Lists, 1695 (1), 1696 (1), 1706 (1).

0409 CLEMENT, William

MP for TCD 1761–8; Dublin B. 1771–6–82

 b. 1707; d. 14 Jan. 1782 (bur. in TCD)
 FAMILY/BACKGROUND: Son of Thomas Clement.
 MARRIED: Mary Cox, wid. of John Montgomery (**1441**) and mother of John Montgomery (**1442**) and Alexander Montgomery (**1436**).
 CHILDREN: *?d.s.p.*
 EDUCATION: School: Mr Fowld, Carrickmacross; entered TCD 28 Apr. 1721, aged 14 years, scholar 1724, BA 1726, MA 1731, Fellow (Physic) 1733, Senior Fellow 1743, 1759–82, Lecturer in Botany 1733, *1759, Professor of Natural Philosophy 1745; MB 1747, MD 1748–d.; Donegal Lecturer 1750–9, Auditor and Vice Provost of TCD 1760–82, *Joint Deputy Vice-Treasurer 1769, Regius Professor of Physic 1761–18 Nov. 1781.
 CAREER/OCCUPATION: Freedom of Dublin July 1764; *Trustee of the Royal Exchange 1774; *Governor of the Foundling Hospital and Workhouse 1773–d.; *Governor of the Hibernian Marine Society 1775–d.; *Commissioner for paving the Streets of Dublin 1778–80.

POLITICAL ACTIVITY: In 1758 Clement stood against Dr Francis Andrews (**0040**) for the post of Provost of TCD. In his support, the Earl of Shannon (**0210**) (Speaker Boyle) wrote to Lord Bedford extolling Clement's suitability for the post, and pointing out that Primate Stone had unofficially made it known that for such a person he would allow 'a dispensation, which is not unprecedented, from that part of the statute which directs that a provost shall be in [Holy] orders'.

In 1750 Mrs Delany described dining with Dr Clements [sic] and meeting Mrs Montgomery (supposed to be his wife but not owned, presumably because Fellows were supposed to be unmarried). In August 1758 she wrote again to her sister, explaining that 'Mr Clements and Mrs Montgomery have been married privately many years, but they are *only called friends – her* fortune *small, his nothing* (if he gave up his fellowship and other advantages that are considerable in the college); the *circumstances* they are under are well known to everybody, but as they are both very agreeable they are *winked* at.'

In a letter to Bedford, Clement pointed out that Dr William Temple had been Provost 'though a layman'. Eventually a dispensation for his marriage was granted by Lord Harcourt against the wishes of the Provost, John Hely-Hutchinson (1001), who was himself neither single nor in holy orders, but was having great difficulty from the hostility of the fellows. Clement's parliamentary politics were influenced by his academic politics and his hostility to both Provost Andrews and his successor, Provost Hely-Hutchinson. His marriage gave both Provosts a hold over him.

On his return for TCD in 1761, Clement refused to give an undertaking to obtain septennial parliaments. He was returned with 68 votes; his opponents Philip Tisdall (2078) and Robert French (0834) received 50 and 19 votes respectively. Clement was not returned for the college in 1768, but Dr Charles Lucas (1276), the MP for Dublin, died in November 1771 and Clement succeeded him. Then in November 1773 the other MP, the Marquess of Kildare (0745), succeeded his father (0734) as Duke of Leinster and was replaced by Redmond Morres (1492). A Parliamentary List of 1773 sums up his position as follows: 'came in by his own interest which he got by his continued opposition to Government. He is Vice Provost of the College. He never was with the Provost [Andrews] but being always against him in Trinity it is thought directed his conduct in the House. A man not apt to laugh or frown. He is thought to be honest and though a fellow of the College he is married contrary to the statutes which keeps him a good deal down. Against.'

Dublin city expected its MPs to be independent of government and attend to its concerns; high among these was the question of quarterage. This concerned fees paid by Catholic merchants and manufacturers to the Protestant guilds so that they might enjoy their economic privileges. The first Quarterage Bill was introduced by Dr Charles Lucas in 1767, and the Marquess of Kildare and Dr Clement subsequently took up the issue. Clement was chairman of a committee of the whole House to consider a bill for establishing a quarterage to be paid to the Dublin guilds, and in February 1778 the heads of a Quarterage Bill did pass the House of Commons, but it subsequently got lost in the elaborate procedure required by Poynings' Law. Quarterage was strongly opposed by the Catholics, and from the accession of George III British policy towards the Catholics had been conciliatory. Clement appears to have been particularly influenced by the Weavers' Guild. He voted almost solidly with the opposition, partly from conviction, partly to please his constituents and partly because both Provost Andrews and Hely-Hutchinson supported the government.

Clement was given a splendid funeral on 18 January 1782. The *Dublin Journal* declared that 'Too much respect could not be paid to the memory of a man who has been all his life a uniform patriot.' The cortege passed through Merrion Street, round St Stephen's Green, and down Grafton Street to the college. The bearers were prominent MPs: Rt Hon. Thomas Conolly (0459), Rt Hon. Sir Capel Molyneaux (1421), Rt Hon. Luke Gardiner (0842), Sir Samuel Bradstreet (0227), Sydenham Singleton (1926), David La Touche (1203), Barry Yelverton (2268), Clotworthy Rowley (1818) and John Fitzgibbon (0749, MP for TCD). They were attended by the dignitaries of the city of Dublin all wearing mourning scarves and hatbands, and the different corps of uniformed Volunteers with muffled drums etc. The Archbishop of Dublin provided a sour note, writing to the Earl of Buckinghamshire that 'Old Dr Clements [sic] was buried this day with great parades. The city has not yet fixed on a successor, but doubtless they will endeavour to choose one who will invariably oppose (as usual) the measures of Government.'

DIVISION LISTS:

1768 (1) voted against army augmentation.

1771 (2) voted for Sir Lucius O'Brien's (**1558**) motion for retrenchment.

1772 (2) voted for a Short Revenue Bill.

1773 (1) voted against the Absentee Tax.

1773 (2) voted for an untaxed press.

1774 (1) voted against the Stamp Bill.

1774 (2) voted against Catholic relief.

1775 (1) voted for the pro-American amendment to the Speech from the Throne.

1777 (1) voted for Grattan's (**0895**) motion for retrenchment.

1777 (2) voted against the trade embargo.

1778 (1) voted for Grattan's motion for retrenchment.

1778 (2) voted against the Popery Bill.

1779 (2) voted for a six-months Loan Bill.

1780 (2) voted for Yelverton's (**2268**) motion to modify Poynings' Law.

1780 (3) voted for the Tenantry Bill.

1780 (4) voted against the Perpetual Mutiny Bill.

1780 (5) voted for the duty on imported sugar.

ADDITIONAL INFORMATION: At his interment it was said that 'In his early youth he was a notable example of brotherly love; in more advanced age a parent to orphans. Many who were in danger of being snatched by an untimely death left him a father to their tender infants, and a faithful guardian to their wants and necessities; to him they looked up for comfort – in his bosum they placed their own hopes and the safety of their children.'

ESTATES/RESIDENCE: Carrickmacross, Co. Monaghan; Park Street, Dublin.

SOURCES: PRONI T/2915/6/1, 6/4/, Bedford Papers; PRONI T/559 vol. 15 p. 342, Burke, extract pedigrees; Ellis thesis; *Alum. Dub.*; Musgrave *Obits*; G. S. Montgomery, *A Family History of the Montgomerys of Ballyleck from whom are descended the Montgomerys of Beaulieu and Convoy* (Belfast, 1887), pp. 36–8; T. P. C. Kirkpatrick, *The Medical School of Trinity College Dublin* (Dublin, 1912), pp. 99–100; Llandover, *Delany Corr.*, vol. 2 p. 559, vol. 3 p. 507; *HMC Lothian* p. 409; T. W. Moody & E. E. Vaughan (eds), *A New History of Ireland*, p. 203, R. B. McDowell, 'Colonial Nationalism, 1760–82'; Johnston, *Gt B. & Ire.*, p. 151;

G. O'Brien (ed.), *Catholic Ireland in the eighteenth century: Collected essays of Maureen Wall* (1989), p. 71, 'Quarterage Dispute'; *Almanacks*; *BNL* 15–18 Jan. 1782 [says he d. 14 Jan. 1782 in his 79th year]; *DJ* 11–14, 14–18 Apr. 1761, 15–17 and 17–19 Jan. 1782; *FJ* 21–24 July 1764, 12–14 Mar. 1772; Parliamentary Lists, 1772 (2), 1773 (1), 1773 (2), 1774 (1), 1775 (1), 1776 (2), (3), 1777 (1), 1778 (1), 1780 (1).

♦♦♦♦ **CLEMENTS**, Francis [n.d.e.]

MP for Carrickfergus Oct.–Dec. 1741

b. *ante* 1700; d. 26 Mar. 1749
FAMILY/BACKGROUND: Son of Edward Clements and Eleanor, dau. of Alexander Dalway.
MARRIED: [   ], dau. of [   ] Pont of Liverpool.
CHILDREN: ?
CAREER/OCCUPATION: Sheriff of Co. Antrim 1721; Searcher of Carrickfergus 22 Oct. 1733; *Magistrate and Mayor of Carrickfergus 1740.
MILITARY: Major of Dragoons.

POLITICAL ACTIVITY: He sat for less than three months before being declared not duly elected; little is known of his activity during this period.

ESTATES/RESIDENCE: Straid, Co. Antrim.

SOURCES: McCracken thesis; Hughes, *Pat. Officers*; S. McSkimin, *The History and Antiquities of the County of the Town of Carrickfergus* (Belfast, 1829); *Almanacks*.

0410 CLEMENTS, Henry

MP for Carrickfergus 1692–3

b. 1644; d. 2 Nov. 1696
FAMILY/BACKGROUND: ?Son of Henry Clements.
MARRIED: ?
CHILDREN: ?
CAREER/OCCUPATION: Mayor of Carrickfergus *c.* 1680; High Sheriff of Co. Antrim 1690.

POLITICAL ACTIVITY: The parliament lasted less than a month before it was prorogued and then dissolved. Nothing is known of his activity during this period.

ESTATES/RESIDENCE: Straid, Co. Antrim.

SOURCES: PRONI D/302; Burke *IFR* (1976) p. 246 [says

the MP for Carrickfergus in 1692 was Robert Clements of Rathkenny, Co. Cavan, born 1664 died 1722 and son of Daniel Clements, but *CJ Ire.* gives Henry Clements]; *Memorials of the Dead*; Simms' cards.

0411 CLEMENTS, Henry

MP for Cavan B. 1729–45

b. 1704; d. May 1745
FAMILY/BACKGROUND: Son of Robert Clements of Rathkenny, Co. Cavan, and Elizabeth, dau. of Gen. Theophilus Sandford of Moyglare, Co. Meath.
MARRIED: ?
CHILDREN: ?
EDUCATION: School: Mr Sheridan, Dublin; entered TCD 17 Mar. 1720, aged 16 years.
CAREER/OCCUPATION: *Magistrate 1739; *Portreeve 1739.
MILITARY: Captain 1733, *Major of Kinsale Fort 1739–41; aide-de-camp to the Lord Lieutenant 1741; Captain 1742; *Major 1742, *Lieutenant-Colonel 1744.

POLITICAL ACTIVITY: A professional soldier. He was listed for 37 committees between 1731 and 1741. By written agreement the Clements family returned one member each for Cavan Borough.

ESTATES/RESIDENCE: Rathkenny, Co. Cavan.

SOURCES: PRONI T/559 vol. 15 p. 344, Burke, extract pedigrees; McCracken thesis; *Alum. Dub.*; Burke *IFR* (1976) pp. 246–7 [does not give a Henry son of Robert Clements and Elizabeth Sandford]; *Musgrave Obits*; *Almanacks*.

0412 CLEMENTS, Rt Hon. Henry Theophilus

MP for Cavan B. 1769–76, 1783–90; Co. Leitrim 1776–83, 1790–5 [n.d.e. Co. Leitrim 1783]

b. 1734; d. 26 Oct. 1795 at his seat in Co. Leitrim
HONOURS: PC, sworn 21 Aug. 1777.
FAMILY/BACKGROUND: Son of Rt Hon. Nathaniel Clements (0414) and Hannah, dau. of Rev. William Gore, Dean of Down.
MARRIED: (1) [2 June 1770] Mary [d. 23 Oct. 1777], dau. and h. of Gen. Webb; (2) [7 Aug.

1778] Catherine [d. 7 Jan. 1836], dau. of Rt Hon. John Beresford (0115).
CHILDREN: (1) Elizabeth; Hannah, m. Sir George Montgomery Bt.; Harriet, m. [July 1789] William Henry Moore Hodder of Co. Cork; Maria Theodosia, m. Rev. Dean Keatinge.
(2) Henry John, m. [1811] Louisa, dau. of James Stewart (2004); John Marcus (b. 4 May 1789; d. 1833; Lieut.-Col., 18 Hussars), m. [1822] Catherine Frances, dau. of Geoffrey Wentworth of Yorkshire; Nathaniel; Anna Barbara (b. 1779; d. yg); Selina (b. 17 Aug. 1780; d. 28 May 1805), m. [13 July 1803] Sir William Mordant Stuart Milner.
CAREER/OCCUPATION: Deputy Vice-Treasurer of the Court of Exchequer 1778–93 (succeeding his father); Sheriff of Co. Cavan 1766, 21 June 1774; High Sheriff of Co. Leitrim 12 Feb. 1773; *Governor of the Foundling Hospital and Workhouse 1769–d.; *Commissioner of the Tillage Act for Munster 1778–85; *Deputy Constable of Dublin Castle 1778–95; *Governor of the Lying-in Hospital 1779–95; Trustee of the Linen Board for Munster Sept. 1779–d.; *Company of Undertakers for the Grand Canal 1783–4; Governor of Co. Leitrim 10 Apr. 1789; *Joint Governor 1789–94; Custos Rot. 9 May 1789; Joint Ranger Phoenix Park 1790; *Governor of the Hibernian Society 1789–d.; Searcher, Packer and Gauger of Dublin; *Receiver and Paymaster General of all Revenues 1795; Army Agent to the regiments serving abroad paid by Ireland, worth £800 p.a. (at his appointment) 1772–95.
MILITARY: *Lieutenant-Colonel of a Regiment of Foot 1764–5; 30th Regiment of Foot 1757–9; Lieutenant-Colonel 69th Regiment; Paymaster of Irish troops abroad *ante* Oct. 1777; Captain of the Ashfield Volunteers 1782; *Agent to the Pensioners of the Civil and Military Establishments 1787–d.; Colonel of the Leitrim Rangers, Volunteers; Recorder General and Paymaster General 25 Dec. 1793; Colonel of Co. Leitrim Militia, 1793.

POLITICAL ACTIVITY: A professional soldier and later an administrator and a major office-holder. He was a younger son of Nathaniel Clements (0414), whom he succeeded as Deputy Vice-Treasurer. His father was a leading mid-century politician and ensured that his son was launched into a promising political career. His first marriage was to an heiress; his second marriage was to Catherine, the eldest daughter of John Beresford (0115)

(Clements was older than her father), and probably did not increase his fortune but added greatly to his influence.

Clements was returned by his father for the Clements seat for Cavan Borough. He sat for Co. Leitrim 1776–83, and although he was declared not duly elected for Co. Leitrim in 1783 on a charge of bribery, he was returned for the safe family seat of Cavan, and in 1790 was again returned for Co. Leitrim, which he represented until his death in 1795. The upset in 1783 was caused by Peter La Touche (**1207**), a member of the Dublin banking family, who stood on the popular interest. Although declared not duly elected, Clements managed to secure the return of his friend and relative John Gore (**0870**).

Co. Leitrim had few resident landlords and a small electorate, but conflicting electoral influences. Clements was a government supporter and followed his father's political lead until the latter's death in 1777. In 1772 he was appointed Agent to the Regiments serving Abroad, £800, and in 1776 he was joined with his father as Deputy Vice-Treasurer. In the course of his viceroyalty Lord Harcourt gave to his recommendation substantial patronage, viz. four boatmen, 11 tidewaiters and four supernumerary gaugers. In 1779 he wrote to Lord Lieutenant Buckinghamshire that every well-wisher to His Majesty's Government and His Excellency's administration must ardently contribute to obtain the Bill for Mutiny and Desertion now to be framed; another former officer, William Burton (Conyngham) (**0303**), wrote to the same effect.

In 1783 Clements was a delegate to the Volunteer National Convention for Co. Cavan. He was absent at the time of the Commercial Resolutions in 1785, when he 'paired' with George Montgomery (**1438**). His father-in-law, John Beresford, commented on the pairing arrangement to Chief Secretary Orde (**1594**): 'Though in ordinary cases it may not be advisable to give up man for man ... I am glad that Montgomery does not go over I never heard anyone so violent.' Clements and his wife were at Spa.

In 1785 it was calculated that as Deputy Vice-Treasurer and Paymaster of Pensions he held government positions worth £2,400 p.a. There was a certain amount of criticism of the way in which he performed his duties, and in 1788 it was noted that his clerk was to be better paid and the Collector's balances were to be regularly brought up. In 1794 he had added to his offices that of Constable of Dublin Castle, possibly as part-compensation for his loss of the Deputy Vice-Treasurership in the Treasury reorganisation of 1793. The two votes in 1791 – on the sale of peerages and free trade – are out of line with the rest of his political behaviour and may be the result of pressure from his brother Robert, Lord Leitrim (**0418**), as Leitrim's son, Nathaniel Clements (**0415**), also voted in this way.

DIVISION LISTS:

1771 (1) voted for Lord Townshend as Lord Lieutenant (called Theophilus in the text).
1771 (2) voted against Sir Lucius O'Brien's (**1558**) motion for retrenchment.
1772 (2) voted against a Short Revenue Bill.
1773 (1) voted for the Absentee Tax.
1774 (2) voted for Catholic relief.
1775 (1) voted against the pro-American amendment to the Speech from the Throne.
1777 (1) voted against Grattan's (**0895**) motion for retrenchment.
1777 (2) a teller for the Trade Embargo.
1778 (2) voted for the Popery Bill.
1779 (1) voted for new taxes.
1779 (2) voted against a six-months Loan Bill.
1780 (1) voted against Grattan's declaration of the rights of Ireland.
1780 (2) voted against Yelverton's (**2268**) motion to modify Poynings' Law.
1780 (4) voted for the Perpetual Mutiny Bill.
1783 (1) voted against Flood's (**0762**) motion for parliamentary reform.
1784 (1) voted against a committee on the Reform Bill.
1785 (1) absent.
1789 (1) voted against a Regency.
1790 (2) voted for Foster (**0805**) on the Election of a Speaker.
1791 (1) voted for Curran's (**0560**) resolution against the sale of peerages.

1791 (2) voted for Grattan's motion for the exercise of free trade.

ADDITIONAL INFORMATION: *A member of RDS from 1777; *a subscriber to the Public Assembly Rooms, 1787. His daughters were listed as nominees in the life annuities of 1779.

ESTATES/RESIDENCE: Ashfield Lodge, Cootehill, Co. Cavan; Woodville, Queen's County; Great George's Street, Dublin. In 1777, on the death of the Rt Hon. Nathaniel Clements, the Ashfield estate passed not to the eldest son, the 1st Earl of Leitrim (0418), but to the second son, Henry Theophilus Clements. The estate lay in the barony of Tullygarvey. The rental was £2,924 a year. In 1798–9, estate maps show that the estate included Corcalvey, parish of Ashfield (also described as in the parish of Killsherdiny), and Tonaghbawn and Corballyguill, parish of Killsherdiny.

SOURCES: PRONI MIC/474 Irish Volunteers; RCBL P80/1/1, Parish Registers of St Thomas, Dublin; Burke *LGI* (1904) p. 95; Burke *PB* (1906) p. 990; Hughes, *Pat. Officers*; Burke *IFR* (1976) pp. 245–6; McNevin, *Volunteers*; *Index to Irish Privy Counsellors, 1711–1910*; Cavan MPs [says he died in early Jan. 1796]; *HMC Lothian* p. 365; Johnston, *Gt B. & Ire.*, pp. 250, 291; T. Bartlett and D. W. Hayton (eds), *Penal Era and Golden Age* (Belfast, 1979) p. 113 f. 1, P. D. H. Smyth, 'The Volunteers and Parliament, 1779–84'; *JRSAI* vol. 38 (1908) pp. 385, 388–9, J. Meehan, 'Catalogue of the High Sheriffs of the County of Leitrim from the Year 1605 to the Year 1800' [calls him Theophilus and Henry Thomas (*sic*) but says correctly that he represented the Borough of Cavan in 1789]; *Ir. Gen.* vol. 1 no. 8 (1940) p. 239, 'A List of Irish Stockholders, 1779'; *Almanacks*; *Pue's Occurrences* 27 Mar. 1742; *FJ* 28–30 Oct. 1777, 16–18 Sept. 1779, 25–27 Apr. 1793, 12 Dec. 1795 [The final interment in the family vault was delayed until 12 Dec., although the newspapers report his death in late Oct. e.g. *DJ* 31 Oct. 1795 says he d. a few days ago.]; *DJ* 23–25 Oct. 1777, 14 Jan. 1797; TCD Clements Papers [Minority accounts for the estate of H. J. Clements, 18 Mar. 1799]; NLI Clements Papers 15 B 24 [Maps *c.* 1775–1804], PC 88, [Maps 1798–9]; NLI MS 3030; Parliamentary Lists, 1772 (2), 1773 (1), (2), 1774 (1), 1775 (1), 1776 (1), (2), (3), 1777 (1), 1778 (1), 1780 (1), 1782 (1), 1783 (1), (2), (3), 1784 (1), (2), (3), 1785 (1), (2), (3), (4), 1787 (1), 1788 (1), 1789 (1), 1790 (1), 1791 (1), 1793 (1), 1794 (1), (2),

0413 CLEMENTS, John

MP for Cavan B. 1777–83

b. 1757; d. 10 July 1817
FAMILY/BACKGROUND: Son of John Clements.
MARRIED: [Mar. 1779] Jane [   ].
CHILDREN: Harriet.
MILITARY: Appointed Captain in the East India Company Service 21 Aug. 1761, resigned *c.* Nov. 1782. He made 7 recorded voyages: to China 15 Nov. 1762 – 3 Sept. 1763, to Bombay, Surat and Mocha 8 Jan. 1765 – 3 Aug. 1767, to Madras and Bengal 12 Oct. 1768 – 16 Aug. 1770, to Bombay, Surat and China 7 Dec. 1771 – 21 Mar. 1774, from Batavia to Bombay and China 22 Mar. 1774 – 19 Sept. 1775, from Bombay(?) to England 12 Feb. – 19 Aug. 1775. His final voyage was probably to China and Bencoolen 8 Mar. 1780 – 27 May 1782. His ship was the *Glatton.*

POLITICAL ACTIVITY: He was part of the extended Clements family and was returned by Robert Clements (0418) following the death of Robert's father, Nathaniel Clements (0414), in May 1777. He was considered an independent, but while he was in parliament he was still in the service of the East India Co., and was absent on a voyage in 1780–82. If Henry Theophilus Clements (0412) had not been declared not duly elected for Co. Leitrim, he might have been returned for Cavan in 1783, although there was the question of the seat traditionally owed by Lord Leitrim for his peerage. However, in the event a seat had to be found for H. T. Clements, who was a major office-holder.

DIVISION LISTS:
1779 (2) voted for a six-months Loan Bill.

ESTATES/RESIDENCE: Milltown, Co. Wicklow.

SOURCES: BL IOR L/MAR/B/150B/C, D, E, F and G; Burke *IFR.* (1976) p. 247; *DJ* 13–16 Mar. 1779; Parliamentary Lists, 1776 (1), 1778 (1), 1780 (1), 1782 (1), 1783 (1).

0414 CLEMENTS, Rt Hon. Nathaniel

MP for Duleek 1728–60; Cavan B. 1761–8; Co. Leitrim 1768–76; Carrick 1776–7 [r. Cavan B. 1768, 1776; Roscommon B. 1768]

b. 1705; d. (bur. 29) May 1777 at Phoenix Park
HONOURS: PC 1757–d. (sworn 17 June 1757, 1 Nov. 1760, 21 Aug. 1761).
FAMILY/BACKGROUND: Son of Robert Clements and Elizabeth, dau. of Gen. Theophilus Sandford.
MARRIED: [31 Jan. 1729] Hannah (b. 1705), dau. of Rev. William Gore, Dean of Down.
CHILDREN: Rt Hon. Robert, 1st Earl of Leitrim (0418); William (0420); Rt Hon. Henry Theophilus (0412); Elizabeth, m. [19 Mar. 1750] Francis Pierpoint Burton, 2nd Earl Conyngham (0299); Hannah, m. George Montgomery (1438); Catherine, m. Eyre Massy, 1st Baron Clarina (1354); Alicia, m. Ralph Gore-St George, 1st Earl of Ross (0881).
CAREER/OCCUPATION: High Sheriff of Co. Cavan 1731, Co. Donegal 1752, Co. Leitrim 1764; Joint Teller and Vice-Treasurer of the Court of the Exchequer 1728–55; Deputy Vice-Treasurer and Receiver General 1756–77; *Clerk of the Wool Accounts 1736–47; Register of the Forfeitures 1750–60; Searcher, Packer and Gauger 1745–77; Agent to the Pensioners on the Civil and Military Establishments 1728–75; Deputy Recorder and Paymaster General 1775; *Commissioner of Tillage and Navigation; Governor of the Workhouse 1733–69; Foundling Hospital and Workhouse 1770–d.; Member of the board of the Incorporated Society for Carrying on the Cambric Manufacture in Ireland 1742; *Subscriber to the Cambrick Manufacture 1743, 1747, 1749, 1751–70, 1772; Customs Collector for the port of Carrickfergus 1742–8; Deputy Constable of Dublin Castle 1738–64; *Trustee of the Linen Board for Munster 1742–d.; Searcher of Skerries, Malahide and Wicklow; Ranger of Phoenix Park and Master of the Game 1750, 1752–d.; Portreeve of Cavan 6 Oct. 1755; *Court of Assistants 1762–3, 1767–69; *Governor of Erasmus Smith's Schools and other Charities 1746–69; *Commissioner of the Tillage Act for Ulster 1749–d.; *Governor of the Blue-Coat Hospital 1750–d.; *Governor of Dr Steeven's Hospital 1755–d.; *Governor of the Lying-in Hospital 1756–d. (Treasurer 1758–d., Committee 1763–4, 1766–8); *Governor of the Royal Hospital (Kilmainham) 1758; *Commissioner of the Infirmary in James' Street 1758–68; *Governor of Co. Leitrim 1758–d.; *Member of the Committee of Fifteen in the Incorporated Society of Dublin (Charter Schools) 1769, 1773; *Governor of the Hibernian Society 1769–d.; member of the Court of Directors of the Grand Canal Company 1772–5; Subscriber to the Marine Society Mar. 1759; partner in the Dublin

bank of Malone, Clements and Gore, which failed after 4 months, July–Nov. 1758.

POLITICAL ACTIVITY: Nathaniel Clements was one of the most prominent politicians of the mid-eighteenth century. He sat in parliament for almost 50 years and was listed for 185 committees in the parliament of George II. His position was partly due to his inherent abilities, partly to his connections in both England and Ireland, and largely to the use he made of his tenure of the offices of Teller of the Exchequer and Deputy Vice-Treasurer. Perhaps the best description of Clements and his position in Dublin society was that given by Mrs Delany to her sister, to whom she wrote in May 1759: '"Not hear of Mr and Mrs Clements!" Why she is finer than the finest lady in England. Dress, furniture, house equipage – *excelling all!* Mr Clements *is – her husband!* They set out in life very young and very humble, though both of good families; he was a favourite of the famous Luke Gardiner's (0841), and has gathered together by degrees an immense fortune, if one may judge by the magnificence of his living; and what is quite surprising, they are both very moderate in their understanding, and yet there is a cleverness and elegance in everything about them that is beyond what could be expected; they are now gone to their house in the park, about four miles from hence – three from Dublin; they keep Wednesdays.' This house is now the residence of the President of Ireland.

Clements, a protégé of Luke Gardiner, was *inter alia* a property speculator and builder. In the 1730s he built eight of the 23 great townhouses in Henrietta Street. Luke Gardiner built the rest, and lived in No. 10. Clements himself lived in No. 7 'in Parisian luxury'; Speaker Ponsonby (1702), Thomas Carter (0360) and Primate Stone were among his neighbours. To what extent Clements actually designed these houses or adapted the designs of Castle, Pearce (1646) and others is uncertain. Clements was not raised to the peerage but his son, Robert (0418), became 1st Earl of Leitrim.

Clements' rise was gradual. On 3 September 1728 Primate Boulter recommended him to succeed Boulter's deceased brother, Thomas, as Agent to the Pensioners, and probably about the same time he became Teller of the Exchequer. This was an important office, as it gave him the use of public money during the period between its receipt and disbursement. He also acted as agent and *de facto* banker for many of those to whom he disbursed money, and he received interest on advances; for instance in 1746/7 he received £670 as agent for 42 individuals and £764 14s 11d as interest on advances to 13 of them. On 10 September 1737, 'being the day of the reduction of the gold coin in this kingdom', he was paid £730 10s 7d for making good the shortfall in public money. At this time the Irish gold coinage was overvalued and, amid a tremendous outcry from the merchants, supported by Dean Swift, the currency was devalued.

Between this and his various building projects, Clements gradually amassed a fortune, and having recourse to such amounts of money gave him great personal power. Sackville (**1835**) wrote to Sir Robert Wilmot on 22 November 1753 that 'They have brought members from all parts of the country that nobody has seen in Dublin for twenty years past, and when we had imagined we had withstood these efforts, our good friend and ally Mr Nathaniel Clements, took a short turn and carried Mr Mitchell the banker (**1414**) with him who, on account of the public remittance, is dependent upon him; so that upon being betrayed, we lost the first division in the Committee by four votes, 119 on our side, 123 on theirs ... Luke Gardiner behaves very well, but Clements being the cashier occasions his influence to be very extensive; for he makes no scruple of lending money very plentifully among those that are distressed.'

In the early 1750s, when Primate Stone attempted to establish a dominant role in the government, he quickly realised the importance of Clements and came to consider that he had been the controlling influence behind the scenes in the Money Bill dispute. In letter after letter he launched a *Carthaga delenda est* type of attack on him. For instance, on 14 January 1754 he wrote to Newcastle (Stone's brother Andrew was the confidential secretary of the Duke of Newcastle and a close friend of both the Pelham brothers) pointing out that in the Lord Lieutenant's letter 'some general means are laid down ... but others

of much greater consequence than any mentioned are omitted. I mean the management of the Treasury ... All [the leading government officials] agreed the treasury was in a state of opposition: and that the loss of the question upon the Money Bill was occasioned by that influence ... the thing is notorious ... in my opinion my lord lieutenant's letter is defective on that point – very materially. The treasury is the strong sinew of the government, here, as well as in other places. The influence of it is very diffuse. The pay of the army remitted monthly into all parts of the country brings a dependence from all the little dealers in money there. Large balances of the King's revenue (which has been the case of late years) are lodged in the hands of favourite bankers. Two of them Mr Macarell (**1298**) and Mr Mitchell had promised to vote for the late question, but they both failed. Four score thousand pounds of the king's money was last year in their hands, for which they had given only a receipt upon account. The receipt was given to Mr Clements, but when he was desired to speak to them, he said he "had no influence"; and they were afraid of a run upon them from their merchants. Other bankers in town, who have no benefit from the government money, but whose business lies solely with those merchants, heard of no such thing, and did not scruple to give their votes for the government. I mean those who were so disposed. Near relations to Mr Clements, his wife's brothers, whom he has maintained and bought seats for them in parliament were against us. And just before the division, Mr Nesbitt (**1523**), a collector and brother to Mr [   ]Albert Nesbitt, who had given some encouragement for hoping that he would stay away, was brought into the house in triumph by Mr Clements' son-in-law. Every day produces some instance of Mr Clements' activity and efficacy. He has the sole direction of the Treasury (very little business being done by Mr Gardiner) and the power of course is solely in him. Mr Gardiner has suffered it to drop into his hands, contenting himself with the share of profit agreed between them. [This resistance will remain so long as Clements is in office] ... His power by it is very distressing to government, and he may be ever depended upon for distressing every administration of which Mr Malone (**1336**) is not the principal ... [the Lord Lieutenant says he will tell HM but] ... Mr Clements having given his single vote for the bill is no sufficient reason for suppressing so material a part of information ... [He, himself, only mentions this to be discharged of any omission] ... until Mr Clements is removed, no administration can be settled so as to be successful ... There is no mystery in this treasury, receiving and paying is the whole operation. Abilities are not requisite; though men of abilities might be found, if they were wanted, at least far superior to this gentleman's who is incapable, if it were necessary, of speaking three sentences in public.'

Part of Stone's trouble was that Clements' tentacles spread right through Irish society, and Stone did not really have a viable alternative. His favourite candidate was Benjamin Burton (0293), who happened to be Lord Bessborough's (1696) son-in-law, and even the ambitious Bessborough could see the problems that this appointment would create. Finally, Lord Lieutenant Dorset was an old and experienced administrator and was not entirely behind Stone, who complained to Lord George Sackville 'that his Grace (in this transaction at least) has declined taking upon him the supporting his own and the Royall authority is too evident to receive any contradiction or colouring. You cannot conceive what use is made of it here to lessen the credit and influence which his Grace is supposed by his friends to have, and consequently to lessen the dependence upon him and those attached to him ... There is not the least falling off of friends, as I can perceive; but there is an apprehension that the Government is falling off from itself.'

Stone's attempts to wrest the Treasury from Clements proved a long-running and unsuccessful saga, and his endless and lengthy repetition of Clements' power – and exculpation of himself – may have been self-defeating, for the ministry wanted peace and quiet, especially in view of the imminence of a major war. Both men were famous for their social qualities and both had excellent connections in London: Stone through his brother, Andrew, and Clements through the king's mistress, the Countess of Yarmouth – Clements was the receiver for her pension on the Irish establishment.

As Mrs Delany indicated, the Clements knew how to make themselves attractive; for instance, on 21 May 1747 he wrote to the recently appointed Chief Secretary Weston (2223) offering his help in settling the Westons into their Castle apartments. In any case, Clements had complied with the essential duty of major office-holders: he had voted with the government, even if his friends had not. In fact Clements wrote to Under-Secretary Wilmot on 18 December 1753 that 'We had a debate yesterday on the altered Money Bill, which lasted until twelve at night, and we lost it by five, which I am heartily sorry for.' A further letter of 16 February 1754 declared that 'I am greatly concerned to hear from some friends in England that my conduct should be called in question as to the Gores, my brothers-in-law voting. I do affirm that I did everything in my power to prevail on them ... and am heartily sorry they did not take my advice. I hope they see their error ...' Waite (2154) wrote a very interesting memorandum on the pros and cons of keeping Clements in office.

At this point the Duke of Dorset was recalled. The parties had fought themselves to a standstill, and the Marquess of Hartington was sent over to resolve the fracas. In a letter to the Duke of Devonshire, 16 July 1755, Hartington reported that 'I had a long conversation with Clements ... he spoke like a man that had considered well the part that he intended to take, and was resolved ... that he thought himself so much obliged to me that he was bound ... to do everything in his power to make my government easy and honourable, and that he had told the Speaker and Malone so, and desired them never to say anything before him that they do not choose I should know, for that he thought it incumbent upon him to acquaint me with everything relative to government that came to his Knowledge. There was also an ease and cheerfulness in his countenance that I have not observed before of [sic] some time.'

Shortly after, Luke Gardiner (0841) died. Clements was his obvious successor and was appointed Deputy Vice-Treasurer; Hartington then appointed his relative, Sir Henry Cavendish (0380), Teller of the Exchequer, doubtless hoping that he would be a safe pair of hands. Sir Henry quickly gave the lie to Primate Stone's statement that 'abilities are not requisite', as very shortly after his appointment his deficiencies were recognised and at his death he had mishandled affairs to the extent that he was considerably in debt to the government.

Clements was made a Privy Counsellor in 1757. In 1758 Malone, now Chancellor of the Exchequer, Clements and Gore (0869) united to found a short-lived bank, which had some innovative features such as the payment of interest, at 2.33%, on deposits. Its collapse led to a statute, 33 Geo. II, c.14, which prohibited persons holding public funds from engaging in banking or discounting notes. Pitt considered that the collapse of this bank had probably contributed to the 1759 anti-Union riot by 'distempering and revolting the minds of the manufacturing multitude'.

Clements now became a senior statesman, and the remainder of his career was honourable and tranquil. In 1768 he ensured his return to parliament by being returned for three constituencies: Co. Leitrim, about which he may have been nervous, and two 'close' boroughs, Cavan and Roscommon, about which he can have had no doubts and which allowed him to play a manipulative role once more. In 1772 a Parliamentary List recorded that 'Mr Clements and his connections have certainly been very steady to Government, and many favours have been asked for them during Townshend's administration', and 'Lord Townshend gave him many small employments in the Revenue'; he gave a similar support to Lord Harcourt. In 1776 he was returned for the 'close' borough of Carrick, which some years previously he had purchased 'of the late General St George (1844) for £5,000'. Although in 1777 he was over 70, it was noted that 'He attends and supports constantly. Does his duty in the Treasury strictly and with great zeal and integrity and is universally respected. Lord Harcourt has given to his recommendation 1 Boatman, 3 Supernumerary Tidewaiters, the Distributor of Stamps for Leitrim county and 1 Hearth Money Collection.' His son (0412) was joined with him and succeeded him in the office of Deputy Vice-Treasurer.

He died in May 1777, and the following October Lord Lieutenant Buckinghamshire wrote to Lord George Germain (Sackville) (1835) that: 'Your Lordship will recollect that since the last Parliament his Majesty has lost three most respectable servants in Mr Malone, Mr Clements and Mr Tisdale (2078), men not easily replac'd.' Remembering the struggles of the early 1750s when he had been Chief Secretary, Lord George may well have smiled.

DIVISION LISTS:
   1749 (1) voted against the election of James Digges La Touche (♦♦♦♦).
   1753 (1) voted for the expulsion of Arthur Jones-Nevill (1125).
   1753 (2) voted for the Money Bill.
   1753 (3) voted for the Money Bill.
   1757 (1) voted against the resolutions on Pensions.
   1768 (1) voted for army augmentation – Deputy Vice-Treasurer and PC.
   1771 (1) voted for Lord Townshend as Lord Lieutenant.
   1771 (2) voted against Sir Lucius O'Brien's (1558) motion for retrenchment – a placeman.
   1772 (2) voted against a Short Revenue Bill.
   1773 (1) voted for Absentee Tax.
   1773 (2) voted against an untaxed press.
   1774 (2) voted for Catholic relief.
   1775 (1) voted against the pro-American amendment to the Speech from the Throne.

ADDITIONAL INFORMATION: *A member of the Dublin Society from 1738. On 7 August 1746 he was granted a pension of £150 p.a. in trust for the children of the late John Clements, presumably the father of 0413. He also looked after another nephew (0417), the son of his brother Robert, whom he launched in the world at the cost of c. £1,000 and had just brought into parliament for Cavan when the young man was killed in 1747, much to Clements' annoyance.

Giving a glimpse of family relations, he refers, in a letter of 21 May 1747 to Chief Secretary Weston, to the death of his sister in Toulon: 'She made a will and died a Papist, and has left all her effects to a priest to pray for her soul, so that I don't think she is any loss – my nephew gets £400 against a jointure she had.'

ESTATES/RESIDENCE: Manor Hamilton and Bohey, Co. Leitrim; Ashfield, Co. Cavan; Woodville, Co. Dublin; 7 Henrietta Street, Dublin. He purchased the Co. Donegal estates of Viscount Boyne in 1743. He is believed to have designed a number of houses in Dublin and elsewhere. When Ranger of the Phoenix Park he designed and build a lodge there as his residence.

In 1755 Clements succeeded Gardiner as Vice-Treasurer and gathered by degrees an immense fortune. He shared with Gardiner an interest in urban development, and was involved for many years in the development of Georgian Dublin. He employed, or worked with, Edward Lovett Pearce and Richard Castle, as contractors and fellow architects.

A 1750 survey of the estate of Nathaniel Clements in the parishes of Mohill and Clune indicates that the Mohill estate contained 2,204 Irish acres of arable, pasture and wood and 1,396 of bog and the Clune estate contained 1,407 and 536. Grand total was 6,112 Irish acres, including 568 of water. One of the neighbouring landowners was Loftus Hume Esq. The Ashfield estate in Co. Cavan, with a rental of *c.* £2,924 p.a., he left to his second son, Rt Hon. Henry Theophilus Clements (**0412**).

SOURCES: PRONI D/302; NLI 14 A 16; *CJ Ire.* (Bradley ed.) vol. 7 p. 258; PRONI T/3158/769 1309 Chatsworth Papers; PRONI T/3019/844 873, 916, / 6456/329 Wilmot Papers; McCracken thesis; Ellis thesis; Hughes, *Pat. Officers*; Burke *IFR* (1976) pp. 246–7; *Index to Irish Privy Counsellors, 1711–1910*; B. De Breffny and Rosemary Ffolliott, *The Houses of Ireland* (Dublin, 1975), pp. 129–32; D. Guinness and W. Ryan, *Irish Houses and Castles* (London, 1971), pp 109–10; J. O'Brien & D. Guinness, *Dublin: a Grand Tour* (1994), pp. 70, 114; S. J. Conolly, *Religion, Law and Power …* (1992), p. 64; D. Dickson (ed.), *The Gorgeous Mask: Dublin 1700–1850* (1987), p. 30; *Boulter Letters* vol. 1 p. 204; Llandover, *Delany Correspondence*, vol. 3 pp. 551–2; *HMC Stopford-Sackville I* pp. 211–2, 213, 223, 225–6, 228–9, 231, 246; *EHR* (Oct. 1905) pp. 736–7, 754–9, C. L. Falkiner, 'Correspondence of Archbishop Stone and the Duke of Newcastle'; Moody & Vaughan (eds) *A New History of Ireland* (1986), p. 70, J. L. McCracken, 'The Political Structure 1714–60', and pp. 155–7, L. M. Cullen, 'Economic Development 1691–1750'; J. Walton, *'The King's Business': Letters on the Administration of Ireland, 1741–61 …* (N.Y.,1996) no. 16, 18, 145, 159, 181 [Waite's memo.]; R. E. Burns, *Irish Parliamentary Politics in the Eighteenth Century*, 2 vols (Washington, 1989) vol. 2 pp. 172, 170–80, 185–7, 190–1, 209, 280–2; G. O'Brien (ed.), *Parliament, Politics and People* (1989), pp. 58, 60, S. Murphy, 'The Dublin Anti-Union Riot of 3 December 1759'; Johnston, *Gt B. & Ire.*, p. 120; *Ir. Gen.* vol. 5 no. 4 (1977) p. 483, H. F. Morris, 'Ramsey's Waterford

Chronicle, 1777'; *JRSAI* vol. 38 (1908) pp. 388, 389, J. Meehan, 'Catalogue of the High Sheriffs of the County of Leitrim from the Year 1605 to the Year 1800' [says incorrectly that he was MP for Cavan Borough from 1763 to 1777]; *Almanacks*; *BNL* 30 Mar. 1759, 20 Feb. 1767; *Pue's Occurrences* 27 Mar. 1742; *DJ* 11–14 Oct. 1755; Parliamentary Lists, 1769 (1), 1772 (2), 1773 (1), (2), 1774 (1), 1775 (1), 1776 (1), (2), 1777 (1).

0415 CLEMENTS, Rt Hon. Nathaniel

MP for Carrick 1790–7; Co. Leitrim 1797–1800 [r. Roscommon B. 1790; Cavan B. and Carrick 1797]; [UK] 1801–4

b. 9 May 1768; d. 31 Dec. 1854
HONOURS: PC, sworn 31 Oct. 1834; Knight of St Patrick 8 Apr. 1834.
PEERAGES: Styled Viscount Clements 1795–1804; suc. as 2nd Earl of Leitrim 1804; cr. Baron Clements [UK] 20 June 1831.
FAMILY/BACKGROUND: Son of Rt Hon. Robert Clements, 1st Earl of Leitrim (**0418**) and Elizabeth, dau. of Rt Hon. Clotworthy Skeffington, 1st Earl of Massereene.
MARRIED: [24 July 1800] Mary (d. 1840), e. dau. and co-h. of William Bermingham of Ross Hill, Co. Galway.
CHILDREN: Robert Bermingham (b. 1805; d. unm. 24 Jan. 1849); William Sydney (b. 1806; murdered 2 Apr. 1878), 3rd Earl of Leitrim; Capt. Charles Skeffington (b. 1807; d. unm. 29 Sept 1877); George Robert Anson RN (d. unm. 1877); Rev. Francis Nathaniel, m. (1) Charlotte (d. 23 Oct. 1868) dau. of Rev. Gilbert King of Langfield, Co. Tyrone, (2) Amelia e. dau. of Sir William Verner, 1st Baronet.
EDUCATION: School: private school, Portarlington; entered Oxford (Oriel College) 22 July 1785, aged 17 years, BA 1788.
CAREER/OCCUPATION: Custos Rot. Counties of Leitrim and Donegal 1795; High Sheriff of Co. Leitrim 1796; Lord Lieutenant of Co. Leitrim 1851.
MILITARY: Colonel of the Donegal Regiment 22 June 1796 until disbanded in 1802.

POLITICAL ACTIVITY: The grandson of Nathaniel Clements (**0414**), he was nicknamed 'The Prophet' by Lord Shannon (**0213**). He came into parliament for the family borough of Carrick but in 1797 was returned for Co. Leitrim, which he also represented at Westminster until 1804, when he succeeded his father (**0418**) as 2nd Earl of Leitrim, although as an Irish peer he could have continued to sit in the UK parliament. He was involved in trying to put down the 1798 rebellion in Wexford. In general he voted the family line (*see* **0412**) but, unlike his father, he opposed the Union, possibly influenced by his friendship with George Ponsonby (**1699**). He was expected to support at Westminster, but he made no mark there. In 1804 he was still thought 'disposed to act with the Ponsonbys and Lord Charlemont'. He aspired to a representative peerage, and the Grenville ministry was disposed to support him. But he was disappointed by ensuing administrations which disliked his opposition politics. His political friends rewarded him with a British peerage in 1831.

DIVISION LISTS:
1790 (2) absent (tied).
1791 (1) voted for Curran's (**0560**) resolution against the sale of peerages.
1791 (2) voted for Grattan's (**0895**) motion for the exercise of free trade.
1799 (1) voted against the Union – Colonel, Donegal Regiment ('Has £4,000 p.a. in landed property or is heir apparent to it').
1800 (1) voted against the Union.

ADDITIONAL INFORMATION: A member of Daly's Club.

ESTATES/RESIDENCE: Killadoon, Celbridge, Co. Kildare; Manor Hamilton, Co. Leitrim; Mary Street, Dublin.

SOURCES: PRONI T/3166/1B Hartnell notes; RCBL P80/1/1 Parish Registers of St Thomas, Dublin [bapt. 10 June 1768]; Jupp thesis; O'Neill thesis; GEC *P*; Burke *PB* (1903) p. 918 (1906) p. 990; *Alum. Oxon.*; *Index to Irish Privy Counsellors, 1711–1910*; *HP 1790–1820*; E. Hewitt (ed.), *Lord Shannon's Letters to his Son* (PRONI 1982) pp. xxii, 122, 132, 177, 207; *FJ* 10 Mar. 1796; Parliamentary Lists, 1790 (1), 1791 (1), 1793 (1), 1794 (2), 1799 (3), 1800 (3).

0416 CLEMENTS, Robert

MP for Newry 1715–22

b. 1664; d. 29 Dec. 1722
FAMILY/BACKGROUND: Son of Daniel Clements of Rathkenny, Co. Cavan (a cornet in Cromwell's army).
MARRIED: Elizabeth, dau. of Gen. Theophilus Sandford of Moyglare, Co. Meath.
CHILDREN: Theophilus (**0419**); Robert; Nathaniel (**0414**); Francis.
CAREER/OCCUPATION: High Sheriff of Co. Cavan 1694; ?Trustee of the Linen Board for Ulster 10 Oct. 1711; Deputy Vice-Treasurer for Ireland.

POLITICAL ACTIVITY: Very little is known about this MP. He was already over 50 years of age when he entered parliament, and was listed as a placeman in 1719.

ADDITIONAL INFORMATION: He was possibly the R. Clements who was listed among the foundation members of the Dublin Philosophical Society.

ESTATES/RESIDENCE: Rathkenny, Co. Cavan.

SOURCES: PRONI T/1075 Canon Leslie's notes [says his will is dated 7 June 1722 and pr. 1 Feb. 1722/3]; PRONI T/3019/916 Wilmot Papers; RCBL GS 2/7/3/44, Prerogative Marriage Licences; PRONI T/559 vol. 15 p. 344, Burke, extract pedigrees; *PB* (1906) p. 990; *LGI* (1904) p. 95; *IFR* (1976) pp. 246–7 [says probably incorrectly that his elder brother was born in 1687]; J. T. Gilbert, *History of the City of Dublin*, 3 vols (1861) vol. 2 p. 174; *Memorials of the Dead*; Parliamentary List, 1719 (1).

0417 CLEMENTS, Robert

MP for Cavan B. 1745–7

b. (bapt. 30 July) 1724; d. (June–July) 1747
FAMILY/BACKGROUND: Son of Robert Clements and Susanna Dobbs.
MARRIED: Unmarried.
CHILDREN: *d.s.p.*
CAREER/OCCUPATION: Military: An officer in Dejean's regiment.

POLITICAL ACTIVITY: During his brief period in parliament he was listed for 14 committees. His uncle Nathaniel (**0414**) lamented his death in the war, writing to Edward Weston (**2223**), Chief Secretary to Lord Lieutenant Harrington, on 14 July 1747: 'I have been very unfortunate in this war. I have lost my nephew that was in Dejean's Regiment. He was a very valuable young man ... I shall lose near £1,000 by his death, for I have constantly paid for his education and bought his commission and he had but just got into the possession of the estate by the death of his aunt and he was only tenant for life. This comes hard upon me, who has so many children to provide for. If he had lived I should have thought myself well paid.' On his death Clements offered his seat for Cavan to Weston, which was 'readily accepted'.

ESTATES/RESIDENCE: Rathkenny, Co. Cavan.

SOURCES: PRONI T/3019/916, Nathaniel Clements to Chief Secretary Weston 14 July 1747, Wilmot Papers; RCBL P277/1/1 Parish Registers of St Mary's, Dublin [says he is Francis Robert and was born (bapt. 30 July) 1724]; McCracken thesis; J. Walton, 'The King's Business': Letters on the Administration of Ireland, 1741–61 ... (NY, 1996), no. 18, 19, 20.

0418 CLEMENTS, Rt Hon. Robert

MP for Co. Donegal 1765–8, 1776–83; Carrick 1768–76 [r. Carrick 1776]

b. 25 Nov. 1732; d. 27 July 1804
HONOURS: PC, sworn 22 Apr. 1802.
PEERAGES: Cr. Baron Leitrim 11 Oct. 1783; Viscount Leitrim 20 Dec. 1793; Earl of Leitrim 6 Oct. 1795; Rep. Peer 1801–4.
FAMILY/BACKGROUND: Son of Rt Hon. Nathaniel Clements (0414) and Hannah, dau. of Rev. William Gore.
MARRIED: [31 May 1765] Elizabeth (d. 29 May 1817), dau. of Rt Hon. Clotworthy Skeffington, 1st Earl of Massereene.
CHILDREN: Rt Hon. Nathaniel, 2nd Earl of Leitrim (0415); Lieut.-Col. Robert Clotworthy (d. 1828); William Thomas; Ann (aged 12 in 1779); Elizabeth (d. 29 Dec. 1859); Louisa (d. unm. 1836); Caroline (d. 1805), m. [27 May 1802] John Thomas Townshend, 2nd Viscount Sydney.
CAREER/OCCUPATION: Commissioner of the Revenue 1772; Comptroller of the Great and Small Customs, port of Dublin 1758–d.; High Sheriff of Co. Leitrim 1759; *Commissioner of the Tillage Act for Ulster 1769–84; *Trustee of the Linen Board for Ulster Aug. 1769–1799 (f.); *Governor of the Foundling Hospital and Workhouse 1769–97; *Governor of the Hibernian Society 1769–1800 (f.); Ranger of Phoenix Park and Master of the Game 1777–d.; Governor of Co. Leitrim 1777; Custos Rot. Co. Donegal 1777–1804; Searcher, Packer and Gauger, port of Dublin 1777–1800 (f.); Foreman of the Grand Jury of Co. Leitrim, Spring Assizes 1780; *Joint Governor of Co. Leitrim 1787–94, *Governor 1795–1800 (f.); Governor of Donegal 19 Apr. 1781 (vice the Earl of Conyngham dec'd), Joint Governor 1784–1800 (f.); *Governor of the Charitable Musical Society 1780; Governor of the Charitable Loan Society 1781–1800 (f.); *Sheriff of Carrickfergus 1789–90, 1792, 1794–5; *Magistrate of Carrickfergus 1795; *Governor and Guardian of the Lying-in Hospital 1797–1800 (f.).

POLITICAL ACTIVITY: He was returned unopposed for Co. Donegal in 1765, for the family borough of Carrick 1768–76 and again for Co. Donegal in 1776–83, when he hedged by also being returned for the family borough of Cavan. At the conclusion of the parliament, in 1783, he was created Lord Leitrim. He submitted to Lord Lieutenant Townshend, in 1769, a paper on the ability of the civil and military establishments to be supported by hereditary revenue alone should the former prorogue parliament. His paper strongly opposed such an idea, arguing that a vast arrear would accrue without the additional duties. A Parliamentary List for 1772 said that he 'follows his father, but is not easily satisfied', and one of 1775 that he 'was a Commissioner of the Revenue but removed on the reuniting of the Boards. He refused his pension of £600, and affected to be offended because there had not been an earlier communication with him upon that measure. He is a peevish, shy, retired man, a bad attender, and the father pretends on some occasions that he cannot influence him. Lord Harcourt gave to his recommendation 2 Boatmen, 1 Tide waiter, and 1 Coast Officer.'

He did not have an employment until 1780, when he was made Searcher of Dublin for life and joined with his brother (0412) as Ranger of Phoenix Park for their lives. In 1782 he sold his share in the Rangership of Phoenix Park, along with the house that his father had built there, to the government for £25,000. He was recommended for a peerage first by Lord Buckinghamshire and then by Lord Carlisle, and was created Lord Leitrim on 11 October 1783. He returned Chief Secretary Pelham for the borough of Carrick. As early as 1784 it was remarked that he wanted further elevation in the peerage, and in the 1783–90 parliament he had a secure following of three in the House of Commons (0650, 0870, 1151). By 1788 he had received 'encouragement' for his ambitions. In 1793 he became a viscount and in 1795 an earl. The British peerage, however, had to wait for his successor (0415). He supported the Union, unlike his son (0415), and was made a representative peer and a Privy Counsellor.

DIVISION LISTS:

1768 (1) voted for army augmentation – Paymaster of the Pensions.

1771 (1) voted for Lord Townshend as Lord Lieutenant.

1771 (2) voted against Sir Lucius O'Brien's (1558) motion for retrenchment.

1773 (1) voted against the Absentee Tax.

1775 (1) voted against the pro-American amendment to the Speech from the Throne.

1777 (1) voted against Grattan's (0895) motion for retrenchment.

1780 (1) voted against Grattan's declaration of the rights of Ireland.

1780 (2) voted against Yelverton's (2268) motion to modify Poynings' Law.

1780 (4) voted for the Perpetual Mutiny Bill.

ADDITIONAL INFORMATION: His daughters were listed as nominees in the life annuities of 1779. He controlled the borough of Carrick and one seat in the borough of Cavan.

His house at Manor Hamilton was attacked by rebels based at Timahoe in the Bog of Allen towards the end of the 1798 rising.

ESTATES/RESIDENCE: Celbridge, Killadoon, Co. Kildare; 36 Sackville Street, Dublin; Manor Hamilton, Co. Leitrim. In 1801, the Mohill and Clune estate contained at least 4,505 Irish acres at a rental of £1,831. All the lands that can be identified are in the parish as well as the barony of Mohill (Annaghderg, Drumdoo, Selton, Roosky, Laheen, Derreen, and others that can be identified): out of a total of 40 townlands, 16 have been identified. This suggests that the whole Mohill estate may have been in that barony.

SOURCES: NLI PC 88 Clements Papers, Rental of Lord Leitrim's estate in the barony of Mohill, 25 Mar. 1801; PRONI T/3019/6459/808 Wilmot Papers; RCBL P80/1/1, Parish Registers of St Thomas, Dublin; Ellis thesis; GEC *P*; Burke *PB* (1903) p. 918; *Index to Irish Privy Counsellors, 1711–1910*; C. Ross (ed.), *Cornwallis Corr.* (London, 1859), vol. 3 p. 109 [says he married 31 May 1765]; Johnston, *Gt B. & Ire.*, p. 173; *JRSAI* vol. 38 (1908) pp. 385, 388–9, J. Meehan, 'Catalogue of the High Sheriffs of the County of Leitrim from the Year 1605 to the Year 1800' [says he is founder of the Irish family of Clements despite making reference to his father Nathaniel (0414)!]; *Ir. Gen.* vol. 1 no. 8 (1940) p. 239, 'A List of Irish Stockholders, 1779'; T. Pakenham, *The Year of Liberty* (London, 1978), p. 313; *Almanacks*; *BNL* 15 Nov. 1765; *FJ* 19–22 Aug. 1769; *DJ* 3–5 May 1781; Parliamentary Lists, 1769 (1), 1772 (2), 1773 (1), (2), 1774 (1), 1775 (1), 1776 (1), (2), (3), 1777 (1), 1778 (1), 1780 (1), 1782 (1), 1783 (1), (2), 1784 (1), 1785 (2), (4), 1787 (1), 1788 (1), 1790 (1), 1791 (1), 1793 (1), 1794 (2), 1799 (2), (3), 1800 (2).

0419 CLEMENTS, Theophilus

MP for Cavan B. 1713–14, 1715–27–8

b. 1687; d. 1728

FAMILY/BACKGROUND: Son of Robert Clements and Elizabeth, dau. of Gen. Theophilus Sandford of Moyglare, Co. Meath.

MARRIED: [*ante* 1723] Elizabeth, eldest dau. of Francis Burton (0296).

CHILDREN: *d.s.p.*

EDUCATION: School: Mr Walls, Dublin; entered TCD 10 July 1703, BA 1708, MA 1711, LLD *spec. grat.* 1718.

CAREER/OCCUPATION: Teller of the Exchequer; Freedom of Drogheda 4 Mar. 1719; High Sheriff of Co. Cavan 1726; Sovereign of Cavan.

POLITICAL ACTIVITY: He was described as 'having been honest in the worst of times' (i.e. under the Tory ministry of 1710–14). He sat on one committee in December 1713 and 62 between 1715 and 1726. In 1719 he was noted as 'a Placeman'. He voted consistently for a national bank and supported the Court candidate in the 1723 Westmeath election dispute. This dispute was heightened by the fact that Speaker Conolly (0460) and Lord Chancellor Midleton (0237) supported opposing candidates. Each side accused the other of bribery. The case went to the vote of the House, and was therefore a trial of strength between Conolly and Midleton. Conolly's candidate, Levinge (**1230**), won by only one vote, 89 to 88.

On 7 September 1723 he complained of being disturbed on part of his lands at Bulrush, Co. Meath, during time of privilege. In 1724 he was one of the Memorialists seeking to revive attempts to explain or revoke the clause in the act of Queen Anne's reign for naturalising foreign Protestants in which favour was given to the children of natural-born subjects. It was felt that the return of the children of papists who had served James II in Ireland before fleeing to Europe might endanger the estates of the present possessors. Following the accession of George II he was one of those responsible for 1 Geo. II, c. 7, an act that continued the life of parliament for six months following the king's death – either the sitting parliament or the previous parliament was to be continued. He was in receipt of a pension of £200 p.a. from Lady Day 1726 until his death in 1728.

DIVISION LISTS:

1721 (1) voted for a national bank.
1721 (2) voted for a national bank.
1723 (1) voted for the court candidate (**1230**) on the Westmeath election petition.

ADDITIONAL INFORMATION: He made an agreement to share the patronage of the borough of Cavan with Thomas Nesbitt (**1525**). It was signed on 22 March 1722, and read as follows. 'Imprimis. That the said Clements; and Nesbitt shall be sovereign, year about, of the said corporation. Mr Clements to be sovereign the next election, Midsummer 1723, and Mr Nesbitt the next year ... Secondly. That no person shall, on any pretences whatsoever be admitted to his freedom of the said corporation, without the joint consent of the said Clements and Nesbitt either personally present, or under their hands. Thirdly. That if any vacancy shall happen either by death or resignation of any burgess then Mr Clements shall first name the succeeding burgess, and then Mr Nesbitt successively, as they are to be sovereigns. Fourthly. That although each has a right to recommend a burgess in his turn in case of any vacancy, yet the vacancy shall not be filled up, unless both ... approve of the person so recommended, either personally, or, in case of absence, under their hands.'

The agreement continued until the political extinction of the borough by the Act of Union, when the £15,000 compensation was divided equally between the two families. This type of agreement was not unique: it precluded the expense of disputed elections.

ESTATES/RESIDENCE: Rathkenny, Co. Cavan. He held eight leases of Church lands in Co. Cavan which were assigned to Arthur Hill after his death. He leased church land called the Termon lands of Clonosyn (Clonosey), Anna and Kilnaleck, Knockbride, Enniskeen, Rantawin, Castlerehan and Lisegny, being lands of the Bishopric of Kilmore; the lease recites that Josiah, Bishop of Kilmore and Ardagh by lease of 2 December 1727, demised the above lands to Theophilus Clements for 21 years at an annual rent of £100 and a consideration of £1,350.

SOURCES: *CJ Ire.* (Bradley ed.) vol. 5 pp. 15, 469–77, 608, 677 (0251); PRONI D/778/64 Dungannon Papers; PRONI T/580 pp. 176g, 176h, TSPI 1723–1724; McCracken thesis; Hayton thesis; Burke *IFR* (1976) p. 246; Simms' cards [says he was Teller of the Exchequer]; Cavan MPs; Johnston, *Gt B. & Ire.*, p. 176; *JRSAI* vol. 38 (1908) p. 389, J. Meehan, 'Catalogue of the High Sheriffs of the County of Leitrim from the Year 1605 to the Year 1800'; *Municipal Corporations, Ireland, Report & App.* (1835) app. II, p. 990; Parliamentary Lists, 1719 (1).

0420 CLEMENTS, William

MP for Baltimore 1761–8

b. 1733; d. 4 June 1770 at Bath
FAMILY/BACKGROUND: Second son of Rt Hon. Nathaniel Clements (**0414**) and Hannah, dau. of Rev. William Gore.
MARRIED: Unmarried.
CAREER/OCCUPATION: Comptroller of Customs, Dublin, 2 May 1758, 17 June 1760, 24 Apr. 1761, 12 Dec. 1780; *Comptroller of Dublin Port 1758–60; Joint Deputy Vice-Treasurer 1766–8; Receiver General; *Commissioner of the Infirmary in James' Street 1766–8; *Banker of Dublin 1756–8.

POLITICAL ACTIVITY: He does not appear to have enjoyed good health or to have been active in parliament. His obituary declared that 'He was a young gentleman endowed with every amiable and good Quality, and perhaps no one more universally regarded.'

ESTATES/RESIDENCE: Dublin.

SOURCES: McCracken thesis; Hughes, *Pat. Officers*; Cork MPs; *DJ* 8–12 June 1770 [says he was the 2nd son of (**0414**)]; *Almanacks.*

0421 CLERE (*alias* CLEARE), John

MP for Fethard (Tipperary) 1727–54

b. *c.* 1690; d. 15 Mar. 1754
FAMILY/BACKGROUND: Son of Thomas Clere, of Kilbury and Ester [   ].
MARRIED: Margaret Clutterbuck.
CHILDREN: Mary, dau. and h., m. [28 June 1754] Sir William Parsons, 4th Baronet (**1639**).
CAREER/OCCUPATION: Burgess of Fethard (Tipperary), 10 June 1718–54, Freeman 6 July 1719, Sovereign 7 Sept. 1720, 28 June 1742, 7 May–25 July 1753.

POLITICAL ACTIVITY: He was indirectly involved in a counterfeiting scandal when Thomas Ridge, subsequently tried at the bar of the House of Commons, 11 February 1732, used Clere's name in the franking of letters. Very little is known about him: he was not a very energetic MP, being listed for only eight committees between 1727 and 1747.

DIVISION LISTS:
1753 (1) voted for the expulsion of Arthur Jones-Nevill (**1125**).

ESTATES/RESIDENCE: Kilbury, Co. Tipperary.

SOURCES: Burke, *Extinct Baronetage* [Cleres of Ormsby, Norfolk]; Michael O'Donnell Esq. [says probably the son of Thomas Clere (**0422**) and also that he died 10 Mar. 1754]; RCBL GS 2/7/3/44, Kilmore Marriage Licence Books [says a John Clere married Catherine Mathias, lic. dated 1686 – he would have been too young]; Burke *PB* (1906) p. 1408; McCracken thesis; *GM* (Exshaw's edition) Mar. 1754; *Ir. Gen.* vol. 4 no. 6 (1973) pp. 616–24, W. G. Skehan, 'Freemen of the Corporation of Fethard, Co. Tipperary' [says he was made Free Burgess *ante* 1718 and was of Drangan]; *DJ* 19 Mar. 1754. In *CJ Ire.* lists, father and son spell their name differently.

0422 CLERE (*alias* CLEARE or CLEERE), Thomas

MP for Fethard (Tipperary) 1692–3

b. *ante* 1658; d. 6 Jan. 1705
FAMILY/BACKGROUND: Eldest son of Col. Thomas Cleere of Dangan and his wife Patience, dau. of [   ] Stone of Cellbridge, Co. Kildare.
MARRIED: Ester [   ].
CHILDREN: Thomas (b. 1680; d. aged 11 1691]; John (**0421**).
CAREER/OCCUPATION: Deputy Governor of Co. Tipperary 1699; Burgess of Clonmel 1695.
MILITARY: Styled Colonel; Lieutenant in William III's army in 1690.

POLITICAL ACTIVITY: A professional soldier, he almost certainly fought at the Battle of the Boyne, and probably in William III's subsequent Irish campaigns. He sought re-election for Fethard in 1695 but was not returned, and his subsequent petition against an undue election was rejected.

ADDITIONAL INFORMATION: Described as 'a person of principal consideration in the town of Clonmel', it was stated that 'He lies under some hardships which are not to be suffered towards such a person.'

ESTATES/RESIDENCE: Kilburry, Co. Tipperary.

SOURCES: Information from Michael O'Donnell Esq.; *CJ Ire.*, vol. 2, 583, 647, 678; Simms' cards; *Memorials of the Dead*; *JRSAI* vol. 55 (1925) pp. 39, 52, H. A. S. Upton, 'A List of Governors and Deputy Governors of Counties in Ireland in 1699' [says he died 6 Jan. 1705].

CLERMONT, Baron, Viscount and Earl of: *see* FORTESCUE

0798 Fortescue, Rt Hon. William Henry, 1st Baron Clermont, Viscount Clermont, Earl of Clermont, MP Co. Louth 1745–60, Monaghan B. 1761–8–70

0797 Fortescue, William Charles, 2nd Viscount Clermont, MP Co. Louth 1786–7–1800, [UK] 1801–6

CLIFDEN, Baron and Viscount: *see* **AGAR**

0016 Agar, Rt Hon. James, 1st Baron Clifden, Viscount Clifden, MP Gowran 1753–60, 1776, Co. Kilkenny 1761–8–76

0013 Agar (-Ellis), Hon. Henry Welbore, 2nd Viscount Clifden, 2nd Baron Mendip [GB], MP Co. Kilkenny 1783–9, [GB] Heytesbury 1793–1802

0423 CLIFFE, John

MP for Bannow 1692–3, 1695–9, 1703–13–14, 1715–27

b. 3 May 1661; d. 1728

FAMILY/BACKGROUND: Son of John Cliffe and Eleanor, dau. of Nicholas Loftus.

MARRIED: [1694] Barbara, eldest dau. and heiress of William Carr of Cork city.

CHILDREN: John, m. [9 Jan. 1728] Jane, e. dau. of his cousin Henry Cliffe of Surrey; William, m. his cousin Eleanor, dau. of Richard Vigors of Co. Carlow; Maj. Anthony; Edward (d. yg); George; Edward; Loftus, m. Anne dau. of William Hore of Co. Wexford; Henry (d. yg); Henry; Eleanor, m. Charles Tottenham (**2086**); Barbara, m. Arthur Gifford of Co. Cork; Anne; Elizabeth; Mary, m. John Leigh (**1220**).

EDUCATION: School: Mr Ryder; entered TCD 21 Aug. 1680.

CAREER/OCCUPATION: 3rd Serjeant-at-Law 29 Nov. 1711; 2nd Serjeant-at-law 12 Feb. 1713; Commissioner for raising money by loan for William III in Co. Wexford 1695 and 1698; Freeman and Burgess of New Ross 16 July 1690 – 29 June 1727; elected Recorder of New Ross 16 July 1690, re-elected 29 June 1695, resigned 2 Jan. 1728 and re-elected 12 Apr. 1728.

POLITICAL ACTIVITY: He was a professional lawyer, who represented the Wexford borough of Bannow continuously for 35 years in parliaments called by three successive sovereigns. He supported the government consistently during that time. In 1695 he voted for Lord Chancellor Porter against the accusations of favouring Catholics made against him by some MPs, and in 1696 he signed the Association for the protection of William III in parliament. He was listed for one committee on

30 August 1695, for 48 during the reign of Queen Anne and for eight between 1715 and 1723, when he would have been over 60 years of age.

In 1705 he introduced what became 4 Anne, c. 7, 'An act for lessening the Duty on Rape Seed to be exported' – it was reduced to 4s a ton. He also introduced 4 Anne, c. 12, which attempted to 'Prevent Disputes and Contraversies concerning Royal Mines'. His interests appear to have been in organised economic development. In 1707, he was one of the 34 Tory MPs who met at the Fleece Tavern in Dublin to consolidate government strategy for the ensuing session. In 1711, when he was appointed Third Serjeant, he was a noted Court supporter, and two years later when he was advanced to Second Serjeant it was stated, correctly, that not only was he a Tory but he probably had a safe seat. Certainly he had a strong sense of local responsibility, for as Recorder of New Ross, with a salary of £8, in January 1710 he is recorded as giving £3 of this salary to the town 'till it is out of debt'.

Following the 1713 election he voted for Sir Richard Levinge (**1230**), the Court candidate for Speaker. At the death of Queen Anne, he was on the black list of Tories. Nevertheless, he sat in the parliament of George I, although he appears to have kept a fairly low profile. His legal offices ceased with the queen's death in 1714.

DIVISION LISTS:

1711 (1) a teller for the Court on the Dublin mayoralty issue.

1713 (1) voted for Sir Richard Levinge (**1230**) for Speaker.

1721 (1) voted against a national bank.

ADDITIONAL INFORMATION: His son John was Magistrate of New Ross, 1739–40, 1753, 1748, 1757–8, 1765, 1767–9; Sovereign, 1739–40; Recorder, 1748, 1757–8, 1765, 1767–9.

ESTATES/RESIDENCE: Mulrankin Hall, Dungulph Castle, New Ross, Co. Wexford. There is a grant of 20 Chas II (1669) to John Cliffe and Daniel Foley of lands of Mulrankin, Ballycormick and Lakes, barony of Bargy. In 1713 the income of John Cliffe, Second Serjeant at Law, was estimated at £400.

SOURCES: *CJ Ire.* (Bradley ed.) vol. 3 pp. 128, 316–7 (0088, 0093); PRONI T/3411 Blenheim Papers; EC 528; Burke

LGI (1904) pp. 95–6; Hughes, *Pat. Officers; Alum. Dub.*; Vicars, *Prerog. Wills*; Simms' cards; *Ir. Gen.* vol. 6 no. 6 (Nov. 1985) pp. 23, 711, A. Dusek, 'Baptisms in St Bride's, Dublin, 1633–1713' [gives a John son of John Cliff baptised 25 Oct. 1664]; *JRSAI* vol. 22 (1892) p. 300, P. D. Vigors, 'Alphabetical List of Free Burgesses of New Ross...1658–1839...'; *JRSAI* vol. 31 (1901) pp. 52–3, 61, 69, P. D. Vigors, 'Extracts from the Old Corporation Books of New Ross, County Wexford'; *Almanacks*; Parliamentary Lists, 1695 (1), 1696 (1), 1706 (1), 1707 (2), 1711 (3), 1713 (1), (2), 1714–15 (1).

CLIFTON, Baron: *see* **BLIGH**
0172 Bligh, John, 1st Baron Clifton, Viscount Darnley, Earl of Darnley, MP Trim 1709–13, Athboy 1713–14, 1715–21
0173 Bligh, John, 3rd Earl of Darnley, MP Athboy 1739–47, [GB] Maidstone 1741–7

CLONBROCK, Baron: *see* **DILLON**
0637 Dillon, Robert, 1st Baron Clonbrock, MP Lanesborough 1776–83–90

CLONCURRY, Baron: *see* **LAWLESS**
1209 Lawless, Sir Nicholas, 1st Baron Cloncurry, MP Lifford 1776–83–9

CLONMELL, Viscount and Earl of: *see* **SCOTT**
1891 Scott, Rt Hon. John, 1st Baron Earlsfort, Viscount Clonmell, Earl of Clonmell, MP Mullingar 1769–76–83, Portarlington 1783–4

CLONMORE, Baron: *see* **HOWARD**
1044 Howard, Rt Hon. Ralph, 1st Baron Clonmore, Viscount Wicklow, MP Co. Wicklow 1761–8–76

1046 Howard, Hon. Robert, 2nd Viscount Wicklow, 2nd Earl of Wicklow, MP St Johnstown (Donegal) 1783–9

0424 CLUTTERBUCK, Rt Hon. Thomas

MP for Lisburn 1725–7–42; [GB] Liskeard 1722–34; Plympton 1734–42

> b. 1697; d. 23 Nov. 1742
> HONOURS: PC 1724, 1733 (sworn 22 Oct. 1724, resworn 19 Nov. 1727, 24 Nov. 1727); [GB] 24 June 1742.
> FAMILY/BACKGROUND: Son of Thomas Clutterbuck of Ingatestone, Essex, and Bridget, dau. of Sir Thomas Exton.
> MARRIED: [4 May 1731] Henrietta Cuffe, dau. of Lionel Tollemache, Lord Huntingtower.
> CHILDREN: 1 s., 3 dau.
> EDUCATION: School: Westminster under Friend; entered Oxford [Christ Church] 20 Oct. 1713, aged 16; Middle Temple 1713.
> CAREER/OCCUPATION: Secretary to Lord Lieutenant 6 May 1724 – 22 June 1730; Lord of Admiralty [GB] 1732–41; Lord of Treasury [GB] 1741–2; Treasurer of Navy [GB] 17 May 1742–d; Freedom of Cork.

POLITICAL ACTIVITY: Clutterbuck was a protégé and a near relation of Lord Lieutenant Carteret, who brought him over as his Chief Secretary. He was nominated for eight committees 1725–6 and for a further eight 1727–30. The Court gossip, Lord Hervey, described him as 'sensible beloved and had a good character, but was lazy indolent and mute, and of no use in parliament but counting one in a division'. Arriving at the height of the Wood's Halfpence furore, his situation was not always easy, particularly as he tried to control some of the literary activities of Dean Swift.

In 1729, immediately following the death of Speaker Conolly (**0460**), the British Privy Council made a few unsubstantial alterations in one of the Revenue Bills – apparently they had previously been discussed in the Irish House of Commons and considered unnecessary. Clutterbuck did not really understand the sensitivity of the Irish parliament on the subject of Revenue Bills, let alone alterations to them made in the British Privy Council, and, moreover, he missed the guidance of Conolly, complaining of the difficulties that ensued from 'serving under a government that has neither power nor party to support it, but is left at the mercy of a parliament.' On his return to England he attached himself to Walpole and the Duke of Newcastle. He was essentially an English politician.

ESTATES/RESIDENCE: Dublin Castle; St Martin's in the Fields, Middlesex.

SOURCES: McCracken thesis; *Alum. Oxon.*; G. F. Russell-Barker and A. H. Stenning (eds), *Record of Old Westminsters: A biographical list* (London, 1928) 2 vols [says he married the dau. of the 4th Earl of Dysart]; R. E. Burns, *Irish Parliamentary Politics in the Eighteenth Century*, 2 vols (Washington, 1989) vol. 1, pp. 162, 179, 181 257; P. McNally, *Parties, Patriots & Undertakers ...* (Dublin, 1997) pp. 137–8; *HP 1715–54*; *Index to Irish Privy Counsellors, 1711–1910*; *Almanacks*.

0425 COBBE, Charles

MP for Swords 1783–90, Jan.–July 1798

> b. 1756; d. 9 July 1798
> FAMILY/BACKGROUND: Son of Thomas Cobbe (0426) and Eliza, dau. of Marcus Beresford, 1st Earl of Tyrone (0118).
> MARRIED: [1778] Anne Power, dau. of Richard Trench (2109).
> CHILDREN: Charles m. [1809] Frances o. dau. of Capt. Thomas Conway of Surrey; Gen. George, m. Amelia, dau. of Rev. Royston Barton; Rev. Henry; Col. Thomas Alexander (HEICS), m. Nuzeer Begum dau. of Azeeze Khan of Kashmir; Capt. William Power RN, m. Elizabeth Bridget, dau. of Richard Fortescue Sharkey (1902).
> CAREER/OCCUPATION: High Sheriff of Co. Louth 1785.
> MILITARY: Captain, 3rd Company of Bath Volunteers.

POLITICAL ACTIVITY: He sat for the potwalloping borough of Swords, which, despite the size of its electorate, was the most notoriously corrupt borough in the Irish parliament. He owed his seat to his uncle, John Beresford (0115), and usually voted with the Beresford party. In 1788 it was noted that 'He seldom attends but would if summoned. For.' In the 1780s there appears to have been a conflict between the Beresford interest and

that of General Massy (1354) for the control of the borough. The two parties settled the 'legions of the army' and the 'locusts of the Revenue' in the town. Ultimately neither was successful; the compensation for the borough's disfranchisement at the Union was claimed by nearly 40 people either singly or collectively and the commissioners allocated the £15,000 plus interest to be invested for the maintenance of a school and other good purposes within the borough. Its oversight was entrusted to a committee of dignitaries, which included the Bishop of Kildare and the Provost of TCD for the time being.

DIVISION LISTS:
> 1783 (1) voted against Flood's (0762) motion for parliamentary reform.
> 1784 (1) voted against a committee on the Reform Bill.
> 1785 (2) absent.

ESTATES/RESIDENCE: Newbridge House, Co. Dublin; Swords, Co. Dublin; Gardiner's Row, Dublin; [?]Dowdstown, Co. Louth, 1785.

SOURCES: PRONI D/302; Information from Hugh Cobbe Esq. of Fox House, East Woodhay, Hampshire; PRONI T/3166/1B Hartnell notes; O'Neill thesis [says he was born 1767]; Burke *LGI* (1912) p. 118, *IFR* (1976) p. 248, *LG* (1846) p. 237; D. Guinness and W. Ryan (eds), *Irish Houses and Castles* (London, 1971) p. 151; *JRSAI* vol. 32 (1902) p. 173, R. Cochrane, 'On Some Monuments and Inscriptions in Bath Relating to Irish Persons'; *FJ* 1–3 Feb. 1785; Parliamentary Lists, 1783 (2), 1784 (1), (2), (3), 1785 (1), (2), 1787 (1), 1788 (1), 1789 (1), 1790 (1).

0426 COBBE, Thomas

MP for Swords 1759–60, 1761–8, 1776–83 [n.d.e. 1768]

> b. 1733; d. 1814
> FAMILY/BACKGROUND: Only surviving son of Charles Cobbe, Abp of Dublin, and Dorothea, dau. of Rt Hon. Sir Richard Levinge (1230).
> MARRIED: [1 May 1755] Elizabeth, dau. of Marcus Beresford, 1st Earl of Tyrone (0118).
> CHILDREN: Charles (0425); Catherine, m. [1788] Hon. Henry Pelham; Elizabeth Dorothea, m. [Nov. 1784] Sir Henry Tuite, 8th Baronet.

EDUCATION: School: Winchester College; entered TCD 25 Sept. 1749, aged 16 years, BA 1753, LLD *hon. caus.* 1754; MA Oxford 14 Jan. 1754.
CAREER/OCCUPATION: *Registrar in the Consistory Court of Dublin 1761–2; Governor of the Workhouse 1755–68; Foundling Hospital and Workhouse 1769–97; *member of the Committee of Fifteen in the High Sheriff of Co. Dublin 1758; Incorporated Society of Dublin (Charter Schools) 1758–63; *Governor of St Patrick's Hospital 1758–88; *Governor of Dr Steevens' Hospital 1758–1800 (f.); Governor of Swift's Hospital for lunatics Jan. 1761; Trustee of the Linen Board for Ulster June 1765–1800 (f.); *elected to Court of Assistants 1766–9; *Governor of the Charitable Musical Society 1780; *Governor of the Charitable Loan Society 1781–3; ?Sheriff of Co. Louth 5 Feb. 1785; elected Librarian of St Sepulchre's Library 1 Feb. 1762; Keeper of the Public Library, Dublin 1763–7.
MILITARY: Colonel of Militia.

POLITICAL ACTIVITY: He sat for the infamous borough of Swords: at the 1761 election he received 76 votes, John Hatch (**0987**) 80, Adam Williams 71, and Hamilton Gorges (**0882**) 69. A number of the votes cast for each of the candidates were declared invalid, and Cobbe and Gorges were duly elected with 56 votes respectively, the others having 35 valid votes each.

The 1768 general election for Swords was disputed between Cobbe, Hamilton Gorges, John Hatch and John Damer (**0576**). Cobbe and Gorges were eventually found not duly elected: 'The returning officer closed the books on Wednesday on account of a riot, but Hatch says none saw the riot but themselves [Gorges and Cobbe] and it will certainly come before the House and be a trial of skill. I do in truth believe Hatch bribed very high.'

Cobbe was returned in 1776 but 'much hurt in his circumstances', although he had 'a good estate' – a subsequent list estimated it at £3–400 (?3,000–4,000) p.a. He was a brother-in-law of John Beresford (**0115**) and the Marquess of Waterford (**0113**). Their influence assisted his return and he tended to follow their political lead, although he could act independently, but he was still 'inclined however to support'. In 1783 his son (**0425**) was elected in his place – also with the Beresford influence.

DIVISION LISTS:

1768 (1) voted for army augmentation.
1777 (1) voted against Grattan's (**0895**) motion for retrenchment.
1778 (2) voted for the Popery Bill.
1779 (2) voted for a six-months Loan Bill.
1780 (2) voted against Yelverton's (**2268**) motion to modify Poynings' Law.
1780 (3) voted against the Tenantry Bill.
1780 (4) voted for the Perpetual Mutiny Bill.

ADDITIONAL INFORMATION: *A member of the RDS from 1754.

ESTATES/RESIDENCE: Newbridge, Co. Dublin; 17 Rutland Square, Dublin.

SOURCES: PRONI D/302; PRONI T/3200/1/14 Arran Papers; RCBL P45/2/3, Parish Registers of St Peter's, Dublin; RCBL P80/1/1, Parish Registers of St Thomas, Dublin; NAI MFCI Reel 13, Parish Registers of Clonegam, Co. Waterford; McCracken thesis; Hughes, *Pat. Officers;* Burke *LG* (1846) p. 237, *IFR* (1976) p. 248; P. and B. Rowan (antiquarian booksellers), *The Eighteenth Century: An Irish Perspective* (Belfast, 1986) no. 80; *Almanacks; DJ* 29 Apr.–3 May 1755, 20–24 Jan., 18–21, 21–5 Apr. 1761, 2–6 Feb. 1762; *FJ* 25–9 June 1765, 1 July 1796; Parliamentary Lists, 1776 (1), 1776 (2), (3), 1777 (1), 1778 (1), 1780 (1), 1782 (1), 1783 (1).

0427 CODDINGTON, Dixie

MP for Dunleer 1762–8–76

b. 1727; d. *c.* (Sept.) 1792
FAMILY/BACKGROUND: Eldest son of Nicholas Coddington of Drogheda and Mary, dau. of Henry Tenison (**2053**).
MARRIED: [1754] Catherine, dau. of Thomas Burgh (**0282**).
CHILDREN: Henry; Dixie (d. 1787); 7 dau. (all d. yg).
EDUCATION: School: Mr Skelton; entered TCD 27 May 1743, aged 16 years, BA 1747.
CAREER/OCCUPATION: Chief Serjeant-at-Arms, 1768–92, 1786–7; Joint Serjeant, with son Dixie Coddington jr (John McClintock (**1314**) was appointed Principal Serjeant 5 May 1789 and reappointed 12 Sept. 1792); High Sheriff of Co. Meath 1754; *Governor of the Charitable Loan Society 1762–3; Vice-President of the Charitable

Musical Society 1763; *Governor of the Foundling Hospital and Workhouse 1769–75; *Governor of the Hibernian Society 1769–6.

MILITARY: Captain, 9th Dragoons, commissioned 1760.

POLITICAL ACTIVITY: Dixie Coddington was brought in by his uncle, Thomas Tenison (**2055**), Second Justice of the Common Pleas. Judge Tenison had half the borough of Dunleer; the Foster (**0804**) family had the other half. Coddington had a strong streak of independence but was controlled by his uncle. The 1775 Parliamentary List sums up his conduct as follows: 'Nephew to Judge Tenison and much connected with Mr Ponsonby (**1702**). Constantly opposed Lord Townshend. During the last session he was as marked in his support of Lord Harcourt. He is independent of Mr Ponsonby.' The reason for this last statement may be that the office of Serjeant-at-Arms, although held for life, was in the gift of the Speaker and by 1775 Ponsonby, who had appointed him, had ceased to be Speaker.

He was probably becoming infirm about 1786 when his son, who died the following year, was joined with him in the office. Although Hughes, *Patentee Officers Ireland 1173–1826*, says that John M'Clintock (McClintock, **1314**) was appointed Principal Serjeant-at-Arms on 5 May 1789 and again on 12 September 1792, it appears probable that in 1789 M'Clintock was joined with Dixie Coddington and took over the active duties of Dixie Coddington Jr. On 30 January 1792 the Commons declared that Dixie Coddington was unable to discharge his duties as Serjeant-at-Arms on account of his infirmities. A motion was passed requesting the king to reward Coddington for 'his very long and dutiful services' and this was resolved *nem. con.* on 1 February 1792, the House offering to make good to His Majesty any provision that he should choose to make. Coddington probably died within the following six months, as M'Clintock was reappointed on 12 September 1792.

DIVISION LISTS:

1768 (1) absent, abroad.
1771 (2) voted for Sir Lucius O'Brien's (**1558**) motion for retrenchment.
1773 (1) voted against an untaxed press.

1773 (1) voted for Absentee Tax.
1774 (2) voted for Catholic relief.
1775 (1) voted for the pro-American amendment to the Speech from the Throne.

ADDITIONAL INFORMATION: *A member of the Dublin Society from 1766. He was appointed one of the commissioners for making a canal from Trim to Drogheda in 1787.

There are problems in sorting out the multiplicity of Dixie Coddingtons: this resolution relies on Hughes, Patentee Officers and Dixie Coddington Jr's obituary notice in the *Dublin Journal*, 28 April–1 May 1787. According to the *Commons Journals*, this MP was definitely alive but very frail in February 1792.

ESTATES/RESIDENCE: Oldbridge and Tankardstown, Co. Meath. In 1703 Lord Ranelagh leased Grange and other lands in the manor of Dorranstown to Dixie Coddington of Holmpatrick, Co. Dublin. In 1707, the manor contained 1,263 acres. This may correspond to the lands of Betaghstown, Neillstown, Dormstown (Dorhamstowne/Dorranstown), Bogstown and Grange, parish of Ardbraccan, which contained 1,377 acres in 1792 and belonged to Henry Coddington. The lands comprising the Oldbridge estate were 1,892 acres in 1711 when they were part of the estate of Henry Moore, 3rd Earl of Drogheda. The lands of Stalleen, Oldbridge, Sheephouse, Donore and Ramullen, 1,892 acres in 1711, were also part of the estate of Henry, Earl of Drogheda. The lands of Tankardstown etc. (470 profitable acres in 1715) were inherited through marriage into the Osborn family of Drogheda. There is also mention of the lands of Ballydugan and Ornelstown in 1737. The lands of Betaghstown, Neillstown and Dormanstown (Dorranstown/Dorhamstowne, Grange and other lands in the manor of Dorhamstowne had been leased to an earlier Dixie Coddington in 1703), Bogstown and Grange, parish of Ardbraccan, 1,377 acres in 1792, were then the property of Henry Coddington – total of 3,739. In 1826, Irishtown, parish of Ardbraccan, 98 Irish acres, was also part of the estate.

SOURCES: *CJ Ire.* (Grierson edition) vol. 15 p. 20; PRONI D/302; PRONI T/559 vol. 15 p. 392, Burke, extract pedigrees; *JRSAI* vol. 25 (1895) p. 161, J. H. Moore, 'Notes on the History of Navan'; *Almanacks*; *DJ* 28–31 Mar. 1778; 28 Apr.–1 May, Sept. 1–4 1787; Malcomson, *Foster*, p. 267 n. 2; Parliamentary Lists, 1769 (1), 1772 (2), 1773 (1), 1774 (1), 1775 (1).

0428 CODDINGTON, Henry

MP for Dunleer 1783–90, 1797–Feb. 1800; [Escheator of Munster Feb. 1800]

b. 1734; d. 21 Sept. 1816

FAMILY/BACKGROUND: Son of Nicholas Coddington of Drogheda and Mary, dau. of Henry Tenison (**2053**).

MARRIED: [1762] Elizabeth, dau. of Latham Blacker.

CHILDREN: Nicholas (**0429**); Henry, m. [1809] Eleanor, dau. of Maj. Henry Hamilton; Dixie (d. yg); Thomas; Rev. Latham, m. [1797] Anne Florentia, dau. of Col. John Bellingham of Co. Louth; Martha, m. [1789] Philip Pendleton; Mary; Elizabeth, m. [14 Apr. 1798] Edward Winder; Mary Jane, m. [1805] George Lendrum.

CAREER/OCCUPATION: *Secretary to the Commissioner of Appeals 1759–94; *Clerk to the Prime Serjeant 1759–60; Clerk in the Court of Common Pleas 1760–7; *listed in Attornies of the Courts of King's Bench, Common Pleas and Exchequer 1789; Deputy Chief Serjeant-at-Arms 1790–1800. *Coroner of Drogheda 1773–80, High Sheriff of Co. Louth 1784, Co. Meath 10 Feb. 1785.

POLITICAL ACTIVITY: Returned for the Coddington seat in the borough of Dunleer, which the Coddingtons inherited from Thomas Tenison (**2055**). A 1784 Parliamentary List declared that 'He attaches himself to Mr Foster (**0805**), but being impatient for office, now and then takes a fit of opposition. Hopeful.' It was said that 'He is not ambitious of parliamentary consequence but in order to secure the place of Chief Serjeant-at-Arms to his brother (**0427**), he was obliged at the last election to come in for it himself. That object being obtained, it will probably, as usual, hereafter go to the highest bidder.' This comment was written some time before 1790, as John McClintock (**1314**) was appointed Chief Serjeant-at-Arms on 5 May 1789. Both the McClintocks and the Coddingtons were relations of Speaker Foster and it is unlikely that Dixie Coddington would have been dismissed.

Dixie Coddington Sr (**0427**) died in 1792, and some time after, Henry Coddington became McClintock's deputy, a position he still held at the Union. In 1790 he did not come into parliament, but his son Nicholas (**0429**) was elected in his place. Coddington returned himself again in 1797, still looking for patronage for his clerical son, as on 6 January 1799 he wrote in reply to Castlereagh's letter requesting his support that 'I shall take an opportunity of waiting on you according to your desire, but at the same time cannot help expressing my surprize that any degree of attachment to Administration should be expected from a man who after having shown such unremitting attention as I and my son have done for upwards of sixteen years was refused so small a favor as the reversion of a living of £400 a year for my son.' This overture must have been rejected, as he reverted to his connection with John Foster, the leading opponent to the Union and his relative and neighbour in Co. Louth, and voted against the Union in 1799.

On 12 February 1800 he accepted the office of Escheator of Munster and sold his seat to Quintin Dick (**0628**), who unsuccessfully tried to claim his money back when compensation was being awarded for the boroughs. Dick, who had wealthy merchant connections in both London and Dublin, went on to sit in the United Kingdom parliament. He was also opposed to the Union.

DIVISION LISTS:

1783 (1) voted against Flood's (**0762**) motion for parliamentary reform.
1785 (1) voted for the Commercial Propositions.
1789 (1) voted against a Regency.
1799 (1) voted against the Union.

ADDITIONAL INFORMATION: He received £350 compensation for the loss of the office of Deputy Serjeant-at-Arms at the Union. He was Deputy Serjeant-at-Arms to John McClintock, who died 23 February 1799, which explains why the Serjeant-at-Arms was not compensated while his Deputy received £350. Henry Coddington also received £7,500 for his share of the borough of Dunleer.

ESTATES/RESIDENCE: Oldbridge, Drogheda, Co. Louth; Dunleer, Co. Louth.

SOURCES: PRONI D/302, PRONI T/3166/1C Hartnell notes; BL Add. MSS 33101 f. 366; NAI M5127, Extracts from the Parish Registers of St Peter's, Drogheda; O'Neill thesis; Burke *IFR* (1976) pp. 252–3; Hughes, *Pat. Officers, Ir. Gen.* vol.1 no. 10 (1941) p. 295, W.

Clare, 'Irish Compensations and Pensions' ; Malcomson, *Foster*, p. 198 n. 1; G. C. Bolton, *The Passing of the Irish Act of Union*, p. 99; *Almanacks*; *BNL* 27 Sept. 1816 [says he died in his 82nd year]; Parliamentary Lists, 1783 (2), 1784 (1), (2), (3), 1785 (1), (2), (3), (4), 1787 (1), 1788 (1), 1790 (1), 1799 (3), 1800 (3).

0429 CODDINGTON, Nicholas

MP for Dunleer 1790–7

b. 1765; d. 31 Aug. 1837
FAMILY/BACKGROUND: Eldest son of Henry Coddington (**0428**) and Elizabeth, dau. of Latham Blacker of Co. Louth.
MARRIED: [13 July 1793] Letitia, dau. of Gaynor Barry of Co. Dublin.
CHILDREN: John; Henry Barry, m. [1827] Maria, e. dau. of William Sharman Crawford; Capt. Joshua William, m. [1840] Agnes Julia, o. dau. of Maj.-Gen. Anthony Emmett; Maj. FitzHerbert (40th Regt.), m. [1841] Jane dau. of Col. Hamelin Trelawny; Anna Elizabeth, m. [1826] John FitzHerbert Ruxton of Co. Louth; Letitia Mary.
CAREER/OCCUPATION: High Sheriff of Co. Louth 21 Feb. 1795, Co. Meath 1798.

POLITICAL ACTIVITY: He was returned by his father (**0428**) in 1790 for Dunleer. Not surprisingly, he supported the claims of his neighbour and relative, John Foster (**0805**), for the Speakership. In 1795 Lord Camden wrote to Chief Secretary Pelham (**1650**) that 'I propose by Lord Lifford's [the former Lord Chancellor Lifford's heir was Dean of Armagh] to get rid of the engagement to Coddington': this probably refers to Coddington's brother, who was in holy orders. Whether this arrangement worked, or was deemed inadequate, Coddington's father, who returned himself in 1797, was still looking for what he considered adequate provision for this son in 1799.

DIVISION LISTS:
1790 (2) voted for Foster (**0805**) on the Election of a Speaker.

ESTATES/RESIDENCE: Oldbridge, Co. Meath.

SOURCES: PRONI D/302; Burke *IFR* (1976) pp. 252-3; Hughes, *Pat. Officers*; *FJ* 1 Mar. 1798; *DJ* 18 July 1793; Parliamentary Lists, 1783 (2), 1791 (1), 1793 (1), 1794 (2).

0430 COGHILL, James

MP for Clogher 1723–7; Newcastle 1727–34

b. *c.* 1677; d. (bur. 6) Sept. 1734
FAMILY/BACKGROUND: Son of Sir John Coghill of Co. Dublin and Hester, dau. of Tobias Cramer of Co. Kilkenny.
MARRIED: [1703] Mary (d. 1734), dau. of John Pearson, of Rathmore, Co. Meath.
CHILDREN: o. dau. and h. Hester, m. (1) Rt Hon. Charles Moore, 1st Earl of Charleville, (2) Maj. John Mayne (-Coghill).
EDUCATION: LLB 1698, LLD 24 Sept. 1717 and LLD *spec. grat.* 1718 of TCD.
CAREER/OCCUPATION: Registrar of the Prerogative Court 1733–4; *Governor of the Workhouse 1733.

POLITICAL ACTIVITY: Like his brother (**0431**), who was a considerable political figure in the years following the Hanoverian succession, James Coghill was a lawyer. On the death in January 1722 of Thomas Ashe (**0060**), he was returned for Clogher, an ecclesiastical borough.

James Coghill was a low-profile MP and probably followed his brother's lead. He was listed for four committees in September 1723 and two in 1727–8.

ADDITIONAL INFORMATION: A foundation member of the Dublin Society, 1731.

ESTATES/RESIDENCE: Castleknock, Co. Dublin.

SOURCES: RCBL T34, Extracts from the Parish Registers of St Andrew's, Dublin; RCBL GS 2/7/3/44, Kilmore Marriage Licence Books; McCracken thesis; Burke *PB* (1903) p. 342; Fermanagh and Tyrone MPs; Berry *RDS* pp 24–7; *Almanacks*.

COGHILL, Sir John, 1st Baronet [GB]: *see* **CRAMER (CRAMER-COGHILL)**, Sir John (**0512**)

0431 COGHILL, Rt Hon. Marmaduke

MP for Armagh B. 1692–3, 1695–9, 1703–13, TCD 1713–14, 1715–27–39

b. 28 Dec. 1673; d. 9 Mar. 1738/9

HONOURS: PC 1722 (sworn 10 Sept. 1722, 19 June 1727, 24 Nov. 1727).

FAMILY/BACKGROUND: Son of Sir John Coghill of Co. Dublin and Hester, dau. of Tobias Cramer of Co. Kilkenny.

MARRIED: Unmarried.

EDUCATION: School: Mr Cox; entered TCD 30 Mar. 1687, BA, LLB 1691, LLD 1695.

CAREER/OCCUPATION: Judge of the Prerogative Court 1699–1739; 1st Revenue Commissioner 1729–12 Sept. 1735 (patent, 20 Nov. 1729); *Pro-Vice Chancellor TCD 1734–9; Chancellor of the Exchequer, patent 6 Oct. 1735–9; Trustee for Impropriated Tithes (for building vicarages, acquiring glebes &c.); Trustee of the Linen Board for Ulster 10 Oct. 1711 (f.); Freedom of Cork 8 Apr. 1732; *Governor of the Workhouse 1732; *Governor of the Blue-Coat Hospital 1732–8; *Commissioner of Oyer and Terminer 1732–8; *Governor of Dr Steevens' Hospital 1733–6, 1738; Commissioner of the Tillage Act for Leinster 1735.

POLITICAL ACTIVITY: Coghill was a lawyer specialising in ecclesiastical law, and was a judge of the Prerogative Court for 40 years. Ecclesiastical law spread widely in the eighteenth century. Cases that came before the court affected people's everyday life, as its jurisdiction included disputes not only over tithes but also over probate and matrimonial affairs. For example, on one occasion Coghill 'was called on to decide a question between a wife and her husband who had given her a good beating. The doctor delivered a grave opinion, that moderate chastisement, with such a switch as he held in his hand, was within the husband's matrimonial privilege. This decision so alarmed a lady to whom he [Coghill] had paid his address, with a prospect of success, that she dismissed the assertor of so ungallant a doctrine.'

His nomination for committee service reflects the development of his political influence. He was listed for one committee on 11 October 1692, 12 in 1695–9, 52 in 1703–11, 78 in 1715–26 and 67 in 1727–38. In 1695 he supported Lord Chancellor Porter against the accusations of favouring Catholics made against him by some MPs, and in 1696 he signed the Association for the protection of William III in parliament. He started Queen Anne's reign in opposition but joined the Court party in 1707 and he remained a Court supporter

for the rest of Anne's reign, voting for the government over the Dublin mayoralty issue in 1711 and against the election of Anderson Saunders (**1878**) to the influential chairmanship of the Committee of Elections and Privileges. In 1713 he was thought to be looking for an opportunity to get his brother (**0430**) returned to parliament, but he did not achieve this until 1723. A declared Tory in 1713, he was on a 'black list' of Tories following the queen's death in 1714.

In 1703 he introduced what eventually became an act for the establishment of Primate Marsh's Library, 6 Anne, c. 19, and he had a genuine interest in education, reflected in his constituency and its affairs. He was also responsible for introducing the Church's business in parliament: 9 Anne, c. 12 which was concerned with parish boundaries, 2 Geo. I, c. 19, the confirmation of the grant of First Fruits given by Queen Anne, and 4 Geo. I, c. 14, which was concerned with the archdiocese of Tuam and the Green Coat School in Cork, came into this category, as did much of his later parliamentary business. More secular matters also concerned him: for instance, 4 Geo. I, c. 5 in 1717 and 8 Geo. I, c. 2 in 1721 were concerned with 'the more effectual prevention of Frauds committed by Tenants'.

During the reign of George I, Coghill, who managed to evade the pogrom on the Tories of Queen Anne's reign, emerged as a supporter of Speaker Conolly's (**0460**) political group and had an increasingly high profile in the House of Commons, becoming one of the political establishment who helped to reconcile the Tories to the new order. He voted solidly for the foundation of a national bank but was hostile to Wood's Halfpence, subscribing to the declaration of High-Sheriffs, justices of the peace, Grand Jury, nobility, clergy, gentlemen and freeholders of Co. Dublin against the patent. The ever-watchful Primate Boulter wrote to the Duke of Newcastle that 'He is a person of abilities and of a fair character, but as determined a supporter of the *Irish* against the *English* interest here, as any body, though with more prudence than many others, and therefore I hope it will be considered whether it be so proper to give him so much authority as seems now putting into his hands by these schemes.' Carteret had entrusted Coghill with announcing certain new professorships to the college without previously informing either the Primate or the Chancellor. Boulter felt that this undermined his influence in the university.

Primate Boulter was jealous of Coghill's authority, and relations between them were not always smooth: for instance, in February 1728, Boulter felt that Coghill was being used to undermine his authority in the university over various appointments. The idea was being mooted that three Vice-Chancellors were to be appointed, one of whom was to be Coghill, and Boulter complained to the Duke of Newcastle that 'What seems pretty much aimed at in this affair, is to give Dr *Coghill* a greater weight and authority in the College than he has already. And as he is the person with whom the affair of the professorships has been settled, as well as who are to be professors, I think his weight is already pretty great.'

Coghill was one of the five executors of Speaker Conolly's will, and on the death of Conolly in 1729, Coghill, with Sir Ralph Gore (**0872**), was appointed to ensure the 'English interest' in the House of Commons. Conolly's death left a vacancy on the Revenue Board, and on 30 October 1729 Boulter wrote to Newcastle that 'As Sir Ralph Gore, the new Speaker, does not care to quit the post of Chancellor of the Exchequer, which he is already possessed of, and which by an addition made to the place by his late Majesty is worth better than £800 *per ann.* and is for life, to be made one of the commissioners, we [Chancellor] join in our opinion that the most proper person here to succeed Mr *Conolly* is Dr *Coghill*, who is already a person of weight and has done service in parliament; and we think by this addition will be more capable of serving his Majesty both in and out of the House.' On 22 November 1729 Boulter wrote expressing his satisfaction to Newcastle at this arrangement: 'Dr *Coghill's* being made commissioner here in the room of Mr *Conolly* is very acceptable here; and I hope that he and Sir Ralph Gore will by degrees get together the friends of Mr *Conolly* and others well disposed, to join heartily in his Majesty's service; but this is more than they will be able to effect this session.' Government hoped that Coghill and Gore would restore the dependability that existed under Conolly.

However, Sir Ralph Gore died shortly after his election to the Speakership and Coghill, Carter (**0360**) and Singleton (**1924**) were among those mentioned as possible successors when Henry Boyle (**0210**) declared his candidature. Meanwhile, Carteret had returned to England and, initially, there was a certain coolness between Speaker Conolly's close associates and the new Lord Lieutenant, the Duke of Dorset, and his advisers. Coghill complained that 'I am not in their confidence', and deplored the new administration's policy of buying off dissidents, which he felt could only lead to future trouble. However, this chill appears to have been overcome, for Coghill, well aware of his value, pointed out to Edward Southwell (**1963**) that 'You know the circumstances of this country and how necessary it is thought for the well-being thereof to have one of the country in the government, in whom there may be a proper confidence placed by the country gentlemen' – and whose recommendations could be relied on.

In 1733 Coghill succeeded Gore as Chancellor of the Exchequer. In the same year he declared that 'I have no other ambition but to go through the world with some sort of credit, to be in such a station only as becomes a private gentleman, to have as much business as may take up a reasonable part of my time and to be able to serve my friends on proper occasions and that I may preserve the character of an honest man.' Reputation and the respect of one's peers were valued in eighteenth-century Ireland.

Coghill shared some of the Primate's worries about the condition of the Established Church. Boulter, like Archbishop King, was concerned that the Church, which aimed at serving the entire nation, had nothing like the resources to achieve this objective. In 1733 he gave as a reason for not repealing the sacramental test that 'It will further the prospect I had of all protestants coming to Church … I durst venture to say, we shall not have a Dissenter of £100 per ann. left in Ireland in twenty years time', and this was partly true. Although a Revenue Commissioner, Coghill, with Lord Lieutenant Dorset's consent, voted against the repeal. However, one of the problems was the uneven distribution of wealth within the Church, between a few very wealthy bishops and a large number of very impoverished clergy. One of Boulter's schemes, which he outlined in February 1728, was the more efficient collection of First Fruits, the sum that bishops paid on entering a new see. In addition he wanted each archbishop and bishop to contribute 2 per cent (self-assessed) of their income for three years, each clergyman whose stipend was above £100, 1 per cent, and those with £50–£100, ten shillings. Those who wished might contribute more. The money was to be 'lodged in the hands of Dr *Coghill*, and to be laid out in purchasing glebes, or impropriations, as the bishops shall direct'.

DIVISION LISTS:

1711 (1) voted for the Court on the Dublin mayoralty issue.

1713 (2) voted against Anderson Saunders (**1878**) for Chairman of the Committee of Elections and Privileges.

1721 (1) voted for a national bank.

1721 (2) voted for a national bank.

ADDITIONAL INFORMATION: In 1722, following the funeral of his mother, Lady Coghill, there was a riot at which the Provost was injured. A student, William Barker (later Sir William Barker, 3rd Bt), drafted an affidavit declaring his innocence.

Coghill was a foundation member of the Dublin Society in 1731. He bequeathed £1,600 for charitable purposes, but his principal heiress was his niece Hester, Countess of Charleville, who *d.s.p.* bequeathed it to her cousin, John Cramer(-Coghill) (**0512**).

ESTATES/RESIDENCE: Capel Street, Dublin; Drumcondra House, Co. Dublin, which he built in 1727. He had lands in the barony of Castleknock which Marmaduke Coghill was sold, or confirmed in, by the Trustees for Forfeited Estates in 1703. In addition he purchased in 1702–3 from the Commissioners for Sale of Forfeited Estates 222 acres in Co. Dublin and 140 acres in Co. Kilkenny.

In 1614, Sir John Coghill was granted fairs at Clanturke, *alias* Neoburrow, and in 36 Chas II (1685) his descendant, Sir John Coghill, was granted fairs at Belgree, Co. Meath.

SOURCES: *CJ Ire.* (Bradley ed.) vol. 3 pp. 246, 390, 433, 447, 841–2, 806; NLI EC 2895; P1/6/1 and 12;

PRONI T/2825 pp. 9, 14, Conolly/Castletown Papers; RCBL T34, Extracts from the Parish Registers of St Andrew's, Dublin [bur. 11 Mar. 1739]; McCracken thesis; Hayton thesis; Burke *PB* (1903) p. 341; *Memorials of the Dead*; Hughes, *Pat. Officers*; *Boulter Letters* vol. 1 pp. 225, 227, 267, 269; J. T. Gilbert, *A History of the City of Dublin*, 3 vols (Dublin, 1861) vol. 2, pp. 265–6; J. H. Lepper and P. Crossle, *History of the Grand Lodge of Free and Accepted Masons of Ireland* (Dublin, 1925), vol. 1; Moody & Vaughan (eds), *A New History of Ireland: Eighteenth-century Ireland*, vol. 4 p. 61, J. L. McCracken 'The political structure, 1714–60'; B. de Breffny and R. Ffolliott, *The Houses of Ireland* (Dublin, 1975), p. 97; L. Boylan, *Castletown and its Owners* [Irish Georgian Society guidebook, c.1970], pp. 22–6; Simms, *Williamite Confiscation*, pp. 125, 150, 184; T. Bartlett and D. W. Hayton (eds), *Penal Era and Golden Age* (UHF 1979), p. 32 *et seq.*, D.W. Hayton 'The Beginnings of the Undertaker System'; S. J. Conolly, *Religion, Law and Power…*(1992), pp. 86, 91, 169; R. E. Burns, *Irish Parliamentary Politics in the Eighteenth Century*, 2 vols (Washington, 1989) vol. 1 pp. 246–7, 265, vol. 2 pp. 14, 18; P. McNally, *Parties, Patriots & Undertakers…* (Dublin, 1997), pp. 116, 139–46, 188, 190; Berry *RDS* pp. 24–7; *Almanacks*; *BNL* 13 Mar. 1738 [says he died 9 Mar. in his 66th year leaving £1,600 for charitable uses]; *The Dublin Gazette* 14 Oct. 1724; *The Dublin Post and General Advertiser* 10 Mar. 1739; Parliamentary Lists 1695 (1), 1696 (1), 1706 (1), 1711 (3), 1713 (1), 1713 (2), 1714–15 (1).

0432 COGHLAN, Joseph

MP for TCD 1689; Limerick B. 1692–3, 1695–7

b. *c.* 1655; d. (bur. 10) Nov. 1697

FAMILY/BACKGROUND: Son and heir of Dermot Coghlan of Limerick and Dorothy [ ]

MARRIED: ?

CHILDREN: ?

EDUCATION: Entered TCD 24 May 1672; Middle Temple 13 July 1674.

POLITICAL ACTIVITY: He was one of the very few MPs who had also sat in the 1689 parliament of James II, when he was returned for the university. He was persuaded to stand with some difficulty. Archbishop King later explained that 'The university must choose and it could not stand with their honour to choose papists.' Coghlan presented to King William the results of the deliberation by the Dublin Committee of Protestants, who had provisionally taken control of the city, in response to the question 'What is fit to be done for drawing in and protecting the Irish and others now in rebellion against their sacred majesties?' The report maintained significant silence about Jacobite land-owners, but recommended a free pardon for the 'lower orders who surrendered their arms'.

On 15 October 1695 he, with Stephen Moore (**1473**), attempted to have Richard Aldworth (**0023**) charged with 'serious crimes and misdemeanours'. However, Moore refused to accept the burden of proof and when Coghlan claimed he could prove one of the articles against Aldworth, the House divided 53 for accepting the articles and 155 against. The result did not please Coghlan, who was charged with disorder, and on a split vote – 144 to 144 – the Speaker found him guilty. At the bar of the House: 'He said, that by what was taken ill from him he designed no affront; either to the House or Chair, and what expressions dropped from him were unadvised, and he was sorry for them and begg'd the pardon of the House and of the Chair.'

Ten days later the Commons heard evidence on the articles against Lord Chancellor Porter, who was accused of favouring Catholics. Eleven MPs including the Solicitor General (**0237**) offered to prove the articles 'notwithstanding anything they had heard the Lord Chancellor say in his own vindication'. Coghlan and Anderson Saunders (**1878**) undertook to prove the truth of Porter's assertions, and the articles against the Chancellor were rejected 123 to 79. In 1696, Coghlan signed the Association for the protection of William III in the country.

ESTATES/RESIDENCE: [?]Limerick.

SOURCES: *CJ Ire.* (Bradley ed.) vol. 2 pp. 720, 750–1; RCBL P154/1/1 Parish Register of St Nicholas Within, Dublin; *Cal. SP Dom. 1695* (London, 1908) p. 59; Simms' cards; *Alum. Dub.*; J. G. Simms, *War and Politics in Ireland, 1649–1730* (London, 1986), pp. 68, 183; Simms, *Jacobite Ireland* (1969), p. 75; *Register of Admissions to the Honourable Society of the Middle Temple*; Parliamentary Lists 1695 (1),1696 (1).

0433 COGHLAN, Thomas

MP for Banagher 1768–76; Castlebar 1776–83; Carlingford 1783–90; Augher 1790–4

b. 1728; d. (Feb.) 1794
FAMILY/BACKGROUND: Son of Felix Coghlan and his 1st wife Elinor (Avelina), dau. of Edmond Malone of Cartons, Co. Westmeath.
MARRIED: Unmarried.
CAREER/OCCUPATION: Principal Storekeeper of the Ordnance Civil Branch 1774–87 £150; Trustee of the Linen Board for Ulster June 1771–93; pension of £300 p.a. 7 June 1776 (additional £350 p.a. 25 Nov. 1783 and further £200 p.a. 8 Aug. 1789).
MILITARY: Colonel of the Cloghan and Garrycastle Union, Volunteers.

POLITICAL ACTIVITY: He came in 1768 and was reputedly under the influence of Lord Ossory (**0322**), although he bought his seat. He first wished to be a Trustee of the Linen Board and, having achieved that, he demanded a place. The 1773 Parliamentary List declares that he: 'purchased from Peter Holmes (**1033**) for £2,100. What is remarkable in this man is [that] he ran out and sold his estate and now rents it and has more profit by it since it was his farm than he originally had when it was his estate. He kept the first whore in Paris, loves to be in the company of great people and expects some favours from Government. La Touche purchased his estate. For.' In fact he appears to have been eccentric to the borders of derangement: one of his particular grievances was the lack of 'pens or paper' available to MPs.

He continued to support government under Lord Harcourt, and was rewarded with the post of Storekeeper to the Ordnance, £200 p.a.; to this was added a pension of £300 p.a. and the nomination of five supernumerary gaugers and the Distributor of Stamps for King's County. The office of Storekeeper may have carried with it a house in lower castle yard, as he was stated as having this perquisite in 1782. In the 1776 general election he stood unsuccessfully for King's County, where he had an encumbered estate. He was returned again by purchase (but possibly at a reduced rate), for Castlebar, through Lord Lieutenant Harcourt's influence, when Sir Charles

Bingham (**0134**), to whom the borough belonged, was raised to the peerage as Lord Lucan. He was a colonel of the local Volunteers.

In 1783, after contemplating standing for King's County, he purchased a seat for Carlingford in the hope of 'further provision'; in 1784 it was admitted that he 'has certainly a claim for further provision'. In 1790 he was returned by Lord Abercorn, who was building up a political party, for Augher. In the meantime his pension appears to have been increased to £850, possibly in compensation for the position of Storekeeper which he appears to have resigned about 1788. Despite his eccentricities, he was a perfect example of a placeman.

DIVISION LISTS:

1771 (1) voted for Lord Townshend as Lord Lieutenant.

1771 (2) voted against Sir Lucius O'Brien's (**1558**) motion for retrenchment – appointed to the Linen Board.

1772 (1) voted against the amendment to the Revenue Bill.

1772 (2) voted against a Short Revenue Bill.

1773 (1) voted for Absentee Tax.

1773 (2) voted against an untaxed press.

1777 (1) voted against Grattan's (**0895**) motion for retrenchment.

1778 (2) voted for the Popery Bill.

1779 (2) voted against a six-months Loan Bill.

1780 (1) voted against Grattan's declaration of the rights of Ireland.

1780 (2) voted against Yelverton's (**2268**) motion to modify Poynings' Law.

1780 (3) voted against the Tenantry Bill.

1780 (4) voted for the Perpetual Mutiny Bill.

1783 (1) voted against Flood's (**0762**) motion for parliamentary reform.

1784 (1) voted against a committee on the Reform Bill.

1785 (1) voted for the Commercial Propositions.

1790 (2) voted for Foster (**0805**) on the Election of a Speaker.

ADDITIONAL INFORMATION: He was known popularly as 'The Man'. 'He was a colourful individual, described as handsome, gallant, eccentric, proud, hospitable in the extreme and of expensive habits. He kept his tenants under stern discipline and although most of them were Coghlans he strictly forbade any of them to use the "Mac" prefix or to claim any relationship with himself.'

ESTATES/RESIDENCE: Cloghan (Strawberry Hill), Banagher, King's County; Co. Leitrim and Dublin Castle. His property was inherited by the Rt Hon. Denis Bowes Daly (**0571**), the son of his sister Rose. In 1702–3 Terence Coghlan had 3,169 acres in King's County forfeited.

In 1684, John Coghlan was granted a market at Cloghan; in 8 Geo. III (1768), Thomas Coghlan was granted fairs at Creggane.

SOURCES: Ellis thesis; PRONI MIC/474 Irish Volunteers; *Alum. Dub.* [gives a Thomas son of Fabius who entered TCD 10 July 1747 aged 20 years but says he was born in Galway]; Fermanagh and Tyrone MPs [says that in 1791 he was excused from attendance on committees being 60 years of age and upwards]; *Ir. Gen.* v. 4 no. 5 (1972) p. 545, L. Cox, 'The MacCoghlans of Delvin Eathra' [says incorrectly that he died 1791]; Simms, *Williamite Confiscation*, p. 178; J. Kelly, *Prelude to Union* (Cork, 1992), p. 219; *Almanacks*; *FJ* 6–8 June 1771; *GM* (Exshaw's edition) Mar. 1794 [says he d. aged 64 years]; Parliamentary Lists, 1769 (1), 1771 (1), 1772 (2), 1773 (1), (2), 1774 (1), 1775 (1), 1776 (1), (2), (3), 1777 (1), 1778 (1), 1780 (1), 1782 (1), 1783 (1), 1784 (1), (2), (3), 1785 (1), (2), (3), (4), 1787 (1), 1788 (1), 1789 (1), 1790 (1), 1791 (1), 1793 (1).

0434 COLCLOUGH, Caesar

MP for Taghmon 1719–26

b. *c.* 1665; d. [*post* 8 Mar.] 1726
FAMILY/BACKGROUND: Son of Anthony Colclough and Mary, dau. of William Esmonde of Co. Wexford.
MARRIED: [lic. 11 Mar.] 1686 Mary, dau. of William Ivory of Co. Wexford.
CHILDREN: Anthony, m. Elizabeth dau. of William FitzGerald; Frances, m. her second cousin Thomas Colclough; Margaret; Eleanor Maria, m. William Sutton; Mary; Mabel; Anne (d. unm.).

POLITICAL ACTIVITY: The Colcloughs were a very old Wexford family: Caesar was a family name, and this one was returned in place of Anderson Saunders (**1878**), the Queen Anne politician, who died in February 1718. Very little is known about him except his support for a national bank and the fact that on 22 February 1726 Lord Lieutenant Carteret recommended to the Duke of Newcastle C. Colclough's application for a private bill in the Imperial parliament to enable him to mortgage or sell part of his estate, which suggests that he may have been in financial difficulties.

DIVISION LISTS:

1721 (1) voted for a national bank.
1721 (2) voted for a national bank.

ESTATES/RESIDENCE: Rosegarland, Co. Wexford.

SOURCES: PRONI T/610 p. 142, TSPI Jan.1725–June 1727; Burke, *IFR* (1976) p. 256.

0435 COLCLOUGH, Caesar

MP for Co. Wexford 1727–60, 1761–6

b. 1696; d. 15 Apr. 1766
FAMILY/BACKGROUND: Eldest son of Dudley Colclough and Mary, dau. of Hon. Francis Barnewell.
MARRIED: (1) [20 Jan. 1718] Frances Muschamp, dau. of Rt Hon. Sir Thomas Vesey, 1st Baronet, Bp of Ossory; (2) [18 July 1721] Henrietta, dau. of Agmondisham Vesey (**2144**).
CHILDREN:(1) Margaret (d. yg).
(2) Caesar, m. [30 Mar. 1767] Ann, dau. of Vesey Colclough of New Ross, Co. Wexford; Vesey, m. Mary dau. of Sir John Bingham, 5th Baronet (**0141**), wid. of Hugh Montgomery; Dudley; Capt. Agmondisham (killed in a duel); Admiral (?) m. [*c.* Jan. 1753] Mary Anne, dau. of John Byrne of Dublin; Rev. Thomas, m. [1 July 1757] Florence, dau. of Hon. Bysse Molesworth (**1417**); Capt. (7th Dragoons) Richard, m. [1771] Mary sis. of Rev. Thomas Moore O'Meara; Frances, m. Joseph Johnstone MD; Anne, m. Caesar Colclough of Athy, Co. Kildare; Harriet, m. William Thomas; Mary; Margaret; Lora.
EDUCATION: LLD of TCD 2 Mar. 1742.
CAREER/OCCUPATION: Free Burgess of Enniscorthy 1718, New Ross 12 Jan. 1722 – 29 June 1731; Portreeve of Enniscorthy 29 Sept. 1733, 1741, 1743, 1745, 1758; Portreeve of St Canice/Irishtown; *Governor of the Workhouse 1732–65; *Commissioner of the Tillage Act for Leinster

1735, 1739–65; *Magistrate of Enniscorthy 1741, 1743, 1745, 1758.
MILITARY: Colonel of Wexford Militia Dragoons.

POLITICAL ACTIVITY: He was a noted Patriot of the ultra-sensitive kind, and in 1730 complained that Lord Lieutenant Carteret 'had taken no notice of the address of the house desiring the prohibition against the exportation of corn might be taken off, but, as he heard, had so little regard for the opinion of the Commons, that he waited to have the opinion of little collectors and customs house officers and that he [Colclough] stood up in behalf of a distressed nation and an injured House of Commons'. The prohibition against the export of corn had been imposed during the severe famine in Ulster at the end of the 1720s. Colclough represented the ultra-sensitivity of the House of Commons to any implied insult to its prestige.

On 3 December 1733 he complained to the House that he had been disturbed in possession of his lands at Staplestown, Co. Carlow, during time of privilege. Although he voted against the election of James Digges La Touche (♦♦♦♦), he belonged to the Country party and supported Speaker Boyle (**0210**) over the expulsion of Arthur Jones-Nevill (**1125**) and at the time of the Money Bill dispute.

DIVISION LISTS:

1749 (1) voted against the elections of James Digges La Touche (♦♦♦♦).
1753 (1) voted for the expulsion of Arthur Jones-Nevill (**1125**).
1753 (2) voted against the Money Bill.

ESTATES/RESIDENCE: Tintern Abbey and Duffrey Hall, Co. Wexford. About 1749 the part of the estate around Taghmon and Dunmain near New Ross etc. was 16,992 acres. On his wife, Henrietta's, death in December 1771 a jointure of £600 p.a. descended to Sir Vesey Colclough, Bt (**0436**). The Colclough grants go back at least to the reign of Edward IV. The Abbey and lands of Tintern were granted (or confirmed) to Anthony Colclough by Queen Elizabeth I in 1577. Patrick Colclough was apparently the head of the family in 1678. In 1687, when Sir Caesar Colclough died intestate, his only sister inherited, as heiress-at-law. Her husband, Robert Leigh, assumed the name Colclough.

In 1629 Sir Adam Colclough, Bt was granted fairs at Nash, in 1684 Patrick Colclough at Mocorry, and in 1747 Caesar Colclough at Tintern.

SOURCES: *CJ Ire.* (Bradley ed.) vol. 6 p. 308, vol. 7 p. 158; EC 3697, EC 4485, EC 7388 [these records include a copy of a Private Member's Bill, the Colclough Estate Act 19 Geo. II (1746) with notes on the family pedigree]; NLI Reps no. 124; McCracken thesis [says he was MP for Taghmon 1719–27]; Burke *LGI* (1904) p. 100; P. McNally, *Parties, Patriots & Undertakers...* (Dublin, 1997), p. 194; *Ir. Gen.* vol. 5 no. 1 (1974) pp. 87–98, H. F. Morris, 'Births, Marriages and Deaths in Ramsey's Waterford Chronicle, 1771'; *Ir. Gen.* vol. 5 no. 5 (Nov. 1984) pp. 606–28, 'Finn's Leinster Journal, 1767, Births, Marriages and Deaths'; *JRSAI* vol. 22 (1892) p. 301, P. D. Vigors, 'Alphabetical List of Free Burgesses of New Ross...1658–1839...'; *Almanacks*; *Pue's Occurrences* 2 Oct. 1733; *The Dublin Gazette* 6 Mar. 1742; *FJ* 29 Apr.–30 May 1766.

0436 COLCLOUGH, Sir Vesey

MP for Co. Wexford 1766–8–76–83–90; Enniscorthy 1790–4

b. 1 July 1745; d. 8 July 1794

HONOURS: Baronet (assumed on a supposed right).

FAMILY/BACKGROUND: Only (and posthumous) son of Vesey Colclough (b. 1722; d. *ante* July 1745) and Mary, dau. of Sir John Bingham, 5th Baronet (**0141**), wid. of Hugh Montgomery.

MARRIED: [2 Aug. 1765] Catherine, dau. of John Grogan (**0906**).

CHILDREN: Caesar (Lincoln's Inn 10 Nov. 1789), m. [1818] Jane Stratford, dau. of John Kirwan; John (d. unm. 30 May 1807, shot by William Congreve Alcock (**0021**) in a duel); Vesey.

EDUCATION: School: Kilkenny College 24 Aug. 1756, aged 10 years.

CAREER/OCCUPATION: Sheriff of Co. Wexford 27 Dec. 1766; High Sheriff of Co. Wexford 1767, ?Co. Carlow 1768; Freeman of Wexford *ante* 1776; Searcher of Kinsale 2 Aug. 1791.

MILITARY: Colonel of the First Volunteers of Ireland 1782; Colonel of the Enniscorthy Rangers, Volunteers, which he formed from his own tenantry and clothed, armed and accoutred.

POLITICAL ACTIVITY: He first came in for Co. Wexford in 1766 on the death of his grandfather (**0435**). He had a large estate and consequently an interest in Co. Wexford, which he enhanced by his alliance with Henry Loftus (**1250**). He was generally in opposition. In 1778 he was said to have 'a good estate in Wexford County. Independent and against Government.' In 1782 his 'good estate' was 'involved' and by 1783 'much distressed', while he himself was considered 'of very weak understanding and addicted to low company'.

In 1766 he bought the borough of Enniscorthy (including the office of Portreeve) from his cousin, Adam Colclough of Duffrey Hall, for £3,000. Nevertheless, Adam and other members of the family remained on the corporation and, from the disputed election report in 1783, obviously considered that they had some rights in it. In 1783 his conduct of the election for Enniscorthy was challenged and the committee on elections resolved that firstly, the election was void and secondly, Sir Vesey Colclough the Returning Officer had conducted the election unduly and irregularly. Apparently he was 'under engagement to return Mr English (**0697**) for one seat if he [Colclough] succeeds in the County, which he probably will and has sold the other to Mr Longfield (**1262**)'. The borough appears to have been a family one, and Sir Vesey had excluded his brothers, among others, from participating in the election. He had ensured, by dubious means, that he was the only burgess present and also the Returning Officer, so he had made out the return as he pleased and had gone off to the Co. Wexford election then in progress, for which he was a successful candidate.

Furthermore, in his enthusiasm as a representative for Co. Wexford at the Volunteer Convention he had 'relinquished his patronage of rotten boroughs for the public benefit'. This self-denial did not last long, as a 1784 Parliamentary List said that 'He has the Borough of Enniscorthy, which he sells but being attacked for bribery at the election, got into a scrape of perjury. He is a very weak man. Has been generally in opposition but is now making advances to Govt, who are coy. Doubtful.' However, by 1785 he was apparently a firm supporter, and by 1788 he had received the disposal of some minor patronage. Throughout the 1783–90 parliament he was an intermittent attender, and after 1790 he appears to have been influenced by his fellow MP for Enniscorthy, Mountifort Longfield.

DIVISION LISTS:

1768 (1) voted against army augmentation.

1771 (2) voted for Sir Lucius O'Brien's (**1558**) motion for retrenchment.

1772 (2) voted for a Short Revenue Bill.

1773 (1) voted against Absentee Tax.

1773 (2) voted for an untaxed press.

1774 (2) voted against Catholic relief.

1775 (1) voted for the pro-American amendment to the Speech from the Throne.

1777 (1) voted for Grattan's (**0895**) motion for retrenchment.

1777 (2) voted against the Trade Embargo.

1778 (2) voted against the Popery Bill.

1779 (2) voted for a six-months Loan Bill.

1780 (2) voted for Yelverton's (**2268**) motion to modify Poynings' Law.

1780 (3) voted for the Tenantry Bill.

1780 (4) voted against the Perpetual Mutiny Bill.

1783 (1) absent.

1784 (1) absent though independent.

1785 (1) voted against the Commercial Propositions.

1790 (2) voted for Foster (**0805**) on the Election of a Speaker.

ADDITIONAL INFORMATION: A member of the RDS from 1766. He is credited with having raised the first corps of Volunteer in Ireland at Enniscorthy in 1773 or 1774: in response to the Whiteboy disturbances in neighbouring counties, Colclough and other Co. Wexford gentlemen formed an Association for the protection of property. The county escaped serious disturbances and the association later developed into the Volunteers. In the early 1780s Colclough was a liberal, and in 1779 he assured his constituents that 'The people are not truly represented in parliament, except their instructions are obeyed by their representatives.'

His son Caesar, who was MP for Co. Wexford 1806, 1818–20, had his early prospects blighted by his profligate father and was later to write: 'I was forced on my coming of age to run off from examination in Trinity College to avoid being arrested for my schooling, diet, lodging and clothing, persecuted by my improvident father to join him to raise money to furnish aliment for his prof-

ligate life with a servant maid, his mistress and her children, whilst my brother, self and mother were pensioners of her five brothers ... Many a day a penny cake ... furnished my dinner and counting the trees my dessert'.

In December 1745, his grandfather, Caesar Colclough, petitioned for leave to implement agreements relating to the estates in counties Wexford and Carlow as well as for the maintenance of his younger children.

He was a member of the Friendly Brothers of St Patrick, a society that attempted to curb 'the barbarous practice of duelling'. He cast off his wife and legitimate children and lived with his mistress and their children in Tintern Abbey, which was falling about their ears.

ESTATES/RESIDENCE: Tintern Abbey, Ross, Co. Wexford; Paradise Row, Dublin. Shortly after his death in July 1794 the estate produced only £1,600 and had 164 freeholders. A decade later, according to Wakefield, the rental was £6,000. By the death of Caesar Colclough's (**0435**) wife in December 1771 a jointure of £600 p.a. descended to him.

SOURCES: PRONI D/302; *CJ Ire.* (Bradley ed.) vol. 7 p. 739; PRONI MIC/474 Irish Volunteers; Ellis thesis; GEC *B*; Burke *IFR* (1976) p. 257; *HP 1794–1820*; Wakefield, *Account of Ire.*, vol. 1, p. 282; Hughes, *Pat. Officers*; McNevin, *Volunteers*; *The Records of the Honourable Society of Lincoln's Inn* (Lincoln's Inn, 1896) vol. 1 p. 532; *The Register of the Parish of St Peter and St Kevin, 1669–1761* (Parish Register Society of Dublin, 1911) p. 273 [records the baptism of Vesey Colclough son of widow Colclough 24 June (?July) 1745]; *JRSAI* vol. 54 (1924) pp. 55–67, T. U. Sadleir, 'The Register of Kilkenny School (1685–1800)'; *Ir. Gen.* vol. 5 no. 1 (1974) pp. 87–98, H. F. Morris, 'Births, Marriages and Deaths in Ramsey's Waterford Chronicle, 1771', *Ir. Gen.* vol. 5 no. 1 (1974) pp. 103–21; D. Goodall, 'The Freemen of Wexford in 1776'; Malcomson, *Foster* (1978), p. 339 [family detail]; McDowell, *Irish Public Opinion, 1750–1800* p. 83; J. Kelly, *'That Damn'd thing called Honour': Duelling in Ireland 1570–1860* (Cork, 1995), pp. 65–6; *Almanacks*; *DJ* 12 July 1794 [died aged 48]; *HP 1660–90* [There was a connection between this family and Sir Caesar Colclough, MP for Newcastle-under-Lyme (Eng.) 1661]; Parliamentary Lists, 1769 (1), 1772 (2), 1773 (1), (2), 1774 (1), 1775 (1), 1776 (1), (3), 1777 (1), 1778 (1), 1780 (1), 1782 (1), 1783 (1), (2), (3), 1784 (1), (2), (3), 1785 (1), (2.), (3), (4), 1787 (1), 1788 (1), 1789 (1), 1790 (1), 1791 (1), 1793 (1).

0437 COLE, Rt Hon. Sir Arthur

MP for Enniskillen 1692–3; Roscommon B. 1695–9

b. 1664; d. 5 Oct. 1754
HONOURS: PC, sworn 9 Nov. 1715, 1733–d.; suc. as 2nd Baronet 1691.
PEERAGES: Cr. Baron Ranelagh 18 Apr. 1715.
FAMILY/BACKGROUND: Son and heir of Sir John Cole, 1st Baronet, and Elizabeth, dau. of Hon. John Chichester.
MARRIED: (1) [8 Sept. 1692] Catherine, dau. of William Byron, 3rd Baron Byron; (2) [1748] Selina, dau. of Peter Bathurst of Wiltshire (she m. (2) 30 Nov. 1775 Sir John Elwill, 1st Baronet).
CHILDREN: *d.s.p.*
CAREER/OCCUPATION: *Commissioner of Oyer and Terminer 1732–d.

POLITICAL ACTIVITY: Returned for the family borough of Enniskillen for both parliaments of William III. In 1695 he was hostile to Lord Chancellor Porter, who was accused of favouring Catholics, and the following year he signed the Association for the protection of William III in parliament. He was listed for a committee on 21 October 1692 and three between 1695 and 1697.

ESTATES/RESIDENCE: Newlands, Co. Dublin.

SOURCES: GEC *B* [d. 12 Sept. 1754]; Fermanagh and Tyrone MPs; Simms' cards; Burke *Ext. P.* (1883) p. 128; GEC *P, Index to Irish Privy Counsellors, 1711–1910* [d. 5 Oct. 1754]; J. J. Howard (ed.), *Miscellanea Genealogica et Heraldica*, vol. 2 (1876) p. 243 [says he died 1 Oct. 1754]; *Almanacks*; Parliamentary Lists, 1695 (1), 1696 (1).

0438 COLE, Hon. Sir Galbraith Lowry

MP for Enniskillen 1797–1800; [UK] Co. Fermanagh 1803–23

b. 1 May 1772; d. 4 Oct. 1842
HONOURS: Knight Grand Cross of the Bath 5 Mar. 1813.
FAMILY/BACKGROUND: Son of William Willoughby Cole, 1st Earl of Enniskillen (**0444**), and Anne, dau. of Galbraith Lowry(-Corry) (**1268**).
MARRIED: [15 June 1815] Frances (d. 1 Nov. 1847), 2nd dau. of Rt Hon. James Harris, 1st Earl of Malmesbury.

CHILDREN: Col. Arthur Lowry (17th Regiment) (b. 24 Aug. 1817; d. 30 Mar. 1885), m. [29 Nov. 1854] Elizabeth Frances (d. 22 May 1889), dau. of Vice Admiral Villiers Francis Hatton; Capt. William Willoughby (27th Regiment) (b. 17 Nov. 1819; d. 4 Apr. 1863); James Henry (b. 15 Dec. 1821 d. unm. 3 Dec. 1888); Florence Mary Georgiana (b. 1817; d. unm. 21 May 1888); Louisa Catherine (b. 1818; d. 14 Oct. 1878); Frances Maria Frederica Virginia; Henrietta (b. 1827; d. 22 Apr. 1888).
CAREER/OCCUPATION: Gentleman-at-Large 1800; Governor of Gravesend and Tilbury 1818–d.; Governor of the Island of Mauritius 1823–8, of the Cape of Good Hope 1828–33.
MILITARY: Cornet 12th Dragoons 31 Mar. 1787; Lieutenant 5th Dragoons 31 May 1791; Captain 70th Foot 30 Nov. 1792; Major 86th Foot 1793; Lieutenant-Colonel, Ward's Foot 26 Nov. 1794, 2nd Foot Guards; Colonel 1 Jan. 1801, 3rd Dragoon Guards, 27th Inniskilling Fusiliers 1803; Brigadier-General 1806; Major-General 1808; Major-General 25 Apr. 1811; Colonel 103rd Foot 13 Jan. 1812; Lieutenant-General 4 June 1813; Colonel 70th Foot 12 Jan. 1814; Colonel 34 Foot 21 May 1816; Colonel 27th Foot 16 Dec. 1826, General 22 July 1830. Cole had a military education and first saw active service at Martinique, where he was aide-de-camp to Sir Charles Grey. He was Deputy Adjutant-General and aide-de-camp to the Commander-in-Chief, Lord Carhampton, in Ireland 1797–1800. He resigned his Deputy Adjutantship 18 Jan. 1800 and was allowed to retire under cover of an appointment as Gentleman-at-Large.

POLITICAL ACTIVITY: He was returned by his father (**0444**). The Cole family were hostile to the Union. He voted against the Union in 1799 and, as serving officers were expected to vote with the government he was ordered abroad with his regiment, and government refused him the Escheatorship of Munster to block any further such vote. This caused a considerable storm and the administration subsequently granted all such requests, probably to its own advantage.

His professional and political career was largely after the Union. In 1803 he succeeded unopposed to his brother's (**0441**) seat for County Fermanagh. His maiden speech of 11 August 1803 criticised the Irish government's handling of the Emmet rising. In 1804 he was reckoned 'against' but tied to Lord Enniskillen, who wanted to be a representative peer, which he achieved. He was listed as a friend of Pitt's. He voted against Catholic relief, 21 May 1816 and 3 May 1819.

DIVISION LISTS:

1799 (1) voted against the Union – Lieutenant-Colonel in the army.

ADDITIONAL INFORMATION: Although he resigned at the Union, he subsequently resumed his military career and fought in the Napoleonic Wars. He was Military Secretary to Lord Hutchinson (1002) in Egypt. In 1805 he took command in Malta and thence went to Sicily, distinguishing himself in action at Maida. In his absence government supported him in the contest for Fermanagh, 1806. In 1807 likewise he received the support of the Portland ministry. In June 1809 he was transferred from Sicily to the Peninsula. On 3 February 1812 he was in the House to acknowledge its thanks for his services at Albuera, but in June he returned to Spain to win further laurels at Salamanca. The House's acknowledgement of his gallant services was delayed on four occasions.

Despite a reminder from the Speaker, Sir Lowry neglected to present himself again for so long that Castlereagh's intervention was necessary to secure the vote of thanks to him on 20 May 1816. He refused the government of Gibraltar, August 1814, and missed Waterloo because of his honeymoon. In December 1815 he refused the Lieutenant Governorship of Corfu; in September 1816 he refused the government of Ceylon.

ESTATES/RESIDENCE: Marlbank, Co. Fermanagh; Granby Row, Dublin. For a younger son he was wealthy: '£4,000, which added to the price of the Borough [Enniskillen] gave him £10,000 besides an estate [Marlbank] worth £230 per annum.'

SOURCES: PRONI T/3166/1B and /1C Hartnell notes; *DNB*; O'Neill thesis; Burke *PB* (1900, 1903) p. 555; Fermanagh and Tyrone MPs; Jupp thesis; *HP 1790–1820*; J. J. Howard (ed.), *Miscellanea Genealogica et Heraldica*, vol. 2 (1876) p. 245 [says he died 5 Oct. 1842]; Parliamentary Lists, 1799 (3), 1800 (3).

0439 COLE, John

MP for Enniskillen 1703–13–14, 1715–26

b. (bapt. 12 Apr.) 1680; d. (*ante* Apr.) 1726
FAMILY/BACKGROUND: Eldest son of Sir Michael Cole (0442) and his 2nd wife Elizabeth, eldest dau. of Sir John Cole, 1st Baronet.
MARRIED: (1) [10 July 1707] Florence, only dau. of Sir Bourchier Wrey, 3rd Baronet of Trebitch, Cornwall; (2) Jane, dau. of Robert Saunderson.
CHILDREN: (1) John, 1st Baron Mount Florence (0440); Capt. Bourchier (Wynard's Regiment), m. Jane dau. of [   ]; Michael, m. Elizabeth dau. of Richard Tenison, Bp of Meath; William, m. [   ]; Florence, m. Arthur Newburgh; Rev. Henry, m. Mary, dau. of Henry Brooke.
(2) Elizabeth, m. (1) William Archdall, (2) Hon. Bysse Molesworth (1417).
CAREER/OCCUPATION: Sheriff of Co. Fermanagh 1723, 1724.

POLITICAL ACTIVITY: For most of Queen Anne's reign he was absent in London. He appears to have returned about 1711, when he was in opposition. It was thought, incorrectly, that he would not be returned in 1713. He was listed as a Whig, but the following year was on the 'black list' of Tories, having voted for the Castle candidate, Sir Richard Levinge (1230), as Speaker.

He was returned again in 1715, and sat for Enniskillen until his death in 1726. In 1719 he was thought to be a Tory, at least as regarded his attitude to Dissenters. He was not a very energetic MP, being listed for a committee in 1711, another in 1713 and three between 1721 and 1723. He was a firm opponent of a national bank.

DIVISION LISTS:

1713 (1) voted for Sir Richard Levinge (1230) for Speaker.
1721 (1) voted against a national bank.
1721 (2) voted against a national bank.

ESTATES/RESIDENCE: Florence Court, Enniskillen, Co. Fermanagh. In 1713 John Cole's income was estimated at £1,000.

SOURCES: PRONI T/3411; Fermanagh and Tyrone MPs; Burke *PB* (1903) p. 555; J. J. Howard (ed.), *Miscellanea Genealogica et Heraldica*, vol. 2 (1876) p. 243 [says he died July 1726, says Elizabeth dau. of first wife and no issue by second wife]; *The Dublin Courant* 17 Nov. 1722; Parliamentary Lists, 1706 (1), 1707 (1), (4), 1711 (1), (3), 1713 (1), (2), 1714–15 (1), 1719 (2).

0440 COLE, John

MP for Enniskillen 1730–60

b. 13 Oct. 1709; d. 30 Nov. 1767
PEERAGES: Cr. Baron Mount Florence 8 Sept.
1760.
FAMILY/BACKGROUND: Son of John Cole (**0439**)
and Florence, dau. of Sir Bourchier Wrey.
MARRIED: [Oct. 1728] Elizabeth, dau. of Hugh
Willoughby (-Montgomery) of Carrow, Co.
Fermanagh (**2236**).
CHILDREN: William Willoughby (**0444**); Arthur
(Cole-Hamilton) (**0445**); Flora Caroline, m.
William Irvine (**1069**); Mary Anne (d. unm.);
Carolina; Catherine, m. Capt. Richard Browne;
Elizabeth (d. unm.).
EDUCATION: School: Mr Gratton, Enniskillen;
entered TCD 27 Sept. 1726.
CAREER/OCCUPATION: Sheriff of Co. Fermanagh
1732, 1733; Governor of Co. Fermanagh 1757–
65; *Joint-Governor of Co. Fermanagh 1764–6.

POLITICAL ACTIVITY: Cole was a member of the
Country or Speaker's party during the 1750s. He
voted against the election of James Digges La
Touche (♦♦♦♦) in 1749 but, in 1753, he voted
for the expulsion of Arthur Jones-Nevill (**1125**)
and against the Money Bill, although in 1752 he
was one of those whom the administration hoped
to detach. He was listed for 42 committees between 1735 and 1759. In 1760 he was elevated to
the peerage as Lord Mount Florence.

DIVISION LISTS:
1749 (1) voted against the election of James
Digges La Touche (♦♦♦♦).
1753 (1) voted for the expulsion of Arthur
Jones-Nevill (**1125**).
1753 (2) voted against the Money Bill.

ESTATES/RESIDENCE: Florence Court, Co. Fermanagh. He
inherited Florence Court on the death of his father in
1726, and an estate of £2,200 p.a. on the death of Lord
Ranelagh in 1754.

SOURCES: McCracken thesis; Fermanagh and Tyrone
MPs; GEC *P*; J. Walton, *'The King's Business': Letters on
the Administration of Ireland, 1741–61 …* (N.Y., 1996),
no. 110; D. Guinness and W. Ryan, *Irish Houses and
Castles* (London, 1971) p. 170; J. J. Howard (ed.), *Miscellanea Genealogica et Heraldica*, vol. 2 (1876) p. 244;
Almanacks; *The Dublin Gazette* 18 Dec. 1731, 28 Nov.
1732; *BNL* 25 Oct. 1754.

0441 COLE, Hon. John Willoughby

MP for Co. Fermanagh 1790–7–1800 [r. Sligo
B. 1790 and 1797]; [UK] 1801–22 May 1803

b. 23 Mar. 1768; d. 31 Mar. 1840
HONOURS: Knight of St Patrick 27 Apr. 1810.
PEERAGES: Styled Viscount Cole 1789–1803; suc.
as 2nd Earl of Enniskillen 1803; cr. Baron
Grinstead [UK] 11 Aug. 1815; Rep. Peer 1804–40.
FAMILY/BACKGROUND: Son of William Willoughby
Cole, 1st Earl of Enniskillen (**0444**) and Anne,
dau. of Galbraith Lowry (-Corry) (**1268**).
MARRIED: [15 Oct. 1805] Charlotte, dau. of
Henry Paget, 1st Earl of Uxbridge.
CHILDREN: William Willoughby (b. 25 Jan. 1707;
d. 12 Nov. 1886), 3rd Earl of Enniskillen, m. (1)
[16 Jan. 1844] Jane, e. dau. of James Archibald
Casamajor; (2) [5 Sept. 1865] Mary Emma, e.
dau. and co-h. of Charles Brodrick, 6th Viscount
Midleton; Henry Arthur (b. 14 Feb. 1809; d.
unm. 2 July 1890); John Lowry (b. 8 June 1813;
d. unm. 28 Nov. 1882); Lowry Balfour (b. 1815;
d. 1818); Jane Anne; Louisa Florence (d. 1831).
EDUCATION: School: Dr Carpenter, Royal School:
Armagh; entered TCD 16 Aug. 1785, BA 1789;
Grand Tour.
CAREER/OCCUPATION: Custos Rot. Co. Fermanagh
1803–d.; Trustee of the Linen Board for Ulster
1806; Lord Lieutenant 1831–d.
MILITARY: Captain of Glenawley Infantry,
Ballyduff Infantry, 1789; Colonel Fermanagh
Militia 1803; Captain Commandant Enniskillen
and Lurgandaragh Infantry 1813.

POLITICAL ACTIVITY: In 1790 it was said that 'So
anxious is the Earl to return his son for this county,
that he has purchased Lord Belmore's (**1269**) interest in it, which is very powerful, at the high
price, it is said, of a seat in his Borough of
Enniskillen.' Actually this is unlikely, as Lord
Enniskillen returned his brother (**0445**) and son-
in-law, Richard Magenis (**1322**), for Enniskillen.
    In the 1790–7 parliament Lord Enniskillen sup-
ported, and Lord Cole did likewise. He was again
returned in 1797, when the results of the poll for
Co. Fermanagh, which showed the division of
interests in the county, were: John W. Cole, 804
votes; Colonel Mervyn Archdall (**0050**), 751;
Henry Brooke (**0249**), 279; Humphrey Butler
(**0318**), 97. In 1790 he supported the election of
John Foster (**0805**) as Speaker rather than W. B.
Ponsonby (**1709**); he voted against Catholic

Emancipation in 1795 and against Sir Laurence Parsons' (**1636**) motion for an investigation into 'the present discontents' in 1798.

Nevertheless, Lord Enniskillen and his sons (**0438** and this MP) were strongly against the Union, and Lord Cole voted against it in both 1799 and 1800. However, at Westminster he was considered a supporter of administration. In 1802 Cole was short of funds and willing to sell the family borough of Enniskillen to government. On 1 March 1803 he informed the Under-Secretary that he began to think the Union 'a good thing after all', although the previous December the Chief Secretary admonished him for asking favours and voting against government at the same time. He succeeded his father in 1803, and in the following year became a representative peer.

DIVISION LISTS:

1790 (2) voted for Foster (**0805**) on the Election of a Speaker.

1795 (2) voted against Catholic emancipation.

1798 (1) voted against Laurence Parsons' (**1636**) motion for an investigation into 'the present discontents'.

1799 (1) voted against the Union.

1800 (1) voted against the Union.

ADDITIONAL INFORMATION: He was nicknamed 'Piggy' by Lord Shannon (**0213**) and was described by Canning in 1794 as a 'very good sort of young man – but very Irish' and by Judge Day as 'the Prince of Orange of County Fermanagh'. In 1797 Lord Shannon referred to him talking 'like the great Bonapart of Fermanagh', but on other occasions he commends his conduct, writing that 'Cole has behaved very well and done much service.' In 1797 he had a narrow escape, as '4 men waylaid him to murder him'. He appears to have first spoken in the United Kingdom parliament on 29 March 1801 to rebut Whitbread's allegations about the severity of a court martial over which Cole had presided during the 1798 rebellion, against which he took an active and energetic part.

ESTATES/RESIDENCE: Florence Court, Co. Fermanagh (inherited in 1803); Granby Row, Dublin. Wakefield calculated that he had a rental of £13,000.

SOURCES: PRONI T/3166/1B Hartnell notes; O'Neill thesis; Jupp thesis; GEC *P*; Burke *PB* (1903) p. 555; Kilkenny MPs; Fermanagh and Tyrone MPs; Vicars, *Prerog. Wills*; Lodge *P*; Young, *A Tour in Ire.*, vol. 1 pp. 277–8; Wakefield, *Account of Ire.*, vol. 1 pp. 259, 277–8; *HP 1790–1820*; *Alum. Dub.*; M. L. Ferrar, *Register of the Royal School: Armagh* (1933); E. Hewitt (ed.), *Lord Shannon's Letters to his Son* (PRONI 1982) pp. xxii, 60, 67; C. Ross (ed.), *Cornwallis Corr.* (London, 1859), vol. 3 p. 50; *FJ* 5 Aug. 1797; Parliamentary Lists, 1790 (1), 1793 (1), 1794 (2), 1799 (3), 1800 (3).

0442 COLE, Sir Michael

MP for Enniskillen (1665–6), 1692–3, 1695–9, 1703–11

> b. 1644; d. 11 Feb. 1711
> HONOURS: Knight.
> FAMILY/BACKGROUND: Only surviving son of Michael Cole and Catherine, dau. of Sir Laurence Parsons of Birr.
> MARRIED: (1) Alice, dau. of Chidley Coote of Killester, Co. Dublin; (2) [20 Feb. 1672] Elizabeth (his cousin) dau. of Sir John Cole, 1st Baronet.
> CHILDREN: (2) John (**0439**); Michael, m. [   ] Chichester; William; Fenton, m. Dorothea, dau. of [   ] Saunderson; Catherine Jane; Mary; Alice and other ch. who all d. yg.
> EDUCATION: School Mr Hill, Dublin; entered TCD 21 June 1659, aged 16 years.
> CAREER/OCCUPATION: Sheriff of Co. Fermanagh 1670 and 1686; Governor of Co. Fermanagh *c.* 1690.
> MILITARY: Lieutenant in Inniskilling Regiment of Foot 1691; Captain in Colonel Abraham Creighton's Regiment of Foot 1692; half-pay 1697.

POLITICAL ACTIVITY: In a list of Irish sheriffs in March 1686, the Lord President described Cole as 'weak and Whiggish'. In reply, Clarendon wrote: 'A sober, loyal gentleman, and no bustling man, but of a very good understanding, and no Whig: all his fortune is old interest, and his father and grandfather were very loyal men.' Clarendon's view was borne out to a certain extent in 1689. The Protestant gentlemen of Ireland had been alarmed at how little support they were receiving from London when, in February 1689, London was greatly excited by rumours that King James had set out for Ireland, and Sir Michael Cole declared that he and others would return to Ireland if James offered them good terms. In the 1692 election he stood unsuccessfully for Co. Fermanagh, before being returned for Enniskillen. Apparently he was a notoriously bad attender; whether for this or another reason, he did not sign the 1696 Association for the protection of William III. He was listed for four committees in October 1692 and one on 5 June 1705.

On 1 March 1706 Robert Johnson (**1101**) wrote to Ormonde that Cole had first contested Co. Fermanagh in the first election after the Revolution (1692) but was so roundly defeated by his great rival James Corry (**0498**) that he never contested that seat again. He continues: 'Sir Michael has been forced to serve for a private borough, that of Enniskillen, which afterwards the Parliament turned him out of for his long absence from duty, and the town then chose the Colonel's son [John Corry (**0499**)] in the other's room.' He was also at odds with another of the local interests: his nephew by marriage, Sir Gustavus Hume (**1052**).

On 2 June 1705 Enniskillen was virtually destroyed by fire. All the houses were thatched, so the fire spread rapidly. Public collections were made from house to house and throughout Ireland. Archbishop King was applied to, to obtain the consent of the Crown for collections to be made in England. In 1706 Cole was one of the commissioners for the rebuilding of Enniskillen.

ADDITIONAL INFORMATION: The 'Writs Issued' section of *CJ Ire.* General Index vol. 2 does not record a writ issued for Enniskillen in Sir Michael Cole's place, but the returns are not always trustworthy in respect of by-elections. The 1704 returns give John Corry sitting for Enniskillen in 'place of Michael Cole' and, to add to the confusion, in 1707 they have him sitting in 'place of Michael Cole, dead', although Michael Cole did not die until 1711. To complete the confusion, the returns at the beginning of the 1711 session, 9 July 1711 (when Cole *was* dead), give 'John Corry in place of Sir Michael Cole'.

ESTATES/RESIDENCE: In 1688 his income was calculated at £1,070 from real estate. He was granted the island of Montserrat estate of the outlawed Terrence Dermot, though as Montserrat was very much an Irish Catholic island he probably did not retain it long.

SOURCES: *Cal. SP Dom. 1691–1692* (London, 1900) pp. 26, 113, 165, 220; King, *A Great Archbishop of Dublin, William King DD*, p. 111 & n.2; Fermanagh and Tyrone MPs; *Alum. Dub.*; Burke *PB* (1903) p. 555; PRONI T/559 vol. 15 p. 421, Burke, extract pedigrees; Fermanagh and Tyrone MPs; C. Dalton (ed.), *English Army Lists and Commission Registers, 1661–1714* (London, 1896), vol. 3 p. 206; *JRSAI* vol. 55 (1925) pp. 38, 40, H. A. S. Upton, 'A List of Governors and Deputy Governors of Counties in Ireland in 1699' [says he died in July 1726]; J. J. Howard (ed.), *Miscellanea Genealogica et Heraldica*, vol. 2 (1876) p. 243; S. W. Singer (ed.), *Clarendon Corr.*, vol. 1 (London, 1828) p. 286, vol. 2 (London, 1828) p. 265; *HMC Ormonde*, (HMC 1920) new ser. vol. 8 pp. 221–2; Parliamentary Lists, 1696 (1).

0443 COLE, Richard

MP for St Canice 1707–13; Enniskillen 1713–14, 1715–27–30

b. (bapt. 8 Dec.) 1671; d. *ante* June 1729
FAMILY/BACKGROUND: Son of Sir John Cole of Co. Dublin and Elizabeth, dau. of John Chichester of Dungannon, Co. Tyrone.
MARRIED: (1) [1698] Penelope, eldest dau. and co-h. of Sir William Evans, 1st Baronet; (2) 1727 Mary, dau. of Maurice Keating (**1132**); (she m. (2) [1730] Maj. Toby Purcell).
CHILDREN: *d.s.p.*
MILITARY: Cornet in Princess Anne of Denmark's Regiment of Dragoons 31 Dec. 1689; ?on 3 Mar. 1692 commissioned a Lieutenant in Captain Holgate's Troop in the Regiment of Dragoons under John, Viscount FitzHarding; Lieutenant of Grenadiers in Colonel Edward Dutton's Regiment in West Indies, 14 Mar. 1695; subsequently served with the fleet as Lieutenant in Dutton Colt's Regiment of Marines; 1st Lieutenant of Grenadiers in Lord Lucas's Regiment of Foot 10 Mar. 1702; Captain in Lucas's Regiment (34th Foot) 25 Sept. 1704; brevet Lieutenant-Colonel 1 Jan. 1712; Lieutenant-Colonel of Chudleigh's Regiment (34th Foot) Aug. 1713; Lieutenant in Wittewrong's Regiment 1716, half pay on latter's reduction in 1718.

POLITICAL ACTIVITY: Cole was originally returned for the government borough of St Canice (Bishop of Ossory's) in place of Sir Christopher Wandesford (**2168**), who succeeded his father

(2167) as 2nd Viscount Castlecomer in September 1707. He was a professional soldier and, as such, expected to support the administration of the day. His support, however, appears to have been less than enthusiastic.

He voted against the Money Bill in 1709, but for Richard Levinge (1230), the government candidate, as Speaker in 1713, and in 1713 he was listed as 'a Tory'. From 1713 until his death in 1729 he sat for Enniskillen. He was named for two committees 1709–11, one in 1717 and one in 1719. In 1721 he was against the proposal for a national bank. In September 1721 he was in receipt of a pension of £301 2s 6d p.a. on the Irish Establishment, which he retained until his death.

DIVISION LISTS:

  1709 (1) voted against a Money Bill.
  1713 (1) voted for Sir Richard Levinge (1230) for Speaker.
  1721 (1) voted against a national bank.

ESTATES/RESIDENCE: Archers' Grove, Co. Kilkenny; Killygreen, Co. Londonderry. In 1713 Richard Cole's income was reputed to be £600.

SOURCES: PRONI T/3411; CJ Ire. (Bradley ed.) vol. 4 p. 744, vol. 5 pp. 304–45, 469–77, vol. 6 p. 70; PRONI T/1075/29 Canon Leslie's notes; McCracken thesis; Cal. SP Dom. 1691–2 (London, 1900) p. 165, 1694–5 (London, 1906) p. 404; Kilkenny MPs; Fermanagh and Tyrone MPs; C. Dalton (ed.), English Army Lists and Commission Registers, 1661–1714 (London, 1896) vol. 3 p. 32 (London, 1898) vol. 4 p. 81; C. Dalton, George the First's Army, 1714–1727; J. J. Howard (ed.), Miscellanea Genealogica et Heraldica, vol. 2 (1876) p. 243; Parliamentary Lists 1711 (3), 1713 (1), (2).

0444 COLE, Hon. William Willoughby

MP for Enniskillen 1761–7

  b. 1 Mar. 1736; d. 22 May 1803 (of influenza while visiting his sister at Hazelwood, Co. Sligo)
PEERAGES: Suc. as 2nd Baron Mount Florence 1767, cr. Viscount Enniskillen 20 July 1776; Earl of Enniskillen 18 Aug. 1789.
FAMILY/BACKGROUND: Son and heir of John Cole, 1st Baron Mount Florence (0440) and Elizabeth, dau. of Hugh Willoughby (-Montgomery) (2236).

MARRIED: [3 Nov. 1763] Anne, dau. of Galbraith Lowry (-Corry) (1268) (sis. of Lord Belmore)
CHILDREN: John Willoughby, 2nd Earl of Enniskillen (0441); Galbraith Lowry (0438); Rev. William Montgomery, Dean of Waterford; Arthur Henry (b. 28 June 1780; d. unm. 1844); Henry (d. yg); Sarah, m. [1790] Owen Wynne (2265); Elizabeth Anne (d. 1807), m. [1788] Col. Richard Magenis (1322); Anne; Florence (b. 1779; d. 1862), m. [1797] Blayney Townly (Townley-Balfour) (2095); Henrietta Frances (d. 2 July 1848), m. [1805] Thomas Philip Weddell, 1st Earl de Grey.
EDUCATION: School: Kilkenny College 15 June 1749, aged 13 years.
CAREER/OCCUPATION: Custos Rot. Co. Fermanagh 1769–1803; Joint *Governor of Co. Fermanagh 1769–?1800 (f.); *Governor of the Charitable Musical Society 1780; *Trustee of the Linen Board for Leinster 1781–1800 (f.); *Governor of the Charitable Loan Society 1782–1800 (f.); *Governor and Guardian of the Lying-in Hospital 1789–1800 (f.).
MILITARY: Colonel of Co. Fermanagh Militia; Captain in the First Enniskillen Volunteers; ?Captain in the Fermanagh Cavalry Oct. 1796.

POLITICAL ACTIVITY: He was only six years in the House of Commons before succeeding his father as 2nd Lord Mount Florence. In 1776, although he was advanced in the peerage, he sold the seats for Enniskillen, as his brother Hon. Arthur Cole-Hamilton (0445) had secured his return for Co. Fermanagh. Lord Lieutenant Harcourt successfully recommended him for a step in the peerage, and in 1776 he was created Viscount Enniskillen. Throughout the 1780s he agitated for a further step in the peerage, and in 1789 he was created Earl of Enniskillen. He took a prominent part in suppressing the 1798 rebellion. Lord Enniskillen and his political followers (0441, 0445, 1322) were solidly hostile to the Union.

ADDITIONAL INFORMATION: He and other officers were publicly rebuked by Cornwallis for their conduct of a court martial which acquitted a yeoman called Wollaghan who had deliberately killed a pardoned rebel in 1798: 'It was a test case for the yeoman had based his defence on the orders given him by his superior, Captain Armstrong ... his orders had been to shoot suspected rebels on sight, whether or not they had been given protections, a practice that was cheerfully continued in some

Irish regiments ... Cornwallis could not reverse the verdict. But he dismissed the yeoman, dissolved the Court Martial, all of whose members were Irish, and banned them from sitting on a new one.' Loyalist opinion was outraged, contrasting Cornwallis' severity to them with the leniency to the rebels whose outrages, it was believed, were being tolerated to terrify the people into a Union.

Cornwallis and Enniskillen were later reconciled, Castlereagh commenting that 'Cornwallis has not a warmer political friend than his Lordship.' However, Enniskillen continued to be ·a strong anti-Unionist. Cornwallis became the patron of his son, Arthur, when he took up a position with the East India Company.

*A member of the RDS from 1774 and of *the Royal Irish Academy, 1790–1800(f.) *A subscriber to the Public Assembly Rooms, 1787. Grand Master of the Orange Lodges 1803.

ESTATES/RESIDENCE: Florence Court, Co. Fermanagh; 38 Rutland Square, Dublin. An estimate of part of the estate in 1776 gives 11,000 Irish acres, at a pre-1752 rental of £981 and a 1776 rental of £3,807. These figures include land in Co. Cavan (the Florence Court estate was on the Fermanagh/Cavan border) and at Ballyshannon, Co. Donegal. However, these figures relate only to some of Lord Enniskillen's farms and are likely to be an underestimate of the acreage and rental of the Co. Fermanagh estate. According to Wakefield, the 2nd Earl of Enniskillen (his son) had a rental of £13,000.

SOURCES: PRONI MIC/474 Irish Volunteers; RCBL P80/1/1, Parish Registers of St Thomas, Dublin; GEC P; Burke PB (1906) p. 593; Fermanagh and Tyrone MPs; D. Guinness and W. Ryan, *Irish Houses and Castles* (London, 1971) p. 170; *Ir. Stat.* 25 George III c. 43 [lists householders in Rutland (Parnell) Square]; C. Ross (ed.), *Cornwallis Corr.* (London, 1859), vol. 3 pp. 193, 198, 333, 507; *JRSAI* vol. 54 (1924) pp. 55–67, T. U. Sadleir, 'The Register of Kilkenny School (1685–1800)'; *Almanacks*; *BNL* 24 May 1803 [says he died 20 May 1803]; *FJ* 20 Oct. 1796; T. Pakenham, *The Year of Liberty*, pp. 390–1; Young, *A Tour in Ire.* vol. 1 pp. 277–8; Wakefield, *Account of Ire.*, vol. 1 p. 259; Parliamentary Lists, 1777 (1), 1782 (1), 1783 (2), 1785 (2), 1787 (1), 1788 (1), 1790 (1), 1793 (1), 1794 (2), 1799 (1), (3).

0445 COLE-HAMILTON, Hon. Arthur

MP for Co. Fermanagh 1783–90; Enniskillen 1790–7–1800, (re-elected after appointment to place of profit 1799), [UK] 1801–2

b. 8 Aug. 1750; d. 1810
FAMILY/BACKGROUND: Son of John Cole, 1st Baron Mount Florence (**0440**) and Elizabeth, dau. of Hugh Willoughby (-Montgomery) (**2236**); assumed additional surname of Hamilton upon the death of his father-in-law in 1782.
MARRIED: 1780 Letitia, dau. of Claude Hamilton (**0917**).
CHILDREN: Claude William Cole-Hamilton, m. [1805] Nichola Sophia, e. dau. of Richard Chaloner of Co. Meath; Letitia, m. [Aug. 1815] Maj. R. Stafford; Elizabeth Anne, m. [1820] Capt. Henry Slade; Isabella, m. James Hamilton.
CAREER/OCCUPATION: High Sheriff Co. Tyrone 15 Feb. 1792.
MILITARY: Captain in Loyal Gorten Infantry Nov. 1796; Barracks Commissioner 19 May 1798, 19 June 1798, 15 Mar. 1799, 9 July 1799 at £400 p.a. – dismissed.

POLITICAL ACTIVITY: He sat for Co. Fermanagh from 1783 to 1790 and he then made way for his nephew, Lord Cole. Thereafter, he was returned for Enniskillen. In the 1780s he pursued the policies of his brother, Viscount Enniskillen (**0444**), who wanted advancement in the peerage, while he himself wanted some 'provision'. He was against the Commercial Resolutions in 1784–5, but thereafter, although no expectations had been held out to him, he gave a moderate support. He was appointed Barracks Commissioner in 1798 with a salary of £400, but his recalcitrance over the Union led to his dismissal in 1799. Like the rest of his family, he voted against the Union in both 1799 and 1800.

DIVISION LISTS:
1783 (1) voted for Flood's (**0762**) motion for parliamentary reform.
1784 (1) voted for a committee on the Reform Bill.
1785 (1) voted against the Commercial Propositions.
1787 (1) absent but had previously voted for a Pension Bill.
1789 (1) voted for a Regency.
1790 (1) voted against Grattan's (**0895**) motion for reducing the influence of the Crown.

1790 (2) voted for Foster (**0805**) on the Election of a Speaker.

1799 (1) voted against the Union – Major Tyrone Militia and Barrack Board.

ESTATES/RESIDENCE: In 1789 his addresses were: Skea, Co. Tyrone; Rutland Square, Dublin (probably his brother's house). His wife was the heiress to Beltuim (Beltrim) Castle, Newtown Stewart, Co. Tyrone – the estate was valued at £3,146 a year. It was compact; the lands were mainly in the parish of Boho, barony of Clanawley, and Rossory, Barony of Magheraboy. He took the name of Cole-Hamilton on inheriting this estate *vice* his wife.

SOURCES: PRONI D/302; PRONI D/1939/14/2/1; PRONI T/3166/1B Hartnell notes; O'Neill thesis; Burke *LGI* (1904) p. 244; Fermanagh and Tyrone MPs; Hughes *Pat. Officers*; C. Ross (ed.), *Cornwallis Corr.* (London, 1859), vol. 3 p. 45 [says he died 25 Apr. 1822]; J. J. Howard (ed.), *Miscellanea Genealogica et Heraldica*, vol. 2 (1876) p. 244; *DJ* Jan. 24–6 1782; *FJ* 24 Nov. 1796; Parliamentary Lists, 1784 (1), 1785 (1), (2), (3), (4), 1787 (1), 1788 (1), 1789 (1), 1790 (1), 1791 (1), 1793 (1), 1794 (2), 1799 (3), 1800 (3).

0446 COLLEY, Henry

MP for Co. Kildare 1698–9

b. 1648; d. 1700
FAMILY/BACKGROUND: Eldest surviving son of Capt. Dudley Colley of Castle Carbery, Co. Kildare, and Anne, dau. of Henry Warren of Grangebeg, Co. Kildare.
MARRIED: (1) Mary, o. dau. of Sir William Ussher; (2) [Aug. 1694] Sarah, dau. of John Boswell of Kilcorey, Co. Wicklow.
CHILDREN: (1) Henry Colley (**0447**); Richard Wesley, 1st Baron Mornington (**2214**); Anne, m. William Pole of Queen's County.
EDUCATION: School: Westminster under Busby; entered TCD 13 Jan. 1663, aged 15 years.
CAREER/OCCUPATION: Sheriff of Co. Kildare 1681; Burgess of Harristown.

POLITICAL ACTIVITY: He was returned for Co. Kildare following the death of the Rt Hon. Robert FitzGerald (**0741**) on 31 January 1698. He took the oaths and subscribed to the declaration and Association for the protection of William III on 24 October 1698. The session ended on 26 January 1699, and little is known of his activity dur-

ing that short period.

ESTATES/RESIDENCE: Castle Carbery, Co. Kildare.

SOURCES: PRONI D/3078/4 Minute book of the borough of Harristown, county of Kildare, 1714–1790; Kildare MPs; Simms' cards; *Alum. Dub.*; G. F. Russell-Barker and A. H. Stenning (eds), *Record of Old Westminsters: A biographical list*, 2 vols (London, 1928); Parliamentary Lists, 1696 (1).

0447 COLLEY, Henry

MP for Strabane 1723–4

b. *c.* 1685; d. 10 Feb. 1724
FAMILY/BACKGROUND: Son of Henry Colley (**0446**) and his 1st wife Mary, dau. of Sir William Ussher.
MARRIED: [Jan. 1719] Mary, dau. of Rt Hon. James Hamilton, 6th Earl of Abercorn (**0933**).
CHILDREN: Henry (d. yg); Elizabeth, m. [   ] Glover; Mary, m. Arthur Pomeroy, 1st Viscount Harberton (**1693**).
CAREER/OCCUPATION: Sheriff of Co. Kildare 1723.

POLITICAL ACTIVITY: He was returned by his father-in-law for Strabane, in place of Oliver McCausland (**1310**) who died before 29 August 1723, when the fifth session of George I's parliament opened. Colley died on the day the session ended some six months later: nothing is known of his activity in the interim.

ESTATES/RESIDENCE: Co. Kildare. His two daughters were his coheirs. In 1702–3 Henry Colley (or his guardians) purchased 52 acres in Co. Kildare from the Commissioners for Sale of Forfeited Estates.

SOURCES: RCBL T/34, Extracts from the Parish Registers of St Andrew's, Dublin; Simms, *Williamite Confiscation*, p. 184; Kildare MPs; Fermanagh and Tyrone MPs; Burke *PB* (1900) under Wellington [d. of b. – father (**0446**) m. (2) in 1694, this MP's yr bro. (**2214**) was an official in Dublin Castle in 1713].

COLLEY, Richard: *see* **WESLEY (COLLEY)**, Richard (**2214**)

COLOONY, Baron Coote of: *see* **COOTE**
0480 Coote, Rt Hon. Charles, 5th Baron Coote of Coloony, 1st Earl of Bellomont, MP Co. Cavan 1761–6

0448 COLTHURST, John

MP for Tallow 1734–56

b. 1678; d. 15 Nov. 1756
FAMILY/BACKGROUND: Son of John Colthurst of Co. Cork and Elizabeth, dau. of Sir Nicholas Purdon; (she m. (2) Nicholas Bromby of Ballynoe, Co. Limerick).
MARRIED: Alice, dau. and h. of James Conway of Cloghane, Co. Kerry.
CHILDREN: Sir John Conway, 1st Baronet (**0449**); James, m. Elizabeth, dau. of Col. Christopher Russell of Co. Cork; Nicholas.
CAREER/OCCUPATION: High Sheriff of Co. Cork 1725, 1738; Weighmaster of Cork Nov. 1756; Freedom of Cork 15 July 1743.
MILITARY: Colonel in the Militia Nov. 1756.

POLITICAL ACTIVITY: He came in in place of William Maynard (**1385**), who died on 3 April 1734. As was to be expected of a Cork MP, sitting for a Boyle (Earl of Cork and Burlington) borough, he belonged to Speaker Boyle's (**0210**) party and supported him in the early 1750s over the expulsion of Arthur Jones-Nevill (**1125**) and the rejection of the Money Bill. He was named for 28 committees between 1735 and 1755.

DIVISION LISTS:
1749 (1) voted against the election of James Digges La Touche (♦♦♦♦)
1753 (1) voted for the expulsion of Arthur Jones-Nevill (**1125**).
1753 (2) voted against the Money Bill.

ESTATES/RESIDENCE: Ardrum, Co. Cork. Residual heir to his eldest brother Nicholas, who left two daughters as his coheirs.

SOURCES: PRONI D/302; PRONI T/581 vol. 3 p. 187; GEC *B* [says d.12 July 1756]; McCracken thesis; Burke *PB* (1903) p. 348; *GM* (Exshaw's edition) July 1754, Nov. 1756; *The Dublin Gazette* 29 Nov. 1724; *DJ* 16–20 Nov. 1756.

0449 COLTHURST, Sir John Conway

MP for Doneraile 1751–60; Youghal 1761–8; Castlemartyr 1768–75

b. *ante* 1720; d. 12 Sept. 1775 at Ardrum
HONOURS: Cr. Baronet 3 Aug. 1744.
FAMILY/BACKGROUND: Eldest son of John Colthurst (**0448**) and his wife, Alice, dau. of James Conway.
MARRIED: [1741] Charlotte (d. 9 Oct. 1774), dau. of Rt Hon. Thomas FitzMaurice, 1st Earl of Kerry (**0753**).
CHILDREN: John Conway (d. unm. 15 Feb. 1787), 2nd Baronet; Sir Nicholas, 3rd Baronet (**0450**); Edward; Rev. Charles; William (at Eton College 1763–70, d. *c.* 1773).
CAREER/OCCUPATION: Freedom of Cork 10 Dec. 1756.

POLITICAL ACTIVITY: He first came into parliament in 1751, at the height of the Money Bill dispute. He was part of Speaker Boyle's (**0210**) party and, in 1753, he voted for the expulsion of Arthur Jones-Nevill (**1125**) and against the Money Bill. In the 1760s he was a friend of the 2nd Earl of Shannon (**0213**) and one of his supporters at the time of the augmentation of the army crisis in 1769. He continued his hostility to Lord Townshend for the remainder of his viceroyalty, but was disposed to support Lord Harcourt.

In 1773 it was reported that he was: 'brought in by Lord Shannon whose Borough and estate this is. He will always obey him. A mere paltry fellow, for he was beat by St Leger Aldworth[-St Leger] (**0026**) and had not spirit to resent it, alleging he was sick. Against.' In 1771 he had refused to call out Aldworth-St Leger after the latter had assaulted him. This comment shows the significance of 'honour' and duelling in Irish society. Actually Colthurst's plea of illness may have had substance, as in 1774 he 'voted for the Stamp Act and Tontine, but came wrapped up in his flannels, ill of the gout, to oppose Popery'. He died in 1775. In 1783 his eldest son attempted unsuccessfully to stand for Co. Cork, against Lord Shannon and in the popular interest.

DIVISION LISTS:
1753 (1) voted for the expulsion of Arthur Jones-Nevill (**1125**).
1753 (2) voted against the Money Bill.

1768 (1) voted against army augmentation.
1771 (1) voted against Lord Townshend as Lord Lieutenant.
1771 (2) voted for Sir Lucius O'Brien's (**1558**) motion for retrenchment.
1774 (1) voted for the Stamp Bill.

ADDITIONAL INFORMATION: *A member of the Dublin Society from 1764. Traditionally the Colthursts had allied with Lord Shannon in Cork politics, but with the death of this MP the situation changed. His son, also called John Conway Colthurst, was one of the gentleman Rightboys who opposed Lord Shannon's political hegemony through Shannon's support of the Established Church and clergy. The vexed subject of tithes enabled them to make common cause with some of the more violent of the underprivileged Catholics. Their opposition was particularly felt at the 1783 election, when Lord Shannon was in some political difficulty. On this occasion Colthurst came bottom of the county poll, which increased his hostility. Subsequently he was killed in 1787 as the result of a duel with Dominick Trant (**2103**). Trant accused Colthurst of collusion with the Rightboys, Colthurst demanded satisfaction and, despite a number of attempts by the authorities to prevent them from duelling, they finally managed to meet. Colthurst refused to accept the outcome of the initial duel, in which neither party was hurt, but demanded further satisfaction and was killed.

ESTATES/RESIDENCE: Ardrum, Co. Cork. There is a deed of grant by the Trustees for Forfeited Estates to Nicholas Colthurst of Ballyally, Co. Cork of lands in the barony of Barretts, Co. Cork, dated 2 March 1702. Deed of lease dated 13 May 1703 by Sir John Mead of Ballintober to Nicholas Colthurst of Ballyany, both in Co. Cork, the lands of Curryleigh and Currybehy, barony of Barretts, Co. Cork. He had lands in the baronies of Barretts and Muskerry West. There is a grant by letters patent to Sir John Conway Colthurst of four fairs at Ballyvourney on the tenth days of May, July, September and December, dated 17 May – 29 Geo. II (1756). In 1764, Sir John Colthurst was granted fairs at Knucknamariff, *alias* Knocknarnariffe, *alias* Knocknarmarave.

The estate of Sir George St John Colthurst, Bt (born 1824, died 1878), his great-grandson, lists lands in the barony of Muskerry West and known as the Ballyvourney Estate, lands in the barony of Duhallow

known as the Boulmore or Rathcoole Estate and lands in the barony of Muskerry East known as the Ardrum and Garryadeen Estates, all in Co. Cork.

There is an extant will and grant, 1776, of Sir John Conway Colthurst, of Ardrum, Co. Cork, Bt, Prerog. (original).

SOURCES: PRONI LC 28; EC 3073, 3074, 4410; PRONI MIC/465/1, R. Ffolliott, Biographical Notices, 1756–1827; PRONI T/559 vol. 16 p. 22, Burke, extract pedigrees; McCracken thesis; GEC *B*; Burke *PB* (1903) p. 348; *Index to Hibernian Chronicle, 1769–1775* (Society of Genealogists, 1936) vol. 2 p. 76 [says he died 12 Sept. 1775]; GEC *B* [says he died 19 Sept.]; *DJ* 19–23 September [says he died 'a few days ago'] R. A. Austen-Leigh (ed.), *The Eton College Register, 1753–90* (Eton, 1921) 3 vols; E. Hewitt (ed.), *Lord Shannon's Letters to his Son* (PRONI 1982), pp. lxiii, lxv; J. Smyth, *Men of no Property* (Dublin, 1992), p. 36; J. Kelly, *'That Damn'd Thing Called Honour': Duelling in Ireland 1570–1860*, pp. 116, 145–6; Johnston, *Gt B. & Ire.*, pp. 129–30; *Almanacks*; Parliamentary Lists, 1769 (1), 1772 (2), 1773 (1), (2), 1774 (1), 1775 (1), 1784 (2).

0450 COLTHURST, Sir Nicholas

MP for St Johnstown (Longford) 1783–90; Clonakilty 1792–5

b. *c.* 1743; d. (*c.* 20) May 1795 at St Stephen's Green
HONOURS: Suc. as 3rd Baronet 1787.
FAMILY/BACKGROUND: Son of Sir John Conway Colthurst, 1st Baronet (**0449**) and Charlotte, dau. of Rt Hon. Thomas FitzMaurice, 1st Earl of Kerry (**0753**).
MARRIED: [8 May 1788] Harriet (d. 1841), dau. of Rt Hon. David La Touche (**1203**); (she m.(2) [1798] Gen. Gray).
CHILDREN: Nicholas Conway, 4th Baronet, m. [1819] Elizabeth, o. dau. of George Vesey (**2146**); Elizabeth (*d.s.p.*), m. Rev. Edward St Lawrence, Archdeacon of Ross; Catherine (*d.s.p.* 7 Mar. 1832), m. Col. William Henry Moore Hodder of Hoddersfield, Co. Cork.
CAREER/OCCUPATION: High Sheriff of Co. Cork 1788; *Town Major of Cork 1789–4.

POLITICAL ACTIVITY: Unlike his fire-eating brother (*see* **0449**), Sir Nicholas resumed his family's friendship with Lord Shannon (**0213**). In 1783 he was returned for St Johnstown, Co. Longford by Lord Granard and formed part of his political following. Lord Granard was a government supporter in 1783 and 1784, and Colthurst was 'hopeful' of obtaining a government post. In 1785 Lord Granard went into opposition and his MPs with him.

In 1788, after his brother John Conway died, a Parliamentary List noted that he 'seldom attends, is well disposed to favour Government notwithstanding [his] connection with Lord Granard', which made his support at best 'doubtful'. The 1790 Parliamentary List alleges that Lord Granard 'leaves his friends to be as free as he desires to be himself, under no influence but that of their own reason, under no other bias than the suggestions of their own understanding. Such liberality of conduct in the proprietors of boroughs is not often experienced': indeed, it would be most unusual. However, in 1788, Colthurst married a daughter of the Dublin banker David La Touche (**1203**) which, in addition to inheriting the family estate, probably eased his financial situation and gave him a greater degree of independence.

In 1789 he voted against the government and for a Regency. In 1790 Lord Shannon reported that he was busy 'canvassing the county against Stawell', who was supported by Lord Bernard, while Colthurst had the support of Lady Riversdale. In the event neither was returned for the county, but Lord Shannon returned Colthurst for Clonakilty. Thereafter he was part of Lord Shannon's following and the old family friendship, broken by his brother, was renewed. In April 1795, Lord Shannon hoped that as Colthurst's wife's confinement was safely over he would attend to vote against Catholic Emancipation. However, the Catholic Emancipation Bill came before the House on 5 May and Sir Nicholas died, at his house in St Stephen's Green, on or about 20 May 1795.

DIVISION LISTS:
1783 (1) voted for Flood's (**0762**) motion for parliamentary reform.
1784 (1) voted against a committee on the Reform Bill.
1785 (1) absent.
1789 (1) voted for a Regency.

ESTATES/RESIDENCE: Ardrum, Co. Cork; St Stephen's Green, Dublin; inherited the estates (est. £3,000 p.a.) of his brother, Sir John Conway Colthurst, who died 15 February 1787, five days after a duel with Dominick Trant (**2103**).

SOURCES: PRONI D/302; PRONI LC 28; EC 3073, 3074, 4410; GEC *B.*; Burke *PB* (1903) p. 348; *GM* (Exshaw's edition) Feb. 1787; Cork MPs; E. Hewitt (ed.), *Lord Shannon's Letters to his Son* (PRONI 1982), pp. lxiii, 10, 21, 34; *Almanacks*; *DJ* 23 May 1795 [reports his death, GEC *B* erroneously gives July]; PRONI Will and Grant, 1795 – Sir Nicholas Conway of Ardrum, Co. Cork, Baronet, Prerog. (Original); Parliamentary Lists, 1783 (2), 1784 (1), (2), (3), 1785 (1), (2), (3), (4), 1787 (1), 1788 (1), 1789 (1), 1790 (1), 1791 (1), 1793 (1), 1794 (2).

0451 COLVILL, Hugh

MP for Co. Antrim 1697–9

b. (*ante* 27 July) 1676; d. 7 Feb. 1701
FAMILY/BACKGROUND: Son of Sir Robert Colvill (**0452**) and his 3rd wife Rose, dau. of William Leslie.
MARRIED: Sarah, dau. of James Margetson; (she mar. (2) Rt Hon. Brabazon Ponsonby, 1st Earl of Bessborough (**1696**)).
CHILDREN: Robert (**0453**); Alicia, m. Stephen Moore, 1st Viscount Mountcashell (**1476**).

POLITICAL ACTIVITY: He sat in parliament very briefly, being returned for Co. Antrim on the death of his father, Sir Robert Colvill (**0452**) – one of the few MPs who had sat in the Restoration parliament of Charles II. Hugh Colvill was sworn and subscribed to the declaration and the Association for the protection of William III on 27 July 1697. He was named for committees on 27 September and 4 and 15 October 1697; nothing else is known of his activity in parliament.

ESTATES/RESIDENCE: Newtownards, Co. Down. The estate comprised Comber, Newtownards (with its parliamentary borough) and Greyabbey. He had also estates in Co. Antrim at Galgorm and Kells.

SOURCES: *UJA* vol. 6 p. 14; Parliamentary List, 1696 (1).

0452 COLVILL, Rt Hon. Sir Robert

MP for (Hillsborough 1661–6), Co. Antrim
1692–3, 1695–7

b. 1625; d. 12 June 1697
HONOURS: PC *ante* 1685, ?1694; Knight 1675–9.
FAMILY/BACKGROUND: Son of Rev. Alexander
Colvill.
MARRIED: (1) Penelope, dau. of Francis Hill of
Hill Hall, Co. Down; (2) Honora, dau. of Thady
O'Hara of Crebilly, Co. Antrim; (3) Rose, eldest
dau. of William Leslie of Prospect, Co. Antrim;
(4) Olive, dau. of Sir Oliver St George, 1st
Baronet; she m. (2) Pierce Butler, 4th Viscount
Ikerrin).
CHILDREN: (1) Hugh; Francis, m. Dorothy, dau.
of Sir John Temple; Hill, m. [17 Mar. 1685]
Hatton, dau. of Rt Hon. Donough Maccarty, 4th
Earl of Clancarty; Ann, m. Sir Maurice Eustace
(**0701**).
(3) Hugh (**0451**); William; Rose, m. [17 Aug.
1697] John Magill (Hawkins) (**1324**).
(4) Penelope m. Sir Robert Adare (**0008**);
Elizabeth, m. Rt Hon. Sir Ralph Gore, 4th
Baronet (**0872**).
EDUCATION: School: Mr Hamilton, Bangor;
entered TCD 25 Jan. 1640, aged 15 years.
CAREER/OCCUPATION: High Sheriff of Co. Antrim
1670.
MILITARY: Captain in army 1651.

POLITICAL ACTIVITY: He was one of the very few
people with parliamentary experience, having sat
in the parliament of Charles II. Colvill was one of
the self-made men who emerged at the Restoration. In January 1686 Sir Robert Colvill was reported by Lord Mount Alexander to Clarendon
for remarks made prior to the succession.
Clarendon sought his prosecution. Lord Chief
Justice Keating, however, urged restraint.
Clarendon wrote: 'Sir Robert Colvill is looked
upon as a very great favourer of Fanatics [Presby-
terians], though he goes to Church himself: he is
a man of a very great estate in the north.' In a
later letter Clarendon wrote to Rochester of 'some
little differences' between Colvill and Lord Mount
Alexander, and that the latter was worried that if
he concealed the information about Colvill's remarks, it would later be used against him. He
wrote that Colvill 'is a man of at least £3,000 per
annum in the north of this Kingdom, and was for
several years of the Privy Council, till the change

upon his Majesty's coming to the crown'.
At the end of February 1686, Clarendon wrote:
'Sir Robert Colvill ... came to me full of professions of duty to the King. He told me ... if I would
give him leave, when he returned into the country, he would give me a constant account of all
things in these parts ... I have scarce ever known a
man more variously spoken of than this Sir Robert.
Some very good men give him a great character;
others as good, shake their heads, and say they
know not what to think of his principles: all agree
that he has a great interest, that is, a great estate.
Some perhaps envy him for that; and some hate
him for the meanness of this birth: indeed, they
say he is come from a very vile beginning.'
In June 1686 David Maxwell sought the protection of the Crown, saying that he had been
molested by Colvill for giving information against
him. Clarendon said no such actions had taken
place against Maxwell.
Colvill was returned for Co. Antrim in 1692
and again in 1695. In 1695 he supported Lord
Chancellor Porter against the accusations of favouring Catholics made against him by some MPs,
and in the following year he signed the Association for the protection of William III in the country.

ADDITIONAL INFORMATION: Colvill sought to arrange a marriage between his son and a daughter
of Sir Thomas Newcomen, niece of Tyrconnel.
This fell through and Tyrconnel was thought to
regard Colvill as a dangerous man, which helped
to inspire Mount Alexander's report. Colvill then
sought a match between his son and Lady Ellen
Carty in an attempt to be made a viscount.
On 29 January 1693, Colvill requested a
baronetage. On 28 February, Sydney advised the
Earl of Nottingham not to sign the warrant until
parliament was dissolved, as Colvill remained of
use to them in the Commons. On 2 December
1693, the Lord Justices asked Sir J. Trenchard to
restore Colvill to the PC.
He features frequently in a contemporary publication: *A Faithful Narrative of the Northern Affairs of Ireland from King James' Accession to the
Crown to the Siege of Londonderry.*

ESTATES/RESIDENCE: Newtown(ards), Co. Down; Mount

Colvill (later Galgorm), Co. Antrim. In 1675 he bought the Co. Down estates of Lord Mount Alexander, Newtown, Comber and Greyabbey. In November 1675 he bought the whole parish of Newtownards from Hugh, 2nd Earl of Mount Alexander for £10,640 and a further part of the estate for £3,000, and finally in 1679 he bought the Comber estate of Mount Alexander for £9,780, the earl reserving for himself only the manor house, farm buildings, certain tithes and townlands. The Co. Down estate comprised 60 townlands. He paid the Earl of Donegall £1,300 for the lately dissolved abbey of Kells, Co. Antrim and its eight townlands.

SOURCES: PRONI T/502/1; J. Stevenson, *Two Centuries of Life in County Down* (Belfast, 1920), p. 103; PRONI T/559 vol. 16 p. 25 Burke, extract pedigrees [says his third wife was Rose Hill]; PRONI T/1765/9; PRONI MIC/315/9/60 Blackwood pedigrees; Lodge *P*; *Cal. SP Dom. 1693* (London, 1903) pp 23, 50–51, 417, *1694–5* (London, 1906) pp 1, 158–9; *UJA* vol. 5, pp 138–145; *UJA* vol. 6 p. 14; *Alum. Dub.*; Simms' cards; S. W. Singer (ed.), *Clarendon Corr.*, vol. 1 (London, 1828) pp. 223, 226, 271, 465–6, 469; Parliamentary Lists, 1695 (1), 1696 (1).

0453 COLVILL, Robert

MP for Killybegs 1719–27; Antrim B. 1727–49

b. *c.* 1697–8; d. 30 Mar. 1749

FAMILY/BACKGROUND: Son of Hugh Colvill (0451) and Sarah, dau. of James Margetson.

MARRIED: Martha Lauders (formerly his mistress).

CHILDREN: *d.s.p.*

CAREER/OCCUPATION: Free Burgess of Newtown(ards) Mar. 1741.

POLITICAL ACTIVITY: He was returned for Speaker Conolly's (0460) borough of Killybegs in the by-election following the creation of Charles Fane, Viscount Fane (0720). He was considered 'wild and indecent' in his conversation and 'disordered in his understanding'. Apart from his voting against a national bank, there is no evidence of his parliamentary activity. He is not listed for any committees.

DIVISION LISTS:

1721 (1) voted against a national bank.
1721 (2) voted against a national bank.
1749 (1) dead.

ADDITIONAL INFORMATION: During his minority he was largely brought up by his stepfather, Brabazon Ponsonby (1696), who also looked after his extensive estates and the parliamentary borough of Newtown(ards). The Parliamentary List for 1790 (Henry Alexander, 0028) says that the Ponsonbys 'purchased it from a certain female friend of Mr Colvill's its proprietor at the commencement of the century'. Considering that Brabazon Ponsonby had already gained control of it as Colville's guardian, this seems unlikely.

ESTATES/RESIDENCE: Newtown(ards), Co. Down; Bishopscourt, Co. Kildare. In 1721 Colvill made a will leaving his Co. Down property to Rt Hon. John Ponsonby (1702), but his mistress turned him against the Ponsonbys and persuaded him to sell the estate for £42,259 to Alexander Stewart. In 1744, the town and manor of Newton in the parishes of Newton and Greyabbey produced a gross rental of £2,241 and a net of £2,160. (The receiver (agent) William Colvill's salary was £54.) Newtown contained 12,409 Cunningham acres in *c.* 1720. According to the deeds of sale, Mount Alexander (Comber) had a gross rental of £1,110 and net rental of £1,098 in 1744; the purchase price was £22,000 British. The Newtown(ards) town and estate was £869, £809 and £18,581. The Newtown(ards) rental was £4,791 in 1789 and Comber £2,080.

His sister Alicia was heiress to his property in Co. Antrim, which may have been entailed, but his residuary heir was a Miss Mary Degge. The will caused a furore and was contested by Alicia (or Alice) and her husband Stephen Moore. It was finally settled in November 1754 'in favour of the said Executors and Guardians and for the validity of said will, by which the said Miss Degge gets a very large fortune in lands in different parts of the Kingdom'.

SOURCES: BL Add. MSS 19997 Newtown(ards) borough book, 1741–75; McCracken thesis; *UJA* vol. 5 (1899) pp. 144–5, *UJA* vol. 6 (1900) pp. 14–15, 138–45; *GM* (Exshaw's edition) Mar. 1749; GEC *P*; *IHS* vol. 18, no. 71 (1973) p. 317; PRONI D/562/1681, Legal notes by Anthony Foster, *c.* 1749, Foster/Massereene Papers [quoted in *IHS* (1973)]; A. P. W. Malcomson, 'The Newtown Act; Revision and Reconstruction' p. 317 [re Colville's personality]; PRONI Newtown rental, 1744; PRONI D/654/R1/1B Londonderry Papers; PRONI T/2493/1 survey of the Colvill estate (*c.* 1720); PRONI D/654/C1/TM A–B and D/654/E1/7 [Indentures between Alex. Stewart and Colvill and Bessborough, 9 July, 14 Sept. and 18 Oct. 1744]; R. E. Burns, *Irish Parliamentary Politics in the Eighteenth Century*, 2 vols (Washington, 1989) vol. 2, pp. 64, 92; *BNL* 26 Nov. 1754.

0454 COLVILL, William

MP for Newtown Limavady 1777–83; Killybegs
1783–90

b. 6 Dec. 1737; d. 5 July 1820
FAMILY/BACKGROUND: Son of William Colvill and
Jane, dau. of John Thompson of Co. Down.
MARRIED: [18 June 1777] Hannah, dau. and h. of
John Chaigneau.
CHILDREN: Edward (d. yg); William Chaigneau,
m. [1812] Hester, dau. of James Lowry of Co.
Tyrone; John Thompson (d. yg); Susanna; Jane;
Margaretta; Hannah, m. [1815] Rev. T. Harper
of Co. Wexford; Arabelle (d. yg).
CAREER/OCCUPATION: A corn merchant. Agent to
Widows of Officers 1780–9, 1793, 1795–9;
*Court of Directors of the Grand Canal Com-
pany, Committee of Works 1772–3, 1775,
Stores, Accounts 1772–3; *on the Committee of
Merchants 1775; *Commissioner for Paving the
Streets of Dublin 1779–80; *Commissioner of
the Tillage Act for Connaught 1779–80; *Trustee
of the Royal Exchange 1775; Director of the
Bank of Ireland 1782, 1784, Deputy Governor
1790–1800 (f.), Governor 1801–2.

POLITICAL ACTIVITY: He was a merchant 'and sensible', a friend of Colonel Burton Conyngham
(**0303**) whose uncle, Lord Conyngham (**0464**),
returned him for Limavady in 1777, when Colonel Burton Conyngham decided to sit for Ennis.
Colvill followed the Conyngham lead and supported. In 1780 he was made Agent to the Widows of Officers, £300 p.a. The 1782 list described
him as 'a Corn Factor and has much information
in that business'; the 1783 list emphasised that he
was 'intelligent in that business'.
  On 6 May 1780 Flood (**0762**) was given leave
to prepare the heads of a bill to encourage and
regulate the corn trade. When his bill was introduced it created conflict over the level at which
the bounties should be set, and thus whether farmers or millers would be the main beneficiaries.
Colvill led the opposition, maintaining on 12 June
that the bill would disadvantage farmers by restricting their access to the Dublin market and by
increasing their dependence on millers. The debate became so heated that some MPs feared that
a duel would ensue. This did not eventuate, but
Colvill's opposition reduced the proposed bounty
on flour and wheat from Flood's suggested level.

In 1783 Colonel Burton Conyngham, having
recently inherited the borough from his uncle,
brought him in for Killybegs. Burton Conyngham
also inherited his uncle's estates in Donegal and
at Slane, Co. Meath, and with them a large flour
mill. Colvill subsequently became Conyngham's
agent. In 1784 he was anxious to be Treasurer of
the Ordnance. In 1788 he was noted as a 'very
good attendant', but there is no evidence that he
achieved his ambition. He did not come in in
1790.

DIVISION LISTS:
  1778 (2) voted against the Popery Bill.
  1779 (2) voted against a six-months Loan
  Bill.
  1780 (1) voted against Grattan's (**0895**)
  declaration of the rights of Ireland.
  1780 (2) voted against Yelverton's (**2268**)
  motion to modify Poynings' Law.
  1780 (3) voted for the Tenantry Bill.
  1780 (4) voted for the Perpetual Mutiny
  Bill.
  1784 (1) voted against a committee on the
  Reform Bill.
  1785 (1) voted for the Commercial Propositions.

ESTATES/RESIDENCE: Bachelor's Walk, Dublin.

SOURCES: Burke *IFR* (1976) p. 263; *JRSAI* vol. 41 (1911)
p. 172, E. M. F.-G. Boyle, 'Records of the Town of
Limavady, 1609–1804'; J. Kelly, *Henry Flood…* (Dublin, 1998), p. 275; *Almanacks*; *FJ* 6 Apr. 1799; *DJ* 19–
21 June 1777; Parliamentary Lists, 1776 (1), 1778 (1),
1780 (1), 1782 (1), 1783 (1), (2), 1784 (1), (2), (3),
1785 (1), (2), (3), (4), 1787 (1), 1788 (1), 1789 (1),
1790 (1).

CONGLETON, Baron: *see* **PARNELL**
1630 Parnell, Rt Hon. Sir Henry Brooke, 1st
Baron Congleton [UK], MP Maryborough 1797–
1800, [UK] Queen's County 1802, 1806–32,
Portarlington 1802, Dundee 1833–41

♦♦♦♦ CONGREVE, Ambrose [n.d.e.]

MP for Co. Waterford Oct.–Dec. 1735; Waterford city Mar. 1738–Nov. 1739

b. 1698; d. 8 Aug. 1741
FAMILY/BACKGROUND: Son of Rev. John Congreve of Co. Kilkenny and Rebecca, dau. of Lieut.-Col. Oliver Jones.
MARRIED: [1725] Elinor, dau. of John Lapp, wid. of [ ] Roche; (she m. (3) John Whitcomb, Abp of Cashel).
CHILDREN: John (0455); Mary.
EDUCATION: School: Mr Fell, Waterford; entered TCD 9 July 1713, aged 15 years.
CAREER/OCCUPATION: Mayor of Waterford 1736; *Magistrate of Waterford 1736.

POLITICAL ACTIVITY: He was twice not duly elected: once for Co. Waterford and once for Waterford city. He belonged to a prominent Waterford family, many of whom represented the city.

ESTATES/RESIDENCE: Waterford.

SOURCES: PRONI T/559 vol. 16 p. 48, Burke, extract pedigrees; NAI MFCI Reel 12, Parish Registers of Christchurch, St Olave and St Patrick, Waterford [bur. 10 Aug. 1741, says his wife is Elizabeth]; McCracken thesis; Burke *IFR* (1976) p. 265; *Alum. Dub.*; R. H. Ryland, *The History, Topography and Antiquities of the county and city of Waterford* (London, 1824), p. 409; *Almanacks*; *The Dublin Gazette* 11 Aug. 1741.

0455 CONGREVE, John

MP for Killyleagh 1761–8; [n.d.e. Co. Waterford 1769]

b. 22 May 1733; d. (bur. 14) Mar. 1801
FAMILY/BACKGROUND: Son of Ambrose Congreve (♦♦♦♦) and Elinor, dau. of John Lapp wid. of [ ] Roche.
MARRIED: [Apr. 1758] Mary, elder dau. of Beverley Ussher (2129).
CHILDREN: John (0456); Ambrose Ussher (d., will proved 1809), m. Anne, dau. of John Jenkins.
EDUCATION: School: private tutor; entered TCD 19 Feb. 1750, aged 16 years, BA 1753.
CAREER/OCCUPATION: High Sheriff of Co. Waterford 1755; *Governor of the Hibernian Society 1769–78.

POLITICAL ACTIVITY: He was returned in 1761 for Sir John Blackwood's borough of Killyleagh and in 1769 was returned for Waterford county with both John Beresford (0115) and Sir James May (1383), much to the annoyance of the Committee on Elections, which was presented with two writs joining Beresford with both candidates. This was illegal, but possibly the Returning Officer was anxious not to offend either candidate. He voted for the augmentation of the army, but he did not come into parliament after 1768.

DIVISION LISTS:
1768 (1) voted for army augmentation.

ADDITIONAL INFORMATION: His son, Ambrose Ussher Congreve, was listed as a nominee in the life annuities of 1779.

He was on friendly terms with Counsellor Power (1717). In his assessment of Co. Waterford in 1775, George Ponsonby (1699) describes him as 'of the independent interest'. An enthusiastic Volunteer, he was one of the delegates for Co. Waterford to the Volunteer National Convention in 1784.

ESTATES/RESIDENCE: Mount Congreve, Co. Waterford. Ponsonby valued it at £2,000 p.a. in 1775.

SOURCES: PRONI D/302; PRONI T/3166/1A Hartnell notes [confuses this and the next MP (0456)]; NAI MFCI Reel 12, Parish Registers of Christchurch, St Olave and St Patrick, Waterford [bapt. 23 May 1733 and bur. 14 Mar. 1801]; Burke *LGI* (1904) p. 106, *IFR* (1976) p. 265; *Alum. Dub.*; Vicars, *Prerog. Wills*, *Ir. Gen.* vol. 1 no. 8 (1940) p. 240 'A List of Irish Stockholders, 1779'; *Waterford Arch. Soc. Jn.* vol. 16 (1913) p. 51, T. U. Sadleir (ed.), 'The County of Waterford 1775'; Parliamentary Lists, 1769 (1), 1783 (3).

0456 CONGREVE, John

MP for Belfast (elected 1 Feb.) 1800

b. 1764; d. 17 Mar. 1801
FAMILY/BACKGROUND: Son of John Congreve (0455) and Mary, dau. of Beverley Ussher (2129).
MARRIED: ?
CHILDREN: *d.s.p.*
EDUCATION: Entered Oxford (Oriel College) 24

Feb. 1781, aged 17 years.
CAREER/OCCUPATION: Sheriff of Co. Waterford 11
Feb. 1792.
MILITARY: Captain of the Waterford Union,
Volunteers.

POLITICAL ACTIVITY: He was a Belfast merchant who
never took his seat, although he was elected in
time for the decisive debate on 5–6 February 1800.
Returned by Lord Donegall, probably as an insurance and to indicate his good intentions towards the government. He replaced George
Crookshank (0532), who had voted against the
Union in 1799.

ESTATES/RESIDENCE: Landscape, Co. Waterford.

SOURCES: PRONI MIC/474 Irish Volunteers; PRONI
MIC/465/1 R. Ffolliott, Biographical Notices, 1756–
1827; Burke *LGI* (1904) p. 106; *IFR* (1976) p. 265;
Alum. Oxon.; Hughes, *Pat. Officers*; G. C. Bolton, *The
Passing of the Irish Act of Union*, p. 176; *BNL* 4 Feb.
1800.

0457 CONNELL, Richard

MP for St Canice 1692–3, 1695–9, 1703–13

b. 1650; d. 1714
FAMILY/BACKGROUND: Eldest son of William
Connell and [   ], dau. of John Bishop of Co.
Kilkenny.
MARRIED: Dorothy, dau. of Robert Lloyd of
Wales.
CHILDREN: Rev. William; Robert, m. Lydia, dau.
of Edmund Ruerke; Judith, m. Jacob [   ]; Anne;
Grissell; Dorothy, m. her cousin William
Connell, Archdeacon of Ossory.
CAREER/OCCUPATION: Registrar of the Diocese of
Ossory; Sheriff of Kilkenny city 1678–9;
Alderman and Mayor 1685–6–7.
MILITARY: Ensign Kilkenny city Militia 1681;
Lieutenant 1691; Captain 1702; Lieutenant-
Colonel 1707 and commanded the Regiment
until death.

POLITICAL ACTIVITY: He was a professional soldier,
but also an official in the diocese of Ossory. He
was returned by the Bishop for St Canice, which
he represented in successive parliaments for over
20 years. In 1695 he supported Lord Chancellor
Porter against the accusations of favouring Catholics made against him by some MPs; in 1696 he

signed the Association for the protection of
William III in the country. During the reign of
Queen Anne he supported the administration, and
in 1703 he introduced 2 Anne, *c.* 18, 'An Act for
the recovery of small debts in a summary way before the Judges of Assize'. He gave a firm support
to the administration over the Dublin mayoralty
issue. He did not come in again in 1713, although
it was thought that he would be returned.

DIVISION LISTS:
    1709 (1) voted against a Money Bill.
    1711 (1) voted for the Court on the Dublin
    mayoralty issue.

ESTATES/RESIDENCE: Kilkenny.

SOURCES: *CJ Ire.* (Bradley edition) vol. 3 p. 30 (0080);
Kilkenny MPs; Parliamentary Lists, 1695 (1), 1696 (1),
1706 (1), 1711 (3), 1713 (1).

CONNER, Arthur: *see* O'CONNOR, Arthur (1565)

0458 CONNER, William

MP for Bandon 1761–6

b. 1701; d. (bur. 9) Jan. 1766
FAMILY/BACKGROUND: Son of Daniel Conner of
Bandon, Co. Cork and Margaret, dau. of [   ]
Sloane.
MARRIED: [Oct. 1721] Anne, dau. of Arthur
Bernard (0123).
CHILDREN: Daniel (*d.s.p.*); William, m. [July
1777] [   ] Grant, dau. of Thos. Grant of
Kilmurry (or Kilworth); Roger, m. [26 Feb.
1753] Anne, dau. of John Longfield; Arthur;
Mary Anne, m. William Dunscomb; Thomasine,
m. Abraham Morris (1495).
EDUCATION: School: Mr Hill, Bandon; entered
TCD 24 Feb. 1718, aged 17 years; Lincoln's Inn
21 Nov. 1720.
CAREER/OCCUPATION: One of the six Clerks in the
Court of Chancery 1759, 1764–5.
MILITARY: An officer in the Cork city Militia.

POLITICAL ACTIVITY: Returned by either Lord Shannon (0213) for the Devonshire interest in Bandon

or by the Bernards (**0125**). His short stay in parliament appears to have been in no way memorable. He possibly hoped to further his legal career.

ADDITIONAL INFORMATION: He was the grandfather of Arthur O'Connor (**1565**), the United Irishman.

ESTATES/RESIDENCE: Connerville, Co. Cork. Daniel Connor purchased 1,311 acres in Co. Cork from the Commissioners for Sale of Forfeited Estates in 1702–3.

When his father died in 1761 his estate was worth £5,000 p.a.

SOURCES: PRONI T/559 vol. 16 p. 64, Burke, extract pedigrees [says his wife's name was Mary]; PRONI MIC/465/1 R. Ffolliott, Biographical Notices, 1756–1827; NAI MFCI Reel 29, Parish Registers of Killrogan, Co. Cork; Burke *LGI* (1904) p. 107, *IFR* (1976) p. 266; *Alum. Dub.*; *The Records of the Honourable Society of Lincoln's Inn* (Lincoln's Inn, 1896) vol. 1 p. 386; *Register of Admissions to the Honourable Society of the Middle Temple* (London, 1949) vol. 1 p. 334 [gives a Daniel Conner son and heir of William of Connerville, Cork, admitted to the Middle Temple 28 June 1744]; C. Dalton (ed.), *English Army Lists and Commission Registers, 1661–1714* (London, 1902) vol. 5 p. 243; Simms, *Williamite Confiscation*, p. 184; *Almanacks*; *FJ* 11–14 Jan. 1766; *DJ* 22–4 July 1777.

0459 CONOLLY, Rt Hon. Thomas

MP for Co. Londonderry 1761–8–76–83–90–7–1800 [r. Ballyshannon 1761]; [GB] Malmesbury 1759–68; Chichester 1768–80; [Escheator of Munster 8 May 1800]

b. 1738; d. 27 Apr. 1803 at Castletown of influenza complicated by asthma
HONOURS: PC, sworn 6 Apr., 8 July 1761–d.
FAMILY/BACKGROUND: Only son of Rt Hon. William Conolly (**0461**) and Anne, dau. of Thomas Wentworth, 1st Earl of Strafford; brother-in-law *inter alia* to the 3rd Duke of Richmond, 1st Duke of Leinster, 2nd Earl of Buckinghamshire, 1st Lord Holland and also of George Robert FitzGerald, executed for murder 1786.
MARRIED: [30 Dec. 1758] Louisa Augusta, dau. of Charles Lennox, 2nd Duke of Richmond.
CHILDREN: *d.s.p.*
EDUCATION: School: Westminster Jan. 1750, aged 12 years, left 1754.

CAREER/OCCUPATION: Joint Governor of City and County of Londonderry and of Coleraine 26 June 1761–95; Sole Governor of the City and County of Londonderry and of Coleraine after the death of his relative and colleague, Earl Conyngham in 1781; Custos Rot. for Londonderry 24 Nov. 1800; Trustee of Linen Board for Ulster Apr. 1764–1803; *on the Court of Directors of the Grand Canal Company (Committee of Works) 1772–3; *Governor of the Foundling Hospital and Workhouse 1777–97; Freeman of Limavady 31 Jan. 1760; Burgess of Limavady 14 Dec. 1781; *Governor and Guardian of the Lying-in Hospital 1788–1803.
MILITARY: Colonel of the Loughinshillen Battalion of Volunteers 1782; Captain Commissioner of the Castletown Union Volunteers 1782, and Celbridge and Bellaghy Volunteers; Colonel of Co. Londonderry Militia, 1793, Kildare Militia (resigned 1797).

POLITICAL ACTIVITY: Thomas Conolly owed his political position to his great possessions as the ultimate Conolly heir of the fortune amassed by Speaker Conolly (**0460**), and to his excellent connections by birth and marriage. Lady Anne Wentworth, his mother, was a daughter of the 1st Earl of Strafford; Lady Louisa Lennox, his wife, was a daughter of the 2nd Duke of Richmond and a sister of Emily, Duchess of Leinster and Caroline, Lady Holland. He had a direct interest in five parliamentary seats – the boroughs of Ballyshannon and, from 1781, Newtown Limavady; his estates and personal interest secured his return for Co. Londonderry. In 1765 he publicly came to blows with his cousin, Henry Conynham (**0464**), over the borough of Newtown Limavady, of which he was the residual heir. In many ways he was the perfect country gentleman and he never sought to be anything else: 'Squire Conolly', a conscientious landlord and a good sportsman.

Conolly was unanimously returned for Co. Londonderry at the 1761 election, and for the next 40 years he represented the county 'faithfully ... [discharging] the duties of that station with credit and advantage to his constituents, and with a dignified spirit becoming a man at the head of the landed interest in Ireland'. He was a British MP for over 20 years, but made little mark on British politics and chose to spend much of his time in

Ireland, where Castletown, his principal residence, was arguably the finest Irish Georgian house. Lady Caroline Dawson, visiting the house in 1778, said that it was 'reckoned the finest in this kingdom. It has been done up by Lady Louisa, and with a very good taste'. Here the Conollys entertained munificently: 'I had no occasion to save money,' he wrote, 'having no children, and I flatter myself that the money I have spent annually was rationally employed by living, not extravagantly, but like a gentleman.' By 1797 his debts stood at £47,667.

His intelligence was limited and his U-turns often illogical. His sister-in-law, Lady Caroline Fox (Lady Holland), said when she first met him that he was 'free and easy and good-humoured', but in a letter to her sister Lady Kildare (Duchess of Leinster) on 17 April 1759, she wrote 'You must indeed be partial to Conolly not to think him immensely silly ... sure he is a tiresome boy, and one feels sorry he is so, he seems so exceeding good natured I can[not] but think how miserable I would have been at Louisa's age to have such a husband.' In fact the Conolly marriage was and remained a happy one. Then on 17 June, Lady Caroline wrote: 'I look upon him as a boy of ten or eleven years old, and treat him as such. I only dread her feeling ashamed of him sometimes.' Both Lady Holland and the Duchess of Leinster were clever women, and the duchess agreed with her sister, writing to her husband on 11 November 1762: 'Conolly was in town yesterday ... talked a vast deal of nonsense about politics in order to make me think him mighty cunning, and that he knew *the way of the world* as well as anybody.'

In 1759 Lord Temple tried 'to engage him to join their party', but he replied 'that he was a young man and could enter into no party'. Initially he became a follower of his brothers-in-law Fox in England and Kildare in Ireland, but he prided himself in his independence: '[He] had a great appetite for Irish politics, but a very poor digestion, full of ideas and opinions, he pursued a will-o-the wisp policy which at times aggravated his friends on both sides of the House, but never himself; for it was his greatest boast that he was always strictly independent.' Frequently this expressed itself in an irrational eccentricity. On 1 May 1768 he moved an Address to His Majesty

against the high estimate of augmentation, which was passed by a committee of the whole House, but he voted for the bill. In 1775 he was one of a group of politicans who had a certain identification and sympathy with the American cause. They included Ponsonby (**1702**) – whom he proposed as Speaker on 18 June 1776, when Pery (**1670**) was elected by 141 to 98 votes – Hussey-Burgh (**1059**), Yelverton (**2268**) and Ogle (**1573**), who argued that if they assisted the British parliament to punish the Americans they would be making a rod for their own backs.

His attitude to the Volunteers was ambiguous. The army was used for defence but, in the absence of a police force, it also undertook policing duties. The withdrawal of troops for the War of American Independence led to a military vacuum which was filled by locally raised and supported (as the treasury was empty) forces known as the Volunteers. They were both a necessity and, in that they were an armed force outside the control of government, a problem.

Conolly was 'unenthusiastic' about the Constitution of 1782: his wife wrote to her sister, Lady Sarah Bunbury, on 26 April 1782 that 'Mr Conolly is one of the few that wished things to remain where they were, as he was quite certain that we had no grievance but imaginary ones, and that attempting to do them away was at a much greater risk than they were worth. However the torrent was against him, and he would not vote against the general opinion of his country, though he said he differed from them in many particulars. The vote that you had heard given for the independency of Ireland was nothing more than acquiescing to the general opinion, upon Mr. Yelverton's bill, which was calculated to quiet the minds of the people upon past transactions respecting property.'

He was often in opposition, but his objective was the maintenance of the *status quo*: for instance, on the proposal of a short Money Bill in November 1779, he declared that 'Three million without doors making 300 do what they please within, is contrary to the principles of the House of Commons, to the principles of representation. Who have the power of voting for members of Parliament? It is those who have property. You represent property, not numbers.' This, of course, was the last bulwark of the Ascendancy.

His basic political motivation, then, was essentially conservative, although it sometimes took an unexpected turn, for instance over the Commercial Resolutions in 1785. On 18 August 1785, the Home Secretary, Lord Sydney, commented to Lord Lieutenant Rutland that 'There are certainly men whose conduct can never excite astonishment, but that of Mr Conolly is not of the number. It is contrary to every part of his former behaviour, and indeed inconsistent with every principle which he has hitherto professed.' His position was certainly not the result of his abilities but of his possessions and probably his good nature. Sir Jonah Barrington wrote of him that 'A few of these country gentlemen had a sort of exclusive privilege of speaking without interruption, whether they spoke good sense or folly ... Of this class was Mr Thomas Conolly. He took a principal lead amongst the country gentlemen ... He was a person of very high family, ample fortune, powerful connexions and splendid establishments; friendly, sincere, honourable and munificent in disposition ... his ideas of politics were limited and confused.' Lady Louisa, however, had something of her sisters' intelligence and was highly respected for her compassion and good sense.

Lord Lieutenant Buckinghamshire, who succeeded Lord Harcourt in 1777, was a brother-in-law of Conolly but denied being influenced by him, writing to Lord George (Sackville) Germain (1835) on 5 February 1780 that 'Mr Conolly has never during my residence in this kingdom attempted to interfere in my councils, or even to talk upon business, professing himself always to stand independent of Government. At this time indeed ... he is a most active and efficient friend to government.' On 24 October 1779 Buckinghamshire had written to Germain that 'The duke of Leinster and Mr Conolly tho' at first disinclin'd to the armed societys at least so far as not to engage in them are now become their great promoters. In the course of the summer upon its being rumour'd that his Majesty might possibly be induc'd to grant commissions to the officers, they both express'd a desire to be honour'd with those of colonel. Mr Conolly went into the North from

whence he was to transmit me a list of gentlemen desirous of having inferior commissions, and the Duke said he would speak to his friends along the same line. From that time his Grace has been totally silent with respect to the measure, and Mr Conolly wrote me a letter from the North declining the idea. During his residence there he engag'd in those societys and contributed very much to give them some systematical regulations ... there are some companies whose principles are determinedly republican ... One very serious regulation is introducing in some of them, that of appointing their officers in rotation.'

Then on 8 June 1780 Buckinghamshire wrote to Germain pointing out that 'The appointment, however, of Lord Charlemont by many of the Northern volunteer Companys to act as their Reviewing General, does not imply a very affectionate disposition to Government, as it was not possible for them to have made a more offensive choice. This circumstance will be far from pleasing to Mr Conolly, but he prudently means to decline shewing any dissatisfaction, and proposes to be present at the Derry Races as usual.'

Conolly's attitude to the Volunteers changed with the shifting emphases within the movement. He was a delegate to the second Volunteer Convention in September 1783, but did not attend the National Convention in Dublin in November, being 'the only delegate who did not attend the meeting or make an apology for non-attendance'. He was opposed to the 'concerting [of] a plan of parliamentary reform' and he loudly denounced this attempt of an armed body to overawe parliament, being the proposer of a motion in parliament to 'preserve our present happy constitution inviolate at the risk of our lives and fortunes'. However, in 1786, during the debates on the Dublin Police Act, he paid tribute to the Volunteers for the way in which they had accepted the authority and direction of parliament 'by their peaceful withdrawal from public affairs'.

The connection between parties in England and opposition groups in Ireland became more pronounced after 1782, and in 1784 a Parliamentary List written at the beginning of the Rutland administration stated that 'The Duke of Leinster (0745) declared himself totally attached to Mr

Fox; Conolly declared the same sentiments, with this reserve, however, that the present times required every man to support Government – that was, in other words, that he would do so until the Reform Bill was rejected.' Rutland, who wanted his support for the Commercial Resolutions in 1784–5, considered that Conolly 'governs his public conduct by the principles of a Newmarket blackleg' – the duke had recently been a guest at Castletown, but Conolly had failed to support the Commercial Resolutions. It was thought that this might have been because Chief Secretary Orde had not paid him sufficient attention.

He supported the administration on the Whiteboy Act of 1787, prompting Lady Sarah (Bunbury) Napier, his sister-in-law, and his nephew Lord Edward FitzGerald (0730) to comment that 'He behaved shabbily' and attribute his actions to his friendship with the Bishop of Cloyne. More probably it was his anxiety about the maintenance of law and order. In 1789, he was a principal member of the opposition in the Regency Crisis, when 'He spoke in favour of Grattan's (0895) motion in February that the Irish Parliament should vote an immediate address to the Prince inviting him to an unrestricted Regency of Ireland.' He was later selected as one of the aborted delegation of MPs to 'wait personally' on the prince. The Lord Lieutenant, the Marquess of Buckingham, refused to transmit their address. He was a founding member of the Whig Club, a mutual support society set up during the Regency Crisis, and was its secretary in 1790.

In the 1790s he did a volte-face from his views in the 1780s and – with his friends the Ponsonbys, who had adopted this issue to the 'unease' of their English patron, the Duke of Portland – took up the cause of parliamentary reform. At the opening of the 1793 session of parliament, he gave notice, along with William Brabazon Ponsonby (1709), that he was bringing forward a measure of parliamentary reform. In a letter to his brother-in-law, the Duke of Richmond, on 30 March 1793, he expressed his opinions at some length: from 'the comparative expenses of government in Lord Townshend's time and at the present day, you will see the enormous increase of every expense, mostly incurred by corruption ... and this

corruption has not procured either a quiet, peaceable or respectable government, but just the reverse. It has been a government working everything in force and coercion, always leading to and giving excuse for further expense ... [the] police, etc. ... When a private man outruns the constable, it is on [sic] no consequence to the state, but when a nation does so, its government loses its energy, and everything goes to confusion ... Don't imagine I wish to recommend one set of men for government in preference to those now in office. I will venture to assert that none of those with whom I am politically connected would undertake any situation of personal responsibility in the present situation of affairs. But I would wish to have our present constitution, though extravagantly worked, go on, in spite of what levellers, republicans and Frenchmen wish to put in the place of it ... You must first get national confidence and credit to get money, and you must leave off extravagance and corruption to get that confidence ... You must alter your system here, or we are undone ... opposition to government has increased here, in proportion to its extravagance, by the adhesion of those Patriots who might wish for a similar distribution of loaves and fishes, and of some from more disinterested motives ... and from the expectation of many to be provided for when once their political champions should come into power. This keeps us in a continual ferment ... Upon that principle I encouraged and supported government in the establishment of a militia which will in time ... get the better of Volunteering, and will preserve us hereafter from Oakboys, Steelboys, Whiteboys, Rightboys, Peep-of-Day Boys and Defenders ... At the time we voted our army here 36,000 men, militia included, our ministry declared their intention of assimilating our constitution with that of Great Britain. Give us therefore the bills in question [Place Bill, Pension Bill, Qualification Bill, and an Election Bill], and you will have the gratitude, thanks and support of this Kingdom ... If not, and if the present system is to be pursued, take all the consequence upon yourselves, and remember that the opposition of Ireland will ultimately be the ruin of Great Britain.'

Conolly was concerned for the plight of the poor, and in the 1790s he, along with James

Stewart (**2004**), wished to ameliorate poverty by the remission of the hearth money tax, illustrating the necessity for this by giving a poor man's budget – excluding beer and meat as the poor could not afford these. His attitude to the Catholic question was conservative. He had strongly supported Luke Gardiner's (**0842**) Catholic Relief Acts of 1778 and 1782, which had given economic and educational equality to Catholics, but his support for political concessions to Catholics was more reluctant, although he said that 'I am ready to give up all the prejudices of my youth to secure peace to my country: I am ready to give up my fortune, and even my life, for the same end.'

He supported Lord Fitzwilliam's administration and subsequently spoke against Fitzwilliam's recall in the debate in the House of Commons. In 1797 he resigned from the Kildare Militia in protest at Lord Camden's disarming of Ulster, but during the crisis of 1798 he offered his 'unconditional service' to the Lord Lieutenant. In 1796 he had sold the two parliamentary boroughs he controlled, Ballyshannon and Limavady, to Lords Belmore (**1269**) and Londonderry (**2008**) for £12,000 each.

He supported the Union, writing, in mid-January 1799, to 'give my love to Lord Cornwallis, and let him be assured that if I am able to speak ten sentences, I will do it on Tuesday next, as nothing ever was, or is, so near my heart as the consolidation of the strength of both islands in one legislative union. If this can be done, in spite of the private interest of one set of men and the non-sensical noisy clamour of the other, I shall die content.' He retired from politics in May 1800, when the Union debate was over. Lord Castlereagh (**2009**) had married his niece, Lady Emily Hobart, and Conolly was succeeded in Co. Londonderry by Colonel Charles Stewart (**2001**), Castlereagh's half-brother. The importance of Conolly's retirement at that time was that it allowed Charles Stewart to represent Co. Londonderry in the United Kingdom parliament.

In 1800 he retired to Castletown suffering from a general depression, apparently as a result of the events of 1798 and a lawsuit with his sisters and Lord Howe, the executor of his mother's will (she died March 1797), over settlements due to them out of his English estates. In March 1799, Lady Sarah Napier, his sister-in-law, wrote that '[He] is hourly in a sort of dispair [*sic*], wishing himself dead, hurting his health, raving of dangers that don't exist saying he is harassed to death because he has not a friend on earth. In short his nerves are gone; it is evident nothing can relieve him from useless agitation ... but to remove to a different scene for some time. For this purpose ... [they are] preparing to leave Ireland next summer for a long time.' Perhaps he sensed that his way of life had gone. He left Castletown in the summer of 1801, and spent some time in Brighton and London until 1802. He died on 27 April 1803 at Castletown, and on 1 May his brother-in-law, Colonel Napier, wrote: 'I never knew a human being whose enemies were more transient and whose friendships were more permanent.'

DIVISION LISTS:

1768 (1) voted for army augmentation – PC.

1772 (1) voted against the amendment to the Revenue Bill.

1773 (1) voted against the Absentee Tax.

1775 (1) teller for the pro-American amendment to the Speech from the Throne.

1777 (1) voted against Grattan's (**0895**) motion for retrenchment.

1778 (2) voted for the Popery Bill.

1779 (2) voted against a six-months Loan Bill.

1780 (1) voted against Grattan's declaration of the rights of Ireland.

1780 (2) voted against Yelverton's (**2268**) motion to modify Poynings' Law.

1780 (4) voted for the Perpetual Mutiny Bill.

1783 (1) voted against Flood's (**0762**) motion for parliamentary reform.

1784 (1) voted against a committee on the Reform Bill – independent member, but owner of a borough or two.

1785 (2) teller against the Commercial Propositions.

1786 (2) voted for Forbes's (**0778**) motion on retrenchment.

1787 (1) voted for a Pension Bill.

1788 (2) voted for Forbes's motion for

limiting pensions.

1789 (1) a teller for a Regency.

1790 (1) voted for Grattan's motion for reducing the influence of the Crown.

1790 (2) voted for Ponsonby (**1709**) on the Election of a Speaker.

1791 (1) voted for Curran's (**0560**) resolution against the sale of peerages.

1791 (2) voted for Grattan's motion for the exercise of free trade.

1793 (1) voted for Knox's (**1180**) motion for Catholic emancipation.

1793 (2) voted against the Convention Bill.

1795 (1) voted for a Short Money Bill.

1795 (2) voted for Catholic emancipation.

1795 (3) voted for Sir Laurence Parsons' (**1636**) resolution against alleged troop removals.

1799 (1) voted for the Union – Privy Counsellor [and] Col. of Militia.

ADDITIONAL INFORMATION: *A member of the RDS from 1760. He was a member of the Kildare knot of the Friendly Brothers of St Patrick, which endeavoured to provide an alternative to duelling for settling quarrels.

He was Master of Foxhounds in Co. Kildare. There is a very Irish legend that after a hard day's hunting Conolly entertained a stranger at dinner who had won his admiration by the way he had ridden during the hunt. At dinner Conolly stooped down to pick up his dropped napkin. In doing so he noticed to his amazement that the stranger had removed one of his shoes to display a cloven hoof. At great length and with much trouble the stranger was evicted.

ESTATES/RESIDENCE: Castletown, Co. Kildare; Stretton Hall, Staffordshire. His principal property was in the North of Ireland, in and around Limavady, the Grocers' proportion at Muff *alias* Eglington, and the Vintners' proportion at Bellaghy, Co. Londonderry, although his estates stretched through Donegal, Londonderry, Leitrim, Fermanagh, Roscommon, Westmeath, Meath, King's County, Kildare and Dublin. The Philips family manor of Limavady was purchased in 1697, the Grocers' proportion leased in 1713 was renewed in 1760 and the Vintner's proportion leased *c.* 1718 was purchased in 1729. However, the Grocers' estate was held on a terminable lease, the Limavady estate passed, until 1781, to his cousin Henry Conyngham after his fa-

ther's death, but a high proportion of the Vintners' and Limavady estates were let in perpetuity. The Limavady rental had been £591 in 1729 but rose to £1,521 by the end of the century; in 1782 the acreage had also reduced to £1,795 (Irish).

His estates were valued at £15,275 p.a. at the time of his marriage in 1758. His wife, Lady Louisa Lennox, brought a dowry of £10,000 for which a jointure of £2,500 was settled on her. In October 1759, they left London and took up residence in Castletown. All his estates were 'heavily encumbered being subject to his father's debts ... and his sisters' portions' – he had at least six married sisters and until 1797 there was his mother's jointure – in all amounting to £124,000. He reduced this sum to £43,000 by 1773, by selling off leases and 'parts not entailed', but added a further £42,000 by his own spending on new property and houses in Dublin and London. He spent £25,000 on alterations and improvements to the house and demesne at Castletown. By 1773 the total rental had also increased to £21,000 p.a. About 1760 the Grocers' Guild owned the manor of Muff surveyed at 8,799 acres and within four miles of Derry city. It was held by Rt Hon. Thomas Conolly, who paid £200 p.a. and had £1,000 profit rent. In 1759 the lease was about to expire, and Lord Abercorn's agent, Nathaniel Nisbitt, reported that Conolly had 'they say, no ready money. Some say the Grocers will take only £600 a year in rent, and the rest as a fine in ready money.' At a rental of £1,200, the estate was 'cheap set'. However, something was worked out, as in 1764 T. Conolly was granted a fair/market at Muff. By 1820, 5,053 acres of the manor was described as arable and pasture. Its rental rose from £476 in 1729 to £4,650 by 1820.

The rental of the Vintners' proportion had been £317 in 1701, rose to approximately £2,322 in 1782 and reached £3,117 by 1791, while the receipt for the chief rent from Conolly to Vintners, 10 July 1798, was only £212. About 1760, the half year's rent for Leixlip was £478, for Castletown £515, for Rodanstown and Co. Meath £533 and £416 respectively. By 1800 the rental of the Ballyshannon estate in Donegal stood at £4,270. The manor of Tymon, including Gallymoystown etc., is mentioned in a settlement of *c.* 1720; it had a rental of £1,068 in 1763, but was down to £918 in 1768 and 1778. Abbotstown is also mentioned in a settlement of *c.* 1720. The lordship of Rathfarnham, and Dunsink, was at a rental of £4,136 in 1768, and £4,548 in 1778. This excluded the Leixlip estate, part of which may have been in Co. Dublin. The 395 statute acres of Marlay were part of the manor of Rathfarnham.

In 1715, the rental of the Castletown estate was £717, rising to £900 in 1727, with the addition of Killadoon, reckoned as 230 Irish acres in 1671, and Castletown as 502 acres in 1705. The Castletown part of the estate was in the barony of Salt. The Leixlip estate appears to have counted as Co. Kildare in the eighteenth century, and the Leixlip rental in 1753 was £955, inc. £218 from the Primate for the castle and demesne, £1,128 in 1768 and £1,440 in 1778. The Castletown rental was £1,594 in 1768 and £1,637 (this last is stated to be for the half year) in 1778, giving an annual rental of £3,274 in 1778. In 1782 a valuation of Newtownlimavady estate stated that it had a rental of £982 4s 9^1/2 d and comprised 1,795 acres, 3 roods, 17 perches. In 1792, Conolly stated the Limavady rental to be 'some £2,200 to £2,300 per annum'. In 1782 the Co. Dublin lands were producing £435 p.a. and Westmeath £590, and were mortgaged to David La Touche (**1203**) and sons for £18,969 (18 years' purchase) subject to a redemption clause which was never acted upon. In 1791, it was reported that Conolly, 'who expected £300,000 by Lord Strafford's death is much disappointed'; in 1798 it was reported that 'the English creditors are proceeding against Conolly, and I hear several ejectments are brought on his estates'. About 1800 the annual rent roll of Newtownlimavady estate recorded £1,521 8s 3d. In 1799, his annual income was approximately £27,000.

On 14 July 1796, Thomas Conolly registered 207 freeholders on his northern estates. In 1822, it was observed: 'With respect to Bellaghy estate, there are around £20 and £50 freeholders who cannot be reckoned in this proportion, as they register independently and pay for their registry. The same observation applies to Mr Ogilby in the Newtownlimivady estate, who are all not only independent of the landlord, but even hostile to him.' There were 220 registered votes on the Bellaghy estate.

On his death his estates went to his great-nephew, Edward Michael Conolly Pakenham (the grandson of his sister, Harriet Staples). In June 1803 Sir Thomas Pakenham (**1623**) (the father of the heir) described the terrible state of Conolly's affairs: 'I crave your pity for all the miseries heaped on me at this damned place, where Conolly has been picking up money by every expedient of promising renewals, which we have not now the power to fulfil. The distress arising of many poor people who have borrowed money for these purposes is not to be described; it is heartbreaking to witness it ... Conolly anticipated by drafts, all his income and Lady Louisa will have at least £10,000 of interest to pay with the half year's rent of this estate ... I see no chance of your legacies being ever paid or of Edward [his son, the residual heir] having one farthing from the property. In my mind there will not be enough to pay, [unless] all except [Castletown House] sells well and soon.'

SOURCES: *IMC Leinster* 3 vols esp. vol. 1 pp. 134, 229, 250, 256–7, vol. 3 pp. x, 146, 239, 369 [these are the letters of the Lennox sisters and contain many refer-ences]; *HMC Rutland III*, p. 234; *Pitt–Rutland Corr.*; PRONI D/3030/513 Castlereagh Papers; PRONI T/2825 Conolly/Castletown Papers, pp. 18–36, C/1/1–98, C/2/1–22, C/10/1–16, C/19/1–13, C/36/1–14; PRONI T/3019/6459/788 Wilmot Papers; PRONI T/3166/1B Hartnell notes; PRONI MIC/238/1, Lady Louisa Conolly to Lady Sarah Bunbury, 26 Apr. 1782; PRONI MIC/474 Irish Volunteers; PRO HO100/43 ff. 169–73; O'Neill thesis; *DNB*; *HP 1754–94*; McDowell, *Irish Public Opinion, 1750–1800* pp. 28 n. 5, 45, 125, 132, 193 n. 1; McNevin, *Volunteers*; G. F. Russell-Barker and A. H. Stenning (eds), *Record of Old Westminsters: A biographical list* (London, 1928), 2 vols; Hughes, *Pat. Officers*; *HMC Stopford-Sackville I* pp. 267, 272, 274; *HMC Lothian* pp. 357–8, 366, 426; Johnston, *Gt B. & Ire.*, pp. 20, 86n, 156, 175, 221–2, 286; T. Bartlett and D. W. Hayton (eds), *Penal Era and Golden Age* (Belfast, 1979), pp. 113 n. 1, 121–2, P. D. H. Smyth, 'The Volunteers and Parliament, 1779–84'; J. Kelly, *Prelude to Union* (Cork, 1992), pp. 40, 166, 196; *Ir. Georgian Soc.* vol. 11 no. 4 pp. 1–46, L. Boylan, 'The Conollys of Castletown'; L. Boylan, *Castletown and its owners* [Irish Georgian Society Guidebook, *c.* 1870] pp. 39–40, 41, 43–44; *Kildare Arch. Soc. Jn.* vol. 2 (1896–9) pp. 373–5, Lord W. FitzGerald, 'Castletown and its Owners'; A. P. W. Malcomson, *The Pursuit of the Heiress* (Belfast, 1982), p. 11; *HP 1754–90*; 'Falkland' (pseudonym of Rev. J. Scott), *The Parliamentary Representation of Ireland* (Dublin, 1790), p. 59; M. O'Connell, *Irish Politics and Social Conflict in the Age of the American Revolution* (Philadelphia, 1965), p. 186; *JRSAI* vol. 41 (1911) pp. 86–8, 168–9, E. M. F.-G. Boyle, 'Records of the Town of Limavady, 1609–1804'; *JRSAI* vol. 52 (1922) p. 176, W. G. Strickland, 'Miscellanea'; J. Barrington, *The Rise and Fall of the Irish Nation* (1833), pp. 75–6; J. T. Gilbert, *History of the City of Dublin*, 3 vols (1861) vol. 3 p. 142; *Almanacks*; *BNL* 22–26 Jan. 1790; *DJ* 10–13 May 1760, 28 Apr.–2 May 1761; *FJ* 21–4 Apr. 1764, 5–7 Mar. 1772, 25–7 Apr. 1793. NLI reps vol. 314; NLI vol. 110, 29 Nov. 1864; TCD /722, Conolly Papers, William Eden to Conolly, 18 Apr. 1781; PRONI T/2541/IB3/3/60, William Conyngham to Abercorn, 6 Nov. 1792; E. Hewitt (ed.), *Lord Shannon's Letters to his Son*, pp. 7, 21, 48, 85, 119; J. Kelly, *'That Damn'd thing called Honour': Duelling in Ireland 1570–1860* (Cork, 1995), p. 66; J. Kelly, *Prelude to Union* (Cork, 1992), p. 40, 78, 152, 166, J. Kelly, *Henry Flood ...* (Dublin, 1998) p. 133; PRONI T/2541/IA1/5/73 Abercorn Papers, Nat. Nisbitt to Abercorn, 9 Mar. 1759, Curraghmore papers, F. 4, James Gregg [Clerk of the Peace] to Sir G. F. Hill, 21 Sept. 1822; PRONI D/2094/61 and 79; Parliamentary Lists, 1769 (1), 1771 (1), 1772 (2), 1773 (1), (2), 1774 (1), 1775 (1), 1776 (1), (2), (3), 1777 (1), 1778 (1), 1780 (1), 1782 (1), 1783 (1), (2), 1784

(1), (2), (3), 1785 (1), (2), (3), (4), 1787 (1), 1788 (1), 1789 (1), (2), 1790 (1), 1791 (1), 1793 (1), 1798 (1), 1799 (1), (3).

0460 CONOLLY, Rt Hon. William

MP for Donegal B. 1692–3, 1695–9; Co. Londonderry 1703–13–14, 1715–27–9 [r. Newtown Limavady 1703, 1713; Ballyshannon 1727]

> b. 1662; d. 30 Oct. 1729 at his house in Capel Street, Dublin, probably after a stroke
> HONOURS: PC appointed 1710, sworn before Apr. 1711, removed 17 July 1711, resworn 9 Oct. 1714, 19 June 1727, 24 Nov. 1727.
> FAMILY/BACKGROUND: Eldest son of Patrick Conolly and Jane [   ].
> MARRIED: [1694] Catherine (b. 1662; d. Sept. 1752, aged c. 90 years) (her dowry was £2,500), dau. of Gen. Sir Albert Conyngham of Co. Donegal.
> CHILDREN: *d.s.p.*
> EDUCATION: LLD *spec. grat.* TCD 1718; qualified as an attorney and attached to the Court of Common Pleas, *ante* 1685.
> CAREER/OCCUPATION: Speaker of the House of Commons 12 Nov. 1715–27, 28 Nov. 1727–13 Oct. 1729; in 1692 obtained employment at £10 p.a. as an agent for Rt Hon. James Hamilton (0933), Keeper of Irish Lighthouses and Master of the King's Alnager; Collector for Coleraine and Londonderry 2 May 1698; Burgess of Limavady 24 June 1701; Freedom of Drogheda 31 Aug. 1719; Commissioner for Forfeited Estates; Revenue Commissioner, Apr. 1709–Sept. 1710; 1st Revenue Commissioner 11 Dec. 1714 – 11 Nov. 1729 (patent, 11 Dec. 1714, 22 Aug. 1727); Lord Justice ten times between 1716–29 (patent, 22 Feb. 1722, 29 Mar. 1723, 8 May 1724, 20 May 1724, 2 Apr. 1726, 23 Dec. 1726, 15 May 1728).
> MILITARY: During the Williamite wars he probably served in Sir Albert Conyngham's Regiment.

POLITICAL ACTIVITY: Early in his career Conolly made a reputation at the Bar, and he was employed as one of the attorneys for the Irish Society in its defence against the claims of William King, Bishop of Derry. He was among those attainted in 1689. Although he had been building his wealth and his power base from the Revolution, Conolly came into his own with the Hanoverian succession. He was an astute and successful land speculator, at a time when there were opportunities for those with strong nerves and, particularly, legal knowledge.

In 1699 the English parliament had set up a commission that focused on the king's use of the prerogative to cut large slices out of the forfeited estates. The majority report was openly critical and the English Commons resumed, initially without compensation, all Irish properties assigned by William over the previous decade and appointed trustees to sell these and the unapportioned remainder of the Jacobite forfeitures. Conolly, modestly described as 'a Donegal lawyer, already famed for an astonishing ascent to riches', was the largest purchaser of the grantees' lands, and in 1701 he rallied about half the other purchasers to urge the gentry of every county to petition the king on the dire effects of the resumption on all Protestants. His campaign did not wholly succeed, but terms were improved, and a modest compensation fund was set up for Protestant purchasers. Conolly and many others were able to reacquire the disputed land on fairly easy terms.

His name appears as one of the petitioners to the Lord Lieutenant in February 1701 for securing the remainder of the purchase money for forfeited estates. He went on to invest heavily in further forfeited estates in 1703. By 1715 he was among the richest men in Ireland. He was named for one committee in 1692, 19 in 1695–9, 231 in 1703–11 and 88 in 1715–17: presumably he did not actually sit on many of these after he became Speaker in 1715.

Although Conolly appears to have been socially adept, inevitably his success created envy and he was rumoured to have come from very humble origins: for instance, on 21 February 1717 Sir John St Leger (1858) wrote to Chief Justice Parker that 'Many people here, especially our quality and old gentry, are much offended at Mr Conolly's being one of them; this gentleman was lately an attorney, his father keeping an ale-house in the north of Ireland, this being too notorious to be stifled, but by making long bills and good bargains, he is now reported to be worth eight thousand a year, and by a generous way of living and adhering to the honest cause in bad times, was chosen Speaker of the House of Commons this Parliament, but has shown himself very unequal to that part, but has still a considerable interest in the House.'

However, his father, Patrick Conolly, was among those attainted by James II's parliament, which suggests that he may not have been that humble, while Conolly's marriage to Catherine Conyngham in 1694 connected him with some of the most influential Protestant families in Ulster: the Leslies, Montgomerys, Hamiltons, Gores, Corrys and Knoxs. In 1696 he signed the Association for the protection of William III in parliament, and during the reign of Queen Anne he was solidly Whig. In fact, given his involvement with the forfeited estates and his land dealing, it would have been difficult for him to have been anything else. He was alleged to have paid Lord Lieutenant Wharton £3,000 for the Revenue Commissionership in 1709, only to be dismissed in the following year; on 28 September 1710 Swift wrote in his *Journal to Stella* 'Conolly is out & Mr Roberts in his place, who loses a better here [London], but was formerly a Commissioner in Ireland. That employment cost Conolly £3,000 to Lord Wharton, so he has made one ill bargain in his life!' But the end was not yet, as Conolly was restored to the Commissionership after the Hanoverian succession.

Despite his numerous activities, Conolly was a busy parliamentarian during the reign of Queen Anne. He had the knack of making himself useful, for instance in 1705 he assisted Sir Richard Buckley in his bill, 4 Anne, c. 9, over the preservation of trees and the prevention of their destruction by 'idle and Lewd Persons'. In 1705 he brought in the heads of a bill, 4 Anne, c. 8, to regulate inland tolls and prevent the hoarding of coal by merchants hoping to drive up the price on the Dublin market by creating a scarcity. He introduced various judicial measures, for instance, 6 Anne, c. 7, limiting Sheriffs' fees on executions, 6 Anne, c. 10, an act for the improvement of judicial administration, and, in 1709, 8 Anne, c. 4, 'An act to enable posthumous Children to take Estates as if born in their Father's Life-time'. Also in 1709, 8 Anne, c. 6 was aimed at 'preventing the counter-feiting the current coin of this Kingdom', while 8 Anne, c. 8 dealt with crimes against

property, offering a reward for apprehending those guilty of breaking, entry and theft. A northern MP, he introduced 9 Anne, c. 3 'for the improvement of the Linen Manufacture and for a further Regulation of the same', while in 1711 he brought in the heads of the ever-popular bill for the 'preservation of the game'.

After the 1713 election he organised Alan Brodrick's (0237) campaign for the Speakership; he was subsequently a member of the Commons committee that reported on the misconduct of Sir Constantine Phipps, the Whigs' *bête noire*. Before the 1713 election he was already acknowledged to have the control of the borough of Killybegs, and on 22 October 1715 he assured the government of his support for Charles Fane (0720), 'who may depend upon being elected to the Irish Parliament' (he was duly returned for Killybegs). Not surprisingly, on 14 December 1715, Charles Delafaye (0611) wrote of 'our Speaker, Mr Conolly, to whose single interest the King is more obliged than to all Ireland besides for the good we have had in this session'.

One of the major issues of the early years of George I was the question of the treatment of Dissenters, who were numerically powerful in the north and had suffered from the Sacramental Test Clause in the 1704 and 1709 penal statutes of Queen Anne. Conolly, on 9 August 1715, wrote to the Earl of Sunderland regarding a letter he had received from Dissenters in the north asking that they should be included in the Commission of Array. He reassured Sunderland that while the government continued to protect the Dissenters from the 'cruel' and 'unjust' Sacramental Test Act, they would make good allies against the pretender and all his followers, and on 7 July 1719 he was one of those summoned by the Lord Lieutenant on the eve of parliament to consider how far the relief of Dissenters should be pressed.

The three major issues that surfaced in the early 1720s were the erection of a Bank of Ireland, the creation of a fire insurance company (early eighteenth-century towns were cramped and fire was always a hazard), and the royal grant of a patent to coin halfpennies in Ireland acquired by an ironmonger called Wood from the grantee, the Duchess of Kendal. These projects, however meritorious in themselves, were complicated in the case of the first two by the government's desire to make money out of them by indicating that substantial fees for their charters would be expected, possibly as much as £100,000, while the copper coinage envisaged in Wood's Halfpence was totally unacceptable to the public. Conolly refused to support the Duchess of Kendal's patent and Wood's Halfpence, and when the patent was withdrawn in 1725, the populace burnt ceremonial bonfires outside his house.

The timing for the bank project was hardly propitious even apart from other considerations and suspicions. It coincided with the financial crisis known as the South Sea Bubble, which caused great economic distress in Ireland as well as Britain. Furthermore, Archbishop King was resolutely opposed to it. As for the fire insurance company, Thomas Brodrick (0243), the expert on the South Sea disaster, did not think that there was the £1,000,000 in Ireland estimated as necessary to float it. Both Alan Brodrick and Conolly disapproved of the fire insurance scheme and came to disapprove of the bank scheme also. Whig solidarity barely survived the Hanoverian succession, and conflict soon broke out between Conolly and Alan Brodrick, appointed Lord Chancellor in 1715.

From 1715 Conolly combined four activities: the Speakership, the control of the Revenue and its patronage as First Commissioner, his frequent appointment as a Lord Justice in the absence of the Lord Lieutenant, and his personal wealth and political influence as a great landowner and borough proprietor. He was the first Speaker to be appointed a Lord Justice, and while this may originally have been to balance Brodrick, the newly appointed Lord Chancellor, his value as Lord Justice was soon realised and he continued to be appointed until his death in 1729. The conflict between Conolly and Brodrick continued, creating difficulties for successive Lords Lieutenant, until Brodrick's resignation in 1725.

Conolly exploited to the full his position as First Commissioner of the Revenue through his capacity for hard and detailed work and the opportunities for new appointments offered by the removal of Tory officials on the Hanoverian succession.

On 20 June 1728, shortly before his death, his wife complained that 'He is every day at least six hours at the Customs House ... I wish some of the [other] Commissioners were ordered to their business, for I think it hard that he should always have the labouring.' Conolly's health was failing from June 1728, and on 11 July the Primate wrote that 'Mr *Conolly* is retired for some time into the country for his health, where I hear he grows better. I believe his indisposition will prevent my visiting my diocese this summer; but as his absence will rob the bankers of one to whom they formerly applied, and on whom they could make some impressions, I believe we shall get easier through this business for his being out of the way.' This was a reference to an adjustment of the price of foreign silver to attract it into the country, for Boulter wrote to Newcastle on 16 July that 'Our want of silver here is such, that it is common to give six-pence for the change of a moidore, and to take a guinea or pistole for part of the change. And I know some in *Dublin*, who have occasion to pay workmen every *Saturday* night, that are obliged to pay four-pence for every twenty shillings in silver they procure.' The bankers naturally did not like the exchange rates to be readjusted as they were, at least in the short term, losers by it.

Conolly collapsed in the House of Commons – probably from a stroke – on 26 September 1729; he resigned on 12 October. On the following day, Sir Ralph Gore (0872), another northerner and Conolly's long-time friend and choice, was elected Speaker without opposition.

Conolly's death brought a period of political instability to the government. On 23 October 1729 Primate Boulter had written to Newcastle that 'There is no doubt but Mr *Conolly's* illness and impossibility of ever acting again, has made things worse than usual, as it must be some time before the several clans that united under him, can settle under a new director *but steadiness* in England, *will, I doubt not by degrees settle us here again.*' An ongoing potential problem of the government of Ireland was the lack of cohesion between the legislature and the executive, and this link was what Conolly successfully 'undertook' to provide. On 30 October Boulter wrote to inform

Newcastle that 'After his death being expected for several days, Mr *Conolly* died this morning about one o'clock. He has left behind him a very great fortune, some talk of £17,000 *per ann.*' The custom of wearing linen scarves at funerals, to encourage the linen manufacture, was first observed at his funeral.

DIVISION LISTS:

1709 (1) spoke for a Money Bill.

ADDITIONAL INFORMATION: On 12 September 1715 he wrote a letter, probably to the Lord Lieutenant, declining the Speakership of the Commons but, obviously, he was persuaded to change his mind. He was paid £500 per session to cover his expenses as Speaker, and warrants were issued to this effect for each session in which he served.

His father appears to have conformed to the Established Church prior to his birth. Although he had no children himself, Conolly had a strong sense of family: for instance, from 1692 he was paying his brother and sisters an allowance out of some leased college lands at Tirhugh. When his brother-in-law Henry Conyngham (0463) died in 1706, and his widow Lady Shelburne married again, he acted as guardian for his two nephews and niece.

In February 1725 a rumour circulated in both London and Dublin that Conolly had borrowed £30,000 of public money from John Pratt (1721), Deputy Vice-Treasurer. Conolly denied this, and had Pratt make a deposition under oath that he had not borrowed the money. Instead, he claimed, the government still owed him £5,000 that he loaned it in 1715 to use against the pretender.

After his death his wife had a monument to his memory, sculpted by Thomas Carter, erected in the old church of Kildrought. He left £500 for the erection of a charity school at Celbridge, Co. Kildare, with a further £250 p.a. from the rents of his Rathfarnham estate as its endowment. The school was reputedly planned by Conolly and the Surveyor-General of Ireland, Colonel Thomas Burgh (0280); his wife, together with his nephew, William Conolly (0461), completed the purchase of the land set aside for it and work commenced shortly after 1733.

A contemporary estimate of Conolly's income was £12–13,000 p.a., but at the time of his death Primate Boulter thought it might be nearer £17,000 p.a., and his Irish estates alone were estimated to be worth £300,000.

His wife was a personality in her own right. At the time of her death in September 1752 Mrs Delany, who was neither a snob nor a fool, wrote that 'We have lost *our great* Mrs Conolly ... her table was open to all her friends of all ranks, and her purse to the poor ... she rose constantly at eight and by eleven was seated in her drawing-room, and received visits till 3 o'clock, at which hour she punctually dined, and generally had *two tables* of eight or ten people each: her own table served with *seven* and *seven* and *a dessert*; and if the greatest person in the kingdom dined with her she never altered her bill of fare ... teas and coffee came exactly at half an hour after five, she then waked, and as soon as tea was over, a party of whist was made for her till ten, then everybody retired. She ... has never made a visit since Mr Conolly died. She was clever at business, wrote all her own letters ... She was a plain and vulgar woman in her manner, but she had very *valuable* qualities.'

ESTATES/RESIDENCE: Rodanstown (1,427 acres), Co. Meath, purchased 1691 (he lived here from 1694 to 1704); Castletown, Co. Kildare (this was to become the showpiece of early Irish Georgian domestic architecture – the centre block was designed by Alessandro Galilei, and when he returned to Italy the work was completed by Edward Lovett Pearce (1646)); Capel Street, Dublin; Rathfarnham, Dunsink, and Scribblestown, Co. Dublin; Roe Park, Limavady, Co. Londonderry (purchased in 1700 from Sir Thomas Phillips' grandson); Stratton Hall, Staffordshire. Before moving to Rodanstown, he had lived in lodgings at Cork Hill, Dublin. He purchased the house in Capel Street in 1707 from a Mr Barry. He bought Castletown on 21 September 1709 for £15,000 from Thomas Dongan, Earl of Limerick, and built the house there in the 1720s. He paid Dongan £9,000, and the remaining £6,000 was used to cover all mortgages, debts and encumbrances on the estate, including £1,624 compensation to the family of the late Nehemiah Donnellan (0652), who had previously purchased the town and lands of Castletown. The acreage amounted to 1,730; the value in yearly income was *c.* £974.

Conolly was a dealer in land: in particular he made 'substantial purchases of forfeited estates'. Thus the Conolly estates, being acquired piecemeal, were extremely complicated. He had estates in North and South Wales and in Counties Meath, Westmeath, Roscommon, Fermanagh, Wexford, Wicklow and Waterford. Among his purchases in 1702–3 was 629 acres in Co. Wexford from the Commissioners for Sale of Forfeited Estates. Further purchases in 1703 included the forfeited lands of the Nugents (998 acres in Meath, 4,819 in Westmeath and 2,182 in Roscommon), the lands of Thomas Plunket in Meath, and the lands of John Itchingham and John Gilligan in Co. Wexford, a total of approximately 10,000 acres. He paid less than £1 per acre on some occasions, and often paid only one-third of the purchase money, making up the rest from Protestant purchasers' debentures.

He purchased the Phillips estate of Limavady in Co. Londonderry in 1697 and the Manor of Castle(town) in 1711. In 1718 he paid £52,000 for the estate of Lord Folliott in Ballyshannon, Co. Donegal, which included the fisheries of Lough Erne – the yearly income of the estate was £2,000, with £450 from the fishery. He also had long leases from the Irish Society (e.g. receipts, May 1727: Limavady, £604; Grocers, £365; Vintners, £353; Church Lands, £132). The 1722 May rental for Ballyshannon was £1,031, and the college lands of Tirhugh, £235. In 1727 the Ballyshannon estate comprised 18,908 Irish acres and Newporton 4,212, valued at £2,364 p.a. and £528 p.a. respectively; also in 1727 the 'College lands' were reckoned at 1,719 acres and valued at £582 p.a. The Ballyshannon Manor had a rental of £493 for the half year in 1687. His college manor of Tirhugh (which was in his possession in 1686) had a rental of £417 in 1686 and £447 in 1706; these lands included Rossnowlagh.

The lands in Co. Dublin were purchased from the Earls of Strafford and Richard Barrett, and the Westmeath properties from the Earls of Westmeath. In 1723 he bought the Manor of Rathfarnham, Co. Dublin for £62,000 from the Duke of Wharton. In 1725 he purchased the estate of Killadoon, Celbridge, Co. Kildare. At the time the Rathfarnham estate consisted of 3,682 arable, meadow and pastoral acres and 2,442 mountainous acres, with a rental of £2,171 p.a. By 1782 its rental stood at £4,084. In June 1728 he purchased for £11,883 the manor, towns and lands of Leixlip, Newtown, Stacumny, Co. Kildare from John Whyte. However, Conolly did not only buy or lease: among his many dealings in land he also sold. In 1719 he conveyed to Robert Lowry of Aghenis, Co. Tyrone the lands of Altedesert (Pomeroy) for £2,850.

By 1691 he had been appointed 'agent for the mayor, commonalty and citizens of Londonderry in connection with a lease of Lord Antrim's forfeited estate'. In 1692 he 'appears as agent for the farming of Sir Patrick Trant's forfeited estate, [and] he complained that as a result of prejudice he was forced to bid unnecessarily

high for it'. He was also agent to Lord Albemarle, 'one of King William's Dutch favourites and a leading grantee of forfeited estates'; he 'admitted taking money for himself from purchasers of Abermarle's grants'. He purchased 8,000–9,000 acres from Abermarle, 'for which he claimed to have paid £3,000'. In 1695, a William Conolly appeared on a list of proprietors who owed arrears of rent for forfeited lands in Co. Dublin (specifically, part of Allen of St Wolstan's forfeited estate). In 1695 he went into partnership with Thomas Brodrick, and 'took vast quantities of land and in great measure governed the cants [auctions] (few daring to bid against them) ... and let afterwards to under-tenants at greater rents'. On 28 June 1703 he leased, jointly with Sir George St George (**1837**), the Manor of Strabane for one year from James Hamilton (**0933**). In addition, in 1709, Conolly had acquired for £1,350 General Frederick Hamilton's mortgage on the manor of Merchant Taylors, originally granted by John Gorges to one Thomas Bridges in 1698.

The fragmented nature and variety of his various holdings is illustrated by the Ballyshannon account for May 1729. This included the Manor of Ballyshannon, £982 13s 9d. College Lands of Bundrews [*sic*], £124 10s. Church lands of Ballyhanna, parish of Inishmacsaint, barony of Tirhugh, £13 0s 6^1/2d. College lands of Tirhugh, £235 12s 6d. Total rent, £1,355 16s 9^1/2d. In the same year, 1729, the rent roll of Manor of Grocers, Co. Londonderry (gale days May and All Saints) showed May receipts £365 19 4^1/2d, All Saints £392 8 4^1/2d. Lands in the Parishes of Cumber Lower, Faughanvale Clondermot, Barony of Tirkeeran; parish of Dungiven, Barony of Keenaght, Co. Londonderry – 31 denominations, all leased for years – 21, 31 or 34. The year's rent was £476. (From 1713 (date of almost all the extant leases) William Conolly was the lessor.) The May rental for the whole of the Londonderry estate in 1727 was £1,654.

On 17 May 1718 he received £500 'as Speaker of the House of Commons, the usual allowance for the session of Parliament'.

In his will, 18 October 1729, he left his wife, Catherine, the estates in Wales, his mansion house in Dublin, Castletown, and all his estates in Kildare, Meath, Westmeath, and Roscommon. The Rodanstown estate and other lands in the barony of Deece were made security for £300 or £350 a year under her marriage settlement (the rental was £1,204 in 1765 and £1,170 in 1778). All his other estates were left to his wife for her lifetime (she was reputed to be in her 90th year at the time of her death in 1752), and thereafter to his nephew William. Mrs Conolly left William Conolly £10,000 in addition to the reversion, and an estate in Wales to Colt Cunningham (Conyngham).

SOURCES: *CJ Ire.* (Bradley edition) vol. 3 pp. 58, 119, 321, 514, 679, 685, 689, 799, 926, vol. 4 p. 542; PRONI D/623 Abercorn Papers; PRONI T/448 pp. 90–3, 102, 138, 175, 1717–19, T/519 pp. 79, 165, T/ 546 p. 36, Jan. 1725–June 1727, T/610 pp. 32–3; PRONI TSPI 1715–16; PRONI T/559 vol. 16 p. 75, Burke, extract pedigrees; PRONI T/2825 pp. 7–16, B/ 5/1–26, C/1/1–98, /2/1–22, /3/1–65, /4/1–11, /11/ 1–18, /20/1–16, /22/1–33, /23/1, /24/1–7, /28/1–25, D/4/1, A. P. W. Malcomson, Introduction to the Conolly/Castletown Papers; McCracken thesis; *Cal. SP Dom. 1695* (London, 1908) p. 143; *DNB*; *Index to Irish Privy Counsellors, 1711–1910*; *Boulter Letters* vol. 1 pp. 195, 263, 267; S. W. Singer (ed.), *Clarendon Corr.* (London, 1828), vol. 2 pp. 348–9; King, *State of Protestants*; King, *A Great Archbishop of Dublin, William King D.D.* p. 145 n. 2; Llandover, *Delany Corr.*, vol. 3 pp. 158–9, 166; R. E. Burns, *Irish Parliamentary Politics in the Eighteenth Century*, 2 vols (Washington, 1989) vol. I pp. 31–4, 120–25, 250–51, vol. 2 pp.1–2; S. J. Conolly, *Religion, Law and Power …* (1992) pp. 64–5, 85, 93, 169; P. McNally, *Parties, Patriots & Undertakers …* (Dublin, 1997) pp. 27, 97; J. Agnew, *Belfast Merchant Families in the Seventeenth Century* (1996), p. 74; D. Guinness and W. Ryan, *Irish Houses and Castles*, pp. 193–209; B. De Breffny and Rosemary Ffolliott, *The Houses of Ireland* (Dublin, 1975), p. 95; T. Bartlett and D. W. Hayton (eds), *Penal Era and Golden Age* (Belfast, 1979), pp. 32–54, D. W. Hayton, 'The Beginnings of the Undertaker System'; *JRSAI* vol. 41 (1911) pp. 160, 166, 171, E. M. F-G. Boyle, 'Records of the Town of Limavady, 1609–1804'; *Irish Georgian Society* vol. 11 no. 4 pp. 1–46, L. Boylan, 'The Conollys of Castletown'; M. Craig, *Dublin 1660–1800*, p. 101; Simms, *Williamite Confiscation*, p. 184; Parliamentary Lists, 1696 (1), 1706 (1), 1711 (3), 1713 (1), (2), (3), 1719 (1); PRONI Conolly Papers [rental, May 1727, Rent Roll for the Manor of Limavady, list of registrations, 1796; PRONI T/788/2 [Deed of assignment, 22 June 1709]; PRONI D/3094/26, D/2094/31–2, D/2094/ 51 [Grocers]; PRONI D/2094/50 (Vintners); NAI M/ 6917/79 Conolly Papers; NLI reps no. 314; EC 4528.

0461 CONOLLY, Rt Hon. William James

MP for Ballyshannon 1727–54; [GB] Aldeburgh 1734–47; Petersfield 1747–2 Jan. 1754

b. *ante* 15 Dec. 1706; d. 2 Jan. 1754
HONOURS: PC, sworn 3 Feb. 1730, 1734–d.
FAMILY/BACKGROUND: Son of Patrick Conolly and Frances [   ].

MARRIED: [2 Mar. 1733] Anne, dau. of Thomas Wentworth, 1st Earl of Strafford.
CHILDREN: Rt Hon. Thomas (**0459**); Catherine, m. [23 Feb. 1754] Ralph Gore, 1st Earl of Ross; Annie, m. [5 Mar. 1761] George Byng; Harriet, m. Rt Hon. John Staples (**1985**); Frances, m. William Howe, 5th Viscount Howe; Caroline, m. [7 Dec. 1770] John Hobart, 2nd Earl of Buckinghamshire; Lucy; Jane (d. Oct. 1779), m. [10 Feb. 1770] George Robert FitzGerald [executed 1786].
CAREER/OCCUPATION: Cursitor of Court of Chancery *c.* Oct. 1720, 1730–54 (at £200 p.a.); Trustee of the Linen Board for Connaught 1733–54; *Commissioner of the Tillage Act for Leinster 1735, 1739–53; Burgess of Limavady 25 July 1740; *Governor of the Workhouse 1743–53; *Governor of City and County of Londonderry and of Coleraine 1746–53; *Commissioner of Oyer and Terminer 1753.

POLITICAL ACTIVITY: A nephew of Speaker Conolly (**0460**), he was a British as well as an Irish MP, and much of his political career was spent in England. As a British MP he described himself as 'an incorrigible Whig', although his father-in-law, who returned him for Aldeburgh in 1734, was a Tory. However, on his return Conolly declared that 'Neither the outcry against the Excise, standing army etc., would change my thought, without the hope of place or pension, which is attributed to be the only excuse of people's steadiness at present.' He voted consistently for the government and was classed an Old Whig in 1746. In the Irish parliament he was listed for 42 committees between 1727 and 1748 and complained, on 21 November 1743, that he had been disturbed in possession of his lands at Rathfarnham by James and Thomas St John, during time of privilege. As his aunt, the Speaker's (**0460**) widow, Catherine Conolly, had a life interest in much of the Conolly estates, including Castletown, he did not come into possession of them until her death in 1752.

During the Money Bill dispute he supported the Castle, and Archbishop Stone said that he was one of the two MPs (the other was H. L. Rowley (**1821**)) who had agreed to move or second the inclusion of the compliment to the Lord Lieutenant should this be omitted in the Address to the King. In fact this proved unnecessary. On 4 November 1753 the Chief Secretary, Lord George

Sackville (**1835**), wrote to Wilmot: 'I fear before this letter goes to the post that I shall have an account of Mr Conolly's death; he has been ill for some time, and very imprudently went to his farm in the mountains; he rode out in the rain, returned home wet through, and could not be prevailed upon to change his clothes; in a few hours he was taken ill of a fever, it has since fallen on his lungs and his life was despaired of last night. He will be a great loss to this country.'

However, Conolly did not die until 2 January 1754 and, writing on 15 December, just before the Money Bill vote, Sackville repeated that 'Mr Conolly's illness is a great drawback to us, as his credit would have been a considerable support.' The Money Bill was rejected two days later. Mrs Delany, writing to her sister, endorsed Sackville's views and in an earlier letter, written at the time of his aunt's death in 1752, described him as 'a very generous good man'. On 29 November 1732, the Hon. Mrs Donnellan wrote to her brother, Lord Strafford: 'I hear Mr Conolly has proposed for one of your daughters ... [He is an] agreeable and a sensible gentleman ... he has a very good fortune and ... is ... a sober man. He has a very good character.' He was listed for 37 committees between 1727 and 1748.

DIVISION LISTS:
    1749 (1) absent, in England.

ADDITIONAL INFORMATION: A foundation member of the Dublin Society, 1731; re-elected following RDS charter, 1750.

ESTATES/RESIDENCE: Rathfarnham, Co. Dublin; Leixlip Castle and Castletown, Co. Kildare; Stratton Hall, Staffordshire. In 1729 he was bequeathed by his uncle, William Conolly (**0460**), the Conolly estates in Donegal, Dublin, Fermanagh, Wexford and Waterford. In 1737 he raised £10,500 on the Vintners' perpetuity lease by mortgage from George Mathews of Thomastown, Co. Tipperary, and others. He helped his aunt to complete the purchase of land set aside by his uncle William for the erection of a charity school at Celbridge, Co. Kildare. Work began on it shortly after 1733. When his aunt died in 1752 he received £10,000 and the rest of the Conolly estates in Wales, Dublin, Kildare, Meath, Westmeath and Roscommon. At the time of his death his income was estimated at £15,000 p.a.

SOURCES: *CJ Ire.* vol. 7 p. 431; PRONI D/2094/24C, D/2094/34; PRONI T/2825 pp 14–16, Conolly/Castletown Papers; PRONI T/3019/6356/322 Wilmot Papers; Burke *LGI* (1904) pp. 107–8; J. Walton, '*The King's Business': Letters on the Administration of Ireland, 1741–61* ... (N.Y.,1996), no. 142; *HP 1715–54* [says ? son of Rev John Conolly]; *Index to Irish Privy Counsellors, 1711–1910*; Berry *RDS* pp. 24–7, *JRSAI* vol. 41 (1911) p. 168, E. M. F-G. Boyle, 'Records of the Town of Limavady, 1609–1804'; Llandover, *Delany Corr.*, vol. 3 pp. 167, 265; *Almanacks*; *EHR* (1905) p. 519 C. L. Falkiner, 'Correspondence of Archbishop Stone and the Duke of Newcastle', *DJ* 16 Feb. 1754, 26–8 Oct. 1779.

CONWAY, Popham: *see* **SEYMOUR-CONWAY**, Popham (**1898**)

0462 CONWAY (SEYMOUR-CONWAY), Rt Hon. Henry

MP for Co. Antrim 1741–61–8; [GB] Higham Ferrers 28 Dec. 1741–7; Penryn 1747–54; St Mawes 1754–61; Thetford 1761–74; Bury St Edmunds 1775–84

    b. (12) Aug. 1719; d. 9 July 1795 at Park Place, Surrey

HONOURS: PC, sworn 5 May 1755.

FAMILY/BACKGROUND: Son of Francis Conway, 1st Baron Conway and his 3rd wife Charlotte, dau. of Sir John Shorter.

MARRIED: [19 Dec. 1747] Caroline, dau. of the Lieut.-Gen. John Campbell, 4th Duke of Argyll, wid. of Charles Bruce, 3rd Earl of Aylesbury.

CHILDREN: Anne, m. John Damer (**0576**).

EDUCATION: School: Eton 1732; studied in Paris and London.

CAREER/OCCUPATION: Chief Secretary under the Duke of Devonshire 2 Apr. 1755 – 2 Jan. 1757; Clerk of the Crown and Hanaper, 15 Jan. 1757, 1766–d.; Groom of the Bedchamber 1757–64; Secretary of State (South) 1765–6; (North) 1766–8; *Bencher of the Honorable Society of King's Inns 1769–d; *Constable of Dublin Castle 1766–84 (f.).

MILITARY: Captain in the 1st Regiment of Foot Guards 1741, with the rank of Lieutenant-Colonel 1742; joined the Army in Flanders, present at Dettingen 27 June 1743 but the

Guards did not engage; aide-de-camp to Marshal Wade 1744; aide-de-camp to the Duke of Cumberland 1745, distinguished himself at Fontenoy 11 May 1745; Colonel of 48th Regiment of Foot 6 Apr. 1746; fought at Culloden 16 Apr. 1746; captured at the Battle of Lauffeld 2 July 1747; Colonel of 34th Regiment 24 July 1749; Colonel of 13th Dragoons Dec. 1751; in Ireland 1752–3; *Colonel of a Regiment of Dragoons 1753; Colonel of 8th Horse 1754–9; Major-General 1756–8; Joint Commander of the expedition to Rochfort, which failed; restored to the Staff as Lieutenant-General 30 Mar. 1759; Colonel of the Royal Regiment of Dragoons 5 Sept. 1759; Dismissed his command 1763 for supporting the Whigs; Lieutenant-General of Ordnance [GB] 8 Sept. 1767; Colonel of 4th Dragoons Feb. 1768; Colonel of the Royal Regiment of Horse Guards Oct. 1770; General 26 May 1772; toured continent to witness the Prussian and Austrian annual reviews 1774; from 1778–81 engaged with the affairs of Jersey (the successful defence of the island was due, to some extent, to his preparations); Commander-in-Chief 1782; Field Marshal 12 Oct. 1793.

POLITICAL ACTIVITY: He was an active parliamentarian and debater, but most of his parliamentary career was in Great Britain. He came over to Ireland with Lord Lieutenant Hartington on the latter's peace mission following the débâcle of the 1753 Money Bill. His dual parliamentary membership and his military career inevitably affected his parliamentary activity in Ireland. Nevertheless, Lord Lieutenant Hartington had chosen his Chief Secretary well for what was a delicate mission in which one false step could bring disaster.

DIVISION LISTS:
1749 (1) absent, in England.
1768 (1) absent, in England

ADDITIONAL INFORMATION: Spoke out, to effect, against the War of American Independence. The army was his chief interest, and he made a number of speeches on it in the British parliament. He had an attractive personality and appeared to be destined for a greatness that never actually materialised, apart from his short tenure, 1765–8, as Secretary of State for the Southern and then Northern Departments.

He was among those, like Robert Waller (2161), who were alarmed and concerned by the Townshend–Bellomont (0480) and Blaquiere (0162)–Bagenal (0071) duels: Waller pointed out that if this went on, then 'As soon as persons receiving appointments take the oath of office, it is expected they should provide good pistols and learn to fence', while Conway considered that there should be a division between public and private actions, as 'Too nice resentment of all words and actions in such cases would make public actions impracticable.'

He constructed the bridge at Henley-on-Thames.

ESTATES/RESIDENCE: Park Place, Surrey. In 1753 he received a legacy of £5,000 as joint heir of his uncle, Captain Erasmus Shorter.

SOURCES: Ellis thesis; *Alum. Dub.*; *HP 1715–54*; *Proc. RIA* vol. 77 c no. 1 (1977) p. 31, J. C. Sainty, 'The Secretariat of the Chief Governors of Ireland, 1690–1800'; *Index to Irish Privy Counsellors, 1711–1910*; Johnston, *Gt B. & Ire.*, pp. 144, 183–4; P. D. G. Thomas, *The House of Commons in the Eighteenth century* (Oxford, 1971), p. 231; R. E. Burns, *Irish Parliamentary Politics in the Eighteenth Century*, 2 vols (Washington, 1989) vol. 2 p. 203; J. Kelly, *'That Damn'd thing called Honour': Duelling in Ireland 1570–1860* (Cork, 1995), p. 112; T. Bartlett, *Macartney in Ireland* (PRONI 1978), p. 165; *DNB*; *Almanacks*; *BNL* 12, 15 May 1761; *DJ* 16–19 May 1761.

CONYNGHAM: *see also* **BURTON (CONYNGHAM)**, Rt Hon. William (**0303**)

CONYNGHAM, Baron: *see* **BURTON (CONYNGHAM)**
0299 Burton (Conyngham), Francis Pierpoint, 2nd Baron Conyngham, MP Killybegs 1753–60, Co. Clare 1761–8–76

0463 CONYNGHAM, Henry

MP for Killybegs 1692–3; Co. Donegal 1695–9, 1703–6

b. (bapt. 2 July) 1664; d. 1706, killed at St Estevans in Spain 1705/6

FAMILY/BACKGROUND: Only surviving son of Sir Albert Conyngham and Margaret, dau. of Robert Leslie, Bp of Raphoe.

MARRIED: [post 1696] Mary, dau. and h. of Sir John Williams, 2nd Baronet of Minster Court, Kent, wid. of Charles Petty, 1st Baron Shelburne; (she m. (3) Robert Dalway (0567)).

CHILDREN: William (0466); Henry, 1st Earl Conyngham (0464); Mary, m. Rt Hon. Francis Burton (0297).

MILITARY: Captain of 9th Foot 1688; Captain in Lord Mountjoy's Regiment, Lieutenant-Colonel 31 Dec. 1691; on 5 May 1692, Lieutenant-Colonel Conyngham was granted a pass to Holyhead; Lieutenant-Colonel in Colonel Echlin's Regiment *ante* 1693; Colonel 8th Hussars 1 Feb. 1693; Colonel of own Regiment of Dragoons 11 Feb. 1693; Embarked for Flanders 1694; Brigadier-General Dec. 1703; Major-General 1704.

POLITICAL ACTIVITY: He was a professional soldier and, when James II desired his army to shift for itself, he, then Captain Conyngham, prevailed on 500 of his regiment to remain united, and with them offered his services to William III. His father was one of the first to support William, and raised a regiment of dragoons at his own expense.

He was returned for Killybegs in 1692 and sat for Co. Donegal from 1695 until he was killed in 1706 during the War of Spanish Succession. In 1695 he voted against Lord Chancellor Porter, who was accused by some MPs of favouring Catholics, and on 28 March 1696 he moved a motion in the House of Commons 'to associate on the account of the late conspiracy against his Majesty's person and Government' and presented the draft of the association 'to stand by and assist each other, to the utmost of our power, in the support and defence of his Majesty's most sacred person, title and government, against the late King James ... and in case his Majesty come to any violent and untimely death ... to unite, associate, and stand by each other, in revenging the same.' This declaration he duly signed in parliament.

On 27 December 1703 Edward Southwell (1962) wrote to Ormonde that 'Brigadier Cunningham seems off his design of selling, "especially now that plots are on foot and there might be an opportunity to show his zeal".' This enthusiasm proved fatal. He was listed for one committee in 1692, 33 in 1695–9 and 25 in 1703–4.

ESTATES/RESIDENCE: Mount Charles and Killybegs, Co. Donegal. His father's death left him in debt. In 1696 he petitioned for a grant of forfeited lands worth £1,400, and a custodiam of other lands. During the 1690s he purchased the Manor of Slane, Co. Meath and other adjacent lands forfeited by Christopher Fleming, Lord Slane and King James. In 1703, Brigadier Henry Conyngham described his purchase of the Slane estate as follows: 'It is one of the noblest seats in the kingdom, which was a great inducement, but I found it so much out of repair that it will cost me a great deal of money before I have it to my mind. It is very good land, and in a country where rents are better paid than in the north. It cost me about £5,000, and I hope will be worth to me £700 per annum, but I pay about £200 a year out of it to two ladies during their lives. I am sorry I cannot tell you it is paid for, for as yet I have paid but about £2,000 of the money.' In 1702–3 he purchased 1,838 acres in Co. Meath from the Commissioners of Forfeited Estates.

On his death in 1705/6, his brother-in-law William Conolly (0460) took overall control of his Mount Charles and Killybegs estates. In 1698, Anna Murray let Colonel Henry Conyngham Lochris and Glenesk for 99 years at £80 a year, and the whole of the rest of the estate for 21 years. In 1700 she granted a separate lease of Carrigrosse and Ballyduff, part of the land included in the 21-year lease, for 80 years from 1719. Total rent payable 1698–1719 was £380; thereafter £80 for Lochris and Glenesk, and £18 for Carrigrosse and Ballyduff. The lands let to the Conynghams, 1719–1790s, contained 15,541 Irish acres and the rest of the Murray estate, 10,473 acres. By 1799, ejectment proceedings by the Murrays were under way.

SOURCES: *CJ Ire.* (Bradley ed.) vol. 2 pp. 820–1; EC 4038 or Memoranda for Mr Murray (1791?) and 10 Nov. 1791; PRONI D/2860/19/4 Murray of Broughton Papers and /20/4; *ibid.* D/2860/5/14, Conyngham to Lady Ann Murray, 2 Oct. 1703; PRONI T/2825/47/1–14 Conolly/Castletown Papers; Burke *PB* (1903) p. 354 (1906) p. 382; *Cal. SP Dom. 1691–2* (London, 1900) pp. 47, 270, *1693* (London, 1903) pp. 33, 334, *1694–5* (London, 1906) pp. 80, 197, 248, 332, *1695* (London, 1908) pp. 94, 135, 249, *1696* (London, 1913) pp. 77, 81, 132, 141, 207, 477; Musgrave, *Obits*; *GEC Complete Peerage*; C. Dalton (ed.), *English Army Lists and Commission Registers, 1661–1714* (London, 1896), vol. 3 pp. 3, 183, 300 (London, 1898) vol. 4 p. 62; *HMC Ormonde* (1920) new ser. vol. 8 pp. 52, 115, 291 [on 13 Mar. 1706/7 Robert Johnson (**1103**) wrote to Ormonde on the subject of deceased MPs and their replacements, 'in the county of Tyrone [?] Gustavus Hamilton's son is to succeed Conyngham']; *Ir. Gen.* vol. 6 no. 6 (Nov. 1985) pp. 711–23, A. Dusek, 'Baptisms in St Bride's, Dublin, 1633–1713'; Simms, *Williamite Confiscation*, p. 184; Parliamentary Lists, 1695 (1), 1696 (1), 1707 (1).

0464 CONYNGHAM, Rt Hon. Henry

MP for Killybegs 1727–53; [GB] Tiverton 1747–54; Sandwich 1756–74

> b. 1705/6; d. 3 Apr. 1781 at Bath, bur. at Slane
> HONOURS: PC, sworn 27 May 1748, 1751, 1753–74.
> PEERAGES: Cr. Baron Mount Charles 3 Oct. 1753; Viscount Conyngham 20 July 1756; Earl Conyngham 4 Jan. 1781.
> FAMILY/BACKGROUND: Posthumous son of Henry Conyngham (**0463**) and Mary, dau. of Sir John Williams.
> MARRIED: [Dec. 1744] Ellen, only dau. and h. of Solomon Merrett of London.
> CHILDREN: *d.s.p.*
> CAREER/OCCUPATION: Joint Governor of Co. Donegal 1746–81; Vice-Admiral of Ulster 1748–79; Joint Governor of City and County of Londonderry and of Coleraine 1754–d.; *Trustee of the Linen Board for Leinster 1769–d.
> MILITARY: Cornet 4th Dragoon Guards, Lieutenant 1725; Captain Royal Irish Dragoons 30 Nov. 1725; *aide-de-camp to the Lord Lieutenant 1738; *Captain 1738–40; Colonel *c.* 1752.

POLITICAL ACTIVITY: He sat in both the British and Irish Houses of Commons. He was a professional soldier and brought up under the guardianship of his uncle, Speaker Conolly (**0460**), from whom, in 1729, he inherited a life interest in the Limavady estate and parliamentary borough. On his death in 1781 this reverted to Thomas Conolly (**0459**). Created Baron Mount Charles, Viscount and finally Earl Conyngham, his main influence in the Irish parliament was exercised through the members he returned. In 1780 these were the Rt Hon. William Burton (**0303**), who appears to have been

his favourite nephew, Henry Hamilton (**0930**), William Colvill (**0454**), Alexander Murray (**1506**) and John Knox (**1183**).

DIVISION LISTS:
    1749 (1) absent, in England.

ADDITIONAL INFORMATION: After his father died in 1705/6, his uncle William Conolly (**0460**) acted as his guardian. He died at Bath in England, but was buried at Slane. The *Dublin Journal* reported his spectacular funeral: on the arrival of his remains in Ireland there was a procession through Dublin, prior to their interment at Slane.
    *A member of the RDS from 1763.

ESTATES/RESIDENCE: Slane, Co. Meath; Mount Charles, Co. Donegal; Limavady, Co. Londonderry; Ramsgate, Kent. On the death of his aunt, Catherine Conolly (William Conolly's wife), he was bequeathed a small estate in Wales. He succeeded his eldest brother William (**0466**) in the family estates on 26 October 1738. But on 17 December 1739 he obtained leave from the Commons to waive privilege 'in any suit commenced, or to be commenced by Mrs Constance Conyngham, for any jointure or thirds by her claimed, or to be claimed, out of any part of the estate of William Conyngham, Esq., her husband, deceased'. His nephew Francis Pierpoint Burton (Conyngham) (**0299**) became his residuary heir and by special remainder succeeded to the barony of Conyngham, but the family estates at Slane and in Co. Donegal were inherited by Francis Pierpoint's younger brother, William Burton Conyngham (**0303**).

SOURCES: PRONI D/2860/19/4, 20/4 Murray of Broughton Papers; PRONI T/2825/C/8/1–12 Conolly/Castletown Papers; Ellis thesis; McCracken thesis; *CJ Ire.* vol. 4 p. 322; *HP 1715–54*; *Index to Irish Privy Counsellors, 1711–1910*; *GEC Complete Peerage*; C. Dalton, *George the First's Army, 1607–1867*; *Ir. Gen.* vol. 1 no. 11 (1941) p. 343 'Testamentary Records' [says he was a posthumous son]; *Almanacks*; *GM* 1787; *DJ* 10–13 May 1760, 10–12 Apr., 19–21 Apr. 1781; Parliamentary List 1780 (1).

0465 CONYNGHAM, Henry

MP for Killybegs 1741–9

> b. *c.* 1693; d. (*ante* 10 Oct.) 1749
> FAMILY/BACKGROUND: Son of Rev. William Conyngham of Co. Donegal.
> MARRIED: Unmarried. (Mistresses: Elizabeth

Massy, Margaret Cruice.)
CHILDREN (ILLEGITIMATE): William; Henry.
EDUCATION: School Mr. Griffith, Elphin; TCD 20
Feb. 1710, aged 18 years, BA 1714, MA 1719.

POLITICAL ACTIVITY: Virtually nothing is known of
this man apart from a few family details.

ESTATES/RESIDENCE: [?]Ballydavid [Ballydevitt], Co.
Donegal.

SOURCES: PRONI T/559 vol. 16 p. 106, Burke, extract
pedigrees; McCracken thesis; *Alum. Dub.*

0466 CONYNGHAM, William

MP for Killybegs 1727–38

b. *c.* 1698; d. 26 Oct. 1738
FAMILY/BACKGROUND: Eldest son of Henry
Conyngham (0463) and Mary, dau. of Sir John
Williams.
MARRIED: (1) [   ], a Dutch lady; (2) Constance,
dau. and co-h. of Thomas Middleton of Essex.
CHILDREN: ?*d.s.p.*
MILITARY: Commissioned as Captain in
Clotworthy Skeffington's Regiment of Dragoons.

POLITICAL ACTIVITY: He was the eldest son of General Henry Conyngham and brought up under
the guardianship of Speaker Conolly, his uncle.
He was listed for seven committees between 1727
and 1733.

ESTATES/RESIDENCE: Slane Castle, Co. Meath; Mount
Charles, Co. Donegal. His brother, Henry (0465), created Earl Conyngham, was his immediate heir and his
nephews Francis Burton Conyngham (0299) and
William Burton Conyngham (0303), the sons of his
sister Mary, his ultimate heirs.

SOURCES: PRONI T/420 pp. 122–8; PRONI T/559 vol.
16 p. 105, Burke, extract pedigrees; McCracken thesis;
CJ Ire. vol. 4, p. 322; Lodge *P.*

0467 CONYNGHAM, William

MP for Dundalk 1776–83

b. 29 Apr. 1723; d. 27 Mar. 1784 at Springhill,
Co. Londonderry
FAMILY/BACKGROUND: Eldest son of George

Conyngham and Anne, dau. of Dr Peacock.
MARRIED: [31 Aug. 1775] Jane, only dau. of James
Hamilton of Co. Donegal, wid. of John Hamil-
ton.
CHILDREN: *d.s.p.*
CAREER/OCCUPATION: Burgess of Limavady 22 Apr.
1757, 7 Apr. 1764; Deputy Governor of Co.
Londonderry 1765; ?Sheriff of Co. Tyrone 1767;
appointed one of the commissioners for building
a canal from Drogheda to Trim 1787.
MILITARY: Colonel of 4th (Black) Regiment of
Horse; commanded Coagh Volunteers 1779; also
Captain Commissioner of the Springhill Union
Volunteers.

POLITICAL ACTIVITY: A professional soldier, and in
1779 a Volunteer. He was returned by the Earl of
Clanbrassill and followed his political lead. His
1778 vote against the Catholic Relief Bill was
probably the decision of Lord Clanbrassill (0936),
as Conyngham, who had his life saved and his
freedom secured in France by the priest of Slane,
the Rev. M. O'Hanlon, built a Roman Catholic
Church at Slane.

When he was first returned he was considered a
government supporter but he appears to have soon
given a general support to the opposition. He did
not come in again in 1783, and died early in the
following year. His obituary in *Dublin Journal,*
3–6 April 1784, refers to his distinguished military career and states that society has 'lost a valuable member, the poor a humane and generous
benefactor, and his tenants a tender hearted and
indulgent landlord'.

DIVISION LISTS:
   1777 (1) voted for Grattan's (0895) motion
   for retrenchment.
   1778 (2) voted against the Popery Bill.
   1780 (1) voted against Grattan's declaration
   of the rights of Ireland.
   1780 (2) voted against Yelverton's (2268)
   motion to modify Poynings' Law.
   1780 (3) voted against the Tenantry Bill.

ADDITIONAL INFORMATION: *A member of the RDS
from 1766.

ESTATES/RESIDENCE: Springhill, Co. Londonderry; lands
in Counties Tyrone, Antrim, Londonderry and Armagh.
Succeeded by his nephew, George Lenox-Conyngham.

SOURCES: PRONI D/302 [says he is from Coagh High];

PRONI D/1449/9/11 and /10/10; PRONI MIC/474 Irish Volunteers; Ellis thesis; Burke *LG* (1846) p. 253; M. Lenox-Conyngham, *An Old Ulster House* (1946); *JRSAI* vol. 41 (1911) pp. 86–8, E. M. F.-G. Boyle, 'Records of the Town of Limavady, 1609–1804'; *JRSAI* vol. 25 (1895) p. 161, J. H. Moore, 'Notes on the History of Navan'; *JRSAI* vol. 31 (1901) pp. 412–13, T. J. Westropp, 'Slane in Bregia, County Meath: Its Friary and Hermitage'; *Almanacks*; *DJ* 3–6 Apr. 1784; Parliamentary Lists, 1776 (1), (2), (3), 1777 (1), 1778 (1), 1782 (1), 1783 (1), 1784 (2), (3).

0468 COOKE, Edward

MP for Lifford 1789–90 (sworn 21 Jan. 1790); Old Leighlin 1790–7–1800 (re-elected after appointment to place of profit, 1795 and 1796)

b. (bapt. 27 June) 1755 at Denham, Buckinghamshire; d. 19 Mar. 1820 in Park Lane, London
FAMILY/BACKGROUND: Third and only surviving son of William Cooke, Dean of Ely, Provost of Eton and Provost of King's College, Cambridge, and Catherine, dau. of Richard Sleech, Canon of Windsor. (In 1746 Dr Cooke had sought a position as one of the Chaplains to the Lord Lieutenant.)
MARRIED: [10 Aug. 1791] (with a portion of £10,000) Isabella, dau. of Hamilton Gorges (**0883**), Joint Housekeeper of Dublin Castle 1794–1835; (she m. (2) Henry Fane).
CHILDREN: ?*d.s.p.*
EDUCATION: School, Eton 27 Nov. 1760, King's Scholar 1768; entered Cambridge (King's College) 16 May 1773, aged 17 years, Fellow 1776–86, BA 1777, MA 1785, Browne's Medal, Fellow Commoner 18 Aug. 1786.
CAREER/OCCUPATION: Private Secretary to the Chief Secretary (Sir Richard Heron) 1778–80; 2nd Chamberlain Exchequer 1778–86; *Clerk of the Stationery Stores 1781–4; 2nd Clerk of House of Commons 18 Jan. 1786 – 9 Sept. 1789, 15 Feb. 1798; Education Commissioner 10 May 1788; Under-Secretary (Military) 7 Apr. 1789–96; Under-Secretary (Civil) 5 June 1796 – 21 Oct. 1801; Keeper of Records 6 Feb. 1802, 26 Dec. 1802–20; Under-Secretary for War and Colonies [UK] 1804–6, 1807–9, Under Secretary for Foreign Affairs 1812–17; Customer for Kinsale 1782, 8 Sept. 1789; Sovereign of Fethard (Tipperary) 1795; *Fethard (Wexford) 1800 (f.); *Magistrate of Fethard (Wexford) 1800 (f.); Ranger of Phoenix Park 5 Nov. 1796–1800

(f.); Customer Baltimore 1801; unanimously voted the Freedom of Dublin 22 Jan. 1796; voted the Freedom of the Guild of Merchants 1798.

POLITICAL ACTIVITY: Cooke was an Englishman who arrived in Ireland in 1778 as private secretary to the then Chief Secretary, Sir Richard Heron. Cooke consolidated his position during the two years following his arrival in Ireland, and remained attached to the Castle secretariat until after the Union, when he returned to England with Lord Castlereagh (**2009**). Chief Secretary Eden (**0681**) described him as 'as a young gentleman of perfect integrity and discretion' and Lord Mornington (**2215**) introduced him to another Chief Secretary, W. W. Grenville, reminding him that they had all met at Eton and writing that 'He bears a very high character and, I believe, very deservedly, not only for his knowledge and talents in his line, but for the integrity of his principles. You will therefore I am persuaded, continue him. No man has had better opportunities than he of knowing the characters of men in this country; the hot-bed of Eden's corruption forced out everyman's principles, and Cooke was witness to the whole process.' The viceroy, Grenville's brother Lord Temple, endorsed this opinion and wished to recommend him to Lord North as Under-Secretary in the Home Department.

During the following viceroyalty, Lord Northington's, Cooke wrote to the retiring Chief Secretary, William Wyndham, pointing out the great difficulty that confronted every man who aspired to a 'civil service' career in the eighteenth century: namely, insecurity of tenure. This was particularly true in the fluid political conditions of the early 1780s. Cooke wrote that 'The little which you must have seen of my situation here must have induced you to consider it not only ineligible in itself, but rendered of late extremely irksome and unpleasant from the changes by which it has been harassed. The difficulty in such times of preserving a right line of conduct, & the impossibility of preventing it being misunderstood & misinterpreted must certainly not have escaped you but I hope you saw *that* in me, which was incapable of playing a game, & acting against the engagements I undertook ... If Lord Northington and your successor in office shall think it worth their while to employ me, they may perhaps find me more use than a stranger and as honourable as a friend.'

In February 1784, on the departure of Northington, Cooke wrote to Eden that 'I can hardly persuade people that I continue as I was. Some conceive me a great minister and others a great rat.' Probably Cooke suffered from not being Irish and from a fear of his abilities, which he did not choose to hide. Even after his departure Lord Chancellor Redesdale wrote to Perceval in 1804 that 'I ought to add that Cooke's character here is not considered as being pure, and perhaps he may have been a little irregular' – this appears to have been a comment on some Union irregularities in his office, and the matter appears to have been debatable.

Cooke continued to act in a confidential secretarial capacity; for instance, he was involved in the Commercial Resolutions. Then in 1786 Lord Lieutenant Rutland appointed him Second Clerk in the Irish House of Commons, an institution with which Cooke was already well acquainted both corporately and individually, as it is highly probable that he had been the government's expert on parliamentary management for some years previously; certainly three years later Lord Lieutenant Buckingham (the former Lord Lieutenant Temple) referred to Cooke and John Lees (Lord Harcourt's private secretary) as 'the old stagers in managing this respectable legislature'.

Cooke was an acute observer of the parliamentarians; for example, in 1783 when Flood (0762) and Grattan (0895) were in violent opposition, he commented on Grattan's personal need 'to justify his conduct'. At the time of the Regency Crisis in 1789, Cooke was appointed Under-Secretary in the Military Department in place of the dismissed Charles Francis Sheridan (1914). He was returned for Lord Erne's (0519) borough of Lifford following the elevation to the peerage of Sir Nicholas Lawless (1209), created Lord Cloncurry. In the 1790 election he entered parliament for Old Leighlin, which he continued to represent until it was disfranchised by the Act of Union.

On 15 January 1795 Cooke and Sackville Hamilton (0945) were both dismissed from office by Lord Fitzwilliam, who had been in the country for less than a fortnight. Fitzwilliam wrote: 'A thousand reasons which I cannot detail have compelled me to make up my mind to this measure.' The reasons were possibly a consequence of Bishop O'Bierne's letters of 25 November when he referred to Hamilton, 'who I trust and hope I shall not see left in his office' and 15 December, when he informed Fitzwilliam that 'Cook [sic] is even worse than Hamilton. Another man you cannot trust is Lees.' Cooke was dismissed on personal as well as political grounds, an action he resisted and resented bitterly. However, shortly after Lord Camden's arrival the new viceroy wrote to Pitt that 'I have reinstated Hamilton & I propose placing Cooke in the War office again. No person will believe that it is done purely because they are the proper & efficient Persons for these offices but no two persons were ever placed in situations more from individual merit than they have been, for I had myself rather a prejudice & wish not to reinstate both and particularly Cooke.' Indeed, Camden had suggested offering the office of Secretary in the Civil Department to William Elliot (0695).

Cooke was never an easy colleague, and as early as 1783 Chief Secretary Windham had been warned that he 'is too intelligent and useful to be neglected – too powerful to be made an enemy ... too ambitious to be made a friend'. Perhaps Lord Cornwallis best understood the root of the ambivalent attitude that Cooke tended to arouse: 'Cooke,' he said, '... although a very clever fellow, is not a man of accommodating temper'; on another occasion he commented on 'a narrow minded jealousy which is inexcusable in so clever a fellow'. This and a failure to delegate responsibility created discontent among the secretariat and resulted in the ordinary business getting behind hand: for instance, in December 1796 Lord Auckland (Eden, 0681) wrote to Beresford (0115) about a pamphlet he wanted: 'I mentioned it twice to Cooke, but he is not attentive in small matters.' Sackville Hamilton had really returned to clear his name and he retired in 1796 with full honours, being made a Privy Counsellor and, after the Union, one of the Commissioners for awarding the compensation authorised under the act. Cooke was appointed in his place. As they surmounted his difficult temperament, most Lord Lieutenants came to like and respect him.

He was one of the government's leading pamphleteers, and following the 1798 rebellion was anxious to create the conditions for a lasting peace: part of this was the plan for the political union of the two countries. Securing a majority for the Act of Union was the joint work of Cooke and Castlereagh, and during the closing years of the Irish parliament a lifelong personal and political friendship was formed between the two men. Cooke believed that concessions should have been made to the Catholics after the passing of the Act of Union: when these did not materialise he resigned from the Civil Department, and in 1801 he returned to England.

As an administrator, Cooke was concerned over the problems associated with the Catholic question, the inferiority of Irish trade and the need to improve the economy. In 1798 he published *Arguments for and against a Union between Great Britain and Ireland Considered.* A year later, he wrote a draft entitled 'Will an Union Make Ireland Quiet'. In February 1801 he wrote 'The sentiments of a sincere friend to the Catholic claims', which argued that if Catholics resorted to violence they would alienate 'those who would otherwise support their cause'. The forces behind the 1798 rebellion were not annihilated but smothered, and flared up again in 1803 with Emmet's rebellion; the government was well aware of this situation. After his return to England he served Lord Castlereagh as under-secretary in the various offices to which he was appointed, and in 1815 he accompanied him to the Congress of Vienna. Two years later he retired, to the great regret of Castlereagh, 'whose entire confidence he possessed'. After a short illness he died on 19 March 1820, 'among the oldest and best of the official servants of the crown'.

DIVISION LISTS:

1790 (2) voted for Foster (**0805**) on the Election of a Speaker.

1795 (3) voted against Sir Laurence Parsons' (**1636**) resolution against alleged troop removals.

1799 (1) voted for the Union – Under-Secretary in the Civil Department, Dublin Castle and Keeper of the Phoenix Park.
1800 (1) voted for the Union.

ADDITIONAL INFORMATION: He received compensation at the Union of £500 for the loss of the Clerk of the House of Commons in reversion, and an annuity of £79 4s 7d for the Under-Secretaryship in the Civil Department.
*A member of the RDS from 1789.

ESTATES/RESIDENCE: Dublin Castle. In 1790 it was estimated that his salary and perquisites as Clerk of the House of Commons made it not less valuable than £800 p.a. He also had the sinecure of Customer of the Port of Kinsale, £350, and two or three other small places, for example in 1799 he was Keeper of the Phoenix Park in Dublin.

SOURCES: PRONI D/3030/1091 G/4 Castlereagh Papers; PRONI T/3019/812 Wilmot Papers; PRONI T/3166/1A Hartnell notes; O'Neill thesis; *DNB*; Hughes, *Pat. Officers*; *Alum. Cantab.*; R. A. Austen-Leigh (ed.), *The Eton College Register, 1753–90* (Eton, 1921), 3 vols; A. P. W. Malcomson (ed.), *Eighteenth Century Irish Official Papers in Great Britain*, 2 vols (PRONI 1973, 1990) vol. 2 p. 404, 315 [drawing of 1815]; McDowell, *Irish Public Opinion, 1750–1800* pp. 243, 250; J. Kelly, *'That Damn'd thing called Honour': Duelling in Ireland 1570–1860* (Cork, 1995), pp. 136, 206; G. O'Brien (ed.), *Parliament, Politics and People* (1989) pp. 110, 141, J. Kelly, 'The Genesis of the Protestant Ascendancy …'; J. Kelly, *Prelude to Union* (Cork, 1992), pp. 53 [Cooke was not an undersecretary until 1789], 78, 122–4, 197; Johnston, *Gt B. & Ire.*, pp. 59–64, 73n, 112–13, 129; *Beresford Corr.* vol. 2 p. 140; E. Hewitt, *Lord Shannon's Letters to his Son* (PRONI 1982) pp. lxxvii–lxxviii; P. and B. Rowan (antiquarian booksellers), *The Eighteenth Century, An Irish Perspective* (Belfast, 1986), no. 83; *Ir. Gen.* vol. 1 no. 10 (1941) p. 295, W. Clare, 'Irish Compensations and Pensions'; *Ir. Gen.* vol. 6 no. 1 (1980) p. 27, H. F. Morris, 'The Waterford Herald 1791' [says incorrectly that he was MP for Lifford 1784–90]; Carlow MPs; *Proc. RIA* vol. 77 C (1977), J. C. Sainty, 'The Secretariat of the Chief Governors of Ireland, 1690–1800'; *Almanacks*; *FJ* 22 Oct. 1795, 23 Jan. 1796, 19 Apr. 1798; *BNL* 25–9 Jan. 1796; Parliamentary Lists, 1790 (1), 1791 (1), 1793 (1), 1794 (1), (2), 1799 (3), 1800 (1), (3).

0469 COOKE, John

MP for Co. Westmeath 1707–13

> b. 1657; d. (1) Oct. 1733
> FAMILY/BACKGROUND: Son of Robert Cooke of
> Moygallen, Co. Westmeath and Anne [   ].
> MARRIED: Elizabeth Foster.
> CHILDREN: Robert m. (1) [   ], (2) Mary, dau. of
> [   ] Standford; Richard; John; Anne, m. [   ]
> Rotton; Elizabeth, m. [1720] Arthur Reynell;
> Cassandra, m. Richard Daniel, Dean of Down;
> Jane, m. James Nugent; Mary, m. William
> Hodson of Co. Westmeath; Rebecca, m. Robert
> Vicars; Elinor, m. Samuel Lucas; Frances;
> Martha.
> MILITARY: ?A Lieutenant John Cooke served at
> Londonderry Apr.–July 1689; ?a Captain-
> Lieutenant John Cooke served in Colonel John
> Courthope's (Courthorpe's) Regiment of Foot in
> 1694; Captain-Lieutenant in the Royal Regiment
> of Fusiliers.

POLITICAL ACTIVITY: A professional soldier, he served
in the siege of Londonderry and for most of his
period in parliament he was probably fighting in
the various theatres of the War of Spanish Succession. He was listed for four committees between
1707 and 1710. He was returned in place of
Robert Rochfort (1806), who was appointed Chief
Baron of the Exchequer, and it was correctly anticipated that he would not be returned for Co.
Westmeath in 1713.

ADDITIONAL INFORMATION: On 8 February 1693, a
John Cooke was granted a pass to Holland.

ESTATES/RESIDENCE: Cooksborough, Co. Westmeath. In
1702–3 he purchased 481 acres in Co. Tipperary from
the Commissioners for Sale of Forfeited Estates and
171 acres in Co. Dublin from [?]Richard Cooke.

SOURCES: PRONI T/559 vol. 16 pp. 141–2, Burke, extract pedigrees; Hayton thesis; *Cal. SP Dom. 1693* (London, 1903) pp. 31, 67, 174, 185, *1694–1695* (London, 1906) p. 111; Vicars, *Prerog. Wills*; *Memorials of
the Dead* [says he died (1) Oct. 1733 in his 77th year];
Ir. Builder, 15 July 1888 'St Audoen's Church, Corn
Market: Its History from its Foundation to the Present
Time' [says he was born 1666]; Musgrave, *Obits*; Simms,
Williamite Confiscation, p. 184; Parliamentary List,
1713 (1).

0470 COOKE, Sir Samuel

MP for Dublin B. 1749–58

> b. *post* 1690; d. 9 Feb.([bur. 13) 1758 'after a
> short indisposition'
> HONOURS: Cr. Baronet 28 Dec. 1741.
> FAMILY/BACKGROUND: Son of Sir Samuel Cooke (d.
> 28 Aug. 1726) and Mary, dau. of Michael
> Christian of Dublin.
> MARRIED: [10 June 1726] Judith (d. 25 Nov.
> 1770), dau. of John Trench, Dean of Raphoe.
> CHILDREN: Samuel (d. unm.); Anne, m. Walter
> Weldon of Kilmorony, Co. Kildare (2202).
> CAREER/OCCUPATION: Sheriff of Dublin 1730,
> Alderman 22 Feb. 1732, 1743–8, Mayor 1740,
> 1749–50; *Commissioner of Oyer and Terminer
> 1742–53; *Governor of the Blue-Coat Hospital
> 1742–57; *Governor of the Workhouse 1745–8;
> *Governor of Erasmus Smith's Schools and other
> Charities 1756–7.

POLITICAL ACTIVITY: He was a brewer and a Dublin
city politician. His election for Dublin city in 1749
was complicated by the Lucas (1276)–La Touche
(♦♦♦♦) fracas. Eventually he was elected along
with La Touche, who was petitioned against by
Sir Charles Burton (0295) and subsequently declared not duly elected by 110 to 54 votes. He
supported the Country party during the Money
Bill dispute and, accompanied by 'about seven or
eight gentlemen, thirty or forty merchants, and
two or three hundred mob who went around the
town and groaned or hurraed as they were directed
at the houses of the principal people. Each of the
Lords Justices were groaned ... They attempted
no violence anywhere.'

Cooke presented an address from the city of
Cork (versified in *HMC Stopford-Sackville I*, pp.
239–43) to the Speaker. In January 1754 he was
thanked by the Corporation of Tailors and Guild
of Merchants for his behaviour in parliament during 'the present session'. In 1751 he introduced
the heads of a bill, 25 Geo. II, c. 15, to ensure
that corn and meal were sold only by weight 'and
for the more effectual preventing the Frauds committed in the buying and selling thereof' – meal
and potatoes were to be sold by weight only at the
public weighbridge in market towns. In 1756 he
introduced the heads of two bills, 29 Geo. II, c.
22 and c. 23, both concerned with the bank failures that marked these years, Willcocks & Dawson

and Dillons. He died in 1758.

DIVISION LISTS:
> 1749 (1) voted against the election of James Digges La Touche (♦♦♦♦).
> 1753 (1) voted for the expulsion of Arthur Jones-Nevill (**1125**).
> 1753 (2) voted against the Money Bill.

ADDITIONAL INFORMATION: *A member of the Dublin Society from 1742. Admitted to the Ouzel Galley before 15 September 1748. Mrs Delany, who visited him in 1754, had a poor opinion of his taste.

His father was Mayor of Dublin during the dispute between the Whig-dominated Corporation and the government in 1711.

ESTATES/RESIDENCE: St Catherine's Park, Leixlip, Co. Kildare; Mary Street, Dublin. Succeeded his father at St James's Street Brewery in August 1726. He bought Aughalane Manor, Co. Fermanagh, in 1739 for £5,980.

SOURCES: *CJ Ire.* (Bradley ed.) vol. 4 p. 259, vol. 8 pp. 383, 422, 479, vol. 9 pp. 639, 845, 915 (0497, 0530, 0531); PRONI T/1185 Genealogies pp. 70–1; RCBL P277/1/2, Parish Registers of St Mary's, Dublin [bur. 13 Feb. 1758]; McCracken thesis; GEC *B*; *Memorials of the Dead* [says his parents married 17 May 1690]; *HMC Sackville I* pp. 209, 239–43; R. E. Burns, *Irish Parliamentary Politics in the Eighteenth Century*, 2 vols (Washington, 1989) vol. 2 pp. 103–4, 110; *Almanacks*; *GM* (Exshaw's edition) Feb. 1758; *BNL* 14 Feb. 1758 [says he died 9 Feb. 1758]; *DJ* 30 Aug. 1726, 15 Jan. 1754, 7–11 Feb. 1758.

He was involved in the long-running saga that followed the failure of Burton's Bank in 1733. In 1751 he brought in a bill, 25 Geo. II, to extend the statute of limitations; an additional clause was added while the heads of the bill were before the House to allow creditors, who wished, to make composition for their several debts at two-thirds of the sum that they were owed. This clause was agreed, 79 to 27. He was a popular barrister, 'much beloved and esteemed for his many good qualities'.

DIVISION LISTS:
> 1749 (1) voted for the election of James Digges La Touche (♦♦♦♦).
> 1753 (1) voted for the expulsion of Arthur Jones-Nevill (**1125**).

ESTATES/RESIDENCE: St Helen's, formerly called Seamount, Booterstown, Co. Dublin, which he rebuilt a few years before his death.

SOURCES: *CJ Ire.* (Bradley ed.) vol. 8 pp. 438–9, 453 (0505); PRONI T/559 vol. 16 p. 157, Burke, extract pedigrees; RCBL P154/1/1, Parish Registers of St Nicholas Within, Dublin; McCracken thesis; Burke *LGI* (1904) p. 502; Burke *LG* (1846) p. 79; *IFR* (1976) p. 978; *IMC King's Inns Admission Papers, 1607–1867*; *Register of Admissions to the Honourable Society of the Middle Temple* (London, 1949) vol. 1 p. 301; *JRSAI* vol. 30 (1900) p. 312, F. E. Ball, 'The Antiquities from Blackrock to Dublin'; *DJ* 16–20 Dec. 1755 [says he died 15 Dec.]; *GM* (Exshaw's edition) Dec. 1755; *Pue's Occurrences* 22 July 1740.

0471 COOLEY, Thomas

MP for Duleek 1747–55

> b. (bapt. 4 Dec.) 1705; d. 15 Dec. 1755
> FAMILY/BACKGROUND: Son and heir of Philip Cooley.
> MARRIED: [18 July 1740] Mary, e. dau. of Abel Ram (**1756**).
> CHILDREN: Thomas; Eleanor, m. Charles Craven; Margaret; Sarah.
> EDUCATION: Middle Temple 4 May 1727; called to the Irish Bar 1732.
> CAREER/OCCUPATION: Practising barrister.

POLITICAL ACTIVITY: He was a member of the Country party and voted with it over the Money Bill.

0472 COOPER, Arthur

MP for Carrick 1695–9

> b. *c.* 1655–60; d. 1710
> FAMILY/BACKGROUND: Second son of Edmund Cooper and Margaret, dau. of Nicholas Mahon of Ballinamulty, Co. Roscommon.
> MARRIED: (settlement 18 May) 1693 Mary, dau. of Sir Joshua Allen.
> CHILDREN: Joshua (**0473**); Richard; Mary, m. (1) Robert Ffolliott of Co. Sligo, (2) Robert Fisher; Elizabeth; Anne, m. [17 Oct. 17??] John Perceval of Co. Sligo; Eleanor; Margaret.
> CAREER/OCCUPATION: Sheriff of Co. Sligo 1698; Deputy Governor of Co. Sligo 1699.
> MILITARY: Arthur Cooper was empowered with his

manor grant to keep a prison, and he also headed a company of dragoons with which he supported the Williamite forces.

POLITICAL ACTIVITY: He sat in William III's second parliament, and signed the Association for the protection of William III in parliament in 1695. For much of the century the dominant political influence in Co. Sligo was held by the Coopers and the Wynnes, who represented the county in successive parliaments.

ADDITIONAL INFORMATION: His father, a Cromwellian soldier, purchased 2,823 acres and 3 roods in Co. Sligo, which had been given to Cromwell's soldiers in discharge of a total debt of £1,387 12s 3d.

ESTATES/RESIDENCE: Markree, Co. Sligo. Markree was erected into a manor for him 27 May 1686, and in 2 Jas II (1687), Arthur Cooper was granted fairs at Tobberscanlan. At the end of the eighteenth century the Coopers had lands in the baronies of Tirerill, Corran, Leyny, Carbury and Tireragh.

SOURCES: PRONI D/302; EC 5293 and EC 6717; PRONI T/559 vol. 16 p. 162, Burke, extract pedigrees; Burke *IFR* (1976) p. 273 [his younger brother Richard was born *c.* 1668]; H. Wood (ed.), *The Register of St Catherine, Dublin, 1636–1715* (Parish Register Society of Dublin, 1908) p. 127; T. O'Rorke, *Parish of Ballysadare*, pp. 154–8 [says his father's name is Edward]; *JRSAI* vol. 5 (1925) pp. 39, 51, H. A. S. Upton, 'A List of Governors and Deputy Governors of Counties in Ireland in 1699'; Parliamentary List, 1696 (1).

0473 COOPER, Joshua

MP for Co. Sligo 1719–27–57

b. *c.* 1694–8; d. 4 Aug. (bur. 6) 1757
FAMILY/BACKGROUND: Son of Arthur Cooper (0472) and Mary, dau. of Sir Joshua Allen.
MARRIED: [1729] Mary, dau. of Rt Hon. Henry Bingham (0136).
CHILDREN: Rt Hon. Joshua (0474); Rt Hon. Richard, m. Anna Maria, dau. of Francis Leigh; Henry.
CAREER/OCCUPATION: High Sheriff of Co. Sligo 1718; Burgess of Sligo B. 1738; *Commissioner of the Tillage Act for Connaught 1739–55; *Governor of Co. Sligo 1746–55.

POLITICAL ACTIVITY: He came into parliament in 1719 as the result of a successful challenge to the election of Francis Ormsby (1599) in the by-election that followed the death of Chidley Coote (0483). In the 1720s he supported a national bank, and he espoused the Country party during the Money Bill dispute. On 30 January 1753 Primate Stone wrote to the Chief Secretary, Lord George Sackville: 'French is a deserving man, and I would not fight my Lady Allen's recommendations [for the cure of Finglas], but in the present system it will operate nothing unless Lady Allen could prevail upon her kinsman Mr Cooper to cease his persecution of poor Owen Wynne (2264) [the other MP for Co. Sligo] in the county of Sligoe, which is undertaken for no other visible reason but on account of Mr Wynne's attachment to the Government.'

DIVISION LISTS:
1721 (1) voted for a national bank.
1721 (2) voted for a national bank.
1749 (1) voted for the election of James Digges La Touche (♦♦♦♦).
1753 (1) voted for the expulsion of Arthur Jones-Nevill (1125).
1753 (2) voted against the Money Bill.

ESTATES/RESIDENCE: Markree, Co. Sligo. In 1729 Joshua Cooper of Markree bought Lord Collooney's Sligo estate at Collooney for £16,945.

SOURCES: PRONI D/302; RCBL P273/1/3, Parish Registers of St Paul's, Dublin [bur. 6 Aug.]; Burke *IFR* (1976) p. 273; McCracken thesis; Cavan MPs; W. G. Wood-Martin, *History of Sligo*, vol. 3 p. 439; *HMC Sackville I* p. 188; *Almanacks*; *GM* (Exshaw's edition) Aug. 1757; Parliamentary Lists, 1755.

0474 COOPER, Rt Hon. Joshua

MP for Castlebar 1761–8; Co. Sligo 1768–76–83

b. 1732; d. 16 Dec. 1800 at Markree, Co. Sligo
HONOURS: PC, sworn 14 Dec. 1776.
FAMILY/BACKGROUND: Son of Joshua Cooper (0473) and Mary, dau. of Rt Hon. Henry Bingham (0136).
MARRIED: [May 1758] Alicia, o. dau. and h. of

Edward Synge, Bp of Elphin.

CHILDREN: Joshua Edward (**0475**); Edward Synge, m. Anne, dau. of Harry Verelst, Governor of Bengal; Richard (Middle Temple 13 June 1767); Robert Arthur; Jane.

EDUCATION: School, Mr Connolly; entered TCD 15 July 1748, BA 1752.

CAREER/OCCUPATION: Joint Governor of Co. Sligo 1758–63; *Commissioner of the Tillage Act for Connaught 1762–84; *Governor of Erasmus Smith's Schools and other Charities 1762–97; High Sheriff of Co. Sligo 1763; Burgess of Sligo B. 1771, resigned 1790.

POLITICAL ACTIVITY: The electoral politics of Sligo were often hard-fought, and at this time were dominated by the Coopers and the Wynnes who were in alliance. Joshua Cooper was a fairly typical country gentleman, and usually in opposition. He had been an unsuccessful candidate for Co. Sligo as early as the by-election of 1757, following the death of his father (**0473**), when Benjamin Burton (the younger) (**0294**) had been returned. In 1769 he was considered to be an 'independent Gentleman of very considerable fortune'. He 'constantly' opposed Lord Townshend, but towards the end of the parliament he supported Lord Harcourt 'without any terms' and 'on almost every material question'.

By 1776 he was judged to be 'a sensible well disposed man in respect to public business', while his large estate made him independent. Lord Harcourt had him made a Privy Counsellor and granted him the disposal of an ensigncy. He was a delegate to the Volunteer National Convention for Co. Sligo. In 1783 he was unseated by Charles O'Hara (**1576**), who belonged to an old Sligo family and had the popular vote. However, the setback was temporary, as Cooper's son (**0475**) was returned in 1790 and 1797.

DIVISION LISTS:

1768 (1) absent, in the country.

1771 (1) voted against Lord Townshend as Lord Lieutenant.

1771 (2) voted for Sir Lucius O'Brien's (**1558**) motion for retrenchment.

1772 (2) voted for a Short Revenue Bill.

1773 (1) voted against Absentee Tax.

1774 (2) voted against Catholic relief.

1777 (1) voted for Grattan's (**0895**) motion

for retrenchment.

1780 (1) voted against Grattan's declaration of the rights of Ireland.

1780 (2) voted for Yelverton's (**2268**) motion to modify Poynings' Law.

ADDITIONAL INFORMATION: A member of the RDS, 1767. He was an experimental farmer.

ESTATES/RESIDENCE: Markree, Co. Sligo. In 1785 the rental appears to have been £3,334 p.a. Some of the lands had head rents payable to the Hon. Paul Gore (**0871**) (formerly to Lord Tyrawley), Rt Hon. Owen Wynne (**2262**), the representatives of the Earl of Carlingford, Lord Palmerston, etc. Rent of £53 a year and annual fine of £38 payable to the See of Elphin. As late as 1824 the Coopers held substantial (£700 clear p.a.) leases of Church land from the See of Elphin, possibly a consequence of his marriage with Alicia Synge.

In 33 Geo. II (1760) Joshua Cooper was granted fairs at Tubberscanavan.

SOURCES: PRONI D/302; RCBL P45/2/3, Parish Registers of St Peter's, Dublin; NLI MS 9738 Cooper of Markree papers; Nat. Army Museum, Wynne of Hazlewood Papers, Access. no. 8504–39; Ellis thesis; Burke *IFR* (1976) p. 273; Hughes, *Pat. Officers*; *Index to Irish Privy Counsellors, 1711–1910*; Johnston, *Gt B. & Ire.*, pp. 113, 218; *Register of Admissions to the Honourable Society of the Middle Temple* vol. 1 (London, 1949) p. 366 [says 'of Mercury' (*sic*), Co. Sligo]; M. Kelleher, *List of Members of the Dublin Society 1731–1800* (Dublin, 1982); W. G. Wood-Martin, *History of Sligo*, vol. 3, pp. 439, 440; T. S. Smyth, *Cavan Members*; *Almanacks*; NLI MS 3050 [Rent-book, 1785–95]; NLI 21 F 27 [Maps, 1767–1849]; PRONI DIO 4/24/2/16/2, Bishop's return [*c.* 1824]; *DJ* 2–6 Aug. 1757; *FJ* 14–16 Oct. 1783. Parliamentary Lists, 1769 (1), 1772 (2), 1773 (1) (2), 1774 (1), 1775 (1), 1776 (1) (2), (3), 1777 (1), 1778 (1), 1780 (1), 1782 (1), 1783 (1), (3), 1785 (2).

0475 COOPER, Joshua Edward

MP for Co. Sligo 1790–7–1800, [UK] 1801–6

b. 5 Mar. 1762; d. 8 June 1837

FAMILY/BACKGROUND: Son of Rt Hon. Joshua Cooper (**0474**) and Alicia, dau. of Edward Synge, Bp of Elphin.

MARRIED: Elizabeth, dau. of Robert Lindsay (**1237**).

CHILDREN: *d.s.p.*

EDUCATION: School, Dr Norris, Drogheda; entered TCD 19 Apr. 1779, aged 17 years, BA 1782.
CAREER/OCCUPATION: *Joint Governor of Co. Sligo 1789–1800 (f.); Governor of Co. Sligo 1802; Governor of Co. Tipperary *post* 1800.
MILITARY: Major Sligo Militia 1793, Lieutenant-Colonel 1795, Colonel 1804–7.

POLITICAL ACTIVITY: In 1790, such was the ferocity of the election for Co. Sligo that the Masonic lodges in the town did not meet for two months, 'the majority of the members being unavoidably engaged in the election'. Cooper was returned. He voted for W. B. Ponsonby (**1709**) for Speaker and until 1794 was in opposition. He then supported for a brief period before becoming a strong opponent to the Union.

After the Union he represented Co. Sligo in the United Kingdom parliament. Here he was at first considered to be 'young – rich – silent', and procurable. In fact by December 1804 he was 'in London, deranged' and by 1811 he was certified insane. His brother was returned at the 1806 election.

DIVISION LISTS:

1790 (2) voted for Ponsonby (**1709**) on the Election of a Speaker.

1791 (1) voted for Curran's (**0560**) resolution against the sale of peerages.

1791 (2) voted for Grattan's (**0895**) motion for the exercise of free trade.

1791 (3) voted for Grattan's motion to abolish the Dublin police.

1799 (1) voted against the Union.

1800 (1) voted against the Union.

ESTATES/RESIDENCE: Markree, Co. Sligo; Kevin Street, Dublin. A brief of affidavits in Chancery in the matter of Joshua Edward Cooper, a lunatic, *post* 6 July 1811, states, on the affidavit of Edward Synge Cooper, his younger brother, that the estate (34,120 acres) had a rental of almost £10,000 a year. About the same time Wakefield estimated the Cooper rental at £5,000–9,000.

SOURCES: NLI MS 10306 Balfour Papers; Wakefield, *Account of Ire.*, vol. 1 p. 275; PRONI T/3166/1C Hartnell notes; O'Neill thesis; *Political History of the County and Borough of Sligo*, vol. 3 p. 38; W. H. Hussey de Burgh, *Landowners of Ireland*; Jupp thesis; NLI MS 3076, MS 9759, Cooper of Markree papers, Register of Freeholders for Sligo Co. 9 Dec. 1817; *HP 1794–*

1820; W. G. Wood-Martin, *History of Sligo*, vol. 3 p. 38; *DJ* 6–9 Mar. 1762, *Almanacks*; Parliamentary Lists, 1791 (1), 1793 (1), 1794 (2), 1799 (3), 1800 (3).

0476 COOPER, William

MP for Hillsborough 1733–60, Apr.–8 Aug. 1761

b. 1689; d. 8 Aug. 1761 at his seat near Templeogue at an advanced age
HONOURS: Cr. Baronet 3 Oct. 1758.
FAMILY/BACKGROUND: Son of Thomas Cooper.
MARRIED: Elizabeth, dau. of [   ] Forster.
CHILDREN: *d.s.p.*; Thomas (b. 1712; d. unm.13 Dec. 1741) (admitted to the Inner Temple 18 Nov. 1732, Middle Temple 27 Oct. 1737).
EDUCATION: LLD of TCD, King's Inns *c.* 1734.
CAREER/OCCUPATION: Chief Examiner in Court of Chancery 1723–43, 1746–56 (patent 24 June 1723); *2nd Examiner 1733; Deputy Register in Chancery 1733; *Deputy Clerk of the Crown and Hanaper 1737–40; Master in Court of Chancery 26 Feb. 1739–54; Seneschal of the King's Manor of Newcastle, Co. Dublin 1736–61 (patent 19 Apr. 1736); *Registrar of the Consistory Court to Dublin 1760–1; ?Sheriff of Co. Sligo 1733; *Commissioner of Oyer and Terminer 1744–54; *Trustee of the Linen Board for Ulster 1753–60; elected a Governor of Swift's Hospital for lunatics, Jan. 1761.

POLITICAL ACTIVITY: In 1731 he was appointed a trustee under an act of parliament to repair the road from Dublin to Dunleer. On 19 October 1733 he and his fellow trustees, including William Aston (**0062**), Arthur Hill (**1015**), Faithful Fortescue (**0790**) and Thomas Fortescue, petitioned for heads of a bill to increase the tolls and broaden their existing powers. He introduced the heads of a bill, 9 Geo. II, c. 5, which was substantially 'for the more speedy Recovery of Rents by distress' in 1735, and an act with the same intent, 25 Geo. II, c. 14, in 1751; he was responsible for bringing in the heads of five Indemnity Bills in 1739, 1745, 1747, 1749, 1757.

He supported the Country party at the time of the Money Bill dispute in the early 1750s, but was absent for the crucial vote on the Money Bill in 1753. He was listed for 162 committees between 1733 and 1760.

DIVISION LISTS:

1749 (1) voted against the election of James Digges La Touche (♦♦♦♦).

1753 (1) voted for the expulsion of Arthur Jones-Nevill (**1125**).

1757 (1) voted against the resolutions on pensions.

ADDITIONAL INFORMATION: [?]Warden of the Freemason lodge that met at the Yellow Lyon.

ESTATES/RESIDENCE: Cypress Grove, Templeogue, Co. Dublin. These estates were inherited by his great-niece, Catherine Rothe (born 1757; died 20 February 1833), who married, 27 December 1774, Hon. Pierce Butler (born 1750, *d.s.p.* 5 May 1826) (**0325**).

SOURCES: *CJ Ire.* (Bradley ed.) vol. 6 p. 626, vol. 7 pp. 69, 431–2, 690, 953, vol. 8 pp. 66–7, 225, 431, vol. 10 p. 238–9; PRONI D/302 [says he is of Lisbusland]; *CJ Ire.* vol. 4 p. 261; McCracken thesis; GEC *B*; *IMC King's Inns Admission Papers, 1607–1867*; GEC *B*. [says only child, Thomas]; *Memorials of the Dead*; *Register of Admissions to the Honourable Society of the Middle Temple* (London, 1949) vol. 1 p. 322; J. Walton, *'The King's Business': Letters on the Administration of Ireland, 1741–61 …* (NY 1996) no. 143; *Almanacks*; *DJ* 13 Mar. 1731, 20–24 Jan. 1761; *The Dublin Evening Post* 23 Oct. 1733.

0477 COOTE, Rt Hon. Algernon

MP for Jamestown 1715–20; [GB] Castle Rising 22 Jan. 1724–34; Hedon 4 Mar. 1742 – 27 Aug. 1744

b. 1688 (bapt. 6 June 1689); d. 27 Aug. 1744
HONOURS: PC, sworn 2 Aug. 1723, 19 June 1727, 6 Aug. 1729, 1732–d.
PEERAGES: Suc. as 6th Earl of Mountrath 27 March 1720.
FAMILY/BACKGROUND: Son of Charles Coote (d. May 1709), 3rd Earl of Mountrath (m. 1675) and Isabella, dau. of Charles Dormer, 2nd Earl of Carnarvon.
MARRIED: [28 Nov. 1721] Diana (b. 1676; d. July 1766), dau. of Richard Newport, 2nd Earl of Bradford. (She d. 'above 90 Years of Age' 18 July 1766 leaving legacies of above £100,000; she left her son £30,000 and an estate of £1,000 p.a.)
CHILDREN: Rt Hon. Charles Henry, 7th Earl of Mountrath (d. unm.1 Mar. 1802).
EDUCATION: School, St Paul's, London; entered

Cambridge (Trinity College) 7 May 1706, aged 18 years.
CAREER/OCCUPATION: Governor of Queen's County ?1723
MILITARY: Guidon and eldest Major of 3rd Troop of Life Guards 24 Dec. 1717; Cornet and Major in same 21 Nov. 1718.

POLITICAL ACTIVITY: His career was largely in England where, despite the efforts of his father-in-law, he failed to secure an English peerage.

ESTATES/RESIDENCE: Co. Roscommon. In 1730 he had 6,719 Irish acres in the baronies of Athlone, Ballintuber and Boyle. In 1770 the estate contained 8,398 Irish acres including land in Co. Leitrim (including lands in the parish of Inishmoyrath) and Co. Westmeath (some lands in the parish of Kilchagh). Of the Co. Roscommon lands, townlands can be traced to the parish of Kilmacumsy, barony of Frenchpark, and parish of Oram, barony of Ballymore (neither of which baronies was mentioned in 1730). The principal concentration (nine townlands) was in the parish of Fuerty in the barony of Athlone and the parish of Rahara. In 15 Jas I (1640), Sir Charles Coote was granted fairs at Fuerty. In 4 Charles I (1629), Sir Charles Coote was granted fairs at Mountrath and Castlecuff. In 11 Geo. III (1771), 'Earl McGrath', later corrected to Earl Mountrath, was granted a market at Jamestown.

SOURCES: NLI MS 2793 vol. of estate maps 1730, 1770; EC 2848, EC 6533; GEC *P*; Burke *PB* (1906) p. 387, *Ext. P* (1883) p. 134; *HP 1715–54*; *Index to Irish Privy Counsellors, 1711–1910*; *Alum. Cantab.*; C. Dalton, *George the First's Army, 1714–1727*; *Almanacks*; *DJ* 22–26 July 1766. *BNL*, 16 March 1802 [this refers to two deaths, Lord Mountrath (MP's son) aged 78 and Lord Bateman aged 81, the ages should possibly be reversed as Lord Mountrath must have been 81 as his mother was 45 at the time of her marriage in 1721].

0478 COOTE, Charles

MP for Castlemartyr 1715–27

b. *ante* 29 Oct. 1694; d. 6 Oct. 1761
FAMILY/BACKGROUND: Only son of Sir Philips Coote (**0485**) and his 2nd wife Elizabeth, dau. and co-h. of Rt Hon. William Brabazon, 3rd Earl of Meath.
MARRIED: [18 Aug. 1714] Catherine, dau. of Sir Robert Newcomen, 6th Baronet (**1532**).
CHILDREN: Chidley, m. Jane, e. dau. of Rt Hon. Sir Ralph Gore, 4th Baronet (**0872**); dau.

POLITICAL ACTIVITY: Very little is known of this MP, apart from the fact that he was of doubtful mental stability and by 1730 he was certified as insane.

ADDITIONAL INFORMATION: On 8 February 1740 his son Chidley petitioned, in case of his marriage, to be enabled to make jointures and settlements. The petition said that his grandfather, Sir Philip Coote, was seized in fee of 1,500 acres in Co. Limerick, which on his father's marriage was placed in hands of trustees to provide for Sir Philip during his life and for Charles thereafter. In 1730 Charles became lunatic and was placed under guardianship. Hence his son, Chidley, required the heads of a bill to arrange the estate during his father's lifetime.

ESTATES/RESIDENCE: Mount Coote, Co. Limerick.

SOURCES: PRONI MIC/465/1 R. Ffolliott, *Biographical Notices, 1756–1827*; Burke *PB* (1906) p. 1474; *LG* (1846) pp. 261–2; Lodge *P*.

0479 COOTE, Charles

MP for Granard 1723–7; Co. Cavan 1727–50

b. 27 Aug. (bapt. 15 Sept.) 1695; d. 6 Dec. 1750
FAMILY/BACKGROUND: Eldest son of Thomas Coote (0487) and his 1st wife Anne, dau. of Christopher Lovet.
MARRIED: [July 1722] Prudence (d. Dec. 1778), dau. of Richard Geering (0845).
CHILDREN: Rt Hon. Charles, 1st Earl of Bellomont (0480); Anne, m. [11 Mar. 1748] William Anketell of Co. Monaghan; Frances, m. [2 June 1755] John Boswell of Co. Wicklow; Catherine, m. [1762] John Corry of Co. Monaghan; Caroline, m. James Uniacke (2121); Elizabeth, m. 23 Oct. 1752 Chidley Coote of Co. Limerick; Mary; Prudentia.
EDUCATION: School, Mr Scott, Dublin; entered TCD 11 July 1710, BA 1714, MA 1737.
CAREER/OCCUPATION: Clerk in Court of Chancery; Sheriff of Co. Cavan 1719; High Sheriff of Co. Cavan 1720, 1725; Trustee of the Linen Board for Ulster 1732–d.; *Governor of the Workhouse 1732–d.; *Commissioner of the Tillage Act for Ulster 1735, 1739–d.; *Subscriber to the Cambrick Manufacture 1743–9; Freedom of the City of Dublin, 14 Oct. 1763.–?d.

MILITARY: Colonel of the Tromtrath Volunteers and Rangers.

POLITICAL ACTIVITY: He was returned for the by-election for Granard in 1723 following the elevation to the bench of John Parnell (1631). On 19 November 1725 he complained of being disturbed in his possession of Killygrany, Co. Monaghan during time of privilege. In the general election of 1727 he was returned for Co. Cavan, which he represented until his death in 1750.

In his capacity as Solicitor General, he was a leading speaker on behalf of the government against the Cork petitions over the realignment of the currency in 1737. There was no Irish mint, and the monetary economy of the country was rudimentary. Coins were supposed to bear a value commensurate with their metallic content and there was an almost perpetual shortage of specie, which encouraged the circulation of all sorts of coins, particularly Spanish and Portuguese gold moidores. The value of these was fixed from time to time by proclamation, and merchants would carry small scales to weigh the coins they were handling. Nevertheless, the proclaimed value was often at variance with their real value. This upset the discounting system and encouraged speculators to play the Irish money market. Finally, in 1737, the overvalued Portuguese moidores were revalued and an $8^{1}/_{2}$ per cent discount between the English and Irish pound established. This continued until 1826, when the currencies were merged. Naturally there was a great furore among the merchants, who considered that they were being robbed by the devaluation. The outcry was particularly loud in Dublin and Cork, the principal commercial centres of the country at this time. On 27 October 1737 Lord George Sackville (1835) wrote to his father, the recently recalled Lord Lieutenant Dorset, that the petitions against the lowering of the gold were considered the previous day in the House. They first proposed a committee and, when that was negatived by 108 to 55, Stannard (1981) moved for a resolution that the lowering was prejudicial to the trade of the country. This was rejected by 11 to 40, and Carter (0360) proposed that the further consideration of the petitions should be postponed to 1 October 1738, which was carried by 118 to 30. 'The chief speakers on the side of the minority were Stannard, Sir Richard Cox (**0508**) (who abus'd the Privy Council very grossly) Mr Morgan (**1487**), Mr Maloun [*sic*] (**1336**). On the other side the Solicitor General (**0196**), Mr Cope (**0489**), Mr Coote, Mr Cuff [*sic*] (**0557**) and Mr Hill (**1015**).'

In December 1745 he introduced the heads of a bill, 19 Geo. II, c. 10, 'An Act for continuing and amending the several acts for the better regulation of Juries'.

DIVISION LISTS:
1749 (1) voted for the election of James Digges La Touche (♦♦♦).

ADDITIONAL INFORMATION: He was 'robbed near St Paul's Church of a gold repeating watch, a gold snuff box, and his purse, by five persons well armed with pistols' on 21 January 1741/2 (*see* **0110**). On 1 February 1741/2 Stephen Jones, Thomas Dowling and Charles MacDaniel were tried for the robbery.

ESTATES/RESIDENCE: Cootehill, Co. Cavan.

SOURCES: *CJ Ire.* (Bradley ed.) vol. 5 p. 288, vol. 7 pp. 747 (0439); PRONI D/302; McCracken thesis; GEC *P*; Burke *Ext. P* (1883) p. 135; Lodge *P* [bapt. 15 Sept. 1695]; Smyth, *Cavan MPs*; *HMC Sackville I* p. 167; *Almanacks*; *GM* (Exshaw's edition) Nov. 1750; *The Dublin Gazette* 29 Nov. 1724; *The Dublin Newsletter* 23 Jan., 2 Feb. 1742; *DJ* 30 Oct. 1750, 15–18 Oct. 1763, 10–12 Dec. 1778.

0480 COOTE, Rt Hon. Charles

MP for Co. Cavan 1761–6

b. 6 Apr. 1738; d. 20 Oct. 1800 in Dublin from complications of a cold caught at the late Curragh [race] meeting
HONOURS: KB 16 Jan. 1764; PC, sworn 19 Dec. 1774; *one of the 15 Knights Companion of the Order of St Patrick 1790.
PEERAGES: Suc. as 5th Baron Coote of Coloony, 10 Feb. 1766; cr. 1st Earl of Bellomont 4 Sept. 1767; Baronet [GB] 12 May 1774.
FAMILY/BACKGROUND: Son and h. of Charles Coote (**0479**) and Prudence, dau. of Richard Geering.
MARRIED: [20 Aug. 1774] Emilia Maria Margaret, dau. of Rt Hon. James FitzGerald, 1st Duke of Leinster (**0734**).

CHILDREN: Charles (d. yg); Mary; Prudentia; Emily Louisa; Charlotte Rebecca; he acknowledged six illegitimate children by four mothers.
EDUCATION: School, Dr Ford; entered TCD 5 July 1754, aged 16 years.
CAREER/OCCUPATION: Joint Post Master General 1789–97; Sheriff of Co. Cavan Feb. 1760; Freedom of the Corporation of Weavers 28 Jan. 1764; *Trustee of the Linen Board for Ulster 1767–d.; *Governor of the Charitable Loan Society 1778–98; *Governor of Co. Cavan 1780–d.; Custos Rot. Co. Cavan 1780–1800.
MILITARY: Deputy Quarter Master General of the Forces Oct. 1766–73; Colonel of the Co. Cavan Militia, 1793.

POLITICAL ACTIVITY: At the end of polling on 19 May 1761, the poll for Co. Cavan stood as follows: Lord Newtown-Butler (**0313**), 506 votes; Hon. Barry Maxwell (**1372**), 467; Charles Coote, 466; George Montgomery (**1438**), 436. It was then urged that the Sheriff, Sir Archibald Acheson (**0001**), should declare Butler and Maxwell duly elected. Acheson said he was of the opinion that his power did not expire with the return of the writ and that he would continue to take the suffrage of each freeholder that should offer himself. As a result the poll did not close until 23 May, when it stood as follows: Lord Newtown-Butler, 612; Charles Coote, 600; George Montgomery, 549; Hon. Barry Maxwell, 477. Butler and Coote were declared duly elected.

He appears to have been a quarrelsome, disagreeable men with a high sense of his own importance. He complained that Lord Townshend had not paid himself and his requests sufficient attention. Finally Lord Townshend, who was not the most patient of viceroys, was provoked into a duel, which took place at the conclusion of his term of office. Bellomont was injured and received considerable public sympathy in Ireland. In England there was concern for the precedent that a viceroy could be subjected to a duel because of his decisions while in office.

Under Lord Harcourt's conciliatory viceroyalty 'he supported very steadily', and was made a Privy Counsellor and given the appointment of various Revenue officers. By 1775: 'His primary object is rank in the Army. His next a Commissioner of the Revenue or any considerable employment.' Lord Harcourt obtained a pension of £800 p.a.

for his wife – this was probably also intended as a compliment to her brother, the Duke of Leinster (0745). By 1782 his estate was 'embarrassed', but his wife's pension had been increased to £1,500. In 1788 he appears to have been allowed to 'dispose' of this pension. He was an advocate of renunciation, i.e. the formal renunciation of Britain's right to 'declare' legislation for Ireland, and was described as 'an eccentric man and a very bombast speaker'.

In 1799 it was reported that 'His lordship is possessed of a strong mind, some reading and much observation. He opposes the Union, although a Member of the Privy Council. As a speaker he is of little consideration. His manner is disgustingly pompous ... His Lordship publishes his own speeches.' He once described Co. Cavan as 'all acclivity and declivity, without the intervention of an horizontal plane; the hills are all rocks, the valleys are all bogs, and the people all savages.'

DIVISION LISTS:
   1763 (1) voted against an inquiry into the
   Pension List.

ADDITIONAL INFORMATION: *A member of the RDS from 1764. Brought to trial in April 1764, along with Lieutenant Edward Mayne, for the killing of 'Alexander McDonald a noted Captain of the Insurgents in the neighbourhood of Castleblayney'. The prosecution case fell apart when the witness it called testified that McDonald had charged against Coote while the latter was in execution of his duty. Coote and Mayne were completely exonerated and he was honoured with the Knight Companion of the Bath in 1764 'for good and laudable service in suppressing the tumultuous and illegal insurrection in the north parts of the kingdom'.

The FitzGerald family fell out with the Cootes because Lord Bellomont wrote a letter to the duke (0745) in 1773 saying that FitzGerald's mother was secretly married to Mr Ogilvie (1571), which was denied. However, they did marry in France the following year. The Bellomont marriage was unhappy, and Lady Bellomont left him in 1794. He was variously described as a man of 'gallantry and high spirits, of the highest refinements and dazzling polish and also as a tyrant, a madman, a person of disgusting pomposity whose actions were a singular mixture of diseased feeling and erroneous reasoning.' A most licentious person, he acknowledged at least six illegitimate children by four different mothers in his will. He was the butt of unkind humour when he was wounded in the groin during his duel with Lord Townshend in 1772.

ESTATES/RESIDENCE: Cootehill, Co. Cavan. His Cootehill estate was over 1,000 acres, including a 500 acre demesne. There is a deed of petition between Chidley and Charles Coote involving the lands of Ballinvana and Darranstown, barony of Coshlea, 1773. He inherited in January 1771 from his cousin Judith, daughter of Richard Coote, 4th Earl of Bellomont, the estates of Birtsmorton and Berrow, Worcestershire.

SOURCES: EC 5577 and 6406; RCBL P45/2/3, Parish Registers of St Peter's, Dublin; RCBL T/34, Extracts from the Parish Registers of St Andrew's, Dublin; O'Neill thesis; *Alum. Dub.*; Burke, *Ext. P,* (1883) p. 135; Ellis thesis; *Index to Irish Privy Counsellors, 1711–1910*; Smyth, *Cavan MPs*; C. Ross (ed.), *Cornwallis Corr.* (London, 1859), vol. 3 p. 41 [says his duel with Townshend took place on 2 Feb. 1773]; J. Kelly, *'That Damn'd thing called Honour': Duelling in Ireland 1570–1860* (Cork, 1995), pp. 107–111; F. G. James, *Lords of the Ascendancy* (1995), p. 152; D. Guinness and W. Ryan, *Irish Houses and Castles* (London, 1971), pp. 43–6; *Almanacks*; *DJ* 19–23 Feb. 1760, 19–23 May, 23–26 May 1761, 28–31 Jan., 24–28 Apr. 1764; *FJ* 25–27 Apr. 1793; *BNL* 31 Oct. 1800; Parliamentary Lists, 1775 (1), 1777 (1), 1782 (1), 1785 (2), 1787 (1), 1790 (1), 1799 (1).

0481 COOTE, Rt Hon. Charles Henry

MP for Queen's County 1776–83, 1797–1800; Maryborough 1783–90–7 (re-elected after appointment to place of profit, 1796); [UK] Queen's County 1801–2 Mar. 1802

   b. 25 Aug. 1754; d. 22 Jan. 1823
   HONOURS: PC, sworn 23 Dec. 1800.
   PEERAGES: Suc. as 2nd Baron Castle Coote 1802; Genealogist to the Order of St Patrick 1783–1804; *Officer of the Order 1799 (f.).
   FAMILY/BACKGROUND: Eldest son of Charles Coote, Dean of Kilfenora, and his 1st wife Grace, dau. of Thomas Tilson, wid. of Thomas Cuffe (0557).

MARRIED: [22 May 1779] Elizabeth Ann, dau. and h. of Rev. Henry Tilson of Eagle Hill, Co. Kildare.

CHILDREN: Charles Henry; William Bushe Conyngham (b. 1786; d. 1799 – midshipman on *Atlas*, d. aged 13); Eyre Tilson, 3rd Baron Castle Coote, m. [1822] Barbara, dau. and co-h. of Sir Joshua Colles Meredyth, 8th Baronet (she m. (2) Joseph Leeson, 4th Earl of Milltown); dau.

EDUCATION: School, Eton 1767–71; entered TCD 7 July 1772, BA 1776; Lincoln's Inn 18 Mar. 1776; called to the Irish Bar 1779.

CAREER/OCCUPATION: Sheriff of Queen's County 1791–2; *Burgomaster of Maryborough 1797; *Magistrate of Maryborough 1797; Governor of Queen's County 1802; Imprest Accounts Commissioner July 1789–95 at £800 p.a.; *listed in Judges and Barristers 1790–1800 (f.); Revenue Commissioner 1802–20; Commissioner of Customs and Port Dues 1820–3 at £1,200 p.a.

MILITARY: Barracks Commissioner Apr. 1788; Captain in Mountrath Cavalry Oct. 1796; Colonel of Queen's County Militia 1799.

POLITICAL ACTIVITY: A lawyer, he was returned for Queen's County at the 1776 general election. He was considered 'an amiable character in the intercourse of private life', but not blessed with sparkling abilities. His father, Dean Coote, was the agent to Lord Mountrath, to whom he was related, and managed his interest in Queen's County. He was at first considered doubtful, although he voted for Pery (**1670**) in the closely contested election for the Speakership. However, Lord Lieutenant Buckinghamshire gave him a pension of £300 p.a. during his wife's lifetime, and Lord Lieutenant Temple made him genealogist to the Knights of St Patrick.

In 1783 he was returned for Maryborough, for which his father had one seat. In 1784 it was noted that 'His wife [has] a pension of £300 p.a. which he wishes to convert into a better thing for himself. Is sometimes a little wavering – borough in Queen's Co. He has a small employment in the Order of St Patrick and even voted for Protecting Duties, but made excuses. Is not entirely to be depended upon.' It was felt that on balance he was 'for', especially as he 'has since professed attachment'. By 1785 he wanted either a bishopric for his father or an office for himself.

In 1788 he was made a Commissioner of Barracks at £400 p.a., and a year later Commissioner

of Accounts at double the remuneration. In 1789 a patriotic reporter considered that 'The two sheet anchors of pension and place prevent all variation in his conduct.' In 1797 he was returned for Queen's County, and in 1798 declared himself not to be against a Union in principle, but that he would like to be an Irish peer. He voted for the Union in 1799 and 1800 and 'obtained a [militia] Regiment, (which was taken from Colonel Warburton), patronage of Queen's County, a Peerage, (Lord Castlecoote,) and £7,500 in cash for his interest at the Borough of Maryborough'.

DIVISION LISTS:

1777 (1) voted for Grattan's (**0895**) motion for retrenchment.

1777 (2) voted against the Trade Embargo.

1780 (1) voted for Grattan's declaration of the rights of Ireland.

1780 (2) voted against Yelverton's (**2268**) motion to modify Poynings' Law.

1780 (3) voted for the Tenantry Bill.

1780 (4) voted for the Perpetual Mutiny Bill.

1783 (1) voted against Flood's (**0762**) motion for parliamentary reform.

1784 (1) voted against a committee on the Reform Bill.

1784 (2) voted for Protective Duties (wool).

1785 (1) absent.

1789 (1) voted against a Regency.

1790 (2) voted for Foster (**0805**) on the Election of a Speaker.

1793 (2) voted for the Convention Bill.

1795 (2) voted against Catholic emancipation.

1798 (1) voted against Sir Laurence Parsons' (**1636**) motion for an investigation into 'the present discontents'.

1799 (1) voted for the Union – A Commissioner of Revenue, a Captain of Yeoman Cavalry but since appointed Commandant of the Queen's County Militia.

1800 (1) voted for the Union.

ADDITIONAL INFORMATION: For his services in promoting the Union he obtained a new barony, with special remainder to himself, for his aged kinsman, the 7th Earl of Mountrath.

He spoke at least twice at Westminster – on 27 May 1801 for the continuation of martial law in Ireland, and on 10 June to disoblige his colleague Parnell (**1630**), in opposition to the latter's proposal to exempt John Beresford (**0115**) from the Irish Members Disqualification Bill. In 1814 he applied for promotion in the peerage. The Chief Secretary, (Sir) Robert Peel, reported: 'I cannot say that I think Lord Castlecoote's a very strong claim. He is an Union peer (of course, according to his own account, not made for Union services) but as he happens to have been made on the same day with 14 others (31 July 1800) one cannot but have a little doubt on that point … If it can, Lord Castlecoote's claim, I fear would rest rather in the length than the efficacy of the service.'

ESTATES/RESIDENCE: Forest Lodge, Mountrath, Queen's County; Leopardstown, Co. Dublin. Wakefield stated that Lord Castle Coote had a good estate.

There is an abstract beginning with the will of Sir Charles Henry Coote, 1864, Rental, 1904.

SOURCES: NAI M/3045 vol. of maps, 1819; EC 494; PRONI T/3166/1C Hartnell notes; O'Neill thesis; Jupp thesis; GEC *P*; *Index to Irish Privy Counsellors, 1711–1910*; *IMC King's Inns Admission Papers, 1607–1867*; *The Records of the Honourable Society of Lincoln's Inn* (Lincoln's Inn, 1896) vol. 1 p. 483; R. A. Austen-Leigh (ed.), *The Eton College Register, 1753–90* (Eton, 1921) 3 vols; P. F. Meehan, *The Members of Parliament for Queen's Co. and its Boroughs, 1585–1800*; *HP 1794–1820*; *Almanacks*; *FJ* 20 Oct. 1796; *DJ* 6 June 1799; Parliamentary Lists, 1776 (1), (2), (3), 1777 (1), 1778 (1), 1780 (1), 1782 (1), 1783 (1), (2), 1784 (1), (2), (3), 1785 (1), (2), (3), (4), 1787 (1), 1788 (1), 1789 (1), (2), 1790 (1), 1791 (1), 1793 (1), 1794 (1), (2), 1798 (1), 1799 (2), (3), 1800 (1), (3).

0482 COOTE, Chidley

MP for Kilmallock 1695–9

b. *c.* 1643; d. 1702

FAMILY/BACKGROUND: Eldest son of Chidley Coote of Co. Limerick and Alice (or Anne), only dau. of Sir Thomas Philips of Co. Londonderry.

MARRIED: [26 June 1675] Catherine, dau. of Col. Robert Sandys (?sis. of **1874**).

CHILDREN: Chidley, DD, m. Jane dau. of Rt Hon. George Evans (**0703**); Anne, m. Bartholomew Purdon (**1745**); Catherine, m. Rt Hon. Henry Boyle, 1st Earl of Shannon (**0210**).

EDUCATION: Entered TCD 22 Feb. 1660.

MILITARY: Captain in the Green Foot Aug. 1670; Captain in Sir Robert Byron's Regiment of Foot 1672; Captain in the Horse July 1680; Captain in the Earl of Ossory's Regiment of Horse 1685; on 4 Feb. 1692 Captain Chidley Coote petitioned for half pay backdated to Jan. 1689, when Sir Henry Ingoldsby's Regiment was disbanded; he was commissioned Captain in Sir Richard Coote's Regiment of Foot 23 Apr. 1692; Lieutenant-Colonel in the Duke of Schomberg's Regiment of Horse 3 Jan. 1694; Lieutenant of the Ordnance (granted in reversion, May 1695) 20 Aug. 1702 at 16s 5 1/2d per day.

POLITICAL ACTIVITY: He sat in the second parliament of William III and may have been on military service during this time as he is listed for only two committees, on 17 October 1695 and 4 September 1697. He supported Lord Chancellor Porter against the accusations of favouring Catholics made against him by some MPs in 1695, and signed the Association for the protection of William III in parliament in 1696.

ADDITIONAL INFORMATION: He was granted, 21 January 1684, £500 for the upkeep of six lighthouses, which he surrendered on 20 February 1691.

ESTATES/RESIDENCE: Kilmallock, Co. Limerick. He had lands in the baronies of Coshlea (lands in Coshlea granted to Coote, 18 Chas II) and in Kilmallock; in 1698, Chidley Coote of Charleville, Co. Cork, let lands in the barony of Coshlea to Rev. Lewis Prytheroh of Charleville.

SOURCES: EC 2138; EC 5098; PRONI T/559 vol. 16 p. 182, Burke, extract pedigrees; RCBL GS 2/7/3/44 Kilmore Marriage Licence Books; *Cal. SP Dom. 1691–2* (London, 1900) pp. 109, 126, 251, 1694–95 (London, 1906) pp. 2, 83, 471; Lodge *P*; Burke *Ext. P* (1883) p. 134; Simms' cards; C. Dalton (ed.), *English Army Lists and Commission Registers, 1661–1714* (London, 1904), vol. 6 p. 230 [says he was Lieutenant of the Ordnance in the reigns of William and Mary and Queen Anne]; Vicars, *Prerogative Wills*; King, *State of the Protestants*; *The Register of the Parish of St Peter and St Kevin, 1669–1761* (Parish Register Society of Dublin, 1911) p. 47; C. Dalton (ed.), *Irish Army Lists, 1661–1685* (London, 1907), pp. 74, 80, 112, 131, 148; Parliamentary Lists, 1695 (1), 1696 (1).

0483 COOTE, Hon. Chidley

MP for Co. Sligo 1713–14, 1715–19

b. *ante* 1677; d. *ante* June 1719
FAMILY/BACKGROUND: Son of Richard Coote, 1st
Baron Coote, and Mary, dau. of Sir George St
George.
MARRIED: (1) [1 Apr. 1698] Elinor, dau. and h. of
Isaac Walkden of Co. Tipperary; (2) Mary, eldest
dau. of Sir Robert King, 1st Baronet (?**1164**).
CHILDREN: John; Chidley (d. yg); Mary, m. (1)
Guy Moore (**1458**), (2) William Gore, Bp of
Limerick; Elinor, m. Robert Moore of Co.
Tipperary; Olivia, m. [1722] Walter Jones of Co.
Leitrim; Catherine, m. Marcus Anthony Morgan
(**1487**).
CAREER/OCCUPATION: Sheriff of Co. Leitrim 1709.
MILITARY: Colonel of Horse.

POLITICAL ACTIVITY: A professional soldier and a
confirmed Whig – considered 'bad' by the government. Neither of his spells in parliament was
long: the 1713 session was very short and he was
dead before the 1719 session began.

ESTATES/RESIDENCE: Coote Hall, Co. Roscommon. In
1713 Chidley Coote, MP for Co. Sligo's income was
estimated at £500, all in Sligo, but this is obviously
questionable – Coote Hall was in Co. Roscommon and
his wife was a Co. Tipperary heiress. (Presumably it
could have referred to his Co. Sligo estates as he was
MP for that county.)

SOURCES: PRONI T/3411; PRONI T/559 vol. 16 p.
183, Burke, extract pedigrees; GEC *B*; Burke, *Ext. P*
(1883) p. 135; *Alum. Dub.*; Vicars, *Prerog. Wills*; *JRSAI*
vol. 38 (1908) p. 387, J. Meehan, 'Catalogue of the
High Sheriffs of the County of Leitrim from the Year
1605 to the Year 1800'; *CJ Ire.* vol. 4 p. 495 [records
the issuing of a writ because he was decd]; Parliamentary Lists, 1713 (1), (2).

♦♦♦♦ COOTE, Sir Eyre [n.d.e.]

MP for Maryborough May–Dec. 1761; [GB]
Leicester 1768–74; Poole 1774–80

b. 1728; d. 2 Sept. 1784 at sea off Madras of
apoplexy
HONOURS: KB 31 Aug. 1771.
FAMILY/BACKGROUND: Fourth son of Rev. Chidley
Coote of Co. Limerick and Jane, dau. of Rt Hon.
George Evans (**0703**).

MARRIED: [6 July 1763] Susana, dau. of Charles
Hutchinson, Governor of St Helena.
CHILDREN: *d.s.p.*
MILITARY: Lieutenant-Colonel 20 Jan. 1759;
Colonel 4 Apr. 1765; Major-General, Colonel
27th Regiment (Inniskillings) Sept. 1771;
Commander-in-Chief India 17 Apr. 1777;
Lieutenant-General 29 Aug. 1777.

POLITICAL ACTIVITY: He sat for eight months before being declared not duly elected, but although
he was returned in May, parliament did not meet
until 22 October, when his election was challenged. John Parnell (**1632**) was sworn on 15
December 1761.

ADDITIONAL INFORMATION: His father died when
he was four years old, and he was brought up by
his uncle, George Evans (**0704**). He served under
Cumberland in Scotland in 1745, and in 1754
was Captain in the 39th Regiment and sent to
India; he was to the fore in the capture of Calcutta and was Governor there until replaced by
Clive. He distinguished himself at Plassey, 23 June
1757, defeating General Count Lally. He again
defeated Lally at Wandiwash, 22 January 1760,
and captured Pondicherry in August 1760. He
commanded the East India Company's forces in
Bengal in 1761. He returned to India in 1769 as
Commander-in-Chief at Madras, but resigned. He
was named Commander-in-Chief for India in
1777, and took over command in Calcutta in
1779. He subsequently had a notorious quarrel
with Lord Macartney (**1302**), Governor of Madras 1780–86. He was successful against Hyder
Ali at Porto Novo, 1 July and at Pollicore, 27 August 1781. William Hickey described his death at
sea whilst being pursued by French warships off
Madras as follows: 'Sir Eyre Coote, who has never
quitted the deck, and had little or no sleep for
two nights, suddenly fell from the chair in which
he was sitting in a fit. In an hour he was so far
recovered as to enquire, with much agitation,
whether the enemy gained upon them ... The enemy gained considerably. Sir Eyre Coote's agitation, if possible, increased; he every minute en-
quired if the ships were seen. About midnight the
man stationed at the bolt sprit end to look out
suddenly called out that a large ship was running
on board of them, whereupon Sir Eyre instantly

fell into a fit of apoplexy, from which he never recovered.'

ESTATES/RESIDENCE: Portrane House, Maryborough, Queen's County, which he built; West Park, Hampshire, purchased in 1762 with money from the HEIC for his Indian services. In 1779, Young reckoned Sir Eyre Coote's rental at £2,000.

SOURCES: *DNB* [d. 1783]; *HP 1754–94* [says he d. 26 Apr. 1783]; Musgrave, *Obits*; P. F. Meehan, *The Members of Parliament for Queen's Co. and its Boroughs, 1585–1800* [says died 28 Apr. 1783]; A. Spencer (ed.), *Memoirs of William Hickey* (1913–25), vol. 3 pp. 94–5; *Ir. Gen.* vol. 3 no. 10 (Oct. 1965) pp. 389–92, Lt Colonel The O'Doneven, 'Two Irish Personalities at War'; *FJ* 17–19 Sept. 1771; Young, *Tour in Ire.*, vol. 2 App. p. 83.

0484 COOTE, Sir Eyre

MP for Ballynakill 1790–7; Maryborough 1797– Jan. 1800; [Escheator of Munster 6 Jan. 1800]; [UK] Queen's County 1802–21 Jan. 1806; Barnstaple 1812–18

> b. (20) May 1759; d. 10 Dec. 1823
> HONOURS: Knight 1800; KB 19 May 1802; Knight Grand Cross of the Bath 2 Jan. 1815 (downgraded 1816); Knight of the Crescent (Turkey) 1801.
> FAMILY/BACKGROUND: Son of Charles Coote, Dean of Kilfenora, and his 1st wife Grace, dau. of Thomas Tilson, wid. of Thomas Cuffe (0557).
> MARRIED: (1) [9 Nov. 1786] Sarah, dau. and co-h. of John Rodard Somerset; (2) Jane, dau. of John Bagwell (0074).
> CHILDREN: (1) 3 dau.
> (2) Eyre Coote, m. [1828] Elizabeth Rosetta, dau. of James Massy Dawson of Co. Tipperary.
> EDUCATION: School, Eton 1767–71; entered TCD 1 Nov. 1774, aged 15 years; LLD of Cambridge (Trinity College) 1811, Fellow Commoner (Trinity College) 30 June 1811.
> CAREER/OCCUPATION: Governor of Jamaica 1806–7.
> MILITARY: Ensign 37th Regiment 1776, aged 14 years?, Lieutenant Aug. 1776, Captain 10 Aug. 1778; Major 47th Regiment 1783; Lieutenant-Colonel 70th Regiment 1788; Colonel 24 Jan. 1794; aide-de-camp to the King 1795; Brigadier-General 1796; Major-General 1 Jan. 1798; Lieutenant-General 1805; Colonel 62nd Foot 1806–10; Colonel 34th Foot 1810–16; General

1814, res. 21 May 1816;*Colonel Lieutenant-Colonel of the 28th Regiment of Foot 1788; *a Regiment of Foot 1789–90, 1792; *Brigadier-General 1796–8.

POLITICAL ACTIVITY: A professional soldier, he was returned for Ballynakill by purchase from Lord Drogheda. He supported the government, voting for Foster (0805) as Speaker, and in 1797 was returned by his brother (0481) for Maryborough. In 1799 he was considered doubtful, but was abroad on active service. He resigned his seat (accepting the office of Escheator for Munster) before the decisive vote on the Union.

DIVISION LISTS:
1790 (2) voted for Foster (0805) on the Election of a Speaker.

ADDITIONAL INFORMATION: Coote carried the colours at the Battle of Brooklyn, 27 August 1776, and served with distinction at the Battles of Yorktown, September–October 1781, Rhode Island and Brandywine, 11 September 1777. He took part in the siege of Charlestown and served under Cornwallis in Virginia. At Yorktown, he was captured by the Americans.

In 1790 he made an unsuccessful attempt to come into Westminster on Lord Camelford's interest as a friend of Pitt's ministry.

At the outbreak of war with revolutionary France he went to the West Indies and distinguished himself at the storming of Guadaloupe, 3 July 1794. In 1798 he was given the command of Dover and was sent to breach the sluice gates at Ostend, and landed with 1,000 troops on 18 May. He completed his mission but, due to bad weather, was unable to return to his ships and, after a conflict in which he was wounded, was captured by the French; he was exchanged shortly afterwards. In 1799 he took part in the expedition to Dan Helder and was successful at Bergen. In 1800 he was given the command of a brigade in the Mediterranean and took part in Sir Ralph Abercromby's disembarkation in Egypt, where he helped capture Alexandria, 21 March 1801.

He was invited to stand for Queen's County in March 1802 but declined because of lack of preparation. However, he was returned in the 1802 general election unopposed and supported government. On 8 December he advocated provision for an expeditionary force in defence proposals, and was seen as a useful counterbalance to Addington's Irish critics, the Hely-Hutchinson family. On 16 March 1803 he spoke in favour of the Irish Militia Bill and praised the militia's services. In 1804 he was put in command at Cork and not expected to attend parliament, although he did turn up, usually to demonstrate his independence of government, March and April 1805, before his departure for Jamaica. In 1807 he was relieved of his Jamaican post because of ill-health. He failed to keep up his interest in Queen's County and was returned for Barnstaple after an expensive contest. Government thought him 'hopeful'. On 2 March and 13 and 24 May 1813 he supported the Catholic claims. He opposed, on 15 March 1813, the abolition of flogging in the army.

In 1809 he took part in the Walcheren expedition and received the surrender of Flushing. 'His proceedings, however, were so eccentric during the expedition that it was obvious, that he could never again be trusted with a command.' In 1815 he was brought before the Lord Mayor of London on a charge of indecent conduct preferred by the officials of Christ's Hospital, who stated that Coote had 'conversed improperly' with a number of boys in the mathematical school and asked them to flog him. After an inquiry it was decided that he was 'eccentric' rather than mad, but he was nevertheless dismissed from the army and lost his Order of the Bath.

ESTATES/RESIDENCE: College Green, Dublin; West Park, Huntingdonshire; Forest Lodge and Portrane, Queen's County. He succeeded to the estates of his uncle, Sir Eyre Coote (♦♦♦) in 1784 and to £200,000 on the death of his father in 1796.

SOURCES: PRONI T/3166/1C Hartland notes; O'Neill thesis; Jupp thesis; *DNB*; *HP 1794–1820*; *Alum. Dub.*; *Alum. Cantab.*; R. A. Austen-Leigh (ed.), *The Eton College Register, 1753–90* (Eton, 1921), 3 vols; P. F. Meehan, *The Members of Parliament for Queen's Co. and its Boroughs, 1585–1800*; *Sotheby's Sale Catalogue* 26–7 June 1987; *Almanacks*; Parliamentary Lists, 1791 (1), 1793 (1), 1794 (1), (2), 1799 (2), (3).

0485 COOTE, Sir Philips

MP for Kilmallock 1713–14

b. (bapt. 10 Mar.) 1659; d. 1715
HONOURS: Knight.
FAMILY/BACKGROUND: Son of Chidley Coote and Alice (or Anne), only dau. of Sir Thomas Philips of Co. Londonderry.
MARRIED: (1) Jane [d. 1677], dau. of Henry Jones, Bp of Meath; (2) Elizabeth, dau. and co-h. of Rt Hon. William Brabazon, 3rd Earl of Meath.
CHILDREN: (1) Alice (d. yg).
(2) Charles (**0478**); Cecilia; Elizabeth.
CAREER/OCCUPATION: Sheriff of Dublin 22 Dec. 1681; Sheriff of Co. Dublin 1682.

POLITICAL ACTIVITY: In 1713 the government wished to bring him in for Killmallock – 'General Webb is to write to Mr Holmes his Deputy Governor to get him elected' – in the hope that he was a Tory, but he turned out to be a Whig. He died in 1715, so he sat only in the one very brief session of the 1713 parliament.

ESTATES/RESIDENCE: Killester and Mountcoote, Co. Limerick. On 17 October 1695 the House appointed a committee to consider his petition for heads of a (private) bill to 'charge his real estate for payment of his debts, he being only tenant for life'. In 1713 Sir Philip Coote, MP for Charlville [*sic*], had an estimated income of £600.

SOURCES: PRONI D/302; PRONI T/3411; *CJ Ire.* (Bradley ed.) vol. 2 p. 727; Lodge *P* [says his first wife d. 1677, i.e. he m. aged 17]; Hughes, *Pat. Officers*; King, *State of the Protestants*; *Ir. Builder* 15 Jan. 1887 'St Audoen's Church, Corn Market: Its History from its Foundation to the Present Time'; Parliamentary Lists, 1713 (1), 1713 (2).

0486 COOTE, Hon. Richard

MP for Co. Kilkenny 1692–3

b. Feb. 1649; d. (13 Feb.) 1703 at Chester
HONOURS: On 3 March 1692 a warrant was issued to swear Coote of the Privy Council.
FAMILY/BACKGROUND: Eldest son of Charles Coote, 1st Earl of Montrath, and his 2nd wife Jane, dau. of Sir Robert Hannay, 1st Baronet.
MARRIED: [July 1666] Penelope, eldest dau. of Rt Hon. Arthur Hill of Co. Down.
CHILDREN: Charles (d. yg); Rose, m. Charles

Boyle, 2nd Viscount Blessington (**0202**); Jane, m. Sir William Evans; 2 other dau.

CAREER/OCCUPATION: Commissioner of Appeals 28 June 1683; Custos Rot. Co. Kilkenny 1675; Deputy Governor of Co. Kilkenny 1699.

MILITARY: Captain in the Foot 1675; left the army as a Captain in the Horse at the accession of James II; Lieutenant-Colonel in Viscount Lisburne's Regiment of Foot 8 Mar. 1689; Colonel (1 Feb. 1692) in the Regiment of Foot of which Lord Lisburne was Colonel; Colonel of his own Regiment of Foot 1694; while quartered at Exeter in 1696 had to convene a court martial to deal with mutiny and desertion in his Regiment; put on half pay 1697 and reappointed Colonel of the Regiment of Foot in Ireland 12 Feb. 1702.

POLITICAL ACTIVITY: On 6 September 1692 the Earl of Longford wrote to Josiah Haydock (**0992**) that Ormonde wanted his tenants to vote for Colonel Richard Coote. Ormonde was all-powerful in Kilkenny, and Coote was duly returned. The parliament was very short, and there is no indication of his activity during that time. He was a professional soldier and appears to have been on active service until 1697.

ESTATES/RESIDENCE: Tullamaine, Co. Kilkenny. He had lands assigned to him by the Acts of Settlement in Counties Kilkenny, Kerry, Roscommon and Limerick. On 6 September 1692 he petitioned for the restoration of Gormanstown, confirmed to his father by the Act of Settlement, as well as the grant of all forfeitures of bonds on the exportation of wool in lieu of the debt of £3,300 owed his father by Charles II. The patent, he claimed, had been seized from him by Tyrconnel in 1688. The debt was £2,833. By 20 November 1694, his petition had still not been allowed, therefore he asked for the grant of £3,500, forfeited to the Crown by the Earl of Clanricarde (originally settled on Clanricarde's daughter, the wife of Patrick Sarsfield). On 1 November 1695, Coote was included on a list of people owing rent for forfeited estates.

SOURCES: *Cal. SP Dom. 1691–1692* (London, 1900) pp. 120, 435, *1693* (London, 1903) pp. 166, 387, *1694–5* (London, 1906) pp. 33, 88, 128, 289, 332, 334, 341, 385, 507, *1695* (London, 1908) pp. 135, 143, 247–8, *1696* (London, 1913) pp. 14, 57, 158, 192, 196, 217–18, 232, 259, 478; Kilkenny MPs; Lodge *P*; GEC *P*; Musgrave, *Obits*; *HMC Ormonde*, (1920) new ser. vol. 8 pp. 33, 291 [a letter of resignation sent by a Colonel Coote, Mar. 1707]; C. Dalton (ed.), *English Army Lists and Commission Registers, 1661–1714* (London, 1896), vol. 3 pp. 7, 75 [says he d. Mar. 1703 at Chester]; C.

Dalton (ed.), *Irish Army Lists 1661–1685* (London, 1907) pp. 100, 136 [says he died Mar. 1703 at Chester]; *JRSAI* vol. 55 (1925) pp. 38, 47, H. A. S. Upton, 'A List of Governors and Deputy Governors of Counties in Ireland in 1699'[says he is a second son]; *Camden Miscellany* 30 (London, 1990) vol. 39 app. p. 408 [gives a Richard Coote Lt. Col. of Lord Lisburne's Foot, 8 Mar. 1789, who had seen service in either the French or Dutch armies prior to 1689, promoted Col. after Lisburne's death at the siege of Limerick, 1691, half-pay 1692, Col. of a newly raised battalion, 1702, died at Chester in Mar. 1703].

0487 COOTE, Hon. Thomas

MP for Dublin city 1692–3; Co. Monaghan 1723–7, 1733–41

b. *c.* 1663; d. 24 Apr. 1741

FAMILY/BACKGROUND: Third son of Rt Hon. Richard Coote, 1st Baron Coote, and Mary, dau. of Sir George St George, Woodford, Essex.

MARRIED: (1) [1680] Anne, dau. of Christopher Lovett, wid. of William Tighe; (2) [?1697] Elinor, dau. and co-h. of Sir Thomas St George; (3) [1701] Frances, dau. and co-h. of Col. Christopher Copeley.

CHILDREN:(1) Charles (**0479**); dau.; dau., m. [1704] Mervyn Pratt of Cabra Castle, Co. Cavan. (2) Thomas; Mary. (3) Chidley.

EDUCATION: Middle Temple 19 Nov. 1683; King's Inns 1684; called to the Bar in 1684.

CAREER/OCCUPATION: King's Counsel 1684; 3rd Justice of the King's Bench (patent 22 Mar. 1693) 1693–9; a Commissioner of the Great Seal 1697; 2nd Justice of the King's/Queen's Bench 1699–1715; Justice of Assize for Munster, Lent 1707; NE Ulster, Summer 1707, Lent 1708, Summer 1708; Munster, Lent 1709; NW Ulster, Summer 1709, Lent 1710; NE Ulster, Summer 1710; Munster, Lent 1711; Leinster, Summer 1711; NW Ulster, Lent 1712, Summer 1712, Lent 1713; NE Ulster, Lent 1714; NW Ulster, Summer 1714. Recorder of Dublin 1692; Sheriff of Co. Dublin 1695; Trustee of the Linen Board for Ulster 10 Oct. 1711–d.; *Governor of Erasmus Smith's Schools and other charities 1739.

POLITICAL ACTIVITY: A lawyer, he was listed for four committees on 11 October 1692. In January 1693 Coote was one of the unsuccessful contenders for the vacant post of Baron of the Exchequer, and on 29 January Sydney recommended him to succeed Sir Henry Echlin on the King's Bench. He was promoted Second Justice in 1699. He visited London about 1710 in order to secure his position on the Queen's Bench, and sought a testimony from Swift as to the soundness of his political principles. He signed a report on the conflict between the government and the aldermen of Dublin 1713–14, and was dismissed in 1715 following the Hanoverian succession.

In the first session of the new parliament called at the accession of George I, the Whigs in the Commons exacted retribution. On 6 June 1716 the Commons found that he, along with seven fellow judges (Sir Richard Cox, Robert Doyne (**0661**), Sir Henry Echlin, Robert Johnson (**1101**), Richard Nutley (**1551**), Robert Rochfort (**1806**) and Anthony Upton), signed a report designed to assuage the doubts of the English Attorney General. In the report they stated that it was usual for the Lord Mayor of Dublin to remain in office beyond his elected tenure if a replacement was not forthcoming, and it was found that in the preparation of the report aldermen had not been consulted and that false precedents had been cited to prove this judgment. In evidence before the Commons in 1716 Coote claimed that he had not acted officiously during the dispute between the government and the Dublin aldermen, and pleaded that all men were liable to make mistakes.

On 16 May 1715 the Earl of Sunderland wrote to Secretary Stanhope that 'Colonel Coote (**0483**) has applied to you to defer the King's letter for making Mr Caulfeild (**0375**) a Judge in the room of his father. I believe Judge Coote was originally an honest man and might privately wish well to the protestant interest; but he was so thoroughly engaged in the measures of the late administration in Ireland particularly those relating to the city of Dublin, that one can not with any reason or justice distinguish him from others who are removed upon that account.' He lived in hard times and paid the penalty for being on the wrong side.

He was returned at the by-election for Co. Monaghan in 1723 following the death of Alexander Montgomery (**1434**) on 25 March 1722,

and was listed for 23 committees between 1723 and 1725. In 1733 he came in again, this time in place of John Montgomery (**1441**), who died in August of that year. He was nominated for 19 committees between 1733 and 1739. In 1725 he introduced the heads of a bill, 12 Geo. I, c. 2, 'to prevent the fraudulent and clandestine importing of goods'; in 1727, 3 Geo. II, c. 16, 'An Act for the better regulating the Fees of Justices of the Peace and for disabling Alderman Thomas Wilkinson and Alderman Thomas Bolton from acting as Justices of the Peace within this Kingdom', and in 1737 he brought in the heads of the recurrent 'Act for the Relief of insolvent Debtors', 11 Geo. II, c. 16. He died on 24 April 1741.

ADDITIONAL INFORMATION: In 1731 he was a foundation member of the Dublin Society. He was interested in the economic development of the country. On 26 January 1692 he was incorporated into the Company of the Royal Fisheries of Ireland, and he was a foundation member of the Linen Board, which met for the first time on 10 October 1711. In 1724 he wrote a pamphlet entitled *Instructions for Cultivating and Raising Flax*. His inheritance from his uncle, Colonel Thomas Coote, included a library, and he was an avid book buyer.

ESTATES/RESIDENCE: Cootehill, Co. Cavan; Smithfield, Dublin. He was heir to his uncle, Colonel Thomas Coote of Cootehill, in 1671. Mrs Pendavers (Delany) visited Coote Hill in 1732 and noted that 'The town of Coote Hill is like a pretty English village, well situated and all the land about it cultivated and enclosed with cut hedges and tall trees in rows. From the town one drives near a mile on a fine gravelled road, a cut hedge on each side and rows of old oak and ash trees, to Mr Coote's house. Within two hundred yards of the house is a handsome gateway, which is built in great taste, with a fine arch to drive through. This house lies on top of a carpet hill, with large lakes on each side which extend four miles and are surrounded by fine groves of well grown forest trees.'

SOURCES: *CJ Ire.* vol. 4 pp. 256–62, vol. 5 pp. 233, 735, vol. 6 pp. 807, 832, 842 (0236, 0287, 0386); PRONI D/2685/14/1 – W. G. S. Tighe, 'The Tighe Story' [unpublished family history, 1959] p. 15; PRONI T/448 p. 35, TSPI 1715–1716; RCBL GS 2/7/3/44, Kilmore Marriage Licence Books; McCracken thesis; Burke *Ext. P.* (1883), p. 135; *Cal. SP Dom. 1691–1692* (London, 1900) p. 112, *1693* (London, 1903) pp. 3, 23, 35, 77,

1696 (London, 1913) pp. 117, 383, 474; Ball, *Judges*; *IMC King's Inns Admission Papers, 1607–1867* [? says called 1690]; *Register of Admissions to the Honourable Society of the Middle Temple* (London, 1949) vol. 1 p. 212; Llandover, *Delany Corr.*, vol. 1 pp. 376–7; D. Guinness and W. Ryan, *Irish Houses and Castles* (London, 1971), p.42 [says he married his third (?second) wife in 1697]; J. J. Howard (ed.), *Miscellanea Genealogica et Heraldica*, vol. 3 new ser. (1880) p. 79 [say he married Elinor, dau. and co-heiress of Sir Thomas St George of Woodford, Essex]; Berry *RDS* pp. 24–7; *Almanacks*; *The Dublin Gazette* 22 Feb., 22 July 1707, 14 Feb., 22 June 1708, 22 Feb., 23 July 1709, 18 Feb. 1710, 26 Feb., 12 July 1712, 14 Feb., 27 June 1713, 20 Feb., 6 July 1714; *The Dublin Intelligence* 27 June 1710, 17 Feb. and 11 Aug. 1711.

0488 COPE, Henry

MP for Donegal B. 1779–83; Philipstown 1783–90; Tulsk 1790–97

b. *c.* 1739; d. 1815
FAMILY/BACKGROUND: Eldest son of Henry Cope and Alice, dau. of Thomas Jones of Co. Meath.
MARRIED: [Jan. 1783] Margaret, dau. of [   ] Knott.
CHILDREN: *d.s.p.*
CAREER/OCCUPATION: Attorney, Court of the Exchequer 1762; Six Clerk in Court of Chancery 7 Apr. 1772–82, 1784–91 (*vice* Francis Hervey, resigned); Accountant General Court of Chancery 7 Apr. 1772, 31 Jan. 1792–1800 (f.); *listed in Attornies of the King's Bench, Common Pleas and Court of Exchequer 1789, 1792, 1794; *Governor and Guardian of the Lying-in Hospital 1786; High Sheriff of Co. Westmeath 1795.

POLITICAL ACTIVITY: He was a lawyer, who purchased his seat and held two legal offices – Six Clerk and Accountant General, both in the Court of Chancery. Despite being a placeman, he was considered to be hostile to government in 1780. However, Lord Carlisle gave his brother a living and subsequently he supported the administration. He married a niece of Colonel Bruen (**0268**), who made a fortune as Quarter-Master General in America. In 1783 Bruen created a 'party' by purchasing three seats for the ensuing parliament, one each for Philipstown, Taghmon and James-

town, from Lord Belvidere (**1800**), Walter Hore (**1037**) and Gilbert King (**1155**) respectively. In the 1783–90 parliament he followed the political lead of his uncle-in-law. By 1788 he was noted as being 'always hostile'.

In 1790 he, or more probably Col. Bruen, bought a seat for Tulsk from Mrs Walcot, the surviving sister of the late Lord Chief Justice Caulfeild (**0371**), who was reputed to be very wealthy. In the 1790–97 parliament Cope supported, and by 1794 was Accountant General of Chancery. Henry Bruen died in 1795, and Cope did not come in again in 1797.

DIVISION LISTS:
1779 (2) voted for the six-months Loan Bill.
1780 (2) voted for Yelverton's (**2268**) motion to modify Poynings' Law.
1780 (3) voted for the Tenantry Bill.
1780 (4) voted against the Perpetual Mutiny Bill.
1784 (1) voted for a committee on the Reform Bill.
1784 (2) voted for Protective Duties (wool).
1784 (3) voted against Foster's (**0805**) Bill to regulate the press.
1785 (1) voted for the Commercial Propositions.
1787 (1) voted for a Pension Bill.
1789 (1) voted for a Regency.
1790 (2) voted for Ponsonby (**1709**) on the Election of a Speaker.

ADDITIONAL INFORMATION: *A member of the RDS from 1768.

ESTATES/RESIDENCE: Castlegal, Co. Sligo; Merrion Square, Dublin; Hightown, Co. Westmeath – he sold this to Henry Dopping. He also had lands (possibly a lease of Church lands) in Armagh.

SOURCES: Information from P. F. Meehan Esq.; Burke *PB* (1903) p. 362; *Memorials of the Dead* [says his parents married 23 Dec. 1738]; Hughes, *Pat. Officers*; *King's Inns Admission Papers, 1607–1867*; *Almanacks*; *DJ* 9–12 May 1772; Parliamentary Lists, 1776 (1), 1780 (1), 1782 (1), 1783 (1), (2), 1784 (1), (2), (3), 1785 (1), (2), (3), (4), 1787 (1), 1788 (1), 1789 (1), 1790 (1), 1791 (1), 1793 (1), 1794 (1), (2).

0489 COPE, Robert

MP for Lisburn 1711–13; Co. Armagh 1713–14, 1727–53

b. 1679; d. 17 Mar. 1753

FAMILY/BACKGROUND: Son of Anthony Cope, Dean of Elphin, and Elizabeth, dau. of Henry Cope of Loughgall, Co. Armagh.

MARRIED: (1) [1 Sept. 1707] Lettice, dau. of Arthur Brownlow (0263); (2) [6 Mar. 1711] Elizabeth, dau. of Sir William Fownes, 1st Baronet (0811).

CHILDREN: (2) Rev. Anthony; Arthur, m. [Jan. 1761] Ellen Osborne; Henry; Robert; William (admitted to Middle Temple 17 May 1732); Barclay; John; Anne, m. John Hadden; Elinor; Mary; Catherine, m. [c. Sept. 1758] Theophilus Clements of Rakenny, Co. Cavan; Emy; Henrietta (d. yg).

EDUCATION: School, Mr Walker, Drogheda; entered TCD 23 Feb. 1696, aged 17 years, BA 1699; Middle Temple 6 May 1702; MA hon. caus. 1707.

CAREER/OCCUPATION: *Governor of the Workhouse 1732–d.; *Trustee of the Linen Board for Ulster 1732–d.; *Commissioner of the Tillage Act for Ulster 1735, 1739–d.; Sheriff of Co. Armagh 1736; *Governor of Erasmus Smith's Schools and other charities 1741–d.

POLITICAL ACTIVITY: He was returned for Lisburn in the by-election following the elevation of Richard Nutley (1551) to be a Justice of the King's Bench. He was a Court supporter and returned for Lisburn by Lord Conway's interest. He supported the government over the Dublin mayoralty issue and, in 1713, voted for Sir Richard Levinge (1230) as Speaker. In 1713 it was considered, correctly, that he was likely to be elected for Co. Armagh. He was classed as a Tory. At the accession of George I he was on the 'black list' of Tories, and on 15 December 1715 he was called before the House to explain his conduct in signing the Armagh address in favour of Sir Constantine Phipps, in opposition to the House of Commons' address for his removal. His excuse was put to the vote and found unsatisfactory, and he was placed in the custody of the Serjeant-at-Arms. He did not come in in 1715, but he came in again in 1727 and represented the county until his death in 1753, which precipitated one of the most bitter elections of the century (see 0265, 0366). On 27 October 1731 he complained that he had been disturbed in possession of his lands of Upper Ballybrine, Co. Roscommon, during time of privilege.

In 1737 he was a leading government speaker in the debate on the Cork petitions against realigning the gold currency. There was no Irish mint and the monetary economy of the country was rudimentary. Coins were supposed to bear a value commensurate with their metallic content and there was an almost perpetual shortage of specie, which encouraged the circulation of all sorts of coins, particularly Spanish and Portuguese gold moidores. The value of these coins was fixed from time to time by proclamation, and merchants would carry small scales to weigh the coins they were handling. Nevertheless, the proclaimed value was often at variance with the real value. This upset the discounting system and encouraged speculators to play the Irish money market. Finally, in 1737, the overvalued Portuguese moidores were revalued and an $8^{1}/_{2}$ per cent discount between the English and Irish pound established. This continued until 1826, when the currencies were merged. Naturally there was a great furore among the merchants, who considered that they were being robbed by the devaluation. The outcry was particularly loud in Dublin and Cork, the principal commercial centres of the country at this time. On 27 October 1737 Lord George Sackville (1835) wrote to his father, the recently recalled Lord Lieutenant Dorset, that the petitions against the lowering of the gold were considered the previous day in the House. They first proposed a committee and, when that was negatived by 108 to 55, Stannard (1981) moved for a resolution that the lowering was prejudicial to the trade of the country. This was rejected by 11 to 40, and Carter (0360) proposed that the further consideration of the petitions should be postponed to 1 October 1738, which was carried by 118 to 30. 'The chief speakers on the side of the minority were Stannard, Sir Richard Cox (0508) (who abus'd the Privy Council very grossly) Mr Morgan (1487), Mr Maloun [sic] (1336). On the other side the Solicitor General (0196), Mr Cope (0489), Mr Coote, Mr Cuff [sic] (0557) and Mr Hill (1015)'.

In 1741 he introduced the heads of a bill, 15 Geo. II, c. 10, 'for the further Encouragement of finding and working Mines and Minerals in this Kingdom'. This was part of the continuing desire to find workable coal mines.

DIVISION LISTS:
1711 (1) voted for the Court on the Dublin mayoralty issue.
1713 (1) voted for Sir Richard Levinge (**1230**) for Speaker.
1749 (1) abstained.

ADDITIONAL INFORMATION: He was a friend of Swift.

ESTATES/RESIDENCE: Loughgall Manor, Co. Armagh. In 1714 his income was estimated at £600 p.a.

SOURCES: *CJ Ire.* (Bradley ed.) vol. 4 p. 127, vol. 6 p. 60, vol. 7 p. 318 (415); PRONI T/559 vol. 16 p. 193, Burke, extract pedigrees; PRONI T/1075/32, 40 Canon Leslie's notes; RCBL T/34, Extracts from the Parish Registers of St Andrew's, Dublin; McCracken thesis; Burke *LGI* (1904) p. 111; *Memorials of the Dead* [says he had sixteen children]; *Register of Admissions to the Honourable Society of the Middle Temple* (London 1949) vol. pp. 251, 313; *Dublin Gazette* 13 Jan. 1736; *HMC Sackville I* p. 167; *Almanacks; GM* (Exshaw's edition) Mar. 1753; *Pue's Occurrences* 20 Mar. 1753; Parliamentary Lists, 1711 (3), 1713 (1), (2), 1714 (1), 1714–15 (1).

0490 COPE, Robert Camden

MP for Co. Armagh 1799–1800, [UK] 1801–2

b. *c.* 1771; d. 5 Dec. 1818
FAMILY/BACKGROUND: Son and h. of Arthur Cope of Clare Street, Dublin, and Ellen Osborne; grandson of Robert Cope (**0489**).
MARRIED: [1811] Mary, dau. of Samuel Elliott, Governor of Antigua.
CHILDREN: O. s. Arthur.
EDUCATION: Entered Cambridge (Trinity College) 10 Feb. 1788.
CAREER/OCCUPATION: Sheriff of Co. Armagh March–Sept. 1799.
MILITARY: Lieutenant-Colonel of the Armagh Militia 1795.

POLITICAL ACTIVITY: He had a majority of 520 over Sir Capel Molyneux in the election for Co. Armagh in 1799. He at first voted against the Union but then changed his mind and was re-warded with 'a Regiment, and the patronage of his County'. Under the terms of the Act of Union (which preserved the two-member county constituency), he was returned to the United Kingdom parliament. At Westminster he made no mark but was listed as a supporter of the ministry. He retired rather than face a contest in 1802.

DIVISION LISTS:
1800 (1) voted for the Union.

ADDITIONAL INFORMATION: A distant relation of the Achesons, he commanded the Armagh Militia under Colonel Walpole, an aide-de-camp sent to reinforce General Loftus' (**1259**) counter-attack into Wexford in 1798. Before attacking the main rebel strength, Loftus ordered that the advance guards, who were nearing Ballymore, should first be destroyed. He split his forces, ordering Walpole to advance inland while he encircled the enemy's flanks along the coast. Walpole's forces were ambushed and cut to pieces. Walpole himself died in the attack.

ESTATES/RESIDENCE: Loughgall Manor, Co. Armagh. The estate had 450 freeholders in 1789 (the largest interest in the county at that time), exclusive of the 70 freeholders on the estate of a cadet branch, the Copes of Drumilly. The Loughgall estate comprised 9,912 statute acres in 1879, valued at £13,574 p.a.

SOURCES: PRONI D/1606/1/139 Gosford Papers [election calculations]; PRONI T/3166/1A Hartland notes; O'Neill thesis; Jupp thesis; Burke *LGI* (1904) p. 111; *HP 1794–1820; Alum. Cantab.*; T. Pakenham, *The Year of Liberty* (1972), pp. 206–8; *BNL* 15, 22 Oct. and 5 Nov. 1799 [election]; *DJ* 22 Oct. 1799 [also gives election details]; Parliamentary Lists, 1791 (1), 1799 (3), 1800 (3).

0491 COPINGER, Maurice

MP for Ardfert 1758–60, 1761–8–76–83; Roscommon B. 1785–90; Belturbet 1790–7

b. 1727; d. 6 Oct. 1802
FAMILY/BACKGROUND: Son and h. of John Copinger of Dublin.
MARRIED: [30 July 1766] Anne, dau. of Henry Mitchell (**1414**).
CHILDREN: John James (d. aged 31 years).

EDUCATION: School, Mr McGill; entered TCD 9 July 1743, aged 16 years; Middle Temple 6 Nov. 1747; BA 1748; called to the Irish Bar 1753.
CAREER/OCCUPATION: King's Counsel; 3rd Serjeant 12 July 1770–d.; 2nd Serjeant 19 July 1774–6; *Bencher of the Honorable Society of King's Inns 1773; *Council at Law for the Port Business 1777–81; Revenue Appeals Commissioner 13 May 1783–97 (21 Aug. 1783, 24 Dec. 1783, 21 Aug. 1789, 14 Apr. 1790, 4 Jan. 1794–Jan. 1797); *Clerk of the Ship's Entries 1783–92; *listed in Judges and Barristers 1789–1800 (f.); *Governor of the Workhouse 1766–8; Foundling Hospital and Workhouse 1769–97; *elected to the Court of Assistants 1767–8; *Commissioner of the Tillage Act for Munster 1767–84.

POLITICAL ACTIVITY: Maurice Copinger entered parliament for Ardfert on the death of Edmond Malone (1337) on 24 January 1758. He was sworn less than a month later, on 22 February, and was returned for Ardfert in successive general elections until 1783. He was a parliamentary lawyer and was nominated for 20 committees between 1758 and 1760.

Ardfert was a Crosbie borough (0540, 0534), and at this time the Crosbies were anxious to establish themselves in the peerage, first as Lords Branden and then as Earls of Glandore; it was thought that Copinger's return might owe something to this ambition and also to the fact that he was related to the Crosbie family. In December 1765 he was appointed to the committee to inquire into the public works necessary to the nation. A 1769 Parliamentary List noted that he was influenced by Lord Branden (Crosbie, 0540) and Mr Mason (1352), and that he 'should be taken notice of. Must be applied to through Mr Mason.' In 1772 he was Third Serjeant-at-Law and in 1774 Second Serjeant-at-Law. In 1775 he was described as 'King's Counsel and Second Serjeant at Law. Connected with Lord Crosbie (0534), Sir Henry Cavendish (0380), and Mr Mason. A very moderate speaker. Seldom takes in [sic – ?any] part in debate.'

In the 1776 general election he was 'returned by purchase' but 'ruined in his fortune'. He had a small estate in which he was 'hurt'. In 1777 it was noted that he was 'a sensible man. Well heard in the House. Very embarrassed in his circumstances. Very constant and uniform in his support'; but

also that he had very little private practice. His financial situation was eased in 1780 when he was appointed Counsel to the Commissioners of the Revenue, worth £1,400 p.a. Then in 1782, on the arrival of the Duke of Portland, whose viceroyalty was in some respects a more experienced and cautious preview of Lord Fitzwilliam's, Copinger was among those dismissed; on 25 May 1782 John Beresford (0115) wrote to Townshend that 'There is something peculiarly cruel and tyrannical in the case of Copinger. Family misfortunes have reduced him in such a manner that his liberty and his absolute existence depended totally upon his office; deprived of that, they had better have hanged him, and yet he is turned out of a place neither ministerial nor confidential, merely to make room for a boy of two years standing at the bar.' A Parliamentary List for that year notes that 'He was removed by the Duke of Portland to make room for Mr George Ponsonby (1699), whose office of Clerk of the Ships Entries £500 p.a., was given to Mr Copinger as some compensation. A quiet heavy man.' A list for 1783 comments that 'His distresses obliged him to accept. His case being taken up by Parliament, he was recommended for further provision to Lord Temple, who made [him] Commissioner of Appeals, £300 p.a. Does not come in again.' However, when Sir Cornwallis Maude (1366) was created Lord Montalt, the government recommended Copinger for his place in the House of Commons and he was elected for Roscommon Borough.

In 1790 he was returned for Belturbet. The borough belonged to Lord Belmore (1269), who brought in his own nominee for one seat and 'the other seat 'tis said he gave Government for being made a Viscount. Mr Copinger has an office.' A 1794 list stated that Copinger and his wife had a pension. He appears to have been essentially an academic rather than a practising lawyer, and he published *A Practical Arrangement of the Laws Relative to the Excise; wherein the Statutes, with reference to similar English Acts of Parliament, are carefully digested. To which are added cases Adjudged in the Court of Appeals, Decisions of the Commissioners for Taxes in England on male servants and windows with the opinions of the judges there on, &c.* (Dublin, 1799).

DIVISION LISTS:

1768 (1) voted against army augmentation.
1771 (1) voted for Lord Townshend as Lord Lieutenant.
1771 (2) voted against Sir Lucius O'Brien's (1558) motion for retrenchment – a placeman.
1772 (2) voted against a Short Revenue Bill.
1773 (2) voted against an untaxed press.
1774 (2) voted for Catholic relief.
1775 (1) voted against the Pro-American amendment to the Speech from the Throne.
1777 (1) voted against Grattan's (0895) motion for retrenchment.
1778 (2) voted for the Popery Bill.
1779 (1) voted for New Taxes.
1779 (2) voted against a six-months Loan Bill.
1780 (3) voted for the Tenantry Bill.
1785 (1) voted for the Commercial Propositions.
1789 (1) voted against a Regency.
1790 (2) voted for Foster (0805) on the Election of a Speaker.

ADDITIONAL INFORMATION: *A member of the RDS from 1764.

ESTATES/RESIDENCE: Glenville, Co. Cork; Harcourt Place, Dublin. In 1702–3 Thomas Coppinger had 158 acres and Walter Coppinger 2,557 acres, both in Co. Cork, forfeited.
In 1766, Maurice Coppinger was granted fairs at Glenville, *alias* Glanfrehane.

SOURCES: PRONI T/3166/1C Hartnell notes; RCBL P30/1/1, Parish Register of St Mark's, Dublin; RCBL P344/11/8 Registry of Monuments, St Anne's Parish Church, Dublin [says he died aged 63 years]; McCracken thesis; Ellis thesis; Hughes, *Pat. Officers*; IMC *King's Inns Admission Papers, 1607–1867*; H. A. C. Sturgess, *Register of Admissions to the Honourable Society of the Middle Temple* (London, 1949), vol. 1 p. 338; P. and B. Rowan [antiquarian booksellers], *The Eighteenth Century, An Irish Perspective* (Belfast, 1986) no. 83; *Kerry Magazine* vol. 3 no. 36 (Dec. 1856) pp. 185–90, 'Parliamentary Representation of Kerry' [says incorrectly that he married Mary Anne Crosbie and that he was later a judge of King's Bench]; *Beresford Corr.* vol. 1 p. 203; Simms, *Williamite Confiscation*, p. 178; *Almanacks; BNL* 27 Dec. 1765; *DJ* 28 June–1 July 1766; Parliamentary Lists, 1769 (1), 1772 (2), 1773 (1), (2), 1774 (1), 1775 (1), 1776 (1), (2), (3), 1777 (1), 1778

(1), 1780 (1), 1782 (1), 1783 (1), (2), 1785 (2), (3), (4), 1787 (1), 1788 (1), 1789 (1), 1790 (1), 1791 (1), 1793 (1), 1794 (1), (2).

CORKE, Earl of: *see* **BOYLE**
0206 Boyle, Hon. Hamilton (styled Viscount Dungarvan 1759–62), 6th Earl of Corke and Orrery, MP Charleville 1759–60, [GB] Warwick 1761–2

0492 CORKER, Edward

MP for Ratoath 1692–3, 1695–9

b. 1645; d. 1702
FAMILY/BACKGROUND: Son of [ ] Corker.
MARRIED: (1) Ann [ ]; (2) Esther, dau. of Sir Daniel Bellingham.
CHILDREN: (2) Daniel; Bellingham (bapt. 29 May 1683); Frances m. [ ] Delany; Annabella; Anna; Hester; Martha, m. Randal Heron; Margaret (d. 2 Sept. 1699, aged 6 months).
CAREER/OCCUPATION: Registrar in Court of Chancery 16 June 1669; Commissioner for Forfeited Estates (at £400 p.a., patent Dec. 1693) 17 Jan. 1694, 29 Mar. 1695.
MILITARY: Ensign in Sir John Edgeworth's Regiment of Foot 1 May 1689; Commissioner for Stating Accounts of the Army *ante* 1693; Captain-Lieutenant in Colonel Frederick Hamilton's Regiment 24 Aug. 1693, Captain 20 Aug. 1694; at the siege of Namur; left regiment *ante* 1702.

POLITICAL ACTIVITY: He was a professional soldier, and probably on active service during both parliaments. He was nominated for a committee in 1692 and for two committees in the following parliament. Captain Corker was one of two named individuals on a draft warrant, December 1693, of Commissioners for Forfeited Estates, who were to receive a salary; he was one of the Commissioners named in the new warrant of 17 January 1694. He supported Lord Chancellor Porter against the accusations of favouring Catholics made against him by some MPs in 1695, and in 1696 he signed the Association for the protection of William III in parliament.

ESTATES/RESIDENCE: Mucktown, Co. Dublin.

SOURCES: PRONI D/3000/27/1 Falkiner Genealogical notes [says his daughter Martha married 28 Apr. 1696 Randal Heron]; PRONI T/559, Burke, extract pedigrees, vol. 16 pp. 222–4; *Cal. SP Dom. 1693* (London, 1903) pp. 91, 96, 101, 109, 442, *1694–5* (London, 1906) pp. 8, 89, 382, *1695* (London, 1908) p. 83, *1696* (London, 1913) p. 61; Simms' cards; C. Dalton (ed.), *English Army Lists and Commission Registers, 1661–1714* (London, 1896), vol. 3 p. 58; H. S. Guinness (ed.), *The Register of the Union of Monkstown, Co. Dublin 1667–1786* (Parish Register Society of Dublin, 1908) p. 52; H. F. Berry (ed.), *The Registers of the Church of St Michan, Dublin, 1636–1700* (Parish Register Society of Dublin, 1909) pp. 145, 146 [says the daughter of his second wife is named Arabella]; *JRSAI* vol. 24 (1894) p. 51, J. H. Moore 'Notes on the History of Navan' [possibly refers to his father or brother, Thomas Corker whose house was burned at Donaghmore, 5 May 1689]; Parliamentary Lists, 1695 (1), 1696 (1).

0493 CORKER, Edward

MP for Rathcormack 1713–14; Midleton 1715–27; Clonmines 1727–34

b. *c.* 1680; d. 27 Jan. 1733/4
FAMILY/BACKGROUND: Son of Robert Corker and Abigail, dau. of Robert Chambre of Co. Louth.
MARRIED: [1701] Margaret, dau. of Peter Wallis.
CHILDREN: Edward, m. [26 Nov. 1734] Esther Cooper.
EDUCATION: ?Member King's Inns 18 May 1698.
CAREER/OCCUPATION: Sheriff of Co. Cork 1719.
MILITARY: Lieutenant-Colonel Cork Militia Dragoons 1729.

POLITICAL ACTIVITY: Not much is known of this MP. He sat for various Cork boroughs from 1713 until his death in January 1734, and he was a Whig in the 1713 parliament and in the early Hanoverian parliaments. Corker was listed for eight committees between 1715 and 1723, and three between 1727 and 1733. He was solidly against the formation of a national bank.

DIVISION LISTS:
1721 (1) voted against a national bank.
1721 (2) voted against a national bank.

ESTATES/RESIDENCE: Mucktown, Co. Dublin; Ballymaloe, Co. Cork. In April 1693 he petitioned for a lease, for 61 years, of Captain Thomas Clifton's forfeited estates in Co. Louth worth £100 p.a. 'as remuneration for service to King'.

SOURCES: PRONI D/3000/27/1 Falkiner Genealogical notes [says he had a son Edward who m. 26 Nov. 1734 Esther Cooper]; PRONI T/559 vol. 16 p. 224, Burke, extract pedigrees; McCracken thesis; *Cal. SP Dom. 1691–2* (London, 1900) pp. 311, 521, *1693* (London, 1903) p.104; Hughes, *Pat. Officers*; Simms' cards; IMC *King's Inns Admission Papers, 1607–1867*; *The Dublin Gazette* 25 Mar. 1729; Cork MPs [says son of Edward (**0492**)]; *Pue's Occurrences* 29 Jan. 1734; Parliamentary List, 1713 (2).

0494 CORNWALL, Robert

MP for Enniscorthy 1795–7–9

b. ?1755; d. 1811
FAMILY/BACKGROUND: Son of [   ] Cornwall.
MARRIED: ?
CHILDREN: ?
CAREER/OCCUPATION: ?Attorney Exchequer 1778; *Deputy Chief Chamberlain 1788; *listed in Attorneys of the Courts of King's Bench, Common Pleas and Exchequer 1789–1800 (f.); Sheriff of Co. Carlow 9 Feb. 1788, 16 Feb. 1799.
MILITARY: Became Barracks Commissioner, 9 July 1799 (in return for vacating his, purchased, seat in favour of a Unionist; however, Lord Lismore succeeded in returning Peter Burrowes (**0288**), a strong anti-Unionist, instead, and the failure of the plan led to cancellation of Cornwall's appointment); officer Union Dragoons (Volunteers) *c.* 1783; Captain in Carlow Cavalry 1796.

POLITICAL ACTIVITY: In October 1780, unanimously, the 'Freedom of guild of merchants [was] voted to Mr Robert Cornwall late sub-sheriff of this city, as a testimony of their high sense of his excellent conduct during the course of his holding the said office.' He came into parliament following the death of Sir Vesey Colclough (**0436**) on 8 July 1794, and was sworn on 22 January 1795. He purchased his seat for Enniscorthy in 1797. He supported government and had the position of Second Chamberlain in the Lord Lieutenant's household.

He voted for the Union in 1799, and was appointed a Commissioner of the Barracks. As this was an office of profit under the 1793 Place Act he had to seek re-election, but the anti-Union borough proprietors refused his re-election and in his place elected Peter Burrowes (**0288**), a strong anti-Unionist. As he had been unable to deliver his seat to the government, his appointment to the Barrack Board was cancelled, but he received £2,700 at the disfranchisement of Enniscorthy – this was probably the price he had given for the seat.

DIVISION LISTS:

1799 (1) voted for the Union – Second Chamberlain, Dublin Castle

ESTATES/RESIDENCE: Myshall Lodge, Leighlin, Co. Carlow; St Stephen's Green, Dublin. Wakefield records that Mr Cornwall let 900 acres in Myshall Parish for 7s 6d the acre in 1787; it would now (1809) bring 50s at 'the common term of three lives or 31 years'. In 1788 Robert Cornwall was granted a fair at Myshall.

SOURCES: Wakefield, *Account of Ire.*, vol. 1 p. 249; PRONI T/3166/1D Hartnell notes; *Prerog. Wills* 1811–58; O'Neill thesis; Hughes, *Pat. Officers*; IMC *King's Inns Admission Papers, 1607–1867*; Musgrave, *Obits*; C. Ross (ed.), *Cornwallis Corr.* (London, 1859), vol. 3 p. 170; *JRSAI* vol. 52 (1922) p. 176, W. G. Strickland, 'Miscellanea'; *Almanacks*; John Stewart Watson, *The Gentleman's and Citizen's Almanack* (1799) [lists him as Attorney of the Courts of Exchequer, King's Bench and Common Pleas and says he is of East Stephen's Green, he does not appear in the *Almanacks* after 1799]; *DJ* 17–19 1780; *FJ* 20 Oct. 1796; Parliamentary Lists, 1783 (2), 1783 (3), 1794 (2), 1799 (2), 1799 (3).

0495 CORRY, Edward

MP for Newry 1774–6 [n.d.e. 1774]

b. 1723; d. 5 May 1792

FAMILY/BACKGROUND: Twin son of Isaac Corry of Newry and Caesarea, dau. (or niece) of Edward Smyth of Newry, Co. Down, wid. of Edward Montgomery.

MARRIED: [Sept. 1752] Catherine (b. 1731 d. 1818), dau. of Capt. Charles Bristow of Crebilly, Co. Antrim.

CHILDREN: Rt Hon. Isaac (**0497**); Edward (**0496**); Catherine, m. [23 July 1775] Daniel Marsden of Dublin; Martha, m. (1) Ross Moore of Carlingford, Co. Louth, (2) John Bingham of Rostrevor, Co. Down; Frances, m. [Feb. 1782] Lieutenant-Colonel William Browne.

CAREER/OCCUPATION: Burgess of Carlingford 29 Sept. 1780.

POLITICAL ACTIVITY: He was a merchant, and returned in a hotly contested election and re-election (as the first election was declared void) in the place of Robert Scott (**1892**), who died on 22 December 1773. In 1774 his son Isaac (**0497**) was agent to Mr Needham, and Edward Corry came in on the Needham interest. He had a majority of 61: 597 votes were cast, which was not a very high turn-out, as in the mid-eighteenth century the electorate for Newry was said to be about 900. Because Newry was a potwalloping constituency, elections were expensive and rough. Both candidates 'gave balls to the ladies ... At the beginning of the hurry, there was a poor man killed by McEvoy ... He stood his trial and by good interest got off, though he did not deny the deed.' The member's expenses did not end with his election, as he was under constant pressure for 'patronage' of all sorts for his constituents. Both Sir Richard Johnston (**1110**) of Guildford, who opposed Corry at the first election, and Captain Benson, who opposed him at the second, were financially straitened by it, and the effect on the Corrys must have been commensurate. The dominant interest in Newry was that of the Needhams, who owned most of the town, but they neglected it and thus encouraged various interlopers. In 1776 Edward Corry stood down in favour of his son, Isaac Corry.

ADDITIONAL INFORMATION: Member of the Down Society for Promoting Agriculture, August 1757, August 1759, 1760.

ESTATES/RESIDENCE: Derrymore, near Newry, Co. Down. Lands in Shinn, Lisnaree and Grynan and the townland of Milltown, Co. Down. These Corrys were a relatively landless branch of the Corrys of Rockcorry, Co. Monaghan.

SOURCES: PRONI T/1075/33 Canon Leslie's notes; PRONI MIC/315/6/24,10/74 Blackwood pedigrees; A. P. W. Malcomson, *Isaac Corry* (PRONI 1974), pp. 1, 33; *Ir. Gen.* vol. 6 no. 2 (1981) p. 166, H. F. Morris, 'The Waterford Herald 1792' [says he died in his 70th year]; *Louth Arch. Soc. Jn.* (1912–15) pp. 273–83, H. Tempest (ed.), 'The Roll of the Sovereigns and Burgesses of Carlingford, 1706–1828'; *BNL* 2 Sept. 1757, 25 Sept. 1759, 7 Oct. 1760; *GM* (Exshaw's edition) May 1792; Parliamentary Lists 1774 (1), 1775 (1).

0496 CORRY, Edward

MP for Randalstown 1794–7

b. c. 1756–60; d. c. 1813
FAMILY/BACKGROUND: Son of Edward Corry
(0495) and Catherine, dau. of Captain Charles
Bristow.
MARRIED: Unmarried.
MILITARY: Captain 49th Regiment of Foot.

POLITICAL ACTIVITY: A younger brother of Isaac
Corry (0497), he was a professional soldier who
sat in parliament for about three years. When
Michael Smith (1938) became one of the Barons
of the Exchequer, he was returned for
Randalstown, an O'Neill borough, probably with
the blessing of government. His brother Isaac was
noted, in 1783, to be 'a great friend of Mr (1592)
and Mrs O'Neill'. Corry was sworn on 9 March
1794. Like his brother, he favoured Catholic
emancipation and voted for it in 1795.

DIVISION LISTS:
1795 (2) voted for Catholic emancipation.

ESTATES/RESIDENCE: Co. Down.

SOURCES: PRONI T/1075/33 Canon Leslie's notes;
PRONI T/1345 [he had four elder siblings, the eldest
of whom was born in 1752, so he was born c. 1756–
60] (There are two conflicting pedigrees: one says he
probably died unmarried ante-1813, the other says he
married and had issue); PRONI MIC/315/6/24
Blackwood pedigrees; A. P. W. Malcomson, Isaac Corry,
(PRONI, 1974) p. 33.

0497 CORRY, Rt Hon. Isaac

MP for Newry 1776–83–90–7–1800 [r.
Randalstown 1797, re-elected after appointment
to place of profit, 1798 and 1799]; [UK] Dundalk
28 Feb. 1801–2; Newry 1802–6; Newport (IOW)
1806–7

b. (15) May 1753; d. 15 May 1813 'in the 61st
year of his age'
HONOURS: PC, sworn 18 Aug. 1795, [GB] 25
Sept. 1799.
FAMILY/BACKGROUND: Son and heir of Edward
Corry (0495) and Catherine, dau. of Capt.
Charles Bristow.
MARRIED: Unmarried (mistress: Jane Symms).

CHILDREN (ILLEGITIMATE): William Isaac Corry, m.
[6 Jan. 1809] Anna, e. dau. of James Holmes of
Inver Lodge, Co. Antrim; Henry Pery Corry;
Charles O'Neill Corry; Jane m. [   ] Syms,
Catherine Jane, m. [1816] Edward Wickham
Dickenson of Cheshire; Selina (Cecilia) (b. 1796
d. 1887); dau. (d. Apr. 1794).
EDUCATION: School, Royal School Armagh, under
Dr Grueber; entered TCD 8 July 1768; Middle
Temple 18 Oct. 1771; BA 1773; called to the
Irish Bar 1779.
CAREER/OCCUPATION: Equerry to the Duke of
Cumberland 1782–9; Trustee of the Linen Board
for Munster 1783–1800 (f.); *Commissioner of
the Tillage Act for Leinster 1783–4; Education
Commissioner 10 May 1788; Surveyor General
of the Ordnance 24 Sept. 1788–1802; *Governor
of Dr Steevens' Hospital 1799 (f.); *Governor of
the Royal Hospital (Kilmainham) 1799 (f.);
Revenue Commissioner 28 Sept. 1789–97 (1
Mar. 1792, 31 Dec. 1793, 27 Oct. 1795–7);
Chairman of Ways and Means 1798–9; Surveyor
General of Lands 24 Jan. 1798, 20 Aug. 1798 for
life; Chancellor of the Exchequer 28 Jan. 1799–
July 1804; Commissioner of the Treasury 1797, 6
Feb. 1799, 5 Aug. 1800, 30 Dec. 1801–4;
Member of Board of Trade 1807; *listed in
Judges and Barristers 1789–1800 (f.); Freedom of
the Corporation of Sheermen and Dyers,
September 1796; Burgess of Carlingford 29 Sept.
1796.
MILITARY: A Volunteer while an MP; member of
the Lawyers Corps of Volunteers; Captain
Commandant of the First Newry Volunteers
1780; Captain of the Mourne Volunteers and
Lieutenant-Colonel of the Newry Regiment,
Volunteers; Commander of New Ross Fencibles.

POLITICAL ACTIVITY: His election for Newry in 1776
had similarities to his father's (0495) in 1774. It
was hard fought and unsuccessfully challenged;
furthermore, it resulted in a duel with Sir Richard
Johnston (1110) in which Sir Richard received a
slight wound. Corry had, like his father, come in
on the Needham interest. In 1791 it was described
as follows: 'This is a potwalloping Borough, the
estate of Mr Nedham, who takes no part in elections. The Members are both Commissioners of
the Revenue. Mr Corry son to a merchant in the
Town, has a good natural interest. Colonel Ross
has an estate in the neighbourhood. There was an
opposition to them last election. Corry is an active man in Parliament and a good speaker. He
was formerly Equerry to the late Duke of

Cumberland. Lord Downshire's Party. Supports.'

Newry, the constituency for which Corry was returned, was the port for one of the earliest industrial canals in the British Isles. Built between 1731 and 1742, it linked Lough Neagh with Carlingford Lough and the Irish Sea. It was intended to bring coal from the Tyrone coalfield to Dublin, but this expectation proved illusory. Nevertheless, Newry flourished, but on Irish linen rather than Irish coal. Commercial interests were therefore a prime concern for its citizens and, given the potwalloping nature of the constituency, for its representatives. Lord Hillsborough, whose interest was next to Needham's in Newry, had supported Robert Ross, the other MP for the town: Hillsborough described the town in 1784 as 'very little short of the factious violence of Belfast'. During the 1776–83 parliament, which coincided with the War of American Independence, Newry had much to be factious about: there was the movement for 'free trade' and the Volunteers. In August 1780, when the Newry Volunteers were reviewed, Captain Isaac Corry was adjutant-general.

In the early 1780s he supported Carlisle's administration, but apart from that was generally in opposition. He also supported parliamentary reform, and was in those days a friend of Grattan (**0895**). In 1783 he opposed the government for not safeguarding the country's interest over Ireland's exclusion from the Methuen Treaty (Portuguese trade), the East India Co. and parts of the 1660 Navigation Act. On the issue of trade, the government feared Corry and Flood's (**0762**) capacity to stir up a national ferment. In March 1785 the *Dublin Morning Post* described Corry as a 'zealous watchman' of Irish interests, and in 1787, at the time of the French commercial treaty, he emphasised that the Irish parliament should exercise its undoubted right and discuss it 'lest in the eyes of the British Minister they should appear altogether ignorant or neglectful'. At the same time he admitted that the ultimate decision had to be made in Great Britain. Corry also pointed out that although France could provide Ireland with a market for her goods – especially, it was hoped, linen – there was 'an opposition of natural interests, an opposition of political constitutions, an opposition of national views and therefore of national councils and conduct'. Like almost all of the Irish opposition, he was anxious to retain the British connection, writing that 'Next to the preservation of our constitution and keeping the country out of debt, the great object of his heart was to support the honour and interests of the British empire'.

In 1783 it was thought that after the election he would 'apply for office, as he lives expensively and does not pursue his profession, which is the law'. The following year a Parliamentary List commented that he was 'Member for the Town of Newry upon the popular interest and is generally in opposition to Government, but is certainly taking that line in view of forcing himself into employment. He is desirous of carrying his point by means of Mr Foster (**0805**), whom he talks with upon many occasions. Mr Foster recommends attention to him, but besides the bad example of giving way to such a mode of application, there is no opening in early prospect, as he looks at more than the employment of a Commissioner of the Revenue. He certainly is more qualified than most in opposition to embarrass Government from very assiduous enquiry and great facility and fluency of expression etc.'

Although they were not always in agreement, in Flood's absence at Westminster, Corry gave leadership to the opposition. However, while his oratorical skills were more than adequate, they lacked Flood's pre-eminence. At this time it was thought that he placed his stakes too high, but by 1788 it was remarked that he 'speaks frequently, has Parliamentary talents, and perhaps among the first in opposition'. No administration could afford to ignore these gifts, and he became Surveyor General of the Ordnance in 1788, which carried a salary of £1,000 p.a. for doing 'virtually nothing': although Corry appears to have been fairly active in putting its affairs in order, much to the chagrin of the inmates. Nevertheless, Corry probably got his instructions from the Marquess of Buckingham who, in both his viceroyalties, was determined to root out any waste or misdemeanours associated with inefficiency. The following year he was appointed a Commissioner of the Revenue. According to Richard Annesley (**0048**), in April 1795 he 'attacked the FitzWilliam administration as vigorously as he had strongly supported it before'.

Corry was made a Privy Counsellor in August 1795. In 1798 he was elected Chairman of the Committee on Ways and Means, and finally in 1799 appointed Chancellor of the Exchequer and a Lord of the Treasury in place of Sir John Parnell (**1633**), who quarrelled violently with Pitt over the projected Union, which he categorically refused to support. Although this decision was taken in London, Corry was blamed for Sir John's dismissal and for succeeding him. This was certainly irrational and probably very unjust, as he was in fact the logical person to succeed Parnell in terms of both abilities and experience. Furthermore, such succession had precedents in the cases of Anthony Malone (**1336**) and John Foster (**0805**). Under the 1793 Place Act he had to seek re-election on his appointment as Chancellor, and on 7 February 1799 the Catholic priest at Newry, Rev. Lennon, wrote to Archbishop Troy that 'Mr Corry was this day re-elected for the town of Newry. Mr Ball, with his partisans, after canvassing the town for eight days, declined the poll, and surrendered yesterday. The Catholics stuck together like the Macedonian phalanx, and with ease were able to turn the scale in favour of the Chancellor of the Exchequer. He is very sensible of the efficacy of your interference, and their steadiness.'

The national finances were in chaos, and to help balance the budget Corry introduced a window tax, similar to that in England. This added to his unpopularity. Then, during a debate on the Union on 18 February 1800, Corry accused Grattan (**0895**) of 'living in familiarity with rebels and being a conniver at this plan to overthrow the country' – an opinion that was not unique to Corry. At the end of the debate Grattan called him out. During the duel Corry was slightly wounded. Nevertheless, the opposition accused him of trying to assassinate Grattan. This was probably part of the hysteria that prompted Mrs Grattan to fear that her husband might meet a fate similar to that of Cornelius Grogan (**0905**). Unfortunate coincidences followed: the Marquess of Downshire (**1016**), a fervent anti-Unionist, committed suicide on 7 September 1801, and the marchioness appears to have blamed Corry, Castlereagh (**2009**)

etc. and vowed vengeance on them. Next, Sir John Parnell died of apoplexy on 5 December. Meanwhile, the representation for Newry had been reduced to one seat by the Act of Union, and Corry was unlucky in the ballot that decided the continuing MP. At the time of the Union he had agreed with Pitt and Castlereagh over the question of Catholic emancipation, and this made it difficult to find him a seat especially in view of the expressed hostility of the king, which brought him unwelcome notoriety. But as Chancellor of the Irish Exchequer he had to present the budget and therefore to be in parliament, and he was returned, at Addington's instigation, for Lord Roden's (**1100**) borough of Dundalk.

In 1802 he was returned unopposed for Newry, but his enemies were gathering, fuelled by a mixture of envy at his abilities and hostility to his origins, which placed him outside the charmed circle, while he lacked the compensation of wealth to get inside. He made his Westminster debut by presenting the Irish budget, 1 April 1801, and continued to confine himself to Irish questions and mostly to financial subjects. He clashed with and got the better of Foster (**0805**) over the plan for Irish finance legislation, arguing for English parliamentary practice. Unlike many Irish members, he appreciated and enjoyed the Westminster scene. He carried the Irish Revenue Acts in the 1802–3 session, but Foster refused to enlist with government while Corry remained. Meanwhile, Wickham, the Chief Secretary, was increasingly exasperated at not being consulted and constantly being upstaged. If Corry was to hold on to Newry he needed ever-increasing patronage, and his continual demands made him unpopular with the Irish administration. Finally, in May 1804, Corry was dismissed by Pitt in favour of Foster, but awarded £2,000 p.a. in compensation. He was not a steady Pitt supporter, and, perhaps not surprisingly, he was critical of Foster's budget. He voted for Catholic relief, 14 May 1805.

Meanwhile the political scene in Newry altered. The Needham estate passed to the senior branch of the family, Viscounts Kilmorey. Newry was a seat in the Imperial parliament and Lord Kilmorey, assisted by Lady Downshire, decided to return Kilmorey's brother, General Francis Needham, at the general election of 1806. Corry was powerless against such 'real' interest and he did not have the above £5,000 necessary to purchase a seat elsewhere. However, Lady Downshire was inclined to support the Grenville ministry and came to a formal agreement with Corry to give him £1,000 towards his expenses should he be successful in Newry and, if not, to bring him in for another borough. Corry was not successful against the Needham interest in Newry, but a seat at Newport, Isle of Wight was purchased for him – Lady Downshire was prepared to contribute £4,000 towards it and Corry was appointed to the Board of Trade. Six months later Grenville's ministry had fallen and there was another general election. Corry stood, again unsuccessfully, for Newry.

He did not come into parliament again. His health was declining and, although he had been given a generous, if erratically paid, pension, he felt bitter at his loss of office and a seat in parliament, for which he blamed Foster. He died at his house in Merrion Square on 15 May 1813.

He was not without personal attractions. It was said in 1789 that 'Possessing from nature, a very pleasing exterior, Mr Corry loses not that advantage, by a slovenly neglect of it ... His voice is remarkably good, clear, distinct, and melodious and equally adapted to thunder in the storm of impetuous eloquence, or to insinuate in the soothing accents of captivating persuasion.' In 1799 it was said that 'Mr Corry was, for a considerable time, a principal favourite at Carlton House and is said to possess at present a great share of the Prince's confidence. He was first introduced into public life in *England* by the Duchess of Cumberland.' The Prince of Wales was not a very reliable friend, and almost invariably at odds with his father. The story of the Corrys in the last quarter of the eighteenth century illustrates the exclusivity of the Ascendancy, for whom wealth and birth counted more than talent. Corry was an isolated figure whose abilities were unable to protect him.

DIVISION LISTS:
1777 (1) voted against Grattan's (**0895**) motion for retrenchment.
1778 (1) a teller against Grattan's motion for retrenchment.

1779 (2) voted for a six-months Loan Bill.
1780 (2) voted for Yelverton's (**2268**) motion to modify Poynings' Law.
1780 (3) voted against the Tenantry Bill.
1783 (1) voted for Flood's (**0762**) motion for parliamentary reform.
1784 (1) voted for a committee on the Reform Bill.
1784 (2) voted for the amendment on the woollen manufacture.
1784 (4) voted against the address to His Grace the Duke of Rutland.
1785 (1) voted against the Commercial Propositions.
1786 (1) voted for the rights of grand juries.
1786 (2) voted for Forbes's (**0778**) motion for retrenchment.
1787 (1) voted for a Pension Bill.
1788 (1) voted for Hartley's (**0979**) motion against the Dublin police.
1788 (2) voted for Forbes's motion for limiting pensions.
1789 (1) voted for a Regency.
1790 (2) voted for Foster (**0805**) on the Election of a Speaker.
1793 (2) voted for the Convention Bill.
1798 (2) voted against Sir Laurence Parsons' (**1636**) motion for an investigation into 'the present discontents'
1799 (1) voted for the Union – A Privy Counsellor, a Commissioner of Revenue, Chairman of Ways and Means and Surveyor General [*sic*] of the Exchequer *vice* Sir John Parnell (**1633**), dismissed.
1800 (1) voted for the Union.

ADDITIONAL INFORMATION: A member of the RDS, 1784–1800; *a member of the Royal Irish Academy, 1790–1800(f.).

He belonged, in the late 1770s, to the constitutional reform society known as the Monks of the Screw. In March 1800 Corry signed a Co. Down petition in favour of discussing the proposed plan of Union.

Apart from his duel with Grattan in 1800 and a near fatal one with Sir Richard Johnston in August 1775, in 1784 he had mortally wounded a Mr Stannis of Carlingford.

He was the executor of his relative, Sir Trevor

Corry Kt and Baron Corry of the Kingdom of Poland, who died in 1780. His legacies included people living in several different countries, and he also left debts. Although the estate was a large one, Sir Trevor's legacies exceeded his assets, and a private member's bill was introduced to secure an equal distribution of the assets among the interested parties. Meanwhile a cross bill was filed against Isaac Corry by Joachim Gabriel Wiechman and John Ernest Schmidt of Danzig, with the aim of restricting claims to those made before the bill came into operation so that the estate could be wound up.

Two of Corry's nephews, Trevor and Smithson, were agents and also friends of the 3rd Marquess of Downshire in the early nineteenth century.

ESTATES/RESIDENCE: Derrymore House, Co. Down; Kildare Street and Merrion Square, Dublin.

SOURCES: PRONI D/607/C/84 Downshire Papers; PRONI T/618/333; PRONI T/3166/1A, Hartnell notes; PRONI T/3229/2/59; PRONI MIC/315/6/24 Blackwood pedigrees; PRONI MIC 474 Irish Volunteers; Ellis thesis; O'Neill thesis; Jupp thesis; Lammey thesis; A. P. W. Malcolmson, *Isaac Corry* (PRONI 1974); *HP 1790–1820* [see also Constituencies vol. 2 pp.185–6, 647–8]; Hughes, *Pat. Officers*; *Alum. Dub.*; *Index to PC*; *IMC King's Inns Admission Papers, 1607–1867*; Johnston, *Gt B. & Ire.* p. 143; J. Kelly, *Prelude to Union* (Cork 1992), pp. 67, 152; J. Kelly, *Henry Flood …* (Dublin, 1998), pp. 348, 368, 391, 438; *Castlereagh Corr.* vol. 2 p. 168; McDowell, *Irish Public Opinion, 1750–1800*, pp. 79, 118, 141; C. Ross (ed.), *Cornwallis Corr.* (London, 1859), vol. 3 pp. 39, 195–6 [says he was born 1755; this would fit with the age 58 estimate at his death but disagrees with the family genealogy]; *Register of Admissions to the Honourable Society of the Middle Temple* vol. 1 (London, 1949) p. 373; T. Bartlett and D. W. Hayton (eds), *Penal Era and Golden Age* (Belfast, 1979), p. 113 fn. 1, P. D. H. Smyth, 'The Volunteers and Parliament, 1779–84'; G. C. Bolton, *The Passing of the Irish Act of Union*, pp. 136–7; J. Kelly, *'That Damn'd Thing Called Honour': Duelling in Ireland 1570–1860*, pp. 137, 140, 211–2; W. A. Maguire, *The Downshire Estates in Ireland, 1801–1845* (1972), p. 187; M. Kelleher, *A List of Members of the Dublin Society 1731–1800* (Dublin, 1982); *Ir. Gen.* vol. 6 no. 2 (1981) p. 166, H. F. Morris, 'The Waterford Herald 1792' [says he was born 1755]; *Louth Arch. Soc. Jn.* (1912–15) pp. 273–83, H. Tempest (ed.), 'The Roll of the Sovereigns and Burgesses of Carlingford, 1706–1828'; *Almanacks*; *BNL* 25 Feb. 1800 [reports the duel], 21 May 1813 [says he died 16 May]; *Drogheda Newsletter or Ulster*

Journal 8–10 Mar. 1800; *FJ* 8 Sept. 1796, 29 Aug. 1799; *BNL* 18–22 Apr. 1794; 15 Jan. 1798, 8 Oct. 1799, 25 Feb. 1800 [gives details of the duel], 21 May 1813 [says 'in the 61st year of his age' which agrees with the family genealogy]; *DJ* 14–16 and 16–18 Oct. 1783; TCD Library, Private Members' Bills OLSX-1-803; Parliamentary Lists, 1771 (1), 1776 (1), (2), (3), 1778 (1), 1780 (1), 1782 (1), 1783 (1), (2), 1784 (1), (2), (3), 1785 (2), (4), 1787 (1), 1788 (1), 1789 (1), 1790 (1), 1791 (1), 1793 (1), 1794 (1), (2), 1798 (1), 1799 (1), (3), 1800 (1), (3).

0498 CORRY, James

MP for Co. Fermanagh 1692–3, 1695–9, 1703–13–14, 1715–18

b. 1634; d. 1 May 1718
FAMILY/BACKGROUND: Son of John Corry and Elizabeth Johnston.
MARRIED: (1) [1 Feb. 1663] Sarah, dau. of Oliver Anketell of Anketell Grove, Co. Monaghan; (2) [1683] marriage arranged with Lucy, dau. of Henry Mervyn (**1406**); (3) [1692] Elizabeth Harryman of London – soon separated.
CHILDREN: (1) s. and h. John (**0499**); Rebecca, m. James Moutray; Elizabeth, m. James Auchinleck; s. or dau.
CAREER/OCCUPATION:. High Sheriff of Co. Fermanagh 1671; Burgess of Enniskillen 2 Oct. 1694, Deputy Governor 20 Dec. 1696 and 1699, Governor 25 June 1705; Freeman of Enniskillen; Free Merchant of Dublin City 1797.
MILITARY: Captain of a Yeomanry company 1666; raised a troop of Horse and a company of Foot at his own expense 1690–91; Colonel of Fermanagh Horse Militia 24 Nov. 1692.

POLITICAL ACTIVITY: 'A Belfast merchant of Scottish origin' who came to Ireland from Scotland in 1649. He was a great political rival of Sir Michael Cole (**0442**), roundly defeating him in the elections to the 1692 parliament. He was listed for five committees in 1692 and 15 in 1695–9. In 1693, he petitioned for recompense for expenses incurred in the upkeep of the Enniskillen garrison, raising and provisioning a troop of horse and a company of foot and the hardship his family had recently endured in England. He was delegated to carry a petition to the king asking compensation for the inhabitants of Enniskillen, of which he was to receive a quarter. Lord Justice Capell advised against compensation, claiming that Enniskillen did not need it and Corry was an 'unworthy' man of 'ill character' and 'low morals'.

In November 1695 he was granted leave to waive his privilege in a cause between him and Mrs Harryman. He supported Lord Chancellor Porter against the accusations of favouring Catholics made against him by some MPs in 1695, and signed the Association for the protection of William III in the country in 1696.

Corry was interested in trade, and in 1703 he carried a bill through the Commons to reduce the rate of interest to 8 per cent – 2 Anne, c. 16. Between 1703 and 1711 he was nominated to 12 committees; by 1711 he was over 70 years of age and his name does not appear on any more committee lists. A strong supporter of the government, he took it as a slight on his character in 1706 when Cole was preferred to him as one of the Commissioners for rebuilding the town of Enniskillen. He was concerned that his interest in Enniskillen would be weakened by his being overlooked, and that this would lead to the return at the next election of Sir Gustavus Hume (1052), Cole's nephew by marriage. However, Cole died on 11 February 1711, and at the ensuing by-election Corry's son John Corry (0499) was returned. In March 1706 Robert Johnson (1101) wrote to Ormonde of Corry and his son, not then in parliament, that despite their disappointment 'I do think they will be serviceable to you.' Corry supported the Court party during the reign of Queen Anne, and attended Ormonde's birthday celebrations in 1706. In 1711 he supported the government over the affair of the Dublin mayoralty, and at the death of Queen Anne he was on the 'black list' of Tories. Nevertheless, he continued to sit for Co. Fermanagh until his death in 1718.

DIVISION LISTS:

1711 (1) voted for the Court on the Dublin mayoralty issue.

1713 (1) voted for Sir Richard Levinge (1230) for Speaker.

ESTATES/RESIDENCE: Castle Coole, Co. Fermanagh. The estate was bought from Roger Atkinson in 1656, for

£860. The original house was burnt on the orders of the Governor of Enniskillen in 1689, and in compensation, on 21 March 1693, Corry petitioned for the grant of a debt of £2,000, due to Sir Robert Scott by the Earl of Tyrone, and the lease of Maguire's small forfeited estate at Fulleville. In 1695, he received the grant of some lands and a 'mortgage of considerable value'. The mortgage amounted to £1,725. The considerations mentioned in his grant are his house being burnt and his having furnished the garrison of Enniskillen with provisions and materials to the value of £3,000 at his own expense, but it gave rise to considerable controversy: '… inquiring into the merits of this gentleman it appeared to us that he gave no assistance to the men of Enniskillen, and that in the town of Enniskillen he publicly declared he hoped to see all those hanged that took up arms for the Prince of Orange, and his house was burned by the said garrison'.

In 1697, Colonel James Corry bought from Mr Fenner 2,600 acres in the baronies of Longford and Granard – Ballagh, Clonbolt, Aghacordrinan, etc. – for £850, and rounded off the purchase in 1707 by buying more land in Aghacordrinan etc. for £135. The rental was £410 in 1740, £1,306 in 1789 and £1,500 in 1800. He made extensive purchases of property in Counties Longford and Fermanagh etc.

A new house was built at Castle Coole in 1709 by John Curld; it was accidentally burnt in 1797.

James Corry's income in 1714 was thought to be £700.

SOURCES: *CJ Ire.* (Bradley ed.) vol. 3 pp. 194, 184 (0078); PRONI D/302; PRONI D/3007/A/5/17–20, D/1/13 Belmore Papers; PRONI T/3411; PRONI T/3365; PRONI T/559 vol. 16 p. 240, Burke, extract pedigrees; *Cal. SP Dom. 1693* (London, 1903) pp. 44, 75, 171, 332, 427, 446, *1695* (London, 1908) pp. 139, 284; Fermanagh and Tyrone MPs; Earl of Belmore, *The History of Two Ulster Manors* (Dublin, 1903), pp. 113, 142, 143, 191–2; *HMC Ormonde* (1920) new ser. vol. 8 pp. 221–2, 226; *JRSAI* vol. 55 (1925) pp. 38, 46 H.A.S. Upton, 'A List of Governors and Deputy Governors of Counties in Ireland in 1699' [says he married Lucy Mervyn 1683]; *FJ* 13 Apr. 1797; *HMC, HC Papers*, new ser. iv 33; PRONI D/3007/B Belmore Papers [giving the history of the Belmore family finances from 1789]; D3007/D/? [1730 survey]; Simms, *Williamite Confiscation*, p. 90; Parliamentary Lists, 1695 (1), 1696 (1), 1706 (1), (2), 1711 (3), 1713 (1), (2), 1714–15 (1).

0499 CORRY, John

MP for Enniskillen 1711–13; Co. Fermanagh 1719–26

b. (bapt. 8 Jan.) 1666/7; d. 11 Nov. 1726
FAMILY/BACKGROUND: Only son of James Corry (**0498**) and Sarah, dau. of Oliver Anketell.
MARRIED: (1) [7 Feb. 1701] Sarah, dau. and co-h. of William Leslie (**1226**) of Prospect, Co. Antrim; (2) [ ].
CHILDREN: (1) Leslie (**0500**); ?James; William; John (d. yg); Martha, m. Edmond Leslie (**1227**) (who assumed the surname of Leslie-Corry); Sarah, m. Galbraith Lowry (Lowry-Corry) (**1268**); Mary, m. Margetson Armar; Elizabeth. (2) 16 children by his 2nd wife; only 3 survived.
EDUCATION: School, Mr Ryder, Kilkenny; entered TCD 5 May 1685, aged 18 years.
CAREER/OCCUPATION: Sheriff of Co. Fermanagh 1711.
MILITARY: Captain in the Inniskilling Regiment of Foot 20 June 1689; Colonel of the Fermanagh Regiment of Foot Militia 17 Sept. 1715; called Captain in the *Commons Journals* and served in both Ireland and Flanders.

POLITICAL ACTIVITY: A professional soldier, there is some confusion about the date of his return. He was definitely returned by 1711, as his predecessor, Sir Michael Cole (**0442**), was dead. He was nominated for a committee on 14 July 1711. He was a government supporter and, in a letter dated 10 August 1705, his father suggested him to Ormonde as a commissioner for the rebuilding of the town of Enniskillen: there was some concern when the Corry interest was by-passed for the Cole/Hume interest in the appointment of the commissioners. John Corry did not come in again in 1713, when Richard (**0443**) and John Cole (**0439**) were returned; they were returned again in 1715, but he succeeded his father as MP for Co. Fermanagh in 1719. He was against the establishment of a national bank, and was listed for three committees between 1721 and 1725. He died in 1726.

DIVISION LISTS:
   1711 (1) voted for the Court on the Dublin mayoralty issue.
   1721 (1) voted for a national bank.
   1721 (2) voted for a national bank.

ADDITIONAL INFORMATION: The returns are not always trustworthy in respect of by-elections. They seem to have been updated in an disorganised fashion, e.g. the 1704 returns give John Corry sitting for Enniskillen and the 1707 return gives him sitting '*loco Michaelis Cole defuncti*' when Sir Michael Cole did not die until 11 Feb. 1710/11, according to 'Fermanagh and Tyrone MPs' and to Burke's *Peerage and Baronetage* (1900 edition), p. 554. In 1709 Sir Michael Cole is resurrected – with the addition of John Corry in place of Michael Cole. However, the returns given at the beginning of the 1710 session, 19 May, give John Corry as MP for Enniskillen, and the returns at the beginning of the 1711 session, 9 July, give 'John Corry in place of Sir Michael Cole'. No writ is recorded as having been issued in the 1711 session, which was the last of the 1703 parliament. The 'writs issued' section of *General Index*, vol. 2 does not record any writ issued for Enniskillen in Sir Michael Cole's place. *HMC Ormonde* does say that he was returned in 1703 for Enniskillen in place of Sir Michael Cole, who had his seat declared void for neglecting to attend the House. But in view of the chaos in the returns it is difficult to work out what actually happened.

ESTATES/RESIDENCE: Castle Coole, Co. Fermanagh. Estates inherited from his father (**0498**).

SOURCES: PRONI D/3007 Belmore Papers; PRONI MIC/315/10/72 Blackwood pedigrees; Burke *PB* (1906) p. 152; Fermanagh and Tyrone MPs; *Alum. Dub.*; Hayton thesis; C. Dalton (ed.), *English Army Lists and Commission Registers, 1661–1714* (London, 1896), vol. 3 p. 122; *HMC Ormonde* (HMC 1920) new ser. vol. 8 pp. 175, 221–2, 226 [this sets out that John Corry was MP for Enniskillen from at least Aug. 1705, he replaced Sir Michael Cole (**0442**) who was dismissed for failure to attend the house]; Earl of Belmore, *The History of Two Ulster Manors* (Dublin, 1903), pp. 113, 165, 167–8 [does not mention a second wife]; *JRSAI* vol. 76 (1946) p. 136, W. E. J. Dobbs, 'A Supplement to the Entrance Register of Kilkenny School, 1684–1800'; Parliamentary Lists, 1711 (3), 1713 (1).

0500 CORRY, Leslie

MP for Killybegs 1739–41

> b. 15 Oct. 1712; d. 20 Feb. 1741
> FAMILY/BACKGROUND: Son of John Corry (**0499**)
> and Sarah, dau. of William Leslie (**1226**).
> MARRIED: Unmarried.
> EDUCATION: School, private tutor; entered TCD
> 11 Nov. 1728, aged 15 years, BA 1732.
> CAREER/OCCUPATION: High Sheriff of Co.
> Fermanagh 1737, Deputy Governor 17 May
> 1740.
> MILITARY: Colonel of Fermanagh Regiment of
> Militia 11 Apr. 1740.

POLITICAL ACTIVITY: He came into parliament for
the Conyngham borough of Killybegs, Co. Donegal, on the death of William Conyngham (**0466**)
on 26 October 1738, but he sat for less than two
and a half years before his own death on 20 February 1741. During that time he was nominated
for six committees.

ESTATES/RESIDENCE: Castle Coole, Co. Fermanagh. Leslie
came into possession of the estate at the death of his
father in 1726 when he was still a minor, and it was
managed until his majority in 1733 by his cousin, later
to become his brother-in-law, Margetson Armar. A survey of Church lands in the county about 1730 states
that Mr Corry held 1,259 profitable acres and 635 un-
profitable acres.

SOURCES: PRONI D/302; PRONI D/3007 Belmore
Papers; McCracken thesis; *Alum. Dub.*

CORRY, Viscount: *see* **LOWRY-CORRY**

1270 Lowry-Corry, Hon. Somerset (styled Viscount Corry 1797–1802), 2nd Earl Belmore, MP
Co. Tyrone 1797–1800, [UK] 1801–2

0501 COSBY, Dudley Alexander Sydney

MP for Queen's County 1703–13–14, 1715–27–9

> b. 2 May 1672; d. 24 May 1729
> FAMILY/BACKGROUND: Eldest son of Alexander
> Cosby and Elizabeth, dau. of Henry Lestrange of
> King's County.
> MARRIED: (1) Anne, dau. and co-h. of Sir Andrew

Owen; (2) Sarah, dau. of Periam Pole (**1689**).
> CHILDREN: Pole, m. Mary, dau. and co-h. of
> Henry Dodwell of Co. Roscommon; Sarah, m. [2
> Mar. 1730] Robert Meredyth of Co. Kildare.
> CAREER/OCCUPATION: High Sheriff of Queen's
> County 1702, 1718.
> MILITARY: Aide-de-camp to Lord Sunderland;
> joined army in 1703 buying Captain's commis-
> sion; in Spain 1704 and fought and was taken
> prisoner at Almanza 25 April 1707; released by
> the French 1709, after touring much of Europe
> on parole; gazetted 3rd Engineer for Ireland 16
> Feb. 1710; Colonel 23 January 1715; left the
> Regiment 22 May 1716.

POLITICAL ACTIVITY: He was a professional soldier,
and for much of the reign of Queen Anne was
fighting in the War of Spanish Succession. He was
listed for three committees 1703–11. Although
he had supported the government over the Dublin mayoralty issue in 1711, in 1713 he was suspected of being 'bad' (i.e. a Whig), and in 1713
he confirmed this by voting against the government candidate, Sir Richard Levinge's (**1230**)
nomination as Speaker. He was in York when he
received the news of Queen Anne's death. The
following day he set out for London to seek preferment. He stayed for about five months, in the
end soliciting a commission as a major in Vesey's
Regiment. His son Pole described him as 'a zealous Wig [*sic*] and voted ever in Parliament for the
good of his country against the high Tory faction'.
In response to his petition of 31 January 1716,
the House recommended that a Committee of
Privy Counsellors request the Lords Justices to
make provision for him in the army because 'by
the discountenance he lay under from the late
Duke of Ormonde, he could not preserve his rank,
both Lieutenant Colonels and Colonels obtaining breviets, who were younger officers than the
petitioner'. Although a lieutenant-colonel at time
of his death in 1729, he was receiving £123 3s 9d
on the half-pay list as a major.

Cosby was against a national bank. He was
nominated for seven committees between 1715
and 1723.

DIVISION LISTS:
> 1711 (1) voted for the Court on the Dublin
> mayoralty issue.
> 1713 (1) voted against Sir Richard Levinge

(1230) for Speaker – half-pay officer, Major in Scotland.

1721 (1) voted against a national bank.

ADDITIONAL INFORMATION: When the death of George I brought a general election in 1727, Ephraim Dawson **(0586)** persuaded Cosby to stand with him once again for Queen's County. However, Cosby was prevailed upon by Richard Warburton **(2176)**, Robert Pigott **(1682)** and others to join Warburton. After three days of polling, Dawson and Cosby were returned. The election cost Cosby £430, whereas it would probably have cost him no more than £100 if he had stuck with Dawson, as no one would have opposed them.

After Cosby's death in 1729, his son Pole saw Warburton's wider scheme. Realising that Cosby was in poor health (he had suffered increasingly from gout since 1711), and assuming that he was not long for this world, Warburton engineered the break with Dawson so that he (Dawson) would be opposed to the Cosby interest ever after, giving Warburton the opportunity to take the county seat when Cosby died. This Warburton duly did.

ESTATES/RESIDENCE: Stradbally Hall, Queen's County. Alexander Cosby let the lands of Ballymaddock, Park, Grange, O'Connell, Rathmore and Carrigine on a long lease at £80 p.a. to John Weaver **(2194)**. Weaver sold his interest in the lease to a Mr Basil. In 1720 Dudley Alexander bought the lease back for £4,000, which he borrowed at 7 per cent interest from Lord Gowran. This brought the debts on his estates to £7,450. In 1713 his income was estimated at £1,200.

In 1609 Richard Cosby was granted fairs at Stradbally, and in 1742 Pole Cosby was granted fairs at Stradbally and Timahoe.

SOURCES: PRONI T/3411; LC 1219; *CJ Ire.* vol. 4 p. 200, vol. 6 p. 71; McCracken thesis; Hayton thesis; Lodge *P* [says Sarah dau. of Periam Pole **(1689)** died unmarried]; Burke *IFR* (1976) p. 282; C. Dalton, *George the First's Army, 1714–1727*; P. F. Meehan, *The Members of Parliament for Queen's Co. and its Boroughs, 1585–1800*; *JRSAI* vol. 54 (1924) pp. 55–67, T. U. Sadleir, 'The Register of Kilkenny School (1685–1800)' [gives a Dudley Cosby entered Kilkenny College 29 June 1687 (?1678) aged 16 years]; *Kildare Arch. Soc. Jn.* vol. 5 1906–8 pp. 87, 88, 91, 175, 180, 182, 319, 'Autobiography of Pole Cosby, of Stradbally, Queen's County, 1703–1737 (?)' [says he was b. 2 May 1672 and that he turned down a Captaincy offered him by the Duke of Ormond for his vote in Parliament, in ?1703]; *Ir. Sword*

vol. 13 (1977–79) p. 121, R. Loeber, 'Biographical Dictionary of Engineers in Ireland, 1600–1730'; Parliamentary Lists, 1706 (1), 1707 (1), (3), (4), 1711 (3), 1713 (1), (2), 1719 (1).

0502 COSBY, Dudley Alexander Sydney

MP for Carrick 1763–8

b. *c.* 1730; d. 22 Jan. 1774 (suicide while insane; last will and testament 14 Dec. 1773)
PEERAGES: Cr. Baron Sydney 14 July 1768.
FAMILY/BACKGROUND: Son and h. of Pole Cosby and Mary, dau. and co-h. of Henry Dodwell of Co. Roscommon.
MARRIED: [10 or 11 Dec. 1773] Isabella, dau. of Rt Hon. Thomas St Lawrence, 1st Earl of Howth.
CHILDREN: *d.s.p.*
EDUCATION: Entered Cambridge (Trinity College) 20 May 1756.
CAREER/OCCUPATION: Ambassador to the Court of Denmark; Joint Governor of Queen's County 1773.

POLITICAL ACTIVITY: He was a diplomat. On 17 May 1760, Primate Stone asked for a civil pension for him of £200 p.a. He was granted a pension of £150 p.a. for 31 years on 31 May 1763, and later that year he was returned for Carrick following the elevation to the peerage of Ussher St George **(1849)**; he was sworn on 8 November 1763. He voted for the augmentation of the army in 1768 and was created a peer later that year.

DIVISION LISTS:
1768 (1) voted for army augmentation – Pensioner.

ADDITIONAL INFORMATION: *A member of the RDS from 1767. 'Our domestic news is first the death of Lord Sydney occasioned by a dose of Danish poison. His lordship to render himself agreeable to his lady upon their marriage stopped two issues he had in his thighs but found no ill effects until the 13th inst. when, after a night of great exercise by dancing, his temper and reason as appears since, was in some sort affected; however, not so much as to make those about him immediately suspect it or the consequence. He complained of indisposition and sent for a physician.

He republished his will leaving his estate to Capt. Cosby of the Navy and added a codicil leaving the jewels he bought for his wife [whom in his delirium he was jealous of] and the family china to his sister Lady Farnham, after which being disappointed in an attempt to shoot himself and one to poison himself, he took on the 23rd the dose which was sufficiently strong to carry him off in a few hours.'

ESTATES/RESIDENCE: Stradbally Hall, Queen's County. Lands in the barony of Maryborough East. His estate was left to Captain Philips Cosby RN, the son of his great-uncle Colonel Alexander, Cosby in tail male. Philips Cosby was unmarried and the estate passed to Thomas Cosby of Vicarstown, Queen's County and his sons in succession in tail male. The Roscommon estate was claimed by Sir John Browne under an entail created by some previous family settlement. Lady Sydney had a jointure of £800 p.a.

SOURCES: PRONI T/2915/9/52 Bedford Papers; LC 1219; GEC *P*; Burke *LGI* (1904) p. 114; *Alum. Cantab.* [says incorrectly married 14 July 1768]; T. Bartlett, *Macartney in Ireland* (PRONI 1978) p. 185 [report of death]; *Almanacks*; BNL 20 Feb. 1767; TCD Library Private Members' Acts 186.s.39.

0503 COTTER, Sir James

MP for Askeaton 1761–8

b. 1714; d. 9 June 1770
HONOURS: Cr. Baronet 11 Aug. 1763.
FAMILY/BACKGROUND: Eldest son and heir of James Cotter (executed 7 May 1720 for high treason in supporting the Jacobite cause) and Margaret, dau. of George Matthew of Thurles, Co. Tipperary.
MARRIED: [1746] Arabella (d. Apr. 1793), dau. and co-h. of Rt Hon. John Rogerson (**1812**), wid. of William Causabon (**0378**).
CHILDREN: Sir James Laurence, 2nd Baronet (**0504**); Edmund; Rogerson (**0505**); Rev. George Sackville, m. Margaret, dau. of Bayly Rogers.
EDUCATION: Entered TCD 26 Nov. 1730; Middle Temple 29 Nov. 1733, BA 1734.
CAREER/OCCUPATION: Freeman of Fethard (Tipperary), admitted 1744, sworn 1755.

POLITICAL ACTIVITY: He was the son of James Cotter, a Jacobite who belonged to a prominent Cork family. Very little is known about him: he trained as a lawyer but whether or not he ever practised is unknown. He had been looking for a seat in parliament certainly since 1755, when he wrote to Lord George Sackville (**1835**) saying that he would give any reasonable sum for a seat provided that if the king should die within five years of his return he would be re-elected. He pointed out that the seat for Midleton was now vacant owing to the death of the Prime Serjeant, Eaton Stannard (**1981**), and asking if Sackville would use his influence with Lord Midleton to have him returned. At the same time he offered to deposit £1,000 with any person whom Lord Midleton should name. Midleton, however, returned the Hon. James Hamilton (**0936**), later second Earl of Clanbrassill. Cotter probably purchased his seat for Askeaton in 1761.

DIVISION LISTS:
1768 (1) absent, in England.

ESTATES/RESIDENCE: Rockforest, Co. Cork. Lands in the barony of Fermoy. Patent to James Cotter of the manor of Cottersborough, 30 Chas II (1679). They also held lands in the baronies of Duhallow, Muskerry E., Fermoy and Barrymore.

SOURCES: LC 879; EC 5850 and EC 5672; *HMC Stopford-Sackville I* p. 238; GEC *B*; Burke *PB* (1903) p. 370; *Alum. Dub.*; *Register of Admissions to the Honourable Society of the Middle Temple* (London, 1949) vol. 1 p. 316; *Ir. Gen.* vol. 4 no. 6 (1973) pp. 616–24, W. G. Skehan, 'Freemen of the Corporation of Fethard, Co. Tipperary'; *Ir. Gen.* vol. 6 no. 3 (1982) p. 337, H. F. Morris, 'Extracts from The Waterford Herald 1793, 1794, 1796'.

0504 COTTER, Sir James Laurence

MP for Taghmon 1771–6; Mallow 1783–90; Castlemartyr 1790–7–1800 [r. Dingle 1797]

b. 1748; d. 9 Feb. 1829
HONOURS: Suc. as 2nd Baronet 1770.
FAMILY/BACKGROUND: Eldest son of Sir James Cotter, 1st Baronet (**0503**) and Arabella, dau. of Rt Hon. John Rogerson (**1812**), wid. of William Causabon (**0378**).
MARRIED: (1) [16 Nov. 1772] Anne (*d.s.p.*1773), o. dau. of James Kearney of Garretstown, Kinsale, Co. Cork; (2) [1785] Isabella (d. 1832), dau. of

Rev. James Kingston of Aglish, Co. Cork, wid. of George Brereton of Carrigslaney, Co. Cork. CHILDREN: (2) Sir James Laurence (b. 1780; d. 31 Dec. 1834), 3rd Baronet, m. [1 Jan. 1820] Helena Trydell; Rev. John Rogerson (*d.s.p.* 31 March 1847), m. (1) Ellen dau. of Rev. Robert Scott, (2) [1840] Ellen, dau. of Rev. T. Hoare, (3) [1845] Caroline, dau. of Sir Robert Shaw, 1st Baronet (**1906**); Rev. George Edmond (b. 2 June 1795; d. 6 Aug. 1880), m. [1828] Grace, dau. of William Digges La Touche; Richard Baillie (d. unm. 1843); Lieut. Henry Johnson (23 Regt) (d. unm. 1830); Nelson Kearney MD, m. [1848] Mary, dau. of R. Nason of Bettyville, Co. Cork; Isabella, m. James Digges La Touche; Henrietta, m. John Wise of Cork city; Catherine; Thomasine, m. Arundel Hill of Graig, Co. Cork. EDUCATION: School, Westminster 1762, aged 14 years; entered Oxford (Christ Church) 18 June 1766, aged 18 years; Lincoln's Inn 2 Aug. 1766, BA 1770. CAREER/OCCUPATION: Freeman of Fethard (Tipperary) 1774; High Sheriff of Co. Cork 1781; Foreman of the Co. Cork Grand Jury 1786. MILITARY: Colonel Mallow Militia; Captain in Mallow Boyne Corps 1796.

POLITICAL ACTIVITY: Cotter came in for Taghmon when John Hatch (**0987**) secured his election for Swords in 1769 and, with the prorogation of parliament, was not able to take his seat until 1771. Taghmon belonged to the Hoare family, and the seats were probably sold. He came in in opposition and was expected to change, but he appears to have been absent for large parts of this parliament. A 1775 Parliamentary List describes him as 'a sensible young man of very independent property. He made one tolerable speech. Did not attend last session.'

He did not come into parliament in 1776 but in 1783 he came in for the Co. Cork borough of Mallow, which belonged to the Jephson family, and was thought to have established a certain popularity in the town which ensured, or at least assisted, his return. In fact the Jephsons' authority was challenged by Richard Longfield (**1263**).

Cotter was part of Lord Shannon's (**0213**) political following and in 1790 was returned for his borough of Castlemartyr. He followed Lord Shannon's lead. In April 1799 he signed a Co. Cork petition in favour of the Union, and he voted for the Union in both 1799 and 1800. It was said that he had been 'privately brought over by cash'. His patron Lord Shannon was also a supporter of the Union.

DIVISION LISTS:

1771 (2) voted for Sir Lucius O'Brien's (**1558**) motion for retrenchment.
1771 (3) teller against the Revenue Bill.
1783 (1) voted against Flood's (**0762**) motion for parliamentary reform.
1785 (1) voted for the Commercial Propositions.
1789 (1) voted for a Regency.
1790 (1) voted for Grattan's (**0895**) motion for reducing the influence of the Crown.
1790 (2) voted for Ponsonby (**1709**) on the Election of a Speaker.
1791 (1) voted for Curran's (**0560**) resolution against the sale of peerages.
1791 (2) voted for Grattan's (**0895**) motion for the exercise of free trade.
1791 (3) voted for Grattan's motion to abolish the Dublin police.
1799 (1) voted for the Union.
1800 (1) voted for the Union.

ADDITIONAL INFORMATION: *A member of RDS from 1772. He was a partner in the Cork bank of Cotter and Kellet, which was responsible for a 'wild and reckless issue of paper currency' in 1803. Some 148,200 notes were issued in that year, and the bank failed in 1807 with a debt of £420,000. Numerous lawsuits followed bankruptcy. The litigation lasted 19 years; the final dividend was paid in 1826.

ESTATES/RESIDENCE: Rockforest, Co. Cork; Grafton Street, Dublin.

SOURCES: PRONI D/302; PRONI D/3000/27/1 Falkiner Genealogical Notes; PRONI T/3166/1A Hartnell notes; PRONI MIC/465/1 R. Ffolliott, *Biographical Notices, 1756–1827*; *The Dublin Hibernian Journal*, 22 Dec. 1772 [says he is married to the dau. of James Kearney. This is supported by the memorial in the *Hibernian Chronicle* and by *DJ* 2–5 Jan. 1773]; NAI, Index to the Marriage Licence Bonds of Cloyne Diocese; O'Neill thesis; Jupp thesis; GEC *B*; *HP 1790–1820* [says he died 9 Feb. 1813]; Burke *PB* (1900) p. 367 [says he m. the dau. of Francis Kearney]; *Alum. Oxon.*; *The Records of the Honourable Society of Lincoln's*

Inn (Lincoln's Inn, 1896) vol. 1 p. 459; J. O'Hart, *Irish Pedigrees* (Dublin, 1892), vol. 1 p. 189 [says Sir Laurence, 3rd Baronet, m. 1 Jan. 1820 Helena dau. of James Lombard of Lombardstown, Có. Cork]; E. Hewitt (ed.), *Lord Shannon's Letters to his Son*, pp. 34, 36, 208; C. Ross (ed.), *Cornwallis Corr.* (London, 1859), vol. 3 p. 49 [says incorrectly that his wife is widow of James Kearney]; G. F. Russell-Barker and A. H. Stenning (eds), *Record of Old Westminsters: A biographical list* (London, 1928) 2 vols; *Index to Hibernian Chronicle, 1769–1775* (Society of Genealogists, 1936) vol. 1 p. 76; *Ir. Gen.* vol. 4 no. 6 (1973) pp. 616–24, W. G. Skehan, 'Freemen of the Corporation of Fethard, Co. Tipperary'; *The Cork Advertiser* 30 Apr. 1799; *Almanacks*; *FJ* 25–27 Apr. 1786, 27 Oct. 1796; Parliamentary Lists, 1772 (2), 1773 (1), (2), 1774 (1), 1775 (1), 1783 (2), 1784 (1), (2), (3), 1785 (1), (2), (3), (4), 1787 (1), 1788 (1), 1789 (1), 1790 (1), 1791 (1), 1793 (1), 1794 (2), 1799 (2), 1799 (3), 1800 (3).

0505 COTTER, Rogerson

MP for Charleville 1783–90–7–1800

b. 1750; d. 19 Feb. 1830
FAMILY/BACKGROUND: Son of Sir James Cotter (**0503**) and Arabella, dau. of Rt Hon. John Rogerson (**1812**), wid. of William Causabon (**0378**).
MARRIED: [Sept. 1794] Jane, dau. of Richard Harrold of Limerick, wid. of William Grady.
CHILDREN: O. child Jane, m. [1822] Gen. le Vicomte de la Hitte, peer of France.
EDUCATION: School, Westminster, KS 1762, aged 12 years, Captain of the School 1766; Lincoln's Inn 2 Aug. 1766; entered Cambridge (Trinity College) 17 June 1767, aged 17 years, Scholar 29 Apr. 1768, minor Fellow 20 Oct. 1771, major Fellow 4 July 1774, 10th Wrangler 1771, BA 1771; called to the Irish Bar 1773; MA 1774.
CAREER/OCCUPATION: *Listed in Judges and Barristers 1789–90; agent to pay, in London, the annuities on the Irish Tontines 1801; Freeman of Fethard (Tipperary) 1774.
MILITARY: Captain of the Mallow Boyne Cavalry and Infantry Volunteers 1782.

POLITICAL ACTIVITY: A lawyer returned for Charleville by Lord Shannon (**0213**). He was a younger brother of James Cotter (**0504**), and both belonged to Lord Shannon's party. Although obviously possessed of considerable ability, Rogerson Cotter appears never to have done anything with

it. In 1797 Lord Shannon wrote to his son indignantly: 'that Rogerson Cotter is a shark. He has written to me to get him employment here, as my application in his favour to the Duke of Portland failed.' He followed Lord Shannon's lead over the Regency Crisis and, in April 1799, signed a Co. Cork petition in favour of the Union. He voted for the Union in both 1799 and 1800.

DIVISION LISTS:
1783 (1) voted against Flood's (**0762**) motion for parliamentary reform.
1784 (1) voted against a committee on the Reform Bill.
1785 (1) voted for the Commercial Propositions.
1789 (1) voted for a Regency.
1790 (1) voted for Grattan's (**0895**) motion for reducing the influence of the Crown.
1790 (2) voted for Ponsonby (**0709**) on the Election of a Speaker.
1791 (1) voted for Curran's (**0560**) resolution against the sale of peerages.
1791 (2) voted for Grattan's motion for the exercise of free trade.
1799 (1) voted for the Union.
1800 (1) voted for the Union.

ESTATES/RESIDENCE: Rock Forest, Mallow, Co. Cork; Anne Street, Dublin.

SOURCES: PRONI T/3166/1A Hartland notes; O'Neill thesis; Burke *PB* (1903) p. 370; *IMC King's Inns Admission Papers, 1607–1867*; McNevin, *Volunteers*; *Alum. Cantab.*; *The Records of the Honourable Society of Lincoln's Inn* (Lincoln's Inn, 1896) vol. 1 p. 459; G. F. Russell-Barker and A. H. Stenning, *Record of Old Westminsters: A biographical list* (London, 1928) 2 vols; E. Hewitt (ed.), *Lord Shannon's Letters to his Son*, p .49; *Ir. Gen.* vol. 4 no. 6 (1973) pp. 616–24, W. G. Skehan, 'Freemen of the Corporation of Fethard, Co. Tipperary'; *Almanacks*; *The Cork Advertiser* 30 Apr. 1799; Parliamentary Lists, 1783 (2), 1784 (1), (2), (3), 1785 (1), (2), (3), (4), 1787 (1), 1789 (1), 1790 (1), 1791 (1), 1793 (1), 1794 (2), 1799 (2), (3), 1800 (3).

COURTOWN, Baron and Earl: *see* **STOPFORD 2017** Stopford, James, 1st Baron Courtown, Viscount Stopford and Earl of Courtown, MP Co.

Wexford 1721–7, Fethard (Wexford) 1727–58
2018 Stopford, Rt Hon. James, 2nd Earl of Courtown, Baron Saltersfield [GB], MP Taghmon 1761–8, [GB] Great Bedwyn 1774, Marlborough 1780–93

0506 COX, Henry

MP for Castlemartyr 1787–90

b. *ante* 8 June 1766; d. 2 Dec. 1821
FAMILY/BACKGROUND: Son of [ ] Cox.
MARRIED: [ ].
CHILDREN: Joshua; Eleanor [unm.]
CAREER/OCCUPATION: Customer Carrickfergus 13 Mar. 1788.
MILITARY: Colonel of the Dunmurray (?Dunmanway) Union Volunteers (Cork).

POLITICAL ACTIVITY: Returned for Castlemartyr when John Bennett (**0112**) was appointed Fourth Justice of the King's Bench, Henry Cox sat in parliament for less than three years – he was sworn on 28 May 1787 and parliament was dissolved on 5 April 1790. He belonged to Lord Shannon's (**0213**) party and followed his direction. Following the 1790 Co. Cork election, he was Abraham Morris' (**1495**) second in his duel with Rt Hon. Robert King, 2nd Earl of Kingston (**1167**). Neither party was hurt.

Lord Shannon, an opponent of Kingsborough, described the election and Lord Kingsborough's unscrupulous conduct in some detail: 'He supports himself with the most infamous, perjured, tutored set of villains that can be conceived: fellows so low as labourers in rags and lice, polled against gentlemen of property and character and he will persist in this while he can get a guinea or a man.' Cox was noted as an active magistrate.

ESTATES/RESIDENCE: Dunmanway, Co. Cork.

SOURCES: PRONI MIC/465/1 R. Ffolliott, *Biographical Notices, 1756–1827*; MIC/474 Irish Volunteers; Hughes, *Pat. Officers*; E. Hewitt (ed.), *Lord Shannon's Letters to his Son* (PRONI 1982) p. 6; Parliamentary Lists, 1783 (2), 1785 (4), 1787 (1), 1788 (1), 1789 (1), 1790 (1).

0507 COX, Richard

MP for Tallow 1703–13–14; Clonakilty 1717–25

b. 27 Oct. 1677; d. 15 Apr. 1725
FAMILY/BACKGROUND: Eldest son of Sir Richard Cox, 1st Baronet (b. 1650; d. 3 May 1733; Lord Chancellor 1703–7) and Mary (b. 1659 d. June 1715), dau. of John Bourne of Carberry, Co. Cork.
MARRIED: (1) [5 Apr. 1698] Susannah (d. 1716), dau. of James French of Cork; (2) [13 Mar. 1719] Mary, dau. of Arthur Pomeroy, Dean of Cork; (3) [9 Feb. 1722] Elinor Jeffreys.
CHILDREN: (1) Sir Richard Cox, 2nd Baronet (**0508**); James, m. (1) Mary Stephens, (2) Catherine Burgh; John; Mary, m. [30 Dec. 1717] Giles Eyre, Dean of Killaloe; Elizabeth; Susannah, m. F. Bisby; Peuiel.
EDUCATION: School, Mr Jones, Dublin; entered TCD 17 Feb. 1692, aged 15 years.
CAREER/OCCUPATION: Sheriff of Co. Cork 1711, 1713.
MILITARY: ?Ensign in Erle's Regiment 1 Mar. 1696; Constable of the Castle of Castlemaine, Co. Kerry; Captain in Brasier's Regiment 1708–9.

POLITICAL ACTIVITY: Richard Cox was politically under his father's shadow. He came into parliament at the beginning of Queen Anne's reign and supported the administration. He was a professional soldier. His father, Lord Chancellor Cox, a Cork lawyer, was assistant to King William's secretary and played a central role in the months after the Boyne, 1 July 1690: he probably helped draft the (unattractive) terms offered to the Jacobites in the royal declaration. He also organised the Co. Cork militia, the Williamite government's most effective militia force outside Ulster. He mobilised a large Protestant force which, between May and October 1691, was alleged to have killed not fewer than 3,000 Tory guerrillas attached to the Jacobite enemy and taken from them £12,000 in cattle and plunder.

Sir Richard Cox was appointed Lord Chancellor in 1703 and was a strong supporter of the Test Clause in the 1704 and 1709 Penal Acts – being quite happy that people should go to heaven by the way of their choice, but only those who conformed to the Church by law established should enter the government. This attitude made membership of the Church of Ireland a desirable, if not essential, 'job card'.

Cox was anxious to promote his son's career: in July 1704 he asked for a troop in Echlin's Regiment and on 29 August a company in the guards for him. In February 1706 he wrote to Ormonde that his son had a great share of his estate. In 1707 this MP was one of the group of MPs who met at the Fleece Tavern to plan the government's strategy for the next session of parliament. His election for Tallow in 1713 was hard-fought and cost him the considerable sum of £131 – his income was estimated at £400 p.a.

He voted for Sir Richard Levinge (**1230**) as Speaker against the successful nominee, the Cork politician Alan Brodrick (**0237**). Cox also signed a county address in favour of Sir Constantine Phipps, although in this he may have been influenced by Cork politics. At the accession of George I he was on the 'black list' of Tories, and he appears to have adopted a low profile for the next few years. In the 1717 by-election, following the death of Sir Ralph Freke (**0825**), he was returned for Clonakilty; he sat for that constituency until his death on 15 April 1725.

DIVISION LISTS:

1709 (1) voted against a Money Bill.
1711 (1) voted for the Court on the Dublin mayoralty issue.
1713 (1) voted for Sir Richard Levinge (**1230**) for Speaker.
1721 (1) voted against a national bank.
1721 (2) voted against a national bank.

ESTATES/RESIDENCE: Dunmanway, Co. Cork. In 1714 his estimated income was £400 p.a.

Sir Richard Cox (father) purchased 381 acres in Co. Cork and 453 acres in Co. Kilkenny from the Commissioners for Sale of Forfeited Estates in 1702–3.

In 1707 the Hollow Blade Company granted Sir Richard Cox in fee farm lands in West Muskerry. In 1693 and 1708 this MP's father, Sir Richard Cox, had been granted a fair/market at Dunmanway. This MP was granted fairs at Killmacganny.

SOURCES: PRONI D/302; EC 3485, EC 3724; LC 2814; TCD MS 4788 (1717 estate map); PRONI D/3000/34/1, 2, 3 Cox Genealogical Charts [says died 15 Apr. 1725, m. 1st 5 Sept. 1698]; GEC *B.*; *Cal. SP Dom. 1696* (London, 1913) p. 63; Simms' cards; Simms, *Williamite Confiscation*, p. 184; *Alum. Dub.*; *Historical Studies* 4 p. 86; Cork MPs; *HMC Ormonde* (1920) new ser. vol. 8 pp. 101, 109, 220; Berry *RDS* p. 28; *The Dublin Gazette* 13 Dec. 1712; Johnston, *Ireland in the Eighteenth Century*, p. 30; D. Dickson, *New Foundations: Ireland 1660–1800* (Dublin, 1987), pp. 35, 37; Parliamentary Lists, 1706 (1), 1707 (2), 1711 (3), 1713 (1), 1713 (2), 1714 (1), 1714–15 (1).

0508 COX, Sir Richard

MP for Clonakilty 1727–60, 1761–6

b. 23 Nov. 1702; d. 2 Feb. 1766
HONOURS: Suc. as 2nd Baronet 1733.
FAMILY/BACKGROUND: Eldest son of Richard Cox (**0507**) and Susannah, dau. of James French of Cork.
MARRIED: [13 Sept. 1725] Catherine (d. Jan. 1768), dau. of Rt Hon. George Evans, Bulgaden Hall, Co. Limerick (**0703**).
CHILDREN: Richard, m. [28 Oct. 1758] Eliza Turner, dau. of John Beecher; Sir Michael, 3rd Baronet (Archdeacon of Cashel), m. [7 Jan. 1762] Elizabeth o. dau. of Hugh Massy, 1st Baron Massy (**1355**), wid. of John Arthur of Seafield, Co. Dublin; George Evans; Mary, m. [Mar. 1750] Joshua Hamilton; Eleanor, m. John Newcomen; Catherine, m. Boyle Moore; Susanna, m. [1757] Daniel Callaghan.
EDUCATION: Entered Oxford (St John's College) 4 May 1720, aged 17 years.
CAREER/OCCUPATION: Sheriff of Co. Cork 1727, 1733; Sheriff of Cork city 1744; Transcriptor and Foreign Apposer in the Court of Exchequer 1750; *Commissioner of Revenue and Excise 1758–65; *Trustee of the Linen Board for Munster 1732; Freedom of Kinsale 9 Jan. 1735; *Collector of the Revenue for the Port of Cork 1750–3; Collector of Customs Cork 1750–53, dismissed Jan. 1754; Commissioner of the Tillage Act for Munster Jan. 1754–65.

POLITICAL ACTIVITY: He was a prominent figure in Cork politics, involving himself on the side of the merchants over the gold currency crisis in 1737, when Lord George Sackville (**1835**) told his father, the Duke of Dorset, that 'The coinage has made a great rout here and the Dean [Swift] has shewn himself more mad and absurd than ever. The poor Primate [Boulter] has been greatly threatened by anonymous letters, so that he has been obliged to have a corporal and six men lye in his house every night to secure him from any insult.' The people at Cork 'have sent to their members [Emanuel Pigott (**1680**) and High Dixon (**0638**)] to desire they would oppose the giving the necessary supplys till the King should think fit to recall his proclamation, which is so prejudicial to the trade and welfare of this kingdom.'

Sackville reported that the petitions against the lowering of the gold were considered the previous day in the House. They first proposed a committee and, when that was negatived by 108 to 55, Stannard (**1981**) moved for a resolution that the lowering was prejudicial to the trade of the country. This was rejected by 11 to 40, and Carter (**0360**) proposed that the further consideration of the petitions should be postponed to 1 October 1738, which was carried by 118 to 30. 'The chief speakers on the side of the minority were Stannard, Sir Richard Cox (who abus'd the Privy Council very grossly) Mr Morgan (**1487**), Mr Maloun [*sic*] (**1336**). On the other side the Solicitor General (**0196**), Mr Cope (**0489**), Mr Coote, Mr Cuff [*sic*] (**0557**) and Mr Hill (**1015**).'

On 24 March 1740 Sir Richard Cox was met outside Cork 'by the Worshipful Company of Clothiers' and a 'numerous cavalcade of citizens on horseback'. They accompanied him to his lodgings where celebrations ensued because Cox had shown 'remarkable zeal for the true interest of his country' while in parliament. Along with Richard Bettesworth (**0130**), in 1735, he was responsible for the heads of a bill, 9 Geo. II, c. 7, 'for encouraging the planting of Timber Trees'. He introduced two road bills, 13 Geo. II, c. 15, from Clonmell through Mitchellstown town to Doneraile, and 25 Geo. II, c. 17, from Clonmell through Fethard to Hurlingford, Co. Kilkenny. In 1756 he brought in the heads of an anti-terrorist bill, 29 Geo. II, c. 12, 'to prevent unlawful Combinations of Tenants, Colliers, Miners and others and the sending of threatening Letters without name or with fictitious Names subscribed thereto; and the malicious destruction of carriages ... maliciously setting Fire to House or Out-houses ... Hay, Corn, Straw or Turf or to Ships or Boats.' The troubles that reached a climax in the late eighteenth century were already starting.

Cox was a pamphleteer with a ready pen. His initial opposition to the Castle had turned to friendship by the time of the Lucas (**1276**) affair, and he wrote a reply to Lucas's London pamphlet attacking the Irish government and the Dublin Corporation. This was officially, though secretly, sanctioned by government; Chief Secretary Weston (**2223**) wrote to Sir Robert Wilmot, the Lord Lieutenant's Secretary in England, 21 March 1750: 'What his Excellency desires of you is that you will contrive (with secrecy and precaution, that it may not be known from whence it comes), to get it [Cox's pamphlet] published in London; and for that purpose I send you herewith the first sheets to go upon immediately ... Pray despatch this business that it may be out here before the secret is cold, or at least by the time that it may be expected to grow hot again by the return of Lucas after the session.' Cox, stung by Lucas's insulting references to his grandfather, directed a Commons inquisition of Lucas and his printers. This resulted in Lucas being declared an enemy of the country and his eventual flight to avoid imprisonment.

He was severely censured by Primate Stone, first over the Cork city by-election in 1751 and subsequently as an active member of the opposition during the Money Bill dispute and an opposition pamphleteer – in 1753 he published a popular pamphlet called *The True History of Betty in Ireland*. In March 1752 Henry Pelham wrote to the Chief Secretary, Lord George Sackville, that 'I am not surprised at the behaviour of Sir Richard Cox. It is of a nature I am too well acquainted with. His ingratitude, if any, to Lord Harrington I can easily account for, but his imprudence in choosing the present manner and time of shewing it is a little extraordinary.' In April 1750, Harrington had decided on an arrangement whereby as a reward for his continuous support of the government Cox would succeed to the post of Collector of Revenue for Cork city, with the then incumbent, John Love, retiring on a pension of £500 p.a. This was one of the very rare occasions when a Lord Lieutenant attempted to interfere directly in Revenue arrangements.

There was a delay in England over the arrangement, which left Chief Secretary Weston writing to Sir Robert Wilmot that 'We begin to be uneasy at the delay of Sir R. Cox's affair, which if it fails will disgrace my Lord Lieutenant and greatly prejudice the King's service. The thing is serious and I cannot use softer terms.' The trouble was that the incumbent, John Love, refused all inducements to resign. Love had been appointed by the Lords of the Treasury in Great Britain over the heads of the Irish Lords Justices, who had recommended Cox. The Revenue Board divided: the 'English' Commissioners, Messrs Bristow (**0236**), Cavendish (**0380**) and Frankland, supported Love, whom they declared to be honest and efficient, while the 'Irish' Commissioners supported Cox. On 10 April 1750 Weston wrote that 'This is a very ugly affair and does infinite prejudice to HM's service.' Eventually Love accepted the pension, Cox was appointed to the Collectorship and Weston wrote to Andrew Stone, the Primate's influential brother, that 'This will put an end to that disagreeable business.'

The sequel occurred at the time of the Cork by-election in 1751 and the Money Bill crisis in 1753. According to Primate Stone in 1751: 'Mr Cavendish (**0380**) was a candidate for the city of Cork and would have been chosen without difficulty. Sir Richard Cox stirred up an opposition to him and prevailed upon the Speaker (**0210**) to think his figure concerned in patronising it. It was carried out with the utmost indecency to Mr Cavendish and with great disrespect to the family to which he has the honour of being related. Sir Richard Cox's motive at all events to bring it to a petition and to draw the Speaker into a measure in which Mr Ponsonby and his friends would be under a necessity of differing from him. The Speaker mention [*sic*] this to me with concern ... he gave me the most solemn assurances that if Mr Cavendish should have a majority in the city and there should be a petition, he would himself oppose it ... [Lord Duncannon] ... received the same assurances from the Speaker, which he desired might be understood as a mark of his respect to the Duke of Devonshire. Soon after Lord Duncannon was gone to England, the Speaker altered his mind, saying that some custom house officers had been busy in soliciting votes, and this was contrary to some resolutions of the House of Commons and the case being now altered he must fight it through. The truth was that the family of Gores would then be offered to him for that service, and he chose to break his then subsisting engagements that he might form new ones with people who he knew would go further with him if there should be occasion. My Lord Lieutenant, in hopes of preventing differences among the King's servants and with marks of high regard for the Speaker, prevailed upon Mr Cavendish to give up the election before the poll [he was returned for the Devonshire borough of Tallow in 1756], by which the Speaker's reputation of power was much enlarged and his following increased.' This whole arrangement bears the marks of the Primate's 'cleverness' in trying to corner the Speaker as the Duke of Devonshire was now in possession of the major Boyle interest in Co. Cork, which had previously been managed by the Speaker.

The next part of the chain, according to the Primate, occurred in 1753 when Jones-Nevill (**1125**), considered a protégé of the Primate, was expelled from the House of Commons for defective maintenance of the barracks that were scattered through the country. In a letter of 3 February 1753, Waite (**2154**) revealed to Wilmot that 'Sir Richard Cox has conducted the whole examination against Nevill, and between ourselves, considering the great obligations he is under to Lord Harrington, he has acted in a very unbecoming and furious manner against a man whom my Lord Harrington thought a proper person to be employed in these works.' At the same time Cox's brother, Michael Cox, was Bishop of Ossory and in 1753 was in line for the vacant archbishopric of Cashel, to which, despite his brother's behaviour, he was appointed in January 1754.

However, Sir Richard had been an active member of the opposition during the Money Bill dispute, and on 24 December 1753 Stone wrote to his brother Andrew, the influential confidant of both Newcastle and his brother Henry Pelham, that 'Sir Richard Cox cannot with any decency be continued.' Secretary Robinson wrote from London on 11 April 1754 that Cox had made himself so obnoxious that he would have to be dismissed from his Collectorship of Cork, and he was dismissed in January 1754. On 14 May 1755 Waite wrote to Wilmot of a ball held by the Lord Lieutenant at Dublin Castle: 'The princes and rulers of those who were called *patriots* have all been at the Castle to pay their respects, except that simpleton Sir R. Cox, who pretends to say that he will not go thither until he is sent for, so that if he perseveres in his resolution, we shall not have the honour of his company.'

He was nominated for no fewer than 332 committees between 1729 and 1760. In the late 1750s Cox changed his approach: a letter from Richard Rigby (**1789**) to the Duke of Devonshire on 18 November 1757 states that 'Sir Richard Cox has behaved handsomely and has never asked but what was my Lord Lieutenant's inclination and that he most steadily abides by, and a more useful or better parliament-man I never saw.' He was described by Bedford in April 1760 as 'a very able and efficient Revenue Officer'. He was again returned for Clonakilty in 1761; he died on 2 February 1766. He had sat in parliament for nearly 40 years.

DIVISION LISTS:

1749 (1) teller against the election of James Digges La Touche (♦♦♦♦).

1753 (1) voted for the expulsion of Arthur Jones-Nevill (**1125**).

1753 (2) voted against the Money Bill.

1757 (1) teller against the resolutions on Pensions.

ADDITIONAL INFORMATION: A foundation member of the Dublin Society, 1731, also elected following RDS charter, 1750. He established a linen manufacture at Dunmanway. He was the author of a letter to Thomas Prior in 1749 'showing from experience a sure method to establish the linen manufacture and the beneficial effects it will immediately produce'.

ESTATES/RESIDENCE: Dunmanway, Co. Cork, 6,891 statute acres in 1858, at a rental of £2,979 and valuation of £4,180. The 1858 sale included the lordship of the manor of Dunmanway, so presumably it related to the entire Cox estate. In 1769, Sir John Cox was granted a market at Ballygurteen, as well as at Dunmanway.

SOURCES: *CJ Ire.* (Bradley ed.) vol. 6 pp. 545, 576, 588–9, vol. 7 pp. 120, 143, vol. 8 pp. 392, 411, 795, vol. 9 pp. 792–3, 892 (350, 0404, 0499, 0520); NLI EEC rental (1858) D/2021/12; D/3000/34/1, 2 Cox Genealogical Charts [says he married first 13 Dec. 1725, and second 4 Mar. 1735 but there were no children by his second marriage. His son, Sir Michael married 1

July 1762 and his dau. was called Elizabeth not Eleanor]; PRONI T/559 vol. 16 p. 805, Burke extract pedigrees; Newcastle MSS T/2863/1/33; PRONI T/2915/9/31 Bedford Papers; T/3019/6455/222, 230, 267, /6456/ 401, /6459/750, Wilmot Papers; PRONI T/3158/1557 Chatsworth Papers; PRONI MIC/338/9 Crossle's notes; PRONI MIC/465/1 R. Ffolliott, *Biographical Notices, 1756–1827* [*Cork Chronicle* says he died 2 Feb. 1766 aged 65 years]; McCracken thesis; GEC *B*; *Alum. Oxon.* [says died 1765]; Berry *RDS* pp. 24–7, 76–7; *HMC Sackville I* pp. 167 182; *EHR* (July 1905) pp. 528, 539, C. L. Falkiner (ed.), 'Correspondence of Archbishop Stone and the Duke of Newcastle'; *Irish Official Papers in Great Britain* vol. 1 pp. 45, 52; *HMC Sackville I* p. 167; *Almanacks*; *BNL* 13, 22, 29 Jan. 1754, 14 Feb. 1766 [says he died 2 Feb. 1766]; *Pue's Occurrences* 11 Jan. 1735; *DJ* 29 Mar. 1740, 26 Jan. 1754, 4–8 Feb. 1766 [says died 2 Feb.]; *Dublin Weekly Journal* 6 Jan. 1750; *FJ* 8–11 Feb. 1766; D. Dickson, *New Foundations: Ireland 1660–1800* (Dublin, 1976) p. 89.

0509 COX, Richard

MP for Charleville 1776–83

b. 15 Jan. 1744/5; d. (*ante* 8) July 1790 'at his house [?] the Green'

FAMILY/BACKGROUND: Only son and heir of Michael Cox, Abp of Cashel, and Anne (d. 1779), dau. of Hon. James O'Brien (**1556**).

MARRIED: [25 Jan. 1766] Mary, eldest dau. of Francis Burton.

CHILDREN: Michael, m. Mary dau. of Henry Prittie, 1st Lord Dunalley (**1742**); Sir Francis, 9th Baronet, m. [1803] Anna Marie, dau. of Sir John Ferns; Rev. Richard, m. Sarah dau. of Ralph Hawtrey; William; Benjamin; Rachel, m. [1801] Ponsonby Moore; Anne, m. [1804] Price Blackwood of Ballyleidy, Co. Down.

EDUCATION: Entered Oxford (Christ Church) 11 Oct. 1762, aged 16 years.

CAREER/OCCUPATION: Freeman of Fethard (Tipperary) 1754.

MILITARY: Ensign Murray's Regiment Dec. 1756: Colonel of Ivirk Volunteers (Kilkenny).

POLITICAL ACTIVITY: He purchased his seat for Charleville in the 1776 election from Lord Cork and, although he was independent with the expectation of a large estate from his father, Archbishop Michael Cox (died 1779), he was inclined to follow the ex-Speaker, John Ponsonby (**1702**), in opposition. In a Parliamentary List for 1783 he was described as 'son to the late Archbishop of Cashel. Has a large fortune but involved. Purchased of Lord Cork. Uncertain and fluctuating in his parliamentary conduct. I know [not] whether he intends bringing himself in again or not at the next election. Does not come in again.' He did not come in again.

DIVISION LISTS:

1777 (2) voted against the Trade Embargo.
1779 (2) voted for a six-months Loan Bill.
1780 (3) voted for the Tenantry Bill.
1780 (4) voted for the Perpetual Mutiny Bill.

ESTATES/RESIDENCE: Castletown, Co. Kilkenny; Hume Street, Dublin. In 1703, Castletown, barony of Iverk, Co. Kilkenny was sold by the Duke of Ormonde to Lord Chancellor Cox. The house was built by David Ducart for Archbishop Cox. The principal component is the townland of Annahely, barony of West Muskerry, where most of the estate lies. In 1800 the Castletown estate comprised 6,877 statute acres.

In 1788 Richard Cox was granted fairs at Cooldorky, *alias* Colderohy, barony of Muskerry.

SOURCES: NLI EEC rental (1853) D/201/30; NLI EC 3485; Cox Genealogical Charts, D/3000/34/1, 2 [says born 19 Jan. 1745, died 18 Apr. 1790]; PRONI T/559 vol. 16 p. 305, Burke, extract pedigrees; PRONI MIC/315/9/51 Blackwood pedigrees; PRONI MIC/474, Irish Volunteers; RCBL P45/2/3, Parish Registers of St Peter's, Dublin; Ellis thesis; Musgrave, *Obits*; Vicars, *Prerog. Wills*; *Alum. Oxon.*; Cork MPs; *Ir. Gen.* vol. 4 no. 6 (1973) pp. 616–24, W. G. Skehan, 'Freemen of the Corporation of Fethard, Co. Tipperary'; D. Guinness and W. Ryan, *Irish Houses and Castles*, pp. 218–223; *DJ* 7–11 Dec. 1756; 6–8 July 1790; Parliamentary Lists, 1776 (1), (2), (3), 1777 (1), 1778 (1), 1780 (1), 1782 (1), 1783 (1).

0510 CRADOCK (CARADOC), Sir John Francis

MP for Clogher 1785–90; Castlebar 1790–7; Midleton 1799–Apr. 1800; Thomastown May–Aug. 1800

b. 11 Aug. 1759; d. 26 July 1839
HONOURS: KB 16 Feb. 1803; Knight Grand Cross of the Bath, Jan. 1815; Knight of the Crescent in Turkey.

PEERAGES: Cr. Baron Howden [I] 19 Oct. 1819, Baron Howden [UK] 10 Sept. 1831.

FAMILY/BACKGROUND: Only son and heir of John Cradock of Dublin and Mary, dau. of William Blaydwin of Co. Lincoln, wid. of Richard St George; assumed the name Caradoc in lieu of Cradock 1831.

MARRIED: [17 Nov. 1798] Theodosia Sarah Frances, dau. of John Meade, 1st Earl of Clanwilliam (**1388**).

CHILDREN: O. s. John Hobart, 2nd Baron Howden, m. [1830] Catherine, Princess Bagration, dau. of Paul, Count Skavronsky.

EDUCATION: School, Dr Norris; entered TCD 31 Oct. 1774; Cambridge (St John's College) 13 Mar. 1775; Middle Temple 9 Feb. 1776; MA 1777.

CAREER/OCCUPATION: Gentleman-at-Large to Lord Lieutenant 12 Apr. 1800; Groom of Bedchamber 1812–19; *Governor of the Royal Hospital, Kilmainham 1789–98.

MILITARY: Cornet 4th Regiment of Horse Dragoons 15 Dec. 1777; Ensign Coldstream Guards 9 July 1779, Lieutenant and Captain 12 Dec. 1781; Major 12th [Prince of Wales's] Light Dragoons 1785; *Major 1786, *Captain 1786; Major 13th [Somerset] Regiment; Lieutenant-Colonel 13th Foot 1787–9, 1792, 1794–5, in West Indies 1790; *Major of the 5th Foot 1789; Quarter Master General Sept. 1792–1803; commanding 2nd Battalion of Grenadiers in West Indies 1793; aide-de-camp to Sir Charles Grey, wounded at Martinique 1794, he was present at the siege of Fort Bourbon, and later thanked by Parliament; Colonel 127th Regiment 1793; Commissioner and Overseer to Barrack Board June 1794–7; Assistant Quarter Master General 1st Oct. 1795, 1798–1800; Brigadier-General (on Irish establishment only) 4 June 1796–8; *Major-General 1797–99; served under Gen. Lake (**1189**) at Vinegar Hill 21 June 1798 and at Wexford, severely wounded at Ballinahinch; Colonel 2nd Battalion 54th Foot 1801–2; second in command to Hutchinson in the advance on Cairo; Commander-in-Chief of the expedition to reduce Corsica; Colonel 71st Light Infantry 1801–9; Commander-in-Chief Madras 1803–7; Lieutenant-General 1st Jan. 1805; commanded the British Army in Portugal 1808, succeeded by Sir Arthur Wesley (Wellesley) (**2210**); appointed Governor of Gibraltar but resigned his command; Colonel of the 43rd Regiment 1809; Governor of the Cape of Good Hope 1811–13; founded the town of Cradock; General 1814.

POLITICAL ACTIVITY: A professional soldier and an aide-de-camp to successive Lords Lieutenant. He was returned for Clogher, normally considered a government borough, in 1785 on the death of Thomas St George (**1850**). He was elected without opposition, although his predecessor had been put forward because of his local popularity and to avoid a conflict.

Captain Cradock was aide-de-camp to the Duke of Rutland and to the Marquess of Buckingham. Under Lord Lieutenant Westmorland, Cradock was first aide-de-camp and Inspector of Recruits – £500 p.a. In 1793 he was Quarter Master General and a lieutenant-colonel of foot. In 1798, he was involved in suppressing the rebellion. He was brought in by government to vote for the Union, first for Midleton in 1799 and then in May 1800 for Thomastown; he voted for the Union in both 1799 and 1800. On 22 May 1804 Lord Clifden wrote indignantly to Pitt: 'I had two boroughs in Ireland, and returned 4 members to the Parliament there. Three of these were unfriendly to the Union. I persuaded them to vacate their seats and returned men devoted to Government, one the brother (**2001**) of Lord Castlereagh (**2009**) – after I came back to England Colonel Stewart was obliged to vacate his seat and Lord Castlereagh had a gentleman returned before he could even communicate with me.' The gentleman in question was presumably this MP, John Francis Cradock, who, in 1819, was raised to the peerage as Lord Howden. He died on 26 July 1839.

DIVISION LISTS:
1785 (1) voted for the Commercial Propositions.
1789 (1) voted against a Regency.
1790 (2) voted for Foster (**0805**) on the Election of a Speaker.
1800 (1) voted for the Union.

ADDITIONAL INFORMATION: Second to Rt Hon. Isaac Corry (**0497**) in his duel with Rt Hon. Henry Grattan (**0895**).

ESTATES/RESIDENCE: Grimston Park, Kirby Wharfe, Yorkshire.

SOURCES: PRONI T/3166/1B and 1A Hartland notes [says born 1762]; O'Neill thesis; GEC *P*, *DNB*; Burke *Ext. P* (1883) p. 605; *Alum. Cantab.*; *Register of Admissions to the Honourable Society of the Middle Temple* vol. 1 (London, 1949) p. 382; Fermanagh and Tyrone MPs; Kilkenny MPs; *Cornwallis Corr.* (London, 1859) vol. 3 p. 195 [says he was born 12 Aug. 1762]; *Almanacks*; *DJ* 22 Nov. 1798; PRO 30/8/123, fol.155; Parliamentary Lists, 1783 (2), 1785 (1), (2), (3), (4), 1787 (1), 1788 (1), 1789 (1), 1790 (1), 1793 (1), 1794 (1), (2), 1799 (3), 1800 (3).

0511 CRAFFORD (*alias* CRAWFORD), William

MP for Belfast 1703–13

b. *ante* 1659; d. (bur. 14 July) 1716
FAMILY/BACKGROUND: Son of [   ].
MARRIED: Janet (d. Dec. 1729), dau. of John Clugston.
CHILDREN: Capt. John, m. [   ]; James, m. Mary, dau. of John Hamilton; Elinor, m. [1709] Roger Haddock.
CAREER/OCCUPATION: Freeman of Belfast 1680, Burgess 4 May 1686, removed 29 Nov. 1707; Sovereign of Belfast 1693, 1694.
MILITARY: As Sovereign of Belfast he was Captain of the Belfast Militia; Commissioner of Array for Co. Antrim 1693.

POLITICAL ACTIVITY: He was among those attainted by James II's parliament in 1689, when he fled to Glasgow. He was a Whig and a Presbyterian, removed from Belfast Corporation on his refusal to take the test oath, decreed in the 1704 penal statute (2 Anne, c. 6). In October 1703 a committee which included Edward Brice (**0233**), Thomas Knox (**1185**) and William Crawford was appointed by the Irish House of Commons to prepare a bill for the encouragement of the linen industry. He was solidly against the Court party during the reign of Queen Anne and, in 1711, signed the loyal address against the Test Act. In 1713 the administration considered that he was 'very bad' and linked to George Macartney's (**1300**) influence in Belfast. He did not come in in 1713, and he died in 1716.

ADDITIONAL INFORMATION: He was among the merchants that lent money to Co. Antrim and Co. Down landlords against the security of their rents.

In 1694 he encouraged the setting up of a printing press, which appears to have been largely used for the production of Presbyterian literature. Second Belfast Presbyterian Church, which he helped to establish, was built in 1708, originally to take the overflow from the first. In the schism over subscription to the Westminster Confession of Faith, the two churches split apart. First Belfast became non-subscribing and part of the Presbytery of Antrim, while Second Belfast subscribed and adhered to the Synod of Ulster; the two churches were rebuilt in the course of the century. They stood side by side in Rosemary Street until Second Belfast was destroyed in 1941 during the air-raids on Belfast in the Second World War.

ESTATES/RESIDENCE: Belfast; Florida, Co. Down, bought in 1692. In 1711 he sold the avowson of Kilmood (the small Church of Ireland church near Florida) to Nicholas Price (1737). He was possibly the William Crawford who purchased the estate of Crawfordsburn, Co. Down, from Lord Clanbrassill.

SOURCES: J. Agnew, *Belfast Merchant Families in the Seventeenth Century* (1996), pp. 46, 48, 58, 74, 87, 89–91, 94, 168, 219–20; PRONI T/559 vol. 16 p. 315, Burke, extract pedigrees; Hayton thesis; Burke *LGI* (1904) p. 115; Simms' cards; Parliamentary Lists, 1706 (1), 1711 (3), 1713 (1).

0512 CRAMER (COGHILL), Sir John

MP for Belturbet 1755–60; 1761–8–76 [r. Ratoath 1768]

b. 14 July 1732; d. 8 Mar. 1790
HONOURS: Cr. Baronet [GB] 31 Aug. 1778.
FAMILY/BACKGROUND: Eldest son of Balthazar Cramer and Judith, only dau. of Rt Hon. Brinsley Butler, 1st Viscount Lanesborough (0312); sometime between 1775 and 1778 he assumed surname Coghill, in lieu of Cramer, pursuant to will of his great-uncle Rt Hon. Marmaduke Coghill (0431).
MARRIED: [17 Oct. 1754] Maria (d. 14 Dec. 1815), dau. of Josiah Hort, Abp of Tuam.
CHILDREN: Sir John Thomas Cramer-Coghill (d. unm.), 2nd Baronet; Vice-Admiral Sir Josiah Coghill Cramer-Coghill (b. 1773; d. 20 June 1850), 3rd Baronet, m. [1803] (1) Sophia (d. 1817), dau. of James Dodson, (2) [27 Jan. 1819]

Anna Maria (d. 8 Mar. 1848), e. dau. of Rt Hon. Charles Kendal Bushe (0309); Mary (d. unm.); Judith, m. Rev. F. W. Michell; Eliza (*d.s.p.*), m. Rev. N. Hinde; Arabella (d. unm.); Frances, m. Lieut.-Col. Sankey; Priscilla (d. 28 Mar. 1860), m. Richard Ottley; Sophia, m. [1801] Lieut.-Gen. Sir Charles W. Doyle; Theodosia Hannah.
EDUCATION: School: private tutor; entered TCD 9 July 1750, LLD *hon. caus.* 1762.
CAREER/OCCUPATION: ?Sheriff of Co. Cavan 1756; *Governor of the Workhouse 1763–8; Foundling Hospital and Workhouse 1769–89; *elected to the Court of Assistants June 1767–8; Freedom of Ennis 1766.

POLITICAL ACTIVITY: He was returned for Belturbet by his mother's family, the Butlers, Earls of Lanesborough, 'whose commands he will implicitly obey'. He was in opposition; in 1774 an opposition list declared that 'He walks in Lanesborough fetters, but would be free if he dared.'

DIVISION LISTS:

1757 (1) voted for the resolutions on pensions.
1768 (1) voted against army augmentation.
1771 (1) voted against Lord Townshend as Lord Lieutenant.
1771 (2) voted for Sir Lucius O'Brien's (1558) motion for retrenchment.
1773 (1) voted against Absentee Tax.
1773 (2) voted against an untaxed press.
1774 (2) voted against Catholic relief.
1775 (1) voted against the pro-American amendment to the Speech from the Throne.

ESTATES/RESIDENCE: Ballyfoyle, Co. Kilkenny (belonged to the Cramers); the Coghill inheritance included Glen Barrahane, Castle Townsend, Co. Cork (seat of the Coghills); Drumcondra, Co. Dublin; Bellaville, Co. Meath. Sir John inherited the estates of his maternal great-uncle Rt Hon. Marmaduke Coghill (0431) in March 1739. By the death of his cousin Hester, Dowager Countess of Charleville, 28 July 1789, he inherited other estates of the Coghill family including Coghill Hall, Knaresborough, West Riding of Yorkshire.

SOURCES: PRONI D/302; McCracken thesis; GEC *P*; Burke *PB* (1903) p. 342; J. Frost, *The History and Topography of the County of Clare, from the Earliest Times to the Beginning of the 18th Century, With Map and Illustrations*, pp. 606–7; *Almanacks*; Parliamentary Lists, 1769 (1), 1772 (2), 1773 (1), (2), 1774 (1), 1775 (1).

0513 CRAWFORD, Thomas

MP for New Ross 1692–3, 1695–9, 1703–6

b. *ante* 1665; d. (*post* Aug.) 1706
FAMILY/BACKGROUND: Son of [   ] Crawford.
MARRIED: Anne [   ].
CHILDREN: John; Elizabeth.
CAREER/OCCUPATION: Free Burgess of New Ross,
13 July 1686 – 30 Aug. 1706; Capital Sovereign
of New Ross, *c.* Feb. 1691; Burgess of New Ross
1692; Collector of the Port.

POLITICAL ACTIVITY: Returned for New Ross for
successive elections until his death in 1706. In
1695 he supported Lord Chancellor Porter against
the accusations of favouring Catholics made
against him by some MPs, and the following year
he signed the Association for the protection of
William III in the country. He appears to have
been under the Duke of Ormonde's influence.

As Sovereign of New Ross, he was confronted
with the aftermath of the Williamite wars. At the
end of the siege of Limerick, New Ross was
swamped by 'Irish inhabitants' who boycotted
Protestant shopkeepers and tradesmen, threatening them with ruin. He sought to have them removed and refused admission to New Ross. The
economic difficulties of the borough were made
worse by the enforced quartering of Dutch troops.
On 16 July 1705 he wrote to Ormonde that the
Commissioners of the Revenue had suppressed the
collection of Ross and Kilkenny and ordered his
removal to Killybegs, the worst collection in the
kingdom: 'This misfortune encourages me to fly
to your Grace's protection and humbly to put your
Grace in mind that I have been a servant to your
family from my youth, that I suffered hardships
for adhering to your Grace's interest in former
Parliaments, particularly for voting for disband-
ing the French forces, and in this last Parliament I
constantly did my duty as I believe Mr Savage
(**1889**) or Mr Portlock (**1715**) can assure your
Grace.'

ESTATES/RESIDENCE: [?]Purchased 202 acres in Co. Kilkenny from the Commissioners for Sale of Forfeited
Estates in 1702–3.

SOURCES: PRONI T/559 vol. 16 p. 339, Burke, extract
pedigrees; Hoare, *History of the Town and County of
Wexford: Old and New Ross*, p. 16; *HMC Ormonde*

(1920) new ser. vol. 8 pp. 166, 291 [Crawford was still
a Free Burgess of New Ross until 30 Aug. 1706. It seems
likely that he died around this last date when he ceased
to be a Free Burgess; certainly he was dead by March
1706/7]; C. Dalton (ed.), *English Army Lists and Commission Registers, 1661–1714* (London, 1892), vol. 1 p.
121 [says a Thomas Craufford, Ensign in Lockhart's
Regiment of Foot 25 July 1672]; *JRSAI* vol. 21 (1892)
p. 301, P. D. Vigors, 'Alphabetical List of Free Burgesses
of New Ross ... 1658–1839'; *JRSAI* vol. 31 (1901) pp.
52–3, P. D. Vigors, 'Extracts from the Old Corporation Books of New Ross, Co. Wexford'; Simms,
Williamite Confiscation, p. 184; Parliamentary Lists,
1695 (1), 1696 (1), 1707 (1).

CRAWFORD, William: *see* **CRAFFORD** (*alias*
CRAWFORD), William (**0511**)

0514 CREIGHTON, Abraham

MP for Co. Fermanagh 1692–3; Enniskillen
1695–9

b. *ante* 1631; d. (bur. 13) Mar. 1706
FAMILY/BACKGROUND: Son of John Creighton of
Crom Castle, Co. Fermanagh, and Mary Irvine.
MARRIED: Mary, dau. of James Spottiswood, Bp of
Clogher.
CHILDREN: Capt. James, m. Hester, dau. of Sir
John Hume Bt (their o. s. John suc. his grand-
father in 1705 and *d.s.p.* 1715); David (**0518**);
Jane, m. John Hamilton; Marian (Mary-Anne),
m. 1706 Hugh Willoughby (Willoughby-
Montgomery) (**2236**); Catherine.
CAREER/OCCUPATION: Sheriff of Co. Fermanagh 19
Dec. 1672; Sheriff of Co. Fermanagh 1673.
MILITARY: Commissioned as an Ensign in Sir
Charles Hamilton's Company of Foot 8 Mar.
1664; Lieutenant-Colonel in Gustavus Hamil-
ton's Inniskilling Regiment of Foot spring 1689;
Colonel in the army (held Crom Castle against
the Jacobite forces 22 March and 28 July 1689),
commanded a Regiment of Foot at the Battle of
Aughrim, 12 July 1691; Colonel 1691–6; put on
half pay 1697; included in list of half-pay
'Reformed Officers' still serving in 1704.

POLITICAL ACTIVITY: He sat in both parliaments of
William III. In 1695 he voted against Lord Chan-

cellor Porter, who was accused by some MPs of favouring Catholics, and the following year he signed the Association for the protection of William III in parliament. He was probably on military service for much of this time.

ESTATES/RESIDENCE: Crom Castle, Co. Fermanagh. The Crom Castle estate was obtained through marriage, his father-in-law, Bishop Spottiswood, having been granted it in 1624. The Knockballymore estate, 2,601 Irish acres, and an Enniskillen estate of 3,673 acres were acquired about 1810. The Crom estate was held in fee farm under the Lanesborough family.

About 1678 he, along with John Johnson of Clare, Co. Tyrone, was foolish enough to secure the purchase of the lordship of Lifford and other lands in Donegal by Hugh Hamill (**0911**). This resulted in a chaotic financial treadmill. Hamill, always short of ready cash, was soon borrowing of one creditor to pay another but, somehow, he convinced Creighton to continue to act as security for loans. Hamill sold part of the Lifford estate, which he had previously mortgaged to Thomas Glascoe for £3,216, and left Creighton to reimburse Glascoe, another of his creditors. Hamill was supposed to pay off, with the £3,216, some of the loans secured by Creighton but instead paid other creditors 'and left the said Crichton in the lurch for at least £10,000 or £12,000 ... Hugh Hamill, his case being so despicable, Dr Maddin commenced suit against Abraham Crichton for his money and interest, which came then to about £1,450; so that the said Crichton was necessitated to purchase the said mortgage from Dr Maddin and pay him down in hand £845 and secure him the remainder of his money; that Mr Thomas Glascoe commenced a suit against the said Abraham Crichton for £5,000 and some odd hundreds of pounds, his estate being seized by elegits for debts owing to Mr Alwith and Mr Savage, and damnified, as he alleges, £700, so that the said Crichton was necessitated to sell and encumber a great part of his own free estate, by which he purchased Glascoe's, which Mr Savage delivered the possession, then in him, to the said Crichton; and ever since the said Crichton has been possessed of the mortgage and the concerns of Hugh Hamill he hath been paying off debts wherein he stood bound for the said Hamill.'

SOURCES: PRONI D/1939/18/9/34, /21/16/1, /21/7/3, /2/14, /21/3 Erne Papers, 'A paper relating to the estate of Lifford' [rentals and surveys, 1719–23 and 1768–9, 1810]; NLI MS 15783 Erne Papers; PRONI D/1939/2/3 A and C, D vols of surveys; PRONI 3000/102 Erne Papers, Carlin Genealogical Notes (the early genealogy of the Creightons is difficult to disentangle) [says son of Abraham Crichton and Nichola ? of Dromoony on Lough Erne, who came to Ireland before 17 Aug. 1616, and d. 1631, also says he m. 1655

and has another son, Abraham; *Alum. Dub.* gives a John son of Abraham Creighton of Fermanagh entered TCD 21 June 1688 aged 19 years; PRONI T/559 vol. 17 p. 2, Burke, extract pedigrees; PRONI MIC/315/8/41 Blackwood pedigrees; RCBL T34, Extracts from the Parish Registers of St Andrew's, Dublin; Burke *PB* (1903) p. 556 [says he was only son of Abraham Creighton and his wife Nicholas (*sic*); *Cal. SP Dom. 1694–5* (London, 1906) pp. 33, 159, *1696* (London, 1913) p. 48; Fermanagh and Tyrone MPs; Hughes, *Pat. Officers*; Simms' cards; C. Dalton (ed.), *English Army Lists and Commission Registers, 1661–1714* (London, 1896), vol. 3 pp. 7, 217; C. Dalton (ed.), *Irish Army Lists, 1661–1685* (London, 1907), pp. 54–5, 57; *Ir. Sword*, vol. 1 (1949–53) pp. 133–5; R. Wyse Jackson, *Queen Anne's Irish Army Establishment in 1704*; Parliamentary Lists, 1695 (1), 1696 (1).

0515 CREIGHTON, Abraham

MP for Lifford 1727–60, 1761–8

b. (bapt. 31 Dec.) 1703; d. 2 June 1772.
PEERAGES: Cr. Baron Erne 15 July 1768.
FAMILY/BACKGROUND: Second and only surviving son of David Creighton (**0518**) and Catherine, dau. of Richard Southwell.
MARRIED: (1) [1 July 1729] Elizabeth (d. 23 Aug. 1761), e. dau. of Rt Hon. John Rogerson (**1812**); (2) [7 Sept. 1763] Jane, dau. of John King (**1160**), wid. of Arthur Acheson.
CHILDREN: (1) David Rogerson (d. yg); Rt Hon. John, 2nd Baron Erne (**0519**); Abraham (**0516**); Meliora; Charlotte, m. Edward King (**1150**); Mary (d. yg).
CAREER/OCCUPATION: Trustee of the Linen Board for Munster 1743–69; Governor of Co. Armagh 1762, *Co. Fermanagh 1756–9, 1762–3; Joint Governor of Co. Fermanagh 1764–70 (f.); Freeman of Dublin 8 June 1738; voted a Freeman of the Guild of Merchant Tailors.

POLITICAL ACTIVITY: Creighton had a half interest and later a full interest in the borough of Lifford, which the Creightons originally shared with Alexander Montgomery (**1435**), and was a full partner, with his father, to the division of Lifford with Alexander Montgomery on 16 June 1727. These formal 'articles of agreement' set out the terms under which the two families were to return to the borough not only during the lives of the two main protagonists but also during Abraham's life and the life of Montgomery's son, if he had one (Montgomery *d.s.p.* in December 1729).

Creighton was indirectly involved in the scandal associated with the failure of Burton's Bank in 1733. On 28 March 1734 Primate Boulter wrote to Sir Robert Walpole regarding the bill before parliament attempting to clear up the bank disaster, and about some reports of objections to it being sent over from Ireland, warning him: 'that Lord Chief Justice *Rogerson* should have written against that bill is not strange, since whatever is taken from *Harrison's* estate towards paying the debts of the bank is taken from Mr *Creighton* who married the Lord Chief Justice's daughter; so that the Chief Justice's letter is not from an indifferent hand. But the truth of our case, and what every man of sense here knows, is, that if this bill miscarries, it must put an end to our paper credit here, by an immediate run upon the bankers, or gradual forbearing to lodge money there: and it is certain we have not cash enough in the nation to carry on our common trade or pay our rents or taxes: and I very much question whether if our paper credit fails, it would not be with the utmost difficulty that our army could be subsisted.'

Creighton was a strong supporter of the Speaker over the Money Bill crisis, but by 1755 there was a general desire to resolve this long-running row, and on 15 February Primate Stone wrote to Sackville (**1835**) that 'Things are in the strangest way that can be conceived. The open language of the opposite party is, that there should be no more fighting. On Thursday I met Lord Carrick [Speaker Boyle's son-in-law], Sir Arthur Gore (**0859**) and Mr Malone (**1336**) at the Board of Navigation: and conversed with them all three separately with the utmost civility and ease. Lord Carrick on Mr Creighton's speaking something before him in the old abusing way, took him short and told him that he hoped never to hear a word more upon those subjects. Sir Ralph Gore (**0873**) told Major Pomeroy (**1695**) that they had gone a great way too far, and he hoped people would soon see their mistake, and all would be quiet. This very new behaviour and conversation is unaccountable, and we, who are left so entirely in the dark, cannot but conceive that these gentlemen know more of the true state of things than we do.'

Creighton continued to take a moderate opposition stand, voting for the resolutions on pensions. He does not appear to have voted on the augmentation of the army in 1768. He was created Lord Erne on 15 July 1768 following the dissolution of parliament on 28 May. He died in 1772.

DIVISION LISTS:
> 1749 (1) voted against the election of James Digges La Touche (♦♦♦).
> 1753 (1) voted for the expulsion of Arthur Jones-Nevill (**1125**).
> 1753 (2) voted against the Money Bill.
> 1757 (1) voted for the resolutions on pensions.

ADDITIONAL INFORMATION: *A member of the RDS from 1765. A Freemason.

ESTATES/RESIDENCE: Crom Castle, Co. Fermanagh. On 9 January 1748 he and William Todd of Haywill, Co. Wicklow petitioned to be enabled to vest the real and personal estate of Francis and Marsh Harrison in trustees in order to reach an agreement over its distribution.

SOURCES: *CJ Ire.* (Bradley ed.) vol. 7 p. 999; PRONI D/1759/3A/7 [says he died 2 June 1772]; PRONI D/1939/21/3 'Articles of Agreement'; PRONI D/3000/102 Carlin Genealogical Notes [says died 2 June 1772, married (1) 31 July 1729 (2) 7 Sept. 1763]; PRONI T/1584 p. 71, 13 Sept. 1763, Pinkerton transcripts; RCBL T34, Extracts from the Parish Registers of St Andrew's, Dublin; McCracken thesis; Burke *PB* (1903) p. 556; *JRSAI* vol. 48 (1918) p. 57, H. F. Berry, 'The Merchant Tailors' Gild – That of St John the Baptist, Dublin, 1418–1841'; *Boulter Letters* vol. 2 p. 94; *EHR* (1905 Oct.) p. 760, C. L. Falkiner, 'Correspondence of Archbishop Stone and the Duke of Newcastle'; *Almanacks*; *DJ* 6–10 Sept. 1763; The *Dublin Weekly Journal* 13 Mar. 1731.

0516 CREIGHTON, Hon. Abraham

MP for Lifford 1768–76–83–90–7–1800

b. c. 1740; d. Sept. 1809

FAMILY/BACKGROUND: Son of Abraham Creighton, 1st Baron Erne (**0515**) and Elizabeth, e. dau. of Rt Hon. John Rogerson (**1812**).

MARRIED: [6 Nov. 1793] Mrs Mary Akinhurst of

Co. Kilkenny.

CHILDREN: dau. (died 1794); Elizabeth Charlotte, m. [1815] Loftus Anthony Tottenham.

CAREER/OCCUPATION: High Sheriff of Co. Fermanagh 3 Mar. 1774; *Surveyor of Excise for Coleraine 1785–7; Registrar of Forfeitures 1792–1800 (f.); *Surveyor of Dingle 1798; voted a Freeman of the Guild of Merchant Tailors or Guild of St John 1769, Master 1779–80, re-elected Master 1780–1.

MILITARY: Ensign, June 1760; Lieutenant in the army; Governor of Hurst Castle in the Solent 1800.

POLITICAL ACTIVITY: In 1768 Lord Erne (0515) returned his two sons for the family borough of Lifford. Although Lord Erne had promised his full support, one of his sons never attended and the other was in opposition. This one was a military officer on half-pay and generally in opposition. In the 1776 election he was returned by his brother (his father died in 1772) and continued with an independent opposition line. He was not solidly in opposition: his voting pattern was erratic. Lord Erne was made a viscount in 1781 and 'He entered into a stipulation to return one Member for Government at the general election. The Duke of Portland released him from the obligation but I do not see with what propriety, as it was not made to his Grace. Lord Erne has returned Mr Creighton.'

After 1783 Creighton appears to have decided to support government, and in 1785 he was a captain in one of the fencible regiments briefly raised to provide an alternative defence to the Volunteers. Creighton was hopeful of office: in 1785 he was Collector of Coleraine. By 1788 he had been promised an office of £200. During the 1790s he acquired a number of minor offices; he was Registrar of Forfeitures. He voted against the Union in 1799 but was persuaded to change his mind in 1800 by being 'privately purchased', and in 1800 he was appointed Comptroller of Dingle, £300 p.a. He took no part in the Union debates.

DIVISION LISTS:

1771 (1) voted for Lord Townshend as Lord Lieutenant.

1771 (2) voted for Sir Lucius O'Brien's (1558) motion for retrenchment.

1772 (1) voted against the separation of the Revenue Board.

1772 (2) voted for a Short Revenue Bill.

1777 (1) voted against Grattan's (0895) motion for retrenchment.

1778 (2) voted against the Popery Bill.

1779 (2) voted for a six-months Loan Bill.

1780 (1) voted against Grattan's declaration of the rights of Ireland.

1780 (2) voted for Yelverton's (2268) motion to modify Poynings' Law.

1783 (1) voted against Flood's (0762) motion for parliamentary reform.

1784 (1) voted against a committee on the Reform Bill.

1785 (1) voted against the Commercial Propositions.

1787 (1) voted for a Pension Bill.

1790 (2) voted for Foster (0805) on the Election of a Speaker.

1799 (1) voted against the Union – Registrar of Forfeitures.

1800 (1) voted for the Union.

ESTATES/RESIDENCE: Crom Castle, Co. Fermanagh; Lifford, Co. Donegal; Capel Street, Mountjoy Square, Granby Row, Dublin. In 1807, the Lifford estate had a rental of £2,895.

SOURCES: PRONI D/302; RCBL P277/1/3, Parish Registers of St Mary's, Dublin; O'Neill thesis; Burke *PB* (1903) p. 556; Ellis thesis; PRONI T/3166/1A Hartnell notes; *JRSAI* vol. 48 (1918) p. 57, H. F. Berry, 'The Merchant Tailors' Gild – That of St John the Baptist, Dublin, 1418–1841'; G. C. Bolton, *The Passing of the Irish Act of Union*, p. 171; *Almanacks*; *DJ* 10–14 June 1760, 1–3 July 1779; PRONI, D/2298/H/1 Wilson & Simms Papers [Survey and rental, 1807]; Wakefield, *Account of Ire.* vol. 1 p. 254; PRONI D/1939/18/9/34, /21/16/1 and /2/14 Erne Papers [rentals and surveys, 1719–23 and 1768–9, 1810]; NLI MS 15783, Erne Papers; Parliamentary Lists, 1769 (1), 1772 (1), (2), 1773 (1), (2), 1775 (1), 1776 (1), (2), (3), 1777 (1), 1778 (1), 1780 (1), 1782 (1), 1783 (1), (2), 1784 (1), (2), (3), (4), 1787 (1), 1788 (1), 1789 (1), 1790 (1), 1791 (1), 1793 (1), 1794 (1), (2), 1799 (2), (3), 1800 (1), (3).

0517 CREIGHTON, Hon. Abraham

MP for Lifford 1790–7

b. 10 May 1765; d. 10 June 1842
PEERAGES: Styled Viscount Creighton 1789–1828;
suc. as 2nd Earl Erne 1828.
FAMILY/BACKGROUND: Son and heir of Rt Hon.
John Creighton, 1st Earl Erne (0519) and his 1st
wife Catherine, dau. of Robert Howard, Bp of
Elphin.
MARRIED: Unmarried.

POLITICAL ACTIVITY: He was brought in by his father and supported, but his parliamentary career
was probably short and little is known of it. He
appears to have been mentally unstable, as his
condition caused some concern during the marriage negotiations between his sister Elizabeth and
James Stuart-Wortley in 1799. 'There has been a
difficulty, owing to old Wortley's [the groom's fa-
ther] fears about Lord Creighton, her [Elizabeth's]
half-brother, who is confined [i.e. insane]. But
Lord Erne (0519) who is in England, cleared it
up to the family, as Lord Creighton's illness was
owing to cold bathing in a course of mercury,
which disordered his head.'

DIVISION LISTS:
1790 (2) voted for Foster (0805) on the
Election of a Speaker.

ESTATES/RESIDENCE: Crom Castle, Co. Fermanagh.

SOURCES: PRONI D/3000/102 Carlin Genealogical
Notes; GEC P; Burke PB (1903) p. 556; A. P. W.
Malcomson, The Pursuit of the Heiress (Belfast, 1982)
p. 33; DJ 11 Apr. 1799; Parliamentary Lists, 1791 (1),
1793 (1), 1794 (2).

0518 CREIGHTON, David

MP for Augher 1695–9; Lifford 1703–13–14,
1715–27–8

b. 1671; d. 1 June 1728
FAMILY/BACKGROUND: Son of Abraham Creighton
(0514) and Mary, dau. of James Spottiswood, Bp
of Clogher.
MARRIED: [1697] Catherine, 2nd dau. of Richard
Southwell of Castle Mattress, Co Limerick (sis. of
1st Lord Southwell).

CHILDREN: James (d. yg); Abraham, 1st Earl Erne
(0515); Anne (d. yg); Elizabeth, m. [19 July
1735] John Todd; Mary; Meliora, m. [Mar.
1742] Nicholas Ward; Belaura.
EDUCATION: LLD of TCD hon. caus. 1709.
CAREER/OCCUPATION: ?Sheriff of Co. Donegal
1702; Master of the Royal Hospital of
Kilmainham 1719–28; Burgess of Lifford until
his death.
MILITARY: ?Commissioned as a Lieutenant of Sir
William Douglas of Caver's Troop in the Royal
Regiment of Dragoons commanded by Sir
Thomas Levingston 16 Jan. 1692; Captain in
Colonel Thomas Brudenell's Regiment of Foot
Mar. 1702; served in Spain; Lieutenant-Colonel
to Colonel Caulfeild [c. Dec.] 1705; Lieutenant-
Colonel ante 1 Dec. 1706 when made Brevet
Colonel by Lord Peterborough at Valencia;
succeeded Colonel Toby Caulfeild as Colonel of a
Regiment of Foot 2 Aug. 1708; Brigadier-
General 12 Feb. 1711; on half pay as Colonel
1712; Master of the Royal Hospital, Kilmainham
1719–28; promoted Major-General by George I
15 Mar. 1727; Brigadier-General 1 June 1728.
According to the accounts of the Irish military
establishment 30 Sept. 1715 – 30 June 1717,
Brigadier Creighton was receiving £547 10s 0d
p.a. On 11 Oct. 1723 he petitioned for his back
pay from June 1720, as half-pay Colonel and
Captain; he was receiving £223 3s 9d half pay at
the time of his death.

POLITICAL ACTIVITY: A professional soldier, he distinguished himself in the defence of Crom Castle
against the Jacobite forces in 1689. He voted
against Lord Chancellor Porter, who had been
accused by some MPs of favouring Catholics, in
1695; he did not sign the Association for the protection of William III in 1696 but was not criticised for it – possibly he was out of the country.
He was listed for nine committees between 1695
and 1698. He fought in the War of Spanish Succession and was absent for much of Anne's reign,
although he was nominated for 16 committees
between 1703 and 1711 and for six in the very
short 1713 parliament.

On his return in 1711 he joined the opposition. In 1713 he was again returned for Lifford,
although at this time the Creighton interest in the
borough was not as absolute as it later became. In
1713 he was a fairly prominent Whig and a member of the Commons committee that reported on
the 'misconduct' of Sir Constantine Phipps. Ac-

cording to the Lord Justices in 1715 he was broken 'out of turn' in his military career because of his Whig principles. He was nominated for 58 committees between 1715 and 1726 and a further five in the period between the general election in 1727 and his death the following year.

On 16 June 1727 Creighton, with his son Abraham, entered into a formal agreement with Alexander Montgomery (**1435**) to divide the representation of Lifford alternately between the two families. These 'articles of agreement' comprised six clauses setting out the terms to apply during the lives of Creighton and Montgomery and also on the succession of Abraham. If Montgomery had a son he was also to enjoy full rights when he came of age and provided he accepted the articles. In fact Montgomery did not have a son.

DIVISION LISTS:

1711 (1) voted for the Court on the Dublin mayoralty issue.

1713 (1) voted for Sir Richard Levinge (**1230**) for Speaker.

1721 (1) voted for a national bank.

1721 (2) voted for a national bank.

ESTATES/RESIDENCE: Crom Castle, Co. Fermanagh. T3411 (Blenheim MSS) reckons David Creighton's income in 1713 at only £300.

SOURCES: PRONI D/302; T/3411; *CJ Ire.* (Bradley ed.) vol. 4 p. 353, vol. 5 p. 100, vol. 6 p. 71; PRONI D/1939/21/3 *Lifford Borough-book, 1716–83*, 'Articles of Agreement'; PRONI D/3000/102 Carlin Genealogical Notes [says married *ante*-1695 Catherine Southwell of Callow and Castle Matrix, Co. Limerick]; RCBL T34, Extracts from the Parish Registers of St Andrew's, Dublin [bur. 3 June 1728]; McCracken thesis; Burke *PB* (1903) p. 556; *Cal. SP Dom. 1691–2* (London, 1900) p. 102; C. Dalton, *George the First's Army, 1714–1727*; Hayton thesis; Musgrave, *Obits*; *HMC Ormonde*, (1920) new ser. vol. 8 p. 199; Parliamentary Lists, 1695 (1), 1696 (1), 1706 (1), 1707 (1), (3), (4), 1711 (3), 1713 (1), (2), (3).

0519 CREIGHTON, Rt Hon. John

MP for Lifford 1761-8–72

b. 1731; d. 15 Sept. 1828
HONOURS: PC, sworn 5 June 1804.

PEERAGES: Suc. as 2nd Baron Erne 1772; cr. Viscount Erne 6 Jan. 1781; Earl of Erne 18 Aug. 1789; Rep. Peer 1801–28.

FAMILY/BACKGROUND: Son and heir of Abraham Creighton, 1st Baron Erne (**0515**) and Elizabeth, dau. of Rt Hon. John Rogerson (**1812**).

MARRIED: (1) [25 Feb. 1761] Catherine (d. 18 June 1775), dau. of Robert Howard, Bp of Elphin (sis. of Viscount Wicklow); (2) [22 Feb. 1776] Mary Catherine, e. dau. of Frederick Augustus Hervey, Bp of Derry, 4th Earl of Bristol.

CHILDREN: (1) Abraham, 2nd Earl Erne (**0517**); Hon. John (**0520**); Elizabeth (d. Feb. 1794), m. [20 Jan. 1783] James King; Catherine. (2) Elizabeth Caroline Mary, m. [30 Mar. 1799] Rt Hon. James Archibald Stuart-Wortley-Mackenzie, 1st Baron Wharncliffe.

CAREER/OCCUPATION: In 1769 voted a Freeman of the Guild of Merchant Tailors; Burgess of St Johnstown (Donegal) 1770; Joint Governor of Co. Fermanagh 1772–1828; *Trustee of the Linen Board for Ulster 1774; High Sheriff of Co. Fermanagh 1814.

MILITARY: Storekeeper of the Ordnance 1768–75; Colonel of the Donegal 1st Regiment, Volunteers, and of the Longford, Ardmor and Royal Volunteers.

POLITICAL ACTIVITY: He and his brother (**0516**) were brought into parliament by their father (**0515**), who was created a peer in 1768. He was appointed Storekeeper of the Ordnance, £200 p.a., in 1768, which he alleged that he owed to Chief Secretary Lord Frederick Campbell 'and no one else'. Despite the father's promises of support, the sons appear to have been either absent or 'doubtful'; it was said in 1772 that 'The one never attends and the other opposes.' He wanted a better place, but at that point his father died and he became Lord Erne. He supported Lord Harcourt 'very steadily'. In 1774 he resigned his appointment as Storekeeper and Lord Harcourt made him a Trustee of the Linen Board and one of his brothers Distributor of Stamps for Galway Co. He was created Viscount Erne in 1781.

Apparently he had promised one seat to government at the 1783 election but had been released from his promise by the Duke of Portland. He controlled the borough of Lifford and, in 1783, returned his brother for one seat and sold the other. His estate was considered only 'moderate', but in

1788 he wanted 'promotion in peerage and mentions his means of bring[ing] two sons into Parliament at the next Election'. In fact he brought in his brother (**0516**) and his eldest son (**0517**). He was created Earl of Erne in 1789. He and his members voted, perhaps reluctantly (especially his brother Abraham), for the Union in 1800, and Lord Erne became a representative peer.

DIVISION LISTS:

1768 (1) voted for army augmentation.

1771 (1) voted for Lord Townshend as Lord Lieutenant.

1771 (3) voted against the amendment to the Revenue Bill.

1772 (1) absent.

ADDITIONAL INFORMATION: He may have had another daughter, Elizabeth (or [?]Patience Elizabeth), referred to in Carlin, who married (1797) Alexander Alexander (a Roman Catholic) of Cloon, probably at Cookstown, Co. Tyrone. They were in America by 1798. But Lord Erne had a daughter Elizabeth who married Stuart-Wortley in 1799, so she could not have been the Elizabeth who married Alexander and styled herself Lady Elizabeth Creighton in the United States.

ESTATES/RESIDENCE: Crom Castle, Co. Fermanagh. Stuart-Wortley-Mackenzie, his daughter Elizabeth's husband, was heir to large estates in Yorkshire, Cornwall and Scotland. 'He will have a property of £18,000 a year from his father, besides MacKenzie's [his greatuncle] … She was to have £15,000 from Lord Erne but I believe he does more in point of present income as old Wortley has a large establishment.' In the 1810s and 1820s the 1st Earl seems to have added, by purchase, 8,700 Irish acres to his inherited 5,759 in Co. Fermanagh.

SOURCES: PRONI D/302; PRONI D/3000/102 Carlin Genealogical Notes [says married (2) Mary Caroline Hervey]; PRONI MIC/474 Irish Volunteers; GEC *P*; Burke *PB* (1903) pp. 556–7 (1906) p. 595; Index to PC; G. C. Bolton, *The Passing of the Irish Act of Union*, pp. 75, 171; A. P. W. Malcomson, *The Pursuit of the Heiress* (Belfast, 1982) pp. 33, 45; *Ir. Gen.* vol. 5 no. 3 (1976) p. 345, H. F. Morris, 'Ramsey's Waterford Chronicle, 1776' [says he married Miss Hervey 5 Feb. 1776]; *JRSAI* vol. 48 (1918) p. 57, H. F. Berry, 'The Merchant Tailors' Gild – That of St John the Baptist, Dublin, 1418–1841'; *Almanacks*; *DJ* 8 Feb. 1794, 11 Apr. 1799; Parliamentary Lists, 1769 (1), 1771 (1),

1772 (1), (2), 1773 (1), (2), 1775 (1), 1777 (1), 1782 (1), 1783 (2), 1787 (1), 1788 (1), 1790 (1), 1793 (1), 1794 (2), 1798 (1), 1799 (2), (3), 1800 (2).

0520 CREIGHTON, Hon. John

MP for Lifford 1797–1800

b. 28 June 1772; d. 10 May 1833

FAMILY/BACKGROUND: Son of Rt Hon. John Creighton, 1st Earl Erne (**0519**) and Catherine, dau. of Robert Howard, Bp of Elphin.

MARRIED: [9 Dec. 1797] Jane, dau. and h. of Walter Weldon (**2202**).

CHILDREN: John, 3rd Earl of Erne, m. 1837 Selina Griselda (b. 1804; d. 6 Sept. 1884), dau. of Rev. Charles Cobbe Beresford; Maj. Henry (6th Dragoons) (b. 31 Oct. 1804; d. 23 Feb. 1864), m. [1849] Elizabeth (d. 30 Oct. 1860), dau. of Lieut.-Col. Hawkshaw; Samuel (b. 9 Jan. 1811; d. 9 Apr. 1863); Jane Anne (d. 1828), m. [1821] Robert Fowler; Catherine (d. 14 Oct. 1860), m. [1825] Rev. Francis Saunderson; Helen (d. 11 Jan. 1875); Charlotte (d. 1895); Mary (d. 7 Nov. 1898), m. [17 Jan. 1856] Rev. J. H. King.

EDUCATION: School: Mr Darby; entered TCD 20 June 1789.

CAREER/OCCUPATION: A Major in the army in 1799.

POLITICAL ACTIVITY: He was brought in by his father (**0519**) in 1797, probably on the incapacity of his older brother (**0517**). He appears to have followed his father's political direction, although like his uncle (**0516**) he voted against the Union in 1799, but was financially persuaded to vote for it in 1800. He took no part in the Union debates.

DIVISION LISTS:

1799 (1) voted against the Union – a Major.

1800 (1) voted for the Union.

ESTATES/RESIDENCE: Crom Castle, Co. Fermanagh. In 1829, the rental of the Kil[?] estate was £1,100, and of the Enniskillen estate, £909. The estate included part of the manor of Anghalane and had belonged to Mrs Anne Weldon in 1775, when it contained 1,845 Irish acres, in the baronies of Coole and Knockninny.

SOURCES: Account between Hon. Colonel John Creighton and David Gumley, 11 Aug. 1830, PRONI D/1939/20/6/8 Erne Papers; RCBL P277/1/3, Parish Registers of St Mary's, Dublin; Burke *PB* (1903) pp.

556–7 (1906) p. 595; *Alum. Dub.*; G. C. Bolton, *The Passing of the Irish Act of Union*, p. 171; Parliamentary Lists, 1799 (2), (3), 1800 (3).

CREMORNE, Baron and Viscount: *see* **DAWSON**

0595 Dawson, Thomas, 1st Baron Dartry, Viscount Cremorne, Baron Cremorne, MP Co. Monaghan 1749–60, 1761–8

0521 CROFTON, Rt Hon. Sir Edward

MP for Boyle 1695–9; Co. Roscommon 1703–13–14, 1715–27–9

> b. *c.* 1662; d. 24 Nov. 1729
> HONOURS: PC, sworn 30 Nov. 1714, 1 Dec. 1727; suc. as 2nd Baronet 1675.
> FAMILY/BACKGROUND: Son of Sir Edward Crofton, 1st Baronet, and his 2nd wife Susanna, dau. of Thomas Clifford of Devon.
> MARRIED: [2 Feb. 1684] Catherine, dau. of Rt Hon. Sir Oliver St George, 1st Baronet (**1842**).
> CHILDREN: Rt Hon. Sir Edward, 3rd Baronet (**0522**); Oliver, m. Catherine Armstrong.
> CAREER/OCCUPATION: Sheriff of Co. Roscommon 1700.

POLITICAL ACTIVITY: He sat in successive parliaments for 34 years, 1695–1729. On 7 May 1688 Sir Edward Crofton was among those attainted by James II's parliament. In 1695 he voted against Lord Chancellor Porter, who was accused by some MPs of favouring Catholics, and the following year he signed the Association for the protection of William III in parliament. During the reign of Queen Anne he was counted as a Whig, although he voted for Sir Richard Levinge (**1230**), the government's candidate for Speaker in 1713. He was listed for four committees 1697–8, and ten 1703–9. On 3 May 1716 he complained to the House that William Westland, merchant, had breached his privilege by bringing an action against him relating to certain lands in Co. Roscommon, and had insulted him 'at the same time knowing him to be a Member'. He was hostile to the idea of a national bank. He sat on nine committees between

1715 and 1723, and two in 1727. He died in 1729.

DIVISION LISTS:
> 1713 (1) voted for Sir Richard Levinge (**1230**) for Speaker.
> 1721 (2) voted against a national bank.

ESTATES/RESIDENCE: Mote, Co. Roscommon. He had land in the baronies of Mohill and Leitrim, and in Longford, Co. Longford, and Roscommon, Co. Roscommon. About 1720 the Galey estates, on the banks of the Shannon, amounted to 649 acres and Sir Edward had also lands in Co. Limerick, about 683 acres of which he apparently wished to sell in the mid-1720s. His estimated income in 1713 was £1,200. In 1703 the Crown rental showed some composition rents in Athlone, Ballintober and Roscommon. His will, dated 1719, was proved in 1730.

There are various interrelated branches of this family, which it is sometimes difficult to sort out. In 1618, William Crofton was granted fairs at Templehouse, *alias* Feagh Temple.

SOURCES: PRONI T/3411; LC 2208, LC 2247 and LC 2254; *CJ Ire.* (Bradley ed.) [3 May 1716]; GEC *B*; McCracken thesis; Burke *PB* (1903) p. 394; PRONI T/3411 Blenheim Papers; *Index to Irish Privy Counsellors, 1711–1910*; C. Dalton (ed.), *English Army Lists and Commission Registers, 1661–1714* (London, 1896), vol. 3 p. 65 [says Edward Crofton, Ensign in Sir Robert Peyton's Regiment of Foot 10 June 1689; this is probably a relative]; *The Dublin Gazette*, 25 Nov. 1729; Parliamentary Lists, 1695 (1), 1696 (1), 1706 (1), 1711 (3), 1713 (2).

0522 CROFTON, Rt Hon. Sir Edward

MP for Roscommon B. 1713–14, 1715–27–39

> b. 25 May 1687; d. 11 Nov. 1739 in Lyons, France
> HONOURS: PC, sworn 26 Oct. 1733, 1734; suc. as 3rd Baronet 1729.
> FAMILY/BACKGROUND: Eldest son of Rt Hon. Sir Edward Crofton, 2nd Baronet (**0521**), and Catherine, dau. of Rt Hon. Sir Oliver St George (**1842**).
> MARRIED: [4 Mar. 1711] his cousin Mary (d. 10 Feb. 1758), dau. of Anthony Nixon of Dublin.
> CHILDREN: Sir Edward, 4th Baronet (**0523**); Catherine m. [9 Sept. 1743] Sir Marcus Lowther-Crofton (**1275**).
> EDUCATION: ?Entered Oxford (Christ Church) 23

Feb. 1704, aged 15 years.
CAREER/OCCUPATION: High Sheriff of Co. Roscommon 1723; *Trustee of the Linen Manufacture for Leinster 1732–d.

POLITICAL ACTIVITY: This MP was not a very active parliamentarian. He came into parliament in 1713 and was designated as a Whig. On 3 October 1723 he complained of being disturbed in his possession of the lands of Tullaroe, Corbally, Balymurry and Corray, Co. Roscommon. He was nominated for only three committees between 1715 and 1726 and four committees between 1731 and 1739.

ESTATES/RESIDENCE: Mote and Galey estate, Co. Roscommon, 649 acres c. 1720.

SOURCES: PRONI D/302; *CJ Ire.* vol. 5 p. 40; NLI 21 F 23 Crofton estate maps; McCracken thesis; *Alum. Oxon.*; Burke *PB* (1903) p. 394; *Index to Irish Privy Counsellors, 1711–1910*; *Almanacks*; *The Dublin Courant* 17 Nov. 1722, 25 July, 22 Aug. 1724; Parliamentary Lists, 1713 (2).

0523 CROFTON, Sir Edward

MP for Co. Roscommon 1735–45

b. 12 Apr. 1713; d. 26 Mar. 1745
HONOURS: Suc. as 4th Baronet 1739.
FAMILY/BACKGROUND: Son of Rt Hon. Edward Crofton, 3rd Baronet (0522) and Mary, dau. of Anthony Nixon.
MARRIED: [17 June 1741] Martha (b. 23 Apr. 1719; d. July 1777), dau. of Joseph Damer (0577); (she m. (2) Ezekiel Nesbitt MD of Bath).
CHILDREN: *d.s.p.*
EDUCATION: School: Mr Hutchinson, Dublin; entered TCD 19 May 1730.
CAREER/OCCUPATION: High Sheriff of Co. Roscommon 1734; Governor of Co. Roscommon Oct. 1735; *Commissioner of the Tillage Act for Connaught 1735, 1739–43.

POLITICAL ACTIVITY: Like his father, he does not appear to have been a very active MP. He was listed for five committees between 1735 and 1740.

ADDITIONAL INFORMATION: A foundation member of the Dublin Society, 1731.

ESTATES/RESIDENCE: Mote, Co. Roscommon.

SOURCES: PRONI D/302; McCracken thesis; *Ir. Gen.*

vol. 5 no. 4 (1977) p. 485, H. F. Morris, 'Ramsey's Waterford Chronicle, 1777'; Berry *RDS* pp. 24–7; *Almanacks*; *GM* (Exshaw's edition) Mar. 1745; GEC B; *Pue's Occurrences* 25 Oct. 1735; *The Dublin Newsletter* 16 June 1741.

0524 CROFTON, Sir Edward

MP for Co. Roscommon 1775–6–83–90–7 [n.d.e. 1769, 1776]

b. 1746; d. 30 Sept. 1797 at Hot Wells, Bristol (where he had gone in a declining state of health and died of a rapid consumption)
HONOURS: Suc. as 2nd Baronet 16 Jan. 1784.
FAMILY/BACKGROUND: Son of Sir Marcus Lowther-Crofton (1275) and Catherine (b. 11 Jan. 1751; d. 12 Aug. 1817), dau. of Rt Hon. Sir Edward Crofton, 3rd Baronet (0522).
MARRIED: [13 Apr. 1767] Anne (d. 1817), o. dau. and h. of Thomas Croker of Co. Kildare (cr. Baroness Crofton 1798).
CHILDREN: Edward (b. 23 Oct. 1778; d. 8 Jan. 1816), 3rd Baronet, m. [1801] Charlotte, dau. of John Stewart, 7th Earl of Galloway; Rev. Henry Thomas Marcus; Vice-Admiral George Alfred (b. 1785; d. 23 Feb. 1858); Capt. William Gorges (Coldstream Guards) (d. 1814, killed at Bayonne); Caroline (d. 1 Sept. 1858); Louisa (d. 1805), m. [1803] Gen. Sir Peregrine Maitland; Frances (d. 1831), m. [1802] St George Caulfeild of Donamon Castle, Co. Roscommon; Harriet (d. 6 July 1837), m. James Caulfeild of Drumcairne; Augusta (d. 1832) m. James Caulfeild RN.
CAREER/OCCUPATION: High Sheriff of Co. Roscommon 1773; Governor of Roscommon Aug. 1782; *Joint Governor 1783–d.; *Commissioner of the Tillage Act for Leinster 1784.
MILITARY: Lieutenant-Colonel of Roscommon Militia 1797; Captain in Roscommon Cavalry Dec. 1796; a delegate for Co. Roscommon to the Volunteer Convention of 1783.

POLITICAL ACTIVITY: He stood unsuccessfully for Co. Roscommon in 1768, when his election was contested on the grounds that he and his followers had provoked a riot; in 1769 the House decided, 94 to 49 votes, that the said riot was 'stirred up and raised by the friends of Edward Crofton or his agent'. He subsequently distinguished himself for his zeal in repressing the rural riots in the counties of Galway and Roscommon.

He was first returned for Co. Roscommon in 1775 in the by-election following the death of John French (**0831**). Returned again in the 1776 general election, he was temporarily declared not duly elected after a colourful double election campaign – the House of Commons declared the first election void. The dominant interests in Co. Roscommon were the Croftons, the Frenchs, the Kings and the Mahons, while the Sandfords controlled the borough of Roscommon – a control that Sir Edward Crofton later challenged. Denis Bowes Daly (**0571**) was called in to adjudicate the respective claims and decided in favour of the Sandfords, although Sir Edward continued to press his claim.

He was a government supporter who, it was alleged in the 1780s, 'does not want anything'. However, a year later he was described as having a 'good property. Moderate, but his support very doubtful'; by 1780 he was definitely 'against'. He appears to have been wooed from his hostility, at least temporarily, by the Duke of Portland.

An enthusiastic Volunteer, he represented the county at the National Convention in 1783. Again returned for Co. Roscommon in 1783, he was declared in 1784 to be 'always in opposition to Government. Violent and intemperate' and, in 1785, he opposed the Commercial Propositions. It was considered that in Co. Roscommon 'The popular interest prevails.' In 1790 an opposition commentator wrote that 'Sir Edward Crofton, Bt, one of the present Members for this County is a respectable County gentleman, of good sense and some information, who speaks in Parliament, not, it will be allowed, with much eloquence, but with firmness and decision, which characters have uniformly marked his parliamentary conduct. What effect they will have in recommending him to the favour of his constituents, it is not easy to conjecture but, most probably, private politics more than public patriotism will determine his future success.' Sir Edward continued to represent the county until his death in 1797.

DIVISION LISTS:

1777 (1) voted for Grattan's (**0895**) motion for retrenchment.

1778 (1) voted for Grattan's motion for retrenchment.

1778 (2) voted for the Popery Bill.

1779 (2) voted for a six-months Loan Bill.

1780 (2) voted for Yelverton's (**2268**) motion to modify Poynings' Law.

1780 (3) voted for the Tenantry Bill.

1783 (1) voted for Flood's (**0762**) motion for parliamentary reform.

1784 (1) voted for a committee on the Reform Bill.

1784 (4) voted against the address to His Grace the Duke of Rutland.

1785 (1) voted against the Commercial Propositions.

1786 (1) voted for the rights of grand juries.

1786 (2) voted for Forbes's (**0778**) motion on retrenchment.

1787 (1) voted for a Pension Bill.

1788 (1) voted for Hartley's (**0979**) motion against the Dublin police.

1788 (2) voted for Forbes's motion for limiting pensions.

1789 (1) voted for a Regency.

1790 (1) voted for Grattan's motion for reducing the influence of the Crown.

1790 (2) voted for Ponsonby (**1709**) on the Election of a Speaker.

1791 (1) voted for Curran's (**0560**) resolution against the sale of peerages.

1791 (2) voted for Grattan's motion for the exercise of free trade.

1791 (3) voted for Grattan's motion to abolish the Dublin Police.

ADDITIONAL INFORMATION: A member of the RDS from 1775. A member of the National Convention in 1784. A member of the Whig Club, 1790.

ESTATES/RESIDENCE: Mote, Co. Roscommon; 14 Henrietta Street, Dublin. Lands in Co. Roscommon and Co. Limerick. About 1783 the Croftons owned Galbally, Keelogues, Askeaton Mill, etc. – 2,768 acres at a rental of £1,393 in Co. Limerick. The 'representatives of Colonel Taylor' were their tenants of Castle Ireland. About 1783 the Galey etc. estate in Roscommon consisted of 5,090 acres of arable and pasture and 1,215 of bog and mountain, at a rental of £2,556. The total rental, including estates in Co. Sligo and Co. Limerick, was £4,483. Sir Edward was said to have married an heiress, Anne Croker, whose father had been a Six Clerk in the Court of Chancery.

SOURCES: PRONI D/302; NLI MS 5904, NLI 21 F 23 Crofton estate maps; Ellis thesis; Burke *PB* (1903) pp. 394–5; McDowell, *Irish Public Opinion, 1750–1800*, p. 107; Johnston, *Gt B. & Ire.*, p. 142; *CJ Ire.* (Grierson ed.) 22 Dec. 1777 [reports the findings of the Election Committee for Co. Roscommon: which are that Edward Crofton is not duly elected and that the Speaker issue a new writ for Co. Roscommon]; D. Englefield, *The Printed Records of the Parliament of Ireland 1613–1800* (1978), p. 45 [this contains a guide to the microfilm records of the Ire. Parl. – the report of the 1777 select committee on the Roscommon election is on microfilm, reel 46 (Trans-Media Publishing Co., New York)]; *BNL* 22–6 Jan. 1790; *FJ* 14–16 Oct. 1783, 22 Dec. 1796; *DJ* 12 Oct. 1797; Parliamentary Lists, 1776 (1), (2), (3), 1777 (1), 1778 (1), 1780 (1), 1782 (1), 1783 (1), (3), 1784 (1), (2), 1785 (1), (2), (3), (4), 1787 (1), 1788 (1), 1789 (1), 1790 (1), 1793 (1), 1794 (2).

ferment. He was known as 'Little Hugh' because he was only 4 feet tall. He was remarkably pious.

ESTATES/RESIDENCE: Mohill, Co. Leitrim. In 1622 James I granted Henry Crofton lands and a market in Mohill. In 1617 Edward Crofton was granted fairs at Ballysodare, Co. Sligo. The MP's son, Sir Morgan Crofton, had *c.* 1760 an estate in Counties Leitrim, Longford and Roscommon, with a rental of £1,270, plus a 349 acre demesne worth £206.

SOURCES: TCD/482 Crofton Papers, Abstract of M. Crofton's estate and fortune (*c.* 1760); McCracken thesis [says he married while still a minor Anne daughter of George Crofton of Lisnadern]; *HMC Ormonde* (1920) new ser. vol. 8 p. 326; *JRSAI* vol. 38 (1908) p. 387, J. Meehan, 'Catalogue of the High Sheriffs of the County of Leitrim for the Year 1605 to the Year 1800'.

0525 CROFTON, Hugh

MP for Co. Leitrim 1743–60

b. ?1690; d. 20 Oct. 1767
FAMILY/BACKGROUND: Only surviving son of Thomas Crofton (d. *c.* 1743) and (m. Nov. 1707) Bridget, dau. of Hugh Morgan of Cottlestown.
MARRIED: [June 1729] Anne, dau. of George Crofton of Lisnadern.
CHILDREN: Thomas (*d.s.p.* Aug. 1759), m. Rachel, dau. of Robert Sandford; Sir Morgan, 1st Baronet (b. 25 Mar. 1733), m. [19 Aug. 1761] Jane (d. July 1797), yst dau. of Lieut.-Col. Henri d'Abzac; Elizabeth, m. William Percy.
CAREER/OCCUPATION: High Sheriff of Co. Leitrim 1737.

POLITICAL ACTIVITY: He was a member of the Country party in the early 1750s, voting for the expulsion of Arthur Jones-Nevill (**1125**) and against the 1753 Money Bill. He was listed for 26 committees between 1745 and 1759.

DIVISION LISTS:
1749 (1) voted against the election of James Digges La Touche (♦♦♦♦).
1753 (1) voted for the expulsion of Arthur Jones-Nevill (**1125**).
1753 (2) voted against the Money Bill.

ADDITIONAL INFORMATION: On 22 January 1711 he wrote to the Duke of Ormonde asking for pre-

0526 CROFTON, Sir Hugh

MP for Tulsk 1786–90

b. 17 July 1763; d. 6 Jan. 1834
HONOURS: Suc. as 2nd Baronet 1802.
FAMILY/BACKGROUND: Son of Sir Morgan Crofton, 1st Baronet, and Jane (d. 1797), dau. of Lieut.-Col. Henri d'Abzac.
MARRIED: [4 June 1787] Frances (d. 27 Mar. 1847), yst dau. of Ralph Smyth of Barbavilla, Co. Westmeath.
CHILDREN: Sir Morgan George, 3rd Baronet, m. [1812] Emily, dau. of Rt Hon. Denis Daly (**0570**); Lieut. Ralph (81st Regiment) (*d.s.p. ante* 1823), m. [1813] Elizabeth, dau. and co-h. of Thomas Ripon of Jersey; Rev. Henry William, m. (1) Marcia Anastasia, dau. and co-h. of Mathias Erberry, (2) [1840] Marianne Amelia (d. 1847), dau. of Rev. James Cazalet; Rev. Augustus (d. 1861), m. [1828] Charlotte, dau. of John Kirwan of Moyne, Co. Galway; Charles (d. unm.); Parsons (b. 1805 d. 1884), m. [2 Aug. 1831] Anne Palmer, dau. of Edward Westby; Frances, m. Rev. Arthur Hyde; Jane, m. [27 Sept. 1838] Ross Mahon; Barbara (d. 1863), m. Edward Rotherman of Crossdrum; Anne Digby, m. (17 Aug. 1836) Vice-Admiral Robert Jocelyn Otway of Castle Otway, Co. Tipperary.
EDUCATION: School: Dr Adamson; entered TCD 12 Nov. 1779, aged 16 years; Lincoln's Inn 5 July 1780; BA 1785, LLD *hon. caus.* 1789.
CAREER/OCCUPATION: *Treasurer of the Charitable Loan Society 1790–4; High Sheriff of Co.

Leitrim 1793, Governor 1795–8; Governor of the Foundling Hospital and Workhouse 1798–1800 (f.).

MILITARY: Captain in Mohill Cavalry Oct. 1796.

POLITICAL ACTIVITY: He was returned in place of William Caulfeild (**0377**), deceased, and sworn on 6 March 1786. During the four years that he was in parliament he was solidly in opposition and reputedly under the influence of Lord Charlemont. He appears to have been a low-key MP, and not much is known of his short parliamentary career.

DIVISION LISTS:

1786 (1) voted for the rights of grand juries.
1786 (2) voted for Forbes's (**0778**) motion on retrenchment.
1787 (1) voted for a Pension Bill.
1789 (1) voted for a Regency.

ESTATES/RESIDENCE: Mohill Castle, Co. Leitrim; Grafton Street, Dublin.

SOURCES: PRONI D/302; Burke *PB* (1903) pp. 396, 425; *Alum. Dub.*; *The Records of the Honourable Society of Lincoln's Inn* (Lincoln's Inn, 1896) vol. 1 p. 497; *Almanacks*, *FJ* 20 Oct. 1796; Parliamentary Lists, 1783 (2), 1785 (4), 1787 (1), 1788 (1), 1789 (1), 1790 (1).

0527 CROFTS, George

MP for Charleville Sept.–Oct. 1692 (expelled 11 Oct. 1692)

b. *c.* 1640; d. 1698
FAMILY/BACKGROUND: Son of George Crofts of Co. Cork and Mary.
MARRIED: Sarah [   ].
CHILDREN: George, m. [1683] Mary, dau. of Capt. Thomas Wills; Mary, m. John Beare of Co. Cork; and other children.

POLITICAL ACTIVITY: Parliament met on 6 October 1692 and he was expelled on 11 October. The background to his expulsion illustrates one of the grey areas of the period. He was said to have fled to England in 1689, but in a petition for pardon of 23 June 1692, he claimed that he and his family were Protestants and that he had sent his only son, George, to England where he became a lieutenant in Sir Edward Dering's Regiment and re-mained so at the date of petition. Crofts claimed that he had remained to protect his property and cattle against the depredations of rapparees, and was a lieutenant of a troop active in suppressing them. He stated that he was 'a great dealer in cattle' and had a stock of between £5,000 and £6,000 on several farms.

Crofts was imprisoned at Cork by the Williamites but, he said, supplied the Williamite army with provisions through his agent. He offered up his commission to the Williamites and had, after the surrender of Cork, 'behaved himself much to the advantage of the Protestants, by guiding all parties for the destruction of the enemy' while serving as a lieutenant of militia. His pardon was issued on 22 September 1692. However, on his return to parliament, Thomas Brodrick (**0243**) with other MPs laid information before the Commons that Crofts had joined 'with the late rebels in many notorious instances'. The evidence against him included a letter from Crofts to one of these Irish rebels in August 1691. The House found him 'a notorious betrayer of the English and Protestant interest and laws of this Kingdom, during the late rebellion'. After being censured before the House 'on his Knees', he was expelled and placed in the custody of the Serjeant-at-Arms. He was released from custody on an apology and payment of fees. He did not come into parliament again.

ESTATES/RESIDENCE: Churchtown, Co. Cork. In his petition for pardon he claimed that he had settled £60 p.a. of free estate on his son at his marriage.

SOURCES: NAI Index to Marriage Licence Bonds of Cork and Ross Diocese; *Cal. SP Dom. 1691–2* (London, 1900) pp. 334, 458, *1695* (London, 1908) p. 212; Burke *LGI* (1904) p. 121, *IFR* (1976) p. 293 (says his father [*sic* – ?he] was born *ante* 1643); Simms' cards; Cork MPs; *CJ Ire.* (Grierson ed.) vol. 2 part 1 p. 13; C. Dalton (ed.), *English Army Lists and Commission Registers, 1661–1714* (London, 1896), [says George Crofts (?son), Lieutenant in Sir David Colyear's Regiment of Foot 1 Aug. 1692. He was out of the regiment *ante*-1694]; J. J. Howard (ed.), *Miscellanea Genealogica et Heraldica*, vol. 3 new ser. (1880) p. 182 [gives a relevant George Crofts of Buttevant, Co. Cork whose daughter Mary married Christopher Waggett in 1696, possibly a granddau. of the MP, and although she would have been very young, such marriages were unusual but not unknown].

0528 CROKER, John

MP for Kilmallock 1723–7

b. c. ?1690; d. 6 Nov. 1751
FAMILY/BACKGROUND: Son of John Croker of
Ballynagard and Mary (m. 10 Dec. 1679), dau.
of John Bucknor of The Grange, Co. Limerick.
MARRIED: Anne, dau. of Andrew Rickards.
CHILDREN: Edward; Elizabeth; Rickards;
Abraham; Andrew; Dillon.
CAREER/OCCUPATION: Sheriff of Co. Limerick
1737.

POLITICAL ACTIVITY: He was returned for Kilmallock
after the death of George King (1152) in July
1722. He was listed for one committee in 1723
and one in 1724. Croker was one of the Memorialists seeking to revive attempts to explain or revoke the clause in the Act of Queen Anne's reign
for naturalising foreign Protestants, which gave
favour to the children of natural-born subjects. It
was felt that this could undermine Protestant interests in Ireland by allowing the return of the
children of papists who had served James II in
Ireland before fleeing to Europe.

ESTATES/RESIDENCE: Ballynagarde (Ballynagrade), Co.
Limerick. In 1724, John Croker was granted fairs at
Croom.

SOURCES: PRONI T/559 vol. 17 p. 34, Burke, extract
pedigrees; PRONI T/580 pp. 176g, 176h, TSPI 1723–
1724; Burke IFR (1976) p. 295 [died 6 Nov. 1751];
Eustace, Abstracts of Wills, vol. 2 p. 48 [gives his will
signed 24 Sept. 1751 and registered Dec. 1751, children, Edward, Rickards, Abraham, Andrew, Dillon];
G. Taylor and A. Skinner, Maps of the Roads of Ireland,
p. 184 [marks Ballynagard off the road from Limerick
to Bruff]; Alum. Dub.; Vicars, Prerog. Wills; King's Inn
Admission Papers, 1607–1867; H. A. C. Sturgess, Register of Admissions to the Honourable Society of the Middle Temple (London, 1949) vol. 1 p. 331; BNL 4 Sept.
1750 [reports the death of another John Croker, a lawyer, on 28 Aug. 1750 at his house at Loughboy, but,
although there is an element of doubt, he is unlikely to
be this MP]; Dublin Gazette 27 Nov. 1736.

0529 CROKER, John

MP for Fethard (Tipperary) 1768–76

b. 6 Apr. 1730; d. 11 Feb. 1795

FAMILY/BACKGROUND: Eldest son of Edward
Croker and Elizabeth, dau. of Henry Prittie of
Dunalley Castle, Co. Tipperary.
MARRIED: [18 Apr. 1753] Mary, dau. of Col.
Richard Pennefather (1654).
CHILDREN: Edward, m. [1783] Margaret Anne,
dau. of Richard Hare of Co. Kerry; Rev. Richard,
m. Mary, dau. of James Gutherie of Co. Limer-
ick; Gen. John, m. Honora, dau. of John
O'Grady of Co. Limerick; William, m. Margaret,
dau. of Col. Christopher O'Brien of Co. Clare;
Henry, m. Harriet o. dau. and h. of Arthur
Dillon of Co. Cork; Sarah, m. [Apr. 1786]
Lancelot Charles Sandys of Queen's County;
Charity, m. [1789] John O'Grady of Co.
Limerick; Eliza, m. Edward Croker of Co.
Limerick.
CAREER/OCCUPATION: Freeman of Fethard
(Tipperary) 1745; High Sheriff of Co. Limerick
1755, of Co. Tipperary 1755; Magistrate of
Cashel 1762; Surveyor of Excise for Galway
1776–8.

POLITICAL ACTIVITY: At the Co. Limerick election
of 1761, Hugh Massy (1355) was returned having polled 453 votes, along with Hon. Thomas
Southwell (1971), who polled 418. The unsuccessful candidates were John Croker and
Windham Quin (1754), who polled 255 and 225
votes respectively. It was said that 'Mr Croker resides in the County of Limerick, has little or no
estate in this county [Tipperary], it is thought he
was brought in to represent Fethard by Mr Prittie
and the Clutterbuck family who have an interest
in the Borough.'

He purchased his seat for Fethard, Co. Tipperary assisted by the influence of his aunt Margaret
(Prittie) Clutterbuck and the Prittie family; his
wife's family, the Pennefathers, were also considered to have some influence in the borough. His
mother and Sir Henry Cavendish's (0380) second
wife Catherine (Prittie) Meade were sisters, and it
was thought that Sir Henry might be able to influence him. Sir Henry was Teller of the Exchequer and Croker was indebted to him. Despite the
fact that Lord Townshend gave his son an ensigncy
and possibly his nephew a commission, he proved
an unreliable government supporter. By 1774 it
was noted that he seldom attended and that 'his
successor to Fethard is already nominated', while
in 1775 a government list declared him to be 'very
unsteady in his support and never to be depended

on'. He did not come in at the general election of 1776.

DIVISION LISTS:

> 1771 (1) voted for Lord Townshend as Lord Lieutenant.
> 1771 (2) voted against Sir Lucius O'Brien's (**1558**) motion for retrenchment.
> 1771 (3) voted against the amendment to the Revenue Bill.
> 1772 (1) absent.

ADDITIONAL INFORMATION: On a list of money borrowed from the government through Sir Henry Cavendish (**0380**), John and Henry Croker are noted as having borrowed on 23 October 1756 a bond of £600. In May 1763 he inherited the fortune of Richard Croker of Limerick.

ESTATES/RESIDENCE: Ballynagarde (Ballynagrade), Co. Limerick.

SOURCES: PRONI D/302; EC 3357; Michael O'Donnell Esq. [says there is some confusion as to who his father was, whether it was John or Edward Croker]; Burke *PB* (1900) [gives Edward]; PRONI T/559 vol. 17 p. 36, Burke, extract pedigrees [says his wife's name was Sarah]; PRONI T/3019/6457/464 Wilmot Papers; PRONI MIC/465/1 R. Ffolliott, *Biographical Notices*, 1756– 1827; Burke *LGI* p. 122, *IFR* (1976) pp. 295–6; M. Lenihan, *Limerick, Its History and Antiquities* (Dublin, 1866), p. 744; *Ir. Gen.* vol. 4 no. 6 (1973) pp. 616–24, W. G. Skehan, 'Freemen of the Corporation of Fethard, Co. Tipperary' [says a family bible gives his date of birth as 6 Apr. 1730]; *Almanacks*; *DJ* 12–16 May 1761; Parliamentary Lists, 1769 (1), 1771 (1), 1772 (1), (2), 1773 (1), (2), 1774 (1), 1775 (1), 1783 (3).

0530 CROMIE, Sir Michael

MP for Ballyshannon 1776–83–90–7

> b. *c.* 1744; d. 14 May 1824 in Paris
> HONOURS: Knight 1772; cr. Baronet 3 Aug. 1776.
> FAMILY/BACKGROUND: Son and heir of William Cromie and Anne, dau. of [ ] Fish.
> MARRIED: [5 Mar. 1774] Gertrude (d. 3 May 1796), O. surviving dau. and h. of Ford Lambert, 5th Earl of Cavan.
> CHILDREN: o. s. and h. William Lambert, m. [1816] Anne Rachael o. surv. dau. and h. of Sir William Hicks, 7th Baronet; dau., m. [1801] [ ] West.

EDUCATION: School: Mr Norris; entered TCD 30 Mar. 1761; Middle Temple 25 June 1764.
CAREER/OCCUPATION: Sheriff of Co. Dublin 1777. In 1790 he was head of a short-lived bank in Liverpool, Sir Michael Cromie, Bt, Pownall and Hartman.

POLITICAL ACTIVITY: He was a protégé and client of Thomas Conolly (**0459**), who returned him for Ballyshannon in 1776. Cromie's manners were considered pleasing and his private character amiable. He spoke seldom but acceptably in parliament, where he followed Conolly's line in politics and, so long as it was in Conolly's possession, he was returned for the borough of Ballyshanon. Conolly sold it in 1797 to Lord Belmore, and Cromie was not returned in the 1797 election.

In 1784 Cromie was described as 'a young man of very small fortune and no occupation and wishes provision ... brought into Parliament by Mr Conolly and hopes through his means to obtain an office at £3 or £400 p.a.' The following year Conolly went into opposition and Cromie with him, who 'forfeits thereby his claim to office and emolument'. He voted against the Commercial Resolutions and thereafter solidly in opposition, following Conolly's lead. In February 1787, following the collapse of the Commercial Resolutions, he proposed unsuccessfully that the expenses due to Edward Cooke (**0468**), Robert Brooke and others for going to London to give information on the state of Irish industry be disallowed. In 1790 he was the head of an ephemeral bank at Liverpool styled 'Sir Michael Cromie, Bt, Pownall and Hartman'. His partners successively went bankrupt, and it came to an end in 1801. Subsequently he took up residence in France.

DIVISION LISTS:

> 1778 (2) voted for the Popery Bill.
> 1779 (2) voted against a six-months Loan Bill.
> 1780 (1) voted against Grattan's (**0895**) declaration of the rights of Ireland.
> 1780 (2) voted against Yelverton's (**2268**) motion to modify Poynings' Law.
> 1780 (4) voted for the Perpetual Mutiny Bill.
> 1783 (1) voted against Flood's (**0762**) motion for parliamentary reform.

1784 (1) voted against a committee on the Reform Bill.

1785 (1) voted against the Commercial Propositions.

1786 (2) voted for Forbes's (**0778**) motion on retrenchment.

1787 (1) voted for a Pension Bill.

1789 (1) voted for a Regency.

1790 (1) voted for Grattan's motion for reducing the influence of the Crown.

1790 (2) voted for Ponsonby (**1709**) on the Election of a Speaker.

1791 (1) voted for Curran's (**0560**) resolution against the sale of peerages.

1791 (2) voted for Grattan's motion for the exercise of free trade.

1791 (3) voted for Grattan's motion to abolish the Dublin police.

1795 (1) voted for a Short Money Bill.

ADDITIONAL INFORMATION: Cromie's father-in-law was Grand Master of the Grand Lodge of Irish Freemasons, 1766–9.

The son and grandson of Dublin merchants. His father was described in the mid-1770s as 'late a wine merchant who made a fortune'. While still a student at TCD, he was made Knight Bachelor at the Castle.

He was a member of the Co. Kildare knot of the Friendly Brothers of St Patrick, an anti-duelling society which included many of the socially prominent in the county, for instance the Duke of Leinster (**0745**) and Cromie's patron, Thomas Conolly.

After the failure of the bank, Sir Michael Cromie, Bt, Pownall and Hartman, Cromie fled the country, and in 1811 had been resident in France for many years. He (long before his death) alienated the estate of Stacunmy. It was reported that 'In the year 1876 [?1806], the said Sir Michael Cromie had been leading a wandering life abroad for many years ... his only son William Lambert was seeking his fortune at the English spas.' The son did elope with and marry an heiress, but such was the parental opposition to the match that he saw little of his wife's money.

ESTATES/RESIDENCE: Stacunmy, Leixlip, Co. Kildare; North Cumberland Street, Dublin.

SOURCES: PRONI MIC315/1/1, 9/52 Blackwood Pedigrees; RCBL P277/1/3, Parish Registers of St Mary's, Dublin; GEC *P* [calls his wife Elizabeth]; *IMC Leinster III* pp. 317, 319; GEC *B.*; *Register of Admissions to the Honourable Society of the Middle Temple* vol. 1 (London, 1949) p. 361; *Alum. Dub.*; Mrs William Hicks Beach, *A Cotswold Family: Hicks and Hicks Beach* (London, 1909), pp. 353–4; J. Kelly, *Prelude to Union* (Cork, 1992), pp. 232–3; J. Kelly, '*That Damn'd thing called Honour': Duelling in Ireland 1570–1860* (Cork, 1995), p. 66; J. H. Lepper and P. Crossle, *History of the Grand Lodge of Free and Accepted Masons of Ireland* (Dublin, 1925), vol. 1; Parliamentary Lists, 1776 (1), (2), (3), 1777 (1), 1778 (1), 1780 (1), 1782 (1), 1783 (1), (2), 1784 (1), (2), (3), (4), 1787 (1), 1788 (1), 1789 (1), 1790 (1), 1791 (1), 1793 (1), 1799 (1).

0531 CROOKSHANK, Alexander

MP for Belfast 1777–83–4

b. 30 June 1736; d. 10 Dec. 1813
FAMILY/BACKGROUND: Eldest son of William Crookshank of Dublin and Rebecca, dau. of John Tandy of Co. Meath.
MARRIED: [July 1768] Esther, dau. of Alderman William Kennedy, Mayor of Londonderry.
CHILDREN: George (**0532**); William; and 'a large family'.
EDUCATION: Middle Temple 1762; called to the Irish Bar.
CAREER/OCCUPATION: Commissioner of Bankruptcy 1772–6; King's Counsel 1781; Justice of the Common Pleas 14 Jan. 1784 in addition to the existing number; 4th Justice 1784–92; 3rd Justice 1794–1800 (f.); *listed in Judges and Barristers 1789–1800 (f.); *Commissioner of Appeals 1795–7; *Bencher of the Honorable Society of King's Inns 1798–d.; *listed in Attornies of the King's Bench, Common Pleas and Court of Exchequer 1798–1800 (f.). A Justice of Assizes for Connaught, Lent 1784; Leinster, Lent 1786; NE Ulster, Lent 1787; Connaught, Summer 1787; Leinster, Lent 1788, Summer 1788; Connaught, Lent 1789; Leinster, Summer 1789; Connaught, Summer 1790, Lent 1790; Leinster, Lent 1791; Munster, Summer 1792; NW Ulster, Lent 1794; Munster, Lent 1796; Connaught, Summer 1797; NW Ulster, Lent 1798, Lent 1799, Lent 1800, Summer 1800.
MILITARY: Second Lieutenant in Attornies Corps, Nov. 1796.

POLITICAL ACTIVITY: Crookshank was a lawyer of moderate abilities returned by Lord Donegall for Belfast at the 1776 election, and he followed his patron's political lead. Lord Donegall opposed Lord Lieutenant Buckinghamshire and supported Lord Lieutenant Carlisle, and Crookshank did likewise. In 1783 he was described as: 'a lawyer and King's Counsel. Returned and guided by Lord Donegall, was in opposition till Lord Carlisle's administration, which Lord Donegall having signified an intention of supporting, he voted with and assisted uniformly. Mr Crookshank speaks in the House but not with much effect. A decent, respectable man. Has a large family and is anxious for preferment in the law line. Will probably be again returned. Is returned. Was insulted and burnt in effigy by the inhabitants of Belfast for not receiving a test from them, although they were not his constituents, the right of election being confined to the sovereign and burgesses. Just made a judge.' This illustrates the power of the patron, the impotence of the inhabitants in a thriving and active community, and the rewards of obedience.

He was one of the earliest judges to take a firm stand against the practice of duelling when, in 1788, the notorious duellist Beauchamp Bagenal (0071) accused his neighbour of challenging *him* to a duel. Bagenal *v.* Weld came before Crookshank, who was the judge at the Carlow assizes, and after he delivered 'an excellent charge' he sentenced Weld to a month in jail and a fine of £70. The challenge had occurred because Bagenal had cropped the tails of some of Weld's trespassing pigs.

DIVISION LISTS:

1777 (2) voted against the Trade Embargo.
1778 (1) voted for Grattan's (0895) motion for retrenchment.
1778 (2) voted against the Popery Bill.
1779 (2) voted for a six-months Loan Bill.
1780 (2) voted for Yelverton's (2268) motion to modify Poynings' Law.
1780 (3) voted for the Tenantry Bill.
1783 (1) voted against Flood's (0762) motion for parliamentary reform.

ADDITIONAL INFORMATION: The sitting member's nominee on the Swords election committee, 6

December 1777. One of the judges on special commission after the rebellion of 1798, resigned 1800. He received £2,000 compensation for the loss of offices at the Union.

ESTATES/RESIDENCE: Newtown Park, Blackrock, Co. Dublin; Cuffe Street and Leinster Street, Dublin.

SOURCES: PRONI T/559 vol. 17 p. 58, Burke, extract pedigrees; PRONI T/1075/27 Canon Leslie's notes; Ellis thesis; Hughes, *Pat. Officers*; IMC *King's Inns Admission Papers, 1607–1867*; Ball, *Judges*; *Memorials of the Dead* [a plaque erected in his memory says he died aged 79 years and his tombstone says he died aged 77 years!]; J. Kelly, *'That Damn'd thing called Honour': Duelling in Ireland 1570–1860* (Cork, 1995), pp. 150, 197; *Ir. Gen.* vol. 1 no. 10 (1941) p. 245, W. Clare, 'Irish Compensations and Pensions'; *Ir. Gen.* vol. 7 no. 2 (1987) p. 269, H. F. Morris, 'Finn's Leinster Journal 1768'; *Almanacks*; FJ 6–9 Dec. 1777, 6–9 Mar. 1784, 9–11 Mar. 1786, 3–6 Mar. 1787, 28–30 June 1787, 9–12 Feb. 1788, 12–14 June 1788, 26–8 Feb. 1789, 2–4 July 1789, 2–4 Mar. 1790, 1–3 July 1790, 10–12 Mar. 1791, 19–21 July 1792, 8 Mar. 1794, 18 Feb., 24 Nov. 1796, 5 Aug. 1797, 1 Mar. 1798, 9 Mar. 1799, 4 Jan., 10 July 1800; Parliamentary Lists, 1776 (1), 1778 (1), 1780 (1), 1782 (1), 1783 (1), (2), 1784 (1).

0532 CROOKSHANK, George

MP for Belfast 1797–1800; [Escheator of Ulster 29 Jan. 1800]

b. 26 Sept. 1770; d. 21 June 1831
FAMILY/BACKGROUND: Eldest son of Alexander Crookshank (0531) and Esther, dau. of William Kennedy of Co. Londonderry.
MARRIED: (1) Letitia, dau. of Rev. Luke Godfrey; (2) Anna Maria, dau. of J. Dyson.
CHILDREN: ?
EDUCATION: School: Mr Austen; entered TCD 2 Oct. 1785; Middle Temple 8 June 1786; BA 2 Oct. 1789; called to the Irish Bar 1792.
CAREER/OCCUPATION: *Listed in Judges and Barristers 1799 (f.).

POLITICAL ACTIVITY: He was returned for Belfast by the 1st Marquess of Donegall. He voted against the Union in 1799, but Lord Donegall died on 15 January 1799 and was succeeded by his spendthrift and erratic heir (0394), who eventually decided for the Union. In July 1799 Henry Alexander (0028), who acted as a go-between, reported that Donegall was 'a unionist, but determined from a variety of grievances to oppose Administration'; however, Alexander thought that he could be won over by being given permission to raise his own yeomanry corps of cavalry. Permission was given, and the following September Lord Donegall backed the pro-Union Co. Antrim address. Both of Lord Donegall's MPs for Belfast resigned. Edward May (**1380**), Lord Donegall's father-in-law and a zealous Unionist, replaced Alexander Hamilton (**0913**); he was sworn on 3 February 1800, while John Congreve (**0456**), a Belfast merchant, who replaced George Crookshank, was elected on 1 February 1800 but does not appear to have taken his seat.

DIVISION LISTS:
1799 (1) voted against the Union.

ESTATES/RESIDENCE: Co. Longford.

SOURCES: PRONI T/3166/1A Hartnell notes; O'Neill thesis; G. C. Bolton, *The Passing of the Irish Act of Union*, pp. 98, 175–6; *King's Inns Admission Papers, 1607–1867*; *Register of Admissions to the Honourable Society of the Middle Temple* (London, 1949) vol. 2 p. 400; Parliamentary Lists, 1799 (3), 1800 (3).

0533 CROSBIE, James

MP for Co. Kerry 1797–1800 [r. Tralee 1797], [UK] 1801–6, 1812–26

b. *c.* 1760; d. 20 Sept. 1836
FAMILY/BACKGROUND: Eldest son of Pierce Crosbie of Ballyheige Castle, Co. Kerry, and Frances, dau. of Rowland Bateman of Co. Kerry.
MARRIED: [1785] his cousin Elizabeth, dau. of Rowland Bateman (**0100**).
CHILDREN: Pierce, m. (1) [1815] Elizabeth Eleanor, dau. of Lieut.-Gen. John Michel of Dorset, (2) Elizabeth, dau. of Thomas William Sandes of Co. Kerry; James; Francis, m. Maria, dau. of Alderman Sir Richard Harte; Thomas; Letitia, m. Capt. William Meredith Twiss; Frances, m. Capt. Rowland Chute.
EDUCATION: School: Harrow 1770.
CAREER/OCCUPATION: Sheriff of Co. Kerry 1792–3, Joint Governor 1803–15, Governor 1815–32, Custos Rot. 1818–32.
MILITARY: Lieutenant-Colonel of Kerry Militia 1797, Colonel 1801.

POLITICAL ACTIVITY: He was the cousin of the 2nd Earl of Glandore (**0534**), who returned him to the Irish parliament. Glandore, a convinced Unionist, made Crosbie toe the line on the issue and he jointly seconded the address, but Glandore was too late in trying to secure an office for him as a reward. Glandore eventually, with some ill grace, resigned his colonelcy of the militia in Crosbie's favour. Crosbie, much to Glandore's chagrin, was appointed joint Governor of Co. Kerry with him in 1803. Glandore then made it clear that he would not support Crosbie again.

Part of Crosbie's intransigence may have been due to the fact that he was impoverished. In the British parliament, although he supported the Catholic cause on 14 May 1805, he was frequently absent and virtually silent. His attendance, always expensive for Irish MPs, improved after he inherited £3,000 p.a. from an uncle. He was pledged to the Catholic cause and would have risked his seat by not supporting it. However, Glandore's hostility ensured that he was not returned in 1826.

DIVISION LISTS:
1800 (1) voted for the Union.

ADDITIONAL INFORMATION: He was given plenary powers to transport rebels during the 1798 rebellion but did not exercise them.

He 'was once wrecked off the coast of Wales when returning from the [school] holidays and thereafter spent the winter holidays in England'. Crossing the Irish sea always entailed a certain amount of risk.

ESTATES/RESIDENCE: Ballyheige Castle, Co. Kerry. On his father's death he inherited an estate worth *c.* £300 p.a., but he received an estate of £3,000 p.a. from an uncle. According to Wakefield, Colonel Crosbie had a rental of £6,000 near Kerry Head. He was able to rebuild Ballyheige Castle 1806–12.

SOURCES: PRONI D/302; PRONI T/3166/1B Hartnell notes; O'Neill thesis; Jupp thesis; Burke *IFR* (1976) p. 302; Wakefield, *Account of Ire.*, vol. 1 p. 263; W. T. J. Gun, *The Harrow School Register, 1571–1800* (London, 1934) [says died 30 Sept.]; *HP 1790–1820*; Parliamentary Lists, 1799 (2), (3), 1800 (3).

0534 CROSBIE, Rt Hon. John

MP for Athboy 1775–6; Ardfert 1776–81 [r. Tralee 1776]

b. 25 May 1752; d. 23 Oct. 1815
HONOURS: PC, sworn 15 Jan. 1785.
PEERAGES: Styled Viscount Crosbie 1776–81; suc. as 2nd Earl of Glandore 1781; Rep. Peer 1801–15.
FAMILY/BACKGROUND: Son of Rt Hon. William Crosbie, 1st Earl of Glandore (0540) and Theodosia, dau. of John Bligh, 1st Earl of Darnley (0172).
MARRIED: [26 Nov. 1777] Diana, dau. of Rt Hon. Lord George Sackville (Germain), 1st Viscount Sackville (1835).
CHILDREN: *d.s.p.*
EDUCATION: School: Kilkenny school 18 Oct. 1763, aged 11 years; entered TCD 7 June 1768, BA 1771, MA *hon. caus.* 1772.
CAREER/OCCUPATION: Joint Master of the Rolls 1789–1801; Governor of Co. Kerry 1790–1800, Joint Governor 1803–15; Custos Rot. for Co. Kerry 1785–15; *Commissioner of the Tillage Act for Munster 1780–4.
MILITARY: Colonel of Co. Kerry Militia, 1793–1801.

POLITICAL ACTIVITY: In 1776 he was returned for the county and for the borough of Tralee. He supported government, and in 1777 was considered to be 'a young man of expectation', but in 1778 he was noted as an infrequent attender. He succeeded his father as 2nd Earl of Glandore in 1781, so that most of his political career was in the House of Lords. He controlled the borough of Ardfert and received £15,000 compensation for its disfranchisement at the Union. Although in 1782 Lord Glandore was considered to have 'a good estate', by 1788 he was reputed to be in such financial difficulties that 'He cannot afford to attend Parliament at present'. He was naturally 'expectant', and in 1789 he was made Joint Master of the Rolls. In 1790 the control of a borough was reckoned to 'bring in a sure £500 p.a.'.

He was 'a tolerable speaker, speaks *often* and *always* in support of administration. His manners are perfectly amiable and pleasing and, from the excellence of his private character, he is held in universal estimation.' In January 1799 he made a speech at the opening of parliament in which he praised the great benefits of the Union that Scotland enjoyed before moving an address in favour of an Irish Union. He became a representative peer at the Union.

DIVISION LISTS:
1779 (2) voted against a six-months Loan Bill.
1780 (1) voted against Grattan's (0895) declaration of the rights of Ireland.
1780 (2) voted for Yelverton's (2268) motion to modify Poynings' Law.
1780 (4) voted for the Perpetual Mutiny Bill.

ADDITIONAL INFORMATION: FRS, 1803; FSA. 1801; *member of the Royal Irish Academy, 1790; *Vice-President, 1799.

When the Master of the Rolls ceased to be a sinecure and became a judicial office, it passed from his hands and he was compensated by a pension of £1,307 6s 9d p.a.

His wife brought him a portion of £10,000 and, being over-fond of gaming and slow at paying her debts, became known as 'Owen (owing) Glendower'. Her proclivity probably contributed to his financial necessity, although her dowry was generous and she subsequently inherited from her father, Lord Sackville (1835).

ESTATES/RESIDENCE: Ardfert Abbey, Co. Kerry; Nassau Street, Dublin. In 1805 the estate had a rental of £3,677 and contained 54 townlands. Shortly after he inherited the earldom he petitioned for a private member's bill to vest lands in the Rt Hon. George, Lord Sackville, the Hon. & Rev. Maurice Crosbie, Dean of Limerick and Robert Day of the City of Dublin to raise £6,000 (plus a maximum of £500 costs) by demise, sale or mortgage of his estates, saving only the mansion house and the demesne lands of Ardfert.
Lands mainly in the baronies of Clanmaurice and Magunihy. In 1805, the estate had a rental of £3,677. According to Wakefield, Lord Glandore's rental was £7,000.

SOURCES: NLI MS 5033 (Glandore rental 1805); Wakefield, *Account of Ire.* vol. 1 p. 261; EC 45, 325, 915; Ellis thesis; GEC *P*; Burke *IFR* (1976) p. 299; *Index to Irish Privy Counsellors, 1711–1910*; A. P. W. Malcomson, *The Pursuit of the Heiress* (Belfast, 1982) p. 11; TCD Library 186s.38, Private Members Bills, no. 0533; *Cornwallis Corr.* vol. 3 [says incorrectly that he was born 25 May 1753 (1752) and died 20 Oct.

1815]; *JRSAI* vol. 45 (1924) pp. 55–67, T. U. Sadleir, 'The Kilkenny School Register (1685–1800)'; *Ir. Gen.* vol. 1 no. 10 (1941) p. 296, W. Clare, 'Irish Compensations and Pensions'; *Almanacks*; *FJ* 21–24 Feb. 1778, 25–27 Apr. 1793; Parliamentary Lists, 1776 (2), (3), 1777 (1), 1778 (1), 1780 (1), 1782 (1), 1783 (2), 1785 (2), 1787 (1), 1788 (1), 1790 (1), 1791 (1), 1793 (1), 1799 (1), (2), (3), (4).

0535 CROSBIE, John Gustavus

MP for Co. Kerry 1794–7

b. *ante* 1749; d. [6] July 1797
FAMILY/BACKGROUND: Eldest son of Lancelot Crosbie (**0536**) and his 2nd wife Mary, dau. of John Blennerhassett (**0167**).
MARRIED: [Oct. 1796] Catherine, dau. of William Blennerhassett of Ballyseedy, Co. Kerry.
CHILDREN: *d.s.p.*
CAREER/OCCUPATION: Sheriff of Co. Kilkenny 1770.

POLITICAL ACTIVITY: With Colonel Henry Arthur Herbert, he contested the county vacancy occasioned by the death of John Blennerhasset (**0169**) in 1794. The contest was nicely balanced and the result for Crosbie doubtful 'when, in the course of his canvass, Mr Crosbie took offence at some real or supposed breach of a promised neutrality on the part of the sitting member Sir Barry Denny (**0618**), a duel followed; the parties met in the demesne of Oakpark, and Sir Barry Denny was killed, being shot through the head at the first fire, and, as was said, by the haphazard aim of a man who had never before discharged a pistol in his life.' The immediate result of this tragedy was the return of Crosbie, but his period in parliament was brief, as 'Within less than a year [*sic* – actually three years] a vacancy again resulted from the death of Mr J. G. Crosbie by a fall from his horse, while riding home at night, a calamity which the enlightened populace did not fail to lay to the charge of "Sir Barry Denny's ghost!"'

ESTATES/RESIDENCE: Tubrid and Dunloe Castle, Co. Kerry. He was succeeded in his estates by his sister Catherine, who married in 1778 John Bayly of Debsborough, Co. Tipperary.

SOURCES: PRONI T/618/329 Crossle Papers; Burke *IFR*

(1976) p. 298; J. Kelly, *'That Damn'd thing called Honour': Duelling in Ireland 1570–1860* (Cork, 1995), p. 147; *Kerry Magazine* vol. 3 no. 36 (Dec. 1856) pp. 185–90 'Parliamentary Representation of Kerry'.

0536 CROSBIE, Lancelot

MP for Co. Kerry 1759–60; Ardfert 1762–8–76

b. *c.* 1723–5; d. (*ante* 15) Aug. 1780 at Tubrid, Co. Kerry
FAMILY/BACKGROUND: Son and heir of Maurice Crosbie and Catherine, dau. of ?Capt. Lancelot Sandes.
MARRIED: (1) Elizabeth, dau. of Sir Maurice Crosbie, 1st Baron Brandon (**0537**); (2) his cousin Mary, dau. of John Blennerhassett (**0167**).
CHILDREN: John Gustavus (**0535**); Catherine, m. [1778] John Bayly of Co. Tipperary; Jane Mary, m. [12 Jan. 1795] Capt. the Hon. Henry Blackwood; Arabella.
EDUCATION: Middle Temple 13 May 1743.
CAREER/OCCUPATION: Sheriff of Co. Kerry 1752; Freedom of Dublin April 1765.

POLITICAL ACTIVITY: Lancelot Crosbie was brought into parliament for Ardfert by his father-in-law, Lord Branden (**0537**), and influenced by him. He was listed for three committees in December 1759. He voted against the augmentation of the army but thereafter supported government. Ostensibly, even ostentatiously, government – while hoping for its defeat – gave a 'free vote' on the Absentee Tax. Like all the Crosbies, he supported Catholic relief.

DIVISION LISTS:
1768 (1) voted against army augmentation.
1771 (1) voted for Lord Townshend as Lord Lieutenant.
1771 (2) voted against Sir Lucius O'Brien's (**1558**) motion for retrenchment.
1772 (2) voted against a Short Revenue Bill.
1773 (1) voted for Absentee Tax.
1773 (2) voted against an untaxed press.
1774 (2) voted for Catholic relief.

ADDITIONAL INFORMATION: *A member of the RDS from 1769.

ESTATES/RESIDENCE: Tubrid, Co. Kerry.

SOURCES: PRONI D/302; PRONI D/3000/27/1 Falkiner Genealogical notes; McCracken thesis; Burke *IFR* (1976) pp. 298–9; *Register of Admissions to the Honourable Society of the Middle Temple* (London, 1949) vol. 1 p. 332; *Kerry Magazine* vol. 3 no. 36 (Dec. 1856) pp. 185–90, 'Parliamentary Representation of Kerry'; *Almanacks*; *BNL* 23 Apr. 1765; *DJ* 15–17 Aug. 1780, 22 Jan. 1795; Parliamentary Lists, 1769 (1), 1772 (2), 1773 (1), 1774 (1), 1775 (1).

0537 CROSBIE, Sir Maurice

MP for Co. Kerry 1713–14, 1715–27–58 [r. Dingle 1727]

b. 1690; d. 13 Jan. 1762
HONOURS: Knight.
PEERAGES: Cr. Baron Branden 6 Sept. 1758.
FAMILY/BACKGROUND: Only son of David Crosbie of Ardfert, Co. Kerry, and Jane, dau. and co-h. of William Hamilton.
MARRIED: [Dec. 1712] Elizabeth Anne, dau. of Rt Hon. Thomas FitzMaurice, 1st Earl of Kerry (0753).
CHILDREN: Rt Hon. William, 2nd Baron Branden (0540); John (at St John's College, Cambridge, 31 Jan. 1741), m. Elizabeth, dau. of [ ] Fisher; Maurice (Dean of Limerick) m. (1) [22 Mar. 1762] Elizabeth, dau. and co-h. of William Gun of Co. Kerry, (2) Pyne, dau. of Rt Hon. Sir Henry Cavendish, 1st Baronet (0380); Jane, m. Thomas Mahon (1334); Anne, m. Bartholomew Mahon of Co. Roscommon; Elizabeth, m. Lancelot Crosbie (0536); Dorothy, m. Rev. Richard Picot.
EDUCATION: School: Mr Condor, Ardfert; entered TCD 8 Apr. 1706, aged 16 years.
CAREER/OCCUPATION: *Commissioner of the Tillage Act for Munster 1743–61; *Governor of Co. Kerry 1747–53.

POLITICAL ACTIVITY: He came in for Co. Kerry in 1713 through his own and his father-in-law, Lord Kerry's interest. He was a Tory and, at the death of the Queen, on a 'black list of Tories'. However, he was returned for Co. Kerry again in 1715 and 1727. In 1719 it was thought that he would be hostile to giving relief to Dissenters. In 1724 he was one of the Memorialists seeking to revive attempts to explain or revoke the clause in the Act of Queen Anne's reign for naturalising foreign Protestants in which favour was given to the chil-dren of natural-born subjects. It was felt that this could undermine Protestant interests in Ireland by allowing the return of the children of papists who had served James in Ireland before fleeing to Europe.

In 1727, with Arthur Denny (0615) and John Blennerhasset (0167), he signed a compact 'partitioning out the [County] representation among themselves and successors by a formal document set forth in all the "pride, pomp and circumstance" of legal phraseology, as if they were doing the most sustainable, constitutional, legal and endurable act in the world.' The compact collapsed with Denny's death, but 'The intention to make the bond of union perpetual is evident.' In the early 1750s he supported the Country party over the expulsion of Arthur Jones-Nevill (1125) and the rejection of the Money Bill. He sat in parliament for 45 years before he was elevated to the peerage as Lord Branden in 1758. He was listed for two committees in 1713, 11 in 1715–25 and 76 in 1728–58.

DIVISION LISTS:
1713 (1) voted for Sir Richard Levinge (1230) for Speaker.
1749 (1) voted against the election of James Digges La Touche (♦♦♦♦).
1753 (1) voted for the expulsion of Arthur Jones-Nevill (1125).
1753 (2) voted against the Money Bill.

ADDITIONAL INFORMATION: 'His influence, both political and personal, was doubtless considerable, he was not only able to obtain one of the County seats – to nominate for his borough of Ardfert – but also, through the marriage of his daughter [his sister] Elizabeth with Maurice FitzGerald, called "the hump-backed Knight of Kerry" [from whence sprung the "nine Geraldines!"] to obtain paramount influence in the borough of Dingle; hence in this Parliament [1713] and the four succeeding, we find him in a position to approach the government with the well known argument "we are four!"'

A foundation member of the Dublin Society, 1731. His horse Crooked Arthur won the £30 purse at Dumanway, Co. Cork, 23 August 1735.

ESTATES/RESIDENCE: Ardfert, Co. Kerry. A contemporary calculated Sir Maurice Crosbie's income in 1713 at £600 p.a.

SOURCES: PRONI T/3411; PRONI T/580 pp. 176g, 176h, TSPI 1723–1724; T/2915/5/34 Bedford Papers; McCracken thesis; GEC *P*; Burke *Ext. P* (1883) pp. 148–9; *Alum. Cantab.*; *The Kerry Magazine* vol. 3, no. 36 (Dec. 1856) pp. 185–90, 'Parliamentary Representation of Kerry'; *DJ* 12–16 Jan. 1762 [says he died aged 73 years]; *Pue's Occurrences* 6 Sept. 1735; Parliamentary Lists, 1713 (1), (2), 1714–15 (1), 1719 (2).

0538 CROSBIE, Thomas

MP for Dingle 1713–14, 1715–27–31 [n.d.e. Co. Kerry 1709]

b. *c.* 1681–8; d. [4] June 1731
FAMILY/BACKGROUND: Son of Sir Thomas Crosbie and his 3rd wife Elizabeth, dau. and co-h. of William Hamilton of Lisclooney, King's County, wid. of [   ] Johnson.
MARRIED: [1711] Margaret, dau. of Richard Barry, 2nd Earl of Barrymore.
CHILDREN: James, m. his cousin Mary, dau. of Pierce Crosbie; Anne Dorothy, m. William Carique of Co. Clare; Harriet Jane.
CAREER/OCCUPATION: High Sheriff of Co. Kerry 1712, 1714.

POLITICAL ACTIVITY: He was thought to be a candidate for Co. Kerry in 1713 – he had been declared not duly elected for the county in 1709 – but instead he sat for Dingle. He was nominated for a committee on 10 December 1713. Crosbie was counted a Tory and, although he had been supported by the Whig interest in Co. Kerry in 1709, he was on a black list of Tories in 1714–15. On 14 June 1716 he complained of a breach of privilege committed by William Eustace, Sovereign of Naas, who, he alleged, arrested his servant Daniel Toole. On 12 March 1728 he alleged that on the preceding Saturday, 9 March, he and Henry Rose (**1813**) were insulted and their servants beaten, the culprits knowing that they were MPs.

He was listed for 11 committees 1716–25 and three in 1727–31. He supported, in 1721, the establishment of a national bank. In 1724 he was one of the Memorialists seeking to revive attempts to explain or revoke the clause in the Act of Queen Anne's reign for naturalising foreign Protestants in which favour was given to the children of natural-born subjects. It was felt that this could undermine Protestant interests in Ireland by allowing the return of the children of papists who had served James II in Ireland before fleeing to Europe.

DIVISION LISTS:
1713 (1) voted for Sir Richard Levinge (**1230**) for Speaker.
1721 (1) voted for a national bank.
1721 (2) voted for a national bank.

ADDITIONAL INFORMATION: The Danish East India Company ship, *Golden Lyon*, was on 7 November 1730 stranded near Ballyheige. The Lord Justices wrote (?on 7 November 1730) thanking Crosbie for looking after the ship and cargo and informing him that the Sheriff and commanding officers of the troops at Dingle and Tralee had been ordered to assist him in this task. On 12 June 1731 the Revenue Commissioners reported a robbery at Ballyheige. One of the robbers was caught and turned king's evidence, and the Danish Asiatic Company offered a reward of 10 per cent of the value of the cargo for its recovery. Buck, a Limerick goldsmith, bought a quantity of the Danish silver, part in coin and part in wedges, for £30. About ten of the robbers were eventually apprehended and charged, and about £7,524 2s was recovered. The total value of the cargo was said to be £9,287 6s. The robbery was alleged to have occurred on 4 June: 'About twelve or one in the night a number of men broke into the house at Ballyheige where the money chests were kept, wounded three of the Danes and carried it off.'

ESTATES/RESIDENCE: Ballyheige, Co. Kerry. By a very peculiar settlement, executed on the marriages of his father Sir Thomas Crosbie and his eldest son (by first wife) David to the two Hamilton sisters on the same day, a new settlement and redistribution of all the family estates was made, by which those of Ballyheige were apportioned to the issue of Sir Thomas' last marriage, i.e. the above. Thomas Crosbie's income in 1713 was reckoned to be £300.

SOURCES: PRONI D/302; PRONI T/3411; *CJ Ire.* (Bradley ed.) vol. 4 p. 272; vol. 5 p. 588; Hayton thesis; McCracken thesis; Burke *IFR* (1976) p. 302 [his father married for the third time in 1680]; PRO SP63/395 ff. 163–70, 194; PRO SP63/398 f. 95, /399 ff 17–20, 38, 40, 50–6; PRONI T/580 pp. 176g, 176h, TSPI 1723–1724; Parliamentary Lists, 1713 (1), (2), 1714–15 (1).

0539 CROSBIE, William

MP for Ardfert 1713–14, 1715–27–43

> b. *c.* 1662; d. 1742 (will registered 24 Nov. 1742)
> FAMILY/BACKGROUND: Son of Sir Thomas Crosbie
> and his 1st wife Bridget, dau. of Robert Tynte of
> Co. Cork.
> MARRIED: Isabella, dau. of Richard Smyth.
> CHILDREN: Anne, m. (1) John Leslie, (2) John
> Blennerhassett (**0168**).
> CAREER/OCCUPATION: High Sheriff of Co. Kerry
> 1699.
> MILITARY: Colonel in the army.

POLITICAL ACTIVITY: He was expected to be, and was, returned for Ardfert in 1713; he was listed for two committees on 10 December 1713. Ardfert was a Crosbie borough, and he sat for it until his death in 1742. In 1713 he was queried as a Whig, but by 1719 he was considered a Tory and likely to oppose the repeal of the Test Clause. He was nominated for 11 committees between 1715 and 1725.

In 1721 he supported the establishment of a national bank, and in 1724 he was one of the Memorialists seeking to revive attempts to explain or revoke the clause in the Act of Queen Anne's reign for naturalising foreign Protestants which favoured the children of natural-born subjects. It was felt that this could undermine Protestant interests in Ireland by allowing the return of the children of papists who had served James II in Ireland before fleeing to Europe. He was nominated for nine committees 1729–41.

DIVISION LISTS:
> 1721 (1) voted for a national bank.
> 1721 (2) voted for a national bank.

ESTATES/RESIDENCE: Tubrid, Co. Kerry. Lands listed in précis of his will. In 1713 William Crosbie's, MP for Ardfert, income was estimated to be £400.

SOURCES: PRONI D/302; T/3411; PRONI T/580 pp. 176g, 176h, TSPI 1723–1724; McCracken thesis; Burke *Ext. P*(1883) p. 148; Burke *IFR*(1976) pp. 298, 301 [His younger brother, Patrick, was born in 1664 and his elder brother was born before 1660]; Eustace, *Abstracts of Wills*, pp. 292–3; Parliamentary Lists, 1713 (1), (2), 1719 (2).

0540 CROSBIE, Rt Hon. William

MP for Ardfert 1735–60, 1761–2

> b. May 1716; d. 11 May 1781 at his house in
> Stephen's Green in his 66th year
> HONOURS: PC 1765–74 (sworn 11 Mar. 1766).
> PEERAGES: Suc. as 2nd Baron Branden 1762; cr.
> Viscount Crosbie 30 Nov. 1771, Earl of
> Glandore 22 July 1776.
> FAMILY/BACKGROUND: Eldest son of Sir Maurice
> Crosbie, 1st Baron Branden (**0537**) and Elizabeth
> Anne, eldest dau. of Rt Hon. Thomas
> FitzMaurice, 1st Earl of Kerry (**0753**).
> MARRIED: [Nov. 1745] Theodosia, dau. of John
> Bligh, 1st Earl of Darnley (**0172**); (2) [1 Nov.
> 1777] Jane, dau. of Edward Vesey, wid. of John
> Ward.
> CHILDREN: Maurice (d. yg); Rt Hon. John, 2nd
> Earl of Glandore (**0534**); Anne, m. May 1775
> John William Talbot of Co. Roscommon;
> Theodosia; Arabella, m. Hon. Edward Ward
> (**2179**).
> EDUCATION: Entered TCD 5 May 1732; Middle
> Temple 17 Mar. 1733.
> CAREER/OCCUPATION: Sheriff of Co. Kerry 1743;
> *Commissioner of the Tillage Act for Munster
> 1755–80; Trustee of Linen Board for Ulster Mar.
> 1759–d.; Governor of the Workhouse Oct.
> 1760–8, Foundling Hospital and Workhouse
> 1769–d.; *elected to the Court of Assistants
> 1766–8; *Governor of the Lying-in Hospital
> 1765–d.; Custos Rot. for Co. Kerry 1770–81;
> *Governor of the Erasmus Smith's Schools and
> other Charities 1772–d.

POLITICAL ACTIVITY: He sat for the family borough of Ardfert from 1735 until he succeeded his father as 2nd Baron Branden in 1762. In 1749 he appears to have avoided the vote on the Dublin city election, as he was 'absent – in town'. In the early 1750s he supported the Country party, voting for the expulsion of Arthur Jones-Nevill (**1125**) and against the Money Bill. From 1762 his career was in the House of Lords where he was steadily advanced: Lord Townshend elevated him to a viscounty and, in 1776, Lord Harcourt successfully recommended that he be created Earl of Glandore.

Along with his support came the further rewards of patronage. He was made a Privy Counsellor and a Trustee of the Linen Board. His brother was made a dean, and his cousin, Maurice Copinger (**0491**), promoted to be Serjeant-at-Law and given several favours in the Revenue. In addition he had the minor patronage of the recommendation to: '2 Coast Officers, a Hearth Money Collection, Distributor of Stamps and 1 Supernumerary Gauger'. He died on 11 May 1781.

DIVISION LISTS:
> 1749 (1) absent – in town.
> 1753 (1) voted for the expulsion of Arthur Jones-Nevill (**1125**).
> 1753 (2) voted against the Money Bill.

ADDITIONAL INFORMATION: *A member of the RDS from 1762.

ESTATES/RESIDENCE: Ardfert, Co. Kerry.

SOURCES: PRONI D/302; PRONI T/618/329 Crossle Papers; PRONI MIC/465/1 R. Ffolliott, *Biographical Notices, 1756–1827* [*Hibernian Chronicle* 14 May 1781 says he died 11 May 1781]; McCracken thesis; GEC *P*, Burke *Ext. P.* (1883) pp. 148–9; *Index to Irish Privy Counsellors, 1711–1910*; *Register of Admissions to the Honourable Society of the Middle Temple* (London, 1949), vol. 1 p. 314; *Ir. Gen.* vol. 5 no. 5 (1978) p. 635, H. F. Morris, 'Ramsey's Waterford Chronicle, 1777'; *Almanacks; The Dublin Gazette* 12 Mar. 1743; *DJ* 4–7 Oct. 1760, 16–18 Dec. 1777, 12–15 May 1781; Parliamentary Lists, 1771 (1).

0541 CROSBIE, William Arthur

MP for Trim 1781–3, 1795–7–1800 (re-elected after appointment to place of profit, 1796 and 1798)

> b. (bapt. 23 Jan.) 1756; d. 19 Feb. 1803
> FAMILY/BACKGROUND: Eldest son of William Francis Crosbie (**0542**) and Francis Colley, dau. of Richard Wesley (Colley), 1st Baron Mornington (**2214**).
> MARRIED: [8 Nov. 1795] Elizabeth, dau. of Sir Frederick Faulkner.
> CHILDREN: William John (d. yg); Maria, m. [1832] Lieut.-Gen. Berkeley Drummond of Hampshire; Frances, m. Maj. Charles George Fairfield.
> CAREER/OCCUPATION: *Listed in Attornies of the Courts of King's Bench, Common Pleas and Exchequer 1789–1800 (f.); Stamps Commissioner 25 May 1798, 19 Jan. 1802, 18 Mar 1802–July 1802 at £600 p.a., Steward of Lord Lieutenant's Household at £506 p.a. 1798–1800

(f.); *listed in Judges and Barristers 1798–1800 (f.); Customer of Waterford and Ross 18 Aug. 1798; Weighmaster of Cork 23 Sept. 1802 at £600 p.a. for life.
> MILITARY: Barracks Commissioner 6 Aug. 1796; resigned in 1798 for a pension of £250.

POLITICAL ACTIVITY: Returned for Trim by his cousin, Lord Mornington (later Marquess Wellesley) (**2215**), whose political leadership he followed. In 1783 it was thought that Lord Mornington would return his brother, Lieutenant William Wellesley-Pole (**2216**), if the latter failed to make his election for Queen's County – this in fact happened. In 1790 Lord Mornington returned his other brother, Arthur (later Duke of Wellington) (**2210**). Lord Mornington appears to have returned one of his family for one seat and, until his death in 1790, General Pomeroy (**1695**) was returned for the other by agreement with both the 1st (**2212**) and 2nd (**2215**) Earls of Mornington. However, in 1795 Crosbie got his opportunity again, as Lord Mornington had provided for the fourth Wellesley brother, Henry (later Lord Cowley) (**2213**), who was no sooner elected than he accepted the office of Escheator of Munster on becoming a précis writer at the Foreign Office in April 1795.

Crosbie sat for Trim until the Union, which he supported in both 1799 and 1800. By 1800 he was 'Commissioner of Stamps, £500 and Steward of the Household, £400 [actually £414 11s] and finally Comptroller to the Lord Lieutenant's Household', and he also had a pension for his wife. All of this appears to be excessively generous even for Union support.

DIVISION LISTS:
> 1799 (1) voted for the Union – Steward of the Household, Dublin Castle, Commissioner of Stamps with a pension for his wife.
> 1800 (1) voted for the Union.

ESTATES/RESIDENCE: Ballyheige, Co. Kerry.

SOURCES: PRONI D/3000/27/2 Falkiner Genealogical notes; PRONI T/3166/1C Hartnell notes; RCBL T34, Extracts from the Parish Registers of St Andrew's, Dublin; McCracken thesis; Burke *IFR* (1976) p. 299 [His father married in 1750]; *Cornwallis Corr.* (London, 1859) vol. 3 p. 76; *Almanacks;* Parliamentary Lists, 1776 (1), 1782 (1), 1783 (1), 1799 (2), (3), 1800 (1), (3).

0542 CROSBIE, William Francis

MP for Trim 1758–60

b. *ante* 1729; d. 7 Jan. 1761
FAMILY/BACKGROUND: Only son of Arthur Crosbie
of Dublin and Elizabeth, dau. of Lancelot
Sandes.
MARRIED: [5 Aug. 1750] Frances (d. 11 Sept.
1768), yst dau. of Richard Wesley (Colley), 1st
Baron Mornington (**2214**).
CHILDREN: William Arthur (**0541**); Elizabeth, m.
[20 Jan. 1775] Maj. the Hon. Clotworthy
Rowley; Mary.

POLITICAL ACTIVITY: In the short time that he was
in parliament he was nominated for seven committees. Apart from this very little is known about
his parliamentary activity. His connection with the
Wellesley family proved valuable to his son (**0541**).

ESTATES/RESIDENCE: Ballyheige, Co. Kerry; 35 St
Stephen's Green, Dublin.

SOURCES: PRONI T/559 vol. 17 p. 64, Burke, extract
pedigrees; RCBL T34, Extracts from the Parish Registers of St Andrew's, Dublin; McCracken thesis; Burke
IFR (1976) p. 299; *DJ* 6–10 Jan. 1761.

0543 CROSSE, Silvester

MP for Callan 1703–13–14; Armagh B. 1715–
27; Clogher 1727–30

b. 1671; d. 1730
FAMILY/BACKGROUND: Only son of Capt. Epinetus
Crosse of Crosse's Green, Co. Cork, and Susanna,
dau. of Edward Worth, Bp of Killaloe.
MARRIED: [1710] Anne, dau. of Anthony Maude
(**1365**), wid. of Jerome Ryves, Dean of St
Patrick's.
CHILDREN: *d.s.p.*
EDUCATION: Entered Oxford (Trinity College) 12
May 1687, aged 16 years; Middle Temple 3 Oct.
1690.
CAREER/OCCUPATION: Private Secretary to the
Duke of Ormonde 1703–7 (on 22 Jan. 1711 he
wrote to Ormonde asking for preferment).

POLITICAL ACTIVITY: He was returned for Callan,
probably through Ormonde's interest, although
in 1713 the election, held on 31 October, was
contested: Crosse received 53 votes, Francis Flood
(**0760**) 47, Captain Thomas Candler 23 and John

Cuffe (**0554**) 7. After 1715 he was returned for
the two government-controlled ecclesiastical boroughs of Armagh and Clogher. As Ormonde's secretary he was a Tory and a solid Court man. In
1713 he was considered a 'good' man for Callan,
and in 1714–15 he was on the 'black list' of Tories. However, he survived the Hanoverian succession and in 1719 was 'thought likely to be an
opponent of the repeal of the Test Clause'.

He was listed on ten committees 1705–11 and
six in 1717–1723, which suggests that he was not
a very active parliamentarian. He voted the Court
line during the reign of Queen Anne, and his
change of vote on the national bank issue may
reflect the effects of the South Sea Bubble.

DIVISION LISTS:
1709 (1) voted against a Money Bill.
1711 (1) voted for the Court on the Dublin
mayoralty issue.
1713 (1) voted for Sir Richard Levinge
(**1230**) for Speaker.
1721 (1) voted for a national bank.
1721 (2) voted against a national bank.

ESTATES/RESIDENCE: Crosse's Green, Co. Cork. In 1714
his estimated income was £180 p.a.

SOURCES: Information supplied by J. Kennedy Esq. [T.
Shelby, Notes on the election of Callan MPs *c.*1870];
McCracken thesis; Hayton thesis; *Alum. Oxon.*; Simms'
cards; Vicars, *Prerog. Wills* [proved 1730]; *Register of
Admissions to the Honourable Society of the Middle Temple* (London, 1949) vol. 1 p. 227; *HMC Ormonde*
(1920) new ser. vol. 8 p. 326; J. Kelly, *Henry Flood …*
(Dublin, 1998), p. 22; Parliamentary Lists, 1706 (1),
1711 (3), 1713 (1), 1713 (2), 1714–15 (1), 1719 (2).

0544 CROWE, Robert

MP for Philipstown 1797–Jan. 1800; [Escheator
of Munster 1800]

b. 1745; d. July 1817
FAMILY/BACKGROUND: Eldest son of James Crowe
of Dublin and ?Mary, sis. of John Hatch of
London.
MARRIED: [1789] [ ] eldest dau. of Anthony
Wolfe.
CHILDREN: ?
EDUCATION: School: Rev. Mr Bluck; entered TCD

1 Nov. 1760; Middle Temple 17 May 1764; entered Oxford (Oriel College) 4 Dec. 1767, aged 22 years; called to the Irish Bar 1770. CAREER/OCCUPATION: *Listed in Judges and Barristers 1789–1800 (f.); *listed in Attornies of the Courts of King's Bench, Common Pleas and Court of Exchequer 1789–1800 (f.).

POLITICAL ACTIVITY: Returned for Philipstown by Lord Belvidere (**1800**). Lord Belvidere usually sold both seats, but whether he did so in 1797 is uncertain. Certainly if he did this would be a complication. Lord Belvidere was a firm supporter of the Union, and obliged both of his members for Philipstown, Francis Knox (**1178**) and Robert Crowe, to resign. Francis Knox was made a KC, and it was apparently made worth Crowe's while to accept the office of Escheator of Munster. A Parliamentary List for 1800 says that Crowe was bribed by Lord Castlereagh (**2009**) to accept the Escheatorship of Munster in order to vacate his seat. The replacement members Robert Johnson (**1103**) and James Mahon (**1328**) were both sworn on 3 February 1800, and both voted for the Union. Crowe was against the Union and had voted with the opposition both in 1798, over Sir Laurence Parsons' (**1636**) motion, and in 1799 against the Union itself. A Parliamentary List for 1800 states that Lord Belvidere was made a Privy Counsellor and given a pension.

DIVISION LISTS:

1798 (2) voted for Parsons' (**1636**) motion for an investigation into 'the present discontents'.

1799 (1) voted against the Union.

ESTATES/RESIDENCE: Temple Street, Dublin; Nutfield House, Ennis, Co. Clare.

SOURCES: Information from P. F. Meehan Esq.; PRONI T/3166/1B Hartnell notes; *Prerog. Wills* 1811–58; O'Neill thesis; *Alum. Dub.*; *Alum. Oxon.*; *Memorials of the Dead* [says a Robert Crow, not this MP, married 28 July 1764 Rachael Goodwin]; Hughes, *Pat. Officers*; *IMC King's Inns Admission Papers, 1607–1867*; *Register of Admissions to the Honourable Society of the Middle Temple* vol. 1 (London, 1949) p. 361; *Almanacks*; The Treble Almanack (1819) [ceases to list him in the 'Judges and Barristers' section]; Parliamentary Lists, 1799 (3), 1800 (3).

0545 CROWE, William

MP for Blessington 1692–3, 1703–11; TCD 1698–9

b. *c.* 1657; d. (*ante* 9 July) 1711
FAMILY/BACKGROUND: Son of Thomas Crowe of Dublin.
MARRIED: ?
CHILDREN: ?
EDUCATION: Entered Cambridge (St John's College) 26 May 1674; Middle Temple 3 June 1674, called to the Bar at the Middle Temple 13 May 1681: LLD (Cambridge) 1706.
CAREER/OCCUPATION: 2nd Master in Chancery 1706; Customer of Waterford and Ross *ante* 1710.

POLITICAL ACTIVITY: He was listed for a committee on 11 October 1692 and for five in 1698–9. He signed the Association for the protection of William III in the country. In the first parliament of Queen Anne he appears to have been in London for much of the time, although on 30 May 1706 he wrote to Ormonde that he was eternally attached to his service, and he came over for Ormonde's birthday celebrations in 1706.

He was listed for 24 committees 1703–9. At the same time he appears to have been divesting himself, as profitably as possible, of his various offices. In 1706 he sold his Commissionership of Appeals to John Jephson (**1089**) for £400. Jephson, finding the transaction too expensive, tried to extricate himself from it. It appears, however, that Sir Richard Cox (**0507**) was determined to hold him to it, owing to Crowe's friendship with Ormonde and to force Jephson's attachment to the government. Similarly, he sold his place as Customer of Waterford and Ross to Jephson in (*c.* February) 1706. The post was worth £100 p.a., but Crowe felt the £400 outweighed the precariousness of this annual sum. He also hoped the bargain would unite the representation of Blessington (for which they were both MPs), Jephson and he having previously been 'dock and nettle to one another'. Crowe felt that he would now 'have the honor of showing him [Jephson] the way out of the House into the lobby upon every division that is material'.

DIVISION LISTS:
1709 (1) voted against a Money Bill.

ESTATES/RESIDENCE: Crowe's Nest, Dublin.

SOURCES: Hayton thesis; *Alum. Cantab.*; *Register of Admissions to the Honourable Society of the Middle Temple* (London, 1949) vol. 1 p. 189; Simms' cards; *HMC Ormonde* (1920) new ser. vol. 8 pp. 268, 277, 282; Parliamentary Lists, 1696 (1), 1706 (1), (2), 1707 (3).

0546 CROWLE, Charles John

MP for Harristown 1781–3; [GB] Richmond (Yorkshire) 1769–74

b. 1738; d. 7 Mar. 1811
FAMILY/BACKGROUND: Only son of Richard Crowle of Hull and Elizabeth, dau. of John Pearman of London.
MARRIED: [Oct. 1770] Hon. Miss Laycock.
CHILDREN: ?
EDUCATION: School: Westminster Jan. 1749, aged 8 years; Inner Temple 1755; entered Cambridge (Trinity College) 30 July 1757, aged 19 years.

POLITICAL ACTIVITY: He was a friend of Lord Lieutenant Carlisle and Steward of the Household. He was brought into parliament very briefly in 1781 by the Duke of Leinster (0745) following the death of Michael Keating (1136). Crowle was sworn on 20 November 1781, and this parliament met for the last time on 27 July 1782. It was subsequently prorogued and then dissolved. His election was a compliment from the Duke of Leinster to Lord Carlisle.

ADDITIONAL INFORMATION: He fought a duel with Lord Hervey (heir of the Earl-Bishop of Derry). He was a member, 1764, and secretary, 1774–8, of the Dilettante Society. In 1762 the Marquess of Tavistock, who had known him at Westminster School, described him to his father as 'not very wise but an inoffensive good humoured lad'. He made no mark on either the British or the Irish parliament.

ESTATES/RESIDENCE: Fryston Hall near Wakefield, Yorkshire.

SOURCES: *HP 1754–94* [does not mention his career in the Irish Parliament and says he died unmarried]; *Alum.*

Cantab.; G. F. Russell-Barker and A. H. Stenning (eds), *Record of Old Westminsters: A biographical list* (London, 1928), 2 vols [calls him John Charles]; Kildare MPs; Parliamentary Lists, 1776 (1), 1782 (1), 1783 (1).

0547 CUFFE, Agmondisham

MP for Co. Kilkenny 1695–9

b. *c.* 1655; d. Dec. 1727
FAMILY/BACKGROUND: Eldest surviving son of Capt. Joseph Cuffe and Martha, dau. of Col. Agmondisham Muschamp.
MARRIED: [1679] Anne, dau. of Sir John Otway of Cumberland, wid. of John Warden.
CHILDREN: John, 1st Baron Desart (0554); Capt. Denny, m. (1) [12 Oct. 1715] Grace, dau. of Ebinezer Wright of Dublin, (2) Anne Cuffe; Maurice (0555); William; Martha, m. John Blunden (0178).
EDUCATION: School: Kilkenny College, entered TCD 9 Aug. 1672.
CAREER/OCCUPATION: Alderman of Kilkenny, Mayor June 1678; Sheriff of Co. Kilkenny 1700.
MILITARY: Captain in the Williamite army.

POLITICAL ACTIVITY: A professional soldier, he supported Lord Chancellor Porter against the accusations of favouring Catholics made against him by some MPs in 1695, and the following year he signed the Association for the protection of William III in the country. On 30 August 1695 he complained to the House of a 'notorious' breach of privilege alleged to have taken place at Callan, Co. Kilkenny, and committed by Lieutenant-Colonel Gorges (0884) and other commissioned and non-commissioned soldiers. The Commons requested that the Lord Lieutenant remove all troops from Callan until the matter was investigated and Gorges was taken into custody. Gorges' supporters reacted, and on 16 September John Langrish, on behalf of himself and other freeholders of Co. Kilkenny, lodged a petition against Cuffe's election. But on 19 September the House found Gorges 'remiss in his care at Callan', reprimanded him and dismissed him from custody on payment of fines. However, Cornet Montgomery, one of his subordinates, received the full displeasure of the Commons and was found guilty of a high misdemeanour for the neglect of his care and duty, on the day of the election of Knights of the Shire for the County of Kilkenny at Callan. Montgomery received the censure of the House, on his knees, from the Speaker.

As a gentleman of Kilkenny, Cuffe was one of the Memoralists who, in August 1700, sought the reopening of the port of New Ross. It had been shut to discourage the woollen trade with England, and this was depressing the industry in Leinster.

During 1693 a Mr Cuffe, who may or may not be the same man, petitioned against Lieutenant Francis Flood (0760) for stealing his wife. On 7 June 1705 Francis Cuffe MP was instrumental in having Francis Flood expelled from the Commons for abuses against Cuffe, his tenants and others in Co. Kilkenny.

ESTATES/RESIDENCE: Castle Inch, Co. Kilkenny. His father was the recipient of one of the largest Cromwellian land grants in Co. Kilkenny, over 3,500 acres. This were followed by a fee farm grant from the Duke of Ormonde of the lands of Aglish, Co. Kilkenny, dated 10 July 1703. Cuffe in turn made leases to the Drews of Ballinlogh.

SOURCES: PRONI D/302; EC 9073; *CJ Ire.* (Bradley ed.) vol. 2 pp. 646, 670, 677; PRONI MIC/338/2 Crossle notes; *Cal. SP. Dom. 1693* (London 1903) p. 166; Kilkenny MPs; *Alum. Dub.*; Burke *PB* (1903) p. 456; Burke *PB* (1857) p. 291; M. A Brennan (St Joseph's College, New York), 'The making of an Ascendancy family: The Blundens of Kilkenny' (Irish-American Conference Paper); J. Kelly, *Henry Flood* ... (Dublin 1998) pp. 21–2; *JRSAI* vol. 31 (1901) p. 57, P. D Vigors, 'Extracts from the Old Corporation Books of New Ross, County Wexford'; *JRSAI* vol. 76 (1946) p. 136, W. E. J. Dobbs, 'A Supplement to the Entrance Register of Kilkenny School: 1684–1800'; Parliamentary Lists, 1695 (1), 1696 (1).

0548 CUFFE, Francis

MP for Co. Mayo 1692–3 [r. Longford B. 1692]

b. *c.* 1654; d. 26 (bur. 28) Dec. 1694
FAMILY/BACKGROUND: Eldest son of Sir James Cuffe and Alice, dau. of Rev. Ambrose Aungier.
MARRIED: Honora, dau. of Michael Boyle, Primate of All Ireland, wid. of Thomas Cromwell, 3rd Earl of Ardglass (she m. (3) Sir Thomas Burdett, 1st Baronet (0278)).

CHILDREN: Francis (0549); Michael (0556); Mary, m. Whitfield Doyne.
EDUCATION: School: Mr Jones, Kilkenny *c.* 1668; entered TCD 1671, aged *c.* 17 years, LLD *spec. grat.* 1694.
CAREER/OCCUPATION: Sheriff of Co. Mayo 8 Dec. 1681; High Sheriff of Co. Mayo 1682; ?appointed one of the Deputy Commissaries-General *c.* Sept. 1693; Commissioner for Forfeited Estates (at £400 p.a. – one of two named individuals on a Dec. 1693 draft warrant of Commissioners for Forfeitures, who were to receive a salary; he was also named on the new warrant of 17 Jan. 1694).
MILITARY: Lieutenant of the Ordnance 2 Mar. 1693 – 26 Dec. 1694, at a salary of £300 p.a.

POLITICAL ACTIVITY: He sat only in the brief 1692 parliament, during which there was little time for any normal parliamentary activity.

ESTATES/RESIDENCE: Ballinrobe, Co. Mayo.

SOURCES: PRONI D/302; *Cal. SP Dom. 1693* (London, 1903) pp. 6, 22, 334, 442, *1694–5* (London, 1906) pp. 8, 38, 42, 382, 393, 471, *1695* (London, 1908) pp. 146, 213; Burke *Ext. P* (1883) p. 149; Simms' cards; *Alum. Dub.*; Hughes, *Pat. Officers*; J. H. Bernard (ed.), *The Register of St Patrick, Dublin, 1677–1800* (Parish Register Society of Dublin, 1907), p. 8; H. F. Berry (ed.), *The Registers of the Church of St Michan, Dublin, 1636–1700* (Parish Register Society of Dublin, 1909), pp. 282, 285 [bur. 28 Dec. 1694]; *JRSAI* vol. 76 (1946) p. 136, W. E. J. Dobbs, 'A Supplement to the Entrance Register of Kilkenny School: 1684–1800'.

0549 CUFFE, Francis

MP for Co. Mayo 1715–17

b. *post* 1675; d. (bur. 13) Nov. 1717
FAMILY/BACKGROUND: Eldest son of Francis Cuffe (0548) and Honora, dau. of Michael Boyle, Primate of Ireland, wid. of Thomas Cromwell, 3rd Earl of Ardglass.
MARRIED: Unmarried.

POLITICAL ACTIVITY: He sat in parliament for the first session of the parliament of George I and probably for part of the second. Apart from the fact that on 5 March 1716 he contracted to build a barracks at Ballinrobe, not much is known about him. The barracks was part of a scheme for building barracks throughout the country. He was to finish by 25 December 1716 but failed to do so; by 19 September 1717 he had received £1,547 14s 7³/₄ d. He died shortly after.

ESTATES/RESIDENCE: Ballinrobe, Co. Mayo. He inherited some of the estates of Ambrose Aungier, last Earl of Longford of that creation.

SOURCES: *CJ Ire.* vol. 4 p. 377; Burke *Ext. P.* (1883) p. 149; J. H. Bernard (ed.), *The Register of St Patrick's, Dublin, 1677–1800* (Parish Register Society of Dublin, 1907), p. 24.

0550 CUFFE, Gerald

MP for Castlebar 1703–13–14

> b. 24 July 1669; d. *post* 1715
> FAMILY/BACKGROUND: Son of Sir James Cuffe and Alice, dau. of Rev. Ambrose Aungier.
> MARRIED: Dorothy, dau. of Col. Owen Wynne of Co. Leitrim.
> CHILDREN: James (0551); Alice, m. John Cuffe; Douglas, m. Rev. James Miller; Catherine, m. George Jones.
> EDUCATION: School: Mr Birbeck, Dublin; entered TCD 29 Apr. 1685, aged 16 years, BA 1687.
> CAREER/OCCUPATION: Customs and Excise Collector for Foxford, Co. Mayo 1714.
> MILITARY: A half-pay Lieutenant on the Irish Establishment at £36 10s p.a. 31 Mar. 1711.

POLITICAL ACTIVITY: A professional soldier, he sat in both parliaments of Queen Anne and supported the administration. In 1706 he attended the Duke of Ormonde's birthday celebrations and in 1711 he was one of a select group of Tories who met to plan government strategy at the Fleece Tavern, Dublin. In the same year he supported the Court over the Dublin mayoralty dispute. In 1713 the Castle considered that he was a 'good' man for Castlebar; he was duly returned at the ensuing election. In 1714 he signed an address in favour of Lord Chancellor Phipps. He did not come into parliament in 1715, although he was, rather surprisingly, suggested as a Whig candidate for Co. Mayo. Possibly he was a 'whimsical' Tory, or excused by his military background, as he does not seem to have attracted the wrath invoked against

many Queen Anne Tories.

DIVISION LISTS:
> 1711 (1) voted for the Court on the Dublin mayoralty issue.

ESTATES/RESIDENCE: Elmhall, Co. Mayo. Patents for fairs were granted to his father, Sir James Cuffe, by Charles II in 1668 and 1670.

SOURCES: *CJ Ire.* (Bradley ed.) vol. 3 pp. 852–3; Hayton thesis; Simms' cards; *Alum. Dub.*; Burke *Ext. P* (1883) p. 149; Parliamentary Lists, 1706 (1), (2), 1711 (1), (2), 1713 (1),1714 (1).

0551 CUFFE, James

MP for Co. Mayo 1742–60

> b. 1707; d. 20 Mar. 1762
> FAMILY/BACKGROUND: Eldest son of Gerald Cuffe (0550) and Dorothy, dau. of Col. Owen Wynne of Co. Leitrim.
> MARRIED: [30 Apr. 1731] Elizabeth, dau. of Sir Arthur Gore, 2nd Baronet (0857).
> CHILDREN: Rt Hon. James (0552); Maj. Michael; Elizabeth, m. Dodwell Browne of Co. Mayo; Anne; Jane, m. George Jackson; Bridget; Sarah, m. John Blake.
> EDUCATION: School Kilkenny College 21 Oct. 1715, aged 8 years; Middle Temple 19 Oct. 1726; entered TCD 12 May 1728, aged 18 years.
> CAREER/OCCUPATION: High Sheriff of Co. Mayo 1736; *Commissioner of the Tillage Act for Connaught 1747–61.

POLITICAL ACTIVITY: He came into parliament in 1742 following the death of Sir Arthur Gore (0857). In the early 1750s, he supported the Country party over the Money Bill dispute. He was listed for 51 committees between 1743 and 1760. He was obviously in some financial distress, as on 15 September 1759 Bedford promised him a pension of £300 p.a. He eventually received a pension of only £250 p.a. in July 1760, but was quite appreciative of 'your grace's seasonable bounty [which] will enable me to keep an old family estate entire, and has relieved me from distress'. He was granted a pension of £500 p.a. for 31 years on 8 Jan. 1761.

He stood unsuccessfully for the county in 1761 and died the following year. At the close of the poll for the Co. Mayo election in 1761 the votes were as follows: Peter Browne-Kelly (**0262**), 454 (237 £10 freehold, 217 40s freehold); Sir Charles Bingham (**0134**), 444 (231 £10 freehold, 213 40s freehold); Hon. Richard Gore (**0874**), 364 (117 £10 freehold, 247 40s freehold); James Cuffe, 333 (120 £10 freehold, 213 40s freehold). Browne-Kelly and Bingham were declared duly elected.

DIVISION LISTS:

1749 (1) absent, in the country.

1753 (1) voted for the expulsion of Arthur Jones-Nevill (**1125**).

1753 (2) voted against the Money Bill.

ESTATES/RESIDENCE: Elm Hall, Co. Mayo. The Elm Hall estate, barony of Cara, and Tyrawley estate, barony of Tyrawley. On 25 November 1747 he, with Sir Arthur Gore (**0859**), petitioned for heads of a bill to sell part of his estate to pay off debts that he had contracted, stating that the sale would be greatly to the benefit of his heir, James Cuffe, then a minor.

SOURCES: PRONI D/302; *CJ Ire.* (Bradley ed.) vol. 7 p. 952; PRONI T/2915/9/53, 10/15 Bedford Papers; RCBL T34, Extracts from the Parish Registers of St Andrew's, Dublin [says Bibby, daughter of James Cuff Esq. bapt. 16 Apr. 1745]; McCracken thesis; Burke *Ext. P* (1883) p. 149; *Alum. Dub.*; *Register of Admissions to the Honourable Society of the Middle Temple* (London, 1949) vol. 1 p. 300; *JRSAI* vol. 54 (1924) pp. 55–67, T. U. Sadlier, 'The Register of Kilkenny School (1685–1800)'; *Almanacks*; *BNL* 20 Feb. 1767; *The Dublin Gazette* 13 Jan. 1736; *DJ* 30 Dec. 1760–3 Jan. 1761, 16–19 May 1761, 22–5 May 1762.

0552 CUFFE, Rt Hon. James

MP for Co. Mayo 1768–76–83–90–7 [r. Donegal B. 1776; Tuam 1783]

b. *ante* 1747; d. 15 June 1821

HONOURS: PC 1765–d. (sworn 17 Sept. 1782).

PEERAGES: Cr. Baron Tyrawley 22 Nov. 1797; Rep. Peer 1801–21.

FAMILY/BACKGROUND: Son of James Cuffe (**0551**) and Elizabeth, dau. of Sir Arthur Gore, 2nd Baronet (**0857**).

MARRIED: (1) [28 Apr. 1770] Mary, only dau. of Richard Levinge (**1232**); (2) Sarah Wewitzer dau. of [   ] Wewitzer, sis. of Ralph Wewitzer.

CHILDREN (ILLEGITIMATE): 2 dau. (d. yg); James

(**0553**).

CAREER/OCCUPATION: Governor of Co. Mayo 1778–80, *Joint Governor 1780–f; *Governor of the Royal Hospital 1743–57, 1770–1800 (f.); Commissioner of the Infirmary 1760; *Governor of the Infirmary in James' Street 1764; *Governor of Dr Steevens' Hospital 1780–1800 (f.); Custos Rot. of Co. Mayo 1786–1800; Foreman of the Grand Jury of Co. Mayo 1792; *Trustee of the Linen Board for Ulster 1795–1800 (f.); Freedom of the City of Dublin Apr. 1797.

MILITARY: Military Ambassador to Portugal 1762; Commissioner of the Barracks 1771–1800 (f.), promoted to Superintendent-General 1772–90; 1st Barrack Commissioner 1783; Commissioner of Board of Works 1784–1803; *Horse (Colonel) 1739–42; *Major-General 1740–2; *Lieutenant-General as Major-General 1744, 1754–7, 1760, *General as Major-General 1764–5; *Colonel of a Regiment of Guards 1743, 1747, 1749–52, 1754–7, 1769–70, 1772; Colonel of the Tyrawley Rangers, of the Kilmaine Horse and Infantry, of the Killala Infantry and of the Crossmolina Infantry and Artillery; Captain in Kilmaine Cavalry Oct. 1796.

POLITICAL ACTIVITY: A professional soldier. He came into parliament in 1769 when he safeguarded his return for Co. Mayo by being also returned for a distant relative, Lord Arran's (**0859**), borough of Donegal. It was thought that his uncle Lord Annaly (**0869**) or Thomas Conolly (**0459**) might have influence with him. In 1772 he was appointed to the Barrack Board, £400 p.a., but in 1773 it was thought that he would follow Lord Arran's lead and vote against. Although in 1774 he had voted for Catholic relief he was later a bitter opponent of further Catholic concessions. In 1776 he was again returned for Co. Mayo and was promoted Inspector General of the Barrack Board, £600 p.a. with a travel allowance. Thereafter he usually supported, but in 1782, despite his 'good estate', he was anxious for further promotion to a position of £1,000 p.a.

In 1775 it was noted that 'He is not less perplexed and embarrassed in his circumstances than he is by his wife and Miss Weitwitser [*sic*]': she was a Canadian singer, a London actress, his longtime mistress and second wife, the mother of his children, and the sister of Ralph Wewitzer, an actor and noted French scholar (*see* **1200**). Miss Wewitzer retired from the stage in 1789. In 1782

he was described as 'a pleasant libertine. He is
parted from his wife who, it was said, had an in-
trigue with the late Attorney General Scott (**1891**)
and there was a duel between him and Mr Cuffe.'

In 1784 he was noted as a determined opponent of (parliamentary) reform; he had successfully resisted George Robert FitzGerald's wild
plans in Co. Mayo. Immediately preceding the
Commercial Resolutions he had a disagreement
with Chief Secretary Orde (**1594**), and neither he
nor the other county MP, Hon. Denis Browne
(**0253**), appeared for the debates on the Commercial Bill. In fact, as a county MP he might have
had difficulties in supporting this, for 'The County
and Grand Jury have been stirring against the
Propositions, but their measures might be kept
down were the Members to co-operate and exert
themselves.' By 1785 he was First Commissioner
of the Barrack Board, £1,000 p.a., and in 1788
he applied for a peerage. In 1790 he was declared
to be 'though not of showy or splendid talents ...
of sound sense and information'. He was reputed
to be a personal, though as an office-holder not a
political, friend of Grattan (**0895**).

He was bitterly opposed to the 1792 Catholic
Relief Bill and stated in the course of the debate
that the administration should make it clear to
'all men of all religions that we have power enough
to protect our establishment in Church and State.
We will protect them on the principles of the Revolution, and we will punish those who seek to disturb the peace and tranquillity of this growing
country.' His view was probably that of the majority, and robbed the Relief Bill of any ameliorating effect. In general his voting pattern, while
usually complying with the administration, had a
strong streak of personal independence. His ambition at the Union was a peerage with remainder
to his illegitimate son (**0553**). He received the
peerage but George III objected to the remainder.

DIVISION LISTS:
> 1771 (1) voted for Lord Townshend as Lord
> Lieutenant.
> 1771 (2) voted against Sir Lucius O'Brien's
> (**1558**) motion for retrenchment.
> 1772 (2) voted against a Short Revenue Bill.
> 1773 (1) voted for the Absentee Tax.
> 1773 (2) voted against an untaxed press.

> 1774 (2) voted for Catholic relief.
> 1777 (1) voted against Grattan's (**0895**)
> motion for retrenchment.
> 1778 (2) voted against the Popery Bill.
> 1779 (2) voted against a six-months Money
> Bill.
> 1780 (2) voted against Yelverton's (**2268**)
> motion to modify Poynings' Law.
> 1780 (3) voted against the Tenantry Bill.
> 1780 (4) voted for the Perpetual Mutiny
> Bill.
> 1783 (1) voted against Flood's (**0762**)
> motion for parliamentary reform.
> 1784 (1) voted against a committee on the
> Reform Bill – Commissioner and Superin-
> tendent of the Barracks.
> 1785 (1) absent.
> 1786 (2) voted for Forbes's (**0778**) motion
> for retrenchment.
> 1789 (1) voted for a Regency.
> 1790 (1) voted against Grattan's motion for
> reducing the influence of the Crown.
> 1790 (2) voted for Foster (**0805**) on the
> Election of a Speaker.
> 1793 (2) voted for the Convention Bill.
> 1795 (2) teller against Catholic emancipa-
> tion.

ADDITIONAL INFORMATION: *A member of the RDS
from 1768; *a subscriber to the Public Assembly
Rooms 1795–f.

ESTATES/RESIDENCE: Deel Castle, Ballina, Co. Mayo;
Elmhall estate and Tyrawley estate, Co. Mayo; Merrion
Square, Dublin. Cuffe leased Castle Gore, Co. Mayo
from the Rt Hon. Sir Arthur Saunders Gore, 2nd Earl
of Arran (**0861**), *post* 1797 (it is given as his address in
the Parliamentary List of 1789), which resulted in a
protracted lawsuit on behalf of Gore's eldest son, Arthur
(**0862**). The 3rd Earl won the case on the grounds that
the lease was invalid under the terms of the then family
settlement. Wakefield estimated that Lord Tyrawley had
a rental of £7,000. His will was proved in 1822. In
1787 James Cuffe was granted fairs at Belcarra.

SOURCES: PRONI T/3200 Arran Papers; PRONI MIC/
474 Irish Volunteers; NLI EC 6958; NLI LC 1589;
NAI MFCI Reel 35, Parish Registers of Ballinrobe, Co.
Mayo [bur. 18 July 1821]; Ellis thesis; Jupp thesis; GEC
P; Burke *Ext. P* (1883) p. 149; *Index to Irish Privy Counsellors, 1711–1910*; J. Kelly, *Prelude to Union* (Cork
1992), p. 192; J. Kelly, *'That Damn'd thing called Hon-*

our': *Duelling in Ireland 1570–1860* (Cork, 1995), pp. 141, 146, 155; G. C. Bolton, *The Passing of the Irish Act of Union* (1966), pp. 39, 206 n. 7; J. Smyth, *Men of no Property* (Dublin, 1992), pp. 62–3; *Cornwallis Corr.* vol. 3 p. 246 [says he was born 1747]; Wakefield, *Account of Ire.*, vol. 1 p. 271; *Almanacks*; *GM*; *FJ* 22–5 Sept. 1792, 20 Oct. 1796, 22 Apr. 1797; *DJ* 21–4 Sept. 1782; Parliamentary Lists, 1769 (1), 1772 (2), 1773 (1), (2), 1774 (1), 1775 (1), 1776 (1), (2), (3), 1777 (1), 1778 (1), 1780 (1), 1782 (1), 1783 (1), (2), (3), 1784 (1), (2), (3), 1785 (1), (2), (3), (4), 1787 (1), 1788 (1), 1789 (1), 1790 (1), 1791 (1), 1793 (1), 1794 (1), (2), 1798 (1), 1799 (2), 1800 (2).

0553 CUFFE, James

MP for Tulsk Feb.–Aug. 1800; [UK] Tralee 29 May 1819 – 29 July 1828

b. 1778; d. 30 July 1828

FAMILY/BACKGROUND: Eldest illegitimate son of Rt Hon. James Cuffe, 1st Baron Tyrawley (0552) and his 2nd wife Miss Wewitzer.

MARRIED: [12 Aug. 1796] Harriet, dau. of Col. John Caulfeild of Co. Roscommon.

CHILDREN: *d.s.p.*

CAREER/OCCUPATION: Custos Rot. Co. Mayo 1801; High Sheriff of Co. Mayo 1818; Governor of Co. Mayo 1818–28; Trustee of the Linen Board.

MILITARY: *Commissioner and Overseer of Barracks 1792; Captain in Tyrawley Cavalry Aug. 1796; *Barrack Master General 1799 (f.); Colonel N. Mayo Militia 1822; Captain Commandant Kilmaine and Rathlacken Infantry 1821; Treasurer of Barrack Board and Board of Works 1800 at £600 p.a.

POLITICAL ACTIVITY: He was brought in to vote for the Union. His father was created Lord Tyrawley but failed to secure a remainder to his son as, although Cornwallis recommended him in June 1800, George III personally objected to his illegitimacy and Portland was reluctant to press it. He was the only exception in the list of recommendations. However, he was made Treasurer of the Barracks, an office that was normally worth about £300 p.a. but was increased to £600.

Such was the influence of the Cuffes, and the lawless state of Co. Mayo, that in 1805 it was suggested that the assizes should no longer be held in Ballinrobe, as it was forecast, in the event incorrectly, that James Cuffe would defend 'his rights' with pistols; his opponents suggested that the town was 'settled on him'. He sat in the united parliament for Tralee from 1819 until his death in 1828. It was thought that he was returned with the support of the Castle.

ADDITIONAL INFORMATION: *A member of the RDS from 1795.

ESTATES/RESIDENCE: Deel Castle, Co. Mayo; Elm Hall and Tyrawley.

SOURCES: PRONI D/302; PRONI T/3166/1C Hartnell notes; NAI MFCI Reel 35, Parish Registers of Ballinrobe, Co. Mayo [says he died 30 July 1828 and was bur. 17 Aug.]; O'Neill thesis; Jupp thesis; *Alum. Dub.*; *HP 1790–1820*; *Memorials of the Dead* [says he died July 1828 aged 50 years]; *Cornwallis Corr.* (London, 1859) vol. 3 pp. 246, 257, 319 [says he died Sept. 1828. Also referred to as Colonel in 1800]; G. C. Bolton, *The Passing of the Irish Act of Union* (1966), p. 206 n. 7; J. Kelly, *'That Damn'd thing called Honour': Duelling in Ireland 1570–1860* (Cork, 1995), p. 268; *Almanacks*; *FJ* 13 Aug., 20 Oct. 1796; *DJ* 18 Aug. 1796; Parliamentary Lists 1800 (1), (3).

0554 CUFFE, John

MP for Thomastown 1715–27

b. 1683; d. 26 June 1749

PEERAGES: Cr. Baron Desart 10 Nov. 1733.

FAMILY/BACKGROUND: Eldest son of Agmondisham Cuffe (0547) and Anne, dau. of Sir John Otway of Cumberland, wid. of John Warden.

MARRIED: (1) [2 Sept. 1707] Margaret (*d.s.p.*), dau. and h. of James Hamilton; (2) [12 Feb. 1726] Dorothea, dau. of Richard Gorges (0884).

CHILDREN: (2) Joseph; Agmondisham; John, 2nd Baron Desart, m. [2 Sept. 1752] Sophia, dau. and h. of Brettridge Badham (0070), wid. of Richard Thornhill; Otway (admitted to Middle Temple 31 Jan. 1756), 3rd Baron and 1st Earl of Desart, m. [18 Aug. 1785] Anne, e. dau. of Hon. Peter Browne-Kelly, 2nd Earl of Altamont (0262); Gorges; Rev. Hamilton (d. 1811), m. [5 June 1766] Esther, dau. and h. of William Williams of Co. Meath; Hon. William (0558); Nichola Sophia (d. 1818), m. [1759] Edward Herbert (1008); Lucy Susanna, m. Sir John Blunden, 1st Baronet (0179); Martha, m. [8 Apr.

1766] Rev. Nicholas Herbert; Margaretta (d. 1742); Catherine.

EDUCATION: School: Mr Coulter, Clonmel; entered TCD 7 Aug. 1697, aged 14 years, BA 1701; Middle Temple 11 Dec. 1702; LLD *hon. caus.* 1718.

CAREER/OCCUPATION: Sheriff of Co. Kilkenny 1708; Burgess of Carlingford *c.* 1711; Mayor of Kilkenny 1722; Clerk of the Crown and Peace for Co. Mayo 1733, *Deputy 1735.

POLITICAL ACTIVITY: He was an unsuccessful candidate for the borough of Callan in October 1713 and again in October 1727, receiving 7 and 52 votes respectively. However, he was returned for Thomastown in 1715. Very little is known of his parliamentary career except for his support for the establishment of a national bank. He was listed for 28 committees between 1717 and 1725.

DIVISION LISTS:
1721 (1) voted for a national bank.
1721 (2) voted for a national bank.

ESTATES/RESIDENCE: Desart, Co. Kilkenny. He built Castle Inch, which was described as 'an elegant mansion'. He purchased the town and liberties of Callan from the Earl of Arran (0859) in 1735 for £11,120.
In 1779 Young reckoned the then Lord Desart's rental at £1,600. According to Wakefield, Lord Desart had a rental of £5,000–£6,000.

SOURCES: Information from J. Kennedy Esq. [T. Shelby, Notes on the election of Callan MPs *c.* 1870]; Burke *PB* (1903) p. 456; *Alum. Dub.*; J. Kelly, *Henry Flood…*(Dublin, 1998) p. 41; Wakefield, *Account of Ire.*, vol. 1 p. 264; Young, *Tour in Ire.*, vol. 2, app. p. 83; *Register of Admissions to the Honourable Society of the Middle Temple* (London, 1949) vol. 1 pp. 252, 350; Kilkenny MPs; *Louth Arch. Soc. Jn.* (1912–15) pp. 273–83, H. Tempest (ed.), 'The Roll of the Sovereigns and Burgesses of Carlingford, 1706–1828'; *Almanacks.*

0555 CUFFE, Maurice

MP for Kilkenny City 1715–27

b. 1681; d. 30 Sept. 1766
FAMILY/BACKGROUND: Second son of Agmondisham Cuffe (0547) and Anne, dau. of Sir John Otway of Cumberland, wid. of John Warden of Burnchurch, Co. Kilkenny.
MARRIED: (1) [6 Feb. 1718] Martha, dau. of John

FitzGerald of Co. Cork, wid. of William Hartpole of Queen's County, and of Richard Power; (2) [8 Jan. 1759] Hannah, dau. of Rt Hon. Thomas Bligh (0174).

CHILDREN: (1) Eleanor, m. [Nov. 1740] John Hely; Mary; Catherine; Anne, m. (1) [1 Mar. 1740] Edward FitzGerald, Knight of Glin, (2) Denny Baker Cuffe (her cousin); 3 other dau.

EDUCATION: School: Mr Coulter, Clonmel; entered TCD, BA 1701; Middle Temple 11 Dec. 1702; called to the Irish Bar 1712; LLD *hon. caus.* 1718.

CAREER/OCCUPATION: King's Counsel 1716, 1748–66; Treasurer to the Honorable Society of King's Inns 1734–5; *Commissioner of Oyer and Terminer 1742–53.

POLITICAL ACTIVITY: He was nominated for 35 committees between 1716 and 1725. He was listed as 'in employment – a placeman' in 1719. In 1721 he supported the establishment of a national bank. At the general election of 1727 he unsuccessfully contested the borough of Callan, receiving 31 votes. The successful candidates were Warden Flood (0765) and Henry Wemys (2205). There was at this time an agreement between the Floods, Agars and Wemyses over this most controversial borough.

DIVISION LISTS:
1721 (1) voted for a national bank.
1721 (2) voted for a national bank.

ESTATES/RESIDENCE: Ballinrobe, Co. Mayo; [?]St Albans, Co. Kilkenny.

SOURCES: Information supplied by J. Kennedy Esq. [T. Shelby, Notes on the election of Callan MPs *c.* 1870]; PRONI MIC/338/2, Crossle notes; J. Kelly, *Henry Flood…*(Dublin, 1998), p. 23; *Alum. Dub.*; IMC *King's Inns Admission Papers, 1607–1867*; *Register of Admissions to the Honourable Society of the Middle Temple* (London, 1949) vol. 1 p. 252; Kilkenny MPs; *Almanacks*; *DJ* 4–7 Oct. 1766; Parliamentary List, 1719 (1).

0556 CUFFE, Michael

MP for Co. Mayo 1719–27; Longford B. 1727–44

b. 1694 (bapt. 1 July 1696); d. 24 (bur. 25) July 1744

FAMILY/BACKGROUND: Second son of Francis Cuffe (**0548**) and Honora, dau. of Michael Boyle, Primate of all Ireland.

MARRIED: [1 Aug. 1718] Frances, dau. of Henry Sandford (**1867**); (she m. (2) Joseph Preston).

CHILDREN: Elizabeth o. dau. and h., m. Thomas Pakenham, 1st Baron Longford (**1622**).

EDUCATION: School: Dr Andrews; Kilkenny College 9 May 1709, aged 14 years; entered TCD 12 May 1712, aged 16 years; Middle Temple 21 Oct. 1715.

CAREER/OCCUPATION: High Sheriff of Co. Longford 1719, Co. Mayo 1723; *Governor of the Workhouse 1733–43; *Commissioner of the Tillage Act for Connaught 1739–43.

POLITICAL ACTIVITY: He was returned for Co. Mayo on petition following the death of his elder brother (**0549**) in 1717. Arthur Ormsby (**1595**) was originally returned but Michael Cuffe successfully petitioned against him. At the 1727 general election he was returned for Longford Borough, which he represented until his death in 1744.

As 'a Tory – [he was] thought likely to be an opponent of the repeal of the Test Clause' in 1719. Cuffe supported the establishment of a national bank in 1721. He was listed for 14 committees between 1719 and 1725 and 33 between 1727 and his death in 1744. He was an heir of the first Earl of Longford and it was through his daughter, Elizabeth, that his (substantial) part of the estate passed to the Pakenhams, in whose family the title was recreated.

DIVISION LISTS:
1721 (1) voted for a national bank.
1721 (2) voted for a national bank.

ADDITIONAL INFORMATION: *A foundation member of the Dublin Society, 1731.

ESTATES/RESIDENCE: Ballinrobe, Co. Mayo. In 1719 Michael Cuffe owned an estate in the parish of Tuam, barony of Clare, of which there is a copy survey of 1808; there are other original or copy maps of lands in the barony of Clare, 1807–9. It was recorded that after his death 'a considerable estate devolves to his son-in-law, Thomas Packenham [Pakenham] Esq.'. In 1720 the Dublin city property of the 1st Earl of Longford was inherited by Cuffe and James Macartney (**1304**). 'The undeveloped southern part of the estate was laid out in large building lots and new streets.' Digges Street and Little Cuffe Street 'were opened through the dunghills at the southern end of Aungier Street. In 1724 the es-

tate was divided equally between Macartney and Cuffe each of whom acquired part of the new building lots and part of the developed land ... Cuffe subsequently assigned his moiety to Boyle Spencer, Esq., and Macartney's moiety was sold in 1747 to repay his share of the mortgage.'

SOURCES: PRONI D/302; EC 3480–3, 6966, 8530; McCracken thesis [says he was born 1694]; J. H. Bernard (ed.), *The Register of St Patrick, Dublin, 1677–1800* (Parish Register Society of Dublin, 1907), p. 45 [bur. 25 July 1744]; H. F. Berry (ed.), *The Registers of the Church of St Michan, Dublin, 1636–1700* (Parish Register Society of Dublin, 1909), p. 282; *Register of Admissions to the Honourable Society of the Middle Temple* (London, 1949) vol. 1 p. 276; *JRSAI* vol. 54 (1924) pp. 55–67, T. U. Sadleir, 'The Register of Kilkenny School (1685–1800)' [says he is aged 14 years in May 1709]; *Ir. Geography* vol. 6 no. 4 (Wexford 1972) pp. 365–85, N. T. Burke, 'An Early Modern Dublin Suburb: The Estate of Francis Aungier, Earl of Longford'; M. Craig, *Dublin 1660–1860: a social and architectural history*, p. 40; *Almanacks*; *GM* (Exshaw's edition) July 1744; *Pue's Occurrences* 20 Dec. 1718; *The Dublin Courant* 17 Nov. 1722, 28 July 1744 [says he died 17 July]; Parliamentary List, 1719 (2).

0557 CUFFE, Thomas

MP for Wexford B. 1735–42

b. 1700 (?1704); d. 9 May 1742

FAMILY/BACKGROUND: Son of Thomas Cuffe and Dorothy, dau. of Edward Jones of Co. Wexford (**1112**).

MARRIED: [12 Jan. 1738] Grace, dau. of Thomas Tilson; (she m. (2) [Aug. 1753] Charles Coote, Dean of Kilfenora).

CHILDREN: ?*d.s.p.*

EDUCATION: School: Mr Sheridan, Dublin; entered TCD 18 Mar. 1720; Inner Temple 1720; called to the Irish Bar 1729.

CAREER/OCCUPATION: King's Counsel; Free Burgess of New Ross 15 Aug. 1741.

POLITICAL ACTIVITY: A lawyer, he was a leading speaker for the government against the Cork petitions opposing the realignment of the gold standard in 1737. On 27 October 1737 Lord George Sackville (**1835**) wrote to his father, the Duke of Dorset, that the petitions against the lowering of the gold were considered the previous day in the House. They first proposed a committee and, when that was negatived by 108 to 55, Stannard (**1981**) moved for a resolution that the lowering was prejudicial to the trade of the country. This was rejected by 11 to 40, and Carter (**0360**) proposed that the further consideration of the petitions should be postponed to 1 October 1738 (when parliament would be in recess), which was carried by 118 to 30. 'The chief speakers on the side of the minority were Stannard, Sir Richard Cox (**0508**) (who abus'd the Privy Council very grossly) Mr Morgan (**1487**), Mr Maloun [*sic*] (**1336**). On the other side the Solicitor General (**0196**), Mr Cope (**0489**), Mr Coote, Mr Cuff [*sic*] (**0557**) and Mr Hill (**1015**).'

He was listed for 35 committees between 1735 and his death in 1742. In 1735 he introduced the heads of a bill, 9 Geo. II, c. 26, 'to repair the Road leading from the city of Kilkenny to the Town of Clonmell', and in 1741 15 Geo. II, c. 8, 'An Act for the more effectual securing the Payment of Rents and preventing Frauds by Tenants'.

ESTATES/RESIDENCE: Grange, Co. Kilkenny.

SOURCES: *CJ Ire.* (Bradley ed.) vol. 6 pp. 603, 611, vol. 7 pp. 299, 339 (0369, 0413); PRONI T/618/323 Crossle Papers; PRONI MIC/338/2 Crossle notes; McCracken thesis; *GM* (Exshaw's edition) May 1742; Eustace, *Abstracts of Wills*; *JRSAI* vol. 21 (1892) p. 301, P. D Vigors, 'Alphabetical List of Free Burgesses of New Ross ... 1658–1839 ... '; *JRSAI* vol. 54 (1924) pp. 55–67, T. U. Sadleir, 'The Register of Kilkenny School (1685–1800)' [gives Thomas Cuffe entered Kilkenny College 10 June 1713 aged 13 years]; *HMC Sackville I* p. 167; *DJ* 11 May 1742.

0558 CUFFE, Hon. William

MP for Kilkenny B. 1783–90–2

b. *c.* 1743; d. 3 Oct. 1792 at Athlone
FAMILY/BACKGROUND: Youngest son of John Cuffe, 1st Baron Desart (**0554**) and Dorothea, dau. of Richard Gorges (**0884**).
MARRIED: Unmarried.
EDUCATION: School: private tutor; entered TCD 26 June 1760.
MILITARY: *Major of Dragoons 1787; *18th Regiment of Dragoons 1790–1; Lieutenant-Colonel 18th Light Dragoons.

POLITICAL ACTIVITY: A professional soldier, he was returned in 1783 for Kilkenny city through the influence of his brother, Lord Desart. However, he voted independently, possibly because of the factions in Kilkenny city, for in 1784 it was thought that although he was still 'doubtful' he was 'more likely now to be in favour of Government as he has quarrelled with the violent party in Kilkenny and as a Colonel of the Volunteers separated himself with his Corps from the Kilkenny Rangers etc.' The Rangers represented the extreme faction in the city and were reputed to have duped the Butlers.

Despite the government's hopes, Cuffe appears to have settled into a solid opposition for the rest of the 1783–90 parliament, voting against the Commercial Resolutions, for a Regency and, after the 1790 election, for W. B. Ponsonby (**1709**) as Speaker. However, his brother Lord Desart was inclined to support. He died in 1792 at Athlone.

DIVISION LISTS:
    1784 (1) voted for a committee on the Reform Bill.
    1784 (2) voted for the amendment on the woollen manufacture.
    1785 (1) voted against the Commercial Propositions.
    1787 (1) absent but had previously voted for a Pension Bill.
    1789 (1) voted for a Regency.
    1790 (2) voted for Ponsonby (**1709**) on the Election of a Speaker.

ESTATES/RESIDENCE: Kilkenny; [?]Athlone, Co. Westmeath.

SOURCES: Kilkenny MPs; *Alum. Dub.*; *Ir. Gen.* vol. 6 no. 2 (1981) p. 176; H. F. Morris, 'The Waterford Herald 1792' [says he was Colonel 13th Light Dragoons]; *GM* (Exshaw's edition) Oct. 1792; Musgrave, *Obits* [says Lieutenant Colonel 13th Light Dragoons]; *Almanacks*; *DJ* 6–9 Oct. 1792; Parliamentary Lists, 1783 (2), 1784 (1), (2), (3), 1785 (1), (2), (3), (4), 1787 (1), 1788 (1), 1789 (1), 1790 (1), 1791 (1).

0559 CUNINGHAME, Rt Hon. Robert

MP for Tulsk 1751–60; Armagh B. 1761–8; Monaghan B. 1768–76–83–90–6; [GB] E. Grinstead 1788–9

b. 18 Apr. 1726; d. 6 Aug. 1801
HONOURS: PC, sworn 7 June 1782.
PEERAGES: Cr. Baron Rossmore 19 Oct. 1796; Rep. Peer Jan.–Aug. 1801. The peerage was granted with remainder to his wife's relations, the Westenras, descendants of Sir Alexander Cairnes (**0334**).
FAMILY/BACKGROUND: Son of Col. David Cuninghame of Stirlingshire and Margaret, dau. of J. Callander of Stirlingshire.
MARRIED: [29 May 1754] Elizabeth, dau. and co-h. of John Murray (**1507**).
CHILDREN: *d.s.p.*
EDUCATION: Edinburgh University.
CAREER/OCCUPATION: *General Governor of the Workhouse 1733–43; *Commissioner of the Infirmary 1758–f.; *Trustee of the Linen Board for Leinster 1794–1800 (f.); *Governor of the Hibernian Society 1769–1800 (f.); *Governor of the Royal Hospital (Kilmainham) 1764–5.
MILITARY: Volunteer with 14th Foot at Culloden; Captain and aide-de-camp to Primate Stone when Lord Justice 1751; aide-de-camp to the Lords Justices 1753–18 May 1754, 1755–61 (reappointed May 1758), to the Adjutant General 1757–70; Colonel Captain 1753, 1755; Lieutenant-Colonel of Foot Nov. 1757; Lieutenant-Colonel 1758–62, 1765–9; Colonel 19 Feb. 1762–4, appointed to command 124th Foot 3 Aug. 1762; *Major-General of the Foot 1759–63, 1769–70, 1772–8, 1780–8; *Commissioner and Overseer of Barracks 1759–61, 1794–6; *1st Colonel 1761; *Colonel of the New Corps 1762, *the 25th Regiment of Foot 1768–9; Adjutant-General, Major-General 25 May 1772; Colonel 14th Foot 18 Oct. 1775; Governor of Kinsale Fort 1770–79; Lieutenant-General 29 Aug. 1777, 1781–9; Colonel (Lieutenant-General) 1788, 16th Foot 1789, of 5th Regiment of Dragoons 1790–1, 1793 (disbanded 1800); Commander-in-Chief 1795–6.

POLITICAL ACTIVITY: He was a professional soldier, a Scot who came to Ireland – possibly encouraged by Lord George Sackville (**1835**), to whom he had been of service in Scotland – as aide-de-camp to Primate Stone. He was returned for Tulsk in 1751 when St George Caulfeild (**0371**), who controlled the borough, was made Chief Justice of the King's Bench. In 1761 he was returned for the Primate's borough of Armagh. He married an heiress, whose inheritance included an interest in the borough of Monaghan, which he represented from 1768 until he was created Lord Rossmore in 1796.

In May 1751 Stone told the Chief Secretary, Lord George Sackville, that he found Cuninghame's conduct and manners thoroughly satisfactory; the following month Stone asked that Cuninghame be promoted as a public mark of his Grace's favour to the Primate. Cuninghame was promoted in 1756 by an arrangement made under Lord Lieutenant Dorset and carried over by Lord Lieutenant Hartington. He appears to have been an obliging and informal link between the British and Irish officials for the next 30 years, conveying a constant stream of information and gossip. For instance, in 1762 Lord George Sackville wrote to General Irwin that 'I expect Cuningham tomorrow he will be so full of politics that his Grace [Dorset] will question him for at least two hours.'

Cuninghame had also a connection with Charles Townshend, Lord Lieutenant Townshend's brother, and in 1771 Lord Townshend said that 'I recommended him for the first Regiment that fell [vacant] during my Administration.' Apparently he opposed the Castle on the division of the Revenue Board and he voted for the Absentee Tax, which was officially an open vote; otherwise he appears to have voted very solidly for the government – the 1774 list declared that 'He voted for popery and tontine.' However, his votes on the division of the Revenue Boards and the Absentee Tax appear to have led to a very critical entry in the 1775 Parliamentary List, which declared that he 'affects independence and great consequence in parliament'.

In 1770 he was Governor of Kinsale, £350 p.a. Lord George Sackville's favour secured him future promotions under Lord Lieutenant Buckinghamshire in 1777. At this time he was anxious to obtain provision for his brother, but whether he succeeded is uncertain. In 1776 it was said that he was 'attached to the King's service only'; this may well have been true as, in 1779, when the Irish Treasury was empty, Sackville (Germain) wrote to the Irish commander-in-chief, General Irwin, that he would be delayed in Ireland unless he could find 'Cuninghame or some such public spirited general who will act as if upon the staff without any pay or consideration whatever. It is the first instance of an officer being sent on duty with instructions to treat all the regiments he reviewed without being allowed even his expenses. I hope he is satisfy'd with the approbation the Lord Lieutenant gives him, as his friends here take the liberty of laughing at his folly.' In 1783 his objective was alleged to be to be commander-in-chief and to have a Regiment of Dragoons.

Cuninghame supported the Commercial Resolutions, but considered that future progress was unlikely in view of the slimness of the majority. He claimed that Orde (**1594**) 'knew little of his ground and less of his members', considering that he paid insufficient attention to men like Conolly (**0459**). Cuninghame himself was reputed to be 'very popular as a *bon vivant* and mixes with all sorts'. In 1790 a verdict was that 'As a public speaker his voice is clear, articulate and well toned ... [but] much injured by a strong Scots accent, a defect from which few natives of Scotland are ever able to get free ... In reasoning he is shrewd, acute and argumentative, severe on the failure of his opponents and careful to leave no room for sharp retorts.'

He was repeatedly accused of military advancement through Court attendance rather than martial valour. Finally, in 1795, he was made commander-in-chief. Two years later he retired and was created Baron Rossmore, and it was said that 'The worthy old gentleman has taken the change in the best way possible ... his full satisfaction with the respect shown to his character and past services by the Duke of York and the Lord Lieutenant.' At the Union Lord Cornwallis recommended him as a representative peer but the Duke of Portland queried this, pointing out that '[His] age and infirmities naturally suggest his unfitness for undertaking a duty which it would be painful to him to fulfill, and to which certainly neither the place of his nativity, nor his hereditary fortune, give him any particular pretention.' Cornwallis responded: 'I feel it my duty to observe that looking to the very high and confidential situation which he en-

joyed in this country, to his long and uninterrupted residence in it, to the Parliamentary influence he has acquired by his connexion with Lord Claremont [brother-in-law], who returns two members to the House of Commons, and to the very considerable property which he possesses, I deemed him qualified for a place in the Representative Peerage.'

DIVISION LISTS:
1753 (1) voted against the expulsion of Arthur Jones-Nevill (**1125**).
1753 (2) voted for the Money Bill.
1768 (1) voted for army augmentation – Colonel of 58th Regiment and Adjutant-General.
1771 (1) voted for Lord Townshend as Lord Lieutenant.
1771 (2) voted against Sir Lucius O'Brien's (**1558**) motion for retrenchment – a placeman.
1771 (3) voted against the amendment to the Revenue Bill.
1773 (1) voted for the Absentee Tax.
1773 (2) voted against an untaxed press.
1774 (2) voted for Catholic relief.
1775 (1) voted against the pro-American amendment to the Speech from the Throne.
1777 (1) voted against Grattan's (**0895**) motion for retrenchment.
1780 (1) voted against Grattan's declaration of the rights of Ireland.
1780 (2) voted against Yelverton's (**2268**) motion to modify Poynings' Law.
1780 (3) voted for the Tenantry Bill.
1780 (4) a teller for the Perpetual Mutiny Bill.
1783 (1) voted against Flood's (**0762**) motion for parliamentary reform.
1785 (1) voted for the Commercial Propositions.
1789 (1) ?voted against a Regency.
1790 (2) voted for Foster (**0805**) on the Election of a Speaker.

ADDITIONAL INFORMATION: He was nicknamed 'Roby' by Lord Shannon (**0213**). The Rossmores are alleged to be followed by a banshee: her terrible wailing was first heard in 1801 when the first baron lay dying. Lord Rossmore lived in some style at Mount Kennedy, and enjoyed giving house parties. Sir Jonah and Lady Barrington lived near by and appear to have been frequent guests. On this occasion they retired at about midnight and slept soundly until two o'clock in the morning, when Sir Jonah was awakened by a wild and unearthly cry, which he described as 'not a natural sound'. He lost no time in rousing his wife, and the scared couple got up and opened the window, which looked over the grass plot beneath. It was a moonlight night and the objects around the house were easily discernible, but there was nothing to be seen in the direction whence the eerie sound proceeded. Now thoroughly frightened, Lady Barrington called her maid, who straight away would not listen or look and fled in terror 'to the servants' quarters. The uncanny noise continued for about half an hour, when it suddenly ceased. All at once a distinct exclamation "Rossmore, Rossmore, Rossmore" was heard and then all was still. The Barringtons looked at each other in dismay, and were utterly bewildered as to what the cry could mean. They decided however, not to mention the incident at Mount Kennedy and returned to bed in the hope of resuming their broken slumbers. They were not left long undisturbed, for at seven o'clock they were awakened by a loud knocking at the bedroom door, and Sir Jonah's servant, Lawler, entered the room, his face white with terror. "Oh, Lord Sir!", "What's the matter?" said I [Sir Jonah] hurriedly "Is anyone dead?" "Oh Sir," answered the man, "Lord Rossmore's footman has just gone by in great haste, and he told me that my Lord, after coming from the Castle, had gone to bed in perfect health but that about half-after two this morning, his own man hearing a noise in his master's bed (he slept in the same room) went to him and found him in the agonies of death, and before he could alarm the other servants all was over!" The banshee, it is said, still follows the family' – presumably the Westenras, as the barony was remaindered to the children of the sisters of Lady Rossmore in succession. The Murray sisters were through their mother, Mary Cairnes, the ultimate heirs of Sir Alexander Cairnes (0334).

ESTATES/RESIDENCE: Mount Kennedy, Co. Wicklow. Cuninghame purchased a vast estate in Co. Wicklow, where he had lands in the baronies of Newcastle and Arklow. Through his marriage he acquired considerable estates at and near Monaghan town (this, the Cairnes/Murray inheritance (0334, 0336), was extremely complicated, involving four sisters). He commissioned a house to James Wyatt's designs. In 1790 it was recorded that 'General Cuninghame ... for a number of years has applied himself to agricultural labours with spirit and perseverance and has not a little adorned the face of the district where he resides both by his buildings and his plantations.'

SOURCES: P. Collins, *County Monaghan Sources in the PRONI* (1998) pp.121–42, 'The Rossmore Papers'; McCracken thesis; Ellis thesis; GEC *P* [says born *c.* 1728]; Burke *IFR* (1976) p. 309; *HP 1754–94*; *Index to Irish Privy Counsellors, 1711–1910*; B. De Breffny and R. Ffolliott, *The Houses of Ireland* (Dublin, 1975), p. 156; *HMC Stopford-Sackville I* pp. 171–2, 219, 224, 233, 239, 244–5; J. Kelly, *Prelude to Union* (Cork, 1992), pp. 191,195; E. Hewitt (ed.) *Lord Shannon's Letters to his Son* (PRONI 1982), p. xxii; *Cornwallis Corr.* (London, 1859) vol. 3 pp. 260, 265 [says incorrectly he was born 1735]; *HMC Sackville I* pp. 171–2; Barrington, *Personal Sketches of his own Times*, vol. 2 pp. 151–5; *Almanacks*; *BNL* 21 May 1754, 19 May 1758; *DJ* 15–19 Nov. 1757; Parliamentary Lists, 1769 (1), 1771 (1), 1772 (2), 1773 (1), (2), 1774 (1), 1775 (1), 1776 (1), (2), (3), 1777 (1), 1778 (1), 1780 (1), 1782 (1), 1783 (1), (2), 1784 (1), (2), (3), 1785 (1), (2), (3), (4), 1787 (1), 1788 (1), 1789 (1), 1790 (1), 1791 (1), 1793 (1), 1794 (1), (2).

♦♦♦♦ CUNNINGHAM, Waddell [n.d.e.]

MP for Carrickfergus Feb. 1784–Mar. 1785

b. 1730; d. 15 Dec. 1797
FAMILY/BACKGROUND: Son of John Cunningham and [ ] Waddell.
MARRIED: 9 Nov. 1765 Margaret, dau. of Samuel Hyde.
CHILDREN: ?
CAREER/OCCUPATION: 1st President of the Belfast Chamber of Commerce, 1788–90.
MILITARY: Captain 1st Company Belfast Volunteers, 1782.

POLITICAL ACTIVITY: This is an example of how long an MP who was afterwards declared not duly elected could sit and vote. Waddell Cunningham, a well-known Belfast merchant 'and somewhat suspected of smuggling' as well as being a 'violent patriot', upset Lord Donegall's control over Carrickfergus. Because Belfast was a close borough, the citizens often expressed their views in the more open county borough of Carrickfergus. The general election of 1783 was particularly turbulent in this respect, and Cunningham was returned by the popular vote against the Chancellor's son, the Hon. Joseph Hewitt (**1012**). Cunningham had a clear majority, 464 against Hewitt's 279. Donegall then returned Hewitt for Belfast.

The election was petitioned against and eventually declared void. Cunningham's being declared not duly elected was in part due to the agitation of the Belfast Constitutional Club, which petitioned that he had used undue influence. The club had appeared at the by-election, consequent on the elevation of Barry Yelverton (**2268**) to the Bench, wearing cockades inscribed 'freedom of election'. At the new election Lord Donegall joined his interest with Lord Hillsborough's in support of Ezekiel Davys Wilson (**2238**), a local landowner and former mayor of Carrickfergus, who had a majority of 36 – 401 against Cunningham's 365. Subsequently, Wilson followed Lord Hillsborough's political lead.

DIVISION LISTS:
    1784 (1) voted for a committee on the
    Reform Bill.

ADDITIONAL INFORMATION: Cunningham spent much of his early life in America, returning to Ireland in 1765. He was in partnership with John Boyle as a general merchant until his retirement from mercantile life in December 1788. In 1767 he started the manufacture of vitriol near Lisburn with his brother-in-law, Thomas Gregg: it was badly located and one of his less successful ventures. In 1770 his house and furniture were burnt by the 'Hearts of Steel' and he was awarded £737 16s 7d by the Irish parliament for the loss sustained. In 1785 he took a prominent part in starting a discount office in Belfast. In the same year he was appointed a member of Belfast Harbour Corporation by act of parliament.

In 1787 he started Cunningham's bank in conjunction with John Campbell, William Brown and Charles Ranken. It was dissolved by mutual consent, 31 December 1793. He was the leading partner of Cunningham, Campbell, Gregg and Co., New Sugar House, Waring Street, and a large shareholder in Cranston and Co., Maltsters and Brewers as well as John Smylie and Co., manufacturers of window glass and bottles. He was suspected of having amassed his fortune early in life in America through the slave trade.

ESTATES/RESIDENCE: Hercules Lane (now Royal Avenue), Belfast; Ballypalliday, Crookedstone, Co. Antrim, 351 Irish acres leased from the Earl of Donegall at a rent of £174 p.a.

SOURCES: *IHS* (Sept. 1979) p. 359; *Memorials of the Dead* [says he died aged 68 years]; McDowell, *Irish Public Opinion, 1750–1800*, p. 97; Benn, *Belfast* (1877), p. 469; *HMC Charlemont II* vii, p. 77; Millin, *Was Waddell Cunningham a Slave Ship Projector?* (1926), pp. 3–4; G. Chambers, *Faces of Change* (Belfast, 1983), pp. 35, 49; McNevin, *Volunteers*; Parliamentary Lists, 1783 (2), 1784 (1), 1785 (2).

0560 CURRAN, Rt Hon. John Philpot

MP for Kilbeggan 1783–90; Rathcormack 1790–7; Banagher 1800

> b. 24 July 1750; d. 14 Oct. 1817
> HONOURS: PC, sworn 25 July 1806.
> FAMILY/BACKGROUND: Eldest son of James Curran of Newmarket, Co. Cork, and Sarah Philpot.
> MARRIED: [16 Oct. 1774] Sarah, dau. of Dr Richard Creagh of Newmarket, Co. Cork.
> CHILDREN: William Henry; Richard; John; James; Sarah, m. Capt. Sturgeon; Gertrude (d. yg); Amelia; Gertrude, m. Rev. Taylor; Henry Grattan FitzGerald (illegitimate) (who assumed the name of Curran).
> EDUCATION: School: Rev. Nathaniel Boyse of Newmarket; Dr Cary at Midleton School; entered TCD 16 June 1769; Middle Temple 4 Nov. 1773; called to the Irish Bar 1775.
> CAREER/OCCUPATION: King's Counsel 1784–d.; *listed in Judges and Barristers 1789–1800 (f.); *Commissioner of Appeals 1796–7; *Bencher of the Honorable Society of King's Inns 1798–1800 (f.); Master of the Rolls 5 July 1806–14 (his pension on retirement was £3,000 p.a.); *Governor of the Royal Hospital 1789–90; Freeman of Fethard (Tipperary) 1783.

POLITICAL ACTIVITY: 'Mr Curran was born in the County of Kerry, of parents in very straitened circumstances. They contrived, however, to give him the rudiments of a liberal education. He was a *sizer* in the College of Dublin, where he obtained a scholarship.' Having decided on a legal career, 'Without fortune he came to the Inns of Court in London, to prepare himself for the Irish Bar. He supported himself during this period by his literary labours and some slender assistance from his friend and patron, now Lord Yelverton (**2268**).' He was called to the bar in 1775; his first brief was for 20 guineas as a counsel in the Ormsby (**1607**) *v.* Wynne (**2265**) Co. Sligo by-election petition of 1778. His success was far from instantaneous, and his reputation was only established in a spectacular court case at the Cork summer assizes in 1780, involving a priest, whom he supported voluntarily, and Lord Doneraile, who had behaved disreputably. After this success, he was brought into parliament for Kilbeggan by Richard Longfield (**1263**), allegedly to provide the party with an orator.

In 1784 a Parliamentary List noted that 'Mr Longfield has brought him [in] for [Kilbeggan], and asks high preferment in the law for him, which cannot be promised. He is inclined to be popular but has been kept out of the way by Mr Longfield upon such questions.' His abilities were already recognised, although, as at the Bar, he made a slow start in parliament which he explained thus: 'I was a person attached to a great and powerful party whose leaders were men of importance in the State, totally devoted to those political pursuits from whence my mind was necessarily distracted by studies of a different description ... After having toiled through the Four Courts for the entire day, I brought to the House of Commons a person enfeebled and a mind exhausted.'

He had an interest in the numerous political debating societies that flourished in both London and Dublin. As a member of the Monks of the Screw, a society that had been founded by Yelverton at the time of the War of American Independence, he had been part of that society's liberal progressive political thinking. In parliament he supported parliamentary reform but he first made his mark in the early opposition to the Com-

mercial Resolutions, which he considered to be contrary to the spirit of 1782. His legal career was retarded by his and Fitzgibbon's (**0749**) mutual dislike. Although they had at least one characteristic in common – namely fearlessness – Curran and Fitzgibbon represented the two sides of the same problem, and because of this looked on it with different emphases and sought diametrically opposed solutions.

In 1788 it was noted that he 'always opposes and speaks frequently and certainly has humour and at times succeeds tolerable well'. By 1789 he had quarrelled with Longfield, who had become a supporter of government and was now looking for a peerage. In order to free himself from Longfield's direction, Curran purchased a seat for a friend of Longfield's, who was content to submit implicitly to his direction. Thereafter Curran followed the straight opposition line, voting for a Regency, for Ponsonby (**1709**) as Speaker and for the various measures proposed for reform and retrenchment. He was always a strong supporter of the Catholic cause, and on 15 February 1792, during the second reading of the Catholic Relief Bill, he warned the House of Commons that 'A disunited people cannot long subsist. With infinite regret must any man look forward to the alienation of three million of our people, and to a degree of subserviency and corruption in a fourth ... the inevitable consequence would be an Union with Great Britain ... It would be the emigrating of every man of consequence from Ireland; it would be the participation of British taxes without British trade; it would be the extinction of the Irish name as a people. We would become a wretched colony, perhaps leased out to a company of Jews, as was formerly in contemplation, and governed by a few tax gatherers and excisemen.'

At the time of the Regency Crisis he took a prominent part with the opposition. Lord Shannon (**0213**), while hardly disinterested, wrote to his son, then on the grand tour, that 'These were three severe days [2, 8, 12 February 1791] and I cannot conceive more ability than was displayed by Ponsonby, Grattan and Curran, with the greatest advantage in point of question, and such torrents of shocking abuse as I never anywhere before heard, on the other side.' In April he was again a leading speaker over the Responsibility [Place] Bill, the fiat business (fixing bail on estimated injuries through slander), pensions, and the terms of Irish trade with the East Indies. Then in 1792–3 he was an ardent supporter of the Catholic Relief Bills, and he voted for Catholic Emancipation in 1793 and 1795.

The following is a contemporary description of him about 1790: 'Mr Curran is not much indebted to nature for external appearance, as his person is rather mean and his countenance by no means expressive. His voice is clear and distinct and though perhaps somewhat too shrill, is not disagreeably toned but, his pronunciation is disgraced by a vulgar provincial accent. His language is correct, copious, elegant and nervous. It is a rich and inexhaustible stream of animated diction, abounding in luminous phrases, poetical allusions and the liveliest turns of fancy ... In wit he abounds and that not far fetched, or laboriously sought, but easy and familiar ... His arguments are peculiarly strong and convincing, rising gradually and with apparent facility one from the other and terminating in the most cogent and powerful whilst his reasonings have more of logical precision, than of the looseness of popular debate ... In irony he is eminently successful, being shrewd, sarcastic and severe and in satire he stands unrivalled by any Member of the House.' Lord Byron considered that 'He has fifty faces and twice as many voices when he mimics.' As an orator he was considered in the same class as Pitt, Canning or the great Dublin preacher Kirwan. Like many people with this mercurial temperament he suffered periodically from acute depression.

Although he was among the more esoteric members of the House of Commons, his knowledge of the Irish peasantry, gained from his childhood in Co. Cork, made Curran among the most realistic of the political thinkers of the 1790s, emphasising to the House of Commons the danger of too great a discrepancy between the rich and the poor. Low wages and high rents were, he felt, as much a cause of social unrest as the dissemination of French ideas. In 1795 Grattan (**0895**), concerned at the growth of Defenderism, had wished to harness extraparliamentary public opinion – meetings were to be held in every county and an aggre-

gate meeting in Dublin was to petition the king. Curran refused to be part of this, considering that 'Nothing should be done to agitate lest pillage and plundering should ensue.' But at the beginning of 1796 Curran moved for the appointment of a parliamentary committee to consider the state of the poor. About 1797 he confessed that, although he had always regarded the war as one of interested ambition, he had refrained from commenting on it lest it encourage the enemy to attack Ireland. Like many of the opposition, he emulated their opposite numbers in England who did not seek re-election in 1797, only to look hurriedly for seats in 1800 in order to oppose the Union. At that time, his reputation can be gauged by the fact that one MP said he was offered £4,000 'for the return in Mr Curran's favour'.

In 1799 it was stated that 'He has uniformly declared against the war with *France* and has strongly combated the coercive system which has been pursued in Ireland. Finding the inefficacy of this opposition, he has seceded from the House of Commons and is now only known to the public as an advocate, in which capacity he has defended many of his unfortunate countrymen.' His integrity and sense of justice were beyond question, as was his courage, both physical and moral, for he defended many of the United Irishmen, from the socially privileged to the underprivileged, and undertook many of the most difficult cases of his day. He was the principal defender of those indicted for offences associated with the 1798 rebellion. Daniel O'Connell declared that 'There never was so honest an Irishman.' He was an excellent cross-examiner, but less happy and less successful as a judge.

He was a noted duellist: among those he fought were Captain Richard St Leger (**1860**), son of the Cork magnate Lord Doneraile (**0026**), John Fitzgibbon (**0749**), later Lord Chancellor, over parliamentary reform in 1785, John Egan (**0694**), Chairman of Kilmainham sessions, and in 1790 Chief Secretary Hobart (**1026**), later Earl of Buckinghamshire.

DIVISION LISTS:
    1783 (1) voted for Flood's (**0762**) motion
    for parliamentary reform.
    1784 (1) voted for a committee on the

Reform Bill.

1784 (2) voted for the amendment on the woollen manufacture.

1784 (4) voted against the address to His Grace the Duke of Rutland.

1785 (1) voted against the Commercial Propositions.

1786 (2) voted for Forbes's (0778) motion for retrenchment.

1787 (1) voted for a Pension Bill.

1788 (2) teller for Forbes's motion for limiting pensions.

1789 (1) voted for a Regency.

1790 (1) voted for Grattan's (0895) motion for reducing the influence of the Crown.

1790 (2) voted for Ponsonby (1709) on the Election of a Speaker.

1791 (1) teller for Curran's (0560) resolution against the sale of peerages.

1791 (2) voted for Grattan's motion for the exercise of free trade.

1791 (3) voted for Grattan's motion to abolish the Dublin police.

1792 (1) voted for the Catholic petition.

1792 (2) voted against resolutions against Napper Tandy.

1793 (1) voted for Knox's (1180) motion for Catholic emancipation.

1793 (2) voted against the Convention Bill.

1795 (2) voted for Catholic emancipation.

1795 (3) voted for Sir Laurence Parsons' (1636) resolution against alleged troop removals.

1796 (1) voted for parity of trade with Great Britain.

1797 (1) voted for Ponsonby's motion for parliamentary reform.

ADDITIONAL INFORMATION: Member of the Royal Irish Academy, 1787. Nicknamed 'Stuttering Jack', he studied divinity with a view to entering the Established Church but gave up the idea on coming of age. At the debating society called 'The Brown Bear', Curran was known as 'the little Jesuit of St Omer' for wearing a brown coat outside a black and making pro-Catholic speeches. Prior of the Order of the Screw, 1779.

ESTATES/RESIDENCE: The Priory, Dundrum, Co. Dublin; Newmarket, Co. Cork; 12 Ely Place, Dublin.

SOURCES: PRONI T/3166/1B Hartnell notes; PRONI MIC/315/1/1,8/38 Blackwood Pedigrees; NAI M2611, Extracts from the Parish Registers of Clonfert and Newmarket, Co. Cork; *IMC King's Inns Admission Papers, 1607–1867*; *Alum. Dub.*; Ball, *Judges*; Johnston, *Gt B. & Ire.*, p. 199; *Register of Admissions to the Honourable Society of the Middle Temple* vol. 1 (London, 1949) p. 377; Cork MPs; Thomas Davis (ed.), *The Speeches of the Rt Hon. John Philpot Curran* (Dublin, 1845) [says he attended Mr Cary's free school at Midleton); *DNB* [a long article]; J. T. Gilbert, *A History of the City of Dublin* (Dublin, 1859), vol. 3, pp. 128, 139, 217, 318; *Ir. Gen.* vol. 4 no. 6 (1973) pp. 616–24; W. G. Skehan, 'Freemen of the Corporation of Fethard, Co. Tipperary'; *JRSAI* vol. 82 (1952) p. 20, M. Quane, 'Midleton School: Co. Cork' [gives Dr Chinnery]; *ibid.* vol. 88 (1958) p. 44 'Charleville Endowed School'; McDowell, *Irish Public Opinion, 1750–1800*, pp. 93, 142, 230, 232, 234; *Beresford Corr.* vol. 2 pp. 72, 77; J. Kelly, *Prelude to Union* (Cork, 1992), p. 62; J. Kelly, '*That Damn'd thing called Honour': Duelling in Ireland 1570–1860* (Cork, 1995), pp. 137–8, 149, 198, 210, 242; J. Kelly, *Henry Flood* … (Dublin, 1998), pp. 346, 354, 438; A. P. W. Malcomson (ed.), *Eighteenth Century Irish Official Papers in Great Britain*, 2 vols (PRONI 1973, 1990) vol. 2 pp. 129, 279, 360, 412; E. Hewitt (ed.), *Lord Shannon's Letters to his Son* (PRONI 1982), pp. 19–20, 30; *Almanacks*; Parliamentary Lists, 1783 (2), 1784 (1), (2), (3), 1785 (1), (2), (3), (4), 1787 (1), 1788 (1), 1789 (1), (2), 1790 (1), (2), 1791 (1), 1793 (1), 1799 (1).

0561 CURTIS, John

MP for Ratoath 1761–8

b. *c.* 1717–19; d. 1775

FAMILY/BACKGROUND: Son of John Curtis and his 2nd wife Mary, dau. of Richard Tighe.

MARRIED: [Feb 1744/5] Martha, dau. of Thomas Towers (♦♦♦♦).

CHILDREN: Richard; Thomas m. [4 June 1768] Deborah Pigott; William; Robert; Mary.

CAREER/OCCUPATION: Surgeon at the Royal Hospital (Kilmainham) 1757–61.

EDUCATION: School: entered Glasgow University 1735.

POLITICAL ACTIVITY: Apart from the fact that he is one of the very few medical MPs, very little is known about this man. Although holding a government post, he voted against the augmentation of the army.

DIVISION LISTS:
1768 (1) voted against army augmentation.

ESTATES/RESIDENCE: Mount Hanover, [?]Co. Wexford.

SOURCES: PRONI T/559 vol. 17 p. 159, Burke, extract pedigrees; *LG* (1846) p. 1415; *Memorials of the Dead* [says his parents married 23 Feb. 1712 and he married 2 Mar. 1744/5]; Vicars, *Prerog. Wills*; W. I. Addison (ed.), *The Matriculation Albums of the University of Glasgow 1728–1858* (Glasgow, 1913); *Almanacks*.

0562 CURTIS, Robert

MP for Carlow B. 1695–9; Duleek 1703–13

b. *ante* 1655; d. 29 July 1726
FAMILY/BACKGROUND: Son of Robert Curtis and his 2nd wife Frances, dau. and h. of William Bull.
MARRIED: [24 July 1676] Maria, dau. of Robert Chambre (**0387**).
CHILDREN: William; Charles; Rev. Robert, m. Anne [   ]; Chambre; Margaret; Elizabeth, m. Francis Heaton; Jane, m. Edward Synge, Bp of Ferns.
EDUCATION: LLD *hon. caus.* 1709.
CAREER/OCCUPATION: Joint 2nd Chamberlain of Court of the Exchequer 1689–1714; Joint Auditor of Foreign Accounts; a member of the Royal Fishery of Ireland.

POLITICAL ACTIVITY: He sat for the second parliament of William III and the first parliament of Queen Anne. He supported Lord Chancellor Porter against the accusations of favouring Catholics made against him by some MPs in 1695, and the following year he signed the Association for the protection of William III in parliament. At the beginning of Queen Anne's reign he supported the Court, but he may have changed sides as in 1713 he was considered 'bad' for Duleek, and he was not returned at the ensuing election.

ESTATES/RESIDENCE: Islandbridge, Co. Dublin; Roscrea, Co. Tipperary – purchased 1703. In 1702–3 he also purchased 1593 acres in Co. Kildare, 11 acres in Co. Louth and 172 acres in Co. Meath from the Commissioners for Sale of Forfeited Estates.

SOURCES: *Cal. SP Dom. 1691–2* (London, 1900) p. 112; Simms' cards; Simms, *Williamite Confiscation*, p. 184; *Alum. Dub.*; Vicars, *Prerog. Wills*; Hayton thesis; PRONI T/559 vol. 17 p. 157, Burke, extract pedigrees; Parliamentary Lists, 1695 (1), 1696 (1), 1706 (1), 1713 (1).

CUSACK, William: *see* **SMITH (CUSACK-SMITH)**, Sir William (**1943**)